The Western Humanities

SEVENTH EDITION

Roy T. Matthews & F. DeWitt Platt

MICHIGAN STATE UNIVERSITY

Thomas F. X. Noble

THE UNIVERSITY OF NOTRE DAME

Mc
Graw
Hill

Connect
Learn
Succeed™

To LeeAnn, Dixie, and Linda

There is nothing nobler or more admirable than when two people who see eye to eye keep house as man and wife, confounding their enemies and delighting their friends, as they themselves know better than anyone.

—HOMER, *Odyssey*

The McGraw-Hill Companies

 Connect
Learn
Succeed™

Published by McGraw-Hill, an imprint of The McGraw-Hill Companies, Inc., 1221 Avenue of the Americas, New York, NY 10020. Copyright © 2011, 2008, 2004, 2001, 1998, 1995, and 1992 by The McGraw-Hill Companies. All rights reserved. No part of this publication may be reproduced or distributed in any form or by any means, or stored in a database or retrieval system, without the prior written consent of The McGraw-Hill Companies, Inc., including, but not limited to, in any network or other electronic storage or transmission, or broadcast for distance learning.

This book is printed on acid-free paper.

1 2 3 4 5 6 7 8 9 0 WDQ/WDQ 0

ISBN: 978-0-07-337662-2 (complete)
MHID: 0-07-337662-0 (complete)
ISBN: 978-0-07-733844-2 (Volume I)
MHID: 0-07-733844-8 (Volume I)
ISBN: 978-0-07-733845-9 (Volume II)
MHID: 0-07-733845-6 (Volume II)

Vice President, Editorial: *Michael Ryan*
Director, Editorial: *William R. Glass*
Publisher: *Chris Freitag*
Associate Sponsoring Editor: *Betty Chen*
Director of Development: *Rhona Robbin*
Developmental Editor: *Arthur Pomponio*
Editorial Coordinators: *Elena Mackawgy & Sarah Remington*
Marketing Manager: *Pamela S. Cooper*
Media Project Manager: *EDP Media Department*
Production Editor: *Leslie Racanelli*

Manuscript Editor: *Margaret Moore*
Design Manager: *Allister Fein*
Text Designer: *Pam Verros*
Cover Designer: *Ashley Bedell*
Photo Researcher: *Brian J. Pecko*
Production Supervisor: *Louis Swaim*
Map Preparations: *Mapping Specialists*
Composition: *9.5/12 Palatino by Thompson Type*
Printing: *65# Sterling Ultra Web Gloss*
  by Worldcolor

Cover: Jan Vermeer. *A Young Woman Seated at a Virginal.* Ca. 1670–72. Oil on canvas, 20¼ × 18". Salting Bequest, 1910 (NG2568). National Gallery, London, Great Britain. © National Gallery.

The credits section begins on page C-1 and is considered an extension of the copyright page.

Library of Congress Cataloging-in-Publication Data

Matthews, Roy T.
    The Western humanities / Roy T. Matthews, F. DeWitt Platt, Thomas F. X. Noble. — 7th ed.
        p. cm.
    Includes bibliographical references and index.
    ISBN-13: 978-0-07-337662-2 (acid-free paper)
    ISBN-10: 0-07-337662-0 (acid-free paper)
    ISBN: 978-0-07-733844-2 (v. I: acid-free paper)
    MHID: 0-07-733844-8 (v. I: acid-free paper)
    [etc.]
    1. Civilization, Western—History. I. Platt, F. DeWitt. II. Noble, Thomas F. X. III. Title.
    CB245 .M375 2010
    909' .09821—dc22

2009051330

The Internet addresses listed in the text were accurate at the time of publication. The inclusion of a Web site does not indicate an endorsement by the authors or McGraw-Hill, and McGraw-Hill does not guarantee the accuracy of the information presented at these sites.

www.mhhe.com

CONTENTS

3
CLASSICAL GREEK CIVILIZATION
The Hellenic Age 59

4
HELLENISTIC CIVILIZATION AND THE RISE OF ROME 87

5
JUDAISM AND THE RISE OF CHRISTIANITY 113

9
THE HIGH MIDDLE AGES
The Christian Centuries   233

10
THE LATE MIDDLE AGES
1300–1500   271

11
THE EARLY RENAISSANCE
Return to Classical Roots
1400–1494   *305*

12
THE HIGH RENAISSANCE
AND EARLY MANNERISM
1494–1564   *335*

13
NORTHERN HUMANISM,
NORTHERN RENAISSANCE,
RELIGIOUS REFORMATIONS,
AND LATE MANNERISM
1500–1603   *369*

**19
THE AGE OF EARLY
MODERNISM
1871–1914   559**

**20
THE AGE OF THE MASSES
AND THE ZENITH
OF MODERNISM
1914–1945   595**

PREFACE

The Western Humanities, in this seventh edition, remains true to its founding vision: to provide an analysis and appreciation of cultural expression and artifacts within an interpretive historical framework. Over many years we have seen how students learn more easily and effectively when the humanities are studied within a historical context. In addition, this vision helps students new to the humanities use their developing historical perspective to enrich and deepen their own contemporary views of our world. They see more clearly that their lives and what is important to them did not emerge in a vacuum, but instead from a long, complex, perhaps exotic, and fascinating past. And, as ever, we offer students a rich array of pedagogical supports that accent critical thinking to help students gain and refine their own vision of the past.

In *The Western Humanities* we also emphasize the universal aspects of creativity and expression. People the world over have the impulse to seek answers to the mysteries of human existence; to discover or invent order in the universe; to respond creatively to nature, both inner and outer; to delight the senses and the mind with beauty and truth; to communicate their thoughts; and to share their visions with others. Thus, another of our intentions is to demonstrate that the desire to express oneself and to create lasting monuments has been a compelling drive in human beings since before the dawn of civilized life. We believe that this emphasis will help students see that they are not isolated from the past but belong to a tradition that began thousands of years ago.

We also aim to help students prepare themselves for the future. When they examine the past and learn how earlier generations confronted and overcame challenges—and managed to leave enduring legacies—students will discover that the human spirit is irre-

pressible. In the humanities—in philosophy, religion, art, music, literature—human beings have found answers to their deepest needs and most perplexing questions. We hope that students will be encouraged by this record as they begin to shape the world of the twenty-first century.

HALLMARKS OF *THE WESTERN HUMANITIES*

A pedagogically-informed organization. Instructors and students have long valued how this text provides a unique balance of history and culture. The chapters follow a consistent organization that reinforces student learning from multiple perspectives, as described below.

An interpretive context for the humanities. The first part of every chapter covers the material conditions of the era—the historical, political, economic, and social developments. We aim to capture the essence of complex periods and to fashion a coherent narrative framework for the story of Western culture.

Cultural expression. The remaining part of each chapter is devoted to cultural expression, both in the realm of ideas (philosophy, history, religion, science) and in the realm of cultural achievements (art, music, drama, literature, and film). In this part we describe and analyze the significant cultural contributions of the age, and we examine how creative individuals responded to the challenges presented to them by their society and how they chose values and forms by which to live.

Cultural legacy. Each chapter ends with a brief section describing the cultural legacy of that era. Students will find that some ideas, movements, or artistic methods with which they are familiar have a very long history. They will also discover that the meaning and ascribed value of cultural objects and texts can change from one time and place to another. Our goal is not only to help students establish a context for their culture but to show that the humanities have developed as a dynamic series of choices made by individuals in one era and transformed by individuals in other eras.

Student Support through Effective Pedagogical Features

Another important goal of ours has been to help students understand cultural expression and achievements by offering a wide range of pedagogical features that make connections and accent important themes. These features enrich the main content of the book by offering additional material or different perspectives on the material. We also take seriously the need to expand the historical picture by including material from nonwestern cultures to show how they have affected each other.

"A Humanities Primer: How to Understand the Arts." Students come to western humanities courses with a wide range of backgrounds. To help students gain a basic literacy in the humanities, we begin the book with "A Humanities Primer," which introduces readers to different ways to appreciate each of the major forms of art: literature, music and visual arts. Through the primer, we offer tools to help students to better understand how to move beyond their initial reactions to artworks towards a more informed understanding. We ask students to consider artists' intentions in creating works of art, to observe the formal elements of their creations, and to appreciate how the artists' cultural and historical contexts influence their work. In this edition, we have added an Interpreting Art feature that is new to the seventh edition (see p. xv).

Encounter boxes. Each **Encounter** describes a meeting between the West and another culture. Through text and art, the Encounter focuses on a critical interchange that influenced both cultures. As we seek to nurture global awareness in today's students, these Encounters demonstrate that cultural encounters and exchanges are an enduring part of history, with both positive and negative consequences.

Slice of Life features. The **Slice of Life** boxes offer students the opportunity to hear voices from the past of eyewitnesses to the historical and cultural events described in the text. These excerpts from primary sources and original documents are designed to bring history to life for the reader.

Learning through Maps. This feature encourages students to develop geographical skills—a highly desirable ability in this age of globalization. By performing map exercises and answering map-related questions, students learn to read maps and understand historical and cultural developments within a specific geographic setting.

Legacy sections. Each chapter ends with a section that conveys the enduring legacy of the traditions described in the chapter. For example, in Chapter 8, the legacy section details the ongoing cultural influence of medieval Islam on both modern Islam and on the West.

In addition to the above, other important features of our textbook include:

Terminology. When a new cultural term is introduced in the main text, it is boldfaced and defined immediately.

Key Cultural Terms are aggregated into a list at the end of each chapter—an important learning tool that provides important words for the student to know.

Glossary. At the back of the book, the **Glossary** provides an alphabetical list of all Key Cultural Terms, along with short definitions and pronunciation guides, as needed.

Suggestions for Further Reading is a list, in alphabetic order by author, of one or two literary works by the major writers discussed in each chapter. Each entry includes a readily available edition along with an assessment of its usefulness—so that students may do some additional reading on their own. The master list, arranged by chapter, is part of the "Suggestions for Further Reading and Listening" section found at the end of the book.

Suggestions for Listening is a list, in alphabetic order by composer, of musical compositions covered in each chapter. The list, with brief annotations, is provided as a follow-up to the music discussion in the chapter, so that students may listen on their own. The master list, arranged by chapter, is part of the "Suggestions for Further Reading and Listening" section found at the end of the book.

CHANGES TO THE SEVENTH EDITION

New Author Thomas F. X. Noble

By far the most significant development in the new edition of *The Western Humanities* is the addition of Professor Thomas F. X. Noble of The University of Notre Dame as co-author. Tom, a preeminent scholar of the late antique and early medieval periods, is author, co-author, editor, or translator of ten books, and nearly fifty articles. As a medievalist with deep understanding of the ancient world, he brings great balance to the author team. All three authors, who have known and respected each other for many years, have refined and freshened all of the chapters, especially, with Tom's help, those on the ancient and medieval worlds. Further, they have unified the text by strengthening the pedagogy across all chapters, namely by adding two new features that encourage the understanding of art and critical thinking, respectively. It is our hope that the seventh edition of *The Western Humanities* will continue to assist instructors in meeting today's teaching challenges, as well as help the next generation of students understand and claim their cultural heritage.

New Features of the Seventh Edition

We remain as committed as ever to listening to our readers for comments and suggestions for improvement. In the seventh edition, we have made significant changes on the basis of numerous in-depth reviews. They include the following:

Reorganization of the time frame for the Hellenistic world and the Roman Republic. The revised Chapter 4 now tells the story of how Rome arose and gained its cultural bearings from the late stages of the Hellenistic world.

Reorganization of Imperial Roman, Byzantine, and Early Medieval periods. In previous editions some material dealing with the Roman Empire was attached to the treatment of the Roman Republic while other material was seen as a gateway to the Middle Ages. With the Roman Republic now anchored in its Hellenistic setting, the revised Chapter 6 ("Roman Imperial Civilization and the Triumph of Christianity") treats Roman imperial civilization from the Age of Augustus to that of Justinian (31 BCE to 565 CE). This chapter also includes the triumph of Christianity and of the Catholic Church. Christianity's triumph was both a critical element in the transformation of the Roman world and a powerful legacy of that world. Finally, Chapter 6 in its new format adopts the "late antique" paradigm as an explanatory framework. As Rome was not built in a day, so it did not fall in a day. The long, slow transformation of the Roman Empire was a dynamic and creative process that extended over several centuries. With the Roman imperial material conveniently gathered into one chapter in this edition, the early Middle Ages can be accorded separate treatment. Chapter 7 ("The Heirs of the Roman Empire: Byzantium and the West in the Early Middle Ages") charts the parallel histories of Byzantium and the early medieval West. This approach permits an expanded treatment of Byzantine civilization in all its aspects and a more detailed treatment of the Age of Charlemagne, a period that was foundational for medieval Europe and for the transmittal of the Western Humanities to later ages.

New feature: Interpreting Art. We have added an **Interpreting Art** feature in response to many review-

ers' requests, but also as part of our continuing mission to bring high culture down to earth for students. This feature is introduced and explained to readers in the "Primer" as part of the overall orientation to the book. Each of the twelve Interpreting Art examples focuses on a great work of art (painting or sculpture) or architecture, using a set of six call-outs that highlight both formal qualities (how it *is* a work of art) and historical context (how it *reflects* the historical moment). We believe that students who master this feature will then be able to apply it to any work of art that they encounter.

New feature: Questions for Critical Thinking. At the end of each chapter, in response to reviewers' suggestions, we have added five **Questions for Critical Thinking.** We have tried to keep the focus in these essay questions on understanding cultural achievements within their historical setting—the basic thrust of our textbook. This pedagogical device, we believe, will assist students in their mastery of the complexities of the humanities story. These chapter-ending questions are in addition to the essay questions on view in the online **Instructor's Manual** (which is not available to students).

Revised art program. As usual, most changes to the art program in this new edition were occasioned by our desire to freshen the text. And, each illustration is discussed both in the text and in a brief caption. In Volume I (Chapters 1–11), thirty-eight art images were added, most notably in Chapters 4, 6, and 7, which cover the period from Hellenistic times to the High Middle Ages—the chapters most reshaped by Tom Noble's expertise. These additions include several floor plans and reconstructions of historic buildings along with many new visual images, including: The Ice Man, a relic from prehistoric times; *Nebamun Hunting Birds*; Ishtar Gate, Babylon; Mask of Agamemnon; Fallen Warrior, East Pediment, Aphaia, Aegina; Grave Stele of Hegeso; Achilles Painter, *Mistress and Maid*; *Sarcophagus of Junius Bassus*; Mount Athos; a page from the *Khludov Psalter*; Silver Denarius of Charlemagne; Oratory at Germigny des Prés; Christ Icon, St. Catherine's; Crucifixion Icon, St. Catherine's; Virgin and Child Apse Mosaic, Hagia Sophia; Virgin and Child Apse Mosaic, Santa Maria in Domnica; Virgin and Child Icon ("Virgin of Vladimir"); David Composing His Psalms, Paris Psalter; Interior of Hosios Loukas; Ardagh Chalice; Virgin and Child, Book of Kells; Prophet Ezra, Codex Amiatinus; Christ in Majesty, Godescalc Evangelistary; Christ in Majesty, Lorsch Gospels; Presentation Miniature, Vivian Bible; Emperor Enthroned, Gospels of Otto III; Westwork of Corvey; Night Journey of Muhammad; and Pietro Perugino, *Christ Giving the Keys to Peter.*

In Volume II (Chapters 12–22), we also added thirty-eight art images, virtually all of which are substitutions for artworks by the same artists or architects.

The new replacement illustrations include: Lucas Cranach's panel portrait of *Martin Luther*; Nicolas Poussin's *Landscape with Orpheus and Eurydice*; Judith Leyster's *Carousing Couple*; Jean-Honoré Fragonard's *The Pursuit*; Francisco Goya's *Hasta la Muerte (Until Death)*; Albert Bierstadt's *The Rocky Mountains, Lander's Peak*; Jean-Francois Millet's *The Gleaners*; Claude Monet's *Waterlilly Pond (Les Bassin des Nympheas)*; Berthe Morisot's *The Harbor at Lorient*; Paul Cezanne's *Mont Sainte-Victoire*; Pablo Picasso's *Man with a Hat* (also known as *Portrait of Braque*); Wassily Kandinsky's *Panel for Edward R. Campbell No. 4* (formerly *Painting No. 201*); Frank Lloyd Wright's Robie House; Henri Matisse's *Decorative Figure in an Oriental Setting*; Romare Bearden's *The Dove*; Jackson Pollock's *White Light*; Mark Rothko's *Orange and Yellow*; Helen Frankenthaler's *Interior Landscape*; Andy Warhol's *Elvis I & II*; and Bridget Riley's *Drift No. 2*. One of the replacement illustrations is the subject of an Interpreting Art feature: Piet Mondrian's *Composition with Blue and Yellow*. We have also introduced students to less well-known artists, such as Hans Burgkmair the Elder, the engraver G. Perelle, the book illustrator Maria Sibylla Merian, the watercolorist Joseph Nash, and the Dadaist artist Hannah Hoch, through whose works we illustrate historical and cultural developments.

TEACHING AND LEARNING RESOURCES

As instructors, we are keenly aware of the challenges encountered in teaching the humanities, especially to large, diverse classes. This text comes with a comprehensive package of supplementary resource materials, designed to help address those challenges.

Readings in the Western Humanities. In the newest edition of this book of readings—the seventh—Matthews and Platt have re-configured the chapters so as to reflect the changes made in *The Western Humanities,* 7e. The selections of primary source materials are arranged chronologically to follow the twenty-two chapters of the text, and are divided into two volumes. Volume I covers ancient Mesopotamia through the Renaissance; Volume II, the Renaissance into the twenty-first century. This anthology gives students access to our literary and philosophical heritage, allowing them to experience firsthand the ideas and voices of the great writers and thinkers of the Western tradition.

Traditions: Humanities Readings through the Ages. For instructors who would like to create their own custom readers, *Traditions* is a new database conceived as both a stand-alone product as well as a companion source to McGraw-Hill's humanities titles. The collection is broad in nature, containing both western and non-western readings, as well as both ancient and contemporary offerings, which were hand-picked from a number of different disciplines, such as literature, philosophy, and science. The flexibility of Primis Online's database allows the readings to be arranged both chronologically and by author. Visit www.primisonline .com/traditions.

Instructor's Manual. The Instructor's Manual has been revised and expanded. For each chapter the manual includes teaching strategies and suggestions; learning objectives; key cultural terms; film, reading, and Internet site suggestions; and a detailed outline revised to accompany the seventh edition of *The Western Humanities*. References to the accompanying anthology, *Readings in the Western Humanities,* are included in each chapter so that primary source material can be easily incorporated into each lesson. In addition to chapter-by-chapter materials, the Instructor's Manual offers five basic teaching strategies and seven lecture models in the preface. The Instructor's Manual is available on the Online Learning Center.

Online Learning Center (www.mhhe.com/ matthews7e). The student content for the Online Learning Center includes a link to **MyHumanitiesStudio,** where students can watch videos about various art techniques and access interactive activities designed to strengthen their understanding of visual art, dance, music, sculpture, literature, theater, architecture, and film. In addition to MyHumanitiesStudio, the Online Learning Center offers the following resources: essay, short answer, and true/false quizzes; chapter outlines; chapter objectives; key terms; and MyHumanitiesStudio exercises. We hope that this online availability will strengthen student understanding of the humanities as well as spark their own creativity.

Image Bank. Instructors can access numerous images featured in *The Western Humanities* and in many other McGraw-Hill art and humanities titles through the Image Bank, a Web-based presentation manager that allows users to easily browse and search for images and to download them for use in class presentations.

Music selections. An audio CD covers the broad spectrum of music discussed in the text and includes pieces by such composers as Hildegard of Bingen, J. S. Bach, Igor Stravinsky, and Philip Glass.

ACKNOWLEDGMENTS

We are grateful to many people for their help and support in this revision of *The Western Humanities*. Roy Matthews and DeWitt Platt continue to appreciate the many insightful comments of students and former students at Michigan State University over the years. Tom Noble is grateful to his thousands of students for all they have taught him over thirty-five years. He is also pleased, and humbled, at being asked to lend a hand in crafting a new edition of a wonderful and successful book.

This seventh edition has been a learning experience for the three of us, but, at the end of the day, we have bonded together into a mutually supportive team. We are grateful to Art Pomponio for his reasonable responses and calming voice. To our McGraw-Hill handlers, we want to single out Rhona Robbin for her leadership on this project. Rhona was easy to work with, and, when there was a question outside her sphere, she knew where to turn to get a quick solution. Kudos, Rhona! We also praise Leslie Racanelli for her wise guidance through a few difficult patches this time around; you have been a great source of wisdom for us authors. And, special thanks to the rest of the McGraw-Hill team—Chris Freitag, Betty Chen, Brian Pecko, Allister Fein, Louis Swaim, Pam Cooper, Elena Mackawgy, Sarah Remington, and to the entire editorial and production crews.

ACKNOWLEDGMENT OF REVIEWERS

This edition continues to reflect many insightful suggestions made by reviewers of the first six editions. The current edition has benefited from constructive and thorough evaluations offered by the faculty listed below. We believe that, because of the changes their reviews inspired, we have produced a better, more usable textbook. Reviewers, we salute you! The reviewers include the following:

Jonathan Austad, Chadron State College
Richard Baskin, Gordon College
Penelope A. Blake, Rock Valley College

Kurt Blaugher, Mount Saint Mary's College
Dan Brooks, Aquinas College–Michigan
John Chamberlain, Saint Petersburg College–Gibbs
Cynthia Clements, Richland College
Kevin DeLapp, Converse College
May Dubois, West Los Angeles College
Andrew J. Grover, Thiel College
Richard Hall, Texas State University–San Marcos
John Hardin, Hillsborough Community College–Brandon
Jason Horn, Gordon College
Luke Howard, Brigham Young University–Provo
Cheryl Hughes, Tulsa Community College
Derek Jensen, Brigham Young University–Idaho
Prudence Jones, Montclair State University
Susan Jones, Palm Beach Atlantic University
Kim Justesen, Utah Career College
Richard Kortum, East Tennessee State University
Barbara Kramer, Santa Fe Community College
Connie LaMarca-Frankel, Pasco-Hernando Community College
Diana Lurz, Rogers State University
Ruth Miller, Diablo Valley College
James Mock, University of Central Oklahoma
Margaret Worsham Musgrove, University of Central Oklahoma
Victoria Neubeck-O'Connor, Moraine Valley Community College
Kaliopi Pappas, San Joaquin Delta College
Douglass Scott, Chattanooga State Tech
Sonia Sorrell, Pepperdine University
Deborah Sowell, Brigham Young University–Provo
Michael Sparks, Wallace State University
Alice Taylor, West Los Angeles College
Margaret Urie, University of Nevada–Reno
Theresa A. Vaughan, University of Central Oklahoma
Paul B. Weinstein, The University of Akron Wayne College
Jason Whitmarsh, St. John's River Community College

INTRODUCTION
Why Study Cultural History?

To be ignorant of what occurred before you were born is to remain always a child.

—CICERO, FIRST CENTURY BCE

Anyone who cannot give an account to oneself of the past three thousand years remains in darkness, without experience, living from day to day.

—GOETHE, NINETEENTH CENTURY CE

The underlying premise of this book is that some basic knowledge of the Western cultural heritage is necessary for those who want to become educated human beings in charge of their own destinies. If people are not educated into their place in human history—five thousand years of relatively uninterrupted, though sometimes topsy-turvy, developments—then they are rendered powerless, subject to passing fads and outlandish beliefs. They become vulnerable to the flattery of demagogues who promise heaven on earth, or they fall prey to the misconception that present-day events are unique, without precedent in history, or superior to everything that has gone before.

Perhaps the worst that can happen is to exist in a limbo of ignorance—in Goethe's words, "living from day to day." Without knowledge of the past and the perspective it brings, people may come to believe that their contemporary world will last forever, when in reality much of it is doomed to be forgotten. In contrast to the instant obsolescence of popular culture, the study of Western culture offers an alternative that has passed the unforgiving test of time. Long after today's heroes and celebrities have fallen into oblivion, the achievements of our artistic and literary ancestors—those who have forged the Western tradition—will remain. Their works echo down the ages and seem fresh

in every period. The ancient Roman writer Seneca put it well when he wrote, in the first century CE, "Life is short but art is long."

When people realize that the rich legacy of Western culture is their own, their view of themselves and the times they live in can expand beyond the present moment. They find that they need not be confined by the limits of today but can draw on the creative insights of people who lived hundreds and even thousands of years ago. They discover that their own culture has a history and a context that give it meaning and shape. Studying and experiencing their cultural legacy can help them understand their place in today's world.

THE BOUNDARIES OF THE WEST

The subject of this text is Western culture, but what exactly do we mean, first, by "culture" and, second, by the "West"? *Culture* is a term with several meanings, but we use it here to mean the artistic and intellectual expressions of a people, their creative achievements. By the *West* we mean that part of the globe that lies west of Asia and Asia Minor and north of Africa, especially Europe—the geographical framework for much of this study.

The Western tradition is not confined exclusively to Europe as defined today, however. The contributions of peoples who lived beyond the boundaries of present-day Europe are also included in Western culture, either because they were forerunners of the West, such as those who created the first civilizations in Mesopotamia and Egypt, or because they were part of the West for periods of time, such as those who lived in the North African and Near Eastern lands bordering the Mediterranean Sea during the Roman and early Christian eras. Regardless of geography, Western culture draws deeply from ideals forged in these lands.

When areas that had been part of the Western tradition at one time were absorbed into other cultural traditions—as happened in the seventh century in Mesopotamia, Egypt, and North Africa when the people embraced the Muslim faith—then they are generally no longer included in Western cultural history. Because of the enormous influence of Islamic civilization on Western civilization, however, we do include in this volume both an account of Islamic history and a description and appreciation of Islamic culture. Different in many ways from our own, the rich tradition of Islam has an important place in today's world.

After about 1500, with voyages and explorations reaching the farthest parts of the globe, the European focus of Western culture that had held for centuries began to dissolve. Starting from this time, the almost exclusively European mold was broken and Western values and ideals began to be exported throughout the world, largely through the efforts of missionaries, soldiers, colonists, and merchants. Coinciding with this development and further complicating the pattern of change were the actions of those who imported and enslaved countless numbers of black Africans to work on plantations in North and South America. The interplay of Western culture with many previously isolated cultures, whether desired or not, forever changed all who were touched by the process.

The Westernization of the globe that has been going on ever since 1500 is perhaps the dominant theme of our time. What human greed, missionary zeal, and dreams of empire failed to accomplish before 1900 has been achieved since through modern technology, the media, and popular culture. The world today is a global village, much of it dominated by Western values and styles of life. In our time, Westernization has become a two-way interchange. When artists and writers from other cultures adopt Western forms or ideas, they are not only Westernizing their own traditions but also injecting fresh sensibilities and habits of thought into the Western tradition. The globalization of culture means that a South American novel or a Japanese film can be as accessible to Western audiences as a European painting, and yet carry with it an intriguingly new vocabulary of cultural symbols and meanings.

HISTORICAL PERIODS AND CULTURAL STYLES

In cultural history, the past is often divided into historical periods and cultural styles. A historical period is an interval of time that has a certain unity because it is characterized by the prevalence of a unique culture, ideology, or technology, or because it is bounded by defining historical events, such as the death of a military leader like Alexander the Great or a political upheaval like the French Revolution. A cultural style is a combination of features of artistic or literary expression, execution, or performance that defines a particular school or era. A historical period may have the identical time frame as a cultural style, or it may embrace more than one style simultaneously or two styles successively. Each chapter of this survey focuses on a historical

Timeline 1   THE ANCIENT WORLD

3000 BCE					1200	800		500	323	146	31		500 CE
Mesopotamian and Egyptian Civilizations; Precursors of Greece								Greek Civilization					
									Roman Civilization				
MAJOR HISTORICAL PERIODS													
Mesopotamian and Egyptian; Minoan and Mycenaean								Greek Archaic	Classical (Hellenic)	Helle- nistic		Imperial Roman	
								Etruscan and Greek Influences		Helle- nistic			
CULTURAL STYLES													

Timeline 2   THE MEDIEVAL WORLD

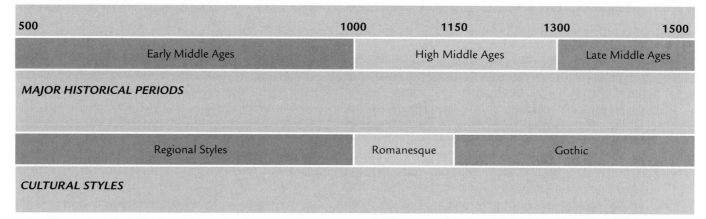

500		1000	1150	1300	1500
Early Middle Ages			High Middle Ages		Late Middle Ages

MAJOR HISTORICAL PERIODS

Regional Styles		Romanesque	Gothic

CULTURAL STYLES

period and includes significant aspects of culture—usually the arts, architecture, literature, religion, music, and philosophy—organized around a discussion of the relevant style or styles appropriate to that time.

The survey begins with prehistory, the era before writing was invented, setting forth the emergence of human beings from an obscure past. After the appearance of writing in about 3000 BCE, the Western cultural heritage is divided into three sweeping historical periods: ancient, medieval, and modern.

The ancient period dates from 3000 BCE to 500 CE (Timeline 1). During these thirty-five hundred years the light of Western civilization begins to shine in Mesopotamia and Egypt, shines more brightly still in Greece and Rome, from the eighth century BCE, until it begins to dim with the collapse of the Roman Empire in 500 CE. Coinciding with these historical periods are the cultural styles of Mesopotamia; Egypt; Greece, including Archaic, classical (or Hellenic), and Hellenistic styles; and imperial Rome.

The medieval period, or the Middle Ages, covers events between 500 and 1500 CE, a one-thousand-year span that is further divided into three subperiods (Timeline 2). The early Middle Ages (500–1000) is typified by frequent barbarian invasions and political chaos so that civilization itself is threatened and barely survives. No single international style characterizes this turbulent period, though several regional styles flourish. The High Middle Ages (1000–1300) is a period of stability and the zenith of medieval culture. Two successive styles appear, the Romanesque and the Gothic, with the latter dominating culture for the rest of the medieval period. The late Middle Ages (1300–1500) is a transitional period in which the medieval age is dying and the modern age is struggling to be born.

The modern period begins in about 1400 (there is often overlap between historical periods) and continues today (Timeline 3). With the advent of the modern period, a new way of defining historical changes starts to make more sense—the division of history

Timeline 3   THE MODERN WORLD

1400	1500	1520	1600	1700	1770	1800	1870	1900	1970	2010
Renaissance		Reformation		Scientific Revolution		Enlightenment	Romanticism		Modernism	Post-modernism

MAJOR MOVEMENTS

Renaissance		Mannerism		Baroque	Rococo	Romantic		Modern	Post-modern
						Neoclassical			

CULTURAL STYLES

into movements, the activities of large groups of people united to achieve a common goal. The modern period consists of waves of movements that aim to change the world in some specific way.

The first modern movement is the Renaissance (1400–1600), or "rebirth," which attempts to revive the cultural values of ancient Greece and Rome. It is accompanied by two successive styles, Renaissance and mannerism. The next significant movement is the Reformation (1500–1600), which is dedicated to restoring Christianity to the ideals of the early church set forth in the Bible. Although it does not spawn a specific style, this religious upheaval does have a profound impact on the subjects of the arts and literature and the way they are expressed, especially in the mannerist style.

The Reformation is followed by the Scientific Revolution (1600–1700), a movement that results in the abandonment of ancient science and the birth of modern science. Radical in its conclusions, the Scientific Revolution is somewhat out of touch with the style of its age, which is known as the baroque. This magnificent style is devoted to overwhelming the senses through theatrical and sensuous effects and is associated with the attempts of the Roman Catholic Church to reassert its authority in the world.

The Scientific Revolution gives impetus to the Enlightenment (1700–1800), a movement that pledges to reform politics and society according to the principles of the new science. In stylistic terms the eighteenth century is schizophrenic, dominated first by the rococo, an extravagant and fanciful style that represents the last phase of the baroque, and then by the neoclassical, a style inspired by the works of ancient Greece and Rome and reflective of the principles of the Scientific Revolution. Before the eighteenth century is over, the Enlightenment calls forth its antithesis, romanticism (1770–1870), a movement centered on feeling, fantasy, and everything that cannot be proven scientifically. The romantic style, marked by a revived taste for the Gothic and a love of nature, is the perfect accompaniment to this movement.

Toward the end of the nineteenth century, modernism (1870–1970) arises, bent on destroying every vestige of both the Greco-Roman tradition and the Christian faith and on fashioning new ways of understanding that are independent of the past. Since 1970, postmodernism has emerged, a movement that tries to make peace with the past by embracing old forms of expression while adopting a global and multivoiced perspective. Although every cultural period is marked by innovation and creativity, our treatment of them in this book varies somewhat, with more space and greater weight given to the achievements of certain times. We make these adjustments because some periods or styles are more significant than others, es-

pecially in the defining influence that their achievements have had on our own era. For example, some styles seem to tower over the rest, such as classicism in fifth-century BCE Greece, the High Renaissance of sixteenth century Italy, and modernism in the mid–twentieth century, as compared with other styles, such as that of the early Middle Ages or the seventeenth-century baroque.

AN INTEGRATED APPROACH TO CULTURAL HISTORY

Our approach to the Western heritage in this book is to root cultural achievements in their historical settings, showing how the material conditions—the political, social, and economic events of each period—influenced their creation. About one third of each chapter is devoted to an interpretive discussion of material history, and the remaining two thirds are devoted to the arts, architecture, philosophy, religion, literature, and music of the period. These two aspects of history do not occur separately, of course, and one of our aims is to show how they are intertwined.

As just one example of this integrated approach, consider the Gothic cathedral, that lofty, light-filled house of worship marked by pointed arches, towering spires, and radiant stained-glass windows. Gothic cathedrals were erected during the High Middle Ages, following a bleak period when urban life had virtually ceased. Although religion was still the dominant force in European life, trade was starting to flourish once again, town life was reviving, and urban dwellers were beginning to prosper. In part as testimonials to their new wealth, cities and towns commissioned architects and hired workers to erect these soaring churches, which dominated the landscape for miles around and proclaimed the economic well-being of their makers.

We adopt an integrated approach to Western culture not just in considering how the arts are related to material conditions but also in looking for the common themes, aspirations, and ideas that permeate the artistic and literary expressions of every individual era. The creative accomplishments of an age tend to reflect a shared perspective, even when that perspective is not explicitly recognized at the time. Thus, each period possesses a unique outlook that can be analyzed in the cultural record. A good example of this phenomenon is classical Greece in the fifth century BCE, when the ideal of moderation, or balance in all things, played a major role in sculpture, architecture, philosophy, religion, and tragic drama. The cultural record in other periods is not always as clear as that in ancient Greece, but shared qualities can often be uncovered that distinguish the varied aspects of culture in an era to form a unifying thread.

A corollary of this idea is that creative individuals and their works are very much influenced by the times in which they live. This is not to say that incomparable geniuses—such as Shakespeare in Renaissance England—do not appear and rise above their own ages, speaking directly to the human mind and heart in every age that follows. Yet even Shakespeare reflected the political attitudes and social patterns of his time. Though a man for the ages, he still regarded monarchy as the correct form of government and women as the inferiors of men.

THE SELECTION OF CULTURAL WORKS

The Western cultural heritage is vast, and any selection of works for a survey text reflects choices made by the authors. All the works we chose to include have had a significant impact on Western culture, but for different reasons. We chose some because they blazed a new trail, such as Picasso's *Demoiselles d'Avignon* (see Figure 19.22), which marked the advent of cubism in painting, or Fielding's *Tom Jones,* one of the earliest novels. Other works were included because they seemed to embody a style to perfection, such as the regal statue called *Poseidon* (or *Zeus*) (see Figure 3.20), executed in the classical style of fifth-century-BCE Athens, or Dante's *Divine Comedy,* which epitomized the ideals of the High Middle Ages. On occasion, we chose works on a particular topic, such as the biblical story of David and Goliath, and demonstrated how different sculptors interpreted it, as in sculptures by

Donatello (see Figure 11.11), Verrocchio (see Figure 11.12), and Michelangelo (see Figure 12.18). Still other works caught our attention because they served as links between successive styles, as is the case with Giotto's frescoes (see Figure 10.19), or because they represented the end of an age or an artistic style, as in the *Colossal Statue of Constantine* (see Figure 6.21). Finally, we included some works, especially paintings, simply because of their great beauty, such as the Byzantine Icon of the Virgin and Child (see Figure 7.11). Through all the ages of Western cultural history, through all the shifting styles and tastes embodied in painting, sculpture, architecture, poetry, and song, there glows a creative spark that can be found in human beings in every period. This diversity is a hallmark of the Western experience, and we celebrate it in this book.

A CHALLENGE TO THE READER

The purpose of all education is and should be self-knowledge. This goal was first established by the ancient Greeks in their injunction to "Know thyself," the inscription carved above the entrance to Apollo's temple at Delphi. Self-knowledge means awareness of oneself and one's place in society and the world. Reaching this goal is not easy, because becoming an educated human being is a lifelong process, requiring time, energy, and commitment. But all journeys begin with a single step, and we intend this volume as a first step toward understanding and defining oneself in terms of one's historical and cultural heritage. Our challenge to the reader is to use this book to begin the long journey to self-knowledge.

A HUMANITIES PRIMER
How to Understand the Arts

INTRODUCTION

We can all appreciate the arts. We can find pleasure or interest in paintings, music, poems, novels, films, and other art forms, both contemporary and historical. We don't need to know very much about art to know what we like, because we bring ourselves to the work: What we like has as much to do with who we are as with the art itself.

Many of us, for example, will respond positively to a painting like Leonardo da Vinci's *The Virgin of the Rocks.* The faces of the Madonna and angel are lovely; we may have seen images like these on Christmas cards or in other commercial reproductions. We respond with what English poet William Wordsworth calls the "first careless rapture," which activates our imaginations and establishes a connection between us and the work of art. However, if this is all we see, if we never move from a subjective reaction, we can only appreciate the surface, the immediate form, and then, perhaps subconsciously, accept without question the values it implies. We appreciate, but we do not understand.

Sometimes we cannot appreciate because we do not understand. We may reject Picasso's *Les Demoiselles d'Avignon*, for it presents us with images of women that we may not be able to recognize. These women may make us uncomfortable, and the values they imply may frighten us rather than please or reassure us. Rather than rapture, we may experience disgust; but when we realize that this painting is considered a groundbreaking work, we may wonder what we're missing and be willing to look deeper. (*The Virgin of the Rocks* and *Les Demoiselles d'Avignon* are discussed in the text on pages 329–331 and pages 584 and 586, respectively.)

LEONARDO DA VINCI. *The Virgin of the Rocks.*

To understand a work of art (a building, a poem, a song, a symphony), we need to keep our "rapture" (our emotional response and connection) but make it less "careless," less superficial and subjective, less restricted to that which we recognize. We need to enrich our appreciation by searching for a meaning that goes beyond ourselves and which involves understanding:

- The intent of the goal of the artist
- The elements of form present in the work
- The ways in which the various elements contribute to the artist's goal
- The context within which the artwork evolved
- The connections of the work to other works

APPROACHES TO THE ANALYSIS OF LITERATURE, ART, AND MUSIC

To analyze a work of art, we want to identify the intent of the work, and we want to evaluate its execution. Thus, we can examine the formal elements of the work—an approach known as formalism—and we can explore its context—known as contextualism.

Formalism

A formal analysis is concerned with the aesthetic (artistic) elements of a work separate from context. This type of analysis focuses on medium and technique:

- A formal analysis of a painting, sculpture, or architectural structure examines its line, shape, color, texture, and composition, as well as the artist's technical ability within the medium used; it is not concerned with anything extraneous to the work itself.
- A formal analysis of a literary work, such as a short story or novel, explores the relationships among theme, plot, characters, and setting, as well as how well the resources of language—word choice, tone, imagery, and symbol—are used to support the other elements.
- A formal analysis of a film explores theme, plot, characters (as developed both verbally and non-verbally), and setting, as well as how the resources of cinematography—camera techniques, lighting, sound, editing, and costumes—support the other elements.

A formal analysis of *The Virgin of the Rocks* examines the artist's use of perspective, the arrangement of figures as they relate to each other and to the grotto that surrounds them, the technical use of color and line,

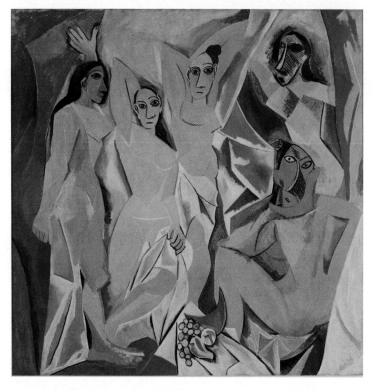

PABLO PICASSO. *Les Demoiselles d'Avignon.*

the dramatic interplay of light and shadow (known as *chiaroscuro*). The same technical considerations are explored in a formal analysis of *Les Demoiselles d'Avignon.* That the two paintings were completed in 1483 and 1907, respectively, is important only in terms of the technology and mediums available to the artists. In a formal analysis, time and place exist only within the work.

Contextualism

Unlike formalism, contextualism requires that a work be understood in its time and place. Contextual analysis focuses on what is outside the work:

- The artistic, social, cultural, historical, and political forces, events, and trends
- The artist's intent and motives in creating the work
- How the work fits in with other works of the same genre of the same or different eras
- How the work fits in with the rest of the artist's body of work

A contextual analysis of the da Vinci and Picasso paintings would include information about where and when each painting was completed; the conditions from which it arose; the prevailing artistic styles of the times; the life circumstances of the artists; and so on. The paintings alone do not provide enough information for contextual inquiry. Similarly, contextual analysis of a novel by Dostoyevsky would consider both his personal circumstances and the conditions in Russia and Europe when he wrote. A contextual analysis of a chorale and fugue by Bach would include information on Bach's life, his religious beliefs, and the political climate of Germany in the eighteenth century.

An Integrated Approach

In a strictly contextual analysis of an artwork, the work itself can sometimes be lost in the exploration of context. In a strictly formal analysis, important knowledge that can contribute to understanding may remain unknown. The most effective analyses, therefore, combine and integrate the two approaches, examining the formal elements of the work and exploring the context within which it was created. A work of art, whether a poem or a painting, a cathedral or a cantata, is a complex entity, as are the relationships it fosters between the artist and the art and between the art and its audience. The integrative approach recognizes these relationships and their complexity. This is the approach to artistic and cultural analysis most frequently used in *The Western Humanities.*

A Variety of Perspectives

Many students and critics of culture are also interested in looking at things from a particular perspective, a set of interests or a way of thinking that informs and influences their investigations and interpretations. Common perspectives are the psychological, the feminist, the religious, the economic, and the historical.

- A *psychological* perspective looks for meaning in the psychological features of the work, such as sexual and symbolic associations—in effect, a kind of retroactive psychological analysis of the artist. This perspective might also examine the facial expressions, gestures, and body positions of Mary and the angel in *The Virgin of the Rocks,* or it might be interested in da Vinci's attitudes toward women and his relationship with them.

- A *feminist* perspective examines the art itself and the context in which it arises from a woman's point of view. This perspective also asks how the work depicts women, what it says about women and their relationships in general, and how it may or

may not reflect a patriarchal society. Many critics have discussed the apparent hatred of women that seems evident in Picasso's *Les Demoiselles d'Avignon.* At the same time, the work, in its size (8 feet by 7 feet 8 inches) and in the unblinking attitude of its subjects, suggests that these women have a kind of raw power. Feminist critics focus on such considerations.

- A *religious* perspective is often appropriate when a work of art originates in a religious context. The soaring spires and cruciform floor plans of medieval cathedrals reveal religious meaning, as do Renaissance paintings depicting biblical characters. Religious analyses look to the use of symbolism, the representation of theological doctrines and beliefs, and intercultural connections and influences for meaning.

- An *economic* perspective on a work of art focuses on its economic content—the roles and relationships associated with wealth. Often drawing upon Marx's contention that class is the defining consideration in all human relationships and endeavors, an economic analysis examines both purpose and content: the artwork created as a display of power by the rich, as a depiction of people of different classes, and as an indicator of the distribution of wealth.

- Perhaps the most encompassing of all perspectives is the historical, because it includes explorations of psychological, religious, and economic issues, as well as questions about class and gender in various times and places. Historical analysis requires an understanding of the significant events of the time and how they affect the individual and shape the culture. *The Western Humanities* most often takes a historical perspective in its views of art and culture.

The Vocabulary of Analysis

Certain terms and concepts are fundamental to the analysis of any artwork:

- **Audience** is the group for whom a work of art, architecture, literature, drama, film, or music is intended. The audience may be a single person, a small group of people , or a special group with common interests or education.

- **Composition** is the arrangement of constituent elements in an individual work. In music, composition also refers to the process of creating the work.

- **Content** is the subject matter of the work; content can be based on mythology, religion, history, current events, personal history, or almost any idea or feeling deemed appropriate by the artist.

- **Context** is the setting in which the art arose, its own time and place. Context includes the political, economic, social, and cultural conditions of the time; it can also include the personal conditions and circumstances that shape the artist's vision.

- A **convention** is an agreed-upon practice, device, technique, or form. A sonnet, for example, is a fourteen-line poem with certain specified rhyme schemes. A poem is not a sonnet unless it follows this formal convention. A convention of the theater is the "willing suspension of disbelief": we know that the events taking place before our eyes are not real, but we agree to believe in them for the duration of the play.

- **Genre** is the type or class to which a work of art, literature, drama, or music belongs, depending on its style, form, or content. In literature, for example, the novel is a genre in itself; the short story is another genre. In music, symphonies, operas, and tone poems are all different genres.

- The **medium** is the material from which an art object is made—marble or bronze, for example, in sculpture, or watercolors or oils in painting. (The plural of *medium* in this sense is often *mediums*; when *medium* is used to refer to a means of mass communication, such as radio or television, the plural is *media*.)

- **Style** is the combination of distinctive elements of creative execution and expression, in terms of both form and content. Artists, artistic schools, movements, and periods can be characterized by their style. Styles often evolve out of existing styles, or in reaction to styles that are perceived as worn out or excessive.

- **Technique** refers to the systematic procedure whereby a particular creative task is performed. For example, a dancer's technique is the way he or she executes leaps and turns; a painter's technique is the way he or she applies paint to a canvas with broad, swirling brushstrokes.

- The **theme** is the dominant idea of a work, the message or emotion the artist intends to convey. The theme, then, is the embodiment of the artist's intent. In a novel, for example, the theme is the abstract concept that is made concrete by character, plot, setting, and other linguistic and structural elements of the work.

These general concepts and terms are supplemented by the more specific terms that will be introduced in the following literary, artistic, and musical sections.

LITERARY ANALYSIS

Literary analysis begins with a consideration of various literary genres and forms. A work of literature is written either in **prose,** the ordinary language used in speaking and writing, or in **poetry,** a more imaginative and concentrated form of expression usually marked by meter, rhythm, or rhyme. Prose is often divided into nonfiction (essays, biography, autobiography) and fiction (short stories, novels).

In literature, *genre* refers both to form—essay, short story, novel, poem, play, film script, television script—and to specific type within a form—tragedy, comedy, epic, and lyric.

- **Tragedy,** according to Aristotle, must have a tragic hero—a person of high stature who is brought down by his or her own excessive pride *(hubris);* this person doesn't necessarily die at the end, but whatever his or her greatness was based upon is lost.

- **Comedy** is a story with a complicated and amusing plot; it usually ends with a happy and peaceful resolution of any conflicts.

- An **epic** poem, novel, or film is a relatively long recounting of the life of a hero or the glorious history of a people.

- A **lyric** poem is a short, subjective poem usually expressing an intense personal emotion.

- **Theme** is the message or emotion that the author wishes to convey. In an essay the theme is articulated as the thesis: the idea or conclusion that the essay will prove or support. In a novel, story, or play, we infer the theme from the content and the development of ideas and imagery.

- **Plot,** in fiction, is the action of the story. There may be a primary plot that becomes the vehicle by which the theme is expressed, with subplots related to secondary (or even tertiary) themes. Plot can be evaluated by how well it supports the theme.

- **Characters** provide the human focus, the embodiment, of the theme; they act out and are affected by the plot. The protagonist, or primary character, of the work is changed by the dramatic action of the plot and thus is a dynamic character; static characters remain unchanged throughout the story. An antagonist is a character in direct opposition to the protagonist. Some characters are stock characters, representing a type rather than an individual human being.

- The **setting** is the background against which the action takes place. It can include the geographical location, the environment (political, social, economic) in which the characters live, the historical time in which the action takes place, and the culture and customs of the time, place, and people.

- The **narrator** tells the story or poem from his or her point of view. The narrator is not necessarily identical with the author of the work. The narrator (or **narrative voice**) can be examined and analyzed like any other element of the work. When a narrator seems to know everything and is not limited by time or place, the work has an omniscient point of view. Such a narrator tells us what everyone is thinking, feeling, and doing. When the story is told from the perspective of a single character who can relate only what he or she knows or witnesses, the work has a first-person point of view. Such a narrator is limited in his or her understanding. Thus, we need to consider the narrator in order to judge how accurate or complete the narrative is.

A literary analysis of a drama, whether a play for the stage or a film script, will consider not only the elements already mentioned—theme, plot, character, setting, language, and so on—but also the technical considerations specific to the form. In theater, these would include the work of the director, who interprets the play and directs the actors, as well as stage design, light and sound design, costumes, makeup, and so on. In film, technical considerations would include direction, editing, cinematography, musical score, special effects, and so on.

Let's turn now to a poem by Shakespeare and see how to approach it to enrich our understanding. Identifying a poem's intent and evaluating its execution is called an *explication,* from the French *explication de texte.* An explication is a detailed analysis of a poem's meaning, focusing on narrative voice, setting, rhyme, meter, words, and images. An explication begins with what is immediately evident about the poem as a whole, followed by a more careful examination of its parts.

William Shakespeare (1564–1616) was not just a great playwright; he was also a great poet. His works portray human emotions, motives, and relationships that we recognize today as well as the conditions and concerns of his time. In this sense, they are an example of aesthetic universality, the enduring connection between a work of art and its audience.

Shakespeare's sonnets are his most personal work. Scholars disagree about whether they are generic love poems or are addressed to a specific person and, if the latter, who that person might be. Formally, an English (or Shakespearean) sonnet is a 14-line poem consisting of three 4-line stanzas, or quatrains, each with its own rhyme scheme, and a concluding 2-line stanza, or couplet, that provides commentary on the preceding stanzas. The rhyme scheme in a Shakespearean sonnet is abab cdcd efef gg; that is, the first and third lines

of each quatrain rhyme with each other, as do the second and fourth lines, though the rhymes are different in each quatrain. The last two lines rhyme with each other.

The meter of most Shakespearean sonnets is iambic pentameter; that is, each line has five feet, or units ("pentameter"), and each foot consists of an iamb, an unaccented syllable followed by an accented syllable (as in *alone*). An example of iambic pentameter is "My mistress' eyes are nothing like the sun"; each foot consists of an unaccented and an accented syllable, and there are five feet. Unrhymed iambic pentameter—the verse of most of Shakespeare's plays—is known as **blank verse.**

Sonnet 130 ("My mistress' eyes are nothing like the sun") is a poem that not only illustrates sonnet form but also showcases Shakespeare's wit and his attitude toward certain conventions of his time. The poem was originally written in Elizabethan English, which looks and sounds quite different from modern English. We reproduce it in modern English, as is customary today for Shakespeare's works.

Sonnet 130

My mistress' eyes are nothing like the sun;
Coral is far more red than her lips' red;
If snow be white, why then her breasts are dun;
If hairs be wires, black wires grow on her head.
I have seen roses damask'd, red and white,
But no such roses see I in her cheeks,
And in some perfumes is there more delight
Than in the breath that from my mistress reeks.
I love to hear her speak, yet well I know
That music hath a far more pleasing sound;
I grant I never saw a goddess go,
My mistress when she walks treads on the ground.
And yet, by heaven, I think my love as rare
As any she belied with false compare.

Because the poet's intent may not be immediately evident, paraphrasing each line or stanza can point the reader to the theme or meaning intended by the poet. Let's begin, then, by paraphrasing the lines:

My mistress' eyes are nothing like the sun;
The speaker's lover's eyes are not bright.
Coral is far more red than her lips' red;
Her lips are not very red, certainly not as red as coral.
If snow be white, why then her breasts are dun;
Her breasts are mottled in color, not as white as snow.
If hairs be wires, black wires grow on her head.
Her hair is black (not blond, as was the conventional beauty standard then, when poets referred to women's hair as "golden wires").
I have seen roses damask'd, red and white,
But no such roses see I in her cheeks,
Her cheeks are not rosy.
And in some perfumes is there more delight
Than in the breath that from my mistress reeks.

> *Her breath doesn't smell as sweet as perfume.*
> I love to hear her speak, yet well I know
> That music hath a far more pleasing sound;
> *Her voice doesn't sound as melodious as music.*
> I grant I never saw a goddess go,
> My mistress when she walks treads on the ground.
> *Although the speaker has never seen a goddess walk,*
> *he knows his lover does not float above ground, as*
> *goddesses are supposed to do, but walks on the ground,*
> *a mortal woman.*
> And yet, by heaven, I think my love as rare
> As any she belied with false compare.
> *His lover is as rare and valuable as any idealized*
> *woman glorified by false poetic comparisons.*

Remember that to analyze a poem, we ask questions like, What is the theme of the poem, the poet's intent? How does Shakespeare support his point with specific images? From the paraphrased lines it is clear that the narrator is stating that his love is a real woman who walks upon the ground, not an unattainable ideal to be worshiped from afar. Idealized qualities are irrelevant to how he feels about her; the qualities he loves are the ones that make her human.

Closely examining each line of a poem helps to reveal the rhyme scheme (abab cdcd efef gg), the meter (iambic pentameter), and thus the form of the poem (sonnet). Explication of the formal elements of the poem would also include examining the use of language (such as word choice, imagery, comparisons, metaphors), the tone of the narrative voice, and so on.

To understand the context of the poem, we would consider the cultural climate of the time (was "courtly love" a prevalent cultural theme?); common contemporary poetic conventions (were many other poets proclaiming their eternal love for idealized women?); and the political, social, and economic conditions (what roles were open to women in Elizabethan England, and how were they changing? What influence might Queen Elizabeth have had on the poet's point of view? What comments about his society is Shakespeare making?).

Finally, we might consider how honest and accurate we find the emotional content of the poem to be, how relevant its truth. Are Shakespeare's observations germane to today, a time when the mass media present us with a nearly unattainable ideal as the epitome of female beauty?

❦ FINE ARTS ANALYSIS

As with literature, knowledge of a particular vocabulary helps us "speak the language" of art critics. The terms introduced here are in addition to those discussed earlier, such as *medium* and *technique*. They apply to all the visual arts, including drawing and painting, sculpture—the art of shaping material (such as wood, stone, or marble) into three-dimensional works of art—and architecture—the art and science of designing, planning, and building structures, usually for human habitation. In architecture, the critic would also pay attention to the blending of artistry and functionality (how well the structure fulfills its purpose).

- **Representational art** is true to human perception and presents a likeness of the world much as it appears to the naked eye.
- **Perspective** is the appearance of depth and distance on a two-dimensional surface.
- **Abstract art** presents a subjective view of the world, the artist's emotions or ideas; some abstract art simply presents color, line, or shape for its own sake.

The formal elements of visual art include the following:

- **Line** is the mark made by the artist, whether with pencil, pen, or paintbrush. Lines can be straight or curved, thick or thin, light or dark, spare or plentiful.
- **Color** is the use in the artwork of hues found in nature; color can enhance the sense of reality presented in a visual image, or it can distort it, depending on how it is used. The primary colors are red, blue, and yellow, and the secondary colors are orange (a combination of red and yellow), green (a combination of yellow and blue), and purple (a combination of blue and red).
- **Composition** is the artist's arrangement of elements within the artwork. Through the composition the artist leads us to see the artwork in a particular way.
- The **setting** of an artwork is the time and place depicted in a representational work, as defined by visual cues, such as the people, their dress, their activity, the time of day, and the season of the year.

New Feature: Interpreting Art

In this seventh edition, we introduce a new feature, Interpreting Art, which will assist students in understanding the visual arts and architecture. Drawing on the analytical terms and categories of the fine arts, which are set forth above, this new feature will serve as a tool to further unify the text. To this end, we include twelve units of the Interpreting Art feature, with six instances each in Volume I and Volume II. Following an integrative approach to an understanding of a work of art or architecture—blending formal analysis with contextual analysis—our Interpreting Art

INTERPRETING ART

Form Verticality is the dominant form, as in the vertical line of the skull, the skull's vertical crack, and the band of black, running from top to bottom. The skull's horns form a horizontal line, thus adding a crosslike shape.

Color The colors are neutral—shades of black, gray, cream, and white. Inside the skull, darker hues—tan and ochre—cause it to stand out from the muted background.

Setting The cow's skull evokes the stark desert landscape of Taos, New Mexico, where the work was painted.

Religious Perspective Renaissance artists used human skulls to remind viewers of their mortality, and, here, the cow's skull suggests the unforgiving nature of the desert.

Psychological Perspective The overall feeling is one of contemplation: the pairing of incongruous objects—cow's skull and artificial flowers—reminds the viewer of the intimate relationships between life and death, beauty and ugliness, art and nature.

Depth Perception The work's surface is shallow and flat, a typical feature of modernist art. The skull appears to float in the foreground, and, at the same time, the black band seems to open into a mysterious space that recedes from the viewer.

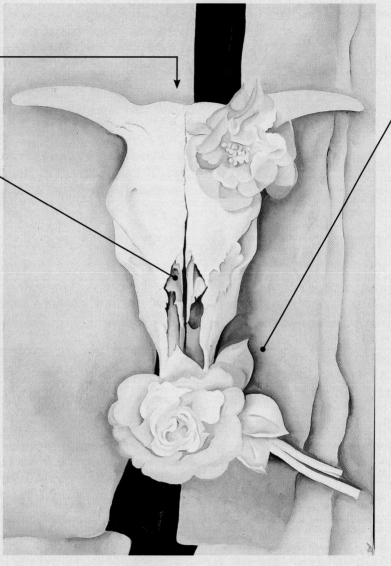

Interpretive Art figure primer 1.1 GEORGIA O'KEEFFE. *Cow's Skull with Calico Roses.* Oil on canvas, 36⁵/₁₆ × 24¹/₈". 1932. *Georgia O'Keeffe's passion for nature was inspired by a childhood on a Wisconsin farm. Her mature artistic style blended realism and abstraction. Her artistic trademark, as shown here: the abstraction of an object from nature, which she then painted according to her inner vision.*

feature offers a model that students can apply to any work of art, whether in the textbook or when they visit art galleries and museums. To demonstrate this new feature, we offer the above example: *Cow's Skull with Calico Roses* by the American artist Georgia O'Keeffe (1887–1986), painted in 1932.

Students, please note: the six categories used in the above illustration are simply "one take" and are not meant to be definitive. Other analytical terms, adapted from the foregoing lists, can and should be applied to the O'Keeffe painting as well as to any other artwork that students encounter in their intellectual endeavors.

❧ MUSICAL ANALYSIS

Like literature and art, music has its own vocabulary, and we need to be familiar with it in order to analyze a composition.

- **Sacred music** refers to religious music, such as Gregorian chants, Masses, requiems, cantatas, and hymns.

- **Secular music** is the term used to describe symphonies, songs, operas, dances, and other non-sacred musical works.

- **Vocal music** is music that is sung and generally has lyrics (words).

- **Choral music** is vocal music performed by a group of singers.

- **Instrumental music** is music that is written for and performed on instruments.

- **Form**, in music, means the particular structure or arrangement of elements by the composer in the musical composition. Musical forms include symphonies, songs, concertos, string quartets, sonatas, Masses, and operas.

- **Tone** is a musical sound of definite pitch (pitch is determined by the frequency of the air waves producing the sound). The term *tone* can also refer to the quality of a sound.

- A **scale** is a set pattern of tones (or notes) arranged from low to high (or high to low). The modern Western scale is the familiar do, re, mi, fa, sol, la, ti, do, with half steps in between the tones. In other cultures, more or fewer tones may be distinguished in a scale.

- **Tempo** is the rate of speed of a musical passage, usually set or suggested by the composer.

- **Texture** describes the number and nature of the voices or instruments employed and how the parts are combined. In music, a theme is a characteristic musical idea on which a composition is built or developed.

- **Melody** is a succession of musical tones, usually having a distinctive musical shape, or line, and a definite rhythm (the recurrent alternation of accented and unaccented beats).

- **Harmony** is the simultaneous combination of two or more tones, producing a chord. More generally, harmony refers to the choral characteristics of a work and the way in which chords interact with one another.

With these basic categories in mind, let's consider a well-known musical work, *Rhapsody in Blue,* by George Gershwin (1898–1937). Even if you don't know this piece by name, it's very likely that you've heard it. It's been used in ads and in the sound tracks of numerous movies, including *Fantasia 2000;* it is also a standard accompaniment to images of New York City.

Imagine that you're seated in a concert hall and hearing this piece performed by a symphony orchestra (probably a "pops" orchestra, one that performs more popular classical music). When listening to a new piece of music or one you're not familiar with, it's a good idea to try to get a sense of its general mood and character—again, focusing on the creator's intent. What emotions or ideas is the composer trying to convey? What musical elements does the composer use to execute that intent?

You'll notice, first of all, that the work is written for a small orchestra and a solo piano, the same instrumental configuration you would expect for a classical piano concerto (a concerto is a work for one or a few instruments and an orchestra, with much of its interest coming from the contrasts between the solo voice and the ensemble voice). But the opening notes of *Rhapsody in Blue* reveal something other than classical intentions: a solo clarinet begins low and sweeps up the scale in a seemingly endless "smear" of sound, finally reaching a high note, briefly holding it, and then plunging into the playful, zigzag melody that becomes one of the major themes of the work. Within moments, the orchestra enters and repeats the theme in the strings and brass, to be followed by the entry of the solo piano. Throughout the work, piano and orchestra alternate and combine to sing out beautiful melodies and create a varied and colorful texture. Variety also comes from different instrumentation of the themes and tunes, played first by a slinky muted trumpet, then by a sweet solo violin, later by a whole lush string section or a brash horn section.

You'll notice too the constant changes in tempo, now slower, now faster, almost as if the work is being improvised. Complex, syncopated, off-the-beat rhythms give the piece a jazzy feeling, and the combination of tones evokes the blues, a style of music in which certain notes are "bent," or lowered slightly in pitch, creating a particular sound and mood. The general feeling of the piece is upbeat, exciting, energetic, suggestive of a bustling city busy with people on the go. It may also make you think of Fred Astaire and Ginger Rogers movies you've seen on late-night TV—sophisticated, playful, casually elegant—and in fact, Gershwin wrote the music for some of their films.

What can we learn about this work from its title? Musical works often reveal their form in their title (Fifth Symphony, Violin Concerto in D, and so on). A rhapsody is a composition of irregular form with an improvisatory character. Although you may have heard themes, repetitions, and echoes in *Rhapsody in Blue,* you probably were not able to discern a regular form such as might be apparent in a classical sonata or symphony. The word *rhapsody* also suggests rapture, elation, bliss, ecstasy—perhaps the feelings conveyed by that soaring first phrase on the clarinet. *Blue,* on the other hand, suggests the melancholy of the blues. The dissonance created by the combination of the two terms—like the combinations and contrasts in the music—creates an energetic tension that arouses our curiosity and heightens our interest.

In making these observations about *Rhapsody in Blue,* we've been noticing many of the formal elements of a musical work and answering questions that can be asked about any composition: What is the form of the work? What kind of instrumentation has the composer chosen? What is the primary melodic theme of the work? What tempos are used? How do the instruments or voices work together to create the texture? What is the overall mood of the piece—joyful, sad, calm, wild, a combination?

Now, at your imaginary concert, there may be notes in the program that will provide you with some context for the work. You'll find that George Gershwin was a gifted and classically trained pianist who quit school at fifteen and went to work in Tin Pan Alley, a district in New York City where popular songs were written and published. His goal in writing *Rhapsody in Blue* (1924) was to blend classical and popular music, to put the energy and style of jazz into a symphonic format. Many listeners "see" and "hear" New York City in this piece. Gershwin created his own unique idiom, a fast-paced blend of rhythm, melody, and harmony that followed certain rules of composition but gave the impression of improvisation. He went on to write musicals, more serious compositions like the opera *Porgy and Bess,* and music for Hollywood films, all in his distinctive style. Information like this can help you begin to compare *Rhapsody in Blue* both with other works of the time and with other works by Gershwin. As in any analysis, integrating the formal and the contextual rounds out your interpretation and understanding of the work.

CONCLUSION

The foregoing materials should give you some ideas about how literature, art, and music can be approached in productive ways. By taking the time to look more closely, we gain access to the great works of our culture. This statement leads us to another issue: What makes a work "great"? Why do some works of art have relevance long beyond their time, while others are forgotten soon after their designated "fifteen minutes of fame"? These questions have been debated throughout history. One answer is that great art reflects some truth of human experience that speaks to us across the centuries. The voice of Shakespeare, the paintings of Georgia O'Keeffe, and the music of George Gershwin have a universal quality that doesn't depend on the styles of the time. Great art also enriches us and makes us feel that we share a little more of the human experience than we did before.

As both a student of the humanities and an audience member, you have the opportunity to appreciate and understand the arts. Despite the formal nature of academic inquiry, an aesthetic analysis is a personal endeavor. In looking closely at a creative work, seeking the creator's intent and evaluating its execution, you enrich your appreciation of the work with understanding; you bring the emotional reaction you first experienced to its intellectual completion. As twentieth-century composer Arnold Schoenberg once wrote, "You get from a work about as much as you are able to give to it yourself." This primer has been intended to help you learn how to bring more of yourself to works of art, to couple your subjective appreciation with intellectual understanding. With these tools in hand, you won't have to say you don't know much about art but you know what you like; you'll be able to say you know *about* what you like.

1 PREHISTORY AND NEAR EASTERN CIVILIZATIONS

The two structures to the left, the Great Sphinx and one of the Great Pyramids, are probably familiar to readers of this book. Why should that be so? After all, they are five thousand years old. The reasons are many, but among the most prominent are history and tradition. These monuments have a history and they have entered the Western tradition. They have become a part of who we are. The story told in this book is therefore partly about who we are and partly about how, century by century, the tradition of which we are the heirs and beneficiaries has grown and changed.

For some two hundred years, it has been customary to speak of "Western civilization" and, for a somewhat shorter time, to speak of the many cultures that have made up Western civilization. What do these terms mean? When people first spoke about "the West," they were referring to western Europe. But western Europe was the product of peoples and cultures who had lived around the Mediterranean Sea in antiquity, and eventually Europe exported its cultures to much of the rest of the globe. "West" is therefore as much an idea as a place. **Civilization** is in a way the largest unit within which any one person might feel comfortable. It is an organizing principle that implies common institutions, economic systems, social structures, and values that extend over space and time. Hence we can feel a connection—however slight—to the Sphinx and the Great Pyramid. **Culture** is a more restricted term. On one very general level, it means high culture: the fine arts and philosophy, for example. On another level, it means the totality of expressions and behaviors that characterize a readily identifiable group of people in a specific place

◄ **Detail** The Great Sphinx. Ca. 2560 BCE. 65' high × 240' long. Giza, Egypt.

and time. Every civilization enfolds many cultures, at any one time and across long periods of time. Mesopotamia and Egypt, like Greece and Rome, were cultures within ancient Western civilization. Although they were not alike, they did have common features and they all contributed powerfully to an enduring tradition.

PREHISTORY AND EARLY CULTURES

Human beings long preceded culture and civilization. The remote ancestors of modern human beings emerged in Africa at least four million years ago. That is a long time, but merely a moment in comparison to the roughly six billion years that planet Earth can boast. To put those huge numbers into perspective, let us imagine a calendar: if Earth appeared on January 1, then human ancestors showed up around the end of August, but civilization, and history, commenced a few minutes before midnight on December 31.

Perhaps two million years ago, the species *Homo,* or the *hominids,* made its appearance whereas *Homo sapiens,* the immediate ancestor of modern humans, emerged around two hundred thousand years ago. For a very long time, therefore, the key story was the development of the human species itself. Unfortunately, knowledge about these hominids is limited and fragmentary. They were hunters and gatherers, lived in natural shelters such as caves, and did not possess complex social structures. Hominids invented crude stone tools, used fire, and probably developed speech—a major breakthrough that enabled them to communicate in ways denied to animals. Their first stone tools were simple choppers and, later, hand axes, pointed tools, and scrapers, all chiseled with care. Double-faced blades became common. Hominids and *Homo sapiens* span the **Paleolithic** period, the Old Stone Age, a time roughly coterminous with the geological Pleistocene, the Ice Age.

Paleolithic Period

The latter millennia of the Paleolithic period are somewhat better known owing to discoveries in widely dispersed places. *Homo sapiens* had migrated across the Eastern Hemisphere and even the Western Hemisphere, reaching the latter by means of a land bridge that connected Siberia and Alaska. People had begun to use more sophisticated tools, such as fishhooks, bows and arrows, and needles (Figure 1.1). Most impressively, however, late Paleolithic peoples began to express themselves in art. Ice Age cave paintings of reindeer, bison, rhinoceroses, lions, and horses in Altamira, Spain, and in Lascaux and the Ardèche region of France date from the Upper Paleolithic (40,000–10,000 BCE) and are the earliest examples of human art (Figure 1.2). The purposes of the paintings in the Chauvet caves in the Ardèche region remain a mystery, but those at Altamira and Lascaux were probably used as part of ceremonies and rituals before hunting. By painting numerous wild animals pierced with arrows, the artists were attempting to ensure a successful hunt.

Another type of Upper Paleolithic art is seen in the carved female figurine found at Willendorf, Austria (Figure 1.3). Made of limestone, the statue is faceless and rotund. The distended stomach and full

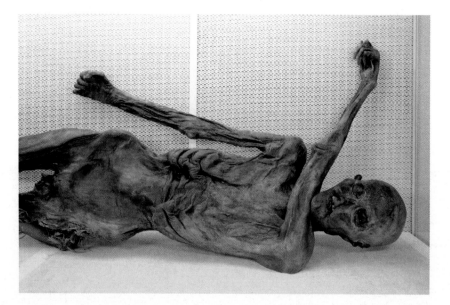

Figure 1.1   The Ice Man. Photo © South Tyrol Museum of Archaeology. *In 1991 hikers in the Alps discovered the body of a man in melting ice. He turned out to be over five thousand years old. He died in a bloody fight after having eaten a last meal of bread and goat meat. He possessed a bow and arrows, a copper hatchet, and several pouches and containers. The Ice Man was about 5 feet 2 inches tall and had lived a very hard life.*

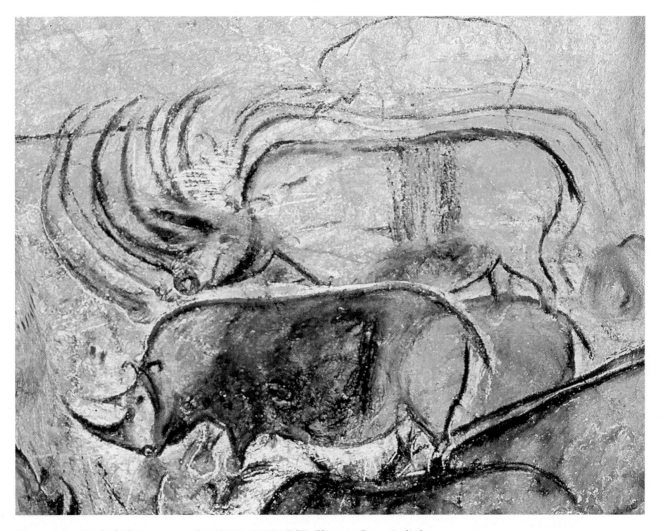

Figure 1.2 Herd of Rhinoceroses. Ca. 32,000–30,000 BCE. Chauvet Cave, Ardèche region, France. *This naturalistic detail of a panel painting includes lions, bison, and a young mammoth (not visible here) moving across a vast expanse of the cave wall. The repeated black lines of the rhinoceroses' horns and backs create a sense of depth and give energy to the work.*

breasts suggest that the figure may have been used as a fertility symbol and an image of a mother goddess, representing the creative power of nature. As a mythological figure, the mother goddess appeared in many ancient cultures, beginning in Paleolithic times; approximately thirty thousand miniature sculptures in clay, marble, bone, copper, and gold have been uncovered at about three thousand sites in southeastern Europe alone. The supremacy of the mother goddess was expressed in the earliest myths of creation, which told of the life-giving and nurturing powers of the female. This figurine from Willendorf, with its emphasized breasts, navel, and vulva, symbolic of creativity, may have been used in religious ceremonies to ensure the propagation of the tribe or to guarantee a bountiful supply of food. The statue also reveals the aesthetic interests of the sculptor, who took care to depict the

goddess's hands resting on her breasts and her hair in tightly knit rows.

The Neolithic Revolution

As the last glaciers retreated from Europe, during the Holocene (Recent) epoch of geological time, humans had to adapt to new living conditions. The Mesolithic period (Middle Stone Age), while brief, proved to be a decisive turning point. In the most important development in human history, hunters and gatherers became farmers and herders. Thus began, some ten thousand years ago, the **Neolithic** period, or New Stone Age. As *Homo sapiens* became farmers and herders, they gained knowledge about agriculture and developed wooden tools and other technologies for managing the

Figure 1.3 Figurine from Willendorf. Ca. 25,000 BCE. Ht. 4⅜". Naturhistorisches Museum, Vienna. *Discovered in about 1908 CE, this female statuette measures just under 5 inches high. Carved from limestone, it still shows evidence of having been painted red. Many other statues like it have been discovered, but this one remains the most famous because of the unusual balance it strikes between symbolism and realism.*

warfare. In construction and building, the discovery and use of kiln-fired bricks made houses, temples, and palaces possible. In the domestic arts, there came five new technologies: weaving, dyeing (using animal and vegetable dyes), tanning, pottery making (both plain and kiln-fired), and the making of oil lamps. In farming, there was now large-scale irrigation in the Near East, with many new plants under cultivation, such as wheat, flax, millet, barley, and spices.

Humans were now well on the road to finding new, faster, and more efficient ways of living and thriving. In Southeast Asia, Central America, parts of South America, and the Near East, humans ceased their nomadic existence and learned to domesticate wild animals. They learned to plow the earth and sow seeds, providing themselves with a much more reliable, predictable food supply, which in turn permitted increased population, permanent settlements, and eventually urban centers. This agrarian pattern of life dominated the West until recently.

The Age of Metals

The Neolithic Revolution expanded across the Near East and probably into Europe and Africa. Between 6000 and 3000 BCE, human beings also learned to mine and use copper, signifying the end of the Neolithic period and ushering in the Age of Metals. In about 3000 BCE, artisans combined copper and tin to produce bronze, a strong alloy, which they used in their tools, weapons, and jewelry.

The Bronze Age extended from about 3000 to about 1200 BCE. A herald of the Age of Metals was the mastery of gold and silver metalworking. Gold and silver were first reduced from their ores after 3500 BCE, but their scarcity made them too precious for general use. The shift from stone tools to bronze tools occurred at first in only a few areas in the Near East, China, and Southeast Asia. Elsewhere, especially in Europe, Mesoamerica, and the Andes of South America, stone continued as the dominant material for tools. Even in the modern world, stone retains its usefulness, as in such products as mortars and pestles, cutting boards, building materials, and flooring.

From Mesopotamia, where the earliest successful bronze was produced by anonymous artisans, this metalworking tradition was transmitted to Egypt, Greece, and elsewhere. It produced a host of new technologies. Writing is the hallmark of this period, with Egyptians putting words on papyrus, a flat writing surface made from pressed reeds, and Mesopotamians incising words on clay tablets. In Egypt, artisans also pioneered the use of vellum, or parchment, a material prepared from animal skin, which was more flexible

processes. Their stone tools became more advanced than those in the Mesolithic period and included knives and hammers. Along with the domestication of animals, the animal-drawn plow was introduced to Mesopotamia, thus increasing the yield of crops. After 3500 BCE, the rise of these new technologies was incredibly rapid, making this one of the most fruitful eras for change that the world has ever known. In transportation the changes included two innovations: the boat (with and without sails) and the wheel—each with enormous potential for commerce, travel, and

Timeline 1.1   GEOLOGICAL TIME AND PREHISTORIC CULTURAL PERIODS   **All dates approximate and BCE**

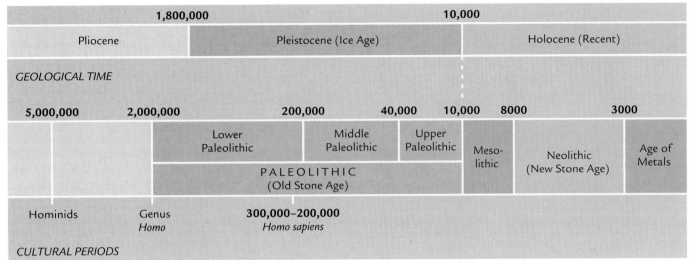

	1,800,000		10,000	
Pliocene	Pleistocene (Ice Age)		Holocene (Recent)	

GEOLOGICAL TIME

5,000,000	2,000,000		200,000	40,000	10,000	8000		3000

		Lower Paleolithic	Middle Paleolithic	Upper Paleolithic	Meso-lithic	Neolithic (New Stone Age)	Age of Metals

PALEOLITHIC (Old Stone Age)

Hominids	Genus *Homo*	300,000–200,000 *Homo sapiens*

CULTURAL PERIODS

and durable than papyrus. With the invention of writing, the silence of the prehistoric period gave way to the voice of the historic period.

Other technologies improved the lives of people during the Bronze Age. Construction methods moved along two different paths: in Egypt, stone building techniques arose, and in Mesopotamia, stepped temples, made of dried bricks, became the chief building style. Advances in transport were made, with sailboats plying their wares on Egypt's Nile and wooden ships maneuvering in the Mediterranean. Copper and tin were in short supply in Egypt and Mesopotamia. To ensure a continuous supply of these metals, complex trading ties and mining operations had to be established. Copper was found in neighboring Anatolia (modern Turkey), but tin was scarce, as it was mined in only a few places, in modern Serbia and Bulgaria at first, and in Cornwall, in modern England, after 2500 BCE. Domestic life made extraordinary advances in Mesopotamia, with many changes that are still part of life today, including the baking of bread in ovens, the brewing of beer, and the distilling of perfumes. In Egypt and Mesopotamia, the making of glass and the fermenting of wine became common, and, in Egypt, the invention of hand mirrors and the sundial lent new perspectives to experience. Urban culture also led to the widespread use of calendars, in both Egypt and Mesopotamia.

The Iron Age began in about 1200 BCE, but the making of iron has been dated to about 2000 BCE. Iron technology soon led to new devices, fashioned from either iron or steel, such as iron-tipped plows, weaponry, buckets, and locks and keys. Warriors quickly realized that sturdy iron defeats fragile bronze every time. Indeed, some wars between 1200 and 1000 BCE are thought by scholars to have had their outcomes determined by which side wielded iron weapons.

THE RISE OF CIVILIZATION: MESOPOTAMIA

Civilization is based on a Latin word meaning "city" and "citizen." It was the Neolithic Revolution that made cities possible. That revolution depended on agriculture and the domestication of animals. Those processes brought in their train the division of labor, government, religion, priestly classes, arts and crafts, and sciences. Taken together, along with writing, these elements add up to civilization. Civilization arose in Mesopotamia and slightly later in Egypt (about 3500–3000 BCE). Both civilizations were ruled by kings who were supported by priestly classes and shared power with a few educated elites. Their economies were slave based; their societies were hierarchical and stratified. Both had elaborate palaces and temples for governmental and ceremonial purposes.

Mesopotamia is a Greek word meaning "between the rivers." The Tigris and Euphrates are the two rivers whose valley forms part of what is known as the Fertile Crescent, which starts at the Persian Gulf, runs slightly northwestward through the region between the rivers (roughly modern Iraq), and then turns westerly to the Mediterranean Sea and curves south along the shoreline toward Egypt (Map 1.1). This arc of land contained some of the most arable soil in the Near East, many heavily traveled trade routes, and most of the early centers of civilization. The hill country and Zagros Mountains rise to the east of the Tigris-Euphrates valley, and the vast Arabian Desert stretches

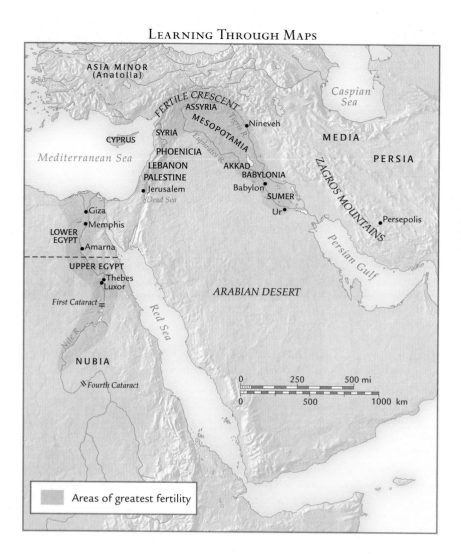

Map 1.1 ANCIENT MESOPOTAMIA AND EGYPT
This map shows the two earliest civilizations of the Near East: Mesopotamia and Egypt. 1. *Notice* that much of Mesopotamia is contained within the area known as the Fertile Crescent and that Egypt is settled mainly along the Nile River. 2. *Locate* the cities in Mesopotamia and Egypt. 3. *Compare and contrast* the role and importance of rivers in these civilizations. 4. *Why* was Egypt less exposed to external influences than was Mesopotamia?

to the west. The twin rivers course down to the Persian Gulf, draining an area approximately 600 miles long and 250 miles wide. Near the mouth of the gulf, in the river delta, human wanderers settled in about 6000 BCE.

The Sumerian, Akkadian, and Babylonian Kingdoms

Three successive civilizations—Sumerian, Akkadian, and Babylonian—flourished in Mesopotamia for nearly fifteen hundred years (Timeline 1.2). Indeed, as historian Samuel Kramer asserts, "History begins at Sumer."

The rulers of Sumer created an exalted image of a just and stable society with a rich cultural life. Sumer's most inspirational king, Gilgamesh [GILL-guh-mesh], ruled during the first dynasty (about 2700 BCE) of Ur, one of the thirty or so cities of Sumer. His heroic adventures and exploits were later immortalized in the poem *The Epic of Gilgamesh.* A later ruler, Urukagina, is known for reforming law codes and revitalizing the economy near the end of the Sumerian period (2350 BCE). But Urukagina's successors were unable to maintain Sumer's power, and the cities became easy prey for the Akkadians of northern Mesopotamia.

Akkadian rulers between about 2350 and 2000 BCE incorporated Sumerian culture into their own society and carried this hybrid civilization far beyond the Tigris-Euphrates valley. According to legends—which are similar to the later story of the Hebrew leader Moses—Sargon (r. about 2334–2279 BCE), the first and greatest Akkadian ruler, was born of lowly origins and abandoned at birth in the reed marshes; yet Sargon survived and rose to prominence at the Sumerian court. Excavated inscriptions reveal that Sargon conquered the Sumerians and founded a far-flung empire to the east and northeast. At its height, Sargon's power was felt from Egypt to India, but his successors, lacking his intelligence and skill, could not maintain the Akkadian Empire.

Timeline 1.2 MESOPOTAMIAN CIVILIZATIONS   **All dates approximate and BCE**

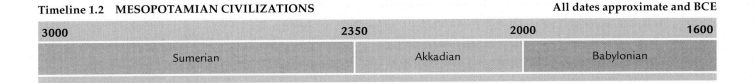

3000	2350	2000	1600
Sumerian	Akkadian	Babylonian	

Babylonia was the third civilization in Mesopotamia. From northern Mesopotamia, their power base, the Babylonians governed the entire valley from about 2000 to 1600 BCE. Under their most successful military leader and renowned lawgiver, Hammurabi [ham-uh-RAHB-e] (r. 1792–1750 BCE), the Babylonians reached their political and cultural ascendancy.

Agriculture dominated the economy of Mesopotamia. Harsh living conditions and unpredictable floods forced the inhabitants to learn to control the rivers through irrigation systems and cooperative tilling of the soil. Farmers eventually dug a complex canal system to irrigate their cultivated plots, which might have been some distance from the river. As production increased, prosperity allowed larger populations to thrive. Villages soon grew into small cities—with populations ranging from ten thousand to fifty thousand—surrounded by hamlets and tilled fields. Trade developed with nearby areas, and wheeled vehicles—perfected by the Sumerians—and sailboats carried goods up and down the Tigris and Euphrates rivers and eventually throughout the Fertile Crescent.

By the beginning of the Bronze Age, the family had replaced the tribe or clan as the basic unit in society. Families now owned their lands outright, and, under the general direction of the religious and secular authorities, they worked their fields and maintained the irrigation ditches. Marriages were arranged by parents, with economics an essential consideration. According to the law codes, women possessed some rights, such as holding property; however, a wife was clearly under her husband's power. Divorce was easier for men than for women, and women were punished more severely than men for breaking moral and marital laws. As peoples fought and conquered each other, government became increasingly military in outlook and function and the roles and status of women declined. In sum, Mesopotamian women were originally able to participate actively in economic, religious, and political life as long as their dependence on and obligation to male kin and husbands was observed, but they progressively lost their relative independence because rulers extended the concept of patriarchy (rule by the fathers) from family practice into public law.

The political structure reflected the order and functions of the social system. At the top stood the ruler, who was supported by an army, a bureaucracy, a ju-

dicial system, and a priesthood. The ruler usually obtained advice from prominent leaders, meeting in council, who constituted the next layer of the social order: rich landowners, wealthy merchants, priests, and military chiefs. The next group consisted of artisans, craftspeople, and petty businesspeople and traders. Below them were small landowners and tenant farmers. At the bottom of the social scale were serfs and slaves, who either had been captured in war or had fallen into debt.

The Cradle of Civilization

The three Mesopotamian civilizations responded to the same geography, climate, and natural resources, and their cultures reflected that shared background. The Sumerians were probably the most influential: from Sumer came writing, the lunar calendar, a mathematical computation system, medical and scientific discoveries, and architectural and technological innovations. However, each civilization, through its religion, literature, law, and art, deeply affected other Near Eastern people.

WRITING Thousands of clay tablets inscribed with the wedge-shaped symbols of Sumerian script have been uncovered in Mesopotamia, indicating that the Sumerians had developed a form of writing by 3000 BCE. With the invention of writing, people no longer had to rely on memory, speech, and person-to-person interactions to communicate and transmit information. Instead, they could accumulate a permanent body of knowledge and pass it on from one generation to the next.

At first, the Sumerians needed a simple way to record agricultural and business information and the deeds and sayings of their rulers. Their earliest symbols were **pictograms,** or pictures, carefully drawn to represent particular objects. To these they added **ideograms,** pictures drawn to represent ideas or concepts. A simple drawing of a bowl, for example, could be used to mean "food." As these pictures became more stylized, meaning began to be transferred from the represented object to the sign itself; that is, the sign began to stand for a word rather than an object.

Later, Sumerian scribes and writers identified the syllabic sounds of spoken words and created **phonograms,**

ENCOUNTER

The Phoenicians and the Alphabet

The small kingdom of Phoenicia taught the alphabet to the ancient Greeks and, thus, to the West. The Phoenicians invented the alphabet, the basis of their writing and reading, to support the interchange of material goods and ideas with their neighbors.

Around 3000 BCE, the Phoenicians, a people of mixed Syrian and Palestinian ancestry, settled along a narrow strip of land on the eastern coast of the Mediterranean in what is modern-day Lebanon. The Phoenicians never became a major political or military force, but they did establish a string of semi-independent and prosperous city-states down the Lebanese coast.

Originally farmers, the Phoenicians turned to manufacturing, trade, and commerce for their survival. They traveled the overland trade routes along the Fertile Crescent and into Mesopotamia and exported many items, including cedar and fir trees for constructing temples and palaces. By 1200 BCE, they had begun redirecting their commercial interests to the sea, building boats and transporting goods around the Mediterranean basin. One of their leading exports was a cloth of purple dye, which the Greeks called *phoinix*—a word that came to identify the Phoenician people. By the seventh century BCE, the Phoenicians had also developed a glass industry, and their fine metal and ivory artworks indicate that they were importing gold, silver, and precious stones from as far away as India and Africa.

By 1100 BCE, the Phoenicians had begun to found colonies on islands and along the Mediterranean coastline—not for conquests but for trade and commerce. These commercial emporiums, at their zenith by 700 BCE, were equipped with port facilities and shipyards, were established close to one another, and served as stopovers for travelers and as marketplaces for traders. Using their seafaring skills and spurred by commercial interests, the Phoenicians sailed down the western coast of Africa and sent ships to the British Isles, in search of tin. In time, the colonies also became outposts for Phoenician culture and intellectual and artistic achievements. Their encounters with other societies led to the spread of the Phoenician alphabetic writing system throughout the classical world.

As early as 1400 BCE, the Phoenicians had created a syllabic writing system, probably based on Egyptian **hieroglyphics**—a system of pictographs—and/or Sumerian cuneiform. Writing, understandably, helped them communicate more effectively and efficiently with their colonies and trading partners. They simplified the pictograms, ideograms, phonograms, and syllabic systems of earlier forms of writing into an alphabetic system. A sign for a particular object, such as one for a cow or tree, was given a Phoenician name and a new symbol, in which the letter was given the initial sound of the name of the object it represented. Thus, the sign became a sound. This collection of signs came to be known as an *alphabet*—the word itself a

symbols for separate speech sounds, borrowing from and building on the earlier pictograms and ideograms. These simplified and standardized symbols eventually resulted in a phonetic writing system of syllable-based sounds that, when combined, produced words (Figure 1.4). It was left to later civilizations to separate vowel sounds from syllables and thus create a true alphabet, based on individual speech sounds (see Encounter).

The Sumerians could now express complex, abstract concepts, and their system could extend to other languages. The Akkadians and the Babylonians adopted and modified the Sumerian script to keep records and preserve their literature. By the end of the Bronze Age (about 1200 BCE), other written languages existed, but Akkadian-Sumerian was the language of diplomacy and trade in the Near East.

The Sumerian writing system is called **cuneiform** ("wedge-shaped"), from the Latin word *cuneus* ("wedge"). Using wedge-shaped reeds or styluses, scribes pressed the symbols into wet clay tablets, and

artists and craftspeople, wielding metal tools, incised the script into stone monuments or cylindrical pillars. Preserved for thousands of years in hardened clay and stone, cuneiform writing has provided invaluable insight into ancient Mesopotamian culture.

RELIGION Sumerian, Akkadian, and Babylonian religions, despite individual differences, shared many basic attitudes and concepts that became the foundation for other Near Eastern belief systems. The underlying beliefs of Mesopotamian religion were that the gods had created human beings to serve them, that the gods were in complete control, and that powerless mortals had no choice but to obey and worship these deities. The hostile climate and unpredictable rivers (flooding in some years, but not in others) made life precarious, and the gods appeared capricious. The Mesopotamians held a vague notion of a shadowy netherworld where the dead rested, but they did not believe in an afterlife as such or any rewards or punishments upon death. Happiness seldom was an earthly goal; pessi-

| NORTH SEMITIC | | | GREEK | | ETRUSCAN | LATIN | |
EARLY PHOENICIAN	EARLY HEBREW	PHOENICIAN	EARLY	CLASSICAL	EARLY	EARLY	CLASSICAL
K	K	≮	⊿	A	A	A	A
9	9	9	9	B	B	9	B
7	1	1	1	Γ	1	1	C
△	◁	◁	△	△	△	⋂	D

Phoenician, Greek, Hebrew, Etruscan, and Roman letters.

Encounter figure 1.1   First Four Letters of the Alphabet—a Comparison. *This table presents, in comparative form, the opening four letters of the Phoenician, Greek, Hebrew, Etruscan, and Latin alphabets. The early Phoenician letters predated the rest, and other peoples adapted those letters into their writing styles.*

combination of the first two letters of the Phoenician system: aleph, or the letter *a*, and beth, or the letter *b*. The Phoenician alphabet consisted of twenty-two letters. It read from right to left, as is typical of Semitic languages, of which Phoenician is one. The letters were all consonants, and later the Greeks turned some of the consonants into vowels. The Greeks passed their modified alphabet to the Etruscans in Italy, to the Copts in Egypt, and to the Slavonic clans in eastern Europe. The Etruscans introduced the alphabet to the Romans, who made it part of their written language, Latin. The Hebrews, Arabs, and other Semitic peoples adapted the Phoenician alphabet for themselves. The alphabet is Phoenicia's lasting contribution to modern civilization.

LEARNING FROM THE ENCOUNTER

1. *Why* did the Phoenicians never become a powerful military kingdom? 2. *How* did the Phoenicians capitalize on their geographic location to become a trading society? 3. *Describe* the colonies founded by the Phoenicians. 4. *What* were the bases of the Phoenician alphabetic writing system, and *how* did the Phoenicians create a new system? 5. *What* impact has this system had on other languages?

Figure 1.4   Sumerian Cuneiform Writing. Ca. 3000–1000 BCE. *The columns illustrate the evolution of Sumerian writing from pictograms to script. Column 1 shows the pictogram: a man, an ox, and the verb "to eat" (represented by the mouth and a bowl). In column 2, the pictographic symbols have been turned 90 degrees, as the Sumerians did in their first writing. Columns 3 and 4 show how the script changed between 2500 and 1800 BCE. Column 5 is an Assyrian adaptation of the Sumerian cuneiform script.*

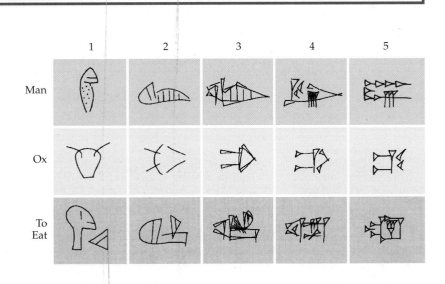

mism ran as a constant theme throughout their religion and literature.

Mesopotamian religion had three important characteristics: it was **polytheistic**—many gods and goddesses existed and often competed with one another; it was **anthropomorphic**—the deities possessed human form and had their own personalities and unique traits; and it was **pantheistic**—everything, whether animate or inanimate, was somehow suffused with divinity. Since Mesopotamians thought of their gods in human form with all the strengths and weaknesses of mortals, they believed their deities lived in the same way as people did, and they were pragmatic in approaching the supernatural powers. For example, they believed that their deities held council, made decisions, and ordered the forces of nature to wreak havoc or to bestow plenty on mortals.

Mesopotamians divided the deities into the sky gods and the earth gods. There were several major deities: Anu, the sky god; Enlil, the air god; Utu the sun god; Enki, the god of earth and freshwater god; Nanna the moon goddess; Inanna (or Ishtar), the goddess of love and war; and Ninhursag, the mother goddess. Enlil emerged as the most powerful god for the Sumerians. He gave mortals the plow and the pickax, and he brought forth for humanity all the productive forces of the universe, such as trees, grains, and "whatever was needful."

Rituals, ceremonies, and the priesthood were essential to Mesopotamian religion. Although the average Mesopotamian might participate in worship services, the priests played the central role in all religious functions. They also controlled and administered large parcels of land, which enhanced their power in economic and political matters. Priests carefully formulated and consciously followed the procedures for rites and rituals, which were written down and stored in their temples. This cultic literature not only told the Mesopotamians how to worship but also informed them about their deities' origins, characteristics, and deeds. Religious myths and instructions constituted a major part of Mesopotamian literature and made writing an essential part of the culture.

LITERATURE   Of the surviving epics, tales, and legends that offer glimpses into the Mesopotamian mind, the most famous is *The Epic of Gilgamesh*. King Gilgamesh, whose reign in about 2700 BCE is well documented, became a larger-than-life hero in Sumerian folktales (Figure 1.5). In all probability, the Gilgamesh epic began as an oral poem and was not written on clay tablets for hundreds of years. The most complete surviving version, from 600 BCE, was based on a Babylonian copy written in Akkadian and dating from about 1600 BCE. Although this poem influenced other Near Eastern writings with its characters, plot, and themes, *The Epic of Gilgamesh* stands on its own as poetry worthy of being favorably compared with later Greek and Roman epics.

Through its royal hero, *The Epic of Gilgamesh* focuses on fundamental themes that concern warriors in an aristocratic society: the need to be brave in the face of danger, the choice of death before dishonor, the conflict between companionship and sexual pleasure, the power of the gods over weak mortals, and the finality of death. Above all, it deals with human beings' vain quest for immortality. As the tale begins, the extravagant and despotic policies of Gilgamesh have led his subjects to pray for relief. In response, a goddess creates from clay a "wild man" of tremendous physical strength and sends him to kill Gilgamesh. But Enkidu, as he is called, is instead tamed by a woman's love, loses his innocence, wrestles Gilgamesh to a draw, and becomes his boon companion.

As the epic unfolds, Gilgamesh chooses friendship with Enkidu rather than the love offered by the goddess Ishtar. Gilgamesh is punished for this choice by being made to watch helplessly as Enkidu dies from

Figure 1.5   Gilgamesh Fighting a Lion. Ca. 2500–2000 BCE. Cylinder seal (left) and modern impression of a cylinder seal (right). British Museum, London. *The separate scenes, rolled out on this impression from the seal, which is about 1 inch high, depict the Sumerian hero in one of his many battles against beasts. The artist heightens the intensity of the physical struggle by placing Gilgamesh, with his legs bent and arms locked around the lion, at a sharp angle under the animal to muster his brute strength against his foe.*

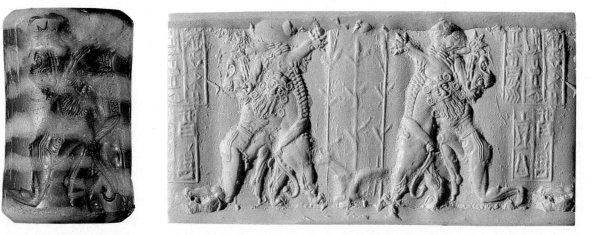

an illness sent by the gods. Forced to confront the fate awaiting all mortals, a grieving Gilgamesh begins a search for immortality.

The next section of the epic, which details Gilgamesh's search, includes the Sumerian tale of the great flood, which parallels the later Hebrew story of Noah and the ark. Although the Sumerian account of the flood was probably a later addition to the original story of Gilgamesh, the episode does fit into the narrative and reinforces one of the epic's major themes: the inescapable mortality of human beings. Gilgamesh hears the story of the flood from its sole survivor. Utnapishtim tells Gilgamesh how he built an ark and loaded it with animals and his family, how the waters rose, and how he released birds from the ark to discover if the waters were receding. The old man then explains how the gods, feeling sorry for the last remaining human, granted him immortality. Utnapishtim refuses to divulge the secret of eternal life to Gilgamesh, but the old man's wife blurts out where a plant may be found that will renew youth but not give immortality. Although Gilgamesh locates the plant, he loses it on his journey home. Gilgamesh, seeing the city of Uruk, which he had built, realizes that the deeds humans do on earth are the measure of their immortality and that death is inevitable.

The Epic of Gilgamesh is essentially a secular morality tale. Gilgamesh's triumphs and failures mirror the lives of all mortals, and the Sumerians saw themselves in Gilgamesh's change from an overly confident and powerful hero to a doubting and fearful human being. Those who, like Gilgamesh, ignore the power of the deities have to pay a heavy price for their pride.

Mesopotamia also gave the world the first known female literary figure, Enheduanna (fl. 2330 BCE), an Akkadian poet who wrote in the Sumerian language. Made priestess of temples in the Sumerian cities of Ur (see Figure 1.9) and Uruk by her father, King Sargon, she used her priestly offices and literary gifts to further his political goal of uniting the Sumerians and the Akkadians. In these posts, she composed hymns to both Sumerian and Akkadian deities, and these hymns—some of which have been identified—became models for later poets. Enheduanna was especially devoted to Inanna, the Sumerian goddess of love, and she made this deity the subject of her best-known literary work, *The Exaltation of Inanna*. In this work, Enheduanna exalted, or raised, Inanna to supremacy in the Sumerian pantheon (all the gods and goddesses), her tribute for what she believed was Inanna's role in Sargon's triumph over a general uprising at the end of his reign.

LAW   The central theme of Sumerian law, whose first existing records date from about 2050 BCE, was justice. From the earliest times, the Sumerian kings understood justice to mean "the straight thing"—that is, dealing fairly with all their subjects and prohibiting the exploitation of the weak by the strong. This concept of equity applied especially to economic matters, such as debts, contracts, and titles to land.

The most important set of laws from Mesopotamian civilization is that of the Babylonian king Hammurabi. Dating from about 1700 BCE, the Code of Hammurabi was found preserved on a seven-foot-high black stone **stele,** or pillar. At the top, Hammurabi is depicted standing in front of Shamash, the Babylonian and Sumerian god of justice. Like other ancient lawgivers (Moses, for example), Hammurabi received the legal code from a deity. Below the two figures are carved the prologue, the collection of laws, and an epilogue (Figure 1.6). The prologue lists Hammurabi's accomplishments and sings his praises while making it clear that the gods are the source of his power to establish "law

Figure 1.6   Code of Hammurabi. Ca. 1700 BCE. Basalt, ht. approx. 3'. Louvre. *Hammurabi stands on the left, his hand raised before his mouth in the traditional Mesopotamian gesture of devotion, and Shamash, the sun god and protector of truth and justice, sits on the right. The cult of Shamash (in Sumeria, Utu) emerged from the earliest times, and this god's representation— flames shooting from the shoulders and hands holding symbols of power—was established in the Sumerian period. The relief, with its incised folds of cloth and ceremonial chair, is carved deep enough into the hard stone stele (7 feet 4 inches) to suggest a three-dimensional sculpture.*

SLICE OF LIFE
A Sumerian Father Lectures His Son

Anonymous
Found on Clay Tablets

In this Sumerian text, dating from about 1700 BCE, a father rebukes his son for leading a wayward life and admonishes him to reform.

"Where did you go?"

"I did not go anywhere."

"If you did not go anywhere, why do you idle about? Go to school, stand before your 'school-father,' recite your assignment, open your schoolbag, write your tablet, let your 'big brother' write your new tablet for you. After you have finished your assignment and reported to your monitor, come to me, and do not wander about in the street. . . .

"You who wander about in the public square, would you achieve success? Then seek out the first generations. Go to school, it will be of benefit to you. My son, seek out the first generations, inquire of them.

"Perverse one over whom I stand watch—I would not be a man did I not stand watch over my son—I spoke to my kin, compared its men, but found none like you among them. . . .

"I, never in all my life did I make you carry reeds in the canebrake. The reed rushes which the young and the little carry, you, never in your life did you carry them. I never said to you 'Follow my caravans.' I never sent you to work, to plow my field. I never sent you to work to dig up my field. I never sent you to work as a laborer. 'Go, work and support me,' I never in my life said to you.

"Others like you support their parents by working. . . .

"I, night and day am I tortured because of you. Night and day you waste in pleasures. You have accumulated much wealth, have expanded far and wide, have become fat, big, broad, powerful, and puffed. But your kin waits expectantly for your misfortune, and will rejoice at it because you looked not to your humanity."

Interpreting This Slice of Life

The key to interpreting this Slice of Life is to determine the tone of the father's speech to his son. *Tone* means "manner of speaking." 1. *What* tone does the speaker manifest here? *List* three words that assist you in identifying the tone of voice. 2. *How* does the father define *family,* and what expectations does the father have for his son? 3. To *which* class do the father and his son belong? *Explain.* 4. *What* are the father's values regarding education, worldly success, and family honor? 5. *Which* values in this Sumerian text are shared by families in American culture?

and justice." The epilogue warns future rulers to carry out these laws or else be subject to defeat and ruin.

The laws concerning punishment for crimes are based on the judicial principle of *lex talionis,* or retaliation, which demands an "eye for an eye," although Hammurabi's code often substitutes payments in kind for damages done. The code constitutes decisions rendered in some three hundred actual cases. Accordingly, the code's provisions are not lofty and abstract but, instead, concrete and specific. Decisions deal with property rights, sales, contracts, inheritance, adoption, prices and wages, sexual relations (much more severely restricted for women than for men), medical malpractice, and personal rights for women, children, and slaves. Hammurabi's code, like other Mesopotamian laws, was only one part of a complex judicial system that encompassed judges, courts, trials, legal proceedings, and contracts.

SCIENCE, MATHEMATICS, AND MEDICINE Mesopotamian science was strongly influenced by the region's polytheistic, anthropomorphic, and pantheistic religion. The Mesopotamians believed that a knowledge and understanding of the natural world was related to their deities' personalities and acts. Priests performed ceremonies and rituals not only to placate the gods and goddesses and to fend off their disruptive powers but also to deal with practical matters, such as land surveys, irrigation projects, sickness, and disease. Thus, Mesopotamia's priests were also astronomers, mathematicians, and purveyors of medicine.

Knowing that the deities were powerful and capricious, the priests were convinced that they could avert some of the divine wrath by observing, studying, and calculating the heavens—the abode of most of the gods. The priests assumed that, by understanding the movements of the stars, moon, and sun, they could forecast natural calamities, such as floods, pestilence, and crop failure, which constantly befell their people. Around 3500 BCE, the priests in Sumer invented a calendar based on the movements of the moon. In this calendar, a "month" equaled twenty-eight days, but the year was divided into thirteen, not twelve, months. They then used this lunar calendar to make plans for the future. Once they were able to calculate the seasonal pattern of nature, they instituted a festival celebrating the New Year, which recognized the end of the growing season and the arrival of the next season.

Mathematics probably developed out of the need to measure and allocate land, build dams, remove dirt, pay workers, and regulate water. The Mesopotamian number system, likely influenced by their system of weights and coinage, used 60, not 100, as its base. Our calculation of degrees, minutes, and seconds evolved from this system. Later societies, like the Babylonian, built on this system to fashion complex formulas, theorems, and equations, which aided shopkeepers in managing their businesses and astronomers in mapping the heavens and plotting navigation charts.

Although the oldest surviving records of Mesopotamian medicine can be dated only to about 1600 BCE, these texts, preserved on stone tablets, represent earlier centuries of medical practice and tradition. In these texts, the authors connected disease with supernatural forces such as deities, ghosts, and spirits. Remedies involved the patient making sacrifices to the gods. At the same time, these texts counseled various treatments, such as administering potions made from herbs or plants. Mesopotamian diagnostic methods and curative practices, while outdated, followed a set of logical steps. First, the patient was examined to determine the nature of the disease and advised how to cure it. Then, the patient was sent to a healer, who prescribed certain medications or applied bandages or plasters. Additional evidence for Mesopotamian medicine comes from the Code of Hammurabi, in which doctors were held accountable for their mistakes and duly fined or punished. What contributions the Mesopotamians made to medicine tended to be lost over the centuries. It was the Egyptians who came to be viewed as the most successful practitioners of medicine during ancient times and influenced later societies, especially the Greeks.

ART AND ARCHITECTURE The art of Mesopotamia also evolved from Sumerian styles to the Akkadian and Babylonian schools. Artisans worked in many forms—small seals, pottery, jewelry, vases, **reliefs** (figures and forms carved so that they project from the flat surface of a stone background), and statues—and in many media—clay, stone, precious gems, gold, silver, leather, and ivory. Artifacts and crafted works from all three civilizations recorded the changing techniques of the producers as well as the shifting tastes of the consumers, whether they were rich individuals decorating their homes or officials issuing commissions for statues to adorn their temples. The

temples, usually the center of the city and set on high mounds above the other structures, were often splendidly ornamented and housed exquisitely carved statues of gods and goddesses.

A fine example of Sumerian artistry is a bull's head carved on the sound box of a lyre (Figure 1.7). Working in gold leaf and semiprecious gems, the unknown artist has captured the vigor and power of the animal in a bold and simple style. Such elegant musical instruments were played in homes and in palaces to accompany the poets and storytellers as they sang of the heroes' adventures and the deities' powers. The bull shape of the lyre reflects Sumerian religion, in which this animal was believed to possess supernatural powers. Religion may also be the inspiration for the varied creatures depicted in the four panels from the front of the sound box (Figure 1.8).

Mesopotamian architecture often seems uninspired. Good building stone was not readily available in Mesopotamia—it had to be brought at great cost from the mountains to the east—so wood and clay bricks were the most common building materials. Even though the Mesopotamians knew about the arch, the vault, and the column, they did not employ them widely; they used primarily the basic **post-and-lintel construction** of two vertical posts capped by a horizontal lintel, or beam, for entryways. The clay bricks used in construction limited the builders in both styles and size. Domestic architecture was particularly unimpressive, partly by design and partly because of unpromising materials. Private homes of clay bricks looked drab from the street; however, they were often attractive inside, with decorated rooms and built around an open courtyard. This is a common feature of ancient societies whereas, for many later peoples, power and status were communicated by impressive personal residences. The exteriors of temples and palaces were sometimes adorned with colored glazed bricks, mosaics, and painted cones arranged in patterns or, rarely, with imported stone and marble.

Although much remains to be discovered, it seems that Mesopotamian cities were surrounded by walls—with a circumference of up to five miles in early Sumer—and characterized by a broad central thoroughfare with a palace at one end and a temple complex at the other. Urban walls, with imposing and elaborately decorated gates, proclaimed the city's wealth and power. The most prominent structure in each Sumerian city was the **ziggurat,** a terraced brick and mudbrick pyramid that served as the center of worship. The ziggurat resembled a hill or a stairway to the sky from which the deities could descend; or perhaps the structure was conceived as the gods' cosmic mountain. A temple of welcome for the gods stood on the top of the ziggurat, approached by sets

Figure 1.8 Inlay from the Front of a Sound Box from Sumerian Lyre. Ca. 2685 BCE. *The four panels, made of ivory-colored shell inlaid onto a black background, depict mythological humans and animals. In the top panel, a man grasps two standing bulls with human heads. He may be either a god associated with the bull or a mythological figure from* The Epic of Gilgamesh. *The other panels show various animals (a hyena, a lion, a bull, and a gazelle), walking upright and behaving as humans, as they carry food and drinks or play musical instruments. In the bottom panel, the figure of the Scorpion Man is typical of the hybrid forms found in Mesopotamian art. Various theories have been offered in interpreting these scenes, including early versions of Aesopian fables, mythological stories, and humans dressed up as animals, but no consensus has been reached as to their ultimate meaning.*

Figure 1.7 Sound Box from Sumerian Lyre, from Ur. Ca. 2685 BCE. Wood with inlaid gold, lapis lazuli, and shell, ht. of bull's head approx. 13″. University Museum, University of Pennsylvania, Philadelphia. *The lyre's sound box, on which the bull's head is carved, is a hollow chamber that increases the resonance of the sound. Music played an important role in Mesopotamian life, and patrons often commissioned the construction of elegant instruments. Thus, even at this early stage of civilization, those with wealth influenced the arts.*

of steps. Shrines, storehouses, and administrative offices were constructed around the base or on the several levels of the massive hill. In the low plain of the Tigris-Euphrates valley, the ziggurat literally and figuratively dominated the landscape. The Tower of Babel, described in the Jewish scriptures as reaching to the sky, may have been suggested by the Sumerian ziggurats, some of which had towers.

Of the numerous ziggurats and temples that have survived, the best preserved is at Ur, in southern Mesopotamia, dedicated to the moon god, Nanna (Figure 1.9). Built in about 2100 BCE, this ziggurat was laid out to the four points of the compass. A central stairway led up to the highest platform, on which the major temple rested. Other cities constructed similar massive podiums in the hope that they would please the gods and goddesses, that the rivers would be kind to them, and that life would continue. Thus, the central themes of Mesopotamian civilization manifested themselves in the ziggurats.

THE CIVILIZATION OF THE NILE RIVER VALLEY: EGYPT

Another great river, the Nile, provided the setting for Egyptian civilization. Whereas Mesopotamian kingdoms were subject to constant external pressures, Egypt was isolated by deserts on both sides and developed an introspective attitude that was little influenced by neighboring cultures. The Egyptians cultivated a sense of cultural superiority and achieved a unified character that lasted for about three thousand years. Subjected to the annual flooding of the Nile and aware of the revolutions of the sun, Egypt saw itself as part of a cyclical pattern in a timeless world.

The regular floods of the Nile made civilized life possible in Egypt. Red sandy deserts stretched east and west of the waterway. Beside the Nile's banks, however, the black alluvial soil of the narrow floodplain offered rich land for planting, although the river's gifts of water and arable land were limited. Irrigation canals and ditches plus patient, backbreaking labor were required to bring the life-giving liquid into the desert.

Because the survival and prosperity of the people depended on the Nile, the river dominated Egyptian experience. About 95 percent of the people lived on the less than 5 percent of Egyptian land that was arable and located along the Nile. People clustered in villages, the fundamental unit of Egyptian civilization. The reward for farm labor tended to be subsistence living, yet the perennial hope that next year's flood would bring a more bountiful harvest created an optimistic outlook that contrasted with the darker Mesopotamian view.

The Nile linked the "Two Lands," Upper and Lower Egypt, two regions whose differing geography made for two distinct ways of life. Since the Nile flows northward, Lower Egypt referred to the northern lands fed by the river's spreading delta, a region made wealthy by its fertile soil. In contrast, the harsh topography and

Figure 1.9 Ziggurat of Ur. Ca. 2100 BCE. Ur (Muqaiyir, Iraq). *A temple to Nanna, the moon god, stood on the top of the ziggurat, which was terraced on three levels. On the first level was an entryway approached by two sets of steps on each side and one in the front. The base, or lowest stage, which is all that remains of this "Hill of Heaven," measures 200 by 150 feet and stands 70 feet high. In comparison, Chartres cathedral in France is 157 feet wide, with each tower over 240 feet high.*

Timeline 1.3   EGYPTIAN CIVILIZATION   **All dates approximate and BCE**

6000	3100	2700	2185	2050	1800	1552	1079	525
Neolithic and Predynastic Periods	Early Dynastic Period	Old Kingdom	First Intermediate Period	Middle Kingdom	Second Intermediate Period	New Kingdom	Late Dynastic Period	Persian Conquest

poor farming conditions of the southern lands made Upper Egypt an area of near-subsistence living. In addition, Lower Egypt, because of its proximity to both Mediterranean and Near Eastern cultures, became more cosmopolitan than the provincial, isolated lands of Upper Egypt.

The earliest Neolithic settlers in the Nile valley probably arrived in about 6000 BCE. These earliest Egyptians took up an agricultural life, wresting control of the surrounding lands, taming the river, and domesticating animals. In the rich alluvial soil, they cultivated barley, wheat, and vegetables for themselves and fodder for their animals. They hunted with bows and arrows and fished with nets, thereby supplementing their simple fare. They also planted flax, from which thread was woven into linen on primitive looms. Most tools and weapons were made of stone or flint, but copper, which had to be imported, became more important after 3500 BCE. The early Egyptians lived in simply furnished, flat-topped houses built of sun-dried bricks. These basic patterns characterized peasant life throughout much of Egypt's history.

Continuity and Change over Three Thousand Years

Manetho, a historian who wrote in the third century BCE, divided Egypt's ruling families into twenty-six dynasties. Egypt stepped from the shadows of its illiterate past in about 3100 BCE, when Menes [MEE-neez] proclaimed himself king and united Upper and Lower Egypt. Modern historians lump Egypt's historical dynasties into three main periods, the Old, Middle, and New Kingdoms. These are preceded and followed by the early and late dynastic periods. Two intermediate periods separate the kingdoms from each other (Timeline 1.3).

In addition to unifying Egypt, the kings of the early dynastic period (about 3100–2700 BCE) brought prosperity through their control of the economy and fostered political harmony through diplomacy and dynastic marriages. These rulers, claiming to be gods on earth, adopted the trappings of divinity and built royal tombs to ensure their immortality.

With the Old Kingdom (about 2700–2185 BCE), Egypt entered a five-hundred-year period of peace and prosperity, as its political institutions matured and its language was adapted to literary uses. The most enduring accomplishment of the Old Kingdom became the pyramid—the royal tomb devised by the Fourth Dynasty kings (Figure 1.10). As the visible symbol of the kings' power, the massive pyramids served to link the rulers with the gods and the cosmos. Yet, although the kings could impress their people with divine claims, they could neither subdue the forces of nature nor make their power last forever. For reasons not fully understood, these rulers loosened their control over the state and thus ushered in an age of political fragmentation called the first intermediate period.

In the first intermediate period (about 2185–2050 BCE), civil war raged sporadically and starvation wiped out much of the populace. Eventually, a family from Thebes, in Upper Egypt, reunited Egypt and initiated the Middle Kingdom (about 2050–1800 BCE). The new dynasty, the twelfth, fortified the southern frontier with Nubia (roughly modern Sudan) and helped bring about a cultural renaissance, especially in literature, but unity was short-lived.

The second intermediate period (about 1800–1552 BCE) was an age of chaos provoked both by repeated failures of the Nile to flood and by a resurgence of local warlords. A weakened Lower Egypt succumbed to the Hyksos, Semitic-speaking invaders from Palestine. Backed by warriors in horse-drawn chariots, the Hyksos with their bronze weapons easily defeated the copper-armed Egyptians. The Hyksos era was crucial in Egypt's history because it ended the isolation that had fed a sense of cultural superiority. Egyptian nobility now joined aristocracies everywhere in employing the horse for war and sport, and Egyptian artisans fully entered the Bronze Age.

Ahmose I [AH-moh-suh], another Theban king, drove out the Hyksos and inaugurated the New Kingdom (1552–1079 BCE), the most cosmopolitan era in Egyptian history. To the south, the pharaohs pushed Egypt's frontiers to the Nile's fourth cataract, conquering the Nubians long in residence there. To the northeast, Egypt's kings, now called pharaohs, pursued imperial ambitions against the cities in Palestine,

Figure 1.10 The Pyramids at Giza. Ground view from the south. Pyramid of Menkure (foreground), ca. 2525 BCE; Pyramid of Khafre (center), ca. 2544 BCE; Pyramid of Khufu (rear), ca. 2580 BCE. *The Fourth Dynasty was the Age of Pyramids, when the pyramid's characteristic shape was standardized and became a symbol of Egyptian civilization. The Great Pyramid, in the rear, was the first structure at Giza; it originally stood 480 feet high but today is only 450 feet high. All three pyramids were originally surfaced with shiny, white limestone, but this covering was stripped in later centuries by builders in nearby Cairo; the only remnant of the limestone surface is the cap on the top of the Pyramid of Khafre, in the center.*

Phoenicia, and Syria, a move that provoked deadly warfare with the Hittites of Anatolia.

The Hittites, the first Indo-European people of historical significance, migrated from southern Russia into Anatolia around 3000 BCE. Gradually they built a powerful kingdom and defeated the kingdoms of Mesopotamia. They made skillful use of horses and chariots and also of iron weapons. In their heyday (about 1450–1180 BCE), they encountered the expanding Egyptians and warred with them continuously. After a great battle at Kadesh in 1274 BCE, itself essentially a draw, the Egyptians and Hittites concluded a treaty that divided Palestine and Syria between them. The treaty survives—the world's oldest international agreement—and its provisions are on display at the United Nations headquarters, in New York City. By about 1200 BCE, both the Egyptian and Hittite Empires were on the decline. Egypt's lack of iron ore probably contributed fatally to its military decline as its neighbors entered the Iron Age.

Just as they dominated the state, so the pharoahs controlled the predominantly agrarian economy, although departments of government or the priesthood of a temple often exploited the land and the king's laborers. In prosperous years, the pharaohs claimed up to half of the farm crops to support their building programs, especially funerary monuments. But in years of famine, dynasties fell and the state splintered into separate units. Politically, ancient Egypt alternated between central and local control.

Foreign trade was a royal monopoly. The government obtained cedar from Lebanon, olive oil from Palestine, and myrrh from Punt, probably on the Somali coast. Since Egypt never developed a coinage, the pharaohs bartered for these imports with papyrus rolls (for writing), linen, weapons, and furniture. The pharaohs also exported gold from the eastern desert and copper from the Sinai peninsula. In addition, Egypt served as the carrier of tropical African goods—ebony, ivory, and animal skins—to the eastern Mediterranean.

Egyptian society was hierarchical, and at the top stood the pharaoh—the king and god incarnate. Because divine blood coursed through the ruler's veins, he could marry only within his own family. Tradition decreed that the chief queen, who was identified with the goddess Hathor, would produce the royal heir. If she failed to produce offspring, the successor pharaoh was selected from sons of the ruler's other wives or royal cousins. On rare occasions, when there was no suitable heir, the chief queen became the pharaoh, as did Hatshepsut [hat-SHEP-soot] in the New Kingdom.

Because there was no provision for a female king in Egyptian culture, the appearance of a female ruler is thought by scholars to signal a political crisis. Only four times in Egypt's three-thousand-year history was the king female; in contrast, there were more than two hundred male kings. Of the four female rulers, three appeared at the end of dynasties: Nitiqret in the Sixth Dynasty, Nefrusobk in the Twelfth, and Tausret in the Nineteenth. Hatshepsut's assumption of power was unique in that it occurred in the midst of a flourishing dynasty, though during the infancy of Thutmose III [thoot-MOH-suh], the heir apparent. Acting at first as regent to the young heir, Hatshepsut soon claimed the kingship in her own right and reigned for about ten years. After her death, Thutmose III obliterated her name and image from her monuments, though the reason for their removal is unclear. He may have been expressing hatred of her, or he may have wanted to erase the memory of a woman who had seized power contrary to *maat*, the natural order of things.

Ranked below the ruling family were the royal officials, nobles, large landowners, and priests, all generally hereditary offices. The pharaoh's word was law, but these groups were delegated powers for executing his will. On a lower level, artists and artisans worked for the pharaonic court and the nobility. Peasants and a small number of slaves formed the bulk of Egypt's population. Personal liberty took second place to the general welfare, and peasants were pressed into forced labor during natural disasters, such as floods, and at harvest time.

A Quest for Eternal Cultural Values

Until the invasion of the Hyksos, Egypt, in its splendid isolation, forged a civilization whose serene values and timeless forms mirrored the religious beliefs of the rulers and the stability of the state. But as contact with other cultures and civilizations grew, Egyptian culture reflected new influences. Writers borrowed words from other languages, for example, and sculptors displayed the human figure in more natural settings and poses than in earlier times. Still, Egyptian culture retained its distinctive qualities, and innovations continued to express traditional ideals.

RELIGION   Mesopotamia's kings were **theocratic:** they believed that they ruled at the behest of the gods. Egypt's pharaohs were gods. Believing that the deities had planned their country's future from the beginning, the Egyptians thought of their society as sacred. From the time when Menes first united Egypt, religious dogma taught that the king, as god on earth, embodied the state. Egyptian rulers also identified themselves with various deities. For example, Menes claimed to be the "two ladies," the goddesses who stood for Upper and Lower Egypt. Other rulers identified themselves with Ra, the sun god, and with Ra's son, Horus, the sky god, who was always depicted as having the head of a falcon. Because of the king's divinity, the resources of the state were concentrated on giving the ruler proper homage, as in the Old Kingdom's massive tombs, designed on a superhuman scale to ensure his safe passage to the next life.

Egyptian subjects worshiped the pharaoh, but the pharaoh could venerate any deity he pleased. Hence, the shifting fortunes of Egypt's many cults depended on the ruler's preference. For example, early pharaohs favored Ptah (who, like the Hebrew God in Genesis, called things into being with words), whereas later ones preferred Ra, the sun god, and they honored this celestial deity by building him temples more impressive than their own royal tombs. Later still, pharaohs worshiped Amen ("hidden one"), and a series of rulers adopted his name, as in Amenemhat [AH-men-EM-hat]. Royal favor to a god generally increased the wealth and influence of the god's cult and priests. Consequently, by the time of the New Kingdom, society had become top-heavy with priests and their privileged religious properties.

Egypt came close to having a national deity during the New Kingdom when Akhenaten [ahk-NAHT-uhn] (r. about 1369–1353 BCE) reshaped the royal religion at his capital, Amarna. Elevating Aten, the god of the sun's disk, to supremacy above the other gods, Akhenaten systematically disavowed the older divinities— a heretical view in tolerant, polytheistic Egypt. This innovation, called **henotheism**—the particular worship of one god without denying the existence of others—aroused the opposition of conservative nobles who supported the powerful priests of the Theban god, Amen. Akhenaten ultimately failed to impose his innovation, and later pharaohs tried to erase his name and memory from history. The Amarna revolution, however, like the religious choices of the pharaohs generally, had little effect on the ordinary Egyptian, who continued to believe that the pharaoh could intervene with the other gods for the benefit of all.

The foremost distinguishing mark of Egyptian religion was its promise of immortality. Because the afterlife was imagined to be a carefree continuation of earthly existence, Egyptians had a more optimistic attitude toward human existence than that found in Mesopotamia. In the Old Kingdom, only the kings were accorded this reward. Eventually, nobles and royal officials were buried in the vicinity of the rulers' tombs, thereby ensuring their immortality as assistants to the risen god in the afterlife. By the first intermediate period, the nobles had claimed their own right to immortality by erecting tombs on which the royal funerary texts were copied. Later, immortality was apparently opened to all Egyptians.

WRITING AND LITERATURE   Late predynastic Egypt borrowed the idea of writing from Mesopotamia. The Egyptians initially drew pictographs, called hieroglyphs, for such words as *hoe, arrowhead,* and *plow.* This early hieroglyphic script could also depict abstract words for which no adequate picture was available, but because such picture writing was time-consuming and clumsy to execute, the scribes soon made the pictographs function as signs, or clusters of consonants, for other words (Figure 1.11).

Egyptian literature produced no single great work that rivals *Gilgamesh,* but the Egyptian experience was rich in its variety of literary **genres,** or types of literature. For example, pyramid texts, the writings inscribed in burial chambers (see the backgrounds in Figures 1.18 and 1.20), formed the chief literary genre in the Old Kingdom. As this era gave way to the first intermediate period, new prose genres, such as prophecies and pessimistic writings, arose that addressed the prevalent political disintegration and social upheaval. Such was the tenor of the times that writers expressed views contradicting Egypt's otherwise optimistic attitudes to death and life. *The Dispute of a Man with His Soul* describes a desperate mortal finally choosing the emptiness of death rather than life in a materialistic and violent world.

The prophecies, **hymns** (songs of praise to the gods), and prose narratives of the Middle Kingdom constitute the classical period of Egyptian letters. The most famous work of the Middle Kingdom, as well as of all Egyptian literature, is the *Story of Sinuhe,* a prose tale that celebrates the ruler Senusert I and his subject, the hero named in the title. Fleeing Egypt, Sinuhe earns fame and fortune in Lebanon yet yearns for his beloved homeland. Sinuhe's exploits smack of the folktale, for in one episode he subdues a taunting giant of a man, much as David defeats Goliath in the Old Testament story. Eventually, a gracious Senusert writes to Sinuhe, forgiving his wandering subject's unnamed crime and inviting him to return home. The travel yarn concludes with a homecoming scene in which a joyful Sinuhe is reintegrated into Egyptian court society.

During the New Kingdom, in addition to songs praising the pharaoh, poets composed lyrics telling of the pain of parted lovers, and new genres included model letters, wisdom literature, and fairy tales. Akhenaten's revolution led to unique forms of literary expression, as in the *Hymn to Aten,* which praised this universal god. The hymn has similarities to Psalm 104 of the Old Testament, which suggests the relatively free flow of ideas during Egypt's imperial years (Figure 1.12).

SCIENCE AND MEDICINE   Natural philosophy, as a separate field of study, did not emerge in ancient Egypt. No term for either philosophy or science existed in the Egyptian language. The Egyptians put their efforts into what would today be called applied science. For example, they invented a convenient decimal number system rendered inconvenient by their cumbersome hieroglyphics. They devised problem-solving methods and related rules for measuring figures and calculating the volumes of solids. They kept accurate records of the annual floods of the Nile and built pyramids

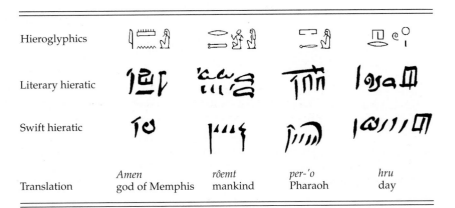

Figure 1.11 Egyptian Writing. *From the Old Kingdom onward, the hieroglyphs (in the top line) constituted the style of formal writing that appeared on tomb walls and in monuments. Religious and governmental scribes soon devised two distinct types of cursive script, a careful manuscript hand (in the middle line) and a more rapid hand (in the bottom line) for administrative documents and letters.*

Hieroglyphics				
Literary hieratic				
Swift hieratic				
Translation	*Amen* god of Memphis	*rôemt* mankind	*per-'o* Pharaoh	*hru* day

and other structures, which required knowledge of measurement and design.

Egyptians studied the movement of the stars, but Egyptian astronomy was not well advanced, being concerned primarily with casting horoscopes and the keeping of the civil calendar. Egypt's lasting contribution in this field was the calendar itself, which priests maintained for the celebration of religious rituals and festivals during the year. They divided the year into twelve months of thirty days each, with five extra days at the end of the year. This calendar began each annual cycle on September 21, the autumnal equinox. Later, the Romans adopted the Egyptian calendar, with its twelve-month, 365-day cycle, and they in turn transmitted it to the modern world.

Medicine was another area of Egyptian scientific achievement, partly from a concern with the health

Figure 1.12   Rosetta Stone. Ca. 197–196 BCE. British Museum, London. *Scholars were unable to decipher hieroglyphics until the nineteenth century. Napoleon's soldiers found this inscribed stone in the Rosetta branch of the Nile—hence its name—when they invaded Egypt in 1799. The text at the bottom is in Greek, which scholars could read. Guessing that all three texts recorded the same event, scholars first solved the hieratic (priestly) cursive in the middle and then moved on to the hieroglyphic at the top. Modern Egyptology began with this discovery.*

Figure 1.13   Imhotep. Step Pyramid of King Djoser. Ca. 2680 BCE. Sakkareh, Egypt. *Although the step pyramid at Sakkareh resembles the Mesopotamian ziggurat, the two structures have different origins. Sakkareh's step pyramid, with its terraced stages, evolved from an Egyptian prototype, which dated from the First Dynasty. Unlike ziggurats, which were made of dried-clay bricks, the step pyramid was made of cut stone, the first buildings to be so constructed in the world. The step pyramid has six levels on a 411-by-358-foot base and stands 204 feet high.*

SLICE OF LIFE
Life's Instruction Book for Egyptians

ANONYMOUS
From a Papyrus Text

Egypt's wisdom literature—aphorisms about the best way to live—culminated in The Instruction of Amenemope, *written in the late New Kingdom. In this work, the author stresses the ethical life rather than the amassing of personal wealth.*

Beginning of the teaching for life,
The instructions for well-being.

. . . .

If you make your life with these [words] in your
    heart,
You will find it a success;
You will find my words a storehouse for life,
Your being will prosper upon earth.

. . . .

Do not move the markers on the borders of fields,
Nor shift the position of the measuring-cord.
Do not be greedy for a cubit of land,
Nor encroach on the boundaries of a widow.

. . . .

Do not set your heart on wealth,
There is no ignoring Fate and Destiny;

. . . .

Do not strain to seek increase,
What you have, let it suffice you.

. . . .

Do not cheat a man (through) pen on scroll,
The god abhors it;
Do not bear witness with false words,
So as to brush aside a man by your tongue.

. . . .

Do not laugh at a blind man,
Nor tease a dwarf,
Nor cause hardship for the lame.

. . . .

Do not sit down in the beer-house
In order to join one greater than you,
Be he a youth great through his office,
Or be he an elder through birth.
Befriend a man of your own measure.

. . . .

Do not revile one older than you,
He has seen Re [the Sun God] before you;
Let (him) not report you to the Aten [the god of the
    sun's disk] at his rising,
Saying: "A youth has reviled an old man."

INTERPRETING THIS SLICE OF LIFE

1. *What* are some of the "words to live by," which are offered in this piece of wisdom literature? 2. *How* should old people be treated by the young? 3. *What* is the author's teaching on wealth and materialism? 4. *Compare* the advice in this work with the Ten Commandments (see Table 5.1). 5. Do you think these rules are useful in today's world? *Discuss.*

of the living and partly from an acute interest in the physical remains of the dead. An ancient medical treatise, dating from about 1600 BCE (but possibly from as early as 3000 BCE), is the world's oldest surviving medical textbook. This surgical treatise offers a comprehensive survey of the human body, detailing the diagnosis, treatment, and outcome of various maladies that can afflict the human organs. A second medical treatise, dating from about 1550 BCE, lists hundreds of magical incantations and folk remedies for numerous illnesses, such as crocodile wounds and ingrown toenails, along with advice on ridding the house of vermin, insects, and scorpions.

ARCHITECTURE   The classic Egyptian building was the pyramid, whose shape seemed to embody a constant and eternal order. During the Old Kingdom, the pyramid became the only building deemed suitable for a ruler-god's resting place preparatory to the afterlife. A modified version of the pyramid appeared first in about 2680 BCE in the step pyramid of King Djoser [ZHO-ser] at Sakkareh, opposite Memphis (Figure 1.13). Later Egyptian rulers preferred the true pyramid form, and this design did not develop further.

The true pyramid appeared in the Old Kingdom when the Fourth Dynasty ruler Khufu [KOO-foo] erected the Great Pyramid at Giza, across the Nile from Cairo (see Figure 1.10). The anonymous architect executed this largest stone building in the world—6.25 million tons—with mathematical precision. Many of the tomb's two million stones were quarried on the site, although most were obtained farther upstream and ferried to Giza during the flooding of the Nile. The infinitesimally small deviation between the two sets of opposing base sides of the pyramid shows the scientific spirit already at work in this early stage of Egypt's history. Later, two of Khufu's successors, Khafre [KAF-ray] and Menkure [men-KOO-ray], added their pyramids to make the complex at Giza the symbol of the Old Kingdom and one of the wonders of the ancient world.

The pyramids eventually gave way to funerary temples when the New Kingdom pharaohs began to construct splendid monuments for themselves that reflected Egypt's new imperial status. The temple of Queen Hatshepsut is perhaps the most beautiful example of this architectural development (Figure 1.14). Designed by the royal architect Senmut, the temple

of Hatshepsut was carved into the face of a mountain across the Nile from Luxor. Senmut, adopting the post-and-lintel style of construction, gave the queen's temple two levels of pillared colonnades, each accessible by long sloping ramps. The most arresting feature of Hatshepsut's temple is its round columns, which are used alongside rectangular pillars in the **porticoes,** or covered entrances. These columns—with their plain tops and grooved surfaces—suggest the graceful columns of later Greek architecture, although some scholars dismiss this similarity as coincidental. Be that as it may, this Egyptian monument, like the later Greek temples, shows a harmonious sense of proportion throughout its impressive colonnades.

SCULPTURE, PAINTING, AND MINOR ARTS   The Egyptians did not understand art as it is defined today. Indeed, they had no word for art. Rather than being art for art's sake, Egyptian painting and sculpture served as a means to a religious end, specifically to house the *ka,* or spirit of a person or deity. Art was more than mere

Figure 1.14   SENMUT. Hatshepsut's Temple. Ca. 1490 BCE. Deir el Bahri, across from Luxor, Egypt. *Hatshepsut's temple was planned for the same purpose as the pyramids—to serve as a shrine for the royal remains. In actuality an ascending series of three colonnaded courtyards, this temple provided a spectacular approach to a hidden sanctuary carved in the steep cliffs.*

Figure 1.15 The Great Sphinx. Ca. 2560 BCE. Sandstone, 65′ high × 240′ long. Giza, Egypt. *Sphinxes, creatures part lion and part human, were often depicted in Egyptian art. The most famous sphinx is the one at Giza, carved from the rock on the site. The sphinx's colossal size prevented the anonymous sculptor from rendering it with any subtle facial expressions. More significant as a monument than as a great work of art, the Great Sphinx had a practical purpose—to guard the nearby pyramid tombs.*

representation; images embodied all of the subjects' qualities.

In the royal graveyard at Giza, artisans of the Old Kingdom carved from the living rock a mythical creature that stirred the imagination of most peoples in the ancient world—a sphinx, a lion with a human head (Figure 1.15). Although this creature often inspired feelings of dread, in actuality there was little mystery to the sphinx, since its original purpose was to guard the royal tombs, perhaps to frighten away grave robbers. Indeed, this first sphinx's face was that of Khafre, the Fourth Dynasty king whose pyramid stood nearby. Today, this crumbling relic stands as a reminder of the claims to immortality of the Old Kingdom rulers.

The sheer size and mythical character of the Great Sphinx set it apart from Old Kingdom sculptures in the round, which favored human-scale figures and realistic images. The life-size statue of King Menkure and his chief queen, found beneath the ruler's pyramid at Giza, shows this art's brilliant realism (Figure 1.16). The sculpture embodies the characteristics of what became the standard, or classical, Egyptian style: their left legs forward, the king's clenched fists, their headdresses (sacred regalia for him and wig for her), their rigid poses, their serene countenances, and the figures' angularity. Designed to be attached to a wall,

Figure 1.16 *King Menkure and His Chief Queen.* Ca. 2525 BCE. Ht. 54½″. Museum expedition. Courtesy Museum of Fine Arts, Boston. *This life-size slate sculpture of Menkure, a Fourth Dynasty ruler, and his chief queen was removed from its resting place beneath the king's pyramid at Giza (see Figure 1.10). In this sculpture, the figures are represented as being of comparable size, unlike the usual depiction of husbands as much larger than their wives, indicating their greater importance. The sizes here probably reflect the royal status of the chief queen. The queen's subordination to the king is subtly shown in her position on his left side, thought to be inferior to the right, and her arm around his waist, an indication that her role was to encourage and support.*

the sculpture was intended to be viewed from the front, so the couple has a two-dimensional quality.

In contrast to practices in the Old Kingdom, the wives of rulers in the New Kingdom acquired claims to divinity in their own right. A statue of Hatshepsut represents her in the clothing and with the sacred pose of pharaoh (Figure 1.17). Having first been chief queen to Thutmose II in the New Kingdom, after his death she seized leadership, probably with the cooperation of the powerful Theban priesthood of Amen. Although more than a thousand years separated this sculpture from that of Menkure (see Figure 1.16), in its expression of dignity and authority the statue of Hatshepsut bears a strong resemblance to the earlier work, thus demonstrating the continuity of the Egyptian style.

A major challenge to Egypt's traditional, austere forms occurred in Akhenaten's revolutionary reign. A low-relief sculpture of the royal family exemplifies the naturalism and fluid lines that this artistic rebellion favored (Figure 1.18). Akhenaten nuzzles one of his daughters in an intimate pose while his wife dandles another daughter on her knees and allows a third to stand on her left arm. The domesticity of this scene is quite unlike the sacred gestures of traditional Egyptian sculpture, but the religious subject of this relief remains true to that tradition, as the rays streaming from the disk of Aten onto the royal family indicate.

The most extraordinary artistic achievement of the Amarna period is the carved portrait head of Queen Nefertiti (Figure 1.19), a life-size sculpture discovered

Figure 1.17 *Hatshepsut.* Ca. 1460 BCE. Marble, ht. 6'5". Courtesy Metropolitan Museum of Art. Rogers Fund and contribution from Edward S. Harkness, 1929 (29.3.2). *This sculpture is one of more than two hundred statues of Hatshepsut intended to adorn her massive and elegant funeral temple at Deir el Bahri in the western hills of Thebes. The authoritative pose and regalia convey her pharaonic status, and she is only subtly represented as a woman.*

Figure 1.18 *Family Scene: Pharaoh Akhenaten, Queen Nefertiti, and Their Three Daughters.* Ca. 1350 BCE. Limestone, 13" high × 15⁵/₁₂" wide. Altes Museum, Berlin. *The religious ideas associated with Akhenaten's reforms are expressed in the lines streaming from the sun's disk above the royal couple. Each ray of the sun ends in a tiny hand that offers a blessing to the royal family.*

Figure 1.19 *Nefertiti.* Ca. 1350 BCE. Limestone, ht. 20". Altes Museum, Berlin. *This portrait head of Nefertiti is characterized by sleekness and charm, a look achieved through the sculptor's fusing of the fluid Amarna style with the formality of Egypt's traditional art. To create the image of sleekness, the sculptor has pushed Nefertiti's face forward like the prow of a ship cutting through the wind. The figure's charm emerges from the tension between the queen's dreamy, deeply hooded eyes (one eye is unfinished) and her lively, arched eyebrows. The artist has succeeded in representing Nefertiti as both a woman and a goddess.*

in 1912 by a team of German archaeologists in the desert sands near the long-lost city founded by Akhenaten for the god Aten. This statue-head with its unfinished left eye, deliberate or accidental, is one of the most arresting images of world art. Painted in flesh tones and natural colors and imbued with the naturalism of the Amarna style, the queen has a vitality that is unsurpassed. Nefertiti's unusual headdress signifies her status as a potent force in this culture. Rising straight up from her forehead, this crown is decorated with the *uraeus*, the image of a cobra ready to strike. By custom, this powerful and protective symbol was part of the kingly **regalia** (tokens of royal authority) and could be worn only by rulers and their great (principal) queens. Nefertiti was the only great, or chief, queen in Egypt's long history to share power with her husband. (Queen Hatshepsut actually ruled alone as pharaoh.) The prevalence of images of Nefertiti in so much of the art that remains from Amarna confirms this queen's importance on the political level and thus underscores her central role in the Amarna revolution.

Just as Egypt's sculpture in the round developed a rigid **canon,** or set of rules, so did two-dimensional representations acquire a fixed formula, whether in relief sculptures or in wall paintings. The Egyptians never discovered the principles of perspective. On a flat surface, the human figures were depicted in profile, with both feet pointing sideways, as in a painting from a New Kingdom funerary papyrus (Figure 1.20). However, the artistic canon required that the eye and the shoulders be shown frontally, and both arms had to be visible, along with all the fingers. The artist determined the human proportions exactly, by the use

Figure 1.20 Opening of the Mouth Scene, Funerary Papyrus of Hunefer. Ca. 1305–1195 BCE. British Museum, London. *Egyptian painters and sculptors always depicted human subjects from the side, with the feet in profile, as in this painting on a papyrus manuscript deposited in a New Kingdom tomb. This painting's treatment of flesh tones of the human figures also typifies the Egyptian style. Egyptian men, represented here by the officiating priests, were consistently shown with red-brown, tanned skins at least partially reflective of their outdoor lives. Egyptian women, such as the mourners directly before the mummy, were usually painted with lighter complexions of yellow or pink or white. The Opening of the Mouth was a burial ritual, preparing the deceased to speak in the afterlife.*

of a grid. The human figure was usually conceived as being eighteen squares high standing and fourteen squares high seated, with each unit equivalent to the width of one "fist"; anatomical parts were made accordingly proportional. The canon of proportions was established by the time of the Old Kingdom, and its continued use, with slight variations, helped Egyptian art retain its unmistakable style. Wall paintings, in contrast to relief sculptures, permitted a greater sense of life and energy, as in the scene of Nebamun hunting birds, but the rules regarding the human figure still had to be observed (Figure 1.21). Given those stringent conventions, the Egyptian artists who worked in two dimensions were amazingly successful in creating the image of a carefree society bubbling with life.

Royal tombs have yielded incomparable examples of Egyptian sculpture, as in the burial chamber of the New Kingdom pharaoh Tutankhamen [too-tahn-KAHM-en]. Of the thirty-four excavated royal tombs, only that of King Tut—as he is popularly known—escaped relatively free from violation by thieves in ancient times. A freestanding, life-size sculpture of the funerary goddess Selket was one of four goddess figures who watched over the gilded shrine that contained the king's internal organs (Figure 1.22). Her arms are outstretched in a protective fashion around

Figure 1.21   *Nebamun Hunting Birds.* Ca. 1400 BCE. From the Tomb of Nebamun, Thebes. Paint on gypsum plaster, ht. 32". British Museum, London. *For the nobleman Nebamun, hunting was a pastime not a necessity. Decorating his tomb with hunting scenes was Nebamun's way of ensuring that there would be plenty of birds to hunt in the afterlife. Note the faces in profile—typical in Egyptian art (see Figures 1.18 and 1.20).*

Timeline 1.4   HEIRS TO THE MESOPOTAMIAN AND EGYPTIAN CULTURES   **All dates approximate and BCE**

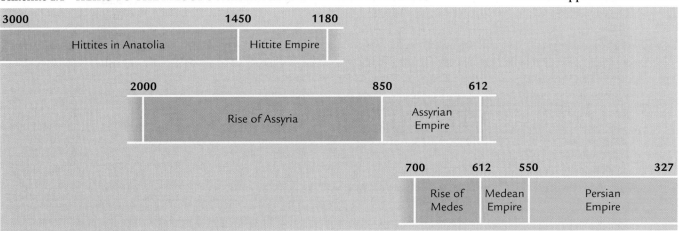

3000		1450	1180
Hittites in Anatolia		Hittite Empire	

	2000		850	612
	Rise of Assyria		Assyrian Empire	

	700	612	550		327
	Rise of Medes	Medean Empire	Persian Empire		

Figure 1.22   *Selket.* Ca. 1325 BCE. Wood, overlaid with gesso and gilded, ht. 53⅝″. Cairo Museum, Egypt. *This statue of the goddess Selket was found in King Tutankhamen's tomb in 1923, one of the great archaeological finds of the twentieth century. Discovered by Egyptologist Howard Carter, the tomb held thousands of royal artifacts and art objects, including the pharaoh's gold funerary mask, a solid gold coffin, a gold throne, chairs, couches, chariots, jewelry, figurines, drinking cups, clothing, weapons, and games. The fascinating story of the discovery is told in Carter's book,* The Tomb of Tutankhamen.

her royal charge's shrine. A unique feature is the turn of Selket's head, a violation of the cardinal rule of two-dimensional Egyptian art that figures face front-ward (see Figures 1.16 and 1.17). The sculpture's style, with its naturalism and fluid lines, reflects the art of Amarna, the revolutionary style that flourished briefly in the fourteenth century BCE before being abandoned and replaced by Egypt's traditional formal style.

HEIRS TO THE MESOPOTAMIAN AND EGYPTIAN EMPIRES

With the decline of the Egyptian and Hittite Empires, the ancient Near East entered upon a confusing period. At first a number of small states emerged and enjoyed periods of independence. Israel (see Chapter 5) and Phoenicia (see Encounter) were the most prominent. Then a series of ever-larger empires arose, the Assyrians, the Neo-Babylonians, and finally the Persians (Timeline 1.4).

The Assyrians

The earliest Assyrian tribes lived in the Upper Tigris region, in present-day Iraq. From about the twentieth to the thirteenth century BCE, they flourished under a series of kings who united their subjects and extended their territories. Over the next three hundred years, the Assyrians conquered Babylon and advanced westward to the Mediterranean Sea. In the ninth century BCE, they moved rapidly against their neighbors, defeating them on the battlefield, sending total populations into exile, and ruling with an iron fist and a policy of terror. At the height of their power, they controlled all the land between the Nile River in

Egypt and the Tigris River in Mesopotamia. A vigorous and warlike people from the beginning, they sent their well-trained and highly disciplined armies to sweep through the enemy ranks. Supplied with the latest iron weapons and supported by swiftly moving chariot legions, they fought to total victory, showing no mercy in executing prisoners and destroying their cities. Yet, just when it appeared the Assyrian Empire would continue for centuries, they were quickly defeated by the Medes and the Neo-Babylonians in 612 BCE, at Nineveh.

The Assyrians' military campaigns and cruel occupation policies manifested themselves in their civilization and art. Their cities were built as fortresses. The temples to their gods were huge and adorned. Their rulers' palaces were constructed on a magnificent and gigantic scale with open courtyards, terraces, and decorations. These royal residences expressed the empire's triumphs and sent a clear message to the Assyrian people and to subjected enemies. Among the ruins of the Assyrian palaces and sculpture, the portal carvings, or "guardians of the gates," and the wall reliefs remain as testaments to the glories and values of a fierce and proud civilization. The stone animals, placed as pairs at the entrances of palaces and temples, were there to impress visitors and to ward off evil forces. The human-headed winged bulls (Figure 1.23), found at several royal palaces, convey the

power, aura, and mystery of the Assyrian kings—and the awe they sought to inspire.

The Neo-Babylonians

One beneficiary of the fall of the Assyrians was the Neo-Babylonian kingdom established in 626 BCE. Although militant and warlike, the Neo-Babylonians were also culturally sophisticated. In addition to helping to defeat the Assyrians, the Neo-Babylonians conquered Jerusalem and exiled the Hebrews of the Kingdom of Judah (see Chapter 5). Under the direction of their greatest king, Nebuchadnezzar (605–562 BCE), the city of Babylon was largely rebuilt (Figure 1.24) and adorned with the famous "hanging gardens," a luxurious, terraced complex built for the queen. The Neo-Babylonians, like the Assyrians, were accomplished in astronomy. Their interests, however, were religious not scientific. That is, they observed the heavens closely to practice astrology. In the end, the Neo-Babylonians were no match for their erstwhile allies the Medes who, having merged with the Persians, conquered them in 539 BCE.

The Medes and the Persians

After their defeat of the Assyrians in 612 BCE, the Medes, an Indo-European people from the southwest Iranian plateau, retained Nineveh, the Assyrian capital. From their homeland in the central Zagros Mountains, the Medes built an empire that eventually covered most of northern and western Mesopotamia and eastern Anatolia. The power of the Medes, however, proved to be short-lived. In about 550 BCE, their empire fell to the Persians, another Indo-European tribe led by the charismatic Cyrus the Great (559–530 BCE). The Persians, under a series of masterful rulers, forged the strongest and largest empire that the eastern Mediterranean had yet seen. At its height, Persian rule extended from Egypt in the south to central Russia in

Figure 1.23 Human-Headed Winged Bull. Eighth century BCE. Gypseous alabaster, ht. 13'10". Louvre. *In Assyrian iconography, human-headed winged bulls—or lions—that guarded the entrances to royal residences and temples combined the characteristics of certain living beings. The head of a man represented intellectual power and the lord of creation; eagle wings were signs of speed and flight; the bull symbolized strength and fecundity, or, if the creature was a lion, then strength and the king of beasts. The carvings' five legs—an unnatural touch—gave each animal the appearance of either walking or standing still, depending on the perspective from which it was viewed. While their purposes are not fully understood, these guardian statues, with their imposing stance and symbolic meanings, made all who approached know that they were in the presence of a powerful ruler and forces.*

Figure 1.24 The Ishtar Gate, Babylon. Ca. 575 BCE. Glazed brick, ht. 48′9″. Staatliche Museen, Berlin. *Nebuchadnezzar dedicated this magnificent processional entryway to Ishtar, the goddess of love and war. It was one of eight gates into the city of Babylon. Excavated by German archaeologists between 1899 and 1914, the gate was reconstructed in Berlin. Dragons and aurochs (now-extinct oxen) are depicted on the gate. The hanging gardens have vanished, so only this gateway survives to convey a sense of Babylon's opulence.*

the north, and from Cyprus in the west to the Indus River in the east. Of its neighbors in the eastern Mediterranean basin, only mainland Greece eluded Persia's grasp. The Persians brought peace to a wide area; granted autonomy to most peoples; instituted common coinage, weights, and measures; and built good roads.

For two hundred years the Persian Empire and its culture had a brilliant run. The Persians created an eclectic style that derived from their own past as well as from the cultures of many of the peoples folded into the Persian Empire. For example, Persian arts had included distinctive vase painting and elegant metalworking but no tradition of stone architecture. Now, under the empire, artists and craftspeople, many of whom were new subjects, built on that heritage and, at the same time, borrowed from their own building traditions. These borrowings included masonry techniques, the finished appearance of buildings, treatment of architectural and sculptural details as decorations, as on columns, and some new building types. In the end, Persian architecture became the first highly decorated style (between India in the east and Syria in the west) to use large dressed stone rather than brick.

Persian art was courtly and ceremonial and focused on heightening the dignity and authority of the king and his court. At the capital, Persepolis, located in the Persian homeland of Parsa (modern Fars, in southern Iran), Cyrus the Great chose the site for a palace. His successor, King Darius I (duh-RYE-us) (r. 522–486 BCE), eventually built the first monumental palace there, and later rulers made splendid additions. Persepolis today is a ruin, having been looted during Alexander the Great's conquest in 330 BCE. Among the ruins, a magnificent decorative relief survives, depicting aristocrats as they offer tribute to the king on New Year's Day. Despite its battered condition, this relief attests to the stateliness of the Persian imperial style (Figure 1.25).

Persian visual arts also stressed contemplative themes with little action, as in the relief sculpture of King Darius (Figure 1.26). In this panel, King Darius is represented on a throne before two fire altars, as he receives a court official. Bending slightly from the waist, the official covers his mouth with the tips of his fingers—a gesture of devotion. These two sculptures illustrate the limited range of subjects, namely, the king and his court duties, employed in the art program of the Persian kings at Persepolis.

The fire altars depicted in the relief panel mentioned above are symbols of Zoroastrianism, the religion of the Persian prophet Zoroaster [ZOHR-uh-was-ter] (about

Figure 1.25 Nobles Marching Up the Stairs. Ca. 512–494 BCE. Persepolis, Iran. *This charming relief sculpture, carved on a wall facing a stairway at the Persian capital, Persepolis, depicts aristocrats mounting stairs to greet the king on New Year's Day, a sacred festival celebrated on the summer solstice and one of the major holidays in Mesopotamia. Each noble bears a flower offering as a tangible sign of his devotion to the monarch. The artist has humanized this courtly ritual by injecting an element of sly humor into the stately scene: one noble (the seventh from the right) sniffs his flower, and a second noble (the third from the right) turns to check on the progress of the procession behind him.*

Figure 1.26 Darius Giving Audience before Two Fire Altars. Found in the Treasury, Persepolis. Ca. 512–494 BCE. Limestone, length 20'. Archaeological Museum, Tehran. *This relief sculpture, carved on the walls of the Treasury at Persepolis, shows King Darius seated before two fire altars. In front of him is the master of ceremonies, with his hand raised to his lips in a gesture of devotion. Two bodyguards, holding spears, stand to the right. The Persian sculptural style is shown by the stylized hair and beards, precise folds in the clothing, and the formal poses of the figures.*

The Legacy of Early Near Eastern Civilizations

Mesopotamia and Egypt provide the earliest models of civilization in the West. In both, large numbers of people were organized into societies characterized by class stratification; a division of labor; complex political, economic, and religious forms; technological advances (in pottery making and glassmaking, the extraction and working of metals, textiles, woodworking, and building techniques); and cultural achievements. They weren't the only ancient civilizations—others developed in China, India, South America, and elsewhere—but they are the ones to which Westerners most directly trace their roots.

Mesopotamia's gifts to Western civilization are impressive. In addition to writing, these societies established urbanism as a way of life in contrast to agrarian or village existence. In more practical matters, they created a mathematical system based on 60 that gave the world the 60-minute hour and the 360-degree circle. They also divided the seasons and devised a lunar calendar to mark off periods of days to aid them in their planting. Trade and commerce forced them to develop methods of counting, measuring, and weighing that became the standard procedures for other Near Eastern peoples for centuries. Mesopotamian myths, legends, and epics found their way into the folktales and literature of other cultures.

Egypt made equally impressive contributions to the West. Egyptian bureaucrats, who wanted to predict the correct date for the annual rising of the Nile's waters, devised a solar calendar that is the basis of the Western calendar. The Egyptian model, which divided the year into twelve months of thirty days each, with five extra days at the end of the year, was conveyed to Western culture by the Romans. In architecture, Egyptian builders devised the column with a decorated capital, which later Greek architects probably adopted. The Greek builders also borrowed the Egyptian tradition of sound engineering principles rooted in mathematics. Similarly, Greek sculptors owed a debt to Egyptian forms and poses. Indeed, the Egyptian idea of an aesthetic canon influenced both sculptors and artists in Greece.

In literature, the Egyptians explored a variety of genres—such as wisdom writing—and folktales that influenced the Hebrews and the Greeks. In science, Egyptian physicians became renowned throughout the Near East for their medical learning and knowledge of drugs. Finally, with its priceless treasures, its mysterious pyramids, and its cult of the dead, Egypt inspired curiosity and excitement in foreigners from ancient times onward. The world's fascination with the culture of ancient Egypt has never diminished.

---

600 BCE), or Zarathustra [zah-ra-THUSH-trah], which became the official faith of the Persian court at the time of Darius I. Zoroastrianism is the most original and enduring of Persia's legacies. Rejecting polytheism, Zoroaster called for a dualistic religion in which the god of light, Ahura Mazda (Persian, "Wise Lord"), engaged in a universal struggle with the god of darkness, Ahriman. According to Zoroaster, not only did those who had led lives of purity gain favored treatment in the afterlife, but their actions also ensured the triumph of the forces of good in the here and now. These teachings later had a profound impact on Western philosophy and religions (see Encounter in Chapter 4).

KEY CULTURAL TERMS

civilization	hieroglyphics
culture	cuneiform
Paleolithic	polytheism
Neolithic	anthropomorphism
pictogram	pantheism
ideogram	stele
phonogram	reliefs
post-and-lintel	genre
construction	hymn
ziggurat	portico
theocracy	regalia
henotheism	canon

QUESTIONS FOR CRITICAL THINKING

1. Define the Neolithic Revolution. What was its importance in the development of institutions and the arts in early civilizations?

2. In what ways did geography expand and constrain the development of Mesopotamian and Egyptian civilizations?

3. What were the general characteristics of Mesopotamian art?

4. Describe the Egyptian religious system. How did Egypt's religion affect developments in art, architecture, and literature?

5. Why is the pyramid the supreme symbol of Egyptian civilization?

2

AEGEAN CIVILIZATIONS
The Minoans, the Mycenaeans, and the Greeks of the Archaic Age

Fascinating and important though they were, the people of Mesopotamia and Egypt nevertheless seem remote, mysterious. The Greeks seem familiar; they seem to be "like us." The most profound and recognizable features of the Western tradition derive from the Greeks. Whether one thinks of political institutions, literary forms, or aesthetic tastes, the Greeks were both original and influential. Greek achievements became the standard against which later ones would be judged. They became "classic," the ideal against which Western societies would judge themselves for more than two millennia. More than all this, however, the Greeks shifted focus from gods and godlike rulers to men and women. Ordinary people were seen as having some control over their destinies and some moral responsibility for their actions. By the fifth century BCE, the Greek philosopher Protagoras could proclaim, "Man is the measure of all things."

The people we refer to as the Greeks were not the first to thrive in the Aegean basin. Two other distinctive civilizations—the Minoan and the Mycenaean—established centers of culture in the area and left their mark on the Greeks of the Archaic Age beginning in about 800 BCE (Timeline 2.1, Map 2.1). On rocky coasts and rugged islands and peninsulas, the peoples of the Aegean basin coaxed a subsistence living from the thin, stony soil and turned to the sea for trade, conquest, and expansion. From the Bronze Age to the Iron Age, Minoans, Mycenaeans, and Greeks interacted with and learned from the cultures that surrounded them, chiefly those of the Hittites and the Egyptians, but whether it be in systems of writing or forms of sculpture, Aegean peoples were never content merely to borrow. They always adapted,

◀ **Detail** Temple of Hera, Paestum. Ca. 560–550 BCE. Limestone.

Timeline 2.1 MINOAN AND MYCENAEAN CIVILIZATIONS   **All dates approximate and BCE**

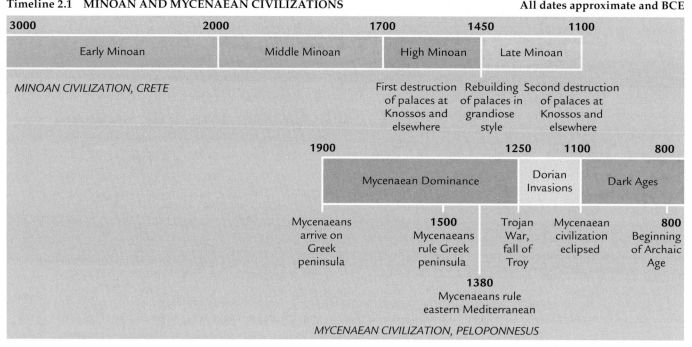

blended, and, finally, superseded. The Greek genius was partly a matter of stunning originality and partly a matter of creative synthesis.

PRELUDE: MINOAN CIVILIZATION, 3000–1100 BCE

While civilizations were flourishing in Egypt and Mesopotamia, another culture was developing among the Neolithic settlements on the island of Crete. By about 2000 BCE, a prosperous and stable mercantile civilization had emerged, and between 1700 and 1500 BCE, it reached its high point in wealth, power, and sophistication. This society, labeled Minoan after the legendary King Minos, was organized into a complex class system that included nobles, merchants, artisans, bureaucrats, and laborers. Noble life was based in palaces, and twentieth-century archaeological excavations of several palace sites indicate that communities were linked in a loose political federation, with the major center at Knossos on the north coast. Remarkably, no fortified walls protected the Minoan palaces, suggesting that the cities remained at peace with one another and that the island itself faced no threats from sea raiders. Crete's tranquil image is further supported by the absence of weapons in excavated remains.

The palace at Knossos is the principal source of knowledge about Minoan Crete. The ruins, though no

longer paved or walled, provide a sense of the grandeur and expanse of this once-magnificent site (Figure 2.1). It included an impressive plumbing and drainage system and a complex layout of rooms and passageways on several levels. Belowground, a storage area contained huge earthenware pots that held grains, oils, and wines, probably collected as taxes from the populace and serving as the basis of trade and wealth. Beautiful **friezes** (bands of designs and figures) decorated the walls of rooms and hallways. **Frescoes,** a process of applying paint to wet plaster, of sea creatures (dolphins and octopuses), of beautiful women, and of intriguing bull-leaping rituals (Figure 2.2) enlivened the palace walls. These remains are highly revealing but, unfortunately, early Minoan writing, called **Linear A,** has not been deciphered. No one knows the language of the Minoans, which adds to the mystery surrounding their origins.

Minoan religion appears to have been **matriarchal,** led or ruled by women, centering on the worship of a mother goddess, or great goddess, creator of the universe and source of all life. Statues of a bare-breasted earth goddess with snakes in her hands show how the deity was portrayed by the Minoans, but the precise purpose of these statues is unknown (Figure 2.3). Minoans also honored numerous minor household goddesses and venerated trees and stone pillars, to which they probably attributed supernatural powers. Near the end of their era, the Minoans began to bury their

LEARNING THROUGH MAPS

Map 2.1   THE AEGEAN WORLD, 479 BCE
This map shows the location of the Minoan, Mycenaean, and Greek Archaic Age civilizations. 1. *Consider* the role of the Aegean and Mediterranean Seas in shaping these three civilizations. 2. *What* were the centers of Minoan and Mycenaean civilizations? 3. *Why* do you think the location of Troy helped to make it a wealthy and strategic city? 4. *Locate* the major city-states of the Greek Archaic Age. 5. *How* did geography influence the origins and strategies of the Persian War?

Figure 2.1   North Entrance, Palace of Minos, Knossos, Crete. Ca. 1750–1650 BCE. *The palace complex, with courtyards, staircases, and living areas, now partially restored, indicates that the royal family lived in comfort and security, surrounded by works of art. When British archaeologist Sir Arthur Evans uncovered these ruins in 1902, he became convinced that he had discovered the palace of the legendary King Minos and labeled the civilization* Minoan.

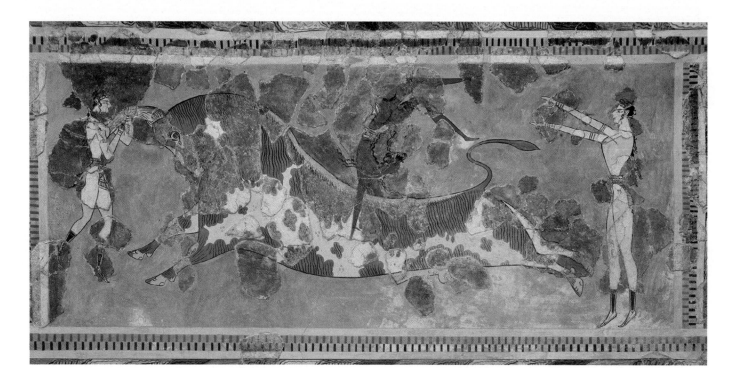

Figure 2.2 *Bull-Leaping.* Ca. 1500 BCE. Archaeological Museum, Heraklion, Crete. *This fresco (approximately 32 inches high) from the east wing of the palace at Knossos is one of the largest paintings recovered from Crete. The association of young men and women with bulls in this scene brings to mind the legend of the Minotaur, in which seven youths and seven maidens were periodically sacrificed to a monster, half-man and half-bull, who lived in an underground labyrinth, supposedly on Crete. A bull cult may have been central to Minoan religion. Scholars have long debated whether the depiction is real or fanciful. Prevailing opinion holds that skilled athletes could have performed the trick of vaulting over a bull's horns and back.*

Figure 2.3 Earth Goddess with Snakes. Ca. 1600–1580 BCE. Faience, ht. 13½". Archaeological Museum, Heraklion, Crete. *This cult figure was discovered in the Treasury of the Knossos Palace. Her triangular dress, with its apron and flounced skirt, is similar to those of Cretan youths in surviving frescoes.*

dead in underground tombs and chambers, but neither the reason for the new burial practice nor its ritualistic meaning has been discovered.

Around 1600 BCE, Crete suffered when a nearby volcanic island erupted. About a century later, the mainland Mycenaeans conquered Crete but did not destroy Knossos. Around 1375 BCE, Knossos was devastated but it is not known how or why. The inhabitants of Crete had always relied heavily on trade, and this did not change under Mycenaean domination down to about 1100 BCE.

The Greeks of the later Archaic Age had no direct knowledge of Minoan civilization, but the Greek attitude toward the Minoans was shaped by mythology. **Myths** are traditional stories told about bygone eras by later peoples who are seeking to explain some of their basic political, social, or religious practices and ideas. They are often communal and comforting in their explanations, and frequently provide insights into peoples' ways of thinking. As an example, Crete is traditionally the birthplace of the god Zeus. The Minoans worshiped a Zeus who was born in a cave, grew to manhood, and died. They venerated the site of his birth and honored him as a child. The later Greeks, however, believed Zeus to be the immortal father and ruler of the Olympian deities, and they were incensed by the Minoan belief that the god had died. The grain of truth in this story may be that, although the Greeks eventually dominated Crete in physical terms, elements of Minoan religion found their way into later Greek beliefs; thus, in a sense, the Olympian gods *were* born on Crete. Cretan influences on Greece may also be detected in language, social organization, and economic pursuits, although the Archaic Greeks did not regard the Minoan past as part of their heritage.

BEGINNINGS: MYCENAEAN CIVILIZATION, 1900–1100 BCE

Mycenaean civilization, named by archaeologists for Mycenae, a prominent fortress city, developed on the rugged lower Greek peninsula known as the Peloponnesus. An aggressive warrior people, perhaps from the plains of southern Russia or from the upper Tigris-Euphrates valley, the Mycenaeans arrived on the peninsula in about 1900 BCE, and, by about 1500 BCE, they ruled the entire Peloponnesus. More is known about the Mycenaeans than about the Minoans. The archaeological record is more abundant, revealing several palace sites and numerous splendid artifacts. But writing is also critical in two distinct respects. First, the Mycenaeans adapted Cretan Linear A writing to their own language, a primitive form of Greek, and produced thousands of **Linear B** tablets. These tablets contain administrative and commercial documents that aid in understanding Mycenaean government. Second, the much later *Iliad* and *Odyssey* are set in the Mycenaean world and contain a good deal of authentic information about it.

Judging from the *Iliad*, Mycenaean society was aristocratic and hierarchical. A confederation of autonomous kings might occasionally accept the leadership of one of their number. For example, in the Trojan War, Agamemnon of Mycenae was the leader of all the Greeks. Excavations at Mycenae, especially its impressive Lion Gate (Figure 2.4), hint at the wealth and power of kings. Literary and artistic depictions suggest a society that prized military prowess. Linear B documents suggest a bureaucratic system that was adept at raising taxes. There were certainly merchants in the Mycenaean world, the majority of whose people were farmers. Slavery existed but its exact significance is not clear.

Excavations show that the Mycenaeans appreciated fine objects and achieved a high level of technical skill. Within the citadel of Mycenae six **shaft graves** (vertical burials) were discovered. In one of them there was a spectacular gold burial mask (Figure 2.5) traditionally called the "Mask of Agamemnon." On discovering it, the famous German archaeologist Heinrich Schliemann telegraphed Berlin, "I have looked on the face of Agamemnon." Probably not—but it is a good story. The graves do reveal the care with which the Mycenaeans attended to the physical remains of their dead. It is tempting to think that they may have learned this from the Egyptians. Near Sparta, archaeologists unearthed a pair of gorgeous drinking cups (Figure 2.6). The energy of the figures depicted is palpable, but no less noticeable is the technical mastery of the unknown artist.

After their conquest of the Minoans, the Mycenaeans extended their raiding and trading activities throughout the eastern Mediterranean. In about 1250 BCE, they attacked the wealthy and strategic city of Troy, on the western coast of present-day Turkey (see Map 2.1). It is delightful to think that the face of the beautiful Helen launched a thousand ships, but the Trojan War was only the culmination of a bitter trade dispute. Although similar expeditions had brought spoils to the Mycenaeans on earlier occasions, this long, exhausting foray weakened them, leaving them open to conquest by more vigorous tribes. In their weakened state, the Myceaneans were no match for the Dorians, who invaded from the north in about 1100 BCE.

Technology in Minoan Crete and Mycenae

The first Aegean civilizations—Minoan and Mycenaean—built on the bronze technology of earlier Near

Figure 2.4 The Lion Gate at Mycenae. Ca. 1300 BCE. *The Lion Gate
is a massive structure of four gigantic
blocks—two posts and a beam forming
the entrance and a triangular block on
which are carved the two 9-foot-high
lions and the central column. So impressive were the megalithic Mycenaean
fortresses to the later Greeks that they
called them "cyclopean," convinced that
only a race of giants, the Cyclopes, could
have built them.*

Figure 2.5 *Mask of Agamemnon.* Ca. 1500 BCE. National
Archaeological Museum, Athens. Thinly beaten gold, c. 12"
across. *Although the only Mycenaean gold burial mask so far
discovered, it is likely that high-status persons, especially kings,
may have had such masks placed in their graves. This is reminiscent of the burial masks on the sarcophagi that held the mummies
of prominent Egyptians.*

Figure 2.6 Vapheio Cup. Ca. sixteenth century BCE. Gold,
3½" high. National Archaeological Museum, Athens. *This
gold cup, one of two discovered in a tomb at Vapheio near Sparta,
Greece, shows a man attempting to capture a bull. At the bottom
of the image, the hunter tries to ensnare the bull by means of the
net held in his outstretched arms. The curved line of the animal's
arched back helps frame the scene, while the bull, with its size
and muscular body, seems to be winning this ferocious struggle
between man and beast. This cup is thought to be from the Mycenaean period, because its execution is less refined than the exquisite artistry of the other cup (not shown here), which is attributed
to the Minoan style. However, both goldsmiths used the same
technique: hammering out the scenes from the inside of the cup.*

Eastern models (see Chapter 1). Bronze was the preferred metal of Mycenaean artisans, as it was for the Minoans before them, but copper, tin, silver, and gold were also used. All these metals were available from mines and deposits in the Mediterranean basin, except tin, which came from the British Isles. Crete and Mycenae used bronze for weapons and everyday objects throughout their time, but both societies collapsed before the onset of the Iron Age, in about 1200 BCE.

In military technology, the Minoans and the Mycenaeans followed the lead of Near Eastern neighbors but made some advances too:

- Bronze weapons: daggers, swords, spears, and javelins; and body armor, such as shields, helmets, and leg and arm coverings
- Introduction of the horse and of horse-drawn chariots by 2000 BCE
- Redesigned chariots by 1300 BCE, with six wheel spokes instead of four and axles under the rear platform, which enhanced stability and maneuverability
- Advances in shipbuilding: extending the height of the mast, enlarging the size of the sails, and redesigning the oar to increase rowing power

THE GREEK DARK AGES

With the fall of the Mycenaeans, a period known as the Dark Ages began, a period about which rather little is known. People lived in isolated farming communities and produced only essential tools and domestic objects. Commercial and social interchange among communities, already made hazardous by the mountainous terrain, became even more dangerous, and communication with the eastern Mediterranean kingdoms nearly ceased.

Yet some fundamental changes were slowly occurring. Political power was gradually shifting from kings to the heads of powerful families, laying the foundation for a new form of government, and iron gradually replaced bronze in tools and weapons, thus ending the Bronze Age and beginning the Iron Age in Greece. Many Mycenaeans fled to the coast of Asia Minor, which later came to be called Ionia, thus paving the way for the formation of an extended Greek community around the Aegean and Mediterranean Seas.

THE ARCHAIC AGE, 800–479 BCE

In about 800 BCE, the Greeks emerged from years of stagnation and moved into an era of political innovation and cultural experimentation. Although scattered and isolated, they shared a sense of identity based on

their common language, their heroic stories and folktales, their myths and religious practices, and their commercial and trading interests. They claimed a common mythical parent, Hellen, who fathered three sons—the ancestors of the three major Greek tribes, the Ionians, the Aeolians, and the Dorians—and thus they called themselves Hellenes and their land Hellas. In the next three centuries, the Greeks reconstructed their political and social systems, developed new styles of art and architecture, invented new literary genres, and made the first formal philosophical inquiries into the nature of human behavior and the universe.

Political, Economic, and Social Structures

By the beginning of the Archaic Age (*archaic* comes from Greek for "ancient" or "beginning"), the isolated farming community was evolving into the *polis* (plural, *poleis*), a small, well-defined city-state. Eventually some two hundred poleis lay scattered over the Greek mainland and abroad. Although each polis was unique, all shared some features:

- An *acropolis* (Figure 2.7): a high, fortified point, often the dwelling place of rulers and location of temples
- An *agora*: essentially a market area where the political, social, and economic life of the polis took place
- A *chora*: the agricultural hinterland that made a true polis a city-state

The polis was a remarkably flexible and creative institution that brought diverse people together into a real community. Poleis generated tremendous pride and loyalty among their citizens.

Simultaneously with the emergence of the polis, in about 800 BCE, the Greek political system underwent a series of changes. The result of these changes was that more and more men were enabled to participate in the political life of the polis. The kings had been deposed by the leaders of noble families, who owned most of the land and possessed the weapons and horses. These wealthy warriors established **oligarchies,** or governments run by the few. Oligarchs looked out for their own interests but also provided exemplary leadership, fostered civic idealism, and supplied cultural and artistic patronage. However, most oligarchies eventually failed because of unforeseen and far-reaching military and economic changes. New military tactics now made obsolete the aristocratic warriors in their horse-drawn chariots. Foot soldiers—armed with long spears, protected by shields and body armor, and grouped in closed ranks called phalanxes—were proving more effective in battles. These foot soldiers,

Figure 2.7 Acropolis, Athens. View from the west. *The Acropolis dominates Athens in the twenty-first century just as it did in ancient times when it was the center of Athenian ceremonial and religious life. Today it is the towering symbol of Athens's cultural heritage as well as the center of the local tourist industry. A landmark in the history of town planning, the Acropolis is the ancestor of all carefully laid-out urban environments from ancient Rome to Renaissance Florence to modern Brasilia.*

or hoplites, were recruited from among independent farmers, merchants, traders, and artisans, who were also profiting from an expanding economy. As their military value became evident, these commoners soon demanded a voice in political decisions.

Rising population and limited land generated acute tensions. Frustrated by the inability of reform efforts to solve deep-seated problems, in the sixth century BCE many poleis turned to rulers whom they entrusted with extraordinary powers to make sweeping economic and political changes. Many of these tyrants, as the Greeks called them, restructured their societies to allow more citizens to benefit from the growing economy, to move up the social scale, and to participate in the political process. However, some tyrants perpetuated their rule through heirs or political alliances and governed harshly for years, thus giving a simple word for ruler its modern negative meaning.

Increasing population and its attendant tensions generated another response: colonization. The Greeks sent citizens to join their earlier Ionian settlements and to establish new colonies along the coasts of Spain, North Africa, southern Russia (or the Black Sea), and Sicily and southern Italy, which became known as

Magna Graecia, or Greater Greece. Colonies were expected to provide resources, especially food, for their *metropoleis* ("mother cities"). Foreign ventures and expanded trade increased the wealth of the new middle class and reinforced their desires for more economic opportunities and political influence, but the entrenched aristocracy and farmer-hoplites tried to deny them access to power. Colonization solved some problems and generated others.

Politically, the Archaic period was important for three reasons. First, it saw the creation of the polis. Second, there was a dramatic expansion of political participation often accompanied by violent conflict between and within poleis. And third, the age of colonization spread Greek ideas, institutions, and artistic achievements all over the Mediterranean world.

The Greek Polis: Sparta and Athens

Among the Greek poleis, Sparta and Athens stand out for their vividly contrasting styles of life and their roles in subsequent Greek history. Dorian Sparta chose to guarantee its integrity and future through stringent

Timeline 2.2   THE ARCHAIC AGE IN GREECE   **All dates BCE**

ca. 800		600	590		508	490	479
Dark Ages	Expansion and Colonization	Solon in Athens	Political, Social, Economic Reforms		Cleisthenes in Athens	Persian Wars	Hellenic Age
Political and cultural activity revives							

and uncompromising policies. Athens created an increasingly open system. Faced by land shortages and population pressures, the Spartans conquered and enslaved their neighbors, making them *Helots*—state slaves. To prevent rebellions and to control the Helots, who outnumbered the Spartans ten to one, a vigilant Sparta was forced to keep its military always on the alert. Spartan boys were trained through the *agoge* (the "upbringing") to be tough, brave, skilled, and self-reliant. All male Spartans over the age of thirty belonged to an assembly that could propose measures to a smaller council made up of Spartans over the age of sixty. There were also two kings and five annually elected officials who pronounced on the legality of legislation. The Spartan system had elements of monarchy, oligarchy, and democracy.

The history of Ionian Athens echoes the general pattern of change in the poleis during the Archaic Age (Timeline 2.2). Aristocrats initially ruled Athens through councils and assemblies. As long as farming and trading sustained an expanding population, the nobles ruled without challenge. But at the beginning of the sixth century BCE, many peasant farmers were burdened with debts and were threatened with prison or slavery. Having no voice in the government, the farmers began to protest what they perceived as unfair laws.

An aristocrat named Draco codified Athens's laws in about 625 BCE. His laws were harsh—"Draconian"—but by issuing them publicly, law (not arbitrary decisions) ruled the state. In about 590 BCE, the Athenians granted an aristocrat named Solon special powers to reform the laws. He abolished debt slavery, guaranteed a free peasantry, and overhauled the judicial system. Solon also restructured Athenian institutions by distributing political participation according to wealth, instead of restricting participation to the wealthy.

Solon's principal successor was Cleisthenes [KLICE-thu-neez], whose reforms established democracy in Athens beginning in 508 BCE. Cleisthenes realized that the great obstacle to civic-minded participation was formed by entrenched class interests. That is, he knew that it would be hard to get small farmers, day laborers, merchants, and landed nobles to cooperate. So he created a new council in which he lumped to-

gether people from each of these groups in such a way as to force them to collaborate.

Cleisthenes' domestic reforms were one of the two major events that heralded the end of the Archaic Age and the coming of Greece's Hellenic (or classical) Age. The other event, the Persian Wars, was pivotal not only for Greece but also for Western civilization. If the autocratic and imperialistic Persians had won these wars, then the democratic institutions, the humanistic values, and the cultural landmarks that the Greeks were establishing would have been lost.

By the mid–sixth century BCE, the Persians ruled a huge empire in the Near East which had gradually incorporated the Greek poleis in Ionia. When Darius, king of the Persians in the late sixth century, demanded taxes from the Ionian Greeks, they revolted and looked to their homeland for support. A few poleis, including Athens, sent an expedition, which Darius defeated. To prevent future uprisings, Darius invaded the Greek peninsula and landed near Athens at Marathon in 490 BCE. The Athenian army defeated a vastly larger Persian force.

However, the Persians soon found a new and determined ruler in Xerxes [ZIRK-seez], son of Darius, who overran much of northern Greece. Under Spartan leadership, the Greeks attempted to trap the Persians at Thermopylae, a northern mountain pass, but they were annihilated by Xerxes' troops. Xerxes moved southward and sacked Athens, whose inhabitants escaped to the island of Salamis. The Athenians drew the Persian navy into narrow waters, where the swifter Greek ships outmaneuvered the more numerous but cumbersome Persian craft. After witnessing the destruction of his fleet, Xerxes returned to Persia. The remainder of the Persian army was routed at Platnea in 479 BCE. The Greeks' final victory over the mighty Persians created a euphoric mood in Athens and set the stage for the ensuing Hellenic Age.

The great service provided by Athens's seamen won them full participation in the political life of the city. After the war, the Athenians even introduced pay for public service so that such service would not be restricted to the idle rich. Athens had a weak executive and a powerful legislative system. Political thinkers in antiquity had very mixed feelings about Athens's government, admiring its massively inclusive character but criticizing its volatility and instability.

One of the most surprising contrasts between Sparta and Athens is the difference in the roles and status of women. In general, Spartan women, though expected to marry, spent their time outside and spoke freely to men; Athenian women were kept in seclusion and rarely talked with their husbands. What made Spartan women so independent was that, above all else, they were to be strong mothers of the vigorous males needed to maintain this warrior society. To that end, Spartan girls, alone among Greek females, were given public education, including choral singing and dancing, and athletics, in which they stripped just as Greek boys did. Spartan women were unique in being able to own land and to manage their own property.

Written sources suggest that the women of Athens pursued respectability as an ideal, which meant they were supposed to marry and stay indoors, overseeing their households and performing domestic chores. It is not clear how strictly this ideal was imposed on them in daily life. Athenian drama contains many instances of female characters complaining about their powerlessness, as when a wife is abandoned or a woman is left behind by her soldier-husband during wartime. But vase painting depicts women actively and positively participating in religious rituals, festivals, weddings, and funerals. Women's engagement in these was deemed necessary to the smooth functioning of society.

Technology in Archaic Greece

The Archaic Greeks were an Iron Age civilization (though a few artisans continued to work with bronze in limited fields, such as sculpture). As the Archaic period opened, the Greeks built on the technology of the earlier cultures of Crete and Mycenae, using mainly iron and steel (a refined form of iron) to build weaponry and body armor. Metalworkers learned to reduce iron from its ore in charcoal-fed furnaces, intensifying the heat by means of a foot bellows. Harder and more readily available than copper and tin, iron drove out the general use of softer metals by 500 BCE.

Also important were the Greeks' improvements in sailing vessels. Between 800 and about 450 BCE, the Greeks developed several modifications of a basic oared ship. At first they used *uniremes* (Latin *remus* means "oar"), small, swift boats with a single row of oars on each side. Gradually the *trireme* developed, a decked ship with three rows of oars on each side (Figure 2.8). From about 700 BCE, the uniremes were outfitted with a beak or a battering ram, to be used in sea battles. This ramming device forever changed the nature of sea warfare. Prior to this time, ships had been designed to transport warriors to fight on land; now, they served as the site for the battles themselves. Greek ships became not only faster but larger as well. Size and speed had important implications for merchants, who could ship more goods farther and more quickly.

THE EMERGENCE OF GREEK GENIUS: THE MASTERY OF FORM

During the Archaic Age, the Greeks explored the natural world, probed human existence, and celebrated life by means of literature, philosophy, and art. These cultural accomplishments, like those of the older Near Eastern civilizations, arose from religious beliefs and practices that played a central role in Greek life and history. In fact, the Greeks believed that creativity it-

Figure 2.8 Greek Trireme. *This type of ship had emerged by 525 BCE and was used by the Ionian Greeks when they revolted against the Persians. It was large and fast but also maneuverable.*

Table 2.1   THE NINE MUSES AND THEIR AREAS OF CREATIVITY

NAME	ART OR SCIENCE
Calliope	Epic poetry
Clio	History
Erato	Erotic poetry and mime
Euterpe	Lyric poetry and music
Melpomene	Tragedy
Polyhymnia	Sacred hymn
Terpsichore	Dance and song
Thalia	Comedy
Urania	Astronomy

self was a divine gift from the **muses,** the nine goddesses of artistic inspiration (Table 2.1). Guided by their muses, they created enduring works of art, literature, and theater, each with a universal appeal. Critical to the Greek experience, however, was a quest for understanding independent of religious explanations.

Religion

For the Greeks, religion was an indispensable part of private and public life. Indeed, the polis and religion could not be separated, for in the eyes of the Greeks the fate of each community depended on the civic deity. Public rituals and festivals forged community, infused civic pride, and recalled common heritage. Greek religion was always more civic than personal. During the Archaic Age, Greek religion—an amalgam of deities derived from the original settlers as well as invaders and foreigners—evolved into two major categories: the Olympian and the chthonian. The **Olympian deities** dwelled in the sky or on mountaintops and were associated with the Homeric heroes and the aristocracy. The **chthonian** [K'THOE-nee-uhn] (from Greek *chthon,* "the earth") **deities** lived underground and were associated with peasant life, the seasons and cycles of nature, and fertility.

Olympian religion shared some traits with the polytheistic cults of the ancient Near East, including the notion that the deities intervene in daily affairs, the belief that they are like humans in many respects, and the idea of a pantheon of gods and goddesses. The Greeks endowed their deities with physical bodies and individual personalities, creating a fascinating blend of charm and cruelty, beauty and childishness, love of justice and caprice. These unruly and willful deities quarreled with one another and played favorites with

their mortal worshipers. Faced with such favoritism among the deities, the Greeks themselves developed a strong moral sense. They came to believe that as long as they recognized the divinities' power and did not challenge them—and thus become victims of **hubris,** or pride—they would survive and often prosper.

Zeus, a sky god and first among the immortals, reigned as king on Mount Olympus, hurling thunderbolts and presiding over the divine councils. Sexually voracious, he sired both immortals and mortals. Hera, probably the great goddess of earlier cultures, was the sister and wife of Zeus. She watched over the women who appealed to her for help and kept a close eye on her wandering husband. Zeus's two brothers controlled the rest of the universe, Poseidon ruling the seas, all waters, and earthquakes, and Hades guarding the underworld. Zeus's sister Hestia protected the hearth and its sacred flame. Zeus's twin offspring, Apollo and Artemis, symbolized the sun and the moon, respectively. Apollo, Zeus's favorite son, personified the voice of reason. Artemis watched over childbirth and guarded wild creatures. Zeus's lying son Ares delighted in fierce battles and, as the war god, possessed a quick temper and few morals. He and Aphrodite—Zeus's daughter and the goddess of love and beauty—were adulterous lovers. Hephaestus, the ugly, lame son of Zeus who was married to Aphrodite in some tellings, was a master smith and the patron of artisans.

Two other children of Zeus rounded out the Olympic roster. Athena, the goddess of wisdom and patron goddess of Athens, was associated with warfare, the arts, and handicrafts. She was worshiped as a virgin goddess. Hermes, the god of trade and good fortune, was also the patron of thieves, although he was best known as a messenger for his fellow deities (Table 2.2).

The chthonian gods and goddesses were probably derived from ancient earth and harvest deities. At first they were worshiped only by the lower levels of society, but as ordinary people grew in influence, chthonian rituals spread and were integrated into civic rituals. Chthonian worship was open only to initiates, who were sworn to silence; hence, they were called mystery cults (from Greek *mystos,* "keeping silent"). Mystery cults constituted the personal element in Greek religion.

The chthonian practices originally invoked the powers of the earth to ensure a successful planting and a bountiful harvest. The "Mediterranean triad" of crops—olives, grapes, and cereal grains—led to two major cults emphasizing grains and grapes, the sources of bread and wine (olives lacked a cult). Demeter, a sister of Zeus, was a harvest goddess. She in turn had a daughter, Persephone, whom Hades abducted to his kingdom belowground. According to her cult legend, Demeter finally rescued Persephone, but not before

Table 2.2	THE OLYMPIAN DEITIES AND THE AREAS THEY RULED
GOD OR GODDESS	**DUTIES AND RESPONSIBILITIES**
Zeus	Chief deity and keeper of order on Olympus
Hera	Mother goddess, protector of women
Poseidon	Ruler of waters
Hades	Keeper of the underworld
Hestia	Protector of the hearth
Apollo	God of wisdom and moderation
Artemis	Virgin goddess who aided women
Ares	Amoral god of violence and warfare
Aphrodite	Goddess of passion, love, and beauty
Hephaestus	Patron of craftspeople
Athena	Goddess of wisdom and warfare
Hermes	God of merchants and thieves; messenger for the gods

Figure 2.9 EXEKIAS. *Dionysus Crossing the Sea.* Ca. 535 BCE. Clay, 12″ diameter. Staatliche Antikensammlungen, Munich. *Painted in the basin of a circular drinking bowl, Dionysus, the god of wine, is depicted sailing in a fish-nosed boat. This work by Exekias, one of the most admired artists of the Archaic Age, illustrates the beautiful mastery of space—placing a convincing pictorial image on a predetermined surface, such as a pot or a tomb—that characterized the best vase painting of the time. Dionysus reclines under a billowing sail, surrounded by gamboling dolphins. Sprouting from the boat is a vine carrying bunches of grapes—the symbol of the god of wine.*

Hades had tricked Persephone into eating a fruit that made her return to the underworld for part of each year. Thus, during the winter months, the earth is bare, but when Persephone and Demeter are together, the earth regains fertility. At Eleusis, a small village in Attica, Demeter was the focus of a mystery cult. Prospective initiates from all over Greece traveled there, apparently to receive her promise of immortal life.

Whereas Demeter's followers honored her in a dignified manner, Dionysus's worshipers, through wild dancing and wine drinking, hoped to be reinvigorated by their god and born again. Dionysus, the god of wine, came to represent the irrational, emotional, and uncontrolled aspects of human nature to the Greeks. In contrast, the rational, conscious, controlled aspects were associated with Apollo. The two aspects—Dionysian and Apollonian—were considered opposing but complementary. Eventually, a Dionysus cult arose in Athens, where Dionysus's followers annually held ceremonies honoring his power as god of the vine (Figure 2.9). Over the years these rituals became civic festivals, which in turn spawned the competitive performances of tragic drama in Athens in the sixth century BCE.

Literature

During the Archaic Age, the Greeks produced some of the greatest literature of the Western heritage, with stories as adventurous, amusing, and heartfelt as they are sophisticated, structured, and rich with many of the values we still hold dear today.

EPIC POETRY   The originator of the major conventions of **epic poetry** is traditionally believed to be Homer, a **bard,** or poet who sang his verses while accompanying himself on a stringed instrument. In the *Iliad* (ca. 750 BCE) and the *Odyssey* (ca. 725 BCE), Homer sang of the events before, during, and after the Trojan War, stories that had circulated among the Greeks since the fall of Mycenae. He entertained an aristocratic audience eager to identify with the Mycenaean past. For many years, his poems were transmitted orally by other bards and probably did not exist in written versions until the sixth century BCE. Homer's authorship and, indeed, even his very existence are established solely by tradition. Nevertheless, by the end of the Archaic Age, the appeal of Homer's poetry had embraced all social levels, and his authority and influence approached that of a modern combination of television, Shakespeare, and the Bible.

The epic genre displays certain features. Always in verse, an epic's language is elevated and its tone is serious. Epic possesses a universalizing quality—what is said is held to be true for all times and places, not for a specific moment. The characters in an epic are deeply human and yet, in their prowess or wisdom or cunning, are greater than most humans. Homer's epics have some distinctive characteristics that recur in Greek culture. Homer delights in verbal play. He revels in competition, sometimes verbal, sometimes physical. And in Homer we can begin to see the characteristic Greek interest in balance, order, harmony, and proportion.

The basic appeal of Homer's epics lies in their well-crafted plots, filled with dramatic episodes and finely drawn characters. Set against the backdrop of the Trojan War, the *Iliad* describes the battle for Ilium, another name for Troy, and the *Odyssey* recounts events after the Greeks defeat the Trojans. The *Iliad* focuses on Achilles, the epitome and paradox of heroic Greek manhood. Achilles was angry and refused for a long time to fight because Agamemnon, the Greeks' leader, had taken away his prize slave girl. Just as the polis was taking shape, Homer invited reflection on participation and allegiance: Where does one draw the line between self-interest and the common good? In contrast to the battlefield heroics of the *Iliad,* the *Odyssey* narrates the wanderings of the Greek warrior Odysseus after the fall of Troy. Moreover, the *Odyssey* celebrates marriage, for Odysseus, despite some amorous adventures, remains fixed on thoughts of his wife, Penelope, who waits for him in Ithaca.

In both poems, the deities merrily intrude into the lives of mortals, changing and postponing the fate of friend and enemy alike. For example, Homer presented Zeus, the nominal protector of the moral order, as forever under siege by other gods seeking help for their favorite mortals. Homer's roguish portraits of the deities remained indelibly imprinted in the minds of the general populace of Greece. So great was Homer's authority that his works made him the theologian of Greek religion. His stories of the gods and goddesses, although not completely replacing other versions of their lives, became the standard that circulated wherever Greek was spoken.

In addition to poetic forms and themes, Homer gave texture to the Greek language. Similes, figures of speech in which two unlike things are compared, help bring the dramatic, exotic events of the stories down to earth. For example, Homer creates a vivid image of Odysseus as a ferocious killer when he compares him to a lion "covered with blood, all his chest and his flanks on either side bloody." In a less violent simile, Homer has Achilles compare his fellow Greeks to "unwinged" baby birds and himself to their nurturing mother. Homer's images also provide a rich repertory of ready phrases and metaphors, known as **Homeric epithets,** such as "the wily Odysseus," "the swift-footed Achilles," and the "rosy-fingered dawn." These phrases constitute ready-made metrical units (think of the beat in music) that permitted the bard to "compose" his poem orally.

Homer also served as a guide to behavior for the Archaic Greeks. Because they became part of the Greek educational curriculum, his poems acquired an ethical function. A young man who took Achilles or Odysseus for a model would learn to maintain his well-being, to speak eloquently in company with other men, to give and receive hospitality, to shed tears in public over the death of his closest friend, to admire the beauty of women, to esteem the material wealth of other nobles, to appreciate songs of bravery, and, above all, to protect his reputation as a man and warrior. On the other hand, a young wife who imitated Penelope, the patient and faithful wife of Odysseus, would inhabit a more circumscribed world as she learned to weave at the loom, to manage a household, to cultivate her physical beauty, and to resist the advances of other men.

LYRIC POETRY   Verses sung to the music of the **lyre** (a stringed instrument), or **lyric poetry,** became the dominant literary expression in the late Archaic Age, and **lyric** verses have dominated Western poetry ever since. Lyric poetry, which originated later than the epic, expressed an author's personal, private thoughts, though the muse Euterpe was credited with the inspiration. The shift from epic to lyric poetry in the sixth century BCE coincided with changes in the polis, where the rising democratic spirit encouraged a variety of voices to be heard.

Of the several types of lyric poetry, *monody,* or the solo lyric, became the most influential in Archaic Greece. Poets of monody achieved relative simplicity by using a single line of verse or by repeating a short stanza pattern. Whereas the Homeric epics survive relatively intact, the solo lyrics exist in fragments. For example, of Sappho's [SAF-oh] nine books of verse, only one complete poem and several dozen fragments survive. And of the music, the whole has been lost. The ancients, however, regarded Sappho (about 600 BCE) as the greatest of lyric poets. The philosopher Plato hailed her as the tenth muse in a short lyric he dedicated to her. A truly original writer, Sappho apparently owed no debt to Homer or any other poet. Her work is addressed to a small circle of aristocratic women friends on her native island of Lesbos in the Aegean. She was deeply personal in her interests, writing chiefly about herself, her friends, and their feelings for one another. In her elegant but restrained verses,

SLICE OF LIFE
The Worlds of Women and Men in Ancient Greece

By pairing these two very different perspectives, it is possible to see the chasm that lay between the worldviews of women and those of men in ancient Greece. Since there are no records of ordinary people from the Archaic Age, human reactions to Archaic life come almost exclusively from famous individuals, such as Sappho and Alcaeus. In the following poems, they express human emotions across time and class but their subjects are rather different. Sappho (about 600 BCE) describes her intensely personal feelings, as in this ode to a lost love. In contrast, Alcaeus [al-KAY-us] (about 620–about 580 BCE) sings of his anguish when he was banished for political activities in the polis of Mytilene on the island of Lesbos—Sappho's hometown too.

SAPPHO
He Seems to Be a God

Sappho's lyrical poems reflect the circumscribed world of Greek women. In this ode, she describes the pangs of jealousy and grief she feels on seeing someone she loves respond to another.

He seems to be a god, that man
Facing you, who leans to be close,
Smiles, and, alert and glad, listens
To your mellow voice

And quickens in love at your laughter
That stings my breasts, jolts my heart
If I dare the shock of a glance.
I cannot speak,

My tongue sticks to my dry mouth,
Thin fire spreads beneath my skin,
My eyes cannot see and my aching ears
Roar in their labyrinths.

Chill sweat slides down my body,
I shake, I turn greener than grass.
I am neither living nor dead and cry
From the narrow between.
But endure, even this grief of love.

ALCAEUS
Longing for Home

Unlike Sappho, Alcaeus wrote about the world of men. His works were collected into ten books in antiquity, but only a few fragments survive today.

Plunged in the wild chaste-woods I live
a rustic life, unhappy me,
longing to hear Assembly called
and Council, Agesilaidas!

From lands my grandfather grew old
possessing, and my father too,
among these citizens who wrong
each other, I've been driven away.

An outland exile: here I dwell
like Onomacles, the Athenian
spear-wolf, out of the fray. To make
peace with . . . is no wise.
So to the precinct of the gods,
treading the dark earth . . .

. . . I live
keeping well out of trouble's reach.
Now Lesbos' long-robed girls are here for the beauty
    contest. All around,
the women's wondrous annual cry,
the holy alleluia, rings.
When will the gods from all my trials
deliver. . . .

INTERPRETING THIS SLICE OF LIFE

1. *What* emotions does Sappho express in her poem?
2. *How* does Sappho describe her body's reaction to jealousy? 3. *What* does Alcaeus long for while he is away from his homeland? 4. *Why* is Alcaeus away from home? 5. *How* does the mood of these poems by Sappho and Alcaeus differ from the mood of Homer's poetry?

Table 2.3	PHILOSOPHERS OF THE ARCHAIC AGE	
PHILOSOPHER	TIME	ACHIEVEMENT
Thales	About 585 BCE	First philosopher and founder of philosophic materialism
Pythagoras	About 580–about 507 BCE	Founder of philosophic idealism
Heraclitus	About 545–about 485 BCE	First dialectical reasoning; belief in continual flux

Sappho sang mostly about moods of romantic passion: of longing, unrequited love, absence, regret, jealousy, and fulfillment. Sappho's willing vulnerability and her love of truth made the solo lyric the perfect vehicle for confessional writing.

Philosophy and Science

The mental attitudes that exemplified the democratic challenge to established authority in the Archaic Age also brought forth thinkers who questioned the power and, ultimately, the existence of the gods. Just as the democrats constructed a human-centered state, so did the philosophers conceive of a world where natural processes operated and human minds could grasp them. These Greek thinkers invented **natural philosophy,** a term that encompasses the fields we now call "philosophy" and "science." The close connection between philosophy and science persisted until the Newtonian revolution of the seventeenth century CE From that point on, science simply demonstrated what happened in nature without speculating about its purpose. The Greeks asked both "how" and "why."

NATURAL PHILOSOPHY   The origins of natural philosophy, like those of lyric poetry, are hidden in the fragmentary historical record, but we can nevertheless say that formal Western philosophy began on the Ionian coast of Asia Minor in the sixth century BCE. There, in the polis of Miletus, thinkers known as the Milesian school speculated that beneath the ever-changing natural world was an unchanging matter (Table 2.3).

Thales [THAY-leez] (fl. 585 BCE), the founder of the Milesian school, reasoned that the fundamental substance of the universe was water—an outlook that made him a materialist, because he thought that everything was made of matter. From the standpoint of modern science, Thales was wrong and so were the rest of his circle, who proposed other elements—earth, air, fire, and "the infinite"—as the underlying essence.

But more important than their conclusions regarding matter were their convictions that there is regularity in the universe and that human reason can ultimately understand the natural order. Their belief in rationality not only determined the direction of speculative thought but also initiated the steps that led to physics, chemistry, botany, and other sciences. Proposing that the universe is governed by natural laws, these first philosophers questioned divine explanations for natural events, a development deplored by those who found satisfactory explanations in religion.

When the Persians conquered Asia Minor near the end of the sixth century BCE, the center of intellectual thought shifted to Athens and to southern Italy and Sicily, where a tradition emerged that challenged the Milesian school. Pythagoras [puh-THAG-uh-ruhs] (about 580–about 507 BCE), the leader of the Italian school, rejected the concept of an underlying substance. Instead, he proclaimed, "Everything is made of numbers," by which he meant that mathematical relationships explained the basic order in nature—an outlook that made him an idealist, because he thought that an immaterial principle was the root cause of things. His musical studies probably led him to this conclusion. He may have observed that a plucked string vibrated, making a certain sound; if the string were cut in half and plucked again, then a new note an octave higher than the first, with twice as many vibrations per second, would be heard. Hence, mathematical ratios determined musical sounds. Pythagoras then concluded that "numbers" explain everything in the "cosmos," his term for the orderly system embracing the earth and the heavens.

A third philosopher, Heraclitus [hair-uh-KLITE-uhs] (about 545–about 485 BCE), appeals more to the modern age than does any other thinker in Archaic Greece. Heraclitus pioneered a philosophic tradition that found truth in constant change, as in his well-known idea that a person cannot step twice into the same flowing river. In addition, he devised the earliest dialectical form of reasoning when he speculated that growth arises out of opposites, a fundamental tenet of dialectic thought.

ENCOUNTER

Near Eastern Art and Greek Pottery

One of the great achievements of the Greek genius was in the minor art of vase painting, which culminated in the black-figure (see Figure 2.9 and Interpreting Art figure 2.1; fl. about 700–530 BCE) and red-figure (see Figures 3.1, 3.10, and 3.11; fl. from late sixth to fourth century BCE) styles. Before black-figure ware made its appearance, the Greeks drew inspiration from the Near East; hence, art historians speak of the **Orientalizing** *period (about 700–625 BCE).*

Trade was the primary vehicle for cultural exchange between the Near East and Archaic Greece, and pottery carried the liquid cargoes, such as oils, perfumes, unguents, and wine. The merchants on Euboea (the largest Greek island in the Aegean Sea) led the way in pottery making in the Greek world, as evidenced in the huge quantity of Euboean pottery discovered at sites in Anatolia (modern western Turkey). The wealthy poleis of Ionia, on the coast of Anatolia, as well as the mainland Greek poleis of Athens and Corinth, profited from this exchange of goods.

In creating the Orientalizing style, Greeks borrowed artistic techniques, vessel forms, decorative motifs, and subjects. The adopted artistic techniques included new ways of representing human and animal figures. They learned to depict a body either by drawing it in outline or by painting it in silhouette with the head drawn in outline, and they learned a more naturalistic method of showing features on figures by painting muscles, ribs, and hair. Some Greek artisans preferred to incise, or cut, the features into their painted figures, and this process, when combined with the use of black paint to make a silhouette, led directly to the black-figure painting style.

Near Eastern motifs, such as sphinxes, sirens, and griffins, now entered the Greek tradition. Hybrid creatures were a beloved feature of Near Eastern art (see Figure 1.23), but Greek tradition normally shunned them, preferring to depict human and animal forms in a natural manner. However, the Greek artists' genius and skills accommodated the exotic and monstrous into their own myths, legends, and folklore. For example, the sphinx—a hybrid of a lion and a man in Near Eastern art—became a riddle-asking winged female in the Oedipus legend. The siren—a bird-woman in Near Eastern myth—became the destructive winged women that lured sailors to their doom in the story of Odysseus. And the griffin—a winged monster with an eagle's head and a lion's body in Near Eastern lore—became part of a tale told by Herodotus about northern barbarians called Arimasps.

A final Near Eastern import into Greek art was the animal frieze, a hallmark of the Orientalizing style. In this frieze, the Greeks divided the vase surface into bands, separated by thin lines, and filled the bands with a linear parade of animals, including antlered beasts, geese, and wild goats (Encounter figure 2.1). The prominence of the wild goat caused these scenes to be called the "wild goat style" of vase painting.

LEARNING FROM THE ENCOUNTER

1. *Explain* how trade led to a cultural exchange involving artistic styles. 2. *Where* did the cultural exchange between Greece and the Near East take place? 3. *What* artistic elements from Near Eastern art were adopted by Greek artists? 4. *Discuss* the way that Greek art was changed by this encounter with Near Eastern traditions.

This original idea led him to argue that "strife is justice" and that struggle is necessary for progress.

Further thinkers began to ask what it means to *know,* how it is possible to know. For example, some questioned whether the five senses—sight, smell, touch, taste, hearing—are actually capable of securing accurate information about the world. Others began to wonder about language: What are the limits of words' ability to articulate and communicate understanding? These philosophers laid the foundations for **epistemology,** the branch of philosophy concerned with the nature of knowledge.

Architecture

The supreme architectural achievement of the Greeks, the temple, became the fountainhead of the building components, decorative details, and aesthetic principles that together have largely shaped Western architecture until today. In its origins during the Archaic Age, the temple, probably made of wood, was a sacred structure designed to house the cult statues of the civic deities. As the Archaic Age gathered economic momentum, each polis rebuilt its wooden sanctuaries in stone.

Encounter figure 2.1 Milesian Oinochoe (the Levy or Marseilles Oinochoe). Ca. 640–630 BCE. Ht. approx. 15½". Louvre. Formerly in the Levy collection, purchased 1891. *This oinochoe [oy-noh-cho-e], or wine vessel, was a popular form of pottery in ancient Greece. Its broad shape and its trefoil, or three-lobed, mouth are typical of the form. This oinochoe depicts both tame and wild animals in the two upper registers and mythic creatures in the five lower zones. The choice of the goat as the central figure reflects the creature's usefulness, as a source for meat, drink, and, ultimately, cheese. Oriental influence also abounds in the plant motifs, with rosettes, lotus blossoms, and intertwined vines. Decorated in a workshop in Miletus, in Ionia, the vessel displays the Orientalizing style the artist used—drawing the figures in black silhouette, incising or cutting details into the image, and adding white and purple colors to enhance the effect.*

A diagram of a typical temple illustrates how much the building has influenced Western architecture (Figure 2.10). Generic Greek architecture is called **post-beam-triangle construction** (also known as post-and-lintel construction). *Post* refers to the columns; *beam* (or lintel) indicates the horizontal members, or **architraves,** resting on the columns; and *triangle* denotes the triangular area, called a **pediment,** at either end of the upper building. Other common features include

- the **entablature**—all of the building between the columns and the pediment,
- the **cornice**—the horizontal piece that crowns the entablature, and

- the **stylobate**—the upper step of the **stereobate,** the base on which the columns stand.

A typical temple had columns on four sides, which in turn enclosed a walled room, called a **cella,** that housed the cult image. Each temple faced east, with the doors to the cella placed so that, when opened, the sunrise illuminated the statue of the deity.

The earliest temple style in Greece was called **Doric,** because it originated in the Dorian poleis and adopted the simplicity of design and scarcity of decorative detail characteristic of the austere Dorian taste (Figure 2.11). The Doric columns have plain tops, or **capitals,** and the columns rest directly on the stylobate without

INTERPRETING ART

Composition Two figures are captured in dynamic action. Achilles is shown mainly in profile thereby drawing the viewer's attention to the frontally depicted Penthesilea. Each figure is identified by name.

Subject Matter Following an unknown source—this episode from the Trojan War is not in Homer—Exekias depicts the moment when Achilles, his arm poised to strike, is moved by the beauty of the Amazon queen Penthesilea and falls in love. He killed her nonetheless but later grieved over her.

Artist's Intent Exekias is only one of many sixth-century vase painters who signed their works, probably to win fame and increase sales.

Style Executed in the black-figure style, the figures are painted in black, details are incised with a stylus. The red background of plain baked clay might be glazed.

Form Despite its modest size, this amphora was probably owned by a prosperous family. Ordinary people would have used ceramic ware without figured decorations or with geometric designs.

Context Vase paintings, such as this, were central to the culture of Archaic Greece, along with the kouros and korē statues (see Figures 2.14 to 2.17); the popularity of Homeric themes, in general; and the winning of greater roles by ordinary men in the life of the polis.

Interpreting Art figure 2.1 SIGNED BY EXEKIAS. *Achilles Killing the Amazon Queen Penthesilea. Ca. 530 BCE. Clay, ht. of jar 16". British Museum, London (B 210). Almost the only painting surviving from ancient Greece is found on ceramic vessels. By the sixth century BCE, black-figure ware emerged as a major art form. Exekias (see Figure 2.9) painted this scene on an Athenian amphora, a vase with an oval body, cylindrical neck, and two handles, used for wine or oil.*

an intervening footing. On the entablature of each Doric temple is a sculptural band, called a *frieze,* which alternates three-grooved panels, called **triglyphs,** with blank panels, called **metopes,** that could be left plain or filled with relief sculptures. The triglyphs are reminders of the temple's origin as a wooden building when logs, faced with bronze, served as overhead beams.

An excellent example of the Doric style in the Archaic Age is the Temple of Hera in Paestum, in southern Italy (Figure 2.12). The Temple of Hera (about 550 BCE) was constructed from coarse local limestone. This large temple has a somewhat ungainly appearance, due in part to the massive architrave and the small spaces between the columns. The builders attempted to remedy this defect (without total success) by introducing refinements into the temple's design. The col-

umns were made to appear strong and solid enough to support the entablature by enlarging the middles of the shafts, a technique known as **entasis.** The artisans also carved vertical grooves, called **flutes,** along the shafts to give the columns a graceful, delicate surface and enhance their visual three-dimensionality.

After much experimentation, Greek architects overcame the awkwardness of the early Doric style by deciding that a temple's beauty was a function of mathematical proportions. The Temple of Aphaia—erected in 510 BCE by the citizens of Aegina, Athens's neighbor and perennial enemy—seems to embody this principle (Figure 2.13). The architect of this temple achieved its pleasing dimensions by using the ratio 1:2, placing six columns on the ends and twelve columns on the sides. The Temple of Aphaia, with its harmonious proportions

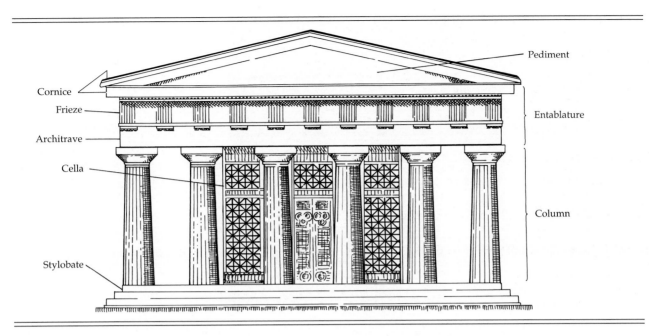

Figure 2.10   Elements of Greek Architecture

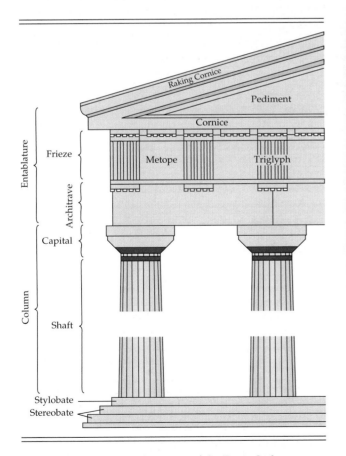

Figure 2.11   Greek Architecture of the Doric Order

Figure 2.12   Temple of Hera, Paestum. Ca. 560–550 BCE. Limestone. *This temple, with its heavy, squat columns, stands not only as a model of Archaic Greek architecture but also as a reminder of Greek wealth and expansion. Colonists from mainland Greece settled in southern Italy, the land they thought of as "Greater Greece," in the seventh and sixth centuries BCE, bringing with them the Olympian gods and goddesses and ideas of how to build temples in their honor.*

Figure 2.13   Temple of Aphaia, Aegina. 510 BCE. *The Temple of Aphaia in Aegina became the standard for the Doric temple style from its creation until it was superseded by the Athenian Parthenon in the 440s. Built of local limestone, covered in stucco, and painted, the Temple of Aphaia gleamed like a jewel in its carefully planned site overlooking the sea. Constructed and decorated with strict attention to artistic refinements, such as the slender columns and the life-like sculptures, this temple represents the climax of Archaic architecture.*

and graceful columns, became the widely imitated standard for the Doric style over the next half century.

Sculpture

Like the art of Mesopotamia and Egypt, Greek sculpture was rooted in religious practices and beliefs. The Greek sculptors fashioned images of the gods and goddesses to be used in temples either as objects of worship or as decorations for the pediments and friezes. Of greater importance for the development of Greek sculpture were the **kouros** (plural, kouroi) and the **korē** (plural, korai), freestanding statues of youths and maidens, respectively. Before 600 BCE, these sculptures had evolved from images of gods, into statues of dead heroes, and finally into memorials of ordinary people, say civic notables or victorious athletes.

What made the **Archaic** statues of youths and maidens so different from Egyptian and Mesopotamian art was the Greek delight in the splendor of the human body. In their representations of the human form, the Greeks rejected the sacred approach of the Egyptians and the Mesopotamians, which stressed conventional, static poses and formal gestures. Instead, Greek sculptors created athletic, muscular males and lively, robust maidens. Health and beauty were as important as religious purpose.

The first Archaic statues of youths owed much to the Egyptian tradition, but gradually Greek sculpture broke free of its origins. An early example of the kouros type of sculpture is the New York Kouros (Figure 2.14), now in New York City's Metropolitan Museum of Art. Artistically, this marble statue of a youth

with the left foot forward, the clenched fists, the arms held rigidly at the sides, the stylized hair, and the frontality—the quality of being designed for viewing from the front—shows the Egyptian influence (see Figure 1.16). The Greek sculptor has moved beyond Egyptian techniques, however, by incorporating changes that make the figure more lifelike, such as by attempting to show the correct shape of the knees and suggesting an actual person's mouth. That the result is not a realistic or idealized human figure is less important than that the sculptor studied the human body with fresh eyes and endeavored to represent it accurately. With such groundbreaking works as the New York Kouros, the Greeks launched a dynamic tradition that later artists continually reshaped.

A generation after the New York Kouros, new sculptors expressed their changed notion of a beautiful living male body in such works as the Anavysos Kouros (Figure 2.15). This sculpture, which was probably a dedicatory offering to a god or a goddess, still shows a powerful Egyptian influence, but it takes a giant step forward to a greater sense of life. The taut body and muscled torso convincingly reproduce the athletic qualities of an Olympic competitor. The legs are flexed and the right arm and shoulder are slightly in advance of the left, suggesting motion. The curious facial expression, known as the "Archaic smile," gives an enigmatic quality to the marble figure.

The korai sculptures, like the statues of youths, evolved from a frozen, lifeless style toward a greater realism, although women were never depicted in the nude at this stage in Greek sculpture. The earliest draped korai sculptures mixed Mesopotamian and Egyptian traditions with Greek ideas, sometimes

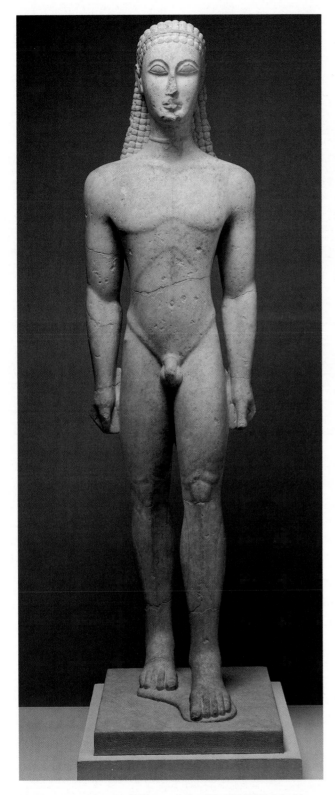

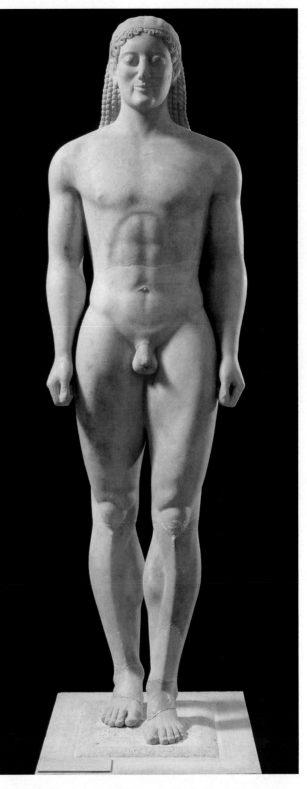

Figure 2.14   New York Kouros. Ca. 615–590 BCE. Marble, ht. 73½". Courtesy Metropolitan Museum of Art. Fletcher Fund, 1932 (32.11.1). *The New York Kouros is one of many similar statues dating from about the beginning of the sixth century BCE. During that century, the male and female statues evolved from stiff and stereotyped models to natural and anatomically correct forms.*

Figure 2.15   Anavysos Kouros. Ca. 540–520 BCE. Marble, ht. 76". National Archaeological Museum, Athens. *The Anavysos Kouros possesses the distinguishing characteristics of all kouroi: frontality, attention to bodily details, and a general formality. However, its subtle innovations—more precise musculature and more liveliness, as contrasted with Figure 2.14—foreshadow the Hellenic sculpture style.*

Figure 2.16   Auxerre Korē. Ca. 675–600 BCE. Limestone. Louvre. *The Auxerre Korē represents a fairly early stage in the development of this female form. The small size of the sculpture (about 29½" high) suggests that it may have been part of a burial rite. Traces of red pigment on the bust indicate that this korē was once painted to make it appear more lifelike.*

Figure 2.17   Peplos Korē. Ca. 535–530 BCE. Marble, ht. 48". Acropolis Museum, Athens. *The korē, a statue of a young draped female, was highly popular during the Archaic phase, which set the standard for later Greek art. The Peplos Korē depicted here—with her beautiful face, elegant dress, and expectant countenance—represents the highest expression of this early style. Like the Anavysos Kouros, this statue conveys a vivid sense of life.*

Figure 2.18 Reconstruction Drawing of the East Pediment of the Temple of Aphaia at Aegina. Glyptotech, Munich, after Janson after Fürtwangler. Marble, ht. ca. 40′. *This drawing displays what pedimental sculpture would have looked like. Notice especially how the sculptor had to fit his figures into a complex triangular space by making each one proportionately larger as they approach the summit of the triangle.*

producing an interesting but awkward effect. Such an early work is the Auxerre Korē (Figure 2.16)—named for the museum in Auxerre, France—whose cylindrical shape is copied from Mesopotamian models and whose stiff pose, wiglike hair, and thin waist are borrowed from Egypt. The Greek sculptor added the broad mouth and the Greek peplos (a loose-fitting outer robe) decorated with a meander pattern, but the Auxerre Korē, despite its charming details, is rigid and inert.

The Peplos Korē (Figure 2.17), dating from about a century later, expresses beautifully the exciting changes that were taking place in late Archaic sculpture. The statue wears a chiton, or tunic, over her upper torso, and a belted peplos. The sculptor has replaced the rigidity of the Egyptian pose with a more graceful one, as shown, for example, by the way the figure holds her right arm. Traces of a painted necklace may be seen, for the Peplos Korē, like all Greek sculpture, was painted to make the figure as true to life as possible. The often-awkward Archaic smile is here rendered to perfection, giving this lovely maiden an aristocratic demeanor.

The Greek tradition of representing males nude and females clothed persisted throughout the Archaic Age and well into the succeeding Hellenic Age. The Greeks readily accepted male nudity, witnessing it in the army on campaigns, in the gymnasium during exercises, and in the games at Olympia and elsewhere, and this acceptance is reflected in their art. But they were much less comfortable with female nudity (except in Sparta, where women exercised in the nude), so women were usually depicted draped or robed.

This discussion of Archaic sculpture may conclude with two figures that pull together the themes already encountered. Figure 2.18 shows a reconstruction of the east pediment of the Temple of Aphaia (see Figure 2.13) depicting Athena presiding over a battle between Greeks and Trojans. Aphaia's sculptures are now in a museum in Munich—virtually no Greek pedimental sculptures are still in place. This reconstruction conveys a wonderful sense of what those many pediments would have looked like. In Figure 2.19, a statue from the east pediment depicts a dying warrior. On the eve of the Persian Wars, the Greeks reminded themselves of an earlier war against an enemy from the East. Notice the beautiful balance, order, and symmetry of the figures as a group in the reconstruction drawing. In looking at the singular dying warrior, notice his nobility and his humanity. Here dies a man carrying out his duty. Of course, his body is superbly crafted—better even than those of the kouroi. In sculpture, as in almost every aspect of life, advances are coming at an accelerating pace.

Figure 2.19 *Fallen Warrior.* East pediment, Temple of Aphaia at Aegina. Ca. 510 BCE. Marble, ht. 72″. Glyptotech, Munich. *This dying soldier commands respect more than pity. Indeed, do we see him falling down or struggling to get up?*

The Legacy of Archaic Greek Civilization

The Archaic Age in Greece was a decisive moment in the story of the arts and humanities. Inheriting survival techniques from Neolithic cultures, continuing the urban ways of Mesopotamia and Egypt, and, more important, drawing spiritual and psychological sustenance from the Minoans and the Mycenaeans, the Archaic Greeks developed a unique consciousness that expressed, through original artistic and literary forms, their views about the deities and themselves and how they interacted. A mark of the creative power of the Archaic Greeks is that at the same time they were inventing epic poetry, lyric poetry, the post-beam-triangle temple, the korē and kouros sculptures, and natural philosophy, they were involved in founding a new and better way to live in the polis.

The new way of life devised by the Archaic Greeks gave rise to what we call, in retrospect, the **humanities**—those original artistic and literary forms that made Greek civilization unique. But the cultural explosion of this brilliant age is inseparable from the Greeks' restless drive to experience life to the fullest and their deep regard for human powers. Having devised their cultural forms, the Archaic Greeks believed passionately that by simply employing these models, either through studying them or by creating new works, the individual became a better human being. In this way,

the Archaic Greeks' arts and humanities were imbued with an ethical content, thus suggesting for some—notably philosophers—an alternative way of life to that offered by religion.

Wherever we look in this age, we see creative energy, a trait that has characterized Western civilization through the ages. Even though the different cultural forms did not develop at the same pace during the Archaic Age—sculpture, for example, was not as expressive as lyric poetry—these early aesthetic efforts were fundamentally different from those of the earlier Near Eastern civilizations. The touchstone of the humanistic style developed by the Archaic Greeks was their belief in human powers, both intellectual and physical. Indeed, the most powerful literary voice of this age, Homer, was quoted again and again for his claim that mortals and divinities are part of the same family. Less confident people, hearing this assertion, might have reasoned that human beings are limited in their earthly hopes. But, for the Greeks of this period, Homer meant that humans are capable of godlike actions. The reverence that the Archaic Greeks expressed for all noteworthy deeds, whether in poetry, in warfare, or in the Olympic games, attested to their belief in the basic value of human achievement.

KEY CULTURAL TERMS

frieze
fresco
Linear A
matriarchy
myth
Linear B
shaft grave
oligarchy
muse
Olympian deities
chthonian deities
hubris
epic poetry
bard
Homeric epithet
lyre
lyric poetry
lyric
natural philosophy
epistemology

Orientalizing style
post-beam-triangle
    construction
architrave
pediment
entablature
cornice
stylobate
stereobate
cella
Doric
capital
triglyph
metope
entasis
fluting
kouros
korē
Archaic
humanities

QUESTIONS FOR CRITICAL THINKING

1. What were the achievements of Minoan civilization? Discuss the impact of Minoan civilization on Archaic Greece.

2. What were the achievements of Mycenaean civilization? Discuss the impact of Mycenaean civilization on Archaic Greece.

3. Discuss the Greek "vision of humanity," and show how this vision made the Greeks different from the Mesopotamians and Egyptians.

4. Compare and contrast epic and lyric poetry. What audiences would be attracted to each of these poetic genres?

5. In what ways did Archaic Greece lay the foundations for Western civilization?

3

CLASSICAL GREEK CIVILIZATION
The Hellenic Age

With the defeat of the Persians at Plataea in 479 BCE, the Greeks entered the **Hellenic,** or Classical, Age, a period that lasted until the death of Alexander the Great of Macedon in 323 BCE. During the Hellenic Age, the Greeks defeated the Persians for a second time and survived a century of destructive civil war, only to succumb ultimately to the Macedonians. But throughout those tumultuous times, the Greeks never wavered in their supreme confidence in the superiority of their way of life.

Although the Greek world consisted of numerous poleis (city-states), spread across the Greek mainland, the Aegean Islands and the Ionian coast of Asia Minor, and the lands bordering the Mediterranean and Black Seas (Map 3.1), Athens became its cultural center. The Hellenic Age was the first stage of classical civilization, the highest achievement of the ancient Greeks. Despite diversity among the poleis, the Greeks of the Hellenic Age shared certain characteristics. Competitiveness and rivalry were certainly dominant features, as was an increasingly urban tone to culture in a still overwhelmingly rural world (Figure 3.1).

Popular attitudes toward the Olympian deities were changing, and public worship began to be assimilated into civic festivals. The great art of the age reflected the fusion of civic and sacred in such works as the Parthenon, the temple of the goddess Athena, protector of Athens (Figure 3.2). With gods and goddesses playing increasingly ceremonial roles in Greek life, religion became demystified and lost some of its personal value in people's lives. Moreover, war, political strife, and challenging new philosophical ideas diminished religion's ability to explain daily realities.

◀ **Detail** *Socrates.* Ca. 200 BCE–100 CE. Ht. 10½". British Museum, London.

LEARNING THROUGH MAPS

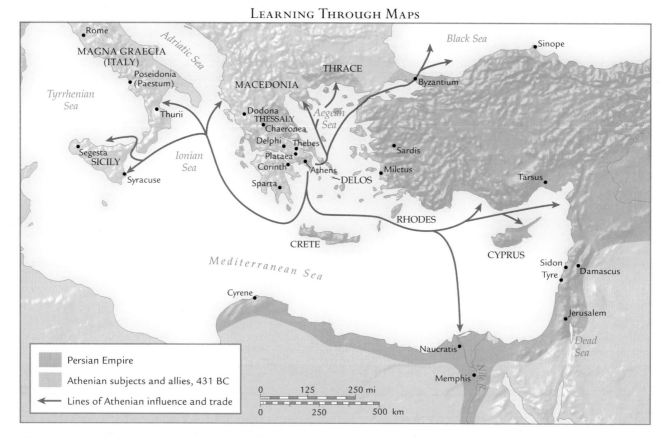

Map 3.1   THE ATHENIAN EMPIRE, 431 BCE
This map shows the Athenian and Persian Empires on the eve of the Peloponnesian War. 1. *Compare* the Athenian and Persian Empires, with respect to size and sea and land configuration. 2. *Notice* the difference between Athenian and Spartan influence in the eastern Mediterranean. 3. *How* did the locations of Athens and Sparta influence their respective naval and military policies? 4. *In what way* did the distance between Sicily and Athens affect the course of the Peloponnesian War? 5. *Observe* that Macedonia's proximity to Greece helped in its conquest of the late fourth century BCE.

Figure 3.1   *Torch Race.* Ca. 430–420 BCE. Clay, ht. 14³⁄₁₆″. Arthur M. Sackler Museum, Harvard University Art Museums, Cambridge, Mass. (Bequest of David M. Robinson.) *From the dawn of the Archaic period, about 800 BCE, sports, especially competitive sports, were integral to Greek life. In Hellenic times, artists used sports contests as subjects, as in this painting depicting a torch race, perhaps during the Panathenaea festival. This vase painting is executed in the red-figure style, a reversal of the black-figure style, which is illustrated in Figure 2.9 and Interpreting Art figure 2.1. The relatively uncluttered design, three figures with sparse details, perfectly fits into the small panel on the krater, a mixing vessel.*

Classical Hellenic civilization sought to define the balanced life and strove for moderation in achieving it. In Athenian tragedy, a recurrent theme is the danger of great wealth and high position. According to the playwrights, riches and status bred pride and led to envy by other citizens or, worse, envy by the gods. A modest life was the safest way to avoid personal calamity.

The Greeks also sought a balance between two opposite aspects of human nature, symbolized by Apollo, god of moderation, and Dionysus, god of excess. Apollo was the god of rational thought, ethical standards, and aesthetic balance (Figure 3.3). Dionysus, on the other hand, was the god of wine, drunken revelry, sexual excess, and madness. Women known as **maenads** followed and worshiped him, sometimes tearing apart beasts in their blind frenzy. By the Hellenic Age, these excesses were confined to rural areas, for the Dionysiac impulse was constantly being tamed by the Apollonian spirit and urban life. In Athens, the drunken worship of Dionysus was transformed into a civic festival, the **Dionysia,** from which tragedy, perhaps the highest expression of the Greek ethical genius, was born (Figure 3.4).

Classic, or **classical,** is a term with varied meanings. *Classic* means, first of all, "best" or "preeminent," and Greek culture has sometimes been seen as the highest moment in the entire history of the Western humanities. *Classic* also means "having permanent and recognized significance"; a classic work establishes a standard against which other efforts are measured. In this second sense, the aesthetic values and forms of Greek culture have been studied and imitated in all later stages of Western history. By extension, "the classics" are the works that have survived from Greece and Rome.

Classic also refers to the body of specific aesthetic principles expressed through the art and literature of Greece and Rome, a system known as **classicism.** The first stage of classicism, which originated in the Hellenic Age, emphasized simplicity over complexity; balance, or symmetry, over asymmetry; and restraint

Figure 3.2 *Athena Parthenos.* Marble replica based on fifth century BCE statue by Phidias. Ht. 3′5⅜″. National Museum, Athens. *Phidias's larger-than-life sculpture, which dominated the inner sanctum of the Parthenon, disappeared in ancient times, but numerous copies, such as this small figurine, have survived. Athena wears a peplos, gathered at her waist, and a helmet, ornamented with a sphinx flanked by two winged horses, and her left hand steadies a shield depicting Greek battle scenes. The statue was composed of gold and ivory sections joined together. A close examination of Athena's head demonstrates the shift from the Archaic to the Hellenic style of sculpture, since it does not have the Archaic smile and its features are idealized.*

Figure 3.3 *Apollo.* West pediment, Temple at Olympia. Ca. 460 BCE. Marble, ht. 10′2″. Olympia Museum. *Apollo's serene countenance in this splendidly crafted head reflects his image as the god of moderation. As the deity who counseled "Nothing in excess," Apollo was a potent force in combating the destructive urges that assailed the Greeks. This sculpture is executed in the Severe style, or the first stage of the Hellenic classical style, which is evident by the turn of the head to the right. However, its wiglike hair indicates the lingering influence of the Archaic style.*

Figure 3.4 *Dionysus and His Followers.* Ca. 430 BCE. Staatliche Museen, Berlin. *Scrolling around a perfume vase, this painting depicts a bearded Dionysus seated on the right with his followers. Of his twelve devotees, eleven are maenads, young female revelers; the last is the bearded Silenus, the foster father and former schoolmaster of Dionysus. Silenus is depicted on the lower left in his usual drunken, disorderly state.*

over excess. At the heart of classicism was the search for perfection, for the ideal form—whether expressed in the proportions of a temple constructed in marble or in the canon of the human anatomy molded in bronze or in a philosophical conclusion reached through logic. Hellenic classicism found expression in many areas: theater, music, history, natural philosophy, medicine, architecture, and sculpture.

DOMESTIC AND FOREIGN AFFAIRS: WAR, PEACE, AND THE TRIUMPH OF MACEDONIA

On the eve of the Hellenic Age, the Greeks, having defeated the Persians, were united only in their continuing opposition to Persia and in their hostility to any polis that tried to control the others. Although they cooperated on short-term goals that served their common interests, goodwill among the poleis usually evaporated once specific ends were met. If the period was marked by division, rivalry, and conflict, it was also generally prosperous. Wealth made possible some aspects of a brilliant culture that sometimes reflected on but that was never deflected by strife.

Political Phases of the Hellenic Age

The Hellenic Age can be divided into four distinct phases:

- The Delian League
- Wars in Greece and with Persia and the ensuing Thirty Years' Peace
- The Peloponnesian War
- Spartan and Theban hegemony and the triumph of Macedonia (Timeline 3.1)

Timeline 3.1 PHASES OF HELLENIC HISTORY   **All dates BCE**

478	460		431	404		323
Delian League	Wars in Greece and with Persia	Thirty Years' Peace	Peloponnesian War	Spartan and Theban Hegemony		Triumph of Macedonia

After defeating the Persians, the Greeks realized that a mutual defense organization was the key to preventing further Persian attack. In 478 BCE, a number of poleis formed the Delian League, a defensive alliance, with Athens at its head. But Athens soon began to transform the voluntary league into an Athenian Empire. As the oppressive nature of Athenian policies emerged, Athens's independent neighbors became alarmed.

Athenian power, however, was restricted by strained relations with Sparta, by the continuing menace of Persia, and by the highly unstable Delian alliance. When a negotiated settlement finally resolved Persian claims, the Delian League fell apart, leaving Athens vulnerable to its enemies on the Greek mainland. First Thebes and then Sparta led attacks on Athens. The war dragged on, but in 445 BCE, when Sparta unexpectedly withdrew, Athens won a quick victory that forced its enemies to negotiate.

The ensuing Thirty Years' Peace (which lasted only fourteen years) brought the Hellenic Age of Athens to its zenith. Athenian democracy expanded so that even the poorest citizens were empowered with full rights (though women continued to be excluded). Artists and sculptors beautified the Acropolis, and the three great Athenian tragedians—Aeschylus, Sophocles, and Euripides—were active in the drama festivals. Drawing on the Delian treasury, Pericles [PER-uh-kleez], the popular leader and general, launched a glorious building program that was essentially a huge public works project (Figure 3.5). In a speech over Athens's war dead, Pericles offered an eloquent summation of Athenian democracy, praising its use of public debate in reaching decisions, tolerance of diverse beliefs, and ability to love beauty without sacrificing military strength. His conclusion boasted that Athens was the model for Greece.

However, those poleis that were not enamored of Athenian aggression became convinced that war was the only way to protect themselves. Athens's foreign policy and its expansionism had given rise to an alliance so delicately balanced that neither side could allow the other to gain the slightest advantage. When Athens's neighbor Corinth went to war with Corcyra (present-day Corfu) in western Greece, Corcyra appealed to Athens for aid. Athens's initial victories

Figure 3.5 *Pericles.* Ca. 440 BCE. Marble, ht. 19¾". Vatican Museum. *Pericles possessed a vision of Athens as the political, economic, and cultural center of the Greek world. Even though this portrait bust is a Roman copy of the Greek original, it conveys Pericles' strong sense of leadership and determination.*

frightened Corinth, whose leaders persuaded the Spartans to join with them in the Peloponnesian League. The Peloponnesian War (431–404 BCE) had begun.

Pericles knew the league was superior on land but thought the Athenians could hold out indefinitely within their own walls and win a war of attrition. However, a plague broke out in Athens in 430 BCE, killing many citizens, including Pericles. The first phase of the war ended in 421 BCE, when a demoralized and defeated Athens sued for peace.

The second half of the Peloponnesian War shifted from the Greek peninsula to distant Sicily and the west—a move that sealed Athens's fate. In 416 BCE, a Sicilian polis begged Athens for military assistance. In trying to conduct a war so far from home, the

Athenians lost their fleet and never recovered their military and economic power.

In the early decades of the fourth century BCE, first Sparta and then Thebes emerged as the preeminent city-state, but these power struggles only further weakened the poleis and made them easy prey for an invader. At the northern edge of the civilized Greek world, that invader was gathering its forces. Macedonia was a primitive Greek state, governed by a king and whose people spoke a rough dialect of the Greek language. Its king, Philip, having been a hostage in Thebes when young, had become a *philhellene*—a lover of Greek civilization. A brilliant soldier, Philip expanded Macedonia to the east as far as the Black Sea. He then moved southward, conquering the poleis of central Greece. The poleis hastily raised an army, but Philip's well-disciplined troops crushed them at Chaeronea in 338 BCE. After establishing a league between Macedonia and the poleis, Philip granted the Greeks autonomy in everything except military affairs. He then announced an all-out war against Persia but was assassinated before he could launch his first campaign.

Philip's nineteen-year-old son, Alexander, succeeded to the throne. Tutored in philosophy by the renowned Aristotle, Alexander nevertheless had the heart of a warrior. When Thebes and other poleis attempted to take control at Philip's death, Alexander burned Thebes to the ground, sparing only the house of the poet Pindar. Placing a general in command of Greece, Alexander turned his sights to the east (Figure 3.6).

Alexander dreamed of a world united under his name and of a culture fused from Hellenic and Persian roots. His armies marched into Asia Minor, Egypt, and Mesopotamia, absorbing the great Persian Empire; then they swept east through Asia to the Indus River in India. As he conquered, Alexander destroyed and looted the great centers of Eastern civilization, but he also founded new cities and spread Greek culture.

Alexander's dream ended abruptly with his death in 323 BCE at the age of thirty-two. Seizing the opportunity presented by his sudden death, the Greeks revolted against the Macedonian oppressors, but they were quickly overwhelmed. The Macedonians then occupied Athens and installed an aristocratic government. Thus ended democracy and Hellenic civilization—in Greece.

THE ARTS OF HELLENIC GREECE: THE QUEST FOR PERFECTION

Throughout this era of shifting political fortunes, artistic and intellectual life flourished. Athens—bursting with creative energy—was the jewel of the Greek world. Atop its Acropolis, perfectly proportioned marble temples gleamed in the brilliant Aegean sun (Figure 3.7). Below, in the agora (market area), philosophers debated the most profound questions of human nature. Hundreds of citizens congregated outdoors to serve in the assembly, where they passed laws or sat on juries that made legal rulings. Citizens who were at leisure cheered on the athletes exercising in the open-air gymnasium (Figure 3.8). During drama festivals, the whole city turned out to share a gripping tragedy or to laugh uproariously at the latest comedy.

Theater

One of the most prominent institutions of Greek civilization was the theater, in which the dramatic form known as **tragedy** reached a state of perfection. Greek theater originally arose in connection with the worship of Dionysus. The word *tragedy* in Greek means "goat song," and this word may refer to a prehistoric

Figure 3.6   *Alexander the Great.* Ca. 200 BCE. Marble, ht. 16⅛". Istanbul Museum. *Alexander's youth and fine features, idealized perhaps in this portrait bust, add to the legends that have accumulated around one of the most famous conquerors in history. Later rulers measured themselves against Alexander, whose dream of a united world was cut short by his early death.*

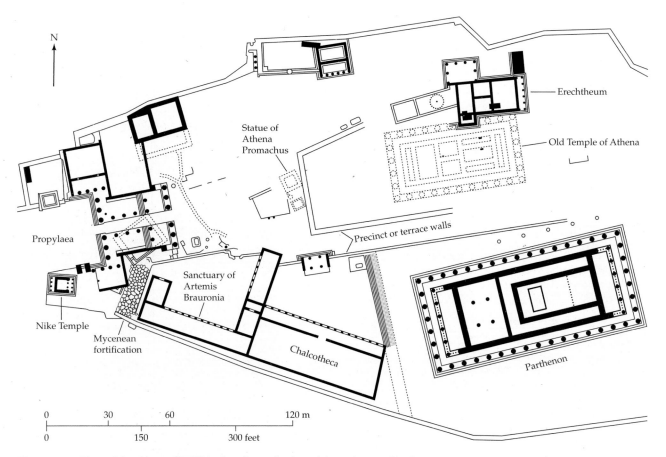

Figure 3.7   Plan of the Acropolis. *This plan shows the sites of the major temples, the Parthenon (Figure 3.15), Athena Nike (Figure 3.16), and the Erechtheum (Figure 3.17). For an overall view, compare Figure 2.7.*

Figure 3.8   *Athletes in the Palaestra.* Second quarter of the fifth century BCE. Marble, ht. 12½". National Museum, Athens. *This low-relief sculpture depicts athletes warming up in the open-air exercise area where spectators would congregate to urge on their favorites. The youth on the left is preparing for a footrace, and the one on the right tests his javelin. The pair in the center has just begun to wrestle. This relief was originally part of a sculptured base built into a wall that the Athenians constructed after the Persian Wars.*

ENCOUNTER

The Representation of Blacks in Greek Art

Starting in the Archaic period, Greek artists began to depict black Africans in their art. For the rest of Greek history and subsequently in Roman history, artists continued this practice, thus making the representation of blacks a significant feature of classical art. This change in classical art is simply one of the ways that, over the centuries, the Western arts have been influenced by non-Western traditions, such as stylistic elements, artistic symbols, and motifs.

The Greeks, over the course of their history, encountered other peoples, but their contact with black Africans left the greatest visual legacy. Starting in the Archaic Age, Greek artists created a black type, which became a persistent theme in their tradition. Features that came to characterize the black type in art included black skin, tightly curled hair, broad nose, full lips, and projecting jaw. Once introduced, the black figure flourished for the rest of Greek history (see Figure 4.1) and became part of Roman art. Few life-size statues and heads of the black type have been found, but hundreds of small works, dating from all periods, reflect the enduring popularity of the type, including images on statuettes, vases, engraved gems, coins, lamps, weights, finger rings, earrings, necklaces, and masks.

The Greek word for a black person was *Ethiopian*, a term originally meaning "one with a sunburned face." As Greeks encountered blacks at home and abroad, the word came to be applied to any dark-skinned person and had no special connection to the land below Egypt.

The black type probably originated in Naucratis, the city founded in Egypt's Nile delta by Greek settlers, in the seventh century BCE. There, artists, impressed by their contacts with black people, may have been the first to portray black figures in Greek art.

A critical date in the evolution of the black type was the arrival in Athens of black troops in the army of Persian king Xerxes in the Persian Wars (479 BCE). The black type had previously emerged in mainland art, but the large number of blacks in Xerxes' defeated army deeply impressed the Greeks who saw them. Some blacks may eventually have been enslaved and thus became a continuing presence in Greek life. Others also made their way to Greece. Most came as prisoners of war, some as soldiers, diplomats, or members of trade delegations, and a few to study. Many black immigrants held menial positions, but others were soldiers, actors, and athletes.

The portrayal of blacks in Greek art arose from artistic and scientific interest, not from racial prejudice. The Greek world, just as the Roman, was free of color bias, unlike the modern world. The numerous images

Encounter figure 3.1   Attic Head-Vase. Sixth to fifth century BCE. Berlin, Staatliche Museen, F4049. Courtesy Staatliche Museen, Berlin. *The head that forms this vase exhibits the typical features of the black type in Greek art, including black skin, curled, short hair, broad nose, and full lips. The vase was fashioned in Athens during the Archaic period.*

Greek artists created provide striking evidence of contacts between Greeks and black Africans throughout most of Greek history.

LEARNING FROM THE ENCOUNTER

1. *What* circumstances enabled Greek artists to encounter black Africans in the Greek world? 2. If we know that the first depiction of blacks may have occurred in the Greek city of Naucratis, in Egypt, *what* does the subsequent spread of the representation of blacks across Greek culture tell us about Greek art and society? 3. *What* are some roles that blacks played in Greek society? 4. *How* did Greek artists depict blacks in their art?

religious ceremony in which competing male **choruses**—groups of singers—sang and danced, while intoxicated, in homage to the god of wine; the victory prize may have been a sacrificial goat. Whatever its precise origins, during the Archaic Age theater in Athens had taken the form of a series of competitive performances presented annually during the Great Dionysia, celebrated in March. Although the names of numerous tragedians are known to us, the plays of only three survive. Eventually comedy took its place alongside tragedy as a public spectacle and as another component of the Dionysiac festival. Only one comedian's plays are extant. All the while, music grew in prominence, in connection with tragedy and independently.

At first, the chorus served as both the collective actor and the commentator on the events of the drama. Then, in the late sixth century BCE, according to tradition, the poet Thespis—from whose name comes the word *thespian*, or "actor"—introduced an actor with whom the chorus could interact. The theater was born. Initially, the main function of the actor was simply to ask questions of the chorus. During the Hellenic Age, the number of actors was increased to three, and, occasionally, late in the fifth century BCE, a fourth was added. Any number of actors who did not speak might be on the stage, but only the three leading actors engaged in dialogue. In the fifth century BCE, the chorus achieved its classic function as mediator between

actors and audience. As time went on, however, the role of the chorus declined and the importance of the actors increased. By the fourth century BCE, the actor had become the focus of the drama.

Because the focus of tragedy was originally the chorus, the need for a space to accommodate their dancing and singing determined the theater's shape. The chorus performed in a circular area called an **orchestra**, or "dancing place," in the center of which was a functioning altar, serving as a reminder that tragedy was a religious rite. The audience sat around two-thirds of the orchestra on wooden bleachers or stone seats under the open sky. The other third of the orchestra was backed by a wooden or stone building called the *skene* [SKEE-nee], which could be painted to suggest a scene and through which entrances and exits could be made (Figure 3.9).

Such simple set decorations may have provided a slight bit of realism, but Greek theater was not concerned with either realism or the expressiveness of individual actors. Instead, ideas and language were crucial. The actors—all men, even in the female roles—wore elaborate masks designed to project their voices, platform shoes, and long robes, which helped give the dramas a timeless, otherworldly quality.

Plays were performed in tetralogies (sets of four) on successive days of the Great Dionysia. Each competing playwright offered three tragedies (a trilogy), not necessarily related in theme or subject, that were

Figure 3.9   Theater at Epidaurus. Ca. 300 BCE. *The best-preserved theater in Greece is the one at Epidaurus. Although tragedy was created only in Athens, the popularity of the art form led to the construction of theaters all over Greece—a telling index of Athens's cultural imperialism. The acoustics in this ancient auditorium were remarkable. Performers' voices could be heard clearly throughout the theater even though it is in the open with fifty-four rows of seats accommodating fourteen thousand spectators.*

performed during the day, and a satyr-play that was performed later. A **satyr-play** usually featured the indecent behavior and ribald speech of the satyrs—sexually insatiable half men, half goats—who followed Dionysus. That the Greeks liked to watch three deeply serious dramas followed by a play full of obscene high jinks demonstrates the breadth of their sensibility.

TRAGEDY   The essence of Greek tragedy is the deeply felt belief that mortals cannot escape pain and sorrow. The dramatists shared with Homer the insight that "we men are wretched things, and the gods . . . have woven sorrow into the very pattern of our lives." Although terrible things happened in the tragedies—murder, incest, suicide, rape, mutilation—the attitude of the play toward these events was deeply moral. And violence was never depicted onstage.

The tragedies were primarily based on the legends of royal families—usually the dynasties of Thebes, Sparta, and Argos—dating from the Age of Heroes of which Homer sang in his epics. Since the audience already knew these stories, their interest focused on the playwright's treatment of a familiar tale, his ideas about its moral significance, and how his language shaped those ideas. The plots dealt with fundamental human issues with no easy solutions, such as the decrees of the state versus the conscience of the individual or divine law versus human law. Humans were forced to make hard choices without being able to foresee the consequences of their decisions. Nonetheless, the dramatists affirmed that a basic moral order existed underneath the shifting tide of human affairs. The political leaders of Athens recognized and accepted tragedy's ethical significance and educative function and thus made the plays into civic spectacles. For example, the audience was composed of citizens seated according to voting precincts, and Athenian warriors' orphans, who were wards of the polis, were honored at the performances.

According to the Greek philosopher Aristotle, whose immensely influential theory of tragedy, the *Poetics*, was based on his study of the dramas of the Hellenic Age, the purpose of tragedy was to work a cathartic, or purging, effect on the audience, to "arouse pity and terror" so that these negative emotions could be drained from the soul. The tragic heroes were warnings, not models; the spectators were instructed to seek modest lives and not aim too high.

Aeschylus   Aeschylus [ES-kuh-luhs] (about 525–about 456 BCE), the earliest of the three dramatists whose plays are extant, won first prize in the Great Dionysia thirteen times. He composed about ninety plays of which only seven are extant. His masterpiece, the *Oresteia*, is the only trilogy that has survived, and even

here the satyr-play is missing. The framing plot is the homecoming from Troy of the Greek king Agamemnon, who had sinned by sacrificing his daughter to gain military success; his murder by his vengeful and adulterous wife, Clytemnestra; and the dire consequences of this killing.

Aeschylus's treatment of these terrible events in the *Oresteia* embodies some of the principles of classicism. In the first place, Aeschylus shows great simplicity by avoiding distracting subplots: The first play, *Agamemnon,* tells the story of the king's death and Clytemnestra's triumph; the second, the *Libation Bearers,* relates the vengeance murder of Clytemnestra by her son, Orestes; and the third, *Eumenides,* halts—with the help of the Olympians Athena and Apollo—the cycle of revenge by instituting an Athenian court to try such cases. The trilogy is symmetrical in that Agamemnon's murder in the first play serves as punishment for the sacrifice of his daughter, Clytemnestra's death in the second avenges her slaying of Agamemnon, and the courtroom drama of the third absolves Orestes of the crime of matricide.

Finally, Aeschylus shows great restraint inasmuch as all deaths occur offstage, and the chorus or messengers only describe them. However, for the Athenian audience, the *Oresteia* had moral significance as well as stylistic power. By transforming the Furies, the blind champions of vengeance killing, into the "Kindly Ones" (*Eumenides*), Aeschylus, in effect, affirmed the ethical superiority of the rational Olympians over the earthbound chthonian divinities (see Chapter 2). In the *Oresteia,* Aeschylus confronts and resolves the opposition between several seemingly irreconcilable polarities—Olympian and chthonian gods, divine and human justice, religious cult and civic ritual, and fate and free will (Figure 3.10).

Sophocles   Sophocles [SOF-uh-kleez] (about 496–406 BCE), the most prolific of the great tragedians, wrote about 125 plays, but only 7 survive. He was popular among the Athenians, who awarded him first prize in the Great Dionysia twenty-four times. Sophocles' *Antigone* (442 BCE) expresses beautifully the principles of classical tragedy. The simple plot treats the conflicts between King Creon and his niece Antigone. The principal, although not the sole, philosophical issue explored by the play is whether human or divine law should take precedence. Antigone's two brothers have killed each other in a dispute over the Theban crown. Creon decrees that Eteocles, who died defending the city, be buried with honor but that the body of the rebel Polyneices be left as carrion for wild beasts. Antigone, whose name in Greek means "born to oppose," defies his order and buries her brother in compliance with religious teachings. Arrested and imprisoned, Antigone hangs

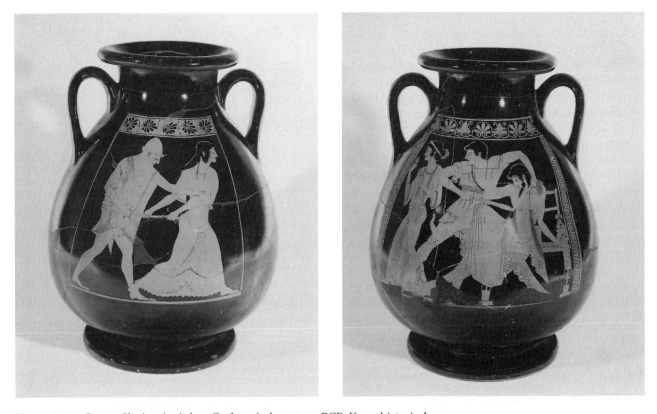

Figure 3.10 *Orestes Slaying Aegisthus.* Ca. late sixth century BCE. Kunsthistorisches Museum, Vienna. *This red-figure vase painting presents a different version of events in Argos from that given by Aeschylus in the* Libation Bearers, *the second play of the* Oresteia. *The vase painter portrays Clytemnestra bearing an ax (left), a detail Aeschylus omitted, and the sister between Orestes and his mother is not named Electra as she is in the* Oresteia. *However, painter and playwright agree that Orestes killed Aegisthus, his mother's lover.*

herself, and Creon's son and wife kill themselves. Too late, King Creon sees the light; he gives up his throne, saying, "There is no man can bear this guilt but I."

Several tensions are at issue here. Creon represents the typical tyrant, concerned only with law and order. His son, Haemon, is the voice of democracy, opposing the tyrannical will of his father. Creon believes in the superiority of public power over domestic life, in the necessity of the state to seek power for its own sake, in the priority of war over the commands of love, and in the right of men to control women. When the king tries to persuade his son to renounce his love for the disobedient Antigone, they argue about all four of these issues. Whether the Athenian citizens sided with Creon or Haemon is unknown, but *Antigone* has become the classic example of a tragic dilemma where two rights confront each other. In his desire for balance, Sophocles gives equally powerful arguments to the play's opposing characters.

Sophocles returned to the history of the Theban dynasty in later plays about Antigone's ill-fated father, Oedipus. In *Oedipus the King,* he tells how the Theban ruler unwittingly kills his father and marries his mother and later blinds himself to atone for his guilt. Though fate has a pivotal role in Oedipus's story, the playwright also emphasizes the part the hero's weakness plays in his downfall. Aristotle's *Poetics* held up this work as a model of Greek tragedy. In *Oedpius at Colonnus,* his last play, Sophocles portrays the former king at peace with himself and his destiny.

Euripides By the time Euripides [yu-RIP-uh-deez] (about 480–406 BCE) was writing for the stage, Athens was fighting for its existence in the Peloponnesian War. Euripides was in tune with the skeptical mood of the later years of this struggle, and, by presenting unorthodox versions of myths and legends, he exposed the foolishness of some popular beliefs and, sometimes, the emptiness of contemporary values. When he staged *The Trojan Women* in 415 BCE, the Athenians could not have missed the parallel between the cruel enslavement of the women of Troy after the Greeks destroyed their city and the fate of the women of the island of Melos, which Athens had just subjugated.

For his ninety or more tragedies (of which eighteen survive), the Athenians awarded the first prize to Euripides only five times, perhaps because his unorthodox plays angered the audience. But later ages, far removed from the stresses of Hellenic times, found his dramas more to their liking. Among the extant works, *The Bacchae* is his masterpiece, a gruesome tale about the introduction of the worship of Dionysus into Thebes. In this play, the bacchae (another name for the drunken followers of Dionysius), blinded by religious frenzy, kill the king of Thebes under the delusion that he is a wild animal. Euripides' dark tragedy may have been a warning to the citizens of Athens about the dangers of both excess and repression in religion and politics.

Euripides followed classical principles in *The Bacchae,* using a single plot, offstage violence, and well-defined conflict, but he also extended the range of classical drama with his unorthodox, even romantic, language and his skeptical treatment of familiar themes. Moreover, Euripides pointed the way toward a different sort of theater by having the severed head of the hero brought onstage at the end of the tragedy. With Euripides, the creative phase of classical theater came to an end.

COMEDY   Comedies were performed in the Great Dionysia just as the tragedies were, and they were also entered in contests in another festival, known as the Lesser Dionysia, celebrated in late winter. Comedies refused to take anyone or anything seriously. Comedies blended exquisite poetry with coarse language. They featured burlesque actions, buffoonery, slapstick, obscenity, and horseplay, and actors wore grotesque costumes with padded bellies or rumps to give a ridiculous effect (Figure 3.11). Comic playwrights invented their own plots and focused on contemporary matters: politics, philosophies, the new social classes, and well-known personalities. Even the deities were ridiculed and portrayed in embarrassing situations.

The freedom of the comic playwrights could exist only in a democracy. And yet the freedom was limited to a highly ritualized setting—the drama festivals—which allowed, even encouraged, the overturning of rules and the burlesquing of traditions. This controlled expression of the unspeakable provided a catharsis that strengthened communal bonds in the polis. At the same time, the comic playwrights demonstrated their faith in the basic good sense of the average citizen.

The comedies of Aristophanes [air-uh-STOF-uh-neez] (about 445–about 388 BCE) are the primary source for what is known as **Old Comedy,** comic Greek plays with a strong element of political criticism. Aristophanes composed forty-four works in all, of which eleven are extant. Like Euripides, he wrote his plays for war-torn Athens, and he satirized famous contemporaries such as the thinker Socrates, depicting him as a hopeless dreamer. Aristophanes must have stepped on many toes, for the Athenians awarded him first prize only four times.

Figure 3.11   Detail, Scene from a Comedy. Mid–fourth century BCE. Ht. of vase 15⅔". British Museum, London. *This scene, painted on a mixing bowl, portrays a situation from a Greek comedy. The actors on the right and left are outfitted in the grotesque costume of comedy with padded rumps and genitals. That these characters are onstage is indicated by the decorations at the bottom of the frame.*

poraries such as the thinker Socrates, depicting him as a hopeless dreamer. Aristophanes must have stepped on many toes, for the Athenians awarded him first prize only four times.

In *Lysistrata,* Aristophanes transcended the limitations of the comedic form and approached the timeless quality of the tragedies. A sexually explicit and hilarious comedy, *Lysistrata* points out the absurdity of the prolonged Peloponnesian War and, by implication, all war. In the play, Lysistrata, an Athenian matron, persuades the women of Athens and Sparta to withhold sex from their husbands until they sign a peace treaty. Filled with sexual innuendos, obscenities, and ridiculous allusions to tragic dramas, the play ends with stirring reminders to the Greeks of their common ancestry, their joint victory over the Persians earlier in the century, and their reverence for the same gods. First staged in 411 BCE, seven years before Sparta won the Peloponnesian War, this play commented on but failed to derail Athens's headlong rush to disaster.

After the Peloponnesian War and the restoration of a restricted democracy in 403 BCE, free speech was severely repressed in Athens. Comedies still relied on burlesque and slapstick, but their political edge was blunted. The great creative age of Greek theater was now over.

Music

Like other peoples of the ancient Near East, the Greeks used music both in civic and religious events and in private entertainment. But the Greeks also gave music a new importance, making it one of the humanities along with art, literature, theater, and philosophy. Music became a form of expression subject to rules, styles, and rational analysis. One reason for this was that the Greeks believed music fulfilled an ethical function in the training of young citizens. They also believed that music had divine origins and was inspired by Euterpe, one of the nine muses (thus the word *music*).

Nevertheless, the vast library of Greek music has vanished. What knowledge there is of that lost heritage, which can be only partially reconstructed from surviving treatises on musical theory and references in other writings, shows a tradition that, despite some differences, became the foundation of Western music. Greek music apparently followed the diatonic system, which had been invented by Pythagoras (fl. 530 BCE), using a scale of eight notes, each of which was determined by its numerical ratio to the lowest tone. The Greek composers also devised a series of scales, called **modes,** which functioned roughly like major and minor keys in later Western music. The modes, however, were not interchangeable the way keys are, because the Greeks believed that each mode produced a different emotional and ethical effect on the listener. Thus, the Dorian mode, martial and grave in its emotional impact, was thought by the Greeks to make hearers brave and dignified; the tender and sorrowing Lydian mode, to make them sentimental and weak; and the passionate and wild Phrygian mode, to make them excited and headstrong. Believing that such emotional manipulation made free citizens difficult to govern, Plato banished virtually all music from his ideal republic. Modern research has been able to reproduce all the Greek modes, but otherwise this music remains a mystery.

Despite music's high ethical status in Greece, it had no independent role in Hellenic culture. Instead, music was integrated with verse, notably in epic and lyric poetry and in tragedy and comedy, with either the lyre (a stringed instrument) or the aulos (a wind instrument) providing accompaniment.

HISTORY, PHILOSOPHY, SCIENCE, AND MEDICINE

The finest poetry of the Hellenic period is to be found in plays. However, new literary forms, especially in prose, became the hallmarks of the age. Historical writing emerged and achieved a high level of skill.

Philosophy soared far above the achievements of the Archaic period and began to differentiate itself from natural science. Medical writers produced works that would be influential for nearly two millennia.

History

The study of history began in the fifth century BCE, when Greeks started to analyze the meaning of their immediate past and to write down in prose the results of their research, or *historia*—the Greek word for "inquiry." The Greeks before the classical period had only a dim sense of their past; what they knew came from Homer, local traditions, and mysterious Mycenaean ruins. Herodotus [he-ROD-uh-tuhs] (about 484 BCE–about 430 BCE) was the first to approach history as a distinct subject and to practice historical writing in anything like the modern sense. He was motivated by the belief that the present has its causes in the past and could be a guide for the future. His *Histories* recorded and analyzed the Persian Wars, which he interpreted as Europe versus Asia, or West versus East. In his desire to be fair to both sides, Herodotus traveled to Persia and recorded what he learned there.

The *Histories* have been criticized for implausible and inaccurate information, but Herodotus's clear prose style, masterful storytelling skills, concern for research, impartiality, belief in cause and effect, and desire to leave a record of the past as a legacy to future generations have justly earned him the title "father of history."

Yet, for all his excellence, Herodotus pales in comparison with Thucydides [thew-SID-uh-deez] (died about 401 BCE). His subject was the Peloponnesian War, of which he was a participant. Thucydides was much more skeptical and analytical than Herodotus, and although he had reservations about democracy, he admired Pericles and strove to be completely fair in his account of Periclean Athens. He saw the weaknesses of his beloved polis and realized the baleful effects of imperialism. In his *History of the Peloponnesian War,* he even wrote objectively of his own role as the losing admiral in a naval battle.

Thucydides also used ordinary events to illuminate human motives and fundamental causes and effects in history. Like the Greek dramatists, he showed that human weaknesses and flaws created the real-life tragedies he observed around him. His insight into human nature was penetrating as he chronicled how individuals shift loyalties and redefine their values to justify their actions. Like a medical writer, he explored the health of the body politic. He rose above his narrative to give lessons to future generations. He argued that events that happened in the past would recur in some way—he did not say they would simply repeat themselves—and thus history, carefully studied, can teach the future.

Philosophy, Science, and Medicine

During the Hellenic Age, philosophy and science experienced a radical transformation. Both types of learning came to focus on the place of humans in society, rather than concentrating on the composition of the natural world. Increasing attention was dedicated to ethics, right conduct, and epistemology, the branch of philosophy that deals with knowledge and cognition.

When the Hellenic Age opened, natural philosophy remained divided into two major camps: the materialists and the idealists (see Chapter 2). The materialists, who continued the inquiries of Thales and the Milesian school, believed that the world is made of some basic physical thing. The idealists, in contrast, whose thought stemmed from Pythagoras and the Sicilian school, were nonmaterialists, reasoning that the physical world is illusory and that behind it lies a realm accessible only by contemplation.

By the mid–fifth century BCE, this simple pattern was being challenged by new philosophies, and by 400 BCE, a revolution in thought had occurred that overshadowed everything that had gone before. The first assault came from Sicily, where a new school of thinkers proposed to reconcile materialism and idealism. Then, in Athens, a group of teachers called the Sophists questioned philosophical inquiry itself and the notion of absolute truth. The corrosive ideas of these figures provoked Socrates, the most revolutionary thinker of the entire ancient world, to respond to their claims. Socrates' life marked a watershed in Greek thought. All Greek thinkers before him are now known as Pre-Socratics, and those who came after him—chiefly Plato and Aristotle in Hellenic Greece—followed his lead in studying the human experience (Table 3.1).

THE PRE-SOCRATICS   The major Pre-Socratic thinkers tried to determine the nature of the physical world. For Parmenides [par-MEN-uh-deez] (fl. after 515 BCE) and his followers in the polis Elea, for example, the world was a single, unchanging, unmoving object whose order could be known through human reason. This attempt to reconcile materialism and idealism was modified by Parmenides' student Empedocles [em-PED-uh-kleez] (about 484–about 424 BCE), who claimed that everything, animate or inanimate, originated in the four elements of earth, water, fire, and air. These elements were unchanging, but the opposing forces of love and strife could combine them in different ways, to the detriment or benefit of humans. This

Table 3.1	PHILOSOPHY IN THE HELLENIC AGE
PHILOSOPHY	**EMPHASIS**
Pre-Socratic	The physical world; nature; debate over materialism and idealism
Sophist	Humanistic values; practical skills, such as public speaking and logic
Socratic	Enduring moral and intellectual order of the universe; the psyche (mind/soul); "Virtue is Knowledge"
Platonist	Ideas (Forms) are the basis of everything; dualism, the split between the world of Ideas and the everyday world; rationalism; severe moderation in ethics
Aristotelian	Natural world is the only world; empiricism, using observation, classification, and comparison; "golden mean" in ethics

essentially metaphysical explanation of change later influenced Aristotle.

The atomists, another school of Pre-Socratic thinkers, believed that everything is composed of atoms—eternal, invisible bodies of varying size that, by definition, cannot be divided into smaller units—and the void, the empty space between the atoms. Atomic theory was developed most fully by Democritus [de-MOK-ruht-us] of Thrace (fl. after 460 BCE). The movement and shape of the atoms were sufficient to explain not only physical objects but also feelings, tastes, sight, ideas—in short, every aspect of the physical world.

THE SOPHISTS   The Sophists—from the Greek word *sophia*, or "wisdom"—scorned Pre-Socratic speculation about atoms and elements as irrelevant and useless. These traveling teachers claimed to offer their students (for a fee) knowledge that guaranteed success in life. Their emphasis on the development of practical skills, such as effective public speaking, led their critics to accuse them of cynicism and a lack of interest in higher ethical values, but the Sophists were deeply serious and committed to humanistic values. Protagoras [pro-TAG-uh-ruhs] (481–411 BCE), the most renowned of the Sophists, proclaimed that "man is the measure of all things." This summed up the Sophists' argument that human beings, as the center of the universe, have the power to make judgments about themselves and their world—that they naturally see everything in relation to themselves. The Sophists helped free the human spirit to be critical and creative. If there was a danger in their teaching, it was a tendency toward unrestrained skepticism. By stressing that human beings have the power to shape the world, the Sophists opened themselves to charges of impiety and undermining traditional values, because the traditional Greek view was that the gods controlled everything. The Sophists' denial of norms, standards, and absolutes registered with the populace because the dramatists responded to them. Sophocles condemned the Sophists while Euripides embraced many of their ideas.

THE SOCRATIC REVOLUTION   Socrates [SAH-kruh-teez] (about 470–399 BCE) launched a new era in philosophy. Given his passionate conviction that an enduring moral and intellectual order existed in the universe, he opposed almost everything the Sophists stood for. But Socrates shared certain traits with them, such as his rejection of philosophizing about nature, his focus on human problems, and his desire to empower individuals to make their own moral choices.

Socrates' method for arriving at true moral and intellectual values was deceptively simple yet maddeningly elusive. At the heart of his thinking was the *psyche* (mind, or soul); being immortal, the psyche was deemed more important than the mortal and doomed body. Those who want wisdom must protect, nourish, and expand their psyches by giving their minds the maximum amount of knowledge. The knowledge the psyche acquired had to be won through stimulating conversations and debates as well as by contemplation of abstract virtues and moral values. Only then could the psyche approach its highest potential.

"Virtue is Knowledge," claimed Socrates; he meant that a person who knows the truth, acquired through personal struggle for self-enlightenment, will not commit evil deeds. And this moral dictum may be reversed: those who do wrong do so out of ignorance. If people used their psyches to think more deeply and clearly, they would lead virtuous lives. Socrates' belief in the essential goodness of human nature and the necessity of well-defined knowledge became central tenets of Western thought.

After having pointed out the proper path to wisdom, Socrates left the rest up to his students. Bombarding inquiring youths with questions on such topics as the meaning of justice, he used rigorous logic to refute all the squirming students' attempts at precise definition. Then—as shown by Plato's dialogues, the principal source for what we know about Socrates—the students, collapsing into confusion, admitted the serious gaps in their knowledge. Socrates' step-by-step questions, interspersed with gentle humor and ironic jabs, honed his students' logical skills and compelled them to begin a quest for knowledge in light of their self-confessed ignorance. Many teachers in Greece and Rome adopted the Socratic method, and it remains an honored pedagogical device.

The Athenians of this era began to perceive Socrates as a threat to their way of life. This short, homely, and rather insignificant-looking man—as surviving statues reveal—aroused suspicion in the polis with his public arguments (Figure 3.12). When Athens fell to the Spartans in 404 BCE, opposition to Socrates swelled. Many citizens now found subversion or even blasphemy in his words and in the behavior of his followers. Five years after the end of the Peloponnesian War, Socrates was accused of impiety and of corrupting the Athenian youth; a jury declared him guilty and sentenced him to die. Plato, a former student, was so moved by

Figure 3.12 *Socrates.* Ca. 200 BCE–100 CE. Ht. 10½". British Museum, London. *This Roman marble copy of the original Greek statue supports the unflattering descriptions of Socrates by his contemporaries. By portraying the philosopher with a receding hairline and a dumpy body, the anonymous sculptor has made one of the world's most extraordinary human beings look very ordinary.*

Socrates' eloquent, though ineffective, defense and by the injustice of his death sentence that the younger man dedicated the remainder of his life to righting the wrong and explaining the Socratic philosophy. Indeed, Plato devoted four works to the last days of Socrates including the *Phaedo*, which is a deathbed scene with an argument in support of immortality.

PLATO   The spirit of Socrates hovers over the rest of Greek philosophy, especially in the accomplishments of his most famous student, Plato (about 427–347 BCE). Plato's philosophy is the fountainhead of Western **idealism,** a thought system that emphasizes spiritual values and makes ideas, rather than matter, the basis of everything that exists. **Platonism** arose out of certain premises that were Socratic in origin—the concept of the psyche and the theory of remembrance. Like Socrates, Plato emphasized the immortal and immutable psyche over the mortal and changeful body. But Plato advanced a new polarity, favoring the invisible world of the Forms, or Ideas, in opposition to the physical world. The psyche's true home was the world of the Forms, which it inhabited before birth and after death—the time when the psyche was lost in wonder among the eternal Ideas. In contrast, the body lived exclusively in the material world, completely absorbed by the life of the senses. Once trapped inside the body, the psyche could glimpse the higher reality, or Forms, only through remembrance.

Nonetheless, Plato thought that through a set of mental exercises the psyche would be able to recall the Ideas to which it had once been exposed. The best training for the psyche was the study of mathematics, since mathematics required signs and symbols to represent other things. After the mastery of mathematics, the student proceeded, with the help of logic, to higher stages of abstract learning, such as defining the Forms of Justice, Beauty, and Love. By showing that wisdom came only after an intellectual progression that culminated in an understanding of the absolute Ideas, Plato refuted the Sophists, who claimed that knowledge was relative.

A major implication of Plato's idealism was that the psyche and the body were constantly at war. The psyche's attempts to remember the lost Ideas met resistance from the body's pursuit of power, fame, and physical comforts. This dualism especially plagued the philosopher, the lover of wisdom; but the true philosopher took comfort in recognizing that at death the psyche would return freely to the world of the Forms.

Plato identified the Form of the Good, the ultimate Idea, with God, yet the Platonic deity was neither the creator of the world nor the absolute and final power. Instead, Plato's deity was necessary for his idealism to function; in his thought, God was the source from which descended the imperfect objects of the natural world. In a related theological notion, he, like Socrates, attributed the presence of evil to ignorance; but Plato added the psyche's misdirected judgment and insatiable bodily appetites as other causes of evil.

Socrates' death provoked Plato to envision a perfect state where justice flourished. The book that resulted from Plato's speculations—the *Republic*—sets forth his model state and, incidentally, launched the study of political philosophy in the West. Plato thought that a just state could be realized only when all social classes worked together for the good of the whole, each class performing its assigned tasks. Because of the importance of the psyche, social status was determined by the ability to reason, not by wealth or inheritance. A tiny elite of philosopher-kings and queens, who were the best qualified to run the state, reigned. Possessing wisdom as a result of their education in the Platonic system, they lived simply, shunning the creature comforts that corrupted weaker rulers.

The two lower ranks were similarly equipped for their roles in society by their intellects and their training: a middle group provided police and military protection, and the third and largest segment operated the economy. In Plato's dream world, both the individual and the society aimed for virtue, and the laws and the institutions ensured that the ideal would be achieved.

ARISTOTLE   Socrates may have been revolutionary; Plato was certainly poetic; but Aristotle [AIR-us-tah-tuhl] (384–322 BCE) had the most comprehensive mind of the ancient world. His curiosity and vast intellect led him into every major field of inquiry of his time except mathematics and music. Born in Macedonia, he was connected to some of the most brilliant personalities of his day. He first studied philosophy under Plato in Athens and then tutored the future Alexander the Great. After Philip's conquest of Greece, Aristotle settled in Athens and opened a school, the Lyceum, that quickly rivaled the Academy, Plato's school.

Although his philosophy owed much to Platonism, Aristotle emphasized the role of the human senses. To Aristotle, the natural world was the only world; no separate, invisible realm of Ideas existed. Nature could be studied and understood by observation, classification, and comparison of data from the physical world—that is, through the empirical method.

Aristotle rejected the world of the Forms because he believed that Form and Matter were inseparable, both rooted in nature. Each material object contained a predetermined Form that, with proper training or nourishment, would evolve into its final Form and ultimate purpose. This growth process, in his view, was potentiality evolving into actuality, as when an embryo becomes a human or a seed matures into a plant. Thus, the philosopher could conclude that everything has a purpose, or end.

Aristotle's thought rested on the concept of God, which he equated with the First Cause. Aristotle's God was a logical necessity not a benevolent figure. Rejecting Platonic dualism and its exclusive regard for the psyche, Aristotle devised a down-to-earth ethical goal—a sound mind in a healthy body—that he called happiness. To achieve happiness, he advised, in his *Nicomachean Ethics,* striking a mean, or a balance, between extremes of behavior. For example, courage is the mean between the excess of foolhardiness and the deficiency of cowardice. Noting that actions like murder and adultery are vicious by their very nature, he condemned them as being unable to be moderated. Although Aristotle disavowed many of Plato's ideas, he agreed with his former mentor that the cultivation of the higher intellect is more important than that of the body.

Aristotle's ethics were related to his politics, for he taught that happiness finally depended on the type of government under which an individual lived. Unlike Plato, who based his politics on speculative thinking, Aristotle reached his political views after careful research. After collecting 158 state constitutions, Aristotle, in his *Politics,* classified and compared them, concluding that the best form of government was a constitutional regime ruled by the middle class. His preference for the middle class stemmed from his belief that they, exciting neither envy from the poor nor contempt from the wealthy, would honor and work for the good of all.

Aristotle's influence on Western civilization is immeasurable. In the Middle Ages, Christian, Muslim, and Jewish scholars studied his writings, regarding them as containing authoritative teachings on the natural world. Today, Aristotelianism is embedded in the official theology of the Roman Catholic Church (see Chapter 9), and Aristotle's logic continues to be taught in college philosophy courses.

MEDICINE   Little is known of the life of Hippocrates [hip-OCK-re-teez] (about 460–377 BCE), the major figure in classical Greek medicine. In his own lifetime, he was highly regarded and apparently traveled extensively through Greece and Asia Minor, healing the sick and teaching aspiring physicians.

Hippocrates was born on the island of Cos in the Aegean Sea and probably taught at the medical school located there. In the second and third centuries CE, scholars collected about seventy works attributed to him, the Hippocratic Collection, which ensured his future reputation. Today, Hippocrates is still the "father of medicine" and identified with the Hippocratic

oath, which most medical students take at the commencement of their medical careers. This oath, which he certainly did not compose, spells out the duties and responsibilities of a physician and sets ethical standards and personal behavior practices.

Regardless of how little is known of Hippocrates, he is still recognized as one of the first physicians to reject supernatural explanations as causes of illness. Instead, he observed and studied the body and its parts from a scientific and clinical point of view. Most specifically, Hippocrates believed that diseases were caused by imbalances of the four "humors," which he identified as the four fluids—blood, phlegm, black bile, and yellow bile—within the physical body. He asserted that disease was not the invasion of evil spirits or controlling deities. If these humors were kept in balance—such as by administering drugs, prescribing diets, or removing excess blood or other humors—then the body would heal itself and the patient would recover.

In one of the works attributed to him, Hippocrates discusses the "sacred" disease, now known as epilepsy. At the time, conventional wisdom explained epilepsy as a "divine affliction," a sign that the patient was favored by the gods. In contrast, Hippocrates argues that epilepsy has natural causes that can be identified and treated. He also comments on the brain, terming it the source of all emotions and senses and the "most powerful organ in the human body."

THE VISUAL ARTS

In architecture, sculpture, and painting, Greeks of the Hellenic Age outstripped their Archaic forebears. Doric architecture was brought to a peak of perfection and then surpassed by a new order, the Ionic. The emerging humanism of the kouroi and korai yielded to classical sculpture of almost inexpressible beauty and naturalism. Finally, the gorgeous black- and red-figure ware of the Archaic period was complemented by exquisite white-ground ware.

Architecture

Although the temple was the supreme expression of Hellenic architecture, there were sanctuaries long before there were temples. These were places considered sacred to a god or a goddess. Apollo's sanctuary at Delphi was the oldest and most famous (Figure 3.13). Delphi, believed to be the center of the earth, was sacred to all Greeks and all poleis contributed to the shrine. Inside the shrine was the priestess of Apollo— the only woman allowed at Delphi—the oracle to whom people came from all over with their questions.

Figure 3.13. The Delphic Sanctuary. Aerial view. Late sixth to fourth century BCE. *The ruins of Apollo's temple—this is an earthquake zone—reveal a rectangular foundation and a few standing columns. A sacred way, or road, zigzagged up the mountain to the shrine. During the fourth century, a gymnasium (boy's school), theater, and stadium were built on the site.*

Figure 3.14 Second Temple of Hera at Paestum. Ca. 450 BCE. Limestone. *This temple of Hera is among the best-preserved structures from the ancient world. Since Hera may have been a chthonian goddess before becoming consort to Olympian Zeus, it is appropriate that this Doric temple, with its ground-hugging appearance, be her monument.*

By Hellenic times, the Greek world was polarized between eastern (the mainland and the Aegean Islands) and western (Magna Graecia) styles of temple design, although in both styles the temples were rectilinear and of post-beam-triangle construction. Influenced by the Pythagorean quest for harmony through mathematical rules, the eastern builders had standardized six as the perfect number of columns for the ends of temples and thirteen, or twice the number of end columns plus one, as the perfect number of columns for the sides. These balanced proportions, along with simple designs and restrained decorative schemes, made the eastern temples majestically expressive of classical ideals.

Architects in western Greece, somewhat removed from the centers of classical culture, were more experimental than those in the Greek mainland. Their buildings deviated from the eastern ideals, as can be seen in the Second Temple of Hera at Paestum, built of limestone in about 450 BCE (Figure 3.14). The best preserved of all Greek temples, this Doric structure does not have the harmonious proportions of the eastern version of this style. Although the Second Temple of Hera owed much to eastern influences, including the six columns at the ends and the porches, it had too many (fourteen) columns on the sides, its columns were too thick, and the low-pitched roof made the building seem squat.

Between 447 and 438 BCE, the architects Ictinus [ik-TIE-nuhs] and Callicrates [kuh-LICK-ruh-teez] perfected the eastern-style Doric temple in the Parthenon, a temple on Athens's Acropolis dedicated to Athena (Figure 3.15). When completed, this temple established a new standard of classicism, with eight columns on the ends and seventeen on the sides and with the numeric ratio 9:4 used throughout, expressed, for example, in the relation of a column's height to its diameter. Inside, the builders designed two chambers, an east room for a forty-foot-high statue of Athena and a smaller room housing the Delian League treasury.

SLICE OF LIFE
Secrets of a Successful Marriage in Ancient Greece

XENOPHON
From *Oeconomicus*

With their boundless curiosity, it is not surprising that the Greeks were concerned with how to have a good marriage, as this piece by Xenophon (about 445–355 BCE) demonstrates. A famous military commander, Xenophon was also a historian, essayist, and student of Socrates. Nonetheless, his discussion of marriage, taken from his essay on domestic economy, or home life, is considered a fairly accurate depiction of the marital ideal among well-to-do Greeks of the time. In this selection, he expounds his ideas through the characters of Socrates and Ischomachus, a rich landowner.

During Hellenic times, literacy increased among the Greeks, as compared with the achievements of earlier peoples of the Near East and Egypt. This growth in literacy was mainly the result of the rise of democracy, in which education became a major goal of the citizenry. Despite the increase, though, the survival of written records by ordinary Greeks is spotty. Hence, this Slice of Life is from the writings of a famous Greek author, not by an ordinary person.

I [Socrates] said, "I should very much like you to tell me, Ischomachus, whether you yourself trained your wife to become the sort of woman that she ought to be, or whether she already knew how to carry out her duties when you took her as your wife from her father and mother."

[Ischomachus replied,] "What could she have known when I took her as my wife, Socrates? She was not yet fifteen when she came to me, and had spent her previous years under careful supervision so that she might see and hear and speak as little as possible. . . .

"[A]s soon as she was sufficiently tamed and domesticated so as to be able to carry on a conversation, I questioned her more or less as follows: 'Tell me, wife, have you ever thought about why I married you and why your parents gave you to me? It must be quite obvious to you, I am sure, that there was no shortage of partners with whom we might sleep. I, on my part, and your parents, on your behalf, considered who was the best partner we could choose for managing an estate and for children. And I chose you, and your parents, apparently, chose me, out of those who were eligible. Now if some day the god grants us children, then we shall consider how to train them in the best way pos-

sible. For this will be a blessing to us both, to obtain the best allies and support in old age. But at present we two share this estate. I go on paying everything I have into the common fund; and you deposited into it everything you brought with you. There is no need to calculate precisely which of us has contributed more, but to be well aware of this: that the better partner is the one who makes the more valuable contribution. . . .

"'Because both the indoor and the outdoor tasks require work and concern, I think the god, from the very beginning, designed the nature of woman for the indoor work and concerns and the nature of man for the outdoor work. For he prepared man's body and mind to be more capable of enduring cold and heat and travelling and military campaigns, and so he assigned the outdoor work to him. Because the woman was physically less capable of endurance, I think the god has evidently assigned the indoor work to her. . . .

"'Because it is necessary for both of them to give and to take, he gave both of them equal powers of memory and concern. So you would not be able to distinguish whether the female or male sex has the larger share of these. And he gave them both equally the ability to practise self-control too, when it is needed. . . .

"[B]ecause they are not equally well endowed with all the same natural aptitudes, they are consequently more in need of each other, and the bond is more beneficial to the couple, since one is capable where the other is deficient.'"

INTERPRETING THIS SLICE OF LIFE

1. Based on this selection, *what* was the role of women in marriage in Hellenic Greece? 2. At *what* age was the wife in the selection married? 3. *What* impact would the wife's youth have on the dynamics of the marriage? 4. *Discuss* the role of material matters (money, property, and other forms of wealth) in Greek marriage, as depicted here. 5. *What* attitude does the speaker, Ischomachus, have toward male and female intellectual abilities? 6. *Why* does such advice on marriage appear in a work on domestic economy? 7. *Compare and contrast* modern attitudes toward marriage with those represented in this selection.

The rest of the Acropolis project, finally finished in 405 BCE, included the Propylaea, the gate leading to the sanctuary; the temple of Athena Nike, a gift to Athens's patron goddess thanking her for a military victory (Figure 3.16); and the Erechtheum, a temple dedicated to three deities.

Ictinus and Callicrates introduced many subtle variations, called refinements, into their designs so that no line is exactly straight, horizontal, or perpendicular. For example, the stepped base of the temple forms a gentle arc so that the ends are lower than the middle; the floor slopes slightly to the edges; and the

Figure 3.15 Ictinus and Callicrates. The Parthenon, Athens. Third quarter of the fifth century BCE. Pentelic marble. *A great humanistic icon, the Parthenon has had a long history since its days as a Greek temple. It served successively as a Christian church, a mosque, and an ammunitions depot, until it was accidentally blown up at the end of the seventeenth century CE. Today, concerned nations are cooperating with the Greek government through UNESCO to preserve this noble ruin.*

columns tilt inward away from the ends. These and other refinements were no accidents but, instead, were intended to be corrections for real and imaginary optical illusions. The Parthenon's fame exerted such authority in later times that these refinements, along with harmonious proportions, became standardized as the essence of Greek architecture.

The second order of Greek architecture, the Ionic, originated in the late Archaic Age and, like the Doric, came to flower in Hellenic times. The **Ionic** style, freer than the Doric and more graceful, reflected its origins in the Ionian world; traditionally, the Ionians contrasted their opulence with the simplicity of the Dorians. In place of the alternating metopes and triglyphs of Doric buildings, the Ionic temple had a running frieze to which sculptured figures might be added. More decorated than the plain Doric, the Ionic columns had el-

Figure 3.16 Callicrates. Temple of Athena Nike, Athens. Late fifth century BCE. Marble. *Designed by Callicrates, one of the Parthenon's architects, this miniature temple was begun after 427 BCE and probably completed before 420 BCE. Like the Parthenon, it was dedicated to the city's patron goddess, Athena, though here she was honored as Nike, goddess of victory. This temple's simple plan includes a square cella with four Ionic columns at the front and back and a sculptural frieze, devoted to scenes of mythic and contemporary battles, encircling the upper exterior walls.*

egant bases, and their tops were crowned with capitals that suggested either a scroll's ends or a ram's horns. What solidified the Ionic temple's impression of elegance were its slender and delicate columns.

The Athenians chose the Ionic style for the exquisite, though eccentric, Erechtheum, the last of the great buildings erected on the Acropolis (Figure 3.17). The artistic freedom associated with the Ionic style may have led the architect, Mnesicles [NES-uh-kleez], to make the floor plan asymmetrical and to introduce so many design variations, but a more likely explanation was Mnesicles' need to integrate three existing shrines into a single building—those of the Olympians Athena and Poseidon and the mythical king Erechtheus [eh-RECK-thee-us], who introduced the horse to Athens. Mnesicles took the unusual step of stressing the site's unbalanced nature by adding two Ionic porches and the temple's crowning feature, the Porch of the Maidens. With his bold design, Mnesicles created a marvelous illusion of harmony that was in keeping with the age's classical ideals.

Sculpture

Equally impressive is the Greek achievement in sculpture. Believing that the task of sculpture is to imitate nature, the Greeks created images of gods and goddesses as well as of men and women that have haunted the Western imagination ever since. They not only forged a canon of idealized human proportions that later sculptors followed but also developed a repertoire of postures, gestures, and subjects that have become embedded in Western art.

During the Hellenic Age, classical sculpture moved through three separate phases: the **Severe style,** which ushered in the period and lasted until 450 BCE; the **high classical style,** which coincided with the zenith of Athenian imperial greatness; and the **fourth-century style,** which concluded with the death of Alexander the Great in 323 BCE.

Sculpture in the Severe style, inspired perhaps by its association with funeral customs, was characterized by a feeling of dignified nobility. The *Kritios Boy*—showing a figure fully at rest—is an elegant expression of this first phase of classicism (Figure 3.18). Kritios [KRIT-ee-uhs], the supposed sculptor, fixed the mouth severely and altered the frontality, a feature of the Archaic style, by tilting the head subtly to the right and slightly twisting the upper torso. The flat-footed stance of the Archaic kouros has given way to a posture that places the body's weight on one leg and uses the other leg as a support. This stance is called **contrapposto** (counterpoise), and its invention, along with the mastery of the representation of muscula-

Figure 3.17 MNESICLES. The Erechtheum. View from the west. Ca. 410 BCE. Marble. Athens. *The Erechtheum was probably built to quiet conservatives who rejected Athena's new temple, the Parthenon, as a symbol of Athenian imperialism. Reflecting its ties with the past, the Erechtheum housed the ancient wooden cult statue of Athena, which pious Athenians believed had fallen from the sky. Its Ionic porches set the standard for the graceful Ionic order. The Porch of the Maidens (above), which was inaccessible from the outside, fronted the southern wall.*

ture, helped to make the classical revolution. Thereafter, sculptors were able to render the human figure in freer, more relaxed poses.

The central panel of the so-called Ludovisi Throne, another sculpture from the same period, conveys an air of quiet gravity (Figure 3.19). The subject is probably the birth of Aphrodite as she rises from the sea, indicated by pebbles under the feet of her attendants, the stooping figures on either side. This relief reflects a perfect blending of late Archaic grace (Aphrodite's stylized hair and the hint of Archaic smile) with the dignity of the Severe style (the delicate transparent draperies and the convincing realism produced by foreshortening the arms of the three figures).

In contrast to the Severe style, which accepted repose as normal, the high classical style was fascinated

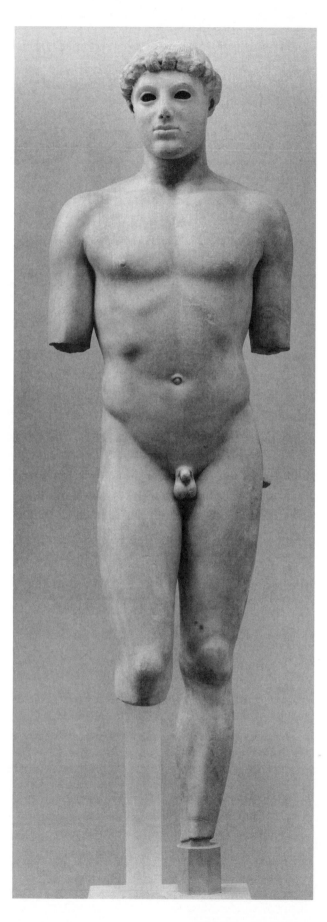

Figure 3.18 *Kritios Boy.* Ca. 480 BCE. Ht. 33". Acropolis Museum, Athens. *This statue is carved from marble probably mined at Mount Pentelicus in Attica. Two features—the treatment of the eyes, which were originally set with semiprecious stones, and the roll of hair—show that the Kritios sculptor was accustomed to working in bronze. The figure's beautifully rendered muscles and sense of inner life announce the arrival of the Hellenic style; the contrapposto, used sparingly here, foreshadows later developments in Greek sculpture.*

with the aesthetic problem of showing motion in a static medium. The sculptors' solution, which became central to high classicism, was to freeze the action, resisting the impulse to depict agitated movement, in much the same way that the tragic playwrights banished violence from the stage. In effect, the high classical sculptors stopped time, allowing an ideal world to emerge in which serene gods and mortals showed grace under pressure. A striking representation of this aspect of high classicism is the bronze statue of Poseidon, or Zeus, found in the Aegean Sea off Cape Artemision. It captures to perfection high classicism's ideal of virile grace (Figure 3.20). The god (whose maturity is signified by the beard and fully developed body) is shown poised, ready to hurl some object. In such sculptures as this, the Greeks found visual metaphors for their notion that deities and mortals are kin.

High classical sculptors wanted to do more than portray figures in motion; some, especially Polykleitos [pol-e-KLITE-uhs] of Argos, continued to be obsessed with presenting the ideal human form at rest. In his search for perfection, Polykleitos executed a bronze male figure of such strength and beauty—the *Doryphoros* ("Spearbearer")—that its proportions came to be regarded as a canon, or set of rules, to be imitated by other artists (Figure 3.21). In the *Doryphoros* canon, each of the limbs bears a numeric relation to the body's overall measurements; for example, the length of the foot is one-tenth of the figure's height. Other principles of high classicism embodied in the *Doryphoros* include the slightly brutal facial features, typical of this style's masculine ideal; the relaxed contrapposto; and the controlled muscles.

Greek architecture reached its zenith in the Parthenon, and, similarly, classical Greek sculpture attained its height in the reliefs and sculptures of this celebrated temple. Under the disciplined eye of the sculptor Phidias [FIHD-e-uhs], craftspeople carved patriotic and mythological subjects destined for various parts of the building. Taken as a whole, the sculptures revealed the Parthenon to be a tribute to Athenian imperialism as much as to the goddess Athena (see Figure 3.2).

On the Parthenon's metopes—the rectangular spaces on the Doric frieze—sculptors portrayed scenes in the prevailing high classical style. In panel after

Figure 3.19 *The Birth of Aphrodite.* Ca. 460 BCE. Ht. 2′9″. Terme Museum, Rome. *The Ludovisi Throne, with its three relief panels, is a controversial work, because scholars disagree about its original function, the interpretation of its panels, and even its date. Discovered in Rome in the late nineteenth century, it probably was carved in Magna Graecia, perhaps for an altar, and brought to Rome in antiquity. The figure of Aphrodite was one of the first naked women depicted in large-scale Greek sculpture. The goddess is rendered in softly curving lines—a marked deviation from the Severe style and a forecast of the sensuous tendency of later Greek art.*

Figure 3.20 *Poseidon (or Zeus).* Ca. 460–450 BCE. Bronze, ht. 6′10″. National Museum, Athens. *The Greek conception of the nobility of their gods is nowhere better revealed than in this magnificent bronze sculpture of Poseidon (or Zeus). Grace, strength, and intellect are united in this majestic image of a mature deity. Poseidon's eyes originally would have been semiprecious stones, and the statue would have been painted to create a more realistic effect. If Poseidon, he hurls a trident; if Zeus, a thunderbolt.*

panel, the metope sculptors depicted perfect human forms showing restraint in the midst of struggle, such as Amazons against men, Greeks against Trojans, and gods against giants. The south metopes portrayed the battle between the legendary lapiths and the half-men, half-horse centaurs (Figure 3.22). For the Greeks, the struggle between the human lapiths and the bestial

centaurs symbolized the contest between civilization and barbarism or, possibly, between the Greeks and the Persians.

Inside the columns, running around the perimeter of the upper cella walls in a continuous band, was a low-relief frieze (Figure 3.23). Borrowed from the Ionic order, this running frieze introduced greater liveliness

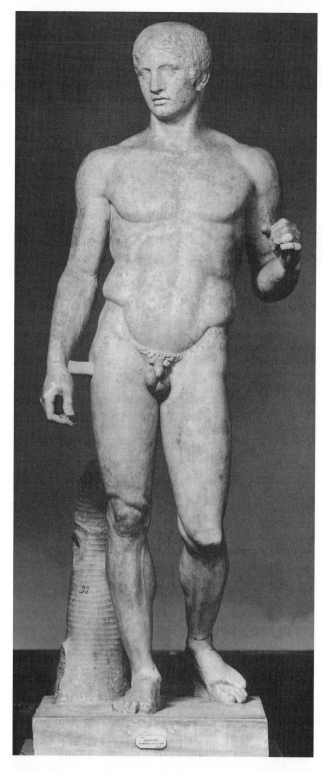

Figure 3.21 *Doryphoros.* Ca. 440 BCE. Marble copy of a bronze original by Polykleitos, ht. 6'6". Museo Nazionale Archeologico, Naples. *The* Doryphoros *expresses the classical ideal of balanced repose. The nude figure rests his weight upon the right leg. The left arm, extended to hold the now-missing spear, balances with the right leg. The left foot, barely touching the ground, balances with the relaxed right arm. Besides representing idealized repose, the* Doryphoros *was also recognized as the embodiment of human beauty with its ordered proportions, well-toned musculature, and rugged features.*

into high classicism. The 525-foot-long band depicts the Panathenaea festival, Athens's most important civic and religious ritual, which was held every four years. This panoramic view of the thrilling procession concluded with a stunning group portrait of the twelve gods and goddesses, seated in casual majesty, awaiting their human worshipers. The entire Parthenon frieze was the most ambitious work of sculpture in the Greek tradition.

The beautiful grave stele of Hegeso (Figure 3.24) is in the Phidian style, the presumed style of Phidias. The deceased lady has selected a necklace from a jewel box held by her attendant. The billowing garments reveal arms, legs, and breasts. These are real people. The figures themselves merge into the background as if it were empty space. Sculptors had by now mastered form and could concentrate on interpretation.

The transition to fourth-century style coincided with the end of the creative phase of tragedy and the disintegration of the Greek world as it passed into the Macedonian political orbit. Sculpture remained innovative, since each generation seemed to produce a master who challenged the prevailing aesthetic rules, and free expression continued as a leading principle of fourth-century style. But sculptors now expressed such new ideas as beauty for its own sake and a delight in sensuality. Earlier classicism had stressed the notion that humans could become godlike, but the last phase concluded that gods and mortals alike reveled in human joys.

This new focus is apparent in Praxiteles' [prax-SIT-uhl-eez] *Hermes with the Infant Dionysus.* This sculpture, perhaps the only original work by a known sculptor that survives from Hellenic Greece, portrays two gods blissfully at play (Figure 3.25). Hermes, lounging in a casual yet dignified pose, probably dangled grapes before the attentive baby god. The contrapposto posture, beautifully defined in Hermes' stance, became widely imitated as the **Praxitelean curve.** Hermes' sensuous body, his intent gaze, and his delicate features are hallmarks of fourth-century classicism; by the next generation, Praxiteles' treatment of the male figure had superseded the more rugged *Doryphoros* canon.

Painting

In the Hellenic period, red-figure ware was more popular than black-figure ware, but both styles continued to be produced (Figures 3.1, 3.10, 3.11). New toward the end of the fifth century was white-ground ware. Surviving examples are almost all painted on lekynthoi (oil jugs, for funeral offerings). Two features of this new style are striking. First, the white-ground ware style shares traits with the period's sculpture, but it is unclear which came first. A look at the Hegeso stele (see Figure 3.24) and the *Mistress and Maid* by the so-called

Figure 3.22 *Centaur Versus Lapith.*
Metope XXX, south face of the Parthenon. Ca. 448–442 BCE. Marble, ht.
56". British Museum. *This struggling
pair was designed to fit comfortably into
the metope frame, and thus the proportions of the figures in relation to each
other and to the small space were worked
out with precision. The intertwined limbs
of the warrior and the centaur visibly
demonstrate the new freedom of high
classicism. The anguished countenance
of the lapith, however, is almost unique
in high classicism and is a portent of
the more emotional faces of the Hellenistic style, the next major artistic
development.*

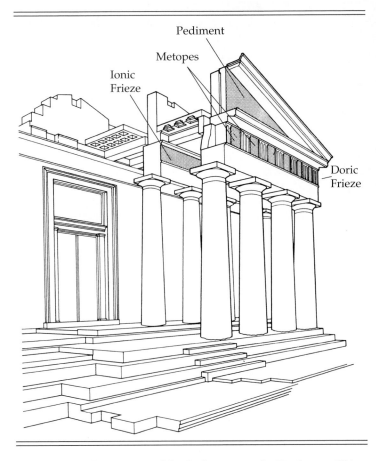

Pediment

Metopes

Ionic
Frieze

Doric
Frieze

Figure 3.23 The Location of the Sculptures on the Parthenon. *This
cutaway view shows the metopes on the Doric frieze, Ionic frieze, and pediments of the Parthenon, which were covered with sculptures celebrating the
glory of Athens.*

Figure 3.24 Grave Stele of Hegeso. Ca. 410–400 B.C.E Ht.
5' 9". National Archaeological Museum, Athens. *Grave markers like this one were produced in profusion in Athens and probably helped to disseminate the Phidian style. Hegeso was a noble
lady and this tomb marker was probably erected by her husband.
As Figure 3.22 shows a lapith in agony, so this stele reveals tenderness, attentiveness, and intimacy. Here is Greek humanism at
its most humane.*

Figure 3.25 PRAXITELES. *Hermes with the Infant Dionysus.* Ca. 350–340 BCE. Marble, ht. 85″. Olympia Museum. *In this statue of Hermes, Praxiteles changed the look of classical art with his rendering of the god's body. For example, Hermes' small head and long legs contributed to the Praxitelean canon for the male figure. The sculptor has also created a dramatic contrast between Hermes' well-muscled body and his soft face. As a direct result of Praxiteles' new vision, sculptors in the Hellenistic Age became interested in more frankly sensual portrayals of the human figure, both male and female.*

Figure 3.26 *Mistress and Maid* by the so-called Achilles Painter. Ca. 440–430 BCE. Ht. 16″. Staatliche Antikensammlungen, Munich. *Probably made in Athens, this white-ground vessel has perhaps the most refined, delicate surviving painting from ancient Greece. Compare the Hegeso stele (Figure 3.24).*

Achilles Painter (Figure 3.26) shows the same melancholy scene interpreted in almost the same way. Second, the white background in the white-ground ware gave the painter the opportunity to draw and color freely, allowing the figures to emerge from seemingly empty space. The painter's command of spatial effects creates a powerful three-dimensionality. In painting, this command of space is corollary to the sense of movement in sculpture.

The Legacy of Hellenic Civilization

Although Athens failed in its dream of political mastery of Greece, the Athenian miracle so impressed its contemporaries that Athenian culture dominated the Hellenic Age. Tragic poets, comic playwrights, and natural philosophers made the Athenian dialect the medium of expression for poetry and prose. The buildings on the Acropolis expressed visually the purity and restraint of the Athenian style. And Athenian democracy, which served as the exciting teacher of its citizens, was the envy of most of the other Greek poleis. After the fall of Greece to Macedonia, however, the idea of democracy fell into disrepute. Almost two thousand years passed before some leaders in Europe were ready to give democracy a second chance.

But **humanism,** the other great creation of Athens, survived as a guide to refined living for the cultivated classes in the West. Athenian culture became the heart of the educational curriculum that was followed in Hellenistic civilization; that model was adopted by Rome and transmitted in the humanistic tradition to Europe. In time, the study and the practice of humanistic learning—literature, philosophy, theater, music, and the arts and architecture—became the crowning glory of Western civilization, affecting private individuals and entire societies.

Moreover, classicism—the style of humanistic achievements in the Hellenic Age—had three great effects on the Western tradition. First, the principles of Greek classicism—balance, simplicity, and restraint—set the standard by which the styles of other times are often measured. Second, the actual works of classicism became basic building blocks of Western culture. In the realm of thought, the works of Plato and Aristotle quickly acquired a luster of authority and retained it until the seventeenth century CE. Aristotle's literary criticism created a new writing genre, and his analysis of tragedy made this type of drama the ultimate challenge to ambitious writers. The Greek tragedies themselves—of Aeschylus, Sophocles, and Euripides—are thought by many people in the West to be unsurpassed.

The comic plays of Aristophanes are less well known today, but their spirit still lives in period comedies and contemporary political satire. The histories of Herodotus and Thucydides retain their vitality as important sources for their respective eras, although modern research has cast doubt on some of their conclusions. Among Greece's accomplishments, architecture has had the most potent effect; the ruins on the Athenian Acropolis and elsewhere are eternal reminders of this Greek heritage. Finally, the idealized statues of men and women, such as the *Doryphoros,* have inspired Western artists with their vision of noble beings alert to the rich possibilities of human life.

The third and perhaps most important contribution of classicism to the Western tradition was a skeptical spirit rooted in democracy. By asserting that the purpose of human life can best be realized in cities that are shaped by the citizens' needs, as Athenian humanism claimed, the humanists declared war on all tyrants, hierarchical societies, and divinely ordered states—in other words, the prevailing order of the ancient world. Because of this critical aspect of humanism, the Greek heritage has sometimes been called into question and, during repressive periods, been subjected to attack. However, the passion for questioning, for inquiry, which characterizes the skeptical spirit, is at the core of Western consciousness.

KEY CULTURAL TERMS

Hellenic
maenad
Dionysia
classic (classical)
classicism
tragedy
chorus
orchestra
skene
satyr-play
Old Comedy

modes
epistemology
idealism
Platonism
Ionic
Severe style
high classical style
fourth-century style
contrapposto
Praxitelean curve
humanism

QUESTIONS FOR CRITICAL THINKING

1. Discuss the impact of the Peloponnesian War on the cultural life of Athens and its citizens.

2. Define classicism and illustrate how Greek tragedy embodies it.

3. Discuss the pivotal role of Socrates in Greek philosophy.

4. Compare Plato's and Aristotle's approaches to truth.

5. What is meant by the high classical style? Discuss examples of this style as found in Greek sculpture.

4

HELLENISTIC CIVILIZATION AND THE RISE OF ROME

The Hellenistic Age extended from the death of Alexander the Great in 323 BCE to the definitive triumph of Rome in the Mediterranean world in 31 BCE. The period is called **Hellenistic** to signal that it was different from the Hellenic Age yet very much its heir and beneficiary. Instead of being purely Greek in culture, the period might be described as "Greekish." The chief dynamic of the Hellenistic world was a remarkable blend of Greek and local cultures from Persia to the western Mediterranean. While the Greek element was everywhere dominant, and gave coherence and unity to the age, Hellenistic culture was **cosmopolitan,** a word that imagines the world (*cosmos*) as a city (*polis*) and the city as a world. The Hellenistic Age was multicultural, open, and tolerant in ways that no preceding cultures had been and that no future ones would be until late in the twentieth century.

The Hellenistic world was large and diverse, but it can be viewed from a series of uniform perspectives. Politically, diplomatically, and militarily, there are three stories to tell. First, three vast new kingdoms formed in the wake of Alexander's conquests. Second, as those kingdoms weakened, new and smaller ones emerged alongside them. Third, the Romans unified Italy and then systematically conquered one people after another until they became totally dominant.

Socially and economically, there are three key issues to consider. The Hellenistic world was rich and luxurious, partly because royal courts spent lavishly and partly because merchants, bankers, and producers grew fabulously wealthy. The tone of life was set by cities, sometimes old ones like Athens or Antioch, and sometimes new ones like Alexandria. There was a general ease

◀ **Detail** *Old Market Woman.* Third or second century BCE. Marble copy of bronze original, ht. 49". Metropolitan Museum of Art, New York.

Figure 4.1 Black Youth. Third–second century BCE. Bronze. Metropolitan Museum of Art, New York. *Beginning in the Archaic Age, Greek artists occasionally depicted black Africans in their works. During the Hellenistic Age, with the migration of peoples and the increased use of slaves, sculptors frequently chose black figures as subjects. This small bronze statue of a young African is an illustration of the racial diversity of the Hellenistic world. Despite the figure's exaggerated half-crouch, the statuette is probably not meant to represent an athlete, as he is not depicted fully nude. Note the sash around the waist, with the end draped down the upper thighs. The figure more likely was intended to represent a worker engaged in some task, as reflected in the object or objects (now lost) that he was holding in his hands.*

of movement, whether of merchants or of soldiers, whether of scholars or of artisans, that tended to make people less rooted in particular cities even though the overall character of life was deeply urban. How very different this was than the polis-bound Greeks of the Hellenic Age! Luxury, rapid change, and constant movement tended, finally, to relax older moral and social conventions.

The culture of the Hellenistic world was extraordinarily complex. It could reflect the majesty of a royal court or the bawdiness of an urban street. Much of the balance, order, and restraint of Hellenic culture was jettisoned. Literature became more theatrical and playful, sculpture more emotional and even sensual. Ordinary people became subjects for plays and poems and statues (Figure 4.1). Whereas Hellenic philosophers tried to understand the natural world, Hellenistic philosophers concentrated on relieving feelings of anxiety and alienation. Their writings have been called therapeutic; they were meant to make people feel better, not to make them know more.

THE CHANGING FRAMEWORK OF POLITICS

Alexander the Great died suddenly in 323 BCE without having made any provision for his succession. Three of his chief generals carved up the vast realm conquered, but never really governed, by Alexander. They built large, reasonably successful kingdoms that eventually fragmented and then succumbed to Rome's legions. By the end of the Hellenistic period, Rome had created an empire larger than Alexander's or Persia's (Timeline 4.1).

The Hellenistic Monarchies

Following a civil war, three resourceful military commanders, Antigonus, Seleucus, and Ptolemy, eventually divided Alexander's empire among themselves. Antigonus took Macedon and Greece as his share. It took him and his successors nearly fifty years to secure power, and even then they had to share rule with various Greek cities in a kind of federal structure. Seleucus took southern Anatolia, Palestine and Syria, Mesopotamia, and the former Persian Empire. The Seleucids warred often on their eastern frontier and gradually lost control of Parthia and Bactria (Map 4.1). They ruled from Sardis in Asia Minor, Antioch in Syria, and Seleucia in Mesopotamia. Under Seleucid rule, Antioch became the second greatest city in the Hellenistic world. Ptolemy took Egypt and the adjoining coast of North Africa. The kings of these lands were some-

Timeline 4.1 THE HELLENISTIC AGE   **All dates BCE**

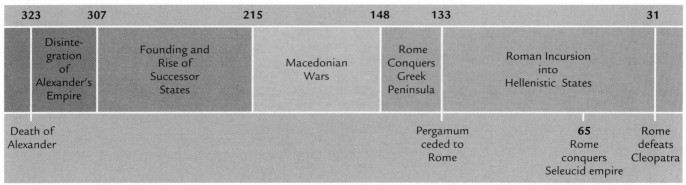

323	307	215	148	133	31
Disintegration of Alexander's Empire	Founding and Rise of Successor States	Macedonian Wars	Rome Conquers Greek Peninsula	Roman Incursion into Hellenistic States	

Death of Alexander   Pergamum ceded to Rome   **65** Rome conquers Seleucid empire   Rome defeats Cleopatra

LEARNING THROUGH MAPS

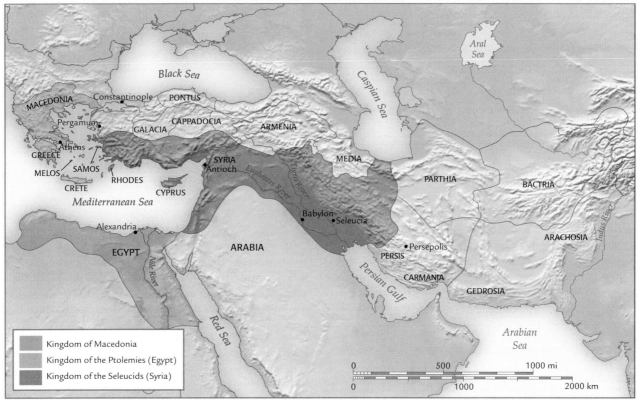

Map 4.1 THE SUCCESSOR STATES AND THE HELLENISTIC WORLD
This map shows the Hellenistic world and the successor states, which emerged after the breakup of Alexander the Great's empire. 1. *Notice* the differing sizes of the successor states and the respective region controlled by each. 2. *Consider* the impact of geography and regional cultural traditions on the three kingdoms. 3. *Locate* the major cities of these kingdoms. 4. *How* did Alexandria's location in Egypt help to make it the dominant city of the Hellenistic world?

times rivals, with the Seleucids and Ptolemies fighting often. Ptolemaic power waxed and waned because the Ptolemies had to make concessions to native Egyptians to get them to fight in their armies and also because some Ptolemaic rulers were incompetent. Neverthe-

less, the Ptolemies built Alexandria into the greatest city of the era.

The large kingdoms could not prevent the emergence of some smaller ones. The most prominent of these was Pergamum in western Asia Minor. The Attalids, the

Figure 4.2 Acropolis at Pergamum. Second century BCE. Reconstruction by H. Schlief. Staatliche Museen, Berlin. *Pergamum architecture was in the Hellenic style, but the city's mixed population and economy made it the commercial and political hub of a Hellenistic kingdom. Under Eumenes II, the capital and the country reached their height of power around 160 BCE.*

ruling dynasty of Pergamum, achieved freedom from the Seleucids in 263 BCE. They decorated their city's acropolis with a splendid palace, a library second only to Alexandria's, and a marble temple to Athena. Scattered on the hillside beneath the acropolis were shrines, markets, and private dwellings of the more prosperous citizens. At the base of the hill, the merchants, artisans, and slaves lived crowded together (Figure 4.2).

The Rise of Rome

The city of Rome arose around 1000 BCE as a cluster of settlements on seven hills overlooking a swampy site about fifteen miles up the Tiber from the sea. The surrounding plain of Latium (whence Latin, the Romans' language) provided fertile farmland, and the river was easily forded near Rome. In Roman tradition the city was founded in the year now denoted 753 BCE. For a long time the Romans were dominated both politically and culturally by two other peoples. To the north were the Etruscans, a creative people whose origins are obscure. Gifted as artists, they were also skilled in the arts of government. They dominated Etruria, roughly modern Tuscany. To the south were the Greeks of Magna Graecia (see Chapters 2 and 3). The emerging Romans had regular commercial and cultural contacts with both peoples, and occasionally fought with them.

Through much of the seventh and sixth centuries BCE, the Romans were actually ruled by the Etruscans.

In 509 BCE, in Roman tradition, the last Etruscan king was expelled and the Romans created an independent republic. Over the next two centuries the Romans gained control of most of central Italy. As they pushed south, they encountered the Greeks and became embroiled with the Carthaginians. Carthage was a Phoenician colony on the coast of North Africa with important diplomatic and trade interests all over the western Mediterranean. Between 264 and 146 BCE, the Romans fought and won three Punic Wars (from *Poeni*, purple, signifying the purple dye for which Phoenicia was famous).

Rome's encounter with Magna Graecia and then with Carthage had three prominent outcomes. First, Rome became dominant in the western Mediterranean region. Second, Rome began acquiring an empire, one that would continue expanding for almost four centuries. Specifically, Rome took the islands of Sicily, Sardinia, and Corsica in 241 BCE, and parts of North Africa in 146 BCE, and began carving out interests in Spain. Third, Rome became involved with the Hellenistic kingdoms.

King Pyrrhus of Epirus (319–272 BCE), whose dynasty created in the western Balkans one of the smaller Hellenistic kingdoms, was called in by the Greeks of the south and he lost a battle to the Romans in 275 BCE.

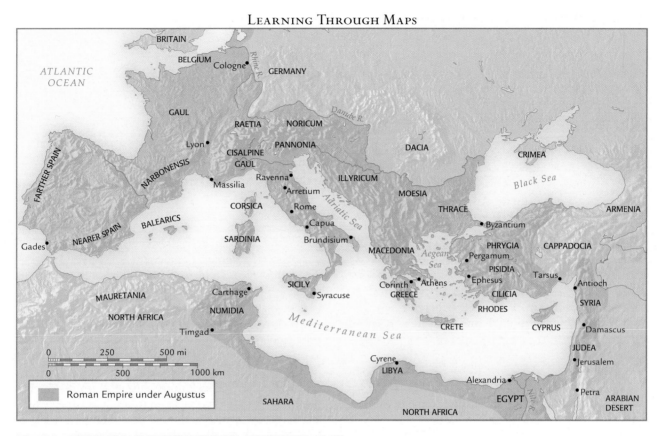

Map 4.2   THE ROMAN EMPIRE UNDER AUGUSTUS, 14 CE
This map shows the Roman Empire at the death of its founder, Augustus. 1. *Notice* the wide-ranging lands incorporated into the Roman world. 2. *Compare* this map with Map 1.1, Ancient Mesopotamia and Egypt, and Map 4.1, The Successor States and the Hellenistic World, and see which ancient civilizations were now included in the Roman Empire. 3. *What* impact did these ancient civilizations have on Roman cultural life? 4. *What* role did the Mediterranean Sea play in the Roman Empire? 5. *How* did Rome's location both help and hinder Rome as a site for the imperial government?

This battle gave rise to the term Pyrrhic victory because the Romans, although victorious, suffered such great losses that they were barely able to continue. During Rome's second and third wars with Carthage (218–201 and 149–146 BCE), the Antigonids lent some support to the Carthaginians. Rome regarded this action as a provocation and began the systematic conquest of Greece and Macedon. The Seleucids and Ptolemies, in turn, lent assistance to the Antigonids, and Rome began a long reckoning of accounts with them too. The future of the whole Mediterranean basin became clear when King Attalus III of Pergamum died without heirs in 133 BCE and willed his kingdom to Rome. At the battle of Actium in 31 BCE the Romans defeated the forces of Cleopatra, the last of the Ptolemies, and secured their dominion in the Hellenistic world. In the meantime, various ambitious Roman politicians undertook the conquest of Spain and Gaul. The latter triumph was the work of Julius Caesar (100–44 BCE). The age of Hellenistic kingdoms was over, and the Roman Empire ruled lands from the Atlantic to Mesopotamia (Map 4.2).

The Nature of Government

The Hellenistic world gave rise to two forms of government, divinized kingship and republicanism, that were to be influential for centuries. Macedonian kings had been essentially warlords. Alexander's successors, however, combined military leadership with theocratic kingship. Kings were either regarded as gods or were thought to be answerable only to the gods. Philosophers equated the happiness and stability of realms and peoples with the fortunes of the kings.

The Romans took a very different path. After expelling the Etruscan kings, the Romans developed a hearty distaste for monarchy. When they created their republic, the Romans instituted a set of magistracies and legislative assemblies. Early Roman society was

Timeline 4.2   THE ROMAN REPUBLIC, 509–31 BCE

509		264		133	31
Early Republic		Middle Republic		Late Republic	
Rome establishes republican form of government, subdues Italian peninsula		**264–241** First Punic War	**219–202** Second Punic War **149–146** Third Punic War	**133–31** Rome acquires Hellenistic kingdoms; social, political unrest	**44** Julius Caesar assassinated **44–31** Civil war

riven by class conflict between plebeians and patricians. The origins of these two groups of people are obscure. The plebeians were small farmers, laborers, artisans, and perhaps merchants. Patricians (from *pater*, "father": patricians were well-fathered men) were landed aristocrats. Initially the patricians reserved virtually all offices and participation to themselves. Three times the plebeians seceded from the state—in effect, they went on strike—to demand reforms. By 287 BCE, almost all formal differences between the two orders had been eliminated and Rome became, at least technically, a democracy.

The Roman Republic was led by two annually elected consuls and two (and then more over time) judicial officers called praetors, as well as financial and public works officers, likewise elected annually. Every Roman belonged to two legislative assemblies. Membership in one was according to wealth and in the other by residence. Finally, there was the Roman senate. Originally this body comprised patricians, but gradually the body came to be made up of former officeholders. The senate could not pass laws, but it could, and did, issue opinions on the great issues of the day. For centuries the Romans paid great deference to the views of the senators. In addition to deferring to the senators, the Romans chose almost all their officers from a small group of families until the end of the second century BCE.

When they were conquering Greece, the Romans captured the historian Polybius (about 200–118 BCE). Acute of mind and fluent of pen, Polybius wrote a history of his times. He wondered how a people "so recently barbarian"—Greeks viewed non-Greeks as barbarians, literally babblers, people who could not speak Greek—and in such a short time conquered the world. He attributed Rome's success to political stability, something that may well have caught the attention of a Greek accustomed to the turmoil of his land. In a section of his history that deeply influenced America's founding fathers, Polybius argued that Rome had a "balanced" constitution. The consuls represented

monarchy. The senate represented oligarchy. The assemblies represented democracy. Rome, Polybius believed, had found a formula that avoided the constant, cyclical political transformations that plagued the Greek world.

Polybius's views notwithstanding, the Roman Republic collapsed in civil war and near anarchy. What happened? Centuries of war and conquest put strains on a society that imagined itself as made up of citizen-soldier-farmers. The empire brought unimaginable wealth. Class conflict between urban and rural dwellers, between farmers and merchants, between rich and poor tore at the stable, deferential fabric of Roman politics. "New men," a Roman term that was not flattering, began to seek the offices that established families had long monopolized. The empire provided scope for personal ambition unthinkable in earlier times. One faction after another tried to gain control of the state by packing the assemblies, by bribery, by violence, by taking over an army, or by some combination of all these means. After decades of civil war, the last man standing was Julius Caesar's adopted nephew, Gaius Julius Caesar Octavianus. It was he who defeated Cleopatra and put an end to the last of the major Hellenistic kingdoms. In 27 BCE what was left of the Roman senate conferred nearly absolute power on Augustus Caesar (see Chapter 6). Ironically, Rome's republic defeated one monarchy after another only to end up with a military despotism of its own (Timeline 4.2).

THE TENOR OF LIFE

This creation of large-scale states under kings destroyed the Hellenic political order in which poleis were guided by their citizens. Everywhere except Rome, citizens became subjects. The Hellenistic economic order rested on specialized luxury crafts and professional occupations, international trade and banking, and an abundant and cheap supply of slaves. The large ports exported and imported basic agricultural commodities such as grain, olive oil, wine, and timber, exchanging them for expensive goods like pottery, silks, jewelry, and spices.

Class divisions in Hellenistic society were pronounced. For the rich, urban life was often luxurious and cosmopolitan, but most of society remained provincial. Those in the middle social ranks, primarily merchants and skilled artisans, struggled to keep ahead and hoped to prosper. However, for the poorest free classes—laborers, unskilled workers, and small landowners—life offered little. Slaves, whose numbers grew during the wars of this period, were expected to bear the brunt of all backbreaking labor.

The Experiences of Women

Hellenistic women were affected by the period's growing cosmopolitanism. Women, along with men, moved to the newly conquered lands and created new lives for themselves in frontier towns. In Alexandria and other large cities, some restrictions of Hellenic Greece were maintained, but others were relaxed or discarded. For example, royal and non-Greek women were able to conduct their own legal and economic affairs, though non-royal Greek women were still forced to use a male guardian in such cases. Dowries remained the custom among Greek families, but unmarried respectable women now had the option of working in the liberal arts, as poets and philosophers, and in the professions, as artists and physicians. Alexander's mother, Olympias, was a powerful, influential woman, and several times women of the Ptolemaic family ruled Egypt. Unmarried women who were unconcerned about their reputations served as courtesans and prostitutes, living outside the norms of respectable society. Hellenistic literature reflects changed mores, portraying women in carefree situations apart from the gaze of their husbands or fathers. In economic matters, some women became prosperous in their own right, and, just as men did, they made charitable bequests and erected impressive gravestones. Despite these changes, Hellenistic society was dominated by masculine thinking (Figure 4.3). The surest sign of women's subordinate role was that the Greek practice of infanticide, which was as old as Greek civilization, continued as a way for families to rid themselves of unwanted females.

Urban Life

Alexander's most enduring legacy to the Hellenistic world was his new image of the city. The city is as old as civilization, since urban life is by definition a component of civilized existence. For Alexander, cities were keystones holding together his diverse and vast

Figure 4.3 *Eumachia.* Mid–first century CE. Marble. Museo Nazionale, Naples. *This statue of Eumachia, which was found at Pompeii, shows that Roman matrons were involved in public life. The inscription on the statue's base praises her for having donated a building in the town's forum for the use of the fullers—workers involved in the making of woolen cloth. Her statue was paid for by the fullers' association in gratitude for her gift. Her idealized face reflects the Hellenic ideal preferred during the reign of Augustus in the first century CE.*

empire—serving as centers of government, trade, and culture and radiating Greco-Oriental civilization into the hinterland. Alexander is reputed to have founded more than seventy cities during his conquests, many of which were named for him.

The burgeoning cities of the Hellenistic world accentuated the period's growing class divisions. As rural folk flocked to the cities seeking jobs and trying to better their economic condition, some succeeded, while others slipped into poverty and despair. Their failures divided the rich from the poor, thus intensifying class conflicts. How the rural migrants adjusted to urban ways also affected the values and beliefs of the times, in particular, the various philosophies and religions (see "Philosophy and Religion"). And, in everyday life, a new survival strategy arose among upwardly mobile city folk as a way to avoid class conflict. That strategy was to shed their provincial ways and ethnic identity and to adopt the ideal of the cosmopolitan—the Greek term for a citizen of a polis having a universal or worldwide view.

Greek migrants constituted a special challenge to Hellenistic culture. Greeks who left their home city-states to seek their fortunes in the successor states of Alexander's empire impacted every phase of life. Drawn to cities and ports across the eastern Mediterranean, Greek would-be traders, bankers, and seamen arrived, spreading their way of life and influencing the local culture—thus further blending the societies of the period. Many became government officials—bureaucrats, advisers, diplomats—or soldiers and sailors. Most, however, pursued business and professional careers or found work in the visual and performing arts. Their numbers and high-profile presence ensured that Greek culture and values would play a preeminent role in Hellenistic thought and art.

The expansion of trade within this diverse culture benefited Greek and non-Greek alike. The period's

kings, seizing the opportunity to enrich themselves and their states, lengthened and improved existing overland trade routes and linked up with routes to India and into parts of Africa. After Egypt's king learned about the monsoon season in the Indian Ocean, regular sea trade with India began, thus ensuring the importance of Coptos, a city on the upper Nile, as the western terminal for this overseas trade.

The premier Hellenistic city was Alexandria at the mouth of the Nile in Egypt, founded by Alexander in 331 BCE (Figure 4.4). Under the Ptolemies, Alexandria grew to be a world city that attracted both the ambitious who sought opportunities and the apathetic who wanted to be left alone. Every desired attraction is said to have existed here, just as in the teeming cities of the twenty-first century. By the end of the first century BCE, Alexandria's population rose to perhaps one million, and the city was divided into five sections, including one reserved for royalty and separate residential quarters for the Egyptians and the Jews, who were attracted by the city's opportunities and tolerant atmosphere. Whereas the polis of the Hellenic Age was self-contained, with a relatively homogeneous population, Alexandria's racially and ethnically diverse groups were held together by economic interests. With busy harbors, bustling markets, and international banks, the city became a hub of commercial and financial enterprises, similar to modern port cities.

Alexandria's economic vitality was matched by the splendor of its cultural achievements. The world's first research institute—a museum, the house of the muses

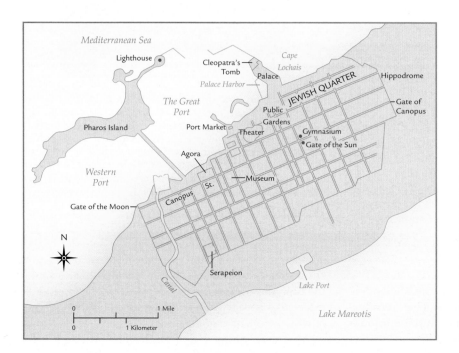

Figure 4.4 Plan of Ancient Alexandria. Third century BCE. *Designed by Deinocrates of Rhodes, Alexander's personal architect, Alexandria was laid out in a grid formed by intersecting avenues and streets. The entire city was enclosed by a wall, accessible by four massive gates at the ends of the major avenues. To the north lay two harbors that made the city the most vital port in the Mediterranean. The harbors were protected by an outer island, at the point of which stood the lighthouse of Pharos—now lost. Remarkable for its colossal size, the lighthouse was considered one of the wonders of the ancient world.*

THE TENOR OF LIFE

(see Table 2.1)—was built here as a place for scholars to study and to exchange ideas. Nearby was the famed library, whose staff, made up of poets and scholars, aimed to collect one copy of every book ever written. At the time of the Roman conquest in the late first century BCE, the library contained nearly seven hundred thousand volumes, the largest collection in the ancient world. By then, Alexandria had become a beacon for great minds, attracted by the city's rich intellectual life and cosmopolitan atmosphere.

Roman Values

The Romans entered the Hellenistic world as a doggedly conservative, inward-looking people. Gradually Roman elites, and then more and more people, adopted aspects of Hellenistic culture. Although Romans were not instinctively cosmopolitan, they became more cosmopolitan as time went by. Rome's encounter with Hellenistic culture led to a centuries-long conflict between those who favored the old ways and those eager for the new.

The Romans were, above all, a practical people, interested chiefly in what was useful. Possessed of a virile moral sense, they were inclined to view intellectual brilliance with suspicion. Furthermore, Roman authority figures cultivated a closely related set of values:

- *Pietas,* piety, but really loyalty, dependability
- *Gravitas,* or gravity, meaning "a deep-seated seriousness"
- *Constantia,* constancy, perseverance, dedication
- *Magnitudo animi,* or magnanimity, "greatness of soul," a lack of concern for wealth and status

By Greek standards, the Romans were a dull lot, too self-controlled and afraid of the imagination. But the Romans were ingenious at adapting borrowed cultural forms and had a gift for governing.

Early Rome was a minor city-state founded by herdsmen and farmers. Over their long rise to world leadership, the Romans changed radically, but they never ceased to honor their agrarian roots. Roman morality and Roman law both echoed a rural ethic by stressing the importance of nature and of living within one's means (Figure 4.5). Roman literary culture was also deeply imbued with a reverence for a rustic past. When Rome became prosperous, many writers bemoaned the corrupting power of luxury and appealed to the homespun values of Rome's founders.

Another important Roman value was the sanctity of the family. Divorce was unheard of until the late republican era, and even then family values continued

Figure 4.5 *Head of a Roman.* Ca. 80 BCE. Marble, life-size. Palazzo Torlonia, Rome. *This Roman head is an excellent example of the highly individualized portraits that flowered in the Late Republic, beginning in about 100 BCE. Note the bald head, deeply lined and scarred face, sunken eyes, and clenched jaw—signs of an extremely realistic style. In cultural terms, the portrait personifies the period's reverence for great age, lack of vanity, and self-discipline—all traditional Roman virtues, greatly admired by the ruling elite. In artistic terms, the individuality of the face reflects the use of a funeral mask, a common custom of the period. With the coming of the empire, after 31 BCE, the realistic style became less pronounced, as the Romans explored earlier phases of Greek art.*

to be eulogized by moralists and honored by leaders. Roles were strictly defined within the Roman family, which was guided by the father, the *paterfamilias,* who exercised legal power of life and death over his entire household, including his spouse, children, relatives, servants, and slaves (Figure 4.6). The Roman father was expected to teach his sons the histories of Rome and of their family, enough agriculture to earn an honest living, and enough law to participate in public life. The paterfamilias wielded greater authority than his Greek counterpart, but, in contrast, the Roman matron was freer and had more practical influence than did the secluded wives of Greece. In general, the Roman matron was conspicuously present in society, attending and presiding at gatherings along with her spouse and supervising the education of both her female and her male offspring.

Figure 4.6 *Patrician with Busts of Ancestors* (*Barberini Togatus*). Early first century CE. Marble, ht. 5′5″. Palazzo dei Conservatori, Rome. *The stern and wrinkled faces of the anonymous patrician and his ancestors convey the quiet dignity and authority of the typical paterfamilias. Some scholars think that these portrait busts, with their unflattering realism, were modeled on death masks.*

HELLENISTIC CULTURES

Hellenistic culture reflected the tastes and needs of the period's diverse states. Greek tragedy lost its vitality when separated from its roots in the independent polis, but comedy appealed to sophisticated urban audiences who were seeking diversion. Nondramatic literature became rather artificial as authors concentrated on perfecting their style or pursuing exotic scholarship. New philosophies and religions arose in response to the urban isolation and loneliness that many people experienced. Roman literature came into being, at first in isolation and then fully in the Hellenistic mainstream. And, finally, grandiose architecture addressed the propaganda needs of autocratic rulers, and realistic sculpture reflected the tastes of an increasingly urban, secular culture.

Nevertheless, the values of Hellenistic culture did not so much replace the standards of Hellenic classicism as they enriched and elaborated the older ideals. Indeed, Greek was the major language across a vast expanse of lands and peoples. Scholars speak of the *Koine* ("common") Greek language of the time. The Koine was a somewhat simplified version of the Attic (i.e., Athenian) Greek that had become dominant in the Hellenic period. The earliest Roman writers even wrote in Greek, partly to attract an audience and partly because they believed Latin too poor for high art. The Hellenistic style emphasized the realities of the physical world rather than finding truth in fantasy or abstraction. And Hellenistic artists and authors agreed with their Hellenic forebears that art must serve moral purposes, revealed through content and formal order.

Drama and Literature

In the Hellenistic Age, Greek comedy began to resemble modern productions. The grotesque padding worn by the actors gave way to realistic costumes; masks were redesigned to be representative of the characters portrayed; and the actors assumed a dominant status over the chorus. Comedies became a form of popular amusement, and Hellenistic playwrights developed a genre known as **New Comedy** to appeal to the pleasure-seeking audiences who were flocking to the theaters. Avoiding political criticism and casual obscenity, New Comedy presented gently satirical scenes from middle-class life.

The plays were generally comic romances on such themes as frustrated first love or marital misunderstandings, and although the endings were inevitably happy and there was much formula writing—somewhat like today's situation comedies on television—

SLICE OF LIFE
Street Scene in Hellenistic Egypt

THEOCRITUS
From *Idylls*, third century BCE

In Hellenistic Egypt, two society matrons, Gorgo and Praxinoa, each with her maid in tow (Eutychis and Eunoa, respectively), make their way through the crowded streets of Alexandria, on their way to the palace of Ptolemy II to hear a singer perform at the festival of Adonis.

[GORGO:] [C]ome, get your dress and cloak on,
  and let's go to King Ptolemy's palace
  and take a look at this Adonis.
  The Queen, I hear, is doing things in style.
PRAXINOA: Oh, nothing but the best. Well, they can
  keep it.
GORGO: But when you've seen it, just think,
  you can tell those who haven't all about it.
  Come on, it's time we were off.
PRAXINOA: Every day's a holiday for the idle.

• • •

[Out in the street.]
Ye Gods, what a crowd! The crush!
How on earth are we going to get through it?
They're like ants! Swarms of them, beyond
  counting!
Well, you've done us many favours, Ptolemy,
since your father went to heaven.
We don't get those no-goods now, sliding up to us
in the street and playing their Egyptian tricks.
What they used to get up to, those rogues!
A bunch of villains, each as bad
as the next, and all utterly cursed!
Gorgo dear, what will become of us?
Here are the king's horses! Take care,
my good man, don't tread on me.
That brown one's reared right up!
Look how wild he is! He'll kill his groom!
Eunoa, you fool, get back!
Thank God I left that child at home.

GORGO: Don't worry, Praxinoa.
  We've got behind them now.
  They're back in their places.
PRAXINOA: I'm all right now.
  Ever since I was a girl, two things
  have always terrified me—horses,
  and long, cold snakes. Let's hurry.
  This great crowd will drown us.

• • •

GORGO: Look, Praxinoa! What a crowd at the door!
PRAXINOA: Fantastic! Gorgo, give me your hand.
  And you, Eunoa, hold on to Eutychis.
  Take care you don't lose each other.
  We must all go in together. Stay close by us.
  Oh no! Gorgo! My coat! It's been ripped
  clean in two! My God, sir, as you hope
  for heaven, mind my coat!
STRANGER: It wasn't my fault. But I'll be careful.
PRAXINOA: What a herd! They push like pigs.
STRANGER: Don't worry, madam, we'll be all right.
PRAXINOA: And may you, sir, be all right
  forever and beyond, for looking after us.
  What a charming man! Where's Eunoa?
  She's getting squashed! Come on, girl, push!
  That's it. "All safely in."

INTERPRETING THIS SLICE OF LIFE

1. *What* is the "plot" in this story of life in the big city? 2. *What* are some of the incidents that happen to the party of women as they move through the streets of Alexandria? 3. *What* is the mood of the women in the story? 4. Based on this vignette, *what* appears to be the position of women in Alexandrian society? 5. *Describe* the relations between the women and their slaves. 6. *Who* was the audience for this poem? 7. *What* modern events are similar to this festival of Adonis? *Explain.*

the plays reflected the comprehensive range of the Hellenistic style. The characters, for example, were familiar types drawn from the rich diversity of Hellenistic society—the courtesan, the grumpy old man, the slave, the fawning parasite. New Comedy remained steadfastly middle-class, however, for the traditional social order always prevailed in the end. For example, a favorite plot device of New Comedy hinged on discovering that a seemingly lowborn character was actually from a respected—and often wealthy—family.

Both ancient and modern critics tend to regard Menander [muh-NAN-duhr] (about 343–291 BCE) as the leading author of New Comedy. He wrote more than one hundred plays for the Dionysia festival in Athens, winning first prize for comedy eight times, and is credited with perfecting the **comedy of manners,** a

Figure 4.7 *The Street Musicians.* Ca. 100 BCE. 16⅞ × 16⅛″. Museo Nazionale, Naples. *This mosaic may portray a scene from a comic play. Two masked figures dance and play the tambourine and the finger cymbals while a masked female figure plays the tibia, or double oboe. This mosaic was found in the so-called Villa of Cicero at Pompeii.*

humorous play that focuses on the way people interact in society. The play reminds us of the Hellenistic focus on ordinary scenes from daily life (Figure 4.7).

The Woman from Samos is a robust example of Menander's work. Dating from about 321 BCE, this comedy concerns the identity of an orphaned baby and features stock characters: a courtesan, a young lover, an old lover, a humorous neighbor, and two comic slaves. Menander first presents a household in which the father believes that he and his son are wooing the same woman, when, in actuality, the son is involved with the girl next door. Then, when a foundling appears, absurd misunderstandings arise and false accusations are made. The play ends happily with all characters reconciled, the son wed to his true love, and the father and mistress married in a joyous ceremony—a typical New Comedy resolution. Western comedy would be inconceivable without Menander. His style was assimilated into Roman comedy,

which passed the spirit of his work into the dramas of the Italian Renaissance and from there into the comedies of Shakespeare and Molière.

Two Alexandrian writers stand out: the poets Theocritus [the-OCK-ruht-us] (about 310–250 BCE) and Apollonius [ah-PO-low-knee-us] (third century). Theocritus created a new poetic form, the **pastoral,** which would influence later classical and modern European literature. Pastoral poems describe the lives of shepherds and farmers in a somewhat artificial, idealized way. Theocritus drew his images from the memory of his earlier years in rural Sicily, and his charming, nostalgic verses appealed to many country folk who had also left the quiet rustic life for the excitement of the Hellenistic cities. Theocritus also wrote what he called **idylls** (from the Greek word meaning "little picture"), which offered small portraits, or vignettes, of Hellenistic life. Some of these poems reveal much about everyday affairs, noting the common concerns and aspirations of all generations—love, family, religion, and wealth. Theocritus created especially sympathetic portraits of a woman's love for a man.

Apollonius's most famous work is the verse romance *The Argonautica*, a tale of Jason and the argonauts' quest for the golden fleece. The story is rich with fantasy, adventure, battles, and love. Jason's lover Medea is in many ways the most compelling character in the story, and Apollonius sets her brains off against Jason's brawn. Apollonius in effect created the romance as a literary genre. *The Argonautica* was immensely popular in Rome.

Gradually the Romans encountered, assimilated, and then contributed to Hellenistic literature. Latin, the Roman language, was at first an unimaginative, functional language, best suited to law, finance, and war. But with the growth of law and oratory in the Early Republic, grammar was standardized, vocabulary was increased, and word meanings were clarified. As the Romans conquered, they made Latin the language of state, except in the Greek-speaking East. Latin literature began to flourish in the middle years of the republic with history, lyric and epic poetry, comedy, and tragedy, initially in the Greek style but gradually in a distinctive Roman style. Early Roman writing was noteworthy for its strongly Greek flavor and, in some writers, its grave moral tone. This period also saw the rise of a Roman theatrical tradition influenced both by roots in boisterous Etruscan religious celebrations and by contact with the Greek theater. Many educated Romans in this period could speak Greek, and many had seen performances of tragedies and comedies during their travels.

Plautus [PLAW-tuhs] (about 254–184 BCE), a plebeian, launched Rome's great age of comic theater with his almost 130 plays. His genius lay in breathing fresh life into the stale plots and stock characters borrowed from Menander and other Hellenistic, New Comedy playwrights. In Plautus's hands, the mistaken identities, verbal misunderstandings, and bungled schemes seemed brand new. Rome's other significant comic playwright was Terence [TAIR-ents] (about 195–159 BCE), a Carthaginian slave who was brought to Rome, educated, and set free. Although he wrote only six plays, he won the acclaim of Rome's educated elite, perhaps because of the pure Greek tone and themes of his works. Terence's highly polished style later inspired the magisterial Cicero.

As Roman comedy began to decline, superseded by the vast spectacles that the masses demanded, two major poets with distinctively different personalities and talents appeared: Lucretius and Catullus. Both were heavily influenced by Greek literature. Lucretius [lew-KREE-shuhs] (about 94–55 BCE) stands in the long line of didactic literary figures dating from Homer. A gifted poet, with his well-turned Latin phrases and imaginative and vivid language, Lucretius wrote *De Rerum Natura (On the Nature of Things)* to persuade the reader of the truth of Epicureanism, the philosophy based on scientific atomism that denied divine intervention in human affairs (see below).

In contrast to Lucretius's lengthy poem, the verses of Catullus [kuh-TUHL-uhs] (about 84–54 BCE) are characterized by brevity, one of the hallmarks of the Alexandrian school of the Hellenistic Age. Catullus's small epics, epigrams, and love poems also closely imitate the scholarly and romantic qualities of Alexandrianism. Catullus is best remembered for his love poems, which draw on the lives of his highborn, free-spirited circle in Rome, and which express his innermost feelings of desire, disappointment, and jealousy. As a typical Hellenistic author, Catullus wrote some poems whose language ranged from sublime to coarse and whose themes extended from the sensual to the frankly erotic.

The efforts of Lucretius and Catullus pale, however, when placed beside those of their contemporary Cicero (106–43 BCE). He dominated Roman letters in his own day so much that his era is often labeled the Age of Cicero. By translating Greek treatises into Latin, he created a philosophical vocabulary for the Latin language where none had existed before.

For centuries, Cicero's collected speeches served as models of both public oratory and written argument. Similarly, his philosophical tracts set the agenda for generations of thinkers and reformers. Today's readers rank Cicero's collection of letters, most by him, some addressed to him (a few written by his son), as his masterpiece. These nearly nine hundred letters, frank in style and language, offer a unique self-portrait of a major public figure in ancient times (Figure 4.8).

Cicero also wrote extensively on law and politics. As a public figure he attained high office but failed in his effort to achieve the *concordia ordinum,* the concord of the orders, that is, peace and understanding among Rome's warring factions.

Philosophy and Religion

As life in Hellenistic cities became more multicultural, the sense of belonging that had characterized life in the Hellenic poleis was replaced by feelings of isolation, of loneliness, even of helplessness. As unsophisticated Roman farmers became world rulers, they experienced cultural disorientation. As a consequence, two seemingly contradictory points of view grew up: individualism and internationalism. Those

Figure 4.8 *Cicero.* First century BCE. Capitoline Museum, Rome. *The anonymous sculptor of this bust of Cicero has caught the character of the man as recalled in literary sources. Honored as one of Rome's finest intellectuals and a patriot devoted to rescuing the state from chaos, he is depicted deep in thought with stern and resolute features. This idealized portrait contributed to the mystique of Cicero as a hero of the Roman Republic.*

Table 4.1	PHILOSOPHY IN THE HELLENISTIC AGE
PHILOSOPHY	*EMPHASIS*
Cynicism	True freedom arises from realizing that if one wants nothing, then one will never lack anything; *autarky* (self-sufficiency) is the goal.
Skepticism	Nothing can be known for certain; question all ideas; *autarky* is the goal.
Epicureanism	Only the atoms and void exist; pleasure is the highest good; death is final in its extinction of consciousness; the gods play no active role in human affairs.
Stoicism	The world is governed by the divine *logos*, or reason, or nature; wisdom and freedom consist of living in harmony with the *logos*; all humans share in the divine *logos*; *autarky* is the goal.

who held these attitudes were searching for continuity in a rapidly changing world; were seeking identity for the individual through common interests, values, and hopes; and were striving to understand events that seemed unpredictable and beyond human control.

Philosophies and religions offered answers that seemed as contradictory as the problems themselves. One philosophy urged a universal brotherhood of all human beings, united regardless of race, status, or birth; another, despairing of the world, excluded most people and appealed to a chosen few. Religions, similarly, provided varying answers. One faith preached salvation in a life after death, and another turned to magic to escape Fate—that blind force that controlled human life. The most enduring of this period's philosophies were Cynicism, Skepticism, Epicureanism, and Stoicism (Table 4.1).

CYNICISM   Of the four schools, **Cynicism** had the least impact on Hellenistic civilization. The Cynics, believing that society diverted the individual from the more important goals of personal independence and freedom, denounced all religions and governments, shunned physical comfort, and advocated the avoidance of personal pleasure. In the Cynics' logic, true freedom came with the realization that if one wanted nothing, one could not lack anything. By isolating themselves from society, they sought a type of self-sufficiency the Greeks called *autarky* [AW-tar-kee].

The most prominent Cynic, Diogenes [die-AHJ-uh-neez] (about 412–323 BCE), openly scorned the ordinary values and crass materialism of his society. His contrary personality so fascinated Alexander the Great that the ruler, upon being insulted by the Cynic, is reported to have said that if he were not Alexander, he would prefer to be Diogenes (Figure 4.9)! The principles of Cynicism offended the educated, and its pessimism offered no hope to the masses.

SKEPTICISM   The proponents of **Skepticism** argued that nothing could be known for certain, an extreme conclusion they were led to by their belief that the senses were unreliable sources of knowledge. Thinking that everything was relative, the Skeptics maintained that all ideas must be questioned and that no single philosophy was true. When their critics pointed out that such unrelenting questioning was clearly not

Figure 4.9 *Diogenes and Alexander the Great.* First century CE. Villa Albani, Rome. *This Roman relief shows that Diogenes and Alexander the Great, two figures of the Hellenistic Age, were living presences for the Romans. The philosopher Diogenes is carved sitting in his famous tub, a symbol of his contempt for creature comforts. The world-conqueror Alexander is on the right, pointing his finger at the Greek thinker. The dog portrayed on top of the tub is a reference to Cynicism (the word* cynic *is from the Greek word for "dog"). Diogenes asserted that humans should live simply—like dogs.*

a practical answer to life's uncertainties, the Skeptics replied that certainty could be achieved only by admitting that truth was unknowable—a circular response. The Skeptics thought that if they recognized that intellectual inquiry was fruitless, then they too could avoid frustration and achieve *autarky,* or self-sufficiency.

The Skeptics, even though they attracted a smaller audience than the Cynics, had a greater impact on Western reasoning. Skepticism appealed to some early Romans, who brought the Greek philosopher and teacher Carneades [kar-NEE-uh-deez] (about 214–129 BCE) to Rome in 155 BCE. Carneades shocked his pious Roman audience, who took his universal doubt as a denial of the stability and permanence of their state and its values. Although Skepticism faded after Carneades' death, the movement was revived during the Roman Empire and eventually passed into the mainstream of Western thought.

EPICUREANISM   The strict and quiet way of life advocated by **Epicureanism** appealed to aristocrats who were more interested in learning than in politics. It be-

gan as the philosophy of the Greek thinker Epicurus [ep-uh-KYUR-uhs] (about 342–270 BCE), who founded a school in Athens where pupils, including slaves and women, gathered to discuss ideas (Figure 4.10). For Epicurus, the best way to keep one's wants simple, and thus to achieve happiness, was to abstain from sex and focus instead on friendship. Friendship was a mystic communion, based on shared need, in which men and men, men and women, rich and poor, old and young, of all nationalities and any class supported each other in trusting relationships. This vision guided Epicurus's school, where life became a daily exercise in friendship. It was an ideal that appealed to women since, in making them men's equals, it showed that there was more to their lives than bearing children and raising families.

Epicurus based his ethical philosophy on the atomic theory of those Greek thinkers who saw the universe as completely determined by the behavior of atoms moving in empty space (see Chapter 3). Epicurus accepted this picture, but with one significant modification: he argued that because atoms on occasion swerved from their set paths and made unpredictable deviations, it

Figure 4.10 *Epicurus.* Ca. 290–280 BCE. Courtesy The Metropolitan Museum of Art. Rogers Fund, 1911. (11.90). *This marble bust of Epicurus, discovered in southern Italy and inscribed with his name, is a copy of the original bronze sculpture. Many busts and likenesses of Epicurus have been found, indicating the popularity of his philosophy in Hellenistic times, especially during the Roman era.*

was possible, even in a deterministic universe, for humans to make free choices. Like the atomists, Epicurus also believed that the senses presented an accurate view of the physical world. Thus, by using the mind as a storehouse for sense impressions and by exercising free will in their choices, individuals could reach moral judgments and ultimately live by an ethical code.

For Epicurus, the correct ethical code led to happiness, which was realized in a life of quiet—separated and withdrawn from the trying cares of the world. Furthermore, those who would be happy should keep their wants simple, not indulge excessive desires, and resist fame, power, and wealth, which only brought misery and disappointment.

Another characteristic of Epicurean happiness was freedom from fear—fear of the gods, of death, and of the hereafter. Although Epicurus believed that the gods existed, he also believed that they cared nothing about human beings, and therefore no one needed to be afraid of what the gods might or might not do. As for death, there was, again, nothing to agonize over because when it did occur, the atoms that made up the soul simply separated from the body's atoms

and united with other particles to create new forms. With death came the end of the human capacity to feel pleasure or pain and thus the end of suffering. Consequently, death, rather than being feared, should be welcomed as a release from misfortune and trouble. Pleasure, in the Epicurean view, was the absence of pain. The happy Epicurean, standing above the cares of the world, had reached *ataraxia,* the desireless state that the Hellenistic Age deemed so precious.

STOICISM Both Epicureanism and **Stoicism** claimed that happiness was a final goal of the individual, and both were essentially materialistic, stressing the importance of sense impressions and the natural world. The Stoics, however, identified the supreme deity with nature, thus making the natural world divine and inseparable from the deity. The supreme being was also another name for reason, or *logos,* and hence nature was also rational. Since the Stoics' God was law and the author of law, this led to the notion that the workings of nature were expressed in divine laws.

The Stoics likewise discovered God in humanity. The Stoics' God, being identical with reason, gave a spark to each mortal's soul, conferring the twin gifts of rationality and kinship with divinity. The Stoics thus believed that reason and the senses could be used jointly to uncover the underlying moral law as well as God's design in the world, proving God's wisdom and power over human life and nature.

There was in Stoicism a tendency to leave everything up to God. Stoics came to accept their roles in life, whether rich or poor, master or slave, healthy or afflicted, and such a resigned and deterministic outlook could (and did) lead to apathy, or unconcern. However, the ideal Stoic, the sage, never became apathetic. The sage escaped Stoicism's fatalistic tendency by stressing a sense of and dedication to duty. Doing one's duty was part of following the deity's plan, and Stoics willingly performed their tasks, no matter how onerous or laborious. The reward for living a life of duty was virtue. Having achieved virtue, the Stoics were freed from their emotions, which they thought only corrupted them. The Stoics had thus achieved *autarky,* the state of existence sought by many Hellenistic philosophers.

Stoicism was unique among the Hellenistic philosophies in holding out the promise of membership in a worldwide brotherhood. Perhaps inspired by Alexander the Great's dream, the Stoics advocated an ideal state, guided by God and law, that encompassed all of humanity of whatever race, sex, social status, or nationality in a common bond of reason. As humans carried out their duties in this larger community, they would rise above local and national limitations and create a better world.

Religion had a firmer hold on most people than philosophy. The belief in Fate, a concept borrowed from Babylonia, gripped the lives of many people in the Hellenistic world. To them, Fate ruled the universe, controlled the heavens, and determined the course of life. Although no one could change the path of this nonmoral, predestined force, individuals could try to avoid the cruel consequences of Fate by various methods. The pseudoscience of astrology, also from Babylonia, offered one alternative. Magic was now revived, and many people tried to conjure up good spirits or to ward off evil ones. Nevertheless, it was the mystery cults—springing from the primitive chthonian religions of Greece (see Chapters 2 and 3) and elsewhere—that eventually emerged as the most popular and effective response to Fate.

Numerous chthonian cults spread from the Seleucid kingdom and Egypt to the Greek mainland, where they were combined with local beliefs and rituals to create religions that fused different beliefs and practices. By the second century BCE, converts were being attracted from all over the Hellenistic world to the well-established mystery cults of Orpheus and Dionysus in Greece and to the new religions from Egypt and the old Persian lands. The growth of these cults in turn sparked an increase in religious zeal after about 100 BCE, resulting in more ceremonies and public festivals and the revival of older faiths.

The Egyptian mystery cults grew, becoming quite popular across the Hellenistic world. The goddess Isis, long known to the Egyptians, became especially prominent. The Egyptians worshiped Isis as the "great lady" who watched over the Two Lands of Egypt and the home. In legend, Isis rescued her husband-brother, Osiris, from his enemies and brought him back to life with her unwavering love. Osiris's resurrection symbolized to the faithful the new life awaiting them at death. Isis herself was identified with the annual flooding of the Nile, thus assuring the Egyptians of another year of survival. Like the pharaohs, the Ptolemies claimed to be the incarnation of her son, Horus (Harpocrates) (Figure 4.11).

The secret rites of the mystery cults, which communicated the thrill of initiation and the satisfaction of belonging, answered deep psychological needs in their Hellenistic converts. This universal appeal cut across class and racial lines and attracted an ever-widening segment of the populace. With their promise of immortality, these rituals contributed to the atmosphere of the Roman world in which Christianity would later be born.

At Rome, religion permeated family life, and each Roman household kept an undying fire burning on its hearth, symbolic of the goddess Vesta, to ensure the family's continuity. The family revered the deceased male ancestors, whose funeral masks adorned the walls and were regularly used in domestic rituals (see Figures 4.5 and 4.6).

The native Roman religion was deeply affected by the cults of neighboring and conquered peoples. **Syncretism,** the blending of religions, began after the

Figure 4.11 Isis with Her Son Harpocrates (left) and God Anubis (right). First century CE. Terra-cotta, ht. approx. 7". British Museum. *This small terra-cotta figurine—probably used as a votive—blends Greek sculptural style with Egyptian symbolism. The goddess is portrayed wearing an Egyptian headdress and is flanked by her son and the jackal-headed Anubis, the god of the dead. Greek features include the goddess's tightly curled hair, her slightly contrapposto pose, and the graceful drapery of her dress. The statue, fired on the Italian peninsula in the first century CE, testifies to the goddess's popularity throughout ancient times and across the Mediterranean world.*

Table 4.2   THE CHIEF ROMAN GODS AND GODDESSES AND THEIR GREEK COUNTERPARTS

ROMAN	GREEK
Jupiter	Zeus
Juno	Hera
Neptune	Poseidon
Pluto	Hades
Vesta	Hestia
Apollo	Apollo
Diana	Artemis
Mars	Ares
Venus	Aphrodite
Vulcan	Hephaestus
Minerva	Athena
Mercury	Hermes

Romans' initial contacts with the Greeks in southern Italy. From the Punic Wars onward, innovative cults sprang up in Rome. From Egypt came the worship of Isis, a religion that promised immortality, and from the Seleucid realm of Asia Minor the cult of Cybele, a mother goddess. Army veterans returning from Persia brought back Mithra, the mortal son of the sun god, whose cult excluded women. Mithra's followers observed each seventh day as Sun Day and December 25 as the god's birthday; the faithful also underwent a baptism in the blood of a sacred bull.

Science and Technology

While Hellenistic scientists owed much to their Hellenic predecessors, they were more practical and less theoretical than the followers of Plato and Aristotle. They were interested in methodologies more than in speculation, and they tended to question, observe, and experiment rather than to offer explanations and quarrel over abstract issues. They focused on day-to-day matters, such as measuring distances, calculating navigation routes, designing war machines, and solving mathematical problems. And, finally, scientists and philosophers worked in isolation, having little contact either as individuals or in groups. They were nonetheless able to make scientific advances and discoveries unequaled in any other age—until Europe's Scientific Revolution in the 1600s (see Chapter 15).

The astronomer Aristarchus of Samos [air-uh-STAR-khus] (fl. about 270 BCE) maintained that the sun was the center of the universe and that the earth rotated on its own axis. His conclusions, though considered correct today, were rejected by other ancient astronomers, who thought his views contradicted common sense. Another astronomer, Eratosthenes [er-uh-TAS-thuh-neez] (about 276–194 BCE) of Cyrene, who at one time headed the library in Alexandria, measured the circumference of the earth by creating a mathematical formula based on the differing angles cast by the sun's rays on the earth, when observed from two sites, separated by a known distance. He also devised a grid for measuring the circumference of the earth, using lines running from north to south and east to west—a system implying that the earth was round.

Euclid [YU-klehd] (fl. about 300 BCE), the most influential mathematician of his time, gave the classic formulations of both plane and solid geometry. His writings laid out mathematical theories, axioms, propositions, and definitions. He was known as the father of geometry, and Euclidean geometry became the basis of mathematical studies until the nineteenth century.

The best-known Hellenistic scientist, Archimedes [are-kuh-MEED-eez] (about 287–212 BCE) was a mathematician, astronomer, and inventor. He made signal contributions in geometry, but he is best remembered for his studies in gravity, mechanics, hydrostatics, the principle of buoyancy, and for his many inventions. Among his inventions were the Archimedean screw for raising water; improved compound pulleys; and engines of war, including catapults and ramming towers. Many legends accrued to his life, including the famous story, undoubtedly apocryphal, in which he discovered the principle of buoyancy—the relation of fluid loss to weight displacement—while seated in his bath. Excited by the discovery, he leaped from his tub and ran naked down the street, shouting "*Eureka!*"— Greek for "I have found it."

Military technology was the cultural sphere in which Rome's practical genius shone. Rome's military was the most technologically advanced in the ancient world. Among its advancements were the following:

- Offensive weapons: swords, daggers, pikes, spears, maces, and bows
- Defensive weapons: shields, helmets, and body armor, including scale (closely fitted pieces in metal, fishlike scales) and chain mail (small metal rings joined tightly together)
- Artillery: the catapult—for hurling iron-tipped wooden javelins to kill enemy troops; for throwing heavy stones to breach walls; and for rapidly firing short, iron-tipped javelins—an ancestor of the machine gun

In addition, the Roman navy adapted the Greek trireme (see Chapter 3) and the Carthaginian quinquereme (an open galley with five banks of rowers) into galleys—floating armies, crammed with sailors and marines. Each galley was outfitted with a grappling *corvus* (hook), for holding fast two battling ships, and a hinged gangplank, which served as a boarding ramp for the marines. The navy also utilized the Liburnian ship, a fully decked bireme, powered by two sets of oarsmen and a single lateen sail.

Architecture

As in Hellenic times, architecture in the Hellenistic Age reflected the central role that religion played in people's lives. Public buildings served religious, ceremonial, and governmental purposes, but the temple continued as the leading type of structure. Hellenistic architects modified the basic temple and altar forms inherited from Hellenic models to express the grandeur demanded by the age's rulers. The altar, which had originated in Archaic Greece as a simple structure where holy sacrifices or offerings were made, now became a major structural form, second in importance only to the temple, because of its use in state rituals.

The **Corinthian** temple embodied Hellenistic splendor. The Corinthian column had first appeared in the Hellenic period, when it was probably used as a decorative feature. Because it was taller, more slender, and more ornamented, with its lush acanthus-leafed capital, than either the Doric or the Ionic column, the Corinthian column was now used on the exterior of temples erected by Hellenistic builders for their kings. In time, Hellenistic taste decreed that the Corinthian column was appropriate for massive buildings. The Corinthian order later became the favorite of the Roman emperors, and it was revived in the Renaissance and diffused throughout the Western world, where it survives today as the most visible sign of Hellenistic influence.

The most outstanding Corinthian temples combined grandeur with grace, as in the Olympieum in Athens, now a ruin (Figure 4.12). Commissioned by the Seleucid king Antiochus IV [an-TIE-uh-kuhs], the Olympieum expressed his notion of a diverse, international culture united under Zeus, his divine counterpart and the lord of Mount Olympus. The temple, the first to use Corinthian columns, was constructed during three different and distinct historical eras. The stylobate, or base, was laid in the late Archaic Age but then abandoned; the Corinthian columns were raised by Antiochus IV in about 175 BCE, after which work was suspended indefinitely; it was finally completed in 130 CE under the Roman emperor Hadrian, a great admirer of Greek culture. The temple is stylistically unified, however,

Figure 4.12 The Olympieum. Various dates: late sixth century BCE; second quarter of second century BCE; completed, second quarter of second century CE. Athens. *The thirteen standing Corinthian columns were part of the original plan of the Olympieum's architect. After the temporary cessation of building in 164 BCE, some of this temple's unfinished columns were transported to Rome and reused in a building there. Their use in Rome helped to popularize the Corinthian style among political leaders and wealthy tastemakers.*

because it was finished according to the surviving plans of its second-century BCE architect. Despite its massive size and lack of mathematical refinements, the Olympieum presented an extremely graceful appearance with its forest of delicate Corinthian columns, consisting of double rows of twenty columns each on the sides and triple rows of eight on the ends.

Before there were temples, there were altars, the oldest religious structure in the Greek world. The earliest altars were simple slabs, made wide enough to allow sacrificial animals to be slaughtered. During the Hellenistic Age, the altars were substantially enlarged. The biggest appears to have been the 650-foot-long altar, permitting the sacrifice of more than one hundred cattle at one time, funded by the ruler of Syracuse in the third century BCE.

The magnificent altar of Zeus at Pergamum has been reassembled in Berlin. It is easy to see why ancient travelers called it one of the wonders of the world (Figure 4.13). The actual altar, not visible in the photograph, stands lengthwise in a magnificent Ionic colonnaded courtyard. The courtyard itself is raised on a **podium,** or platform; below the courtyard, the sides of the structure are decorated with a sculptured frieze depicting the deities at war. The overall design—with the frieze below the columns—appears to be an inversion of the usual temple plan. This altar was but one part of a concerted effort to transform Pergamum into another Athens. Thus, the idea of a "new" Athens—a recurrent motif in the humanistic tradition—had already been formulated by the Hellenistic Age.

Sculpture

Like Hellenistic architects, Hellenistic sculptors adapted many of the basic forms and ideas of the Hellenic style to meet the tastes of their day. The Hellenistic sculptors perpetuated such Hellenic principles as contrapposto and proportion as well as the Hellenic emphasis on religious and moral themes. But Hellenistic art increasingly expressed a secular, urban viewpoint, and Hellenic restraint often gave way to realism, eroticism, and violence, expressed and enjoyed for their own sake. Some of these Hellenistic qualities are apparent in the refreshingly naturalistic sculpture *Boy Struggling with a*

Figure 4.13   Altar of Zeus at Pergamum. (Reconstruction.) 170s BCE. Pergamum Museum, Berlin. *This masterpiece of Hellenistic architecture was erected in the 170s BCE by Eumenes II, the king of Pergamum, to commemorate his victories over various barbarian states in Asia Minor. Eumenes believed himself to be the savior and disseminator of Greek culture, and this altar with its giant frieze was meant to suggest Hellenic monuments, such as the Athenian Parthenon.*

ENCOUNTER

The Invention of Parchment and the Birth of the Secular Library

The Hellenistic kingdom of Pergamum in northwestern Anatolia (modern Turkey) gave birth to an improved technology for writing surfaces—parchment—and a new civic institution—the secular library. Both achievements played a defining role in the heritage of the West.

Founded in the fifth century BCE by Greek settlers, Pergamum emerged as an important state during the Hellenistic period. Under the Attalid dynasty, beginning in 263 BCE, Pergamum reached its zenith, holding sway over most of Anatolia. The Pergamenes constituted a rich ethnic mixture. With differing languages, religions, and traditions, the Pergamenes were typical of the ethnic variety of the time. Faced with polyglot subjects, divided into many minorities and lacking a coherent majority, Pergamum's kings responded with creative cultural projects. Perhaps as a unifying point, they launched a building program to beautify their acropolis (see Figures 4.2 and 4.13). What was especially new about this project, and appealing to Pergamum's multicultural ethos, was the inclusion of a monumental library (now lost), which can be claimed as one of the first secular libraries in the world.

Egypt's king, Ptolemy II Philadelphus (285–246 BCE), founded his own library at Alexandria. A repository of papyrus scrolls, it formed part of the research complex called the Alexandrian Museum. This library inspired envy in Pergamum's ruler, Eumenes II [YOU-muh-neez] (r. 263–241 BCE), who desired to establish his own library. To defeat his Pergamene rival, Ptolemy II banned the export of papyrus from Egypt. In retaliation, Eumenes II encouraged anonymous craftspeople to develop parchment as a writing surface—an innovation that proved more durable and cheaper than papyrus. The word *parchment* evolved from its Latin name, *pergamena*, signaling its invention in Pergamum. **Parchment** is made from calf-, sheep-, or goatskins that have been treated to make a writing surface.

Pergamum's library was a truly secular building, even though it housed a statue of Athena, the goddess of wisdom (Encounter figure 4.1). The link to Athena was for symbolic, not religious, reasons. The library's was simply a repository for books. Pergamum's library, with its writings on parchment, set the standard for the secular libraries that followed.

LEARNING FROM THE ENCOUNTER

1. *Describe* the population mixture of Hellenistic Pergamum. 2. *What* cultural impact did the diverse population of Pergamum have on the rulers? 3. *How* did the Pergamene library differ from earlier libraries in the ancient world? 4. *What* event led the Pergamene ruler to the use of parchment for manuscripts in his library? 5. *Consider* the impact of technological changes on the act of reading, from reading a scroll to reading a book to reading a computer screen.

Encounter figure 4.1 *Athena*. From library at Pergamum. Second century BCE. Copy of fifth-century BCE original. Marble. Antikensammlung, Staatliche Museen, Berlin. *This statue of Athena is freely adapted from one that stood in the Parthenon (see Figure 3.2). The statue at Pergamum symbolized learning and had no strictly religious meaning. The statue is executed in the round, which emphasizes its status as a secular work of art. Hellenistic artists often created secular interpretation of religious sculptures.*

Goose (Figure 4.14). At the same time, this work of art relates ironically to the age's values because it can be understood on two levels: its subject is both an everyday scene and a mock-heroic battle; its playful nature masks a sense of violence; and its twisting forms and shifting planes seem overdone on such a small scale.

Between 230 and 220 BCE, King Attalus I of Pergamum dedicated in Athens a group of bronze sculptures that celebrated his recent victory over the barbarian Gauls. By donating these bronzes to Athens, which was outside of Pergamum's political orbit, the Attalid ruler hoped to establish his cultural credentials as a defender of Greek culture and thus further his claims to rule over the entire Hellenistic world.

One of these pieces, *Dying Gaul* (which survives only in a Roman marble copy), shows a mortally wounded barbarian warrior (Figure 4.15). The torque, or twisted necklace, he wears identifies him as a Gaul. Lying close by are his sword and trumpet. The sculptor demonstrates his keen eye for realistic details in

Figure 4.14 *Boy Struggling with a Goose.* Roman copy of a Greek original, dating from second half of second century BCE. Marble, ht. 33½". Capitoline Museum, Rome. *When Hellenistic sculptors freed themselves from the ideals of Hellenic art, one of the results was the production of works on unhackneyed themes, as in* Boy Struggling with a Goose. *So popular was this genre scene that several versions of it are known from antiquity. Its popularity reflects the age's delight in childhood and its joys—perhaps an outgrowth of the rising status of women in Hellenistic times.*

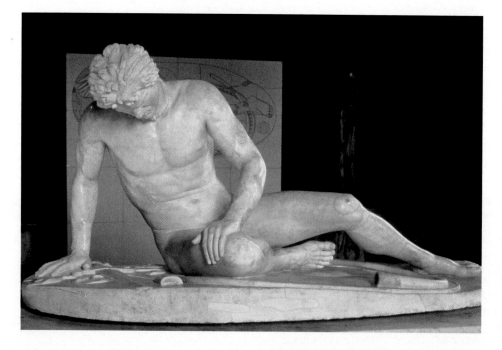

Figure 4.15 *Dying Gaul.* Ca. 230–220 BCE. Roman marble copy of a bronze original, ht. 3'. Capitoline Museum, Rome. *The rulers of the Hellenistic kingdom of Pergamum preferred art that was showy and overwrought, a taste that perhaps stemmed from their insecurity at being a new dynasty. A Pergamene style of sculpture developed under these kings, in which gestures were theatrical and anatomical features were portrayed in exaggerated depth. The* Dying Gaul *is a superb example of this style.*

INTERPRETING ART

Literary Source In Virgil's *Aeneid*, Laocöon (lay-OK-oo-ahn) warns the Trojans not to bring the wooden horse inside Troy, even though he did not know it was full of Greek soldiers, hence the famous line "Beware Greeks bearing gifts." Two serpents emerged from the sea and killed Laocöon and his sons.

Form The sculptural group brims with energy, as may be seen in the tormented faces of the victims, in their twisted, muscular bodies, in the serpent's coils that frame the scene, and in the deep folds of the draperies.

Composition Laocöon and his sons—depicted larger than life—are being crushed and perhaps devoured by two huge serpents. The sculptors have made an extraordinarily close study of human anatomy.

Moral Perspective Virgil's story of Laocöon had two different morals: (a) Apollo, whose cult demanded priestly chastity, sent the serpents to punish the priest and his sons; and (b) Athena, who favored the Greeks in the Trojan War, sent the serpents to silence Laocöon's warnings about the horse.

Context The dynamic, agitated, theatrical figures in this group reveal the ways in which the arts of the Hellenistic era jettisoned the stately grace and reserve of the Hellenic period.

Influences This sculptural group vanished in antiquity and was rediscovered in 1506, when it profoundly influenced Michelangelo and the subsequent rise of baroque art (see Chapters 12 and 14).

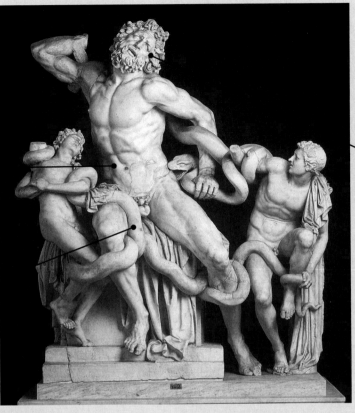

Interpreting Art figure 4.1 Hagesandros, Polydoros, and Athanadoros, *The Laocöon Group.* Ca. 50 CE. Roman copy (?) of a Hellenistic work. Marble, ht. 8'. Vatican Museum. *This statue is probably a Roman copy of the original executed on the island of Rhodes.*

the open wound oozing blood from the warrior's rib cage and by the blank stare as he faces death. The Hellenistic style's appreciation of the melodramatic is evident in the tension between the warrior's sagging body and his efforts to prop himself up. But by treating a foreign enemy with such nobility, the anonymous sculptor perpetuated the deep moral sense that was central to Hellenic art. After 146 BCE, an outstanding sculptural school flourished on the Island of Rhodes for more than two hundred years. Probably the most stunning sculpture of Rhodian and Hellenistic art is *The Laocöon Group* (Interpreting Art figure 4.1).

A radically different subject is treated in the *Old Market Woman*, which, like a stock character from New Comedy, depicted a well-known social type (Figure 4.16). The old woman, who might have strolled out of the marketplace of any Hellenistic city, represented a **genre subject,** or a scene taken from everyday life. The original third-century BCE bronze portrayed a stooped figure, straining under the combined weight of her groceries and her advancing years. In this Roman marble copy, the left arm is missing, but she car-

ries a fowl and a brimming bucket. Her deeply lined and wrinkled face and her sagging breasts express the realism of Hellenistic style.

The sculpture of the Hellenistic Age is also characterized by a frank appreciation of female beauty, a famous example of which is the *Aphrodite of Melos*, perhaps better known as the Venus de Milo (Figure 4.17). This original sculpture, carved from Parian marble, shows many borrowings from the tradition of Praxiteles (see Figure 3.25). Both Aphrodite and Hermes exhibit exaggerated contrapposto; a sensuous, even erotic, modeling of the body; and a serene countenance with an unmistakable gaze. However, the Hellenistic sculptor, demonstrating a playful flair with the rolled-down draperies, calls attention to Aphrodite's exposed lower torso. The *Aphrodite of Melos* was part of the growing influence of **neoclassicism,** which swept the disintegrating Hellenistic world in the wake of Rome's rise to greatness. Neoclassicism, developing first in Athens in the late third century BCE and later in Pergamum and other cities, was a kind of nostalgia for the glory days of the fifth and fourth centuries BCE.

Figure 4.16 *Old Market Woman.* Third or second century BCE. Roman marble copy of a Hellenistic bronze, ht. 49". Metropolitan Museum of Art, New York. *Many Hellenistic sculptors depicted old women in pathetic situations, tired, drunk, or begging. Scholars are divided in opinion about whether these statues were meant to be admired for their truthfulness or whether they represented disdain for what Hellenistic aristocrats considered an ugly social phenomenon.*

Figure 4.17 *Aphrodite of Melos (Venus de Milo).* Ca. 160–150 BCE. Marble, ht. 6'10". Louvre. *This celebrated statue represents the classicizing tendency, derived from Greek tradition, in Hellenistic art. The head is executed in the pure Hellenic style, as seen in the serene countenance, the exquisitely detailed hair, and the finely chiseled features. However, the body, with its frank sensuality and its rumpled draperies, is clearly in the Hellenistic style.*

The Legacy of Hellenistic Civilization and the Rise of Rome

The Hellenistic world left a substantial bequest to the future course of Western civilization. Its austere, remote, godlike kings provided a model for later Roman and Persian emperors. Rome's republican institutions and ideals were adopted or emulated in medieval and Renaissance cities and in modern states, not least the United States. Perhaps the urban legacy of the Hellenistic era was its greatest. For centuries after the rise and then decline of Rome, the great cities of Antioch, Alexandria, and Rome itself served as hubs of government, commerce, and culture.

The Hellenistic world was more cosmopolitan and multicultural than the eras that preceded and followed it, but its openness, mobility, and tolerance created conditions long conducive to the spread of ideas and art forms. The period also saw the dissemination of two "world" languages, Greek and Latin. Of course, the Hellenistic world was not the whole world. But the Greeks, and later the Romans too, tended to think of their world as the whole world or, at any rate, as the only world that mattered. The broad dissemination of Greek and Latin facilitated the spread of literary forms, motifs, and stories. Something like a "world" literature grew up in Hellenistic times.

Hellenistic philosophies in general, but especially Epicureanism and Stoicism, were influential until modern times. Hellenistic science held sway until the seventeenth century in many fields, and in a few fields even after that. Hellenistic aesthetics deeply influenced the Romans, who in turn handed that aesthetic to the earliest Christian artists.

In almost every field of human endeavor, the Hellenistic world erected the framework on which life would be lived in and beyond the Mediterranean world for the next thousand years.

KEY CULTURAL TERMS

Hellenistic
cosmopolitan
Koine
New Comedy
comedy of manners
pastoral
idyll
Cynicism
autarky
Skepticism

Epicureanism
ataraxia
Stoicism
logos
syncretism
Corinthian
podium
parchment
genre subject
neoclassicism

QUESTIONS FOR CRITICAL THINKING

1. How did the rise of Hellenistic cities affect Hellenistic cultural and artistic developments?

2. Discuss the changes made to classicism by Hellenistic writers and artists. What was retained from Greek classicism, and what became the hallmarks of Hellenistic classicism?

3. Identify the four major philosophies that dominated the Hellenistic period, and compare and contrast their differing principles and goals. Indicate the relative long-term importance of each of these philosophies to the Western tradition.

4. When a civilization expands successfully, it often encounters new challenges and problems. What were some of Rome's problems as a result of its expansion, and how did these problems affect Roman values?

5. In what ways was early Roman literature indebted to Hellenistic norms and tastes?

5

JUDAISM AND THE RISE OF CHRISTIANITY

The great civilizations discussed so far—Mesopotamian, Egyptian, Greek, Hellenistic, and Early Roman—were all wealthy, powerful, and culturally dynamic, and durable contributors to the Western heritage. Yet an even greater contribution, one that cannot be measured in buildings or governments, came from a politically insignificant people who lived in a tiny corner of the eastern Mediterranean during ancient times—the Jews. This people created a religion that helped to shape the character of the civilizations of the Western world. Through the Hebrew Bible—the Old Testament to Christians—Judaic beliefs were passed on to both Christianity and Islam and spread around the world. In addition, the fruitful interaction of the Judeo-Christian heritage with the Greco-Roman classical ideals enriched and transformed the Western humanities.

JUDAISM

Judaism is one of the oldest living religions in the world. It originated in the third millennium BCE among a tribal Middle Eastern people who placed themselves at the center of world history and created sacred texts for passing on their heritage. Unlike the history and religion of other ancient peoples, the history and religion of the Jews are so inextricably connected that they cannot be separated.

The People and Their Religion

◄ **Detail** *Christian Good Shepherd.* Second century CE. Marble, ht. 39". Vatican Museum.

In about 2000 BCE, many displaced tribes were wandering throughout the Middle East because of the political upheavals that accompanied the collapse

113

Timeline 5.1 JEWISH CIVILIZATION

2000 BCE	1500	1250	1020	926		586	538		168	63	70 CE
Hebrews in Canaan	Hebrews in Egypt	Hebrews Return to Canaan	United Monarchy	Division of Kingdom and Wars with Neighboring Empires		Babylonian Captivity	Postexilic Period, Reestablishment of Jewish State		Maccabean Kingdom	Roman Rule in Judea	
		Moses		**722 BCE** Assyrians destroy Israel	Babylonians conquer Judah		**332 BCE** Alexander the Great conquers Judah			Pompey conquers Judah	Romans destroy Jerusalem

of the Akkadian kingdom and the coming of the Babylonians. Some of these nomads eventually settled along the eastern coast of the Mediterranean Sea that is part of the Fertile Crescent. These patriarchal tribes, under the guidance of the oldest and most respected male members, founded communities united by bloodlines, economic interests, and folk traditions. One of these tribes, known as the Hebrews and led by the patriarch Abraham, occupied territory called Canaan, a region identified loosely with ancient Israel (Timeline 5.1). Primarily shepherds, they settled in the hill country (Map 5.1).

The Hebrews considered themselves unique, a belief based on the relationship between Abraham and a supernatural being who spoke to him and whom he obeyed. This deity made a **covenant,** or solemn agreement (the outward sign of which was the circumcision of all male children), with Abraham to protect his family and bring prosperity to his offspring if they agreed to obey his divine commands. Although this Hebrew deity was associated with nature, he differed from other Mesopotamian deities in his commitment to justice and righteousness. He was an ethical god and sought to impose ethical principles on humans.

EGYPT, EXODUS, AND MOSES The Hebrews prospered for decades in Canaan, but around 1500 BCE, in a time of famine, a group migrated south into the more prosperous Egypt, which had recently been overrun by the Hyksos, a Semitic people with whom the Hebrews shared language and cultural traits. The Hebrews thrived over the next few centuries, until the Egyptians overthrew the Hyksos and enslaved the Hebrews. In about 1250 BCE, the extraordinary leader Moses rallied the Hebrews and led them on the Exodus from Egypt—one of the most significant events in Jewish history.

As the Hebrews wandered in the desert on the Sinai peninsula, Moses molded his followers into a unified people under a set of ethical and societal laws, which they believed were received from God. The laws of Moses were unique among ancient peoples because they were grounded in the covenant between the Hebrews and God and because no distinction was made between religious and secular offenses. All crimes were seen as sins and all sins as crimes. Those who committed crimes could not simply make reparation to their victims; they also had to seek forgiveness from God. There were some crimes, such as murder, that were so offensive to God that they could not be forgiven by human beings alone. Furthermore, human life was seen as sacred because it was given by God, who created and owned all things; individual humans were precious because they were made in God's image.

The core of Mosaic law was the Ten Commandments, which set forth the proper behavior of human beings (Table 5.1). The commandments became the basis of a renewed covenant, which was now extended beyond Abraham and his descendants to include the entire people. The Hebrew God tolerated no rivals; he was seen as the sole, omnipotent creator and ruler of the universe. If individuals followed his laws and worshiped him alone, they would be rewarded, and if they strayed, they would be punished. Likewise, if the tribe followed the divine commands, they would prosper, and if they disobeyed, they would meet with adversity. As the mediator of the covenant between God and the Hebrew people, Moses played a crucial role in shaping Judaism into a comprehensive system of ethical **monotheism,** the belief that there is only one God.

As they wandered through the Sinai desert, the Hebrews carried with them a sacred decorated box called the Ark of the Covenant. Within it were the stone tablets on which the Ten Commandments were carved. Details of how to craft the Ark and all the other sacred objects used in worship were dictated to Moses by God (Figure 5.1). In the desert, the deity also revealed a new name for himself—YHWH, a name so sacred that pious Jews never speak or write it. In the Middle Ages, European scholars rendered YHWH as

LEARNING THROUGH MAPS

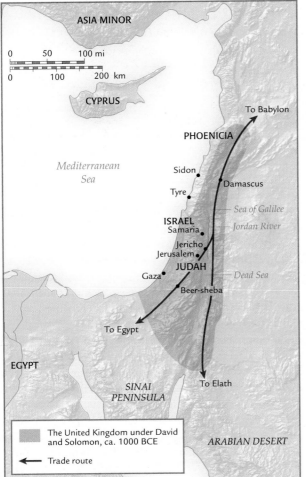

Map 5.1   ANCIENT ISRAEL
This map shows the Hebrews' ancient kingdom, known as the United Monarchy, forged by the rulers David and his son Solomon. The map also shows the kingdoms of Israel and Judah, the two Hebrew states that emerged when the United Monarchy split on the death of Solomon, in 926 BCE. 1. *Locate* the capitals of these two kingdoms. 2. *How* was the cultural life and religious faith of the nation of Israel influenced by foreign neighbors? 3. *What* impact did Israel's size and location have on its history and religious faith? 4. *Notice* the scale of the map and compare it with the scale of Map 4.2, The Roman Empire under Augustus.

Table 5.1   THE TEN COMMANDMENTS

1. You shall have no other gods before me.
2. You shall not make for yourself a graven image, or any likeness of any thing that is in heaven above, or that is on the earth beneath, or that is in the water under the earth. . . .
3. You shall not take the name of the Lord your God in vain. . . .
4. Observe the sabbath day, to keep it holy, as the Lord your God commanded you. . . .
5. Honor your father and your mother. . . .
6. You shall not kill.
7. Neither shall you commit adultery.
8. Neither shall you steal.
9. Neither shall you bear false witness against your neighbor.
10. Neither shall you covet your neighbor's wife . . . or anything that is your neighbor's.

Source: The Bible, Revised Standard Version, Deuteronomy 5:6–21.

Jehovah, but today this term is generally considered a false reading of the sacred letters. In modern English, YHWH is usually rendered as Yahweh. In biblical times, Jewish priests called the deity Adonai, the Semitic term for Lord.

After forty years of wandering, followed by Moses's death, the Hebrews finally returned to Canaan, the Promised Land pledged by Yahweh to their forefathers. Over the next two centuries, the Hebrews won Canaan and became known as the Israelites.

Figure 5.1   Stone Menorah. Second century CE. Ht. 18". Israel Museum, Jerusalem. *Although this particular menorah dates from the second century CE, the seven-branched candelabrum had been in use as a religious symbol for centuries. According to Jewish beliefs, God gave Moses explicit instructions on how to craft the menorah, which was made for the tabernacle, or house of prayer. Later the menorah came to symbolize knowledge and understanding as well as the light of God protecting the Jews.*

Table 5.2   HISTORICAL STAGES OF THE TEMPLE IN JERUSALEM

NAME	CONSTRUCTION DETAILS	DATE DESTROYED
Solomon's Temple. Also called First Temple	Completed under King Solomon, 957 BCE	587/586 BCE, by the Babylonians
Second Temple. Also called Herod's Temple after being rebuilt in 26 CE	Completed 515 BCE. Rebuilt at order of King Herod (d. 4 BCE) between 20 BCE and 26 CE.	70 CE, by the Romans. A section of the western wall (also called the Wailing Wall) survived; it was incorporated into the wall around the Muslim Dome of the Rock and al-Aqsa mosque in 691 CE.

THE KINGDOM OF ISRAEL   In about 1000 BCE, the Israelites established a monarchy, and from the late eleventh century to the end of the tenth century BCE, the nation flourished under a series of kings—Saul, David, and Solomon. The popular king David rallied the scattered Israelite tribes, centralized the government, and shifted the economy away from herding and toward commerce, trade, and farming.

Solomon, David's son, brought the Israelite kingdom to its pinnacle of power and prestige. He signed treaties with other states, expanded Israel's trade across the Middle East, and raised the standard of living for many of his subjects. He completed the building of Jerusalem begun by David, which, with its magnificent public structures and great temple, rivaled the glory of other Middle Eastern cities. The Temple of Solomon, also known as the First Temple, housed Israel's holy relics, including the Ark of the Covenant, and became the focal point of the nation's religion, which required pilgrimages and rituals, based on the religious calendar (Table 5.2; Figure 5.2). The Hebrew religion required ritual offerings (sacrifices of animals on large altars and wine, incense, and grain mixed with oil on small altars) twice daily. These offerings were conducted by priests in the Temple in Jerusalem as a community ritual for the entire Hebrew nation; individuals could also arrange for sacrifices to be made on their own behalf.

King Solomon considered himself a patron of literature and the arts, and under his rule Hebrew culture

Figure 5.2 Horned Altar. Tenth century BCE. Carved limestone, ht. 26½". Oriental Institute, University of Chicago. *Middle Eastern peoples made sacrifices to their deities on altars, but the small horned altar, as pictured here, was unique to the Hebrews. Horned altars are described in the Bible, especially as a ritual object in the Temple in Jerusalem, built in the tenth century BCE. However, this horned altar was discovered at Megiddo, one of the cities of the Hebrew kingdom. Originally, then, sacrifices could be performed away from the Temple in Jerusalem.*

northern and southern tribes. When Solomon died in 926 BCE, the tensions between the regions intensified and the United Monarchy separated into two states: Israel in the north, with its capital at Samaria, and Judah in the south, with its capital at Jerusalem.

During the period of the two Hebrew kingdoms, a new type of religious leader, known as a prophet, appeared. The prophets warned of the fatal consequences of breaking Yahweh's commandments. The prophets also demanded social justice for the helpless and the downtrodden. In the face of a widening gulf between rich and poor, the prophets predicted that if the well-off did not aid the less fortunate, Yahweh would bring down the evil rulers and, in the future, punish the selfish and reward the sufferers. But the words of the prophets, such as Hosea and Amos in Israel and Isaiah and Jeremiah in Judah, seemed to go unheeded. Finally, the prophets began to insist that the Hebrew religion was universal.

THE BABYLONIAN CAPTIVITY AND THE POSTEXILIC PERIOD
Although Israel enjoyed its moments of prosperity and power, the larger empires, especially Egypt and Assyria, wanted to control the military and trade routes crossing this part of the Fertile Crescent. In 722 BCE, the tiny nation of Israel was destroyed by the Assyrians. Judah, to the south, endured for another one hundred fifty years, but in 586 BCE, the Babylonians conquered Judah, destroying Solomon's Temple in Jerusalem and deporting most of the Hebrews to Babylonia. The approximately forty years of exile, known as the Babylonian Captivity, became one of the major turning points in Jewish history.

At the end of the sixth century, the Jews (as the Hebrews are called after the Babylonian Captivity) were freed by the triumphant Persians, who were sweeping across the ancient world under Cyrus (see Chapter 2). Returning to Judah, the Jews rebuilt their Temple, now known as the Second Temple, and their towns. Believing that God had rescued them, they established a theocratic state—a government ruled by those who are recognized as having special divine guidance and approval—and dedicated themselves to the correct formulation and observation of their religious beliefs. Many exiles remained outside the homeland and became known as Jews of the **Diaspora,** or the Dispersion.

After their return from Babylon, the Jews expanded their views of Yahweh. Probably under the indirect impact of the increasingly popular Persian religion, Zoroastrianism—and its description of the twin forces of good and evil or light and dark—the Jews began to envision a cosmic dualism in their own beliefs. The Hebrews' earlier perception of themselves as a chosen people under a universal deity was reinforced as they

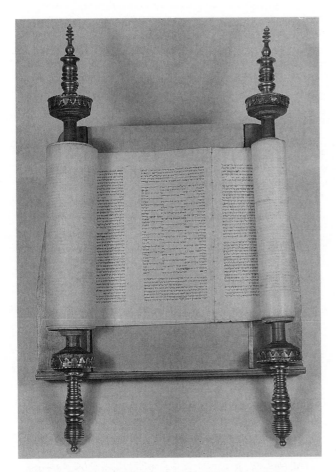

Figure 5.3   Scroll of the Pentateuch. *The ancient Hebrews recorded their scriptures on parchment scrolls. The scroll of the Pentateuch was wound on two staves. The scrolls were not decorated or illuminated with designs, animals, or humans because the Bible forbade any likeness of Yahweh and artistic expressions were not encouraged. However, some sacred books were illustrated and ornamented at various stages of Hebrew history. The carved staves on which the Pentateuch was wound were often embellished. Evidence exists that by the fifth century CE, the scrolls might have been encased in a container of precious metal, and by the fifteenth century, they were enclosed in containers adorned with reliefs and Hebrew lettering.*

expanded, notably in law, writing, music, and dance. As the Hebrews' oral traditions gave way to written records, Hebrew authors wrote down their laws and their earliest histories, which are preserved in the first books of the Bible (Figure 5.3). These Hebrew works predate by five centuries the writings of the great Greek historians Herodotus and Thucydides, but, unlike the Greek writers, the Hebrew historians made God the central force in human history and thus transformed the unfolding of earthly events into a moral drama with cosmic significance.

Solomon's achievements came at a heavy price, for they undermined his people's religious foundations, intensified class divisions, and tended to divide the

Figure 5.4   Model of the Reconstructed Second Temple (Herod's Temple) in Jerusalem. *This model of the Second Temple shows the strong influence of Hellenistic-style architecture, particularly in the colonnaded arcades, the decorative frieze, and the tall, slender Corinthian columns flanking the main entryway. The Second Temple was destroyed by Roman legions in 70 CE, but one wall was left standing.*

concluded that Yahweh had used the Persians to free them. Furthermore, the Jews started to incorporate two new features into their religion: **eschatology,** or the concern with the end of the world, and an interest in **apocalypse,** prophecies about the coming of God and a day of judgment. This future world would be led by a **Messiah,** or Anointed One, who would bring peace and justice to all.

THE HELLENISTIC AND ROMAN PERIODS   Alexander the Great conquered Judah in 332 BCE, and after his death the area became part of the Seleucid kingdom, centered in Syria. Hellenistic culture and ideas proliferated and deeply affected Jewish life. Growing tensions between

Figure 5.5   Masada, Israel. *This outcropping of rock in the forbidding terrain outside Jerusalem was a natural fortress. King Herod had built one of his palace-fortresses here in the years just before the birth of Christ. For three years the Zealots occupied its ruins, holding out against the Romans after the end of the First Jewish War in 70 CE.*

Figure 5.6   *Moses Giving Water to the Twelve Tribes of Israel.*
Fresco. Synagogue. Third century CE. Dura Europos, Syria.
Reconstructed in the National Museum, Damascus, Syria.
*This fresco is from a house-synagogue (a place of worship set up
within a private residence) that was discovered in the early twentieth century, after having been filled with rubble in 256 CE, as
part of a defense plan for the city of Dura Europos. Only sections
of the walls survive. The room featured benches running around
the walls and a niche for the Torah scrolls in the western wall.
The paintings depict various events from the Hebrew Bible, most
having to do with national salvation, such as Samuel Anointing David, the Ark Brought to Jerusalem, and the Exodus from
Egypt. Painted by anonymous artists, these works were executed
in tempera, a medium made of pigments blended with egg yolks
and water, applied to dry plaster. This fresco was part of the
Exodus group and was based on Numbers 2:2–12. It portrays
Moses seated and holding a staff, as he delivers life-giving water
(via "tubes") to the tribes, symbolized by twelve huts, each with a
single figure. A menorah stands in the center rear.*

the Jews and the Hellenistic leaders erupted in 168
BCE when the Seleucid king Antiochus IV tried to impose the worship of Greek gods on the Jews, placing
a statue of Zeus in the Second Temple in Jerusalem.
Antiochus's violation of the sacred place enraged the
Maccabean clan, whose inspired leadership and bravery led to a successful revolt and the recapture of the
Second Temple. The Maccabean family ruled Judah
as an independent commonwealth for approximately
one hundred years. Then, in 63 BCE, the Romans conquered most of the Middle East. They subsequently
incorporated Judah (in what was now called Palestine)

into their empire as Judea and placed the Jewish lands
under client kings (loyal, pliable dependents).

The Romans ruled through the Jewish Herodian
dynasty. Herod the Great, who ruled from 37 to 4 BCE,
rebuilt Jerusalem, including the Second Temple, and
promoted Hellenistic culture (Figure 5.4). But conditions under the Romans became unbearable to the
Jews, and in 66 CE a rebellion broke out. After the
First Jewish War (66–70), the Romans captured Jerusalem and destroyed the Second Temple. The western
wall, or Wailing Wall, of the Second Temple in Jerusalem remained standing and came to symbolize the
plight of the Jewish people. A revolutionary group
known as Zealots held out until 73 at Masada, a sheer-
sided mesa on the shores of the Dead Sea (Figure 5.5).
When their cause became hopeless, they committed
suicide rather than surrender to the Romans. To make
sure the Jews would no longer be a problem for them,
the Roman government in the late first century CE
ordered the dispersal of the Jews throughout the empire. However, this second Diaspora did not end the
Jews' cultural, intellectual, and religious existence. On
the contrary, the Jewish way of life continued, though
it changed. With the fall of the Temple in Jerusalem,
Jews worshiped in synagogues, or congregations,
which eventually were headed by rabbis, or teachers
(Figure 5.6). Over the centuries, the rabbis' teachings
evolved into Rabbinic Judaism, based on the Torah and
the Talmud (from Hebrew, "learning"), a collection of

SLICE OF LIFE
A Jewish Eyewitness to the Destruction of the Second Temple

FLAVIUS JOSEPHUS
A Jewish Soldier in the Roman Army

The Jewish historian Josephus (about 37–100 CE) was an eyewitness to one of the darkest days in Jewish history: the destruction of the Second Temple in Jerusalem on September 8, 70 CE. Earlier, in 67 CE, he had been made a captive of the Romans, but through his ingenuity, he had been given his freedom. He became an admiring, though sometimes reluctant, soldier in the Roman cause. Assigned to General Titus, he was among the troops that sacked and burned the temple on that fateful day. The following account is taken from Josephus's History of the Jewish War *(75–79 CE).*

At this moment one of the [Roman] soldiers, not waiting for orders and without any dread of such an act but driven on by some frenzy, snatched a brand from the blazing fire and, lifted up by a comrade, hurled the torch through the golden door which gave access to the buildings of the Temple Precinct from the north side. As the flames surged up, a great cry to match their feelings arose from the Jews, and they rushed to the defence, reckless of their lives and prodigal of their strength once they saw that the purpose of their previous watch was gone. . . .

As the fire gained strength, Titus found that he could not restrain the surge of his enthusiastic soldiers. . . .

Most were driven on by the hope of loot, for they thought that the inside of the building must be full of money if the outside, which they could see, was made of gold. One of those who had got in forestalled the attempts of Titus, who had rushed in to check them, and hurled a brand against the hinges of the door. Suddenly flames appeared from within, which forced back Titus and his officers, leaving those outside to kindle the blaze unhindered. In this way, though much against Titus's will, the Temple was burnt. . . .

INTERPRETING THIS SLICE OF LIFE

1. *What* was the source of conflict between the Romans and the Jews? 2. *Do* you find Josephus's account credible, given that he was both a Jew and a Roman soldier? 3. *Analyze* his account of the Temple's fall. 4. *What* role does General Titus play in the assault? 5. *How* are the Roman soldiers depicted? 6. *How* does Josephus depict the Jewish rebels? 7. *Are* there modern parallels to this type of eyewitness history?

---

legal rulings and commentaries. Rabbinic Judaism established a mode of worship and moral code that Jews worldwide have followed down to modern times.

SOCIETAL AND FAMILY RELATIONSHIPS   From earliest times to the founding of the monarchy, Jewish families survived in an agrarian economy and society. Although the patriarchal structure set the pattern of life and ensured the dominance of the tribal chieftains, men and women shared duties and responsibilities because in a rural society a family's continuation and the preservation of its property required the efforts of all its members. Within the family, women exercised some freedom, mothers' and sisters' roles were taken seriously, and the family rights (divorce, property ownership, inheritance) of wives and mothers were protected by law.

However, with the coming of the kingdom of Israel and during and after the Babylonian Captivity, the male leaders, in their efforts to protect the new political system, the integrity of their religion, and the Hebrew way of life, formally and informally limited the rights and powers of women. This trend accelerated in the Hellenistic period as urbanism and commercialism made inroads into the Jewish social order and

family. Work was increasingly divided according to gender, with women being assigned domestic duties and subordinated and restricted within the economic, social, legal, and cultural system. The changing, and often conflicting, roles for women were reflected in the Hebrew Bible and other literature, which recorded instances of women serving as priestesses or influencing Hebrew officials, defined the qualities of a good wife, justified women's subservient status in a patriarchal order, and blamed women for human transgressions.

The Bible

The Jews enshrined their cultural developments in the Bible, their collection of sacred writings, or **scriptures.** Known as the Old Testament to Christians, the Hebrew Bible (from the Greek word for "book") contains history, law, poetry, songs, stories, prayers, and philosophical works. Evolving out of a rich and long oral tradition, parts of the Bible probably began to assume written form during the United Monarchy in the tenth century BCE. By then the Hebrews had an alphabet, which, like that of the Greeks, was probably derived

Table 5.3   BOOKS OF THE HEBREW BIBLE AND THE CHRISTIAN BIBLE OLD TESTAMENT

HEBREW BIBLE		CHRISTIAN BIBLE OLD TESTAMENT	
The Law (Torah)		**The Pentateuch**	
Genesis	Numbers	Genesis	Numbers
Exodus	Deuteronomy	Exodus	Deuteronomy
Leviticus		Leviticus	
The Prophets		**The Historical Books**	
(Early Prophets)		Joshua	2 Chronicles
Joshua	2 Samuel	Judges	Ezra
Judges	1 Kings	Ruth	Nehemiah
1 Samuel	2 Kings	1 Samuel	Tobit*
(Later Prophets)		2 Samuel	Judith*
Isaiah	Micah	1 Kings	Esther
Jeremiah	Nahum	2 Kings	1 Maccabees*
Ezekiel	Habakkuk	1 Chronicles	2 Maccabees*
Hosea	Zephaniah		
Joel	Haggai	**The Poetical or Wisdom Books**	
Amos	Zechariah	Job	
Obadiah	Malachi	Psalms	
Jonah		Proverbs	
		Ecclesiastes	
The Writings		Song of Solomon (Songs)	
Psalms	Esther	Wisdom*	
Proverbs	Daniel	Sirach*	
Job	Ezra		
Song of Songs	Nehemiah	**The Prophetical Books**	
Ruth	1 Chronicles	Isaiah	Obadiah
Lamentations	2 Chronicles	Jeremiah	Jonah
Ecclesiastes		Lamentations	Micah
		Baruch*	Nahum
		Ezekiel	Habakkuk
		Daniel	Zephaniah
		Hosea	Haggai
		Joel	Zechariah
		Amos	Malachi

*Roman Catholics include these books in the canon and refer to them as deuterocanonical ("second canon"); Protestants sometimes place them in an appendix with other Apocrypha.

from the Phoenicians. Having acquired a written language and a unified political state, the Hebrews shared a consciousness of their past and desired to preserve it. They assembled and recorded various historical accounts, songs, and stories, plus the sayings of the prophets. Sometime in the fifth century BCE, Jewish scholars and religious leaders canonized (declared official) parts of these writings as divinely inspired. They became the first five books of the Bible, known as the Torah or the Pentateuch. The Hebrew Bible's ultimate form was reached in 90 CE when a council of Jewish rabbis added a last set of writings to the **canon.**

Another important development in the transmission of the Hebrew scriptures was their translation into other languages. In the third century BCE, after many Jews had been influenced by Hellenistic culture,

a group of Alexandrian scholars collected all the authenticated Jewish writings and translated them into Greek. This Hebrew Greek Bible was called the Septuagint, from the Latin word for "seventy," so named because of the legend that it was translated by seventy scholars.

The final version of the Hebrew Bible is divided into three parts: the Law, the Prophets, and the Writings (Table 5.3). (Christians divide the Old Testament into four parts.) The Law, also called the Torah (from Hebrew, "instruction"), recounts the story of God's creation of the world and the early history of the Hebrews. More important, it details the establishment of the covenant and the foundation of the moral and ritualistic codes of personal and societal behavior that underlie Judaism.

Figure 5.7 The Dead Sea Isaiah Scroll (detail). First century BCE–first century CE. *The Dead Sea Scrolls are believed to be the work of a Jewish sect known as the Essenes. Living in a monastic community called Qumran, this radical group rejected the leadership of the Jews in Jerusalem and practiced a militant, separatist form of Judaism. The scrolls represent their copies of the Hebrew Bible as well as previously unknown works. The Dead Sea Isaiah Scroll preserves all sixty-six chapters of the Bible's longest book.*

The Prophets, canonized in the first century BCE, provide records about Israel and Judah and expand the Hebrews' ideas about God's nature and their relationship to him. They recount the conquest of Canaan, the events of the era of the Judges and the period of the United Monarchy, and the fate of Judah after the Babylonian Captivity.

The Writings reflect diverse viewpoints and contain many types of literature, including poetry, wise sayings, stories, and apocalyptic visions of the end of time. Some of these books, such as Job, Ecclesiastes, and Proverbs, reflect the influence of other cultures on Jewish beliefs. The Writings were not deemed canonical until 90 CE, with the exception of Psalms, a collection of poems, which was given sacred status by 100 BCE because of their role in the prayer life of the Jews.

There is also a body of Jewish literature outside the canon. The Apocrypha are books written between 200 BCE and 100 CE that include wisdom literature, stories, and history, including the history of the Maccabees. Though not part of the Jewish canon, these books were included in the Septuagint, the Greek translation of the Hebrew Bible, and accepted by the Roman Catholic Church as part of the Christian Old Testament.

Copies of many Jewish works, both canonical and noncanonical, were found in a cave near the Dead Sea in 1947. These documents, dating from about 200 BCE to 100 CE and known as the Dead Sea Scrolls, were almost a thousand years older than any other existing manuscripts of the Bible and confirmed that the books had been transmitted faithfully for centuries (Figure 5.7).

The Hebrew Bible provided Judaism with many of its beliefs and values and much of its worldview. It contrasted a changing view of God with a consistently negative opinion of human nature. In light of Yahweh's strict demands, the Bible implied that few humans would attain happiness. While awaiting the coming of Yahweh's kingdom on earth, the faithful were encouraged to keep God's commandments and hope for God's forgiveness should they fail.

Early Jewish Art and Architecture

Jewish culture was profoundly shaped by the Second Commandment, which forbids the making of images or likenesses of God. In art, this meant that Yahweh could not, by definition, be depicted in any recognizable form. Furthermore, creation and creativity are considered the exclusive domain of God and reserved for him alone. Thus, there is no official Jewish sculpture or painting.

The scattered surviving artifacts of the Hebrews from the period before the United Monarchy can seldom be distinguished from the works of their neighbors. Because of the early Hebrews' nomadic existence, what sacred objects they had were transportable and kept in tents. These early works were not for public display because of the very holiness of Yahweh and the Hebrews' sense of their deity's power. Only a few persons were even permitted to see or be in the vicinity of these sacred objects. Once the tribes were united, however, Solomon enshrined the Ark of the Covenant and other ritualistic items in the splendid Temple that he built in Jerusalem. Solomon meant the Temple to be the central national shrine of the Hebrews and a symbol of his dynasty.

Solomon's Temple was destroyed by the Babylonians when they carried off the Jews in the early sixth century BCE. The description of the Temple in 1 Kings makes it sound similar to the "long-house" temples found in other civilizations of that time and probably indicated the influence of foreign neighbors. According to the Bible, Solomon's Temple was a rectangular building comprising three sections: a porch, a sanctuary, or main hall, and an inner sanctum that housed the Ark of the Covenant. Artists and craftspeople decorated the interior with carvings of floral designs and cherubs, highlighting these with gold. The building was made of ashlars, and two large freestanding columns were placed at the entryway. The Temple may have been raised on a platform. A court surrounded the Temple, and a large altar stood inside the court.

When the Jews were released from the Babylonian Captivity by the Persians, they returned to their homeland and reconstructed the capital city of Jerusalem and its Temple. The Second Temple, completed in the late sixth century BCE, exhibited a simpler design and decoration scheme than did Solomon's Temple. Meanwhile, the Jews of the Diaspora gathered in Hellenistic cities to read the Torah and to pray in buildings that became synagogues, or houses of worship. No record survives of how these synagogues looked or how they might have been decorated until the third century CE.

Greek influences became apparent in Jewish architecture during Hellenistic times. One Maccabean ruler, John Hyrcanus [hear-KAY-nuhs] (135–106 BCE), constructed a fortress-palace at present-day Araq el Emir in Jordan that shows this influence clearly. The facade of the palace blended Greek columns and oriental carvings, typical of the Alexandrian architectural and decorative style. The edifice and its carvings were probably similar to the Second Temple in Jerusalem. One of the few decorations remaining from this palace is a lion fountain (Figure 5.8). Carved in high relief, the lion is well proportioned and conveys a sense of power with its raised front paw and open mouth.

The lingering influence of late Greek architecture on Jewish structures is also seen in a set of tombs dug out of the soft limestone rocks east of Jerusalem in the Kidron Valley. According to the inscription, these tombs contained the remains of priests from the Hezir family (Figure 5.9). The tomb on the left displays Doric columns, and the one in the center fuses Greek Ionic columns and an Egyptian pyramidal roof. Several other tombs in the vicinity reveal a similar melding of styles.

During the reign of King Herod the Great (r. 37–4 BCE), architecture in Judea exhibited a further mix of Greek styles with Jewish motifs. King Herod's magnificent fortress-palace at Masada may have been a conscious blending of the two cultures in an effort to bridge the gap between the Roman and Jewish worlds (see Figure 5.5). The various buildings in Herod's complex contained many representative Greco-Roman features, including fluted Corinthian columns and marble facings (Figure 5.10). In Herod's palace, classical patterned mosaics were combined with traditional Jewish decorations of flowers, fruits, and intertwined vines and branches (Figure 5.11).

Figure 5.8 Lion at the Palace of John Hyrcanus. Second century BCE. Araq el Emir, Jordan. *This lion, Greco-Oriental in style, was carved deeply into the stone's surface to create a high-relief work. The lion's tail, wrapped around its right rear leg, is balanced by the raised left front leg, creating a feeling of strength and agility.*

Herod also built palaces at Jericho and in Jerusalem, but they were destroyed, and their remains have not been uncovered. He also supervised the rebuilding of the Second Temple in Jerusalem (see Figure 5.4), whose large dimensions and impressive features were recorded in the writings of the Jewish historian Josephus in his works *The Jewish War* and *Jewish Antiquities*. Like the First Temple, this one contained many rooms, including the inner sanctuary, the Holy of Holies, with the menorah (see Figures 5.1 and 5.2) and the table where the priests placed the consecrated, unleavened bread eaten during Passover, the festival that commemorates the exodus from Egypt. Whatever may have been Herod's motives in constructing this new Temple, the results were short-lived. When the Romans finally crushed the Jewish revolt in 70 CE, the Temple, except for the western wall, was destroyed, and its sacred objects were transported to Rome.

In about 20 CE King Herod Antipas, son of Herod the Great, founded the city of Tiberias, named for the Roman emperor Tiberius, on the Sea of Galilee. Initially, Jews refused to live in Tiberias, but by the third century Tiberias became a center of learning. Jewish officials moved the Sanhedrin—the civil and religious supreme court—there and the local Jews built a synagogue. Destroyed by an earthquake in 363 CE, this synagogue was replaced by a more splendid edifice decorated with mosaics reflective of Greco-Roman influences. The mosaics in this synagogue included forbidden images such as human figures and non-Jewish themes, as well as depictions of sacred Hebrew symbols and objects (Figure 5.12).

Figure 5.9 Tomb of Bene Hezir. Early first century BCE. Kidron Valley, Israel. *The Tomb of Bene Hezir (on the left) shows the influence of Greek architecture in its post-and-lintel construction and its Doric columns. Even though the area was subject to Roman impact at this time, Roman influence is not apparent in the architecture. The members of the priestly Hezir family, as recorded in 1 Chronicles 24, were buried in what has been determined to be the oldest tomb in Israel's Kidron Valley. Scholars disagree over whether the structure in the center with the pyramidal roof belonged to the Bene Hezir tomb.*

Figure 5.10 Hall of Herod's North Palace. Late first century BCE. Masada, Israel. *These Corinthian columns were originally plastered over and painted. Carved directly out of the hill's rock, they formed a natural corridor around the banqueting hall. Herod built this and other splendid palaces to impress the Jews and win their political sympathy, but he failed to do either.*

Figure 5.11 Mosaic from Herod's Palace. Late first century BCE. Masada, Israel. *The Greek practice of mosaic making was adopted by both the Romans and the Jews. The patterned designs around the borders of this mosaic from Herod's Palace are typically Greek, and the more organic image in the center is typically Jewish.*

Figure 5.12 Decorative Mosaic Floor Panel. Synagogue. Fourth century CE. Hammat, near Tiberias, Israel. Israel Antiquities Authority, Jerusalem. *This decorative mosaic includes many objects associated with Jewish religious rites, tradition, and history. In the center stands the Ark, a cabinet partly covered by a draped curtain, which contained the Torah, the sacred scrolls on which were written the Pentateuch, the first five books of the Hebrew scriptures. The Ark is the focal point of prayer in houses of worship, because it symbolizes the Holy of Holies of the Temple in Jerusalem. Other sacred objects in this mosaic include the menorah (seven branched candelabrum), which was used in the Temple in Jerusalem; the shofar (ram's horn), which is blown at certain religious festivals, as a call to prayer; and an incense shovel, used in making offerings on altars (see Figure 5.2) in ancient Judaism. The two tall palm branches and the flowering citrons are agricultural symbols of the Festival of Tabernacles (in Hebrew, "Sukkot").*

ENCOUNTER

Baal, a Rival to the Israelites' God

The Israelites were tempted by the religion of Baal, the Canaanite deity, and for many centuries Baal was Yahweh's most threatening rival for the hearts and minds of the people of Israel.

The origins and evolution of the Baal cult are similar to those of many other ancient polytheistic religions. According to texts on clay tablets discovered at Ugarit (modern Ras Shamra, Syria), which are dated from the second millennium BCE, Baal evolved into a fertility deity, the protector and guarantor of life for crops, animals, and humanity. As a fertility deity, Baal controlled the weather, planting, and harvests. His followers addressed him as Lord of Heaven (Baal means "master," "owner," or "lord"). Baal, according to one myth, ultimately became king of the gods, having challenged and defeated several deities, including Mot (death) and Yamm (the sea god). Many tribes across the Fertile Crescent, including the Canaanites, worshiped Baal, building temples and altars to him, paying homage in rituals and sacrifices, fabricating his image and symbols (human or animal), and incorporating the name Baal into individual names as a protection from evil.

The Israelites, led by Moses and his followers, wrested control of Canaan from the Canaanites and set up the kingdom of Israel with a moral and legal code based on Yahweh's teachings. Some Israelites, living among the conquered Canaanites, found Baal a satisfying alternative to Yahweh. They were drawn to the Baal cult's emotional practices, such as dancing and other frenzied rites, rather than to the staid ritu-

als of Yahweh. Others were attracted to the Baal cult's use of visible images, whereas Yahweh denounced this practice as idol worship. And a number of Israelite farmers and herdsmen found Baal's role as a fertility god, with a fairly lax moral code, more appealing than Yahweh's more distant status as Creator God and stern moral judge.

From the time of King Saul through the United Monarchy under Solomon, the Israelites tended to be loyal to Yahweh, though Baal's presence loomed in the background. With the fall of the United Monarchy in 926 BCE, Baal worship resurfaced in the northern kingdom of Israel and also in Judah, the southern kingdom. The Hebrew prophets, who were then emerging as a moral force, preached against the cult and its images, usually a bull or calf. Their message was that Yahweh, as Creator God, controlled all natural forces but was not a nature god. Rather, Yahweh was the transcendent and universal deity, influencing historical events and affecting the lives of all peoples everywhere.

The prophet Elijah angrily denounced this movement, predicting that drought and famine would stalk the land until the Israelites gave up Baal and returned to Yahweh. Thereafter, the worship of Baal in Israel tended to subside until the Assyrians overran the kingdom in 722 BCE.

LEARNING FROM THE ENCOUNTER

1. *How* was the origin and evolution of Baal similar to that of other ancient deities? 2. *Why* were the Israelites attracted to Baal? 3. *What* role did the prophets

CHRISTIANITY

Like Judaism, Christianity rose from obscurity and gained much of its power from the tremendous moral force of its central beliefs and values. But Christianity went on to become the dominant religion of Western culture. From its origins among the Jews of Judea, Christianity slowly spread until, by the end of the fourth century CE, it had become the official faith of Rome. When Rome lost control of the western provinces at the end of the fifth century CE, Christianity's ideas and institutions survived as tutors to the emerging European kingdoms. Christianity's triumph was powerfully symbolized in the early Middle Ages when church authorities revised the old Roman calendar to make the birth of Christ the pivotal event in history. Thus, the period before Jesus's birth is known as BC, or "before Christ," and the era after his birth is

termed AD, or *anno Domini,* Latin words meaning "in the year of the Lord," the title of respect given to Jesus by Christians. Although Christianity and the church have declined from their zenith in the Middle Ages, the Christian calendar remains in effect throughout the West as well as in many other parts of the world—a symbol of the continuing power of this creed. In this textbook, reflecting today's multicultural world, the term BCE, "before common era," replaces BC, and the term CE, "common era," replaces AD.

The Life of Jesus Christ and the New Testament

The surviving primary sources for the origin of Christianity are writings in Greek by early believers who were openly partisan. According to them, Christianity

play in the rivalry between Baal and Yahweh? 4. *How does the story of Elijah's defeat of the Baal support-ers symbolize larger issues in the Hebrews' religion? 5. *What* other religions have faced similar threats to their gods throughout history—and even today?

Encounter figure 5.1   Baal. Ca. 1700–1400 BCE. Louvre. Limestone, ht. 55″. *This statue of Baal, discovered at Ugarit, shows the god, with his right arm raised, standing on a pedestal—a typical depiction of a weather god. The wavy lines below may represent mountains. He is dressed in a kilt fastened by a broad belt and cord from which hangs a sheathed dagger and a sharp pointed helmet with a pair of bull horns on the front. In his right hand, he holds a club or mace and in his left a spear with its top sprouting into a plant—a fertility symbol. In front, a miniature figure, who may be a Syrian king, pays homage. Although he was a Middle Eastern deity, Baal's deli-cate features and slim body hint at Egyptian influences.*

began within the Jewish faith among the followers of Jesus, a deeply pious and charismatic Jew who failed to purify his own faith but succeeded in founding a dynamic new religion.

Jesus was born to Mary and Joseph in Judea in about 4 BCE (a date that reflects errors in early Christian time-reckoning). After narrating the events surrounding his birth, the accounts of Jesus's life are almost silent until he reaches the age of about thirty, when he commenced a teaching mission that placed him squarely in conflict with prevailing Jewish beliefs and authorities. Jews of various social classes heard Jesus's message, and he soon had a small group of followers who believed that he was the Messiah, the Anointed One who would de-liver the Jews, promised by God to the prophets. He was also termed the Christ, taken from the Greek for "the anointed one." Performing miracles and healing the sick, he preached that the apocalypse, or the end of

the world, was near. In anticipation of what he called the coming of the kingdom of God, he urged his fol-lowers to practice a demanding and loving ethic.

Growing discord between the Jewish establish-ment and this messianic band caused Roman leaders to classify Jesus as a political rebel. In about 30 CE, Je-sus was crucified by the Romans (Timeline 5.2). Three days later, some of his followers reported that Jesus had risen from the dead and reappeared among them. His resurrection became the ultimate miracle associ-ated with his teachings, the sign that immortal life awaited those who believed in him as the son of God and as the Messiah. After forty days, Jesus ascended into heaven, though not before pledging to return when the world came to an end.

The outline of Jesus's life is set forth in the first three books, called **Gospels,** of the Christian scriptures. The early Christian community believed that the writers,

Timeline 5.2   CHRISTIANITY TO 284 CE

4 BCE	30 CE	70	100		284
Life of Jesus	Age of Apostles	Scriptures Written	Age of the Church Fathers (to **476**)		

| | 38–65 Paul's missionary travels and letters | | | 200 Tertullian flourished | 250 Persecutions by Decius; Origen flourished |

known as Matthew, Mark, and Luke, were witnesses to Jesus's message; hence they were called **evangelists** after the Greek word *evangelion*—for those who preached the gospel, or the good news. The Gospels, although providing evidence for the historical Jesus, were not intended as histories in the Greco-Roman sense because they were addressed to Christian converts. Mark's Gospel was the earliest, dating from about 70; the Gospels of Matthew and Luke are dated a little later. They made use of Mark's narrative and added the *logoi*, the "sayings" of Jesus. These three works are known as the synoptic Gospels (from the Greek words *syn*, for "together," and *opsis*, for "view") because they take essentially the same point of view toward their subject. Between 90 and 100, a fourth, and somewhat different, Gospel appeared—that of John—which treats Jesus as a wisdom teacher, a revealer of cosmic truths. The author of the Fourth Gospel has Jesus teach the possibility of being born again to eternal life.

Despite their similarities, the synoptic Gospels reflect a schism, or split, in the early Christian church. Peter, one of Jesus's original disciples, headed a Judaizing group that stressed the necessity of first becoming a Jew before becoming a Christian. Paul, a Jew who converted to Christianity after the death of Jesus, led a group that welcomed gentile, or non-Jewish, members. Mark's Gospel was written in part to support Paul's gentile faction and therefore takes a negative tone toward Jews. Matthew was written in part as a corrective to Mark and made Peter, according to Roman Catholic doctrine, the "rock" on which the church was founded—the biblical source for the belief that Peter was the first pope.

Luke's Gospel was an effort by the early Roman church to deny, after the fact, that a schism had ever existed. Luke also wrote the Acts of the Apostles, the earliest account of the fledgling Christian community. This work records the activities of Jesus's followers immediately after his resurrection and defines some of the church's first rituals and beliefs, including a rejection of Jewish dietary laws and the practice of circumcision. Acts also affirmed the opening of Christianity to gentiles, a policy that in the future would aid in the spread of Christianity. At the time Acts was written,

however, Paul and other missionaries were preaching mainly to Greek-speaking Jews and Jewish converts scattered across the Roman Empire. Paul's Roman citizenship enabled him to move about freely.

The meaning of Jesus's life and teachings was further clarified by Paul, who had persecuted the Christians of Judea before joining the new faith. Between 50 and 62, Paul, who was familiar with Greek philosophy, addressed both local issues and broader theological concerns in epistles, or letters, the earliest writings among the Christian scriptures, although only seven of the fourteen so-called Pauline epistles are generally recognized as having been written by him. These epistles constitute Christianity's first **theology,** or the study of the nature of religious truth. Paul directed his letters to churches he either founded or visited across the Roman Empire: Ephesus and Colossae (Galatia), Philippi and Thessalonica (Macedonia), Corinth (Greece), and Rome (Map 5.2).

Paul's interpretation of the life of Jesus was based on the "Suffering Servant" section of the book of Isaiah in the Old Testament. The Suffering Servant was described as noble and guiltless but misunderstood and suffering on behalf of others. Paul set forth the doctrine of the Atonement, whereby a blameless Christ suffered on the cross to pay for the sins of humankind. Christ's life and death initiated a new moral order by offering salvation to sinful human beings who otherwise were doomed to eternal death and punishment by Adam's first sin. But, according to Paul, human redemption was not automatically given, for a sinner must have faith in Jesus Christ and his sacrifice.

Paul's teachings also stressed that Christ's resurrection, which guaranteed everlasting life for others, was the heart of Christian beliefs, an argument that echoed the synoptic Gospels. Pauline Christianity made a radical break with Judaism by nullifying the old law's authority and claiming that the true heirs of Abraham were not the Jews but the followers of Christ. Paul also affirmed that obedience to Christ led to righteousness. Such righteousness demanded ascetic living, with particular stress on sexual chastity.

The final section of the Christian scriptures was the book of Revelation, dating from about 95. This apoca-

LEARNING THROUGH MAPS

Map 5.2   THE EARLY CHRISTIAN WORLD
This map shows the spread of Christianity after the death of Jesus. 1. *Identify* the major churches in existence by the end of Paul's ministry. 2. *Which* of these churches did St. Paul found or visit? 3. *Which* church was best positioned to become the mother church of Christianity? *Why?* 4. *Consider* the impact of geography on the location of these churches. 5. *Is* there a connection between the major cities on Map 4.2, the Roman Empire under Augustus, and the location of the Christian churches on this map?

lyptic scripture projected the end of the world and the institution of a new moral order on the occasion of Jesus's return and final judgment. Revelation's picture of Rome as a corrupt Babylon destined for destruction reflected the early church's hatred of the existing political and social order. But the book, filled with enigmatic sayings and symbols, proved controversial, and not all ancient church communities accepted its authority.

By the mid–second century, the four Gospels, the Acts of the Apostles, the fourteen Pauline epistles, the seven non-Pauline epistles, and Revelation were accepted as the canon of Christian scriptures, or the New Testament (Table 5.4). Believing themselves to be the new Israel, the early Christians also retained the He-

brew scriptures, called the Old Testament. Although the spoken language of the Jews in Palestine was Aramaic, a Semitic tongue, the Christian canon was composed in Koine Greek, like the Hebrew Septuagint. The use of Greek reflected the triumph of Paul and the gentile party as well as the pervasive Hellenistic culture.

Christians and Jews

Despite the distinctive features of early Christianity, many Jewish ideas and rituals contributed to the new religion. The Christian vision of Yahweh was rooted in Judaism: a single, creating, universal God who spoke through sacred texts (the canon) and who demanded

Table 5.4 BOOKS OF THE NEW TESTAMENT

Gospels

Matthew	Luke
Mark	John

Acts of the Apostles

Acts

Epistles

Romans	Titus
1 Corinthians	Philemon
2 Corinthians	Hebrews
Galatians	James
Ephesians	1 Peter
Philippians	2 Peter
Colossians	1 John
1 Thessalonians	2 John
2 Thessalonians	3 John
1 Timothy	Jude
2 Timothy	

Apocalypse

Revelation

moral behavior from all humans. Both Jewish and Christian ethical standards required social justice for individuals and for the community. Likewise, the Christian image of Jesus as Messiah was framed within the context of Jewish prophetic literature. Christian apocalyptic writing, such as Revelation, also shared a common literary form with Jewish models such as the book of Daniel.

Even when Christians rejected specific Jewish ideas, such as the sanctity of the Mosaic law, the early church continued discussions on human righteousness and sin in terms familiar to Jews. The Christians probably adapted their rite of baptism from a ceremony similar to that of the Jews of the Diaspora. Christians also kept the idea of the Sabbath but changed it from Saturday to Sunday, and they transformed the festival of Passover (a celebration of the Hebrews' escape from Egypt) to Easter (a festival celebrating Jesus's resurrection). The church sanctuary as a focal point for prayer and learning evolved out of the Jewish synagogue, as did Christian priests from the Jewish elders. And the Christian **liturgy,** or the service of public worship, borrowed heavily from the Jewish service with its hymns, prayers, and Bible reading.

Judaism also influenced Christian thought by transmitting certain ideas from Zoroastrianism, including such dualistic concepts as Satan as the personification of evil, heaven and hell as the two destinies of humankind, and a divine savior who would appear at the end of time.

Despite their common heritage, relations between Christians and Jews were stormy. After the Council at Jamnia in Judea in 90, when the Jews established the final version of their sacred canon, there was no place in Judaism for the Christian message. As revealed in Paul's letters, the Jews viewed the followers of Jesus Christ as apostates, people who had abandoned or renounced their true religion. Accordingly, the Jews tried to deny the Christians the protection that Jewish leaders had negotiated with Roman authorities regarding their distinctive religious beliefs. For example, Jews were not required to worship the emperor as a god. Until the end of the second century, Jews and Christians occasionally engaged in violent clashes.

Christianity and Greco-Roman Religions and Philosophies

Christianity also benefited from its contacts with Greco-Roman mystery cults and philosophies. Whether or not the rituals of the cults of Cybele, Isis, or Mithra directly influenced Christianity, they did share religious ideas—for example, salvation through the sacrifice of a savior, sacred meals, and hymns. Christianity, as a monotheistic religion, paralleled movements within the cults of the second and third centuries that were blending all deities into the worship of a single divinity. Among the Greco-Roman philosophies, both Stoicism and Neoplatonism influenced Christianity as the church shifted from its Jewish roots and became hellenized; the Stoics taught the kinship of humanity, and the Neoplatonists praised the spiritual realm at the expense of the physical world.

Christians in the Roman Empire

The Romans initially regarded the Christians as a Jewish sect, but during the First Jewish War, the Christians evidently held themselves aloof. The Christian attitude seemed to be that the Jews had brought calamity upon themselves through their rejection of Christ. Similarly, Christians remained untouched during later persecutions of Jews by Romans in 115–117 and in 132–135. As their faith expanded during the first century, individual Christians encountered sporadic persecution, though there was no state policy of persecuting Christianity.

As the empire descended into chaos in the third century, Christians were sometimes blamed for its troubles. The emperor Decius [DEE-see-us] (r. 249–251) mounted a wide-ranging political test that required all citizens (men, women, and children) to make a token sacrifice to him. When the Christians refused to honor the emperor in this manner, hundreds of them were killed, including several of their local leaders, or bishops. Decius's sudden death ended this assault, but in 257 Valerian (r. 253–260) renewed it, which resulted in the martyrdom of the bishop of Rome and the leading intellectual, Cyprian. The killings eventually ceased, but for the rest of the century the survival of the Christian church was uncertain and depended on a muted existence.

Despite persecutions by the authorities, the Christian church drew much sustenance from Roman culture. The language of the church in the western provinces became Latin, and in the eastern provinces the religious leaders adopted Greek. The canon law that governed the church was based on the Roman civil law. Most important, the church modeled itself on the Roman state: bishops, the chief Christian officers in cities, had jurisdiction over territories called dioceses just as the secular governors controlled administrative dioceses.

In addition, the church was moving toward a monarchical form of government. Because the authority of the officeholders was believed to descend from Jesus's faithful supporters, those bishoprics (territory ruled by a bishop) established by apostles—such as the one in Rome that tradition claimed was founded by both Peter and Paul—emerged as the most powerful.

From an insignificant number of followers at the end of the first century, the church had attained a membership of perhaps five million, or about a tenth of the population of the empire, by the end of the third century. The smallest communities were scattered along the frontiers, and the largest congregations were in Rome and the older eastern cities. Social composition of the church came to include progressively higher classes. By the late second century, the middle classes, especially merchants and traders, were joining the church. Aristocratic women sought membership, but men of the highest classes tended to remain unconverted.

Christianity's appeal to women was complex, though all seemed to respond to its promise of salvation and the apostle Paul's egalitarian vision (Galatians 3:28): "There is neither Jew nor Greek, there is neither bond nor free, there is neither male nor female: for ye are all one in Christ Jesus." Female converts also found the Christian community to be a refuge from the anonymity and cruelty of Roman society; the church formed a secret underworld of close relationships among people drawn together by an ascetic but loving way of life. It offered power by allowing them to influence others by their faith; it widened their horizons through intimate contacts with spiritual leaders; it gave them new identities through foreign travel and involvement in a cause that was life sustaining; and, for those who chose lives of chastity, it could serve as a means of birth control and freedom from the constraints of marriage and family life.

Early Christian Literature

By the late second century, the status of the church had attracted the attention of leading Roman intellectuals, such as the philosopher Celsus and the physician Galen. Celsus ridiculed the Christian notion of the resurrection of the body and the new religion's appeal to women and slaves. On the other hand, Galen found merit in Christianity because of its philosophical approach to life and its emphasis on strict self-discipline (see Chapter 6).

In the second century, postbiblical Christian literature, generally unremarked by the secular world, took two forms. **Apologists,** vigorous, principled defenders of Christianity, offered arguments that Christians were loyal, dependable subjects of Rome; that Christianity and Judaism were different; and that living a Christian life in a pagan world was difficult, but possible. Theologians, for example Tertullian [tehr-TULL-yuhn] (about 160–230) and Origen [OHR-uh-juhn] of Alexandria (about 185–254), began to define basic Christian teachings, to create a distinctive Christian vocabulary, and to relate Christian thought to humanistic learning.

Tertullian's life and writings showed the uncompromising nature of Christianity. Trained in Stoic philosophy in Roman Carthage, Tertullian later converted to the new faith after he witnessed the serenity of Christians dying for their religion. The strength of his beliefs made him a spokesperson for North Africa, where a cult of martyrs made the area the "Bible belt" of the Roman world. Writing in Latin, he helped to shape the Western church's voice in that language. His diatribes against the pleasures of the theaters and arenas and his intense denunciation of women as sexual temptresses became legendary. In the severest terms, Tertullian rejected the Greco-Roman humanistic heritage, preferring the culture of Christianity.

Origen of Alexandria shared Tertullian's puritanical zeal, but he did not repudiate humanistic learning. In his mature writings, composed in Greek, Origen brought Christian thought into harmony with Platonism and Stoicism. Origen's Jesus was not the redeemer of the Gospels but the *logos* of Stoicism (see

SLICE OF LIFE
A Christian Mother Faces Death from Roman Authorities

VIBIA PERPETUA
A Martyr in the Early Christian Church

Vibia Perpetua, an educated young woman from a wealthy Carthaginian family and a convert to Christianity, defied an edict against proselytizing issued by the non-Christian emperor in 202. She was jailed and died in the arena of Carthage in 203. This excerpt is part of her personal account of her last days before martyrdom.

A few days later we were moved to a prison [in Carthage]. I was frightened, because I had never been in such a dark place. A sad day! The large number of prisoners made the place stifling. The soldiers tried to extort money from us. I was also tormented by worry for my child. Finally, Tertius and Pomponius, the blessed deacons responsible for taking care of us, bribed the guards to allow us a few hours in a better part of the prison to regain our strength. All the prisoners were released from the dungeon and allowed to

do as they wished. I gave suck to my starving child. . . . I was permitted to keep my child with me in prison. His strength came back quickly, which alleviated my pain and anguish. The prison was suddenly like a palace; I felt more comfortable there than anywhere else.

INTERPRETING THIS SLICE OF LIFE

1. *Why* was Vibia Perpetua being held captive by the Romans? 2. *Describe* the conditions of her imprisonment. 3. Since the Roman guards were eager for bribes, *what* does this reveal about their attitude toward Christians? 4. *How* does Vibia Perpetua's faith sustain her in prison? 5. *Compare and contrast* the religious conflict depicted here with religious conflicts in modern times. 6. *Compare and contrast* conditions of prisons and prisoners then and now.

Chapter 4). The *logos,* or reason, liberated the human soul so that it might move through different levels of reality to reach God. Origen's Platonism led him to reject the notion of the resurrection of the body as described in the Gospels and Paul's letters and to assert instead that the soul is eternal. Although some of Origen's ideas were later condemned, his philosophic writings, which were read secretly, helped free Christianity from its Jewish framework and appealed to intellectuals. Origen also initiated the allegorical method of reading the scriptures. Behind the plain words on the page, Origen taught, there were layers upon layers of deeper meaning.

Christian women writers in this earliest period were very rare, because intellectual discourse was dominated by men. Women did play important roles in the new faith—such as Mary Magdalene, who waited at Jesus's empty tomb, and Lydia and Priscilla, whom Paul met on his travels—but their voices are almost always heard indirectly. In their theoretical writings, men often addressed women's issues, such as Tertullian's "The Apparel of Women." Nevertheless, the voice of one Christian woman from this period has come down to us: that of Vibia Perpetua (about 181–203 CE) of Carthage in North Africa, one of the first female saints. An anonymous account of the Christian martyrs' struggles includes a verbatim reproduction of Perpetua's writings in prison. Filled with heartbreaking detail, the account describes her prison ordeal as she awaited death while nursing her child. The sen-

tence was imposed because she refused to renounce her faith (see Slice of Life).

Early Christian Art

Had Christians obeyed the Second Commandment, no Christian figurative art would have been produced. Indeed, the earliest Christian writers, including Tertullian and Origen, condemned the depiction of religious subjects as blasphemous. But pious Christians, attracted by the pull of humanism, commissioned frescoes for underground burial chambers and sculptures for their **sarcophagi,** or marble tombs. Christian painters and sculptors slowly fused their religious vision with the Greco-Roman tradition, a style that would dominate the art of the late empire. Religious values and themes were central to Western art for almost a thousand years, until the Italian Renaissance.

In imperial Rome, citizens had the legal right to bury their dead in catacombs (underground rooms) alongside the roads leading out of Rome (Figure 5.13). By the late second century, some of the tombs displayed Christian symbols and subjects. Some images were purely symbolic, for example, crosses, chi-rho's, evangelist symbols, and fish (*ichthus,* the Greek word for fish, makes an anagram interpreted as "Jesus Christ, Son of God, Savior") (Figure 5.14). In the Catacomb of Priscilla, a second- or third-century fresco depicts a shepherd as a symbol of Jesus (Figure 5.15). This

Figure 5.13 The Roman Catacombs: A Narrow Corridor with Niches for Burials. *Because of their belief in a bodily resurrection, proper burial loomed large in the minds of early Christians. Roman Christians joined with other citizens in burying their dead along subterranean passages underneath the city. In 400, when Christianity triumphed in Rome, the custom of catacomb burial ceased. Knowledge of the catacombs passed into oblivion until 1578, when they were rediscovered and became subjects of study and veneration.*

Figure 5.14 Symbolism and Early Christian Art. *Early Christians had some aversion to figural representations and used symbols, such as chi-rho and alpha-omega. Chi and rho are the first two letters of "Christ" in Greek. Alpha and omega are the first and last letters of the Greek alphabet, signifying God as the beginning and end. The evangelist symbols—man, lion, bull, and eagle—were derived from the book of Revelation; however, the four symbols have numerous antecedents, for example, in Assyrian iconography.*

Figure 5.15 Christ as the Good Shepherd. Second–third century CE. Fresco. Catacomb of Priscilla, Rome. *This fresco shows one of the popular religious symbols used by early Christians to disguise evidence of their faith from prying and perhaps hostile eyes. The "Good Shepherd" as an image of Jesus persisted in Christian art until the end of the fifth century.*

Figure 5.16 *Calf Bearer.* Ca. 570 BCE. Marble, ht. 65". Acropolis Museum, Athens. *This sixth-century BCE Greek statue shows a young man carrying a calf probably intended for a ritual sacrifice. The statue is executed in the kouros style, popular in the Archaic Age, as indicated by the frontality, stiffness, and stylized beard. The shepherd image later became associated with Jesus in the early Christian period.*

Figure 5.17 *Christian Good Shepherd.* Second century CE. Marble, ht. 39". Vatican Museum. *This graceful statue blends Greek influences with a Christian subject. The casual pose of the shepherd with his easy contrapposto and dreamy gaze shows that the influence of Praxiteles, the fourth-century BCE Greek sculptor, was still active after more than five centuries. The short cloak worn by the figure was a typical costume of shepherds in the art of the times.*

Figure 5.18 *Three Hebrews in the Fiery Furnace.* Chamber of the Velatio. Mid–third century CE. 19½ × 34″. Cemetery of Priscilla, Rome. *This catacomb painting of* Three Hebrews in the Fiery Furnace *illustrates the practice of early Christian artists drawing on Jewish stories to symbolize their beliefs. The rescue of the Hebrew youths, who refused to bow down to the golden image set up by the Babylonian king, becomes a symbol of Christian refusal to engage in worship of Rome's emperor. However, the Christian artist has changed the story so that, instead of being rescued by an angel, as recorded in Daniel 3:28, the Hebrews are promised salvation by means of a bird bearing leaves in its beak (above). This symbol probably derives from the Jewish story of Noah and the Flood, in which a dove with an olive leaf was a sign that the dry land had reappeared (Genesis 8:11)*

depiction, the most popular figural image in early Christian art, is based on the idea of Jesus as the shepherd of his flock of followers, an image derived from many biblical sources, including the Twenty-third Psalm: "The Lord is my shepherd." Holding a sheep across his shoulders with his right hand, the shepherd stands in the center of a circle, flanked by two sheep. This circle in turn is surrounded by eight panels with alternating depictions of orants (praying figures) and scenes from the life of the prophet Jonah.

Even though the shepherd and sheep convey a Christian message, the image adapts a familiar Greco-Roman theme—known in both art and literature—that identified such diverse figures as the philosopher Pythagoras and the Orphic cult leader Orpheus with shepherds. The pose of the youth carrying an animal on his shoulders appeared in Archaic Greek sculpture as early as the sixth century BCE (Figure 5.16). The painter of the Good Shepherd ceiling fresco portrays the shepherd as a beardless youth without distinctive, godlike traits (see Figure 5.15). A statue of a shepherd

from the second century attests to the widespread use of this image (Figure 5.17). By such representations as these, the artists in effect declared the limits of their art in penetrating the mystery of Jesus as both God and man.

Catacomb paintings were rich in images, however disguised, of Christian resurrection, salvation, and life after death. The Jewish Bible was a source of subjects for Christian artists, as can be seen in Figure 5.18, *Three Hebrews in the Fiery Furnace.* The youths, Shadrach, Meschach, and Abednego, were rescued from certain death by divine intervention and thus symbolize redemption (Daniel 3). In the painting, they are depicted impressionistically, floating in abstract space. Their feet are hidden in swirls of red paint, representing the fiery torment of the furnace. Their arms are upraised as if praying and constitute an additional symbol: the invocation of God's blessing. These images, found so often in Christian funerary art, attest to the saving power of their God.

The Legacy of Biblical Judaism and Early Christianity

The entire Jewish tradition has evolved from the early history of the Hebrews—their wandering without a homeland, their role as outsiders in other cultures, their brief period in control of the promised land of Canaan, and, above all, their deep and abiding sense of being the chosen people of the almighty God, Yahweh. Under the Romans, the Jews were punished for their religious views, a portent of the anti-Semitism and violent attacks that have dogged their existence down to the twenty-first century. Despite adversity, the Jews have survived and today have the longest continuous history of any group of people in Western civilization.

Unlike the Greco-Roman deities, who were seen as encouraging and supporting human achievement and excellence in many areas of life, the God of the Hebrews was primarily concerned with the ethical conduct of human beings and their obedience to his laws. Yahweh's jealousy extended to all forms of human expression insofar as they detracted from his worship. As a consequence, the arts and humanities, when allowed in Judaism, tended to be subordinated to religious concerns. Ultimately, Jewish culture found its voice in the ideals of the Bible, among the highest moral standards of any ancient people. The Jewish ethical vision, which even today drives Western reformers and revolutionaries, demanded social justice for every person, no matter how poor or powerless, within the human community.

Inheriting this conception of God and culture, the Christians reinterpreted it and gave it their distinctive stamp. After the fall of Rome, when Christianity emerged as the religion of the West, the Judeo-Christian tradition merged with the Greco-Roman heritage to form the basis of Western civilization. Following the teaching of Jesus, the early Christians perpetuated the Jewish emphasis on God's unity and omnipotence as well as the demands for stringently ethical behavior. Accordingly, Jesus's golden rule—to treat others as one would like to be treated—became the goal of devout Christians. The first Christians also laid great emphasis on taking care of the sick, the impoverished, and the homeless—a tradition that has given rise in Western civilization to a wide variety of private and public social relief programs.

The early Christians, rejecting the relatively closed nature of Judaism, turned their religion into a missionary faith; in the first generation of missionaries, Paul and other church leaders took Jesus's message to all people, addressing them as individuals regardless of their racial and ethnic backgrounds. Today, after two thousand years, nearly one-third of the world's population subscribes—at least nominally—to Christian beliefs.

Under the early Roman Empire, Christian thought also became a transnational, or international, belief system that expressed uncompromising hostility to Greco-Roman culture and to the Roman state. Those Christian writers who, like the author of the book of Revelation, described Rome as "the great whore" and forecast that city's destruction simply expressed the collective yearnings of the faithful in the early church. Under the onslaught of the Roman persecutions, the Christians anticipated a new order ruled by God's values. Thus, early Christians adopted Greco-Roman ideas not for their own sake but for their usefulness to the Christian religion.

The hostility of the early church to humanism and secular thought was but the opening assault in a running battle between two ways of looking at the world. For the moment, in imperial Rome humanism was triumphant among the people who counted—the aristocrats, the intellectuals, and the ruling class. But by the end of the fourth century, the balance had swung in favor of Christianity, and the non-Christian intellectuals were rapidly disappearing. This state of affairs prevailed until the Italian Renaissance; then, artists, writers, and intellectuals challenged the reigning Christian worldview by reviving humanistic learning and the Greco-Roman past. As the modern world has taken shape, Christianity has found itself assaulted from many sides and has never regained the preeminence that it held from the time of the fall of Rome to the coming of the Renaissance.

KEY CULTURAL TERMS

covenant	canon
monotheism	Gospels
Diaspora	evangelists
eschatology	theology
apocalypse	liturgy
Messiah	apologists
scripture	sarcophagi

QUESTIONS FOR CRITICAL THINKING

1. Discuss the major historical periods of Hebrew history, and note how each period influenced the evolution of Hebrew religion.

2. Identify the key beliefs of Judaism, and indicate the ones that were later integrated into the Western tradition.

3. Compare and contrast the stages and evolution of the Hebrew Bible and the Christian Bible, noting their various parts, subjects, and sources.

4. Compare and contrast Judaism and Christianity using the following terms: covenant, law, messiah, social justice, and canon.

5. Discuss early Christian art, its themes, symbols, and style. What was the relationship of Christian art to Greco-Roman art?

6 ROMAN IMPERIAL CIVILIZATION AND THE TRIUMPH OF CHRISTIANITY

A historian once said that the mystery of Rome's empire is not that it fell, but that it lasted so long. Indeed, Rome acquired its first provinces in 241 BCE and the empire continued expanding until 117 CE. The Roman Republic collapsed amid civil wars but the Augustan Principate ushered in the *Pax Romana,* two centuries of good rule and great prosperity. In the third century, the Roman Empire plunged into crisis only to be revived and reformed by two remarkable rulers, Diocletian and Constantine. Their reforms eventually had different outcomes in the eastern and western halves of the empire. By the end of the fifth century the western empire had vanished, replaced by several barbarian kingdoms. The eastern empire commenced a long evolution that would result in a new regime called "Byzantine," which lasted for another millennium.

Rome's institutional transformations are only one part of the story of Roman imperial civilization. Beginning in the era of Augustus Caesar, Rome emerged from the Hellenistic world with a distinctive culture of its own—albeit Rome's debts to all the cultures that had preceded it were immense. In the Golden and Silver Ages, Rome produced a brilliant Latin literature. In the later imperial period, a triumphant Christianity developed a literature of its own in genres ranging from history to theology to poetry. Roman architecture came into its own, and the Christian church adapted Roman buildings for its own uses. Roman sculpture attained its highpoint of development, and then Christians accommodated Roman styles to new subject matter. In every area of life, the Roman Empire was dynamic and productive. Forces of continuity and change were in constant tension. And yet, the Roman world in 500 CE would have been barely recognizable to Augustus and his contemporaries.

◀ **Detail** Colossal Statue of Constantine. Ca. 313. Marble. Palazzo dei Conservatori, Rome.

Timeline 6.1   THE ROMAN EMPIRE FROM AUGUSTUS TO JUSTINIAN, 31 BCE–565 CE

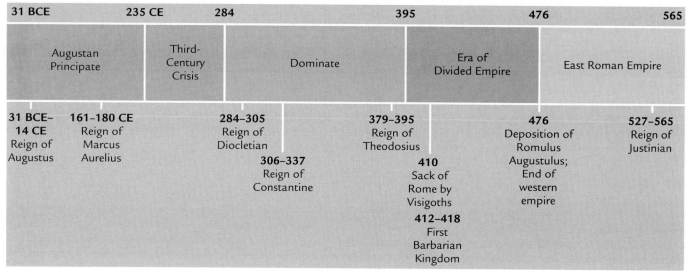

31 BCE	235 CE	284	395	476	565
Augustan Principate	Third-Century Crisis	Dominate	Era of Divided Empire	East Roman Empire	

| 31 BCE–14 CE Reign of Augustus | 161–180 CE Reign of Marcus Aurelius | 284–305 Reign of Diocletian 306–337 Reign of Constantine | 379–395 Reign of Theodosius 410 Sack of Rome by Visigoths 412–418 First Barbarian Kingdom | 476 Deposition of Romulus Augustulus; End of western empire | 527–565 Reign of Justinian |

THE AUGUSTAN PRINCIPATE

The reign of Augustus Caesar (r. 31 BCE–14 CE) inaugurated a new phase of Roman history. The regime itself, called the **principate** [PRIN-chuh-pate] (from *princeps*, "first citizen"), lasted until the death of Marcus Aurelius in 180 CE. These two centuries were marked by institutional stability, imperial expansion and then consolidation, and widespread prosperity.

The Principate

After a century of civil war, it was the genius of Augustus that brought order out of chaos. The senate voted him virtually all power in the state, which he used with discretion. He was content to be hailed as princeps, first citizen. He sometimes held one of the republican magistracies (consul, praetor), but usually let others hold them; this satisfied ambitious individuals and created the impression that power was shared. Augustus permitted the senate to control many provinces, but he retained the militarily threatened and economically prosperous ones (especially Egypt) in his own hands. Above all, he controlled the military; he was the *imperator*, the commander, hence the emperor. In truth, the principate was a thinly disguised military dictatorship, but Augustus made it look like a largely civilian regime with military backing.

For two centuries the principate worked remarkably well. Some emperors were gifted while others were feckless and foolish. The senate was at once prestigious and powerless. The emperors effected a working compromise with the urban elites of the empire. These

people—the Herods of Judea (see Chapter 5)—are a good example: they went Roman not because of coercion but because it was in their interest to do so. Rome propped them up and they served Roman interests. The entire empire was governed by a few hundred aristocratic amateurs who served brief tenures as provincial governors. Rome required little from people: peace, good order, and taxes.

The Pax Romana

Augustus and his successors down to Trajan [TRAY-jun] (r. 98–117) basically rounded off the conquests of the late republic and ushered in the **Pax Romana,** the Roman Peace, an age of public order and military stability. They added Britain while establishing the Rhine and Danube rivers as the frontiers in the west, the northern edge of the Sahara Desert in the south, and Mesopotamia in the east. Rome briefly pushed north of the Danube into Dacia (Map 6.1; see Encounter). It is important to remember that "Roman Peace" is how the Romans looked at things. Those millions of people did not ask to be conquered. The wily historian Tacitus (discussed later in the chapter) said the Romans "made a vast desert and called it peace."

The world-historical significance of the Pax Romana may be grasped by thinking of it as the Hellenistic world with several key differences. Geographically, Rome's empire extended vastly farther to the west but somewhat less far to the east. The Hellenistic world was, however, a congeries of political entities whereas the Roman Empire was one. The Hellenistic world was prosperous but unevenly so. All evidence suggests

Roman Empire by death of Augustus, 14 AD

Roman territory added by death of Hadrian, 138 AD

Map 6.1   THE ROMAN EMPIRE IN THE TIME OF HADRIAN (117–138)
This map presents the Roman Empire at its greatest territorial extent. Compare this map
to Map 4.2: 1. *Where* had the Roman Empire expanded after Augustus? 2. *What* major
cultural zones can you identify within this empire? 3. *What* major strategic problems did
this empire present?

that the Roman Empire was more prosperous and
more widely so. Hellenistic culture was fundamentally Greek; indeed, even Roman Republican culture
was Greek at its roots. Imperial culture added Latin
as an essential component. The Romans added urban
amenities—aqueducts, baths, theaters—wherever they
went (Figure 6.1). This "rhetoric in stone," as it has been
called, was powerfully alluring to provincial populations. The ease with which Christianity spread and
communicated is one excellent gauge of the effective-
ness of the Pax Romana.

THE CRISIS OF THE
THIRD CENTURY

Between 235 and 284, Rome had twenty-two emperors. Many reigns lasted only a year or two, and few
emperors died a natural death. The military side of

the principate had completely trumped the civilian
side. Civil war was endemic, with one military commander after another trying to get his troops to back
his claim on the imperial office.

Institutional chaos could not have come at a worse
moment. For the first time, Rome faced threats along
multiple frontiers simultaneously. A revived Persian
Empire threatened Mesopotamia. Germanic peoples
pressed hard against the Rhine and Danube. And Berber tribesmen raided the North African frontier.

The economy was in shambles. Inflation was rampant and the government's usual response was to
debase the currency—to reduce the amount of pure
silver and gold in coins. Disparities between rich and
poor were growing greater by the year. The uncertainty of the military situation led farmers to flee from
exposed, but fertile, territories.

There was a spiritual and cultural crisis too. The
government lashed out against Christians as never

ENCOUNTER

Roman Conquests and Romance Languages

As the Romans expanded their empire, they encountered the Dacians and other peoples, making them part of the Roman world. Over time, political, commercial, and military needs led to the creation of hybrid languages that blended Latin with native tongues. Thus, in the sounds, words, and syntax of these new hybrid languages, the legacy of ancient peoples survives in the world today.

The Romans of the early empire, envisaging Cicero's call for "imperial glory," began to conquer neighboring peoples who threatened the Roman way of life. A superb example of this policy was Trajan's wars (101, 105–106 CE) against the Dacians, a people living in a territory roughly equivalent to modern Romania. With their strong, loyal tribal system and distinctive advanced material culture based on iron products and weapons, the Dacians refused to succumb to the Romans. Succeeding where other emperors had failed, Trajan conquered the Dacians and colonized the region, bringing in merchants, traders, and government officials.

The Romans, in varying degrees of success, followed their usual patterns of colonization in Dacia, transforming villages into provincial towns, constructing villas or country estates, and settling their veterans in the civic centers and rural areas. The colonizers set examples of the Roman way of life for the local populations, persuaded the tribal leaders to adopt Roman dress and other habits, encouraged them to finance and build amphitheaters, and made Latin the official language.

Among the Dacians, a new language soon emerged, based on Latin but different from the Latin spoken by the invaders. The new tongue was a mingling of the local languages with the Latin spoken by the common Roman citizen—known as the vulgar, or ordinary, tongue—as opposed to the classical Latin used in official documents and writings. However, when the Western Roman Empire disintegrated, this new language lost its links to Rome and gradually evolved to become what is known as Romanian.

Romanian belongs to the Romance language family, which includes French, Spanish, Italian, Catalan, and Portuguese. These languages, though separate, share some vocabulary and grammar. As Europeans contacted and conquered many parts of the globe, the Romance languages spread so that today nearly 400 million people speak a Romance language. Romanian, which had it origins under Trajan, is still spoken by about 23 million inhabitants in Romania and by 2.5 million in Russia plus a half million others scattered across the Balkans and southeastern Europe.

LEARNING FROM THE ENCOUNTER

1. *Why* did the Romans initially have difficulty in conquering the Dacians? 2. *Describe* the Roman pattern of colonizing newly conquered territories. 3. *What* were the basic characteristics of the new language? 4. *How* has American English been transformed by the introduction of other languages? 5. *Which* languages seem to have been the most influential on American English?

Encounter figure 6.1   Rome's War Against Dacia (modern Romania). *Trajan's victory over the Dacians was represented in Trajan's Column, which stands in the ruins of Trajan's forum in Rome. The continuous frieze narrates Trajan's two campaigns against the Dacians. The bottom scenes depict the Dacians attacking a Roman fort (left), the Dacians crossing the Danube (center), and the Romans ferrying troops over the Danube (right); the top scene shows the Romans attacking Dacian supply wagons.*

Figure 6.1 Timgad, Algeria. Ca. 100 CE. *Timgad, strategically located at the intersection of six Roman roads in North Africa, was typical of the towns built from scratch by the Romans during the Pax Romana and populated by ex-soldiers and their families. The town was planned as a square with two main avenues crossing in the middle where the forum stood and all other streets intersecting at right angles. The so-called Arch of Trajan in the foreground marked one of the main thoroughfares, which was lined with columns. Temples, baths, fountains, markets, a theater, and private homes gave the city the reputation of being a pleasant place to live.*

before, casting about for scapegoats. The literature of the age, and there is not much of it, is grim and pessimistic. Almost no major buildings were built. Despair reigned.

THE REFORMS OF DIOCLETIAN AND CONSTANTINE

During more than fifty years of rule, Diocletian (284–305) and Constantine (306–337) completely transformed the Roman state. They responded to the central issues in the third-century crisis and laid the foundation on which the late Roman Empire stood.

To address the irregularity in the imperial succession, Diocletian instituted the **tetrarchy,** or the rule by four (Figure 6.2). The empire was divided into two halves, east and west. Each half of the empire was to be ruled by an Augustus with a subordinate Caesar. The senior Augustus was to have ultimate authority, and the Caesars were to gain experience and then succeed the Augustuses. Constantine, however, shared rule with three of his sons, and for the rest of Roman history the tetrarchal and dynastic systems coexisted. Diocletian and Constantine also created an elaborate administrative hierarchy in the empire with four prefectures, fourteen dioceses, and more than one hundred provinces. The number of imperial officials

Figure 6.2 *Diocletian's Tetrarchy. Ca. 300. Porphyry, approx. 51". St. Mark's cathedral, Venice. In this group portrait of the tetrarchs, the four rulers—two Augustuses, or leaders, joined by their two Caesars, or successors—stand clasping shoulders to signify their unity and loyalty. By this time, the political leaders were no longer wearing imperial togas, as can be seen in the figures' cloaks, tunics, and hats; but the eagle-headed swords and decorated scabbards show that fine workmanship in armor was still practiced in late Rome. Despite the solidarity suggested by the sculpture, the tetrarchy was not a successful reform of the imperial administration.*

Diocletian and Constantine, and their successors, abandoned the idea of the principate. The regime they inaugurated is called the **dominate,** from *dominus* ("lord and master"). The emperors increasingly adopted Persian and Hellenistic customs such as sprinkling gold dust in their hair, appearing infrequently in public, and requiring people to bow before them. These rulers unquestionably enhanced the power and prestige of the imperial office, but they did so at a cost: there was no longer any pretense that the emperor was a magistrate who ruled with the consent of the people and senate.

The two reformers treated Christianity very differently. In 303, Diocletian launched the last and greatest persecution of Christianity. At Milan in 313, Constantine issued an edict that made Christianity a legal faith, on a par with all other faiths. Near the end of his life, Constantine openly embraced the new faith. During his reign, however, he conferred privileges on the church, for example, freeing the clergy from military service and some taxes. In addition, he facilitated the construction of three major Christian churches in Rome: the Lateran Basilica, St. Peter's, and St. Paul's outside the Walls.

THE LATER ROMAN EMPIRE IN WEST AND EAST

The western empire eventually vanished while the eastern empire regrouped and reformed once again. Except for a few years in the 390s, the Roman Empire was never again ruled by a single emperor. The western court was occasionally at Rome but more often at Milan, Arles, Trier, or Ravenna. The eastern court was always at Constantinople. The courts were often fierce rivals.

The End of the Western Empire

Although the western empire in the later imperial period, usually called "late antiquity" today, generally had less effective leadership than the East, the West's great challenge came from the barbarians. Who were these people and how did Rome try to deal with them?

Barbarians is a catch-all term for a host of Germanic peoples–so called because they spoke Germanic languages—who lived beyond the Rhine and Danube frontiers. The barbarian peoples were not coherent ethnic groups but, instead, loose confederations. Through diplomacy, war, and commerce, the Romans had dealt with these peoples for centuries. Contemporaries called them Franks, Lombards, Goths, Vandals, and other names, but each group was a loose band of different peoples organized under a leader usually

rose from a few hundred to tens of thousands. Both emperors substantially increased the size of the Roman army. Constantine developed flexible mobile field armies stationed near cities behind the frontiers to meet threats more effectively. Both emperors also took steps to get control of spiraling prices and to stabilize the currency. Constantine, finally, created a new capital for the East. He chose the old Greek colony of Byzantium, which he renamed for himself, Constantinople ("Constantine's polis"). Across the fourth century, emperors built Constantinople into the greatest city in the empire, more important even than Rome, although Rome kept much of its historical and psychological significance (Map 6.2).

LEARNING THROUGH MAPS

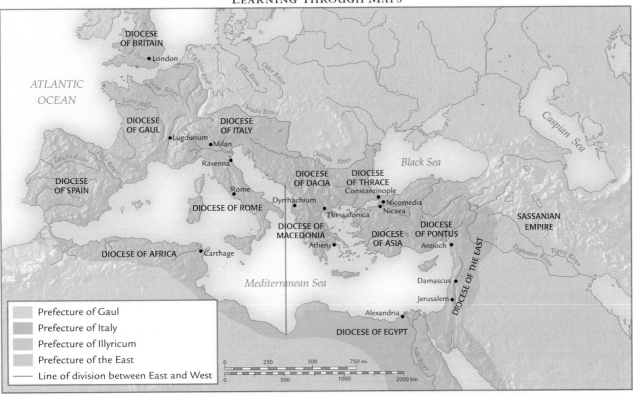

Map 6.2   THE ROMAN EMPIRE IN THE FOURTH CENTURY
This map shows the Roman Empire after the reforms of Diocletian and Constantine.
1. *Notice* the role of rivers and bodies of water in determining the empire's frontiers.
2. *What* was the impact of geography on establishing the pattern of governmental dioceses? 3. *Notice* also the dividing line between the eastern and western halves of the empire. 4. *Compare* the location of the Hellenistic kingdoms in Map 4.1, the Hellenistic World, with the location of the same regions in this map.

called a king. In 300 CE all of these peoples were outside Rome's frontiers, but by 500 several of them had secured kingdoms inside the former western provinces. There was never a single, coordinated movement that can be called "the barbarian invasions." Some people did indeed invade the empire, but most were settled by the Romans themselves inside the empire. One historian spoke of "an imaginative experiment that got a little out of hand."

Beginning with Constantine, emperors often made treaties with barbarian groups. Usually the aim was to have these federates (from *foedus*, "treaty") defend a section of the frontier. Building on this model, the Romans assigned some barbarians lands inside the empire and allotted them specific tasks—policing brigands, defending frontiers, guarding coastlines, administering territory. The Visigoths, as an example, crossed the Danube in 376, defeated a Roman army in 378, and threatened Italy for a generation in a complex game aimed at securing them official recognition. They actually sacked Rome in 410 and, in the end, received most

of southern Gaul. Later, the Ostrogoths held Italy under nominal Roman authority. The Vandals, on the contrary, forcibly seized North Africa. The system worked reasonably well for a time. A coalition of barbarians in Gaul serving under a Roman general defeated the invading Huns in 451. By the middle of the fifth century, however, the western government lost virtually all of its territory and tax revenues. By 476, the traditional date for Rome's "fall," the western empire had no meaningful authority and a barbarian general sent the imperial insignia to Constantinople, saying that there was no longer any need for an emperor in the West. The key point is that the western empire gradually shifted from provinces to kingdoms in a process which, for a long time, the Romans thought they controlled (Map 6.3).

The Eastern Empire

Ruling from Constantinople, the eastern emperors had two fundamental objectives: to defend the empire's

Map 6.3   THE ROMAN WEST CA. 500

This map represents the former western provinces of the Roman Empire after the end of direct imperial authority. Compare this map to Map 6.2: 1. *What* had changed? Had anything remained the same?

Figure 6.3   The Theodosian Walls. *During the reign of Theodosius II (408–450), massive brick and masonry walls were erected across the landward side of the peninsula at whose end Constantinople is sited. Outside the walls there was a complex network of moats and ditches. The city withstood all attacks until western crusaders took it in 1204.*

SLICE OF LIFE
A Roman Delegate at a Barbarian Banquet

PRISCUS

In the fifth century, the Roman world was ravaged by Attila the Hun, the barbarian king who ruled a vast state in central and southeastern Europe (r. 434–453). Demanding tribute and holding prisoners for ransom, Attila and his fierce army invaded the Balkans and Greece in the east, and Italy and Gaul in the west. In 448, Theodosius II (r. 408–450), the Eastern Roman emperor, sent ambassadors to Attila's court to address certain issues, such as subsidies. The Greek historian Priscus (fl. 450–475), who was part of the Roman delegation, gives an eyewitness account of a banquet meeting.

When [three o'clock] arrived [Maximin, the head ambassador and I] went to the palace. . . . [A]ll the chairs were ranged along the walls of the room. . . . Attila sat in the middle on a couch; a second couch was set behind him, and from it steps led up to his bed, which was covered with linen sheets and wrought coverlets for ornament. . . . The places on the right of Attila were held chief in honour, those on the left, where we sat, were only second. . . . [A] cup-bearer . . . handed Attila a wooden cup of wine. He took it, and saluted the first in precedence, who . . . stood up, and might not sit down until the king, having tasted or drained the wine, returned the cup to the attendant. All the guests then honoured Attila in the same way. . . . [T]ables, large enough for three or four . . . were [then] placed next [to] the table of Attila. . . . A luxurious meal, served [by attendants] on silver plates, had been made

ready for us . . . but Attila ate nothing but meat on a wooden trencher. In everything else, too, he showed himself temperate; his cup was of wood, while to the guests were given goblets of gold and silver. His dress, too, was quite simple, affecting only to be clean. The sword he carried at his side, the latchets of his . . . shoes, the bridle of his horse were not adorned, like those of the other[s] . . . with gold or gems or anything costly. . . . When evening fell torches were lit, and two barbarians coming forward in front of Attila sang songs they had composed, celebrating his victories and deeds of valour in war. When the night had advanced we retired . . . , not wishing to assist further at the potations [drinks].

INTERPRETING THIS SLICE OF LIFE

1. *Why* was Priscus able to observe Attila the Hun in such an intimate setting? 2. *Describe* the seating arrangement at the banquet. 3. *Why* do Attila's personal dress and accessories differ from those of the other barbarians? 4. *Is* there any evidence in this account of Attila's taste for personal luxury? 5. Contemporaries of Priscus greatly feared Attila the Hun, giving him the nickname "the Scourge of God," because of the savagery of his military campaigns. 6. That being the case, *how* do you account for Priscus's rather different picture of the barbarian king? 7. Do you *detect* any cultural bias in Priscus's account? *Explain.*

Balkan and Mesopotamian frontiers; and to ensure tax revenues and food supplies. The Balkans were threatened by barbarian peoples and by Slavs, whereas Mesopotamia stood face-to-face with a revived Persia. Constantinople was primarily provisioned by Egypt, so controlling that province was critical. A stunning symbol of the East's resolve and resources is the vast set of landward walls built by Theodosius II (408–450) to protect Constantinople (Figure 6.3).

Most of Rome's eastern rulers were hardened military men. In Justinian (527–565) the greatest of them took the throne. Called "the emperor who never sleeps," Justinian launched a series of wars to recover Rome's former western provinces. His generals recaptured North Africa and Italy and took a strip of land on Spain's Mediterranean coast. Justinian substantially revised the imperial administration, jettisoning the traditional split between military and civilian control in favor of a system that placed most authority in mili-

tary hands. He also issued the definitive codification of Roman law, the *Corpus Iuris Civilis* (529–532) and built the vast and magnificent church of Hagia Sophia (Figure 6.4).

By the middle of the sixth century, the western half of the Roman Empire was gone forever but the eastern half appeared to be a going concern. As the Byzantine Empire, the Roman east survived for a millennium, although it would experience several major transformations of its own over the years. The slowly transforming western empire provided a stable framework for the emergence of the successor kingdoms, and the eastern empire remained a bulwark of Hellenistic and of Greco-Roman civilization for centuries. East or West, however, the Roman Empire from Augustus to Justinian knit together the peoples and cultures of the ancient world, gave definitive shape to a new late antique culture, and transmitted that culture to the Middle Ages.

Figure 6.4 ISIDORE OF MILETUS AND ANTHEMIUS OF TRALLES. Hagia Sophia, Exterior. 532–537. 270' long × 240' wide, ht. of dome 180'. Istanbul. *The Byzantine emperors transformed their capital into a glittering metropolis that easily outshone ravaged Rome. The most magnificent building in the city was Hagia Sophia ("Holy Wisdom"), originally built by Justinian as a church. The building's 101-foot-diameter dome makes it the largest domical structure in the world. Two half-domes at either end double the interior length to more than 200 feet. The beauty of Hagia Sophia made the domed church the ideal of Byzantine architecture.*

THE TRIUMPH OF CHRISTIANITY

The Roman administration persecuted, then tolerated, and finally supported both the Christian faith and the church. The most influential bequest of the Roman Empire to the subsequent history of Western civilization was Christianity and the Catholic Church.

The Growth of the Catholic Church

After Constantine granted toleration to Christianity in 313, the church could function as a legal, public institution with leaders and structures of its own. As an institution, the church developed an empire-wide structure that no pagan religion had ever possessed. In virtually every significant city of the empire, the Christian bishop became a prominent local figure, partly a function of his growing social prominence. For a long time bishops were men of obscure or middling status, but by the fifth century it was common for them to have aristocratic backgrounds. As Christians gradually became the majority of the population in all towns and increasingly in the countryside too, bishops came to have influence over and responsibility for more and more people. Bishops looked out for the poor, and for widows and orphans, and in some cities they had thousands of people on their charity rolls. Bishops intervened in legal disputes between citizens and interceded with the state for Christians caught in the web of judicial conflict. Especially in the West, where the imperial regime was slowly disappearing, they looked after urban amenities and tended to the food supply. On numerous occasions, bishops assembled from throughout the empire in councils to debate points of theology and to settle matters of daily religious practice.

Among all the bishops, the bishops of Rome gradually achieved a leading position. In Rome, the bishops, called popes, based their claims to authority on two key ideas. First of all, they believed, Christ has uniquely assigned leadership among the apostles to Peter. Second, Christian communities everywhere tried to trace their origins to one of the apostles in order to claim an authentic tradition of teaching and authority. **Apostolic succession,** the idea that the authority of the apostles descended to their successors, was in Rome coupled with the **Petrine Idea,** the doctrine that special authority fell to Peter's successor. Peter died as bishop of Rome, so it was believed that Peter's successors continued to possess authority over the church. Leo I (pope, 440–461) was the greatest exponent of the idea of Roman leadership in the church.

The root meaning of *catholic* is universal. In 325 the bishops gathered at Nicaea to define a creed, an authoritative and uniform statement of belief. With minor modifications that creed is still recited in many Christian churches to this day. The need for a creedal statement arose because of the teaching of an Alexandrian priest, Arius (about 250–336). Arius taught that Jesus Christ was not "one in being with the Father" as the creed still has it and, to preserve strict monotheism, that "there was when he [Christ] was not." The larger problem was that Christians were arguing over how God could be a Trinity, three persons—Father, Son, and Holy Spirit—in one. Arius's teachings were widely accepted, including by a Gothic priest, Ulfilas (310–383), who converted many barbarians to Arian Christianity.

In the fifth century, another ferocious quarrel arose over how to explain that Jesus Christ was true God and true man, as Catholic Christianity taught. Monophysites (literally, one-nature-ites) held that Christ was fundamentally divine. Arianism and Monophysitism were the most significant **heresies** of antiquity, beliefs chosen by large numbers of people despite official condemnation.

Christian Monasticism

A fascinating and durable achievement of late antique Christianity was monasticism. There was always a tension in Christianity between those who wished to flee the world and those who wished to change it. Some Christians after 313 felt life had become too pleasurable. Whatever their motivations, in the fourth century, first in Egypt and then everywhere, thousands of men and women abandoned city, family, jobs, sex, food—indeed, all life's pleasures—to join monasteries.

Anthony of Egypt (251–356) came from a wealthy, Christian family. Around 270 he gave up all he had and went into the desert to live as a solitary, to pray, and to discipline his bodily desires. Gradually he attracted followers who wanted to learn from his austere way of life. Somewhat later, Pachomius (292–348) also went into the desert. A convert to Christianity and a former soldier, he too attracted followers. Unlike Anthony, however, Pachomius organized his followers into communities that ate, worked, and prayed together. Such communities were called monasteries where, ironically, groups of men or women lived alone together. The leaders of such communities were called abbots or abbesses.

Christianity and the Roman State

Relations between the Roman state and the Catholic Church were complex. On the one hand, emperors conferred many privileges upon the church. They passed laws effectively outlawing paganism and demanding that all Christians have the same beliefs as the bishop of Rome. On the other hand, emperors meddled in the selection of bishops and intervened in the increasingly bitter doctrinal quarrels that cropped up among rival Christian groups. At the end of the fifth century, Emperor Anastasius I (r. 491–518) issued a decree to settle a doctrinal quarrel. Gelasius I [juh-LAY-zee-us] (pope, 492–496) wrote him a letter saying that emperors had *power* whereas priests had *authority*. These words had powerful resonance in Latin language and Roman culture. Gelasius argued that the authority of priests was superior to the power of emperors because priests were concerned with immortal souls but emperors only with mortal bodies. What-

ever his authority, Gelasius did not have the power to coerce the emperor. But Leo I within the church and Gelasius within the Roman Empire had made claims that would echo down through the centuries.

ROMAN IMPERIAL CIVILIZATION

The Roman world produced magnificent literature, attractive philosophies, impressive architecture, glorious sculpture, a durable legal culture, medical and scientific writings of immense influence, and both music and music theory that were long influential. Distinctively, Roman writing was in Latin, but Greek made important contributions too. The most original aspect of imperial culture was the emergence of the arts of Christianity.

Secular Latin Literature

The reign of Augustus is considered the Golden Age of Roman letters. This period's three greatest poets, Virgil, Horace, and Ovid, captured the age's euphoric mood as peace and stability once more returned to Rome. Of the three writers, Virgil best represented the times through his vision of Rome and his stirring verses. In prose, Livy (59 BCE–17 CE) captured the spirit of the age.

The works of Virgil [VUR-jill] (70–19 BCE), a modestly born Italian from Mantua, were inspired by Greek literary forms—idylls (or vignettes), didactic (instructive) poems, and epics—yet his use of native themes and his focus on the best traits in the Roman people give an authentic Roman voice to his work. Deeply moved by Augustus's reforms, he put his art in the service of the state. Virgil's pastoral poetry, the *Eclogues* and *Georgics,* celebrated rural life and urged readers to seek harmony with nature in order to find peace—advice that became a significant moral theme of the Western heritage. But Virgil is best known for the *Aeneid,* an epic poem in twelve books that he wrote in imitation of Homer. In this work, infused with Roman values and ideals (see Chapter 4), Virgil gave full voice to his love of country, his respect for Augustus, and his faith in Rome's destiny.

The *Aeneid* tells of Aeneas, the legendary Trojan hero who wandered the Mediterranean before founding Rome. In the first six books, Virgil models his tale on the *Odyssey,* writing of travel and love. The second half is modeled on the *Iliad,* stressing fighting and intrigue. The *Aeneid* became Rome's bible and its literary masterpiece. Children were often required to memorize passages from the poem to instill in them the values that had made Rome great. Aeneas served as the prototype of the faithful leader who would not be diverted from his destined path. The work's rich language led later poets to mine the *Aeneid* for expressions and images. As Homer inspired Virgil, so Virgil became the model for Western poets.

The second major poet of the Golden Age was Horace (65–8 BCE), another humble Italian who welcomed Augustus as Rome's savior and offered patriotic sentiments in his verses. His poems, which were written to be read aloud, use Alexandrian forms such as odes and letters in verse. A master and even innovator with poetic forms, Horace was playful and creative with language. He helped to create a new poetic genre, the **satire,** which rebuked the manners of the age. Horace was at his best in addressing the heartbreaking brevity of life: "what has been, has been, and I have had my hour."

Ovid [AHV-uhd] (43 BCE–about 17 CE), the third voice of the Golden Age, was a wealthy Italian who did not devote his verses to patriotic themes or pay lip service to conventional morality. Ovid's love poems speak of the purely sensual and fleeting quality of sex and ignore the enduring value of committed love. His *Art of Love* offers advice, in a manner bordering on the scientific, on how to seduce women. Such advice contrasted with Virgil's and Horace's attempts to raise the moral level of the Romans. And the austere Augustus exiled Ovid.

Ovid's masterpiece was the *Metamorphoses,* or *Transformations.* Somewhat irreverently, he breathed new life into more than two hundred Greek and Roman myths and legends that centered on the transformation of people into other forms. This work is the source of our knowledge of many classical myths, and medieval and Renaissance poets turned to it continually for inspiration.

A fourth writer, the historian Livy (59 BCE–17 CE), also embodied the spirit of the times. He wrote a massive history of Rome in 142 books of which only 35 survive, basically telling in prose the story Virgil told in verse. But where Virgil ended with the age of Aeneas, Livy came down to his own times; albeit all the contemporary material has disappeared. An accomplished Latin stylist, Livy tells stories about Rome's real or legendary heroes to instruct his contemporaries about proper beliefs and conduct.

The literary period from the death of Augustus to the end of the second century is called the Silver Age. In this period, the patriotic style of the previous era was replaced by the critical views of writers who often satirized Roman society and the state. Lacking the originality of the Golden Age, the writers of this era looked to their predecessors for models while they polished their phrases and reworked earlier themes.

This shift in literary taste reflected a new educational ideal, which stressed skills in debate and oratory. As a result, moral considerations became secondary to aesthetic effects, with writers using rhetorical flourishes and exaggerated literary conceits.

An outstanding Silver Age talent was Seneca [SEN-e-kuh] (4 BCE–65 CE). Born into a wealthy family in Spain, Seneca became a powerful senator and one of the age's chief thinkers. He is best remembered as a dramatist, though his works failed to measure up to the Greek heritage. His ten extant plays relied on emotionalism, rhetorical excess, and stage violence—the perennial traits of Roman tragedy. After his day, the staging of tragedies ceased, not to be revived for more than fifteen hundred years.

The Silver Age produced a great Latin poet, Juvenal [JOO-vuh-nall] (about 60–140 CE), who trained his censorious gaze on the follies of the empire. Juvenal expressed his outraged observations in sixteen satires, the literary form originated by Horace and others. The voice that speaks in Juvenal's satires is embittered, perhaps a reflection of his obscure social origins. But the carefully crafted language—obscene, bilious, and evocative but always just right—made him the master of this genre in Rome, if not in world letters.

The leading historian of the Silver Age was Tacitus [TASS-uh-tus] (about 55–117 CE), famed also as an orator and politician. Like the greatest of Greek historians, Tacitus was a superb stylist, wrote about his own times, and stressed human responsibility. But the values he stressed, and often found lacking, were wholly Roman. Tacitus acquired his knowledge of statecraft as the governor of the province of Asia (present-day southwestern Turkey). Among his works are two that have earned him the front rank among Roman historians. The *Annals* focus on the rulers after the death of Augustus in 14 CE until the murder of Nero in 68. The *Histories* then pick up the story of Rome and carry it through 96, when the tyrannical Domitian was assassinated. A master of the Latin language, Tacitus had a flair for dramatic narrative. Like other Roman historians, he wrote history with a moral purpose, but his critical spirit set him apart from those who had nothing but glowing praise for Rome. Tacitus's perspective was that of a proud senator who could not conceal his distaste for Rome's loss of political freedom. He concluded that tyranny was an innate flaw in the imperial system.

Philosophy

Although Stoicism was introduced to Rome by Greek philosophers in the late republic, its greatest influence was achieved later, through the writings and teaching of Seneca, Epictetus, and the emperor Marcus Aurelius. Seneca's fame as a philosopher rests on his *Letters on Morality.* These letters, which were usually written in response to pressing ethical problems, are filled with good advice, even though they break no new philosophical ground. In one letter, for example, Seneca counseled a grieving acquaintance to maintain dignity and inner strength in the face of a loved one's death.

Epictetus [ep-ik-TEET-uhs] (about 55–115 CE) not only preached but also lived his Stoic creed. According to tradition, Epictetus, though a slave in Rome, won his freedom because of his teachings. He subsequently founded a school in Asia Minor and attracted enthusiastic converts. He did not write anything, but Arrian, a pupil, composed the *Discourses* and the *Handbook,* both in Greek, which together preserved the essence of his master's ideas. Epictetus's philosophy reflected his own victory over personal misfortune. He advised patience in the face of trouble, indifference to material things, and acceptance of one's destiny. Although these ideas represented a rehash of basic Stoic beliefs, his moral wholeness gave them a special appeal.

Stoicism's finest hour arrived in 161 CE when Marcus Aurelius (Figure 6.5) became emperor. Converted to Stoicism in his youth, the emperor wrote an account (in Greek) of his daily musings—called *Meditations*—while he was engaged in almost continuous warfare against barbarian invaders. His journal came to light after his death and was soon recognized as a masterpiece of Stoicism. Like all Stoics, Marcus Aurelius admonished himself to play with dignity the role that providence had assigned: if a divine plan guides the universe, then he must accept it; if, however, the world is ruled by chance, then a well-regulated mind is the best defense. Such reasoning enabled him to avoid moral confusion. His death in 180 signaled the end of ancient Stoicism.

Some Roman thinkers adopted Stoicism in either its Greek or Latin manifestations; others were interested in blending the various Greek schools—Platonic, Aristotelian, and Stoic, among others—into a philosophic synthesis. The outstanding example of this latter trend was **Neoplatonism,** a school of thought founded primarily by Plotinus [plo-TIE-nuhs] (205–270). Neoplatonism was the last major school of philosophy in the ancient world. The movement began as an attempt to correct the problem at the heart of Plato's system—the seemingly irreconcilable split between the absolute world of Ideas and the perishable material world. This Platonic dualism could and did lead to the notion that the everyday world has little purpose in the overall scheme of things. Plotinus now succeeded in bridg-

Figure 6.5 *Marcus Aurelius.* Ca. 173 CE. Bronze, ht. 16′8″. Piazza del Campidoglio, Rome. *The unknown artist has represented Marcus Aurelius as a warrior-emperor, but the militaristic image is offset somewhat by the Stoic ruler's face. Here we see revealed a human being lost in thought and far removed from pomp and power. This magnificent equestrian statue marked the climax of sculpture in the Roman Empire. In the eighteenth and nineteenth centuries, sculptors would copy this statue's militaristic image to glorify European rulers.*

ing the two worlds with his theories, and his writings later influenced Christian thinkers in the Middle Ages and the Italian humanists of the Renaissance.

Plotinus resolved Platonic dualism not with logical analysis but with mystical insight, claiming that the union of the physical and spiritual worlds could be grasped only through an ecstatic vision. His retreat from philosophy into mysticism occurred during the crisis of the third century, when many people fled from urban violence to the relative peace of their villas and estates in the countryside.

Science and Medicine

Unlike the Greeks, the Romans made few original contributions to science. However, in medicine the Romans made some original contributions. The scientific aspect of Roman medicine went through three stages. The first stage grew out of Rome's agricultural heritage: remedies for sick farm animals, such as applying salves soaked in wool, had been widely used on humans for generations. The powerful paterfamilias acted as a physician, using ancestral expertise and home remedies. Roman medicine entered its second stage when Greek doctors finally gained acceptance among the Romans, many of whom harbored suspicions of all things Greek. By the start of the empire, in 31 BCE, Roman medicine had entered a third stage, as Greek and Roman medicine merged into a hybrid form—ranging from diagnostic procedures to pharmacology. The Roman army, with its hospitals and surgeons, carried Roman medicine throughout the empire.

Based on their lasting influence, the two most important doctors from this period are Celsus and Galen. The reputation of Celsus [KEL-suhs] (fl. first century CE) as a knowledgeable physician was enhanced by the encyclopedia he compiled, which included articles on philosophy, agriculture, and the military, as well as medicine. Much of what is known about early medical history and Roman medicine, such as surgical procedures, hygienic practices, and treatment of various diseases, is found in this work. It was rediscovered in the early Renaissance (see Chapter 11) and influential for several centuries, but only the section *On Medicine* has survived into modern times.

Galen [GAY-len] of Pergamum (129–about 216 CE) was Rome's most famous medical authority. After studying medicine in Pergamum, Smyrna (modern Izmir, Turkey), and Alexandria, Galen settled in Rome. He soon became a fashionable physician, catering to Rome's elite. Several emperors, including Marcus Aurelius and Commodus, made Galen their court physician. Galen wrote more than five hundred medical treatises, covering such topics as anatomy, physiology, hygiene, exercise and diet, and pharmacology. In general, he followed scientific guidelines: collecting data, relying on experience and observation, and keeping to a set of general principles. His vast erudition and imperious writing style made him the West's chief authority on medicine, until about 1650. Later, his commanding status became a burden, when some of his findings on human anatomy, based on his dissection of dogs rather than humans, impeded the progress of medical knowledge.

Law

The most original contribution of the Roman mind was law. Rome's law created a notion of justice founded on such ideals as fairness for both citizens and subjects, as well as the presumption of innocence in criminal cases. These principles later became central to the Western legal tradition. But the most important facet of Roman law was born in Stoicism: the idea of **natural law,** or a justice higher than any human rule or concept. This doctrine of natural law is the basis of the American Declaration of Independence.

Rome's law evolved over many centuries, starting in 450 BCE with the first written code, the Twelve Tables. These tables, which represented a plebeian victory over the patricians, treated basic aspects of civil life such as personal and property rights, religious practices, and moral behavior. But this milestone did not rid Rome of class distinctions; it merely recognized conflicting rights and the necessity of a judge above both parties. Through the years, class divisions continued to affect the way the law was applied, since the dispensing of justice always favored the rich.

Under the empire, there were three important developments in the history of Roman law. First, the emperors themselves could make law; that is, law no longer had to be made in assemblies. "What pleases the prince has the force of law" was a favorite motto of imperial supporters. Second, building on republican precedents, the *jurisconsults,* or *jurisprudentes,* became more prominent. These were specialists in the theory and science of the law—which is what jurisprudence means. Third, Theodosius II (in 438) and then Justinian (from 529 to 532) codified Roman law by gathering together and systematizing the writings of the jurisconsults and the legislation of earlier emperors. Justinian's codification has proved to be the most influential law book in human history.

FROM THE SECULAR TO THE SPIRITUAL: CHRISTIAN LITERATURE

In the later empire, secular and Christian writers competed for the hearts and minds of educated Romans through poems, treatises, letters, and essays. The secular authors, who felt threatened by Christian activity and thought, preserved classical forms and values in their writings. They turned to the humanistic tradition for inspiration and guidance because they believed that their morals and culture were undergirded by Rome's old religion and farmer-soldier values. Nonetheless, these writers' romantic views of the past were distorted by nostalgia and veneration for a Rome that either was no more or had never been.

Secular literature declined in the late empire, and writers did not experiment with new styles or attempt to modify established forms. No one wrote plays or epics. As a group, the secular Roman authors reflected a growing sense of a lost age. With the exception of a few poets, they seemed unable to define or to analyze the profound changes occurring in their own lifetime.

In contrast, Christian writers looked to the future and a new world to come. With their eyes firmly fixed on heaven, they were indifferent to Rome or to any worldly state. They believed in eternal life but not, like Virgil and his readers, in Rome's eternity. After Constantine decreed toleration for Christians in 313, these authors moved into the mainstream and slowly began to overshadow their pagan rivals. The bitter differences of opinion between them and the pagans, which characterized the late fourth century, faded in the early fifth century. By then Christian literature had triumphed, though it remained deeply indebted to Greco-Roman thought and letters. Christian literature represented the last great achievement of ancient literature.

The Fathers of the Church

By about 300, Christian writers began to find a large audience as their religion continued to win converts among the educated. Although they extolled the virtues and benefits of the new faith, they did not necessarily abandon classical philosophy and literature; they believed that some of these writings conveyed God's veiled truth prior to the coming of Christ, and thus they combined classical with biblical learning. Revered later for their personal lives and public deeds, superior talents, resolute convictions, and commanding personalities, the fathers, as these Christian writers were known, not only were powerful figures within the church but also often intervened in secular matters, instructing the local authorities and even the emperors. Moreover, their writings laid the foundation of medieval Christian doctrine and philosophy. The three most renowned were Ambrose, Jerome, and Augustine.

Ambrose (about 339–397), the son of a high Roman official, embarked on what would doubtless have been a distinguished public career. Unexpectedly, however, the citizens of Milan elected him bishop. Ambrose vigorously opposed the Arian heresy, and as bishop of Milan he aided the urban poor and the victims of bar-barian assaults. In scholarly sermons, he condemned the emperors for the social injustices of their reigns. His letters shed light on problems of church government, and his treatises analyzed controversies dividing the church. His biblical commentaries brought Origen's allegorical method to the West and to Latin (see Chapter 5). Ambrose's hymns, perhaps his most memorable contribution, introduced to the Western church another way for Christians to praise their God and enrich their ceremonies (Figure 6.6).

The second major church father, Jerome (about 345–420), wrote extensively on religious issues, but his most enduring work was his preparation of the **Vulgate** (from *vulgus,* "common people") Bible. Jerome used his knowledge of Greek and Hebrew to revise the existing Latin texts and to translate anew many biblical books. The mark of his Bible's success is that, with some revisions, it remains the standard of the Roman Catholic Church today. Like Ambrose, Jerome received a classical education. Later, after settling in Bethlehem, he founded a monastery, where he devoted most of his days to his biblical studies. His reclusive habits and his harshly critical opinions of Roman society made him controversial.

Of all the church fathers, Augustine (354–430) exercised the greatest influence on Christianity. In his youth in North Africa, he studied classical literature and thought, including Neoplatonism. Augustine then journeyed, via Rome, to Milan, where he met Ambrose, whose persuasive sermons assisted in his conversion. Augustine, convinced of Christianity's intellectual integrity and spiritual vitality, retired to North Africa and dedicated himself to the spread of his new faith. However, his winning personality and administrative skills soon propelled him into church politics.

Augustine joined the debates raging in the church. During his lifetime, his writing came to represent the voice of orthodox beliefs. He opposed the Donatists, who claimed that a priest's sin would make the sacraments invalid. Augustine's position—that each sacrament worked in and of itself and depended on the grace of God, not the worthiness of the priest—became the church's official stance. But his greatest fury was against Pelagianism, which asserted that good works could earn salvation for a sinner. Augustine's argument—that salvation can be achieved only by God's grace—rested on his rejection of free will and his insistence on original sin, the belief that all humans are tainted by a sin inherited from Adam.

During a long, active life, Augustine wrote many kinds of religious works, but looming over them all are his two major achievements: *The Confessions* and *The City of God. The Confessions,* written at the end of the fourth century, traces his search for intellectual and spiritual solace and details his dramatic conversion. In

Figure 6.6 *Ambrose.* Ca. 470. Church of Sant'Ambrogio, Chapel of San Vittore in Ciel d'Oro, Milan. *This portrait of Ambrose conveys some of the spiritual intensity of the powerful fourth-century bishop of Milan. The work is one of few mosaics that survived the destruction brought by Germanic assaults in northern Italy. Although the artist shows some feeling for the shape and movement of the body, the mosaic strongly reflects the artistic ideals developing in the eastern provinces: frontality, flatness, enlarged eyes, and stylized pose.*

this spiritual autobiography, he castigates himself for living a sinful, sensual life. Although he was remorseful and laden with guilt for not having found God sooner, he came to believe that his efforts to understand the world by studying Greco-Roman philosophy, literature, and religion affirmed his desire to search for life's ultimate truths.

Augustine's conversion occurred in a garden in Milan, where a child's voice commanded him to read the scripture. Opening the Bible at random, he read from a letter of Paul, which directed him to arm himself with Jesus Christ as a way of combating the sins of the flesh. Upon reading this passage, Augustine wrote: "The light of confidence flooded into my heart and all the darkness of doubt was dispelled." Now certain of his faith, he dedicated himself to his new mission, adopted an ascetic style of life, and, ultimately, accepted church leadership as the bishop of Hippo, in North Africa. Augustine's convictions, so forcefully expressed, helped to raise the standards of Christian literature in the final years of the Roman Empire.

Shortly after the Visigothic sack of Rome in 410, Augustine began *The City of God,* a theological interpretation of human history. In this work Augustine addresses the central question confronting the Romans of that generation: Why was their empire subjected to so many catastrophes? To those who blamed the Christians, he replied that the decline of Rome was part of God's plan to prepare the world for the coming of a divine kingdom on earth. If the city fell, it was best for the human race. Augustine expounded and reinforced this argument in the first ten books of *The City of God* as he attacked Greco-Roman philosophies and religions.

In the concluding twelve books of the work, Augustine elaborated his view of world history, which relied on the Hebrew experience and Christian sources. At the heart of his argument lay what he called the two cities in history, the City of God and the City of Man. The City of God was the realm of the redeemed. The course of history traced the slow redemption of the City of Man, the realm of sinful humans, by the City of God. History would end when the City of God triumphed. In the City of God, the saved would enjoy an eternal happiness that paganism had promised but could not deliver. Augustine also abandoned the cyclical view of history in favor of a linear, providential version: history had a purpose, it was going somewhere—namely, to God's final judgment.

Church History

In addition to theology, early Christian writing included a new literary genre—church history. Eusebius [you-SEE-be-uhs] (about 260–340), bishop of Caesarea in Palestine from 314 until his death, made no claims to impartiality in his *History of the Christian Church*. It makes the bishops the heroes, for Eusebius believed that they ensured the truth of Christianity. His story is organized church by church and bishop by bishop, revealing the importance then attached to apostolic succession. He also charted the church's spiritual, intellectual, and institutional life in its martyrs, thinkers, and leaders from its earliest days until 324. When his account can be corroborated, Eusebius has been found to be reliable.

Written in Greek, Eusebius's history was inspired by the secular Greco-Roman historians, and he followed them in quoting from written sources. He consulted both the Old and the New Testaments, Christian scholars, and the Greek classics, including Homer and Plato. Eusebius's historical account of the early church gained authority from his background. Having been jailed twice and having survived the Great Persecution (Diocletian's attempt to stamp out Christianity), he appeared to prove God's power in the world. He also baptized Constantine and delivered the opening oration at the Council of Nicaea.

Poetry

During the fourth and fifth centuries, a number of Christian poets showed how this most typical of ancient literary arts could be adapted to Christian purposes. The Roman senator turned monk, Paulinus of Nola (342–431), was born in Gaul but lived much of his life in southern Italy. He was taught by Rome's last great pagan poet, Ausonius (310–395), who became Christian at the end of his life. Paulinus is best known for a series of poems on the life of St. Felix of Nola and on the monastic life. Prudentius (348–about 413) was a Spaniard who wrote theological works, hymns, and many poems. His *Psychomachia* is an allegory in which Christian virtues and human vices wage a cosmic battle for souls. Prudentius was a master of the poet's art. Caelius Sedulius (fl. early fifth century), a third Christian poet, had learned his Virgil at school and

took it to heart. He wrote the *Paschal Song*, which is a retelling in epic verse of the story of Christ's life and crucifixion. Sedulius was not the equal of his model, but his aspirations are revealing.

THE VISUAL ARTS

Architecture and sculpture dominated Rome's visual arts, but they were pressed into the service of practical needs. The Romans commissioned buildings and statues to serve the state, religion, or society, but they recognized that the practical did not exclude the beautiful, and the functional did not rule out the elegant. When Christianity became free and public, the church adapted basic Roman building styles and techniques for its churches. Through the church, therefore, Roman architecture was transmitted to succeeding centuries.

Architecture

Over the years, the Romans used many types of materials in their public and private buildings. The architects of the early republic built with sun-dried bricks and used terra-cotta, a fired clay, for roofs and decorations. As Rome's wealth grew and new materials were imported, the bricks retained an important though less visible role in buildings, chiefly in foundations and walls. By the late republic, two new products had been adapted from the Greeks, mortar and **ashlars** (massive stones hewn into rectilinear shapes with even surfaces and square corners), which, in time, revolutionized the face of Rome.

Much of the impetus for the building revolution sprang from the Romans' improvement of mortar. They produced a moldable concrete by mixing lime, sand, small rocks, and rubble, but because the concrete was visually unappealing, the builders began to cover it either with slabs of expensive and highly polished marble and granite or with the off-white, marble-like travertine easily available around Rome.

The Romans' most significant innovations in architecture were made with the rounded arch, which already had a long history by the time they began to experiment with it. The Mesopotamians probably invented this arch, the Greeks knew about it, and the Etruscans used it in their drainage systems. The arch's basic round form is created with wedge-shaped stones called **voussoirs**. A **keystone** at the center of the semicircle locks the arch in place. The installed arch is amazingly strong, diverting the weight of the upper walls both outward and downward onto columns or other supports (Figure 6.7).

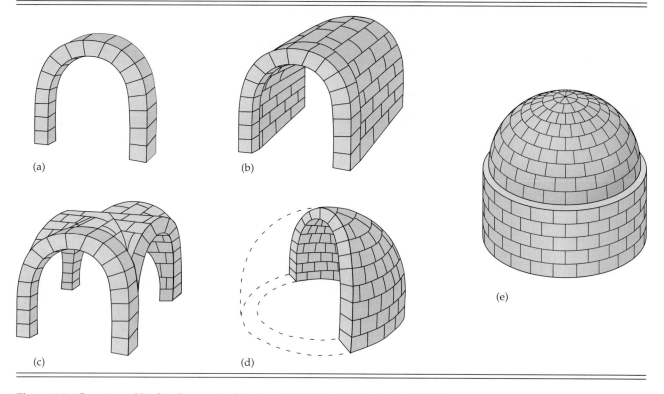

(a)

(b)

(c)

(d)

(e)

Figure 6.7 Structures Used in Roman Architecture. *Beginning with the basic arch (a), the Romans created the barrel vault (b) and the cross vault (c). These structural elements, along with the dome (d), which they formed by rotating a series of arches around a central axis, and the dome on a drum (e), gave the Romans the architectural elements they needed to construct their innovative temples and monuments.*

Figure 6.8 Maison Carrée. Ca. 16 BCE. Base 104′4″ × 48′10″. Nîmes, France. *This temple was probably modeled on temples in Rome, since buildings with Corinthian columns and similar overall designs were being constructed in the capital at this time. Reproducing architecture in the provincial cities was another way in which the Romans spread civilization throughout their conquered lands.*

The Romans demonstrated their inventive genius by creating ceilings, or **vaults,** from arches—by transforming the simple rounded arch into barrel vaults, groined vaults, and domes. They created the **barrel vault**—named because it looks like a barrel divided lengthwise—by building a series of contiguous arches. They intersected two barrel vaults at right angles to produce a **groined,** or **cross, vault.** Finally, the dome, the crown jewel of Rome's architectural vocabulary, was constructed essentially by rotating an arch in a full circle. It was then placed on a drum or enclosed cylinder. The Romans were also able to build arches more safely after they discovered the correct mathematical ratio (1:2) between the height of an arch and the width of its base.

The prototype of imperial temples is the well-preserved Maison Carrée in Nîmes, France, a major provincial city. Built in about 16 BCE, the Maison Carrée incorporated Etruscan and Greek ideas (Figure 6.8). Raised on a platform in the Etruscan manner, this temple shows other Etruscan borrowings in the central stairway, the deep porch, and the engaged columns—that is, the columns built into the walls of the cella, the inner sanctum housing the cult statue. Greek influences are visible in the low gable—the triangular end of the building's roof—and the Corinthian columns. The Greek notion that beauty lies in mathematical harmony is also expressed in the predetermined ratio of the area of the cella to the area of the temple's porch. In the eighteenth century, Thomas Jefferson would use the Maison Carrée as the model for the statehouse in Richmond, Virginia.

Besides perfecting their version of the rectilinear temple, the Romans also invented the round temple, as seen in the Pantheon, a sanctuary dedicated to all their deities. The Pantheon consists of three different units: the entrance porch, or portico, with its supporting columns; the huge drum, housing the sanctuary proper, which is attached to the porch; and the dome, set on top of the drum (Figure 6.9). This design showed the Romans' reliance on a native heritage, because the rounded shape was probably inspired by the circular

Figure 6.9 Pantheon Exterior. 126 CE. Rome. *In modern Rome, the Pantheon is crowded into a piazza where it faces a monument topped by an Egyptian obelisk. However, when built under the emperor Hadrian, the Pantheon was part of a complex of structures that complemented one another, and the temple's facade faced a set of columns in an open forecourt. Its original setting reflected the Roman sense that urban space should be organized harmoniously.*

Figure 6.10 Pantheon Interior. 126 CE. Rome. *The inner diameter of the dome is 144 feet. The height of the dome is 72 feet, or one-half of the total height (144 feet) of the building. The sunlight sweeps around the interior and plays on the dome's decorations as the earth turns, creating constantly changing patterns of light and design.*

religious shrines of the pre-Romans, as modern archaeology has shown. The Pantheon also combined a religious with a secular image: the dome symbolized both the heaven of the deities and the vastness of the empire.

But the Pantheon did more than reflect the deep longings of the Roman people; its rich interior illustrated the Roman genius for decoration (Figure 6.10). A polychrome marble floor and a dome with recessed panels created a dazzling interior, and statues, decorative columns, triangular pediments, niches, and other architectural details alternated around the circular room. The most unusual effect of all was the round hole, thirty feet in diameter, called the **oculus,** or eye, which opened the dome to the sunlight and the elements. As the oldest standing domed structure in the world, the Pantheon is the direct ancestor of St. Peter's Basilica in Rome and St. Paul's cathedral in London.

Rome's architecture consisted of more than beautiful temples. The city of Rome was the center of government for the Mediterranean world, the nucleus of the state's religious system, and the hub of an international economy. And at the heart of the city was its

forum, which functioned like the agora of Greek city-states. In the forum, citizens conducted business, ran the government, and socialized among the complex of public buildings, temples, sacred sites, and monuments. As part of his reforms, Augustus rebuilt and beautified much of the republican forum. Indeed, Augustus boasted that he had found a city of brick and left it one of marble.

Later emperors, such as Trajan, constructed their own forums, which not only served as new centers for trade and government but also immortalized their names. Trajan's forum, which originally included a library, law courts, and plazas for strolling, has vanished except for one of the most significant monuments of the Roman Empire, a column commemorating Trajan's conquest of Dacia (modern Romania) (Figure 6.11).

In addition to forums, columns, and arches, the emperors commissioned amphitheaters as monuments to themselves and as gifts to the citizens. The amphitheaters were the sites of the gladiatorial contests and other blood sports that were the cornerstone of popular culture in the empire. The most famous of these structures was called the Colosseum, actually the

Figure 6.11 Trajan's Victory Column. 106–113 CE. Ht. 125',
including base. Rome. *Borrowing the idea of a victory column
from Mesopotamia, the pragmatic Trajan used art to enhance his
power in the eyes of the citizens. This work commemorated his
conquest of Dacia—present-day Romania. The marble column,
set on a foundation, enclosed a winding stairway that led to an
observation platform and a statue of Trajan. Spiraling around the
column's shaft was a stone relief sculpture that told the story of
Trajan's victory in lively and painstaking detail.*

Figure 6.12 Colosseum. Ca. 72–80 CE. Ht. 166'6". Rome.
*Although the Flavians were a short-lived dynasty, starting with
Vespasian in 69 CE and ending with Domitian in 96, they left
Rome this structure, one of its most enduring landmarks. The
Romans created the oval amphitheater (literally, "theater on both
sides") by joining two semicircular Greek theaters, another
example of their ingenuity and practicality.*

Flavian amphitheater, named in honor of the dynasty
that built it (Figure 6.12). The name Colosseum, dating from a later time, referred to a large (i.e., colossal)
statue of the emperor Nero that stood nearby.

The exterior of the Colosseum was formed by stack-
ing three tiers of rounded arches on top of one another;
Greek columns were then inserted between the arches
as decorations—Doric columns on the first level, Ionic
on the second, and Corinthian on the third. A concrete
and marble block foundation supported this immense
amphitheater. The playing area, or arena (Latin for
"sand"), was made of wood and usually covered with

sand. A honeycomb of rooms, corridors, and cages ran underneath the wooden floor. The Colosseum's vast size and unusual features, such as its retractable overhead awning, made it one of the triumphs of Roman engineering, but the spectacular and brutal contests between men, and sometimes women, and wild beasts, in varied combinations, that took place there symbolized the sordid side of Rome.

Like modern urban centers, Roman towns needed a continuous supply of water. In meeting the water demands of the cities, the Romans displayed their talent for organization and their preference for the practical by creating an elaborate network of aqueducts, sluices, and siphons that ran by gravity from a water source in nearby hills and culminated in a town's reservoirs and fountains.

The Romans started building underground aqueducts in about 300 BCE and constructed the first elevated aqueduct in 144 BCE. Under Augustus, they completed an aqueduct to serve the city of Nîmes that crossed the Gardon River in southern France (Figure 6.13). Known as the Pont du Gard, this section of the aqueduct has a beautiful and functional design. Six large arches form the base, and above them are eleven smaller ones supporting a third tier of thirty-five even smaller arches. Atop the third tier is the sluice through which the water flowed, by gravity, to Nîmes. This graceful structure is a reminder of how the Romans transformed an ordinary object into a work of art.

After the third-century crisis, Diocletian revitalized architecture. As a part of his efforts to restore centralized rule, he used art, specifically architecture, as a sign of his new power. He constructed the last great public baths in Rome, large enough for thousands of people to use at one time. As part of his imperial reforms—indeed, as a propaganda statement that all was well again—Diocletian built a palace on the Dalmatian coast (modern Croatia), where he spent the last twelve years of his life. Strategically located halfway between the western and eastern centers of power, his residence resembled a Roman camp in its symmetrical layout. The palace serves as a fitting monument for this soldier who restored law and order to a world racked by civil war and incompetent rulers.

Visitors entered the palace by the main gate on the north side and walked along a path lined with columns across the central intersection and into the **peristyle,** or colonnaded courtyard (Figure 6.14). Those who traveled this far would be reminded of the emperor's presence by such architectural features as the long entryway, the domed vestibule, and the grandiose courtyard. Beyond the vestibule, on the south side bordering the sea, were the imperial apartments, the guards' barracks, rooms for private audiences, and banquet halls. This residence incorporated nearly all

the major designs and techniques, including the arch and mortar mixtures, known to Roman builders. More important, its impressive splendor symbolized divine authority combined with secular political power.

Just as Diocletian's palace was one of the last pagan edifices, the Arch of Constantine was the last pagan triumphal arch (Figure 6.15). The Romans had built triumphal arches since republican times. They usually had single openings whereas Constantine's arch has three. It was erected to celebrate the emperor's victory in 312, which led to the issuing of the Edict of Milan. The circular **medallions** set between the detached columns on the side arches help to balance these smaller arches with the central arch. The decorated **attic,** or crown of the arch, with its statues of barbarian peoples, blends well with the lower sections. The senate and the Roman people, according to the inscription, gratefully dedicated this arch to Constantine for his deeds as their liberator from civil war and as their new emperor.

Much of the arch's decoration was borrowed from other monuments; for example, some of the reliefs and carvings came from works honoring the victories of Trajan, Hadrian, and Marcus Aurelius; and where a likeness of the emperor is intended, the original has been remodeled to resemble Constantine. Despite Constantine's celebrated conversion to Christianity, however, the arch clearly reflects a strong pagan influence. The symbols and figures stress human action, and only one small frieze hints at divine intervention.

A shift from pagan to Christian architecture began after 313 under Constantine's inspiration and patronage. He ordered the building of churches as places of worship for congregations and as memorials at holy spots in Rome, Palestine, and other parts of the empire. Financed and supported by the state, this ambitious enterprise resulted not only in the spread of Christianity but also in the founding of new artistic values and architectural forms. The basic design of the churches that Constantine had constructed was derived from the **basilica,** a large enclosed rectangular structure that dated back to the second century BCE and, by the early empire, was often built to house marketplaces or public assembly halls.

Although basilicas varied in detail, the basic form used for churches was simple: an oblong hall with an **apse,** or curved extension, at the eastern end. Two or four rows of parallel columns usually divided the hall into a central area, or **nave,** and side **aisles.** The roof was taller over the nave section with a **clerestory**— windows were set high in the outside nave walls to let in light. The apse, where ceremonies were performed or where holy relics—physical remains of martyrs and saints—were placed, was often screened off from the worshipers, who stood in the nave. In some structures

Figure 6.13 Pont du Gard. Ca. late first century CE. Ht. 161'. Gardon River, near Nîmes, France. *This aqueduct spanning the river was only one segment of the 50-mile system that supplied water to Nîmes. Between 8,000 and 12,000 gallons of water were delivered daily, or about 100 gallons per inhabitant.*

Figure 6.14 Diocletian's Palace. Ca. 300. Split, Croatia. *The peristyle, or colonnaded courtyard, screened off the buildings on the left and right, enhanced the enclosed atmosphere, and focused attention on the vestibule. Behind the peristyle, on the left, stood Diocletian's tomb (now a church) and, on the right, the Temple to Jupiter (now the Baptistery of St. John).*

Figure 6.15 Arch of Constantine. 312–315. Ht. 68'10". Rome. *The frieze that winds around the monument narrates the emperor's preparations for war, his victory, and his triumphant entry into Rome. The scenes depicted on the Arch of Constantine, like those on Trajan's Column, memorialized the Roman ruler's presence at every stage of a military campaign.*

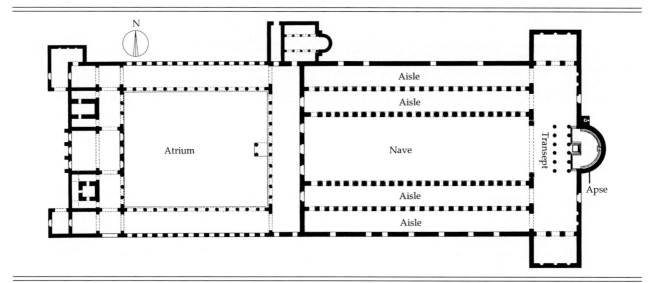

Figure 6.16 Floor Plan of Old St. Peter's Basilica. Ca. 330. Rome. *Old St. Peter's Basilica was the most important structure in Christian Europe until it was demolished in the early sixteenth century to make way for the present St. Peter's. Constantine dedicated Old St. Peter's on the spot believed to be the burial site of Peter, whom the church considered the successor to Jesus. Of the original basilica nothing remains, but sixteenth-century drawings show that it was cruciform (cross shaped), had a wide central nave with two aisles on either side, and was fronted by an atrium, where worshipers washed their hands and faces before entering the sanctuary.*

there was an **atrium,** or open courtyard, in front of the main hall.

No fourth-century Roman basilica churches remain, but drawings, such as that of the floor plan of the basilica of Old St. Peter's, suggest their appearance (Figure 6.16). St. Peter's Basilica, built to mark the grave of the apostle who, by tradition, founded the church in Rome, included a **transept,** or crossing section, that intersected the nave at the apse end of the building,

making it **cruciform** (cross shaped). This first St. Peter's Basilica attracted pilgrims for centuries.

Sculpture

The reign of Augustus was important in the development of Roman sculpture. Under his rule, imperial portraiture reverted to the idealism of Hellenic

Figure 6.17 *Augustus,* from Prima Porta. Ca. 14 CE. Marble, ht. 6'7½". Vatican Collection. *This statue of Caesar Augustus (r. 31 BCE–14 CE), the founder of the Roman Empire, was uncovered at Prima Porta, the villa of his wife, Livia. The statue closely resembled the ruler yet presented him as godlike. Augustus's imperial successors commissioned similar sculptures to convey a sense of their dignity and power.*

Greece, displacing the realistic art of the late republic. But Augustus's pure idealism did not prevail for long, for under his successors sculpture became more propagandistic—that is, more symbolic of imperial power. This move to symbolic idealism reflected the later emperors' need to find a highly visible way in which to overawe, and thus draw together, Rome's increasingly diversified masses.

Two major sculptural works associated with Augustus, the Prima Porta portrait and the Ara Pacis, or the Altar of Peace, helped to popularize the idealistic style. Augustus's statue, commissioned after his death, stood in a garden on his widow's estate, Prima Porta, just outside Rome (Figure 6.17). The pure Hellenic style is evident in Augustus's relaxed stance and idealized face, both of which were modeled on the *Doryphoros* by Polykleitos (see Figure 3.21). However, the accompanying symbols reveal the propagandistic intent of the sculpture and were portents of the path that imperial portraits would take. For example, the cupid represents Venus, the mother of Aeneas, and thus Augustus is symbolically connected to the legendary origins of Rome.

The second idealistic sculpture, the marble Ara Pacis, was funded by the senate as an offering of thanks to Augustus for his peacekeeping missions. The entire structure was set on a platform and enclosed by three walls. On the fourth side, an entrance with steps led to the altar (Figure 6.18). Relief sculptures decorated the interior and exterior walls, some in an idealized style and others in a realistic style (Figure 6.19). The resulting tension between realism and idealism marked this altar as an early work in the imperial style.

This type of sculpture reached its highest potential as a propaganda tool on triumphal arches and victory columns, such as the Arches of Titus and Constantine and Trajan's Column (Encounter figure 6.1). One of the reliefs from the Arch of Titus, the *March of the Legions,* portrays the army's victory march into Rome after the destruction of the Temple in Jerusalem in 70 CE (Figure 6.20).

During Diocletian's reign and before Christianity's assimilation of the Roman arts, the late empire produced some unique and monumental works, such as the group portrait of Diocletian's tetrarchy, carved in red porphyry (see Figure 6.2) and the colossal statue of Constantine, a composite of marble and metal (Figure 6.21). The generalized features of these figures show the trend to symbolic representation characteristic of the art of the late empire and the movement away from the idealized or realistic faces of classical sculpture.

Christian sculpture was undergoing aesthetic changes similar to those taking place in secular art. By the end of the third century, Christian art was symbolic in content and impressionistic in style (see Chapter 5). Simple representations of Jesus and the apostles had become common in the underground church. After 313, artists began to receive the support of the Roman state and also of bishops and wealthy Christians.

Christian Rome's reshaping of the humanistic tradition can be seen in the carvings on sarcophagi. The Roman anxiety about life after death and the pursuit of intellectual matters easily evolved into Christian images and themes. The growing acceptance of burial rather than cremation and the resultant increased demand for sarcophagi afforded many artists new opportunities to express themselves. After the second century, rich Roman families commissioned artists to

Figure 6.18 Ara Pacis. 9 BCE. Marble, width 35'. Rome. *Like the Prima Porta statue, the Ara Pacis became a model for later emperors, who emulated its decorations, symbols, and size. The altar was rediscovered in the six-teenth century, excavated in the nineteenth and early twen-tieth centuries, and restored in 1938.*

Figure 6.19 *Family of Augustus*, Ara Pacis relief. 9 BCE. Marble, ht. 63". Rome. *The figures in low relief, moving from right to left, are separated yet linked by their placement and clothing. The child to the right of center is given great prominence: he faces right while all the adults in the foreground are looking left and a man places his hand on the child's head. This singling out of the child may be an act of endearment or of recognition that he is to be the emperor.*

Figure 6.20 *March of the Legions*, from the Arch of Titus. Ca. 81 CE. Marble relief, approx. 6 × 12½′. Rome. *This rectangular marble relief occupies the south side of the Arch of Titus. It commemorates the Roman victory in the Jewish War of 66–70 CE, when the Romans put down a rebellion by the Jews in Judea and subsequently dispersed them across the Roman world. In the relief, the Roman soldiers hold aloft the Jewish holy relics from the Temple as they seem to press forward and pass under the arch on the right.*

Figure 6.21 Colossal Statue of Constantine. Ca. 313. Marble. Palazzo dei Conservatori, Rome. *Like Diocletian, Constantine consciously nurtured the image of the emperor as a larger-than-life figure. To enhance this image, he commissioned a huge statue of himself, perhaps ten times life size, to stand in the gigantic basilica (which he had also built) in the Roman Forum. All that remains of the statue today are the head, which measures over eight feet tall, a hand, and some pieces of the limbs. The monument signaled the climax of the emperor cult and the beginning of its decline. With the spread of Christianity, rulers were no longer viewed as gods.*

INTERPRETING ART

Style The sculpture is late classical style, with ideals of harmony and balance. Some of the deeply carved figures give the impression of sculpture in the round.

Subject The biblical scenes depict: (top, left to right) Abraham and the sacrifice of Isaac, the arrest of Peter, Christ enthroned between Peter and Paul, Christ as a prisoner, and Christ before Pontius Pilate; (bottom, left to right) the patience of Job, Adam and Eve, Christ's entry into Jerusalem, Daniel in the lion's den, and Paul led to martyrdom.

Theological Perspective The Old Testament scenes are prophetic of New Testament events and all scenes point to Christ. Scenes of sacrifice dominate, but Christ's sacrifice on the cross is not depicted.

Pagan Elements Amid the Christian symbols, pagan remnants

remain. In the top center, Christ appears above, and with his feet on, a personification of a pagan sky god, implying that Christ is now the ruler of the universe. Christ appears bearded and Apollo-like—as philosophers were depicted.

Setting This sarcophagus was created in that dynamic moment when Christianity was coming to dominate the Roman world. The wealthy could afford the finest artists who adapted classical modes to Christian subjects.

Symbolism The sarcophagus shows Christian beliefs in: (on its front) scenes from the Old and New Testaments—the two parts of the Christian Bible; (on its ends) putti (small children) harvesting grapes (left end) and grain (right end)—symbols of bread and wine, the elements in the Christian Eucharist, or Holy Communion.

Interpreting Art figure 6.1 The Sarcophagus of Junius Bassus. After 359. Marble, 4′ × 4′ × 8′. St. Peter's Treasury, Vatican City. *Junius Bassus (d. 359), a Roman aristocrat, served as prefect of the city of Rome. His sarcophagus was discovered in 1595 under the floor of St. Peter's near the tomb of the apostle.*

decorate the sides of these marble coffins and tombs with images of classical heroes and heroines, gods and goddesses, military and political leaders, and scenes of famous events and battles. Christians adapted existing funerary styles to new subject matter with Christian themes (Interpreting Art figure 6.1).

Painting and Mosaics

Murals, or wall paintings, the most popular type of painting in Rome, have been found in private dwellings, public buildings, and temples. Surviving works hint at a highly decorative, brightly colored art. Originally the Romans applied **tempera,** or paint set in a binding solution, directly onto a dry wall. However, this quick and easy method produced a painting that soon faded and peeled. Later they adopted fresco painting (see Chapter 2) as the most practical and lasting technique. The Romans were drawn to many subjects: Greek and Roman myths, architectural vistas,

religious stories, ritual performances, genre scenes (everyday events), and landscapes.

Among the many landscapes painted by Roman artists are the splendid garden frescoes from the Villa of Livia at Prima Porta (Figure 6.22). This fresco, depicting a distant garden, is framed by twin horizontal walls at its bottom and a jagged border at the top. Roman artists never mastered mathematical perspective; instead, they used the placement of objects, animals, and human figures to create a sense of space, as in this fresco. The patterned fence (foreground) and the stone wall (in the rear), with a walkway in between and a tree in the center, create the illusion of depth. The placement of the bushes, smaller trees, shrubs, fruits, and flowers behind the walls further augments the fresco's perspective. The vast array of identifiable plants and birds typifies two themes of Augustan art, as the art of the reign of Augustus is called. Those themes are prosperity and peace, thus suggestive of the propagandistic nature of the art of the period.

Figure 6.22 *Garden Scene.* Villa of Livia, Prima Porta. Ca. 20 BCE. Fresco. Museo di Palazzo, Massimo, Rome. *This garden scene represents a particular style of Roman fresco painting that began in the first century BCE and was still popular in the Age of Augustus. Labeled* architectural, *these paintings were often divided into three horizontal planes and framed by columns to give the sense of a wall opening or looking through a window onto a bucolic view of the world beyond the villa or house.*

In the fourth century, Christian frescoes flourished in the Roman catacombs and continued the symbolic, impressionist style of the previous era (see Chapter 5). Non-Christian paintings are extremely scarce from the fifth century, except for a few works such as a collection of **miniatures**—small illustrations—for Virgil's *Aeneid,* probably painted for a wealthy patron. This extensive picture cycle (Figure 6.23), more than 225 scenes, recalls the style of earlier paintings, but it is also an early example of a new medium, the illustrated book. Books were now written on vellum, a parchment made from animal skins, and bound in pages rather than written on scrolls. In the Middle Ages, this type of decorated, or illuminated, book would become a major art form. In the late empire, however, the form was in its infancy.

A more vital art form was the mosaic, which, as in other art forms, Christians ultimately turned to their own ends. The Romans learned to make **mosaics,** assemblages of tiny bits of stone, glass, or metal, from the Hellenistic Greeks in the third century BCE, but by the third century CE, several local Roman mosaic styles had sprung up across the empire. Although subjects varied, certain ones seemed always to be in vogue, such as still lifes, landscapes, Greek and Roman myths, philosophers and orators, and scenes from the circus and amphitheaters. A mosaic from Tunisia (North Africa) shows the intricacy of design and variety of color that artisans achieved even in the Roman provinces (Figure 6.24). Pagans continued to place mosaics on both floors and walls, but Christians more

Figure 6.23 Illumination from Virgil's *Aeneid.* Fifth century. 6 × 6″. Vatican Library, the Vatican. *This page from an illustrated manuscript of Virgil's* Aeneid *shows Dido, the Queen of Carthage (center), flanked by Aeneas (left) and a guest. The scene depicts the banquet, described at the end of Book I, that Dido gave in honor of the newly arrived Trojans. After the meal, Aeneas recounted his escape from Troy and seven subsequent years of wandering. Faithful to the* Aeneid's *description, the painting represents Aeneas speaking to Dido while she appears to be calling for the attendant, in the lower right corner, to wash the hands of the diners. That such works were being commissioned in fifth-century Christian Rome showed that not everyone was partaking of the new religion and its symbols.*

Figure 6.24 Calendar Mosaic. Late second–early third century CE. From the Maison des Mois at El Djem. Detail of 5 × 4′ mosaic. Sousse Museum, Sousse, Tunisia. *The El Djem Calendar comprises twelve small scenes, each representing a month, the name of which is inscribed in Latin. The Roman year began with March (top middle) and ended with February (top left corner). The months are symbolized by either religious or rural activities, such as in the September panel, which shows two figures standing in a vat crushing grapes.*

often put them on the walls. Christian artists also replaced the stone chips with bits of glass or metal that reflected light, thus adding a glittering, ethereal quality to the basilicas and other buildings.

In late Roman mosaics, the subject matter for pagan and Christian works stands in sharp contrast. Among the many pagan mosaics that survive are those at the Villa Romana del Casale, a Roman estate near the town of Piazza Armerina in central Sicily. The villa, built in the early fourth century on the ruins of a second-century structure, was the residence of either a rich Roman aristocrat or a high-ranking Roman official. The estate operated for more than one hundred fifty years until the buildings fell into disuse when the Vandals and the Visigoths invaded Sicily. This partially restored villa contains the largest, most valuable collection of late Roman mosaics in the world.

Over thirty-five thousand square feet of mosaic flooring covers a complex of rooms, including baths, a gymnasium, guest quarters, peristyles or open courts, and long hallways. One of the hallways, the Corridor of the Great Hunt, over two hundred feet long, depicts the hunting, capturing, and transporting of wild animals, which were typically found in the five provinces of the empire's diocese (administrative division) of Africa. These animals—antelopes, kids, lions, boars, and wild horses—were destined for Rome's Colosseum or arenas in other cities. Composed of two hunts, the narrative scene begins at either end of the corridor, with scenes of the hunters trapping or caging their prey. Then there are scenes at the ports where soldiers and slaves load the animals onto a ship, which is laden with crates, and, in the center of the hallway, the same ship is depicted as having arrived in Rome, where slaves unload the boxes and lead the animals away (Figure 6.25). The soldiers, slaves, and officials can be clearly identified by their dress and armor and their roles in the narrative. Their diverse facial features and multicolored skin tones indicate the diversity of the Roman Empire in the fourth century.

Among the many examples of life in the late Roman Empire recorded in the pagan mosaics at the Villa Romana del Casale were various scenes of children, including young boys hunting animals and young girls gathering roses. These scenes, found in a floor decoration in the bedroom of the son of the owner, confirm that the pagans liked pictures of young children, or *putti*, in the role of adults at work or play or even in religious scenes. In the very first Christian art, some artists adopted this playful genre for scenes of grape harvesting, as in a mosaic from the Church of Santa Costanza, Rome (Figure 6.26). In Christian art, however, the scene was a disguised representation of the Christian communion, in which wine made from grapes became the blood of Christ (see Interpreting Art figure 6.1).

In the fifth and sixth centuries, the apses of almost all Christian basilicas acquired majestic mosaics, most of them depicting Christ. In Rome's church dedicated to Saints Cosmas and Damian, there is a particularly good example from the fifth century (Figure 6.27). After Justinian's reconquest of Italy, Ravenna became a showplace for patrons and mosaicists. In the small, cruciform mausoleum of Galla Placidia, a daughter of Emperor Theodosius I (r. 378–395), there is an especially attractive Good Shepherd in the space above the entry door (Figure 6.28). The nearby church of San Vitale has numerous mosaics. Flanking the altar are two, one depicting Justinian and his courtiers and the other depicting the emperor's wife, Theodora, and her courtiers (Figure 6.29). These fifth- and sixth-century styles would have a long life in medieval Rome and in the Byzantine Empire.

MUSIC

The absorption of the Greek tradition in music was so complete that for a long time Roman music, in effect, simply perpetuated Greek forms and ideas. And yet the Romans originally used music only for practical purposes and rejected the Greek notion that music performed an ethical role in educating the soul or mind.

Not until imperial times did music come to play an important role in Roman life. Under the emperors, music became wildly popular, as all classes succumbed to its seductive charms. **Pantomimes**—dramatic productions with instrumental music and dances—became the spectacle favored by the Roman masses. In the long run, the pantomimes became a symbol of music's decadent trend under the empire. The largest of these productions featured three thousand instrumentalists and three thousand dancers, but the more common size was three hundred performers in each category. A more serious sort of music was kept alive by the wealthy classes, who maintained household orchestras and choruses for their private amusement. An even more cultivated audience encouraged poets such as Horace to set their verses to music, thus continuing the Greek tradition of lyric poetry.

Although what Roman music actually sounded like remains a subject of conjecture, Roman musical instruments, borrowed from across the Mediterranean world, can be identified with some certainty. From Greece came the stringed instruments, the lyre and the kithara, along with such woodwinds as the single aulos, or oboe, and the double aulos—called by the Romans the tibia. From the Etruscans came the brasses. The Romans delighted in the harsh sounds made by these instruments, incorporating them into their military music just as the Etruscans had done. The hydraulic organ, or water organ, was probably perfected in

Figure 6.25 Loading the Wild Animals. Detail from mosaic. Early fourth century. Villa Romana del Casale near Piazza Armerina, Sicily. *This detail from the Corridor of the Great Hunt expresses the energy and activity found in nearly every mosaic on this site. Two workers struggle with the antelope on the gangplank, as sailors on deck prepare for the sailing. These mosaics were probably created by North African artists whose skills were well known during the late Roman period. Many motifs and scenes, in particular those of the Great Hunt, were standard design elements employed in North Africa and across the Roman Empire. Given the repetition of some of the decorations and motifs, and the uniform quality of the mosaics, the entire project was likely done over a five- to ten-year period by the same design crew and skilled workers. Some stones were quarried locally, but the colored ones were imported from Africa.*

Figure 6.26 Putti *Harvesting Grapes.* Mosaic. Fourth century. Church of Santa Costanza, Rome. *Besides alluding to communion, this scene illustrates the Christian scripture John 15:1, in which Jesus says, "I am the true vine, and my Father is the vinedresser."* Putti *are depicted trampling grapes and loading grapes into carts pulled by oxen; the rest of the scene is a labyrinth of vines, making up an arbor, amid which other* putti *are gathering grapes. This scene harkens back to representations of the cult of Dionysus; we know it is Christian only because it is in a Christian church.*

Figure 6.27 *Christ in Glory.* Mid to late fifth century. Mosaic. Church of Saints Cosmas and Damian, Rome. *The scene depicts Christ's Second Coming wreathed in clouds of fire. The biblical text depicted here is from the book of Revelation. Compare the representation of Christ here with the one on the sarcophagus of Junius Bassus (see Interpreting Art figure 4.1). There, Christ is shown as an ancient philosopher. Here, he takes on the "Jewish" features that would be common for a millennium: long, dark hair, heavy beard, olive skin.*

Figure 6.28 *The Good Shepherd.* Ca. 450. Mausoleum of Galla Placidia, Ravenna, Italy. *The young, beardless Christ, which was still the accepted image of the Christian savior in the fifth century, supports himself with the cross and feeds the sheep, the symbol of the church, with his right hand. Foliage and plants in the background tie in with similar decorations on the mausoleum's ceilings and walls. Upon entering the small tomb, worshipers would immediately be confronted with this large figure of Christ.*

Figure 6.29   *Theodora and Her Attendants.* Ca. 547. Church of San Vitale, Ravenna, Italy.
This mosaic featuring the empress Theodora faces a panel of her husband, Justinian, with his
courtiers. Together, these mosaics communicate the pageantry and the luxury of this age. The
man on Theodora's right draws back a curtain, inviting the imperial party into some unseen
interior. His gesture may mean that this scene was part of a religious procession.

Hellenistic Alexandria, but in imperial Rome it became a crowd pleaser, adding deep, voluminous sounds to the pantomimes. The taste of the imperial Roman audience is evident in the water organ, which was impressive not for its musical qualities but as a feat of engineering expertise.

While the pagan music of late Rome was in decline, Christian music was just beginning to take shape. The Christians took the principles of Greco-Roman music and integrated them into the Jewish tradition of singing the psalms and the liturgy to make music a dynamic part of their worship. In later times, this Christian practice gave birth to a rich body of sacred music that utilized both singers and instrumentalists.

In late Rome, however, sacred music was limited to chanting and unaccompanied singing. The Antioch church, inspired by the congregational singing in Jewish synagogues, developed a new musical genre, the hymn, a song of praise to God. From Antioch the practice of hymn singing spread to Constantinople and Milan and eventually was integrated into the Christian liturgy everywhere. Ambrose, bishop of Milan and a powerful influence at the imperial court, stands out among the earliest hymn writers as one of the founders of the Western sacred song. Ambrose's Latin hymns were probably meant to be sung **antiphonally**—that is, with lines sung alternately between a leader and a chorus.

The Legacy of Roman Imperial Civilization

The Hellenistic world, and then the Roman Empire, provided a stable framework for historical development across a huge geography and for more than eight centuries. This stability and longevity helps to explain why there are discernible similarities in art and architecture in places ranging from Britain to Afghanistan. Across that same span, boys once learned Greek and Latin epics and later learned the Psalms. The laws and institutions of every state that emerged within lands that had once been Rome's betray their origins in Roman ideas and practices.

Where the Western world is concerned, the Roman legacy has been deep, direct, and durable. It is interesting, but perhaps not crucial, that today's superhighways in western Europe lay right on top of Roman roads. In 1970 Rome's daily water supply was about what it was in the time of Augustus. More important is, for example, the impact of Roman law, indirectly on every Western legal system and directly on France, Louisiana, Quebec, and Scotland. Alfred, Lord Tenny-son, the nineteenth-century English poet, called Virgil the "wielder of the stateliest measure ever formed by the mouth of man." Virgil's influence has never waned; the great Dante took him as guide and model. Rome's interpretations of Greek architecture formed a style that has been revived again and again.

The Christianity of the Roman world is another durable legacy. The papacy is the world's oldest functioning institution, and monks and bishops still serve the church. Directly or indirectly, Christians have been indebted to the church fathers for fifteen hundred years. The Christian achievement in the textual and visual arts has been influential and inspiring for just as long. Roman science, medicine, and technology—transmitted directly by the Christian church and indirectly through the world of medieval Islam (see Chapter 8)—empowered the West in the High Middle Ages (see Chapter 9) to begin its rise to world-historical significance.

KEY CULTURAL TERMS

principate
Pax Romana
tetrarchy
dominate
apostolic succession
Petrine Idea
heresy
satire
Neoplatonism
natural law
Vulgate Bible
ashlars
voussoir
keystone
vault
barrel vault
groined, or cross, vault
oculus

forum
peristyle
medallions
attic
basilica
apse
nave
aisles
clerestory
atrium
transept
cruciform
tempera
miniatures
mosaics
pantomime
antiphonal

QUESTIONS FOR CRITICAL THINKING

1. What were the most important changes in the structure and organization of the Roman Empire from the reign of Augustus to that of Justinian?

2. What were the most important aspects of the growth of the Catholic Church as an institution in the Roman world?

3. How did Golden Age and Silver Age writers differ? What did the writers of each period owe to the Hellenistic world? In what ways were these writers distinctively Roman?

4. What did the church fathers have in common with each other? What did they have in common with the secular writers who preceded them?

5. What did the Christian visual arts owe to pagan art? In what ways did Christian and pagan art differ?

7

THE HEIRS TO THE ROMAN EMPIRE: BYZANTIUM AND THE WEST IN THE EARLY MIDDLE AGES

If the late Roman world were envisioned as a long evening, the early Middle Ages might be seen as a long morning. The years between 600 and 1000 saw the Eastern Roman Empire evolve into a Byzantine Empire that would last until Constantinople was conquered by the Ottoman Turks in 1453. In the West, small kingdoms gave way to the huge empire of Charlemagne, which, in turn, dissolved into the realms of France and Germany. The surprising development in the early Middle Ages was the emergence of the Islamic caliphate, the subject of Chapter 8.

Compared to imperial Rome, everything now happened on a smaller scale. Governments employed fewer people, controlled smaller territories, and provided fewer services. Population was contracting everywhere until the ninth century, and cities were shrinking in both size and importance. Rome, for example, probably had fifty thousand people in 600, a dramatic drop from the roughly half-million in the time of Constantine.

Government was less bureaucratic than it had been in late Roman times. In Byzantium there were more remnants of the old Roman system. In the West, those remnants gradually disappeared. Everywhere, but more so in the West, government came to depend on personal relationships between rulers and landed aristocrats. While cities remained the basis for ecclesiastical administration, secular government was increasingly based in the countryside.

The economy was, as in antiquity, overwhelmingly rural and agricultural. In the wake of the disappearance of Rome's crushing tax regime, the life of the peasants may have improved slightly. By the end of the tenth century, some modest technological gains may have improved rural living standards.

◀ **Detail** Charlemagne's Palace Chapel. 788–806. Aachen, Germany.

Timeline 7.1   **THE BYZANTINE EMPIRE**

476	641	867	1081	1261	1453
	Revival of Empire	Withdrawal and Renewal	The Golden Age	The Challenge from the West	Palaeologian Emperors
Fall of Rome		**726–843** Iconoclastic Controversy	**1054** Schism between Orthodox and Roman churches		Fall of Constantinople

But this was no golden age for, paradoxically, slavery and freedom were declining simultaneously. In both East and West, slaves tended to gain personal freedom while free men and women were sinking into serfdom. A broad class of dependent peasants existed almost everywhere. As for trade, the other key component of the economy, the absence of the Roman state and the diminished capacity of the Byzantine Empire, made all the difference. Imperial Rome's had been a command economy. The state could, for example, command that bulky foodstuffs be transported uneconomically from North Africa or Egypt to Rome or Constantinople to feed the populace. This activity was not trade; it was politics. By the seventh century, this system was gone and what remained was fairly modest long-distance trade in high-value luxury goods.

Religion was a decisive feature of both East and West in the early medieval world. The church helped to stabilize political, social, and economic life. Church schools provided for the preservation of ancient learning and the training of the clergy. The church continued to function as a key patron for art and architecture, and Christian subject matter dominated the pictorial arts. During this period, moreover, East and West began to develop ever more distinctive patterns of religious life. By 1000 it is possible to speak of Orthodox Christianity and Roman Catholic Christianity. In addition, warriors, merchants, and missionaries carried Christianity far beyond the boundaries of the old Roman world, especially to those areas that constitute Europe today.

In the seventeenth century, a Dutch scholar used the Latin phrase *medii aevi*, the "Middle Ages," to define the period between the end of antiquity and the Renaissance. Already in the fourteenth century, some Italian writers had begun to claim that their contemporaries were more like the people of antiquity than the people of the thousand years—the Middle Ages—that preceded them. The claim was not true, as later chapters will demonstrate, but the claim prevailed. Western civilization is still divided into three periods: ancient, medieval, and modern. The term was once exclusively pejorative; medieval implied backward,

ignorant, superstitious. Today the term is only a label. In the Middle Ages, human folly raised its head from time to time, but so did stunning achievements in every area of life. For present purposes, it is important to keep in mind only that no one who lived in the Middle Ages knew that he or she was medieval.

THE BYZANTINE WORLD

Between the sixth and eighth centuries, the Eastern Roman Empire evolved into a distinctive regime that can be called *Byzantine*—called Byzantine by modern scholars, that is. The name derives from Byzantium, the old Greek colony on which Constantine erected his new city, Constantinople. Byzantines, however, always called themselves Romans, albeit they did so in Greek. Three themes dominated the history of Byzantium: foreign threats, institutional reforms, and religious change.

The Birth of Byzantium: War and Government

After the death of Justinian in 565, the eastern Roman world faced severe challenges. The Persians were a menace, and Slavs, Bulgars, and Avars pressed against the Danube frontier. The Lombards conquered most of Italy. Berber tribesmen rendered the reconquest of North Africa almost meaningless. Until Heraclius (her-ah-KLI-us) came to the throne in 610, most emperors were poor leaders.

Heraclius (r. 610–641) restored the treasury and went to war with Persia. In brilliant campaigns, he defeated Rome's old foe but suddenly faced a new threat from the Arabs (see Chapter 8). Exhausted from Rome's wars with Persia, Constantinople had no answer for the Arabs and lost Syria, Palestine, and most of North Africa. Heraclius's successors in the eighth century created a shaky frontier with the Arabs in Anatolia (modern Turkey), which held until the lightning campaigns of

Map 7.1 EARLY MEDIEVAL BYZANTIUM
This map shows the Byzantine Empire as it existed from the eighth century until western crusaders captured Constantinople in 1204. In Anatolia the frontier often moved
back and forth slightly according to the politics and diplomacy of the day. In the eleventh century, the Seljuk Turks conquered vast stretches of eastern and central Anatolia.
1. Based on this map, *why* did Byzantium have little interest in the West?

the Seljuk Turks in the eleventh century. Those same
successors could not prevent Avar raiding in the Danube basin, Slavic settlement in the Balkans, and the
creation of a Bulgarian kingdom. Northern Italy was
abandoned; no resources could be spared to hold it.
Byzantium profited from Charlemagne's destruction
of the Avar kingdom (788–796) (see below). After years
of gains and losses along the frontier with Bulgaria,
Basil II "the Bulgar Slayer" (r. 976–1025) eliminated
the first Bulgarian kingdom. Nevertheless, the basic
geographic outline of the Byzantine Empire had taken
shape by 800 (Map 7.1).

Because of these wars, Byzantium's institutions
were reformed several times. Rome's wars had been
fought by professional standing armies financed by
tax revenues. With the exception of some troops in immediate attendance on the emperor, Byzantium gradually developed armies that were settled on the land, in
lieu of pay, under the leadership of local officers. The

zones within which these armies were settled were
called **themes** (see Map 7.1). The theme system provided troops that could be mobilized locally to face
threats and did not constitute a continuous draw on
the treasury. Local military commanders combined
civil and military authority in their hands. Justinian
had begun the process of joining civil and military authority, and by the end of the eighth century the process was complete.

The large and intrusive late Roman government
was simplified. There may actually have been more
branches of government, but they employed fewer
men and the great officials were less powerful and
prestigious than their predecessors had been. The emperors lived in a magnificent palace complex in Constantinople and rarely left the city. In the 720s Leo III
issued a new law code, the *Ekloga*, which, as an ab-
breviation of Justinian's code, testifies to the empire's
contraction.

The Birth of Byzantium: Culture and Religion

A reduced geography and transformed institutions were not the only changes experienced by the east Roman regime as it became Byzantine. At the most fundamental level, Greek replaced Latin as the underlying basis for culture. This happened notwithstanding the fact that only about one-third of Byzantium's population were native speakers of Greek. Leo's *Ekloga,* for example, was issued in Greek whereas Justinian's code had been published in Latin. The emperors called themselves "emperors of the Romans" but did so in Greek, *Basileus tōn Romaiōn.*

From a territorial point of view, the Byzantine Church was smaller than the church of late Roman times. The great cities of Alexandria, Jerusalem, and Antioch were in Muslim hands and thus were isolated from Christian Constantinople. The patriarch of Constantinople often had trouble gaining assent from the bishops in the lands that remained to the empire. The emperor was literally the patriarch's next-door neighbor and frequently involved himself in church affairs.

Monasticism was important in both East and West, but in the East monks were often seen as counterweights to the imperial regime. Monasteries had acquired great wealth and immense prestige. Numerous patriarchs came from the monastic order. Many bright and capable young men were drawn to the monastic life instead of to the imperial service. From its Egyptian origins, monasticism had two prominent forms, eremitic and cenobitic. The former, from *heremos,* Greek for "desert," was austere and solitary; think of hermits. The latter, from *koinos bios,* Greek for "common life," was communal. Byzantine monasticism was primarily cenobitic with eremitic aspects. Monasteries could be found throughout the empire. In 963 a major monastic complex arose on Mt. Athos, eventually comprising numerous monasteries and more than eight thousand monks (Figure 7.1).

The manifestation of the Christian faith that can be called Orthodoxy emerged over several centuries. It

Figure 7.1   Mount Athos. *In 963 Athanasius the Athonite founded a monastery on the Athos peninsula of Chalcidice in the Greek part of Macedonia. Eventually, twenty monasteries clustered on the peninsula. The buildings shown here date from various periods but reveal the isolated setting.*

was rooted in the Greek scriptures, the Septuagint (see Chapter 5), and the writings of the Greek church fathers (whereas the Vulgate and Latin fathers were predominant in the West). There were differences in basic practices. For instance, Latin clergy were generally celibate whereas Eastern clergy could marry. The two communities celebrated Easter, the feast commemorating Christ's resurrection from the dead, on different days. There were also some theological differences; East and West recited the Nicene Creed slightly differently, for example. In 1054 the pope and the patriarch excommunicated each other inaugurating a schism—a split—that lasted a thousand years.

A famous incident in Byzantine religious history reveals some of the tensions and characteristics of the age. In 726 Emperor Leo III began agitating against icons. As small, detached, frontal, and timeless images, icons had a history reaching back to at least the fifth century. As images that were believed by some to have miraculous powers, icons were of much more recent vintage, no older than the seventh century. Leo, a rugged military man, not an urban sophisticate, believed that icons violated the biblical prohibition of graven images, that they were blasphemous, and that their growing prominence explained why God was punishing the empire. Leo's son Constantine V (741–775) was a knowledgeable theologian himself and persuaded a number of bishops to write against icons. Irene, serving as regent for her son Constantine VI, convoked a council at Nicaea in 787 and restored the veneration of icons. What did this mean? It meant that people could kiss icons or approach them with candles and incense—and carry them around as protection against demons or illness. In 815 the emperor instituted a milder form of opposition to icons, but in 842 this was also overcome.

This struggle over icons is called the Iconoclastic Controversy. Iconoclasts were those who broke, effaced, or destroyed icons. Iconodules were those who venerated icons. Almost all surviving evidence on the controversy comes from iconodules who had no interest in representing their opponents' views fully or accurately. Even art was mobilized by the iconodules. The Khludov (CLUE-doff) Psalter, for example, has an image depicting a Roman centurion piercing Christ's side with a lance while, below, a figure is portrayed whitewashing an image of Christ. The message is clear: harming an image of Christ is like harming Christ himself (Figure 7.2). In reality, little art was destroyed and few people suffered physically although many were exiled. The controversy was a battle over how to read the Bible and how to understand the traditions of the church. The popes resolutely opposed Byzantine iconoclasm as did everyone else in the West. Both the existence of icons and the controversy over

Figure 7.2 Khludov Psalter, folio 51 verso. Ca. 843. Constantinople. 7.67 × 5.9". Moscow State Historical Museum. *Most of the images in this book of psalms pertain to standard theological issues, but some, like this one, are polemical. The key verse here is (Septuagint or Vulgate 51.9 or RSV 52.7): "See the man who would have none of God's help but relied on his store of riches and found his strength in his folly." A psalter like this would have been a book for private devotions, so this one gives a sense of the depth of feeling surrounding the image debates.*

them illustrate some of the ways in which Orthodoxy was tracing its own path.

THE EARLY MEDIEVAL WEST

Most of the earliest kingdoms established within Rome's former western provinces had relatively brief runs on history's stage. Justinian conquered the Vandal kingdom in Africa and the Ostrogothic kingdom in Italy as part of his effort to recapture Rome's glorious imperial past (see Chapter 6).

The Visigoths' story is different. Settled in Gaul by the Romans, they created a successful kingdom despite their Arianism. After the collapse of Roman authority in the West, the Visigoths found themselves face-to-face with the Franks, who defeated them decisively in 507 and confined them to Spain, where they had been expanding their influence for decades. They built an impressive kingdom in Spain and in 589

Timeline 7.2 THE EARLY MEDIEVAL WEST

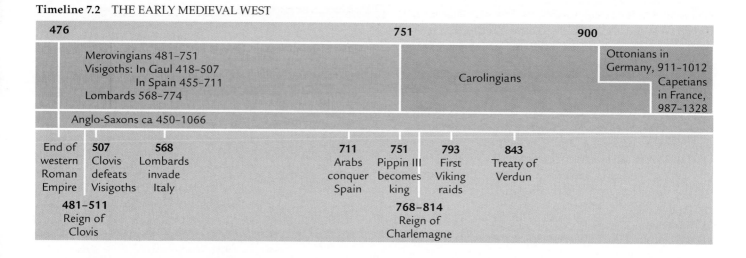

LEARNING THROUGH MAPS

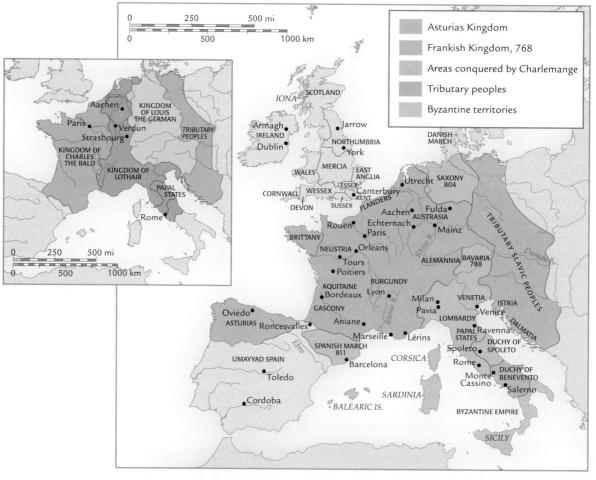

Map 7.2 THE CAROLINGIAN EMPIRE, THE BRITISH ISLES, AND THE TREATY OF VERDUN

This map shows three areas: (a) small kingdoms in the British Isles; (b) the vast extent of the Carolingian Empire, including old Frankish territories and the new lands added by Charlemagne; and (c) the division of Charlemagne's empire by his grandsons in 843. In comparing this map to Map 6.1: 1. *What* lands did the Carolingians rule that the Romans did not? 2. *How* does this map aid in understanding the Carolingian foundations of European civilization? 3. *What* is the significance of the location of Charlemagne's capital in Aachen rather than in Rome?

embraced Catholicism. Unfortunately, the defeat of 507 so damaged the prestige of the Visigothic monarchy that it was never able to create strong central institutions. As a result, between 711 and 716, Visigothic Spain fell to a Muslim army from North Africa.

The future of the West fell into the hands of the Anglo-Saxons and Franks (Timeline 7.2). The Anglo-Saxons were a conglomeration of peoples from what is today southern Denmark and northern Germany. By 410 the Romans had withdrawn their troops from Britain to deploy them elsewhere. Within a generation, bands of Angles and Saxons began settling in Britain. They settled slowly and, for the most part, peacefully across most of eastern and southern Britain. By 600 there were several small independent Anglo-Saxon kingdoms (Map 7.2). For two or three centuries, leadership within Britain passed from one kingdom to another as aggressive kings expanded at the expense of their neighbors. Anglo-Saxon kings issued law codes, held court in impressive wooden halls (Figure 7.3), and adopted some of the symbolic trappings of rulership such as wielding scepters. The greatest of the early kings, Offa of Mercia (757–796), issued laws, presided at church councils, and negotiated with the pope and with Charlemagne. In the latter endeavor he revealed his aspirations when he tried—unsuccessfully—to arrange a marriage between his son and Charlemagne's daughter. Offa was the first ruler to be called "king of all the English."

While political consolidation was slowly taking shape, ecclesiastical organization proceeded at a quicker pace. The British had been nominally Christian when the Romans departed, and their fate is difficult to grasp. The Anglo-Saxons were pagan. England's conversion to Catholicism had two roots. Irish missionaries from the Isle of Iona began working in the north, in what is now lowland Scotland. In 597 Gregory I (pope, 590–604) sent Augustine (d. 604/09) and a group of monks to evangelize the southern kingdom of Kent. The king of Kent had a Catholic Frankish wife, so there must have been some antecedent work of conversion. Augustine and his successors established a base at Canterbury (the burgh or fortress of the Kent men) and began pressing their missionary work to the north. All the while, Irish missions had been pressing south. In 664, at Whitby, a council decided in favor of Roman over Irish practices. The archbishops of Canterbury became the leaders of England's church although another archbishopric was set up at York in the eighth century. England had a small number of rather large bishoprics, so monks played a key role in evangelizing the countryside.

The Franks were a confederation of peoples first visible in the historical record around 250, and by about 400, living along the lower Rhine in what is now the Netherlands. For two or three generations, they ex-

panded south across what is now Belgium and northern France. Under their king Clovis (r. 481–511), the Franks consolidated their power in the Paris region and defeated the Visigoths. Clovis was the most powerful and famous member of the Merovingian family, named for a legendary ancestor, Merovech. Clovis embraced Catholicism and collaborated with the influential bishops of Gaul. On his death, Clovis treated the kingdom as if it were a personal patrimony and divided it among his sons. For more than two centuries, there was rarely a unified Frankish kingdom. Nevertheless, the idea of a single kingdom of the Franks persisted. All the Franks identified common enemies in the Saxons and Bavarians, and common laws were observed. Royal courts were centers of political action and intrigue. Kings ruled, supported by aristocrats,

Figure 7.3 Yeavering Hall. Ca. 600. Reconstruction. Kirknewton Parish, Northumberland, England. *Yeavering is the modern name for Gefrin, a British word meaning "hill of the goats." Archaeological excavations beginning in 1953 and continuing to today have identified several buildings and numerous burials on the site. The hall pictured here was in use around the year 600. From this site, kings ruled the surrounding territory. The site overall reveals British, Anglo-Saxon, Frankish, and Roman influences. Yeavering Hall is one of four nearly contemporary halls discovered in Northumbria. Readers of the Old English epic* Beowulf *(discussed later) will be reminded of Heorot, the great hall of King Hrothgar, where powerful men drank and deliberated while Queen Waltheow passed out mead.*

whose privileges were guaranteed in return. Factional squabbles among the aristocrats finally led to a weakening of the effective power of the Merovingian kings and the rise to prominence of the Carolingian family. The name Carolingian derives from *Carolus,* Charles, the name of several members of the dynasty but especially of *Carolus Magnus,* Charles the Great, or Charlemagne.

THE WORLD OF CHARLEMAGNE

The Carolingians rose to prominence by varied means. Some members of the family were clever and ruthless. The family had vast landholdings—land was wealth in that world—and they made strategic marriage alliances with other key families. Several members of the family were great warriors. Charles Martel (the Hammer) (about 684–741) defeated near Poitiers in 733 a Muslim raiding party that had begun in Spain. The victory vastly enhanced the Carolingians' reputation. For almost a century the Carolingians dominated the office of Mayor of the Palace, a sort of prime minister to the Merovingian kings.

In 749 Pippin III, son of Charles Martel and father of Charlemagne, asked the pope if it were right that in the land of the Franks the one who had the royal title had no power while the one who lacked the royal title had real power. The pope said that this situation contravened the divinely instituted order, and in 751 the Franks made Pippin their king. In 754 the pope visited the Franks to enlist their help against the Lombards. Pippin defeated the Lombards and forced them to give the pope all the lands they had, technically, conquered from Byzantium. In these actions lay the origins of the Papal States, then about one-third of Italy, but today only the 108 acres of Vatican City. The pope crowned and anointed Pippin, his wife, and their sons. Royal anointing, based on the anointing of Saul by Samuel in the Old Testament (1 Samuel 10:1), was new here, although it had been widely practiced in the ancient Near East. The rite of anointing added divine approval to that of the pope and the Franks. When Pippin died in 768, his two sons divided his kingdom. One of them died in 771 leaving the older brother, Charles, who would be known to history as Charlemagne.

The Reign of Charlemagne

The greatness of Charlemagne (r. 768–814) is legendary. In the forty-six years of his reign, commanders acting in his name fought fifty-three campaigns. Yet Charles did not always accompany his armies and is not remembered as a brilliant strategist or charismatic

Figure 7.4   Silver Denarius of Charlemagne. Munz-kabinett, Staatliche Museen zu Berlin. *This coin was struck at Frankfurt in about 806. Although it adopts certain Roman imperial conceits—the bust profile, laurel wreath, and gathered cloak—the image is thought to represent Charlemagne accurately. His biographer, Einhard, commented on his long nose and short neck. The legend on the coin reads KAROLUS IMP(erator) AUG(ustus): Charles Emperor Augustus.*

leader. He was deeply pious but sired a dozen children out of wedlock and slaughtered 4,500 Saxons in a fit of rage. He could read and speak several languages but never learned to write. Nevertheless, Charles, who had a tidy, almost fastidious mind, fostered a massive program of educational renewal. He reformed secular and ecclesiastical institutions, took a keen interest in theological controversies, and raised the intellectual level of his clergy (Figure 7.4).

The most famous event in Charlemagne's reign was his coronation as emperor by Leo III (pope, 795–816) on Christmas day in 800 at St. Peter's Basilica in Rome. The pope had been attacked by a Roman mob and fled to the Franks for protection. Charles traveled to Rome to investigate. For more than a decade, men around Charles had been calling him emperor or insisting that he deserved to be emperor. Some said that the imperial throne was vacant because Irene, a woman, was ruling in Constantinople. The coronation was Leo's own idea and upset Charlemagne. Charlemagne never called himself a Roman emperor, and in 813 he crowned his son Louis (r. 814–840) as his successor in the chapel at Aachen, his capital, before the assembled Franks. After a lapse of more than three centuries, there was again an emperor in the West (see Map 7.2).

Pippin, Charlemagne, and Louis enjoyed almost a century (751–840) of unified rule over most of western Europe. By following consistent policies, they laid the foundation on which European civilization would be built. Once or twice per year they gathered the several hundred counts, the key local officials appointed by the ruler, in a great assembly where issues were debated and decisions made. The decisions took the form of **capitularies,** edicts issued in chapters (*capitula*). Each year, officials—*missi dominici,* envoys of the king—were sent two by two, one layman and one cleric, through specified territories to investigate whether the capitularies were being applied. Sons of powerful aristocrats regularly spent some time at the royal court to learn the ways of the regime, and great churchmen frequently gathered in councils that legislated for the Frankish church as a whole. Charlemagne and Louis sought to impose uniformity in canon law, monastic practices, and church worship on all their lands.

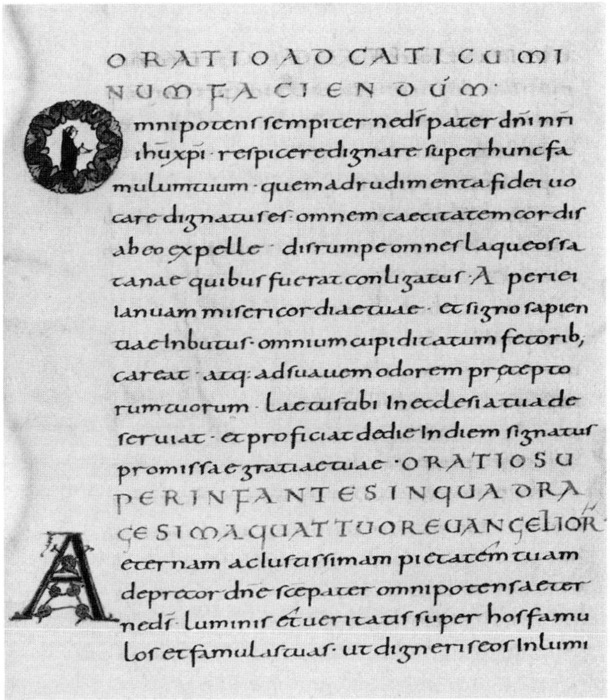

The Carolingian Renaissance

As long ago as 1839, a scholar spoke of the "Carolingian Renaissance." The phrase was intended to capture the spirit of rebirth, renewal, and reform that characterized the age. The Renaissance was born in the hearts and minds of the Carolingian rulers. Charlemagne had both the vision and the resources to promote a mighty movement, and he saw himself in some ways as an Old Testament king. People around him compared him to David, the simple yet learned warrior, and to Solomon, the wisest of kings. Charles compared himself to Josiah in his duty to visit, to admonish, and to correct, and also saw himself as something like a bishop. He was deeply influenced by a book, *The Pastoral Rule,* written by Pope Gregory I. Although Gregory had written it as a guide to bishops' behavior, Charles took to heart the idea that rule was not a privilege or a benefit to the ruler but, instead, a massive responsibility conferred on some by God for the benefit of everyone else.

As for resources, Charlemagne's wars brought plunder and tribute and also created peace and prosperity in his lands. Charles did not hesitate to use his vast wealth to promote the church, which, in turn, became the great patron of scholarship and the arts. In the Carolingian period, several dozen cathedral churches and more than three hundred monasteries were built or rebuilt. Charles also used his resources to attract the best minds from all over Europe. About one of them, Alcuin, who came from England, a scholar said, "He landed on the Continent with a bag of books and died the lord of twenty thousand men."

Charlemagne was concerned about the low level of education that prevailed and the lack of teachers,

Figure 7.5 Carolingian Minuscule. Ninth century. Bibliothèque Nationale, Paris. *Because Christianity relied heavily on written works, legible texts were important; but the prevailing style of writing, which used separately formed lowercase letters, was almost impossible to read. To overcome this difficulty, scribes during Charlemagne's reign perfected a new style of writing—the Carolingian minuscule—characterized by clearly formed letters linked into words, spaces between words, and capital letters at the beginning of sentences, as shown here. All subsequent Western handwriting styles follow from this tradition.*

schools, and libraries. In capitularies, therefore, he commanded that cathedrals and monasteries should establish schools (even sons of laymen not destined for clergy were permitted to attend). Only well-trained men—the schools were restricted to boys and men—should be permitted to teach. Copies of important books were to be secured and then multiple copies made for dissemination. To avoid mistakes, only the most experienced scribes were to be employed. By the middle years of Charlemagne's reign, a new script, **Carolingian minuscule** (Figure 7.5), began to spread from one church or monastery to another. This was an extremely clear and legible script characterized by simple letter forms. Carolingian minuscule is actually the script that is at the base of most modern typefaces. So comprehensive and systematic were the efforts of Carolingian scholars that the oldest surviving manuscript of over 90 percent of all Latin classical works is Carolingian. Ironically, Renaissance humanists of the fourteenth and fifteenth centuries emulated this handwriting because they mistakenly believed the manuscripts they kept finding were Roman.

The curriculum in Carolingian schools was the same as in the schools of antiquity: **the seven liberal arts.** The arts were grammar, rhetoric, dialectic, arithmetic, geometry, astronomy, and music. Grammar involved the acquisition of basic skills in Latin. Rhetoric had for a long time been less focused on speaking well than on a kind of literary criticism, the ability to identify and also to write figures of speech. Dialectic meant formal logic. Medieval students before the thirteenth century had few ancient logic treatises, but enough were available that they could make and recognize logically sound arguments. Arithmetic and geometry were practical, useful for doing sums, building, and measuring property. Astronomy was useful for navigation but also included elements of astrology. Music was more like musicology, the science of music, than the skill of performance.

Overall the Carolingian program was limited, practical, and functional. It was also intelligently designed and remarkably effective across Charlemagne's empire. While the program was designed to achieve basic literacy among the religious and secular leaders of society, it also produced a number of astonishingly learned and gifted scholars.

The Post-Carolingian World

The Carolingian Empire began breaking up in the middle of the ninth century. One man ruled the realm from 751 to 840, but thereafter there were always rival claimants. In 843 Charlemagne's grandsons divided the empire with the Treaty of Verdun. Although no one could have seen it at the time, that treaty established the foundations for the later kingdoms of France and Germany. In addition to familial strife, the sheer size and complexity of the Carolingian realm militated against its long-term cohesion. Finally, the ninth century saw a return of external attacks unseen since the fifth century. Vikings, Magyars, and Muslims ravaged Europe's coasts and frontiers. These raids were psychologically damaging, economically disruptive, and politically destabilizing.

In what was becoming France, the Carolingian family finally succumbed to a rival, Hugh Capet (r. 987–996), who secured the throne definitively for his family. The Capetians would rule France until 1328, but between 987 and 1328, they had direct control over a smaller and smaller portion of the realm. From one point of view, government was failing and anarchy was ascendant. From another point of view, however, small territorial principalities—Normandy, Anjou, Champagne, for example—were emerging on the local level with extremely effective government. Ironically, these counties and duchies looked like miniaturized ver-

sions of the former Carolingian state. They preserved both memory and practices that later French kings would draw upon to rebuild the monarchy.

In what was becoming Germany, the dukes of Saxony worked hard to create an effective state. They controlled their own lands in Saxony with an iron fist and led successful military campaigns against the Slavs and the Magyars. The three greatest Saxon kings, all named Otto, supported the church and drew it into their government. They were also great patrons of culture. And in 962, Otto I was crowned emperor in Rome, which added great prestige to the dynasty.

In England, the Vikings first appeared in 793 and they were a real menace for a century after that. Effective government whether secular or ecclesiastical virtually ceased, and intellectual life ground to a halt. In 871 Alfred (r. 871–899) became king of Wessex (see Map 7.2). Although at that time he was confined to a swamp in the south of England, little by little he rallied his forces and then went on the offensive. He faced a major threat: a Viking army was trying to conquer England. Alfred won several victories in the south and then marched north, rolling back the Viking forces as he did so. When he died in 899, the south of England was entirely free of Viking threats and the tide had turned. Alfred, who shared Charlemagne's interest in education and culture, attracted scholars and patronized churches and schools. He lamented the fact that Charlemagne had turned to England for scholars while he had to go to the Continent to find them. Alfred personally translated various works from Latin into Old English so that their contents would be available in a devastated England.

THE LITERARY ARTS IN THE EARLY MIDDLE AGES

Some early medieval writers were prodigiously learned, and a few were capable of achieving real originality. Most writers, whether from the East or West, devoted most of their energy to preserving and explicating the ancient heritage in both its secular and Christian manifestations. The culture of Byzantium was almost exclusively Greek and looked back to the Greek classics and the writings of the Greek church fathers. Similarly, in the West, culture was Latin and drew inspiration from the Latin classics and Latin church fathers.

Byzantine Writers

Throughout the early Middle Ages there were Byzantine writers who sought to preserve a fragile heritage.

For example, John Moschus (550–619) wrote *The Spiritual Meadow* as a collection of brief lives of famous eastern ascetics. He tried to transmit a sense of their habits and customs to later ages. The work was widely read both as a historical guide and as spiritual instruction. In the ninth century, Photius (FOH-shus) (810–893) compiled his *Library,* a collection of 280 extracts from a wide array of classical authors. In many cases, the extracts found in the *Library* are all that survive of some ancient works. Photius, who was one of the great figures of his age and twice patriarch of Constantinople, seems to have felt that a tradition was slipping away.

Two works had more practical aims. The *Strategikon* (struh-TEE-juh-kon), a manual of military science, appeared around 600. It was either written or commissioned by the emperor Maurice (r. 581–602). In twelve books, mainly on mounted soldier warfare, the book provides a wealth of strategic, tactical, and logistical details. Incidentally, the books contain brief ethnic studies of many of the peoples living along Byzantium's northern frontier. In the tenth century, the emperor Constantine VII Porphyrogenitus (PORE-fear-oh-gen-uh-tus) (905–959) wrote two treatises, *On the Administration of the Empire* and *On Ceremonies.* Designed as handbooks to guide governmental and court procedures, the books contain a great deal of information on, for example, officials and rituals, that is invaluable to modern historians.

Other writers produced works that were both original and influential. Maximus the Confessor (580–662) was a profound theologian who entered the fray during the Christological controversies over Christ's divine and human natures in the seventh century. He was the greatest Neoplatonist among Byzantine theologians. John of Damascus (about 676–749) is best known today for *Three Orations against Those Who Attack Holy Images,* which he wrote after Emperor Leo III began campaigning against icons. These works are immensely learned and were highly influential in Byzantium after the final restoration of images in 842. In the Byzantine tradition, however, John's most important work was *Fountain of Knowledge,* a compendium of theology organized and argued by means of acute dialectical reasoning drawn mainly from Aristotle. John laid down in this work a great deal of the technical terminology that was subsequently used in Orthodox theology and philosophy. And, as Maximus was the great Neoplatonist, so John was the great Aristotelian.

Byzantium produced two historians of note. Michael Psellos (SELL-us) (1018–about 1081) was a prolific author who wrote on law, philosophy, theology, and history. His *Chronography* is a history of the period 976 to 1078. Michael was an eyewitness to much of the story he told and, as an adviser to several emperors, he was unusually well informed. His account

brims with fascinating details, but its most memorable feature is its credible character sketches of powerful Byzantines.

The other Byzantine historian of note was a woman: Anna Comnena [kawm-NEE-nuh] (1083–about 1153), daughter of Emperor Alexius I Comnenus. Anna's *Alexiad* was one of the first known works of history by a woman. Joining Christian and classical knowledge and following the rigorous method pioneered by the Greek historian Thucydides (see Chapter 3), the *Alexiad* is a scholarly study of the reign of Anna's father, Alexius. Despite the author's obvious bias toward her father and confused chronology, the work is the best source for this period in Byzantine history. Especially valuable for Western readers is its portrait of the soldiers, saints, and hangers-on of the First Crusade (1096) passing through Constantinople on the way to Jerusalem. To Anna Comnena's non-Western eyes, the European Crusaders were a crude, violent bunch, more greedy for loot than concerned about salvation.

The Latin West

Several figures stand out as preservers of the old ways and ideas. In Italy there were three. Boethius (BOW-ee-thee-us) (480–525) hailed from an ancient Roman family and served the Ostrogothic king Theodoric until he was suspected of treason, imprisoned, and executed. Versatile, Boethius wrote a treatise on music and planned to translate the whole of Aristotle into Latin. He managed only to finish some of Aristotle's logic treatises, and for the next several centuries the logic taught in schools was based on these Boethian translations. While he was in prison awaiting death, Boethius wrote a work that was extremely popular and influential for centuries, *The Consolation of Philosophy.* Cast in dialogue form, this **prosimetric**—sections alternate between verse and prose—treatise probes the questions of why fortune seems so fickle, why good people are afflicted with misfortune, what consolation there may be for poor mortals. Boethius and Lady Philosophy go back and forth, she saying to him at one point "no man can ever be truly secure until he has been forsaken by Fortune." Happiness, in other words, is a fleeting thing. Although deeply imbued with Christian values, the text makes no explicit appeal to Christian teachings. Happiness, the work suggests, can be found only in philosophical contemplation.

Cassiodorus (CASS-ee-oh-DOR-us) (about 490–585), another aristocrat, was like Boethius a servant of Theodoric. Unlike the philosopher, however, Cassiodorus was loyal to the end. He held high office three different times and, for some years, kept the court's official

ENCOUNTER

Globalization: The Silk Road

Globalization occurred before the modern world through trade, warfare, and travel. The greatest catalyst for globalization was the Silk Road, the network of roads linking China with the Mediterranean and involving all the states in between these two distant points.

Not a single route, the Silk Road was a system of links connecting China to the West. Merchants and their pack animals (horses, camels, and/or asses), organized into caravans for safety, stopped at the towns and watering holes along the 4,000-mile road. A fully loaded caravan could travel fifteen to twenty miles per day. Encounter map 7.1 shows the Silk Road over the long course of its history.

China's Han dynasty (206 BCE–8 CE) established this long-distance trade route. In China, the terminal points of the Silk Road changed according to political circumstances. Under the Han emperors, embassies were sent to the western regions, hoping to forge trading and military ties. The embassies discovered flourishing contacts between Central Asia and the Mediterranean. As Rome absorbed the Hellenistic states, the old trade routes passed under Roman control, including the western entry points to the Silk Road: the Mediterranean ports of Alexandria in Egypt, Gaza, Tyre, and Antioch; and the Black Sea port of Trebizond. Through them, silk (yarn and cloth) entered the Roman world, becoming a prized luxury, comparable to gold and silver.

In Latin, silk is *ser,* derived possibly from the Chinese term for silk; the Romans called the Chinese *Seres,* the "people who make silk." The English word for silk production, *sericulture,* memorializes this encounter between the West and China.

Sericulture was ancient in China and the rulers made its production a state secret. Rome first encountered silk in 53 BCE, when the shimmering silk tents of Parthian enemies dazzled the Roman soldiers. In 46 BCE, Julius Caesar, who awed the masses with silk banners during a parade in Rome, sparked a fad for silk in upper-class families. In 14 CE, the senate, fearing for public morals, tried unsuccessfully to forbid men to wear silk, claiming that it shamed them, and reserved its use exclusively to women. Sericulture was introduced into the Byzantine world in the sixth century. In the early Middle Ages, European silk came from Byzantium.

The Silk Road brought other luxuries to the Mediterranean world: aromatic and pungent spices—used for seasoning foods, as burnt offerings in temples and homes, as ingredients in medicines and perfumes, and in embalming—were imported from Arabia (myrrh and frankincense); from India (black pepper, cardamom, fennel, ginger, and turmeric); and from Southeast Asia (cinnamon, cloves, and cassia). From India came two other luxury goods: pearls and cotton muslin textiles. The West offered exports in exchange: wool, coral, amber, red cinnabar, colored glass, perfumes, copper and tin, linen, and wines. Slaves were also a constant commodity on the Silk Road.

Learning from the Encounter

1. *What* was the Silk Road? 2. *Why* was it termed the Silk Road? 3. *Explain* how the Silk Road came into being. 4. *What* role did the Chinese play in establishing the Silk Road? 5. *What* brought the Romans into Silk Road commerce? 6. *What* influence did silk have on the Roman people? 7. *Describe* the spices imported into Rome and *explain* their various uses.

---

records. These letters, the *Variae,* are written in an elegant Latin and provide crucial information for modern scholars. Cassiodorus also wrote a history of the Goths that does not survive, although a Gothic writer paraphrased and built upon it. Cassiodorus had longed for a durable reconciliation between Goths and Romans, and, when that proved impossible, he retreated to his family estates at Squillace in southern Italy and established a school of Christian studies. There, Cassiodorus wrote biblical commentaries and the work for which he is best known, *Institutes of Divine and Human Readings.* The divine institutes is arranged according to the books of the Bible and lists the best commentators on each book. The human institutes is arranged according to the seven liberal arts and lists the best manuals and commentaries on each art. This work of stupendous learning was in every medieval library and often served as a kind of wish list for librarians.

Contemporary with Boethius and Cassiodorus was the great monastic father, Benedict of Nursia (480–543/5). Born into a family of modest means in Rome, Benedict withdrew from the secular world and went out into the wilderness to live an ascetic life. Around 520, he established his own community about eighty miles from Rome at Monte Cassino. There he wrote a *Rule* for his monks. In seventy-three chapters, based largely on the Bible, Benedict set forth a comprehensive guide to life. Its three guiding principles were

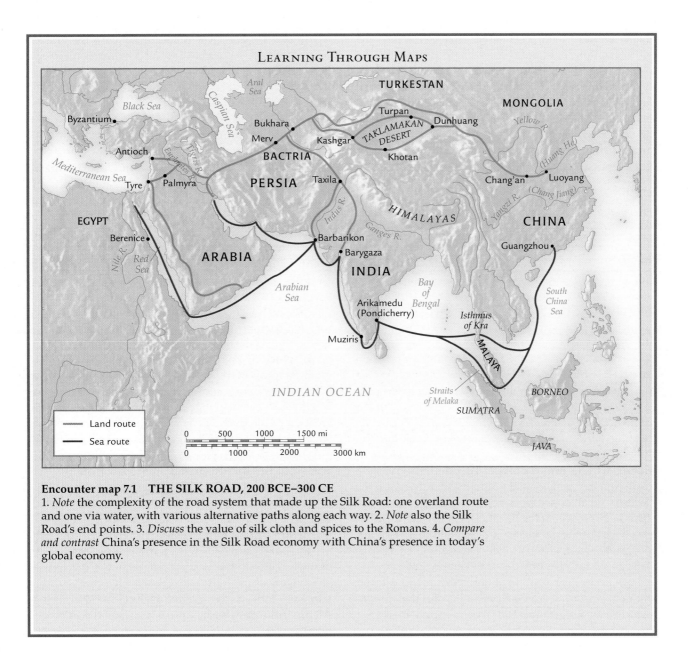

LEARNING THROUGH MAPS

Encounter map 7.1   THE SILK ROAD, 200 BCE–300 CE
1. *Note* the complexity of the road system that made up the Silk Road: one overland route and one via water, with various alternative paths along each way. 2. *Note* also the Silk Road's end points. 3. *Discuss* the value of silk cloth and spices to the Romans. 4. *Compare and contrast* China's presence in the Silk Road economy with China's presence in today's global economy.

obedience, stability, and conversion. The first involved absolute obedience to the abbot, to the father figure in the monastery, a renunciation of the willfulness of the individual monk. Stability meant a pledge to remain in a monastery after one had entered; Benedict despised wandering holy men. Finally, monks were to undertake a complete change of their way of life—a conversion. Benedict wrote his *Rule* for Monte Cassino alone, but Pope Gregory I admired it and wrote approvingly about it. The Anglo-Saxons had a special fondness for Benedict's *Rule,* and Charlemagne considered it the ideal expression of monasticism. He issued capitularies demanding that all monasteries adopt the *Rule.* Ironically, Benedictine monasticism, although based

on Benedict's *Rule,* was actually created by men who came long after him.

In Spain, the Bishop of Seville Isidore (560–636) was a commanding figure. Highly educated, Isidore wrote histories, biblical commentaries, a book on offices and duties within the church, and his *Etymologies* in twenty books. In this latter work, Isidore's aim was to create an encyclopedia of all knowledge organized according to the principle that the origins and meanings of words reveal a tremendous amount of practical information. Throughout the Middle Ages, Isidore's book was copied and studied.

At the court of Charlemagne, Alcuin (AL-kwin) (about 730–804) was the architect of the academic and intellectual revival. Charlemagne attracted him to court with a promise of support for a broad program of reform. He had been trained in the excellent schools in the north of England and was one of the most learned men of his time. Alcuin was a good poet, a sound theologian, and a solid biblical scholar but is best remembered as a teacher. He wrote elementary texts and taught Charlemagne's children, including his daughters. Although Alcuin did not leave behind a body of original scholarship or beautiful literary works, he was supremely influential. Some two dozen of his pupils founded schools in the ninth century.

One individual above all others exemplifies the best of the Carolingian Renaissance: Theodulf of Orléans (about 750–821), a Visigoth. Charlemagne called Theodulf to court in about 790. His first task was to write *The Book of King Charles Against the Synod*, which constituted Charlemagne's official rejection of the Second Council of Nicaea in 787. The work, a brilliant dismantling of every argument raised both for and against images at Nicaea, argued the basic Carolingian position on sacred art: it was legitimate to possess such art for commemoration or decoration and heretical to worship or to destroy sacred art. Theodulf's language ranged from wickedly polemical to serenely philosophical. His learning, particularly his command of the Bible and the church fathers, was impressive, and he knew Hebrew, which was unusual in his age. Theodulf also wrote a treatise on baptism, a set of guidelines for priests in his diocese, and an angry work deploring the corruption of officials. He was also the finest poet of his age, a craftsman with both form and language. As if that were not enough, he was a gifted architect and designed a beautiful chapel at Germigny-des-Prés (Figure 7.6).

In a period when new states were being created and new peoples were being brought into the church, historical writing flourished. Writers tried their best to get a sense of where they themselves, or their peoples, or their time, fit in the grand sweep of time. The idea of history in Augustine's *City of God* had made such questions urgent: if history had begun when God created the world and would continue until God returned to judge the world, people wondered where they stood at the moment.

Gregory (538–594), the bishop of Tours, who came from an old, distinguished family, was a prolific author. In addition to voluminous writings about the lives of the saints, he wrote *Ten Books of Histories*. Gregory began at the beginning—with the Creation. He quickly brought his account up to the Roman conquest of Gaul and then to the rise of the Franks. He portrays long-term historical continuities, not ruptures. The largest part, more than eight books, of Gregory's *Histories* treats the sixth century, but it would be a mistake to say that Gregory was preoccupied with the Franks. In fact, Gregory sketches out an implicit comparison between his own world and the world of the biblical kings. His overall intention is moral and didactic: he aims to teach lessons about good and bad behavior and the consequences of each. His Latin is not elegant and, by classical standards, is often clumsy, but Gregory is a wonderful storyteller with a sharp eye for detail.

Bede (BEED) (672/3–735) was a product of the cultural crosscurrents of northern England. That is, he was heir to the Irish, English, and Roman traditions. From the age of five, he lived in the monasteries of Monkwearmouth and Jarrow. Bede was a prolific author who wrote on time reckoning, for example, and popularized the use of AD (*anno Domini*, "in the year of the Lord") dating. He wrote many biblical commentaries and was the first to use a system of references that anticipates the modern footnote. Bede is best known for his *Ecclesiastical History of the English People*, a work modeled on Eusebius's *Ecclesiastical History* (see Chapter 6), which he knew in Latin translation. For the "English People," Bede imagines a common history long before they had a common polity—that history was religious. Instead of beginning his history with the creation of the world, he starts with Christianity's first stirrings in Britain. Here again was an homage to Augustine. Bede was trying to show how the City of God, at least in Britain, was being built apart from the City of Man. Bede's Latin is clear, graceful, and correct.

Bede lived in a world where no one spoke Latin. It had to be acquired in school. Consequently, Latin was learned in Britain more precisely than it was in Gregory of Tours' Gaul, where the Latin people spoke every day was close to the written language. As the spoken language was evolving into French, so too the written language looked less like old-fashioned Latin. It was Alcuin, from Bede's England, who urged the reform of language that Charlemagne implemented. Ironically, by correcting Latin, the Carolingians killed it; they began turning it into a dead language. The Romance languages—French, Italian, Spanish—continued to evolve while Latin did not. It remained the language of learning, church, and government for a long time, but it was no longer the language in daily use.

Another highly regarded historian was Einhard (about 770–840), who came from a noble family in the Main River region of what is now western Germany. His family sent him to a monastery for his education but the abbot, recognizing his talent, sent him to court. Although a generation younger than Charlemagne, Einhard became his good friend. Einhard wrote a good deal but is best known for the most successful and popular of all medieval biographies, *The Life of the Emperor Charles*. Einhard wrote this work about 828,

Figure 7.6   Oratory, Germigny-des-Prés, France. 806. *Theodulf designed this oratory as part of a palace complex. Everything except this building was later destroyed by Vikings. Internally the building is a Greek cross. Externally the building is almost square with single apses on the north, south, and west sides, and a triple apse on the east side. A high tower covers the central bay while barrel vaults cover the N, S, E, and W side bays. The corners have shallow domes supported by* **squinches** *(projecting arches placed diagonally at the internal angles of towers to support round superstructures; compare pendentives—see Figure 7.13). Centrally planned churches were rare in the Carolingian world. Theodulf adopted a style that would become normative later in Byzantium but that had never previously appeared in the West.*

fourteen years after Charlemagne died, in a beautiful, classicizing Latin. Near the beginning, Einhard professed his admiration for Cicero (see Chapter 4) and said that Ciceronian eloquence was necessary to the subject at hand. He used Stoic virtues—self-restraint and magnanimity, for example—to craft his portrait of Charlemagne and took his basic structure from Suetonius, the Roman historian who wrote *The Lives of the Twelve Caesars.* In consequence, Einhard's portrayal is not chronological but instead thematic—wars, private affairs, public affairs, personal qualities, and so forth. Several things are striking about Einhard's *Life.* First, its author was a layman. Second, learning was not ex-

clusive to the clergy. And third, the book was the first secular biography; for the past five hundred years, all biographies had been about saints. Einhard's learning and his literary aspirations reveal the achievements of the Carolingian Renaissance.

In the tenth century, one historian towered over all the others—and there were a good many. Liudprand [LOOD-prand] of Cremona (922–972) traveled widely and observed much. He spent time in Constantinople, where he learned Greek along with a sharp dislike for all things Byzantine. Liudprand wrote accounts of his journeys to Constantinople and the *Deeds of Otto I.* Although an Italian, Liudprand admired Otto. Primarily,

---

SLICE OF LIFE
Marriage Diplomacy Nets a Diplomatic Insult

LIUDPRAND OF CREMONA

Bishop Liudprand (about 920–972) of Cremona, emissary of the German ruler Otto I (the Great), traveled (968) to Constantinople to arrange a marriage between Otto's son and a Byzantine princess. Here, he describes his strained meeting with the emperor to King Otto.

On the fourth of June we arrived at Constantinople, and after a miserable reception, meant as an insult to yourselves, we were given the most miserable and disgusting quarters. . . .

On the sixth of June, which was the Saturday before Pentecost, I was brought before the emperor's brother Leo, marshal of the court and chancellor; and there we tired ourselves with a fierce argument over your imperial title. He called you not emperor, which is Basileus in his tongue, but insultingly Rex, which is king in yours. I told him that the thing meant was the same though the word was different, and he then said that I had come not to make peace but to stir up strife. Finally he got up in a rage, and really wishing to insult us received your letter not in his own hand but through an interpreter. . . .

On the seventh of June, the sacred day of Pentecost, I was brought before Nicephorus himself in the palace called Stephana, that is, the Crown Palace. He is a monstrosity of a man. . . . He began his speech as follows:—

It was our duty and our desire to give you a courteous and magnificent reception. That, however, has been rendered impossible by the impiety of your master, who in the guise of an hostile invader has laid claim to Rome; . . . has tried to subdue to himself by massacre and conflagration cities belonging to our empire. . . .

To him I made this reply: "My master did not invade the city of Rome by force nor as a tyrant; he freed her from a tyrant's yoke, or rather from the yoke of many tyrants. . . . Your power, methinks, was fast asleep then; and the power of your predecessors, who in name alone are called emperors of the Romans, while the reality is far different. . . .

INTERPRETING THIS SLICE OF LIFE

1. *What* was the purpose of the mission of Bishop Liudprand to the Byzantine court? 2. *Why* was a churchman entrusted with this mission? 3. *Discuss* church-state relations in both Byzantine and early medieval culture, based on the evidence of this Slice of Life. 4. *Why* was Liudprand insulted by being addressed as the ambassador of a king? 5. *What* were the issues at stake in this argument between Liudprand and the emperor's brother Leo? 6. *Speculate* on the reaction of Otto to this report from his ambassador Liudprand.

---

however, he intensely disliked the petty squabbling among the Italian princes of his day. A shrewd judge of character despite a penchant for caricature, Liudprand created memorable portraits of the characters who crossed his path.

The one original philosopher in the early Middle Ages was an Irishman, John Scottus Eriugena (air-ee-oo-GAY-nuh) (815–877), who accepted the invitation of Charles the Bald, one of Charlemagne's grandsons, to come to his court and pursue his studies. An excellent Greek scholar, Eriugena translated works by Greek church fathers into Latin. His most important work, the *Periphyseon,* was an attempt to reconcile Platonic philosophy and Christianity. He argued that nature could be divided into four categories:

- Nature which is not created, but creates (God)
- Nature which is created and creates (the Platonic forms or ideas—see Chapter 3)
- Nature which is created and does not create (things perceived by the senses)

- Nature which neither creates nor is created (God, to whom all must return)

In the thirteenth century, Eruigena's work was declared heretical because he had not drawn sufficient distinction between the Creator and his creation. His philosophical achievement was nevertheless considerable.

Two women writers, working against overwhelming odds, left their mark on this virile age: Dhuoda (DOO-oh-duh) (fl. 840s), a laywoman, and Hrotsvitha (RAWTS-vee-tuh) (935–about 975), a nun. About Dhuoda herself little is known. A noblewoman from the Rhineland, she married a Frankish count from the south of France. In the early 840s she wrote a manual of advice for his son William, whom his father had taken to the Frankish court. While not particularly original, the work urges William to attend to religious duties, honor family members, and learn the ways of the court. Of perhaps greater interest, the book shows Dhuoda in command of a fine Latin style in her prose and verse. She knew the Bible, and also several texts by church fathers, extremely well. Surely, Dhuoda's learning and writing ability were not unique to lay-women in her era, but only hers have been recovered.

A century later, Hrotsvitha, who came from a noble Saxon family and lived in a convent in Gandersheim, made an even greater impression than Dhuoda. She was an exceptionally skilled poet, well versed in the Bible, and familiar with Horace, Virgil, Ovid, Plautus, and Terence (see Chapters 4 and 6). Taking Terence as her model, Hrotsvitha wrote six plays, which survive. In these plays, she held up Christian women—virgins, ascetics, and martyrs—as exemplary figures in opposition to Terence's fickle and immoral women. Hrotsvitha is hailed as Germany's first woman poet.

The Vernacular Achievement

Vernacular writings are those written in a language other than Latin. The earliest vernacular writings appeared in lands outside the boundaries of the former Roman Empire. In Wales around 600, Aneirin (un-NEE-run) wrote the *Gododdin* (guh-DOTH-un), which is about a fierce battle between the advancing Saxons and the British. In Ireland, a great many legal, religious, and literary works were written in Old Irish. One remarkable tale, the *Tain* (toyne), centering on the epic-scale cattle raid of Cooley, was set down in its extant form in the eighth century. In this tale, Queen Maeve of Connaught (kuh-NOTT) raids Cooley to capture the brown bull, but the hero Cuchulian (KOO-hull-un) defeats her. *Tain* is a rich and intriguing tale full of universal themes and Irish peculiarities.

The Anglo-Saxons too were precocious in developing an impressive literature in Old English. In addition to legal, historical, and religious material, there survive thousands of lines of verse. Some of the lyric and elegiac poetry of Anglo-Saxon England is beautiful and moving. Best known, however, is the extraordinary anonymous epic *Beowulf*. Probably a work of the tenth century, this poem of 3,182 lines features a series of verbal and physical combats. Men fight monsters and one another, and loyalties are pledged and strained. The work is set in a remote past but clearly deals with contemporary issues. Although *Beowulf* makes no reference to Christianity or the church, some scholars see in it an implicit struggle between Christian and heroic values. The poem is dominated by a sense of gloom and foreboding—perhaps a poignant comment on human life itself.

On the Continent the German lands of the Carolingian world produced some interesting material in Old Saxon and Old High German. The most important work in Saxon is the *Heliand* (HAY-lee-ahnd) (*Savior*), an imaginative recasting of the Gospels. Almost certainly this ninth-century work was intended as an aid in evangelizing the militant Saxons. In this version, Jesus and the twelve apostles form a war band and Jerusalem becomes a hill fort.

THE VISUAL ARTS IN THE EARLY MIDDLE AGES

Brilliant visual display was a constant feature of the early medieval environment. Royal and imperial courts were major centers of patronage, but the church was the most generous patron. Accordingly, most art had religious themes and subject matter. If significant secular art existed, little has survived. Freestanding sculpture became very rare, although relief sculpture sometimes appeared in churches and some very fine ivory carvings survive. Large-scale mosaics were less common than in late Roman times, but in a few places, works of great beauty and high technical proficiency did appear. Painting regularly occupied two sites: the walls of churches and the pages of books.

East and West, a blending of cultural traditions is in evidence. In Byzantium, the late antique heritage mixed with the visual culture of frontier regions. In the West, late antique, barbarian, and Celtic traditions fused in a new art of beauty, energy, and originality.

Byzantine Art

Byzantine styles became relatively fixed in the age of Justinian. The Ravenna mosaics (see Chapter 6) are illustrative of the dominant style. Far off in the Sinai peninsula, however, monks at the monastery of St. Catherine painted or imported stunning icons. The majestic icon of Christ (Figure 7.7), perhaps painted in the sixth century in Constantinople, makes Christ present to the viewer both immediately and timelessly. The naturalistic style evokes a sense of reality: this is not a picture of Christ; this is Christ. The picture attracts the reverence and awe of the viewer. Perhaps painted in the early eighth century, the crucifixion scene from St. Catherine's is quite different (Figure 7.8). Here, Christ is erect and garbed like a royal figure. His head is slightly tilted, he bears the crown of thorns, and his eyes are closed. He has suffered and died. This picture both evokes reverence and teaches a central truth of Christianity.

The iconoclastic era was probably less damaging to art than heretofore thought. Some images were removed, painted over, or replaced with simple crosses. But on the whole, the early Byzantine environment was not as richly decorated as the post-iconoclastic world would be. In Hagia Sophia, for example, there

Figure 7.7 Icon of Christ. Constantinople, sixth century. Encaustic on wood, 33 × 18″. *This icon, preserved in the extremely remote monastery of St. Catherine on the Sinai peninsula, is an early example of what became a traditional way of representing the mature Christ in medieval art. Most icons were executed in an abstract, illusionistic style, but this one has a high degree of naturalism. The unknown artist uses naturalism to convey the religious message: this is both the son of God (signaled by the golden halo) and the son of man (indicated by the precise rendition of hand gestures and facial hair and features). The use of gold, an artificial touch, is a defining feature of Byzantine style.*

Figure 7.8 Icon of the Crucifixion. Ca. 700. Monastery of St. Catherine, Sinai. Tempera, 18.25 × 10″. *The Virgin (left) and St. John (right, the beloved disciple) stand on either side of the crucified Christ and in front of the two crucified thieves (the painting in its current state shows only the thief in the left rear). Beneath the cross, two Roman soldiers, oblivious to the meaning of the Crucifixion, cast lots for Christ's garments upon his death. The diminished size of the soldiers in relation to the central figures is typical of Byzantine style. This icon, based on John 19:18–26, represents a biblical narrative, unlike other icons that focus on a single, isolated figure (see Figure 7.7).*

is very little evidence of pre-iconoclastic images. In 867, however, the patriarch Photius installed a large mosaic of Mary and Jesus in the apse (Figure 7.9). There are earlier examples of this particular image—for example, the one commissioned by Pope Paschal I in Santa Maria in Domnica in Rome in the 820s (Figure 7.10). Subsequently this became one of the two dominant ways of depicting Mary with the baby Jesus. The Virgin of Vladimir, painted in Constantinople around 1100 (Figure 7.11), is the second. The former is called a *hodegetria* (hoe-duh-GEE-tree-uh), from Greek, "one who points the way," which means Mary essentially presents Jesus to the viewer. The latter is an *eleousa*

(ELL-ay-oo-sah), from Greek, "a tenderness," which means that the viewer sees Mary and Jesus in intimate relation with each other.

In the middle of the tenth century, amid other historicizing and classicizing efforts, an anonymous

Figure 7.9 *Virgin and Child.* Mosaic, Apse, Hagia Sophia, Constantinople, 867. *Between the ninth and twelfth centuries, Hagia Sophia received a vast program of figural mosaics. It appears that the church had mainly floral or geometric designs before that. The final victory of the iconodules in 842 may have encouraged them to begin putting images everywhere. As Figure 7.10 indicates, Rome and Constantinople may have been in some competition over claiming Mary's patronage.*

Figure 7.10 *Virgin and Child.* Mosaic, Apse, Santa Maria in Domnica, Rome, 817–824. *During his reign, Pope Paschal I donated several large mosaics to Roman churches as one way of registering his disapproval of Byzantine policies. This one has a special resonance. Since the seventh century, both Constantinople and Rome had claimed Mary as their special patroness. Here, Paschal presents himself as Mary's humble attendant, and he looks out to the assembly as if to remind them that he alone intercedes for them with Mary. His square nimbus (or halo) signifies a living person, and his face may reflect what he actually looked like.*

painter in Constantinople produced the magnificent Paris Psalter. This book has fourteen full-page images (Figure 7. 12) that exude a classicizing style which contrasts with the polemical messages and conventional style of the Khludov Psalter (see Figure 7.2).

Byzantine Architecture

Justinian's Hagia Sophia had a profound impact on all that would follow in Byzantium. Scholars now know that placing a dome on a square or elongated nave was not so much started as perfected in Hagia Sophia; there were earlier examples in Asia Minor. It is the sheer scale of Hagia Sophia that is novel. The Byzantines developed the **pendentive,** an inverted concave triangle

that permitted the placement of a round dome over straight walls (Figure 7.13). Another critical feature of Hagia Sophia and of churches influenced by it is that it is centrally planned. In other words, it abandoned the traditional Roman basilican plan.

With Hagia Sophia showing the way, the success of the octagonal, or eight-sided, church of San Vitale in Ravenna helped to make the centrally planned church the signature Byzantine style (Figures 7.14 and 7.15). Although quite different in feel and effect, both San Vitale and Hagia Sophia add a vertical dimension that further escapes the horizontality of the basilican form preferred in Rome and generally in the Catholic West. The impact of this new style can be seen in the eleventh-century monastic church of Hosios Loukas (St. Luke) (Figure 7.16).

194

Figure 7.11 *Icon of the Virgin and Child.* Constantinople. Ca. 1100. 30.7 × 21.65". Tretyakov Gallery, Moscow. *This icon depicts a loving moment between Mary and Jesus: their faces are pressed together, his face tilted upward and his gaze fixed upon her eyes. Painted in Constantinople, this icon was sent to Kiev as a gift to the new Russian church. Later it was moved to Vladimir and eventually to Moscow. The faces are original, but the rest of the work has been refurbished several times. Legend attributed this painting to St. Luke, and the faithful believed it to be miraculous.*

Figure 7.12 *David Composing His Psalms,* from Paris Psalter. Ca. 950. Constantinople. 14.75 × 10.4". Bibliothèque Nationale de France. (Ms. Gr 139 fol 1 v.) *This most richly decorated of all Byzantine psalters puts Byzantine classicism on vivid display. The scene is portrayed in receding three-dimensionality. David sits with his harp, but Melodia—the personification of song—and the nymph Echo attend him. In the lower right, Bethlehem is personified as a classical river god. David's presence in this painting has a dual purpose. First, in religious terms, he points to the coming of Christ (Matthew traces Christ's lineage from David). Second, David is the symbol of perfect rulership—a just and learned ruler (his learning based on his supposed authorship of the Psalms).*

Figure 7.13 Isidore of Miletus and Anthemius of Tralles. Hagia Sophia, Interior. 532–537. Istanbul. *Hagia Sophia was the mother church of the Orthodox faith. After the Ottoman conquest, the church became an Islamic mosque, and some of the trappings, such as the calligraphic writings, survive from this stage of the building's life. Today, Hagia Sophia is a museum, and its striking mixture of Byzantine and Islamic elements makes it a vivid symbol of the meeting of West and East. The pendentive is clearly to be seen in the center of the picture.*

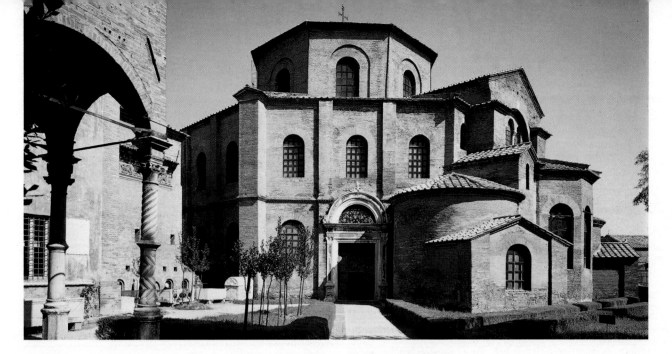

Figure 7. 14 San Vitale. 526–547. Ravenna, Italy. *The centrally planned, octagonal church has antecedents in both East and West but, apart from Hagia Sophia, San Vitale is considerably larger than any predecessors. The exterior creates visual interest and complexity. The cupola is octagonal on the outside but domed on the inside. Construction was completed under Bishop Maximian (546–557), and the building was financed by Julianus Argentarius, a local financier. The church was built over the presumed grave of St. Vitalis as a thank-offering for the defeat of the heretical (Arian) Ostrogoths and the restoration of Justinian's authority.*

Figure 7.15 Plan of San Vitale. Ravenna, Italy. *This ground plan brings out the distinctive design elements of the church. The external octagon envelops a series of internal semicircular bays. The aisle is circular instead of horizontal. Above the aisle is a gallery, originally reserved to women for worship. The mosaics portraying Justinian and Theodora were on the sides of the apsidal sanctuary at the center right (for the one depicting Theodora, see Figure 6.29).*

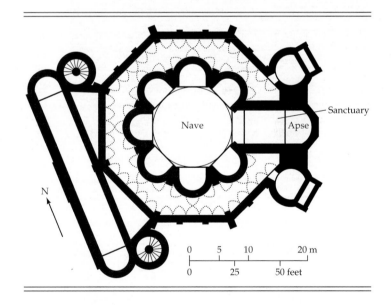

Western Art

In the British Isles, images which artists saw in old books or perhaps during their travels combined with native tradition to produce a style that was playful and pleasing. The Ardagh (ARR-daw) Chalice—the cup used for the distribution of wine in Holy Communion—is a splendid example of Irish metalwork (Figure 7.17). The plain surfaces show a restraint appropriate to a liturgical vessel, but handles, rim, edges, and medallions provided the artist with an opportunity to give full vent to his flair for decoration. The extraordinarily intricate interlace designs fashioned from thin gold wire are thoroughly Irish in inspiration and exceptionally beautiful.

Manuscript illumination is another artistic realm in which the Irish excelled. The astonishing Book of Kells, probably made at Iona around 800, has been

Figure 7.16 Hosios Loukas. Ca. 1020. Phokis, Greece. *The Katholikon Church (the principal church in a monastery) was built on the site of the tomb of a local, wonder-working saint, Blessed Luke of Stiris. The use of pendentives and **squinches** creates a dome-over-square internal space of elegance and fine proportions. The interior has a rich array of mosaics and of decorative marble fittings.*

called "the chief relic of the Western world." In the page displayed in Figure 7.18, a Mary and Jesus scene, decoration and color are prominent. The elaborate interlace border is full of animal heads. Within the image, there are interlaces, gemlike sections, and complex geometric designs. While the reds and greens are vivid, blues are noteworthy too, along with gold. The figures are delightfully abstract yet recognizable. The scene has an overall balance and harmony that is pleasing to the eye.

In England, in many manuscript paintings, the Irish influence may be seen in decorative patterns, along with other artistic and scholarly conceits, as in, for example, the Ezra Portrait from the Codex Amiatinus (Figure 7.19). Painted at the monasteries of Monkwearmouth and Jarrow in the north of England, this painting is framed much in the manner of the Irish style. And its illusionistic appearance—modeled in light and dark and with naturalistic colors—is reminiscent of late antique art. The subject matter is biblical: Ezra, a Jewish prophet, copying the law after the exile. The setting, a library with books in a cabinet, perhaps suggests the quest in early medieval Europe to recapture the classical heritage.

On the Continent, in the Carolingian era, many traditions flowed together not least because the kings could attract the best scholars and artists to the royal court from all over Europe. Book painting began under Charlemagne with the Godescalc Evangelistary, an illuminated manuscript containing the Gospel readings for the mass. Made between 781 and 783 by the court scribe and painter Godescalc, it contained five decorated figures, including Christ in majesty (Figure 7.20). This figure, which became common in medieval art, shows Christ enthroned as the ruler of the world.

Figure 7.17 Ardagh Chalice. Ca. 800. 7" high × 7.67" wide × 4" deep. National Museum of Ireland. *This chalice was found by two boys digging in a potato field in 1868 in the village of Ardagh in County Limerick. Assembled from 254 separate pieces of silver, gold, bronze, brass, pewter, glass, and enamel, this chalice is the supreme example of early Irish metalwork. The artist combined several different techniques including engraving, casting, filigree, cloisonné, and enameling. There are more than forty separate designs on the chalice with motifs ranging from prehistoric European, to Roman, Byzantine, and Celtic.*

Figure 7.18   *Virgin and Child,* from Book of Kells. Ca. 800. 13 × 9.5". Trinity College, Dublin. (Ms. 58 fol 34 r.) *A mother holding an infant was a common scene in classical art and one early adopted by Christian artists. But here classical values have been left behind. The immobile faces and the modeling of the figures are so stylized that it is difficult to see what space they occupy. The painter took real delight in bright, arresting colors and in amazingly complex geometric and animal designs. Pictures like this one represent something new in medieval art. It is instructive to compare this image with Figures 7.9, 7.10, and 7.11.*

In such figures as this one, local, Celtic, late antique, and Byzantine styles merge to make the Carolingian style. Despite the otherworldly subject, the artist has given the scene a natural feel with his use of natural colors and the sense of depth, which is conveyed by his use of light and dark.

A significant advance in artistic technique and style occurred about twenty years later in the Lorsch Gospels, an illuminated manuscript of the Gospels produced at the scriptorium of Lorsch (in modern Germany) around 800. The unknown artist produced a series of arresting images, such as *Christ in Majesty* (Figure 7.21), in which the enthroned figure seems to float in a blue sky. Christ's facial features are more clearly delineated than in the Godescalc image (see

Figure 7.19   *Prophet Ezra,* from Codex Amiatinus. Before 716. Monkwearmouth-Jarrow. 19.8 × 13.6". Biblioteca Medicea Laurenziana, Florence. (Ms. Amiatinus 1 fol 5 r.) *Bede's monasteries produced three complete (that is, both Old and New Testaments) Bibles, of which the Codex Amiatinus (so named because in the Middle Ages it was kept at the monastery of Monte Amiata in Italy) alone survives. It is the oldest surviving witness to Jerome's Vulgate. The portrait of Ezra copying out the Law after the Jews returned from exile (see Chapter 5) was placed at the front of the book—perhaps to symbolize the copying out of the Law in far-off England.*

Figure 7.20), but the overall effect here is more ordered and precise. The circle surrounding Christ consists of symbols of the four evangelists (each within a circlet) and eight angels, which alternate with two geometric designs. The circle itself floats above a purple field. Purple is the imperial color (Charlemagne has just become emperor). The intricate border has something of the insular tracery and knot-work already observed, but also adds luxurious gold, jewels, and pearls. Classical references are unmistakable. Carolingian art, like the writings of the age, synthesized traditions rather than choosing among them.

Carolingian painting reached a glorious climax with the images in the spectacular Vivian Bible, produced by the monks at Tours (in modern France) and presented to Charles the Bald at Christmas, 845. The last image

Figure 7.20 *Christ in Majesty,* from Godescalc Evange-listary. 781–783. 12.63 × 8.25". Bibliothèque Nationale, Paris. (Ms nouv. acq. lat 1203, fol 3 r.) *Commissioned by Charlemagne as a gift for Pope Hadrian I, this book of gospel readings is written in Carolingian minuscule—one of the earliest surviving examples of this new script. The image of Christ in majesty portrays a youthful Christ, much as had been done in early Christian art but unlike the mature, bearded Christ that was emerging in Byzantine art.*

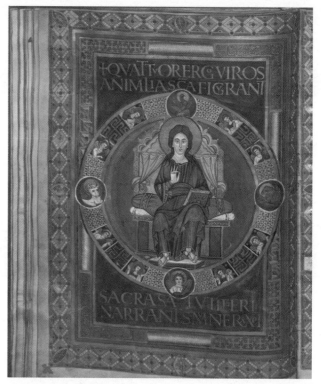

Figure 7.21 *Christ in Majesty,* from Lorsch Gospels. After 800. Middle Rhine. 14.625 × 10.625". Batthyaneum Library, Alba Julia, Romania. (Ms. R II 1 fol 18 v.) *The illustrations in the Lorsch Gospels show the skills of the talented artists attached to the Carolingian court and their growing confidence in adapting various styles to create a new tradition. This famous book has had a checkered career. At some point it was divided: two gospels wound up in Romania and two in the Vatican Library. Its beautiful ivory covers ended up in the Victoria and Albert Museum, London, and in the Vatican Museum.*

(Figure 7.22) in this Bible depicts the book's presentation to Charles—one of the first portrayals of an actual event in the Middle Ages. One of the arresting aspects of this image is its political and theological message: the right hand of God (above the enthroned Charles) is a clear signal of the source of the king's authority to rule. The figures are arrayed in a circle suggesting a procession (the artist had to work within his space!). The faces in the picture have a certain sameness about them but are nevertheless lifelike. The king is flanked by two of his officials and then by two soldiers in Roman military gear. The references may be Roman or imperial or both. Charles, although enthroned, seems to float in space. The whole scene is bounded by an architectural frame.

Another grand era in the history of book painting happened during the reign of Otto III (r. 982–1002). A fine example of Ottonian art, taken from his tenth-century Gospel Book, produced at the monastery of Reichenau (in modern Germany), is the image that depicts Otto enthroned (Figure 7.23). In the manuscript, this image is one of two facing images. In the other one, Otto is depicted receiving homage from the provinces that comprised his realm—Slavinia, Germania, Gallia, and Roma. In contrast to the naturalism of Carolingian art, Otto is represented in a stiff, erect pose that suggests eminence and power. Staring without seeing, he meets no one's gaze. Flanking Otto are secular and ecclesiastical officials, the former holding swords and the latter Bibles, symbolizing the dual nature of Otto's imperial rule. That Otto's mother was a Byzantine princess may account for the presence of Byzantine features in these paintings.

Figure 7.22 *Presentation Miniature,* from First Bible of Charles the Bald (Count Vivian Bible). 845. Paris, Tours. 19.5 × 14.75″. Bibliothèque Nationale de France. (Ms. Lat. 1 fol 423 r.) *This presentation scene, depicting the Carolingian ruler, comes from one of four complete Bibles produced by the monastery of Tours in the time of Charles the Bald (r. 838–877). While Charlemagne, the dynasty's greatest figure, left no contemporary portraits (except maybe Figure 7.4), his heirs fared much better, as can be seen in this splendid likeness. This vivid scene, with its natural colors, has a sense of depth, created by the modeling in light and dark. The painter stresses the ruler's status by enhancing his size at the expense of his officials. Thus, the seated Charles is as tall as Count Vivian of Tours, standing on the left.*

Western Architecture

For two hundred years, nothing was built in the Christian West on anything like the scale of Hagia Sophia or San Vitale. Then, in the eighth century, the return of peace and prosperity awakened aspirations. In the south of Italy at the monastery of San Vincenzo al Volturno and in England at Winchester, huge—about 300-foot-long—basilicas were built. In Rome, Pope Hadrian I (772–795) built and rebuilt one church after another, and his successor, Leo III (795–816), erected two large **triclinia**—rectangular, multi-apsed banqueting and reception halls—for the papal court. At Aachen, Charlemagne began building his palace complex in about 788. He took up residence there in 794, and the structures were largely completed by 806.

Figure 7.23 *Emperor Enthroned,* from Gospels of Otto III, perhaps Reichenau. 997–1000. 13 × 9.375″. Bayerische Staatsbibliothek, Munich. (Ms. Clm. 4453 fol 24 r.) *The drawing and modeling of the figures in this image are simple. The painter attains sophistication by the use of brilliant colors and plentiful gold. The scale (as in Figure 7.22) is hieratic, not natural; that is, figures are scaled according to their importance.*

The essential components of the original palace complex were a basilican hall, a long porticus, and a chapel (Figure 7.24). The hall, nearly 175 feet in length, was two stories high and contained official and residential quarters. The building was a **triconch,** that is, with an apse at one end and **conches** (apse-like extrusions) on each long side. Triconch buildings had become very prestigious in late antiquity. The **porticus,** or covered gallery, ran more than 350 feet from the hall to the chapel. The chapel was modeled somewhat on San Vitale, or perhaps on the Lateran baptistery in Rome (Figure 7.25). The exterior is sixteen sided and the interior core is an octagon (Figure 7.26). The massive piers and powerful arches create alternating triangular and rectangular bays in the ambulatory at ground level. The piers then rise to create a gallery twice as high as the main floor. The gallery is surrounded by slender columns brought from Rome and Ravenna and by exquisite bronze **balustrades,** vertical posts connected by metal grillwork, apparently cast on the site. The piers reach to the base of the cupola, which is octagonal like the central core of the building. The overall effect of the chapel is stunning: the chapel is both massive and powerful,

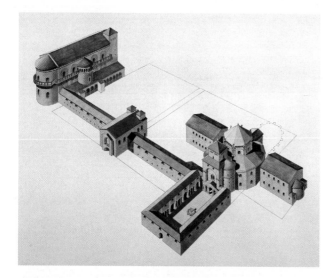

Figure 7.24   Model of Charlemagne's Imperial Complex at Aachen. By Leon Hugot. Cathedral Museum, Aachen. *This model makes clear the basic components of the palace complex. The basilican royal hall and octagonal chapel align north-south with the hall to the north. The porticus—basically a covered passageway—joins the two main structures.*

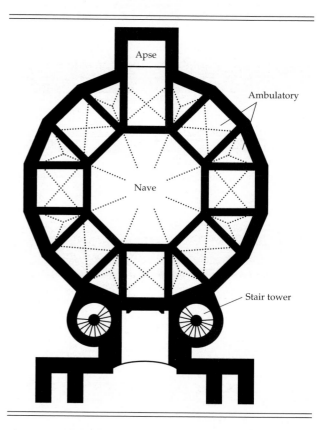

Figure 7.26   Ground Plan, Aachen Chapel. *This plan illustrates the architectural complexity of the building. Comparing this plan with that of San Vitale in Ravenna (see Figure 7.15) reveals San Vitale's influence and shows how the Carolingian builders innovated.*

Figure 7.25   Palace Chapel. Aachen. Ca. 788–806. *This chapel is the chief work of Carolingian architecture. The work is impressively complex in its mathematical proportions. For instance, each of the octagonal **bays** (vertical divisions of the interior or exterior of a building marked not by walls but by architectural features such as windows, columns, or vaulting) measures 18 feet across for a total of 144 feet, which is almost exactly the width of the building. The building may imitate San Vitale, but it is a significant reinterpretation. One late source says that the "master" responsible for the building was the otherwise completely unknown Odo of Metz. Most scholars think Einhard played a major role in its design and construction.*

but, at the same time, it appears to spring from the ground and soar vertically to the heavens.

Aachen was spectacular, but its centrally planned design was not influential. The longitudinal basilica triumphed in the Carolingian world and after. To the traditional rectangular Roman basilica, Carolingian builders added two new features. At the monastery of Fulda (in modern Germany), and at some other places, for example, Cologne cathedral, basilicas were double apsed—they had an apse at each end (Figure 7.27). The Carolingian innovation with the brightest future however was the **westwork,** a tall, multistoried structure on the western end of a church. Divided into multiple interior chambers, westworks had both ceremonial and practical uses. Only one example of Carolingian westwork survives, at the monastery of Corvey in Saxony (in modern Germany) (Figure 7.28).

TECHNOLOGY

The early Middle Ages saw some playful developments. For example, Liudprand, the envoy of Otto I to Constantinople, tells of Byzantine thrones that rose hydraulically and of magical golden trees in which artificial birds sang pretty tunes. But practical advances were more important in the military and agricultural fields.

Military Technology: Byzantine

- The Byzantine navy improved on Roman models with the *dromon,* a warship manned by a crew of up to three hundred men and capable of carrying bowmen, catapults, and the metal tubes for Greek fire (see below).
- By 700 the lateen sail was in use, allowing ships to be more responsive to the winds.
- Greek fire, probably a mixture of crude oil, sulfur, and resin, which would burn on water and stick to a surface, was first employed in 678 against the Arabs at the siege of Constantinople. Heated and then pushed through a metal tube, by means of a pump, or thrown from catapults in breakable containers, Greek fire became a very effective weapon in naval battles.

Military Technology: Western European

- The war saddle was adapted from contacts with invading peoples and provided greater stability for the rider.

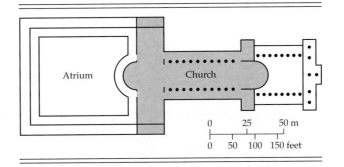

Figure 7.27 Plan of the Monastic Basilica of Fulda. 791–802. The double apses are clearly visible in the plan.

Figure 7.28 The Westwork of the Monastic Basilica of Corvey. Saxony. 883–885. *This massive, yet flat, simple, and elegant western entry to the monastic church of Corvey is the largest standing example of Carolingian architecture. The rounded windows at the top with columns were added in the twelfth century during restorations.*

- The curb bit, inserted in the horse's mouth, gave the rider greater control of his mount.
- The stirrup, probably borrowed from the Avars, further enhanced the rider's stability and control.
- The larger, more powerful war horse was imported from the Arab world, through Spain.

- Mounted infantry, drawing on the technologies just listed, gave the Carolingians the capacity to move larger forces to more distant battlefields.

Agriculture

- The bipartite estate (later called the manor) divided lands in such a way that 25 to 40 percent of the land was reserved to a lord while the remainder of the estate was worked by the peasants for themselves. This type of estate permitted lords to remunerate vassals, and vassals to support themselves profitably.
- Vastly more land was brought under cultivation by clearing forests and draining marshes.
- Many areas switched from two- to three-field systems: two thirds of an estate were planted each year, usually one in spring and one in winter crops, with one third lying fallow. Previously it had been common to farm only half an estate per year.
- Heavy iron plows, with a mould board that turned the soil dug up by the plowshare, were used on large estates (but may not have spread to ordinary peasants).

MUSIC

Einhard reports that Charlemagne loved the "old barbarian songs." Unfortunately, neither he nor anyone else wrote them down. All the music that survives from East or West is religious and, at that, connected with the liturgy. Moreover, almost everything known pertains to vocal music.

Music became integral to the church's liturgy during the early Middle Ages and kept alive the Greek heritage of music as an art form. From this religious foundation ultimately arose all of the sacred and secular music of the modern West. The name of Pope Gregory the Great is preserved in the early medieval musical form the **Gregorian chant,** which became the official liturgical music of the early church—used in the Mass (the celebration of the Eucharist) and other services of the yearly cycle of public worship. The chants consisted of a single melodic line sung by male voices in unison—called **monophony**—without instrumental accompaniment. They had an impersonal, nonemotional quality and served religious rather than aesthetic or emotional purposes. Notwithstanding this aim, the chants cast a spell over their listeners, evoking in them feelings of otherworldliness, peace, and purity.

The ninth century saw two of the most important advances in music history: the rise of **polyphony**—two lines of melody sounded at the same time—and musical notation. Polyphony, unlike the monophonic Gregorian chants, gave music a richer, more textured quality. Musical notation owed much to Charlemagne's desire for uniformity in worship. He sought to impose Gregorian chant, but how might this be possible? Only by developing a system of written musical notation could anything approaching uniformity be achieved. First, at the monastery of Saint Amand in northern France, **neumes**—inflected marks—began to be placed above the lines of text, to help singers follow shifts in the melody. Next, a four-line staff was devised to accommodate these marks. Eventually, books showing the neumes and lines could be copied, and, with training, singers could learn to read marks as notes.

The Legacy of Byzantium and the West in the Early Middle Ages

To look in the sixth and seventh centuries at what had been the Roman Empire might lead one to think that all order had vanished. And yet, on closer inspection, one might well see the birth of new and promising political realms. Byzantium was reinventing itself as one more Roman Empire; how many had there already been, under Augustus, Diocletian, Justinian? In the West, weak and ineffective kingdoms were being eliminated in a kind of Darwinian survival of the fittest. The fittest, as it happened, were initially the Anglo-Saxons and the Franks. Among the latter a new imperial dynasty emerged that laid the foundations for faith and order and for a European culture. Christendom is the name often applied to the Carolingian creation.

Schools preserved, assimilated, and handed on the classical heritage, albeit with a distinctly Christian coloration. In Celtic and Germanic regions, people began to write in their own tongues. Byzantium transmitted the classical and Christian heritages to the Slavic world. The arts in Byzantium remained closer to their late antique foundations, whereas in the West sparkling innovation appeared in many areas. The decorative exuberance of the Celts and the Carolingian penchant for blending numerous traditions are key examples. In architecture, the Byzantines continued to develop the dome-over-square model that had been so effective in Hagia Sophia. The centrally planned church became normative in the East. In the West, the basilican plan remained normative, and influential for centuries, but the Carolingians demonstrated that some innovation was possible—for instance, the use of multiple apses and the introduction of a vertical dimension. The Carolingian era was critically important in the development of Western music. Synthesis and innovation mark the cultural life of the early Middle Ages.

KEY CULTURAL TERMS

themes
capitularies
Carolingian minuscule
the seven liberal arts
prosimetric
vernacular
pendentive
squinch
triclinia
triconch

conch
porticus
balustrade
bay
westwork
Gregorian chant
monophony
polyphony
neumes

QUESTIONS FOR CRITICAL THINKING

1. What were the chief dynamics in the development of Byzantium?

2. What steps did Carolingian rulers take to try to ensure uniformity across their vast realm?

3. What similarities and differences do you observe in the literary interests of the Byzantine and the western Europeans of the early Middle Ages?

4. Thinking about the figural arts of the early Middle Ages, what carried over from late antiquity and what was new?

5. Discuss the fate of the basilica in Byzantium and western Europe.

8 THE WORLD OF ISLAM
630–1517

Islamic civilization was the third heir to the Roman Empire. The word *islam* is Arabic for "submission" (to God); a *Muslim* is "one who has submitted," or accepted the beliefs and practices of Islam. At its largest, the Islamic Caliphate, or Empire, stretched from Spain to the frontiers of China (Map 8.1). Islamic civilization built on the culture of the Arabs, the teachings of the prophet Muhammad, and the traditions of many of the peoples folded into the caliphate. Creative and international, Islamic civilization was the source of numerous scholarly advances as well as a wealth of artistic achievements.

The date 630 marks the year when Muhammad's call for a new religion was accepted by the Arab leaders of Mecca and surrounding areas. The date 1517 marks the triumph of the Ottoman Turks, who had converted to Islam, and the beginning of a new era in Islamic history. Modern Islam is no longer identified with a particular country or region or with any one ethnic or racial group. The world's fastest-growing religion, with over one billion adherents around the globe, it is second in numbers only to Christianity (Figure 8.1).

The pre-Islamic Arabs inhabited the Arabian peninsula, a dry land wedged between the Red Sea and the Persian Gulf. In the north, nomadic Bedouin tribes herded sheep and goats across the higher plateaus and deserts. In the south, Arabs lived in farming communities and cities. Merchants prospered from trade on the southern caravan route, which began in India, crossed southern Arabia, and then followed the west coast plateau along the Red Sea into the Roman Empire.

◀ **Detail** The Dome of the Rock. Ca. 687–691 Jerusalem.

LEARNING THROUGH MAPS

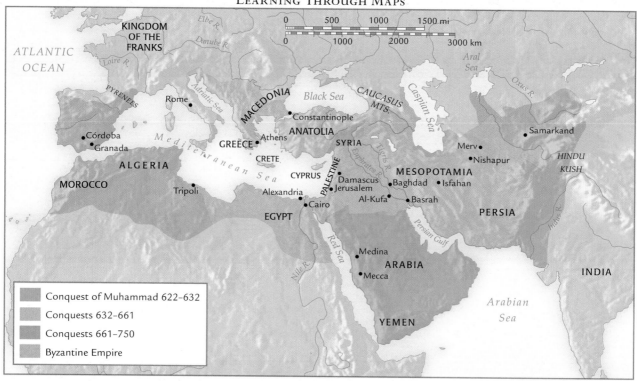

Map 8.1   THE WORLD OF ISLAM, 622–750
This map shows the successive expansion of the Islamic world, between 622 and 750.
1. *Notice* the three phases of expansion. 2. *Consider* how the expansion of Islam threatened the Byzantine Empire and the Kingdom of the Franks. 3. *Identify* the three successive capitals of the Islamic Empire. 4. *What* problems would the Muslims face in conquering so much land so quickly and ruling such diverse peoples? 5. *Compare* the size of the Islamic holdings in 750 with the size of the Roman Empire under Augustus in Map 6.1.

Neither the Romans nor the Persians ever dominated the Arabian peninsula. By the early seventh century, the Arabic language had spread throughout the peninsula, binding the inhabitants with a common tongue and oral literary tradition. Jews and Christians, lured by the prospects of wealth and trade, migrated into southern Arabia. From them the Arabs acquired additional knowledge of weaponry, textiles, food and wine, and writing. In Mecca, the leading commercial city on the southern trade route, Jews, Christians, and Arabs not only exchanged products and wares but also shared ideas and values.

MUHAMMAD, THE PROPHET

Muhammad, the founder of Islam and one of the most commanding figures in history, was born in the city of Mecca in 570. His father was from a minor but respected clan within the city's most powerful tribe, the Quraysh. Orphaned when quite young, Muhammad was reared by grandparents and an uncle. He entered

the caravan trade, acquired a reputation for honesty, and became financial adviser to a wealthy Quraysh widow, Khadija [kah-DEE yah], whom he married. Their only surviving child, Fatima [FAT-uh-mah], was to become a revered religious figure (Figure 8.2).

In 610 Muhammad experienced a spiritual transformation that convinced him Allah had called him to be his prophet to the Arab people. Other revelations soon followed. Inspired by these encounters, Muhammad slowly gathered a small band of converts. As his fame grew, he became known simply as "the Prophet."

At first, Mecca's leaders paid scant attention to Muhammad. However, he became a controversial figure when, in the name of Allah, he declared that there was only one God, attacked the polytheistic beliefs of his fellow Arabs, and condemned as idolatrous the *Kaaba* ("cube"), a local pagan shrine that housed a sacred black rock. Since the Kaaba was not only a holy place but also a source of revenue generated by the thousands of pilgrims who visited it each year, Mecca's leaders feared that they were in danger of losing one of their most profitable attractions. They also

Figure 8.1   The Pilgrimage to Mecca and the Circling of the Kaaba. J. Allan Cash photograph. *All Muslims are required to make a pilgrimage to Mecca at least once in their lives. There they circle the* Kaaba, *a sacred shrine, seven times in a counterclockwise direction, trying to touch or kiss its walls. On the ninth day of their pilgrimage, worshipers assemble on the plain of Arafat outside Mecca to make their stand before God. This ten-day journey and its ceremonies often mark the climax of a devout Muslim's life.*

Figure 8.2 *Fatima.* Chester Beatty Library, Dublin. *Fatima, veiled and dressed in white, kneels beside two of Muhammad's wives. Although Fatima is not mentioned in the Qur'an, her reputation grew over the years among the Shiite Muslims. She became the ideal woman, possessing extraordinary powers similar to those of the Virgin Mary for Roman Catholics. Devout Shiite women appeal to her for guidance and protection, and worship at her shrines.*

considered Muhammad to be socially inferior and uneducated. Soon hostility turned to persecution. Fearing for his life, Muhammad and a few followers fled, in 622, to Yathrib, a neighboring city. This historic flight, or Hegira (*hijra*), transformed Muhammad's message of reform into a call for a new religion. And the date, 622 in the Christian Western calendar, marks the year 1 for Muslims.

According to tradition, Muhammad was welcomed into Yathrib and quickly made a name for himself by settling several disputes that had divided its citizens. He emerged as a judge and lawgiver as well as a military leader. In Yathrib, Muhammad was able to found his ideal community, where religion and the state were one. Yathrib became known as Medina, or "the City," a name that denoted its position as Islam's model city.

Before the Hegira, Muhammad had formulated the basic doctrines of Islam. In Medina, he put them into practice to solve social and legal problems and to offer guidelines for everyday life and social interactions. Muhammad, it is believed, also drew up a charter defining relations among the Medinese people, his own followers, and the Jews, who were influential in the city. Most important, this charter established several fundamental principles. Faith, not blood or tribe, unified the believers; Muhammad, as the voice of Allah, was a ruler and not a consensus builder; and Islam was the only source of spiritual and secular authority. In essence, a theocracy was in the making in Medina, as political and religious objectives blurred into one, and a unified, faith-based state government was envisioned. Eventually, tensions between the Jews and the followers of Muhammad reached the point where Muhammad exiled the Jews. At the same time, he expunged any rituals that might have had Jewish associations. Specifically, he changed the direction for praying from Jerusalem to Mecca, he called for pilgrimages to the Kaaba, and he moved the day of collective prayer from Saturday to Friday.

While Muhammad held sway in his newly adopted home, conflicts between Medina and Mecca grew as Medinese raiders attacked the caravans traveling over the trade routes from Mecca. Desert warfare soon erupted. From 624 to 628, the two cities fought three major battles. The last one resulted in a victory for Muhammad's forces. Now in full control of Medina and having repelled the Meccan army, Muhammad was ready to return to Mecca.

Muhammad and about one thousand of his followers set out as pilgrims to the Kaaba shrine. Mecca's Quraysh leaders faced a dilemma. If they attacked or tried to prevent the pilgrims from worshiping, they would be violating their role as protectors of the shrine. But if they did nothing, they risked turning their city over to Muhammad and his supporters. As a way out of this impasse, a Quraysh delegation negotiated a treaty that allowed Muhammad to visit Mecca the next year as a pilgrim in exchange for his returning to Medina. This peaceful solution convinced many Arab tribes that Muhammad's new faith and tactics were legitimate, and they soon converted to Islam.

In 629 Muhammad made his pilgrimage, winning new converts during a three-day visit. The next year, when the Quraysh attacked one of Muhammad's allied tribes, he raised an army of ten thousand to march on Mecca. Faced with these odds, the Quraysh opened the city, their leaders accepted the new faith, and the Prophet entered triumphantly. He destroyed the pagan idols at the Kaaba, and he forgave his enemies if they became Muslims. Nearby tribes sent delegations to Mecca, from which contacts Muhammad constructed a network of personal and political alliances across the Arabian peninsula based on recognition of Mecca's power and agreement not to attack Muslims and their allies. On the eve of his death in 632, Muhammad had achieved what no Arab leader before him had done: he had brought peace to Arabia and united its inhabitants; and, at the same time, he had given the Arabs a new faith based on revelation, an ethical code of conduct, and a monotheistic deity. Muhammad's personality, dedication, and resolve had ignited a unification movement that now was energized and directed by a vigorous and resourceful religion.

IMPERIAL ISLAM

Islam evolved through a series of dynasties in the first nine hundred years of its history. They can be divided into five major periods, which sometimes overlapped (Timeline 8.1).

The Post-Muhammad Years

A leadership crisis followed Muhammad's death until the Meccan elite chose Abu Bakr [AH-bu BAK-er] (573–643) as caliph. (*Caliph* means "representative" or "successor.") Abu Bakr and his three successors were Meccans, early converts to Islam, and relatives of the Prophet by marriage. Islamic tradition calls them the *rashidun*, or "rightly guided," to distinguish them from the caliphs of later dynasties. The first three rashidun caliphs were great warriors. The last three rashidun caliphs were all murdered. Ali, killed in 661, was Muhammad's cousin and son-in-law, having married the Prophet's daughter, Fatima. Centuries later the *Shia*, the party of Ali, looked back to Ali as the divinely appointed. To this day, that Islamic world is divided between the Shiites and Sunnis.

Timeline 8.1   THE WORLD OF ISLAM, 630–1517

632	661	750		1050		1250		1517
Post-Muhammad Years	Umayyad Dynasty		Abbasid Dynasty				Imperial Decline	
					Seljuk Turk Empire			

Capital moved to Damascus

762 Capital moved to Baghdad

Muhammad dies

632–641 The four "rightly guided" caliphs

1258 Mongols sack Baghdad

1260 Defeat of the Mongols

1169–1250 Saladin founds Ayyubid dynasty

Ottoman Turks conquer Egypt and Syria

During his brief rule, Abu Bakr suppressed a revolt of Arab tribes and launched numerous raiding parties beyond the Arabian peninsula—a step that inaugurated Islam's imperial period. Although the Arabs took their share of loot, they neither destroyed towns or villages—indeed, they tended to build new ones—nor tried to convert their new subjects to Islam. "People of the book" (*dhimmis*)—initially, Christians and Jews but later Buddhists too—were allowed to keep their religion as long as they paid taxes and obeyed the local Muslim authorities.

The Umayyad Dynasty

Muawiyah [mu-A-we-ya] (about 602–680) founded the Umayyad dynasty in 661, which lasted until 750. Muawiyah moved the capital of his new empire from Medina to Damascus—a cosmopolitan trade center located more centrally in the Middle East—signifying an important shift in Arab politics and worldviews. Under this dynasty, territorial expansion continued. As more people came under Arab control and converted to Islam, intense social and political conflicts arose in the caliphate. Old converts looked down on new ones, and Meccan elites lorded it over everybody.

The Abbasid Dynasty

During the 740s, a series of uprisings by frontier peoples and recent converts undermined the Umayyad regime. In 750 an army led by a member of the Abbasid clan defeated the last Umayyad ruler. The Abbasids, who claimed to be descendants of Abbas, the uncle of Muhammad, moved the capital from Damascus to Baghdad in modern Iraq—an old trading city that now became Islam's cultural center and the home of the caliphs. During the Abbasid period, Islamic peoples from other traditions began to play prominent roles in government, society, and culture. The Persians, a people with a centuries-old civilization, now exerted a strong influence in the arts and learning and set the tone and atmosphere at the Abbasid court. Persians also staffed the state bureaucracy and ran the government. Persian prime ministers, who ruled in the name of the caliph, made day-to-day decisions. Turks, Kurds, and other hired mercenaries gradually replaced Arabs in the imperial armies.

The Fragmentation of the Caliphate

The rulers in Baghdad proved incapable of holding the vast caliphate together. By the late ninth century, the Abbasids controlled a glittering court but had little effective power elsewhere. They had gradually handed military authority to Turkish mercenaries, and, when marauding Seljuk Turks burst on the scene in the eleventh century, Abbasid rule ended, even though there were caliphs until 1258. The Seljuks also dealt the Byzantines a crushing defeat in 1071 that resulted in the emperor's eventual request for Western assistance; that assistance took the form of the Crusades.

In their empire, the Seljuks generally ruled through local sultans, and, as the central power weakened, some of the sultans became especially influential. One was the charismatic Saladin (1137–1193), a Kurd and

Figure 8.3   Courtyard and Mosque. Sultan Han Caravanserai. Aksaray, Turkey. 1229, heavily restored. *This caravanserai, or way station for merchants, pilgrims, and other travelers, was built by the Seljuk sultan 'Ala' ad-Din Kayqubad.* Han *is Turkish for "caravanserai." Located along well-traveled caravan routes, at distances about a day's travel apart (about twenty-five miles), caravanserais were usually heavily fortified and offered amenities, such as food and lodging for travelers, fodder and stables for the animals, and protection to all. The courtyard of the Sultan Han caravanserai is surrounded by an arcade that opens to a series of rooms on one side and covered places on the other. A small mosque stands in the center of the courtyard.*

the founder of the Ayyubid dynasty that ruled Egypt as well as much of Palestine, Syria, and Iraq from 1169 to 1250. Saladin is best known for defeating the largest crusading army ever assembled in 1187, but he is more important for his governmental acumen and his elevation of Cairo into a center of learning. By the 1250s the fearsome Mongols, who had been conquering Muslim lands in central Asia since the 1220s, reached Mesopotamia and seized Baghdad—thus putting an end to the Abbasids and to what was left of Seljuk power.

The idea of a caliphate, embracing the Muslim world, reflected a central teaching of Islam: the *umma Muslima*—the belief in a single community of believers. Until the 750s, the Umayyad Caliphate did realize that dream. Fragmentation began with the Abbasids. Spain was never part of the Abbasid Caliphate but stayed loyal to its Umayyad conquerors. Then, in 956, Spain emerged as the Western Caliphate of Córdoba, a period of great intellectual achievement. Córdoba maintained unified rule only until 1031 after which date Spain broke down into numerous independent principalities. At the same time, North Africa was falling prey to a series of rival Muslim dynasties. And Egypt was ruled by no fewer than three dynasties in this period: the Shiite Fatimids, the Ayyubids (just discussed), and the Turkish Mamelukes. The Mamelukes, in turn, defeated the Mongols in 1260, causing further splintering of the Islamic lands. Unity in the Muslim world was reestablished by the Ottoman Turks in the early 1500s, but by the early twentieth century the Ottoman Empire had crumbled (Figure 8.3).

ISLAM AS RELIGION

Islam's fundamental characteristics—monotheism and revelation—are founded on its two central beliefs: there is but one God and Muhammad is his Prophet. Muslims worship the same God as Jews and Christians, but Muslims alone recognize Muhammad as the final prophet of a tradition that dates from Abraham and Moses in Judaism, and that recognizes Jesus Christ, not as the son of God, but as the giver of the Christian prophecy. However, for devout Muslims, it is Muhammad's voice, above all others, that is the culminating revelation and perfects God's earlier message to Jews and Christians.

Muhammad's prophecies make up the text of the *Qur'an,* a word that literally means "recitation" (Figure 8.4). These prophecies were given final form in the generation after the Prophet's death. Nevertheless, for pious Muslims, the Qur'an is the uncreated or eternal word of God revealed through the angel Gabriel to the Prophet. In the historical context, however, the Qur'an was created by a committee of Muslims between 640 and 650. They gathered the fragments of texts and sayings of Muhammad and compiled them into an official version of the word of God as had been revealed to the Prophet. They then destroyed all other sources or collections of sayings that might constitute rival texts. The

Qur'an was now the only text, and it could not be questioned. Over time, Muslims came to believe that the Qur'an should be read only in Arabic. (Most Muslims today cannot read classical Arabic, the language of the Qur'an, so translations may be used for instructional purposes. For devotion, only the Arabic is allowed.)

The text of the Qur'an is arranged in 114 chapters, each called a *sura,* with the chapters printed according to length, from the longest to the shortest. Each chapter is divided into *ayas,* or verses. The style resembles a type of rhymed prose. Muhammad's utterances reveal him to be a master of literary expression and rhetoric. Many converts came to Islam because they were swayed as much by the Qur'an's evocative language as by its message. Its elevated tone and poetic qualities appeal to the faithful's soul, or inner being.

Within a century of Muhammad's death, a collection of the Prophet's sayings, proclamations, and instructions appeared in the Hadith, or "the Tradition." Likewise, there emerged written collections of the Sunnah, the religious customs and practices of the prophet. Muslims use the *Hadith* and Sunnah as a supplement to the Qur'an and regard it as a source to explain their laws, rituals, and dogma. Today, the Hadith, Sunnah, Qur'an, commentaries on the Qur'an, and the Arabic language make up the core curriculum taught in Islamic religious schools.

Figure 8.4 Kufic Calligraphy from the Qur'an. Ninth–tenth centuries. Ink and gold leaf on vellum, 8½ × 21". Nelson-Atkins Museum of Art, Kansas City, Missouri. Purchase: Nelson Trust. *Kufic calligraphy, which originated in the city of al-Kufa in Iraq, was used in mosque decoration and the writing of early copies of the* Qur'an. *Because Islam opposed the representation of figures in most art, calligraphy was one of the major forms available to Muslim artists.*

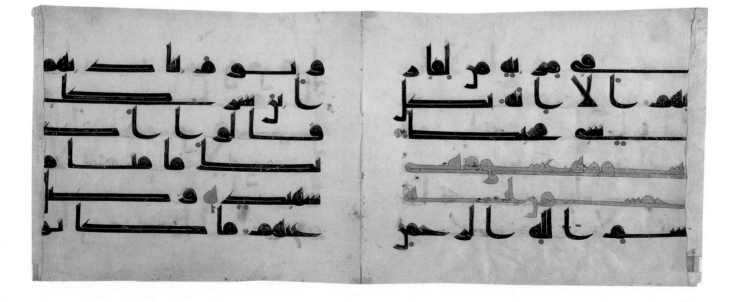

In early Islam, two types of schools soon emerged. The elementary school, maintained by a mosque (house of worship), offered boys basic religious education, along with training in how to read and interpret the Qur'an. Advanced learning took place in a ***madrasah,*** or university, the first of which was established in the ninth century in Fez, in modern Morocco. By the twelfth century, these universities had spread to most of the major cities of Islam. At first, their curriculum included only law, literature, philosophy, and theology, but, over time, mathematics, astronomy, and medicine were added (Figure 8.5). Some *madrasahs* became famous for particular areas of study, and local rulers often supported these schools in order to attract scholars and improve the university's reputation.

The Qur'an and the Hadith, as noted above, offer truth and guidance to the faithful. However, the core of Muslim religious life rests on the Five Pillars, or Supports, of the Faith—which include one verbal affirmation and four required devotional practices. The affirmation of faith states: "There is but one God, Allah, and Muhammad is his Prophet." The four acts of devotion are to pray five times a day facing Mecca (Figure 8.6), to fast from dawn to sunset during the month of Ramadan, to give alms to the poor, and to make a pilgrimage to Mecca at least once in one's life (see Figure 8.1).

Not one of the Five Pillars but central to the faith is the idea of ***jihad.*** *Jihad* basically means "to strive," or "to struggle," or "to make the utmost effort." Muslims "struggle" against sinning, or doing evil, and strive to follow the demands of the Qur'an and the Five Pillars of the Faith. Thus, *jihad* is a moral or spiritual striving or fight within the individual to do the right thing.

Figure 8.5 Scene from a *Madrasah.* Bibliothèque Nationale de France. (Ms. Arabe 5847 fol 5v.) *This manuscript page, with Arabic writing at the top and bottom, shows a Muslim scholar, the second person to the right holding an open book, explaining a particular text to his students. Behind the students and teacher are stacks of books set on open shelves, suggesting a library setting for the classroom. All students are male and have beards—as required by Islamic law. Adorning the room's upper level are typical decorative motifs of Islamic art, such as intricate foliage patterns and designs.*

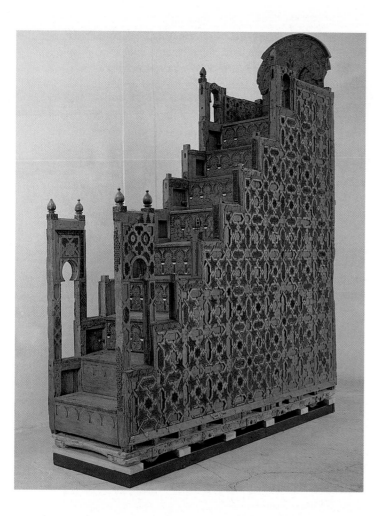

Figure 8.6 Kutubiyya *Minbar.* Ca. 1137–1145. Bone and colored woods, ht. 12′10″, width 2′10¼″, depth 11′4¼″. Kutubiyya Mosque, Marrakesh, Morocco. Islamic. Three-quarter view from the right. Photography by Bruce White. Photograph © 1998, The Metropolitan Museum of Art. *Richly decorated* minbars, *or portable pulpits, were used by local prayer leaders to address worshipers during Friday services. A* minbar *is basically a wooden staircase on wheels, with a seat at the top of the stairs for the prayer leader. This intricately detailed example was assembled from perhaps a million pieces of bone and fine African woods.*

However, *jihad* has other meanings, such as "holy war," a definition often found in the Western media. Many modern Muslims reject the linkage between *jihad* and holy war, but certain groups within Islam consider *jihad* to be a Sixth Pillar of the Faith. The belief that *jihad* means holy war can lead, and has led, to military action on the part of individuals, of groups, or of states to protect the community, to defend the faith, or to promote Islam.

In the eighth century, Muslim orthodoxy, also known as Sunni Islam, was challenged by the rise of Sufism, a mystical movement. Sufism emerged as both a reaction to the worldliness of the Umayyad dynasty rulers and a desire, on the part of some especially dedicated Muslims, to return to what they perceived to be the simpler faith that Muhammad had taught and practiced. Sufis rejected the legalism and formalism that had crept into Islam, and they challenged the power and influence of the *ulama,* or those men who interpreted the Qur'an and guarded the tradition of the faith. A majority rejected the Sunni position that all revelations from Allah were now complete, for they felt that religious truths were to be found in many places, even in other faiths. The word *Sufi* comes from

the Arabic word *su,* which means "wool," in reference to the coarse woolen garment worn by the Sufis as a symbol of their ascetic life and in memory of the simple garb worn by Muhammad. In some ways, Sufism resembled monasticism, which became so important in shaping Christianity's early growth and development (see Chapter 9).

Like most societies where codes of law are rooted in religious practice and tradition, the Muslim world established the holy law of Islam—the *Sharia*—on their faith. For Muslims, this body of sacred laws was derived, in its earliest forms, from the Qur'an, Sunnah, and Hadith. Although Muslim jurists, intellectuals, and scholars have added to the Islamic law over the centuries, the basic purpose remains the same—to tell the faithful what to believe and how to live their daily lives.

MEDIEVAL ISLAMIC CULTURE

From the ninth to the twelfth century, Islamic scholars, intellectuals, and inventors made significant advances in medicine; in the humanities, including mathematics, philosophy, and history; and in technology. Muslim scholars tended to be highly versatile, often making contributions in more than one field of study. At the time of the Arabic expansion, they became the saviors and successors of the Greek learning tradition by translating Greek philosophy, mathematics, and science into Arabic, which they then passed on to other cultures (see Chapters 7 and 9). In addition, they used the classical heritage as a foundation for numerous advances (see Encounter).

Medicine

Muslim doctors, whose skills were far superior to those of their Western contemporaries, obtained their knowledge from Greek texts that were translated into Arabic about the middle of the ninth century. In addition, Islamic medicine had a practical approach to the curing of disease, namely, through the use of observation and experimentation. Islamic medicine also made advances in ophthalmology, added new drugs to the pharmacopoeia, stressed the role of diet in the treatment of various maladies, and made the first clinical distinction between measles and smallpox. Surgeries, such as amputations, trepanning, or opening the skull, and cesarean sections were occasionally performed (Figure 8.7).

Muhammad al-Razi [al-RAY-zee] (about 865 to between 923 and 935) set the standard for medicine, both as a practicing doctor and as a scholar. A prolific writer, he compiled a twenty-volume medical encyclopedia in which he noted his own findings and took issue with the ancient Greeks and their medical tradition. Al-Razi also treated childhood diseases and wrote a treatise on them, earning the title "Father of Pediatrics." Most of his writings were translated into Latin and became part of the curriculum in Western medical schools until the nineteenth century.

Philosophy and History

The two most creative Muslim thinkers were Ibn Sina [IB-en SEE-nah] (980–1037), known in the West as Avicenna [av-ah-SEN-ah], and Ibn Rushd [IB-en RUSHT] (1126–1198), known in the West as Averroës [uh-VER-uh-weez]. Both were well educated in the liberal arts, and although both were trained in medicine and became highly respected physicians, they wrote extensively not only in the area of medicine but also in metaphysics, theology, and religion.

Figure 8.7   A Doctor Performing an Operation. Edinburgh University Library. *Muslim physicians normally did not operate on patients, preferring to use medicines and noninvasive procedures. Sometimes operations were necessary, as in this illustration of a woman having a cesarean section. The surgeon is helped by several attendants; on the right, one is holding the patient's head, while the one on the left is handing instruments to the doctor.*

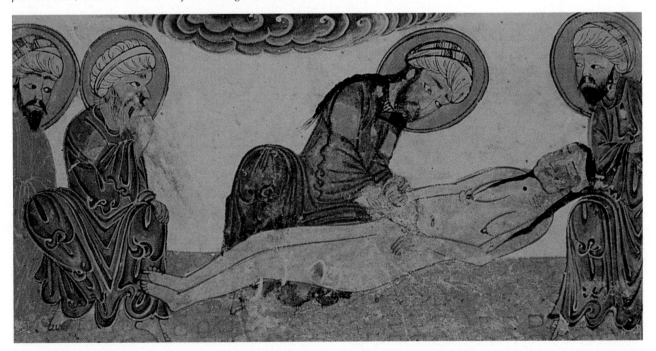

ENCOUNTER

An International Community of Scholars

Islamic scholars during the Abbasid dynasty (750–1258), which is known as the Golden Age of Islam, preserved the works of Greek mathematicians, adopted and transmitted the contributions of the Hindus, and made original discoveries in mathematics and the sciences. They and western European scholars, often working together, passed this accumulated knowledge to western Europe during the twelfth and thirteenth centuries through oral communication and the creation of many new illuminated manuscripts.

Under the Abbasid dynasty, learned men gathered at Islamic centers of study scattered throughout the western reaches of the Islamic Empire. In Spain the university at Córdoba, famed for its tolerance and diversity, attracted monks and scholars from western Europe who studied the Arabic writings, made copies, and brought them back to their monasteries and schools. There, they were translated into Latin and studied by others.

Islam's Golden Age was the work of an international community of scholars. Al-Khwarizmi [al-KWAHR-iz-me] (780–850) advanced the field of algebra; he also introduced Hindu numerals, which became known as Arabic numerals, and used them to make calculations. His near-contemporary al-Battani [al-ba-TAN-e] (about 858–929) corrected errors in the Ptolemaic planetary system and constructed an elaborate astronomical table. His writings on equinoxes and eclipses, in which he showed the possibility of solar eclipses, were translated by European scholars into Latin, making him the best-known Arab astronomer in medieval Europe. Both al-Khwarizmi and al-Battani were associated with the "House of Wisdom" in Baghdad, the capital of the Abbasid dynasty. Another scholar, Ibn al-Haytham [IB-en al-hi-THAM] (965–1039), who spent his life in Cairo, studied the Ptolemaic system of planetary motions, expanded on the mathematical work of Euclid, and developed new ideas about optics and light rays. His works, available in Latin in the thirteenth century, later influenced the German astronomer Johannes Kepler and the French mathematician and philosopher René Descartes.

Western scientists and mathematicians during the Renaissance of the fifteenth and sixteenth centuries studied the Islamic works in translation and built upon their discoveries. By 1700 the West had assimilated the knowledge generated by Islamic civilization and applied it to their study of nature, especially the exploration, navigation, and mapping of the earth. Then Europeans, for the first time since the fall of Rome, took the lead in mathematics and science.

LEARNING FROM THE ENCOUNTER

1. *Name* three cities in the Islamic world associated with Islam's Golden Age, and the achievements made in each of them. 2. *Which* dynasty ruled in Baghdad during Islam's Golden Age? 3. *What* was special about the atmosphere in Córdoba, Spain? 4. In *what* way was Islam's Golden Age produced by "an international community of scholars"? 5. *What* Islamic achievements were transmitted into the Western tradition? 6. *Compare and contrast* Islam's "international community of scholars" with the situation in the Western world today.

PHILOSOPHY Avicenna and Averroës served at the courts of Islamic rulers, where their careers rose and fell and where they engaged in heated controversies with other Muslim scholars. Avicenna, a Persian, spent most of his life in what is present-day Iran. By the age of twenty-one, he had mastered logic, metaphysics, and Islamic law and religion as well as medicine. Appointed court physician, he advised and served numerous Persian rulers. Over the years he wrote nearly two hundred works on medicine and other sciences, languages, philosophy, and religion. His *Canon of Medicine*, one of the most important books in the history of medicine, surveyed the achievements of Greek and Roman physicians, Arabic doctors, and his own findings. As Avicenna's reputation grew, Arabic and Western medical schools used his encyclopedia of classical and Arabic medicine as their authoritative source for centuries. His philosophical works addressed Aristotelian philosophy and Neoplatonism and attempted to reconcile both to Islam, including the Qur'an and other holy writings. Through these works, Avicenna strived to understand the essence of God in the physical and metaphysical worlds. His writings on the nature of God later influenced Western medieval thought, especially scholasticism (see Chapter 9).

Averroës, Islam's foremost thinker and one of the world's greatest minds, had even more of an impact on the West than did Avicenna. Born and reared in Córdoba, Spain, in a distinguished family, Averroës held important government positions, including chief judge of the judiciary system and personal physician to the caliph. Among his vast works, which he wrote while

Encounter figure 8.1 *In the 1570s, Arab astronomers, under the guidance of Taqi al-Din, the head astronomer of the Ottoman Empire, studied the heavens with various instruments at an observatory in Istanbul. To make their observations and calculations, they used astrolabes, hourglasses, globes, and a mechanical clock built by Taqi al-Din. Many of their instruments were similar to those later used by Western astronomers in the explorations of the universe.*

performing judicial duties, were comprehensive commentaries on Aristotle's writings, effectively reconciling the Greek thinker's ideas with Islamic thought. Western scholars used his Arabic versions of Aristotle, translated into Latin, to help reconcile Aristotelian and Christian thought. Averroës's writings were studied in Western schools and universities until modern times.

HISTORY   The study of history first played a role in Islamic thought because of the supreme significance of Muhammad's life to Islam. Biographies of the Prophet and histories of his time appeared soon after his death. Later generations developed a taste for diverse historical genres, including accounts of territorial conquests, family genealogies, and town histories. However, Islamic history—and, indeed, the study of history—

took a giant step forward in the works of Ibn Khaldun [IB-en kal-DOON] (1332–1406).

Ibn Khaldun's fame rests on a multivolume history of the world, especially the *Muqaddima* or *Prolegomena,* which serves as the introduction to his lengthy study. Ibn Khaldun examined ancient societies with an eye to identifying their characteristics and the stages of their evolution. He was one of the first thinkers to deal with supply and demand, the role and value of currency, and stages of economic development as a society evolves from an agricultural to an urban economy. In Ibn Khaldun's view, which echoes that of the Greek writer Thucydides, the best historical studies downplay the role of religion or divine forces and focus on the role of human activity. Historians, by probing beneath the surface explanations of human behavior, would discover that humans are governed not by religion or idealism but rather by status concerns and the desire to identify with certain groups. Ibn Khaldun also offered a theory explaining the rise and fall of civilizations: As a civilization decays, its social bonds weaken, and it falls victim to a more vigorous people from outside its frontiers. The outsiders overthrow the weakened civilization, become powerful, and then cycle into a state of decay, to be invaded by more powerful intruders—an outlook that reflected his knowledge of the dramatic impact of Seljuk Turk, Mongol, and other nomadic forces on Muslim life.

Technology

Islamic technology, like Islamic science and philosophy, continued and expanded the Greco-Roman heritage. As Islamic civilization spread from its Middle Eastern home, its technology borrowed new features from the Far East, Iran, and India. While making no dramatic breakthroughs, Muslim artisans were skilled at perfecting the achievements of others. And, over time, Muslim technology served as a bridge to Western technology. Medieval Muslim civilization made noteworthy technological advances in three areas: papermaking, hydraulics, and mechanical engineering.

PAPERMAKING   The art of papermaking originated in China, perhaps in the second century CE.

- The first paper was made from old rags and organic fibers, softened by soaking in water, dried, pressed, and cut into sheets.
- China kept papermaking a royal monopoly and largely secret until the eighth century, when supposedly, a Chinese prisoner of war revealed the secret of making paper to his Islamic captors.
- Paper mills began to be built on rivers.
- In 793, Baghdad, on the Tigris River, became the site of the first paper mill in the Islamic world.
- In 1151, papermaking reached Muslim Spain. From Spain, European cities learned the art of papermaking.

HYDRAULICS   From the Greek word meaning "water organ" or "water hollow tube," hydraulics is the branch of engineering concerned with water flow and the use of liquids to power machines. It has been at the forefront of Muslim technology since the eighth century.

- Hydraulics was important for irrigation, powering mills (for grinding grain into flour, crushing sugarcane, and sawing wood), and raising water from a lower to a higher level.

- Hydraulics enhanced prosperity; for example, Baghdad had a system of dams, canals, and mills that tapped the waters of the Tigris River.
- A huge dam, 1,400' wide, at Córdoba, in Spain, served an irrigation system and mills.
- Valencia, Spain, had an elaborate desilting process for purifying water.
- The water clock—powered by water moving through interlocking hollow tubes, which activated cams, shafts, pulleys, wheels, and wheels within wheels—became a hallmark of Muslim technology (erected in Toledo, Spain, Damascus, Baghdad, and Fez, Morocco), in the eleventh through fourteenth centuries.

MECHANICAL ENGINEERING   Muslim artisans worked in two distinctly different areas of mechanical engineering:

- Development of utilitarian devices employed in daily life, such as pumps (to remove water from mines) and the astrolabe (for telling time and navigation—it permitted determination of the position of the sun or stars relative to the horizon).
- Development of automata, self-regulating machines, designed to entertain courtly audiences by controlling fountains and clocks.

Literature

In pre-Islamic Arabia, Arabic was basically a spoken language, developed by desert Bedouins and spread into urban areas by traders, who adapted it to their needs. Within this tribal culture, poets played a critical role, because they were thought to be wizards inspired by a *jinn*, or spirit. They eventually created a body of works that were transmitted orally by *rawis*, professional reciters of poetry. The preferred poetic form was the *qasida* ("ode"), composed in varied meters with a single rhyme. These poems, celebrating tribal life, personal glory, and love and wine, helped create a community identity and became the preferred model for poetic expression. Between 800 and 1300, Arabic became standardized as a written language. Called literary Arabic, or classical Arabic, it took the basic form of the language of the Qur'an, though modified to suit changing needs.

Critical to understanding Islam's literary culture is the concept of *adab*, an Arabic word initially meaning "rules of conduct," "manners," or "good habits." *Adab* first appeared in the eighth century as a literary genre, with the translation into Arabic of a Persian work on statesmanship. Among the elite, *adab* came to mean "refinement," which included having certain skills, such as the ability to swim and to ride horses, and, especially, having deep knowledge of Islamic poetry, prose, and history and of the Arabic language. In modern Arabic, *adab* simply refers to the whole of literature.

POETRY Pre-Islamic poetry did not disappear with the advent of Islam. The most famous surviving works are *al-Mu'allaqat* ("The Hanged Poems," or "The Seven Odes"), which, according to tradition, were suspended on the walls of the Kaaba while it was still a pagan shrine. The Prophet, though rejecting the pagan themes, recognized the poetry's power and called for poets to adapt the ode for religious ends.

Another genre that survived from pre-Islamic times was the elegy, or lament, especially for the dead. Usually composed by a woman, most often the dead hero's sister, the elegy became a favorite of Islamic poets. The best of these pieces were those by the female poet al-Khansa [al-kan-SAH] (d. after 630), who lived into the early Islamic period.

A new literary genre, the *ghazal,* a short lyric usually dealing with love, emerged in early Islamic Arabia. Composed in rhyming couplets, the *ghazal* often drew on the poet's personal life. Of these early poets, Jamil (d. 701) set the standard for later writers. His usual theme was impossible love: star-crossed lovers devoted to each other unto death. Persian, Turkish, and Urdu poets, adapting the *ghazal* into their languages, made it a popular genre in the Islamic world.

Two centuries later in Islamic Spain, Ibn Hazm [IB-en KAZ-um] (994–1064) produced the highly influential *The Ring of the Dove,* which blends poetry with prose and focuses on the art of love. In this work, he argues that the "true" lover finds happiness in pursuit of rather than in union with the beloved—a central idea of Arabic poetry that may have influenced Provençal poetry (see Chapter 9).

The Persian-speaking region of the Islamic world produced the gifted poet Rumi (1207–1273), active in Afghanistan, Persia, and Anatolia (modern Turkey). A Sufi mystic, Rumi greatly influenced Muslim ascetic thought and writing and, most important, Turkish religious life. As part of prayer ritual, the Sufi order of Whirling Dervishes created a whirling dance. Rumi's literary legacy is twofold: the *Diwan-e Shams,* a collection of poems addressed to a Sufi holy man and the poet's master; and the *Masnavi-ye Ma'navi* ("Spiritual Couplets"), a complex work, part Sufi handbook, part anthology of proverbs and folktales. The theme of the *Diwan-e Shams* is the poet's deep love for his master, a metaphor for the Sufi idea of an all-consuming love for God. The *Masnavi,* written in rhyming couplets, a Persian genre, presents the Sufi "way" through pointed stories and anecdotes.

PROSE Literary prose in Arabic originated at the Abbasid court in Baghdad, mainly as the creation of clerks and translators. A vast literature gradually emerged, but the genres were limited because of Islam's moral objection to drama and pure fiction—drama because it "represented" reality and was thus not real, and fiction because it made no claim to truth. Early writings from the Abbasid court were collections of proverbs; tales of tribal warfare known as *ayyam al-'Arab,* or "The Days of the Arabs"; and, especially, "night conversations," or *musamarah,* which evoked lively communal evenings around desert campfires. Organized loosely about a well-worn theme, filled with puns, literary allusions, and colorful vignettes of tribal life, and, above all, animated by love of the Arabic language, the "night conversations" reminded urban Arabs of their past and inspired the *maqamah* genre, a major prose achievement.

The **maqamah** ("assembly") genre was created by al-Hamadhani [al-HAM-uh-tha-NE] (969–1008). Blurring the line between fact and fiction, his *maqamahs* are entertaining works, focusing on rogues, dreamers, and lowlifes, written in rhymed prose to display his learning and literary art.

The foremost writer in the *maqamah* genre was al-Hariri [al-ka-RE-re] (1054–1122), a government official in Basra and a scholar of Arabic language and literature. Al-Hariri's poems are noted for verbal fireworks, humor, and exquisite usage of Arabic language and grammar. In the *Maqamat,* or *The Assemblies of al-Hariri,* he focuses on the adventures of the learned rogue and vagabond Abu Zayd, as reported by a narrator, al-Harith. Abu Zayd, who resembles the author in his poetic powers and lively intelligence, repeatedly uses his skills as a storyteller to charm presents from wealthy victims.

During this time, the collection of stories known as *The Thousand and One Nights,* first translated into Arabic from Persian, was circulating in the Muslim world. It is perhaps the most famous example of the "tale within a framing tale" literary genre in all of literature. The framing tale, probably from an Indian source, tells of the woman Shahrazad (Scheherazade), who devises a storytelling plan to keep the vengeful king Shahryar from his mad scheme of murdering a wife a day because an earlier wife had betrayed him. The tales come from many lands, including India, Iran, Iraq, Egypt, Turkey, and possibly Greece, and represent various genres—fairy tales, romances, legends, fables, parables, anecdotes, and realistic adventures. Originally, fewer than a thousand tales existed, but as the stories grew in popularity, new ones were added to make the number exact. This collection has supplied the West with many legendary figures, such as Aladdin, Ali Baba, and Sinbad the Sailor. In the Arab world,

Figure 8.8 The "Ardebil" Carpet. Formerly in the Mosque of Ardebil, Iran. 1539–1540. Woolen knotted carpet, 37'9½" × 17'6". Victoria and Albert Museum, London. *Arabesque leaves fill the yellow medallion at the center of this exquisite carpet. The medallion is surrounded by sixteen ogees (pointed ovals), which also contain arabesques. A section of this design is repeated in the corners of the interior rectangle. Praised as "the greatest example of carpet weaving in the world," this carpet of silk and wool was woven for a Persian mosque. At least thirty-two million knots were needed to complete it.*

however, Islamic scholars have not accepted *The Thousand and One Nights* as classical literature, criticizing it for colloquial language and grammatical errors.

Art and Architecture

Islamic art and architecture developed within a cultural setting dominated by the Qur'anic ideal that religion should govern all aspects of living. In an effort to sanctify human life, this ideal made no distinction between the artistic and the practical, the private and the public, the secular and the divine. Thus, art and architecture, like the rest of Islamic culture, had no purpose beyond serving religious faith. Reality, of course, never fully realized this ideal, but it helped to define what Islamic artists and architects could and, of equal importance, could not do.

The Qur'an forbade the worship of idols. In time, this ban was extended to mean that artists were prohibited from representing all living things. Accordingly, large-scale paintings and sculptures were not produced, and lifelike figures, whether of humans or of animals, largely disappeared from art. Artists became abundantly inventive in the use of nonrepresentational forms. The **arabesque**—a complex figure made of intertwined floral, foliate (leaf shaped), or geometric forms—emerged as a highly visible sign of Islamic culture (Figure 8.8). Geometric shapes, floral forms, and **calligraphy,** or beautiful writing, decorated walls, books, and mosaics (see Figure 8.4).

Islamic tenets allowed borrowing from other cultures, so long as what was borrowed was adapted to the teachings of the Qur'an. From Greco-Roman architecture came the column and the capital, the rib and the vault, and the arcade. From Byzantine architecture came the dome, the most prominent feature of the Islamic style, and the pendentive, the support feature that made the dome possible. From Persian art and architecture came miniature painting, the vaulted hall, the teaching mosque, the pointed arch, and floral and geometric ornamentation. And from Turkish art and architecture came a grand artistic synthesis, which raised Persian influence to a dominant role in Islamic art and architecture, in the zone stretching from Egypt eastward, after 1200.

ARCHITECTURE The oldest extant Islamic monument is the Dome of the Rock in Jerusalem, a shrine for pilgrims dating from between 687 and about 691 (Figure 8.9). Located in a city already sacred to Jews and Christians, and built over a rock considered holy by Muslims and Jews, the shrine proclaimed by its presence that Islam was now a world religion. For Mus-

Figure 8.9   The Dome of the Rock. Ca. 687–691. Diameter of dome approx. 60′; each outer wall 60′ wide × 36′ high. Jerusalem. *This Islamic shrine is filled with theological symbolism. The dome itself is a symbol of the heavens, and the dome's thrusting shape represents the correct path for the faithful to follow. The eight-sided figure on which the interior drum rests is an image of the earth, and the rock enclosed within this sacred space is the center of the world—a traditional Islamic belief. This belief arises, in part, because the Dome of the Rock stands on the Temple Mount—the location of Solomon's Temple and its successors. Thus, this building symbolizes Islam's claim to be the successor to and fulfillment of the Judaic and Christian faiths.*

lims, the shrine's rock marked the spot from which the founder of their faith, Muhammad, made his "night journey" to heaven. For Jews, it was identified with Abraham's planned sacrifice of his son Isaac. Because Muslims also claim Abraham as their ancestor, the site was thus given added meaning. Today, the Dome of the Rock remains one of Islam's holiest places, after Medina and Mecca.

The architecture of the Dome of the Rock draws mainly on Roman and Byzantine sources, but the aesthetic spirit reflects the new Islamic style. Its basic plan—an octagon covered by a dome—was rooted in Roman and Byzantine tradition, and the dome's sup-

port system—a tall **drum** or wall, resting on an **arcade,** or a series of arches supported by columns—was derived from Byzantine models. But, unlike the stone domes of Byzantine churches, this dome is made of wood covered with gold. The dome's splendor reflected the opulent aesthetic emerging in the Muslim world, as well as the ambitions of the Umayyad caliph who commissioned it.

The architectural aesthetic of the Dome of the Rock is echoed in its art program. Unlike Byzantine churches, whose plain exteriors contrasted with brilliant interiors, the Dome of the Rock is a feast for the eyes throughout. Everywhere there are mosaics, tiles, and marble, much of which was added later. In obedience to the Qur'anic ban, there is no figural art. Arabesques, foliated shapes, scrolls, and mosaics of purple and gold, inspired by Byzantine and Persian designs, animate the surfaces, and more than seven hundred feet of Arabic script—repeating passages from the Qur'an—are written on both interior and exterior surfaces. Sixteen stained-glass windows allow muted daylight to play across the interior surfaces.

The Dome of the Rock did not set the standard for Islam's dominant building type, the **mosque,** or, in Arabic, *masjid,* "place for bowing down." The Prophet himself established the basic plan with the house of worship he constructed in Medina. This first mosque, now lost, reflected the simple values of early Islam. It consisted of a rectangular courtyard, covered by a roof that rested on palm trunks and enclosed by walls made of raw bricks. The wall facing Mecca, the direction for prayer, was designated the *qiblah* wall, and a pul-

pit was erected from which Muhammad led prayers, preached, decreed new laws, and settled disputes. The courtyard also functioned much as the Greek *agora* and the Roman forum, providing a public meeting space. In huts opening onto the courtyard lived the Prophet and his wives. With its varied activities—judicial, political, social, and religious—this first mosque expressed the Islamic ideal of the unity of life.

Later mosque builders followed the example set by the Prophet. Plain in exterior ornament and rectangular in shape, mosques were distinguished from secular buildings by their interior features and spaces—basins and fountains for ritual hand washing, porticoes for instruction, a screened enclosure to shield the prayer leader, and an open area for the group prayers (Figure 8.10). Sometimes the mosque was crowned with a dome, as in the Byzantine churches, but the Islamic dome's high melon shape distinguished it from the spherical Byzantine form. A thin pointed tower, or **minaret,** from whose top a Muslim official, the *muezzin,* called the faithful to prayer five times a day, also identified the mosque. Inside the mosque, from the earliest times, rich decorations reminded worshipers of the beauty of paradise: brilliant mosaics and oriental carpets emblazoned the floors, facings and calligraphic friezes beautified the walls, metal or ceramic lamps cast a twilight glow onto the faithful at night, and richly decorated *minbars,* or pulpits (see Figure 8.6), elevated the prayer leader above the worshipers. The mosque type inspired by Muhammad's example is called the **congregational mosque,** or **Friday mosque,** a horizontal structure that houses the Friday worshipers in a central courtyard with a domed fountain for ablutions. With the Arab conquests, mosques of this type were built across the Islamic world, from southern Spain and Morocco to China.

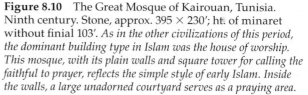

Figure 8.10   The Great Mosque of Kairouan, Tunisia. Ninth century. Stone, approx. 395 × 230'; ht. of minaret without finial 103'. *As in the other civilizations of this period, the dominant building type in Islam was the house of worship. This mosque, with its plain walls and square tower for calling the faithful to prayer, reflects the simple style of early Islam. Inside the walls, a large unadorned courtyard serves as a praying area.*

Figure 8.11.   Arches of the Great Mosque. Stone and brick columns, ht. 9'9", exterior 590 × 425'. Eighth–tenth centuries. Córdoba, Spain. *The Great Mosque, nearly as large as St. Peter's Basilica in the Vatican, contains 850 pillars with nineteen aisles running north to south and twenty-nine going east to west. Although Spanish Christians, in 1236, converted it to a cathedral and constructed a high altar in the interior and, in the sixteenth century, added chapels around the quadrangle, the Great Mosque still stands as a monument to the Umayyad kingdom in southern Spain and a crowning achievement of Islamic architecture and decorative art.*

Early in the history of Islam, Abd al-Rahman (731–788), a member of the Umayyad dynasty who survived the Abbasid revolt, made his way to southern Spain, where he founded a new kingdom. In 786, he began to build the Great Mosque—an awe-inspiring example of the congregational mosque style. Constructed on the site of a Roman temple and a Christian church, the mosque was laid out in the traditional rectangular plan. During the next century, local rulers enlarged the Great Mosque four times to make it the largest sacred building in the Islamic world. The second expansion added an elaborately decorated *qiblah* and three domed

chambers of Byzantine-inspired mosaics and gold ornamentation. But the most striking feature of the Great Mosque is the row after row of double-tiered horseshoe arches (Figure 8.11). The slender lower columns were salvaged from Roman buildings and Christian churches, and double-height arches were then placed on them. These rounded arches of red brick and yellow stone produce alternating patterns of light and color down the seemingly endless aisles.

The ninth-century Ibn Tulun mosque at Cairo is an imposing example of the congregational mosque (Figure 8.12). Four rows of arcades stand between the

SLICE OF LIFE
Fears of Assimilation in a Multicultural Society

PAUL ALBAR

In early-ninth-century Spain, the Umayyad rulers in Córdoba extended certain religious, legal, and civic rights to Christians, known as Mozarabs, and to Jews, who as dhimmis, or "people of the book," shared some religious beliefs with the Muslim community. However, in the 850s, peaceful relations between Muslims and Christians broke down after the government executed about fifty Christians for disrespecting Islam. In a contemporary account, the Christian layman Paul Albar laments how some young people in the Christian community were reacting to the government's crackdown. His account reveals the fear of assimilation to another culture and faith, and the subsequent loss of cultural and religious identity—a timeless issue in our multicultural society today.

The Christians love to read the poems and romances of the Arabs; they study the Arab theologians and philosophers, not to refute them but to form a correct and elegant Arabic. Where is the layman who now reads the Latin commentaries on the Holy Scriptures, or who studies the Gospels, prophets or apostles? Alas! all talented young Christians read and study with enthusiasm the Arab books; they gather immense libraries at great expense; they despise the Christian literature as unworthy of attention. They have forgotten their own language. For every one who can write a letter in Latin to a friend, there are a thousand who can express themselves in Arabic with elegance, and write better poems in this language than the Arabs themselves.

INTERPRETING THIS SLICE OF LIFE

1. *Why* were the Spanish Muslims tolerant of Jews and Christians? 2. *What* was the background to the conflict between the Muslims and Mozarabs? 3. *Why* should we be careful in accepting Paul Albar's views on the Arabization of young Christians? 4. *Why* were these young people attracted to Islamic culture? 5. *Would* you be interested in joining another religion or culture? *Why or why not?*

Figure 8.12 Ibn Tulun Mosque, Cairo. 876–879. Red brick covered with white stucco, exterior 531 × 532½'. *The finest surviving example of the congregational style, the Ibn Tulun mosque was imitated throughout the Islamic world. This view, from inside the courtyard, shows a domed fountain used for ritual washing. Outside the walls rises the spire of a four-story minaret, set on a square base with a cylindrical second story and an exterior staircase.*

faithful and the east wall (the direction of Mecca), and portals of pointed arches open into the arcaded area. A minaret with a winding stair rises just beyond the mosque, which is built of brick faced with stucco. In later Islamic mosques, the pointed arches and decorated stucco work became basic features of this style. During the Christian Middle Ages, Western architects borrowed the pointed arch and adapted it to their own needs, using it to perfect the Gothic style of architecture.

In the twelfth century in the eastern Islamic lands ruled by the Seljuk Turks, a new type of mosque, inspired by Persian architecture but retaining the basic rectangular plan of the Friday mosque, emerged. The new mosque type was called a teaching mosque, because it provided distinctive areas for the *madrasah,* the religious school for advanced study. The teaching mosque proved to be a popular innovation, and, between the twelfth and eighteenth centuries, architects built similar structures in Egypt, central Asia, and India.

The most famous example of a teaching mosque is the Masjid-i Jami, or Great Mosque, in Isfahan (in modern Iran), the capital of the Seljuk dynasty in the eleventh and twelfth centuries (Figure 8.13). Four huge vaulted halls, or **iwans,** open into a central courtyard. Prayers are said in the *iwan* that opens toward Mecca, and the other three serve as areas for study, school, and rest. Viewed from the courtyard, the opening in each *iwan* constitutes a huge arch set into a rectangu-

lar facade, faced with blue tiles—a specialty of Persian artisans and the signature color of the Seljuk rulers.

Islamic builders also excelled in palace architecture, as exemplified by the Alhambra in Granada, the residence of the last Muslim rulers of Spain. Its exterior of plain red brick contrasts dramatically with its fantastic interior. The presence and sound of water everywhere—fountains, pools, and sluices—enhance the serenity and pleasure of the gardens and buildings. The Court of the Lions illustrates vividly the meaning of the term *arabesque,* with its calligraphic carvings, slender columns, geometric and floral shapes, and lacy decoration (Figure 8.14). The fountain surrounded by stone lions is a rare example of Islamic representational sculpture.

PAINTING   Notwithstanding the Qur'anic prohibition, one branch of Islamic art—book painting, or the art of the book—usually depicted realistic scenes. A few surviving examples show that the art of the book was practiced in the early days of Islam. However, after

Figure 8.13 Masjid-i Jami (Great Mosque). Eleventh and twelfth centuries. Isfahan. *The view of the central courtyard and* iwan *(vaulted hall) of this teaching mosque is framed by the arched opening of the facing* iwan. *Various mosque facilities, including living quarters for teachers and students, are located in the areas around the* iwans.

Figure 8.14 Court of the Lions. The Alhambra. Thirteenth and fourteenth centuries. Granada, Spain. *The Alhambra is the only Islamic palace surviving from the medieval period. A popular destination for European and American tourists, the ornate Alhambra has played a pivotal role in developing a taste for the arabesque among many Westerners.*

1100, in rapid succession, two brilliant schools of book painting emerged, each devoted to representational scenes. Little known in the West, the first school flowered in Syria and Iraq, and its artists were probably Arab, strongly influenced by Persian tradition. The second was the world-famous school of **Persian miniatures,** which flourished in Persia from the thirteenth to the seventeenth century.

Of the Arab painters whose works survive, Yahya ibn Mahmud al-Wasiti [YAK-yah IB-en mak-MOOD al-WAH-see-tee] (fl. 1230s) is generally recognized as the best. Working in Baghdad, he illustrated al-Hariri's *maqamat,* a twelfth-century work. Each picture depicts a colorful episode in the life of the con artist Abu Zayd, rendered with an eye to detail (Figure 8.15). The typical format of the page includes arranging the scene's focus into the frontal plane, keeping the background neutral in color, and creating a setting with the barest of details, such as a small hill or a single tree. Near

Eastern tradition is apparent in the very large eyes, the dark outline of the figures, and the bunched drapery folds.

The Persian miniatures were produced under the patronage of the Mongol sultans, who had replaced the caliphs as rulers. Although the Mongols brought Chinese influences to the Persian miniatures, the Muslim artists rejected the openness of Chinese space and created their own ordered reality, as shown in a superb example from the early sixteenth century (Interpreting Art figure 8.1). Like all Persian miniatures, this exquisite work is characterized by fine detail, naturalistic figures and landscape, and subtle colors.

Music

Music has historically been a controversial topic in Muslim culture. Only a few musical genres have gained

Figure 8.15 Yahya ibn Mahmud al-Wasiti. *Abu Zayd Preaching.* Book painting. 1237. *Abu Zayd, here disguised as a religious official, preaches to a group of pilgrims. Islamic touches include the beards of male pilgrims and head coverings of both men and women. The artist creates a lively scene, in the manner of street theater, in the way he shows the pilgrims' varied eye and facial movements, including an exchange of glances, stares into the distance, heads lifted upward, and a head looking down.*

universal approval, such as the call to prayer (*adhan*), the chanting of the Qur'an, and the chanting of poems and prayers during certain religious events, including the Prophet's birthday, pilgrimages, and Ramadan. Clerics often question other musical forms, especially instrumental music, claiming such music undermines faith. And yet, music traditionally has thrived in the Muslim world.

Music was a constant presence in Muslim life, as heard in the five daily calls to prayer, echoing loudly from minarets in towns and cities across the Muslim world. A single male voice chants the call to worship, according to fixed rules, in which each phrase is followed by a longer pause. As the prayer unfolds, each phrase grows progressively longer and more ornamented in style. In each day's first prayer, the phrase "Prayer is better than sleep" is inserted into the sequence, before the last two statements. The Islamic call to prayer, in English translation, is

"God is great" (repeated four times)

"I bear witness that there is no god except God" (twice)

"I bear witness that Muhammad is the Messenger of God" (twice)

"Hasten to the prayer" (twice)

"Hasten to real success" (twice)

"Allah is the Greatest" (twice)

"There is none worthy of worship but Allah"

Early Islamic music employs a microtonal system, in which the intervals, or distances between sounds

INTERPRETING ART

Subject Matter Qur'an 1:17 may be paraphrased: A journey of a single night was made by a servant of God from the "sacred place of worship" to the "further place of worship."

Theological Perspective Traditionally, the "servant of God" was Muhammad and the "sacred place of worship" was Mecca. The early commentators interpreted the "further place of worship" as heaven (*miraj*) and believed that the ascension of the prophet took place from Mecca. Under the Umayyads, the "further place of worship" was interpreted as Jerusalem. The versions were later reconciled such that the *Isra* was taken to be a night journey to Jerusalem with the ascension to heaven occurring from there.

Content Muhammad is portrayed riding the *buraq,* a mythical winged horse, and being accompanied by the angel Gabriel amid a host of angels.

Cross-Cultural Influences The *buraq* has parallels in the winged beasts of ancient Mesopotamia and later central Asian art. The biblical story of Elijah riding into the sky on a fiery chariot (2 Kings 2: 7–12) is also a source.

Style The image blends Christian, Persian, central Asian, and Chinese motifs. The faces in particular betray Buddhist features, and the fiery halos around Muhammad and Gabriel are Chinese. The image reveals superbly the extraordinary melting pot of Islamic culture.

Composition The surface is virtually flat, the picture two-dimensional. The absolute centrality of Muhammad to the scene creates a sense of perspective that is not geometric but is still effective. By ringing Muhammad and Gabriel with angelic figures, the artist achieves an effect of great energy and movement. The artist took sheer delight in rich colors of many hues.

Interpreting Art figure 8.1 *The Night Journey of Muhammad.* Persia. Sixteenth century. British Library, London. *This Persian miniature represents a key Muslim belief: Muhammad made a night journey (Isra) from Mecca to Jerusalem before his ascension to heaven. His face was left blank because it was deemed blasphemous to depict his visage. This painting was executed during the Mongol period, as the Asian invaders, though converts to Islam, did not share the Arabs' abhorrence of figural art.*

(pitches) on a scale, are **microtones,** or intervals smaller than a semitone—the smallest interval in mainstream Western music before jazz.

Vocal music initially was dominant in Muslim culture, with instrumental music used only to support singing. Instrumental music later won its freedom under Spain's Umayyad rulers, who were great patrons of musicians and, most notably, of secular music (Figure 8.16). Meanwhile, religious music was given a new direction by the Sufi sect, who, in their pursuit of religious emotion, encouraged singing, chanting, and **recitative,** or vocal passages delivered in a speechlike

Figure 8.16 Pyxis. Córdoba. 968. *The image on this pyxis—* ▶ *a vessel to hold cosmetics or perfumes—testifies to the high status held by instrumental musicians at the Umayyad court in Córdoba. At the center stands a musician, holding an* ud, *or lute, as he performs for the two young men flanking him. The listening youths, seated Muslim style, are royalty, as symbolized by the two lions below. The youth on the left holds a vessel and a flower, and the one on the right holds a fan. Executed in the style of Islamic art, the surrounding space is enlivened with human, animal, and vegetal figures and abstract, meandering scrolls. An inscription identifies the* pyxis *as a gift to al-Mughira, the younger son of Abd al-Rahman III (r. 912–961), the first caliph of the West.*

manner. A major change arose in Turkey, where the Sufi order of Whirling Dervishes introduced music into their mosques.

Musicians across the Muslim world played many instruments, representing three groups of instruments and drawn from varied traditions. These included, from the string group, the *ud* (lute), the pandore (a bass lute), the psaltery (a trapezoidal-shaped zither), the harp, the *qithara* (guitar), and the *rabab* (rebec, a lute-shaped fiddle); from the wind group, the flute, the reed pipe, and the horn; and from the percussion group, tambourines (square and round), castanets, and various drums, such as *naqqara* (nakers, or small kettledrums) and *tabla* (a pair of wooden drums). Most of these instruments were adopted into Western music, especially as a result of cultural encounters during the Crusades.

The Legacy of Medieval Islam

The legacy of medieval Islam remains potent in the modern Muslim world. That medieval presence is apparent in distinctive architecture, which uses domes, vaulted halls, arcades, and pointed arches; in decorative patterns made with nonrepresentational designs, such as arabesques, calligraphy, and geometric, floral, and abstract forms; in a music tradition based on a microtonal system; in classical Arabic as a literary and scholarly language; in traditional clothing styles, along with beards for men and headscarves, and sometimes veils, for women; and in daily readings from the Qur'an on radio and television.

Medieval Islam also transmitted a legacy of suspicion toward the Christian West as a result of the Crusades in the eleventh through thirteenth centuries; indeed, in parts of Islamic society today, the word *crusader* is a hate-charged term for a Westerner on Muslim soil. When the Greek heritage fell into disrepute in the Muslim world, medieval Islam changed the intellectual climate for scholars. As a result, the Muslim world, which after the fall of Rome had been the leader in scientific knowledge, began to lag behind the West, so that by 1800, Muslim science and universities had become irrelevant. Medieval Islam also transmitted a vision of a unified Islamic Empire, stretching from Spain to China, inhabited by millions of Muslims, all worshiping Allah and obeying the Qur'anic laws— a vision that appeals to those dissatisfied with their place in today's Western-dominated world. Probably the major legacy of medieval Islam, and the feature of Islamic life that so differs from Western life, is the intermingling of religion and state. In the Muslim world, except for the secular state of Turkey, religion's dominant role is expressed in varied ways from law codes based on the Qur'an, mandating severe punishments for crimes such as adultery and theft, to separation of the sexes in public and private life.

Though perhaps not as strong as its impact on modern Islam, the influence of medieval Islam on the civilization of the modern West has been significant—ranging from architecture to literature to philosophy to mathematics to technology. Islam's direct legacy to Western civilization includes the pointed arch, which made the Gothic style possible; musical instruments from the string, the wind, and the percussion groups; poetic forms and themes that may have been imitated by the Provençal poets; love poetry, which inspired modern imitators; the poetry of the Sufi mystic Rumi, much admired by contemporary artists including the writer Doris Lessing and the composer Philip Glass; the tradition of reconciling religion with Aristotle's philosophy, which became the goal of Europe's scholastic thinkers; algebra and other original mathematical concepts, which became part of the Western educational curriculum; and a pump with suction pipes, a necessary feature used later in the steam engine.

Besides direct influence, medieval Islam has also had an indirect impact on the West by transmitting legacies from other cultures. Of these mediated legacies, the classical heritage was probably the most important. Islamic scholars produced Arabic versions of most of the Greek and Roman scholarly writings, which Christian scholars then translated into Latin and used as the textbooks in medieval Europe's schools and universities. From the study of those textbooks, the West's modern scientific tradition was born. Other notable transmitted legacies include, from China, papermaking; from Greece, the astrolabe and various automata with intricate components; and, from India, the Hindu-Arabic numeral system along with other mathematical knowledge and probably the basic form of the *Arabian Nights*, though embellished with stories from various cultures.

KEY CULTURAL TERMS

madrasah

jihad

qasida

adab

ghazal

maqamah

arabesque

calligraphy

drum

arcade

mosque

qiblah

minaret

minbar

congregational mosque
  (Friday mosque)

iwan

Persian miniature

microtone

recitative

QUESTIONS FOR CRITICAL THINKING

1. What forces contributed to the cohesion and to the disunity of the Islamic Empire?

2. Islam has been called a religion of "orthopraxy" (right conduct) more than of "orthodoxy" (right belief). Comment.

3. Discuss some of the ways in which Islam, Judaism, and Christianity are both alike and different.

4. Describe the two main kinds of mosques. How are mosques like and unlike churches?

5. To what extent do Western concepts such as realism, illusionism, and naturalism apply to the Islamic arts?

9

THE HIGH MIDDLE AGES
The Christian Centuries

The three centuries between about 1000 and 1300—the period called the High Middle Ages—were among the most dynamic in all of European history. The word that captures a sense of this time period is *expansion*. In every aspect of life, things got bigger and better. There was more of everything, too—people, food, products, government, literature, art, theology.

The most significant political changes were the creation of new monarchies, the consolidation of central power in the states that had already existed in the early Middle Ages, and the formation of city governments. In addition, Scandinavia, the Slavic world, and Rus (Russia's ancestor) all emerged during this period.

Economic expansion was the hallmark of the age. The population doubled, and millions of acres of new land were put into cultivation. Cities grew and played more important roles in European commerce, politics, and culture, while many new towns appeared. Old trade routes carried more goods and new ones emerged. All signs pointed to rising prosperity.

Expansion is an apt characterization of cultural life too. There were more and bigger schools, and also more scholars with wider interests. Alongside the Latin writings of the learned, vernacular writing flourished in Europe's native languages. And two new styles of art and architecture graced the environment—first the Romanesque and then the Gothic.

All these kinds of expansion spurred each other on. In culturally diverse regions such as Spain, Sicily, and the crusader principalities in the eastern Mediterranean, warriors, merchants, artisans, scholars, and pilgrims encountered and influenced each other, and enriched each other's worldviews.

◀ **Detail** Nave, Amiens Cathedral. Ca. 1220–1236. France.

POLITICS AND SOCIETY

King Alfred the Great of England (r. 871–899) once said that a kingdom needed "men of war, men of prayer, and men of work." A little later, two French bishops spoke in exactly the same terms. This tripartite scheme is helpful as a way of thinking about how medieval society and politics functioned—and it is contemporary. Nevertheless, this view is too tidy. Those who work, for example, were, in this landed and aristocratic way of looking at things, the peasants, but not the townspeople, who were increasingly numerous and prominent. In addition, the scheme did not include women and minorities, such as Jews.

Lords and Vassals: Those Who Fight

The term **feudalism** is almost synonymous with medieval social and political practices, although the term itself never appeared in the Middle Ages. Like all modern words that end in *ism*, feudalism is tricky and has been used in different ways. Feudalism can mean a kind of government with shared, segmented power and authority; a set of relationships between free men bound to each other in both personal and material ways; or the exploitation of the peasantry by the nobility. While each of these definitions grasps a part of the truth, none grasps it whole, and it is impossible to speak about a feudal "system." People from Iceland, through Britain and France, to Russia, over many centuries, had numerous ways of organizing politics and government.

The best way to understand feudalism is to examine the mutual, honorable relationships between lords and vassals. Lords were those who held both public and private power in their hands. They could be kings, or the powerful local officers of kings, or self-serving regional leaders who profited from the breakup of the Carolingian Empire. The great problem of government in the Middle Ages was harnessing the numerous lords to peaceful and productive purposes. Vassals, who were the retainers of lords, swore homage and fealty to a lord, and promised aid and counsel. Homage involved a public, ceremonial acknowledgment of allegiance. Fealty implied loyalty. Aid usually took the form of military service. Counsel meant giving advice, whether privately and intimately or publicly in hall or court. Lords agreed to protect their vassals in judicial troubles or against the attacks of others and usually provided them with something of material value, such as clothing and weapons, housing, money, or land. When land was involved, it was called a fief (*feudum* in Latin, whence feudalism). A fief was an estate—typically of the bipartite kind (see Chapter 7)—that was already developed and inhabited. The fief was supposed to support the vassal and free him—almost without exception, only men were involved—to perform his service (Figure 9.1).

This was a violent society whose leaders were men trained to fight, ideally their lord's enemies but sometimes each other. These warrior-aristocrats shared a guiding ethos: **chivalry,** from the French *cheval*, horse; so chivalry—*chevalerie*—means "horsiness," the way

Figure 9.1 *Count Eckhart and Uta.* Naumburg cathedral. Ca. 1245. Limestone, life-size. Naumburg, Germany. *In this representation of a feudal lord and lady, the most striking features are the woman's chaste beauty, reflecting her role as the queen of chivalry and linking her to the Virgin Mary, and the man's great heraldic shield and sword, symbolizing his position as an aristocratic warrior and defender of honor. These two figures are among several that stand in Naumburg cathedral, representing noble men and women associated with the founding of the cathedral. The Naumburg statues are considered among the most beautiful sculptures from this period.*

of life for men who fought on horseback. The word also meant "knighthood." The essential values of the chivalric knight were prowess—a knight who cannot fight is a contradiction in terms; courage; loyalty, an ideal that was often violated; and generosity, open-handed giving.

Originally, chivalric values were male and martial and did not pertain to relations between the sexes. Later, in the twelfth century, female influences began turning rough-and-ready warriors into gentlemen. But as early as the tenth century, the church began to try to ameliorate and redirect the worst excesses of the warriors' behavior. In the Peace and Truce of God, a movement that began in France and then spread widely, the church tried to civilize violence. Fighting was forbidden on religious feasts (more than 150 days per year) or near churches, and noncombatants and their property were to be protected. Framed more positively, knights were to protect the weak and the poor, women, widows, and children. Instead of fighting other Christians, knights were to direct their violence against pagans and infidels. Ironically, though, church teachings against violence served as one spur to crusading.

Peasants: Those Who Work

The routine of the serfs and the free peasants—rural slaves were comparatively rare—was dictated by custom and regulated by daily and seasonal events (Figure 9.2). Men and women worked together in the fields, eking out a bare subsistence from their tiny plots of land; they lived in wooden huts, reared their children, and found relief in the church's frequent holy days (the source of the modern term *holiday*). Some of the farming innovations (such as three-field crop rotation, which allowed the land to replenish itself, and improved plows) introduced in the Carolingian period began to be more widely used, and the plight of the peasants improved. Increasing the productivity of the soil brought economic benefits to the lord, who could then, if he wished, pay the peasants in coin and sell them tracts of land. Moreover, the expanding commercial economy led many lords to desire more money to buy luxuries. To acquire such money, they often permitted peasants to exchange labor services for money payments. In general, the lot of the peasant in France and England improved while, in some areas of central and eastern Europe, serfs continued to be exploited for centuries.

The Rise of Towns (and the Rest of Those Who Work)

Although rural estates included about 90 percent of all people at the beginning of the High Middle Ages, Europe's population nearly doubled between 1000 and 1300, rising to around seventy million, and an increasing number of people sought economic opportunities in the new and revitalized urban areas (Figure 9.3). From then on, the future of the West lay with town dwellers.

As towns grew larger and urban life became more competitive, the residents formed associations, called

Figure 9.2 Agricultural Laborers at Work. Aelfric writings, Canterbury. Eleventh century. *In the top panel, four men are depicted harvesting grain with various handheld tools, and, in the lower panel, five men carry bundles of grain. The scribe who painted these panels, as part of his copying duties, must have witnessed such scenes often in the harvest season. The laborers' costume—a loose-fitting tunic or gown, reaching below the knee, belted at the waist, and with long sleeves and a round neck—was typically worn by both sexes in Europe, from the fall of Rome until fitted garments emerged, after 1340.*

Figure 9.3 AMBROGIO LORENZETTI (active ca. 1319–1347). *Street Scene in Medieval Siena.* Detail from *Allegory of Good Government in the City.* 1338–1339. Fresco in the Sala della Pace, Palazzo Pubblico, Siena. *Although an idealized image, this painting is nevertheless an accurate representation of medieval Siena as a bustling country town built on a hill. Signs of prosperity abound. In the middle right and center, farmers, perhaps from the nearby countryside, lead pack animals loaded with sacks of wool and other goods. Nearby, three weavers are making textiles. On the lower right, a goatherd coaxes his flock, probably to the city market. In the middle left foreground, a shopkeeper arranges his wares. Through the large opening on the left may be glimpsed a classroom, where a seated teacher addresses his students. On the extreme right, two women, perhaps servants, carry objects, one, most noticeably, with a large bundle balanced on her head.*

guilds, to protect their special interests. The artisan and craft guilds, for example, regulated working conditions, created apprenticeship programs, and set wages; merchant and banking guilds developed new businesses and supervised trade contracts. These guilds often quarreled over issues inside the town walls, but they joined hands against the intrusions of the church and the local nobility.

Because urban economic life often conflicted with the interests of popes, bishops, kings, counts, and others who dominated the towns, urban dwellers, led by the guilds, founded self-governing regimes, called communes, often with written charters that specified their rights in relation to their various lords. Italy led the way but, by about 1200, many towns in northern and western Europe had charters, and their political independence spurred economic growth.

Artisans and merchants needed buyers, secure trade routes, and markets for their products. The earliest trade routes were the rivers and the old Roman roads, but as demand increased in the West for luxury items from the East, new trade routes opened. Italian cities led this international commerce, trading the luxurious woolen cloth of Flanders for the silks of China and the spices of the Middle East (Map 9.1). Along the overland routes in Europe, local lords guaranteed traders safe passage through their territory for a fee. In the twelfth and thirteenth centuries, the fairs of the Champagne region in France brought virtually all of Europe's commerce together.

As on the estate, the position of women in the medieval urban world was subordinate to that of men, even though urban women often worked closely with their husbands in trade or crafts. In this hierarchical society, gender roles became increasingly differentiated through custom and legislation. The few women with economic power, such as those directly involved in manufacturing and trade or the occasional rich widow who kept her husband's business afloat, were exceptions to this general exclusionary rule. Some aspects of the cloth and brewing industries were such exceptions.

LEARNING THROUGH MAPS

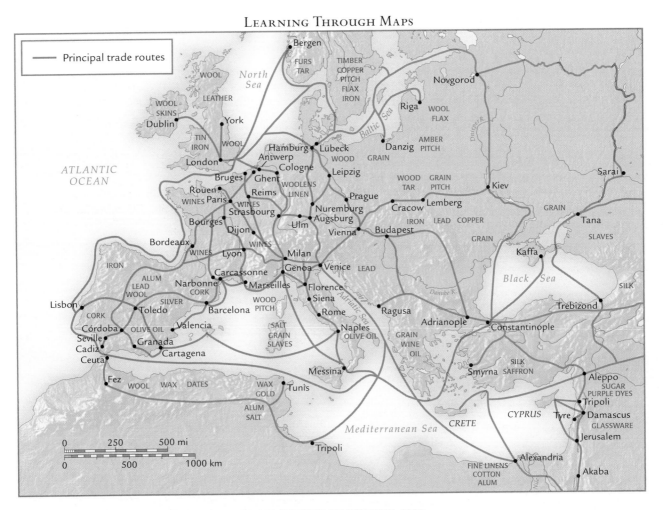

Map 9.1   PRINCIPAL TRADING ROUTES AND TOWNS OF EUROPE, 1300
This map shows the major towns and trading routes in Europe at the end of the High Middle Ages. 1. *Note* the important role played by sea trade. 2. *Identify* some key crossroads of trade. 3. *How* did the location of the north Italian cities help to make them leaders in trade? 4. *Consider* the extensive nature of the long-distance trade between Europe and its neighbors. 5. *Consider* also the impact of climate on the products made and produced in various regions.

Medieval Government

During the High Middle Ages, four impressive governments emerged in western Europe: France, England, Germany, and the papacy. However, their political fortunes varied. Germany was the most powerful state in tenth-century Europe and the weakest in the thirteenth. The papacy rose steadily in power and influence to about 1200 and then declined. France and England both developed strong, effective central governments but took very different paths to that destination (Timeline 9.1).

THE FRENCH MONARCHY Patience, luck, fame, feudalism, and faith all contributed to the development of

the French monarchy. When Hugh Capet came to the throne in 987, he established a dynasty that ruled until 1328. The Capetians followed similar policies, patiently wearing down and overcoming one rival after another, first in northern France and then toward the south. They saw two-thirds of their land fall into English hands and then got almost all of it back. They scrupulously insisted on feudal rights when it suited their purposes—seizing lands from recalcitrant vassals, for example, then retaining them. They also built up effective institutions. By the end of the thirteenth century, King Philip IV "the Fair" (r. 1285–1314) could issue laws for all of France.

During this time, the French established themselves as the cultural leaders of Europe. France had the best

Timeline 9.1   THE FEUDAL MONARCHIES IN THE HIGH MIDDLE AGES

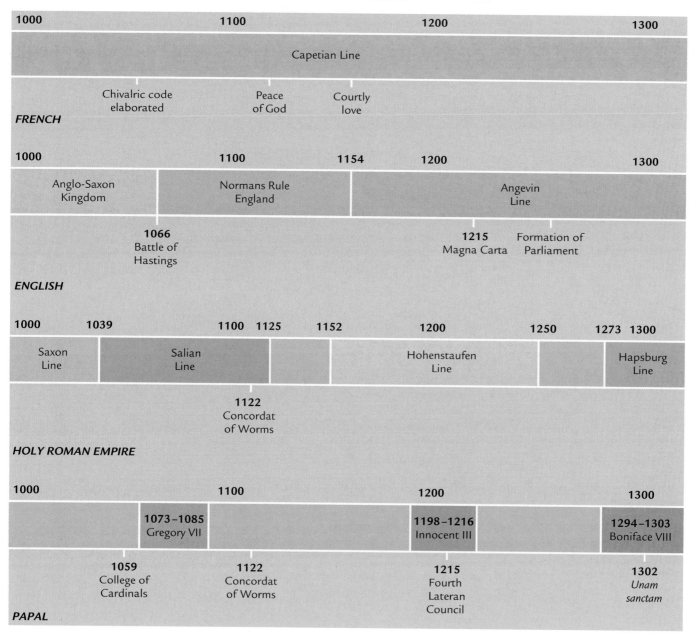

university and the most famous scholars. Its architecture was dominant, and its literature was emulated. The Capetians, alone among all their contemporaries, produced a saint: King Louis IX (r. 1226–1270), or Saint Louis, revered for his crusading zeal and personal piety. France and its monarchy were going to face severe challenges in the late Middle Ages, but in 1300 France was a formidable force in Europe and vastly stronger than it had been in 1000.

THE ENGLISH MONARCHY   Unlike the French, the English suffered several invasions, their ruling families were short-lived, and their monarchs were forced to

relinquish some of their power. In the tenth century the Vikings savaged England; in 1016 the country was overrun by Cnut of Denmark and, in 1066, conquered by William of Normandy (Figure 9.4). In 1135 and 1154 the crown changed hands, and in the thirteenth century the English experienced one domestic crisis after another. Yet, in spite of the turmoil, England's kings managed to construct an effective kingdom.

As conquerors, Cnut and William the Conqueror in the eleventh century, and later Henry II of Anjou (r. 1154–1189), possessed some political advantages: they had opportunities to redraw the political map. Each of these kings was politically astute, however,

Figure 9.4   *These Men Wonder at the Star. Harold.* Panel from the Bayeux Tapestry. Third quarter of the eleventh century. Wool embroidery on linen, ht. 20″. Bayeux, France. *Today housed in the cathedral of Bayeux, this famous embroidery provides an important historic record of the events leading up to the Battle of Hastings in 1066 and presents a justification for the Norman conquest of England. Harold is cast as a villain who breaks his oath of allegiance to William and loses the English crown as a result of this treachery. Halley's comet, interpreted as an evil omen, appeared over England in February 1066. The comet is shown in the center of the upper border. On the left, men point to the comet, and on the right Harold also seems upset by the comet. Beneath Harold and his adviser are outlines of boats, implying a possible invasion by the Normans.*

and managed to expand royal power while keeping the barons quiescent. Each had vast overseas interests that were sometimes distracting but that also provided wealth for the rulers and outlets for restless nobles. Henry II, especially after his marriage to Eleanor of Aquitaine (1122–1204), controlled directly or indirectly some two-thirds of France. Nominally he was a vassal of the French king, but the reality was not in French favor. King John (r. 1199–1215), a weak ruler, managed to lose most of England's French holdings. With his prestige fatally damaged, John's key vassals forced him to sign the Magna Carta in 1215. The king was compelled to admit that he was not above the law, had to observe due process of law, and had to take baronial advice.

One thing the English barons wanted to advise about was the stunning growth of royal institutions across the twelfth century. England's financial ministry was efficient and incorruptible and its judicial system, effective and fair. Through a system of well-ordered courts, England began operating with a common law—a single law applicable to all. During the thirteenth century, the barons and townsmen challenged the crown over how to institutionalize criticism and dissent. The crisis was resolved with the founding of Parliament (a "talking together," from the French *parler*, "to speak"), a venue for the king and the elite to meet, negotiate, and make decisions.

THE GERMAN EMPIRE   In contrast to France and England, the German Empire did not become unified but slowly disintegrated because of frequent dynastic changes and conflicts with the church. In the tenth century, the Ottonian kings built Europe's strongest realm. These fierce warriors, the conquerors of the Magyars and of neighboring Slavs, were, after 962, once again emperors. They controlled the church, with its substantial wealth and educated personnel, and were heirs to the Carolingian ideology that they ruled by the grace of God and were answerable to God alone.

In the eleventh century, under more peaceful conditions in the east, Germany's rulers no longer won prestige and plunder, and could not distract the nobles with profitable wars. There were also repeated changes of dynasty. In 1056 a powerful king died and left a child as his heir—always a dangerous situation in a dynastic state. Unexpectedly, a major crisis in relations with the church broke out.

The **Investiture Controversy,** ostensibly a struggle over the right to invest—appoint and install—churchmen by laymen, was one of the most significant events

Figure 9.5 Pope Urban II Consecrates the Great Abbey Church of Cluny (III). Book of Offices. Late twelfth century. Bibliothèque Nationale de France, Paris. *In this small manuscript painting, Pope Urban II (r. 1088–1099) consecrates the third version of the Great Abbey Church at Cluny. In the consecration service, the church is transformed into sacred ground and thus dedicated to the service of God. Framed by architectural features suggestive of the church's interior, the pope (the large standing figure on the left) offers a papal blessing before the high altar (under the domed center section). The artist has skillfully suggested a crowded church of worshipers, including Cluniac monks and nuns and various church officials. Pope Urban II, a member of the Cluniac order, preached the First Crusade in 1095.*

of the Middle Ages. For centuries, powerful lords had been investing bishops and abbots with their offices; this was a way to extend their authority through the church, and sometimes they received payments for making appointments. Where kings were concerned, however, the matter was more complicated. Insofar as they considered themselves God's chosen agents on earth, they imagined the clergy, even the popes, to be their natural helpers and subordinates. The clergy came to regard its freedom from lay control as crucial and also to view the buying and selling of church offices as a serious sin, called simony. And, finally, the papacy, which had reformed its worldliness, emerged under a series of resolute popes who saw themselves as the chief earthly representatives of heavenly power, and considered kings and other rulers to be their helpers and subordinates. The struggle raged for more than fifty years. In the end, secular rulers lost the right to invest clerics with the symbols of their religious offices although they could still draw them into their governments.

Germany suffered a damaging blow to its prestige and power during the Investiture Controversy because several emperors who confronted the papacy had to make humiliating concessions. Simultaneously, the rulers faced a restless nobility that took advantage of the situation to strengthen its political power. Finally, the emperors, attempting to resurrect a new Roman Empire, became embroiled in Italy. By the thirteenth century—when France and England were achieving unity—German rulers were more interested in Italy than in Germany. And, when they invaded Italy, they found themselves facing the formidable Papal States, which generated new struggles with the papacy. By 1300 Germany's once powerful monarchy was shattered.

THE PAPAL MONARCHY   The medieval church was a hierarchical institution, and in the High Middle Ages the popes reached the highpoint of their power and influence. Consequently, historians speak about "the papal monarchy." Papal power rested on several foundations. In 910 at Cluny in Burgundy, William of

Aquitaine founded a monastery, declared it free of all lay control, and placed it under the protection of the pope (Figure 9.5). Over the next two centuries, Cluny became a powerful force for reform in the church as its monks insisted on the moral and intellectual reform of the clergy, and on freedom for the church. Eventually, Cluny's zeal for reform penetrated Rome and the papacy placed itself at the head of a broad reform movement—the Investiture Controversy was but one aspect of this movement. In the curia—the papal government—the papacy built complex institutions and, during the High Middle Ages, the judicial and financial branches of the papal government expanded. By 1200 the popes had the most complex government in Europe. The legal system, the canon law, of the church was unrivaled. The popes had disciplinary tools that gave them influence all over: They could excommunicate an individual—declare him outside the community of the faithful. They could impose an interdict on a region—a suspension of religious services. They could send legates, in effect ambassadors, to conduct inquiries or to represent them. And they could institute courts of Inquisition, strict judicial forums that operated on the basis of Roman law. Finally, popes could call councils. In the Fourth Lateran Council of 1215, the largest council since antiquity, Innocent III (pope 1198–1216) presided like the uncrowned king of Europe.

By 1300 secular forces were gaining strength in Europe and many rulers thought the popes had claimed too much. Both French and English kings defied the pope's refusal to let them tax the clergy. The king of France summoned a French bishop before his court, much to the pope's chagrin. Boniface VIII (pope, 1294–1303) issued a papal bull (from *bullum,* "seal"), *Unam Sanctam,* with a powerful affirmation of papal primacy in both church and state. However, very few rulers honored the bull and some reacted by force. For example, the king of France sent his lawyers and a military force to arrest the pope. Boniface fled but died soon thereafter.

MEDIEVAL CHRISTIANITY AND THE CHURCH

Christianity and the church touched every aspect of life in medieval Europe. Important moments of life— birth, marriage, death—were attended by Christian rituals, and the Christian calendar regulated life from farming to government. Rulers imagined themselves to be divinely appointed and inspired. Literature and art had Christian themes, and music lifted praises to God. Neither before nor since the High Middle Ages

have Christianity and the Catholic Church exercised so profound and pervasive an influence.

Christian Beliefs and Practices

The immense authority of the church sprang from the belief shared by the overwhelming majority of medieval people that the church held the keys to the kingdom of heaven and provided the only way to salvation. By attempting to adhere to the Christian moral code and by participating in the rituals and ceremonies prescribed by the church and established by tradition, Christians hoped for redemption and eternal life after death.

These rituals and ceremonies were inseparable from the religious doctrines. They derived from the teachings of Jesus and Paul, the church fathers, particularly Augustine, and were further defined by medieval theologians. Finally, the Fourth Lateran Council of 1215, under Pope Innocent III, officially proclaimed the sacraments as the outward signs of God's grace and the only way to heaven.

As established by the council, the sacraments numbered seven: baptism, confirmation, the Eucharist (Holy Communion), penance, marriage, last rites, and ordination for the priesthood. Baptism, the Eucharist, and penance were deemed of primary importance. In baptism, the parents were assured that the infant had been rescued from original sin. In the Eucharist, the central part of the Mass, the church taught that a miracle occurred whereby God, through the priest, turned the bread and wine into the body and blood of Jesus. That the outer appearance of the bread and wine remained the same while their inner substance changed was explained by medieval theologians in the doctrine of transubstantiation.

Penance evolved into a rather complicated practice. First, sinners felt contrition—sorrow—and then they confessed their sins individually to a priest; the priest conveyed God's forgiveness for the mortal penalties of sin so that hell could be avoided; the priest then directed that an earthly punishment—the penance—be carried out in an effort to erase the effects of the sin. Depending on the severity of the sin, penance could range from a few prayers to a pilgrimage or a crusade. This sacrament was made even more complex by its association with purgatory.

With the groundwork laid by Augustine in the fifth century and Pope Gregory the Great in the sixth century, the doctrine of purgatory was given more explicit form by thinkers of the High Middle Ages. Neither hell nor heaven, purgatory was a third place, where those who had died in a state of grace could avoid damnation by being purged, or purified, from all stain

ENCOUNTER

Pagan Vikings versus Christian Europeans

The ethnic composition of Europe changed dramatically during the Middle Ages (500–1500), with the assimilation of numerous barbarian peoples. These included various Germanic tribes, such as Angles and Saxons (in England), Franks (in France), Alemanni (in Germany), Visigoths (in Spain), and Lombards and Ostrogoths (in Italy); several Slavic groups, including Poles, Czechs, Slovaks, and Wends or Sorbs (in central and eastern Europe); and Magyars (in Hungary). The Vikings, a Germanic people, are the classic example of a barbarian people who not only were forever changed by assimilation but also effected indelible changes on European civilization.

The Vikings, the last Germanic people to be assimilated into European life, began the early Middle Ages as pagans, linked by trade with Christian Europe but otherwise isolated, living in Norway, Denmark, and Sweden. Starting about 789, that changed, as peaceful coexistence gave way to sometimes violent encounters with European neighbors. For more than three hundred years, the Vikings launched hit-and-run raids, pillaging monasteries, churches, and other unfortified sites along the coasts and rivers of Britain, Ireland, northern France, and occasionally Italy; conquering Normandy, Sicily, and large parts of Russia and Britain; trading with Constantinople and Baghdad; discovering and colonizing Iceland and Greenland; and being the first Europeans to set foot in North America, on the coast of Newfoundland. Any hope for a far-flung Viking culture ended in the tenth and eleventh centuries, mainly because the Vikings converted to Christianity and thus lost their distinctive Scandinavian identity. By 1100 the Viking Age was over; the Vikings were now Christian Europeans.

The word *Viking* originally meant only those Scandinavians who went *vikingr,* or plundering, and it probably originated in Britain, where the first raids began about 789. Today, it is applied to all early medieval Scandinavians, whether they went "plundering" or not. However, the Viking Age was more than a time for looting. It was a period of migration of peoples, propelled by varied motives, including overpopulation, worsening climate and food supply, infighting among rival chieftains in which the losers were driven overseas, and the search for lucrative trading opportunities.

The Vikings unquestionably altered Western culture. They established the first towns in Ireland, Russia, and Scandinavia and made Iceland part of Europe by opening it to settlement. In France, they hastened the breakup of the Carolingian Empire and deeply influenced the history of France, England, and Italy by founding the duchy of Normandy. They set up the first state in Russia; the word *Russia* is derived from *Rus,*

Encounter figure 9.1   Viking Raid. Tombstone. Lindisfarne (Holy Island). Ninth century. *This tombstone vividly depicts a Viking raid, through simple forms and expressive gestures. The ferocity of the attack is manifest in the massed warriors, each with one leg bent at the knee to suggest movement and one arm brandishing a battle-ax. Found in the monastery of Lindisfarne, on the northeastern coast of England, this image probably depicts the actual sacking of this monastery in 793. The attack on Lindisfarne, a major monastic center, caused some people to believe that God was using the Vikings to punish Christians for some terrible sin.*

the name given Scandinavians by the Slavic majority. They contributed about six hundred loanwords to modern English, including "cast," "knife," "window," and "egg," as well as certain plural pronouns, such as "they," "them," and "their." The Vikings' greatest impact was probably on Britain, where their small states, though short-lived, destroyed old governing units and thus prepared the way for the founding of the unified kingdoms of England and Scotland.

LEARNING FROM THE ENCOUNTER

1. *What* is the popular stereotype of a Viking? 2. *Assess* the truth of the Viking stereotype. 3. *What* reasons led the Vikings to leave their homeland? 4. *What* prompted the end of Viking culture? 5. *How* were the Vikings changed by the process of assimilation? 6. *List* five significant changes to European culture as a result of the Vikings' raids. 7. *What* lessons may be learned from the assimilation of the Vikings into Western culture? 8. *Is* there any modern non-Western people related to the West in the manner of the Vikings to the medieval West? *Explain.*

of sin. All souls in purgatory were ultimately destined for heaven; penance was a means of reducing time in purgatory. Thus the living could do penance on earth in hope of spending less time in purgatory.

Religious Orders and Lay Piety

The clergy were the most visible signs of the church's presence in everyday life. The "secular" clergy (from *saeculum,* Latin for "world") moved freely in society, and the "regular" clergy lived apart from the world in monasteries under a special rule (*regula,* in Latin). The monasteries served as refuges from the world, as schools, and as places of study where manuscripts could be copied and traditional learning maintained. They also gave rise to the reform movements that periodically purged abuses and enhanced piety.

As noted earlier, the Cluniac monks originated the reform movement that helped to establish the moral and political authority of the medieval church. Other waves of reform followed, the most important of which was represented by the founding of the Cistercian order in the twelfth century. Bernard of Clairvaux [klair-VOH] (1090–1153), a saint, a mystic, and one of the most forceful personalities of the period, founded over 160 Cistercian abbeys. The Cistercians believed that the Cluniacs were too rich and powerful and that they failed to observe the Rule of St. Benedict strictly. They adopted an austere life and often lived in isolated monasteries where the brothers worked with the local peasants. Whereas the Cluniacs understood the Benedictine motto "To Labor Is To Pray" in such a way that they turned prayer into work and accordingly had elaborate and lengthy worship, the Cistercians understood work as manual labor and simplified their worship.

In convents, women could devote themselves to Christ and follow ascetic lives filled with prayer, contemplation, and service. And they could live in community with other women, under the authority of women. In some houses, they had opportunities for education. Convents had existed since the early Middle Ages, although seldom with the large endowments monasteries enjoyed or with as much influence in local affairs.

Convent life nurtured several gifted women who influenced this age, most notably Hildegard of Bingen (1098–1179), founder and abbess of the Benedictine house of Rupertsberg near Bingen (modern Germany). Her writing and preaching attracted scores of supporters in Germany, France, and Switzerland, including most of her male superiors. She was highly influential with major figures of the time, as evidenced by her correspondence with Eleanor of Aquitaine, the emperor Frederick Barbarossa, and various popes. Hildegard

Figure 9.6 Hildegard's Awakening: A Self-Portrait from *Scivias.* Ca. 1150. *Hildegard's description of the moment when she received the word of God is effectively captured in this illumination: a "burning light coming from heaven poured into my mind." The Holy Spirit inflames her mind as she etches the word of God on a tablet; Volmar, the priest of the abbey and her loyal secretary, gazes at the event. The simplistic sketch of the towers and building is typical of twelfth-century illuminated manuscripts.*

wrote in the medical arts, music, theology, and the history of science, but her visionary tracts had the most impact on her contemporaries. Her first book, titled *Scivias (Know the Ways of the Lord),* included descriptions of her visions, the texts of liturgical songs, and a sung morality play, *Ordo Virtutatum (The Company of the Virtues),* the first of its kind. She also illuminated manuscripts (Figure 9.6) and composed sacred poetry, which has survived in monophonic musical settings and has found new audiences today. Hildegard was a bold talent and left a superb legacy, especially given the belief of the time that it was dangerous to teach a woman to read and write, because it could lead to independent-mindedness and thus upset the social order.

Figure 9.7 ATTRIBUTED TO GIOTTO. *St. Francis of Assisi's Trial by Fire Before the Sultan.* Before 1300. Fresco. Basilica of St. Francis, Assisi, Upper Church, nave. *This painting, from a cycle of twenty-eight frescoes detailing the life and miracles of St. Francis of Assisi, shows the saint (center, with a halo around his head) preaching before the enthroned sultan al-Malik Kamil (r. 1218–1238), the last of the Ayyubid dynasty (right). The setting is Egypt, the center of the sultan's holdings, which included Syria and Palestine. Trying to convert the sultan to Christianity, St. Francis, backed by a second Franciscan friar, challenges the sultan's Islamic clergy to join in a walk through the blazing fire on the bottom left, as a test of their respective religious faiths. The sultan gestures toward the fire with his right hand, as four Muslim clergy prepare to leave on the far left. This fresco, completed perhaps seventy years after the saint's death, was painted during a time when Franciscan missionaries were active in Egypt and other Middle Eastern lands.*

Another type of religious order appeared in the thirteenth century with the rise of two major mendicant, or begging, orders, the Franciscans and the Dominicans, whose members were called **friars** (from Latin *fratres*, "brothers"). The Franciscans had an urban ministry, working among the poor and sick, and the Dominicans were preachers, working among heretics. Although both orders made important contributions, the Franciscans had a greater impact on medieval society, largely because of the attractive nature of the order's sainted founder, Francis (1182–1226), and their urban work. Francis's piety, selflessness, and legendary humility remain inspiring (Figure 9.7).

Alongside monastic reform, in the thirteenth century a wave of lay piety swelled up from all ranks of society, triggered by a mixture of religious fervor and social protest. Typical of these novel movements were the beguines, independent communities of laywomen dedicated to good works, poverty, chastity, and religious devotion. Unlike nuns, who isolated themselves from the world, the beguines had regular contact with society—caring for the sick at home and in hospitals, teaching in both girls' and boys' schools, and working

in the textile industry. The beguines first established themselves in northern France and then, along with male lay brethren called beghards, spread to Germany and the Netherlands, usually in proximity to Dominican monasteries. Some members of these communities became influential spiritual guides. For example, Mechthild of Magdeburg (about 1207–1282) wrote *The Flowing Light of the Godhead*, a mystical account of her religious odyssey. The beguine and beghard communities also provided the audience for medieval Germany's finest devotional writer and a great mystic of the Christian tradition, Meister Eckhart (about 1260–1328).

Beguines, beghards, and mendicants won approval from religious authorities, but other lay groups were condemned as heretics because they refused to submit to ecclesiastical authority. The most prominent of these heretical sects was the Albigensian, which was centered at Albi in southern France. The Albigensians were also known as Cathars (from the Greek for "pure"). Their unorthodox beliefs were derived partly from Zoroastrianism (see Chapter 1), the source of their concept of a universal struggle between a good God and an evil deity, and partly from Manichaeism, the source of their notion that the flesh is evil. The Albigensians stressed that Jesus was divine and not human, that the wealth of the church was a sign of its depravity, and that the goal of Christian living was to achieve the status of Cathari, or perfection.

These unorthodox beliefs spread rapidly across much of southern France, permeating the church and the secular society. After they murdered his legate in 1208, Pope Innocent III called for a crusade against the Albigensians. His call appealed to the feudal nobles eager to seize the heretics' land, kings eager to extend their authority in the south, and persons of faith who were offended by heresy. It took decades but the Albigensians were finally rooted out. The heretics were treated with cruelty, and, as the thirteenth century proceeded, many of them were summoned before courts of Inquisition—ecclesiastical tribunals charged with identifying heresy. The crusade against the Albigensians reflected a shared medieval belief: those who rejected Catholic beliefs were traitors.

There were also groups that were less obviously unorthodox. The Waldensians, for example, followers of Valdes (or Peter Waldo; about 1180–1210), from Lyons in France, wished to follow what they believed to be the apostolic life: they wanted to embrace poverty and preaching. The church grudgingly accepted the former but refused the latter. Some Waldensians were reconciled but others were declared heretics.

The Crusades

The **Crusades** were a defining feature of the High Middle Ages. To free the Holy Land, or Palestine, from the Muslims, whom Christians then regarded as unbelievers, the Christian church preached nine Crusades between 1095 and 1272, none of which succeeded in the long run. Attracted by a complex set of motives—Christian zeal, the papal promise that all sins would be pardoned, and the anticipation of wealth from plunder—kings, bishops, and nobles, along with peasants, priests, workers, and prostitutes, sewed a cross on their garments (Crusader, *crucesignatus*, "signed by the cross") and walked or sailed the arduous and dangerous journey to the Holy Land. Crusader victories proved to be temporary, as in the brief capture of Jerusalem from 1099 to 1187. Otherwise, the many sieges, sackings of cities, and pitched battles that marked the Crusades heightened hatred between the two sides, which resulted in mutual atrocities (Figures 9.8 and 9.9). Still, the crusading movement led to economic, social, intellectual, and cultural interchanges, which made Europe less provincial and enhanced medieval thought and learning.

Figure 9.8 and Figure 9.9 (top) Crusaders Attacking a Muslim Fortress. Twelfth century. Bibliothèque Nationale de France, Paris. Copyright The Bridgeman Art Library. (bottom) Muslims Burning Crusaders at the Stake. Twelfth century. Copyright Erich Lessing/Art Resource, N.Y. *In the painting on the top, Crusaders, dressed in chain mail, catapult severed enemy heads into a Muslim fortress. Note the identifying cross on the banner at the top. In the painting on the bottom, Muslim warriors burn Christian captives at the stake. Mutual atrocities, such as depicted in these manuscript paintings, fueled horror stories of the Crusades and helped engender a legacy of mistrust that still complicates Western and Muslim relations today.*

THE AGE OF SYNTHESIS: EQUILIBRIUM BETWEEN THE SPIRITUAL AND THE SECULAR

Between 1000 and 1300, Christian values permeated European cultural life. The Christian faith was a unifying agent that reconciled the opposing realms of the spiritual and the secular, the immaterial and the material—as symbolized in many cities and towns by the soaring spires of the local **cathedral**—a bishop's church, named after his *cathedra,* or chair, the seat of his authority (Figure 9.10). Medieval culture drew from the humanities of the classical world, the heritage of the various European peoples, and, to a lesser extent, the traditions of Byzantium and Islam. Because of these diverse influences, the culture of the High Middle Ages was never uniform. What many writers, thinkers, and artists shared was a set of common sources, concerns, and interests.

A historical watershed occurred in the mid–twelfth century that was manifested in architecture, sculpture, music, learning, and literature. Before 1150, Western culture reflected the rugged virtues of the feudal castle and the cloistered monastery; the militant warrior and the ascetic monk were the social ideals; and

women were treated as impure and inferior. After 1150, urban values became prominent, and attitudes toward both men and women became courtly. Logic came to dominate the academic curriculum with decisive results for thought and letters.

Theology and Learning

From about 1000 onward, scholars revived the school system that had flourished briefly under the Carolingians. These monastic schools—along with many new cathedral schools—appealed to an age that was hungry for learning and set Europe's intellectual tone until about 1200. During these two centuries, the only serious rival to the schools was a handful of independent scholars who drew crowds of students to their lectures in Paris and elsewhere. By 1200 new educational institutions had arisen—the universities—that soon surpassed both the monastic and cathedral schools and the independent masters. Since then, universities have dominated intellectual life in the West.

THE DEVELOPMENT OF SCHOLASTICISM **Scholasticism** is a term applied to the style and substance of learning in the High Middle Ages. The arts curriculum remained dominant in this period, but whereas grammar had been the focus in the Carolingian period, logic came to dominate after about 1100. During the eleventh century, several thorny theological problems had arisen and scholars began to approach them in a new way. Instead of appealing to authorities—the Bible, the church fathers, decisions of church councils, papal decrees—theologians began to apply logical analysis, human reasoning, to the solution of problems.

Across the High Middle Ages, more of the work of Aristotle became available to scholars. Some of Aristotle's logical tracts had been available for a long time in the translations of Boethius (see Chapter 7), but now more of his logical work plus a host of his other writings were accessible. Most of this work entered Europe via Latin translations from medieval Arabic translations of the Greek originals. Aristotle was a pagan, so his immense learning posed an acute problem: How

Figure 9.10 Auxerre Cathedral. Begun ca. 1225. Auxerre, France. *Looming over the town and dominating the countryside for miles around, the Gothic cathedral symbolized the preeminent role of the Christian church in medieval life. No other building could soar past its spires, either literally or figuratively. People worshiped inside it, built their houses right up to its walls, and conducted their business affairs within the shadows of its towers. Thus, the cathedral also symbolized the integration of the secular and the sacred in medieval life.*

SLICE OF LIFE
When Love Knows No Boundaries

HELOISE
The Abbess of Le Paraclete, Founded by Abelard

The letters of Abelard, a monk, and his student Heloise (about 1101–1164), who later became a nun, are still read because they offer glimpses into the hearts of lovers whose devotion transcends any historical period or social context. In this letter, Heloise writes to Abelard after they have been forced to separate. His scholarly reputation has been tainted, and, for his transgression, Abelard has been castrated by men in the hire of Fulbert, Heloise's uncle and protector.

You know, beloved, as the whole world knows, how much I have lost in you, how at one wretched stroke of fortune that supreme act of flagrant treachery robbed me of my very self in robbing me of you; and how my sorrow for my loss is nothing compared with what I feel for the manner in which I lost you. Surely the greater the cause for grief the greater the need for the help of consolation, and this no one can bring but you; you are the sole cause of my sorrow, and you alone can grant me the grace of consolation. . . . God knows I never sought anything in you except yourself;

I wanted simply you, nothing of yours. I looked for no marriage-bond, no marriage portion, and it was not my own pleasures and wishes I sought to gratify, as you well know, but yours. The name of wife may seem more sacred or more binding, but sweeter for me will always be the word mistress, or, if you will permit me, that of concubine or whore. I believed that the more I humbled myself on your account, the more gratitude I would win from you, and also the less damage I should do to the brightness of your reputation.

INTERPRETING THIS SLICE OF LIFE

1. *What* are the relationships among Abelard, Heloise, and Fulbert? 2. *What* is the treachery to which Heloise refers in her letter? 3. *In what ways* does Heloise think Abelard can console her? 4. *How* does Heloise describe her love and relationship to Abelard? 5. *Why* do we still read their correspondence and love letters? 6. *Does* this letter have a modern tone and message? *Why or why not?*

---

could the potentially competing claims of faith and reason, of natural and of divine truth, be reconciled?

The Scholastic method used deductive logic to clarify existing issues and to explore the intellectual ramifications of a topic. A Scholastic thinker would pose a problem, argue for and against various possible solutions to the problem, and then draw a conclusion, which itself led to a new problem. The arguments deployed might come from Christian or pagan sources, but the aim was to achieve synthesis and reconciliation, not to prove that one kind of learning was superior to another. Anselm (1033–1109), the most accomplished logician since Aristotle and the formulator of an ingenious proof for the existence of God, expressed the early scholastic view this way: "Faith Seeking Understanding."

PETER ABELARD   Among the daring independent masters who challenged the standing of the great cathedral schools, the greatest, and most controversial, was Peter Abelard (AB-uh-lard) (1079–1142). Intellectually gifted and instinctively argumentative, Abelard quarreled with his own teachers and with other influential scholars. He was one of the first medieval thinkers to proclaim a clear distinction between operative realms of reason and faith. Eventually, Abelard began his

own lecture series. He quickly became the sensation of Paris and his words found eager listeners.

What divided Abelard and his teachers was the problem of universals, an intellectual issue that arose between 1050 and 1150 and attracted attention for centuries. This controversy revolved around the question of whether or not universals, or general concepts, such as "human being" and "church," exist in reality or only in the mind. At stake in this dispute between the two schools of thought, known as **realism** and **nominalism**, were basic Christian ideas, such as whether Jesus's sacrifice had removed the stain of original sin from each individual. The realists, following Plato, reasoned that universals do exist independently of physical objects and the human mind. Hence, "humanity," for example, is present, albeit imperfectly perceived, in every individual. In opposition, the nominalists said that universals are merely names (from Latin *nomen*, name) and claimed that only particular objects are real. Hence, "church" and "human being" exist only in particular instances.

In these debates, Abelard showed that extreme realism denied human individuality and was thus inconsistent with church teachings. For his part, Abelard taught a moderate realism that held that the universals existed, but only as mental concepts and as mental devices to sharpen and focus thinking. When new translations of Aristotle became available, thinkers discovered that Abelard and the Greek genius agreed in part about universals, a discovery that further enhanced Abelard's fame.

THE RISE OF THE UNIVERSITIES   The university—called a *studium generale* because it was a place where almost everything could be studied—emerged around 1200 in the towns where numerous masters and pupils converged. Imitating the practices of secular guilds, the masters organized, in the north, and the students, in the south, especially in Italy. Irrespective of who organized the university, the central issues were faculty appointments, curricula, examinations, and fees. The universities secured charters from both royal and ecclesiastical authorities. Universities typically had an arts faculty and then one or more higher faculties in law, medicine, and theology. Paris was especially famous for theology, Bologna for law, Montpellier for medicine. Students came from all over Europe to attend universities and, as foreigners, life was often hard for them; they were overcharged for food and housing and were mistreated by the local townspeople. The baccalaureate degree was earned after four to six years of intense engagement with the liberal arts. Higher degrees in specialized subjects could take years and followed upon the production of a serious piece of scholarship and a rigorous public examination.

INTELLECTUAL CONTROVERSY AND THOMAS AQUINAS   The Scholasticism of the thirteenth century differed in degree, not in kind, from that of the twelfth. Resting on systematization and controversy, it culminated in the magisterial works of Thomas Aquinas.

Already in the twelfth century, some scholars had begun to organize learning across whole fields. Gratian (d. by 1160), a monk from Bologna, produced the *Decretum,* a systematic manual of canon law containing more than four thousand entries drawn from the Bible, church fathers, and conciliar and papal decrees. It became the standard reference and textbook for canon law. Peter Lombard (1100–1160) wrote *Four Books of Sentences* (a "sentence" is a conclusion in a Scholastic disputation) treating in thorough and orderly fashion virtually the whole of the Christian faith under the headings the Trinity, the Creation and Sin, the Incarnation and the Virtues, and the Sacraments. For centuries the *Sentences* was the standard text in theology.

Islamic thinkers, among them Ibn Rushd (IB-en RUSHT]), known in the West as Averroës (uh-VER-uh-weez) (see Chapter 8), contributed to the development of Scholastic thought. Averroës was a major Aristotelian scholar who wrote vast commentaries—detailed explanations and interpretations—on the master's writings. He took from Aristotle certain ideas such as the eternity of matter and the denial of individual immortality. As more of Aristotle's works became available, and as Averroës's commentaries circulated, some scholars at the University of Paris, called Latin Averroists, believed they could reconcile those writings with Christian doctrines. Differences of opinion became more acute when in 1255 the Parisian masters assigned the teaching of Aristotle's *Metaphysics* and writings on natural science. The Latin Averroists wished to keep philosophy and theology distinct, and they were accused of teaching a double truth. When those in charge of the curriculum realized the challenges posed by Averroës and his disciples, they condemned many Averroist propositions.

Parisian theologians devised two ways to relate the new learning to orthodox beliefs. The more traditional view was set forth by the Franciscan Bonaventure [bahn-uh-VEN-chur] (1221–1274). Denying that knowledge was possible apart from God's grace, Bonaventure, following Augustine's mode of reasoning, argued that truth had to begin in the supernatural world and thus could not arise in the senses, as Aristotle had argued. A new and brilliant theological view, and the one that carried the day, was set forth by Thomas Aquinas [uh-KWI-nus] (1226–1274), a Dominican friar who taught at the University of Paris for many years. In 1874 the papacy declared his thought the official basis of Roman Catholic theology. Avoiding the pure rationalism of the Latin Averroists and the Augustinianism of Bonaventure, Thomas Aquinas steered a middle path, or *via media,* which gave Aristotle a central role in his theology while honoring traditional Christian beliefs. This theological system—called Thomism—in its complex design and sheer elegance remains one of the outstanding achievements of the High Middle Ages.

Of Thomas Aquinas's two monumental *summas*—comprehensive summaries of human thought—the *Summa Theologica* is his masterpiece. In this work, he showed that God had given human beings two divine paths to truth: reason and faith. Following Aristotle, he made the senses a legitimate source for human knowledge—a bold step that sharpened the difference between reason and faith. At the same time, Thomism escaped the strict rationalism of the Latin Averroists by denying that philosophy, or reason, could answer all theological questions. Aquinas claimed that natural reason, based on sensory knowledge, could prove certain truths—that God and the soul exist—but that spiritual reason (or revealed truth) alone could prove that the soul was immortal, that Jesus had been born of a virgin, and that God was Triune, or had three aspects.

Thomas Aquinas's contributions to medieval thought extended beyond theology into political and economic matters. He followed Aristotle in seeing the secular state as natural and necessary. For Aquinas, politics and society had "natural" ethical roots, and this allowed him to write about, for example, law, marriage, and economic issues such as usury (the practice of charging exorbitant interest) and setting a just price for consumer goods.

Science and Medicine

Medieval science inherited classical works and interpreted them within the framework of Christian theology. As noted above, by 1200, many Latin translations of Arabic versions of Greek scientific and philosophical works, as well as original writings by Muslim scientists and thinkers, were available in the West. Their arrival coincided with the birth of the universities. The spread of these writings encouraged scientific-minded scholars to explore the natural world. Once again, conflicts and differences arose as natural truths confronted Christian teachings.

SCIENCE Scholastic thinkers faced the daunting challenge of reconciling Aristotelian science and its Muslim commentaries with Christian thought. For Thomas Aquinas, the study of nature was not an end in itself but a means to understand God and his creation. Thus, any question about the natural world, such as motion, light, cosmology, or matter, would include Aristotle's and other thinkers' explanations, but the reason to explore these topics was to discover God's purposes, such as for creating the universe (cosmology) or living things (matter). Often the pursuits of medieval science were in direct relationship to their theological importance, such as studying light in order to account for a particular characteristic of God ("God is Light") or trying to understand the process of creation found in the biblical book of Genesis. Even though the role of reason was carefully circumscribed within the context of Christian thought and often had to give way to revelation, a genuine rational tradition persisted throughout this period—one that originated in ancient Greece and passed through medieval Islam, then would be transmitted into Renaissance thought, and, finally, would help bring about the Scientific Revolution, which would inaugurate modern times.

MEDICINE Medieval medicine also inherited beliefs and practices from the past while making significant advances. The preservation of ancient medical texts and the teaching of these works in the newly founded universities and hospitals paved the way for modern medicine.

Included in the vast number of Greek and Roman texts now made available to the learned were the writings of Hippocrates and Galen (see Chapters 3 and 6). Their works, along with *The Canon of Medicine,* by the Muslim scholar Avicenna (see Chapter 8), became the basis of the curricula in the new medical schools. The first prestigious medical schools were in Salerno, Italy, dating from the ninth century, and Montpellier, France, founded in about 1200; they were eclipsed in the late Middle Ages by new medical schools in Paris, and in Bologna and Padua, in Italy.

In these schools, aspiring doctors read medical works, attended lectures by scholars and practicing physicians, dissected human bodies (after the mid-thirteenth century), and learned to identify and treat certain disorders and diseases. Students were taught that the body is composed of four humors—black bile, phlegm, blood, and yellow bile—a belief of the ancient Greeks. Patients who suffered from certain maladies would be treated to correct the imbalance of humors by means of herbs, diet, or bleeding. Of the many teachers in these schools, perhaps the most influential was William of Saliceto [sah-le-CHAY-toe] (1210–1277), an Italian who taught at the University of Bologna and, later, was city physician (appointed medical officer) in Verona, Italy. In his book, *Cyrurgia,* or *Surgery,* the most advanced study on this subject in his day, he discussed surgical anatomy and advocated a union between medicine and surgery—a view that ran contrary to the prevailing medical wisdom that relegated surgery to the status of a craft. In the twelfth century, an anonymous author compiled three lengthy medical texts that came to be called the *Trotula.* The second of these treatises, "On the Cures of Women," was probably written by a woman named Trota.

The physicians formed guilds to set standards and regulate the profession; many became rich. Cities also built the first hospitals in the West, often founded by religious orders or by secular guilds. These hospitals were one of the few places women could be involved in medicine as nurses, since they were barred from medical school. Poorer city dwellers relied on untrained doctors or barbers who performed simple operations. Apothecaries sold drugs that were usually herbal or derived from animals or from minerals believed to possess healing powers.

Literature

Latin remained the language of learning, but not all Latin writings were confined to the fields of law, philosophy, and theology. There were numerous histories sometimes treating the ancient world or the age of King Arthur but more often chronicling the contemporary period. Latin poetry—especially Latin lyric poetry—flourished as well. These poems were rich in metric subtleties, extremely learned in content, and filled with classical and Christian allusions. Some of the poets, the **goliards,** or roaming scholars, were probably young clerics who addressed both church intellectual and secular audiences with poems ranging from sophisticated intellectual topics to lighthearted themes of love.

The most surprising development of the age was the explosion of writing in the vernacular, or popular, spoken language. Lay poets at the feudal courts of northern France developed a new literary genre, the **chanson de geste,** or "song of brave deeds," the majority of which were composed in Old French. The *chansons de geste* honored the heroic adventures of warriors who had lived in the time of Charlemagne. These medieval epics often memorialized a minor battle or, more rarely, even a defeat. The epics were based on Christian values, but supernatural and magical elements were commonly a part of their plots. Of the many *chansons de geste,* the masterpiece is the *Song of Roland,* which became the standard for the genre (Figure 9.11).

The basis for *Song of Roland* was passed down orally for three hundred years and did not reach its final written form until about 1100. The narrative is based on a historical event, the destruction of a troop of Frankish warriors, led by Count Roland, a vassal of Charlemagne, and of Charlemagne's revenge for this massacre. Superimposed on this supposedly Carolingian tale are later chivalric values, militant Christianity, and primitive nationalism. For example, Roland and his men are brave, loyal, pious, and honorable—exaggerating the ideals of Charlemagne's day. Charlemagne never fought Muslims in Spain, and Roland was killed by Basques in the Pyrenees, but the poem breathes the spirit of the First Crusade. Finally, this poem portrayed the Franks as ready to die for "sweet France," a notion unthinkable in Charlemagne's time but emerging in the twelfth century.

COURTLY WRITING Inspired by Latin lyric verse, and perhaps by the love poetry of Islamic Spain (see Chapter 8), vernacular lyric poetry began to appear in the eleventh century in the Provençal tongue of southern France. Its supreme expression was the **canzone,** or love poem, the ancestor of all later Western love poetry. At the educated feudal courts of southern France, professional **minstrels,** or entertainers, sang the songs before the assembled court; the poems' composers, called **troubadors** (from Provençal *trobar;* compare French *trouver,* "to find"—thus troubadors were "finders," "inventors") came from various social classes, including nobles. Addressed to court ladies whose identities were thinly disguised in the poems, troubadors made devotion to a highborn, probably unattainable, woman the passionate ideal of the chivalrous knight. In the mature Provençal lyrics, adulterous passion was the central theme, and women were idolized and made the masters over men. Where previously adoration had been reserved for God, the troubadour lyrics now celebrated the worship of women.

Figure 9.11 Charlemagne Panels. Ca. 1220–1225. Stained-glass window, Chartres cathedral. Chartres, France. *The* Song of Roland *was so well known and well loved that scenes from the poem were depicted in the stained-glass windows of Chartres cathedral, constructed in the thirteenth century. Even though the Charlemagne panels were inspired by a secular poem, they were situated in the ambulatory behind the main altar, one of the cathedral's most sacred areas. In one scene, Charlemagne is shown arriving too late to save Roland's life. Other panels depict him donating a church and traveling to Constantinople.*

After 1150, courtly **romances** replaced the feudal *chansons de geste* in popularity. The romances were long narratives, usually in verse, of the chivalric and sentimental adventures of knights and ladies. The name *romance* arose from *mettre en romanz,* Old French for "to put into the vernacular." Their subjects derived from stories of ancient Troy and Celtic legends from the British Isles, the most enduring of which proved to be the stories of King Arthur and his knights of the Round Table.

The first poet to make Arthur and his court his subject was Chrétien de Troyes [KRAY-tyan duh TRWAH], who set the standard for later romances. Chrétien (fl. 1165–1180) was the court poet of Marie de Champagne, the countess of Champagne. His treatment of the adulterous love of the knight Lancelot and Arthur's queen, Guinevere, is characteristic of the way romances combined aristocratic, courtly, and religious themes. In this version, Lancelot rescues Queen Guinevere after experiencing many adventures and personal humiliations for her sake; this humbling of Lancelot is necessary to teach him to love Guinevere with unquestioning obedience. But Lancelot has to cope with his loyalty to Arthur, his lord and Guinevere's husband.

Another literary genre that flourished simultaneously with the romance was the **lay** (French, *lai*), a short lyric or narrative poem meant to be sung to the accompaniment of an instrument such as a harp. The oldest lays are the twelve surviving by Marie de France (fl. about 1170), a poet from Brittany who lived most of her life in England. Based on Arthurian stories, Marie de France's lays were stories of courtly love, often adulterous (for instance, a young wife kept under close watch by a jealous old husband), usually faced with conflict, always with a moral lesson. Writing in Old French, Marie addressed the French-speaking nobility of post–Norman Conquest England, an audience that may have included King Henry II and Queen Eleanor of Aquitaine. Marie's lays were part of the outpouring of writing that made Old French literature the most influential in Europe until the rise of Italian literature in the age of Dante Alighieri.

This **vernacular literature** gave rise to a new ethos called **courtly love.** The product of courts, this ethos envisioned "fine love" as the love of an unattainable lady and male refinement in manners and behavior. It is difficult to know how seriously to take the conventions of courtly love. Perhaps it was ironic or even satirical: men became love vassals. Certainly it flew in the face of Christian morality. It is not clear that hearty lords and vassals became gentlemen. But courtly love marked medieval and later literature deeply.

DANTE Vernacular writing appeared late in Italy; not until the thirteenth century did Italian poetry begin to emerge. But, despite its later start, Italy had brought forth by 1300 the greatest literary figure of the High Middle Ages, Dante Alighieri [DAHN-tay ah-legg-ee-AIR-ree] (1265–1321). A native of Florence, in Tuscany, Dante was the first of a proud tradition that soon made the Tuscan dialect the standard literary speech of Italy (his impact is comparable to Luther's Bible in German and the King James Bible in English).

Born into a minor aristocratic family, Dante was given an excellent education with a thorough grounding in both Greco-Roman and Christian classics. Attracted to the values of ancient Rome, he combined a career in public office with the life of an intellectual—a tradition of civic duty inherited from the ancient Roman republic. When Dante's political allies fell from office in 1301, he was exiled from Florence for the rest of his life. During these years, poor and wandering about Italy, he composed the *Commedia,* or *Comedy,* which stands as the culmination of the literature of the Middle Ages. As in antiquity, comedy means a story with a happy ending. The *Comedy*'s sublime qualities were immediately recognized, and soon its admirers attached the epithet "Divine" to Dante's masterpiece.

Divided into three book-length parts, the *Divine Comedy* narrates Dante's fictional travels through three realms of the Christian afterlife. Led first by the ghost of Virgil, the ancient Roman poet, Dante descends into hell, where he hears from the damned the nature of their various crimes against God and the moral law. Virgil next leads Dante into purgatory, where the lesser sinners expiate their guilt while awaiting the joys of heaven. At a fixed spot in purgatory, Virgil is forced to relinquish his role to Beatrice, a young Florentine woman and Dante's symbol of the eternal female. With Beatrice's guidance, Dante enters paradise and rises to a vision of God, for him "the love that moves the sun and all the stars."

The majestic complexity of Dante's monumental poem, however, can scarcely be conveyed by this simple synopsis. Written as an allegory, the *Divine Comedy* was meant to be understood on several levels. Read literally, the poem bears witness to the author's personal fears as a mortal sinner yet affirms his hope for eternal salvation. Read allegorically, the poem represents a comprehensive synthesis of the opposing tendencies that characterized medieval culture, such as balancing the classical with the Christian, Aristotle with Aquinas, the ancient with the new, the proud with the humble, the profane with the sacred, and the secular with the spiritual.

Of the great cultural symbols that abound in the *Divine Comedy,* the richest in meaning are the central figures of Virgil and Beatrice, who represent human reason and divine revelation, respectively. In the poem, Virgil is made inferior to Beatrice, thus revealing Dante's acceptance of a basic idea of Thomas Aquinas—reason can lead only to awareness of sin; revelation is necessary to reach God's ultimate truth. Besides this fundamental Christian belief, the two figures convey other meanings: Virgil stands for classical civilization and the secular literary life; Beatrice (Italian for "blessing") symbolizes spiritualized love and Christianized culture. By turning Beatrice into an image of God's grace and love, Dante revealed that the High Middle Ages were open to new paths to Christian truth. Alongside faith and reason, pure love might lead to God.

Dante's vision of the afterlife underscored his belief that humans have free will. Predestination had no place in his system, as his picture of hell shows. With one exception, all of the damned earned their fate by their deeds on earth. Excepted were the people consigned to limbo—the virtuous pagans who lived before Jesus and thus were denied his message of hope. Moreover, those in limbo, such as Aristotle and Plato, were not subjected to any punishment other than being denied God's presence.

The intricate structure of Dante's massive poem owes much to numerology, a pseudoscience of numbers that absorbed the medieval mind. The numbers three and nine, for example, occur prominently in the *Divine Comedy*. Three is a common symbol of the Christian Trinity (the union of the Father, the Son, and the Holy Ghost in one God), and the poem is written in a three-line verse form called *terza rima* (an interlocking rhyme scheme in three-line stanzas, as *aba, bcb, cdc, ded,* and so on, ending in a rhyming couplet), which was Dante's invention. Dante identified the number nine with the dead Beatrice, whose soul lived on in the ninth heaven, the one nearest to God. He also divided hell, purgatory, and paradise into nine sections each.

Despite its allegorical and theological features, the *Divine Comedy* is a deeply personal poem. Dante rewards and punishes his Florentine friends and foes by the location that he assigns each in the afterlife. He also reveals his private feelings as he enters into discussions with various saints and sinners along the way. Above all, he sought harmony between the church and the secular state on earth and peace in his beloved Florence.

Architecture and Art

Just as scholars and writers devoted their efforts to exploring religious concerns and Christian values, artists, artisans, and architects channeled their talents into glorifying the Christian house of worship. Because the dominating physical presence of the church made it a ubiquitous symbol in both the countryside and the towns, architecture ranked higher than the other arts in medieval life. Indeed, the arts lacked an independent status, for they were regarded as mere auxiliary sources of church decoration—wall paintings, statues, and **stained-glass** windows, most of which portrayed saints and biblical heroes (Figure 9.12). In this respect, these art forms conformed to the church's teaching that the purpose of art was to represent Christian truth.

In about 1000, an international style called the **Romanesque** emerged. The first in a succession of uniform styles to sweep over Europe, the Romanesque was carried along by the monastic revival until about 1200. But by 1150, the **Gothic style** was developing in Paris; it was to become the reigning style of the towns for the remainder of the Middle Ages, succumbing finally to Renaissance fashion in about 1500.

ROMANESQUE CHURCHES AND RELATED ARTS   *Romanesque* is a term invented in the nineteenth century to describe the dominant architectural style after the Carolingian and before the Gothic. Although based on the architectural language of ancient Rome, Romanesque was not a pure Roman style but rather embraced elements inspired by Christianity, along with innovations beginning in the Carolingian period and continuing for some two centuries. Romanesque builders adapted the Roman basilica plan, rounded arches, vaulted ceilings, and columns for both support and decoration (see Figure 6.16). Inspired by Christian beliefs, they pointed the basilicas toward Jerusalem in the east and curved each building's eastern end into an apse to house the altar. A transept, or crossing arm, was added at the church's eastern end to achieve a cross shape (Figure 9.13). Other Christian beliefs dictated such practices as having three doorways in the western facade—to symbolize the Trinity. To Roman and Christian elements, Romanesque builders added innovative design features, such as the **narthex** (a porch or vestibule, usually enclosed, leading into the nave), vaulting techniques, and a wealth of ornamental detail, to create the most expressive and disciplined architectural style since the fall of Rome. Romanesque had many points of origin and spread through the international order of Cluny; along pilgrimage routes; and in imitation of Roman and German imperial churches. Comparatively few Romanesque churches can be viewed today in anything like their original condition. Some were torn down and replaced by later styles, but most have been substantially modified. Romanesque appears to have moved through two phases.

The **First Romanesque style** originated in Germany and along the Mediterranean, in the zone ranging from Dalmatia (modern Croatia), across northern Italy

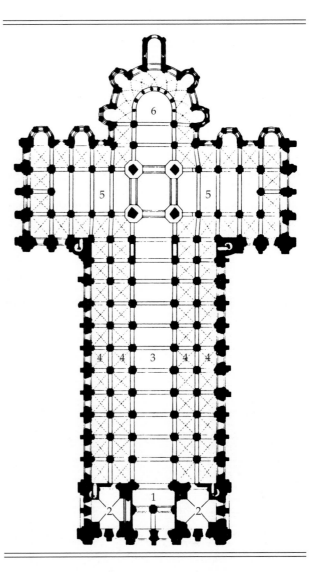

Figure 9.12 Scenes from the Life of Christ. Detail. Ca. 1150–1170. Stained-glass windows, each panel 40⅛" wide × 41⅓" high. West facade. Chartres cathedral. *The stained-glass windows of Chartres cathedral are renowned as the most beautiful examples of this craft to survive from the Gothic period. Of Chartres' windows, those in the west facade have been much praised for the brilliant effects created by their jewel tones of red, blue, and gold, as well as white, with small areas of green and lemon yellow. Taken from the central window of the west facade, this detail shows eighteen of its twenty-four panels, treating the life of Christ. Visible in the detail are panels depicting the annunciation (bottom left row), the visit of the three wise men (left and right, third row from bottom), and the flight into Egypt (left and right, sixth row from bottom). In the design, square panels alternate with roundel forms to frame each scene; red is the ground color for the squares and blue for the roundels. The windows can be awe inspiring, as in the reaction of the scholar Henry Adams, who described the cathedral's interior as a "delirium of coloured light."*

Figure 9.13 Floor Plan of a Typical Romanesque Church. *This floor plan identifies the characteristic features of a Romanesque church with its cruciform floor plan: (1) narthex, (2) towers, (3) nave, (4) side aisles, (5) transept, and (6) apse.*

and Provence (southern France), to Catalonia (northeastern Spain). Simple in design, the First Romanesque churches were built of stone rubble, a Roman technique, and covered with flat, wooden roofs. With high walls and few windows, they resembled fortresses, a trait that came to characterize both Romanesque styles.

The defining exterior features of the First Romanesque churches were a web of vertical bands or buttresses along the sides and a sequence of small arcades below the eaves (Figure 9.14). Because these features may have been born in Lombardy (north central Italy), they are usually called **Lombard bands** and **Lombard arcades.** Later builders experimented with the Lombard bands and arcades, creating spectacular churches, such as the Speyer cathedral in Germany (Figure 9.15). At Speyer, Lombard bands establish a rhythmic, vertical sequence on the walls of the apse. Variations on the Lombard arcade form include, on the lower part of the apse, the elongated, relatively windowless arcade attached to the wall; on the top part of the apse, the open, or "dwarf," arcaded gallery; and, on the wall above the

Figure 9.14 Santa Cruz de la Seros (Aragon), church of San Caprasio, Spain. View from the north. Last quarter of the eleventh century. *This church, though simple in the extreme, embodies the basic elements of the First Romanesque style. These elements include stone rubble walls, which have not been faced; a small number of windows; a flat, wooden roof; and both Lombard bands and Lombard arcades.*

Figure 9.15 Speyer Cathedral. View from the east. Speyer, Germany. Begun about 1030, completed before 1150. *Speyer cathedral, whose massive size rivals that of the great mother church at Cluny, the home of the Cluniac order of monks, represents the climax of the First Romanesque style.*

apse, the arched niches arranged in stairstep fashion and the line of Lombard arches below the roofline.

The **Second Romanesque style** derived from Cluny III, founded 1088 and the third church built on this site (see Figure 9.5). Cluny III (destroyed in the 1800s) was greatly admired in its day for its vast scale, including double transepts and crossing towers, towers at the ends of the transepts, a double-aisled nave covered with a barrel vault, and a rich decorative program of religious art, both inside and out. The spectacular success of the Cluniac movement in the eleventh and twelfth centuries led to the spread of the Second Romanesque style throughout Europe (Figure 9.16). These churches were richly decorated and earth hugging, with massive walls and few windows, though more and larger windows than in the First Romanesque. Their castle-like exteriors made them spiritual fortresses. Many Second Romanesque churches were pilgrimage churches—destinations for pilgrims traveling vast distances to see and venerate holy relics, the supposed bones of saints.

A celebrated pilgrimage church in the Second Romanesque style is Sainte-Marie-Madeleine in Vézelay, France. Attached to a Cluniac convent, this church attracted penitents eager to view the bones of Mary Magdalene. Vézelay's builders followed a basilica design with a cruciform floor plan. Inside, the most striking feature is the nearly 200-foot-long nave, which could hold a large number of pilgrims and accommodate religious processions (Figure 9.17). Typical of Romanesque architecture, the nave is divided into bays, each framed by a pair of rounded arches constructed from blocks of local pink and gray stones. These colors alternate in the overhead arches and create a dazzling effect for which this church is famous. The ceiling of each bay is a groin vault—a Roman building technique. The support system for the tall nave walls—an arcade, or series of arches resting on clusters of columns—was also taken from Roman architecture. Vézelay's builders used sculpture to provide "sermons in stone" to remind illiterate visitors of the stories they heard in sermons. Instead of copying Greco-Roman columns, the artisans created their own style of decorated column. The capitals, or tops, of the interior columns are sculptured with religious scenes and motifs, such as one that shows Jacob, one of the Hebrew patriarchs (on the left), wrestling with the angel (Figure 9.18). The angel, clutching his robe in his left hand, raises his right hand to bless Jacob. The simple figures with their dramatic gestures and expressive faces accurately convey the message in Genesis (32:24–30) that Jacob has been chosen by God to lead the Hebrew people. The art is typically Romanesque: the feet point downward, the limbs are placed in angular positions, and the drapery folds are depicted in a stylized manner.

A more mature Romanesque style appears in the carvings on the **tympanum**—the triangular area—over the south portal of the tower porch at Moissac, one of the two extant elements of the twelfth-century abbey church. The other surviving element is a **cloister,** a covered arcade (where the monks walked to say their daily prayers) surrounding a quadrangle, which originally connected the church to the monastic community. The tympanum carvings probably depict a vision of the Christian apocalypse, much of which is based on the book of Revelation (Figure 9.19). Jesus is portrayed in glory, indicated by the cross-shaped symbol behind his head and the oval in which he sits enthroned, and he wears a crown. Surrounding him are the four evangelist symbols, namely, man (Matthew), winged lion (Mark), winged bull (Luke), and eagle (John) (see Chapter 5). Jesus and the four symbols are, in turn, encircled by ten of the twenty-four elders listed in Revelation 4, while fourteen other elders sit in a line below, gazing up at the Savior. The elders hold cups and musical instruments as described in Revelation 5. This tympanum sculpture served as a warning about life's ultimate end to those who passed through the south portal.

Besides church building and church decoration, the Romanesque style was used in manuscript illumination, which had originated in late Rome and flourished

Figure 9.16 Basilica of Sacre-Coeur, formerly Abbey Church of the Virgin and St. John the Baptist, Paray-le-Monial, France, view of nave, looking east. Begun 1110s–1120s, completed mid–twelfth century. Nave height approx. 147'7½"; length approx. 72'2⅛". *The monastery at Paray-le-Monial became part of the Cluniac system in 999. Tradition links St. Hugh, abbot of Cluny (1049–1109), with the building of the Paray-le-Monial basilica. As head of the Cluniac order, Hugh commissioned Paray to be a scaled-down version of the great mother church, Cluny III. It replicates Cluny III's vaulting techniques, using barrel vaults in the nave and groin vaults in the aisles, combined with pointed arches—derived from Muslim architecture. (The pointed arches used at Cluny III and Paray-le-Monial were not related to the development of Gothic-style architecture.) As in Cluny III, the east end culminates in a semi-circular arcade resting on slender columns. The nave, consisting of only three vaulted sections, is markedly shorter than Cluny III's nave, reflecting the lack of pageantry associated with the small monastic community at Paray-le-Monial.*

Figure 9.17 View of Nave, Looking East. Church of Sainte-Marie-Madeleine, Vézelay, France. Ca. 1089–1206. *Vézelay's nave was made unusually long so that religious pilgrims might make solemn processions along its length. A reliquary, or an area for displaying holy relics, was later set aside in the choir. Within the choir, the design of the ambulatory provided ample space for masses of pilgrims to view all the relics at one time.*

Figure 9.18 *Jacob Wrestling with the Angel.* Decorated column capital. Church of Sainte-Marie-Madeleine, Vézelay, France. Ca. 1089–1206. *The Vézelay capitals survive in near-immaculate condition. Late medieval moralists considered their vivacity and gaiety inappropriate in God's house, and the offending sculptures were plastered over. When they were uncovered during a nineteenth-century restoration of the church's interior, the capitals were revealed in their charming originality.*

in the early Middle Ages. During the High Middle Ages, new local styles arose, inspired by regional tastes and by a knowledge of Byzantine painting brought from the East by crusaders. English monks probably developed the finest of these local styles.

The Bury Bible, painted at Bury St. Edmunds monastery, reflects an English taste that is calmer and less exuberant than Continental styles. Two panels from the Bury manuscript, set off by a border of highly colored foliage, show an episode in Moses's life (Figure 9.20). Borrowings from Byzantine art may be detected in the elongated figures, the large eyes, the flowing hair, and the hanging draperies. The naturalness of

these scenes presents a vivid contrast with the spirited agitation of French Romanesque art.

GOTHIC CHURCHES AND RELATED ARTS   The word *Gothic* was a critical term invented by later Renaissance scholars who preferred Greco-Roman styles and imagined that Gothic architecture was so ugly that only the ferocious Goths could have been responsible for it. In fact, the Gothic grew out of the Romanesque and was not a barbarian art. Today the term *Gothic* has no negative connotations.

Gothic architecture sprang from multiple impulses. Dawning Scholasticism, the recovery of Euclid's geometry, and faintly emerging Platonism induced builders to adopt extravagant geometrical designs and to incorporate light symbolism. Prosperous townsmen demanded larger, more magnificent churches. Increasing wealth made larger projects possible.

Two problems with the Romanesque stood in the way: the groin vaults were so heavy that the nearly

Figure 9.19 *Christ in Glory with Four Evangelist Symbols and the Twenty-four Elders.* Tympanum over south portal. Church of St. Pierre, Moissac, France. Ca. 1125. *The jam-packed imagery in this tympanum and surrounding space is typical of the allover patterns used in the Romanesque style. Nevertheless, there is artistic order here. Stylized floral forms are aligned rhythmically along the lintel and around the tympanum frame, and human and animal shapes encircle the seated Jesus, who is rendered four times larger than the elders. The tympanum itself is divided into three zones by the horizontal lines of clouds below Jesus's feet and above the second row of elders.*

windowless walls had to be extremely thick to support their great weight, and the rounded arches limited the building's height. Between 1137 and 1144, the Gothic style was created by Suger [sue-ZHAY] (about 1081–1151), the abbot of the royal Abbey Church of St. Denis, near Paris. Suger's startling originality resulted from his combining a number of elements that had long been in use—three in particular: First a **pointed arch** (adapted from the Muslim world) is more elegant than a round one; it also permits the joining of two arches of identical height but different widths, which, in turn, permits complex shapes and sizes. Second, the **ribbed vault** is lighter and more graceful than the barrel and groin vaults characteristic of Romanesque architecture; it also exerts less stress and facilitates experimentation with shapes. Third, point support—basically, the sup-

port of structural elements at only certain points—permits the replacement of heavy, stress-bearing walls with curtains of stained glass. The points of support might be massive internal piers or intricate skeletal frameworks, called **buttresses,** on the outside of the church. These three elements—pointed arch, ribbed vault, and point support—produce a building that is characterized by verticality and translucency (Figure 9.21). The desired effect is one of harmony, order, and mathematical precision—Scholasticism in stone.

The glory of the Gothic church—the **choir**—was all that remained to be built. The plan and inspiration for the choir (the part of the church reserved to the clergy) were the pilgrimage churches, such as Vézelay, that had enlarged their apses by creating ambulatories, zones where people could mill about without disrupting the

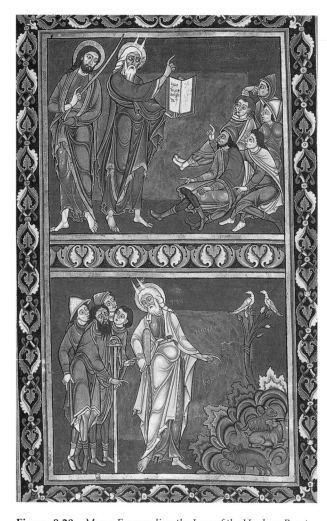

Figure 9.20 *Moses Expounding the Law of the Unclean Beasts.* The Bury Bible. 1130–1140. Approx. 20 × 14″. Bury St. Edmunds, England. Master and Fellows of Corpus Christi College, Cambridge. *These panels depict Moses delivering the dietary laws to the ancient Hebrews. The responses of his audience reveal the sure hand of the artist, known only as Master Hugo. For example, in the upper panel one figure pulls at his nose, while a nearby companion looks skeptical. Moses's head is depicted with horns, which reflected a biblical mistranslation of the term for the radiance that surrounded Moses after receiving God's law.*

Figure 9.21 Principal Features of a Typical Gothic Church. *In this schematic drawing, the features are numbered from the nave outward: (1) nave arcade, (2) pointed arch, (3) vault, (4) clerestory, (5) flying buttress, (6) buttress, and (7) gargoyle.*

services, to accommodate pilgrims. In Suger's skillful hands, the east end of St. Denis was now elaborated into an oval-shaped area—the choir—ringed with several small chapels (Figure 9.22). At the heart of the choir was the apse, now arcaded; a spacious ambulatory area divided the apse from the chapels (Figure 9.23).

Between 1145 and 1500, the Gothic style presented an overwhelming image of God's majesty and the power of the church. A Gothic exterior carried the eye heavenward by impressive vertical spires. A Gothic interior surrounded the daytime worshiper with colored, celestial light; the soaring nave ceiling, some-

times rising to more than 150 feet, was calculated to stir the soul. In its total physicality, the Gothic church stood as a towering symbol of the medieval obsession with the divine.

During the High Middle Ages, the Gothic style went through two stages, the Early and the High. The Early Gothic style lasted until 1194 and was best represented by Notre Dame cathedral in Paris. The High Gothic style flourished until 1300 and reached perfection in the cathedral at Amiens, France.

Early Gothic Style, 1145–1194   The cathedral of Notre Dame ("Our Lady," the Virgin Mary) in Paris made popular the Early Gothic style, making it a fashion for other cities and towns. Begun in 1163, the cathedral was the most monumental work erected in the West to that time. Its floor plan was cruciform, but the length of the transept barely exceeded the width of the aisle walls (Figure 9.24). Part of Notre Dame's beauty stems from the rational principles applied by the builders, notably the ideal of harmony, best expressed in the integration of sculpture and decorative details with building units. For instance, the west facade is divided into three equal horizontal bands: the three doorways, the **rose window** and **blind arcades** (walled-in windows), and the two towers (Figure 9.25). Within each subdivision of this facade, figurative sculpture or architectural details play a harmonizing role, from the rows of saints flanking each of the portals to the **gargoyles,** or grotesque demons, peering down from the towers.

Inside Notre Dame, which can hold ten thousand people, the spectacular nave reveals the awe-inspiring effects of Early Gothic art at its best (Figure 9.26). The strong vertical lines and the airy atmosphere represent the essence of this taste. With its ribbed vaults and pointed arches, the nave rises to a height of 115 feet from the pavement to the vaulting. Like the harmonious west facade, the nave is divided into three equal tiers: the nave and double aisles, the open spectator **gallery** above the aisles, and, at the top, the clerestory—the luminous window zone.

Notre Dame reveals that the choir was coming to dominate the Early Gothic church. Notre Dame's choir is almost as long as the nave, so that the transept virtually divides the church into two halves. At first, the choir's walls had no special external supports, but as cracks began to appear in the choir's walls during the thirteenth century, flying buttresses were added to ensure greater stability—a feature that would later characterize High Gothic churches (Figure 9.27).

The Gothic sculptures that decorate Notre Dame differ from the exuberant Romanesque style. The Romanesque's animated images of Jesus have given way to the Gothic's sober figures. In addition, the Gothic figures are modeled in three dimensions, and their draperies fall in natural folds (Figure 9.28). At the same time, the rise of the cult of the Virgin meant an increased number of images of Mary as well as of female saints. The name "Notre Dame" itself testifies to the appeal of the cult of the Virgin.

Before Notre Dame was finished, its architects began to move in new directions, refining the traditional features into a new style, called **Rayonnant,** or Radiant. In the Rayonnant style, the solid walls gave way to sheets of stained glass framed by elegant **traceries,** or rich ornamentation, of stone. This radiant effect was especially evident in the north transept facade, which

Figure 9.22   Ambulatory. Church of St. Denis, Paris. Ca. 1145. *This view of the choir of St. Denis shows a portion of the ambulatory that allowed pilgrims to view the chapels in the apse. The evenly spaced support columns and the pointed arches create this flowing, curved space. The ribbed arches in the ceiling are also central to the Gothic skeletal construction.*

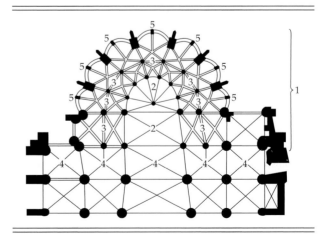

Figure 9.23   Floor Plan, Ambulatory. Church of St. Denis, Paris. Ca. 1145. *This floor plan, based on a similar design used in the pilgrimage churches, became the basis for the reordering of interior space in the Gothic choirs. The features include (1) choir, (2) apse, (3) ambulatory, (4) transept, and (5) chapel.*

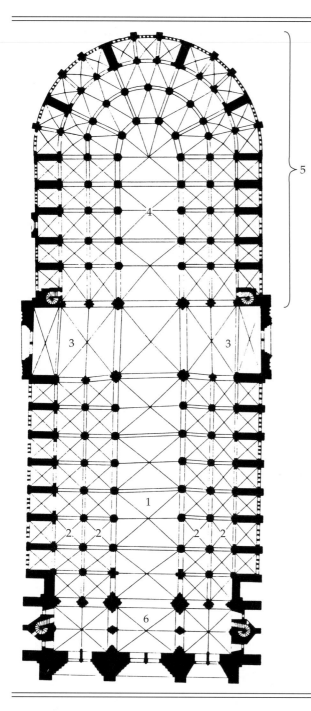

Figure 9.24 Floor Plan of Notre Dame. Paris. 1163–ca. 1250. *This drawing shows the principal features of Notre Dame cathedral: (1) nave, (2) aisle, (3) transept, (4) apse, (5) choir, and (6) narthex, or vestibule.*

Figure 9.25 Western Facade. Notre Dame. Paris. 1220–1250. *In the gallery above the western portals are twenty-eight images of the kings of Judah, including David and Solomon. These sculptures, which are typical of Gothic churches, are more than decorations: they are reminders that Mary and Jesus were descended from royalty. In the medieval mind, this religious idea was meant to buttress the monarchical style of government.*

was rebuilt in this new style. With the addition of this transept's imposing rose window, designed to suggest the rays of the sun, the cathedral's interior was bathed in constantly shifting colors, giving it a mystical atmosphere (Figure 9.29).

High Gothic Style, 1194–1300 The High Gothic style is a tribute to the growing confidence of the builders of the thirteenth century. These builders took the Gothic ingredients and refined them, creating grander churches than had been erected earlier. In comparison with Early Gothic architecture, High Gothic churches were taller and had greater volume; artistic values now stressed wholeness rather than the division of space into harmonious units. Rejecting the restrained decoration of the Early Gothic style, the High Gothic architects covered the entire surface of their churches' western facades with sculptural and architectural designs.

The cathedral in Amiens is a perfect embodiment of the High Gothic style. Amiens was planned so that flying buttresses would surround its choir and march along its nave walls (Figure 9.30). Instead of trying to disguise these supports, the architect made the exterior skeleton central to his overall plan. As a result, more spacious window openings could be made in the nave and the choir walls than had been the case in Notre Dame. Furthermore, the design of Amiens' nave was also changed so that the entire space was perceived as a homogeneous volume. The division of the nave walls into three equal horizontal bands was eliminated, and

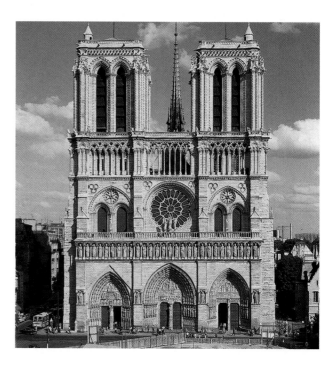

Figure 9.26 Nave. Notre Dame. Paris. View from the height of the western rose window. 1180–1250. Ht. floor to summit of roof 115'. *The nave is clearly not aligned properly. The choir bends perceptibly to the north, which probably reflects the different building times for various parts of the cathedral. The transept and the choir were finished first, after which the nave and the double aisles were added. The western facade was completed last.*

the system of arches and bays overhead became less emphatic (Figure 9.31). Amiens' overall floor plan was conservative, however, for it resembled that of Notre Dame; for example, its transept bisected a choir and a nave of equal length (Figure 9.32).

The western facade of Amiens shows how decoration changed in the High Gothic style (Figure 9.33). Amiens' western wall and towers are pierced with rich and intricate openings. The elegant tracery has the effect of dissolving the wall's apparent solidity. What surface remains intact is covered with an elaborate tapestry of architectural devices and sculptural figures (Figure 9.34).

The finest stained glass from the High Gothic era is from the cathedral in Chartres, a town fifty miles south of Paris. Chartres has 176 windows, and most are the thirteenth-century originals. Outstanding examples of this art are the Charlemagne panels depicting scenes from the *Song of Roland*, illustrated earlier in this chapter (see Figure 9.11). Each figure is precisely rendered, though many are cropped off at the edge of the pictorial space. The glass itself is brilliant, notably in the dominant blue tones.

High Gothic painting survives best in the manuscript illuminations of the late thirteenth century. By that time, these small paintings were being influenced by developments elsewhere in Gothic art. The Gothic illuminators abandoned the lively draperies of the Romanesque and instead showed gowns hanging in a natural manner. More important, they sometimes allowed the architectural frame to dominate the painting, as in the *Psalter of St. Louis IX* of France. Commissioned by the sainted French king, this book contains seventy-eight full-page paintings of scenes from the Old Testament. Of these paintings, *Balaam and His Ass* is a typical representation of the anonymous painter's style (Figure 9.35). The scene unfolds before a High Gothic church; two gables with rose windows are symmetrically balanced on the page. Although this

Figure 9.27 Notre Dame. Paris. View from the east. 1163–1182. *Notre Dame's choir, shown on the right, was originally built without chapels and flying buttresses—a sign of its Early Gothic origins. Paris's greatest church caught up with the High Gothic style in the fourteenth century, when these architectural features were added.*

Figure 9.28 *The Last Judgment.* Central portal, west facade, Notre Dame, Paris. Ca. 1210. *This tympanum represents Jesus enthroned and presiding over the Last Judgment. Surrounding him are the apostles, the prophets, the church fathers, and the saints—arranged in descending order of their importance in relation to Jesus. Like all the sculptures of Notre Dame's first story, the entire scene was gilded with gold paint until the mid–fifteenth century.*

painting owes much to changes in Gothic sculpture, the animated figures of the men, the angel, and the ass are reminiscent of the exuberant Romanesque style.

Music

As with the other arts, the purpose of music during the High Middle Ages was the glorification of God. At first, the monophonic (single-line) Gregorian chants were still the main form of musical expression, but two innovations—the introduction of tropes and the development of polyphony—led the way to a different sound in the future.

Among the compositions of sacred music written during this period, the works of Hildegard of Bingen have a lasting appeal. Hildegard composed within the tradition of Gregorian chant (see Chapter 7), though she, a devout mystic, claimed ecstatic visions as the inspiration for her musical ideas. The words for her texts were drawn from the Bible, her theological writings, and the church's liturgy.

Hildegard's works were unusual not only because they were written by a woman but also because they were performed by women singers before audiences of women—Hildegard's fellow nuns. Besides the previously mentioned sung morality play *Ordo Virtutatum* (*The Company of the Virtues*), she composed seventy-seven songs, chants, and hymns for the church's liturgy, including such works as "O Pastor Animarum" ("O Shepherd of Souls"), "Spiritui Sancto" ("To the Holy Spirit"), and "O Jerusalem." She also wrote a kyrie (a chant sung during the Mass asking the Lord for mercy) and an alleluia (a chant sung during the Mass offering praise), as well as two longer works composed specifically for women, one dedicated to virgins and the other to widows.

Hildegard's "O Pastor Animarum" is one of the seventy-seven songs in the collection known as the *Symphonia* (full title: *Symphonia armonie celestium revela-*

Figure 9.29 North Rose Window of Notre Dame. Paris. Ca. 1255. *This masterwork by Jehan de Chelles is the only original of Notre Dame's three rose windows. The nineteenth-century restoration genius Viollet-le-Duc re-created the other two. Measuring forty-three feet in diameter, the window was installed after workers first removed sections of the existing wall. The bits of predominantly blue glass, encased in iron settings, were then placed inside the stone frame.*

tionum, or *Symphony of the Harmony of Celestial Revelations*). *Symphony* here means simply "collection" and should not be confused with the modern symphony, a musical form. "O Pastor Animarum" is an **antiphon,** a short prose text, chanted by an unaccompanied voice or voices during the liturgy. Addressed to God the Father, this antiphon reads, in Latin: "*O Pastor animarum, / et o prima vox, / perquam omnes creati sumus, / nunc tibi, / tibi placeat, / ut degneris nos liberare / de miseries et languoribus nostris*" (in English, "O Shepherd of souls, / and o first voice, / through whom all creation was summoned, / now to you, / to you may it give pleasure and dignity, / to liberate us / from our miseries and languishing)." Typically, Hildegard's antiphon is composed in **plainsong,** the Christian chant that dominated the period. The music shows her personal style: wide leaps of melody and ornamental features, especially **melismas** (groups of notes sung to the same syllable) and, to a lesser extent, **syllabic** singing (one note per syllable).

The **tropes,** or turns, were new texts and melodies inserted into the existing Gregorian chants. Added for both poetic and doctrinal reasons, these musical embellishments slowly changed the plainchants into more elaborate songs. Culminating in about 1150, this musical development coincided with the appearance of the richly articulated Gothic churches. The tropes also gave a powerful impetus to Western drama. From the practice of troping grew a new musical genre, the **liturgical drama,** which at first was sung and performed in the church but gradually moved outdoors. From the twelfth century onward, these works were staged in the area in front of the church as sacred dramas or mystery plays (from Latin *mysterium,* "secret" or "hidden"—i.e., the plays revealed deep truths). As their popularity increased, they began to be sung in the vernacular instead of Latin. Ultimately, the liturgical drama supplied one of the threads that led to the revival of the secular theater.

Gregorian chants were also being modified by the development of **polyphony,** in which two or more lines of melody are sung or played at the same time. In the early eleventh century, polyphony was extremely simple and was known as **organum.** It consisted of a main melody, called the *cantus firmus,* accompanied by an identical melody sung four or five tones higher or lower. By about 1150, the second line began to have its own independent melody rather than duplicating the first. During the thirteenth century, two-voiced organum gave way to multivoiced songs called **motets,** which employed more complex melodies. In the motets, the main singer used the liturgy as a text

Figure 9.30 Amiens Cathedral. Amiens, France. Ca. 1220–1270. *This photograph shows the brilliantly articulated exterior skeleton of Amiens cathedral. Gothic churches openly displayed the exterior support system that made their interior beauty possible. In the Renaissance, this aspect of Gothicism was decried for its clumsiness. Renaissance architects preferred classical structures that hid their stresses and strains.*

while up to five other voices sang either commentaries or vernacular translations of the text. The result was a complex blend of separate voices woven into a harmonious tapestry. By about 1250, the motet composers had laid the foundations of modern musical composition.

Notwithstanding these developments in sacred music, the church could not stop the rise of secular music any more than it could prevent the spread of courtly love. Indeed, the first secular music was associated with the same feudal courts where the *chansons de geste* and the troubador songs flourished in the twelfth century. At first, France was the center of this musical movement, but in the early thirteenth century, German poets took the lead. At the same time, music began to be practiced not just by aristocratic poets but also by middle-class minstrels, and new musical

instruments—some, such as the **lute** (a multistringed instrument with neck and soundbox) and the bagpipe, banned by the church—started to find their way into secular music (Figure 9.36).

The High Middle Ages also gave rise to some innovations that made modern music possible. Guido of Arezzo [GWEE-doe / uh-RET-so] (about 995–1050), an Italian monk, modernized musical notation by his invention of the music staff, the set of five horizontal lines and four intermediate spaces on which notes may be drawn. Guido also began the practice of naming the musical tones by the syllables *ut* (or *do*), *re*, *mi*, *fa*, *sol*, and *la*, a step that greatly simplified the teaching of music. The music composed according to Guido's system can be reproduced by today's music historians; thus, Western music may be said to descend in an unbroken line from the music of this period.

Figure 9.31   Nave. Amiens cathedral. View from the west. Amiens, France. Ca. 1220–
1236. Ht. floor to summit of vault 139′. *Gothic architecture was built to appeal to the emotions.
The overwhelming height and the celestial light were intended to create a spiritual environment.
This spiritual feeling may be sensed even in a photograph. The dramatic contrast between the
human elements—the chairs—and the voluminous space is a reminder of the frailty of mortals.*

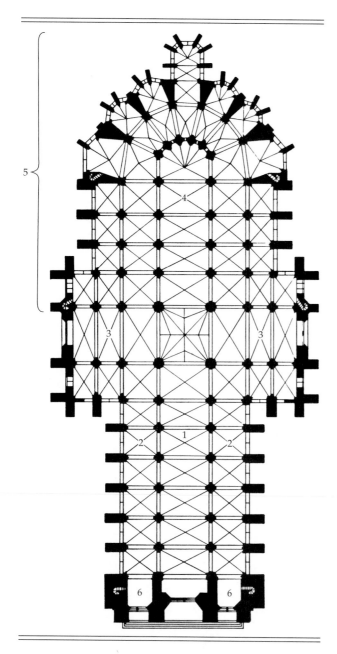

Figure 9.33 Western Facade. Amiens cathedral. Amiens, France. Ca. 1220–1236. *Comparison of Amiens' facade with that of Notre Dame in Paris (see Figure 9.25) shows how the High Gothic differs from the Early Gothic. The basic form remains the same, but Amiens' surface is richer in detail and more splendid overall. The pointed features, such as the arches over the portals and over the openings in the towers, are the most characteristic visual element in the High Gothic style.*

Figure 9.32 Floor Plan of Amiens Cathedral. Amiens, France. Ca. 1220–1236. *This drawing shows the principal features of Amiens cathedral: (1) nave, (2) aisle, (3) transept, (4) apse, (5) choir, and (6) narthex.*

Figure 9.34 *Golden Virgin.* Amiens cathedral. Ca. 1260. Amiens, France. *The Golden Virgin of Amiens, so called because it was originally covered with a thin layer of gold, is one of the most admired works of Gothic art. The artist has depicted Mary as a loving earthly mother with fine features, a high forehead, and a shy smile. This sculpture shows the new tenderness that was creeping into art during the High Middle Ages as part of the rise of the cult of the Virgin.*

Figure 9.35 *Balaam and His Ass.* Psalter of St. Louis IX. 1252–1270. Bibliothèque Nationale de France, Paris. *The architectural details in this miniature painting show a correspondence with the Rayonnant architectural style: the two gabled roofs, the two rose windows with exterior traceries, the pointed arches, and the pinnacles. Just as Gothic architects emphasized the decorative aspects of their buildings, so did this anonymous painter of miniatures. The story of Balaam and his ass (Numbers 22:22–35 in the Old Testament) was a beast fable—a popular literary genre in the Middle Ages. In the biblical story, the ass could speak and see things of which his master, Balaam, was ignorant. In the painting, the ass turns his head and opens his mouth as if to speak.*

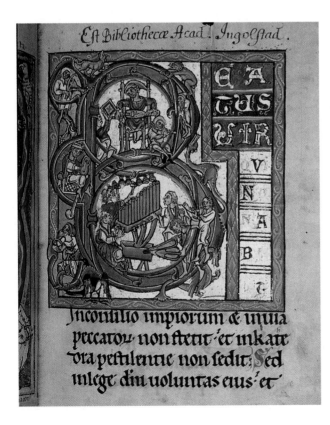

Figure 9.36 Embellished Letter *B.* Psalter from Würzburg-Ebrach. Early thirteenth century. Universitäts Bibliothek, Munich. *In illuminated manuscripts, the initial letter of a sentence was often embellished with intricate details, drawn from the artist's imagination and experience. In this example from a thirteenth-century German psalter, the letter B is interwoven with a band of musicians playing instruments typical of the era: organ (with bellows), bells, ivory horn, flute, stringed instruments, and an instrument for bows. The artist who painted this miniature scene has captured the liveliness of a musical performance, depicting several players singing.*

Technology

Technology during the High Middle Ages recovered many valuable techniques from ancient Rome, and, by improving on this heritage and borrowing from Islam, the West was able to sustain Europe's burgeoning economy and society, as well as, in a few cases, to take steps forward. Among the largest steps forward were the adoption of papermaking and the astrolabe, both introduced from the Islamic world (see Chapter 8). However, the impact of these new technologies was relatively limited. Technology's strongest impact on the wider culture was made by further advances in warfare, the rise of watermills and windmills in the North, and new tools in farming.

Advances in military technology included

- larger, more powerful warhorses, imported from Spain;
- widespread use of better saddles, stirrups, and spurs, which enhanced the knight's stability on his mount;
- better armor, including head-to-toe chain mail, metal gauntlets (gloves), and helmets;
- the introduction of the powerful, accurate crossbow; and
- the introduction of gunpowder (probably from China), used mainly as an explosive in siege warfare to topple walls.

Advances in agricultural productivity included

- water-driven mills that significantly expanded milling capacity—more grain could be milled faster, producing more flour, and increasing food supplies;
- the proliferation of windmills, probably introduced from the Muslim world, perhaps by crusaders; and
- a widespread shift from the ox to the horse and a plow and draft animal, facilitated by the horse-collar.

The Legacy of the Christian Centuries

The grandeur of this age of synthesis declined after 1300, when the secular and the spiritual began to go their separate ways. But the legacy of the Christian centuries survives, particularly in the writings of Dante, the theology of Thomas Aquinas, and the Gothic cathedrals. The *Divine Comedy* is Dante's most enduring gift to world literature; his poetic style and literary forms influenced Italian writers for centuries. Furthermore, Dante's love for Beatrice has deeply influenced Western literature by encouraging poets to seek inspiration from a living woman.

The Roman Catholic world is the most significant beneficiary of the philosophy of Thomas Aquinas. Since the late nineteenth century, Thomism has been regarded as the basis of orthodox beliefs. As for the Gothic style, it ceased to be practiced after about 1500, although it was revived in the nineteenth century as part of the romantic movement, and even today universities often adopt Gothic elements in their architecture.

Besides these great gifts, the Christian centuries have left the modern world other significant cultural legacies. First and foremost was the birth of the courtly-love movement that glorified individual romantic affection—the idea that *this* man loves *this* woman. Vernacular literature finally found its voice during this time in the first European poetry. Of special note, the vernacular writers created one of the richest literary traditions in the West through the stories of King Arthur and the knights of the Round Table. The basic theoretical system for composing music was developed during this period under the auspices of the church. Outside the church, the ancestor of all Western love songs was invented by the Provençal poets. In Gothic sculpture, artists began to move away from symbolic representation to a more realistic art. In medicine, the hospital made its first appearance in the West.

Notwithstanding these innovations, the Christian centuries transmitted many of the legacies that had been received from ancient and other sources. The liberal arts; the Christian religion; the rationalist tradition; schools, universities, and medical schools; water and wind technologies; cavalry warfare; Muslim science; and the entire Greco-Roman heritage are only the major ingredients of this invaluable legacy to later ages.

KEY CULTURAL TERMS

feudalism
chivalry
Investiture Controversy
friars
Crusades
cathedral
scholasticism
realism
nominalism
via media
goliard
vernacular language
chanson de geste
vernacular literature
canzone
minstrel
troubador
romance
lay
courtly love
terza rima
stained glass
Romanesque style
Gothic style
narthex
First Romanesque style

Lombard arcades
Lombard bands
Second Romanesque
    style
tympanum
cloister
pointed arch
ribbed vault
flying buttress
choir
rose window
blind arcade
gargoyle
gallery
Rayonnant style
tracery
antiphon
plainsong
melismas
syllabic
trope
liturgical drama
polyphony
organum
motet
lute

QUESTIONS FOR CRITICAL THINKING

1. What are some of the chief signs that Europe was expanding in the High Middle Ages?

2. Discuss the relationship of the Romanesque style to the Gothic style, showing how the latter grew from the former.

3. What were some of the key problems faced by governments in the High Middle Ages?

4. What roles did faith and reason play in the intellectual life of Europe in the High Middle Ages?

5. What was courtly love and why is it important?

10

THE LATE MIDDLE AGES
1300–1500

Many who lived during what a modern historian has termed the "calamitous" fourteenth century believed that the biblical apocalypse had arrived, attended by plague, famine, war, and death. The Black Death ravaged the population. The economy suffered one shock after another. The church had to relinquish its dream of a united Christendom when faced with the reality of warring European states. New military tactics and weapons rendered chivalry obsolete, and the chivalric code began to seem a romantic fiction. In the universities, new intellectual currents drove a wedge between philosophy and theology, which had been so carefully integrated by Thomas Aquinas. Vernacular literature took off in bold new directions. And the balanced High Gothic style in art and architecture gave way to the florid late Gothic style.

HARD TIMES COME TO EUROPE

Shortly after the opening of the fourteenth century, Europe entered a disastrous period of economic depression, accompanied by soaring prices and widespread famine. Against the backdrop of the Hundred Years' War between England and France (1337–1453), social unrest increased and renegade feudal armies ravaged much of western Europe. The church, in disgrace and disarray for much of this period, was unable to provide moral or political leadership. As old certainties evaporated, the optimistic mood of the High Middle Ages gave way to a sense of impending doom.

◀ **Detail** Giovanni Pisano. Nativity Scene. Pulpit in the Pisa cathedral. Ca. 1302–1310. 33½ × 44½". Pisa, Italy.

LEARNING THROUGH MAPS

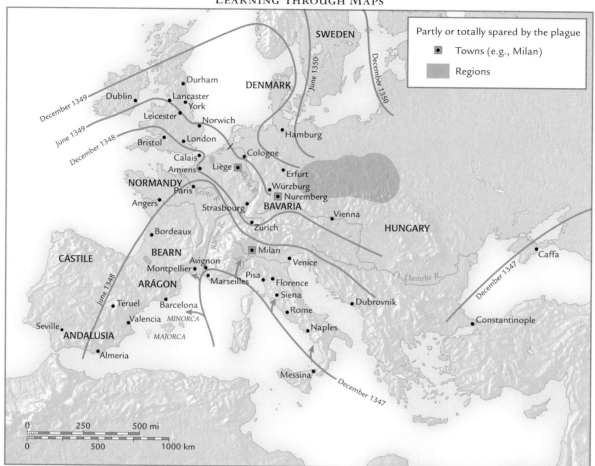

Map 10.1   PROGRESS OF THE BLACK DEATH ACROSS EUROPE IN THE FOURTEENTH CENTURY
This map shows the spread of the plague across Europe in the mid–fourteenth century. 1. *Notice* how the dark lines mark the progress of the plague at a specific time. 2. *Where* and *when* does the Black Death appear in Europe? 3. *Where* and *when* does it end? 4. *What* regions and cities were partly or totally spared the plague? 5. *Consider* the role of various types of travelers in spreading the Black Death.

Ordeal by Plague, Famine, and War

Of all Europe's calamities, the worst was the bubonic plague, an animal-to-human illness, carried over sea and land by fleas. In the sixteenth century, writers began to label the epidemic the "Black Death," which has become the common term. The plague first appeared in northern Italy in 1347 (Map 10.1). From Italy, the disease spread rapidly over most of Europe, halted by the frost line in the north. A few cities and areas—such as Milan and central Germany—were free of plague, but elsewhere it raged from 1348 until 1351, and further onslaughts occurred into the next century. So deadly was the disease that more than a third of Europe's seventy million people died in the first epidemic alone. The mechanism of disease transmission was not fully understood, and the plague created panic.

The Black Death cast a long shadow over the late Middle Ages. Many writers and artists reflected the melancholy times, occasionally brightening their dark works with an end-of-the-world gaiety. The age's leading image became the Dance of Death, often portrayed as a skeleton democratically joining hands with kings, queens, popes, merchants, peasants, and prostitutes as they danced their way to destruction. This symbol forcefully portrayed the folly of human ambition and the transitory nature of life (Figure 10.1).

The plague was compounded by growing famine conditions across the European continent. Starting in 1315, agricultural harvests failed with some regularity for more than a century. These famines braked centuries of steady population growth and weakened the populace by making them more susceptible to diseases.

Figure 10.1 *The Dance of Death.* Fifteenth century. *In the wake of the Black Death, art and literature became filled with themes affirming the biblical message that life is short and death certain. A vivid image of this theme was the* Danse Macabre, *or Dance of Death, which took many artistic and literary forms. In this example, a miniature painting taken from a fifteenth-century Spanish manuscript, the corpses are shown nude, stripped of their human dignity, and dancing with wild abandon.*

War also disrupted the pattern of social and economic life. Princes from France and Aragon (northeastern Spain) struggled to control southern Italy. Northern Italian cities waged war among themselves for commercial and political advantage. England and France fought the seemingly endless Hundred Years' War, while the dukes of Burgundy attempted to carve out a "middle kingdom" between France and the German Empire. Farther east, from 1347 on, the Ottoman Turks occupied Greece and the Balkan peninsula, conquered Constantinople in 1453, and menaced eastern Europe. Amid all this constant warfare, bands of mercenaries and marauding renegades only made things worse.

Depopulation and disruption, therefore, were the chief results of the plague and the wars that accompanied it. Old areas, such as France, lost population and prosperity, while new areas, such as eastern Europe and Scandinavia, gained population and prosperity. Florence and Venice, which were initially devastated by the plague, rebounded by the fifteenth century. Disparities between rich and poor grew greater. Wages fluctuated wildly as workers moved about in search of opportunities and employers competed for their services. Between 1296 and 1381 in Flanders, Florence, France, and England, workers and peasants rose up violently, albeit without durable effect (see Slice of Life). Ironically, in the long term those who survived experienced an elevated standard of living. Political and social unrest did not, however, bring much real change. Serfdom continued to decline in western Europe, but in eastern Europe the lot of peasants grew worse. Urban middle classes still fought with each other and with their royal and ecclesiastical overlords.

THE SECULAR MONARCHIES

France and England maintained their leading positions in Europe, but they exhausted their economies with wasteful wars. The Hundred Years' War, as the group of conflicts between the mid–fourteenth and the mid–fifteenth centuries is called, had three root causes: England's conquest in 1066 by a Norman duke; Henry II's (r. 1154–1189) "Angevin Empire"; and John of England's defeat in 1212 by the French king Philip II (r. 1179–1223) (Timeline 10.1). The war was fought entirely on French soil. The Valois dynasty—successor to the Capetians in 1328—had to contend not only with England but also with the dukes of Burgundy, who threatened to break their ties with the French crown and establish an independent kingdom on France's eastern border. The Burgundian court at Dijon was the most brilliant in northern Europe, attracting the leading artists and humanists of the age. A heroic figure who emerged from this war was Joan of Arc (1412–1431), who rallied the French to victory, only to be burned at the stake by the English; in modern times, she became one of France's national heroines and a Roman Catholic saint.

Despite the ravages of the Hundred Years' War, the Valois kings ultimately increased their territory. Except for the port of Calais in northern France, England was forced to cede its overseas lands to the French crown.

Timeline 10.1 ROYAL DYNASTIES IN LATE MEDIEVAL FRANCE AND ENGLAND

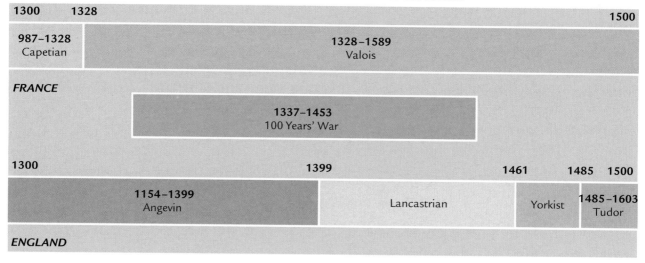

The dukes of Burgundy were brought under French control. And the northwestern region of Brittany, the last major territory that had escaped the French crown, was acquired through marriage. The contour of modern France was now complete (Figure 10.2).

While the Hundred Years' War raged on the Continent, life in England was disrupted by aristocratic factionalism, peasant unrest, and urban strife. Like France, England was emerging from feudalism, but it was moving in a different direction. The English Parliament, which represented the interests of the nobles, the towns, and the rural counties, gained power at the expense of the king. Parliament also reflected popular feeling when it passed laws curbing papal power in England.

When Henry VII (r. 1485–1509) became king, however, it became apparent that a key reason for the dominance of Parliament had been the weakness of the kings. This founder of England's brilliant Tudor dynasty avoided the quarrels his predecessors had had with Parliament by abandoning foreign wars, living off his own estates, and relying on his own advisers. Henry VII's policies deflated parliamentary power and made him as potent as his contemporaries in France.

The success of the French and the English kings in centralizing their states attracted many imitators. Their ruling style—with royal secretaries, efficient treasuries, national judiciaries, and representative assemblies—was adopted in part by other states. Spain was the most successful in achieving unity. Dynastic politics and civil war kept central Europe and Scandinavia from becoming strong and centralized. The Holy Roman Empire was the least successful of these political entities, and Germany remained divided into

combative states. And, in the eastern Mediterranean, the Ottoman Turks, devout Muslims, posed a threat to the whole of Christian Europe. Having consolidated rule over southeastern Europe and Anatolia (modern Turkey) by 1481, the Ottoman Empire now reached its height of power and wealth, and, at the same time, the Ottoman rulers began a century of expansive wars against European neighbors.

THE PAPAL MONARCHY

From its pinnacle of power and prestige in 1200 under Pope Innocent III, the church entered a period of decline in about 1300, and for the next century it was beset with schism and heresy. From 1309 to 1377, the seat of the papacy was located in Avignon, a papal fief on the Rhône River, chosen initially to allow negotiations with the king of France after the disastrous conflict between Boniface VIII and Philip IV (see Chapter 9). Opponents of the relocation of the papacy, claiming the popes were in the pocket of the French king, tagged it the "Babylonian Captivity." The Avignon popes were exceptionally effective administrators, especially in the financial realm, but often worldly and dissolute.

The Avignonese papacy had barely ended in 1378 when a new calamity, the Great Schism, threw the church into even more confusion. Gregory XI (pope 1370–1378) returned to Rome in 1377 but he died in 1378, and, in the ensuing election of an Italian pope, some French cardinals alleged intimidation and returned to Avignon. When the French cardinals elected a new pope, Western Christendom was divided into two obediences (as the area under papal control is

Figure 10.2 *An Archbishop before a King of France. The Grand Coutumes of Normandy, the Coutumes of France.* Fifteenth century. Law Library, Library of Congress, Washington, D.C. *In addition to wars and marriage, the kings of France consolidated their power by establishing legal and judicial control over their newly acquired regions and territories. One of their tactics was to collect and codify the* coutumes, *or local customary laws. For centuries, provincial lawyers and regional courts had formulated and interpreted these local laws, and, by the fifteenth century, the* coutumes *had become the basis and the structure of the legal rulings and procedures in each province. Charles VII (r. 1422–1461), who, with the help of Joan of Arc, drove the English out of France during the Hundred Years' War, ordered in 1453 that the* coutumes *be codified and brought before him and his grand council for their examination and approval. Unlike other compilations,* The Grand Coutumes of Normandy *(ca. 1450–1470) were embellished with seven miniature paintings depicting various examples of the application and execution of the laws, which were common in Normandy and in England. In this example, the French king gives a document or charter to the archbishop of Normandy. Since such agreements between kings and church leaders were renewed many times in the fourteenth and fifteenth centuries, this miniature is likely symbolic, not representing an actual event. However, its message is clear—the crown holds the real power.*

called) with two popes, two colleges of cardinals, and two papal courts. The rising power of the secular states became evident as rulers cast their support for one side or the other: France, Sicily, Scotland, Castile, Aragon, and Portugal rallied behind the Avignon pope; England, Flanders, Poland, Hungary, Germany, and the rest of Italy stayed loyal to the Roman pope. The papal office suffered the most; the pope's authority diminished as pious Christians became bewildered and disgusted.

The worst was yet to come. In 1409 both sets of cardinals summoned a church council in Pisa to heal the fissure. The Pisan Council elected a new pope and called on the other two to resign. They refused, and the church was faced with *three* rulers claiming papal authority. The Great Schism was finally resolved at the Council of Constance (1414–1418), which deposed the Avignon ruler, accepted the resignation of the Roman claimant, ignored the Pisan Council's choice, and elected a new pope, Martin V.

With the success of the Council of Constance, conciliar rule (rule by councils) as a way of curbing the power of the popes seemed to be gaining support in the church. But Martin V (pope 1417–1431) rejected this idea as soon as he was elected to the papal throne. Nevertheless, the conciliar movement remained alive until the mid–fifteenth century, when strong popes reasserted the monarchical power of their office. Although powerful, these popes failed to address pressing moral and spiritual concerns, for they were deeply involved in Italian politics and other worldly interests, ruling almost as secular princes in Papal States.

TECHNOLOGY

As farming life changed because of the growth of urban life, so did Europe's fledgling industrial life, and new technology, for instance the suction pump, increased productivity in some industries. Older inventions, such as eyeglasses, mechanical clocks, and gunpowder, were improved in this age of rapid change. However, the most significant technological innovation of the late Middle Ages was the development of printing with movable metal type in the mid–fifteenth century.

The Rise of Industries

Hand-loomed textile manufacturing remained the leading industry, but its production and distribution centers shifted. The greatest change in textile manufacturing, however, was precipitated by England's shift from the export of raw wool to the export of finished cloth, a change that disrupted the traditional rural way of life.

Wool merchants organized the new textile industry in England. The merchants, who bought and owned the raw wool, created the "putting-out system," the assigning of tasks (shearing, carding, combing, spinning, weaving, fulling, felting, dyeing, and cutting) to families who worked at home—which came to be defined as the cottage industry. The spinning wheel—imported from India via the Middle East, perhaps during the Crusades—streamlined the spinning of wool into thread, or yarn. It replaced the ancient method, involving two handheld sticks, called a distaff and a spindle. With the spinning wheel the worker stretched wool from a distaff onto a spindle, turning the wheel constantly so as to create a continuous thread. Women traditionally performed the spinning, hence the medieval terms *spinster* and *distaff side,* meaning "woman's work."

In England, merchant entrepreneurs invested in sites based on available grazing land for sheep and access to fast-flowing streams—the latter to power fulling mills, where wooden paddles washed and beat the cloth before it was stretched to dry outdoors. In some textile-producing areas, merchants recruited skilled workers from Flanders (modern Belgium). The importation of foreign workers could provoke social unrest, as in 1381, during the Peasants' Revolt, when the rioters massacred Flemish workers, accusing them of taking work from the local populace.

Other new industries also emerged. Rag paper, a Chinese invention improved by the Arabs, was manufactured widely in Spain, Italy, France, and Germany. Silk fabrics were woven in impressive patterns in Florence, Venice, and Lucca, from the 1300s and, in England and France, from the late 1400s. Salt was now distributed by Venice and Lisbon and used in the industries of tanning leather and preserving food. The iron industry expanded to meet the demand for weapons, armor, and horseshoes.

The Printing Press

The German craftsman Johannes Gutenberg (1397–1468) is often credited with the invention of the printing press, in about 1450, even though his achievement rests on numerous earlier developments. That is, the model for his printing press came from similar devices used to bind books and to make wine and paper. Gutenberg also had knowledge of printing from wood blocks (though without a printing press), invented in China in perhaps the sixth century CE and developed in the West after 1350, whereby pictures along with a brief text could be impressed onto a paper surface (see the section "The Print," later in the chapter).

Gutenberg's invention gave rise to the printing and publishing industries, with a host of related occupations, such as printers, engravers, compositors, typefounders (designers of typefaces), booksellers, editors, proofreaders, and librarians. Because it was cheaper to print a book than to have a text copied as a manuscript, books became agents of democracy, with huge repercussions for education, literature, and society. Hints of the changes to come may be glimpsed in a survey of the perhaps forty thousand books, known as **incunabula** (from the Latin, "cradle"), which were printed before 1500: a mass of Christian texts, especially Bibles, prayer books, and lives of saints, in both Latin and vernacular languages; a flood of "how-to" manuals on topics such as etiquette; a horde of fictional works calculated to appeal to literate laypeople; a few books of music, showing lines and notes; and from Jewish-owned presses, an outpouring of works in Hebrew, including Bibles, prayer books, and almanacs.

THE CULTURAL FLOWERING OF THE LATE MIDDLE AGES

The calamitous political, social, and economic events of the late Middle Ages were echoed in the cultural sphere by the breakdown of the medieval synthesis in religion, theology, literature, and art. New secular voices began to be heard, challenging traditional views, and the interests of the urban middle classes started to influence art and architecture. Although the church remained the principal financial supporter of the arts, rich town dwellers, notably bankers and merchants, were emerging as the new patrons of art (Figure 10.3).

Religion

The waves of monastic reform that had repeatedly brought renewed life to the medieval church largely

Figure 10.3 Jacques Coeur's House. 1443–1451. Bourges, France. *Coeur was an immensely successful entrepreneur who at one point bankrolled the French kings. His magnificent mansion at Bourges spawned many imitations among wealthy businessmen across Europe. The building's spiky turrets, fanciful balconies, and highly decorated windows are all secular adaptations of the late Gothic style more commonly seen in church architecture. Coeur conducted his Europe-wide financial and commercial dealings from this house, sending messages by carrier pigeons released through holes in the roof.*

ceased in the late Middle Ages. Lay piety thus became one of the most significant developments in the religious landscape. By 1400 the Brethren and Sisters of the Common Life and the Friends of God were rising in the Rhineland, the Low Countries, and Flanders. This lay movement constituted the *devotio moderna,* or the "new devotion," with its ideal of a pious lay society. Disappointed with traditionally trained priests, members of these groups often rejected higher education and practiced the strict discipline of the earlier monastic orders, but without withdrawing into a monastery. Among the most important expressions of this new devotion was *The Imitation of Christ,* by Thomas à Kempis (1380–1471). His manual, with its stern asceticism, reflected the harsh ideals of the Brethren of the Common Life, the group of which Thomas was a member. For others, however, sober reflections on the life of Christ were not enough. The flagellants, for example, who regarded the plague as God's way to judge and punish an evil society, staged public processions in which they engaged in ritual whippings in an attempt to divert divine wrath from the general population (Figure 10.4).

The flagellants managed to escape official censure, but those more openly critical of the church did not. The leaders who attempted to reform the church in England and Bohemia met stout resistance from the popes. The English reform movement sprang from the teachings of John Wycliffe (about 1320–1384), an Oxford teacher whose message attracted both nobility and common folk. Wishing to purify the church of worldliness, Wycliffe urged the abolition of ecclesiastical property, the subservice of the church to the state, and the denial of papal authority. The most lasting achievement of Wycliffe's movement was the introduction of the first complete English-language Bible, produced by scholars inspired by his teaching. After his followers (known as Lollards, because during religious frenzy, their tongues were said to "loll" out of their mouths) were condemned as heretical, the secular officials launched savage persecutions.

The Bohemian reformers in the Holy Roman Empire were indebted to Wycliffe, whom some had met at Oxford; but, more important, their strength was rooted in the popular piety and evangelical preachers of mid-fourteenth-century Prague. The heresy became

Figure 10.4 *Flagellation Scene. Annales of Gilles Le Muisit.* Bibliothèque Royale Albert Ier, Brussels. *This miniature painting represents a familiar scene across Europe during the plague years. The penitents, depicted with bare backs and feet, marched through towns scourging themselves with whips. By this self-punishment, they hoped to atone for their own and society's sins and thus end the plague.*

identified with Jan Hus (about 1369–1415), a Czech theologian who accepted Wycliffe's political views but rejected some of his religious teachings. Hus was invited to the Council of Constance in 1415, where his ideas were condemned, and he was burned at the stake by state authorities. His death outraged his fellow Czechs, many of whom, including the powerful and wealthy, now adopted his views. Hussite beliefs became a vehicle for Czech nationalism, as Hus's ethnic comrades fought against German overlords. Because of the backing of powerful lay leaders, the Hussites survived into the next century. They gained more followers during the Protestant Reformation and exist today as the Moravian Brethren.

Although the secular authorities, instigated by the church, could usually be counted on to put down the heresies, the church had a more powerful internal weapon at its disposal: the Inquisition (from the Latin *inquisitio,* "inquiry"). Born in the aftermath of the Albigensian heresy in the twelfth century (see Chapter 9), the Inquisition reached its cruel height during the late Middle Ages, particularly in Italy and Spain. Following the basic ideals of Roman law, this church court allowed suspects to be condemned without facing their accusers and accepted evidence gained under torture. Forbidden by the Bible to shed blood, the leaders of the Inquisition turned convicted heretics over to the state authorities, who then executed them by burning. By modern estimates, hundreds of men and women perished in this way.

Theology and Philosophy

Alongside all the strife in the wider world, scholars in Europe's universities engaged in intellectual combat. The major disputes were over Thomism, the theological system of Thomas Aquinas, which in the late Middle Ages was drawing increasing criticism. The old philosophical struggle between realism and nominalism finally ended with a nominalist victory. In the long run, those who questioned Thomism and those who accepted nominalism set philosophy and theology on separate paths and contributed to the Renaissance and the Scientific Revolution.

THE *VIA ANTIQUA* VERSUS THE *VIA MODERNA*   The opening round in the theological war against Thomism be-

SLICE OF LIFE
A Gossip Columnist of the Late Middle Ages

HENRY KNIGHTON
A View from the Provinces

The Chronicle *of Henry Knighton (?–1396) is an excellent source for the late Middle Ages in England. An attentive observer of public affairs, Knighton recorded the gossip about the political and religious unrest of his age. He lived mainly in Leicestershire, far from London, but he had well-placed contacts and reliable sources. In the first excerpt, Knighton reports on the 1381 rebellion of Wat Tyler. In the second excerpt, he passes along a rumor about religious unrest, which may be related to the Lollards, who believed that women could be priests.*

1

The next day, which was Saturday [15 June 1381], they all came together again in Smithfield, where the king [Richard II] came early to meet them, and showed that although he was young in years he was possessed of a shrewd mind. He was approached by their leader, Wat Tyler, who had now changed his name to Jack Straw. He stood close to the king, speaking for the others, and carrying an unsheathed knife, of the kind people call a dagger, which he tossed from hand to hand as a child might play with it, and looked as though he might suddenly seize the opportunity to stab the king if he should refuse their requests, and those accompanying the king therefore greatly feared what might come to pass. The commons asked of the king that all game, whether in waters or in parks and woods should become common to all, so that everywhere in the realm, in rivers and fishponds, and woods and forests, they might take the wild beasts, and hunt the hare in the fields, and do many other such things without restraint.

And when the king wanted time to consider such a concession, Jack Straw drew closer to him, with menacing words, and though I know not how he dared, took the reins of the king's horse in his hand. Seeing that, [William] Walworth, a citizen of London, fearing that he was about to kill the king, drew his basilard and ran Jack Straw through the neck. Thereupon another esquire, called Ralph Standish, stabbed him in the side with his basilard. And he fell to the ground on his back, and after rising to his hands and knees, he died.

2

A woman in London celebrates mass. At that time there was a woman in the city of London who had an only daughter whom she taught to celebrate the mass; and she privily set up and furnished an altar in her own bedroom, and there she caused her daughter on many occasions to dress as a priest and in her fashion to celebrate mass, though when she came to the sacramental words she prostrated herself before the altar and did not complete the sacrament. But then she would rise for the rest of the mass and recite it to the end, her mother assisting her and showing her devotion.

That nonsense went on for some time, until it was revealed by a neighbour who had been admitted to the secret, when it came to the ears of the bishop of London. He summoned them to his presence and showed them the error of their ways, and compelled them to display the child's priestly tonsure in public, for her head was found to be quite bald. The bishop greatly deplored and bewailed such misconduct in the church in his time, uttering many lamentations, and put an end to it by enjoining penance upon them.

INTERPRETING THIS SLICE OF LIFE

1. *What* particular demand did Wat Tyler make of Richard II, the English King? 2. *Why* do you think Knighton singled out this demand in his account? 3. *Why* might Wat Tyler have taken the pseudonym Jack Straw? 4. *How* reliable is Knighton as a reporter? 5. *Why* were the unnamed mother and daughter punished by the bishop of London? 6. *What* bias may have motivated Knighton to report this London gossip to his patron? 7. *What* modern parallel can you draw to Henry Knighton and his *Chronicle*?

gan soon after the death of Thomas Aquinas in 1274. In 1277 church officials in Paris condemned the Latin Averroists for their rationalism. As part of their attack on extreme rationalism, the church authorities rejected some of Aquinas's arguments. The censure of Thomism led to a heated controversy that raged for much of the late Middle Ages among university scholars. In particular, Thomas's fellow Dominican friars waged an acrimonious battle with the Franciscan masters, their great rivals in theological studies.

During these theological debates, new labels were invented and assumed by the opposing sides. Aquinas's *via media* came to be termed by his opponents the *via antiqua*, or the "old-fashioned way." Broadly speaking, the *via antiqua* followed Thomism in urging that faith and reason be combined as the correct approach to divine truth. In contrast, the **via moderna**, or the "modern way," made a complete separation of faith and reason. In time the *via moderna* prevailed, driving the *via antiqua* underground until it was rescued from oblivion in the modern period.

DUNS SCOTUS AND WILLIAM OF OCKHAM   The conflict between the *via antiqua* and the *via moderna* was best exemplified in the writings of John Duns Scotus and William of Ockham, respectively. The first of these commentators was sympathetic to the theology of Thomas Aquinas, but the second scholar was unmistakably hostile and tried to discredit Thomism.

Duns Scotus [duhnz SKOAT-us] (about 1265–1308), the most persuasive voice of the *via antiqua,* was a Scottish thinker who was trained as a Franciscan and lectured at the universities in Oxford, Paris, and Cologne. Even though he was a supporter of Thomism, Duns Scotus unwittingly undermined Aquinas's synthesis by stressing that faith was superior to reason, a shift in focus that arose from his belief in God's absolute and limitless power. Pointing out that God's existence could not be proven either through the senses or by reason, he asserted that only faith could explain the divine mystery. Furthermore, Duns Scotus concluded that because the theologian and the philosopher have different intellectual tasks, theology and science (that is, the study of nature) should be independent fields of inquiry.

What Duns Scotus unintentionally began, William of Ockham (about 1300–1349) purposely completed. Under the assaults of Ockham's keen intellect, the Thomist theological edifice collapsed. An Oxford trained theologian, he recognized the importance of both reason and faith; but, like Scotus, he did not see how reason could prove God's existence. Both thinkers believed that only personal feelings and mystical experiences could reveal God and the divine moral order. Yet Ockham went further than Scotus by asserting that reason, the senses, and empirical evidence could enable human beings to discover and hence understand the natural world. To Ockham, faith and reason were both valid approaches to truth, but they should be kept apart so that each could achieve its respective end.

In the seemingly endless medieval debate between the realists and the nominalists, Ockham's reasoning swept nominalism to its final victory. Like the nominalists of the twelfth century, Ockham denied the existence of universals and claimed that only individual objects existed. He concluded that human beings can have clear and distinct knowledge only of specific things in the physical world; no useful knowledge can be gained through reason or the senses about the spiritual realm. Ockham's conclusion did not mean that human beings were cast adrift without access to the world of God. A corollary of his approach was that understanding of the spiritual realm rested solely on the truths of faith and theology.

In his reasoning, William of Ockham asserted a principle of economy that stripped away all that was irrelevant: arguments should be drawn from a minimum of data and founded on closely constructed logic. "It is vain to do with more what can be done with fewer," he says in one of his works. Ockham's "razor" of logic eliminated superfluous information that could not be verified, thus enabling a student to cut to the core of a philosophical problem. The Ockhamites, following their mentor's logic and empiricism, challenged the realists and dominated the intellectual life of the universities for the next two hundred years.

Science

Ockham's ideas broadened the path to modern science that had been opened by two thirteenth-century thinkers. In that earlier time, Robert Grosseteste [GROAS-test] (about 1175–1253), a Franciscan at Oxford University, had devised a scientific method for investigating natural phenomena; using step-by-step procedures, he employed mathematics and tested hypotheses until he reached satisfactory conclusions. Roger Bacon (about 1220–1292), another Franciscan and a follower of Grosseteste, advocated the use of the experimental method, which he demonstrated in his studies of optics, solar eclipses, and rainbows and in his treatises on mathematics, physics, and philosophy.

In the fourteenth century, other thinkers, with Grosseteste and Bacon as guides and Ockham's logic as a weapon, made further contributions. Outstanding among these men was one bold Parisian scholar who took advantage of the growing interest in the experimental method, Nicholas Oresme [O-REM] (about 1330–1382). Oresme answered all of Aristotle's objections to the idea that the earth moved. Using pure reason and applying theoretical arguments, he concluded that it was as plausible that the earth moved around the sun as that it was fixed. Having used reason to show that the earth may move, however, Oresme then chose to accept church doctrine, denying what he had demonstrated. Nevertheless, Oresme's arguments, along with Ockham's separation of natural philosophy from theology and Bacon's formulation of the experimental method, foreshadowed the approaches of modern science (Figure 10.5).

Figure 10.5 DOMENICO DI BAR-TOLO. *Distribution of Alms.* 1440–1441. Fresco. Hospital of Santa Maria della Scala, Siena. *Hospitals, which originated in the High Middle Ages, continued to be founded across Europe. By the fourteenth century, in Siena, Italy, Santa Maria della Scala, which was located on the square of the cathedral, had grown into a highly reputable and richly endowed hospital. The friars and, later, the city of Siena managed it, nursing the sick, taking in orphans and abandoned children, and caring for the numerous pilgrims who traveled through the city on their way to Rome. Domenico di Bartolo's fresco, the* Distribution of Alms, *illustrates the life of this hospital, as it nurses its patients and performs its civic responsibilities. On the left, the rector (the hospital head) tips his hat to a well-dressed man, probably one of the wealthy donors; in the center, a man puts on clothes while other poor people wait in line, and, in the far right background, children receive bread. Above the figures, the facades of the cathedral and the bishop's residence may be seen. The painter's credible treatment of space and volume indicates his familiarity with the art innovations under way in Florence, where he probably studied.*

Literature

The powerful forces that were reshaping the wider culture—the rising new monarchies, the growing national consciousness among diverse peoples, the emerging secularism, and the developing urban environment—were also transforming literature in the late Middle Ages. The rise of literacy produced a growing educated class who learned to read and write the local languages rather than Latin, and a shift to vernacular literature began to occur (see Chapter 9). Two new groups—the monarchs and their courts, and the urban middle class—started to supplant the nobility and the church as patrons and audiences. And, most important, Gutenberg's printing press enabled a wider and faster dissemination of knowledge than ever before.

NORTHERN ITALIAN LITERATURE: PETRARCH AND BOCCACCIO
Petrarch and Boccaccio, both Florentines, like Dante, grew up in a Christian world that was urban, rapidly secularizing, and had little experience with chivalry. These two writers captured the mood of this transition era as Florence and the other Italian city-states shed their medieval outlook. Both authors looked back to the classical world for inspiration; yet both found, in the bustling world of the nearby towns, the materials and characters for their stories. Of the two, Petrarch was the more dedicated classicist and often used ancient themes in his writings.

Francesco Petrarch [PAY-trark] ("Petracco" in Italian) (1304–1374), though Florentine by birth and in spirit, grew up in the south of France where his father worked at the papal court. As a diplomat for popes and Italian princes, he won fame and wealth, but his reputation arose from his career as a professional man of letters. Petrarch unleashed a torrent of superb Latin scholarship on classical subjects and themes but also earned wide renown for a collection of 366 love lyrics and sonnets called *Canzoniere,* or *Songbook,* in beautiful Italian.

ENCOUNTER

A New Look at the Spread of Byzantine Scholarship in the West

It used to be thought that after the capture of Constantinople by the Ottoman Turks in 1453 numerous Greek scholars fled to the West, bringing with them knowledge of long-lost books and, thus, ushering in the Renaissance. Sudden and calamitous events are often seen by contemporaries as major turning points in history with both immediate and far-reaching consequences. But careful historical scholarship eventually demonstrated that the Renaissance had Italian roots unconnected to Byzantium and that Italy long enjoyed contact with Greek scholars.

As early as the end of the fourteenth century, Manuel Chrysoloras [kris-uh-LOR-uhs] (about 1353–1415), a Byzantine aristocrat and scholar, came to Florence, at the invitation of the city's government, to teach Greek (Encounter figure 10.1). Over the next few decades, more and more Byzantine scholars settled in Rome and Venice, where they taught Greek and rhetoric and translated Greek texts into Latin. They also brought ancient Greek and Latin philosophical, literary, and scientific works and treatises by learned Byzantine writers, which had never been available in the West. In Venice, some of these scholars later worked with the famous Aldine Press, which printed many Greek and Latin classics, only four decades after Gutenberg's invention.

Another encounter between Byzantine and Italian scholars occurred when church leaders from Rome and Constantinople held ecumenical councils in Ferrara and Florence (1438–1445). The Eastern Orthodox Church, based in Constantinople, which felt threatened by the Ottoman Turks and their Islamic faith, wanted to settle past disagreements with the papacy and reunite the two branches of Christianity. However, fundamental differences over ecclesiastical governance, dogmas, and liturgical practices doomed any hope for reconciliation (see Figure 11.21).

Although the church union failed, numerous intellectual exchanges took place between the conference delegates. Several Byzantine churchmen and scholars remained in Italy to teach and to translate. The most influential of these men, John Bessarion (1403–1472), was made an archbishop in the Eastern Church by the Byzantine emperor in 1437. Bessarion first settled in Rome, where he founded an academy that translated Greek books and taught Greek philosophy. Recognizing his piety and learning, the pope, in 1439, made him a cardinal in the Western Church and sent him on several diplomatic missions. Later, he withdrew to Venice, where his reputation grew. When he died, he willed his personal library of Greek works to his beloved city of Venice.

Petrarch, despite a clerical training, reveals the complementary Latin and vernacular, secular and spiritual interests of his time.

Petrarch touched on religious themes in *Secretum*, or *Secret Book*, which deals with the state of his soul. In this dialogue, "Augustinus," or St. Augustine, hounds "Franciscus," or Petrarch, about his innermost thoughts and desires, charging him with all the deadly sins. Freely admitting his moral lapses, Franciscus pleads that he is the same as any other man—driven by a love of learning, a weakness for fleshly attractions, and an appetite for personal comforts. Despite this confession, with its modern overtones, the dialogue shows that Petrarch could not liberate himself fully from medieval values. Classicism inspired much of his scholarship, but Augustine's *Confessions* called forth the *Secretum*.

Even more than his lifelong friend Petrarch, Giovanni Boccaccio [bo-KACH-e-o] (1313–1375) was a man of the world. The son of a banker, Boccaccio began his literary career by penning prose romances along with poetic pastorals and sonnets, many of which were dedicated to Fiammetta, a young woman who was both his consuming passion and his literary muse. His early efforts, however, are overshadowed by his Italian prose masterpiece, *The Decameron*. Written in about 1351, this work reflects the grim conditions of the Black Death, which had just swept through Florence. In *The Decameron* (from the Greek word for "ten days"), Boccaccio describes how ten young men and women, in their efforts to escape the plague, flee the city to a country villa, where they pass the time, each telling a story a day for ten days. Most of their one hundred tales were based on folk stories and popular legends. Although some tales deal lightly with social mores and a few contain moral messages, the majority simply entertain. Boccaccio, speaking through a cross section of urban voices and relying on well-known stories, helped develop a form of literature that eventually led to the modern short story.

ENGLISH LITERATURE: GEOFFREY CHAUCER Like its Italian counterpart, English literature rapidly matured into its own forms during the late Middle Ages. The development of an English literary style was aided immensely by the evolution of a common language. Until this time, most educated English people read and spoke

Encounter figure 10.1   ANONYMOUS. *Manuel Chrysoloras Teaching Greek in Florence.* Drawing. Louvre. *Although Chrysoloras's classroom teaching techniques are not known, today's scholars believe he would read aloud, in front of his students, a passage in Greek from some classical text and then analyze the work, drawing on sources from other Byzantine writers, a pedagogical device used in Constantinople. This portrait of Chrysoloras, perhaps done by one of his students, shows him teaching the Greek alphabet at the Florentine* studium, *or school, at which he taught.*

French, but a rising sense of national consciousness, triggered by the Hundred Years' War and an emerging educated urban class, hastened the spread of English as the native tongue.

By 1300 important works in English were beginning to appear, such as *The Vision of Piers Plowman,* a moral allegory, by William Langland (about 1332–1400), that graphically exposes the plight of the poor and calls for a return to Christian virtues. This work provides insight into England's social and economic system and, through the author's anguish, reveals the social tension around the time of the Peasants' Revolt in 1381.

English literature was still establishing its own identity and a common language was slowly emerging when Geoffrey Chaucer (about 1340–1400) appeared on the scene. He wrote in an East Midland dialect of English that became the standard form for his generation as well as the foundation of modern English. The son of a wealthy London merchant, Chaucer spent his professional life as a courtier, a diplomat, and a public servant for the English crown. The profession of "writer" or "poet" was unknown in Chaucer's day. But his poetry brought him renown, and when he died he

was the first commoner to be buried in Westminster Abbey, a favored burial spot for English royalty.

Chaucer began composing his most famous work, *The Canterbury Tales,* in 1385. He set the tales in the context of a pilgrimage to the tomb of Thomas à Becket, the twelfth-century martyr. Even though the journey has a religious purpose, Chaucer makes it plain that the travelers intend to have a good time along the way. To make the journey from London to Canterbury more interesting, the thirty-one pilgrims (including Chaucer himself) agree to tell tales—two each going and returning—and to award a prize for the best story told.

Chaucer completed only twenty-three tales and the general Prologue, in which he introduces the pilgrims. Each person on the pilgrimage not only represents an English social type but also is a unique and believable human being. In this poetic narrative about a group of ordinary people, the spiritual is mixed with the temporal and the serious with the comic.

Chaucer drew his pilgrims from nearly all walks of medieval society. The Knight, in this late stage of feudalism, personified much that was noble and honorable in the chivalric code; his bravery could not be questioned, but he was also a mercenary and cruel to his enemies. Certain representatives of the church are also somewhat skeptically treated. The Prioress, the head of a convent and from the upper class, is more concerned about her refined manners and polished language than the state of her soul. Similarly, the Monk lives a life of the flesh and enjoys good food, fine wines, and expensive clothing. The Friar seems the very opposite of his sworn ideals; he is eager to hear a confession for a fee, and he never goes among the poor or aids the sick. However, in the country Parson, Chaucer portrays a true servant of God who preaches to his parish, looks after the infirm and dying, and lives as simply as his church members. Among the secular travelers, the most vivid is the Wife of Bath. A widow five times over, this jolly woman is full of life and loves to talk. She has been on many pilgrimages and not only knows about foreign places but also has a keen insight into people (Figure 10.6).

As for the tales they tell, the pilgrims' choices often reflect their own moral values. The worthy Knight tells a chivalric love story, but the Miller, a coarse, rough man well versed in lying and cheating, relates how a young wife took on a lover and deceived her husband. Thus the pilgrims' stories, based on folk and fairy tales, romances, classical stories, and beast fables, are entertaining in themselves and function as a kind of *summa* of the storyteller's art.

FRENCH LITERATURE: CHRISTINE DE PIZAN Christine de Pizan [kris-teen duh pee-zahn], among the leading French writers of the day, began to explore in her works the status and role of women, giving voice in the process to one of the most prominent issues in the postmodern world (see Chapter 22). She also contributed to the triumph of vernacular over Latin language by writing in a graceful French with the learnedness of Latin.

Christine de Pizan (1364–about 1430) was by birth an Italian from Pisa whose literary gifts blossomed under the patronage of the French kings and dukes of Burgundy. She began a life of study and learning after the death of her husband, a royal official, in 1389, left her with a family to support. The first known Western woman to earn a living through her writings, de Pizan was a pioneer who blazed the trail for women authors.

Christine wrote on diverse topics, working within the well-established literary genres of her day, including love poems, lays, biography, letters, political tracts, and moral proverbs. Two themes dominate her writing: calls for peace and appeals for the recognition of women's contributions to culture and social life. Both themes reflect the era in which she lived—an age beset by civil strife because of the Hundred Years' War

Figure 10.6 *The Wife of Bath.* Ellesmere Manuscript. Early fifteenth century. Bancroft Library, University of California at Berkeley. *In the Ellesmere Manuscript, an early edition of* The Canterbury Tales *issued soon after Chaucer's death, each story was accompanied by a sketch of the pilgrim who was narrating it. This portrait of the Wife of Bath shows her riding an ambler, a horse that walks with an easy gait, and wearing a wimple, the typical headdress of nuns as well as laywomen of the period.*

and a time in which women were scarcely allowed to express an opinion in public.

The work of Christine's that has excited the most interest among modern readers is *The Book of the City of Ladies* (1405), a book that forcefully tries to raise the status of women and to give them dignity. Offering one of the first histories of women and arguing that women have the right to be educated, based on her premise that women are moral and intellectual equals of men, this book seems almost feminist in a modern sense; however, a close reading shows that Christine is writing within a medieval framework. Nowhere in this book or in any other writings does she advocate that women abandon their traditional roles and strike out on a new path. It is proper, nevertheless, to claim that Christine de Pizan is the first Western writer to raise the issue of women's rights in society and culture.

Art and Architecture

The Gothic style continued to dominate architecture (see Chapter 9), but the balanced and unified High Gothic of the thirteenth century was now replaced with the ornate effects of the **late Gothic style.** Virtuosity became the chief aesthetic goal, as the architects took basic forms and pushed them to the stylistic limits. Virtuosity bordering on excess marked painting and sculpture too. Statues and sculptured figures were given willowy, swaying bodies, rendered in exquisite detail, and illuminated manuscripts and painted wooden panels became more refined. At the same time, in Florence around 1300, Giotto was revolutionizing art with a new approach to painting. The trend toward naturalism embodied in his works was the most significant new artistic development of this period and was destined to be the wave of the future.

LATE GOTHIC ARCHITECTURE   France—the home of the Gothic style—remained a potent source of architectural innovation. French architects now abandoned the balanced ideal of the High Gothic and made extravagance their guiding principle, creating a late Gothic style typified by ever greater heights and elaborate decoration. In the fifteenth century, this tendency culminated in the **Flamboyant style,** so named for its flamelike effects. French churches built in this style had sky-piercing spires, and their facades were embroidered with lacy or wavy decorations that obscured the buildings' structural components (Figure 10.7). During the fourteenth century, the late Gothic spread, becoming an international style, although with almost infinite local variations.

In England, the late Gothic was called **Perpendicular** because of its dramatic emphasis on verticality. This Perpendicular style was characterized by an

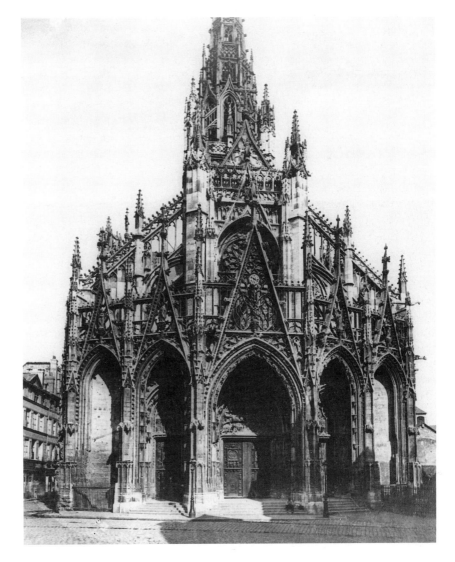

Figure 10.7   The Church of St. Maclou. 1435–ca. 1514. Rouen, France. *St. Maclou's exterior illustrates the ornate late Gothic style. Its west facade, unlike a square High Gothic front, fans out to form a semicircular entrance. There are five portals (rather than the usual three), two of which are blind, and set above them are steeply pitched stone arches of intricate design.*

Figure 10.8 Choir of Gloucester Cathedral. Ca. 1330–1357. Gloucester, England. *The choir and apse of Gloucester cathedral were rebuilt in the Perpendicular Gothic style in about 1330, when King Edward III chose the church as the burial shrine for his murdered father, Edward II. The architects made the earlier Norman apse into a square and filled the east end with glass panels. Inside, the builders redesigned the support system, using thin vertical piers; these piers were attached to the walls and laced together on the ceiling, creating elaborate patterns that complemented the glass decorations.*

increased use of paneled decorations on the walls and overhead vaults, resulting in a variation of rib vaulting, called **fan vaulting,** in which stone ribs arch out from a single point in the ceiling to form a delicate pattern. This style also increased the number of window openings, which necessitated additional flying buttresses. The best example of the English Perpendicular is the cathedral in Gloucester. In the choir, the vertical lines, extending from the floor to the ceiling, where the tracery is interwoven, unite the building's interior into an upward-moving volume (Figure 10.8). Just as impressive as the interior is the nearby cloister with its fan vaulting that weaves a pattern overhead while tying the walls and ceiling into a complex unit (Figure 10.9).

A key example of the late Italian Gothic is the cathedral in Siena. Filled with civic pride, Siena's citizens urged their leaders to build a cathedral more splendid than those of their neighbors. Begun in the mid–thirteenth century, the cathedral was constructed over the next one hundred fifty years, and, as a result, the building complex shows a mixture of styles: the **campanile,** or bell tower, is executed in the Italian Romanesque, but the overall cathedral complex is Italian Gothic (Figure 10.10). The facade, for the first time in Italy, incorporated nearly life-size figures into the total design, thus heightening its resemblance to the French Gothic. However, many features distinguish the style of Siena from the French style. For example, the decorative statues on Siena's facade were placed

Figure 10.9 South Cloister of Gloucester Cathedral. Ca. 1370. Gloucester, England. *Fan vaulting, an intricate pattern in which ribs arch out from a single point in the ceiling, first appeared at Gloucester cathedral and inspired many imitations. Although the ribs may appear to be structurally necessary, they are really a richly decorative device carved from stone. In Gloucester's south cloister, the tracery fans out from the top of each column and then merges in the center of the ceiling, giving the impression of a delicate screen.*

Figure 10.10   Siena Cathedral. 1250–1400. Siena, Italy. *Extant records and floor plans show that the Sienese changed their minds several times before deciding on the cathedral's final shape. At one time, in about 1322, a commission of architects advised that the existing cathedral be demolished because the foundations and walls were not strong enough to support new additions. Nonetheless, construction went forward, and the cathedral is still standing after more than six hundred years.*

above the gables, not set in niches. Furthermore, the Sienese builders put mosaics into the spaces in the gables and above the central rose window.

Florence, Siena's greatest military and trade rival, refused to be outdone by its nearby competitor. The Florentine city fathers asked Giotto [JAWT-toe] (about 1276–1337), the city's most renowned painter, to design a campanile for their own cathedral. Today, the first story of the bell tower—with its carvings, interlaced patterns of pink and white marble, and hexagonal inlays—still stands as conceived by Giotto (Figure 10.11). Giotto's plan, as left in a drawing, called for an

Figure 10.11   GIOTTO. Campanile of the Florentine Cathedral. Ca. 1334–1350. Ht. approx. 200'.
Florence, Italy. *Giotto's Tower, as this campanile is
known in Florence, is one of the city's most cherished
landmarks. Today, its bells still toll the time. The two
sets of windows in the central section and the taller
openings at the top give the campanile a strong sense
of balanced proportion. Thus, despite being built in
the fourteenth century, the tower anticipates the classical ideal that was revived in the Renaissance.*

open tower with a spire on top, as in a French Gothic tower. But later architects constructed a rectangular top instead and decorated it with marble—making it distinctively Italian rather than reminiscent of the French.

LATE GOTHIC SCULPTURE   During the late Middle Ages, sculpture, like architecture, continued to undergo stylistic changes, among which two general trends may be identified. One trend centered in Italy, notably in Siena, where the Pisano [pee-SAHN-o] family began to experiment with sculptural forms that foreshadowed Renaissance art, with its return to classical themes and values (see Chapter 11). Outstanding among the members of the gifted Pisano family was Giovanni Pisano (1245–1314), who designed the intricate late Gothic facade of the Siena cathedral (see Figure 10.11). Giovanni's great artistic reputation is largely based on the massive marble pulpit that he carved for the cathedral at Pisa. Using classical themes derived from Roman art (as Renaissance artists were to do), he designed the pulpit to rest on acanthus leaves at the top of eight Corinthian columns (Figure 10.12). The lions that support two of the columns were modeled on those on an ancient Roman sarcophagus. Just as late Roman art blended Christian and classical symbols, so Giovanni's treatment of the pulpit's base mixed images of the cardinal virtues, such as Justice and Temperance, with the figure of the Greek hero Herakles.

Pisano's octagonal pulpit includes eight panels in high relief that depict scenes from the lives of either John the Baptist or Christ. Of these panels, the scene depicting the Nativity ranks as his finest work. In this scene, he portrays a natural vitality through the careful balance and orderly spacing of the animals and people (Figure 10.13). The placement and the calm actions of the surrounding figures frame the Virgin and child so that the viewer's attention is focused on these two central figures. Giovanni's swaying figures with their smooth draperies were rooted in Late Gothic art, but their quiet serenity attested to his classicizing manner.

The other trend in sculpture during this time centered in Burgundy, where Philip the Bold (r. 1364–1404) supported scholars and artists at his ducal court in Dijon. Preeminent among these was Claus Sluter [SLUE-tuhr] (about 1350–1406), a sculptor of Netherlandish origin who helped to define this last phase of Gothic art. Sluter's masterly sculptures are still housed in a monastery near Dijon, and his most famous work, *The Well of Moses,* was commissioned for the cloister of this monastic retreat.

The Well of Moses, which was designed as a decorative cover for an actual well in a courtyard, is surrounded at its base with Old Testament prophets symbolizing the sacraments of communion and baptism. The most beautifully rendered of the surviving life-size statues is Moses, encased in a flowing robe and standing erect with a finely chiseled head (Figure 10.14). Sluter's sense of the dramatic moment, of the prophet's personal emotions, and of the individual features makes the statue nearly an individual portrait. Sluter rendered Moses's beard and the unfurled scroll in precise detail and carved the figure with the head turned to the side, eyes looking into the future.

LATE GOTHIC PAINTING AND THE RISE OF NEW TRENDS   Of all the arts, painting underwent the most radical changes in the late Middle Ages. Illuminated manuscripts maintained their popularity, but their themes became more secular under the patronage of titled aristocrats and wealthy merchants. At the same time, painters of frescoes and wooden panels introduced new techniques for applying paint and mixing colors. Stylistically, painters preferred to work in the extravagant late Gothic manner with its elegant refinement and its undulating lines. Nevertheless, Giotto and other Italian painters discovered fresh ways of depicting human figures that started to revolutionize art.

Illuminated Manuscripts   The Burgundian court played a pivotal role in the production of one of the outstanding illuminated manuscripts of the medieval period, the *Très Riches Heures du Duc de Berry.* This famous collection of miniatures was painted by the three Limbourg brothers for the duke of Berry, brother of Philip the Bold of Burgundy. These illustrations stand above the others of their time for their exquisite detail, general liveliness, and intricately designed crowd scenes—some of the marks of the late Gothic style.

The *Très Riches Heures,* or the *Very Rich Hours,* represents a type of small prayer book that was a favorite of nobles and businessmen. These personal books of worship, with their litanies and prayers, were often handsomely hand-illustrated to enhance their value. The duke of Berry's prayer book contained some 130 miniatures, including scenes from the life of Christ and the calendar cycle. In the calendar series, each tiny painting, finely detailed and colored in jewel-like tones, notes a seasonal activity appropriate for the month. Some represent the brilliant court life of the duke, and others depict the drudgery of peasant life, sharply differentiated from the court scenes by their action and color. The illustration for January shows the duke of Berry surrounded by his well-dressed courtiers and enjoying a sumptuous feast (Figure 10.15).

The Print   The print, a new artistic medium, developed in the late Middle Ages in the Austrian-Bavarian regions, eastern France, and the Netherlands. Sparked

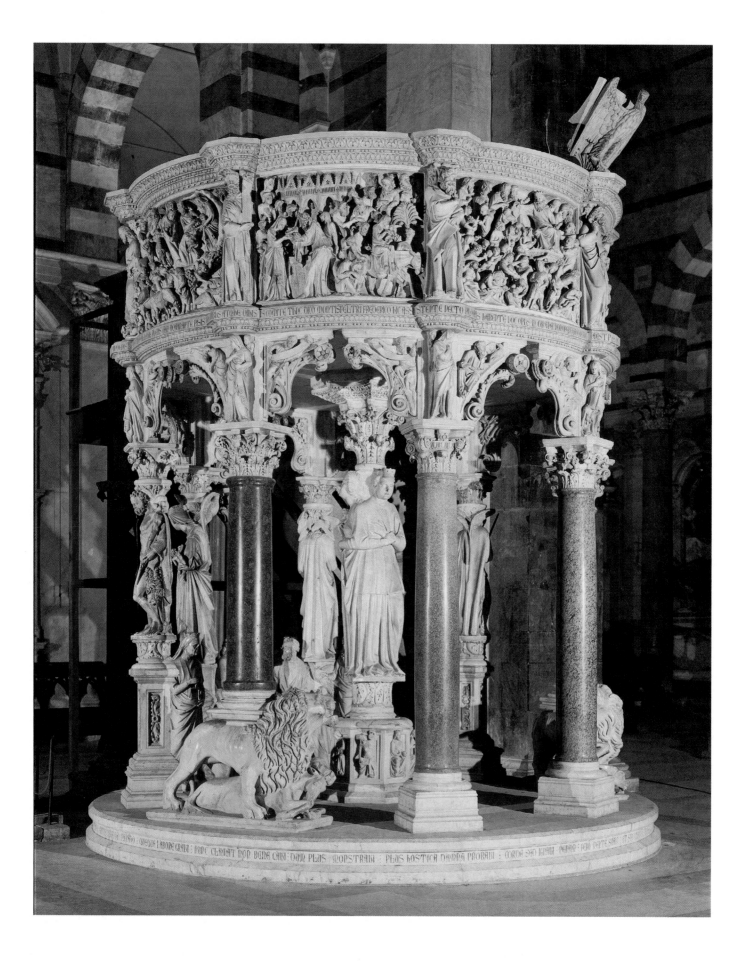

◀ **Figure 10.12**   GIOVANNI PISANO. Pulpit in the Pisa Cathedral. Ca. 1302–1310. Pisa, Italy.
*Pisano built and carved this massive (17-foot-high) pulpit at the height of his reputation. A superb
artist but a quarrelsome man, Pisano recorded his frustrations in the lengthy inscription around
the pulpit's base. In it he claimed that he had achieved much, had been condemned by many, and
took full responsibility for this work of art. Pisano's advance from anonymity to a position of
great artistic repute was typical of a new breed of artist appearing in fourteenth-century Italy.*

Figure 10.13   GIOVANNI PISANO. Nativity Scene. Pulpit in the Pisa cathedral. Ca. 1302–
1310. 33½ × 44½". Pisa, Italy. *In this late Gothic sculpture, Pisano cut deeply into the marble's
surface to give a nearly three-dimensional effect. His many figures seem involved in their own
tasks but are nevertheless linked with one another around the Madonna and child. For example,
the two shepherds (the head of one has been lost) in the upper-right corner appear to be listening
to the angels approaching from the left, while at the far right, sheep rest and graze. Such balanced
placements are evidence of Pisano's classicizing tendencies. Pisano's relief retains a prominent
Gothic feature, however, by presenting the Virgin and child twice—in the central scene and in
the lower-left corner, where a seated Mary, balancing the baby Jesus on her right leg, stretches
her left hand to test the temperature of the water in an elaborate basin.*

by the growth of lay piety, the earliest prints were devotional woodcuts to be used as aids to personal meditation. The prints initially featured scenes from the lives of the Virgin and Christ. For the **woodcut print,** the artist drew an image on a woodblock, which was then cut by a woodcutter and printed by the artist; some were then hand-tinted by a colorist. By 1500 the new techniques of **engraving** (using a sharp tool to draw an image onto a metal plate overlaid with wax, dipping the plate in acid, and then printing it) and **drypoint** (marking an image onto a copper plate with a metal stylus and then printing it) were becoming increasingly popular.

Probably the outstanding set of prints dating from this period was that in the Medieval Housebook, a late-fifteenth-century German manuscript. The so-called Medieval Housebook was a gathering of 192 prints, of which only 126 remain. Most of the prints are in black and white, though a few are partially colored. The printing techniques vary from drypoint and engraving to simple drawings on vellum. Stylistic differences indicate that at least three artists contributed to the work, thus suggesting that the Housebook may have been produced in a workshop. For convenience, however, the artist is called simply the Housebook Master. Of the surviving 126 prints, the subjects range over late medieval life, from the workaday world to jousting scenes to court life. Some offer realistic views of medieval buildings, including barnyards, private dwellings, and palaces; most are highly detailed, showing hair and clothing styles. Others are lively and playful, depicting relations between the sexes and the classes (Figure 10.16).

New Trends In Italy: Giotto   While the illuminated manuscript and the print were popular in northern Europe, a revolution in painting was under way in Italy. The paintings of Giotto are generally recognized as having established a new direction in Western art, one that led into the Renaissance. In Giotto's own day, Dante praised him and the citizens of Florence honored him.

Giotto's revolution in painting was directed against the prevailing **Italo-Byzantine style,** which blended late Gothic with Byzantine influences. He turned this painting style, with its two-dimensional, timeless quality, into a three-dimensional art characterized by naturalism and the full expression of human emotions. Partly through the innovative use of light and shade and the placement of figures so as to create nonmathematical **perspective,** or depth, Giotto was able to paint realistic-looking figures, rather than the flat, ornamental depictions found in most illuminated manuscripts or the Italian altar paintings.

A painting by one of Giotto's contemporaries, Cimabue [chee-muh-BU-ay] (about 1240–1302), the *Ma-*

Figure 10.14   CLAUS SLUTER. *Moses*, from *The Well of Moses*. Ca. 1395–1406. Ht. of full figure approx. 6'. Chartreuse de Champmol, Dijon, France. *Sluter followed the allegorical tradition of medieval art in this portrait of the Hebrew prophet Moses. The book in Moses's right hand and the scroll over his left shoulder symbolize the Word of God. Sluter also depicted Moses with "horns" growing out of his forehead, as was characteristic in medieval representations.*

donna Enthroned, reveals the state of Italian painting at this time (Figure 10.17). The angels on the side are rendered stiffly, aligned vertically without any sense of space between them, and placed flat on the wood panel without any precise relationship with the four prophets below them. Although Cimabue's angels were balanced in their placement and the depiction of the figures of the Madonna and Christ child offered some sense of rounded form, the overall effect of the work confirms its debt to the two-dimensional tradition of Italo-Byzantine art.

In contrast, Giotto's *Madonna Enthroned,* painted about thirty years after Cimabue's, shows how Giotto

Figure 10.15 LIMBOURG BROTH-ERS. *Month of January,* from the *Très Riches Heures du Duc de Berry.* 1413–1416. Approx. 8½ × 5½". Mu-sée Condé, Chantilly, France. *This miniature painting provides insightful social history in its exquisite details. The duke, seated in the right center, is dressed in a blue patterned cloak and is greet-ing his guests for what was probably a New Year's celebration. Behind the duke stands a servant, over whose head are written the words "aproche, aproche," a welcome that is the equivalent of "come in, come in." Above this festive scene, the zodiac signs of Capricorn and Aquarius identify the month as January.*

was transforming Florentine art (Figure 10.18). His Madonna seems to be actually sitting on her throne, and the four angels on either side of her chair are placed to give a sense of spatial depth, or perspective. The angels' distinctive gazes are highly expressive, suggesting feelings of wonder. The Virgin resembles an individual woman and Christ a believable child, not a shrunken adult. Although Giotto uses Gothic touches—the pointed arch, the halos, and the applied gold leaf—the natural rendering of the figures fore-shadows great changes in art.

Giotto was a prolific artist whose paintings adorned churches in Florence and cities all over Italy. At the Arena Chapel in Padua, Giotto painted his masterpiece, two sets of frescoes, one of the life of the Virgin and the other of the life of Christ. These thirty-eight scenes

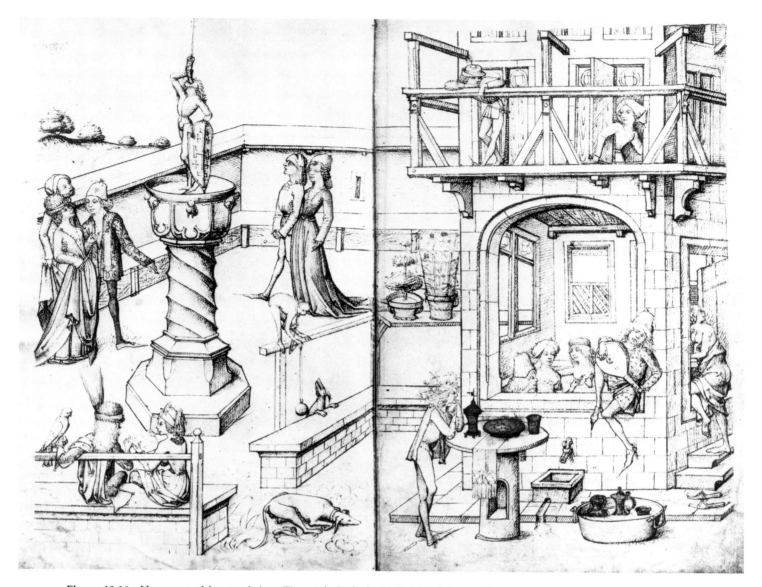

Figure 10.16   HOUSEBOOK MASTER. *Leisure Time at the Bath.* Ca. 1475–1490. Ink on vellum drawing, partially colored. Private collection. *This print reveals the upper classes at play as well as the strict social order. On the left, young couples converse or flirt around a fountain in a courtyard; the pets (a falcon, two dogs, and a monkey) are indicators of the high status of their owners; a lady-in-waiting holds the skirt of her mistress. On the right, young aristocrats (a man and two women) enjoy bathing, while a third woman is entering the bathhouse. A servant serenades the bathers on a stringed instrument, as another waits in attendance. On the balcony, two servants enjoy a flirtatious moment. This Chaucerian-like scene, with its frank sensuality, indicates that within the increasingly secular world of the late Middle Ages the pleasures of the flesh could be a fit subject for an artist.*

show Giotto at the height of his powers, rendering space with a sense of depth and organizing figures so as to create dramatic tension. An outstanding scene from the Padua frescoes is the *Pietà*, or *Lamentation* (Figure 10.19). This scene, which portrays the grief for the dead Christ, expresses total despair through the mourners' faces and gestures, from Mary, who cradles the body

of Jesus, to John, who stands with arms outstretched, to the hovering angels. In the fresco's stark and rugged landscape, even nature seems to mourn, notably in the barren tree that symbolizes the wood of the cross on which Jesus was crucified. After Giotto died in 1337, no painter for the rest of the century was able to match his remarkable treatment of nature and human emotions.

Figure 10.17 CIMABUE. *Madonna Enthroned.* Ca. 1280. Tempera on panel, 12′7½″ × 7′4″. Uffizi Gallery, Florence. *Although Cimabue was experiencing the same desire for freedom in art as the sculptor Giovanni Pisano, this painting of the Madonna shows that he was still strongly under the spell of the Italo-Byzantine tradition. Rather than showing the intense feeling of Giotto's portraits, Cimabue's Virgin and Christ child remain medieval and mystical.*

Flemish Painting: Jan Van Eyck and Hans Memling
When Philip the Good (r. 1419–1467) became duke of Burgundy, he expanded his territories to include the wealthy counties of Holland, Zeeland, and Luxembourg, known as Flanders. Philip was the greatest secular patron of the arts of his day. Of the artists encouraged by his patronage, the brothers Jan and Hubert van Eyck are the most famous, and their religious works and portraits established the Flemish style of art. Little is known of Hubert, but Jan van Eyck [YAHN van IKE] (about 1370–1441) is considered the founder of the Flemish school.

Figure 10.18   GIOTTO. *Madonna Enthroned.* Ca. 1310. Tempera on panel, 10'8" × 6'8". Uffizi Gallery, Florence. *Giotto's* Madonna Enthroned, *so revolutionary in its composition and spatial dimensions, has been called the most influential painting of the fourteenth century. Especially innovative in this altarpiece is the realistic treatment of the Virgin's eyes: they are shaped like ordinary eyes and peer out at the viewer rather than gazing into the distance, as in the Italo-Byzantine style.*

As a general principle, Flemish art sought reality through an accumulation of precise and often symbolic details, in contrast to Italian art, which tended to be more concerned with psychological truth, as in Giotto's frescoes in the Arena Chapel. This national style, expressed primarily through painting with oils on wood panels, turned each artwork into a brilliant and precise reproduction of the original scene. The finest detail in a patterned carpet, the reflected light on a copper vase, and the wrinkled features of an elderly patron were laboriously and meticulously recorded. The Flemish style, with its close attention to detail, was widely appreciated and quickly spread to Italy and England.

THE CULTURAL FLOWERING OF THE LATE MIDDLE AGES

Figure 10.19   GIOTTO. *Pietà,* or *Lamentation.* Ca. 1305–1310. Fresco, 7'7" × 7'9". Arena
Chapel, Padua, Italy. *Such works gained Giotto his reputation as the modern reviver of realistic
art—a tradition that had been lost with the fall of ancient Rome. In this fresco, he created three-
dimensional space in ways that even the Greeks and the Romans had not used. Giotto's illusion of
depth was conveyed by surrounding the dead Christ with numerous figures and, in particular, by
placing two mourners in the foreground with their backs to the viewer. Giotto's use of perspective
was convincing to his generation even though it lacked mathematical precision.*

Figure 10.20   Hubert and Jan van Eyck. *Ghent Altarpiece.* Ca. 1432. Oil on panel, 11'3"
× 14'5". St. Bavo cathedral, Ghent, Belgium. *This large altarpiece may seem to be a collection
of separate paintings, but the work is united in themes and symbolism. What links the panels
is their portrayal of Christ's redemption of humanity. From* The Sin of Adam and Eve *to the
mystic* Adoration of the Lamb, *all the paintings touch in some manner on Christ's sacrifice.*

Jan van Eyck, probably with his brother's help,
painted an altarpiece for the cathedral at Ghent, Belgium (Figure 10.20). This large work—originally commissioned to beautify the main altar—still remains
in its original place. The twenty panels are hinged together so that when opened twelve are visible. These
twelve panels are divided into two levels—heavenly
figures and symbols on the upper level and earthly figures on the lower level. On the ends of the upper level
are nude portraits of Adam and Eve, next to angels
singing and playing musical instruments. Mary on the
left and John the Baptist on the right flank a portrayal
of God the Father, resplendent in a jewel-encrusted
robe and triple crown. Below, on the lower level, are

human figures who are depicted as moving toward
the center panel. On the left, knights and judges ride
on horseback, while, on the right, pilgrims and hermits
approach on foot.

The focus of the *Ghent Altarpiece,* when opened, is
the lower center panel, the *Adoration of the Lamb.* In
this work, the sacrificial death of Jesus is symbolized
by the cross, the baptismal font in the foreground, and
the blood issuing from the lamb into the communion
chalice. The surrounding worshipers include holy
virgins, martyrs, and prophets, plus the four evangelists and the twelve apostles, who stand and kneel in
groups amid plants and trees (Figure 10.21). Besides
mystical subjects, van Eyck could paint secular works,

Figure 10.21   Hubert and Jan van Eyck. *Adoration of the Lamb.* Detail of the *Ghent Altarpiece.* Ca. 1432. St. Bavo cathedral, Ghent, Belgium. *This lower center section of the opened altarpiece dramatically shows how the Flemish school could use religious symbolism to evoke a mystical effect. The refined details, which derive from the tradition of manuscript painting, make this scene both credible and otherworldly.*

though still filled with symbolism, as in *Arnolfini Wedding Portrait* (Interpreting Art figure 10.1).

A second outstanding artist working in Flanders during the late Middle Ages was Hans Memling (about 1430–1494), the most popular painter of his day in Bruges. Long a northern commercial center, Bruges was now entering a period of decline, hastened by the displacement of the Burgundian ruling house by that of the Hapsburgs. Before settling in Bruges, the German-born Memling studied painting in Cologne and the Netherlands, where he fully absorbed the northern tradition. Memling's painting style, which borrowed heavily from that of Jan van Eyck and his generation, was characterized by serenity and graceful elegance, traits that stand in marked contrast to this turbulent era. After starting his workshop in Bruges, Memling grew wealthy from commissions, mainly for altarpieces and portraits, paid for by church leaders, local businesspeople, and resident foreign merchants. More than eighty of his works have survived.

Memling was particularly celebrated for the piety of his Madonna paintings, such as the *Madonna and Child with Angels* (Figure 10.22). Following the Flemish tradition, this painting is filled with religious symbolism, which reinforces the message that Christ died to atone for the sins of humankind. The baby Christ reaches for an apple held by an angel, the fruit symbolizing original sin. The second angel, dressed in a vestment associated with the High Mass, plays a harp, possibly a reference to heavenly music. A carved vine of grapes, depicted on the arch, is an emblem of Holy Communion. On the left column stands David, an ancestor of Christ, and on the right column stands Isaiah, a prophet who foretold the birth of the Messiah.

The format and the details of Memling's enthroned Madonna harken back to Jan van Eyck, but without the intensity or sense of reality. Memling's style is static and somewhat artificial. The painting space is clearly arranged, but the landscape and architectural background function as a stage set; the figures are so

INTERPRETING ART

Date The inscription on the rear wall reads *Johannes de Eyck fuit hic* [Latin for "Jan van Eyck was here"] *1434.*

Subject Traditionally, this painting was thought to portray the 1434 wedding of Giovanni Arnolfini and Giovanna Cenami. But this pair did not marry until 1447. So, rival theories abound over the painting's subject: the Arnolfinis at their betrothal or some other legal transaction; or Giovanni's marriage to an undocumented wife; or a memorial to Giovanni's first wife, Costanza Trenta (d. 1433).

Style Van Eyck used wet-on-wet paints to achieve subtlety and variety of color. Layers of translucent glazes cause the surface to shimmer with light. The use of color, light, and shadow creates three-dimensionality, an effect heightened by the way outside light streams into the room. Van Eyck was the first painter to master photo-like realism.

Religious Symbols The single burning candle functions as a sanctuary lamp in a church, signaling the constant presence of God.

Around the mirror are medallions with scenes of Christ's passion—promises of salvation to the persons represented. The couple do not wear shoes—they are standing on holy ground. The dog symbolizes (marital) fidelity: the common dog's name Fido comes from Latin *fido,* "I trust."

Secular Symbols The lavish attire signifies prosperity, but the bride wears no jewelry—a symbol of the restraint of the merchant classes as opposed to the ostentatious display of the nobles. The man raises his hand in a sign of authority; the woman's hand is shown in a submissive pose—conforming to the period's marriage roles.

Historical Interest This painting is the oldest extant representation of real people in an authentic setting. A historic fashion note: the woman is not pregnant; she wears a stomacher—a fashion of the era that emphasized a woman's stomach. Other items in the room exude wealth: the oriental carpet on the floor; the oranges, a rarity in this period; and the intricate chandelier.

Interpreting Art figure 10.1 JAN VAN EYCK. *Arnolfini Wedding Portrait* or *Arnolfini Double Portrait.* 1434. Oil on wood, 33 × 22½". Reproduced by permission of the Trustees, National Gallery, London. *The Arnolfinis, originally from Lucca (Italy), were agents of the Medici family. The painting was executed in Bruges, where there was an Italian community. Flanders, like Italy, had banking, commercial, and industrial centers. This work is an expression of the symbolic realism that dominated northern European painting in the late Middle Ages.*

composed that they constitute a veritable *tableau vivant,* a staged scene in which costumed actors remain silent as if in a picture. Each of the three figures is treated in similar fashion—thin bodies; oval faces; blank, emotionless stares. Adding to the air of artificiality is the absence of shadows, for the painting is bathed in unmodulated light.

Music

The forces of change transforming Europe in the 1300s also had an impact on the field of music (Figure 10.23). Sacred music began to be overshadowed by secular music, with the rise of new secular forms—such as the ballade and rondeau—based on the **chanson,** a song

Figure 10.22   HANS MEMLING. *Madonna and Child with Angels.* After 1479. Oil on panel, 23⅛ × 18⅞″. Andrew W. Mellon Collection. National Gallery of Art, Washington, D.C. (1937.1.41) Photograph © Board of Trustees. *Memling, though part of the Flemish tradition, appears to have been aware of developments in Renaissance Italy. He introduced some Italian elements into this painting, such as the* putti, *or small angels (used as decorations on the columns and arch), and the stringed musical instruments held by the angels.*

Figure 10.23 *Music and Her Attendants.* Fourteenth century. From Boethius, *De Arithmetica. This miniature painting, using both secular and religious imagery, artfully surveys the state of music in the late Middle Ages. Court music, which flowered during this period, is represented by the seated lady playing a portable pipe organ, in the center, while around her other ladies perform with various instruments, including, starting from the top right and going clockwise: a lute; clappers; trumpets; nakers, or kettledrums; a shawm, an ancestor of the oboe; bagpipes; a tambourine; and a rebec, a precursor of the viol. Religious music, which had kept the legacy of ancient music alive after the fall of Rome, is represented by King David, visible in the circle at the top center, who is depicted playing a psaltery, a handheld type of harp, which is named after the Psalms—the book attributed to his authorship. As to the source of the instruments on view, Greco-Roman tradition supplied only the pipe organ, clappers, trumpets, and bagpipes, while all the others, including the psaltery, were imports from the Islamic world, either from Muslim Spain or from the Middle East during the Crusades.*

set to a French text and scored for one or more voices, often with instrumental accompaniment. Polyphony remained the dominant composing style, but composers now wrote secular polyphonic pieces that were not based on Gregorian chants. These changes were made possible by innovations that coalesced into what came to be called the *new art* (**ars nova** in Latin), particularly in Paris, the capital of polyphonic music. The innovations included a new system of music notation, along with new rhythmic patterns such as **isorhythm**—the

use of a single rhythmic pattern from the beginning to the end of a work, despite changes in the melodic structure. The chief exponent of *ars nova* was the French composer and poet Guillaume de Machaut [gee-yom duh mah-show] (about 1300–1377).

Machaut, who trained as a priest and musician, first made his mark as a court official to the king of Bohemia. For his services, he was rewarded with an appointment to the cathedral in Reims (1337), where he worked for much of the rest of his life. His music circulated widely in his day, largely because he made gifts of his music manuscripts to wealthy patrons. Thus, he became one of the first composers whose works have survived. Reflecting the decline in church music, his output consists mainly of secular love themes. His verses influenced Chaucer.

Although Machaut was famous for secular music, his reputation rests on his *Notre Dame* Mass, the first polyphonic version of the Mass Ordinary by a known composer. "Ordinary" refers to the five parts of the Mass that remain unchanged throughout the liturgical year, namely the kyrie ("Lord, have mercy"), gloria ("Glory"), credo ("the Nicene Creed"), sanctus and benedictus ("Holy" and "Blessed"), and Agnus Dei ("Lamb of God"). Written for four voices, some of which may have been performed by instrumentalists, Machaut's Mass made liberal use of isorhythm in most of its parts. Following his lead, composers for more than six hundred years made the Mass Ordinary the central point of choral music.

A short analysis of Machaut's Agnus Dei, from the *Notre Dame* Mass, shows the new polyphonic style. Its complex composition—four voices singing four parts simultaneously and using varied rhythms—means that the lead melody (sung by the tenor and based on an existing plainsong) is lost in a web of shifting sounds. The two lower voices, including the tenor, provide the ground for this piece. The two upper voices are the more inventive, ornamenting the text with melismas and syllabic singing, along with shifting rhythms, including **syncopation**—the accenting of a weak beat when a strong beat is expected. A prayer for mercy and peace, Agnus Dei is highly repetitive—a typical practice in the Christian liturgy. And it is divided into three parts, the symbol of the Trinity. Thus, Agnus Dei furthers Christian beliefs through words, musical sounds, and structure.

Agnus Dei reads, in Latin, *"Agnus Dei, qui tollis peccata mundi: misere nobis / Agnus Dei, qui tollis peccata mundi: Miserere nobis / Agnus Dei, qui tollis peccata mundi: dona nobis pacem,"* and, in English, "Lamb of God, who taketh away the sins of the world, have mercy on us / Lamb of God, who taketh away the sins of the world, have mercy on us / Lamb of God, who taketh away the sins of the world, grant us peace."

The Legacy of the Late Middle Ages

All historical eras are periods of transition, but the changes of the late Middle Ages were especially momentous. The medieval world was dying, and the modern era was struggling to be born. Dating from this turbulent period were many of the cultural tensions that defined the history of Europe for the next four hundred years.

The most revolutionary happening in the late Middle Ages was the release of a powerful secular spirit that began to make its presence felt everywhere. The upsurge of vernacular literature, the rise of literary themes questioning the low status of women, the increasing popularity of secular music, and the divergence of philosophy and theology are four examples of this new development. But the greatest impact of the rise of secularism on cultural life was that painting and sculpture began to be liberated from the service of architecture. The first stirrings of this change were expressed in the works of Giotto and other Italian and Flemish artists. By the next century, painting in Italy had freed itself from the tutelage of architecture and become the most important artistic genre in the West.

This period also saw the emergence of a new breed of secular ruler who was prepared to mount a sustained drive against the church's combined political and spiritual powers. The victories of the English and the French kings over the papacy—each ruler was able to secure control over his national church—were signs of the breakup of Christendom.

Another important legacy of these years is that the towns, led by their bourgeois citizens—the beginning of the middle class—began to exercise their influence over the countryside. From today's perspective, the growth of the middle class as a dominant force in society was perhaps the most critical development of this age. The first stirrings of industrialism, what has been called *protoindustrialism,* may be detected in the spread of pockets of manufacturing—paper, textiles, and books—over the face of Europe. This age also saw a strong upsurge in the West's continuing love affair with machines, with the inventions of the printing press and the spinning wheel. Finally, this period witnessed the unusual spectacle of the common people revolting against the aristocratic control of the culture and society. Their sporadic efforts failed, but the seeds of future revolution were planted.

KEY CULTURAL TERMS

incunabula
devotio moderna
via antiqua
via moderna
late Gothic style
Flamboyant style
Perpendicular style
fan vaulting
campanile

woodcut print
engraving
drypoint
Italo-Byzantine style
perspective
chanson
ars nova
isorhythm
syncopation

QUESTIONS FOR CRITICAL THINKING

1. The word *crisis* often comes up in discussions of the late Middle Ages. How does it apply?

2. How do the philosophy and theology of the late Middle Ages differ from those of the High Middle Ages?

3. In what respects might Petrarch and Boccaccio be called medieval, and how did they break with medieval precedents?

4. What are the essential characteristics of late Gothic architecture?

5. What is new in the paintings of Jan van Eyck and Hans Memling?

11

THE EARLY RENAISSANCE
Return to Classical Roots

1400–1494

Since the nineteenth century, it has been customary to refer to the period from about 1300 to 1550 as "the **Renaissance**" (from a French word meaning "rebirth"). In *that* understanding, the age looked back to the medieval past for inspiration. Viewed as a *rebirth*, the period looks back to classical antiquity and also seems to anticipate what came next, to inaugurate the modern world. The Renaissance was a process, not an event. Accordingly, Chapter 10 opened the discussion by looking at Petrarch and Boccaccio and Chapter 12 will look at the grand culmination of the Renaissance.

THE RENAISSANCE: SCHOOLS OF INTERPRETATION

In 1860 the Swiss historian Jacob Burckhardt published his masterpiece *The Civilization of the Renaissance in Italy*. By emphasizing the themes of individualism, humanism, and classicism, Burckhardt attempted to capture the spirit of the Renaissance period as a whole in all its aspects. He believed that the Renaissance had liberated individuals from their medieval shackles, that art should be seen as a key expression of life and not merely as an aesthetic achievement, and that classical humanism, far from being an elitist and antiquarian exercise, changed people and states for the better. Decades later, the influential art historian Erwin Panofsky said that people in the Renaissance "look back as from a fixed point in time." They believed they were different from their medieval predecessors and more like the people of Greek and Roman antiquity, whom they sought to emulate. Curiously, then, Renaissance figures made something new out of their encounter with something old.

◀ **Detail** DONATELLO. *David.* Ca. 1430–1432. Bronze, ht. 62¼". Bargello, Florence.

Timeline 11.1 STAGES OF THE ITALIAN RENAISSANCE

1400		1494	1520	1600
Early Renaissance		High Renaissance	Late Renaissance	

Today it is generally conceded that the late medieval, or Renaissance, centuries achieved few innovations in government or the economy. The church, beset by turmoil, was criticized but remained a powerful force. Ironically, despite humanism and classicism, many great Renaissance buildings were churches, many churchmen patronized artists, and religious subjects still provided the majority of artistic themes. Intellectual and artistic life unquestionably took some steps forward. But Renaissance novelty emerged from a subtle blending of the forces of continuity and change (Timeline 11.1).

EARLY RENAISSANCE HISTORY AND INSTITUTIONS

Two great themes dominated the history of Italy during the fifteenth century. One of these was the intense and destructive, but sometimes creative, competition among several Italian powers. The other was a series of international developments that had mainly negative consequences in Italy. It is intriguing to think that Italy's spectacular cultural achievements took place amid war, political strife, and economic upheaval.

Italian City-States during the Early Renaissance

During the early Renaissance, five Italian states competed for dominance: the Republic of Venice, the Duchy of Milan, the Republic of Florence, the Papal States, and the Kingdom of Naples (Map 11.1). Other small states, such as the artistic and intellectual centers of Ferrara and Modena, played minor but occasionally crucial roles. In the first half of the fifteenth century, the Italian states waged incessant wars among themselves, shifting sides when it was to their advantage.

The continuous warfare, against a background of economic uncertainty, provided the conditions for the emergence of autocratic rulers called *signori*, who arose from prominent families or popular factions. Taking advantage of economic and class tensions, these autocrats pledged to solve local problems, and in so do-

ing they proceeded to accumulate power in their own hands. What influence the guilds, the business leaders, and the middle class had wielded in the thirteenth and fourteenth centuries gave way to these despots, ending the great medieval legacy of republicanism in Venice, Milan, and Florence.

Under the *signori,* the conduct of warfare also changed. Technological developments improved weaponry, and battles were fought with mercenary troops led by *condottieri,* soldiers of fortune who sold their military expertise to the highest bidder. But the most significant change in Renaissance warfare was the emergence of diplomacy as a peaceful alternative to arms, a practice that gradually spread throughout the Continent. The Italian regimes began sending representatives to other states, and it soon became customary for these diplomats to negotiate peace settlements. In turbulent fifteenth-century Italy, these agreements seldom lasted long—with the notable exception of the Peace of Lodi. This defensive pact, signed in 1454 by Milan, Florence, and Venice, established a delicate balance of power and ensured peace in Italy for forty years.

Before the Italian city-states were eclipsed by other European powers, however, upper-class families enjoyed unprecedented wealth, which they used to cultivate their tastes in literature and art and thus substantially determine the culture of the early Renaissance (Figure 11.1). One reason for the importance these families gave to cultural matters is that they put high value on family prestige and on educating their sons for their predestined roles as heads of family businesses and their daughters as loyal wives and successful household managers (Figure 11.2). The courts of the local rulers, or *grandi,* became places where educated men—and, on occasion, women—could exchange ideas and discuss philosophical issues.

Although the status of women did not improve appreciably, more were educated than ever before. Many ended up behind the walls of a convent, however, if their parents could not afford the costly dowry expected of an upper-class bride. The few upper-class women with an independent role in society were those who had been widowed young. The women at the ducal courts who exercised any political influence did so because of their family alliances. One of the

LEARNING THROUGH MAPS

Map 11.1   THE STATES OF ITALY DURING THE RENAISSANCE, CA. 1494
This map shows the many states and principalities of Italy in the early Renaissance. 1. *Consider* how the size of each state affected its role in competing for dominance of the Italian peninsula. 2. *Notice* the large number of states in the north as compared with the small number in the south. 3. *Notice* also the four forms of government—duchy, republic, kingdom, and papal states. 4. *Identify* the major ports of the Italian state system. 5. *What* geographic advantage made the Papal States such a force in Italian politics?

most powerful of these women was Lucrezia Borgia [loo-KRET-syah BOR-juh] (1480–1519), the illegitimate daughter of Pope Alexander VI. Married three times before the age of twenty-one, she held court in Ferrara and was the patron of many writers and artists. Most women who tried to exercise real power, however, found it unattainable.

Florence, the Center of the Renaissance

Amid the artistic and intellectual centers throughout Italy, Florence, the capital of the Tuscan region, was the most prominent of the city-states. After 1300 Florence's political system went through three phases, evolving from republic to oligarchy to family rule. Despite political turmoil, however, Florentine artists and writers made their city-state the trendsetter of the early Renaissance (Timeline 11.2).

The republic, which began in the fourteenth century with hopes for political equality, fell into the hands of a wealthy oligarchy. This oligarchy, composed of rich bankers, merchants, and successful guildsmen

and craftsmen, ruled until the early fifteenth century, when the Medici family gained control. The Medicis dominated Florentine politics and cultural life from 1434 to 1494, sometimes functioning as despots.

The Medicis rose from modest circumstances. Giovanni di Bicci de' Medici [jo-VAHN-nee dee BEET-chee day MED-uh-chee] (1360–1429) amassed the family's first large fortune through banking and close financial ties with the papacy. His son Cosimo (1389–1464) added to the Medicis' wealth and outmaneuvered his political enemies, becoming the unacknowledged ruler of Florence. He spent his money on books, paintings, sculptures, and palaces, and, claiming to be the common man's friend, he was eventually awarded the title *Pater patriae*, Father of His Country—a Roman title revived during the Renaissance.

Cosimo's son, Piero, ruled for only a short time and was succeeded by his son Lorenzo (1449–1492), called the Magnificent because of his grand style of living. Lorenzo and his brother Giuliano controlled Florence until Giuliano was assassinated in 1478 by the Pazzi family, rivals of the Medicis. Lorenzo brutally executed the conspirators and then governed autocratically for

Figure 11.1   Pedro Berruguete (?). *Federico da Montefeltro and His Son Guidobaldo. Ca. 1476–1477. Oil on panel, 4'5⅛"* × 2'5⅞". Galleria Nazionale della Marche, Urbino. *Urbino, under the Montefeltro dynasty, was transformed from a sleepy hill town with no cultural history into a major center of Renaissance life. Federico, the founder of the dynasty and one of the greatest condottieri of his day, was named duke of Urbino and captain of the papal forces by Pope Sixtus IV in 1474. Federico then devoted his energies to making Urbino a model for Italian Renaissance courts. In this portrait, the seated Federico wears the armor of a papal officer while reading a book—symbols that established him as both a soldier and a scholar, later the ideal of Baldassare Castiglioni's (1478–1529) Courtier (1528). At the duke's right knee stands his son and heir, Guidobaldo, wearing an elaborate robe and holding a scepter, a symbol of power. Federico's dream ended with his son, the last of the Montefeltro line. At the Urbino court, artists combined Flemish and Italian styles, as in this double portrait. The internal lighting, emanating from some unseen source on the left, is adopted from the tradition pioneered by Jan van Eyck; the profile portrait of the duke follows the Italian practice, based on portrait heads rendered on medals. This double portrait was probably painted by Pedro Berruguete, Spain's first great Renaissance artist, who studied painting in Naples and worked briefly in Urbino before returning to his homeland.*

the next fourteen years. His brutality notwithstanding, in some years Lorenzo spent half of Florence's budget buying books.

Within two years of Lorenzo's death, the great power and prestige of Florence began to weaken and the buoyant spirit of the early Renaissance was eclipsed. Two events are symptomatic of this decline in Florence's spirit and authority. The first was the iconoclastic crusade against the city led by the Dominican monk Fra Savonarola [sav-uh-nuh-ROH-luh] (1452–1498). He opposed the Medicis' rule and wanted to restore a republican form of government. And he hated everything that the Renaissance stood for. In his fire-and-brimstone sermons, he denounced Florence's leaders and the city's infatuation with the arts. He eventually ran afoul of the papacy and was excommunicated and publicly executed, but not before he had had an enormous effect on the citizens—including the painter Botticelli, who is said to have burned some of his paintings while under the sway of Savonarola's reforming zeal. The second event was the destructive invasion of Italy by Charles VIII of France (r. 1483–1498) in 1494.

The Resurgent Papacy, 1450–1500

The Great Schism was ended by the Council of Constance in 1418, and a tattered Christendom reunited under a Roman pope (see Chapter 10). By 1447 the so-called Renaissance popes were in command and had turned their attention to consolidating the Papal States

and securing their interests among Italy's competing powers. Like the secular despots, these popes engaged in war and, when that failed, diplomacy. They brought artistic riches to the church but also lowered its moral tone by accepting bribes for church offices and filling positions with kinsmen. But above all, these popes patronized Renaissance culture.

Three of the most aggressive and successful of these popes were Nicholas V (pope 1447–1455), Pius II (pope 1458–1464), and Sixtus IV (pope 1471–1484). Nicholas V, who had been librarian for Cosimo de' Medici, founded the Vatican Library, an institution virtually unrivaled today for its holdings of manuscripts and books. He also continued the rebuilding of Rome be-

Timeline 11.2   THE EARLY RENAISSANCE IN FLORENCE, 1400–1494

1400							**1494**
Early Renaissance							

1403–1424	1425	1424–1452	1438–1445	1461	1473–1475	1480s	1483
Ghiberti's north doors, Florentine Baptistery	Invention of linear perspective (Brunelleschi)	Ghiberti's east doors, Florentine Baptistery	Fra Angelico's *Annunciation*	Completion of Pazzi Chapel by Brunelleschi	Verrocchio's *David*	Botticelli's *Primavera* and *The Birth of Venus*	Leonardo da Vinci's *The Virgin of the Rocks*
	1425–1428	1430–1432		1462			
	Masaccio's frescoes for Santa Maria Novella	Donatello's *David*		Founding of Platonic Academy, Florence			
		1435					
		Alberti's *On Painting*					

gun by his predecessors. Pius II, often considered the most representative of the Renaissance popes because of his interest in the Greek and Roman classics and authorship of poetry, rose rapidly through the ecclesiastical ranks. This clever politician practiced both war and diplomacy with astounding success. As a student of the new learning and as a brilliant writer in Latin, Pius II attracted intellectuals and artists to Rome. His personal recollections, or *Commentaries,* reveal much about him and his turbulent times. Sixtus IV came from a powerful family and increased his personal power through nepotism, the practice of giving offices to relatives. He continued the papal tradition of making Rome the most beautiful city in the world. The construction of the Sistine Chapel, later adorned with paintings by Botticelli, Perugini, and Michelangelo, was his greatest achievement (see Chapter 12).

Figure 11.2 DOMENICO GHIRLANDAIO. *Giovanna degli Albizzi Tornabuoni.* Ca. 1489–1490. Tempera and (?) oil on panel, 29½ × 19¼″. Madrid, Thyssen-Bornemisza Collection (cat. no. 46). *This likeness of Giovanna degli Albizzi Tornabuoni (1468–1486) embodies the Florentine ethos of family, city, and church. Her husband, Lorenzo Tornabuoni, a member of a prominent Florentine family, commissioned it as a memorial. Probably painted after his wife's death, it was much admired by Lorenzo, who, according to household records, kept it hanging in his bedroom, even after his remarriage. The subject's gold bodice is decorated with emblems—interlaced Ls and diamonds—which are symbolic of Lorenzo and his family. The brooch, the coral necklace, and the prayer book allude to Giovanna's high social status and piety. In the background, the Latin epigram "O Art, if thou were able to depict conduct and the soul, no lovelier painting would exist on earth" evokes the Renaissance ideal that equates physical beauty with moral perfection. It is based on a line from an ancient Roman poet.*

International Developments

For Italy, the chief consequence of Charles's invasion in 1494 was that it shattered the forty-year-old Peace of Lodi. Charles was pressing a somewhat dubious hereditary claim to the Kingdom of Naples, where he was crowned in 1495. His invasion of the north owed much to the connivance of the ruling family of Milan, the old enemies of Florence.

Outside Italy, three events further weakened the region's prospects for regaining its position as a major economic power: the fall of Constantinople in 1453, Portugal's opening of the sea route around Africa to India at the end of the century, and Columbus's Spanish-sponsored voyage to the New World. These events shifted the focus of international trade from the Mediterranean to the Atlantic. The fall of Constantinople to the Ottoman Turks in 1453 temporarily closed the eastern Mediterranean markets to the Italian city-states. At the same time, by virtue of the wide-ranging global explorations they sponsored, some European powers—most notably Portugal and Spain—were extending their political and economic interests beyond the geographic limits of continental Europe. Alone among Italian powers, the Venetians managed to negotiate the new realities.

THE SPIRIT AND STYLE OF THE EARLY RENAISSANCE

Drawing inspiration from ancient Greek and Roman models, the thinkers and the artists of the early Renaissance explored such perennial questions as, What is human nature? How are human beings related to God? and What is the best way to achieve human happiness? Although they did not reject Christian explanations outright, they were intrigued by the secular and humanistic values of the Greco-Roman tradition and the answers they might provide to these questions. They also rightfully claimed kinship with certain fourteenth-century predecessors such as the writer Petrarch and the artist Giotto (see Chapter 10).

Those artists, scholars, and writers who are identified with the early Renaissance and who embodied its spirit were linked, through shared tastes and patronage, with the entrepreneurial nobility, the progressive middle class, and the secular clergy. Until about 1450, most artistic works were commissioned by wealthy patrons for family chapels in churches and for public buildings; later, patrons commissioned paintings and sculptures for their private dwellings.

Even though artists, scholars, and writers stamped this age with their fresh perspectives, some of the old cultural traits remained. Unsettling secular values emerged in the midst of long-accepted religious beliefs, creating contradictions and tensions within the society. In other ways, however, the past held firm, and certain values seemed immune to change. For example, early Renaissance thought made little headway in science, and church patronage still strongly affected the evolution of the arts and architecture, despite the growing impact of the urban class on artistic tastes.

Humanism, Schooling, and Scholarship

Inspired by Petrarch's interest in Latin literature and language, scholars began to collect, copy, disseminate, and comment upon Roman texts uncovered in monastic and cathedral libraries. There was a shift in emphasis from the church Latin of the Middle Ages to the pure Latin style of Cicero, the first-century BCE Roman writer whose eloquent letters and essays established a high moral and literary standard (see Chapter 4). For centuries Greek works, if they were known at all, were read in Latin translations. Petrarch, who knew no Greek, sponsored a Latin translation of Homer. Gradually, however, the humanists studied Greek and began to acquire and study works in the original. Already in the 1300s, these scholars spoke of their literary interests and new learning as *studia humanitatis*. They coined this term, which may be translated as "humanistic studies," and we call them "humanists."

Humanism, as used in the Renaissance and even today, is a multifaceted term. It may imply a concern with the literary culture of Greco-Roman antiquity. And it may suggest an interest in the humane disciplines: history, rhetoric, poetry, philosophy, for example. And it may connote a tendency to look for natural as opposed to theological explanations. In response to the demand for humanistic learning, new schools sprang up in most Italian city-states. In these schools was born the Renaissance ideal of an education intended to free or to liberate the mind—a liberal education.

Coluccio Salutati (Kuh-LOOTCH-ee-o Sahl-u-TA-tee) (1331–1406), who was chancellor of Florence, founded and endowed many schools; Florence had no university. He himself wrote letters, orations, and histories praising his city's past. He took Cicero as his ideal, arguing that family life and public service, not penance and retreat from the world, should be held up as exemplary ideals. He also argued that the liberty of free, educated citizens created an environment in which people could flourish.

A little later, Guarino (Gwa-REE-no) of Verona (1374–1460) stressed the importance of learning Latin and Greek in their classical purity. He believed that

SLICE OF LIFE
Battle of the Sexes, Fifteenth-Century Style

LAURA CERETA
In Defense of the Education of Women

In this letter, dated January 13, 1488, eighteen-year-old Laura Cereta (1469–1499) responds fiercely to a male critic whose praise she finds patronizing to her as a woman. She then sets him straight about the intellectual needs of women of that time. There were a few women humanists, but the movement's participants were overwhelmingly male, as were their interests.

My ears are wearied by your carping. You brashly and publicly not merely wonder but indeed lament that I am said to possess as fine a mind as nature ever bestowed upon the most learned man. You seem to think that so learned a woman has scarcely before been seen in the world. You are wrong on both counts. . . .

I would have been silent, believe me, if that savage old enmity of yours had attacked me alone. . . . But I cannot tolerate your having attacked my entire sex. For this reason my thirsty soul seeks revenge, my sleeping pen is aroused to literary struggle, raging anger stirs mental passions long chained by silence. With just cause I am moved to demonstrate how great a reputation for learning and virtue women have won by their inborn excellence, manifested in every age as knowledge. . . .

Only the question of the rarity of outstanding women remains to be addressed. The explanation is clear: women have been able by nature to be exceptional, but have chosen lesser goals. For some women are concerned with parting their hair correctly, adorning themselves with lovely dresses, or decorating their fingers with pearls and other gems. Others delight in mouthing carefully composed phrases, indulging in dancing, or managing spoiled puppies. Still others wish to gaze at lavish banquet tables, to rest in sleep, or, standing at mirrors, to smear their lovely faces. But those in whom a deeper integrity yearns for virtue, restrain from the start their youthful souls, reflect on

higher things, harden the body with sobriety and trials, and curb their tongues, open their ears, compose their thoughts in wakeful hours, their minds in contemplation, to letters bonded to righteousness. For knowledge is not given as a gift, but [is gained] with diligence. The free mind, not shirking effort, always soars zealously toward the good, and the desire to know grows ever more wide and deep. It is because of no special holiness, therefore, that we [women] are rewarded by God the Giver with the gift of exceptional talent. Nature has generously lavished its gifts upon all people, opening to all the doors of choice through which reason sends envoys to the will, from which they learn and convey its desires. The will must choose to exercise the gift of reason. . . .

I have been praised too much; showing your contempt for women, you pretend that I alone am admirable because of the good fortune of my intellect. . . . Do you suppose, O most contemptible man on earth, that I think myself sprung [like Athena] from the head of Jove? I am a school girl, possessed of the sleeping embers of an ordinary mind. Indeed I am too hurt, and my mind, offended, too swayed by passions, sighs, tormenting itself, conscious of the obligation to defend my sex. For absolutely everything—that which is within us and that which is without—is made weak by association with my sex.

INTERPRETING THIS SLICE OF LIFE

1. *Describe* the ways Cereta responds to her critic.
2. *What* are some of the types of women she lists?
3. *How* does she portray herself? 4. According to Cereta, *what* are some of the talents God has given to women? 5. *Compare and contrast* Cereta's arguments with those used by modern feminists.

constant reading of and reflection on classical texts would inculcate their values in modern people. He also emphasized the importance of rhetoric, the art of speaking elegantly and persuasively, as opposed to the stress on logic and grammar that had dominated in the Middle Ages.

Finally, Vittorino da Feltre [veet-toe-REE-no dah FEL-tray] (1378–1446) made the most significant contributions. Vittorino favored a curriculum that exercised the body and the mind—the ideal of the ancient Greek

schools. His educational theories were put into practice at the school he founded in Mantua at the ruler's request. At this school, called the Happy House, Vittorino included humanistic studies along with the medieval curriculum. A major innovation was the stress on physical exercise, which arose from his emphasis on moral training. At first, only the sons and daughters of Mantuan nobility attended his school, but gradually the student body became more democratic as young people from all social classes were enrolled. Vittorino's reforms were slowly introduced into the new urban schools in northern Europe, and their model—the well-rounded student of sound body, solid learning, and high morals—helped to lay the foundation for future European schools and education.

Two products of this educational program will serve to illustrate its many effects. Leonardo Bruni (1374–1444) typifies the practical, civic humanist—the kind of man who believed that properly educated individuals would make for a better civic community. A one-time chancellor, or chief secretary, of Florence's governing body, or *signoria*, Bruni also worked for both the Medicis and the papacy and wrote *History of the Florentine People*. This work reflected his humanistic values, combining as it did his political experience with his knowledge of ancient history. To Bruni, the study of history illuminated contemporary events. Bruni and the other civic humanists, through their writings and their governmental service, set an example for later generations of Florentines and helped infuse them with love of their city. Moreover, by expanding the concept of humanistic studies, they contributed new insights to the ongoing debate about the role of the individual in history and in the social order. The textual and linguistic interests of the humanists met to perfection in Lorenzo Valla (1406–1457)—the second product of Vittorino's educational program. Valla exposed the Donation of Constantine as a forgery by noting that its vocabulary and grammar could not date from the fourth century. Occasionally during the Middle Ages, this famous document, probably written in the eighth century, had been cited by the popes as proof of their political authority over Christendom. Supposedly, the Roman emperor Constantine, after he departed for Constantinople, gave the popes his western lands and recognized their power to rule in them.

Thought and Philosophy

The Italian humanists were not satisfied with medieval answers to the perennial inquiries of philosophy because those answers did not go beyond Aristotelian philosophy and Christian dogma. Casting their scholarly nets wider, Renaissance thinkers fell under the influence of a richer array of ancient authors than had been known in the Middle Ages. Some Renaissance scholars advocated a more tolerant attitude toward unorthodox religious and philosophical beliefs than in the past. A few Renaissance thinkers began to stress individual fulfillment instead of social or religious conformity. During the Renaissance, a growing emphasis on the individual resulted in a more optimistic assessment of human nature and capability—a development that led to a diminution of Christianity's stress on human sinfulness and weakness.

Beginning in the late 1300s, a small number of Byzantine scholars, living and working in Rome, Florence, and Venice, added an important new dimension to the Renaissance. As teachers of Greek, these scholars introduced Italy's first generation of humanists to many ancient works not seen in the West for nearly a thousand years. Then, in 1453, with the fall of Constantinople to the Ottoman Turks, a fresh wave of Byzantine scholars, teachers, and intellectuals arrived in Italy, bearing countless manuscripts (see Encounter in Chapter 10). Thereafter, the humanists began to focus increasingly on Greek language, literature, and, eventually, philosophy. The philosophy of Plato found a home in Italy in 1462 when Cosimo de' Medici established the Platonic Academy at one of his villas near Florence. Here, scholars gathered to examine and to discuss the writings of Plato as well as those of the Neoplatonists, as Plato's followers in late antiquity are called. The academy was under the direction of the brilliant humanist Marsilio Ficino [mar-SILL-e-o fe-CHEE-no] (1433–1499), whom Cosimo commissioned to translate Plato's works into Latin.

In two major treatises, Ficino made himself the leading voice of Florentine Neoplatonism by harmonizing Platonic ideas with Christian teachings. Believing that Platonism came from God, Ficino began with the principle that both thought systems rested on divine authority. Like Plato, Ficino believed that the soul was immortal and that complete enjoyment of God would be possible only in the afterlife, when the soul was in the divine realm. Ficino also revived the Platonic notion of free will—the power of humans to make of themselves what they wish. In Ficino's hands, free will became the source of human dignity because human beings were able to choose to love God or to reject him.

Ficino had the most powerful impact on the early Renaissance when he made Plato's teaching on love central to Neoplatonism. Following Platonism, he taught that love is a divine gift that binds all human beings together. Love expresses itself in human experience by the desire for and the appreciation of beauty in its myriad forms. Platonic love, like erotic love, is aroused first by the physical appearance of the beloved. But Platonic love, dissatisfied by mere physical enjoyment, cannot rest until it moves upward to the highest spiritual level, where it finally meets its goal of union with the Divine. Under the promptings of Platonism, the human form became a metaphor of the soul's desire for God. Many Renaissance writers and artists came under the influence of Ficino's Neoplatonism, embracing its principles and embodying them in their works. Sandro Botticelli (baht-tuh-CHEL-lee) (1445–1510), for

Figure 11.3 SANDRO BOTTICELLI. *The Birth of Venus.* 1480s. Tempera on canvas, 5′8″ ×
9′1″. Uffizi Gallery, Florence. *With the paintings of Botticelli, the nude female form reappeared
in Western art for the first time since the Greco-Roman period. Botticelli's* Venus *contains
many classical echoes, such as the goddess's lovely features and her modest pose. But the artist
used these pre-Christian images to convey a Christian message and to embody the principles of
Ficino's Neoplatonist philosophy.*

example, created several allegorical paintings in which
divine love and beauty are represented by an image
from pre-Christian Rome—Venus—the goddess of love
(Figure 11.3).

Ficino's most talented student, Pico della Mirandola [PEE-koh DELL-lah me-RAHN-do-lah] (1463–
1494), surpassed his master's accomplishments by the
breadth of his learning and the virtuosity of his mind.
Pico—a wealthy and charming aristocrat—impressed
everyone with his command of languages, his range of
knowledge, and his spirited arguments. His goal was
the synthesis of Platonism and Aristotelianism within
a Christian framework that also encompassed Jewish, Arab, and Persian ideas. Church authorities and
traditional scholars attacked Pico's efforts once they
grasped the implication of his ambitious project—that

all knowledge shares basic common truths and that
Christians could benefit from studying non-Western,
non-Christian writings.

Pico's second important contribution—the concept of individual worth—had been foreshadowed by
Ficino. Pico's *Oration on the Dignity of Man* gives the
highest expression to this idea, which is inherent in
the humanist tradition. According to Pico, human beings, endowed with reason and speech, are created as
a microcosm of the universe. Set at the midpoint in
the scale of God's creatures, they are blessed with free
will, which enables them either to raise themselves to
God or to sink lower than the beasts. This liberty to
determine private fate makes human beings the masters of their individual destinies and, at the same time,
focuses attention on each human being as the measure

ENCOUNTER

The Influence of Islam on the European Renaissance

Christian Europe and the Islamic world, despite mutually antagonistic religions, did engage in artistic borrowings in the period from 1300 to 1600. These borrowings, though modest for both cultures, were stronger and more enduring in Christian Europe, where Islamic influences helped give shape to the visual and decorative arts in the Renaissance, then in full flower.

During the early Italian Renaissance, Europe and Islam were locked in a centuries-old struggle. For Christian Europe, Islam was a false faith, whose leaders had unjustly conquered lands, such as Spain and the Holy Land. For Islam, Christian Europe was the home of the infidel who refused to accept Muhammad's revelation.

Trade offered the best opportunity for cultural interchange, given Europe's taste for Islam's luxury goods. Each culture acquired prized objects from the other which, in turn, inspired artistic exchanges between Islam and Europe. Venice led the way, followed by other Italian cities, along with Sicily and southern Italy. These commercial centers imported textiles—silks, embroidered cloth, carpets—metalwork, and other luxury goods from the Ottoman Empire (after 1453), Egypt, Syria, Iraq, and Persia.

Islamic goods slowly changed the personal style of Europe's powerful and rich. For example, in 1003, Pope Sylvester II (pope 999–1003) was buried in a shroud made of Persian silk cloth. Islamic ceramic and metal-

work goods became prestige objects, serving ritual purposes in churches and denoting the social aspirations of those who displayed them in their homes. The floors of royal and noble courts, along with those of wealthy households, shifted from rush matting to woven carpets, especially in the Turkish and Persian styles. Carpets also were used as table covers and wall hangings.

As Islamic luxury goods grew in popularity, Europe's decorative arts began to imitate them. In ceramics, southern Italian artisans copied Islamic models and motifs, such as geometric patterns, arabesques, and calligraphy that imitated Arabic writing. Venetian guildsmen imitated Ottoman models and designs in metalwork, varnished ware, and saddle decoration.

In the visual arts, painters began to incorporate motifs and design features from Islamic imported goods into both their secular and religious works—as symbols of opulence and high status. Italian painters started this trend, in the early 1300s, introducing images of carpets and some decorative motifs and patterns into their works. Others followed: For example, Hans Memling, in his painting *Madonna and Child with Angels,* depicts the Virgin and baby Christ, enthroned, with a Turkish carpet, identified as a "wheel carpet," placed before them (see Figure 10.22).

Islam's borrowing from the West was more limited, confined to a few luxury goods, such as textiles, in-

of all things—a classical belief now reborn. Yet Pico's magnificent *Oration* begins as a commentary on Psalm 8: "What is man that thou art mindful of him?"

Architecture, Sculpture, and Painting

It was in architecture, sculpture, and painting that the Renaissance made its most dramatic breaks with the medieval past. The **early Renaissance style** was launched in Florence by artists who rejected the excesses of the late Gothic style (compare Figures 11.4 and 10.7). Led by the architect Filippo Brunelleschi [brun-uh-LESS-kee] (1377–1446), this group studied the ruins of classical buildings and ancient works of sculpture to unlock the secrets of their harmonious style. They believed that once the classical ideals were rescued from obscurity, new works could be fashioned that captured the spirit of ancient art and architecture without slavishly copying it.

ARTISTIC IDEALS AND INNOVATIONS   Inspired by Brunelleschi's achievement, architects, sculptors, and painters made the classical principles of balance, simplicity, and restraint the central ideals of the early Renaissance style. Sculpture and painting, freed from their subordination to architecture, regained their ancient status as independent art forms and in time became the most cherished of the visual arts. Renaissance sculptors and painters aspired to greater realism than had been achieved in the Gothic style, seeking to depict human musculature and anatomy with a greater degree of credibility. Whereas architecture and sculpture looked back to ancient Greek and Roman traditions, developments in painting grew from varied sources, including the Islamic world (see Encounter) and the late medieval world, though the most important inspiration was the art of the Florentine painter Giotto.

Two technical innovations—linear and atmospheric or aerial perspective—forever changed painting and,

Encounter figure 11.1 GENTILE BELLINI. *Mehmet II.* Ca. 1480. Oil on canvas, 27¾ × 20⅝". National Gallery, London. *Bellini's commission for this portrait grew out of a diplomatic exchange between Venice and the Ottoman Empire. As a condition of making peace with Venice after a war, the sultan requested that a Venetian portrait painter be sent to his court. Bellini's portrait blends Western technique—the oil medium, the seated subject in profile, and the perspective—with Islamic touches—the rounded arch with an elaborate design, the sumptuous fabric draped over the balustrade, the turban and fur-lined robe, and the black background.*

cluding velvets and cloths with gold and silver threads and pearls, from Florence, and undecorated glass, from Venice, to be finished with Islamic designs. However, one outstanding interchange between Islam and the West did occur during this time: the portrait of the Ottoman sultan who conquered Constantinople, Mehmet II (r. 1444–1446 and 1451–1481), painted in about 1480 by the Venetian artist Gentile Bellini (Encounter figure 11.1). Knowledge of the Renaissance art style was little known in Islam. Therefore, this portrait is a landmark, because it introduced Western perspective to the Ottoman court and its workshop of miniature painters.

LEARNING FROM THE ENCOUNTER

1. *Why* did Europe and Islam hold negative images of each other during the European Renaissance? 2. *Compare and contrast* the economies of Europe and the Islamic world between 1300 and 1600. 3. *Summarize* the influence of Islam on Europe during the Renaissance.

4. *What* impact did the West have on Islam during the Renaissance? 5. *Discuss* the interaction between the West and the Islamic world today.

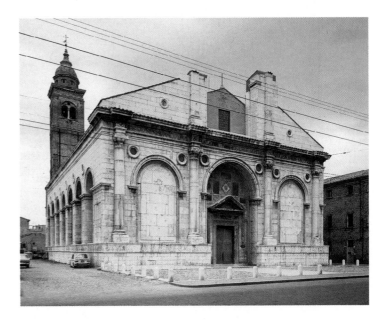

Figure 11.4 LEONE BATTISTA ALBERTI. Tempio Malatestiano (Malatesta Temple) (Church of San Francesco). Ca. 1450. Rimini, Italy. *Although unfinished, this church strikingly demonstrates the revolution in architecture represented by early Renaissance ideals. Nothing could be further from the spires of late Gothic cathedrals than this simple, symmetrical structure with its plain facade, post-and-lintel entrance, rounded arches, and classical columns. Designed by the leading theoretician of the new style, the Malatesta Temple served as a model for artists and architects of the later Renaissance.*

to a degree, architecture and sculpture too. The invention of linear perspective was another of Brunelleschi's accomplishments. Using principles of architecture and optics, he conducted experiments in 1425 that provided the mathematical basis for achieving the illusion of depth on a two-dimensional surface (and, coincidentally, contributed to the enhancement of the status of the arts by grounding them in scholarly learning). Brunelleschi's solution to the problem of linear perspective was to organize the picture space around the center point, or **vanishing point.** After determining the painting's vanishing point, he devised a structural grid for placing objects in precise relation to each other within the picture space. He also computed the ratios by which objects diminish in size as they recede from view, so that pictorial reality seems to correspond visually with physical accuracy. He then subjected the design to a mirror test—checking its truthfulness in its reflected image. Pietro Perugino's (pair-oo-GEE-no) (about 1450–1524) *Christ Giving the Keys to St. Peter* is a splendid example of the new technique (Figure 11.5).

When the camera appeared in the nineteenth century, it was discovered that the photographic lens "saw" nature according to Brunelleschi's mathematical rules. After the 1420s, Brunelleschi's studies led to the concept of Renaissance space, the notion that a composition should be viewed from one single position. For four hundred years, or until first challenged by Manet in the nineteenth century, linear perspective and Renaissance space played a leading role in Western painting (see Chapter 18).

Atmospheric, or aerial, perspective was perfected by painters north of the Alps in the first half of the fifteenth century, although the Italian painter Masac-

Figure 11.5 Pietro Perugino. *Christ Giving the Keys to St. Peter.* 1480–1482. Fresco. North Wall, Sistine Chapel, Vatican City. *Pope Sixtus IV renovated an old chapel—now known after him as "Sistine"—between 1477 and 1480. He attracted many of the best painters of the day to execute frescoes for the side walls. They were first to make preliminary frescoes to see if their work and subject matter was satisfactory. By early 1482, it was clear that the works were in fact excellent. Perugino took as his theme a topic of great ideological interest to the papacy, namely the "Petrine Text" (Matthew 16:16–18; see Chapter 6). Perugino not only displays virtuosity in his ostentatious use of linear perspective, but he combines this with ideological, theological, and historical perspectives. Christ tells Peter he is the rock on which the church will be built. So here the church is directly above Peter. The church itself stands between two triumphal arches inspired by the Arch of Constantine (see Figure 6.15). The church has triumphed over the state, it seems. The vast expanse of the background suggests that Peter's authority, conferred by Christ, is limitless.*

cio was the first to revive atmospheric perspective in the 1420s, based on the Roman tradition. Through the use of colors, these artists created an illusion of depth by subtly diminishing the tones as the distance between the eye and the object increased; at the horizon line, the colors become grayish and the objects blurry in appearance. When atmospheric perspective was joined to linear perspective, as happened later in the century, a greater illusion of reality was achieved than was possible with either type used independently.

Leone Battista Alberti (ahl-BAIR-tee) (1404–1472) published a treatise in 1435 that elaborated on the mathematical aspects of painting and set forth brilliantly the humanistic and secular values of the early Renaissance. Alberti was an aristocratic humanist with a deep knowledge of classicism and a commitment to its ideals. In his treatise, he praised master painters in rousing terms, comparing their creativity to God's—a notion that would have been considered blasphemous by medieval thinkers. He asserted that paintings, in addition to pleasing the eye, should appeal to the mind with optical and mathematical accuracy. But paintings, he went on, should also present a noble subject, such as a classical hero, and should be characterized by a small number of figures, by carefully observed and varied details, by graceful poses, by harmonious relationships among all elements, and by a judicious use of colors. These classical ideals were quickly adopted by Florentine artists eager to establish a new aesthetic code.

ARCHITECTURE   The heaviest debt to the past was owed by the architects, for they revived the classical orders—Doric, Ionic, and Corinthian. The new buildings, though constructed to accommodate modern needs, were symmetrical in plan and relied on simple decorative designs. The theoretician of early Renaissance style was Alberti, who wrote at length on Brunelleschi's innovations. Alberti believed that architecture should embody the humanistic qualities of dignity, balance, control, and harmony and that a building's ultimate beauty rests on the mathematical harmony of its separate parts.

In the High Middle Ages, most architects were stonemasons and were regarded as artisans, like shoemakers or potters. But by the fifteenth century, the status of architects had changed. Because of the newly discovered scientific aspects of their craft, the leading architects were now grouped with those practicing the learned professions of medicine and law. By 1450 Italian architects had freed architecture from late Gothicism, as well as from the other arts. Unlike Gothic cathedrals adorned with sculptures and paintings, these new buildings drew on the classical tradition for decorative details. That is, Renaissance architects revived the practice of using simple architectural el-

ements as parts of a building's decoration but not of its structure (see Figure 11.8 and compare Figure 6.12). This transformation became the most visible symbol of early Renaissance architecture.

Although Brunelleschi established the new standards in architecture, most of his buildings have been either destroyed or altered considerably by later hands. However, the earliest work to bring him fame still survives in Florence largely as he had planned it—the dome of the city's cathedral (Figure 11.6). Although the rest of the cathedral—nave, transept, and choir—was finished before 1400, no one had been able to devise a method for erecting the projected dome until Brunelleschi received the commission in 1420. Using the learning he had gained from his researches in Rome as well as his knowledge of Gothic building styles, he developed an ingenious plan for raising the dome, which was virtually completed in 1436.

Faced with a domical base of 140 feet, Brunelleschi realized that a hemispheric dome in the Roman manner, like the dome of the Pantheon, would not work

Figure 11.6 FILIPPO BRUNELLESCHI. Cathedral Dome, Florence. 1420–1436. Ht. of dome from floor 367'. *After the dome of the Florence cathedral was erected according to Brunelleschi's plan, another architect was employed to add small galleries in the area above the circular windows. But the Florentine authorities halted his work before the galleries were fully installed, leaving the structure in its present state.*

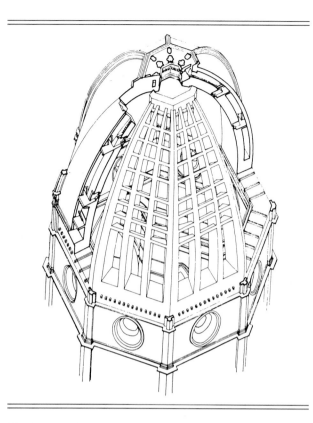

Figure 11.7 FILIPPO BRUNELLESCHI. Design for Construction of Dome of Florence Cathedral. *Brunelleschi designed the dome of the Florence cathedral with an inner and an outer shell, both of which are attached to the eight ribs of the octagonal-shaped structure. Sixteen smaller ribs, invisible from the outside, were placed between the shells to give added support. What held these elements together and gave them stability was the lantern, based on his design, that was anchored to the dome's top sometime after 1446.*

Figure 11.8 FILIPPO BRUNELLESCHI AND OTHERS. Exterior, Pazzi Chapel, Santa Croce Church. 1433–1461. Florence. *The Pazzi Chapel's harmonious facade reflects the classical principles of the early Renaissance style: symmetry and simplicity. By breaking the rhythm of the facade with the rounded arch, the architect emphasizes its surface symmetry so that the left side is a mirror image of the right side. Simplicity is achieved in the architectural decorations, which are either Greco-Roman devices or mathematically inspired divisions.*

(see Figure 6.10). Traditional building techniques could not span the Florentine cathedral's vast domical base, nor could the cathedral's walls be buttressed to support a massive dome. So he turned to Gothic methods, using diagonal ribs based on the pointed arch. This innovative dome had a double shell of two relatively thin walls held together by twenty-four stone ribs, of which only eight are visible. His crowning touch was to add a lantern that sits atop the dome and locks the ribs into place (Figure 11.7). The dome's rounded windows echo the openings in the upper nave walls, thereby ensuring that his addition would harmonize with the existing elements. But the octagonal-shaped dome was Brunelleschi's own creation and expresses a logical, even inevitable, structure. Today, the cathedral still dominates the skyline of Florence, a lasting symbol of Brunelleschi's creative genius.

Brunelleschi's most representative building is the Pazzi Chapel, as the chapter house, or meeting room,

of the friars of Santa Croce is called. This small church embodies the harmonious proportions and classical features that are the hallmark of the early Renaissance style. In his architectural plan, Brunelleschi centered a dome over an oblong area whose width equals the dome's diameter and whose length is twice its width and then covered each of the chapel's elongated ends with a barrel vault. Double doors opened into the center wall on one long side, and two rounded arch windows flanked this doorway. A loggia [LOH-je-uh], or open porch, which Brunelleschi may not have designed, preceded the entrance (Figure 11.8). Inside the chapel, following the classical rules of measure and proportion, Brunelleschi employed medallions, rosettes, **pilasters** (or applied columns), and square panels. In addition to these classical architectural details, the rounded arches and the barrel vaults further exemplify the new Renaissance style (Figure 11.9). His classical theories were shared by Florence's humanist

Figure 11.9 FILIPPO BRUNELLESCHI. Interior. Pazzi Chapel, Santa Croce Church. Ca. 1433–1461. 59'9" long × 35'8" wide. Florence. *Decorations on the white walls of the Pazzi Chapel's interior break up its plain surface and draw the viewer's eye to the architectural structure: pilasters, window and panel frames, medallions, capitals, and dome ribs. The only nonarchitecturally related decorations are the terra-cotta sculptures by Luca della Robbia (1399/1400–1482) of the four evangelists and the Pazzi family coat of arms, mounted below the medallions.*

elite, who found religious significance in mathematical harmony. Both they and Brunelleschi believed that a well-ordered building such as the Pazzi Chapel mirrors God's plan of the universe.

The other towering figure in early Renaissance architecture was Alberti. Despite the influence of his ideas, which dominated architecture until 1600, no completed building based on his design remains. A splendid unfinished effort is the Tempio Malatestiano in Rimini (see Figure 11.4), a structure that replaced the existing church of San Francesco. Rimini's despot, Sigismondo Malatesta (1417–1468), planned to have himself, his mistress, and his courtiers buried in the refurbished structure, and he appointed Alberti to supervise the church's reconstruction.

Alberti's monument represents the first modern attempt to give a classical exterior to a church. Abandoning the Gothic pointed arch, Alberti designed this church's unfinished facade with its three rounded arches after a nearby triumphal arch. He framed the arches with Corinthian columns, one of his favorite decorative devices. Although the architect apparently planned to cover the church's interior with a dome comparable to Brunelleschi's on the Florentine cathedral, Malatesta's fortunes failed, and the projected temple had to be abandoned. Nevertheless, Alberti's unfinished church was admired by later builders and helped to point the way to the new Renaissance architecture.

SCULPTURE   Like architecture, sculpture blossomed in Florence in the early 1400s. Sculptors, led by this period's genius, Donatello [dah-nah-TEL-lo] (about 1386–1466), revived classical practices that had not been seen in the West for more than a thousand years: the free-standing figure; the technique of contrapposto, or a figure balanced with most of the weight resting on one leg (see Figure 3.21); the life-size nude statue; and the equestrian statue. Donatello was imbued with classical ideals but obsessed with realism. He used a variety of techniques—expressive gestures, direct observation, and mathematical precision—to reproduce what his eyes saw. Donatello accompanied Brunelleschi to Rome to study ancient art, and he adapted linear perspective as early as 1425 into a small **relief**—figures carved to project from a flat surface—called *The Feast of Herod* (Figure 11.10). The subject is the tragic end of John the Baptist, Florence's patron saint, as recounted in Mark 6:20–29. In Donatello's square bronze panel, the saint's severed head is being displayed on a dish to King Herod at the left, while the scorned Salome stands near the right end of the table. A puzzled guest leans toward the ruler, who recoils with upraised hands; two children, at the left, withdraw from the bloody head; and a diner leans back from the center of the table—all depicted under the rounded arches of the new Brunelleschian architecture. The sculpture's rich details and use of linear perspective point up the horror of the scene and thus

Figure 11.10   DONATELLO. *The Feast of Herod.* Ca. 1425. Gilt bronze, 23½" square. Baptismal font, San Giovanni, Siena. *The first low-relief sculpture executed in the early Renaissance style,* The Feast of Herod *is a stunning example of the power of this new approach to art. Its theatrical force arises from the successful use of linear perspective and the orderly placement of the figures throughout the three rooms.*

achieve the heightened realism that was among the artistic goals of this era. The scene's vanishing point runs through the middle set of arches, so that the leaning motions of the two figures in the foreground not only express their inner turmoil but also cause them to fall away from the viewer's line of sight.

Donatello also revived the freestanding male nude, one of the supreme expressions of ancient art. Donatello's bronze *David,* probably executed for Cosimo de' Medici, portrays David standing with his left foot on the severed head of the Philistine warrior Goliath—a pose based on the biblical story (Figure 11.11). This sculpture had a profound influence on later sculptors, who admired Donatello's creation but produced rival interpretations of David (Figure 11.12). Donatello and his successors used the image of David to pay homage to male power—a major preoccupation of Renaissance artists and intellectuals.

Like other Renaissance masters, Donatello owed debts to classical artists, but he also challenged them by adapting their principles to his own times. For example, the Roman statue of Marcus Aurelius (see Figure 6.5) inspired Donatello's bronze called the *Gattamelata,* the first successful equestrian sculpture in over twelve hundred years (Figure 11.13). As Donatello's *David* portrays the subtleties of adolescent male beauty, his *Gattamelata* pays homage to mature masculine power. This work honored the memory of Erasmo da Narni, a Venetian *condottiere* nicknamed Gattamelata, or "Honey Cat." The warrior's pose resembles the Roman imperial style, but, in almost every other way, the sculptor violates the harmonious ideas of ancient art.

Most significant, the rider's face owes its sharp realism—firm jawline, bushy eyebrows, widely set eyes, and close-cropped hair—to fifteenth-century sources, especially to the cult of the ugly, an aesthetic attitude that claimed to find moral strength in coarse features that did not conform to the classical ideals (Figure 11.14). Since this work was commissioned after the hero's death and since Donatello had no way of knowing how the soldier looked, he sculptured the face to conform to his notion of a strong-minded general. The massive horse, with flaring nostrils, open mouth, and lifted foreleg, seems to be an extension of the soldier's forceful personality.

The only serious rival to Donatello in the early Renaissance was another Florentine, Lorenzo Ghiberti [gee-BAIR-tee] (about 1381–1455), who slowly adapted to the new style of art. In 1401 he defeated Brunelleschi in a competition to select a sculptor for the north doors of Florence's Baptistery. The north doors consist of twenty-eight panels, arranged in four columns of seven panels, each depicting a New Testament scene. These doors, completed between 1403 and 1424, show Ghiberti still under the influence of the International

Figure 11.11 DONATELLO. *David.* Ca. 1430–1432. Bronze, ht. 62¼". Bargello, Florence. *The David and Goliath story was often allegorized into a prophecy of Christ's triumph over Satan. But Donatello's sculpture undermines such an interpretation, for his* David *is less a heroic figure than a provocative image of refined sensuality, as suggested by the undeveloped but elegant body, the dandified pose, and the incongruous boots and hat. Donatello's* David *is a splendid modern portrayal of youthful male power, self-aware and poised on the brink of manhood.*

Figure 11.13 Donatello. *Equestrian Monument of Erasmo da Narni, Called "Gattamelata."* 1447–1453. Bronze, approx. 11 × 13′. Piazza del Santo, Padua. *This equestrian statue of the condottiere was funded by his family but authorized by a grateful Venetian senate in honor of his military exploits. Conceiving of the dead military leader as a "triumphant Caesar," Donatello dressed him in classical costume and decorated his saddle and armor with many allusions to antique art, such as flying cupids and victory depicted as a goddess.*

Figure 11.12 Andrea del Verrocchio. *David.* 1473–1475. Bronze, ht. 4′2″. Bargello, Florence. *Verrocchio's* David *inaugurated the tradition in Renaissance Florence of identifying the Jewish giant-killer with the city's freedom-loving spirit. A masterpiece of bravado, Verrocchio's boyish hero stands challengingly over the severed head of Goliath. In its virility, this work surpasses the sculpture that inspired it, Donatello's* David *(see Figure 11.11). Florence's ruling council liked Verrocchio's statue so much that they placed it in the Palazzo Vecchio, the seat of government, where it remained until Michelangelo's* David *(see Figure 12.19) displaced it. Verrochio's* David *was restored in 2003, bringing back to the original the gold patina in the locks of hair, the borders of the clothes and boots, and the pupils of the eyes. With the restoration of the gold leaf gilding, restorers have concluded that the statue originally was intended for display indoors.*

Figure 11.14   DONATELLO. Detail of *"Gattamelata."* 1447–1453. Piazza del Santo, Padua. *Donatello deliberately designed the monument's stern, deeply lined face to conform to the Renaissance ideal of a strong military commander.*

Gothic style that prevailed in about 1400. Illustrative of this tendency is the panel *The Annunciation* (Luke 1: 26–38), which depicts the moment when Mary learns from an angelic messenger that she will become the mother of Christ (Figure 11.15). The Gothic quatrefoil, or four-leafed frame, was standard for these panels, and many of Ghiberti's techniques are typical of the Gothic style—the niche in which the Virgin stands, her swaying body, and the angel depicted in flight. Nevertheless, Ghiberti always exhibited a strong feeling for classical forms and harmony, as in the angel's well-rounded body and Mary's serene face. Ghiberti's early work reveals the Renaissance synthesis of the Christian and classical, of the classical and the medieval.

The artistic world of Florence was a rapidly changing one, however, and Ghiberti adapted his art to conform to the emerging early Renaissance style of Donatello. Between 1425 and 1452, Ghiberti brought his mature art to its fullest expression in the east doors, the last of the Baptistery's three sculptured portals. These panels, larger than those on the north doors, depict ten scenes from the Old Testament. Most of the Gothic touches have been eliminated, including the framing quatrefoils, which are now replaced with square panels (Figure 11.16).

One of the sublime panels from the east doors depicts the story of the brothers Cain and Abel (Figure 11.17), taken from Genesis 4: 1–16. This panel shows, in many ways, Ghiberti's growing dedication to classical ideals, seen, for example, in the graceful contrapposto of the standing figures and their proportional

Figure 11.15   LORENZO GHIBERTI. *The Annunciation.* Panel from the north doors of the Baptistery. 1403–1424. Gilt bronze, 20½ × 17¾". Florence. *Ghiberti's rendition of the Annunciation was typical of his panels on the north doors. Mary and the angel are placed in the shallow foreground and are modeled almost completely in the round. The background details, including a sharply foreshortened representation of God on the left, are scarcely raised from the metal. The contrast between these design elements enhances the illusion of depth.*

◀ **Figure 11.16** LORENZO GHIBERTI. *Gates of Paradise.* East doors of the Baptistery. 1424–1452. Gilt bronze, ht. approx. 17′. Florence. *The ten scenes depicted on these doors are based on Old Testament stories, taken from the books of Genesis through Kings. Reading from top left to right, then back and forth, and ending at bottom right, the panels begin with an illustration of the opening chapters of Genesis followed by others representing events in the lives of Cain and Abel, Noah, Abraham, Isaac and Jacob, Joseph, Moses, Joshua, David, and Solomon. Taking heed of medieval artistic tradition, Ghiberti placed several dramatic episodes from the life of each biblical character in a single panel. Each panel was formed into a wax model, then cast in bronze, and gilded with gold. According to Giorgio Vasari, the Renaissance artist and writer, Michelangelo, on first seeing the doors, described them as "worthy of Paradise"—the name by which they are still known—the* Gates of Paradise. *In 1991 Ghiberti's original doors were moved inside to Florence's Duomo Museum and duplicate doors replaced them on the Baptistery.*

relationships. This work translates Albertian aesthetics into bronze by creating an illusion of depth. According to Ghiberti's *Commentaries,* the sculptor's purpose was not illusion for illusion's sake but, rather, an articulate visual presentation of the biblical story. Five incidents from the story of Cain and Abel are illustrated: (1) Cain and Abel as children with their parents, Adam and Eve, at the top left; (2) Cain and Abel making sacrifices before an altar, at the top right; (3) Cain plowing with oxen and Abel watching his sheep, in the left foreground and left middle, respectively; (4) Cain slaying Abel with a club, in the right middle; and (5) Cain being questioned by God, in the right foreground.

PAINTING   In the early fourteenth century, Giotto had founded a new realistic and expressive style (see Chapter 10), on which Florentine painters began to build at the opening of the fifteenth century. Much of Giotto's genius lay in his ability to show perspective, or the appearance of spatial depth, in his frescoes, an illusion he achieved largely through the placement of the figures (see Figure 10.20). Approximately one hundred years after Giotto, painters learned to enhance the realism of their pictures by the use of linear perspective.

The radical changes taking place in architecture and sculpture were minor compared with the changes in

painting. Inspired by classicism though lacking significant examples from ancient times, painters were relatively free to experiment and to define their own path. As in the other arts of the 1400s, Florentine painters led the way and established the standards for the new style—realism, linear perspective, and psychological truth (convincing portrayal of emotional states). This movement climaxed at the end of the century with the early work of Leonardo da Vinci.

After 1450 Florence's dominance was challenged by Venetian painters, who were forging their own artistic tradition. Venice, not having won its freedom from the Byzantine Empire until the High Middle Ages, was still in the thrall of Byzantine culture (see Chapter 7). As a result, Venetian painters and their patrons showed a pronounced taste for the stylized effects and sensual surfaces typical of Byzantine art. However, a distinct school of Venetian painters emerged, which eventually would have a major impact on the course of painting in the West.

North of the Alps, a third early Renaissance development was taking place in Burgundy and the Low Countries. There, compared with Italians, painters kept more closely to religious themes and images and departed less from the Gothic. The northern artists concentrated on minute details and landscapes rather than on the problems of depth and composition that concerned Italy's painters.

The guiding genius of the revolution in painting in the earlier Florentine school was the youthful Masaccio [mah-ZAHT-cho] (1401–1428), whose career was probably cut short by the plague. He adopted mathematical perspective in his works almost simultaneously with its invention by Brunelleschi. In the history of Western painting, Masaccio's *Holy Trinity* fresco is the first successful depiction in painting of the new

Figure 11.17 LORENZO GHIBERTI. *The Story of Cain and Abel.* Detail from the east doors of the Baptistery (the *Gates of Paradise*). 1424–1452. Gilt bronze, 31¼ × 31¼″. Florence. *This exquisite panel from the Florence Baptistery's east doors is a testament to Ghiberti's absorption of early Renaissance taste. Ghiberti followed Brunelleschi's new rules for linear perspective by placing the vanishing point in the middle of the tree trunks in the center of the panel, and he adhered to Alberti's principle of varied details by adding the oxen, sheep, and altar.*

Figure 11.18   MASACCIO. *The Holy Trinity.* 1427 or 1428. Fresco, 21'10½" × 10'5". Santa Maria Novella, Florence. *Masaccio achieved a remarkable illusion of depth in this fresco by using linear and atmospheric perspective. Below the simulated chapel, he painted a skeleton in a wall sarcophagus (not visible in this photograph) with a melancholy inscription reading, "I was once that which you are, and what I am you also will be." This* memento mori, *or reminder of death, was probably ordered by the donor, a member of the Lenzi family. His tomb is built into the floor and lies directly in front of the fresco.*

concept of Renaissance space. His design for this fresco in the church of Santa Maria Novella, Florence, shows that he was well aware of the new currents flowing in the art of his day. The painting offers an architectural setting in the style of Brunelleschi, and the solidity and vitality of the figures indicate that Masaccio had also absorbed the values of Donatello's new sculpture.

Masaccio's fresco portrays the Holy Trinity—the three divine persons in the one Christian God—within a simulated chapel (Figure 11.18). Jesus's crucified body appears to be held up by God the Father, who stands on a platform behind the cross; between the heads of Father and Son is a dove, symbolizing the Holy Spirit and completing the Trinitarian image. Mary and Saint John, both clothed in contemporary dress, flank the holy trio. Mary points dramatically to the Savior. Just outside the chapel's frame, the donors kneel in prayer—the typical way of presenting patrons in Renaissance art.

In the *Holy Trinity* fresco, Masaccio uses a variety of innovations. He is the first painter to show light falling from a single source, in this instance, from the left, bathing the body of Christ and coinciding with the actual lighting in Santa Maria Novella. This realistic feature adds to the three-dimensional effect of the well-modeled figures. The use of linear perspective further heightens the scene's realism. Finally, the perspective, converging to the midpoint between the kneeling donors, reinforces the hierarchy of beings within the fresco: from God the Father at the top to the human figures at the sides. In effect, mathematical tidiness is used to reveal the divine order—an ideal congenial to Florence's intellectual elite.

A second fresco by Masaccio, *The Tribute Money*, painted in the Brancacci Chapel of the church of Santa Maria del Carmine, Florence, is recognized as Masaccio's masterpiece (Figure 11.19). This fresco illustrates the Gospel account (Matthew 17:24–27) in which Jesus advises Peter, his chief disciple, to pay the Roman taxes. Because this painting depicts a biblical subject virtually unrepresented in Christian art, it was probably commissioned by a donor to justify a new and heavy Florentine tax. Whether the fresco had any effect on tax collection is debatable, but other artists were captivated by Masaccio's stunning technical effects: the use of perspective and **chiaroscuro,** or the modeling with light and shade.

The Tribute Money fresco follows the continuous narrative form of medieval art. Three separate episodes are depicted at the same time—in the center, Jesus is confronted by the tax collector; on the left, Peter, as foretold by Jesus, finds a coin in the mouth of a fish; and, on the right, Peter pays the coin to the Roman official. Despite this Gothic effect, the fresco's central section is able to stand alone because of its spatial integrity and unified composition. Like Donatello, Masaccio could synthesize several traditions masterfully. Jesus is partially encircled by his apostles, and the tax gatherer, viewed from the back, stands to the right. In this central group, the heads are all at the same height, for Masaccio aligned them according to Brunelleschi's principles. Fully modeled in the round, each human form occupies a precise, mathematical space.

Figure 11.19 MASACCIO. *The Tribute Money.* Ca. 1425. Fresco, 8′2⅜″ × 19′8¼″. Santa Maria del Carmine, Florence. *This fresco represents the highest expression of the art of Masaccio, particularly in his realistic portrayal of the tax collector. This official, who appears twice, first confronting Christ in the center and then receiving money from Peter on the right, is depicted with coarse features—a typical man of the Florentine streets. Even his posture, though rendered with classical contrapposto, suggests a swagger—a man at home in his body and content with his difficult occupation.*

Painters such as the Dominican friar Fra Angelico (about 1400–1455) extended Masaccio's innovations. Fra Angelico's later works, painted for the renovated monastery of San Marco in Florence and partially funded by Cosimo de' Medici, show his mature blending of biblical motifs in Renaissance space. The *Annunciation* portrays a reflective Virgin receiving the angel Gabriel (Figure 11.20). Mary and Gabriel are framed in niches in the Gothic manner, but the other elements—the mastery of depth, the simplicity of gestures, the purity of colors, and the integrated scene—are rendered in the new, simple Renaissance style. The painting's vanishing point is placed to the right of center in the small barred window looking out from the Virgin's bedroom. The loggia, or open porch, in which the scene takes place was based on a new architectural fashion popular among Florence's wealthy elite. Religious images abound in this painting; the enclosed garden symbolizes Mary's virginity, and the barred window attests to the purity of her life. Because of his gracious mastery of form and space, Fra Angelico's influence on later artists was pronounced.

One of those Fra Angelico influenced was Piero della Francesca [PYER-o DAYL-lah frahn-CHAY-skah] (about 1420–1492), a great painter of the second Florentine generation, who grew up in a Tuscan country town near Florence. His panel painting *The Flagellation* shows the powerful though mysterious aesthetic effects of his controversial style (Figure 11.21). The sunlight flooding the scene unites the figures, but the composition places them in two distinct areas. At the extreme left sits Pilate, the judge, on a dais. The painting's subject—the scourging of Christ before his crucifixion—is placed to the left rear. Reinforcing this odd displacement are the figures on the right, who are apparently lost in their own conversation. Aesthetically this strange juxtaposition arises because Piero has placed the horizon line around the hips of the figures beating Christ, causing the three men on the right to loom in such high perspective; thus the men in the foreground appear to be indifferent to Christ and unaware of his importance. The effect is distinctly unsettling in a religious scene. The modern world, which loves conundrums, has developed a strong passion for the private vision of Piero della Francesca as represented in his art.

Botticelli is the best representative of a lyrical aspect of this second generation and one of the most admired painters in the Western tradition. One of the first Florentine artists to master both linear and atmospheric perspective, he was less interested in the technical aspects of painting than he was in depicting languid beauty and poetical truth.

Until the 1480s, Botticelli's art was shaped by the Neoplatonic philosophy of the Florentine Academy,

Figure 11.20   Fra Angelico. *Annunciation.* 1438–1445. Fresco, 7′6″ × 10′5″. Monastery of San Marco, Florence. *Fra Angelico's portrayal of the Virgin at the moment when she receives the news that she will bear the baby Jesus is a wonderful illustration of the painter's use of religious symbols. Mary's questioning expression and her arms crossed in a maternal gesture help to establish the painting's subject. Moreover, the physical setting of the scene, bare except for the rough bench on which Mary sits, suggests an ascetic existence—an appropriate detail for the painting's original setting, a monastery.*

and thus he often allegorized pagan myths, giving them a Christian slant. Especially prominent in Neoplatonic thought was the identification of Venus, the Roman goddess of love, with the Christian belief that "God is love." Botticelli, with the support of his patrons, notably the Medici family, made the Roman goddess the subject of two splendid paintings, *The Birth of Venus* (see Figure 11.3) and the *Primavera.* In this way, female nudes once again became a proper subject for art, though male nudes had appeared earlier, in Donatello's generation (see Figure 11.11). Botticelli's *Primavera,* or *Allegory of Spring,* presents Venus as a Christianized deity, dressed in a revealingly transpar-

ent gown (Figure 11.22). At first glance, the goddess, standing just slightly to the right of center, appears lost amid the general agitation, but on closer view she is seen to be presiding over the revels. Venus tilts her head coyly and holds up her right hand, establishing by these commanding gestures that this orange grove is her garden and the other figures are her familiars, or associates, all of them symbolically linked with divine love.

Even though the *Primavera* is one of the most beloved works of Western art, in technical terms the painting shows that Botticelli was out of step with the early Renaissance. He has placed the scene in the

Figure 11.21 PIERO DELLA FRANCESCA. *The Flagellation.* 1460s. Oil on panel, 23 × 32″. Galleria Nazionale della Marche, Palazzo Ducale, Urbino. *A secondary religious message may be found in this work. In 1439 the Orthodox Church discussed union with Rome at the Council of Florence but later repudiated the merger when the Byzantine populace rioted in favor of Turkish rule. The hats on Pilate (seated at the left) and the third man from the right are copies of Greek headdresses that were worn at the council. In effect, these figures suggest that the Greek Church is a persecutor of true Christianity, for the papacy regarded the Greek Orthodox faith as schismatic.*

near foreground, stressing this area's extreme shallowness by the entangled backdrop of trees and shrubs. The figures are flattened, and the background appears more decorative than real.

In the 1480s, Florentine art was moving toward its culmination in the early works of Leonardo da Vinci (1452–1519). Leonardo is the quintessential representative of a new breed of artist: the Renaissance man, who takes the universe of learning as his province. Not only did he defy the authority of the church by secretly studying human cadavers, but he also rejected the classical values that had guided the first generation

of the early Renaissance. He relied solely on empirical truth and what the human eye could discover. His notebooks, encoded so as to be legible only when read in a mirror, recorded and detailed his lifelong curiosity about both the human and the natural worlds. In his habits of mind, Leonardo joined intellectual curiosity with the skills of sculptor, architect, engineer, scientist, and painter.

Among Leonardo's few surviving paintings from this period, the first version of *The Virgin of the Rocks* reveals both his scientific eye and his desire to create a haunting image uniquely his own (Figure 11.23). In this

Figure 11.22   Sandro Botticelli. *Primavera*. Ca. 1482. Tempera on panel, 6′8″ × 10′4″. Uffizi Gallery, Florence. *Botticelli's lyricism is evident in his refined images of human beauty. His figures' elegant features and gestures, such as the sloping shoulders and the tilted heads, were copied by later artists. The women's blond, ropelike hair and transparent gowns are typical of Botticelli's style.*

scene, set in a grotto or cave, Mary is portrayed with the infant Jesus, as a half-kneeling infant John the Baptist prays and an angel watches. The plants underfoot and the rocks in the background are a treasure of precise documentation. Nevertheless, the setting is Leonardo's own invention—without a scriptural or a traditional basis—and is a testimony to his creative genius.

Leonardo's plan of *The Virgin of the Rocks* shows the rich workings of his mind. Ignoring Brunelleschian perspective, he placed the figures his own way. He also developed a pyramid design for arranging the figures in relation to one another; Mary's head is the pyramid's apex, and her seat and the other three figures anchor its corners. Within this pyramid, Leonardo creates a dynamic tension by using gestures to suggest a circular motion: The angel points to John the Baptist, who in turn directs his praying hands toward Jesus. A second, vertical, line of stress is seen in the gesturing hands of Mary, the angel, and Christ. Later artists so

admired this painting that its pyramidal composition became the standard in the High Renaissance.

No prior artist had used chiaroscuro to such advantage as Leonardo does in *The Virgin of the Rocks*, causing the figures to stand out miraculously from the surrounding gloom. And unlike earlier artists, he colors the atmosphere, softening the edges of surfaces with a fine haze called **sfumato.** As a result, the painting looks more like a vision than a realistic scene. Leonardo's later works are part of the High Renaissance (see Chapter 12), but his early works represent the fullest expression of the scientific spirit of the second generation of early Renaissance painting.

While the Florentine painters were establishing themselves as the driving force in the early Renaissance, a rival school was beginning to emerge in Venice. The Venetian school, dedicated to exploring the effects of light and air and re-creating the sensuous effects of textured surfaces, was eventually to play a major role in the history of painting in Italy and the West. Founded by Giovanni Bellini, a member of a dynasty of painters, the Venetian school began its rise to greatness.

Giovanni Bellini (about 1430–1516), who trained in the workshop of his father, the late Gothic painter Jacopo Bellini (about 1400–1470), made Venice a center of Renaissance art comparable to Florence and Rome. Ever experimenting, always striving to keep up with the latest trends, he frequently reinvented himself. Nevertheless, there were constants in his approach to painting. He combined the traditions of the Florentine school (the use of linear perspective and the direct observation of nature) and the Flemish school (the technique of oil painting, the use of landscape as background, and the practice of religious symbolism). Made aware of the importance of atmosphere by the Venetian setting, Bellini also experimented with a range of colors, variations in color intensity, and changes in light. In particular, Bellini perfected the landscape format as a backdrop for foreground figures. A great teacher, Bellini founded a workshop where his methods were taught to young painters, including Giorgione and Titian (see Chapter 12).

An excellent example of Bellini's use of landscape may be seen in *St. Francis in Ecstasy* (Figure 11.24). This work, which depicts an ecstatic St. Francis displaying the stigmata (spontaneous appearance of open wounds, similar to those of the crucified Christ), shows Bellini's typical treatment of landscape: he divides the painting surface into zones, beginning with the area around the saint in the foreground, continuing through a second zone occupied by a donkey and a crane, to a third zone featuring Italian castles nestled into a hillside, and concluding with a fourth zone marked by a fortress and the sky. To heighten the realism, Bellini uses both a rich palette of colors and numerous objects to lead the viewer's eye into the vast distance. He adds to the realism by suffusing the scene with natural light. The landscape, with its vivid rendering of flora and fauna, expresses the Franciscan belief that humankind should live in harmony with the natural world (see Chapter 9).

Music

The changes affecting the cultural life of fifteenth-century Europe naturally also affected the music of the time. The impetus for a new musical direction, however, did not spring from classical sources, because ancient musical texts had virtually perished. Instead, the new music owed its existence to meetings between English and Continental composers at the church councils that were called to settle the Great Schism (see Chapter 10) and the Continental composers' deep regard for the se-

Figure 11.23   LEONARDO DA VINCI. *The Virgin of the Rocks.* 1483. Oil on panel, approx. 6′3″ × 3′7″. Louvre. *Two slightly different versions of this work exist, this one dating from 1483 and a later one done in 1506 and on view in the National Gallery in London. The Louvre painting, with its carefully observed botanical specimens, is the culmination of the scientific side of the early Renaissance. The painting's arbitrary features—the grotto setting and the unusual perspective—point ahead to the High Renaissance; the dramatic use of chiaroscuro foreshadows the "night pictures" of the baroque period (see Figure 14.10).*

ductive sound of English music. The English composer John Dunstable [DUHN-stuh-bull] (about 1380–1453) was a central figure in the new musical era that began with the opening of the fifteenth century. Working in England and in France, he wrote mainly religious works—motets for multiple voices and settings for the Mass—that showed his increasingly harmonic approach to polyphony. The special quality of his music is its freedom from the use of mathematical proportion—the source of medieval music's dissonance.

Dunstable's music influenced composers in France, in Burgundy, and in Flanders, known collectively as

Figure 11.24 GIOVANNI BELLINI. *St. Francis in Ecstasy.* 1470s. Oil in tempera on panel, 49 × 55⅞". Frick Collection, New York. *In the foreground, Bellini renders his vision of the grotto at Alvernia, a mountain retreat near Assisi, where St. Francis went to pray and fast for forty days, in imitation of Christ's forty days in the wilderness. The artist reinforces the scene's religious significance through various symbols, such as the grapevine and the stigmata, alluding to the sacrifice of Christ, and the donkey (in the middle distance), emblematic of Jesus's entry into Jerusalem before the Crucifixion.*

Figure 11.25 Mass at the Court of Philip the Good in Burgundy. Bibliothèque Royal Albert Ier, Brussels. Fifteenth century. *This miniature painting shows a Mass being conducted at the court of Philip the Good of Burgundy (r. 1419–1467). Philip's patronage of the arts and music attracted leading painters and musicians to his court, which he conducted in cities across his holdings in modern-day Holland, Belgium, and France. John Dunstable, a composer of the Franco-Netherlandish school, was, on occasion, at the duke's court. In the painting, the priest prepares the sacraments at the altar, with his attendant behind him. On the right, the choir, dressed in white robes and gathered in front of the music stand, sings the Latin Mass. In the center background, dressed in black, stands a member of the Burgundian royal court, attended by two servants.*

the Franco-Netherlandish school. This school, which became the dominant force in fifteenth-century music, blended Dunstable's harmonics with northern European and Italian traditions. The principal works of this group were Latin **Masses** (Figure 11.25), or musical settings of the most sacred Christian rite; motets, or multivoiced songs set to Latin texts other than the Mass; and secular chansons, or songs, with French texts, including such types as the French ballade and the Italian madrigal, poems set to music for two and six voices, respectively. Together, these polyphonic compositions established the musical ideal of the early Renaissance: multiple voices of equal importance singing **a cappella** (without instrumental accompaniment) and stressing the words so that they could be understood by listeners.

Between 1430 and 1500, the Continent's musical life was guided by composers from the Franco-Netherlandish school, the most important of whom was the Burgundian Josquin des Prez [zho-SKAN day PRAY] (about 1440–1521). Josquin was influential in his day and is now recognized as one of the greatest composers of all time. He was the first important composer to use music expressively so that the sounds matched

the words of the text, thereby moving away from the abstract church style of the Middle Ages. One of his motets was described at the time as evoking Christ's suffering in a manner superior to painting. Josquin also began to organize music in the modern way, using major and minor scales with their related harmonies. All in all, he is probably the first Western composer whose music on first hearing appeals to modern ears.

Josquin's motet *Ave Maria . . . Virgo Serena (Hail, Mary . . . Serene Virgin;* 1502), a musical setting of a prayer to the Virgin Mary, shows the new expressive Renaissance style as it breaks away from the abstract music of the Middle Ages. Based on a Gregorian chant, the opening section quickly gives way to an innovative melody. Divided into seven sections, the motet employs shifting voice combinations in each part. The opening section uses polyphonic **imitation,** a musical technique that functions like a relay race. The soprano begins with the phrase *Ave Maria*, which, in turn, is restated by the alto, tenor, and bass. Next, there follows the second phrase, *gratia plena* ("full of grace"), sung to a different melody, which is also repeated among the voices. The musical effect in the first section is to create an overlapping tapestry of sound. The second section uses a duet of two upper voices, which is then imitated by the lower voices. Next, there is a four-voice ensemble, using expressive music that reflects the text, *nova laetitia* ("new joy"). Then, there follow four sections that shift voice groupings along with alterations in rhythms, ending with a brief pause. The motet ends with the group singing together in sustained chords: *"O mater Dei / memento mei. Amen,"* or "O Mother of God / remember me. Amen."

The Legacy of the Early Renaissance

Today, modern times are considered to begin with the early Renaissance in Italy. This period saw the rebirth of the study and practice of the arts and the humanities and the rise of the idea of the "Renaissance man"—a term used today to define the supreme genius who makes all of human knowledge his province. Under the powerful stimulus of humanism, the liberal arts were restored to primacy over religion in the educational curriculum, a place they had not held for a thousand years, since the triumph of Christianity in the fourth century. With humanism also came a skeptical outlook that expressed itself in a new regard for the direct role of human causality in history and the rise of textual criticism. A new ingredient in Renaissance humanism was the drive to individual fulfillment, perhaps the defining trait of Western civilization from this point onward.

The greatest cultural changes took place in the arts and in architecture, largely under the spell of humanistic learning. Now freed from subordination to architecture, sculpture and painting became independent art forms. Fifteenth-century architects, inspired by the Greco-Roman tradition, adapted classical forms and ideals to their own needs. For the next four hundred years, until the Gothic revival in the nineteenth century, classicism was the ruling force in a succession of architectural styles. Sculpture also used its classical roots to redefine its direction, reviving ancient forms and the practice of depicting male and female nudes. Of all the visual arts, painting was least influenced by the classical tradition, except for its ideals of simplicity and realism. Perhaps as a consequence of its artistic freedom, painting became the dominant art form of this era and continues to hold first rank today.

KEY CULTURAL TERMS

Renaissance	chiaroscuro
studia humanitatis	sfumato
humanism	Mass
early Renaissance style	motet
vanishing point	a cappella
pilaster	imitation
relief	

QUESTIONS FOR CRITICAL THINKING

1. What connections can be identified between Italy's political and social life and the Renaissance?

2. Define *civic humanism* and show how it was a feature of the Italian Renaissance.

3. What were the key intellectual characteristics of the early Renaissance?

4. Was there a radical break between the Middle Ages and the early Renaissance?

5. Trace the evolution of early Renaissance painting from Masaccio to Leonardo da Vinci noting specific artists, their achievements, and the guiding themes of their works.

12

THE HIGH RENAISSANCE AND EARLY MANNERISM
1494–1564

Between 1494 and 1564, one of the most brilliantly creative periods in Western history unfolded in Italy. During this span of seventy years, there flourished three artists—Leonardo da Vinci, Raphael, and Michelangelo—and a writer—Machiavelli—whose achievements became legendary (Figure 12.1).

The **High Renaissance,** lasting from 1494 to 1520, was a time when the classical principles of beauty, balance, order, serenity, harmony, and rational design reached a state of near perfection. The center of culture shifted from Florence, the heart of the early Renaissance, to Rome, where the popes became the leading patrons of the new style. After 1520, however, the Renaissance veered away from the humanistic values of classicism toward an antihumanistic vision of the world, labeled **mannerism,** because of the self-conscious, or "mannered," style adopted by its artists and intellectuals. Mannerist art and culture endured from 1520 until the end of the century, when the style was affected by religious controversy. This chapter covers the High Renaissance style and the mannerist style through the end of its first phase in 1564, with the death of Michelangelo.

THE RISE OF THE MODERN SOVEREIGN STATE

The most important political development during this period was the emergence of powerful sovereign states in France, England, and Spain. This process, already under way in the late fifteenth century (see Chapter 10), now began to influence foreign affairs. The ongoing rivalries among these three states led to the concept of the balance of power—a principle that still dominates politics today.

◀ **Detail** MICHELANGELO. *Pietà.* 1498–1499. Marble, ht. 5′8½″. St. Peter's, the Vatican.

From 1494 to 1569, Europe's international political life was controlled, either directly or indirectly, by France and Spain. France's central role resulted from the policies of its strong Valois kings, who had governed since the early 1300s. Spain's fortunes soared during this era, first under the joint rule (1474–1504) of Ferdinand V and Isabella and then under Charles I (r. 1516–1556). In 1519 Charles I was elected Holy Roman emperor as Charles V (he was of the royal house of Hapsburg), thus joining the interests of Spain and the Holy Roman Empire until his abdication in 1556. England kept aloof from Continental affairs during this time.

After 1591 the French and the Spanish rulers increasingly dispatched their armies into the weaker states, where they fought and claimed new lands. As the sovereign monarchs gained power, the medieval dream of a united Christendom—pursued by Charlemagne, the popes, and the Holy Roman emperors—slowly faded away. These new states were strong because they were united around rulers who exercised increasing central control. Although most kings claimed to rule by divine right, their practical policies were more important in increasing their power. They surrounded themselves with ministers and consultative councils, both dependent on the crown. The ministers were often chosen from the bourgeois class, and they advised the rulers on such weighty matters as religion and war and also ran the developing bureaucracies. The bureaucracies in turn strengthened centralized rule by extending royal jurisdiction into matters formerly administered by the feudal nobility, such as the justice system.

The crown further eroded the status of the feudal nobles by relying on mercenary armies rather than on the warrior class, a shift that began in the late Middle Ages. To pay these armies, the kings had to consult with representative bodies, such as Parliament in England, and make them a part of the royal government.

Figure 12.1 MICHELANGELO. *Dying Slave.* 1513–1516. Marble, approx. 7'5". Louvre. *Michelangelo's so-called* Dying Slave *embodies the conflicting artistic tendencies at work between 1494 and 1564. The statue's idealized traits—the perfectly proportioned figure, the restrained facial expression, and the body's gentle S-curve shape—are hallmarks of the High Renaissance style. But the figure's overall sleekness and exaggerated arm movements—probably based on one of the figures in the first-century CE Laocoön Group (see Interpreting Art Figure 4.1), which had recently been rediscovered—were portents of early mannerism.*

The Struggle for Italy, 1494–1529

Italy's relative tranquility, established by the Peace of Lodi in 1454, was shattered when the French invaded in 1494, to assert a hereditary claim to land. For the next thirty-five years, Italy was a battleground where France, Spain, and the Holy Roman Empire fought among themselves, as well as with the papacy and most of the Italian states. The French repeatedly invaded Italy in these years, only to be repelled by varied combinations of local states and foreign rulers. Ironically, the French kings, during these campaigns, grew enamored of the Italian Renaissance, bringing its artistic and intellectual ideals to their court (Figure 12.2).

A far-reaching political effect of this fight for Italy's future was to launch a series of wars between France and the Holy Roman Empire, a struggle that pitted the old Europe against the new. The Holy Roman Empire, ruled by Charles V of the Hapsburg line, was a decentralized relic from the feudal past. France, led by the bold Francis I (r. 1515–1547) of the royal house of Valois, was the epitome of the new sovereign state.

The first Hapsburg-Valois war (1522–1529) was the only one fought in Italy. In 1527 the troops of Charles V ran riot in Rome, raping, looting, and killing. This notorious sack of Rome had two major consequences: (1) it cast doubt on Rome's ability to control Italy—long a goal of the popes—for it showed that secular leaders no longer respected the temporal power of the papacy; and (2) it ended papal patronage of the arts for almost a decade, thus weakening Rome's role as a cultural leader. It also had a chilling effect on artistic ideals and contributed to the rise of mannerism.

In 1529 the Treaty of Cambrai ended the first phase of the Hapsburg-Valois rivalry. And, after years of warfare, Italy was divided and exhausted. Some cities suffered nearly irreparable harm. The Florentine republic fared the worst; in the 1530s, its Medici family resumed control of the city, but they were little more than puppets of foreign rulers who now controlled much of the peninsula. The only Italian state to keep its political freedom was Venice, which became the last haven for artists and intellectuals in Italy for the rest of the sixteenth century.

Charles V and the Hapsburg Empire

By 1530 the struggle between the Valois and the Hapsburgs had shifted to central Europe. The French felt hemmed in by the Spanish in the south, the Germans to the east, and the Dutch to the north—peoples all ruled by the Hapsburg emperor Charles V. In French eyes, Charles had an insatiable appetite for power and for control of the Continent. In turn, the Hapsburg

Figure 12.2 JEAN CLOUET. *Francis I.* Ca. 1525. Oil on panel, 37¾ × 29⅛". Louvre. *During his thirty-two-year reign, Francis I embarked on an extensive artistic program, inspired by the Italian Renaissance, to make his court the most splendid in Europe. Under his personal direction, Italian artworks and artists, including Leonardo da Vinci, were imported into France. Ironically, this rather stylized portrait by Jean Clouet, Francis's chief court artist, owes more to the conventionalized portraits of the Gothic style than it does to the realistic works of the Italian Renaissance.*

ruler considered the French king a land-hungry upstart who stood in the way of a Europe united under a Christian prince. In 1559, after a number of exhausting wars and a series of French victories, the belligerents signed the Treaty of Cateau-Cambrésis, which ushered in a brief period of peace (Map 12.1).

Charles V, the man at the center of most of these events, lived a life filled with paradoxes (Figure 12.3). Because of the size of his empire, he was in theory one of the most powerful rulers ever to live; but in actuality, again because of the vastness of his lands, he never quite succeeded in gaining complete control of his empire. In some ways, he was the last medieval king; in other ways, he foreshadowed a new age driven by sovereign kings, standing armies, diplomatic agreements, and strong religious differences.

LEARNING THROUGH MAPS

Map 12.1   EUROPEAN EMPIRE OF CHARLES V, CA. 1556
This map shows the extensive holdings of the Holy Roman emperor Charles V, also
known as King Charles I of Spain. 1. *Notice* the lands inherited and the lands gained by
Charles V. 2. *Identify* the boundaries of the Holy Roman Empire. 3. *Who* were Charles V's
enemies within the Holy Roman Empire and elsewhere? 4. *Consider* the challenges
Charles V faced in governing his widely scattered and culturally diverse empire.
5. *What* impact did geography have on France's attitude toward Charles V's empire?

Charles V's unique position at the center of Europe's political storm was the result of a series of timely deaths and births and politically astute arranged marriages. These circumstances enabled the Hapsburg rulers to accumulate vast power, wealth, and land. Charles was born in 1500 to a German father and a Spanish mother, and he was the grandson of both the Holy Roman emperor Maximilian I and the Spanish king Ferdinand V. He held lands in present-day Spain, France, Italy, Germany, and Austria—along with much of the New World. By 1519 Charles V—simultaneously Charles I of Spain—ruled the largest empire the world has ever known.

For most of his life, Charles traveled from one of his possessions to another, fighting battles, arranging peace treaties, and attempting to unify his empire of disparate holdings. His attention was often divided, and he found himself caught between two powerful foes—especially the French to the west and the Ottoman Turks in the east—who drained both his personal energies and his imperial resources.

Within the Holy Roman Empire, the princes of the German principalities often took advantage of his prolonged absences and his preoccupation with the French and the Turks. Their ability to gain political power at the emperor's expense increased after Martin Luther's revolt and the beginning of the Protestant Reformation (see Chapter 13). Charles also weakened his own position by his contradictory policies. At times he angered the disaffected German princes by meddling in their affairs and condemning Lutheran doctrines, and at other times he angered the popes by making concessions to the Protestants.

Exhausted and disillusioned by his inability to prevail in Europe, Charles abdicated in 1556 and retired to a monastery. His brother Ferdinand (r. 1558–1564) took control of the German-Austrian inheritance and was elected Holy Roman emperor. His son Philip (r. 1556–1598) assumed control of the Spanish Hapsburg holdings, including Spain, the New World territories, and the Netherlands. Thus ended Charles's vision of a united Christendom, which had turned into a nightmare of endless meetings, gory battles, and false hopes of peace and unity.

ECONOMIC EXPANSION AND SOCIAL DEVELOPMENTS

Figure 12.3 TITIAN. *Charles V with a Dog.* Ca. 1533. Oil on canvas, 6′3″ × 3′8″. Prado, Madrid. *Titian's full-length, standing portrait of Charles V was painted when the Hapsburg emperor was at the height of his power. By rendering the "ruler of the world" in contrapposto, his fingers casually holding the collar of his dog, Titian endows the emperor with a natural grace. The lighting that illuminates Charles from the dark background and the breathless hush that seems to envelop the man and dog are trademarks of Titian's style.*

By 1500, Europe had nearly recovered from the plague; the sixteenth century continued to be a time of growing population and increasing prosperity. The center of trade shifted from the Mediterranean to the Atlantic coast, making cities like London and Antwerp financial and mercantile capitals. Skilled craftspeople turned out quality products, and enterprising merchants distributed these finished goods across much of northwestern Europe. The daring sailing expeditions of this period provided new raw materials from

America. Innovative manufacturing methods spurred economic growth and expanded worldwide markets.

Demographics, Prosperity, and the Beginning of a Global World

Modern research indicates that the population of Europe increased from about forty-five million in 1400 to sixty-nine million in 1500 and to about eighty-nine million by 1600. Society grew more urban, as people migrated from the countryside to urban areas and the number of cities with populations over one hundred thousand rose from five to eight between 1500 and 1600. Rome, for example, grew from about fifty thousand in 1526—the year before the sack—to one hundred thousand by the end of the century.

Prosperity brought a higher standard of living for the urban middle class, but throughout much of the century prices rose faster than wages. Those who were not profiting from increased economic growth, such as poor peasants and impoverished nobles living on unproductive farms, suffered the most. In areas of Europe hardest hit by inflation or agricultural and commercial stagnation, economic crises often became intertwined with social and religious issues that intensified longstanding regional and local differences.

Yet the boom offered economic opportunities to some. Many merchants made fortunes and provided employment for others. These merchants and the bankers who offered loans were also accumulating capital, which they then invested in various commercial activities. The wars of Charles V were financed by wealthy bankers operating in a well-organized money market. The amassing of surplus capital and its reinvestment ushered in the opening phase of commercial capitalism, which laid the foundation for Europe's future economic expansion.

Until 1550, the New World's abundant raw materials and its vast market potential were just beginning to affect Europe's economy. After 1650, that changed; South American gold and silver began to play an important role in the upward price spiral, and the New World's farm products, such as tobacco, cotton, and cocoa, were used in new manufactured goods, thereby profoundly altering consumer habits.

Central to these economic changes was slavery. Some European traders, taking advantage of the institution of slavery and the existing slave trade in western Africa, mercilessly exploited the local Africans by buying and shipping them to the colonies in the New World. The Africans were forced to work in the gold and silver mines of Central and South America and on the cotton and sugarcane plantations in the West

Indies, where they became a major factor in the production of these new forms of wealth.

Technology

The High Renaissance was a period of economic and social transformation, stimulated by advances in technology. Two groups who contributed to this dynamic period were the inventors and tinkerers whose devices and discoveries opened the world for exploration. An especially powerful agent of change was improved firearms, which rendered old forms of warfare obsolete and, gradually, altered the balance of power among the rising nation-states.

SAILING Europe, starting in 1492, began to explore and then conquer much of the world. The pretext was the spread of the Christian faith, but the motivation was gold, commodities, and other riches. Based on knowledge of the sea and the winds, sailing technology was now advanced for navigational instruments, ships, and sails. Europe had entered the Age of Exploration and, in rapid order, came to dominate the globe until the mid–twentieth century.

The historic developments in navigational instrument technology and seamanship were

- the magnetic compass, to determine direction,
- the astrolabe, to determine latitude, and
- an increased understanding of the path of prevailing winds and currents in the ocean.

These advances empowered mariners to sail farther and farther from Europe. In 1522 a heroic milestone was reached when the first Westerners circumnavigated the globe: the surviving crew of the ships commanded by the Portuguese navigator Fernao de Magalhaes [mah-GAHL-yeesh] (in English, Ferdinand Magellan) (about 1480–1521).

The dramatic innovations in sailing ship technology included the following:

- The *galley* (a long warship powered by oars and sails; loaded with armed boarding parties) became dominant in naval warfare, after 1400.
- The galley was modified into a square-rigged ship fitted with deck cannons, after 1450.
- The Portuguese and the Spanish perfected a cargo-carrying galley called the *caravel* (a three-masted vessel with a small roundish hull and a high stern and bow).
- The caravel was replaced by the larger *galleon,* with greater maneuverability and firepower—the mainstay of Europe's global commerce and navies, from 1550 to 1700.

So successful were the galleons that the outcome of Europe's wars was often determined by battles at sea, as in England's triumph over the Spanish Armada in 1588.

WARFARE   One of the most far-ranging agents of technological change occurred with firearms, including

- the cannon (early 1300s); first, as siege cannons, packed with gunpowder and stones or bits of metal—used to batter down walls of castles and towns,
- the lightweight, rustfree bronze cannon, which quickly replaced the iron cannon, and
- arsenals and foundries, turning out guns and shot.

As these advances unfolded, Europe's first arms race began: the Spaniards held the lead, from about 1500, but the Dutch and English moved ahead after 1600. Amassing weapons became a central need for each sovereign state, while new strategies and tactics were reshaping the nature of warfare.

Among those who understood how new weaponry was transforming warfare was the artist-scientist Leonardo da Vinci (see the section "Painting"). He designed catapults, giant crossbows, and cannons. He calculated the trajectories of missiles fired by mortars and cannons and drew plans for armed land vehicles, underwater craft, and flying machines. As a military engineer, he advised city planners on fortifications. Leonardo's quest for knowledge led him not only to invent engines of war but also to speculate on how these destructive devices brutalized humans and destroyed nature (Figure 12.4).

Science and Medicine

While less pronounced in their immediate impact than the technological innovations, advances in science during this age would have long-lasting effects.

In the natural sciences, Leonardo again led the way, in observation, in practices, and in understanding. His genius was directed toward the study of nature in all of its forms, especially the human body. In what he learned, he perhaps surpassed all those who had gone before him. He dissected human cadavers and took meticulous notes, describing organs, bones, and muscles, and drawing detailed anatomical studies. Although his writings and anatomical drawings were not made public during his lifetime, Leonardo's contributions to the understanding of the human body

Figure 12.4   LEONARDO DA VINCI. *Men Struggling to Move a Large Cannon. Ca. 1488. Pen and ink, drawing. Windsor, Royal Library. Leonardo's drawing is more than just a scene of a sixteenth-century iron foundry. While much can be learned from its details—the use of winches and pulleys, the tools and equipment, and the differing types of cannons—the artist is also showing how machines are coming to control human life. Leonardo was fascinated by the machines of war, but he also understood their destructive force, as when he wrote: "With its breath it will kill men and ruin cities and castles."*

Timeline 12.1   ITALIAN CULTURAL STYLES BETWEEN 1494 AND 1564

1494	1520	1564
High Renaissance	Early Mannerism	

| French invasion of Italy | 1508–1512 Michelangelo's Sistine Chapel ceiling frescoes | 1519 Death of Leonardo da Vinci **1520** Death of Raphael | 1532 Publication of Machiavelli's *The Prince* | 1536–1541 Michelangelo's *Last Judgment* fresco | 1550 Palladio's Villa Rotonda | 1564 Death of Michelangelo |

and the function of its skeleton, muscles, and organs reflected the Renaissance's desire to understand ourselves and the world.

Between 1400 and 1600, Italy's schools of medicine continued to be among the best in Europe. During this time, Italy took another innovative step in medical care through the creative work of local administrators in the largest cities, officials who personified another characteristic of the Italian Renaissance, **civic humanism.** Civic humanism was an outgrowth of the Renaissance's cultivation of the culture of ancient Greece and Rome. Italy's civic administrators—dedicated men who were trained in the Greek and Latin classics—saw themselves as modern equivalents of civil servants in an ancient *polis,* or city. As such, they tried to establish responsible and efficient city governments. One of their projects, for example, which had a strong impact on medical care, was the setting up of citywide health boards composed of physicians and medical personnel, to deal with public health issues, especially plague and other contagious diseases. Although lacking knowledge of the germ theory of disease, the health boards could build on practices that had worked in the past. For example, starting in the 1400s, they used controls and quarantines to isolate plague and prevent the spread of this and other contagious diseases among the populace. The new city health boards had jurisdiction over such matters as keeping records of each death and its cause, inspecting food markets, regulating city health conditions, and supervising burials, cemeteries, hospitals, and even beggars and prostitutes.

FROM HIGH RENAISSANCE TO EARLY MANNERISM

The characteristics of High Renaissance style were largely derived from the visual arts. Led by painters, sculptors, and architects who worshiped ancient clas-

sical ideals, notably those of late-fifth-century BCE Greece, the High Renaissance was filled with images of repose, harmony, and heroism. Under the spell of classicism and the values of simplicity and restraint, artists sought to conquer unruly physical reality by subjecting it to the principle of a seemingly effortless order.

The visual arts dominated the High Renaissance, but literary figures also contributed to this era. From classicism, the High Renaissance authors appropriated two of their chief aesthetic aims, secularism and idealism. Like their ancient predecessors, historians showed that contemporary events arose from human causes rather than from divine action—unmistakable evidence of a mounting secular spirit. Actually, secularism more deeply affected the writing of history than it did the arts and architecture, where church patronage and religious subjects still held sway. A rising secular consciousness can also be seen in the popular handbooks on manners that offered advice on how to become a perfect gentleman or lady. Although they have no counterpart in ancient literature, these books have the classical quality of treating their subject in idealized terms.

What distinguished the High Renaissance preoccupation with the classical past from the early Renaissance's renewed interest in ancient matters was largely a shift in creative sensibility. The early Renaissance artists, in the course of growing away from the late Gothic style, had invented new ways of recapturing the harmonious spirit of ancient art and architecture. The geniuses of the next generation, benefiting from the experiments of the early Renaissance, succeeded in creating masterpieces of disciplined form and idealized beauty. The High Renaissance masters' superb confidence allowed them to produce works that were in harmony with themselves and the physical world—a hallmark of classical art.

In spite of its brilliance, the High Renaissance existed for only a fleeting moment in the history of Western culture—from the French invasion of Italy in

Figure 12.5 *Pope Clement VII Besieged in Castel Sant'Angelo.* 1554. Engraving, 6⅙ × 9″. Kunsthalle, Hamburg. *This engraving shows the imperial army of Charles V besieging Castel Sant'Angelo, one of the pope's palaces, during the sack of Rome in 1527. The engraver's sympathies with the pope are revealed by the huge statues of St. Peter (with keys, on the right) and St. Paul (with sword, on the left), who look on disapprovingly. Pope Clement VII, imprisoned in his own fortress, peers down on the scene from a balcony at the center top.*

1494 until the death of Raphael in 1520 (preceded by the death of Leonardo in 1519) (Timeline 12.1). In this era, the Renaissance popes spared no expense in their patronage of the arts and letters. After the disasters of the fourteenth century, the papacy seemed to have restored the church to the vitality that it had enjoyed in the High Middle Ages. In reality, however, the popes of the early sixteenth century presided over a shaky ecclesiastical foundation. To the north, in Germany, a theological storm was brewing that would eventually split Christendom and destroy the papacy's claim to rule over the Christian world. This religious crisis, coupled with increasing tendencies to exaggeration in High Renaissance art and with the sack of Rome in 1527, contributed to the development of mannerism and its spread through Italy and later across western Europe (Figure 12.5).

Mannerist painters, sculptors, and architects abandoned two of the guiding principles of the High Renaissance: the imitation of nature and the devotion to classical ideals. In contrast to High Renaissance masters, mannerist painters deliberately chose odd perspectives that called attention to the artists' technical effects and their individual points of view. Mannerist sculptors, rejecting idealism, turned and twisted the human figure into unusual and bizarre poses to express their own notions of beauty. Likewise, mannerist architects toyed with the emotions and expectations of their audience by designing buildings that were intended to surprise. Behind the mannerist aesthetic lay a questioning or even a denial of the inherent worth of human beings and a negative image of human nature, along with a sense of the growing instability of the world.

Literature

The leading writers of the High Renaissance in Italy drew their themes and values from the Greco-Roman classics. Their artistic vision sprang from the classical virtue of *humanitas*—a term coined by Cicero in antiquity that can be translated as "humanity," meaning the wisdom, humor, tolerance, and passion of the person of good sense. With some reservations, they also believed in classicism's basic tenet that human nature is inherently rational and good. One of the finest expressions of High Renaissance literature was the poetry of the artist Michelangelo, whose love poems and other lyrical verses adhered closely to the classical tradition. But, even as High Renaissance literature was enjoying its brief reign, the mannerist works of the Florentine author Niccolò Machiavelli began to appear, and at the heart of his thought is an anticlassical spirit. Despite his education in classicism and his strict rationalism, Machiavelli concluded that the human race was irremediably flawed. The contrast between the idealizing spirit of the High Renaissance and the antitraditionalist views of mannerism can be clearly seen by placing the work of the diplomat and courtier Baldassare Castiglione beside that of Machiavelli. Each wrote a book that can fairly be described as a manual of behavior—but there the resemblance ends.

MICHELANGELO   Like Leonardo da Vinci, Michelangelo embodied the "Renaissance man," the well-rounded cultural ideal of this period. Along with remarkable achievements in architecture, painting, and sculpture, Michelangelo was a dedicated poet. More than three hundred of his short (usually fourteen-line) poems

ENCOUNTER

Portuguese Exploration Sets the Stage for a New World

Portugal led the first wave of Europeans to export their peoples, traditions, and culture overseas. The Portuguese poet Luis Vaz de Camoes, following the ancient poet Virgil, wrote an epic poem celebrating his adventurous countrymen and heralding the new Age of Exploration.

Portugal's arrival in Africa, India, and the Far East launched a new phase of international trade and commerce, stimulated racial, ethnic, and cultural interchanges, and altered the course of world history. The Portuguese explored islands in the Atlantic and traded along the west coast of Africa for gold and slaves. By the 1490s, they were at the southern tip of Africa—the Cape of Good Hope—searching for sea routes to Asia, which would bypass the Muslim trade system in the Middle East. In 1497 Vasco da Gama [VAS-co da GAH-ma] (about 1460–1524) sailed from Lisbon, rounded the Cape of Good Hope, came up the east coast of Africa, crossed the Indian ocean—with the aid of a Muslim mariner—and landed at Calicut (modern Kolkata, formerly Calcutta), India. Da Gama returned to Portugal two years later, his ships laden with pepper and spices. The Portuguese set up trading posts and forts along the coasts of Africa, throughout the East Indies, and in China. They monopolized the spice and pepper markets and tried to control the sea routes between Europe and the Far East. For most of the 1500s, this country, small in size and population,

was the richest nation in Europe. However, the Portuguese soon overextended their empire and found themselves challenged by the Spanish, Dutch, French, and English, who were entering the European Age of Exploration.

Portugal's age of greatness, personified by Vasco da Gama's daring exploits, was recorded and praised by the country's first renowned poet, Luis Vaz de Camoes [LU-ees VAZH th KAE-moish] (about 1524–1580) (Encounter figure 12.1), in his epic poem *The Lusiads*. Descended from the lesser nobility, Camoes's father was a sea captain whose travels probably inspired the son. Camoes attended a Portuguese university, which was just coming under the influence of Renaissance thought, where he studied the Greek and Latin Classics. After 1546, he led an adventurous life: soldiering in North Africa, traveling to India, serving his government in the Far East, and returning home in 1570. *The Lusiads*, which he composed over the years of his wandering, was published in 1572. In recognition of his epic poem, he received a small stipend from the state and lived in modest circumstances until his death, in 1580.

The Lusiads, named for *Lusus*, the mythical founder of Portugal, was modeled on Virgil's *Aeneid*. In ten cantos, Camoes recounts Vasco da Gama's voyage to India. In this epic, da Gama and his men encounter various enemies (usually Muslims), meet a friendly

---

survive, written mainly between 1532 and 1548. His poems, although virtually unknown in his day, did circulate among friends and patrons. In one instance, one poem reached a larger audience, when it served as the focus of an admirer's address to the Florentine Academy, in 1547.

In his poetry, Michelangelo adopted either the Petrarchan sonnet (see Chapter 11) or the **madrigal**—an irregular verse form, not to be confused with the English madrigal (see "Music," Chapter 13). Classicism in his High Renaissance style included the Petrarchan sonnet and the Neoplatonic philosophy that he had absorbed as a youth in Florence, at the Medici court. In his verses, Platonic love, while originating in physical beauty, ultimately leads to the divine. A product of his era, Michelangelo also wrote verses about his life as a working artist and as a man facing aging and death.

CASTIGLIONE   The reputation of Castiglione [kahs-teel-YOH-nay] (1478–1529) rests on *The Book of the Courtier* or,

simply, *The Courtier*, one of the most influential books of the High Renaissance. Intended for Italian court society, *The Courtier* was published in 1528. Translated into most Western languages, it quickly became the bible of courteous behavior for Europe's upper classes until about 1800.

A Mantuan by birth, Castiglione (Figure 12.6) based his guide to manners on life at the north Italian court of Urbino, where, between 1504 and 1517, he lived under the patronage of its resident duke, Guidobaldo da Montefeltro (see Figure 11.2). Impressed by the graceful conversations of his fellow courtiers and especially taken with the charms of Urbino's duchess, Elisabetta, Castiglione was moved to memorialize his experiences in writing. *The Courtier* is composed as a dialogue, a literary form originated by Plato and favored by Cicero. Castiglione's dialogue is set in Urbino and peopled with actual individuals for whom he invents urbane and witty conversations that suit their known characters. Despite this realistic touch, his book's overall tone

Encounter figure 12.1 *Luis Vaz de Camoes.* Frontispiece from *The Lusiads.* 1655. *In this anonymous portrait, Luis Vaz de Camoes is dressed as a soldier and wears the laurel crown of the poet—an honorific symbol from classical culture. The loss of his eye, he wrote, taught him about the expense of war and reminded him of the price he paid for his personal heroism and his country's empire.*

king to whom da Gama recounts the glorious history of Portugal, establish trading outlets in India, and return home with their prizes and as heroes. As in the *Aeneid*, the author opens his tale *in medias res* (in the middle of events), with da Gama sailing up the east coast of Africa. Camoes then introduces the Greek and Roman deities, who play significant roles: Venus and Mars in aiding da Gama, and Bacchus (the god of wine) in thwarting the explorer's journey.

Camoes was more than an accomplished storyteller: he was the voice of sixteenth-century Portugal and Europe. To him, Portugal had established itself as a great nation, acting as a harbinger for Europe's future, saving Europe from enemies abroad, and helping spread the Christian faith around the world. And, from a multicultural perspective, he linked Portugal's future and, by extension, all of Europe's to the hitherto little-known worlds overseas.

LEARNING FROM THE ENCOUNTER

1. *What* advantages enabled Portugal to become a nation of explorers? 2. *What* were some consequences of the encounter between Portugal and the Far East? 3. *Compare The Lusiads* with Virgil's *Aeneid*. 4. *Discuss* the relationship between *The Lusiads* and the birth of a kind of multiculturalism in Europe.

is definitely idealistic and hence expressive of High Renaissance style.

Castiglione's idealism shines forth most clearly in the sections in which the invited company try to define the perfect courtier, or gentleman. Under Duchess Elisabetta's eye, the guests debate which aspect of the ideal gentleman's training should take precedence: education in the arts and humanities or skill in horsemanship and swordplay. Eventually, both sides agree that the ideal courtier should be proficient in each of these areas. A sign that the Renaissance had raised the status of painting and sculpture was the group's expectation that a gentleman be knowledgeable about both of these art forms.

The Courtier also describes the perfect court lady. In the minds of the dialogue participants, the ideal lady is a civilizing influence on men, who would otherwise be crude. To that end, the perfect lady should be a consummate hostess, charming, witty, graceful, physically attractive, and utterly feminine. She ought to be well versed in the same areas as a man, except for athletics and the mastery of arms. With these social attributes, the cultivated lady can then bring out the best in a courtier. But she must not seem his inferior, for she contributes to society in her own way.

Castiglione's book turned away from medieval values and led his followers into the modern world. First, Castiglione argued that social relations between the sexes ought to be governed by Platonic love—a spiritual passion that surpassed physical conquest—and thus he rejected medieval courtly love and its adulterous focus. Second, he reasoned that women in society should be the educated equals of men, thereby sweeping away the barrier that had been erected when women were excluded from medieval universities. In the short run, the impact of Castiglione's social rules was to keep women on a pedestal, as courtly love had done. But for the future, his advice allowed women to participate actively in every aspect of society and encouraged their education in much the same way as men's.

Figure 12.6 RAPHAEL. *Baldassare Castiglione.* 1514. Oil on canvas, 32¼ × 26½". *Castiglione, author of* The Book of the Courtier, *was memorialized in this handsome portrait by the High Renaissance painter, Raphael. Elegantly groomed and completely at ease, Castiglione appears here as the age's ideal courtier—an ideal that he helped to establish.*

MACHIAVELLI   In contrast to Castiglione's optimism, the Florentine Machiavelli [mak-ee-uh-VEL-ee] (1469–1527) held a negative view of human nature and made human weakness the central message of his writings. If *The Courtier* seems to be taking place in a never-never land where decorum and gentility are the primary interests, Machiavelli returns the reader to political reality. His mannerist cynicism about human weakness sprang from wounded idealism, for life had taught him that his early optimism was wrong. In his writings, the bleak view of human nature is meant to restore sanity to a world that he thought had gone mad.

Except for Martin Luther (see Chapter 13), Machiavelli left a stronger imprint on Western culture than any other figure who lived between 1494 and 1564. Machiavelli's most enduring contribution was *The Prince,* which inaugurated a revolution in political thought. Rejecting the medieval tradition of framing political discussions in Christian terms, Machiavelli treated the state as a human invention that ought not necessarily conform to religious or moral rules. He began the modern search for a science of politics that has absorbed political thinkers and policymakers ever since.

Machiavelli's career in sixteenth-century Italy, like that of many writers in antiquity, was split between a life of action and a life of the mind. Between 1498 and 1512, he served the newly reborn Florentine republic as a senior official and diplomat, learning statecraft firsthand. During these turbulent years, he was particularly impressed by the unscrupulous Cesare Borgia, Pope Alexander VI's son. In 1512, after the fall of the Florentine republic to the resurgent Medici party, Machiavelli was imprisoned, tortured, and finally exiled to his family estate outside the city. There, in exile, he wrote the small work known as *The Prince* (1513), which circulated in manuscript until after his death. In 1532 it was finally published.

Machiavelli had several motives in writing this masterpiece. Despairing over Italy's dismemberment by the French and the Spanish kings, he hoped the book would inspire an indigenous leader to unify the peninsula and drive out the foreigners. Enlightened by his personal experience in Florence's affairs, he wanted to capture in writing the truth of the politics to which he had been a witness. And, of equal importance, by dedicating *The Prince* to the restored Medici ruler, he hoped to regain employment in the Florentine state. Like other writers in this age, Machiavelli could not live by his wits but had to rely on secular or religious patronage.

Machiavelli's work failed in its immediate objectives: the Medici despot brushed it aside, and Italy remained fragmented until 1870. But as a work that exposed the ruthlessness needed to succeed in politics, *The Prince* was an instant, though controversial, success. The book was denounced by religious leaders for its amoral treatment of political power and read secretly by secular rulers for its sage advice. In the prevailing worldview of the 1500s, an era still under the sway of Christian ideals, the name "Machiavelli" became synonymous with dishonesty and treachery, and the word **Machiavellianism** was coined to describe the amoral notion that "the end justifies any means."

From the modern perspective, this negative valuation of Machiavelli is both too simplistic and too harsh. Above all else he was a clear-eyed patriot who was anguished by the tragedy unfolding in Italy. *The Prince* describes the power politics that the new sovereign states of France and Spain were pursuing in Italian affairs. Machiavelli realized that the only way to rid Italy of foreigners was to adopt the methods of its successful foes. Seeing his countrymen as cowardly and greedy, he had no illusions that a popular uprising would spring up and drive out Italy's oppressors. Only a strong-willed monarch, not bound by a finicky moral code, could bring Italy back from political chaos.

The controversial heart of Machiavelli's treatise was the section that advised the ruler on the best way to govern. He counseled the prince to practice conscious duplicity, since that was the only way to maintain power and to ensure peace—the two basic goals of any state. By appearing virtuous and upright while acting as the situation demanded, the prince could achieve these fundamental ends.

Painting

In the arts, the period between 1494 and 1564 was preeminently an age of painting, though several sculptors and architects created major works in their respective fields. The classical values of idealism, balance, and restraint were translated by High Renaissance painters into harmonious colors, naturally posed figures with serene faces, realistic space and perspectives, and perfectly proportioned human bodies. After 1520, mannerist tendencies became more and more evident,

reflected in abnormal subjects, contorted figures with emotionally expressive faces, and garish colors.

LEONARDO DA VINCI   The inauguration of the High Renaissance in painting is usually dated from Leonardo's *The Last Supper*, which was completed between 1495 and 1498 (Figure 12.7). Painted for the Dominican friars of the church of Santa Maria delle Grazie in Milan, *The Last Supper* heralded the lucidity and harmony that were the essence of High Renaissance style. In executing the fresco, Leonardo unfortunately made use of a flawed technique, and the painting began to flake during his lifetime. Over the centuries, the work has been touched up frequently and restored seven times, with the most recent restoration completed in 1999. Nevertheless, enough of his noble intention is evident to ensure the reputation of *The Last Supper* as one of the best-known and most beloved paintings of Western art.

Leonardo's design for *The Last Supper* is highly idealized—a guiding principle of the High Renaissance. The fresco depicts the moment when Jesus says that one of the twelve disciples at the table will betray him (Matthew 26:21). Ignoring the tradition that integrated this symbolic meal into an actual refectory, Leonardo

Figure 12.7   LEONARDO DA VINCI. *The Last Supper.* (Restored.) 1495–1498. Oil-tempera on wall, 13'10″ × 29'7½″. Refectory, Santa Maria delle Grazie, Milan. *Classical restraint is one of the defining characteristics of this High Renaissance masterpiece. Instead of overwhelming the viewer with distracting details, Leonardo reduces the objects to a minimum, from the austere room in which the meal is being celebrated to the simple articles on the dining table. The viewer's gaze is thereby held on the unfolding human drama rather than on secondary aspects of the scene.*

separated the scene from its surroundings so that the figures would seem to hover over the heads of the clergy as they ate in their dining room. Idealism is also evident in Leonardo's straightforward perspective. The artist makes Jesus the focal center by framing him in the middle window and locating the vanishing point behind his head. In addition, the arrangement of the banqueting party—Jesus is flanked by six followers on either side—gives the painting a balanced effect. This harmonious composition breaks with the medieval custom of putting the traitor Judas on the opposite side of the table from the others.

A final idealistic touch may be seen in the way that Leonardo hides the face of Judas, the third figure on Jesus's right, in shadow while illuminating the other figures in bright light. Judas, though no longer seated apart from the rest, can still be readily identified, sitting cloaked in shadows, reaching for the bread with his left hand, and clutching a bag of silver—symbolic of his treason—in the other hand. For generations, admirers have found Leonardo's fresco so natural and inevitable that it has become the standard version of this Christian subject.

Leonardo's setting and placement of the figures in *The Last Supper* are idealized, but his depiction of the individual figures is meant to convey the psychological truth about each of them. Jesus is portrayed with eyes cast down and arms outstretched in a gesture of resignation, while on either side a tumultuous scene erupts. As the disciples react to Jesus's charge of treason, Leonardo reveals the inner truth about each one through bodily gestures and facial expressions: Beneath the visual tumult, however, the artistic rules of the High Renaissance are firmly in place. Since neither biblical sources nor sacred tradition offered an ordering principle, Leonardo used mathematics to guide his arrangement of the disciples. He divides them into four groups of three figures; each set in turn is composed of two older men and a younger one. In his conception, not only does each figure respond individually, but also each interacts with other group members.

Besides mastering a narrative subject like *The Last Supper,* Leonardo created a new type of portrait when he painted a half-length view of the seated *Mona Lisa* (Figure 12.8). As the fame of this work spread, other painters (and, later, photographers) adopted Leonardo's half-length model as a basic format for portraits. Avoiding the directness of *The Last Supper,* Leonardo hints at the sitter's demure nature through her shy smile and the charmingly awkward gesture of having the fingers of her right hand caress her left arm. In her face, celebrated in song and legend, he blends the likeness of a real person with an everlasting ideal to create a miraculous image. Further heightening the painting's eternal quality, the craggy background isolates the figure in

space and time, in much the same way that the grotto functioned in Leonardo's *Virgin of the Rocks* (see Figure 11.23). Finally, he enhances the *Mona Lisa*'s mystery by enveloping the subject in the smoky atmosphere called *sfumato*—made possible by the oil medium—which softens her delicate features and the landscape in the background.

During the High Renaissance, Leonardo's great works contributed to the cult of genius—the high regard, even reverence, that the age accorded to a few select artists, poets, and intellectuals. *The Last Supper* earned him great fame while he was alive. The history of the *Mona Lisa* was more complicated, since it was unseen while he lived and found among his effects when he died in 1519. After his death, as the *Mona Lisa* became widely known, first as a possession of the king of France and later as a jewel in the Louvre collection, Leonardo was elevated to membership among the immortals of Western art.

MICHELANGELO   While Leonardo was working in Milan during most of the 1490s, Michelangelo Buonarroti [my-kuh-LAN-juh-lo bwo-nahr-ROH-tee] (1475–1564) was beginning a career that would propel him to the forefront of first the Florentine and later the Roman Renaissance, making him the most formidable artist of the sixteenth century. Michelangelo's initial fame rested on his sculptural genius, which manifested itself at the age of thirteen when he was apprenticed to the early Renaissance master Ghirlandaio and then, one year later, taken into the household of Lorenzo the Magnificent, the Medici ruler of Florence. In time, Michelangelo achieved greatness in painting and architecture as well as in sculpture, but he always remained a sculptor at heart.

Michelangelo's artistic credo was formed early, and he remained faithful to it over his long life. Sculpture, he believed, was the art form whereby human figures were liberated from the lifeless prison of their surrounding material. In this sense, he compared the sculptor's creativity with the activity of God—a notion that would have been judged blasphemous in prior Christian ages. Michelangelo himself, unlike the skeptical Leonardo, was a deeply pious man given to bouts of spiritual anxiety. His art constituted a form of divine worship.

Central to Michelangelo's artistic vision was his most celebrated image, the heroic nude male. Like the ancient Greek and Roman sculptors whose works he studied and admired, Michelangelo viewed the nude male form as a symbol of human dignity. In the High Renaissance, Michelangelo's nudes were based on classical models, with robust bodies and serene faces. But in the 1530s, with the onset of mannerism, the growing spiritual crisis in the church, and his own failing

Figure 12.8 Leonardo da Vinci. *Mona Lisa.* 1503. Oil on panel, 30¼ × 21″. Louvre. *Leonardo's* Mona Lisa, *a likeness of the wife of the wealthy Florentine merchant Giocondo, illustrates the new status of Italy's urban middle class. This class was beginning to take its social cues from the fashionable world of the courts, the milieu described by Castiglione. Leonardo treats his middle-class subject as a model court lady, imbuing her presence with calm seriousness and quiet dignity.*

health, Michelangelo's depiction of the human figure changed. His later nudes had distorted body proportions and unusually expressive faces.

In 1508 Michelangelo was asked by Pope Julius II (pope 1503–1533) to decorate the Sistine Chapel ceiling. Michelangelo tried to avoid this commission, claiming that he was a sculptor and without expertise in frescoes, but the pope was unyielding in his insistence. The chapel had been built by Julius II's uncle, Pope Sixtus IV (pope 1471–1484), in the late 1400s, and most of the walls had already been covered with frescoes. Michelangelo's frescoes were intended to bring the chapel's decorative plan closer to completion.

The challenge of painting the Sistine Chapel ceiling was enormous, for it was almost 70 feet from the floor, its sides were curved downward, necessitating numerous perspective changes, and its area covered some 5,800 square feet. Michelangelo overcame all these difficulties, teaching himself fresco technique and working for four years on scaffolding, to create one of the glories of the High Renaissance and unquestionably the greatest cycle of paintings in Western art (Figure 12.9).

Michelangelo, probably with the support of a papal adviser, designed a complex layout (Figure 12.10) for the ceiling frescoes that combined biblical narrative, theology, Neoplatonist philosophy, and classical allusions. In the ceiling's center, running from the altar to the rear of the chapel, he painted nine panels that illustrate the early history of the world, encompassing the creation of the universe, the fall of Adam and Eve, and episodes in the life of Noah. Framing these biblical scenes were nude youths, whose presence shows Michelangelo's belief that the male form is an expression of divine power.

On either side of the center panels, Michelangelo depicted Hebrew prophets and pagan sibyls, or oracles—all foretelling the coming of Christ (Interpretive Art figure 12.1). The pagan sibyls represent the Neoplatonist idea that God's word was revealed in the prophecies of pre-Christian seers. At the corners of

Figure 12.9 MICHELANGELO. Sistine Chapel Ceiling. (Restored.) 1508–1512. Full ceiling 45 × 128'. The Vatican. *Michelangelo's knowledge of architecture prompted him to paint illusionistic niches for the Hebrew prophets and the pagan sibyls on either side of the nine central panels. Neoplatonism inspired his use of triangles, circles, and squares, for these geometric shapes were believed to hold the key to the mystery of the universe. These various framing devices give visual order to the more than three hundred figures in his monumental scheme.*

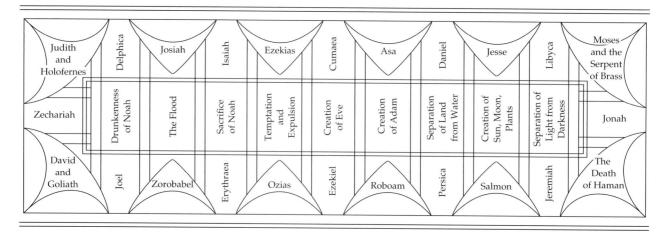

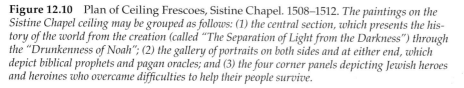

Figure 12.10 Plan of Ceiling Frescoes, Sistine Chapel. 1508–1512. *The paintings on the Sistine Chapel ceiling may be grouped as follows: (1) the central section, which presents the history of the world from the creation (called "The Separation of Light from the Darkness") through the "Drunkenness of Noah"; (2) the gallery of portraits on both sides and at either end, which depict biblical prophets and pagan oracles; and (3) the four corner panels depicting Jewish heroes and heroines who overcame difficulties to help their people survive.*

the ceiling, he placed four Old Testament scenes of violence and death that had been allegorized as foreshadowing the coming of Christ. Michelangelo unified this complex of human and divine figures with an illusionistic architectural frame, and he used a plain background to make the figures stand out.

The most famous image from this vast work is a panel from the central section, *The Creation of Adam* (Figure 12.11), based on a passage in the book of Genesis. Michelangelo reduces the scene to a few details, in accordance with the High Renaissance love of simplicity. Adam, stretched out on a barely sketched bit of ground, seems to exist in some timeless space. Depicted as a pulsing, breathing human being, he possesses wondrous vitality in human flesh, the likes of which had not been seen in Western art since the ancient Greeks. In a bold move, Michelangelo ignored the Genesis story that told of God's molding Adam from dust. Instead, the artist painted Adam as half-awakened and

reaching to God, who will implant a soul with his divine touch—an illustration of the Neoplatonic idea of flesh yearning toward the spiritual.

By the 1530s, Michelangelo was painting in the mannerist style, reflecting his disappointment with Florence's loss of freedom and his own spiritual torment. In this new style, he replaced his heroic vision with a fearful view of the world. A compelling example of this transformation is *The Last Judgment,* painted on the wall behind the Sistine Chapel's altar. This fresco conveys his own sense of sinfulness as well as humanity's future doom (Figure 12.12). Executed twenty-five years after the ceiling frescoes, *The Last Judgment,* with its images of justice and punishment, also reflects the crisis atmosphere of a Europe divided into militant Protestant and Catholic camps. In the center of the fresco, Michelangelo depicts Jesus as the divine and final judge, with right arm raised in a commanding gesture. At the bottom of the fresco, the open graves yield up the dead,

INTERPRETING ART

Composition Three figures (a female, in foreground, and two boys, in midground), a draped chair, and a large open book are crowded into an illusionistic niche.

Architectural Elements The niche, defined by decorated columns on either side and a running band of lines in the rear, provides a space to frame the central figures.

Female Body The muscular shoulders and back reflect Michelangelo's practice of using male models for female subjects. The resulting image deviates from classical ideals of feminine beauty.

Anatomy Michelangelo was fascinated by the way muscles and bones interacted beneath the skin. In this image, he presents the sibyl, with her back to the viewer, her upraised arms holding her book of sayings, and her lower body balanced on her toes.

Religious Perspective Michelangelo's overall plan, blending Christian theology and Neoplatonic thought, is meant to validate the Christian view of creation and human history.

Color Color is used to heighten the image's three-dimensional look, by using primary colors for the bodies, clothing, and draperies so that they will stand out against the muted hues of the background.

Interpreting Art figure 12.1 MICHELANGELO. *The Libyan Sibyl.* (Restored.) Detail of the Sistine Chapel ceiling. 1508–1512. 12′11½″ × 12′6″. The Vatican. *Michelangelo's subject—the Libyan Sibyl—was an ancient oracle, based in Libya. Neoplatonic thought—which contributed to the plan for the Sistine Chapel ceiling—taught that God, however imperfectly, spoke to all peoples. Thus, the voice of God could be heard in the sibyl's utterances. By 1500 the church had accepted the Libyan Sibyl, along with eleven other pagan seers, as divinely inspired prophetesses foretelling the coming of Christ.*

and the saved and the damned (on Jesus's right and left, respectively) rise to meet their fate.

In this painting, Michelangelo abandons the architectural framework that had given order to the ceiling frescoes. Instead, the viewer is confronted with a chaotic surface on which a circle of bodies seems to swirl around the central image of Jesus. Michelangelo elongates the bodies and changes their proportions by reducing the size of the heads. There is no classical serenity here; each figure's countenance shows the anguish provoked by this dreaded moment. Faced with

judgment, some figures gesture wildly while others look beseechingly to their Savior. In this mannerist masterpiece, simplicity has been replaced by exuberant abundance, and order has given way to rich diversity.

RAPHAEL The youngest of the trio of great High Renaissance painters is Raphael [RAFF-ee-uhl] Santi (1483–1520). Lacking Leonardo's scientific spirit and Michelangelo's brooding genius, Raphael nevertheless had such artistry that his graceful works expressed the ideals of this style better than did those of any other

Figure 12.11   MICHELANGELO. *The Creation of Adam*. Detail (restored) of the Sistine Chapel ceiling. 1511. 9′5″ × 18′8″. The Vatican. *One of the most celebrated details of this fresco is the outstretched fingers of God and Adam that approach but do not touch. By means of this vivid symbol, Michelangelo suggests that a divine spark is about to pass from God into the body of Adam, electrifying it into the fullness of life. The image demonstrates the restraint characteristic of the High Renaissance style. The Vatican's restoration of the Sistine Chapel frescoes has revealed the brilliant colors of the original, apparent in this detail.*

painter. Trained in Urbino, Raphael spent four years (1504–1508) in Florence, where he absorbed the local painting tradition, learning from the public works of both Leonardo and Michelangelo. Inspired by what he saw, Raphael developed his artistic ideal of well-ordered space in which human beauty and spatial harmony were given equal treatment.

Moving to Rome, Raphael had an abundance of patrons, especially the popes. The secret of Raphael's success was his talent for blending the sacred and the secular, and in an age when a pope led troops into battle or went on hunting parties, this gift was appreciated and rewarded. Perhaps Raphael's most outstanding work in Rome was the cycle of paintings for the *stanze*, or rooms, of the Vatican apartment—one of the finest patronage plums of the High Renaissance. Commissioned by Julius II, the *stanze* frescoes show the same harmonization of Christianity and classicism that Michelangelo brought to the Sistine Chapel ceiling.

Raphael's plan for the four walls of the Stanza della Segnatura in the papal chambers had as its subjects philosophy, poetry, theology, and law. Of these, the most famous is the fresco devoted to philosophy called *The School of Athens* (Figure 12.13). In this work, Raphael depicts a sober discussion among a group of ancient philosophers drawn from all periods. Following Leonardo's treatment of the disciples in *The Last Supper*, Raphael arranges the philosophers in groups, giving each scholar a characteristic gesture that reveals the essence of his thought. For example, Diogenes sprawls on the steps apart from the others—a vivid symbol of the arch Cynic's contempt for his fellow man. In the right foreground, Euclid, the author of a standard text on geometry, illustrates the proof of one of his theorems. In his careful arrangement of this crowd scene, Raphael demonstrates his mastery of ordered space.

The School of Athens has a majestic aura because of Raphael's adherence to classical forms and ideas. The architectural setting, with its rounded arches, medallions, and coffered ceilings, is inspired by classical ruins and also perhaps by contemporary structures. Perfectly balanced, the scene is focused on Plato and Aristotle, who stand under the series of arches at the painting's center. Raphael reinforces their central position by placing the vanishing point just above and between their heads. The two thinkers' contrasting gestures symbolize the difference between their philosophies: Plato, on the left, points his finger skyward, suggesting the world of the Forms, or abstract thought, and Aristotle, on the right, motions toward the earth, indicating his more

Figure 12.12 Michelangelo. *The Last Judgment.* 1536–1541. 48 × 44'. Sistine Chapel, the Vatican. *This* Last Judgment *summarizes the anticlassicism that was sweeping through the visual arts. Other painters studied this fresco for inspiration, borrowing its seemingly chaotic composition, its focus on large numbers of male nudes, and its use of bizarre perspective and odd postures as expressions of the mannerist sensibility. This fresco has been restored, its colors returned to the vivid primary colors of Michelangelo's original design and the draperies removed (they had been added during the Catholic Reformation).*

Figure 12.13   RAPHAEL. *The School of Athens.* 1510–1511. Fresco, 18 × 26′. Stanza della Segnatura, the Vatican. *Much of Raphael's success stemmed from the ease with which he assimilated the prevailing ideas of his age. For instance, the posture of the statue of Apollo in the wall niche on the left is probably derived from Michelangelo's* Dying Slave *(see Figure 12.1). For all his borrowings, however, Raphael could be very generous, as indicated by the conspicuous way he highlights Michelangelo's presence in this fresco: the brooding genius sits alone in the foreground, lost in his thoughts and oblivious to the hubbub swirling about him.*

practical and empirical method. Raphael also uses these two thinkers as part of his ordering scheme to represent the division of philosophy into the arts and sciences. On Plato's side, the poetic thinkers are gathered under the statue of Apollo, the Greek god of music and lyric verse; Aristotle's half includes the scientists under the statue of Athena, the Greek goddess of wisdom.

Of even greater fame than Raphael's narrative paintings are his portraits of the Virgin Mary, or his Madonna series—admired for their exquisite sweetness and harmonious composition. Raphael's Madonnas clearly show the influence of Leonardo, whose Virgin and Christ child paintings were well known by then (see Figure 11.23). Like many of the Madonna series, Raphael's *Madonna of the Chair* (Figure 12.14) is organized in a pyramidal structure, a design borrowed from Leonardo. The Virgin and Christ child are not enthroned, as in the traditional setting, but are sitting, lovingly cuddled together, in a chair, as is

hinted by the carved spindle (on the left). To the right stands the child John the Baptist, who looks up adoringly at the Virgin and her son. The Virgin's simple piety comes through in the way Raphael captures her beauty and tenderness in a lovely image. Unlike many religious paintings, the *Madonna of the Chair* does not deliver a theological message, preach a sermon, or tell a story. Because of its domestic setting, this image is considered one of the most natural of Raphael's Madonnas and remains one of his most popular paintings today.

THE VENETIAN SCHOOL: GIORGIONE AND TITIAN   Venice maintained its autonomy during the High Renaissance both politically and culturally. Despite the artistic pull of the Roman and Florentine schools, the Venetian artists stayed true to their Byzantine-influenced tradition of sensual surfaces, rich colors, and theatrical lighting. The two greatest painters of the Venetian

Figure 12.14 RAPHAEL. *Madonna of the Chair.* Ca. 1515. Oil on wood panel, diameter 2′5″. Pitti Palace, Florence, Italy. *The Christ child caresses the Virgin's cheek—a conventional pose used by Renaissance artists for depicting the baby Jesus and Mary. Mary gazes at the viewer and seems to be contemplating her son's fate. Her head is covered in an oriental-inspired headdress (see Encounter in Chapter 11), and she wears a shawl over a red bodice. The Christ child sits on a blue pillow, the color mystically associated with the Virgin. The circular composition makes the three figures appear even more intimate, as it narrows the spaces between their bodies. Raphael probably painted the* Madonna of the Chair *for a church official.*

Figure 12.15 GIORGIONE. *The Tempest.* 1505. Oil on canvas, 31¼ × 28¾″. Galleria dell'Accademia, Venice. *Giorgione's mysterious painting evokes the moment—called an "anxious hush"— that sometimes attends the prelude to a violent thunderstorm. He creates this tense mood through atmospheric effects that suggest a gathering storm: billowing clouds; a flash of lightning and its watery reflection; and, in particular, the stark color contrasts between the harshly lighted buildings and the somber hues of earth, sky, and river. The mood is also heightened by the presence of two vulnerable figures, especially the nursing mother who gazes quizzically at the viewer, about to be engulfed by the storm. The painting has a typical Venetian feature in its carefully rendered textures— flesh, cloth, wood, stone, and foliage.*

High Renaissance were Giorgione [jor-JO-na] (about 1477–1510), who was acknowledged to be Venice's premier artist at the end of his life, and Titian [TISH-uhn] (about 1488–1576), who in his later years was revered as Europe's supreme painter.

Little is known of Giorgione's life until the last years of his brief career. A student of the Bellini workshop, he won early fame, indicated by the rich private and public commissions he was awarded. Although only a few of his works survive, Giorgione's influence on the course of European art was substantial. His two major innovations, the female nude and the landscape, contributed to the growing secularization of European painting. These developments helped to make Venetian art distinctive from that of Rome and Florence.

The Tempest (Figure 12.15) is probably his best-known work. Breaking free of the Bellinis' influence, Giorgione created a dramatic landscape, framed on the left by a soldier and on the right by a partly clothed mother nursing a child, that did not allude to mythology, the Bible, or allegorical stories. Whereas Bellini's *St. Francis in Ecstasy* (see Figure 11.24) made the saint the focus of the painting, in *The Tempest* the framing figures are overshadowed by the menacing storm. Thus, Giorgione's landscape, freed of storytelling elements, becomes the subject and should be appreciated on its own terms.

Titian's paintings were prized not only for their easy grace and natural lighting—characteristics of the Venetian Renaissance—but also for their dramatic use of color (see Figure 12.3). Titian's adherence to the principles of High Renaissance style is evident in such narrative paintings as his *Martyrdom of St. Lawrence* (Figure 12.16). According to tradition, Lawrence, a Spaniard, served as a deacon in charge of the church's treasures in Rome. When commanded to turn this wealth over to the civil authorities, he instead assembled the poor and distributed the treasures to them. For this act of defiance, the Romans condemned and executed him in 258. Later, as St. Lawrence, he became the patron saint of the poor and downtrodden.

Titian's careful arrangement of this scene of torture and martyrdom reflects his commitment to the principle of simplicity. In the foreground, he shows St. Lawrence being roasted on a grill; to the right, he depicts a pagan temple, rendered in sharply receding perspective, thereby framing the saint's death scene. The juxtaposition of the dying St. Lawrence and the classical temple reminds the viewer that the pagan Romans had failed to eradicate Christianity. Titian's subtle modulations of color, which create a sense of harmony, made him a leading "colorist"—an artist concerned more with color than with form—and an inspiration to future generations of painters.

Figure 12.16   Titian. *Martyrdom of St. Lawrence.* 1550s. Oil on canvas, 16'5½" × 9'2". Chiesa dei Gesuiti, Venice. *Even though Titian worked within the classical rules required by the High Renaissance style, he sometimes deviated from its strict regularity, as in this painting. The temple's columns recede along a diagonal line, creating a sense of deep space in the foreground; within this space, he arranged objects in a triangular outline with the celestial light source at the apex. By using diagonal and triangular lines, as he often did in his religious works, Titian was able to achieve dramatic and emotional effects without forfeiting coherence or meaning. He heightened this effect by bathing the human figures in the light from the sky and the glow from the torches and the fire underneath St. Lawrence.*

THE SCHOOL OF PARMA: PARMIGIANINO   Parma, in northern Italy, was another center of High Renaissance art, but the city's best-known artist is a founder of mannerism, Parmigianino [pahr-mee-jah-NEE-noh] (1503–1540). The *Madonna with the Long Neck* shows Parmigianino's delight in ambiguity, distortion, and dissonance and his love of eccentric composition (Figure 12.17). Mary is portrayed with sloping shoulders

Figure 12.17 Parmigianino. *Madonna with the Long Neck.* 1534–1540. Oil on panel, 7′1″ × 4′4″. Uffizi Gallery, Florence. *This Madonna by Parmigianino is one of the landmark works in the mannerist style. Ignoring classical ideals, Parmigianino exaggerates the Virgin's body proportions, especially the slender hands and long neck, and elongates the body of the sleeping Jesus. This anticlassical portrait was greatly at odds with the prevailing High Renaissance image of the Madonna established by Raphael.*

and long arms in the manner of Botticelli, and her sensuous figure is not quite hidden under diaphanous draperies—a disturbing mix of sacred and profane love. A similar confusion exists in the depiction of the infant Christ: The bald baby Jesus appears more dead than alive, so that the subject invokes the Pietà image of the dead Christ stretched on his mother's lap along with the image of the Virgin and Christ child. On the left, five figures stare in various directions. In the background, unfinished columns and an old man reading a scroll, perhaps an allusion to biblical prophecies of Jesus's birth, add to the feeling of multiple focuses and contradictory scales. Unlike the art of the High Renaissance, which offered readily understood subjects, this mannerist painting, with its uneasy blend of religious piety and disguised sexuality, is enigmatic.

Figure 12.18 Michelangelo. *Pietà.* 1498–1499. Marble, ht. 5′8½″. St. Peter's, the Vatican. *This Pietà is the only one of Michelangelo's sculptures to be signed. Initially, it was exhibited without a signature, but, according to a legend, when Michelangelo overheard spectators attributing the statue to a rival sculptor, he carved his signature into the marble strap that crosses Mary's chest.*

SLICE OF LIFE
Artists and Their Critics: Michelangelo's Strategy

GIORGIO VASARI
From *Life of Michelangelo*

Medieval artists were guild members, that is, skilled crafts-people with little social status. In the following vignette, Michelangelo is portrayed as a confident Renaissance artist: proud and ready to take on critics, even the head of the Florentine republic. The vignette's author, Giorgio Vasari (1511–1574), who studied painting with Michelangelo, is known today primarily as a biographer of Renaissance artists, sculptors, and architects.

Some of his [Michelangelo's] friends wrote to him from Florence urging him to return there as it seemed very probable that he would be able to obtain the block of marble that was standing in the Office of Works. Piero Soderini, who about that time was elected Gonfalonier for life [head of the Florentine republic], had often talked of handing it over to Leonardo da Vinci, but he was then arranging to give it to Andrea Contucci of Monte Sansovino, an accomplished sculptor who was very keen to have it. Now, although it seemed impossible to carve from the block a complete figure (and only Michelangelo was bold enough to try this without adding fresh pieces) Buonarroti had felt the desire to work on it many years before; and he tried to obtain it when he came back to Florence. The marble was eighteen feet high, but unfortunately an artist called Simone da Fiesole had started to carve a giant figure, and had bungled the work so badly that he had hacked a hole between the legs and left the block completely botched and misshapen. So the wardens of Santa Maria del Fiore (who were in charge of the undertaking) threw the block aside and it stayed abandoned for many years and seemed likely to remain so indefinitely. However, Michelangelo measured it again and calculated whether he could carve a satisfactory figure from the block by accommodating its attitude to the shape of the stone. Then he made up his mind to ask for it. Soderini and the wardens decided that they would let him have it, as being something of little value, and telling themselves that since the stone was of no use to their building, either botched as it was or broken up, whatever Michelangelo made

would be worthwhile. So Michelangelo made a wax model of the young David with a sling in his hand; this was intended as a symbol of liberty for the Palace, signifying that just as David had protected his people and governed them justly, so whoever ruled Florence should vigorously defend the city and govern it with justice. He began work on the statue in the Office of Works of Santa Maria del Fiore, erecting a partition of planks and trestles around the marble; and working on it continuously he brought it to perfect completion, without letting anyone see it. . . .

When he saw the David in place Piero Soderini was delighted; but while Michelangelo was retouching it he remarked that he thought the nose was too thick. Michelangelo, noticing that the Gonfalonier was standing beneath the Giant and that from where he was he could not see the figure properly, to satisfy him climbed on the scaffolding by the shoulders, seized hold of a chisel in his left hand, together with some of the marble dust lying on the planks, and as he tapped lightly with the chisel let the dust fall little by little, without altering anything. Then he looked down at the Gonfalonier, who had stopped to watch, and said:

"Now look at it."

"Ah, that's much better," replied Soderini. "Now you've really brought it to life."

And then Michelangelo climbed down, feeling sorry for those critics who talk nonsense in the hope of appearing well informed.

INTERPRETING THIS SLICE OF LIFE

1. *Why* was Michelangelo eager to work on this particular block of marble? 2. *What* does this story reveal about the character of Michelangelo? 3. *What* trick did Michelangelo play on Soderini? 4. *Speculate* as to the motive behind Michelangelo's behavior. 5. *Do* artists today show some of the same traits as those of Michelangelo in this piece? *Explain.*

Sculpture

Michelangelo's sculptures, just like his paintings, helped to define High Renaissance style. An early sculpture that helped to inaugurate this style was the *Pietà* executed when he was twenty-one (Figure 12.18). The touching subject of the **Pietà**—Mary holding the body of the dead Christ—struck a responsive chord in

Michelangelo, for he created several variations on the Pietà theme during his lifetime.

The first *Pietà*, executed in 1498–1499, about the same time as Leonardo's *Last Supper*, shows Michelangelo already at the height of his creative powers. He has captured completely a bewildering sense of loss in his quiet rendering of Mary's suffering. Everything about the sculpture reinforces the somber subject: the superb

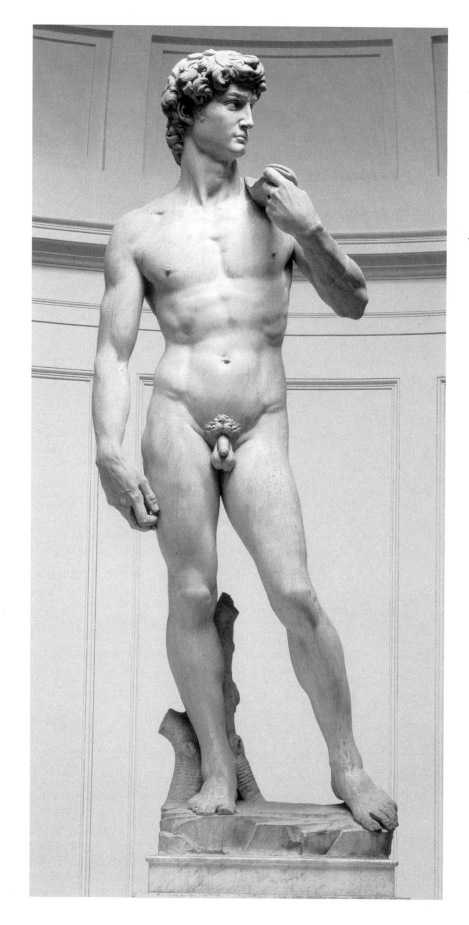

Figure 12.19 MICHELANGELO. *David.* 1501–1504. Marble, ht. 14′3″. Accademia, Florence. *Michelangelo's colossal* David—*standing more than 14 feet tall—captures the balanced ideal of High Renaissance art. The "closed" right side with its tensed hanging arm echoes the right leg, which supports the figure's weight; in the same way, the "open" left side with its bent arm is the precise counterpart of the flexed left leg. Further tension arises from the contrast between David's steady stare and the readiness of the right fist, which holds the stone. Through these means, Michelangelo reinforces the image of a young man wavering between thought and action.*

modeling of Jesus's dead body, with its heavy head and dangling legs; Mary's outstretched gown, which serves as a shroud; and Mary's body, burdened by the weight of her son. Like some ancient funeral monument, which the *Pietà* brings to mind, this sculpture of Mary and Jesus overwhelms the viewer with its sorrowful but serene mood.

In 1501, two years after finishing the *Pietà*, Michelangelo was given the commission by the city of Florence for the sculpture that is generally recognized as his supreme masterpiece, the *David* (Figure 12.19). He was eager for this commission because it allowed him to test himself against other great sculptors who had tackled this subject, such as Donatello in the early Renaissance (see Figure 11.11). Moreover, Michelangelo, a great Florentine patriot, identified David with the aggressive spirit of his native city. His *David* was instantly successful, and the republic of Florence adopted the statue as its civic symbol, placing the work in the open square before the Palazzo Vecchio, the town hall. Damage to the statue through weathering and local unrest caused the civic leaders eventually to house Michelangelo's most famous sculpture indoors, where it remains today.

Michelangelo's *David*, rather than imitating Donatello's partly clothed and somewhat effete version, portrays the young Jewish warrior as a nude, classical hero. Taking a damaged and abandoned block of marble, Michelangelo carved the colossal *David* as a muscular adolescent with his weight gracefully balanced on the right leg, in classical contrapposto. The *David* perfectly represents Michelangelo's conception of sculpture; imagining a human figure imprisoned inside marble, he simply used his chisel to set it free.

Michelangelo also made minor deviations from classical principles in his rendition of David in the name of higher ideals, just as ancient artists had done. David's large hands, for example, are outside classical proportions and suggest a youth who has yet to grow to his potential. And David's furrowed brow violates the classical ideal of serene faces but reflects his intense concentration.

Michelangelo's later sculpture is mannerist in style, as are his later paintings. A second *Pietà*—with Christ, Mary, Mary Magdalene, and Joseph of Arimathea—shows the change in his depiction of the human form (Figure 12.20). In this somber group, Michelangelo's anticlassical spirit is paramount. Jesus's body is elongated and unnaturally twisted in death; the other figures, with great difficulty, struggle to support Jesus's dead weight. But rather than detracting from the sculpture's impact, the awkward body adds to the scene's emotional interest—an aim of mannerist art, which did not trust the viewer to respond to more orderly im-

Figure 12.20 MICHELANGELO. *Pietà.* Before 1555. Marble, ht. 7′8″. Santa Maria del Fiore, Florence. *The rage that seemed to infuse Michelangelo's mannerist vision in* The Last Judgment *appears purged in this* Pietà—*the work he was finishing when he died at the age of eighty-eight. Mannerist distortions are still present, particularly in the twisted body of the dead Christ and the implied downward motion of the entire ensemble. But the gentle faces suggest that serenity has been restored to Michelangelo's art.*

ages. Joseph, the rich man who, according to the Gospel, donated his own tomb to Jesus, has Michelangelo's face—a face that is more a death mask than a human countenance.

Architecture

The architectural heir to Alberti in the early sixteenth century was Donato Bramante [brah-MAHN-tay] (1444–1514), who became the moving force behind the High Renaissance in architecture. Trained as a painter, Bramante rejected the reigning building style, called **scenographic,** in which buildings are composed of discrete, individual units. Instead, by concentrating on space and volume, Bramante created an architecture that was unified in all its components and that followed the rules of the classical orders.

The clearest surviving expression of Bramante's architectural genius is the Tempietto, or little temple, in Rome (Figure 12.21). This small structure was designed both as a church, seating ten worshipers, and as a building marking the site of the martyrdom of St. Peter. Copied from the circular temples of ancient Rome, this small domed building became the prototype of the central plan church popularized in the High Renaissance and later.

Bramante's design for the Tempietto sprang from ancient classical principles. Foremost was his belief that architecture should appeal to human reason and that a building should present a severe appearance, not seek to please through specially planned effects. Bramante also thought that a building should be unified like a piece of sculpture and that ornamentation should be restricted to a few architectural details.

In accordance with this artistic credo, the Tempietto functions like a work of sculpture; it is raised on a pedestal with steps leading up to its colonnaded porch. In the absence of sculptural decorations, the temple's exterior is accented with architectural details: the columns; the **balustrade,** or rail with supporting posts; and the dome with barely visible ribs. The proportions of its various features, such as the ratio of column widths to column heights, were based on ancient mathematical formulas. Unfortunately, the plan to integrate the small temple into a circular courtyard of a nearby church was never completed—thus deviating from the classical rule that buildings should relate to their surrounding space. Despite the absence of this crowning touch, the Tempietto is one of the jewels of the High Renaissance.

Bramante had been commissioned by Pope Julius II to rebuild St. Peter's Basilica, the world's most famous church, but he died before his plans could be carried out. The supervision of the rebuilding of the church fell to other architects; eventually Michelangelo, at the age of seventy-one, was given this vital task. From 1546

Figure 12.21 BRAMANTE. Tempietto. After 1502. Marble, ht. 46'; diameter of colonnade 29'. San Pietro in Montorio, Rome. *Bramante's Tempietto is the earliest surviving High Renaissance building and an exquisite example of this style. Fashioned from pure classical forms, the building is almost devoid of decoration except for architectural features, and the separate parts—dome, cylindrical drum, and base—are brought into a harmonious whole.*

until his death in 1564, Michelangelo, among his other artistic duties, was occupied with St. Peter's, especially with the construction of the dome. Although the dome was completed after his death and slightly modified, it remains Michelangelo's outstanding architectural monument and a splendid climax to his career.

Michelangelo's sculptural approach to architecture was similar to that of Bramante. To integrate the dome with the rest of St. Peter's, Michelangelo used double Corinthian columns as a unifying agent. Because the facade was altered in the 1600s, Michelangelo's dome is best observed from the southwest (Figure 12.22). Beginning at ground level, the Corinthian order serves as an artistic feature that gives harmony to the building. Sometimes as columns, sometimes as pilasters, and sometimes as ribs, the double Corinthian units move up the walls, eventually up the dome's drum, and up the dome itself.

St. Peter's plan shows that Michelangelo the architect differed from Michelangelo the painter and sculptor. In painting and sculpture, he had by the 1530s become a mannerist in his use of exaggeration and expressive effects. But in architecture, he stayed faithful to the High Renaissance and its ideal of harmonious design.

The preeminent architect of the mannerist style was Andrea di Pietro (1508–1580), known as Palladio [pah-LAHD-yo], whose base was Vicenza, in northern Italy. The name Palladio derives from Pallas, a name for Athena, the goddess of wisdom. Palladio's artistic creed was rooted in classicism, but his forte was the richly inventive way in which he arranged the classical elements of a building to guarantee surprise. He played with the effects of light and shadow, adding feature on top of feature, to create buildings that possess infinite variety in the midst of a certain decorative solemnity.

Palladio's most influential domestic design was the Villa Capra, more commonly called the Villa Rotonda because of its central circular area and covering dome (Figure 12.23). Inspired by ancient Roman farmhouses, the Villa Rotonda is a sixteenth-century country house built of brick and faced with stucco and located on a rise overlooking Vicenza. A dome provides a central axis from which four symmetrical wings radiate. Each of the four wings in turn opens to the outdoors through an Ionic-style porch raised on a pedestal. The porticoes, or covered porches supported by columns, then lead to the ground level through deeply recessed stairways. Statues stand on the corners and peak of each of the four pediments, and others flank the four stairways.

Figure 12.22 MICHELANGELO. Dome of St. Peter's. View from the southwest. 1546–1564. (Completed by Giacomo della Porta, 1590.) Ht. of dome 452′. Rome. *Its harmonious design and its reliance on classical forms made Michelangelo's dome an object of universal admiration when it was completed in 1590, after his death. From then to the present day, other architects have used his dome as a model, hoping to reproduce its classical spirit.*

Figure 12.23 PALLADIO. Villa Rotonda (Villa Capra). Begun 1550. (Completed in about 1592 by Vincenzo Scamozzi [1548–1616].) Ht. of dome 70′; villa 80′ square. Vicenza. *Despite its classical elements, the Villa Rotonda is a mannerist building. Unlike High Renaissance buildings, which were designed to be integrated with their settings, this boxlike country house stands in an antagonistic relationship to its surrounding garden space. Furthermore, the mannerist principle of elongation is apparent in its four long stairways. But the Villa Rotonda's most striking mannerist feature is the surprise inherent in a plan that includes four identical porches.*

Palladio's mannerist spirit can be seen at work in the design of this building. Although the coldly formal porches are classical in appearance, no Greek or Roman temple would have had four such identical porches, one on each side of the building (Figure 12.24). Palladio's design incorporates the unexpected and the contradictory within an apparently classical structure.

Besides designing buildings, Palladio wrote the treatise *Quattro libri dell'architettura,* or *The Four Books of Architecture.* This work, in English translation, gained wide currency and led to the vogue of Palladianism in the English-speaking world. English aristocrats in the 1700s commissioned country houses built on Palladian principles, as did plantation owners in America's antebellum South.

Music

No radical break separates High Renaissance music from the music of the early Renaissance.

CHORAL MUSIC Josquin des Prez, the leading composer of the dominant Franco-Netherlandish school, had previously brought to a climax the early Renaissance style while he was employed in Italy by the popes and the local aristocrats (see Chapter 11). His sixteenth-century pieces, which consist chiefly of religious Masses and motets along with secular *chansons,* or songs, simply heightened the ideal already present in his earlier works: a sweet sound produced by multiple voices, usually two to six, singing a cappella

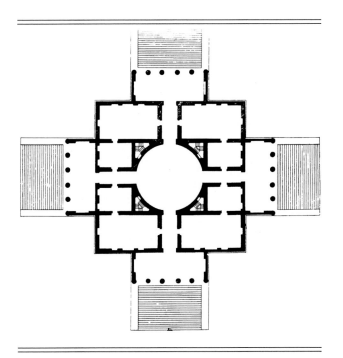

Figure 12.24 PALLADIO. Floor Plan of the Villa Rotonda. *Palladio designed the Villa Rotonda to further the social ambitions of its wealthy Venetian owner, making its most prominent interior feature a central circular area, an ideal space for concerts, parties, and other gatherings. He surrounded this space with four identically shaped sets of rooms on two levels—to house family and guests. Passageways led to the four porches, where residents could obtain relief from the summer's heat and enjoy diverting views of the countryside.*

and expressing the feelings described in the text. Despite his interest in music's emotional power, Josquin continued to subordinate the song to the words—thus reflecting the needs of the church, the foremost patron of the age. The clearly sung texts also show the classical restraint of his High Renaissance style. A striking feature of this style was the rich multichoral effect produced when the singers were subdivided into varied groups of voices.

Experimentation with choral effects was carried into the next generation by Adrian Willaert [VIL-art] (about 1490–1562), a member of the Netherlandish school and a disciple of Josquin's. After the latter's death, Willaert became Europe's most influential composer. Appointed the chapel master of the cathedral of St. Mark's in Venice, Willaert is considered the founder of the Venetian school of music. Taking advantage of St. Mark's two organs and the Venetian practice of blending instruments with voices, he wrote music for two choirs as well. By various musical techniques, such as alternating and combining voices, contrasting soft and loud, and arranging echo effects, Willaert created beautiful and expressive sounds that were the ancestor of the splendid church concertos of the baroque era. A benefit of Willaert's innovations was that the organ was released from its dependence on vocal music.

Missa Christus resurgens (Mass, the Risen Christ, about 1536), composed for four voices, shows Wil-

laert's beautifully expressive style. Based on a short polyphonic work by the Franco-Flemish composer Jean Richafort (about 1480–1547), Willaert's Mass creates an appealing tapestry of sound, using melismas and imitation, but ensuring faultless understanding of the text—the essence of "modern" sacred polyphony, his legacy. The short Agnus Dei (Lamb of God) begins with all four voices forming an ever-shifting ground, from which the tenor voice emerges, soaring above the rest, giving an ethereal sound and acting as a musical metaphor for Christ's rebirth.

OTHER DEVELOPMENTS   Instrumental music still played a secondary role to the human voice. However, Josquin and Willaert composed a few pieces for specific instruments, either transposing melodies originally intended for singers or adapting musical forms from dance tunes.

Another important step forward occurred with the birth of the violin, an instrument with strings and a bow, which evolved from the Arabic *rebec* and the medieval fiddle and its Italian cousin (Figure 12.25). By 1600, Italian artisans had fixed the violin's basic size and shape, but the number of strings continued to vary for decades. The tradition of making violins of great distinction began with Andrea Amati (about 1520–1578), who founded a workshop in Cremona in the mid–sixteenth century. Antonio Stradivari (about

Figure 12.25 Giovanni di Lutero, Known as Dosso Dossi. *Apollo and Daphne.* Ca. 1538. Oil on canvas, 6'2" × 3'9". Galleria Borghese, Rome. *Dosso Dossi (about 1490–1542) painted many allegorical and mythological scenes. His sense of color and understanding of light—adapted from the Venetian art of Giorgione and Titian—added to the magic and fantasy of his works. In this painting, Apollo, the patron of poetry and music and leader of the Muses, is placed in the foreground, while Daphne, whom he constantly chased, is in the middle ground, fleeing from her pursuer. An Italian city, perhaps Bologna (identified by its Twin Towers), fills in the background. Apollo, rather than playing the lyre, an ancient Greek string instrument, is holding a violin. This painting may be one of the first to feature the violin, since the violin did not appear until about 1510.*

1644–1737) and Andrea Guarneri (about 1626–1698), two of the most famous violin makers in history, were apprentices of Niccolò Amati (1596–1684), Andrea's grandson. Antonio Stradivari brought violin making to its highest level of perfection, building 540 violins along with many other string instruments. Today, a Stradivari violin is considered one of the most precious musical instruments in the world.

A further development, holding great future promise, was the invention of the **consort,** a family of musical instruments, ranging from the low bass to the high treble, initially made up of either recorders or viols. The consort represented the principle of the mixed instrumental ensemble, and from this start would emerge the orchestra. And, when human voices were added to the mixture, the conditions were ripe for opera.

The Legacy of the High Renaissance and Early Mannerism

The seventy-year period during which the High Renaissance and early mannerism flourished is the golden age of the West in certain artistic and humanistic areas. In the visual arts—painting, sculpture, and architecture—standards were set and indelible images created that have not been surpassed. In political theory, this age produced the mannerist thinker Machiavelli—the founder of modern political thought.

Beyond those achievements, three other important steps were taken on the road to the modern world. On a political level, the origins of the modern secular state may be seen in the examples of France, Spain, and England. What was innovative, even revolutionary, for these countries has become second nature to the states of the twenty-first century, both in the Western world and beyond. On a social level, a new code of behavior appeared in the Italian courts and was in time adopted throughout Europe. Not only did the rules of courtesy finally penetrate into the European aristocracy and alter their behavior, but this code also trickled down to the middle classes. Until about 1945, this code, with many variations, became the model for all Western people with social aspirations. On the international level, the first stirrings of multiculturalism were being felt, as Portugal, followed by Spain, England, France, and the Netherlands, began to initiate contacts with societies beyond Europe—thus beginning the process of globalization that defines our world today.

Perhaps the greatest change inaugurated during this period concerned the role of the individual in society. The classical and the medieval worlds had praised what was corporate and public, in conformity with traditional, universal values. But in the High Renaissance a few artists and humanists, along with their patrons, began to revere what was individual and private. Early mannerism carried individual expression to greater extremes by finding merit in personal eccentricities and unrestrained behavior. That patrons supported the new works of these artists and humanists demonstrates the rise of the belief that free expression is both a social and a private good. Both the High Renaissance and early mannerism encouraged the daring idea of individualism and thus introduced what has become a defining theme of Western culture.

KEY CULTURAL TERMS

High Renaissance
mannerism
civic humanism
madrigal
Machiavellianism

Pietà
scenographic
balustrade
consort

QUESTIONS FOR CRITICAL THINKING

1. Discuss the causes of the rise of the new nation-states—France, Spain, and England—using one of them as your focus. What impact did the new nation-states have on the arts and humanities?

2. What conditions led to the brief flowering of the High Renaissance, 1494–1520? What events contributed to the rise of mannerism, after 1520?

3. Compare and contrast the High Renaissance and mannerism as cultural styles.

4. Select a painting, a sculpture, and a building from both the High Renaissance and early mannerism and compare and contrast the two artworks, with the goal of setting forth the distinguishing characteristics of these two artistic styles.

5. What was the single most important cultural development in this period? Explain.

13

NORTHERN HUMANISM, NORTHERN RENAISSANCE, RELIGIOUS REFORMATIONS, AND LATE MANNERISM

1500–1603

As the High Renaissance and early mannerism were unfolding in Italy (see Chapter 12), the rest of Europe was being transformed by three developments: a literary movement, two new artistic styles, and a religious crisis. The literary movement and the new artistic styles were partially inspired by the cultural changes in Italy. However, the religious crisis was unique to northern Europe; but by midcentury, it had become intertwined with local and international politics. The literary movement, known as northern (or Christian) humanism, was inspired by the Italian Renaissance, with its emphasis on classical studies, and late medieval lay piety, with its focus on a simpler Christianity. Two distinct artistic styles appeared in Europe: the northern Renaissance, from 1500 until about 1560, and late mannerism, enduring for the rest of the century. The course of these literary and artistic developments was affected by the religious crisis that soon engulfed all of Europe (Timeline 13.1).

Germany became the epicenter of the spiritual earthquake called the **Reformation,** a movement that forever shattered the religious unity of the West. The Reformation, like the Renaissance, looked to the past for inspiration and ideas, but rather than focusing on the classical world of Greece and Rome, the Reformation's religious leaders looked to the early Christian church before it became hierarchical and bureaucratic. Almost immediately, the reformers met with unbending resistance from church officials. These hostile groups became what are known today as the Protestants, who wanted a complete renovation of the church, and the Roman Catholics, who were largely satisfied with the church as it was.

◀ **Detail** HANS HOLBEIN THE YOUNGER. *Erasmus of Rotterdam.* Ca. 1523–1524. Oil on panel, 16½ × 12⅝". Louvre.

Timeline 13.1   THE SIXTEENTH CENTURY

1500				1545		1563		1600
The Reformation and Founding of the Protestant Order					Council of Trent		The Counter-Reformation	

| **1509**
Erasmus's
The Praise of Folly | **1517**
Luther's
Ninety-five
Theses | **1521**
Independent
Lutheran
churches
founded | **1533**
Church of
England
founded | **1540**
Jesuit order
founded | | **1564**
Death of
Michelangelo | | **1586**
El Greco's
*Burial of
Count Orgaz* | **1592–1594**
Tintoretto's
Last Supper |
| **1513**
Dürer's *Knight,
Death, and
the Devil* | | | | **1541**
Independent
Calvinist
churches
founded | | **1566**
Bruegel's
Wedding Dance | | **1590–1610**
Shakespeare's
plays performed | |

The Roman Catholics did not oppose all change. In the second half of the sixteenth century, they conducted the **Counter-Reformation** and set the church on the path that it followed until the 1960s. In contrast, the Protestants disagreed over basic Christian doctrines and soon split into separate sects.

In the 1560s, the Counter-Reformation began to have a strong impact on culture. In Spain and Italy late mannerism in the arts, architecture, and music flourished, until the baroque style arose at the end of the century. One exception to this late mannerist trend was Spanish literature, which entered its golden age in about 1500 and reached its zenith with the works of Cervantes.

NORTHERN HUMANISM

Northern humanism, also known as **Christian humanism,** shared some of the aesthetic values of the High Renaissance: idealism, rationalism, and a deep love for classical literature. Unlike the Italian humanists, the northern humanists were preoccupied with the condition of the church and the wider Christian world. These northern thinkers researched and studied both Christian writings and the Greco-Roman classics, and their scholarship was meant to further the cause of ecclesiastical reform.

Like the lay pietists of the late Middle Ages (see Chapter 10), from whom they drew inspiration, the northern humanists approached their faith in simple terms. They taught that any Christian who had a pure and humble heart could pray directly to God. These scholars furthered the appeal of this simple creed by claiming that it was identical with Christ's scriptural message, which they were discovering in their vernacular translations of the New Testament.

The thinking of some German Christian humanists was tinged with national feeling and hostility toward Italian interference in their local religious affairs. Their Christian humanism led them to believe that by imitating the early church—freed of corrupt Italian leaders—they could revitalize Christianity and restore it to its original purpose.

A notable French humanist, François Rabelais [RAB-uh-lay] (about 1494–1553), wrote a five-part satire collectively titled *The Histories of Gargantua and Pantagruel* in which he vigorously attacked the church's abuses and ridiculed the clergy and theologians. Beneath the satire, Rabelais affirmed the goodness of human nature and the ability of men and women to lead useful lives based on reason and common sense. However, his skepticism and secularism, as well as the ribald humor, obscene references, and grotesque escapades of his heroes, put Rabelais well outside the mainstream of northern humanism.

Another northern humanist outside the mainstream was Marguerite of Angoulême, queen of Navarre (1492–1549), sister of King Francis I. Her court was a safe haven for Rabelais, Protestant reformers, and other free spirits. Marguerite of Navarre—her usual name—was associated with the *Heptameron* (from the Greek word for "seven"), a collection of seventy frankly sexual tales in the style of Boccaccio's *Decameron* (see Chapter 10). Whether or not Marguerite actually wrote these tales is uncertain, although scholars generally agree that the stories were written for the French court. Based on the evidence of the stories, the French nobility welcomed outspokenness in sexual matters (the tales deal with rape, seductions bordering on rape, incest, and trespasses of the sexual and marital codes of aristocratic life) and condoned Protestant-like religious views (the villains are often members of monastic orders who are portrayed as gluttons, parasites, and rapists). The social matrix that spawned the *Heptameron* was northern humanism, a world hostile to the dying ethos of medieval monasticism.

The outstanding figure among the northern humanists—and possibly among all humanists—is the Dutch scholar Desiderius Erasmus (Figure 13.1). Erasmus (about 1466–1536) was fully prepared for the influential role that he played in the Christian humanist movement. He studied in the pietistic atmosphere of a school run by the Brethren of the Common Life, where he was introduced to the Greek and Roman classics. He later completed his education at the University of Paris. His training was supposed to lead to a church career, but Erasmus never wore clerical garb or lived as a priest, although he was ordained. On the contrary, with the aid of patrons he patiently pursued a writing career, enjoying the comforts of a scholarly life. He also traveled widely throughout western Europe, eventually finding a second home in England among the intellectual circle gathered around Sir Thomas More, England's lord chancellor and another well-known humanist.

As a humanist, Erasmus believed in education in the *humanitas* tradition advocated by Cicero, emphasizing study of the classics and honoring the dignity of the individual. As a Christian, he promoted the "philosophy of Christ" as expressed in the Sermon on the Mount and in Jesus's example of a humble and virtuous life. Erasmus earnestly felt that the church could reform itself and avoid division by adopting the moderate approach that he advanced.

Despite a prodigious output of books that include treatises, commentaries, collections of proverbs, a manual for rulers, and a definitive edition of the Greek New Testament, Erasmus's fame rests on his most popular work, *The Praise of Folly* (1509). This lively book, filled with learned humor, captures the gentle grace and good sense of the Christian humanists. Even this work's Latin title, *Encomium Moriae*, reflects a lighthearted spirit, for it is a punning reference to the name of Sir Thomas More—the English friend to whom the book is dedicated.

Erasmus pokes fun at the human race by making his mouthpiece a personified Folly—an imaginary creation who symbolizes human foolishness. In a series of sermons, Folly ridicules every social group, from scholars and lawyers to priests and cardinals. Erasmus's satire, especially in its exposure of clerical hypocrisy, struck a responsive chord among educated people. But with the rapid growth of Protestantism, such cultivated criticism got Erasmus into trouble. Roman Catholics felt betrayed by his mild barbs, and Protestants accused him of not going far enough. In the end, this mild re-

Figure 13.1 HANS HOLBEIN THE YOUNGER. *Erasmus of Rotterdam.* Ca. 1523–1524. Oil on panel, 16½ × 12⅝″. Louvre. *This sensitive likeness of the great humanist was painted by one of the most successful northern Renaissance portraitists, Hans Holbein. The artist conveys his subject's humanity and intellectual authority by depicting him engaged in writing one of his many treatises. The realistic detail, warm colors, and dramatic lighting are typical of Holbein's work.*

former and gentle scholar sadly witnessed the breakup of his beloved church while being denounced by both Roman Catholics and Protestants.

For a time, Luther had hoped for the support of Erasmus in his reforming crusade. But that changed in 1524 when Erasmus asserted, contrary to Luther, that the human will was free; otherwise, according to Erasmus, the Bible would not have urged sinners to repent. Erasmus's argument so enraged Luther that he countered with a tract in which he declared that the human will was irrevocably flawed; in Luther's view, only God's free grace could save any man or woman from the fires of hell. So intemperate was Luther's reply that the two scholars never communicated again. Erasmus's calm voice went unheeded amid the wild rhetoric and religious mayhem that characterized this age.

THE NORTHERN RENAISSANCE

While Italy was experiencing the High Renaissance and early mannerism, northern Europe was bursting with cultural vitality. The cultural scene was affected by events in and outside northern Europe and by the last phase of the medieval era. The religious upheavals—the Reformation and the Counter-Reformation—split Europe into two camps and triggered wars across the Continent and within some of the emerging sovereign states. Late medieval trends, such as Gothic forms and mysticism, manifested themselves in art and religion, while northern humanism shaped the minds and hearts of many thinkers, writers, and artists. The result of the religious and political conflicts and the dissimilar artistic tendencies meant that the **northern Renaissance**—the term used to describe the culture of sixteenth-century northern Europe—was a period marked by competing styles. By midcentury, however, early mannerism was encroaching on the ideals of Renaissance painting and literature north of the Alps.

Northern Renaissance Thought and Science

The northern Renaissance produced new attitudes for understanding the world, ranging from analyzing the characteristics and functions of political institutions to analyzing the structure and organization of the human body. Jean Bodin's analysis of political systems and Andreas Vesalius's discoveries about the human body, while seemingly unrelated, were indications of how the Renaissance was changing Europe. Both men were products of the new learning in the universities, they shared the Renaissance's goal of seeking to understand the worlds of nature and humanity, and they were heavily influenced by the political and religious events swirling around them.

JEAN BODIN   Jean Bodin [ZHAHN bo-DAN] (1530–1596), the French political philosopher and author, lived through eight civil and religious wars that threatened to end the monarchy and to divide France into two religious factions. The Huguenots, or French Protestants, who coalesced into a political union composed of some of the French nobility and the rising middle class, fought the Catholic faithful and those loyal to the kings—mainly the peasants and the city of Paris. The wars—complicated by royal marriages, dynastic

rivalries, and shifting alliances—lasted from about 1562 to 1598.

Bodin studied philosophy in Paris and civil law at the University of Toulouse. While teaching at that university, he came to appreciate and advocate an education based on Renaissance humanism. Later, he returned to Paris, where he entered royal government service, acting as a councilor and adviser on religious and political issues. In 1583 he moved to Laon, where he worked for the municipal government and wrote his tracts on political systems.

As a participant and observer of the period's wars and as a student of history and law, Bodin made it his life's mission to understand the ideal state, which he set forth in his masterpiece, *Six Livres de la République (Six Books of the Commonwealth,* or *Republic)* (1576). According to Bodin, the basic issue in politics is sovereignty, that is, the political entity that has control of a state's internal and external affairs. Sovereignty, he asserted, is absolute and perpetual and resides always in the office of the monarchy. By claiming sovereignty to be inalienable—cannot be shared, given away, or lost—Bodin, in effect, made an argument for absolute monarchy. Within the context of absolute monarchy, Bodin allowed for three different forms of government: the rule of one, or monarchy; the rule of the few, or aristocracy; and the rule of all, or democracy. Monarchs, by virtue of being naturally invested with absolute power, might choose those who were the richest and from noble families to participate in government—thus creating an aristocracy. Similarly, monarchs might give certain rights, including the ability to hold public office, to all subjects—thus making a democracy. Nevertheless, in both an aristocracy and a democracy, power ultimately remained in the hands of the monarch.

According to Bodin, the absolute monarch, while not bound to the civil law, was bound to natural and divine law, and monarchs who went against those laws—such as by enslaving a people or seizing subjects' property—were tyrannical and should be opposed. Monarchs rule by divine right, because the Divine is looking out for the well-being of humanity—their lives and their property. Having witnessed the wars between Huguenots and Catholics, Bodin concluded that in a monarchy a uniform religious faith would be best, because it would flourish and this would help ensure peace and harmony in the state. He concluded that a unity of religion and of country was the only way for a people to live.

Bodin, along with Machiavelli, was one of the first political philosophers to focus on the ideal state in the modern world. While attacking the last vestiges of the feudal system that stand in opposition to royal power, Bodin's book is also forecasting the future debate about the meaning of sovereignty. Over the next two centuries, until the Age of Democratic Revolutions (see Chapter 17), political thinkers made sovereignty the central issue, raising questions about who possessed it and how best to use it in a civil society.

ANDREAS VESALIUS   Andreas Vesalius [va-SAIL-yas] (1514–1564), like Bodin, personified the humanistic traits of the Renaissance. Both observed and analyzed the world around them, both looked to history for guidance, and both offered new ways to understand the human condition. However, Vesalius made his contributions in the sciences, while Bodin furthered the study of political science (a term attributed to him).

Vesalius came from a family of physicians who served at the court of the Holy Roman emperor. He studied at the elite universities of Europe: Louvain (in modern Belgium), Paris, and Padua. The Paris years were critical, as he learned to dissect human cadavers and to analyze human bones. At the University of Padua, he discovered errors in the teachings of Galen, the renowned Roman physician whose findings in human anatomy had been the standard in medical training for the previous 1,300 years (see Chapter 6).

The young Vesalius, convinced that Galen's observations were incorrect and that humans and animals do not share the same anatomy, first circulated some of his classroom drawings. Later, in 1543, he published his findings, *De Humani Corporis Fabrica (The Seven Books on the Structure of the Human Body)* or, as it was commonly known, *Fabrica*.

Fabrica's detailed and accurate descriptions, especially illustrations of the human body, which were based on human dissections, transformed the study of anatomy (Figure 13.2). At the same time, Vesalius stirred up a fierce controversy among two groups: fellow scientists who thought Galen was right; and Catholic Church officials who believed dissection of human cadavers flouted canon law. By proving Galen wrong, Vesalius did for anatomy what Copernicus did for astronomy in showing Ptolemy to be in error (see Chapter 15). Within a short time, Vesalius's writings were accepted in nearly all European medical schools, and his work came to influence other sciences—physiology, biology, and the study of medicine.

Northern Renaissance Literature

The sixteenth century was an amazing period in literature, for the vernacular tongues now definitively showed that they were the equals of Latin as vehicles for literary expression. In the High Middle Ages, Dante led the way with his *Divine Comedy*; now, other authors writing in the vernacular found their voices.

Figure 13.2   ANDREAS VESALIUS. Drawing from *De Humani Corporis Fabrica*. 1543. *Vesalius wrote, illustrated, and supervised the drawing, engraving, and printing of the first comprehensive illustrated textbook on anatomy. The drawings of his dissections were engraved on wooden blocks and are considered to be some of the finest engraved art of the sixteenth century. Fabrica exceeded all previous medical texts in its clear and accurate illustrations, high standard of craftsmanship, and printing, layout, and organization. Vesalius, following a tradition of Renaissance anatomical drawings, placed his "muscle-men" in a landscape—with a village or classical ruins in the background. He also gave each subject a classical pose. None of his figures is a cadaver lying on a dissecting table. By rendering the human body in such settings, Vesalius made it easier for the viewer to accept what he had done, and, at the same time, these drawings also demonstrate that even medical illustrations are subject to the same cultural forces as the rest of a period's creative achievements.*

Montaigne, writing in French, and Shakespeare, writing in English, left such a rich legacy that, by common consent, each is revered as the outstanding writer of his respective tradition.

MICHEL DE MONTAIGNE Michel de Montaigne [mee-SHEL duh mahn-TAYN] (1533–1592) balanced a public career with a life devoted to letters. While serving as a judge and a mayor, he worked on his lifelong project, which he called *Essays*. This collection of discursive meditations is the autobiography of his mind and is thus representative of the individualistic spirit of the Renaissance. A self-portrait emerges of a man who is intellectually curious and fascinated by his own mental processes and personality. He describes his contradictions, accidental as well as deliberate, though he writes that his loyalty is always to truth. What keeps the *Essays* from falling into sterile self-absorption is Montaigne's firm sense that in revealing himself he is speaking for others.

But the *Essays* are more than an early example of confessional literature. They also constitute, in the French tradition, the earliest work of *moralisme*, or moralism, and the beginning of modern skepticism. In terms of morality, Montaigne attached little importance to Christian ethics, since cruelty and barbarism in the name of religion were justified equally by Protestant and Catholic. His musings reflected France's chaotic condition during the religious wars, causing him to question the Renaissance's natural optimism. Montaigne searched vainly for a moral code that was centered on a human world and that no one could deny. In his skeptical outlook, Montaigne rejected the Renaissance view of humanity as a microcosm of the universe. Indeed, he claimed that he saw nothing except vanity and insignificance in human beings and their reasoning. Montaigne, however, avoided total skepticism, for although he denied that humans could ever achieve perfect knowledge, he held that practical understanding was possible.

WILLIAM SHAKESPEARE Montaigne wrote during a period when religious wars were disrupting France, but England at the same time was enjoying a relatively calm period of cultural exuberance, the Age of Elizabeth. Under Queen Elizabeth I (r. 1558–1603), London rose to an eminence that rivaled that of Florence of the early Renaissance. English playwrights rescued tragedy and comedy from oblivion, and they again became part of popular culture. A secular and commercial theater now emerged, with professional playwrights and actors, playhouses, and a ticket-buying public (Figures 13.3 and 13.4).

The revived popularity of the theater represented a dramatic reversal of a cultural outlook that had pre-vailed in the West since the time of Augustine in the fifth century (see Chapter 6). Christian scholars had condemned the stage as wicked and immoral. On occasion, medieval culture had spawned morality plays and dramas with biblical themes, but those edifying works remained primitive in form, with little attention given to language, character, or plot. The fifteenth-century play *Everyman,* for example, was intended mainly to reinforce Christian values and only incidentally to entertain or to provoke thought. Under Elizabeth I, many able dramatists began to appear, such as Thomas Kyd (about 1557–1595) and Christopher Marlowe (1564–1593). These playwrights revolutionized drama in a single generation. However, first honors must be given to William Shakespeare, the greatest dramatist in the English language.

Shakespeare (1564–1616) was born in Stratford-upon-Avon, a market-town, and educated in its grammar school. By 1590 his plays were being performed on the London stage, and his active public career continued until 1610, when he returned home to Stratford to enjoy country life. His early retirement reflected the success that he had achieved as an actor, a theater owner, and a playwright. But he earned undying fame as the age's leading dramatist, mastering the three different genres of history, comedy, and tragedy. His thirty-seven dramas constitute his legacy to the world. Just as tragedies ranked higher than comedies in ancient Greece, so have Shakespeare's tragedies enjoyed a reputation superior to that of his other writings. Of the eleven tragedies, many are regarded as masterpieces; *King Lear, Othello, Julius Caesar, Macbeth,* and *Romeo and Juliet* are constantly performed on the stage and often presented in films, in English as well as other languages. Perhaps the Shakespearean tragedy that stands above the rest, however, and that is reckoned by many to be his supreme achievement, is *Hamlet.*

Hamlet is a **revenge tragedy,** among the most popular dramatic forms in the Elizabethan theater. The revenge play had its own rules, consisting chiefly of a murder that requires a relative of the victim, usually with the prompting of a ghost, to avenge the crime by the drama's end. The origin of this type of play, with its characteristic violence and suspense, has been obscured by time, although Seneca's Roman tragedies, which were known and studied in England, are almost certainly a source.

The basic plot, characters, and setting of *Hamlet* are drawn from a medieval chronicle of evildoings at the Danish court. Elizabethan theatergoers had seen an earlier dramatized version (now lost) before Shakespeare's play was performed in 1600–1601. Shakespeare thus took a well-known story but stamped it with his own genius and feeling for character. In its basic conception, *Hamlet* is a consummate expression of

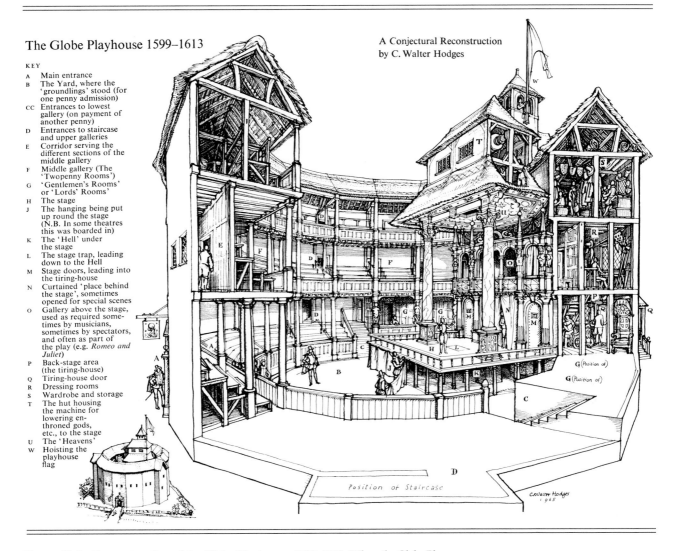

The Globe Playhouse 1599–1613

A Conjectural Reconstruction by C. Walter Hodges

KEY

A   Main entrance
B   The Yard, where the 'groundlings' stood (for one penny admission)
CC Entrances to lowest gallery (on payment of another penny)
D   Entrances to staircase and upper galleries
E   Corridor serving the different sections of the middle gallery
F   Middle gallery (The 'Twopenny Rooms')
G   'Gentlemen's Rooms' or 'Lords' Rooms'
H   The stage
J   The hanging being put up round the stage (N.B. In some theatres this was boarded in)
K   The 'Hell' under the stage
L   The stage trap, leading down to the Hell
M   Stage doors, leading into the tiring-house
N   Curtained 'place behind the stage', sometimes opened for special scenes
O   Gallery above the stage, used as required sometimes by musicians, sometimes by spectators, and often as part of the play (e.g. *Romeo and Juliet*)
P   Back-stage area (the tiring-house)
Q   Tiring-house door
R   Dressing rooms
S   Wardrobe and storage
T   The hut housing the machine for lowering enthroned gods, etc., to the stage
U   The 'Heavens'
W   Hoisting the playhouse flag

Figure 13.3 Reconstruction of the Globe Playhouse, 1599–1613. *When the Globe Playhouse of London was razed in 1644 to make way for new buildings, one of the most significant monuments of Renaissance England disappeared: the theater where most of Shakespeare's plays were first performed. This cutaway drawing, made by C. W. Hodges, a leading expert on the theaters of the period, attempts to depict the Globe Playhouse as it appeared in Shakespeare's day. As shown in the drawing, the Globe was a sixteen-sided structure with the stage erected in an open courtyard bounded on three sides by three tiers of seats.*

Figure 13.4 The Reconstructed Globe Playhouse. 1996. London. *Spurred by the vision of the American actor Sam Wanamaker, an international effort resulted in the construction of a modern Globe Playhouse, near the site of the original theater of Shakespeare's time. This theater, which staged its first performances in August 1996, is true to Elizabethan design and construction methods, including wooden nails and thatched roof. Performances are staged in the daytime, when weather permits— just as they were four centuries ago.*

mannerist principles. Shakespeare presents Hamlet from shifting perspectives, preferring ambiguity, rather than portraying him from a single vantage point in accordance with the classical ideal. By turns, Hamlet veers from madman to scholar to prince to swordsman, so that a unified, coherent personality is never exposed to the audience. Because of Hamlet's elusive character, he has become the most frequently analyzed and performed of all Shakespeare's heroes.

Another aspect of this play reminiscent of the mannerist aesthetic is the self-disgust that seems to rule Hamlet's character when he is alone with his thoughts. Whereas the High Renaissance reserved its finest praise for the basic dignity of the human being, Hamlet finds little to value in himself, in others, or in life. Instead, he offers a contradictory vision:

> It goes so heavily with my disposition that this goodly frame, the earth, seems to me a sterile promontory; this most excellent canopy, the air . . . this majestical roof fretted with golden fire, why, it appears no other thing to me but a foul and pestilent congregation of vapours. What a piece of work is a man, how noble in reason, how infinite in faculty; in form and moving how express and admirable, in action how like an angel, in apprehension how like a god! the beauty of the world, the paragon of animals! And yet to me what is this quintessence of dust? Man delights not me. (Act 2, Scene 2)

In its construction, the tragedy of *Hamlet* is typical of Shakespeare's plays. All his dramas were written for commercial theater troupes and were not intended especially for a reading public. Only after Shakespeare's death were his plays published and circulated to a general audience and thus regarded as "literature."

Northern Renaissance Painting

The northern Renaissance emerged during an era of cultural crisis. The late Gothic style of the Flemish school was losing its appeal, except for one extraordinary artist, Hieronymus Bosch. At the same time, growing numbers of artists were attracted to the new Italian art, especially to mannerism. In the 1520s, the influence of the Protestant Reformation also began to become apparent in the arts. Individual tastes and styles became important, and secular subjects were acceptable, in part because some of the more fervent Protestants looked on enjoyment of the visual arts as a form of idol worship. They destroyed some paintings, statues, and stained glass that portrayed religious subjects. The combined influences of mannerism and Protestantism produced three artists of unique stature who reflected the turbulent world of post-Lutheran

Europe in quite different ways: Dürer, Grünewald, and Bruegel.

ALBRECHT DÜRER Albrecht Dürer [AHL-brekt DURE-er] (1471–1528), the son of a goldsmith, pursued a career as an engraver and painter. After studying in Germany, he traveled throughout Italy, to absorb the lessons of Renaissance art. Between 1510 and 1519, he earned fame for the works that he executed for the Holy Roman emperor, but he also discovered that his true artistic talent was engraving, either on wood or on metal. The multiple editions of his engravings enhanced his reputation, and as a result he received many commissions throughout Germany and the Netherlands. Near the end of his life, Dürer became a Lutheran, and some of his last paintings indicate his new faith.

Fully aware of himself and his place in the world, Dürer showed a Renaissance sensibility in introspective self-portraits, especially in the famous work in which he depicts himself as a Christ figure (Figure 13.5). In this stunning image—the intense stare suggests he painted while looking in the mirror—Dürer blends a dandified likeness of himself with a standard Flemish representation of Christ. Conflating his artistic self with Jesus's divine power would have been unthinkable before the Renaissance. Nevertheless, Dürer incorporated the spirit of the Middle Ages, for he was also following the tradition of mysticism in which he saw himself as striving to imitate the example of Christ.

Although Dürer's paintings brought him recognition and wealth in his day, his engravings constitute his greatest artistic legacy. At the time of Luther's revolt, Dürer engraved the *Knight, Death, and the Devil* (Figure 13.6). This magnificent engraving shows a knight riding through a forest, ignoring both the taunts of Death, who holds up an hourglass to remind him of his mortality, and the Devil, who watches nearby. The knight is probably meant as a symbol of the Christian who has to live in the practical world.

Dürer's *Knight, Death, and the Devil* combines late Gothic and Renaissance elements to make a disquieting scene. From the northern tradition are derived the exquisite details, the grotesque demon, and the varied landscape in the background. From Renaissance sources comes the horse, which Dürer copied from models seen during his travel in Italy.

MATTHIAS GRÜNEWALD A second major German artist in this period is Matthias Grünewald [muh-THI-uhs GRU-nuh-vahlt] (about 1460–1528), who was less influenced by Italian art and more northern in his techniques than Dürer. His paintings represent a continuation of the late Gothic style rather than a northern Renaissance tendency.

Figure 13.5 ALBRECHT DÜRER. *Self-Portrait*. 1500. Oil on panel, 26¼ × 19¼". Alte Pinakothek, Munich. *The northern Renaissance shared with the Italian Renaissance an emphasis on the individual, as shown in this self-portrait by the German artist Albrecht Dürer—one of the first artists to make himself the subject of some of his paintings. In a series of self-portraits, starting at the age of thirteen, he examined his face and upper torso and rendered them in precise detail, recording his passing age and moods. An unusual aspect of Dürer's self-portrait is that it suggests that he has taken on the role of artist in much the manner that Jesus had taken on the role of Savior.*

Grünewald's supreme achievement is the *Isenheim Altarpiece*, painted for the church of St. Anthony in Isenheim, Germany. The altarpiece includes nine painted panels that can be displayed in three different positions, depending on the church calendar. When the *Isenheim Altarpiece* is closed, the large central panel depicts the Crucifixion (Figure 13.7). In crowding the five figures and the symbolic lamb into the foreground and enlarging Christ's body, Grünewald followed the late Gothic style. This style is similarly apparent in every detail of Christ's tortured, twisted body: the gaping mouth, the exposed teeth, the slumped head, and the torso raked by thorns. And late Gothic emotionalism is evident in his treatment of the secondary figures in this Crucifixion panel. On the right, John the Baptist points toward Jesus, stressing the meaning of his sacrificial death. John the Baptist's calmness contrasts with the grief of the figures on the left, including Mary Magdalene, who kneels at Jesus's feet, and the apostle John, who supports a swooning Mary. The swaying bodies of these three figures reinforce their anguished faces. One Renaissance feature in this Gothic painting is the low horizon line, which shows Grünewald's knowledge of Italian perspective.

Figure 13.6 ALBRECHT DÜRER. *Knight, Death, and the Devil*. 1513. Engraving, approx. 9⁵⁄₆ × 7⁷⁄₁₂". The Fogg Art Museum, Harvard University. Gift of William Gray from the Collection of Francis Calley Gray. *Dürer's plan for this work probably derived from a manual by Erasmus that advised a Christian prince on the best way to rule. In his version, Dürer portrays the Christian layman who has put on the armor of faith and rides steadfastly, oblivious to the various pitfalls that lie in his path. The knight is sometimes identified with Erasmus, whom Dürer venerated.*

Figure 13.7 MATTHIAS GRÜNEWALD. *The Crucifixion,* from the *Isenheim Altarpiece.* 1515. Oil on panel, 9'9½" × 10'9". Musée d'Unterlinden, Colmar, France. *Jesus's suffering and death was a central theme in northern European piety, particularly after the plague of the fourteenth century. Northern artists typically rendered Christ's death in vivid and gory detail. Grünewald's* Crucifixion *comes out of this tradition; Christ's broken body symbolizes both his sacrificial death and the mortality of all human beings.*

HIERONYMUS BOSCH Hieronymus Bosch [hi-uh-RAHN-uh-muhs BOSH] (about 1450–1516), whose personal life is a mystery, painted works that still puzzle modern experts. Treating common religious subjects in bizarre and fantastic ways, he earned a reputation even among his contemporaries for being enigmatic.

Much of Bosch's distinctive art may be explained by the changes under way in northern Europe. In the late fifteenth century, political upheavals in Burgundy caused aristocratic patronage to decline, and a feeling of dread, born perhaps of the periodic ravages of the plague, stalked the land. In the early sixteenth century, serious religious trouble that would end with the revolt of Martin Luther was brewing. Influenced by these forces and also perhaps subjected to his own private demons, Bosch created a body of works that defies strict classification in the stylistic sense.

In his paintings, Bosch seems torn between the declining late Gothic style and the soon-to-be-born mannerist style. His addiction to precise detail and his frequent use of sweeping landscapes are clear signs of the debt he owed Flemish art and, in particular, illuminated manuscripts; but his tendency to endow his works with ambiguous, or even cynical, moral messages foreshadows later Dutch artists, such as Pieter Bruegel the Elder. Perhaps the best way to look at Bosch is as an artist whose originality has placed him outside any historical period.

Of Bosch's thirty or more paintings, the best known and most controversial is *Garden of Earthly Delights,* a work in oil on three wood panels, called a **triptych** (Figure 13.8). When open, the triptych displays three separate but interrelated scenes, organized around the theme of the creation, fall, and damnation of the

Figure 13.8 HIERONYMUS BOSCH. *Garden of Earthly Delights.* Ca. 1510–1515. Oil on wood, center panel 86⅝ × 76¾"; each side panel 86⅝ × 38¼". Prado, Madrid. *Careful study of the minute details of this triptych has uncovered the major sources of Bosch's artistic inspiration— namely, medieval folklore, common proverbs, exotic learning, and sacred beliefs. For example, folklore inspired the ravens and owl (left panel), traditional emblems of nonbelievers and witch- craft, respectively; the Flemish proverb "Good fortune, like glass, is easily broken" is illustrated by the lovemaking couple under the glass globe; allusions to exotic learning may be seen in the egg shapes (all three panels), symbolic of the world and sex in the pseudoscience of alchemy; and Christian belief is evident throughout the triptych, but especially in the right panel, showing the punishment of sinners.*

human race. The center and right panels are crowded with tiny figures—mostly human, though some are grotesquely monstrous—performing various peculiar acts. Although no scholarly consensus exists as to the ultimate meaning of this work, certain features can be identified and explained.

The left panel of *Garden of Earthly Delights* shows the Garden of Eden, with Adam and Eve in the fore- ground, along with the first plants and animals (in- cluding "natural" animals but also weird monsters). Contrary to the story in the Bible, Jesus holds Eve's hand and introduces her to Adam. Many scholars in- terpret this panel as making Eve the source of origi- nal sin.

The center panel—the focus of the triptych—depicts the sins of the flesh in lurid and metaphorical detail. In the top horizontal band, the waters of the earth converge to make a fountain, an image that has been identified as a false symbol of human happiness. In

the middle band, naked young women cavort in a pool while a parade of naked youths riding animals—partly realistic, partly fantastic—encircles them. In the lower band, more naked men and women engage in various sex acts or are involved with huge birds, fruits, flow- ers, or fish. The diverse images in this central panel symbolize Bosch's perspective on the human condi- tion: perpetual enslavement to the sexual appetite unleashed by Adam and Eve's first sin. This crowded scene also includes many black males and females, an early instance of nonwhites in Western art.

The triptych's right panel is a repulsive vision of hell that details the pains human beings must suffer for their sins. In this horrific scene, the fiery ruins and grisly instruments of torture proclaim Bosch's vision of the futility of life on earth. For the artist, human beings cause their own destruction through wicked desires. Nowhere in the entire work is there a hint of salvation.

A few scholars reject this gloomy view of Bosch's message by trying to link the triptych to the beliefs of the Adamites, an underground, heretical sect. If their interpretation is correct, then the central panel may be understood as the Adamites' unusual vision of paradise. Most scholars reject this view, however, and hold instead that Bosch was a stern moralist, mocking the corrupt society of his day.

PIETER BRUEGEL THE ELDER   The life and work of Pieter Bruegel [BREW-gul or BROY-gul] the Elder (about 1525–1569) indicate the changes in northern European art by about 1550. The great German artists Dürer and Grünewald were now dead, and German art, which

had dominated northern Europe in the early 1500s, was in decline. Protestant iconoclasm had taken its toll, and the demand for religious art had markedly diminished. Within this milieu, Bruegel, by choosing a novel set of artistic subjects—landscapes, country-life scenes, and folk narratives—became the first truly modern painter in northern Europe. Bruegel's subjects, rooted in the Flemish tradition, were often devoid of overt religious content and presented simply as secular art, although Bruegel painted a number of pictures on standard religious themes such as the adoration of the Magi.

Bruegel's scenes of peasant life and folk narratives are his most memorable works. In them, he always de-

Figure 13.9   PIETER BRUEGEL THE ELDER. *Netherlandish Proverbs.* 1559. Oil on panel, 3'10" × 5'4½". Staatliche Museen, Berlin. *Bruegel's satirical, ironic, and, ultimately, pessimistic view of human nature permeates his* Netherlandish Proverbs. *In Bruegel's "world turned upside down," human stupidity, folly, and vanity are depicted in nearly every scene. Many of these proverbs, or versions of them, have come down to modern times, such as the man in the lower left ("Don't butt your head against a brick wall"); the man in the center foreground ("Don't throw your roses before swine"); in the water ("Big fish eat the little fish"); and in the lower right corner ("Don't cry over spilled milk"). Many of the proverbs have sexual references, such as the woman in red (center foreground) who is putting a blue cloak on her husband. This act signifies she is unfaithful, and thus he is a cuckold.*

Figure 13.10 PIETER BRUEGEL THE ELDER. *Wedding Dance.* 1566. Oil on panel, 47 × 62″. Detroit Institute of Arts. *Bruegel has made a sensuous arrangement out of the dancers and bystanders at this country wedding. The line of dancers winds from the foreground back through the trees, where it reverses itself and returns to its original starting point. The sense of lively movement is reinforced by the vivid red colors in the hats and vests and by the stomping feet and flailing arms.*

picted his peasant subjects in their natural settings, neither romanticizing nor patronizing them. He portrayed the common folk as types, never as individuals, and often as expressions or victims of the blind forces of nature. His scenes of country weddings and dances conveyed pessimism tinged with grudging admiration about human nature, as reflected in the peasants' simple, lusty behavior. He seemed more inspired by the timeless attitudes of the ordinary folk around him than by the prevailing intellectual thought of his times. This is most evident in *Netherlandish Proverbs,* a depiction of proverbial sayings and moralizing allegories (Figure 13.9). **Proverbs** embody folk wisdom and, through repetition, have come to be regarded as wise sayings.

Bruegel's fascination with landscapes and village scenes is the backdrop for the sayings and stories he illustrates in *Netherlandish Proverbs.* Bruegel views his subjects from above and they are loosely scattered across the tilted picture plane—a typical format for

him. The nearly one hundred figures, either singly or in groups, represent a saying or a moral tale based on the Bible, folktales, or popular culture. As in his other narrative paintings, he creates an organic harmony with splashes of color—yellows, browns, reds, blues, whites, and greens. And he uses the bold reds, blues, and greens to draw attention to a particular scene, as, for example, the man in the red cloak and red stockings (right foreground), who has a spinning globe on his left thumb ("He has the world on a string"). The painting also shows that Bruegel was, at the time, under the influence of Bosch (see Figure 13.8). Bosch's influence is evident in the complex narrative, the grotesqueness of some figures and scenes, and the general moralizing about the foolishness, absurdity, and sinfulness of life.

A painting that illustrates Bruegel in a less dark attitude toward country folk is his lively *Wedding Dance* (Figure 13.10). He records the exuberant revelers—the lusty men and their energetic partners. The bride and

Figure 13.11 PIETER BRUEGEL THE ELDER. *The Painter and the Connoisseur.* Mid-1560s. Pen and gray-brown ink, with touches of light brown ink, 10 × 8½″. Graphische Sammlung Albertina, Vienna. *Bruegel's drawing was probably intended as an inside joke about the artistic community, not as an artwork to be engraved or sold. The painter, with his skullcap and bushy hair and beard, is depicted as a dreamer, his mind lost in thought as he stares into the distance. Behind him stands an art expert, who clutches the "money" pouch at his waist and stares in a different direction from that of the painter.*

groom cannot be distinguished from the other dancers. Typical of Bruegel's style, there is a high horizon and an elevated point of view, so that we look at the scene from above. This effect, along with the crude faces of the peasants, underscores the impression that these are types, not individuals. The painting's composition reinforces the sense of peasant types in the way that the swirling figures in the foreground are repeated in the background in ever-diminishing size.

Bruegel is also known for his sixty-one drawings, which were devoted to either fantastic or naturalistic subjects. About half of the drawings were made as preparations for engravings, and, as such, they establish Bruegel as the heir to the Netherlandish artists who developed the print as a new artistic medium in the late Middle Ages (see Chapter 10). One of his drawings, *The Painter and the Connoisseur* (Figure 13.11), which was not intended for printmaking, pioneered a new subject in art: a satiric view of the relations between an artist and an art expert. Bruegel depicts the painter as an eccentric visionary, and the connoisseur as a self-deluded ignoramus who wears glasses and a ridiculous cap that covers his ears. Other details confirm this negative image of the connoisseur: the hairless face, the nonexistent lips, and the pinched expression.

THE BREAKUP OF CHRISTENDOM: CAUSES OF THE RELIGIOUS REFORMATIONS

Although the reasons for the breakup of Europe's religious unity are complicated, two basic causes are clear: the radical reshaping of Western society and culture that began about 1350 and the timeless spiritual yearnings of human beings. After 1500 these two forces came together in Germany to make conditions ripe for religious revolution. What made changes inevitable were several historical trends under way since the late Middle Ages: the corruption inside the church, the beginning of the sovereign state, the decay of medieval thought, and the revival of humanism.

The church had been in disarray since the Avignon papacy and the Great Schism of the fourteenth century; corruption charges, doctrinal issues, and questions about papal authority were raised by heretical groups like the Hussites (see Chapter 10). Many clergy led less than exemplary lives, particularly those inside the monasteries. Lay writers, now unafraid of the church, delighted in describing clerical scandals, and the populace gossiped about their priests' latest sins. Everywhere anticlericalism seemed on the rise.

LEARNING THROUGH MAPS

Map 13.1   THE RELIGIOUS SITUATION IN EUROPE IN 1560
This map shows the religious divisions in Europe in the middle of the sixteenth century.
1. *Notice* the line that separates Protestant Europe from Catholic Europe. 2. *Which* of the
two areas is larger? 3. *Identify* the three major Protestant religions and their locations.
4. *Which* Protestant religion covered the largest land area? 5. *What* region was the most
likely battleground between Protestants and Catholics? 6. *Which* area of Charles V's empire (see Map 12.1) was most affected by the Protestant Reformation, as seen in this map?

Perhaps the church could have reformed the clergy
and stemmed the tide of anticlericalism if the papacy
had been morally and politically strong, but by 1500
the popes were deeply distracted by Italian politics and
fully committed to worldly interests. The church was
also losing power to secular rulers, who were striving
to bring their subjects under state control. By 1500 the
English and the French kings, to the envy of other European rulers, had made their national churches relatively free of papal control.

In Germany, however, where no unified kingdom
was developing, the local secular leaders had no say
about clerical appointments and were unable to control the ecclesiastical courts or prevent the church from
collecting taxes—conditions that intensified anticlericalism and hatred of Rome. The German princes, who

were already struggling to be free from the control
of Charles V, made church reform a rallying cry and
turned against Rome as well as the Holy Roman emperor. As events unfolded, the popes were incapable
of preventing these princes from converting their
lands into independent states outside papal jurisdiction (Map 13.1).

The Protestant Order

Protestantism first appeared in Germany, where Martin Luther led the founding of a new religious sect in
the 1520s. In the 1530s a second generation of Protestants acted on the opportunity created by Luther.
John Calvin, a French scholar, formed an independent

ENCOUNTER

Indigenous Peoples and New Spain

The rise of European colonies in the New World, often inspired by religious motives, was changing the geography of Western culture during the sixteenth century. Spain led the way with its vast overseas empire and, in 1535, organized its overseas possessions into four viceroyalties, or regional governments. New Spain, the northernmost viceroyalty, included all Spanish territories from the isthmus of Panama into what is now the southwestern United States, California, and Florida, along with the Philippine Islands. The viceroyalty of New Spain administered these territories until 1821, when it collapsed in the wake of the wars of revolution (see Chapter 17).

New Spain brought its lands and peoples into the Western orbit, but with a distinctive character that reflected the ideas, rituals, beliefs, imagery, and traditions of indigenous populations. Spain's encounter with native peoples was reminiscent of how ancient Rome was gradually conquered by the Greeks, whom they had conquered. Native cultures slowly permeated nearly all aspects of colonial life in New Spain, especially art and religion.

The Spanish conquerors built the capital of New Spain, Mexico City, on the ruins of the Aztec capital, Tenochtitlán, which became the grandest city of Spanish North America. From there, the viceroyalty imposed Western values and institutions on the native peoples: converting them to the Christian faith, establishing schools and universities, and constructing an economy based on mining, ranching, and farming. These policies were enforced with such a harsh rigor that, between 1500 and 1600, the native population declined from twenty-five million to one million.

Although exploited by the Spanish ruling class, the descendants of the Native Americans quickly became the backbone of New Spain and the new emerging culture. The large numbers of *mestizos* (Spanish, "mixed"), persons of both European and Amerindian ancestry, with a 50:50 ratio—the result of intermarriage—stimulated a cross-cultural exchange. Modern Mexico has embraced its mestizo heritage and looks upon the Spanish conquest as "the painful birth of the mestizo nation." The ethnic traditions have been further enriched by the *indigenas*, purebred indigenous peoples, who adhere to their own dress, customs, and languages.

Although Western styles were in the ascendant in the arts and crafts—ceramics, embroidery, weaving, clothing, and pottery—indigenous and mestizo influences were highly visible in subject matter, themes, and techniques. Glyph (symbolic figures or characters) writing, which had been developed by indigenous peoples, was now transformed into an alphabetic script and adorned with figural decoration as can be seen in surviving manuscripts from the postconquest period.

The architecture also reflected a blend of Western and local traditions. The conquerors dismantled the Indian temples, recycled the stones into public and private buildings, and constructed churches, monastic complexes, and schools for the converts. Indian influence on these new churches was often determined by a church's location. Wealthy churches in Mexico City might import artists from Spain, but poor rural parishes would employ local artists. The church had strict rules governing religious images, but indigenous artists often followed their own taste.

---

church in Geneva, Switzerland, and King Henry VIII removed the English church from the pope's control (see Timeline 13.1).

LUTHER'S REVOLT One of the church's more glaring abuses was the selling of indulgences—pardons that reduced the amount of penance that Christians had to perform to atone for their sins—a practice that dated from the High Middle Ages. In 1517, in response to the archbishop of Mainz's sale of indulgences to raise money, Martin Luther (1483–1546), a monk teaching at nearby Wittenberg University, published his famous Ninety-five Theses (Figure 13.12). These questions and arguments about the legitimacy of indulgences implicitly challenged the sacraments of confession and penance and the authority of the pope. Luther had hoped

to arouse a debate in the university, but instead he ignited criticism against the church and placed himself in the vanguard of a reform movement.

The church's response to Luther was initially hesitant, but in 1520 Pope Leo X excommunicated him. When Luther burned the papal document of excommunication in public, the church branded him a heretic and an outlaw. Luther survived because he was under the protection of his patron, Elector Frederick the Wise of Saxony (r. 1486–1525), who had led the German princes opposed to the Holy Roman emperor (Figure 13.13).

Luther's Beliefs Luther's attack on indulgences arose from his spiritual quest to understand sin and salvation that had led him to become a monk. Through

The Catholic Church strengthened its hold over new converts by embracing certain practices of pagan religion. The major example of this blending of religions happened when the church appropriated the hill of Tepeyac—a holy site to the Aztec people, who believed it to be the home of Tonantzin, Mother of the Gods. There, in 1531, a series of miracles occurred, following an appearance of the Virgin Mary to an Indian convert. The Church of the Virgin of Guadelupe was soon built there, transforming an Aztec holy site into a Christian shrine. Today, the Virgin of Guadelupe (Encounter figure 13.1) is honored as the patron saint of Mexico, and her shrine is the most visited pilgrimage site in the Western Hemisphere.

Learning from the Encounter

1. *Why* were indigenous peoples able to have such a strong impact on society and culture in New Spain? 2. *Discuss* the influence of indigenous peoples on the art of New Spain. 3. *What* was the significance of the blending of Christianity with elements of indigenous faiths that occurred in New Spain?

Encounter figure 13.1 Anonymous. *Our Lady of Guadelupe. Our Lady of Guadelupe has captured the imagination of the faithful, many of whom crawl for miles on their knees to worship at her shrine. The image's meaning is twofold. For indigenous peoples, it represents the Virgin Mary defeating the chief Aztec gods (symbolized by the sun behind her and the moon at her feet). And for Christians, it depicts the Virgin as the woman in Revelation 12:1: "adorned with the sun, standing on the moon, and with the twelve stars on her head for a crown."*

long study of the scriptures, he reached the understanding that salvation comes not from good works but from God's unmerited love, or grace, or, as Luther phrased it, "justification by faith alone." According to Luther, salvation is achieved by faith in Jesus's sacrificial death; thus, buying indulgences is trying to buy salvation—a direct contradiction of the biblical truth Luther had gleaned from his theological studies.

In his theology, which became known as **Lutheranism,** he tried to revive a Christianity based on biblical precedents and reminiscent of the early church. He believed that the sole source of religious authority was the Bible, not the pope or church councils, and that any Christian could lead a simple life of piety and repentance, could be his or her own priest and, thus, could mediate with God, without the need of a priest.

Luther also repudiated the mystical definition of the sacraments, the notion of purgatory, the adoration of the saints, and Masses for the dead; he retained only baptism and the Lord's Supper, as he called the Eucharist. Preaching in German became the heart of the liturgy, replacing the Latin Mass.

Luther's voluminous writings constitute the largest legacy of any German author. Of all his tracts, essays, and letters, his German translation of the Bible has had the most enduring influence. His biblical scholarship was based on translating the original languages of the scriptures, the technique that had been developed by the northern humanists, particularly Erasmus. He also set the path followed by subsequent Protestant reformers regarding what books to include in the Bible: Rejecting the Apocrypha of the Jewish Septuagint,

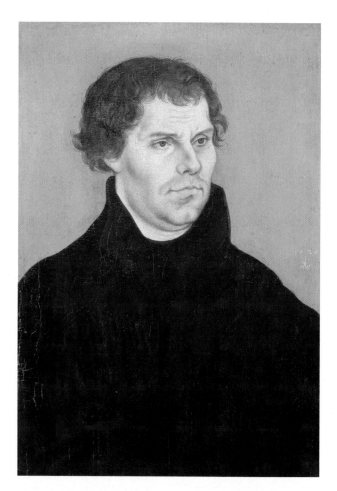

Figure 13.12   Lucas Cranach the Elder. *Martin Luther.* 1533. Panel, 8 × 5¾". © Nationalmuseum, Stockholm, Sweden. *This portrait of Martin Luther, with its vivid rendering of his steel jaw and piercing eyes, shows some of the qualities that made him such a force during the Reformation. The admiring likeness was done by the German artist Lucas Cranach, a supporter of the new faith and a close friend of Luther's. At the time of this painting, the Reformation was well under way.*

Figure 13.13   Albrecht Dürer. *Elector Frederick the Wise.* 1524. Copper engraving, 7⅜ × 4¾". Print collection, Miriam and Ira D. Wallach Division of Art, Prints, and Photographs, The New York Public Library, Astor, Lenox, and Tilden Foundations. *Dürer's portrait captures the princely bearing of Frederick the Wise, the ruler of Electoral Saxony and Luther's great patron. Ironically, Frederick owned one of the largest collections of relics in Christendom. It has been estimated that the 17,443 artifacts in Frederick's collection in 1518 could reduce the time in purgatory by 127,799 years and 116 days.*

Luther chose the canonical books of the Hebrew Bible, or Old Testament, and the New Testament. Luther's version of the Bible outlived its competitors (nineteen by 1518) and left its stamp on the German language. His pithy style engaged the reader's emotions with realistic images and idiomatic speech.

Social and Political Implications of Luther's Revolt
The Ninety-five Theses circulated widely throughout Germany, and in 1521 Lutheran churches sprang up in most German towns. Simultaneously, radical followers of Luther fomented new problems, causing riots, driving priests from their homes, closing monasteries, and destroying religious images. Luther rejected this violence and advocated moderation. He did accept the abolition of monasticism, however, dropping the

monk's habit in 1523 and marrying Katherine von Bora (1499–1552), a former nun, in 1525 (Figure 13.14). When he and Katherine had children, they created a familial tradition for Lutheran clergy. Lutheran women thus seemed to make gains with the closing of convents and the giving of new respectability to married life, but these steps proved illusory, since Luther affirmed male rule and female submission within the family.

Another area altered by Luther's beliefs was education. His supporters set up schools and universities, replacing Catholic foundations. Unlike church-run Catholic schools, the Lutheran schools were financed by taxes, so that teachers became state employees— a reflection of Luther's belief that church and state should work hand in hand. For Lutheran women, the changes in education created a dilemma. Women were denied access to these schools, but they were expected to know the Bible, in order to supervise their children's moral education.

Luther distanced himself from the antigovernment political and social reforms espoused by some followers. In 1523 a brief Peasants' War erupted under the banner of Luther's faith, but Luther urged its suppres-

Figure 13.14 WORKSHOP OF LUCAS CRANACH. *Katherine von Bora. Ca. 1526. Oil on panel, 7½ × 5". Wartburg-Stiftung, Germany. Katherine von Bora was one of a dozen nuns liberated from a convent near Wittenberg in the heady days of 1523. She joined the mixed collection who lived with Luther in the Black Cloisters, his old monastery given him by Frederick the Wise. Despite Luther's protests, she determined to become his wife, and she did. He treated her with great deference, calling her "My lord Kate," though he poked fun at her supposed greed for property. This small portrait was executed in the workshop of Lucas Cranach the Elder, who was also a witness to the marriage of Martin Luther and Katherine von Bora.*

sion by the nobility, clearly showing his preference for the status quo. His reliance on Saxony's rulers for protection set the model for his religion; in the Lutheran faith, the church acted as an arm of the state. Luther's revolt did not embrace individual rights in the political or social arena; indeed, the Protestant princes were more powerful than their predecessors, since Rome could not control them.

THE REFORMS OF JOHN CALVIN   Among the second generation of Protestant reformers, the most influential was John Calvin (1509–1564) (Figure 13.15). After earning a law degree in Paris, he experienced a religious

Figure 13.15 ANONYMOUS. *John Calvin. 1550s. Bibliothèque Publique et Universitaire de Geneva. This anonymous portrait of Calvin shows the way that he probably wanted to be viewed rather than a natural likeness. Still, the angular features, the intense gaze, and the set mouth suggest that the reputation Calvin had for strict discipline was justified. The well-trimmed beard and somewhat extravagant fur collar, although typical of middle-class fashion of the era, create an ironic contradiction in this otherwise austere portrait.*

SLICE OF LIFE

The Conscience of Sixteenth-Century Christian Europe

BARTOLOMÉ DE LAS CASAS
A Short Account of the Destruction of the Indies

Bartolomé de las Casas (1484–1576), a Dominican friar, was an eyewitness to Spain's quest for empire. Outraged by the massacres committed during the 1502 conquest of Cuba, he denounced Spain's entire overseas mission as misguided and even genocidal, in A Short Account of the Destruction of the Indies *(1542). By "Indies," he meant the lands of the Indians in the New World. In his short book, las Casas called for justice for indigenous peoples.*

New Spain was discovered in 1517 and, at the time, great atrocities were committed against the indigenous people of the region and some were killed by members of the expedition. In 1518 the so-called Christians set about stealing from the people and murdering them on the pretence of settling the area. And from that year until this—and it is now 1542—the great iniquities and injustices, the outrageous acts of violence and the bloody tyranny of these Christians have steadily escalated, the perpetrators having lost all fear of God, all love of their sovereign, and all sense of self-respect. . . . This was . . . the pattern they followed in all the lands they invaded: to stage a bloody massacre of the most public possible kind in order to terrorize those meek and gentle peoples. What they did was the following. They requested the local lord to send for all the nobles and leading citizens of the city and of all the surrounding communities subject to it and, as soon as they arrived and entered the building to begin talks with the Spanish commander [Hernán Cortés (1485–1546)], they were

seized without anyone outside getting wind of what was afoot. Part of the original request was that they should bring with them five or six thousand native bearers and these were mustered in the courtyards when and as they arrived. One could not watch these poor wretches getting ready to carry the Spaniards' packs without taking pity on them, stark naked as they were with only their modesty hidden from view, each with a kind of little net on his shoulders in which he carried his own modest store of provisions. They all got down on their haunches and waited patiently like sheep. Once they were all safely inside the court-yard, together with a number of others who were also there at the time, armed guards took up positions covering the exits and Spanish soldiers unsheathed their swords and grasped their lances and proceeded to slaughter these poor innocents. Not a single soul escaped. . . . The Spanish commander gave orders that the leading citizens, who numbered over a hundred and were roped together, were to be tied to stakes set in the ground and burned alive.

INTERPRETING THIS SLICE OF LIFE

1. *What* is las Casas's description of the indigenous people? 2. *What* is his attitude toward the Spanish invaders? 3. *What* appears to be las Casas's motives for writing? *Justify* your answer. 4. *Why* do you think las Casas's call for justice went largely unheeded in his lifetime?

---

conversion and cast his lot with the Reformation. Coming under the suspicion of the French authorities, he fled to Basel, Switzerland, a Lutheran center, where he began to publish *The Institutes of the Christian Religion.*

Calvin, like Luther, advocated beliefs and practices having biblical roots. He differed from Luther over the nature of God, church–state relations, and Christian morals. Calvin's religious thought, called **Calvinism,** rested on his concept of an awesome, even angry, God, which led him to make predestination (the belief that God predestines certain souls to salvation and others to damnation) central to his faith. Calvin also espoused a theocratic state in which the government was subordinate to the church. He favored strict ethical demands, regulating everything from laughter in

church to public shows of affection between the sexes. Because of such rules, which later became associated with **Puritanism,** Calvinism acquired the reputation for being a joyless creed.

Calvin's theology also had an impact on political, social, and economic life. Calvinism encouraged thrift, industry, sobriety, and discipline—the same traits that made for business success. Calvin's teachings spurred the Christian capitalist to accumulate wealth, so that gradually there developed the idea that worldly success was tantamount to God's approval and that poverty was a sign of God's disfavor. Of all the new sects, Calvinism was the most international, and reformed congregations spread across Europe, especially in Scotland and the Netherlands (see Map 13.1).

Figure 13.16 HANS HOLBEIN THE YOUNGER. *Henry VIII.* Ca. 1540. Oil on wood panel, 34¾ × 29½″. Galleria Nazionale d'Arte Antica, Rome. *Hans Holbein the Younger, like Erasmus, established his reputation in Europe before making his way to England. In 1537 Holbein became the court painter to Henry VIII, for whom he executed murals (now lost), designed jewelry, silver plate, and state robes, and painted easel portraits of the court, including the king. In this portrait, Holbein captured the power and majesty of his patron by centering him in a three-quarter, frontal pose so that the king's figure completely fills the frame with no props or objects to distract the viewer. The king's right upper arm is pushed out in an assertive manner, and he holds a glove in his clenched right hand. His Majesty's direct gaze and assured stance radiate self-confidence and speak of a sense of power and self-importance, which are reinforced by the bejeweled coat, puffed sleeves, decorated hat, and elaborate chain necklace. Holbein's painting sends a clear message about his subject's personal authority and high status, which contrasts nicely with his more intimate portrait of Erasmus, the Dutch scholar and man of ideas (see Figure 13.1).*

THE REFORM OF THE ENGLISH CHURCH   A second major religious reformer in the 1530s was Henry VIII (r. 1509–1547), who founded the Church of England (also called the Anglican Church). In 1529 Henry asked the pope to annul his marriage to Catherine of Aragon, who, though she gave birth to a daughter, had not produced a male heir. In more favorable times, the pope might have given Henry a dispensation, but the troops of Holy Roman Emperor Charles V, Catherine's nephew, had just sacked Rome and imprisoned the pontiff. Charles also opposed any step that would nullify his aunt's marriage and make her daughter a bastard. In 1533 Henry pushed through Parliament the laws setting up the Church of England with himself as the head and granting him a divorce (Figure 13.16).

Although **Anglicanism** was founded by Henry VIII, the ground had been prepared locally by Christian humanists and English Lutherans. The work of both groups led to the so-called Reformation Parliament (1529–1535), which had begun to reform the Catholic Church in England even before Henry made the decisive break with Rome.

Religious turmoil followed Henry's death in 1547, and the fate of the English Reformation stayed in doubt until his daughter Elizabeth (r. 1558–1603) became queen and the head of the Anglican Church (Figure 13.17). In 1559 Elizabeth I, with the aid of Parliament, steered a middle course between Catholicism and Calvinism, which had gained many English converts. Anglican beliefs were summarized in the Thirty-nine Articles, and those who wished to sit in Parliament, earn university degrees, or serve as military officers had to swear allegiance to them. Hence, Calvinists and Catholics were excluded by law from English public life and remained so for about 275 years.

The Counter-Reformation

Before Martin Luther took his stand in Germany, a Roman Catholic reform movement had begun quietly in isolated parts of Europe. Confronted with the surprising successes of the various Protestant groups, the Roman Catholic Church, as it was now called, struck back with a Counter-Reformation. By 1600 this superbly organized campaign had slowed Protestantism and won back many adherents. The Catholics held on to southern and most of central Europe, halting Protestantism's spread in Poland, France, and Switzerland and limiting the movement to northern Europe. The

Figure 13.17 MARCUS GHEERAERTS THE YOUNGER. *Elizabeth I.* Late sixteenth century. Oil on panel, 7'11" × 5'. National Portrait Gallery, London. *The so-called Ditchley portrait presented Queen Elizabeth in all her Renaissance finery. Following the Spanish fashion, the queen wears a neck ruff and yards of pearls, and she carries a fan. She stands atop a map of England, which she ruled for forty-five years with compassion and firmness, until her death in 1603.*

Counter-Reformation, with a revitalized papacy, new monastic orders, and a reforming council, confronted the Protestant threat, purified the church of abuses, and reorganized its structure.

THE REVITALIZED PAPACY With the reign of Paul III (pope 1534–1549), a series of reform-minded popes reinvigorated the church. To counter the inroads made by Protestantism, Paul enlisted the support of the full church by convening a council representing Roman Catholic clergy from all over Europe and launched new monastic orders.

Paul and his successors reclaimed the moral leadership of the church and reorganized the papal bureaucracy so that discipline was now enforced throughout the ecclesiastical hierarchy. Sensing that Protestantism would not go away and recognizing the increasing availability of written material due to the printing press, these popes tried to isolate the church from deviant ideas. A committee of churchmen drew up an Index of Forbidden Books, which listed writings that were off-limits to Roman Catholics because they were considered prejudicial to faith or morals. The first Index included the works of Luther, Calvin, and other Protestants. This tactic failed to suppress threatening ideas, but the Index continued to be updated until the 1960s.

NEW MONASTIC ORDERS Since the High Middle Ages, monastic reform had played a small role in the life of the church. Suddenly, in the sixteenth century, new monastic groups arose to fill a variety of needs, such as preparing men and women to minister directly to the masses and reclaiming lapsed believers to the faith.

Typical of monastic reform for women in Counter-Reformation Europe was the fate of the Company of St. Ursula, or the Ursulines, founded in 1535 in Brescia, Italy, by Angela Merici [ma-REE-chee] (about 1470–1540). The Ursulines were named after a legendary British princess who, with eleven thousand virgin companions, was martyred on the way to her wedding. Reflecting the same ideals as contemporary early Protestantism in stressing individual grace and keeping apart from clerical rule, the Ursulines were originally intended to be for laywomen, without any intrusion by male church officials. Merici's followers, divided into "daughters" and "matrons," were to live in their own homes, practice chastity without taking formal vows, serve the sick and the poor, and educate the young. In 1540, after Merici's death and under pressure from Protestantism, church leaders cloistered the order and placed its members under male control.

The most significant new order was the Society of Jesus, commonly known as the **Jesuits.** Recognized by Pope Paul III in 1540, the Jesuits had emerged by 1600 as the church's leading monastic order. The dedicated members helped to curb Protestantism in Europe, and their missionary efforts abroad represented the first steps in making Roman Catholicism a global faith. After a shaky beginning, their rise to power was quick, and their success was largely due to the order's founder, the Spaniard Ignatius Loyola (about 1493–1556) (Figure 13.18).

Loyola's life was imbued with more than a touch of medieval knight errantry. His first calling was as a professional warrior, defending his country from invaders. When in 1521 Loyola suffered a battle injury which crippled him for life, he underwent a religious conversion that led him to become a "soldier" in the army of Christ. Eventually, he founded the Society of

Jesus, which resembled a military company in its rigid hierarchy, close discipline, and absolute obedience to the founder.

The Jesuits were initially concerned with working among the unchurched and the poor, focusing especially on teaching their children. But that mission was modified in the 1540s. Guided by the Spaniard Francis Xavier (1506–1552), they established outposts in the Far East and converted thousands to the Christian faith. Other Jesuits had similar success in missions to North and South America.

Because of the Jesuits' unique vow of loyalty to the pope, which set them apart from other monastic orders, and their emphasis and expertise in education, the Jesuits soon became the church's chief weapon against the Protestants. In their writings, the Jesuits answered the church's critics, setting forth their orthodox beliefs in a clear and persuasive manner.

THE COUNCIL OF TRENT The Counter-Reformation's third force was the council held at Trent in northern Italy, over three separate sessions between 1545 and 1563. Dominated by papal supporters, Italian delegates, and the Jesuits, the Council of Trent offered no overtures to the Protestants and thus solidified the split in Christian Europe. The council reaffirmed all the practices condemned by the Protestants, such as monasticism, the sale of indulgences, and the veneration of holy relics, although mechanisms were set in motion to eliminate their worst abuses. The council also initiated some education and training reforms for the clergy.

The council's unyielding position toward the Protestants was based on its belief that both the Bible and church tradition—not the Bible alone as advocated by the Protestants—were the bases of authority and the word of God. The only official Bible was the Vulgate (including the Apocrypha of the Jewish Septuagint); all other versions were rejected. The council reaffirmed that salvation should be sought by faith *and* by good works, not by faith alone; it also reaffirmed the seven sacraments. The council's doctrinal and disciplinary decisions laid the foundations for present-day Roman Catholic policies and thought.

Warfare as a Response to Religious Dissent, 1520–1603

As religious dissent spread, the secular rulers watched with mounting concern. Until 1530, compromise between the Lutheran rebels and the dominant faith seemed possible, but with the constant growth of mutually hostile sects, secular rulers increasingly relied on warfare to deal with the crisis.

Figure 13.18 JACOPINO DEL CONTE. *St. Ignatius Loyola.* 1556. Curia Generalizia, or Headquarters, of the Society of Jesus, Rome. *This portrait captures Loyola's humanness at the end of an active life. His energetic youth a distant memory, he now wears a serene and contemplative countenance. Not a life portrait, Jacopino del Conte's work was painted soon after Loyola's death. The artist probably had access to Loyola's death mask, so this portrait—unlike many that were painted years later—is as accurate a likeness of the founder of the Society of Jesus that exists.*

War between Charles V's armies and the Lutheran forces erupted on German lands in 1546, the year Luther died, and lasted until 1555, when the Religious Peace of Augsburg brought hostilities to an end. This agreement granted toleration to the Lutheran states, but on strict terms. The ruler's religion became the official faith of each territory; members of religious minorities, whether Roman Catholic or Lutheran, could migrate and join their coreligionists in nearby lands. But because the rights of other minority sects, such as the Calvinists, were ignored, the Peace of Augsburg contained the seeds of future wars.

In 1556 Philip II (r. 1556–1598) inherited the Spanish crown from Charles V and became the head of the Roman Catholic cause. Besides Spain, Roman Catholic regimes now ruled Italy, Portugal, and Austria; Protestants reigned in Scandinavia. Elsewhere the religious rivals vied for supremacy. For the rest of the century, until 1603, Germany was at peace, but western Europe suffered religious violence.

Financed by gold and silver from Mexico and Peru, Philip dominated European politics. His well-prepared armies enabled him to control much of Europe. He expelled suspected Muslims from Spain and defeated the Turks in the Mediterranean; he invaded Portugal and joined that country to Spain. But his fortunes declined when he launched a costly campaign against the United Provinces in the northern Netherlands. As the Dutch war was winding down, Philip turned his attention to Protestant England, a supporter of the Dutch revolt. In Philip's eyes, only England stood between him and a reunited Christendom; moreover, Spain and England were rivals for the precious metals of the New World. Philip's attempt to invade England in 1588 ended in a disaster when the Spanish Armada was defeated by English sea power and a violent storm.

Philip II's dream of a reunited Christendom had been impossible from the beginning. The Protestant faith was too entrenched, the growth of national consciousness too widespread, and the rise of a system of sovereign states too far advanced for any one monarch to unify Europe under a single religious or political system. When Philip died in 1598, Spain was declining and Europe was divided into independent states and several religions.

LATE MANNERISM

The strongest impact of the Counter-Reformation on the arts, architecture, and music began after the Council of Trent, in 1563. Spain and the Italian states, the areas least attracted to Protestantism, were greatly influenced by the council's decisions. The council decreed that the arts and music should be easily accessible to the uneducated. In sacred music, for example, the intelligibility of the words should take precedence over the melody, and in architecture the building should create a worshipful environment. The church council also decreed that paintings and sculptures should be simple and direct as well as unobjectionable and decent in appearance. Guided by this principle, the Counter-Reformation popes declared that some of Michelangelo's male nudes in *The Last Judgment* were obscene and ordered loincloths to be painted over them. General church policy returned to the medieval ideal that the sole aim of art and music was to serve and clarify the Christian faith.

Since the Roman Catholic Church after Trent wanted a simplified art that spoke to the masses, its artistic policy tended to clash with mannerism, which embodied a self-conscious vision that was elitist and deliberately complex. Only with the rise of the baroque after 1600 was there a style that could conform to the church's need for art with a mass appeal. In the meantime, the general effect of Trent on the last stage of mannerism was to intensify its spiritual values.

Late mannerism, which emerged across Europe after 1564, dominated Spanish painting, but it had little influence on Spanish literature. Under the influence of the Renaissance, Spanish literature flourished with the revival of the theater and the birth of new literary genres.

Spanish Painting

No Catholic artist expressed the spirit of the Counter-Reformation better than El Greco (1541–1614) in his Spanish paintings after 1576. These visionary works epitomize the spirit of late mannerism. El Greco's real name was Domenikos Theotokopoulos [doh-me-NEEK-os TAY-o-toh-KOH-pooh-lohs]. A native of Crete, he had lived in Venice, where he adopted the colorful style of Venetian painting. Unsuccessful in Venice, he also failed to find rich patrons in Rome, though he learned from the works of Michelangelo and the mannerists. He arrived in Toledo, Spain, about 1576, where he found an appreciative public among the wealthy nobility. But he never became a favorite of the Spanish ruler, Philip II, who faulted El Greco's works as too bizarre.

For his select audience of aristocrats and Roman Catholic clergy, however, El Greco could do no wrong. They believed that his paintings of saints, martyrs, and other religious figures caught the essence of Spanish emotionalism and religious zeal—the same qualities that had led Loyola to found the Jesuits. El Greco's extravagant images gave visible form to his patrons' spiritual yearnings. He rejected a naturalistic world with conventional perspective, and his spiritualized vision came to be distinguished by elongated bodies, sharp lines in the folds of cloth, and luminous colors.

El Greco's masterpiece is *The Burial of Count Orgaz,* painted to honor the founder of the church of Santo Tomé in Toledo (Figure 13.19). This painting, designed to fit into a special place beside the church's high altar, depicts the miraculous scene that, according to legend, occurred during the count's burial, when two saints, Augustine and Stephen, appeared and assisted with the last rites.

The painting is divided into two halves, with the lower section devoted to the count's actual burial and the upper section focused on the reception of his soul in heaven. Except for a few men who tilt their faces upward, the town dignitaries seem unaware of what is

Figure 13.19 El Greco. *The Burial of Count Orgaz.* 1586. Oil on canvas, 16′ × 11′10″. Church of Santo Tomé, Toledo, Spain. *A manneristic invention in* The Burial of Count Orgaz *was the rich treatment of the robe of St. Stephen, the first Christian martyr and, in this painting, the beardless figure supporting the body of the dead count. Sewn onto the bottom of this robe is a picture of the stoning of St. Stephen, an episode narrated in the New Testament. By depicting one event inside another, El Greco created an illusionistic device—a typical notion of mannerist painters, who were skeptical about conventional reality.*

happening just above their heads. The dignitaries below are rendered in realistic terms, showing fashions of El Greco's era, such as the neck ruffs, mustaches, and goatees. The heavenly spectacle is depicted in the ethereal manner that he increasingly used in his later works. El Greco had devised two distinct styles to deal with these different planes of reality.

El Greco also painted several portraits of church officials; the best known is *Cardinal Guevara* (Figure 13.20). This painting portrays the chief inquisitor, dressed in his splendid red robes. El Greco has captured the personality of this austere and iron-willed churchman who vigorously pursued heretics and sentenced them to die in an *auto-da-fé* ("act of faith")—a public cer-

emony in which heretics were executed, usually by being burned at the stake. El Greco's likeness of Cardinal Guevara seems to suggest much about the inner man: an uneasy conscience, as betrayed by the shifty expression of his eyes, the left hand clutching the chair arm, and the general sense that the subject is restraining himself.

Another mannerist artist-in-exile working in Spain in the late sixteenth century was Sofonisba Anguissola [an-gwee-SOL-uh] (about 1532–1625), a northern Italian from Cremona who, with El Greco, helped introduce the Italian school of painting into Spanish culture (Figure 13.21). Praised and encouraged by the aging Michelangelo, Anguissola began her rise to international

Figure 13.20 EL GRECO. *Cardinal Guevara.* 1596–1600. Oil on canvas, 67¼ × 42½". Courtesy of the Metropolitan Museum of Art. The H. O. Havemeyer Collection. Bequest of Mrs. H. O. Havemeyer, 1929. (29.100.5). *El Greco's painting of Cardinal Guevara illustrates his mastery of mannerist portraiture. Disturbing details are visible everywhere. Guevara's head is almost too small for his large body, made even grander by the cardinal's red robe, and the divided background—half wooden panel, half rich tapestry—sets up a dissonant effect. Even the cardinal's chair contributes to the air of uneasiness, for its one visible leg seems barely to touch the floor.*

fame when Philip II of Spain chose her to be his court painter from 1559 to 1579. She painted mainly portraits, including the *Portrait of Don Carlos* (Figure 13.22). In this three-quarter-length likeness of Spain's crown prince, Anguissola shows her mastery of the mannerist style, including the challenging gaze of the young subject and the painting's highly polished surface and dark olive background. Such portraits made Anguissola a celebrity, the first internationally acclaimed Italian woman artist. Her painting career at the Spanish court ended in 1580, when she married a Sicilian nobleman and moved to Palermo, Sicily, where she lived and worked for much of the rest of her life.

Anguissola's international acclaim was due, in part, to her aristocratic breeding and her education in Renaissance learning, rare for women of the times. Her background, coupled with rich artistic gifts, enabled her to overcome the prejudices and guild restrictions that had previously kept women from pursuing careers in the arts. Sofonisba Anguissola was the ablest of the women artists who began to emerge in sixteenth-century Europe.

Figure 13.21 SOFONISBA ANGUISSOLA. *Bernardino Campi Painting Sofonisba Anguissola.* Ca. 1550. Oil on canvas, 43¹¹/₁₆ × 43⁵/₁₆". Pinacoteca Nazionale, Siena. *Unusual for her time, the aristocratic Sofonisba Anguissola pursued a painting career, and, even rarer, she studied painting apart from her parents' household, under the artist Bernardino Campi (1522–1591), living in his home as a paying guest. From him, she learned the mannerist style, as in this double portrait of herself and her mentor, both presented in three-quarter length. Within the painting, she depicts her likeness on a canvas supported by an easel. Campi, standing before her likeness, holds a paintbrush in his right hand, which is steadied by a hand rest (a device used to prevent smudges). The sharp contrasts of light and dark and the characteristic "square-U" shape to the hands are typical of Anguissola's mannerist style. By depicting Campi at work, she also broke new ground in the portrait genre, which hitherto had focused on subjects seated or standing, but always in static situations (see Figures 12.2 and 12.8).*

Figure 13.22 SOFONISBA ANGUISSOLA. (Formerly attributed to Alonzo Sánchez Coello.) *Portrait of Don Carlos.* Ca. 1560. Oil on canvas, 42¹⁵⁄₁₆ × 34³⁄₁₆". Prado, Madrid. *This painting of Prince Don Carlos shows typical features of the artist's personal style. Like most women of the period, Anguissola was skilled in the needle arts, and she reveals this knowledge in the painstaking detail she has lavished on the prince's court costume—her trademark, according to one scholar. She also had a signature way of rendering hands—in a "square-U" shape so that the index and little fingers are parallel and act as the raised portions of a "U" connected by an imaginary line—which may be seen in both of Don Carlos's hands.*

Spanish Literature

Known in Spanish as *Siglo de Oro,* or Golden Century, the sixteenth century is the high point in Spain's literary history. The writings, characterized by direct observation of life, satiric treatment of earlier epics and ballads, religious zeal, and Spanish themes, values, and subject matter, also reflected minor influence from Renaissance humanism. Plays and novels were the most popular forms of literary expression.

As in England, theater was now revived in Spain for the first time in centuries. Spanish playwrights began to write dramas, including tragedies and comedies, and invent new dramatic forms, such as allegorical religious plays. The dramatist Lope de Vega [BAY-gah] (1562–1635), author of 426 secular plays and 42 religious dramas, is generally credited with almost single-handedly founding the Spanish national theater.

The **chivalric novel,** a late medieval literary form that presented romantic stories of knights and their ladies, was now challenged by the more realistic picaresque novel. The **picaresque novel** (Spanish *picaro,* "rogue"), which recounted the comic misadventures of

a roguish hero who lived by his wits, often at the expense of those above him in society, became immensely popular in Spain. The first picaresque novel was the anonymous *Lazarillo de Tormes,* published in 1554, in which the poor hero, Lazaro, encounters several masters, each of whom is a shady character suffering from self-deception. In translation, *Lazarillo de Tormes* found a wider audience across Europe and influenced the writing of novels in England, France, and Germany for about two hundred years.

The Spanish novel was raised to new heights by Miguel de Cervantes Saavedra [sir-VAN-tez SAH-uh-VAY-drah] (1547–1616). Poet, playwright, and novelist, Cervantes is the greatest figure in Spanish literature and one of the most respected writers in the world. In his masterpiece *Don Quixote* (part I, 1605; part II, 1615), he satirized the chivalric novel, mocking its anachronistic ideals. Although the long, rambling structure was borrowed from the chivalric novel, *Don Quixote* is the prototype of the modern novel, with its psychological realism, or probing into the motives of the main characters. These characters—the hero, Don Quixote, and his servant, Sancho Panza—whose lives are intertwined, embody the major themes of the work. The tormented Don Quixote, driven half-mad by his unreachable quest, represents the hopeless visionary, while the plodding Sancho Panza, never taken in by his master's madness, stands for the hardheaded realist. At one level, the characters signify the dual nature of the Spanish soul, the idealistic aristocrat and the down-to-earth peasant. At a higher level, the characters personify a universal theme, that idealism and realism must go hand in hand.

Late Mannerist Painting in Italy: Tintoretto

With the death of Michelangelo in 1564, Venice displaced Rome as the dominant artistic center in Italy, and until the end of the century, Venetian painters carried the banner of the Italian Renaissance, bringing mannerism to a brilliant sunset. The leading exponent of late mannerism in Italy was Tintoretto [tin-tuh-RAY-toe] (1518–1594). With his feverish, emotional style that reflected impetuosity in its execution, Tintoretto was reacting against Titian, who had been noted for extraordinary discipline. But in other respects, he followed Titian, adopting his love of color and his use of theatrical lighting. The special quality of Tintoretto's art, which he achieved in his earliest paintings, was his placement of human figures in arrangements that suggest a sculptural frieze.

Tintoretto's rendition of the familiar biblical account of the Last Supper shows his feverish style

Figure 13.23   TINTORETTO. *The Last Supper.* 1592–1594. Oil on canvas, 12′ × 18′8″. San Giorgio Maggiore, Venice. *Nothing better illustrates the distance between the High Renaissance and mannerism than a comparison of Leonardo's* Last Supper *(Figure 12.7) with that of Tintoretto. Everything about Tintoretto's spiritualized scene contradicts the quiet classicism of Leonardo's work. Leonardo's painting is meant to appeal to the viewer's reason; Tintoretto's shadowy scene is calculated to stir the feelings.*

(Figure 13.23). Unlike the serene, classically balanced scene that Leonardo had painted (see Figure 12.7), Tintoretto portrays an ethereal gathering, illuminated by eerie light and filled with swooping angels. The diagonal table divides the pictorial space: on the left side is the spiritual world of Jesus and his disciples, and on the right is the earthly realm of the servants. Tintoretto's depiction of the two levels of reality is reminiscent of a similar division in El Greco's *The Burial of Count Orgaz* (see Figure 13.19). Especially notable is Jesus's body, including the feet, which glows as if in a spotlight. *The Last Supper,* finished in Tintoretto's final year, is a fitting climax to mannerist painting.

Music in Late-Sixteenth-Century Italy and England

Unlike painting, Italian music remained under the sway of High Renaissance ideals, keeping to the path pioneered by Josquin des Prez (see Chapter 12). However, the Council of Trent, along with other forces, led to the decline of the High Renaissance style and created the conditions for the rise of the baroque style. For example, the council decreed that the Gregorian chant was preferable to polyphony (two or more lines of melody sung or played at the same time) for church liturgy and that the traditional chants should be simplified to ensure that the words could be easily understood. Most composers, considering the chants to be barbarous, continued to use polyphony but pruned its extravagant effects. The best of these composers and the chief representative of Counter-Reformation music was Giovanni Pierluigi da Palestrina [pal-uh-STREE-nuh] (about 1525–1594). His controlled style established the Roman Catholic ideal for the next few centuries—polyphonic masses sung by choirs and with clearly enunciated and expressive texts.

Nevertheless, the future of Italian music lay outside the church as secular vocal music was moving toward an ideal in which the words took precedence over the sound. But secular composers, unlike those in the church, rejected polyphony because it did not allow the text to be fully understood. The move to make the words primary in secular music was triggered by Renaissance humanists who were convinced that ancient music's power stemmed from the expressive way that the setting suited the clearly articulated words of the text. The most evident signs of this humanistic belief were in the works of the Florentine Camerata, a group of musical amateurs. Rejecting polyphony, the Florentine musicians composed pieces for a text with a single line of melody accompanied by simple chords and sung in a declamatory (speechlike singing) style.

The trend to expressive secular music in Italy was reflected most completely in the **madrigal,** a song for four or five voices composed with great care for the words of the poetic text. The novelty of this vocal music was that it vividly illustrated the meanings and emotions in the words, rather than the structure of the music. Madrigals were first written in the 1520s, but their heyday was the second half of the sixteenth century. They were imported to England and quickly be-

came the height of fashion. The success of madrigals in England had to do with the popularity of Italianate things, as is evident from the settings and sources of Shakespeare's plays and the translation of Castiglione's *The Book of the Courtier.*

England's leading madrigal composer was Thomas Weelkes [WILKS] (about 1575–1623), whose works often made use of the technique called **word paintings,** or word illustrations, a musical illustration of the written text. For example, in the madrigal "As Vesta was from Latmos hill descending," Weelkes uses a descending scale for the word "descending," an ascending scale for the words "a maiden queen ascending," and a hill-shaped melodic phrase for the words "Latmos hill descending." Such clever fusing of music and lyrics appealed to listeners, many of whom, in the spirit of the Renaissance, were amateur musicians themselves (Figure 13.24).

Madrigals eventually achieved a European-wide popularity, but they ended with the Renaissance. Nevertheless, the technique of word painting continued to be a favorite of composers, down through Bach and Handel in the baroque age (see Chapter 14).

Figure 13.24 Hans Burgkmair the Elder. *Maximilian with His Musicians.* Illustration from *Der Weisskunig.* Sixteenth century. Woodcut. Courtesy of the Metropolitan Museum of Art. Gift of William Loring Andrews, 1888. (88.1 fol. 142b). *This woodcut shows the Holy Roman emperor Maximilian I being educated in music and music-making by his court musicians. The youthful emperor is surrounded by ten musicians, either singing or playing instruments, and eleven different types of musical instruments are visible: organ, drum, sackbut (an early trombone), tromba marina (a one-stringed fiddle), lute, a keyboard instrument, viola da gamba, recorder, cornet, crumhorn, and flute. Burgkmair's woodcut was part of a series used to illustrate* Der Weisskunig, *an idealized biography of the Hapsburg ruler.*

The Legacy of Northern Humanism, Northern Renaissance, Religious Reformations, and Late Mannerism

The period from 1500 until 1520 in northern Europe witnessed important developments in painting and literature. The German painters Grünewald and Dürer and the Flemish painter Bosch brought the late Gothic style to its final flower, though Dürer was also influenced by the methods of the Italian Renaissance.

In the Netherlands, Erasmus launched Christian humanism, and in France, Rabelais and Marguerite of Angoulême followed in this tradition. The movement was undermined by Luther's break with the Roman Catholic Church and was finally ended by the wars of religion.

The period from 1520 until 1603 brought to a close the third and final phase of the Renaissance. This eighty-three-year period, framed by the deaths of Raphael and Queen Elizabeth I, saw the foundations of early modern Europe move firmly into place. A world culture and economy, in embryo, began during this period. This momentous development was foreshadowed in the shift of Europe's commercial axis from the Mediterranean to the Atlantic, as well as in the start of Europe's exportation of peoples, technology, religions, and ideas to colonies in Asia, Africa, and the Americas.

Probably the most important material change during this era was the rise of a system of sovereign and mutually hostile states. No single state was able to assert its authority over the others; the pattern set by their struggles would govern Western affairs until the emergence of global politics in the twentieth century. The European state system also spelled the doom of a united Christendom.

The religious reformations further split Christian Europe, dividing it into Protestant and Catholic armed camps. As a result, religious wars afflicted this century and the next, fading away only by about 1700. On a local level, religious differences led to intolerance and persecution. Although Europe's religious boundaries today remain roughly the same as they were in 1600, it took more than three hundred years for Protestants and Catholics to accept that they could live together in harmony.

The reformations also left different cultural legacies to their respective Christian denominations. From Protestantism came a glorification of the work ethic, Puritanism, and a justification for capitalism. At the heart of the Protestant revolution, despite its insistence on the doctrine of original sin, was the notion that human beings can commune directly with God without church mediation. Whereas Protestantism tended to view human beings as adrift in the universe, the Catholic Church tried to control the spiritual and moral lives of its members and to insulate them from the surrounding world. This policy eventually placed the church on a collision course with the forces of modernity, but it nevertheless was followed by most of the popes until after World War II.

In the aftermath of the religious crisis, the legacy of northern humanism—rational morals allied to a simple faith—went unheeded by Protestants and Catholics alike. Not until the eighteenth century and the rationalist program of the Enlightenment did Christian humanist ideas find a willing audience.

In the arts and humanities, however, the legacy was clear: this period left a rich and varied inheritance, including the work of Cervantes and the rest of Spain's golden age authors and the work of Shakespeare, the most gifted and influential individual writer in the history of Western civilization.

KEY CULTURAL TERMS

Reformation
Counter-Reformation
Christian humanism
northern Renaissance
revenge tragedy
triptych
proverb
Lutheranism
Calvinism

Puritanism
Anglicanism
Jesuits
late mannerism
chivalric novel
picaresque novel
madrigal
word painting

QUESTIONS FOR CRITICAL THINKING

1. What were the basic characteristics of northern humanism, and how did they differ from those of Italian humanism?

2. Discuss the religious and political changes in Europe between 1500 and 1603. How were these changes reflected in the map of Europe?

3. Compare and contrast Lutheranism and Calvinism, noting key doctrines, the role of the Bible in doctrine, and the relationships between church and state.

4. Trace the Catholic Church's response to the rise of Protestantism. How successful was the church in its encounters with the new movement?

5. As Protestantism and Roman Catholicism emerged, how did they respond to the arts, especially painting, and culture in general? In what ways did their responses come to define and identify Protestant and Roman Catholic Europe?

14

THE BAROQUE AGE I
Glamour and Grandiosity
1600–1715

A new European age—the **baroque**—dawned in 1600. The Roman Catholic Church continued its march against Protestantism, and powerful sovereign secular states became the norm across the land. Baroque art and architecture—driven by the ideals of grandeur, opulence, and expanding horizons—provided spectacular and compelling images with which the church could reassert its presence and dazzle the faithful. The baroque also offered secular rulers a magnificence and vastness that enhanced their political power. Baroque art took on a propagandistic role, in contrast to the individualistic art of the mannerist period, which had been focused on the distorted and the eccentric (see Chapter 13).

The term *baroque* was coined by eighteenth-century artists and scholars whose tastes were attuned to classical ideals. To them, much seventeenth-century culture was imperfect, or "baroque," a term probably derived from the Portuguese word *barroco,* meaning "irregular pearl." Not until about 1850 did the word acquire a positive meaning. Today, "baroque" is a label for the prevailing cultural style of the seventeenth century.

The baroque period was an era of constant turmoil, and until 1650, Europe was plagued by religious warfare, a legacy of the Reformation. The conflicts of the second half of the century had secular motivations: territorial expansion and the race for overseas empires. This century was also a period of great scientific discoveries and intellectual change. Because the Scientific Revolution, as this intellectual movement is called, so keenly influenced the making of the modern world, it is covered separately in Chapter 15, along with related philosophical ideas. This chapter focuses on the art, literature, and music of the baroque age and their historical, political, and social contexts.

◀ **Detail** HYACINTHE RIGAUD. *Louis XIV.* 1701. Oil on canvas, 9′2″ × 7′10¾″. Louvre, Paris. Réunion des Musées Nationaux/Art Resource, NY.

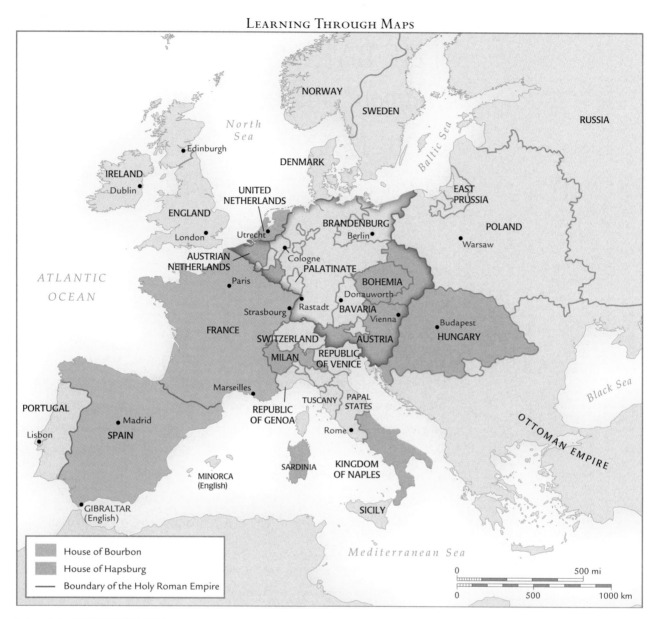

Map 14.1   EUROPE IN 1714
This map shows Europe in the early eighteenth century. 1. *Compare* the lands of the
Hapsburg dynasty in this map with the holdings of Hapsburg emperor Charles V in
Map 12.1. 2. *Compare* the Holy Roman Empire's size in this map with its size on Map 12.1.
3. *Which* of the two dynasties—Bourbon or Hapsburg—had the larger landholdings in
1714? 4. *How* did the size and location of England and the United Netherlands help make
them major maritime powers? *Note* the large number of small states in central Europe
and northern Italy.

ABSOLUTISM, MONARCHY, AND THE BALANCE OF POWER

Although the baroque style originated in Rome and
from there spread across the Continent, the Italian
city-states and the popes were no longer at the center
of European political life. By the time Europe had recovered from the first wave of religious wars in 1600,

a new system of sovereign states had replaced the old
dream of a united Christendom. By 1715 there was a
balance of power in Europe among five great military
states—England, France, Austria, Prussia, and Russia
(Map 14.1). The rise of these states was due to a new
breed of ruler fascinated with power. Known as *ab-
solutists*, these rulers wanted complete control over
state affairs, unlike medieval monarchs, who had to

Figure 14.1 Hyacinthe Rigaud. *Louis XIV*. 1701. Oil on canvas, 9'2" × 7'10¾". Louvre, Paris. Réunion des Musées Nationaux/Art Resource, NY. *Hyacinthe Rigaud (1659–1743), a master of the baroque style, painted this theatrical portrait, when Louis XIV was sixty-three years old. In the portrait, the monarch wears his coronation robes, his ceremonial sword at his side and the royal scepter in his hand; the crown rests on the stool beside him. Two details underscore the king's vanity: his stocking-clad legs are exposed to midthigh and he wears high-heeled shoes (about two inches high) to compensate for his short stature. Although commissioned as a gift of a grandson, Philip V of Spain, the painting so pleased Louis XIV that it became part of the royal collection.*

share authority with the church and the feudal nobles. Steeped in the ideas of Machiavelli, the new monarchs buttressed their claims to power with theories of divine right and natural law. France's greatest monarch, Louis XIV, was the most extreme in his claims, glorifying himself as the Sun King—a title derived from the late Roman emperors (Figure 14.1).

In their bid for absolute power, these monarchs founded new institutions and reformed old ones. For example, administrative bureaucracies, which had existed since the High Middle Ages, were reformed to become the exclusive domain of university-trained officials drawn from the middle classes. These career bureaucrats began to displace the great lords who had previously dominated the kings' advisory councils. As a consequence, the authority of the feudal nobility began to diminish.

The absolute monarchs also established permanent diplomatic corps to assist in foreign policy. The great states of Europe set up diplomatic missions in the major capitals, staffed with trusted officials who served as their rulers' eyes and ears away from their homelands. Another new institution was the standing army funded from state revenues, led by noble officers, and manned by lower-class soldiers.

France: The Supreme Example of Absolutism

As the century opened, France was ruled by Henry IV, the first of the Bourbon dynasty, who had converted from Calvinism to Catholicism to restore peace to his largely Roman Catholic state. Like a medieval king, Henry shared authority with the feudal nobles, though he began to reward middle-class supporters with high office. A pragmatist, Henry felt no need to force his adopted faith on the Huguenots, as the French Calvinists

Timeline 14.1   RULERS OF FRANCE AND ENGLAND DURING THE BAROQUE PERIOD

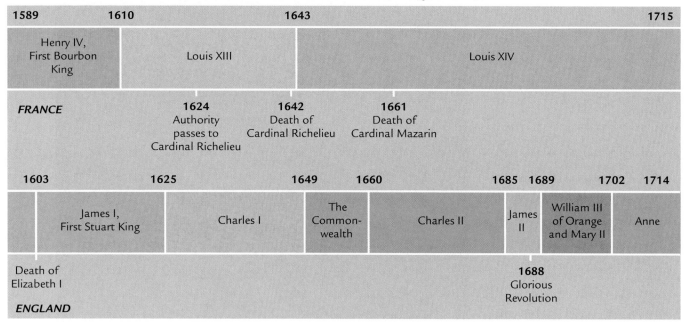

were called, and allowed them limited freedom of worship. The atmosphere changed when Henry was assassinated in 1610. Between then and 1715, France became the model absolutist state (Timeline 14.1).

Henry IV was succeeded by Louis XIII, but real authority passed to Cardinal Richelieu [REESH-lew] (1585–1642), who was the virtual ruler of France from 1624 until his death. Gifted with political acumen, Richelieu worked tirelessly to wrest power from the nobles. An opportunist in religious matters, Richelieu restricted the freedom of French Protestants at home, but abroad he allied himself with Swedish Protestants. His pragmatic policies were continued by his protégé and iron-fisted successor, Cardinal Mazarin [maz-uh-RAN] (1602–1661), who served as regent for the young Louis XIV. Mazarin's rule, during the 1640s and 1650s, moved France closer to absolutism, but it also coincided with the beginning of a golden age in France. Until 1790, French politics and culture dominated Europe, and French became the language of diplomacy.

When Mazarin died, Louis XIV, aged twenty-three, decided to rule France in his own right. Throughout his fifty-four-year reign, Louis made his private and public life the embodiment of the French state: "*L'État c'est moi*"—"I am the state"—is what he allegedly said about his concept of absolute government. Determined that nothing should escape his grasp, Louis XIV canceled what freedom remained to the Huguenots, persecuting them until they converted to Roman Catholicism, fled into exile, or were killed. As king, he perfected the policies of his Bourbon predecessors, becoming the chief of

a bureaucratic machine that regulated every phase of French life, from economics to culture. His economic policy was called mercantilism, a system that rested on state control. Through his ministers, Louis XIV regulated exports and imports, subsidized local industries, and set tariffs, customs duties, and quotas.

Louis XIV waged a spectacular campaign of self-glorification, and in so doing he made France the center of European arts and letters. His palace at Versailles became the symbol of his regal style (Figure 14.2). He also encouraged the work of the emerging academies, particularly the French Academy, founded in 1635 by Cardinal Richelieu to purify the French language and honor the state's most distinguished living authors, and the Royal Academy of Painting and Sculpture, founded by Cardinal Mazarin in 1648 to recognize the country's best artists. France's academies became the models for similar institutions in other Western states.

England: From Monarchy to Republic to Limited Monarchy

Like France, England turned toward absolutism in the early 1600s. Following the death of Elizabeth I, the new Stuart dynasty assumed the throne. King James I claimed to rule by divine right, but certain aspects of English life held royal power in check. Specifically, the English property-owning classes served together in Parliament, with the upper nobility in the House of Lords and lesser lords and middle-class members

Figure 14.2 Louis Le Vau and Jules Hardouin-Mansart, architects; André Le Nôtre, landscape architect. Aerial View of Park and Palace of Versailles. Print based on Pierre Patel (called Le Père). View of Versailles. 1668. Oil on canvas. Châteaux de Versailles et de Trianon, Versailles, France. *As the seat of government and the center of fashionable society, Versailles was the greatest symbol of this age of kings. Here, nobles competed for Louis XIV's favors and a royal post. He shrewdly rewarded them with menial positions and lofty titles and thus undermined their political influence. At the height of Louis's power, this complex of buildings could house ten thousand people—members of the royal court, hangers-on, and servants.*

in the House of Commons; Parliament met regularly and considered itself the king's partner rather than his enemy; and the country's Calvinist minority, called Puritans, were not despised by the Anglican majority, many of whom shared their religious zeal. When England became embroiled in a constitutional crisis between Parliament and the headstrong Charles I, Puritan leaders in Parliament led a successful civil war, toppling the monarchy and setting up a republic, called the Commonwealth, in 1649. But the Commonwealth soon lost its allure when its leader, the Puritan Oliver Cromwell, turned it into a military dictatorship.

After the failed republic, the English restored monarchy in 1660, recalling Charles I's son from exile in France to become Charles II. During the Restoration— as the period 1660–1688 is known—the king's powers were hedged in by vague restrictions, but lack of clarity about the arrangement soon led to renewed conflicts between crown and Parliament. In 1688 King James II, brother of Charles II, was expelled in a bloodless coup known as the Glorious Revolution, and his daughter and son-in-law, Mary II and William III of the Netherlands, became England's joint sovereigns. England's constitutional crisis was finally resolved, for William and Mary understood that they could rule only if they recognized citizens' rights and Parliament's power over most financial matters. By 1715, England had become the classic example of limited monarchy under written laws. In later years, political philosophers cited England's experience as a successful example of the principle that government should rest on the consent of the people.

Warfare in the Baroque Period: Maintaining the Balance of Power

Warfare was crucial in establishing the great power system, because the most successful states were those in which the king could marshal his country's resources behind his military goals. Warfare and diplomacy now became means for keeping the existing state system in check—that is, using balance-of-power principles to prevent any state from controlling the rest. A side effect of this system was to relegate many countries, such as Spain and Poland, to secondary-power status and end any significant role for lesser states, such as Florence and Venice.

THE THIRTY YEARS' WAR, 1618–1648 While England was distracted by its constitutional crises, the Continent endured the destructive Thirty Years' War (actually a series of four wars), the last great European-wide struggle between Protestants and Roman Catholics. Besides the great powers of Austria, France, and Bran-

denburg (soon to be Prussia), states involved at one time or another included Denmark, Sweden, Spain, Venice, the United Provinces of the Netherlands, and Poland. Germany suffered the most because the war was fought largely on its soil, wiping out a generation of Germans and inaugurating more than a century of cultural decline.

The Treaties of Westphalia, also known as the Peace of Westphalia, which ended the war in 1648, forced Protestants and Roman Catholics to recognize each other's existence and also created the conditions for the rise of Brandenburg-Prussia to great-power status. Germany itself remained divided; Calvinism was now tolerated, but true religious freedom did not appear, for the principle established at Augsburg in 1555 was retained: The religion of each state was to be dictated by its ruler (see Chapter 13). A divided Germany served the interests of Brandenburg-Prussia and its rulers. Commencing with the Treaties of Westphalia, these Calvinist leaders began to amass additional territories, becoming kings of Prussia in 1701 and finally emperors of a united Germany in 1871.

The Thirty Years' War also had major consequences for the emerging system of great powers. The peace conference was the first in which decisions were arranged through congresses of ambassadors. Both the war and the conference revealed Spain's impotence, showing that it had fallen from its peak in the 1500s. In contrast, Sweden and the Netherlands gained advantages that made them major powers for the rest of the century (Figure 14.3). The Hapsburg rulers were forced to accept that Protestantism could not be turned back in their German lands; henceforth they concentrated on their Austrian holdings, ignoring the Holy Roman Empire, which now seemed a relic of the feudal age.

France profited the most from the Thirty Years' War. By shifting sides to support first Roman Catholics and then Protestants, the French rulers demonstrated a particularly shrewd understanding of power politics. Even after the religious wars were over, France continued to struggle against Roman Catholic Spain until 1659. Having taken control of France in 1661, Louis XIV launched a series of aggressive wars four years later against various coalitions of European states that lasted until 1713.

THE WARS OF LOUIS XIV, **1665–1713** Louis XIV used various means, including marriage and diplomacy, to assert French might on the Continent, but it was chiefly through warfare that he left his enduring mark. In his own mind, he strove for *la gloire* ("glory"), an elusive term that reflected his image as the Sun King but that in practice meant the expansion of France to imperial status.

Louis XIV fought the states of Europe in four separate wars and was finally defeated by a coalition that included virtually all of Europe's major and minor powers. Because of its wide-ranging nature, Louis's last struggle, the War of the Spanish Succession, is generally regarded as the first of the world wars—a new type of war. The Treaty of Utrecht, signed in 1713, not only settled this last war but also showed that the great-power system was working.

The peace constructed at Utrecht was a reaffirmation of the balance-of-power principle. The victors set aside Louis's most extravagant acquisitions of land, but they granted those additions that still serve as France's borders today. Brandenburg-Prussia gained territory, and England emerged with the lion's share of the spoils, acquiring Gibraltar and the island of Minorca from Spain and areas of Canada from France. From this augmented base, England became the leader of world trade in the 1700s.

Technology

No dramatic technological breakthroughs occurred, but the baroque period did witness a consolidation of inherited trends, along with a few important advances. The age's innovations, especially in warfare and household technologies, led to changes in both public and private life. While widespread, the scope of these changes was limited by climate, ingrained habits, and availability of materials.

WARFARE TECHNOLOGY By 1600, when the baroque period began, the cannon had already revolutionized artillery warfare (see Chapter 12). By 1700, when the period ended, a few new and/or improved firearms and a tactical strategy had done much the same for infantry warfare, including

- the arquebus, or harquebus, a shoulder-fired gun (in Spain, after 1450);
- the musket, a muzzle-loading shoulder gun (in Spain, 1500s);
- the rifle—an improved musket, using a flintlock instead of a matchlock for ignition (about 1630);
- the paper cartridge, for holding the gunpower (about 1670);

◄ **Figure 14.3** GERARD TER BORCH. *The Swearing of the Oath of Ratification of the Treaty of Muenster, 15 May 1648.* 1648. Oil on copper, 17⅞ × 25⁵⁄₁₆″. National Gallery, London. *The Treaty of Muenster, part of the Peace of Westphalia, ended the eighty-year war between the Spanish crown and the Dutch people. In the treaty, the United Provinces of the Netherlands was recognized as an independent republic, giving the Dutch their freedom and strengthening their position as a maritime power. In the painting, the Dutch Protestant delegates, left center, take the oath of allegiance by holding up their right hands, with two raised fingers, while the Catholic Spanish, right corner, place their hands on the Bible and a cross. More than seventy people are crowded into the foreground, which is enclosed by three walls, while above stand three other groups of observers. The artist, depicted at the far left, gazes out to the viewer. Gerard Ter Borch [ge-RART ter BORK] (1584–1662), a very successful Dutch portrait painter and a master of domestic life scenes, helped establish, in this work, the tradition of painting contemporary historical events. Paintings commemorating important happenings, such as coronations (see Figures 17.6 and 19.6) and wars (see Figures 17.22 and 19.8), became popular later with the rise of nationalism and the emergence of art patrons who preferred secular to religious subjects.*

SLICE OF LIFE
Two Views of Power
Master (Louis XIV) and Servant (the Duke of Saint-Simon)

Louis XIV was the West's most powerful monarch during this age of kings. He made France the envy of other rulers, centralizing political power in his own hands, creating an efficient bureaucracy, fielding a well-armed army, and setting the cultural and artistic standards for the period. In con- *trast, the soldier and courtier Duke of Saint-Simon, though an aristocrat, was little more than a servant to Louis XIV when both were in residence at Versailles, Louis's palatial home outside Paris.*

LOUIS XIV
Reflections on Power

Kings are often obliged to do things against their natural inclination and which wound their natural goodness. They ought to love making people happy, and they must often chastise and condemn people whom they naturally wish well. The interest of the state must come first. One must overcome one's inclinations and not put oneself into a position of reproaching oneself, in something important, for not having done better because personal interests prevented one from doing so and distorted the views which one should have had for the grandeur, the good, and the power of the state. . . .

One must guard against oneself, guard against one's inclinations, and ever be on guard against one's own nature. The king's craft is great, noble, and extremely pleasant when one feels oneself worthy of carrying out everything one sets out to do; but it is not exempt from pain, fatigue, cares. Uncertainty sometimes leads to despair; and when one has passed a reasonable amount of time in examining a matter, one must decide and choose the side believed to be best.

When one keeps the state in mind, one works for oneself. The good of the one makes the *gloire* of the other. When the former is happy, eminent and powerful, he who is the cause as a result is *glorieux* and consequently must savor more than his subjects, if the two are compared, all of the most agreeable things in life.

DUKE OF SAINT-SIMON
Memoirs

In everything [Louis XIV] loved splendor, magnificence, profusion. He turned this taste to a maxim for political reasons, and stilled it into his court on all matters. One could please him by throwing oneself into fine food, clothes, retinue, buildings, gambling. These were occasions which enabled him to talk to people. The essence of it was that by this he attempted and succeeded in exhausting everyone by making luxury a virtue, and for certain persons a necessity, and thus he gradually reduced everyone to depending entirely upon his generosity in order to subsist. . . . This is an evil which, once introduced, became the internal cancer which is devouring all individuals—because from the court it promptly spread to Paris and into the prov-

inces and the armies, where persons, whatever their position, are considered important only in proportion to the table they lay and their magnificence ever since this unfortunate innovation.

INTERPRETING THIS SLICE OF LIFE

1. *What* is Louis XIV's thinking about his role as king? 2. *How* does he think he should carry out his responsibilities? 3. *In what ways* does Louis XIV see himself as the embodiment of the state? 4. *How* does the duke of Saint-Simon view the king and his policies? 5. *Why* does the duke have his own point of view? 6. *Which* of the two do you believe is telling the truth? *Explain.*

- the tactic of affixing of bayonets to rifles (about 1670)—thus ending the medieval practice of employing pikemen for close combat.

As these advances were adopted across Europe, the last vestiges of medieval warfare disappeared. The feudal host was replaced by standing armies, and these armies, fighting with rifles, bayonets, and small and light artillery—all supplied by the rulers—grew more and more divorced from general society.

HOUSEHOLD TECHNOLOGY   In contrast to warfare technology, changes to household technology moved at a glacial pace. Yet between 1500 and 1700, significant innovations occurred in the household interiors of wealthy people in the West, including

- the replacement of a Gothic look—rough, large scale, and painted in showy colors—by a refined Italian look, characterized by splendidly carved and polished furniture in elegant shapes;

Figure 14.4 NICOLAES MAES. *The Eavesdropper.* 1657. Oil on canvas, 36⅜ × 48″. The Netherlands Institute of Cultural Heritage, on loan to Dordrechts Museum, Dordrecht. *This Dutch painting accurately depicts the layout of a wealthy household. The high ceilings, tall banks of windows, rich draperies, and abundant use of carved wood for doors, columns, and arches attest to the owner's affluence. At the foot of the stairs, the lady of the house calls for silence, signaled by her slightly raised right forefinger. Having left the party upstairs (behind her), she has overheard her kitchen maid in an intimate moment with a young man. The guest's outer clothing is visible on the right. This satiric scene plays on the period's notion that maidservants had loose morals, thus necessitating close monitoring. As a respectable matron, the lady of the house was expected to keep a watchful eye on her household. Privacy was not a concern of this period, as reflected in this scene as well as the openness of the house's interior. Note the map on the wall (right), which may be interpreted as a sign of the globalism embraced by Holland's middle-class elite.*

- a fashion for imported Oriental products, such as lacquered furniture and household goods (china, vases, and precious objects);
- new furniture for specific purposes, such as wardrobes, for clothing; dressers, for displaying valued objects; cupboards, for china and silver; and small cabinets, for writing materials, playing cards, and jewelry.

Inspired by the Italian Renaissance and attracted to lavish furnishings imported from overseas, Europe's elite opted for formal interiors with high ceilings and opulent displays, in effect, using their dwellings to assert their social status, real or imagined. Louis XIV's Versailles Palace is the best example of this period's lavish baroque style. Lesser royalty, nobility, and the bourgeoisie followed Louis XIV's lead as befitting their wealth and status (Figure 14.4).

Similarly, the baroque era brought changes in the methods used to heat palaces, courts, and residences. Taking a long view—from 1100 to 1700—the following list shows the heating options available in baroque times.

- Until 1100: open hearths for cooking, located in the center of a room, thus making the kitchen the center of family life in winter; braziers, or charcoal-fired portable heaters, in other rooms.
- After 1100: wood-burning fireplaces, built into walls, with chimneys to vent the smoke, introduced

in Venice; fireplace usage spreads across Europe except to Germany and Spain.
- Early 1500s: shift to coal-burning fireplaces in England, because of a shortage of wood.
- Early 1600s: fireplaces with carved mantles become furniture; used to display status objects.
- The 1630s: an improved fireplace, with air ducts and vents, invented in France.

Despite these improvements, fireplaces remained notoriously inefficient, as a 1695 letter reports on conditions inside Versailles' Hall of Mirrors: "At the king's table the wine and water froze in the glasses." The Hall of Mirrors being the period's most palatial room, it is no surprise that people living in cold climates wore furs and heavy robes indoors in winter.

THE BAROQUE: VARIATIONS ON AN INTERNATIONAL STYLE

The baroque mentality originated in a search for stability and order in a restless age. Encouraged by the Catholic Church, artists and writers sought to reveal the order they believed lay beneath the seeming chaos of life. In this, they shared certain aims with the artists of the High Renaissance. But although both styles were devoted to order, they differed in their concept of how harmony was best achieved. High Renaissance artists valued repose, a single, static perspective, and designs that were complete in themselves. Baroque artists, on the other hand, created dynamic, open-ended works that threaten to explode beyond their formal boundaries. These exuberant works are characterized by grand, sweeping gestures; flowing, expansive movement; and curving lines and oval and elliptical shapes. Reflecting the excitement of overseas explorations and of the new discoveries in astronomy, baroque artists were fascinated with the concept of infinite space.

Despite religious differences among various regions of Europe, the baroque style spread readily from its origin in Rome to the entire Continent and to England. Lines of communication—through trade, diplomacy, and marriage—facilitated its spread, as did the persistence of Latin as the common language of scholarly works and diplomatic exchanges. Travel was also a factor in the export of baroque ideals to the rest of Europe. Many Protestant families in northern and western Europe sent their sons, and sometimes their daughters, on grand tours of the Continent to "complete their education." English travelers to Rome and other Catholic bastions included such faithful Protestants as poet John Milton and architect Christopher Wren.

Although the baroque was an international style, it was reinterpreted in different regions, so that three distinct manifestations of the style emerged. The florid baroque, dominated by Roman Catholic religious ideals and motivations, was a product of the Counter-Reformation. This style developed in Italy and flourished there and in Spain and central Europe. The classical baroque, aristocratic and courtly, was a more subdued interpretation of baroque ideals. This style was associated with French taste, which had been guided by the values of simplicity and harmony since the early 1500s, when Renaissance culture was first introduced into France. The French preference for the classical fit well with the absolutist policies of Louis XIV, who promoted the adoption of strict rules in all aspects of cultural life as a way to reinforce his own obsession with order and control. The third manifestation of this style, the restrained baroque, arose in the middle-class United Provinces of the Netherlands and aristocratic England. Repelled equally by Catholicism and French absolutism, the artists and writers of the restrained baroque cultivated a style in keeping with their own Protestant values, a style simpler and less ornate than either the florid or the classical baroque.

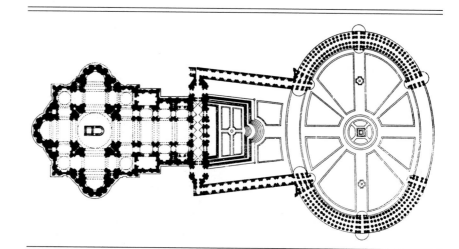

Figure 14.5 CARLO MADERNO AND GIANLORENZO BERNINI. Plan of St. Peter's Basilica with Adjoining Piazza. 1607–1615 and 1665–1667. *This plan of St. Peter's Basilica shows the design of Maderno for the church (left), dating from 1607 to 1615, and the adjoining piazza and colonnade (right) by Bernini, dating from 1665 to 1667.*

The Florid Baroque

The most important formative influence on the evolution of the baroque style in the arts and architecture was the Council of Trent (see Chapter 13). In this series of sessions held between 1545 and 1563, church leaders had reaffirmed all the values and doctrines rejected by the Protestants and called for a new art that was geared to the teaching needs of the church and that set forth correct theological ideas easily understood by the masses. To achieve these goals, the popes of the late sixteenth century began to hold a tighter rein on artists and architects and to discourage the individualistic tendencies of the mannerist style.

The seventeenth-century popes used their patronage powers to bring to life the **florid baroque style.** Once again, as in the Middle Ages, aesthetic values were subordinated to spiritual purposes. The popes enlisted architects, painters, and sculptors to glorify the Catholic message. Architects responded with grand building plans and elaborate decorative schemes that symbolized the power and richness of the church. Painters and sculptors represented dramatic incidents and emotion-charged moments, particularly favoring the ecstatic visions of the saints and the suffering and death of Jesus. They portrayed these subjects with a powerful realism intended to convey the physical presence and immediacy of the church's holiest figures. In everything, vitality and theatrical effects were prized over such classical elements as restraint and repose.

ARCHITECTURE   The church of St. Peter's in Rome became the age's preeminent expression of the florid baroque building style. First conceived in the early 1500s by Donato Bramante (see Chapter 12) as a High Renaissance temple in the shape of a Greek cross, St. Peter's was now redesigned to conform to the ideals of the Council of Trent. Rejecting the Greek cross as a pagan symbol, Pope Paul V commissioned Carlo Maderno [mah-DAIR-noh] (1556–1629) to add a long nave, thereby giving the floor plan the shape of a Latin cross (Figure 14.5). Not only did the elongated nave satisfy the need to house the large crowds drawn to the mother church of Roman Catholicism, but also the enormous size of the building signified the church's power.

St. Peter's exterior was basically finished after Maderno designed and built the building's facade, but the popes wanted to integrate this huge church into its urban setting—a classical ideal that was now adapted to baroque taste. For this task, Pope Alexander VII commissioned Gianlorenzo Bernini [bayr-NEE-nee] (1598–1680). Bernini's solution was a masterstroke of florid baroque design in which he followed the principle of abolishing all straight lines. He tore down the buildings around St. Peter's and replaced them with a huge public square where the faithful could gather to see and hear the pope. Bernini then outlined this keyhole-shaped space with a sweeping colonnade topped with statues of saints (Figure 14.6). For worshipers assembled in the square, the curved double colonnade stood as a symbol of the church's welcoming arms.

Figure 14.6   GIANLORENZO BERNINI. Piazza of St. Peter's. 1665–1667. The Vatican. *Bernini's plan for the piazza leading up to St. Peter's was instrumental in making exterior space a major concern of baroque architects. The ancient Romans had integrated buildings into their urban settings, as had High Renaissance planners, but no architect had ever achieved such a natural blending of a monumental structure with its surroundings as Bernini did in this design.*

ENCOUNTER

Japan Closes Its Doors, Nearly

When societies feel threatened by contact with foreigners, they often react in self-defense, which may be more intense if the society is already under stress, as was the case when Westerners arrived in Japan, in about 1550. Japan initially welcomed them, but after about a century, it closed its doors to the world, concluding that Western customs and thought threatened the Japanese way of life.

Sixteenth-century Japan was embroiled in a costly and bloody civil war, which undermined the old feudal order, challenged the power of regional military governors, or *shoguns,* and further weakened an already-moribund imperial system. New military technology, adopted during the war, reduced the role of the warrior class and made way for the rise of a new feudal system dominated by regional lords, or *daimyos.* With the support of vassals, the daimyos controlled the local economy and kept the peace.

After 1550, power was seized by a few daimyos until Japan was unified under three successive shoguns—the final victor being Tokugawa Ieyasu [toekug-ah-wah ee-yas-u] (r. 1603–1616). Ieyasu moved the capital from Heian (modern Kyoto) to Edo (modern Tokyo) and assumed full control of the country, opening trade with the West and giving access to Christian missionaries. And, most important, he established the Tokugawa *shogunate,* or government, which lasted until 1867, though its zenith was from the 1640s to the 1750s.

The Tokugawa shogunate's goals—to prevent civil war and to stabilize the country—were achieved by controlling domestic and foreign affairs. At home, it brought the daimyo class under its supervision by interfering in local disputes, organizing the daimyo domains, and requiring each daimyo to attend the shogun's court in Edo every other year—a practice called "alternate attendance." Like France's Louis XIV, Japan's Tokugawa rulers kept watch over their aristocratic supporters, looking for signs of rebellion and forcing them to spend their wealth on a lavish lifestyle. The shogunate also created a class of elite warriors, known in the West as *samurai,* whose mission was to protect the rulers in Edo.

At the height of the civil war, in 1543, the first Westerners—Portuguese traders (see Encounter, Chapter 12)—arrived in Japan, bringing Roman Catholicism and guns. At first, the Japanese did not see Christianity as a threat, and the Jesuit missionaries were usually welcomed in the ports. By 1603, the year of the founding of the Tokugawa shogunate, nearly three hundred thousand Japanese had converted to Christianity. However, some leaders within the shogunate began to see the Christians as a threat. These critics reasoned that Christian missionaries and traders might be only the first wave of Europeans, who would destabilize their recently unified country. Starting with a few isolated persecutions, the Tokugawa regime, in 1612, inaugurated a campaign to drive out the Christian missionaries and to force converts to renounce their new faith or face execution. In 1638 the persecutions reached a climax when about twenty thousand peasants, in revolt against the persecutions, were put to death.

Meanwhile, the shogun issued a series of Exclusion Decrees (1633, 1636), curtailing trade and foreign travel. Rules were also laid down regarding treatment of foreign vessels in Japanese ports. Only Chinese and Dutch traders were permitted to trade, and then only through the port of Nagasaki (Encounter figure 14.1). By allowing the Dutch to keep a center at Nagasaki, the Japanese were able to receive news from the outside world. Thus, a small circle of Japanese thinkers began to focus on "Dutch Learning"—their name for Western culture. These scholars and writers advocated more contacts between Japan and the West and imported some Western knowledge, particularly in science and technology.

LEARNING FROM THE ENCOUNTER

1. *What* were some consequences of the civil wars in sixteenth-century Japan? 2. *How* and *why* did the Japanese come to see the Westerners as threats? 3. *How* has the United States, during its history, reacted to outside threats? Give an example. 4. *Evaluate* the American policy you offered as an example.

From its origin in Rome, the florid baroque style in architecture spread to Spain, Austria, and southern Germany. By 1650 this lush style had appeared in Spanish and Portuguese colonies in the Americas, and there it flourished until well into the nineteenth century.

SCULPTURE   During the baroque period, sculpture once again became a necessary complement to architecture, as it had been in medieval times. This change was has-

tened by the Council of Trent's advocacy of religious images to communicate the faith as well as the need to decorate the niches, recessed bays, and pedestals that were part of building facades in florid baroque architecture. The demand for sculpture called forth an army of talented artists, of whom the most outstanding was Bernini, one of the architects of St. Peter's.

Bernini brought the florid baroque to a dazzling climax in his sculptural works. His pieces, executed

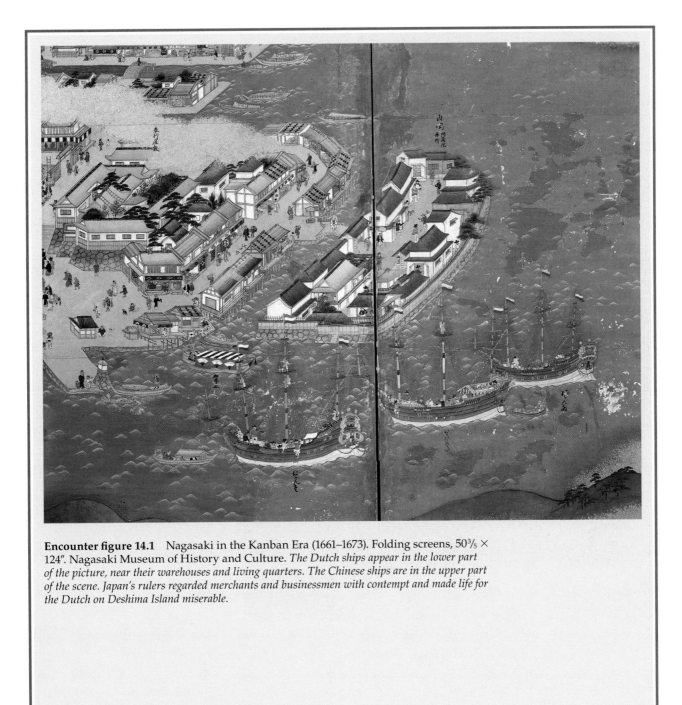

Encounter figure 14.1   Nagasaki in the Kanban Era (1661–1673). Folding screens, 50³/₅ × 124″. Nagasaki Museum of History and Culture. *The Dutch ships appear in the lower part of the picture, near their warehouses and living quarters. The Chinese ships are in the upper part of the scene. Japan's rulers regarded merchants and businessmen with contempt and made life for the Dutch on Deshima Island miserable.*

for such diverse projects as churches, fountains, and piazzas, or squares, often combined architecture with sculpture. His sculptural ideal was a dynamic composition that used undulating forms to delight the eye. His sensuous sculptures with their implicit movement were the perfect accompaniments to florid baroque structures with their highly decorated walls.

Bernini's most famous sculptures are those he made for the interior of St. Peter's—including altars, tombs,

reliefs, statues, and liturgical furniture—during a fifty-year period, commencing in 1629. His masterpiece among these ornate works is the **baldacchino** [ball-duh-KEE-no], the canopy, mainly bronze and partly gilt, that covers the spot where the bones of St. Peter are believed to lie—directly under Michelangelo's dome. Combining architectural and sculptural features, the baldacchino is supported by four huge columns whose convoluted surfaces are covered with climbing vines

Figure 14.7 GIANLORENZO BERNINI. The Baldacchino. 1624–1633. Ht. approx. 100'. St. Peter's, Rome. *This magnificent canopy reflects the grandiose ambitions of its patron, Pope Urban VIII, a member of the Barberini family. The Barberini crest was the source for the huge stylized bees displayed on the flaps of the bronze canopy. In his desire for worldly immortality, this pope shared a common outlook with the secular rulers of the baroque age.*

(Figure 14.7). Bernini crowned this colossal work with a magnificent display of four large angels at the corners, four groups of cherubs in the centers of the sides, and behind the angels four scrolled arches that rise to support a ball and cross at the top.

The baldacchino's twisting columns were modeled on the type that by tradition supported Solomon's Temple in Jerusalem and had been used in the old St. Peter's Basilica. Thus, these columns symbolized the church's claim to be the true successor to the Jewish faith. So popular was Bernini's Solomonic canopy that in southern Germany it inspired many imitators and became the standard covering for altars for the next two centuries.

The sculpture that marks the highest expression of Bernini's art is *The Ecstasy of St. Teresa* (Figure 14.8). Using marble, metal, and glass, he portrayed the divine moment when the saint receives the vision of the Holy Spirit—symbolized here by the arrow with which the angel pierces her heart. In his conception, Bernini imagines the pair floating on a cloud and bathed by light from a hidden source; the light rays seem to turn into golden rods that cascade onto the angel and the saint. The intensity of the saint's expression, the agitation of the draperies, and the billowing clouds all contribute to the illusion that the pair are sensuously real. By depicting St. Teresa's supernatural experience in physical terms, Bernini intended to force the viewer

Figure 14.8 Gianlorenzo Bernini. *The Ecstasy of St. Teresa.* 1645–1652. Marble, glass, metal, life-size. Cornaro Chapel, Santa Maria della Vittoria, Rome. *Even though this sculpture captures an ecstatic vision, its portrayal reflects the naturalism that was central to the baroque style. Bernini based this work on the saint's personal account, in which she described how an angel pierced her heart with a golden spear—a mystical moment the tableau faithfully reproduces. The sculpture's subject, St. Teresa of Avila (Spain) (1515–1582), founded the Carmelite order of nuns (1562); she recorded her mystic visions in works such as* Camino de perfección (The Road to Perfection).

to suspend disbelief and accept the religious truth of the scene.

PAINTING   In the baroque period, painting once again became an essential part of church decoration. In pursuit of church ideals, the painters of this tradition tended to use rich color and unusual lighting effects to depict spectacular or dramatic moments. They represented nature and the human form realistically to make art intelligible and meaningful to the ordinary viewer.

The earliest great florid baroque painter was Michelangelo Merisi (1573–1610), better known as Caravaggio [kahr-ah-VAHD-jo]. Caravaggio rejected the antinaturalism of mannerism in favor of a dramatic realism. His concern with realism led him to pick his models directly from the streets, and he refused to idealize his subjects. To make his works more

dramatic and emotionally stirring, he experimented with light and the placement of figures. His paintings offer startling contrasts of light and dark—a style of chiaroscuro called **tenebrism**—in which he banished landscape from his canvases and focused on human figures grouped tightly in the foreground.

A superb example of Caravaggio's work is *The Conversion of St. Paul* (Figure 14.9), which is paired with his *Crucifixion of St. Peter* in a Roman church. The two works were part of a commission to paint the founders of the Church of Rome, who, according to the New Testament, preached in the city. Caravaggio's revolutionary use of chiaroscuro emphasizes the dramatic event of Paul's conversion. The light, coming from the upper right, focuses on St. Paul and part of the horse's body. This makes the background nearly indistinct except for the groomsman, on the right, who holds the

Figure 14.9 CARAVAGGIO. *The Con-version of St. Paul.* 1600–1601. Oil on canvas, approx. 7'5" × 5'8". Cerasi Chapel, Santa Maria del Popolo, Rome. *Caravaggio's paintings made monumentality an important feature of the florid baroque. By presenting St. Paul's figure in close-up, and giving full weight and presence to both him and the horse, the artist filled the canvas not only to capture a turning point in St. Paul's life and in the history of Christianity but also to teach the faithful a lesson about forgiveness and the power of God. Saul of Tarsus, the persecutor of Christians, will now become St. Paul, the convert who has been chosen to bring Jesus's message to the Gentiles.*

reins of the horse. St. Paul's head is thrown toward the viewer, and his eyes are shut as he is blinded by the light of the presence of Jesus, who, as recorded in the New Testament (Acts 9:3–9), did not appear in human form but only as light.

Caravaggio had an enormous influence on other painters both in Italy and elsewhere, notably France, Spain, and the Netherlands. Perhaps the most original of Caravaggio's Italian disciples—known as Caravaggisti—was Artemisia Gentileschi [ahrt-uh-MEEZe-uh jain-teel-ESS-key] (1593–1653), his only female follower. Unlike most women artists of the early modern period, who limited their art to portraits, such as the late-sixteenth-century painter Sofonisba Anguissola (see Chapter 13), Gentileschi concentrated on biblical and mythical subjects, as many male artists did. Trained by her painter-father Orazio, himself a disciple of Caravaggio, Gentileschi adapted the flamboyant and dramatic style of Caravaggesque realism and made it her own. In almost thirty surviving paintings, she followed this style's preference for "night pictures," dark scenes whose blackness is illuminated by a single internal light source.

What distinguishes Artemisia Gentileschi's art from that of the rest of the Caravaggisti is its female assertiveness, a highly unusual quality in the baroque period, when women artists were still making their way without guild support or access to nude modeling. Female assertiveness is expressed throughout her works in an androgynous (having female and male characteristics) ideal, as may be seen in *Judith and Her Maidservant with the Head of Holofernes* (Figure 14.10), which depicts a scene from an apocryphal book of the Old Testament, the book of Judith. The painting's cen-

Figure 14.10   ARTEMISIA GENTILE-SCHI. *Judith and Her Maidservant with the Head of Holofernes.* Ca. 1625. Oil on canvas. Detroit Institute of Arts. *Gentileschi's style in this painting is strongly indebted to the style of Caravaggio: The natural background is painted black and thus virtually eliminated, the central figures are shown in tight close-up, and the action is frozen like a single frame in a film sequence. The aesthetic impact of this cinematic method is to draw viewers into the scene and to personalize the figures. The artist's interest in the personal psychology of her characters is part of the trend toward naturalism that characterized baroque culture in general.*

tral figure—Judith—is decidedly female (as shown in the vulnerable throat and fleshy body) and yet exhibits masculine strength (as shown in the commanding gesture accentuated by the firmly grasped sword). Judith, often treated in Italian painting and sculpture in the Renaissance and baroque eras, is a perfect subject for Gentileschi, since the biblical story describes a woman of destiny. In the story, Judith saves the Jewish people by beheading their enemy Holofernes after having seduced him. In the painting, Holofernes' bloody head, partly visible in the basket, starkly dramatizes the point that Judith is a forthright woman who plans and acts, just as men do. Gentileschi's Judith typifies a heroic female ideal who is endowed with the traits of that fuller humanity that by tradition had been allowed only to male figures. Through such dramatic works as this, Gentileschi helped to spread the Caravaggesque style in Italy.

About the same time that Caravaggio was creating his dramatic works, a new form caught the imagination of painters in the florid baroque tradition—the illusionistic ceiling fresco. In these paintings, artists constructed imaginary continuations of the architectural features already present in the room, expanding up through layers of carefully foreshortened, sculptured figures and culminating in patches of sky. Looking up as if at the heavens, the viewer is overawed by the superhuman spectacle that seems to begin just overhead.

The superb example of this **illusionism** is the nave ceiling of the church of Sant'Ignazio (St. Ignatius) in Rome, painted by Andrea Pozzo [POE-tzo] (1642–1709). In this fresco, titled *Allegory of the Missionary Work of the Jesuits,* Pozzo reveals a firm mastery of the technique of architectural perspective (Figure 14.11). The great nave ceiling is painted to appear as if the viewer

Figure 14.11   Andrea Pozzo. *Allegory of the Missionary Work of the Jesuits.* Ca. 1621–1625.
Ceiling fresco. Sant'Ignazio, Rome. *The meaning of Pozzo's fresco is based on* ignus, *Latin for
"fire," a pun on the name of St. Ignatius (Loyola), the founder of the Jesuit order. In church tradition, the saint and the Jesuit mission are linked with the power of fire and light. At the fresco's
center, Christ, holding the cross, emits rays of light from his wounded side, which pierce the figure
of Ignatius (sitting on the cloud bank nearest Christ), who acts as a mirror; from him the light
then radiates to the four corners, symbolic of the four continents. Thus, Ignatius and his missionary followers mediate Christ's saving light to the whole earth, as commanded by the scriptures.*

were looking up through an immense open colonnade.
Figures stand and cling to the encircling architectural supports, and, in the center, an expansive vista
opens to reveal St. Ignatius, the founder of the Jesuit
order, being received by an open-armed Christ. The
clusters of columns on either side are labeled for the
four continents—Europe, Asia, America, and Africa—
symbolizing the missionary zeal of the Jesuits around
the globe. Pozzo was motivated by spiritual concerns
when he painted this supernatural vision. He believed
that the illusion of infinite space could evoke feelings
of spiritual exaltation and even religious rapture in
the viewer. Illusionism, infinite space, and spectacular
effects make this a masterpiece of the florid baroque.
To see the dramatic differences between baroque and
High Renaissance ideals, compare this ceiling fresco
with the ceiling of the Sistine Chapel by Michelangelo
(see Figure 12.9).

Outside Italy, the principal centers of florid baroque
painting were the studio of Velázquez in Spain and
the workshop of Rubens in Flanders (present-day Belgium). Whereas Velázquez softened the florid baroque
to his country's taste, Rubens fully embraced this sensual style to become its most representative painter.

The work of Diego Velázquez [vuh-LAS-kus] (1599–
1660) owes much to the tradition of Caravaggio but
does not have the intense drama of the Italian's painting. Velázquez also used chiaroscuro, but he avoided
the extreme contrasts that made Caravaggio's paintings
controversial. Velázquez's greatest work is *Las Meninas,*
or *The Maids of Honor* (Figure 14.12). In his role as official artist to the Spanish court, Velázquez painted this
group portrait of the infanta, or princess, surrounded
by her maids of honor (one of whom is a dwarf). What
makes this painting so haunting is the artful play of
soft light over the various figures. In the background, a

Figure 14.12 VELÁZQUEZ. *Las Meninas (The Maids of Honor).* 1656. Oil on canvas, 10'5" × 9'. Prado, Madrid. *Velázquez uses the mirror on the back wall, reflecting the Spanish king and queen, to enhance the dynamic feeling of the scene. This illusionistic device explodes the pictorial space by calling up presences within and outside the painting.*

man is illuminated by the light streaming through the open door, and even more abundant sunshine falls on the princess from the window on the right.

Velázquez also plays with space and illusion in this painting. On the left side, he depicts himself, standing before a huge canvas with brush and palette in hand. The artist gazes directly at the viewer—or is he greeting the king and queen, who have just entered the room and are reflected in the mirror on the rear wall? The princess and two of her maids also look attentively out of the picture, but whether at the artist painting their portrait, at the royal couple, or at the viewer is left unclear. This fascination with illusion and with the effects of light and shade reveals Velázquez's links with Caravaggio and the art of the florid baroque.

In contrast to Velázquez's devotion to the ideal of grave beauty, the work of Peter Paul Rubens (1577–1640) is known for its ripe sensuality and the portrayal of voluptuous female nudes. Rubens had already forged a sensuous style before he sojourned in Italy for eight years, but his encounters with Caravaggio's tradition impressed him deeply, causing him to intensify his use of explosive forms and chiaroscuro. From the Venetian painters, especially Titian, he derived his love and mastery of gorgeous color. In his mature works, he placed human figures in a shallow foreground,

bathed them in golden light with dark contours, and painted their clothes and flesh in sensuous tones.

As the most sought-after artist of his day, Rubens was often given commissions by the kings of the great states, and he produced works for royalty, for the church, and for wealthy private patrons. As official painter to the French court before the ascendancy of Louis XIV, who preferred the classical style, Rubens was commissioned to paint a cycle of works glamorizing the life of Queen Marie de' Medici, widow of Henry IV and powerful regent for her son, Louis XIII. One of the typical works from this series is *The Education of Marie de' Medici* (Figure 14.13). In this huge canvas, Rubens used Roman mythological figures to transform a mundane episode in the life of a queen into a splendid pageant of the French monarchy. All action is centered on the kneeling future queen. Minerva, the goddess of wisdom, offers instruction in reading and writing; Mercury, the god of eloquence, hovers overhead and offers his blessing; Apollo (or Orpheus, or Harmony) plays a stringed instrument, thereby inculcating a love of music; and the three Graces, attendants of the goddess Venus, encourage the perfection of feminine grace. A waterfall cascades in the background, a drapery billows above, and various images of Greco-Roman culture (a mask of tragedy and a musical instrument) are displayed in

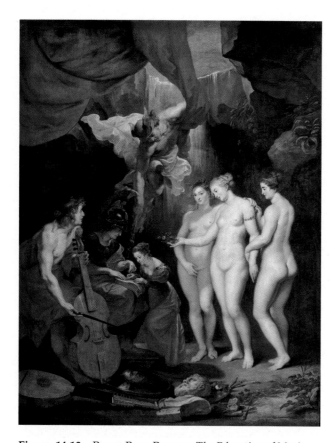

Figure 14.13   PETER PAUL RUBENS. *The Education of Marie de' Medici.* 1621–1625. Oil on canvas, 12'11" × 9'8". Louvre. *The Medici cycle, of which this work is a superb example, not only established the artist's European-wide reputation but also defined historical narrative—the combining of a historical event with mythological motifs—as one of the great themes of baroque art. By 1715 the French Academy had created a ranked set of painting subjects, of which historical narrative occupied the highest level.*

the foreground. Rubens's mastery of both spiritual and secular subjects and the turbulent drama of his works made him the finest artist of the florid baroque.

The Classical Baroque

Although the Baroque originated in Rome, the pronouncements of the church had little effect on the art and architecture of France. Here, the royal court was the guiding force in the artistic life of the nation. The rulers and the royal ministers provided rich commissions that helped to shape the **classical baroque,** giving this style a secular focus and identifying it with absolutism. A second powerful influence on the baroque in France was the pervasiveness of the classical values of simplicity and grave dignity. Accord-

ingly, after Louis XIV became king, French artists and architects found the florid baroque alien and even offensive; their adaptation of the baroque was more impersonal, controlled, and measured.

ARCHITECTURE   The palace at Versailles was the consummate architectural expression of the classical baroque. Versailles, a former hunting lodge, was transformed by Louis XIV into a magnificent royal residence that became the prototype of princely courts in the West. At Versailles, where all power was concentrated in the royal court, were collected the best architects, sculptors, painters, and landscape architects as well as the finest writers, composers, and musicians that France could produce. The duty of this talented assemblage was to use their gifts to surround Louis XIV with the splendor appropriate to the Sun King.

The redesign of Versailles gave Louis XIV the most splendid palace that has ever been seen in Europe. The chief architects of this revamped palace were Louis Le Vau [luh VO] (1612–1670) and Jules Hardouin-Mansart [ar-DWAN mahn-SAR] (1646–1708), but the guiding spirit was the Sun King himself. When finished, the palace consisted of a huge central structure with two immense wings (see Figure 14.2). The architecture is basically in the style of the Renaissance, with rounded arches, classical columns, and porticoes inspired by Roman temples, but the overall effect is a baroque style that is dignified yet regal.

The most striking aspect of Versailles is its monumentality: The palace is part of an elaborate complex that includes a royal chapel and various support structures, all of which are set in an elaborate park over two miles long. The park, designed by André Le Nôtre [luh NOH-truh] (1613–1700), is studded with a rich display of fountains, reflecting pools, geometric flower beds, manicured woods, exotic trees, statues, urns, and graveled walks—a gorgeous outdoor setting for royal receptions and entertainments (Figure 14.14).

The most famous room in the palace at Versailles is the Hall of Mirrors, a central chamber with a tunnel-vaulted ceiling (Figure 14.15). The grandiose design of this hallway reflects its original function as the throne room of Louis XIV. Named for its most prominent feature, this long hall is decorated with baroque profusion, including, in addition to the mirrors, wood parquetry floors of intricate design, multicolored marbles, ceiling paintings depicting military victories and other deeds of Louis XIV, and gilded statues at the base of the paintings. In modern times, major political events have taken place in the Hall of Mirrors: The Germans proclaimed their empire from here in 1871 after having vanquished the French, and the peace treaty that ended World War I was signed here in 1919.

Figure 14.14 ANDRÉ LE NÔTRE, LANDSCAPE ARCHITECT, AND VARIOUS SCULPTORS. Versailles Gardens. The Pool of Latona with adjacent parterres. 1660s. Versailles, France. *This fountain, composed of four concentric marble basins, is named for its crowning statue of Latona, the mother of the sun god Apollo, who was the inspiration for Louis XIV's reign. On either side of the fountain are parterres, or flower gardens with beds and paths arranged into patterns. Beyond the fountain stretches an avenue flanked by wooded areas that culminates in the grand canal, which extends the view into infinity. The rich profusion of this scene is a hallmark of baroque design.*

Figure 14.15 CHARLES LEBRUN AND JULES HARDOUIN-MANSART. Hall of Mirrors, Palace at Versailles. 1678–1684. Versailles, France. *The French architects Lebrun and Mansart designed this enormous hall to overlook the vast park at Versailles—the court and showplace of the French king, Louis XIV, the most powerful ruler in seventeenth-century Europe. Viewed through the floor-to-ceiling windows, which are placed along the width of the room, the majestic park outside becomes an extension of the interior space. The inside space in turn is enlarged by the tall mirrors that match the windows, echoing the exterior views.*

Figure 14.16   NICOLAS POUSSIN. *Landscape with Orpheus and Eurydice.* Oil on canvas,
48⅞″ × 78¾″ (enlarged at the bottom by about 2″). 1640s. Louvre, Département des Pein-
tures (Inv. 7307). *Poussin here demonstrates his mastery of the baroque landscape, especially
in these features: the drama created by juxtaposing a catastrophe in the midst of calm; the small-
scale figures versus the vast distances of the overall composition; the sensual tones and rich
colors; and the use of chiaroscuro, which makes the bare limbs and the faces stand out vividly
from the background. The building burning has been identified as Rome's Castel Sant'Angelo, a
papal fortress—which has given rise to many interpretations, but none persuasively for a scholarly consensus.*

PAINTING   Classical values dominated baroque painting in France even more completely than architecture.
In pursuit of ancient Roman ideals, classical baroque
artists painted mythological subjects, stressed idealized human bodies, and cultivated a quietly elegant
style. The outstanding classical baroque artist was Nicolas Poussin [poo-SAN] (1594–1665). Ironically, except
for two disappointing years in Paris, Poussin spent his
professional life in Rome, the home of the florid baroque. Although he was inspired by Caravaggio's use
of light and dark, the style that Poussin forged was
uniquely his own, a detached, almost cold approach
to his subject matter and a feeling for the unity of human beings with nature.

An intriguing example of Poussin's detached style
is *Landscape with Orpheus and Eurydice,* a painting in
which human figures are integrated into a vast, atmospheric landscape (Figure 14.16). In ancient mythology,
the legend of Orpheus and Eurydice was a tragic tale

of true love lost twice: once, when the mortal Eurydice was bitten by a poisonous snake on her wedding
day, and, secondly, when her lover, the poet-musician
Orpheus, failed in his bid to rescue her from the underworld. Poussin, in his version of the legend, depicts
the doomed pair's wedding day. Eurydice, kneeling in
the center foreground, appears to have been startled
by something nearby (unseen to the viewer). Behind
her, a fisherman turns around, presumably startled by
her cry. On the right, a seated Orpheus, holding a lyre,
continues to sing, having neither heard nor seen anything. Similarly, the other people in the painting—the
nymphs before Orpheus (including the standing figure dressed as Hymen, the goddess of marriage), along
with the bathers and workmen—are equally oblivious. In this idyllic world, the rising clouds of smoke
over the castle offer a visual metaphor of the looming
tragedy. The magnificent stillness, the mythological
subject, and the gentle melancholy evoked by this re-

minder of death were central to Poussin's art and evidence of his classical spirit.

The Restrained Baroque

The Protestant culture of northern and western Europe created simpler works that humanized baroque exuberance, appealed to democratic sentiments, and reflected common human experience. This style of art is called the **restrained baroque,** and it was founded by the painters and architects of the Netherlands and England.

PAINTING The Calvinist Netherlands pointed the way in the arts in Protestant Europe until 1675. The Dutch Republic was ruled by a well-to-do middle class whose wealth was based largely on their dominant role in international shipping. Led by these sober-minded burghers, as the townspeople were called, the Netherlands was briefly one of Europe's great powers. During the middle of the century, the Dutch controlled northern Europe, using their military and naval might to fight England, check French ascendancy, and destroy Spanish sea power. Amsterdam became one of Europe's largest cities, and an important school of painting flourished there. In about 1675, a series of military disasters ended the Netherlands' economic expansion, and the state's fortunes declined sharply. By this time, the great days of Dutch art were over.

During the heyday of the Dutch Republic, a school of painters arose whose works defined the restrained baroque. Attuned to the sober values of their religion and sympathetic to the civic ideals of the republic, these artists created a secular style that mirrored the pious outlook of the ruling middle class. An important development that helped to shape the course of Dutch painting was the rise of an art market. Venice had shown some tendencies in this direction in the 1500s, but in the Netherlands in the 1600s the first full-fledged art market made its debut. The impact of this market on the Dutch school was instantaneous and dramatic. Driven by a demand for home decoration, especially small works to hang on the wall, the market responded with specific subjects—still lifes, landscapes, portraits, and genre, or "slice-of-life," scenes. Paintings were sold by dealers as wares, and buyers speculated in art objects. The market dictated success or failure; some painters pursued other careers as a hedge against financial ruin.

The greatest artist of the Dutch school and probably one of the two or three greatest painters of Western art was Rembrandt van Rijn (1606–1669). His early genius lay in his subtle and dramatic use of lighting and his forceful expressiveness—both qualities that reflected the distant influence of Caravaggio. He also was supremely gifted in his ability to portray the range of moods and emotions he found in humanity, as expressed through the ordinary people he used as models.

The culmination of Rembrandt's early style is a painting titled *The Militia Company of Captain Frans Banning Cocq* but commonly known as *The Night Watch* (Figure 14.17). The painting was commissioned by one of Amsterdam's municipal guard troops in a typical display of Dutch civic pride. Instead of painting a conventional group portrait, however, Rembrandt created a theatrical work filled with exuberant and dramatic gestures and highly charged chiaroscuro effects. He gave the composition added energy by depicting the guardsmen marching toward the viewer. The militia is led by Captain Cocq, the black-suited figure with the red sash and white ruff who marches with arm outstretched in the center foreground. On his left marches his attentive lieutenant, dressed in yellow, with his halberd in his hand. Behind them, the members of the surging crowd, engaged in various soldierly activities and looking in different directions with expressive faces, seem ready to burst forth from the space in which they are enclosed. Of Rembrandt's vast repertory, this painting is one of his most representative.

However, by 1647, five years after *The Night Watch*, Rembrandt's reputation was in decline, and by 1656 he was bankrupt. During these years, his paintings and etchings, which often had a religious theme, began to express his deepest emotions and convictions. He also often illustrated moral lessons, as he did in *Susanna and the Elders* (Figure 14.18).

The story of Susanna is found in chapter 13 of the biblical book of Daniel, a chapter considered canonical by Roman Catholics and Greek Orthodox, but part of the noncanonical Apocrypha by Protestants. Jews also consider this chapter of Daniel outside their biblical canon. In Susanna's tale, Daniel is presented as a young, learned Jew who is deported from Israel to Babylon. There, through his storytelling ability and predictions, he becomes an adviser to Babylon's ruler, Nebuchadnezzar. As the story unfolds, Daniel challenges two powerful Jewish elders, who are also jurists, to save the life and reputation of an innocent young Jewish married woman, Susanna, who is charged with adultery—a capital offense under the old Jewish law code. The two elders, filled with lust, spy on Susanna while she is bathing in an enclosed garden. They demand that she yield to them or they will swear that they have seen her having sex with a young man. Susanna refuses to succumb to their advances and calls for her servants. The next day, in a jumped-up trial, the

Figure 14.17 REMBRANDT VAN RIJN. *The Night Watch (The Militia Company of Captain Frans Banning Cocq)*. 1642. Oil on canvas, 12'2" × 14'7". Rijksmuseum, Amsterdam. *Because of its murky appearance, this painting acquired its nickname,* The Night Watch, *in the nineteenth century. But a cleaning of the painting's deteriorated surface showed that it was actually set in daylight. Restored to its original conception, this work now reveals Rembrandt's spectacular use of light and dark.*

elders repeat their accusation against her. Because of their standing in the community, the crowd believes them until Daniel appears and demands a new trial for Susanna. Daniel shows, through his cross-examining of the witnesses, that the elders have lied. The men are condemned to death and Susanna is exonerated. Innocence and honor are vindicated, and false testimony given by the powerful is proven worthless when exposed to the truth and God's sense of right and wrong. Rembrandt, the devout Protestant, understood the meaning of the story and, in his painting, captured the climactic moment when the elders startle the naked Susanna, who appears vulnerable and helpless.

In the later work painted in the mid-1640s, Rembrandt's style became more personal and simpler. His paintings now expressed a stronger naturalism and an inner calm, a change that paralleled the rise of the quieter classical baroque. This final stage of his art is most beautifully and movingly rendered in his last self-portrait (Figure 14.19). During his career, he had often painted his own likeness, coolly revealing the effects of the aging process on his face. The last self-portrait is most remarkable for the expressive eyes, which, though anguished, seem resigned to whatever happens next. Rembrandt's pursuit of truth—inspired by his own meditations—is revealed here with clarity and acceptance. Looking into this time-ravaged face, the viewer recognizes the universality of growing old and the inevitability of death.

Besides being a master painter, Rembrandt was a giant in printmaking, creating thousands of extant prints and influencing the field for generations to come. Beginning in the 1640s, when he was beset with personal woes (the death of his first wife, Saskia) and a

Figure 14.18   REMBRANDT VAN RIJN. *Susanna and the Elders.* 1647. Oil on mahogany panel, 2′5″ × 4′. Gemäldegalerie Staatliche Museen, Berlin. *The scene is the garden of Susanna's wealthy husband, Joacim, whose palace looms in the upper left background. As Susanna steps into the pond, the two elders appear. The first one lunges after her, trying to disrobe her, while the other stands nearby and leers. Rembrandt's masterful command of chiaroscuro, his placement of the three figures so as to make the scene more threatening, and his deployment of light on Susanna's body heighten the dramatic incident.*

Figure 14.19   REMBRANDT VAN RIJN. *Self-Portrait.* 1669. Oil on canvas, 23¼ × 20″. Mauritshuis, The Hague. *In this last self-portrait, Rembrandt's eyes reveal the personal anguish of a man who has outlived wife, beloved mistress, and children. By this means, Rembrandt expresses one of the most popular themes of baroque art, that of pathos—the quality that arouses feelings of pity and sorrow.*

series of financial crises, he was able to keep himself afloat financially through sales of his prints. While prints generally sold for lower prices than paintings, Rembrandt, through his mastery of the print medium, was able to command higher prices for his prints than for his paintings, which were not selling. Fashioned with a deft hand and a clinical eye, the prints showed the same mastery of chiaroscuro and understanding of character as his paintings. The methods Rembrandt used were either etchings or drypoint—both techniques from late medieval times (see Chapter 10)—and his subjects included landscapes, Amsterdam street scenes, self-portraits, and religious scenes.

The religious prints reflected his personal faith, which was centered on a compassionate, personal savior rather than a stern, distant God. Rembrandt's simple religious scenes, in sharp contrast to the grandeur and splendor of the Italian florid baroque, often portray Christ, dressed in simple clothes, mingling with the common folk, as he heals, preaches, and brings hopes to the poor and downtrodden (Figure 14.20). Pious Protestants, who bought religious art for their homes, found Rembrandt's prints appealing because of their simple treatment of Christian themes.

Another great Dutch artist was Jan Vermeer [yahn ver-MEER] (1632–1675), who specialized in domestic genre scenes. His works reveal a calm world where ordinary objects possess a timeless gravity. Color was important for establishing the domesticity and peacefulness of this closed-off world; Vermeer's favorites

Figure 14.20 REMBRANDT VAN RIJN. *Christ Preaching. Ca. 1648–1650. Etching, 11 × 15½″. Rijksmuseum, Amsterdam. Rembrandt's command of the etcher's tools shines forth in this scene, based on a verse from the biblical book of Matthew, depicting Christ preaching in the street. Christ stands in the center, bathed in light, while surrounded by the poor and the lame, their figures fading into the shadows on the right. On the left are gathered the Pharisees—a sect that interpreted Jewish laws strictly. Recognizable by their finery and showy hats, the Pharisees engage in conversation, perhaps debating what to make of this street preacher. Rembrandt created characters not from his imagination but from real people he encountered in the streets of Amsterdam. This etching is often called the Hundred Guilder Print, because of the high price (est. $1,300, today) it brought at an auction in the seventeenth century.*

were yellow and blue. These serene works evoked the fabled cleanliness of Delft, the city where he lived and worked.

One of the most beautiful of Vermeer's domestic scenes is *The Lacemaker* (Figure 14.21). Like most of his thirty-five extant paintings, *The Lacemaker* depicts an interior room where a single figure is encircled by everyday things. She is lit by a clear light falling on her from the side, another characteristic of Vermeer's paintings. The composition (the woman at the table and the rear wall parallel to the picture frame), the basic colors (yellow and blue), and the subject's absorption in her task typified Vermeer's works. *The Lacemaker* also has a moral message, for a woman engaged in household tasks symbolized the virtue of domesticity for Vermeer.

One of the few Dutch female artists was Judith Leyster (1609–1660), who, like her male colleagues, was a member of an artists' guild (in Haarlem) and painted

for the art market. Beginning in about 1300, women were able to join artists' guilds in the Netherlands—working in embroidery and other crafts—but it was the explosive growth of the art market in the 1600s, with the increased demand for artworks in the home by the Dutch burghers, that made artistic careers such as Leyster's possible. Leyster opened her own studio, where she also instructed aspiring artists. Leyster's specialties were genre scenes, portraits, and still lifes. Her *Carousing Couple* (Figure 14.22), painted when she was about twenty, demonstrates early mastery of artistic technique. Leyster's skill at genre painting, such as this, enabled her to experience modest success in her profession.

England also contributed to the creation of the restrained baroque, but conditions there led to a style markedly different from that of the Dutch school. Unlike the Netherlands, England had no art market, was dominated by an aristocracy, and, most important,

Figure 14.21 JAN VERMEER. *The Lacemaker.* Ca. 1664. Oil on canvas, 9⅝ × 8¼". Louvre. *Unlike Rembrandt, Vermeer was not concerned with human personality as such. Rather, his aim was to create scenes that registered his deep pleasure in bourgeois order and comfort. In* The Lacemaker, *he gives his female subject generalized features, turning her into a social type, but renders her sewing in exquisite detail, giving it a monumental presence. The painting thus becomes a visual metaphor of a virtuous household.*

Figure 14.22 JUDITH LEYSTER. *Carousing Couple.* 1630. Oil on panel, 26¾ × 22⅝". Louvre. *Leyster's* Carousing Couple *shows her command of the painting tradition in which she was trained. The woman, holding a pitcher of beer and a half-filled glass, gazes at her male companion, who is playing a stringed instrument. Both revelers, with their rosy cheeks, are clearly enjoying themselves. The straitlaced ruling class of the Netherlands viewed genre scenes such as this as cautionary tales, depicting public rowdiness of which they disapproved.*

had as yet no native-born painters of note. Painting in England was controlled by aristocratic patrons who preferred portraits to all other subjects and whose taste was courtly but restrained. The painter whose style suited these aristocratic demands was a Flemish artist, Anthony van Dyck [vahn DIKE] (1599–1641). A pupil of Rubens, van Dyck eventually settled in England and became court painter to Charles I.

Van Dyck's elegant style captured the courtly qualities prized by his noble patrons. He depicted his subjects' splendid costumes in all their radiant glory, using vibrant colors to reproduce their textures. He invented a repertory of poses for individual and group portraits that showed his subjects to their greatest advantage. But van Dyck did more than cater to the vanity of his titled patrons. With superb sensitivity, he portrayed

their characters in their faces, showing such qualities as intelligence, self-doubt, and obstinacy. His psychological insights make his courtly portraits genuine works of art.

Van Dyck's fluent style is clearly shown in his double portrait of Lords John and Bernard Stuart, two of the dandies of the court of Charles I (Figure 14.23). This painting indicates the artist's mastery of the society portrait. The subjects' fashionable dress and haughty expressions establish their high social status. Van Dyck skillfully renders the play of light on the silk fabrics of their clothing. He creates an interesting design by placing their bodies opposite each other, but this positioning also offers psychological insight into their characters as the mirrorlike pose suggests that they are vain young men. Van Dyck's deftness at creating elegant likenesses set the standard for English portraiture and influenced French artists well into the eighteenth century.

ARCHITECTURE   Perhaps the most famous architect of the restrained baroque was an Englishman, Sir Christopher Wren (1632–1723). His diverse career personified the baroque age: astronomer and professor at Oxford University, mathematician, engineer, friend of Isaac Newton, architectural advisor to Charles II, and a founding member of the Royal Society. Although influenced by English architects, Wren, over the course of his travels, observed at first hand the classical baroque of Versailles and Paris, as well as the High Renaissance style in Italy with its classical forms such as the dome and the column orders.

After the devastating fire of 1666, Wren was commissioned by Charles II to supervise the rebuilding of much of central London, including the old Gothic church of St. Paul. Wren's St. Paul's cathedral, built between 1675 and 1710, was modified during construction (Interpreting Art figure 14.1). In its final configuration St. Paul's cathedral—the crowning achievement of Wren's illustrious career—represented the climax of the restrained baroque. Today, St. Paul's cathedral is one of the dominant landmarks of the London skyline.

Literature

The Council of Trent's decrees, which had played a powerful role in shaping baroque art and architecture, had little impact on seventeenth-century literature. Nevertheless, a baroque literary style now arose, which became international in scope.

The most enduring legacy of baroque literature is drama. Audiences of the period delighted in works that blended different forms, and baroque drama mixed literature, costume design, set painting, and

Figure 14.23 Anthony van Dyck. *Lords John and Bernard Stuart.* Ca. 1639. Oil on canvas, 7'9⅓" × 4'9½". National Gallery, London. *Van Dyck has depicted these dandies in the carefully disheveled style preferred by the era's aristocrats. Their doublets (jackets) are of plain, muted colors and slashed on the chest and sleeves to allow a contrasting color to show. The deliberately casual look is especially prominent in the unbuttoned doublet worn by Lord John (left) and the cloak thrown over the shoulder of Lord Bernard (right). Both men wear the soft leather boots, partly rolled down the legs, that were now replacing the shoes of an earlier time.*

theatrical spectacle. Tragedy, based on Roman models, was the supreme achievement of the baroque stage, but comedies of all types, including satires, farces, and sexual comedies, were also important. After centuries of neglect, tragedy and comedy had been brilliantly revived in Elizabethan England (see Chapter 13), and their revival in France in the 1600s was evidence of the continuing growth of secular consciousness. Another ancient literary genre that returned to favor was the epic, a reflection of the love of power typical of the age. Finally, baroque literature began to acknowledge the world outside Europe, as may be seen in the rise of writings with a non-Western dimension, such as settings (for example, Mexico, in the poetry of the Mexi-

can nun Sor Juana Inés de la Cruz [1648–1695]) (Figure 14.24); characters (for example, the Aztec ruler Montezuma, the hero of the play *The Indian Emperor* [1665], by John Dryden [1631–1700]); and themes (for example, comparison of Western and non-Western customs in travel literature, as in *Travels in Persia* [1686], by Jean Chardin [1643–1713]).

Despite the variety of their works, baroque writers shared certain traits, including a love of ornate language; a fascination with characterization, either of individuals or of types; and a tendency to choose plots loaded with emotional extremes, such as gross sensuality versus pangs of conscience. With such emotionally charged works, baroque writers could and did

INTERPRETING ART

Personal Vision The design for St. Paul's, Wren's masterpiece, united the architect's sense of beauty with his mathematical training and religious faith. Wren's tomb lies under the cathedral's dome, where a plaque reads, in Latin: "*Si monumentum requires, circumspice*" ("If you are seeking his monument, look around you").

Religious Perspective Members of the Church of England worship here, observing their rituals and ceremonies and professing their beliefs. Like medieval cathedrals, St. Paul's was designed to awe and inspire worshipers by affirming God's power and glory.

Setting St. Paul's, built on the site of old St. Paul's, stands on a slight rise on the north side of the Thames River, in the heart of what was medieval London. Although tucked in among commercial buildings, it remains aloof and alone, thanks to the orientation of the building, the surrounding gardens, and the imposing dome.

Mixed Stylistic Elements Medieval: the floor plan has the cruciform shape that typified

Interpreting Art figure 14.1 CHRISTOPHER WREN. St. Paul's Cathedral. 1675–1710. London. *As King's Surveyor of Public Works, Christopher Wren designed and built St. Paul's, along with more than fifty other London churches after the Great Fire of 1666. St. Paul's, the first cathedral to be built for the Church of England, was meant to be a Protestant rival to St. Peter's in Rome. Over time, members of England's royal family and well-known commoners have been married and mourned here.*

Romanesque and Gothic churches—nave, transept, and choir—though the transept is placed slightly closer to the east end, near the choir and the high altar. Classical: the west facade, as seen here, has two symmetrical towers, the pairs of columns on two levels, the elaborate pediment, and classical decorations. Baroque: the exterior has a lively appearance, with its ornate facade punctuated by niches, the robust twin steeples with their shadowy recesses and staggered columns, and the dramatic play of light across the building's surface.

Materials Brick, wood, lead, marble, and stone were used in construction. A brick structure supports both the lantern and the wooden framework of the outer dome, which is covered with lead. Most of the exterior is sheathed in slabs of marble. The front steps, exterior columns, and interior floor are marble.

Echoes of St. Peter's Wren adapted elements of Michelangelo's design for St. Peter's (see Figure 12.22), including the magnificent dome with its encircling colonnade, and the use of the Corinthian order as a unifying motif.

---

employ dramatic rhetoric, slipping occasionally into empty bombast.

BAROQUE LITERATURE IN FRANCE Drama was France's greatest contribution to baroque literature. Secular drama revived in the 1630s under the patronage of Louis XIII and reached a climax during Louis XIV's reign. Strict control—a defining feature of the absolutist policies of the king—was exercised over the plays staged at the royal court, although comic playwrights were given more freedom, as long as they did not offend common decency or good taste.

France's tragic playwrights were expected to obey the rules of literary composition identified by the French Academy and based on the theories of Aristotle

(see Chapter 3). The ideal play had to observe the unities of time, place, and action—that is, it had to take place during a twenty-four-hour time span, have no scene changes, and have a single uncomplicated plot. Furthermore, the plays were supposed to use formal language and to focus on universal problems as reflected in dilemmas experienced by highborn men and women. Because of the playwrights' strict adherence to these rules, it is sometimes claimed that the dramas of this period are expressive of a classical style. But the French obsession with order, gravity, and severity was evidence of a baroque sensibility—just as was the case in the French style of baroque painting and architecture.

France's two great baroque tragedians were Pierre Corneille [kor-NAY] (1606–1684) and Jean Racine [ra-

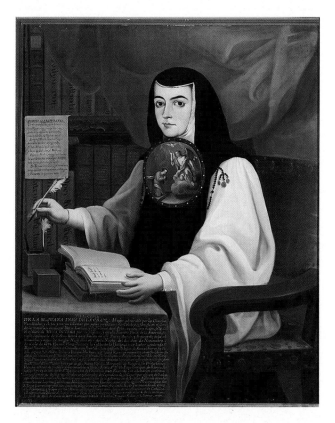

Figure 14.24 ANDRES DE ISLAS. *Sor Juana Inés de la Cruz.* 1772. Museo de America, Madrid. *This portrait, painted seventy-seven years after the subject's death, is based on an earlier (now lost) likeness. Sor Juana is depicted in a conventional pose for a writer-intellectual (see Figure 13.1)—seated before an open book, writing implement in hand. She wears the Hieronymite habit of the Order of St. Jerome—a white tunic under a full-length scapular in a color that varied by region. In Mexico City, the scapulars were black or blue. Around her neck is a nun's shield—in Spanish,* escudo de monja—*typically a painting on copper of a religious scene of spiritual importance to the wearer. Sor Juana's shield shows the Annunciation, the moment when the Angel Gabriel reveals to Mary her destiny as the Mother of God. This painting is by the Mexican artist Andres de Islas (active 1753–1775), whose specialty was the documentation of the ethnic life of colonial Mexico.*

SEEN] (1639–1699). Corneille composed tragedies in verse, which were based on Spanish legends and Roman themes. Drawing on the Hellenistic philosophy of Stoicism, his dramas stressed the importance of duty, patriotism, and loyalty—ideals that mirrored the values of his courtly audience. His finest work is *Le Cid,* based on the legendary Spanish patriot, who must choose between personal feelings and honor.

Racine, perhaps France's greatest playwright, wrote tragedies characterized by refined language and penetrating psychological insight. Preoccupied with the moral struggle between the will and the emotions, he created intensely human characters in classically constructed plays. A subject that intrigued Racine was the doomed woman who was swept to her destruction by obsessive sexual passion. This baroque theme was most perfectly expressed in his masterpiece, *Phèdre (Phaedra),*

his version of the Greek tale of incestuous love first dramatized by Euripides in the fifth century BCE. Where Euripides makes fate a central reason for his heroine's downfall, Racine portrays Phèdre as the unfortunate victim of uncontrolled passion for her stepson. Even though Racine explored other types of love in his plays, such as mother love and even political passion, it was in his study of sex as a powerful motive for action that he was most original.

Baroque drama in France also produced one of the comic geniuses of the Western theater, Jean Baptiste Poquelin, better known as Molière [mole-YAIR] (1622–1673). Molière analyzed the foibles of French life in twelve penetrating satirical comedies that had the lasting impact of tragedy. He peopled his plays with social types—the idler, the miser, the pedant, the seducer, the hypochondriac, the medical quack, the would-be gentleman, the pretentiously cultured lady—exposing the follies of the entire society. To create his comedic effects, Molière used not only topical humor and social satire but all the trappings of farce, including pratfalls, mistaken identities, sight gags, puns, and slapstick, as well.

Molière was appointed official entertainer to Louis XIV in 1658; even so, he made many enemies among those who felt they were the butt of his jokes. When he died, for example, the French clergy refused to give him an official burial because they believed some of his plays to be attacks on the church. The testament to Molière's enduring brilliance is that many of his comedies are still performed today, including *Tartuffe, The Miser, The Would-Be Gentleman,* and *The Misanthrope,* and they are still enormously entertaining.

BAROQUE LITERATURE IN ENGLAND   England's outstanding contribution in English to baroque literature was made by John Milton (1608–1674), a stern Puritan and a high-ranking official in Cromwell's Commonwealth. The deeply learned Milton had a grand moral vision that led him to see the universe as locked in a struggle between the forces of darkness and the forces of light. Only an epic was capable of expressing such a monumental conception.

His supreme literary accomplishment was to Christianize the epic in his long poem *Paradise Lost.* Inspired by Homer's and Virgil's ancient epics, but also intended as a Protestant response to Dante's *Divine Comedy,* Milton's poem became an immediate classic. His grandiose themes in *Paradise Lost* were the rebellion of the angels led by Lucifer, the fall of Adam and Eve in the Garden of Eden, and Christ's redemption of humanity.

An astonishing aspect of *Paradise Lost* is Milton's portrait of Lucifer, which some critics have seen as a baroque glamorization of evil. Lucifer is characterized as a creature of titanic ambition and deceitful charm. Despite his powerful presence, however, this epic story has moral balance. At the end, Adam, the author of original sin, is saved instead of being condemned to hell. Adam's redemption occurs when he accepts Jesus as Lord. Adam's choice reflected Milton's belief in free will and the necessity of taking responsibility for one's actions.

In addition to its grand theme, *Paradise Lost* is baroque in other ways. The mixing of Christian legend and ancient epic, for example, is typical of baroque taste. Milton's convoluted style is baroque with its occasionally odd word order, Latinisms, and complex metaphors. Most of all, Milton's epic is baroque in its lofty tone and exaggerated rhetoric—literary equivalents, perhaps, of Rubens or Rembrandt.

A secondary achievement of the literary baroque in England was that literature began to reflect the West's overseas expansion, as in the publishing of travel books, memoirs, and letters describing real and fictional contacts with peoples and lands around the globe. Part of a European-wide trend, the growth of English literature with a non-European dimension expressed the baroque theme of pushing against the boundaries of life and art. A pioneering work on this baroque theme was the short prose story *Oroonoko* (1688) by Aphra Behn (1640–1689), an English writer who exploited her firsthand experiences as a resident of Surinam (modern Suriname) to provide a vivid, exotic setting. Situated in South America and told with a blend of realism and romance, *Oroonoko* condemns the culture of slavery through the story of the doomed love affair between a black slave-prince and a slave woman. The author portrays the black hero as untutored in Western ways yet polished and educated on his own terms and, above all, superior to the natural depravity of the European characters. This is an early version of the myth of the noble savage, the cultural archetype that reached its climax in the romantic era (see Chapter 17). England's first woman to earn her living as a writer, Behn also wrote about twenty comedies for the stage and a poem collection, but *Oroonoko* is her chief claim to renown.

Music

Unlike the Renaissance, when a single musical sound prevailed (see Chapter 12), the baroque had no single musical ideal. Nonetheless, four trends during the baroque period give its music distinctive qualities. First, the development of major and minor tonality, which had been prefigured in Josquin des Prez's music in the early 1500s, was a central feature of the works of this time, making it the first stage in the rise of modern music. Second, the mixing of genres, which has been noted in literature and the arts, also occurred in baroque music. Third, the expressiveness that had entered mu-

Figure 14.25 Concert with Baroque Era Instruments. Seventeenth century. The Granger Collection, New York. *In the baroque period, professional musicians often performed with amateurs in various venues, such as university musical societies, taverns, coffeehouses, and private homes. In this print, the venue is unclear, though the setting is a richly paneled, Italianate room and the musicians are wearing court dress and powdered wigs. The musical instruments include flute, bassoon, recorder, violin, harpsichord, and cello.*

sic in the late 1500s now became even more exaggerated, being used to stress meanings and emotions in the musical texts that otherwise might not have been heard. And last, this was an age of **virtuosos,** master musicians, especially singers, who performed with great technical skill and vivid personal style, and of a growing variety of musical instruments (Figure 14.25). The musical form that drew these trends together was **opera,** making it the quintessential symbol of the age.

OPERA   Opera originated in Italy in the late sixteenth century among a group of Florentine musicians and poets with aristocratic ties. The first great composer of opera was Claudio Monteverdi [mon-teh-VAIR-dee]

(1567–1643), whose earliest opera, *Orfeo* (1607), was based on the legend of the ancient Greek poet-musician Orpheus. *Orfeo* united drama, dance, elaborate stage mechanisms, and painted scenery with music. Monteverdi wrote melodic arias, or songs, for the individual singers, and he increased the opera's dramatic appeal by concluding each of its five acts with a powerful chorus. His setting truly mirrored the text, using musical phrases to serve as aural symbols and thus to enhance the unfolding of events.

By the 1630s, opera began to shed its aristocratic origins and become a popular entertainment. This change did not affect opera's focus on ancient myths and histories about noble men and women, nor did it halt the trend to brilliant singing called **bel canto,** literally "beautiful song." However, to appeal to a wider audience, operatic composers added elements from Italy's popular comic theater, such as farcical scenes and stock characters, notably humorous servants. By the end of this age, the operatic form was stylized into a recipe, including improbable plots, inadequate motivations for the characters, and magical transformations—signs of its baroque nature.

Opera became immensely popular in Europe, especially in Italy, where it remains so today. By 1750, opera houses had been built in many major cities; Venice led the way with more than a dozen establishments. The rise of opera in Italy during the 1600s, like the founding of a commercial theater in London in the 1500s, presaged the downfall of the aristocratic patronage system and the emergence of entertainments with mass appeal.

The winding down of the Thirty Years' War allowed Italian opera to be exported to the rest of Europe. Only in France were composers able to defy the overpowering Italian influence and create an independent type of opera. This development was made possible by the grandeur of Louis XIV's court and by French taste, which was more restrained than the opulent Italian. Nevertheless, French opera was founded by an Italian, Jean-Baptiste Lully [loo-LEE] (1632–1687), who later became a French citizen and Louis's court composer. Under Lully's direction, French opera developed its identifying features: dignified music, the full use of choruses, the inclusion of a ballet, and, most important, a French text. Lully's patron, the Sun King, sometimes performed in the opera's ballet sequences himself, dancing side by side with the composer. Lully's works, which dominated French music until 1750, ensured a powerful role for French music in the Western tradition.

BACH, HANDEL, AND VIVALDI   Baroque music reached its climax after 1715. Three composers were responsible for this development: in Protestant northern Europe, the Germans Bach and Handel, and in Roman Catholic Italy, Vivaldi.

Johann Sebastian Bach   The greatest of these late baroque masters was Johann Sebastian Bach (1685–1750). A devout Lutheran who worked for German noble courts and municipalities far from the major cities, Bach created a body of sacred music that transcends all religious creeds and nationalities. Employing all the baroque musical genres, his works are distinguished by their inventiveness and complete mastery of major and minor tonality. His most memorable achievements are the Passions, the musical settings of the liturgy to be performed on Good Friday—the most tragic day in the Christian calendar. Composed in about 1727, the *St. Matthew Passion* expresses the collective grief of the Christian community for the death of Jesus. Bach used a German text with arias and choruses, making the music bring out all the emotional implications of the words. Thus, the *St. Matthew Passion* is more dramatic than most operas and a sublime religious experience in itself.

Although Bach's religious music is his greatest legacy, he also left a body of secular music, including orchestral works and works for various instrumental groups. A musician's musician, Bach composed *The Well-Tempered Clavier* as an ordered set of studies in all the major and minor keys. The forty-eight preludes and fugues in this work set a heroic challenge for keyboard performers and are still an essential part of the piano repertoire today. (A **clavier** is an early keyboard instrument; a **fugue** is a polyphonic composition in which a theme is introduced by one instrument and then repeated by each successively entering instrument until a complicated interweaving of themes, variations, imitations, and echoes results.) This work contributed to the standardization of the pitches of the notes of the musical scale and of the tuning of keyboard instruments.

Bach's Organ Fugue in G Minor ("Little Fugue"; about 1709) is a classic of the fugue genre. A fugue may be written for a group of instruments, voices, or a single keyboard instrument, in this instance, an organ. Bach's organ fugue is scored for four melodic lines: soprano, alto, tenor, and bass. It opens with the "voices" playing "follow the leader": the soprano line announces the **subject**—the main musical theme, followed by its imitation in the alto, tenor, and bass lines. However, before the alto line can complete its part, the soprano line begins the **countersubject**—a variation of the subject that will now be played in tandem with the subject, either above it or below it. The bass line, recognizable by its deep plush tones, concludes the opening sequence.

A short transitional section, known as an **episode,** leads to another round of follow the leader, with each melodic line taking a turn. Episodes may be fresh music or phrases taken from the subject. Throughout the remainder of this piece, the subject and countersubject are in constant dialogue, with episodes added after each recurrence of the subject. Sustained notes and **trills**—rapid alternation of two notes, a step apart—are two means Bach used to embellish the increasingly active melody. The Little Fugue, though in a minor key, has some episodes and restatements of the subject in a minor key, and it concludes with a glorious major chord—a typical baroque ending.

Of Bach's secular works, the most popular today are probably the six *Brandenburg Concertos* (written for the duke of Brandenburg), whose tunefulness and rhythmic variety the composer rarely surpassed. The concertos were composed for the type of ensemble found in the German princely courts of the time—a group of string players of average ability along with a few woodwind and brass instruments, perhaps a total of twenty to twenty-five musicians. Bach's dominant idea in these concertos was to demonstrate the interplay between individual soloists and the larger group. As in most of his work, the composer wove different melodic lines and different harmonies into elaborate, complex structures of tremendous variety, power, and scope.

George Frideric Handel The other great late baroque German master, George Frideric Handel (1685–1759), was renowned for his Italian-style operas. More cosmopolitan than Bach, Handel eventually settled in London, where he composed thirty-six operatic works. His operas succeeded in their day because of the brilliant way in which the music allows the singers to show their virtuosity, but they are generally not to the taste of modern audiences and have not found a place in the standard operatic repertory. In contrast, his mastery of sacred music, particularly the **oratorio**—an opera-like form but without any stage action—which he perfected, has made his name immortal. Of the oratorios, *Messiah,* based on biblical texts and sung in English, holds first place. Its popularity stems from its baroque qualities: the emotionally stirring choruses and the delightful embellishments the soloists are permitted in their arias. As a result, *Messiah* is probably the best-known work of sacred music in the English-speaking world.

One of *Messiah's* great arias, which shows Handel's expressive music to perfection, is "Ev'ry Valley Shall Be Exalted," for tenor, strings, and basso continuo. Handel's exuberant music matches the exuberant text, based on Isaiah 40:4, a verse that envisions an earth transformed by the coming of the Messiah.

> Ev'ry valley
> Ev'ry valley shall be exalted,
> and ev'ry mountain
> and hill made low,
> the crooked straight,
> and the rough places plain.
> Ev'ry valley shall be exalted,
> and ev'ry mountain and hill

> made low, the crooked straight,
> and the rough places plain.
> The crooked straight,
> And the rough places plain.

Through word painting, a popular baroque musical technique, Handel makes the text come alive. For example, the word *exalted* ("raised up"), in line 2, becomes a rising musical phrase made up of forty-six rapid notes. High tones are used to depict *hill* and *mountain,* and certain words are given musical equivalents, such as *crooked* (two notes a half step apart, repeated), *straight* (sustained tone), and *plain* (long sustained note). The aria begins and ends in the baroque style with a **refrain** (in Italian, *ritornello*), a short instrumental passage.

Antonio Lucio Vivaldi Antonio Lucio Vivaldi (1678–1741), the late baroque Italian composer and violinist, set a new standard for instrumental music. Unlike Bach and Handel, who worked almost exclusively within secular settings, Vivaldi supported himself through church patronage, serving as both a priest (briefly) and a musician and composer (mainly) at a church orphanage for females in Venice. He also was a freelance composer, producing works for patrons and customers across Europe. Employing diverse musical genres, he wrote nearly fifty operas, of which about sixteen survive complete; about forty cantatas; fifty sacred vocal works; ninety **sonatas** (a sonata is a work for a small group of instruments); and nearly five hundred **concertos** (a concerto is a piece for solo instrument and orchestra), of which nearly half were written for solo violin. Vivaldi's music is little performed today except for the concertos, whose innovations and style raise him to the first rank of composers. His innovations include a three-movement form, arranged in a fast-slow-fast pattern, and, most important, the use of a refrain, that is, a recurring musical phrase, in combination with brief passages performed by a solo instrument, which together provide a unifying thread to the work. Vivaldi's concerto form influenced the late baroque works of Bach and helped to set the standard for classical music in general (see Chapter 16).

The best known of Vivaldi's concertos are those collectively titled *The Four Seasons* (1725), a set of four violin concertos, each named after a season of the year, beginning with spring. Using both major and minor tonality, Vivaldi's music passionately evokes a feeling of each passing season. This work established the tradition of **program music,** or music that represents a nonmusical image, idea, or story without the use of words. Later, Beethoven made program music a central feature of his music (see Chapter 17).

Vivaldi's lively "La Primavera" ("Spring"), from *The Four Seasons,* is a masterful evocation of springtime. A work in a major key usually conveys optimism, and this concerto certainly does. Typical of baroque concertos, "Spring" opens with an orchestral refrain, expressed in two phrases, which are repeated twice, first loudly and then softly. The refrain theme, or at least parts of it, becomes a recurring motif. After the opening, violin solos alternate with the orchestral refrain. To conjure up the complex sounds of spring, Vivaldi uses word painting, for both solo violin and the orches-

tra's string section: bird songs (high trills and repeated high notes), murmuring brooks (running notes alternating with sustained notes), and thunder and lightning (string **tremolos**—the rapid repetition of a pitch or chord) and upward rushing scales. "La Primavera" is probably Vivaldi's most popular single work.

The Legacy of the Baroque Age

The baroque period left a potent legacy to the modern world in politics, economics, religion, and the arts. The system of great states governed by a balance of power dominated European affairs until 1945. Standing armies, divorced from general society, became a central feature of life among Europe's great powers until 1790. From the baroque period date the roles of France and England as Europe's trendsetters, both politically and culturally. The concept and practice of "world war" also date from this period. The economic system known as mercantilism originated during the baroque period and prevailed in Europe into the nineteenth century. The religious orientation of the European states became well established in the seventeenth century, along with the division of the vast majority of Westerners into Protestant and Catholic camps. In the Netherlands, artists operated in an open market, painting works for wealthy citizens, thus launching the trend toward today's commercial art world. The baroque idea of spectacle is a thread that runs throughout the cul-

ture of this period and helps to explain not only the propagandistic aspects of politics and religion but also the theatrical elements in the arts and entertainment. Culturally, the baroque is still with us, even though much about this style seems excessive to modern taste. Although baroque operas are not often performed, the idea of opera originated in this age of spectacle. Other baroque musical works, notably the majestic oratorios of Handel and the powerful compositions of Bach for church and court, are part of the regular concert repertoire in the West today. Some of the most admired and enduring artworks in Western history were created during this time, including Bernini's *Ecstasy of St. Teresa* and the paintings of Rembrandt. Many cities of Europe are still showcases of baroque splendor. The church of St. Peter's in Rome, St. Paul's cathedral in London, and the palace and gardens at Versailles are but three of the surviving monuments of this period, reminding us of the grand religious and political ideals of a very different age.

KEY CULTURAL TERMS

baroque
florid baroque style
baldacchino
tenebrism
illusionism
classical baroque style
restrained baroque style
virtuoso
opera
bel canto
clavier

fugue
subject
countersubject
episode
trill
oratorio
refrain
sonata
concerto
program music
tremolo

QUESTIONS FOR CRITICAL THINKING

1. Take an artwork from each of the three variations of the international baroque style, discuss their characteristics, and show how each reflected its historical setting.

2. Discuss the reign of Louis XIV of France as a personification of the type of government known as absolutism. Why did Louis determine to become an absolute ruler? Explain Louis's use of propaganda in achieving his political aims.

3. What influence did religion have on the baroque style? What values in Protestantism and Catholicism made for different developments?

4. What classical features and ideals survived in the baroque style? Where was classicism strongest in baroque culture? Why?

5. What are the characteristics of baroque literature? What literary forms flourished during the baroque period? Compare and contrast literary developments in England and France during this period.

15

THE BAROQUE AGE II
Revolutions in Scientific and Political Thought
1600–1715

The baroque age witnessed not only political upheavals and artistic spectacles, but also the Scientific Revolution. The era challenged centuries-old beliefs, especially in the fields of astronomy and physics, and created a whole new way of viewing the universe. In England, political philosophers asserted that governments were not the products of divine rule but, instead, were created by humans and their deeds. These scientific discoveries and political ideas added to the baroque age's pervasive restlessness.

The term *Scientific Revolution* applies chiefly to astronomy and physics, although major advances were made in medical science, and changes occurred in chemistry, biology, and embryology. The Scientific Revolution also gave rise to a type of literature that considered the impact of the new science on secular and religious thought. A few scholars composed literary works that redefined the place of human beings in the cosmos and the purpose of human life. This furthered the separation of philosophy from theology, a gap that had been widening since the 1300s (see Chapter 10). Philosophy now began to address secular concerns, and theology was relegated to a minor cultural role.

The climax of this revolutionary age occurred between 1685 and 1715, a period that witnessed what one historian called "the crisis of the European conscience," as the balance tipped from traditional ideas to modern views. These early modern scientists and philosophers countered faith with reason, dogma with skepticism, and divine intervention with natural law. They accepted as true what could be proven mathematically and rejected as untrue those things that could not. They eventually concluded that the universe was

◀ **Detail** MARIA SIBYLLA MERIAN. *Insect Metamorphoses in Surinam.* 1705. Hand-colored engraving. (Reprinted in F. Schnack, *Das Kleine Buch der Tropenwander.* Leipzig: Insel-Verlag, 1935. Plate 11. 4¾ × 7".)

Timeline 15.1　REVOLUTIONS IN SCIENTIFIC AND POLITICAL THOUGHT

1543	1600	1700 1715

The Scientific Revolution and Early Modern Political Philosophy

1543	1570–1600	1609	1625	1637	1651	1687	1690
Copernicus's *Revolutions of the Heavenly Bodies*	Brahe's observations	Kepler's *On the Motion of Mars*	Grotius's *The Law of War and Peace*	Descartes' *Discourse on Method*	Hobbes's *Leviathan*	Newton's *Mathematical Principles*	Locke's *Two Treatises of Government* and *An Essay Concerning Human Understanding*

1610	1632
Galileo sights four moons of Jupiter	Galileo's *Dialogues on the Two Chief Systems of the World*

like a great clock that operated according to universal laws. Although this clockwork image has been discarded today, we still owe a debt to these thinkers, who set Western culture on its present course and brought modernity into being (Timeline 15.1).

THEORIES OF THE UNIVERSE BEFORE THE SCIENTIFIC REVOLUTION

The Scientific Revolution was both an outgrowth and a rejection of Aristotelian cosmology that had held Western thinkers in its grip for two thousand years. The ancient Greeks built upon the Aristotelian system, which was transmitted to the West through Roman and Islamic culture and into the European medieval scholastic tradition. The cosmology's fundamental principle is **geocentrism,** the theory that the universe is earth centered. Around the stationary earth, which was not considered a planet, revolved the five known planets (Mercury, Venus, Mars, Jupiter, and Saturn) and the sun and the moon, each held aloft by a crystalline sphere. Nearest the earth was the moon (Figure 15.1). In the supralunar world, or the region beyond the moon, the planets moved in circular orbits and were made of an incorruptible element, aether; in the sublunar world, or the region beneath the moon, change was constant, motion was rectilinear, and matter was composed of the four elements, earth, air, fire, and water. This system had an absolute up and down: "up" referred to the area beyond the spheres inhabited by the Unmoved Mover—Aristotle's term for the source of all celestial motion—and "down" referred to the center of the earth.

In the second century CE, the Egyptian scholar Ptolemy updated Aristotle's geocentric theory with

new astronomical data and improved mathematical calculations. During the golden age of Muslim culture (800–1100 CE), Arab intellectuals preserved this geocentric legacy, improving and refining it to reflect new planetary sightings. In the High Middle Ages (1000–1300), Western scholars recovered the Ptolemaic heritage—with its Muslim additions—and integrated it into a Christian context: the Unmoved Mover was God and the space beyond the spheres was heaven. The church also became attached to the geocentric theory because it seemed to validate the doctrine of original sin: the corrupt earth—inhabited by fallen mortals—corresponded to the sublunar world of decay and constant change.

At the University of Paris in the 1300s, a more skeptical outlook arose among a few thinkers who began to question these assumptions. Unconvinced by Aristotle's solution to the problem of motion (which was to attribute the forward motion of a projectile to air movement), the Parisian scholars offered an alternative explanation. They asserted that a projectile acquired "impetus," a propulsive quality that gradually diminished as the projectile moved through space. The theory of impetus commanded scholars' attention for about three centuries, leading them to consider a new range of scientific problems.

Although the theory of impetus was later proven untrue, it was a first step away from the Aristotelian tradition because it made Western scientists aware that the great Greek thinker was not always right. And scholars at Paris and other universities began to advocate applying mathematics to practical problems as well as directly observing nature—in other words, collecting data (**empiricism**) and framing hypotheses from observable facts (**inductive reasoning**).

Aristotle had also used empirical data and inductive logic, but his writings had become so revered, for

Figure 15.1   PETER APIAN. Geocentric Diagram of the Universe, from the *Cosmographia*. 1539. The Bancroft Library, University of California, Berkeley. *This schematic diagram illustrates the geocentric universe in the pre-Copernican era. The unmoving earth is at the center and is surrounded by ten moving spheres, containing, in sequential order, the moon, Mercury, Venus, the sun, Mars, Jupiter, Saturn, the fixed stars, the aqueous or* crystalline heaven, *and the empty sphere called the* primum mobile. *The ninth sphere, the crystalline heaven, was added by medieval scholars to address a problem raised by the account of creation in Genesis. The tenth sphere, the* primum mobile, *was logically necessary in Aristotle's theory because it moved first and brought the other nine spheres into motion. Beyond the tenth sphere was the Empyrean, home of the Unmoved Mover in philosophy or of God in theology.*

generations scholars did not examine his methodology and were afraid to tamper with his conclusions. Indeed, his followers relied on **deductive reasoning;** that is, they only explored the ramifications of accepted truths. But with the new critical spirit that appeared in the late Middle Ages, scholars began to look at the world with fresh eyes. In time, this spirit led to the Scientific Revolution, which overturned the geocentric Ptolemaic system and established **heliocentrism,** the theory that the universe is centered on the sun.

THE MAGICAL AND THE PRACTICAL IN THE SCIENTIFIC REVOLUTION

The Scientific Revolution is notable for its paradoxes and ironies, some of which will be discussed later in this chapter. A paradox that should be noted at the outset, however, is that this revolution in human thought, which ushered in modern science, was rooted in both magical beliefs and practical technological achievements. With one or two exceptions, the Scientific Revolution was motivated by two divergent and contradictory sets of beliefs. On the one hand, it followed the lead of late medieval science by collecting empirical data, reasoning inductively, and using mathematics to verify results (Figure 15.2). Significantly, the most startling changes occurred in those areas where mathematics was applied to long-existing intellectual problems, namely, in astronomy, physics, and biology.

On the other hand, the Scientific Revolution was entranced by Neoplatonism, the philosophy that revived the ancient Greek philosophy in the early Renaissance (see Chapter 11). Like late medieval science, Neoplatonism stressed the role of mathematics in problem solving, but Neoplatonism also had a mystical streak—a legacy from Pythagoras—that led its devotees to seek harmony through numbers (see Chapter 2). Thinkers who followed Neoplatonism believed that simplicity was superior to complexity in mathematical figuring because simplicity was the supreme sign that a solution was correct. This belief has become a guiding ideal of modern science, although other aspects of Neoplatonism are rejected today, such as the attribution of mysterious powers to the sun. One effect of Neoplatonism's occult side was to tighten the link between astronomy and astrology, a connection as old as Greek science. Most of those thinkers who advanced the Scientific Revolution supported this linkage, and a few even cast horoscopes for wealthy clients.

Many of the Scientific Revolution's achievements would have been impossible without the telescope and the microscope, both of which were invented in about 1600 in the Netherlands. Without them, scholars would have simply remained thinkers, as they had been since the time of the ancient Greeks. But with the new technology, they could penetrate deep into hitherto inaccessible areas—outer space and the inner workings of the human body. Henceforward, those scholars with scientific interests allied themselves with the crafts tradition, becoming experimenters and empiricists.

Figure 15.2 MARIA SIBYLLA MERIAN. *Insect Metamorphoses in Surinam.* 1705. Hand-colored engraving. (Reprinted in F. Schnack, *Das Kleine Buch der Tropenwander.* Leipzig: Insel-Verlag, 1935. Plate 11. 4¾ × 7″.) *A painter and a scientist, the German-born Maria Sibylla Merian (1647–1717) traveled to the South American Dutch colony of Surinam, where, for two years, she collected and raised insects and made notes and illustrations. Her illustration of the metamorphosis of a moth, from caterpillar through pupa (covered by a cocoon) to mature adult, along with a flowering branch of an orange tree, captures the exotic character of the New World, adds to the growing body of scientific knowledge, and reflects the high standards of seventeenth-century Dutch art.*

Astronomy and Physics: From Copernicus to Newton

The intellectual shift from the earth-centered to the sun-centered universe, which lasted almost one hundred fifty years, involved an international community of scholars. Heliocentrism, the new model of the world, was first broached by the Polish thinker Copernicus in 1543, and, in 1687, the English scholar Isaac Newton proved this view with his incontrovertible mathematical calculations. Between those dates, major steps in science were taken by Tycho Brahe of Denmark, Johannes Kepler of Germany, and Galileo Galilei of Italy (see Timeline 15.1).

NICOLAUS COPERNICUS   When Nicolaus Copernicus (1473–1543) published *Revolutions of the Heavenly Bodies* in 1543, he was reviving the discarded heliocentric theory of the third-century BCE Greek thinker Aristarchus (see Chapter 4). In this highly technical work, Copernicus launched a head-on assault against Ptolemaic geocentrism. The main issue between Copernican astronomy and the older worldview was not one of mathematical precision, for both were mathematically solid and thus equally able to predict planetary positions and solar and lunar eclipses. Rather, the basic question between the two systems was which one was simpler. Copernicus reasoned that a more convincing picture of the universe could be achieved by transposing the positions of the sun and the earth. Instead of the Ptolemaic notion of a finite world centered on a fixed earth, Copernicus envisioned a vastly expanded, but not infinite, universe with the planets orbiting the sun (Figure 15.3).

Recognizing the revolutionary nature of his hypothesis, Copernicus delayed printing his ideas until he was dying. In an attempt to mollify clerical critics, he dedicated his book to the pope, Paul III. Later religious leaders, concluding that heliocentrism was dangerous and contrary to scripture, condemned it as a false system. What disturbed them was that if the earth were to be removed from the center of the universe, the place of human beings in the divine order would be reduced. In effect, human beings would no longer be the leading actors in a cosmic drama staged for them alone.

Catholics and Protestants alike denounced the ideas of Copernicus. Lutheran and Calvinist authorities condemned his views as unbiblical, and in 1610 the pope placed *Revolutions of the Heavenly Bodies* on the Index, the list of forbidden books created during the Counter-Reformation. Eventually, the two religious groups parted ways over Copernican ideas. For more than two hundred years, until 1822, the Roman Catholic Church opposed the sun-centered theory, thus reversing a centuries-old tradition of being open to innovative scientific thought. However, in Protestantism—where authority was less centralized than in Roman Catholicism—some sects slowly accepted and adapted their beliefs to the new astronomy.

JOHANNES KEPLER   The reception of Copernican astronomy by the scientific community was neither immediate nor enthusiastic. For example, the great Danish astronomer Tycho Brahe [TEE-ko BRAH-hee] (1546–1601) adopted a modified Copernicanism, believing that the other planets moved around the sun but that the earth did not. Brahe nevertheless contributed to the ultimate triumph of heliocentrism through his copious observations of planetary movement. So accurate were his sightings (without the aid of a telescope)

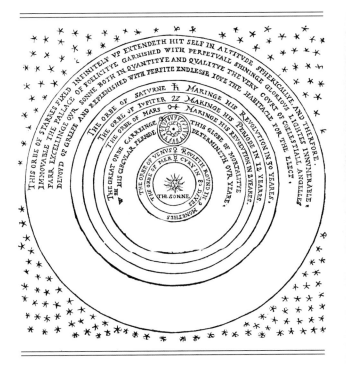

Figure 15.3 THOMAS DIGGES. The Sun-Centered Universe of Copernicus, from *A Perfit Description of the Celestiall Orbes*. 1576. The Huntington Library, San Marino, California. *This diagram drawn by the Englishman Thomas Digges agrees with the Copernican system except in one major way: Copernicus believed the universe was a finite, closed system, but Digges represents it as infinite, expressed in the stars scattered outside the orbit of fixed stars.*

Figure 15.4 *Tycho Brahe in His Observatory*. Engraving, from Brahe's *Astronomiae Instauratae Mechanica*. 1598. Joseph Regenstein Library, University of Chicago. *Tycho Brahe, the Danish astronomer who contributed to the Scientific Revolution, is shown in his observatory at Uraniborg, on the island of Ven, in Denmark. With right hand pointing upward, he instructs his assistants in the use of the wall quadrant, the semicircular, calibrated instrument (on his left) he developed for measuring the positions of stars. In the background, other assistants work with various astronomical instruments and perform chemical experiments.*

that they set a new standard for astronomical data (Figure 15.4).

Among Brahe's assistants was Johannes Kepler (1571–1630), a brilliant mathematician who dedicated his life to clarifying the theory of heliocentrism. When Brahe died, Kepler inherited his astronomical data. Inspired by Neoplatonism to make sense of the regular and continuous sightings of Brahe, Kepler in 1609 published *On the Motion of Mars*, setting forth his solution to the problem of what kept the planets in their orbits. His findings were expressed in two scientific laws that were elegant in their simplicity. In the first planetary law, Kepler substituted the ellipse for the circle as the descriptive shape of planetary orbits. And his second planetary law, which was set forth in a precise mathematical formula, accounted for each planet's variable speed within its respective orbit by showing that nearness to the sun affected the planet's behavior—the closer to the sun, the faster the speed, and the farther from the sun, the slower the speed. Together, these laws validated sun-centered astronomy.

Kepler continued to manipulate Brahe's undigested data, convinced that other mathematical laws could

be derived from observations of the heavens. In 1619 he arrived at a third planetary law, which relates the movement of one planet to another's. He showed that the squares of the length of time for each planet's orbit are in the same ratios as the cubes of their respective mean distances from the sun. Through this formula, he affirmed that the solar system itself is regular and organized by mathematically determined relationships. This was the first expression of the notion that the universe operates with clocklike regularity, an idea that became an article of faith by the end of the baroque age. Kepler took great pride in this discovery,

because it confirmed his Neoplatonist belief that there is a hidden mathematical harmony in the universe.

GALILEO GALILEI   While Kepler moved in the rarefied realm of theoretical, even mystical, science, one of his contemporaries was making major breakthroughs with experiments that relied on mathematics, logic, and instruments. This patient experimenter was Galileo Galilei (1564–1642), whose most valuable contributions were his accurate celestial observations and his work in terrestrial mechanics, the study of the action of forces on matter. Inspired by news that Dutch lens grinders had made a device for viewing distant objects, in 1609 Galileo made his own telescope, which enabled him to see stars invisible to the naked eye.

With these sightings, Galileo demonstrated that the size of the universe was exponentially greater than that computed on Ptolemaic principles. Further, his observations of the moon's rough surface and the sun's shifting dark spots provided additional proofs against the ancient arguments that the heavenly bodies were perfectly formed and never changed. But his most telling discovery was that the planet Jupiter has moons, a fact that contradicted the Ptolemaic belief that all celestial bodies must move about a common center. Galileo's observations, affirming that Jupiter's four satellites rotate around it in much the same way the six planets orbit the sun, hastened the demise of geocentrism.

Similarly, Galileo's research in terrestrial mechanics proved conclusively that both Aristotle and his fourteenth-century critics in Paris were wrong about one of the central questions of earthly motion—that is, the behavior of projectiles. Aristotle had claimed that projectiles stayed in flight because of the pushing mo-

tion of the air, and the Parisian scholars had countered with the theory of impetus. Through experimentation, Galileo showed that a mass that is moving will go on moving until some force stops it—the earliest expression of the modern law of inertia.

Galileo was probably the first scientist to make a clock a basic means for measuring time in his experiments. Like his contemporary Kepler, he reported his findings in the form of simple mathematical laws. Galileo's work was later validated by Newton, who proved that the laws of mechanics on earth are the same as the laws of mechanics in the sky.

At the same time Galileo was conducting the experiments that would make him a hero of modern science, he ran afoul of the religious authorities, who brought his career to a humiliating end. The church had by now abandoned its relative openness to ideas and was moving to stifle dissent. In 1633 Galileo was arrested by the Inquisition, the church court created in the 1200s to find and punish heretics. The renowned astronomer was charged with false teachings for his published support of the idea that the earth moves, a notion central to Copernicanism but untrue according to Aristotle and the church. Threatened with torture, Galileo recanted his views and was released. Despite living on for several years, he died a broken man. This episode abruptly ended Italy's role in the burgeoning revolution in science (Figure 15.5).

ISAAC NEWTON   Building on the research of the heirs to Copernicus, including Kepler's laws of planetary motion and Galileo's law of inertia, the English mathematician Isaac Newton (1642–1727) conceived a model of the universe that decisively overturned the Ptolemaic scheme and finished the revolution in astronomy begun by Copernicus. In Newton's world picture, there is uniform motion on earth and in the heavens. More significant, Newton presented a satisfactory explanation for what held the planets in their orbits: the force of gravity, the force that forms the heart of his theory of the universe (Figure 15.6).

In a precise mathematical formula, Newton computed the law of universal gravitation, the formula whereby every object in the world exerts an attraction on all other objects. By this law, the sun holds tightly in its grip each of the six planets, and each in turn influences to a lesser degree the sun and the other planets. The earth and its single moon as well as Jupiter and its four satellites similarly interact. Because of gravity, the heavenly bodies form a harmonious system in which each attracts the others.

Having described gravity and asserted its universal nature, Newton declined to speculate about what caused it to operate. For him, the universe behaved precisely as a machine, and his law was nothing but a description of its operation. Newton refused to speculate

◀ **Figure 15.5** PIETRO DA CORTONA. *Glorification of the Reign of Urban VIII.* 1633–1639. Fresco. Palazzo Barberini, Rome. *Pope Urban VIII (pope 1623–1644), born Maffeo Barberini, a member of the powerful Barberini family of Italy's Tuscan region, was active in state and church affairs, a patron of the arts (he supported Bernini's projects to beautify Rome), a poet and man of learning, and a longtime friend of Galileo. However, Galileo could not rely on his friend when he found himself before the Inquisition. Indeed, Pope Urban VIII sanctioned the Inquisition's second condemnation of Galileo. In this illusionistic ceiling painting, Pietro da Cortona (1596–1669) depicted Urban VIII's reign as a golden age—in the tradition of art used as propaganda. The ceiling design is a complex blend of religious, artistic, and dynastic symbols. Mythological figures, whose heyday predated the Christian era, are portrayed in the shadows—symbolic of their pagan roots. And the illuminated figures in the center represent people who have been exposed to the truth of Christianity. Near the top of the frame floats the personification of Religion, holding symbols of the papal office—the triple crown and two crossed keys. Below Religion, angelic figures and cherubs carry a giant laurel wreath—the Roman emblem of triumph—and inside the wreath are three huge bees—part of the Barberini coat of arms.*

German thinker, invented a more useful version of calculus. By 1800 Leibniz's symbols had become the universally accepted language of calculus. Even though Newton's work culminated in the birth of modern science, he continued to cling to many older attitudes—manifested, for example, by his extensive researches in alchemy and theology. Indeed, Newton's theological writings outnumber in length those of his scientific writings. At the same time that he pursued truth about the natural world, using mathematics and careful observation, he cared little for his own scientific achievements. Newton believed his lasting monument would be his religious writings, and as a pious Christian, he devoted his last years to demonstrating that the biblical prophecies were coming true.

Medicine and Chemistry

While Western understanding of the universe at its outer limits was being radically altered, breakthroughs were also occurring in medical knowledge and the foundations of modern chemistry were being laid.

MEDICINE In 1600 anatomical knowledge was extremely limited, primarily because Christians forbade the violation of corpses, as they believed that the body would be resurrected. Biological research, which had been limited to the dissection of animals and then equated to parts of the human body, led to misinformation and half-truths. Also, the authority of ancient Greek thinkers reigned supreme in biology. Aristotle's investigations of the natural sciences and Galen's research and findings in medicine were lost in the fall of Rome, but some works were preserved by Arab scholars and then translated from Arabic into Latin by Western scholars from the eleventh century onward (see Chapter 8). Though offering rival theories, Aristotle and Galen shared many false ideas: air moves directly from the lungs into the heart, blood flows from the veins to the outer part of the body, and different types of blood course in the arteries and the veins.

The debate over how blood circulated was resolved in the early 1600s by scientists at the University of Padua in Italy, the most prominent of whom was Andreas Vesalius. Vesalius's anatomical studies first proved Galen's explanation of the body's structure and muscle system to be incorrect (see Chapter 13). Later, Vesalius concluded that Galen's theory about the circulation of the blood—that it passed from one side of the heart to the other through the septum, an impermeable membrane—was also erroneous (Figure 15.7).

The research of Vesalius and his successors paved the way for William Harvey (1578–1657), an English scientist who studied medicine at the University of Padua

Figure 15.6 GODFREY KNELLER. *Sir Isaac Newton.* 1702. Oil on canvas, 29¾ × 24½". National Portrait Gallery, London. *As the most celebrated intellectual of his generation, the middle-class Newton was given star treatment in this portrait by the reigning society painter in England. Decked out fashionably in an elaborate baroque wig, Newton peers somewhat uncomfortably at the viewer. The likeness tends to support Newton's reputation for vanity and ostentation.*

beyond what mathematics could prove, and modern scientists have followed his lead, preferring to ignore the why of things and to concentrate on the how and what.

Newton's views were set forth in his authoritative work *Mathematical Principles of Natural Philosophy.* Known more familiarly as the *Principia* (the first word of its Latin title), this book soon gained an authority that made Newton the modern world's equivalent of Aristotle. By the eighteenth century, the English poet Alexander Pope could justifiably write:

> Nature and Nature's Laws lay hid in Night;
> God said, *Let Newton be!* and All was *Light.*

Newton also invented a form of calculus, a mathematical method of analysis that uses symbolic notation. This breakthrough had huge potential for solving problems in physics and mechanics by providing a tool for computing quantities that had nonlinear variations. Simultaneously and independently of Newton, Gottfried Wilhelm von Leibniz [LIBE-nits] (1646–1716), a

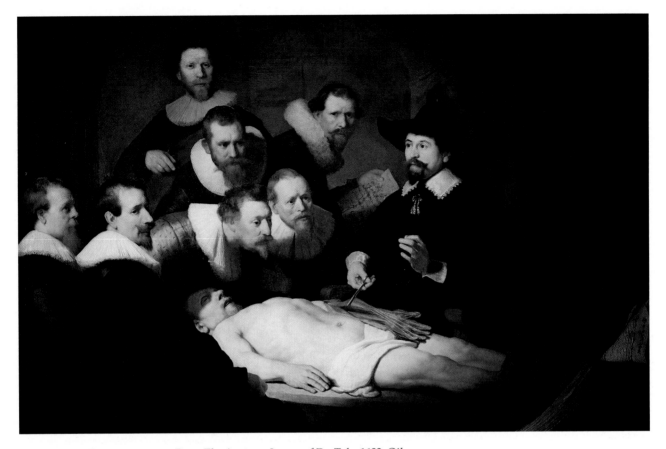

Figure 15.7 REMBRANDT VAN RIJN. *The Anatomy Lesson of Dr. Tulp.* 1632. Oil on canvas, 66¾ × 85¼". Mauritshuis, The Hague. *The pioneering work of Vesalius made the study of anatomy a central concern of medical science in the seventeenth century. In this painting, Rembrandt depicts Dr. Nicholas Tulp of Amsterdam as he demonstrates the dissection of the left arm. Rembrandt's use of baroque effects, such as the dramatic light on the corpse, the contrast between Dr. Tulp's calm demeanor and the inquisitive faces of his pupils, and the flayed arm of the corpse, makes this an arresting image.*

(1597–1602), to offer the correct view of the circulation of the blood. Using arithmetical calculations, as had Newton, Harvey proved that a constant quantity of blood continuously circulates throughout the body, thereby invalidating Galen's ebb-and-flow theory. However, Harvey lacked knowledge of the capillaries, the connectors between the arteries and the veins. Later, in 1661, the Italian scientist Marcello Malpighi [mahl-PEE-gee] (1628–1694), with the aid of a microscope, identified the capillaries, which made possible an accurate and complete account of the blood's circulation.

CHEMISTRY   The English physicist Robert Boyle (1627–1691) established the groundwork for modern chemistry. Like Newton, Boyle believed that the universe is a machine, and he was also convinced that the workings of nature could be revealed only through experimental study—that is, the inductive method. His zeal for experimentation led him to study the behavior of

gases and to formulate the famous law that bears his name.

Boyle also attempted to separate chemistry from alchemy, a set of magical practices that had been associated with chemistry since the time of the ancient Greeks. Medieval European scholars, who were often alchemists, searched vainly for the "philosopher's stone" that would turn lead into gold. Boyle rejected alchemy's assumptions and methodology, and sought to understand only those chemical reactions that happened naturally and could be analyzed in mathematical terms.

Technology

Galileo's studies of celestial and terrestrial motion and Newton's explanation of gravity may be difficult to understand, but their experiments led to inventions, in particular, the pendulum clock, that impacted life in seventeenth-century Europe. This clock, which measured time more precisely and accurately than any other clock heretofore, soon determined how people conducted business, performed religious duties, and planned their daily lives. The clock became a metaphor for the human condition, symbolizing the brevity of life and its graduated moments filled with unexplored potential.

Humans had built instruments for measuring time for millennia, such as sundials, water clocks, and hourglasses, but none of them could keep accurate time. In medieval Europe, pressure to measure time more precisely came from the church because, with its monasteries, nunneries, schools, and cathedrals, it needed devices to set schedules for prayer, work, lessons, and daily activities. Records confirm that the earliest clocks were installed in English cathedrals by the thirteenth century. By 1335 Milan, Italy, had the first public clock and during the fourteenth century several cities, including Paris and Rouen, France, erected municipal tower clocks. These clocks were operated by heavy weights attached to cords around a drum and regulated by a circular escapement mechanism and sets of gears.

A German locksmith, Peter Henlein (1480–1542), invented the coil spring clock, which reduced the size and weight of the timekeeping mechanism—thus allowing for table clocks and eventually watches. Henlein's early timepieces could be carried around or placed on a table. Further advances during the sixteenth and seventeenth centuries improved clocks' accuracy and dependability. By 1600 clocks were all given an upright design, though they remained bulky and difficult to regulate.

The development of the pendulum clock came in two stages: the work of Galileo and that of Christian Huygens [HOI-genz] (1629–1695). In the 1580s, Galileo, while studying the properties of motion, observed that the period of oscillation of a swinging pendulum was always the same. Although he recognized the importance of the pendulum, he failed to design a pendulum clock. Huygens, a Dutch mathematician, physicist, and astronomer, while studying the heavens, realized he needed an accurate time instrument to calibrate his findings. Upon discovering that a swinging pendulum could regulate a clock, he built a vertical clock with a pendulum, which kept time more accurately than any existing clock. The pendulum clock's error rate of less than a minute a day meant that the time required for a "natural" period of oscillation was constant and dependable (Figure 15.8).

A few years later an English clockmaker devised the seconds pendulum and improved the escapement mechanism. The two pendulums—one for the hours,

Figure 15.8 A Reconstruction of Huygens's 1656 Clock. Science Museum, London. *Huygens's clock used the old-fashioned escapement mechanism, but he added a pair of gear wheels to adjust for the precise swinging of the pendulum, to ensure accurate timekeeping. On the main dial, the hours hand is the shorter one, rotating twice every day. The longer hand was the seconds hand, and it required five minutes to revolve. This reconstruction also shows a minutes hand in the small dial at the bottom, which rotated counterclockwise once every hour.*

the other for the seconds—and other parts of the clock were encased in wood, thus creating the so-called grandfather clock. This invention made it possible to place clocks anywhere—in palaces, courts, homes, offices, businesses, shops, laboratories, and schools. Mechanical clocks were now on their way to becoming part of the collective consciousness of modern life.

The Impact of Science on Philosophy

The Scientific Revolution's profound influence on Western thought also gave rise to a type of literature that reflected the impact of science on the nonscientific culture. Three prominent contributors to this literature were the English jurist and statesman Francis Bacon and two French mathematicians, René Descartes and Blaise Pascal, whose writings continued the French rationalist tradition begun by Montaigne in the 1500s (see Chapter 13).

FRANCIS BACON   Francis Bacon (1561–1626) possessed the ability to write lucid prose about science and its methodology, which appealed to a curious and educated public. In clarifying the techniques and the aims of the new science, he became the spokesman for the "experimenters," those who believed that the future of science lay in discarding Aristotle. Condemning Aristotle for relying on deductive reasoning and unproven axioms, Bacon advocated the inductive method, the procedure that embraced the conducting of experiments, the drawing of conclusions, and the testing of results in other experiments. His claims were not new, but they were forcibly and memorably expressed. Bacon was convinced that scientific discoveries would lead to mastery over the natural world, a view summarized in the famous phrase attributed to him, "Knowledge is power."

RENÉ DESCARTES   An outstanding critic of the belief that the experimental method was the correct path to knowledge was René Descartes [day-KAHRT] (1596–1650), a philosopher who urged a purely mathematical approach in science (Figure 15.9). Descartes' love of numbers came from a mystical side of his personality, which inspired his belief that mathematics holds the key to nature. Descartes founded analytic geometry,

the branch of mathematics that describes geometric figures by the formulas of algebra, and authored a widely influential philosophical treatise, *Discourse on Method*, published in 1637.

In the *Discourse on Method*, Descartes outlined four steps in his approach to knowledge: to accept nothing as true unless it is self-evident; to split problems into manageable parts; to solve problems starting with the simplest and moving to the most complex; and to review and reexamine the solutions. He used deductive logic in his method, making inferences only from general statements. But more important than his emphasis on deductive reasoning was his insistence on mathematical clarity: he refused to accept anything as true unless it had the persuasiveness of a proof in geometry.

Descartes' most influential contributions to Western philosophy were skepticism and a dualistic theory of knowledge. Descartes rejected the authoritarian method of medieval scholasticism and began with universal doubt in order to determine what was absolutely certain in the universe. Step-by-step, he questioned the existence of God, of the world, and of his own body. But he soon established that he could not doubt the existence of his own doubting self. He reached this absolute conclusion in the oft-quoted *"Cogito ergo sum"* ("I think, therefore I am"). Having first destroyed the

Figure 15.9   FRANZ HALS. *René Descartes.* After 1649. Oil on canvas, 30¾ × 26¾". Louvre. *In this likeness, Frans Hals, the great Dutch portrait artist and contemporary of Rembrandt, has captured the complex personality of the great French philosopher and mathematician. Descartes' piercing gaze shows his skeptical spirit. His disdainful presence and rough features reveal his early background as a soldier. Hals apparently felt no need to flatter his sitter in this compelling portrait.*

age-old certainties, he then, through deduction, re-established the existence of his own body, the world, and, finally, God.

Descartes' speculations were aimed at identifying clear and distinct ideas that were certain for everyone, but his efforts had a deeply ironic result: his thought fostered the growing awareness among the educated elite that absolute truth is not possible. Many who read his *Discourse* were unimpressed by his rational arguments, but they nevertheless accepted his radical doubt, and some even became atheists. That his work contributed to the rise of atheism would have horrified Descartes since, to his own way of thinking, he had proven the existence of God. He had used skepticism merely as a means of achieving certainty.

Descartes' other great legacy, dualism, made a division between the material world and the human soul or mind. According to Descartes, mathematics permitted natural truths to be revealed to the human understanding. He thought, however, that the mind itself was beyond mathematical knowing and hence was not a fit subject for study. From this dichotomy arise two contrasting traditions: the scientists, who reduce the natural world to order through mathematics; and the thinkers, who focus on human psychology. The second group—the psychologists—represent another ironic legacy, for through the study of such topics as depth psychology and alienation, they want to prove that Descartes was wrong and that the human self is knowable in all its irrationality.

Even though Descartes' speculations were aimed at achieving certainty, his focus on deductive logic has not withstood the test of time. This is because modern scientists think that inductive reasoning—building a model of truth on the facts—is more valid. But Descartes was proven correct in assigning to mathematics its paramount role in establishing precision and certainty in science. Today, those sciences that have the greatest degree of mathematical rigor have better reputations for accuracy and believability than those sciences whose formulations cannot be achieved mathematically.

Descartes made another contribution to the Scientific Revolution when he applied his method of inquiry to terrestrial mechanics. It was he, rather than Galileo, who gave final expression to the law of inertia. He concluded that a projectile would continue to move in a straight line until it was interrupted by some force. With this language Descartes finally debunked the myth of circular motion, and his definition of the law of inertia became part of the scientific synthesis of Newton.

BLAISE PASCAL   Descartes' work was barely published before it elicited a strong reaction from Blaise Pascal [BLEHZ pas-KAHL] (1623–1662), an anguished thinker who made radical doubt the cornerstone of his beliefs.

Like Descartes, Pascal left his mark in mathematics, notably in geometry and the study of probability. Pascal was a Jansenist, a member of a Catholic sect that to some observers was Calvinistic because it stressed original sin and denied free will. Pascal's Jansenism permeates his masterpiece, the *Pensées,* or *Thoughts,* a meditative work of intense feeling published in 1670, eight years after his death.

In the *Pensées,* Pascal went beyond Descartes' skepticism, concluding that human beings can know neither the natural world nor themselves. Despite this seemingly universal doubt, Pascal still reasoned that there are different levels of truth. Regarding science, he thought that what he called the geometric spirit—that is, mathematics—could lead scholars to a limited knowledge of nature. Pascal's most controversial opinions, however, concerned human psychology. He felt that the passions enabled human beings to comprehend truths about God and religion directly. He summed up this idea in his oft-quoted "The heart has reasons that reason does not know." In another passage, he justified his continued belief in God, not by intellectual proofs in the manner of Descartes, but by a wager—a notion he derived from his probability studies. Pascal claimed his faith in God rested on a bet: if God exists, then the bettor wins everything, but if God does not exist, then nothing is lost. Pascal's fervent belief in God in the face of debilitating doubt makes him a forerunner of modern Christian existentialism (see Chapter 21).

Ironies and Contradictions of the Scientific Revolution

Ironies abound in the Scientific Revolution. To begin with, only a handful of thinkers contributed to the scientific changes. The vast majority of the populace remained unaware of the new findings; besides, they could not have understood the changes even if they had been informed of them. Furthermore, those who made the scientific discoveries were engaged primarily in solving practical problems rather than in trying to build a new model of the universe. They also believed that what they were doing was entirely within an orthodox Christian framework (although some were aware that religious leaders might think otherwise), and few foresaw that their efforts would eventually lead to a conflict between religion and science.

Another irony was that not all of the scientific advancements were original creations; some were rooted in late medieval rationalism and the Renaissance revival of Classical learning. Indeed, the new thinkers were often more concerned with working out minor inconsistencies in the calculations of medieval scholars than in overturning the accepted picture of the universe. Not only did seventeenth-century science have roots in medieval science, but it was also influenced by superstitions and mystical beliefs. During the Scientific Revolution, even the greatest intellectuals still held firmly to nonrational medieval views. Brahe and Kepler, for example, supported their research by pursuing careers as court astrologers. Harvey imagined that the heart restored a "spirituous" quality to the blood during circulation. Newton and Boyle were both involved in secret experiments with alchemy. A mystical experience lay behind Descartes' mathematical zeal, and Neoplatonism motivated the thought of Copernicus, Kepler, and Galileo. Many scholars were conventionally devout in their religious convictions, and Newton tried to correlate biblical prophecy with history. Despite their medieval heritage, these scholars did point European thought in a new direction.

THE REVOLUTION IN POLITICAL PHILOSOPHY

Political philosophy reflected the nature of the shifting political, economic, social, scientific, and religious institutions of the seventeenth century. The Thirty Years' War, the wars of Louis XIV, and the English civil war (see Chapter 14) forced political theorists to reconsider such basic themes as the nature of government, the relations between rulers and subjects, the rivalries among sovereign states, and the consequences of war on society and the individual.

Political writers, stimulated by the rise of sovereign states in the 1500s, addressed themselves in the 1600s to the fundamental questions of who holds the final sovereignty in a state and how power should be exercised. Realizing that new states were rapidly extinguishing the rights held by the feudal estates, these theorists tried to define the best form of government. They all supported their arguments with the same sources—the Bible, the concept of natural law, scientific discoveries, and their own views of human nature—but they came to widely differing conclusions.

Natural Law and Divine Right: Grotius and Bossuet

Hugo Grotius [GRO-she-us] (1583–1645) thought that natural law should govern the relations between states. He arrived at this belief chiefly because of his personal sufferings during the Thirty Years' War and the intolerance that he observed in religious disputes. A Dutch citizen but also an ambassador for Sweden, he

saw at first hand the ambiguity of diplomatic relations between the great military powers—England, France, Austria, Prussia, and Russia.

Drawing on the idea of natural law as set forth by the ancient Stoic thinkers, Grotius urged the states to follow a law that applied to all nations, was eternal and unchanging, and could be understood by human reason. Like the Stoics, Grotius was convinced that natural law was founded on human reason and was not the gift of a loving God. He rejected original sin, believing instead that human beings are not motivated merely by selfish drives. He thought that because all mortals are rational, they want to improve themselves and to create a just and fair society. In his treatise *The Law of War and Peace*, Grotius applied this rational view of human nature to his description of sovereign states. He concluded that nations, like individuals, should treat each other as they would expect to be treated. Today, the writings of Grotius are recognized as the starting point of international law.

Taking a contrary point of view to Grotius was Bishop Bossuet [bo-SWAY] (1627–1704), who defended the theory that kings rule by divine right. This French church leader echoed the opinions of James I of England, who maintained that God bestowed power on certain national monarchs. The French bishop avowed that absolutism, as ordained by God in past societies, was now manifested in the rule of Louis XIV, king of France. Louis XIV, as God's chosen vessel on earth, had the power to intervene in the lives of his subjects, not because of natural law, but by divine right. According to this theory, for corrupt and sinful humans to rebel against the king was to go against God's plan. The bishop believed that the age's conflicts made autocratic rule a political necessity. Bossuet's belief in autocracy was shared by the Englishman Thomas Hobbes, although Bossuet explained absolute rule in different terms.

Absolutism and Liberalism: Hobbes and Locke

Thomas Hobbes (1588–1679) grew up in an England increasingly torn by religious, social, and political discord. A trained classicist and a student of the new science, Hobbes came to believe that everything, including human beings and their social acts, could be explained by using mechanistic, natural laws to describe various states of motion or movement.

Hobbes's efforts to synthesize a universal philosophy founded on a geometric design and activated by some form of energy culminated in his best-known work, *The Leviathan*, published in 1651 (Figure 15.10). *The Leviathan* sets forth a theory of government based

Figure 15.10   Frontispiece of *The Leviathan*. 1651. The Bancroft Library, University of California, Berkeley. *The original illustration for Hobbes's* Leviathan *conveys the political message of this controversial work in symbolic terms. Towering over the landscape is the mythical ruler, whose body is a composite of all his subjects and in whose hands are the sword and the scepter, symbols of his absolute power. Below this awesome figure is a well-ordered and peaceful village and countryside—Hobbes's political dream come true.*

on the pessimistic view that individuals are driven by two basic forces, the fear of death and the quest for power. Hobbes imagined what life would be like if these two natural inclinations were allowed free rein and there were no supreme power to control them. Hobbes described human life under these circumstances as "solitary, poor, nasty, brutish, and short."

Hobbes thought that rational human beings would recognize their miserable situation in a state of nature, give up such an existence, and form a civil society un-

der the rule of one man. The first step to create a civil society was to draw up a **social contract** between the ruler and the subjects. By the terms of this covenant, the subjects surrendered all their claims to sovereignty and bestowed absolute power on the ruler. The sovereign's commands were to be carried out by all those under him, including the religious and civic leaders. Always prepared for war, the sovereign would keep peace at home and protect the land from its enemies abroad.

SLICE OF LIFE
Innocent or Guilty? A Seventeenth-Century Witch Trial

SUZANNE GAUDRY
Trial Court Records, June 1652

Suzanne Gaudry, an illiterate old woman, was accused of witchcraft, including such crimes as renouncing "God, Lent, and baptism," worshiping the devil, attending witches' Sabbaths, and desecrating the Eucharist wafer. Questioned by the court at Rieux, France, she confessed to some charges but later recanted. Because confession was necessary for conviction, she was subjected to torture, and once again she confessed. She was then condemned and sentenced to be tied to a gallows, strangled, and to have her body burned.

On [June 27], . . . this prisoner [Suzanne Gaudry], before being strapped down, was admonished to maintain herself in her first confessions and to renounce her lover [the devil].

—Said that she denies everything she has said, and that she has no lover. Feeling herself being strapped down, says that she is not a witch, while struggling to cry.[1] . . .

—Says . . . she is not a witch. And upon being asked why she confessed to being one, said that she was forced to say it.

Told that she was not forced, that on the contrary she declared herself to be a witch without any threat.

—Says that she confessed it and that she is not a witch, and being a little stretched [on the rack] screams ceaselessly that she is not a witch, invoking the name of Jesus and Our Lady of Grace, not wanting to say any other thing. . . .

The mark having been probed by the officer, in the presence of Doctor Bouchain, it was adjudged by the aforesaid doctor and officer truly to be the mark of the devil.[2]

Being more tightly stretched upon the torture-rack, urged to maintain her confessions.

—Said that it was true that she is a witch and that she would maintain what she has said. Asked how long she has been in subjugation to the devil.

—Answers that it was twenty years ago that the devil appeared to her, being in her lodgings in the form of a man dressed in a little cow-hide and black breeches. . . .

Asked if her lover has had carnal copulation with her, and how many times.

—To that she did not answer anything; then, making believe that she was ill, not another word could be drawn from her.

---

[1]Not crying was thought to be a sign of witchcraft.
[2]Perhaps a birthmark or other skin blemish. It was commonly believed that witches were marked by the devil, as a sign of their intimate union, and when the mark was pricked, no pain would occur nor any blood flow out.

INTERPRETING THIS SLICE OF LIFE

1. *What* were the charges against Suzanne Gaudry? 2. *How* did she respond to the charges? 3. In *what* ways does the official court record reveal the attitudes and reactions of that time and place? 4. *Did* Suzanne Gaudry receive a fair trial? *Explain.* 5. *Compare and contrast* this trial with the treatment of suspect criminals today.

Hobbes made no distinction between the ruler of a monarchy and the head of a commonwealth, for he was less concerned with the form of government than with the need to hold in check destructive human impulses. In the next generation, Hobbes's pessimistic philosophy provoked a reaction from John Locke, who repudiated absolutism and advocated a theory of government by the people.

Despite their contradictory messages, Hobbes and John Locke (1632–1704) had been subjected to similar influences. Both adapted ideas from the new science, witnessed the English civil war, and sought safety on the Continent because of their political views. But Locke rejected Hobbes's gloomy view of humanity and his theory of absolutism; he taught instead that

human nature is potentially good and that human beings are capable of governing themselves. The two thinkers originated opposing schools of modern political thought: from Hobbes stems the absolutist, authoritarian tradition, and from Locke descends the school of liberalism. Their works represent two of the most significant legacies of the baroque age to the modern world.

Locke set forth his political theories in his *Two Treatises of Government,* which he published anonymously in 1690. In the *First Treatise* he refuted the divine right of kings, and in the *Second Treatise* he laid out the model for rule by the people. The latter work has become the classic expression of early **liberalism.** In it Locke described the origins, characteristics, and purpose of the ideal political system—a government limited by laws, subject to the will of its citizens, and existing to protect life and property.

Locke shared some of Hobbes's ideas: humans possess reason, human life is violent and disorderly in the state of nature, human beings must form civil governments to protect themselves, and a social contract is the necessary basis of civil society. But Locke believed that basic rights, including life and property, exist in the state of nature. He also believed that human beings are fundamentally decent, law abiding, and slow to want change. From these principles, he concluded that human beings would contract together to create a limited government that had no other purpose than the protection of the basic natural rights of life and property.

Locke rejected the idea that by making a social contract citizens surrender their sovereignty to a ruler. He argued instead that the people choose rulers who protect their rights in a fiduciary trust; that is, they expect their rulers to obey the social contract and govern equitably. If the rulers break the agreement, then the people have the right to revolt, overthrow the government, and reclaim their natural rights. Unlike Hobbes, Locke asserted that rulers possess only limited authority and that their control must be held in check by a balanced governmental system and a separation of powers. Locke's tract influenced American and French political thinkers and patriots, who used its ideas to justify the right to revolt against a tyrant and to establish a government of checks and balances.

Locke was not only a political theorist but also the preeminent English philosopher of his day. He grappled with many of the same problems as Descartes, although his conclusions were radically different from the French thinker's. Locke's significant philosophical work, *An Essay Concerning Human Understanding,* published in 1690 (the same year *Two Treatises of Government* was published), addressed the question "How is knowledge acquired?" Descartes had proposed that the germs of ideas were inborn and that people were born knowing certain truths, such as mathematical principles and logical relationships; education required nothing more than the strenuous use of the intellect without concern for new information from the senses.

Locke repudiated these views and described the mind at birth as a **tabula rasa** ("blank tablet") on which all human experiences were recorded. Locke maintained that everything human beings can know must first be received through their senses (a basically Aristotelian viewpoint) and then recorded in their minds. The raw sensory data are manipulated by the mental faculties, such as comparing and contrasting, so that abstract concepts and generalizations are formed in the mind. As a result, reason and experience are united in human thought and together determine what is real for each person. Locke's explanation of the origin of ideas is the basis of modern-day empiricism—the theory that all knowledge is derived from or originates in human experience. His influence has been so great that many of his ideas seem to the modern reader to be just common sense.

EUROPEAN EXPLORATION AND EXPANSION

Explorations begun in the late 1400s had led to a series of encounters with new peoples that slowly eroded the isolation and self-absorption of Europe. In the 1500s, the pace of explorations quickened and the globe was circumnavigated—events that intensified rivalries among the European states, increased the Continent's economic power, and diffused European culture and customs around the world.

Europe's success overseas was achieved through a series of permanent settlements in North and South America and by the opening of new trade routes to the Far East (Map 15.1). Expansion and colonization affected Europe in numerous ways: the introduction of new foodstuffs and other products, the establishment of innovative business methods, the disruption of old economic and social patterns, the introduction of novel ways of looking at the world, and the adoption of new symbols and themes in the arts. Whatever may have been the beneficial or harmful effects of these changes on European life, the negative effects of the introduction of Western culture on non-Europeans tended to outweigh the good. In Africa, the Europeans expanded the slave trade; in North, Central, and South America and the Caribbean, they annihilated many native tribes; and everywhere they forced trade agreements favorable to themselves on the local people.

The earliest leaders in the European penetration of the Western Hemisphere were Portugal and Spain (see Encounters in Chapters 12 and 13). Since the 1500s, these two states had claimed South and Central America and the southern reaches of North America. Where possible, they mined the rich gold and silver veins, flooding Europe with the new wealth and gaining power and influence for themselves. But Spain's and Portugal's ties with the New World languished during the baroque age. At the same time, England, France, and the Netherlands accelerated their explorations, especially in North America (Table 15.1). In 1607 English farmers settled along the Atlantic seaboard in Virginia, ready to exploit the land, and in 1620 English Puritans

LEARNING THROUGH MAPS

Map 15.1 EXPANSION OF EUROPE, 1715

This map shows the presence of Europeans around the globe in the early eighteenth century. 1. *Notice* the overseas holdings of the five European countries identified on the map. 2. *Observe* the differing encounter patterns—coastal and inland—on the various continents. 3. *Which* country has the largest number of overseas holdings? 4. On *which* continent is there the greatest European presence? 5. *Where* are conflicts among European powers most likely to occur? 6. *Which* areas of the world seem less touched by European expansion?

emigrated to New England in search of religious freedom (Figure 15.11). To the north, French explorers, missionaries, and fur traders founded Quebec in 1608 and then spread along the St. Lawrence River valley and southward into the Great Lakes region. At the same time, the French moved into the Caribbean basin, occupying many islands in the West Indies. After 1655 the English worked their way into the southern part of the Atlantic coast and the West Indies. These newly arrived colonists eventually either drove out the Spaniards or drastically reduced their influence. Meanwhile,

Table 15.1 SETTLEMENTS IN THE NEW WORLD DURING THE BAROQUE AGE

LOCATION	DATE OF FOUNDING	SETTLERS
Jamestown (Virginia)	1607	English
Quebec (Canada)	1608	French
Plymouth (Massachusetts)	1620	English
Saint Kitts (West Indies)	1623	English
New Amsterdam (New York)	1624	Dutch
Barbados	1627	English
Brazil	1632–1654	Dutch
Curaçao (West Indies)	1634	Dutch
Martinique (West Indies)	1635	French
Saint Lucia (West Indies)	1635	French
Honduras (Belize)	1638	English
Saint Domingue (Haiti)	1644	French
Bahamas (West Indies)	1648	English
Jamaica (West Indies) (captured from Spain)	1655	English

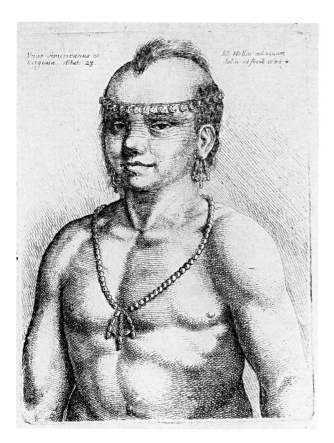

Figure 15.11   HOLLAR. *Indian of Virginia, Male.* 1645. Etching, 4 × 3″. Courtesy of the New York Public Library. *This engraving portrays a Native American male, who was probably one of many brought to London in the early seventeenth century. Whether his presence abroad was voluntary or involuntary is unknown, but the artist depicts him as a proud man with dignity. A translation of the Latin inscription reads, in part: at the upper left, "An American from Virginia. Age 23," and, at the upper right, "W. Hollar . . . made from Life 1645." W. Hollar is Wenceslaus Hollar (1607–1677), an artist from what is now the Czech Republic, who lived in London in the mid–seventeenth century and worked for aristocratic patrons with ties to the English court.*

Figure 15.12   ANONYMOUS. *Dutch Shipyard.* Engraving. Seventeenth century. *The Dutch were successful traders, explorers, and colonists because of their business practices and maritime technology. In the Dutch Republic, leaders encouraged entrepreneurial projects such as the Dutch East Indies Company, founded in 1602. This joint stock company—a trading company of investors who pooled their funds and shared the risk to make money in an overseas venture—made many very rich. To transport their cargoes overseas, the Dutch built spacious and fast merchant ships. Dutch sailors and crews ranked at the top, rivaled only by the English. Dutch naval vessels, or men-of-war, were well constructed, seaworthy, and armed. Although they were smaller than the heavier Portuguese and Spanish galleons, they were easier to maneuver, required less wind to sail, and subsequently drove those ships off the high seas.*

Figure 15.13 *A Chinese Interpretation of Dutch Traders.* Porcelain. Ch'ing dynasty, K'ang-hsi period, seventeenth century. Formerly owned by the Dutch East Indies Company. *As Europeans spread Western culture around the globe in the seventeenth century, they were sometimes confronted with images of themselves created by artists in other cultures, as in these Chinese representations of Dutch traders. These figures express a stereotype of a European man, dressed in the costume of the day (long coat, knee breeches, and hat) and with distinctive features (marked cheekbones, curly hair [wig?], and smiling face). Dating from the reign of China's Emperor K'ang-hsi (1661–1722), these porcelains were made as "curiosities" for the European market. They are enameled glaze porcelains, in which green, yellow, purple, and white enamels were applied to a prefired, or biscuit, body and then given a second firing.*

the Dutch set up their own colonies in North America, on the banks of the Hudson River and in scattered areas of the mid-Atlantic region (Figure 15.12).

The English, French, and Dutch recognized the economic advantages of financing more explorers and sending families abroad to establish permanent colonies. Relying chiefly on state or royal charters, they created large overseas settlements that soon led to a brisk trade in which raw products from the New World were exchanged for finished goods from the Old World. William Penn (1644–1718) founded Pennsylvania in 1681 on the basis of such a charter from England.

In the Far East, Europeans relied less on charters than on joint-stock companies, a private enterprise technique exploited by both England and the Netherlands. The English East India Company and the Dutch East India Company opened trade routes and secured markets in the Far East (see Encounters in Chapters 14 and 15). The two companies made lucrative contracts

with Indian princes and Japanese and Chinese state officials (Figure 15.13).

RESPONSES TO THE REVOLUTIONS IN THOUGHT

The scientific discoveries, the growth of skepticism, the new political theories, and the overseas explorations provoked a variety of responses among the artists, intellectuals, and educated public. Among the aristocracy, for example, a new social type arrived—the **virtuoso,** a person who dabbled in the latest science and gave it respectability. A new type of literature also evolved, in which scientific concepts and discoveries were popularized for the consumption of an educated elite. The seventeenth century found ample creative expression among those who embraced the innovations and change and their implications.

Figure 15.14 J. GOYTON after a painting by S. Leclerc. *Louis XIV at the Academy of Science.* 1671. Engraving. Bibliothèque Nationale, Paris. *Science became fashionable during the baroque age, and rulers provided funds to advance the new discoveries. Louis XIV, king of France, is shown here visiting the Royal Academy of Science, the premier organization of scientists in France. From this period dates the close alliance between science and government, a linkage based on mutual self-interest.*

The Spread of Ideas

In the dawn of the Scientific Revolution, some scientists and intellectuals realized that new scientific findings needed to be given the widest dissemination possible, since the information would be of inestimable value to others who were engaged in their own research. At first, they exchanged information informally through personal contacts or by chance encounters in the universities. But by midcentury, the scientific societies were spreading new knowledge through their corresponding members and by publishing journals. The first one was in England, where Charles II granted a charter to the Royal Society in 1662. In 1666 Louis XIV supported the creation of the Royal Academy of Science (Figure 15.14), and in 1700 German scientists instituted the Berlin Academy of Science.

At the same time, many intellectually curious men and women, who wanted to learn more about the changes taking place in the sciences and mathematics but who lacked specialized training, turned to writers who could demystify the new discoveries and explain them in popular language. One who responded to this interest was the French thinker Bernard de Fontenelle [fon-tuh-NELL] (1657–1757), the long-lived secretary of France's Royal Academy of Science. His *Conversations on the Plurality of Worlds* set the early standard for this type of popular literature. With learning and wit, Fontenelle created a dialogue between himself and an inquiring countess in which Newtonian physics and the new astronomy were explained in an informative and entertaining way. Through publicists like Fontenelle, the new theories and ideas became available to the general reading public.

ENCOUNTER

The Sinews of Trade

In 1616 Sir Thomas Roe (about 1581–1644), King James I's ambassador, paid homage, with gifts, to Emperor Jahangir [je-HAN-ger] (1569–1627), or the Great Mogul, at his court in Agra, India (Encounter figure 15.1). Roe, through his strong personality, patience, and palace intrigues, negotiated a trade outlet, or "factory," the East India Company at Surat on India's west coast. This seemingly insignificant encounter linked one of the richest, most powerful empires in the world and a small island kingdom until the mid–twentieth century.

The English, as the Portuguese and the Dutch before them, were interested in turning a profit from Indian goods and products, not establishing a colony. They held in contempt or viewed with amazement the rich, eclectic Mogul civilization built on Persian, Indian, and central Asian cultures that had emerged after the Mongol invasions of the thirteenth century. As Christians they were offended by many Hindu and Muslim practices and beliefs. Although unimpressed with the Moguls' achievements in architecture and technology, in the metal arts, and in much of their fine arts and jewelry, they immediately recognized the economic value of Indian textiles, especially cotton goods. English merchants began importing linen cloth from the Gujarat area of western India to be made into household goods and, in the seventeenth century, into clothes. Madras cotton cloth, from the town of Madras, and chintz, a type of printed cotton cloth, along with Persian silks also became popular.

During the 1600s, the East India Company forced more concessions from the Mogul rulers, and as the Mogul Empire collapsed in the early 1700s, the English meddled in local political affairs. In the mid–eighteenth century they drove out their remaining rival, the French, and gained control of the country through a network of princes and by economic pressures. In the nineteenth century the Industrial Revolution in Europe ruined the Indian textile industry, for the Brit-ish could now ship their own finished cotton goods to India and sell them at a profit. India still remained vital to British interests for her raw materials and as a market for English manufactured products. Her indispensable position in the British Empire became more evident in 1876 when Queen Victoria was made empress of India. Yet, within seventy-five years, in 1947, India, led by the Indian nationalist and spiritual leader Mahatma Gandhi [ma-HAT-ma GAN-de] (1869–1948), gained its independence, emerging as the most populous democracy in the world. India's independence also initiated the beginning of the dismantling of the British Empire (see Encounter in Chapter 20).

LEARNING FROM THE ENCOUNTER

1. *Why* did the Portuguese, Dutch, and English go to India? 2. *What* did India gain from its encounter with the English? 3. *How* did the English react to the Indian culture and religions? 4. In *what* ways did the original trade agreements between the English and India evolve into an imperial relationship? 5. *Discuss* how trade affects relationships between the United States and other countries.

Encounter figure 15.1 BICHITR. *Allegorical Representation of the Emperor Jahangir.* Seventeenth century. Color and gold on paper, ht. 10½". Courtesy of the Freer Gallery, Smithsonian Institution, Washington, D.C. (42.15V). *In this delicate miniature painting, Jahangir (r. 1605–1627), whose name means "world seizer," sits on an hourglass throne, perhaps a reference to the fleeting of time and the brevity of his reign. Jahangir's head is encircled in a halo with the sun and the moon. Before him stands a mullah, or Islamic teacher, to whom the ruler is handing a book. The two figures who are placed below the mullah—a symbolic ranking to show Jahangir's preference for spiritual over worldly matters—have been identified by art historians as the Ottoman sultan (with a black beard) and James I of England (with the neck ruff). At the lower left, the man holding a painting may be Bichitr, the famous court artist who painted this miniature.*

Another French publicist, Pierre Bayle [BEL] (1647–1706), launched the intellectual fashion for arranging ideas in systematic form, as in dictionaries and encyclopedias. Bayle's influential and popular work, called the *Historical and Critical Dictionary,* was probably the most controversial book of the baroque age. Bayle wrote articles on biblical heroes, classical and medieval thinkers, and contemporary scholars, many of which challenged Christian beliefs. Each article was a short essay accompanied by lengthy footnotes. His aim was to set forth rival and contradictory opinions on each topic; if the essay was offensive to the pious, Bayle pointed out that he himself was only following the Bible and the teachings of the Christian faith. Many readers responded to the articles by becoming skeptical about the subjects. Others questioned Bayle's motives and accused him of atheism. Despite the controversy, by 1750 Bayle's *Dictionary* had been reprinted many times and spawned many imitations.

Bayle's *Dictionary* marked a new stage in the history of literature for two reasons. First, the work was sold to subscribers, which meant that royal, aristocratic, or ecclesiastical patronage was no longer necessary to publish a book. Second, the extravagant success of his venture showed that a literate public now existed that would buy books if they appealed to its interests. Both of these facts were understood very well by authors in the next generation, who freed writing from the patronage system and inaugurated the world of modern literature with its specialized audiences.

Impact on the Arts

The innovations in science and philosophy coincided with and fostered a changed consciousness not only in the educated public but also among artists and writers. New attitudes, values, and tastes reflecting these ideas are evident in the creative works of the baroque period, many of which are discussed and illustrated in Chapter 14. Central to the new ideas was the belief that there is a hidden harmony in nature that may be expressed in mathematical laws. In the arts, this belief was expressed by order and wholeness beneath wild profusion, such as the geometric order that organizes the gardens and grounds of Versailles or the theme of redemption that unifies Milton's sprawling epic, *Paradise Lost.*

A second reflection of the Scientific Revolution, particularly of the discoveries in astronomy, is the feeling of infinite space that pervades baroque art. The love of curving lines, elliptical shapes, and flowing contours may be related to the new, expansive views of the planets and the universe. The ultimate expression of these interests and feelings, of course, is the illusionistic ceiling painting (see Figure 14.11).

A final effect of the Scientific Revolution was the elevation of analytic reasoning skills to a position of high esteem in the arts. Just as Newton's genius led him to grasp concepts and laws that had eluded others, so artists and humanists were inspired to use their powers of analysis to look below the surface of human life and search out its hidden truth. Racine's plays, for example, reveal acute insight into human psychology, as do the political philosophies of Hobbes and Locke; and Rembrandt's cycle of self-portraits shows his ability and desire to reveal his innermost feelings. Baroque art and literature demonstrate that although the Scientific Revolution may have displaced men and women from the center of the universe, an optimistic view of the human predicament was still possible.

The Legacy of the Revolutions in Scientific and Political Thought

One historian of science claims that the Scientific Revolution "outshines everything since the rise of Christianity and reduces the Renaissance and Reformation to the rank of mere episodes . . . within the system of medieval Christendom." Although other scholars hesitate to go that far in praise of this singular event, enough evidence exists to show that the revolution in science caused a dramatic shift in the way people viewed themselves and their world. The Newtonian system became the accepted view of the universe until the twentieth century. Likewise, the new methodology—collecting raw data, reasoning inductively to hypotheses, and verifying results with mathematics—remains the standard in modern science. This method of reasoning gradually spread and laid the foundation for the modern social sciences. Even certain disciplines in the humanities—such as linguistics, the study of language—use scientific methods to the extent that is possible.

At the same time science held out the promise that it could unlock the secrets of nature, it was contributing to a dramatic upsurge in skepticism. Since the baroque age, virtually everything in Western culture has been subjected to systematic doubt, including religious beliefs, artistic theories, and social mores. Although many causes besides science lie behind this trend to question all existing standards, the Scientific Revolution created a tried-and-trusted model and ready tools for universal doubt. Because Aristotle's and other ancient thinkers' ideas were proven false, modern schol-ars were inclined to question all other beliefs received from the past. This trend has encouraged an intellectual restlessness that is perhaps the most prominent feature of modern life.

Although the innovations in baroque political thought and the expansion of European culture cannot compare with the effects of the rise of modern science, the changes in political theory and in the relations of Europe with the rest of the world did have strong consequences for modern life. In general, the new political theories gave rise to two rival heritages: the authoritarian tradition, which claims that a strong centralized government is the best way to ensure justice for all citizens, and the liberal tradition, which holds that citizens are capable of ruling themselves. Since then, politics in the West has tended to be organized around the conflicting claims of these two points of view.

The colonizing efforts in the New World during the 1600s served to extend the geographic limits of the West. As a result, Western ideas and technology may be found today even in the most far-flung reaches of the globe. A negative consequence of the opening of the New World was that slavery, an institution that had virtually died in Europe in the early Middle Ages, was reintroduced, with destructive consequences for the non-Western people who became enslaved. We in the modern age are reaping the harvest of this development.

KEY CULTURAL TERMS

Scientific Revolution   heliocentrism
geocentrism   social contract
empiricism   liberalism
inductive reasoning   *tabula rasa*
deductive reasoning   virtuoso

QUESTIONS FOR CRITICAL THINKING

1. What was the long-term impact of the Scientific Revolution on the study of philosophy and theology?

2. Discuss the discoveries and contributions of Copernicus, Kepler, Galileo, and Newton to astronomy and physics. How did their discoveries threaten the existing views of the universe?

3. Who was more important to the Scientific Revolution, Bacon or Descartes? Explain the reasons for your choice.

4. Define the term "social contract" and illustrate how Hobbes and Locke used the term in their political writings. Which of the two thinkers' assessments of human nature do you think correct? Why?

5. Do you think the Scientific Revolution was more important than the Renaissance and the Reformation? Defend your position. Compare and contrast the impact of all three movements on Western thought.

16

THE AGE OF REASON
1700–1789

The scientific discoveries and philosophic ideas that made the seventeenth century so intellectually exciting bore fruit in the eighteenth century, a period often referred to as the Age of Reason. The advances of the Scientific Revolution led thinkers in the 1700s to believe they were living in a time of illumination and enlightenment. Committed to scientific methodology, mathematical reasoning, and a healthy skepticism, they fervently believed their knowledge could lead to the improvement of both the individual and society.

The Age of Reason was marked by four major trends. The first trend, dating from the 1600s, was the growing power of sovereign centralized states: France, Great Britain (formed from the union of England and Scotland in 1707), Prussia, Austria, Russia, and the Netherlands (Map 16.1). The second trend was the return of the aristocracy to prominence after a century or more of decline; the ostentatious culture of this resurgent class proved to be its swan song, as the French Revolution of 1789 destroyed the aristocracy's power base (see Chapter 17). The third trend was the rise to political and cultural eminence of the middle class, which, in turn, supported those thinkers who advocated social equality, social justice, and a thorough restructuring of society. The intellectual and cultural movement spawned by these progressive thinkers is called the **Enlightenment,** which constitutes the fourth and most important trend in the 1700s.

As these four trends evolved, two new styles in art, architecture, and music were developing in reaction to the baroque. Rococo, the first of the new styles, originated in France and was more informal and graceful, less ponderous and oppressive than the baroque (Figure 16.1). After about 1750, in

◀ **Detail** BALTHASAR NEUMANN AND OTHERS. Kaisersaal, the Residenz. View toward the south wall. 1719–1744. Würzburg, Germany.

LEARNING THROUGH MAPS

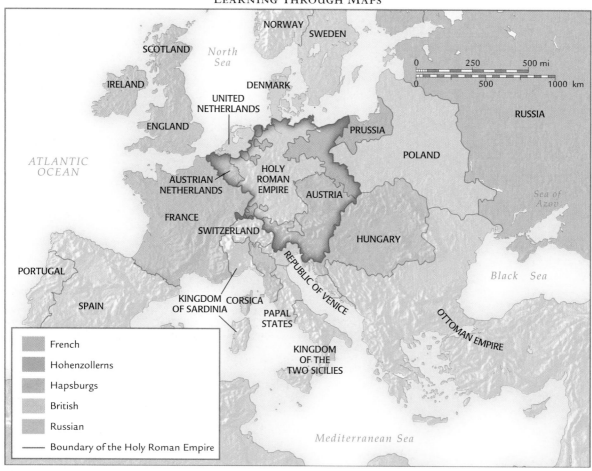

Map 16.1   EUROPE, 1763–1789
This map shows the political divisions of Europe in the mid–eighteenth century. 1. *Locate* the territories of France, Great Britain, Russia, the Hohenzollern dynasty, and the Hapsburg dynasty—the five great powers. 2. *Which* great power has the most compact state? 3. *Which* great power has the most widely dispersed lands? 4. *How* would geography and cultural diversity influence a state's ability to maintain great-power status? 5. *Notice* the vastness of the Ottoman Empire, a Muslim state, in the southeast corner of Europe.

reaction to both the rococo and the baroque, a second new style—the neoclassical—began. Unlike the rococo, the neoclassical style in art and architecture spread widely across Europe and into British colonial America. The new style in music—known as the classical—was marked by refinement and elegance, as embodied in the works of Mozart, arguably the greatest musical genius who ever lived.

THE ENLIGHTENMENT

The Age of Reason thinkers derived their ideals and goals from varied sources. Following the example of ancient Greece and Rome, they rejected superstition, sought truth through the use of reason, and viewed the world from a secular, human-centered perspective. Drawing on the Renaissance, they embraced humanism—the belief that a human being becomes a better person through the study and practice of literature, philosophy, music, and the arts. And from the seventeenth-century revolutions in science and philosophy, particularly the works of Newton, Bacon, Descartes, and Locke, they derived a reliance on rationalism, empiricism, skepticism, and the experimental method, along with a belief in human perfectibility through education and unlimited progress.

The Enlightenment changed the worldview of only a small number of Westerners, mainly those living in the cultural capitals of Paris, London, and Edinburgh.

Timeline 16.1   THE AGE OF REASON

1700	1714		1740	1748	1756	1763		1776		1783	1789
War of Spanish Succession			War of Austrian Succession		Seven Years' War			American Revolution			

			1740 Richardson's *Pamela*	1750 First volume of the *Encyclopédie*	1759 Voltaire's *Candide*			1776 Smith's *Wealth of Nations*		1786 Mozart's *Marriage of Figaro*
						1762 Rousseau's *Social Contract*				1785 David's *Oath of the Horatii*
							1771–1773 Fragonard's *The Pursuit*			

Few workers and peasants were touched by the movement, but some aristocrats and many middle-class readers—such as educators, lawyers, journalists, and clergymen—were drawn to the new ideas. Ultimately, enough influential people were converted to the goals of the Enlightenment to have an impact on the revolutionary events that occurred later in the century (Timeline 16.1).

The Philosophes and Their Program

The leaders of the Enlightenment were a small band of writers known as **philosophes,** the French word for "philosophers." Not philosophers in a formal sense, the philosophes were more likely to be popularizers who wanted to influence public opinion. They avoided the methods of academic scholars, such as engaging in philosophical debates or writing only for colleagues, and tried to reach large audiences through novels, essays, pamphlets, plays, poems, and histories. In this

Figure 16.1 SIR JOSHUA REYNOLDS. *Mrs. Siddons as the Tragic Muse.* 1784. Oil on canvas, 7'9" × 4'9". Huntington Art Gallery, San Marino, California. *The rococo portrait painter Sir Joshua Reynolds painted many English personalities of his day, including Sarah Siddons. Mrs. Siddons, who came from a theater family, won the applause of England's knowledgeable and discerning audiences to emerge as the most famous actress of tragic drama in the late eighteenth century. Reynolds distances Mrs. Siddons from the viewer and surrounds her with elaborate scenery as if she were on a proscenium stage in a darkened theater. The two figures behind her represent Aristotle's definitions of tragedy—pity and terror.*

they were following the lead of Fontenelle, who had popularized the new astronomy in his *Conversations on the Plurality of Worlds* (see Chapter 15). When possible, they openly attacked what they deemed to be the evils of society and supported those rulers who favored change, the so-called enlightened despots. When the censors threatened, however, the philosophes either disguised their radical messages or published their criticisms in the Netherlands—the most liberal state in Europe at the time.

The Enlightenment was essentially a product of French cultural life, and Paris was its capital. The principal philosophes were Voltaire, Diderot, Montesquieu—all French—and by adoption the French-speaking Swiss writer Rousseau. But major philosophes appeared elsewhere in Europe, notably in Great Britain, and in Britain's North American colonies. The most influential of these voices were the English historian Edward Gibbon, the American writer Benjamin Franklin, and two Scottish thinkers, the economist Adam Smith and the philosopher David Hume.

The philosophes, though never in complete agreement and often diametrically opposed, shared certain assumptions: they had full confidence in reason; they were convinced that nature was orderly and fundamentally good and could be understood through the empirical method; they believed that change and progress would improve society, since human beings were perfectible. Faith in reason led them to reject religious doctrine, in particular Roman Catholic dogma; to denounce bigotry and intolerance; and to advocate freedom of religious choice. Maintaining that education liberated humanity from ignorance and superstition, the philosophes called for an expanded educational system independent of ecclesiastical control.

The philosophes thought that the political, economic, and religious institutions should be reformed to bring "the greatest happiness for the greatest numbers"—a phrase that expresses a key Enlightenment ideal and that, in the nineteenth century, became the battle cry of the English thinker and reformer Jeremy Bentham (see Chapter 18). These theorists anticipated a general overhaul of society, leading to universal peace and a golden age for humanity. In effect, they preached a secular gospel that happiness need not be delayed until after death but, instead, could be enjoyed here on earth.

Envisioning a rejuvenated society that guaranteed natural rights to all citizens, the philosophes were almost unanimous in thinking exclusively in terms of men. They still considered women their intellectual and physical inferiors and thus in need of male protection or guidance. Not until the late eighteenth century were voices raised on behalf of women's rights and only then under the inspiration of the French Revolution.

One of those thinkers moved by the revolutionary winds blowing from France was the English writer Mary Wollstonecraft (1759–1797), who, in *A Vindication of the Rights of Woman* (1792), used Enlightenment ideals to urge the liberation of her own sex. Like Rousseau, Wollstonecraft was a democrat and opposed to hierarchy in all forms: in the aristocracy, the military, and the clergy to the extent that promotion was based on pleasing those in higher positions. Unlike Rousseau, she was dedicated to the rights of women, whom she repeatedly called "one-half of the human race." Rejecting the "Adam's rib" explanation of women's inferiority as being simply a male fabrication, she claimed that women are as rational as men and thus should be treated the same. The heart of this latter-day philosophe's argument was that women should abandon feminine artifice and cunning, especially the all-consuming need to be socially pleasing, and through education become equal partners with educated men. In the nineteenth century, reformers began to take up Wollstonecraft's challenge, particularly her call for female education and women's suffrage.

Religion

During the Age of Reason, two divergent religious trends emerged: the Deist faith, which appealed to a small, but influential group of thinkers; and new Protestant sects, which attracted followers across all classes in Europe and the New World. Both trends generated controversy at the time, and their lingering effects are still felt in the West today.

DEISM   Newtonian science implied that God set the universe in motion and then left it to run by its own natural laws. Taking this metaphor of God as a clockmaker, some thinkers rejected traditional Christianity and, instead, adopted a natural Christianity called **Deism.** Deists worshiped a Supreme Being, a God who created the universe and set the laws of nature in motion but who never again interfered in natural or human affairs. Believing in the concept of a clockmaker God, the Deists rejected the efficacy of prayer and downgraded Jesus's role from savior to good moral example.

Deism was espoused by a small band of public figures, such as Benjamin Franklin in the British colony of Pennsylvania and Jean d'Alembert, coeditor of the influential *Encyclopédie* (see below). Deism's appeal, though limited, marked another shift in religious attitudes and was added evidence of the growing secularization of European consciousness in the 1700s.

POPULAR RELIGION   The two most important popular religious movements of the 1700s were **Pietism** in Europe and the **First Great Awakening** in Britain's American colonies. Both movements emerged from mainline Protestantism, and the two were loosely interconnected and shared certain traits. They both thought established churches had lost contact with their membership, by becoming too closely identified with the rich and powerful. Both movements also believed that the church's mission should be to help resolve pressing social and economic issues, such as poverty and social inequality, rather than accepting the status quo, as seemed to be the case with established churches in England and Germany. And both also urged a personal living faith based on strict adherence to the Scriptures, rather than a focus on ritual and liturgy, as was done in the established churches.

Pietism began in Germany among the Lutherans in the late 1600s and flourished until the 1760s. In the early 1700s it spread into central Europe, where it spawned several new sects. One sect, the Moravians (in the modern Czech Republic), sent a missionary to Britain's American colonies, founding settlements there. The Moravians also sent missions to England, where they had a ready audience among disaffected members of the Church of England. John Wesley (1703–1791), the founder of Methodism, was influenced by the Moravians both in England and in the Georgia colony, which he visited in his early life. Wesley called for a spiritual renewal, demanding that followers be "born again," that is, renounce their sinful ways and choose Jesus Christ as their personal savior—a belief that remains central to the evangelical movement today. Wesley's movement, which had special appeal to the rural poor as well as urban workers in this first Industrial Age, grew rapidly in England and America. Although initially unwilling to secede from the Church of England, Wesley gradually acknowledged the irreconcilable difference between his teachings and those of the Church of England. A formal break between the churches did not come until 1784, the founding date of the Methodist Church.

Methodism and German Pietism became catalysts for the First Great Awakening in colonial America. A wave of preaching and revivalism swept over the English colonies, from New England to Georgia. As in the Protestant Reformation (see Chapter 13), this movement stressed human sinfulness and the gift of God's grace, the central role of Jesus Christ as savior, the Bible as the ultimate source of religious authority, and the need to be "born again." Two key leaders were Jonathan Edwards (1703–1758), the theologian and spellbinding preacher, operating in New England, and George Whitfield (1714–1770), a fire-and-brimstone preacher and member of Wesley's inner circle, who led revivals in Georgia and other southern colonies, as well as in cities along the East Coast.

While the First Great Awakening soon died out in New England, it showed great staying power along the westward-moving frontier, in the countryside, and throughout the southern colonies—laying the foundation for what became the Bible Belt of the United States. By reaching out to the poor, to women, and to slaves and free blacks, this movement tended to democratize religion in colonial life. It also led to the founding of a number of colleges, which, by educating young men and training ministers, ensured that the religious, moral, and cultural values of the First Great Awakening would be perpetuated for generations. As a strong rival to the Church of England and other mainline Protestant sects, the movement tended to weaken the ties of the established churches with local British officials. This development had social and political implications, which surfaced on the eve of the American Revolution (see Chapter 17). The First Great Awakening peaked in the 1760s, but its influence remained strong, and it became the prototype of religious revivals in America's later history.

The *Encyclopédie*

The message of the philosophes was communicated by various means: pamphlets, essays, and books; private and public discussions and debates; the new journalistic press; and, especially in France, the salon—the half-social, half-serious gatherings where fashionable people met to discuss ideas. But the principal work of the philosophes was the *Encyclopédie*—the monumental project that remains the summation of the Enlightenment. Two earlier works, Chambers's *Cyclopedia* in England (1728) and Bayle's *Dictionary* in France (1697) (see Chapter 15), paved the way for the *Encyclopédie*. Begun in 1750 and completed in 1772, the project comprised seventeen text volumes and eleven books of plates and illustrations (Figure 16.2). More than 161 writers wrote articles for this venture, which was intended as a summary of existing knowledge in the arts, crafts, and sciences.

The editor of the *Encyclopédie* was Denis Diderot [DEED-uh-roh] (1713–1784), a key figure of the Enlightenment. Diderot was constantly in trouble with the French authorities because of the work's controversial essays, which he claimed were meant "to change the general way of thinking." Publication was halted in 1759 by the state censor but resumed secretly with the collusion of other government officials. Unlike most publications of the period, the project was funded by its readers, not by the crown or the church, and private circulating libraries rented the volumes to untold numbers of customers.

The Physiocrats

Under the broad umbrella of Enlightenment ideas, the philosophes were joined by a group of French writers

Figure 16.2 Illustration from the *Encyclopédie: Cotton Plantation in the French West Indies. 1751–1765. As principal editor of the* Encyclopédie, *Diderot adopted Francis Bacon's notion that all knowledge is useful. Thus, the articles and illustrations for this reference work focused on practical data such as soapmaking, human anatomy, and military drill. In this drawing, for example, the readers could peruse the romanticized plantation scene to discover how raw cotton was prepared for shipment to European mills.*

concerned with economic matters—the **Physiocrats,** as they called themselves. (The term is a coined word, from Greek, meaning "rule of, or from, the earth.") The Physiocrats examined the general nature of the economy and, in particular, the strengths and weaknesses of mercantilism, the prevailing economic system, in which the state regulated trade and production for its own benefit. In their eyes, this state-run system hindered economic growth: mercantilism, contrary to its goals, lowered the productivity of workers, especially farmers, and led to labor unrest and riots.

Guided by Enlightenment doctrine that natural laws govern society, the Physiocrats assumed that similar laws applied to economic growth and decline. After a thorough analysis of the French economy, they concluded that certain fundamental economic principles did exist, such as the law of supply and demand, and that these laws operated best when free from governmental interference. Accordingly, they recommended the dismantling of mercantilism and the adoption of *laissez-faire,* French for "to let alone"—in other words, an economy where the self-regulating laws of free trade were in effect. In addition, they argued that unrestricted enjoyment of private property was necessary for individual freedom. These French thinkers concluded that both the individual and the entire society automatically benefited when all people were allowed to serve their own self-interest instead of working for the good of the state.

At about the same time, the Scottish economist Adam Smith (1723–1790) was developing similar ideas. His conclusions, reported in *An Inquiry into the Na-* *ture and Causes of the Wealth of Nations* (1776), became the bible of industrial capitalism and remains so today. In this work, Smith blamed mercantilism for the economic woes of his time, identified the central role played by labor in manufacturing, and called for open and competitive trade so that the "invisible hand" of a free-market economy could operate. Smith's ideas were quickly absorbed by budding entrepreneurs and had an immediate impact on the changes being generated by the Industrial Revolution (see Chapter 17).

THE GREAT POWERS DURING THE AGE OF REASON

In comparison with the turbulent 1600s, Europe between 1715 and 1789 enjoyed peace and prosperity. Wars between sovereign states were few and brief; economic growth was slow, but steady; and a continuing population increase supported the economic expansion. The period's prosperity fueled the rise of the middle classes, especially in Great Britain and Holland. However, in France, the middle class made only modest gains, and, in central and eastern Europe, it formed only a small fraction of the population.

Society: Continuity and Change

A major consequence of the century's modest economic growth was the growing urbanization of society. Although most Europeans still followed traditional liveli-

Figure 16.3 ÉTIENNE AUBRY. *Paternal Love*. Ca. 1775. Oil on canvas, 30 × 39″. The Trustees of the Barber Institute of Fine Arts, The University of Birmingham, England. *Paternal Love is a symbol of French rural bourgeois life. It depicts a father, probably returned home from a trip, greeting his three children, wife, and father (the children's grandfather). Although the room's amenities—stone floor, fireplace, and solid walls—signal financial security, the simple and sturdy furniture and the scanty display of household effects indicate that the family is merely middle class and not upper class (see Figure 16.5). Nevertheless, the painter's moral lesson is evident: parental love makes a family strong—a sentiment that would appeal to moralistic middle-class taste. Aubry (1745–1781) was a popular artist, praised by the writer-critic Diderot and famous for his "moral genre" paintings, such as this.*

hoods on farms and in villages, cities and towns offered increasing opportunities for ambitious folk. The rural-to-urban shift originated in England, the home of the Industrial Revolution, and to a lesser extent in France. Only in the next century did it slowly spread to some parts of central and eastern Europe.

The traditional social hierarchy kept each class in its place. The aristocracy constituted only about 3 percent of the total population, but it possessed tremendous power and wealth. The upper middle class—encompassing rich merchants, bankers, and professionals—normally resided in the rapidly expanding urban areas

and influenced business and governmental affairs. In the broad middle class were the less wealthy merchants, shopkeepers, skilled artisans, bureaucrats, and well-to-do rural families (Figure 16.3). In the lower middle class were the lesser artisans and craftspeople, and below them, the metropolitan poor, who performed menial labor and were often unemployed, and rural laborers. In the countryside, the nobility and the prosperous farmers owned large sections of the land and controlled the rural populace. The small cultivators, tenant farmers, landless workers, and indentured contract laborers constituted a complex group whose legal, social, and personal rights varied widely across Europe. Next were the peasants, whose status ranged from freedom in western Europe to serfdom in Russia. (Serfs were bound to the land they worked, but they had customary rights and, strictly speaking, they were not slaves.) These impoverished people often bore the brunt of the taxes and the contempt of the other classes.

With few exceptions, such as the upper-middle-class women who played influential roles in the salons, women remained subordinate to men. As mentioned earlier, the philosophes, who thoroughly critiqued society, failed to recognize women's contributions or champion their rights. Even Jean-Jacques Rousseau, who was often at odds with his fellow writers, agreed with the philosophes that women were inferior to men and should be submissive to them.

Another group who gained little from the Enlightenment were the African slaves in Europe's overseas colonies. During the eighteenth century, ships from England, France, and Holland carried about six million Africans to enslavement in the New World. Efforts to abolish the slave trade or even to improve the conditions of the slaves proved futile despite the moral disapproval of the philosophes and the pleas of English Christians.

Absolutism, Limited Monarchy, and Enlightened Despotism

The eighteenth century was the last great age of kings in the West. In most countries, the royal rulers followed traditional policies even in the face of criticism or opposition. Supported by inefficient bureaucracies and costly armies, they controlled the masses through heavy taxes and threats of brutality while holding in check the privileged groups. Although a few rulers attempted reforms, by the end of the century most of the monarchies were weakening as democratic sentiments continued to rise.

In France, the kings struggled to hold on to the power they inherited from Louis XIV. In Great Britain, the kings fought a losing battle against Parliament and the restrictions of constitutional monarchy. In Prussia and Austria, so-called enlightened despots experimented with reforms to strengthen their states, while in Russia the czars found new ways to expand absolutism. By midcentury, the Continent had undergone a series of brief wars that ended the several relatively peaceful decades Europe had enjoyed (see Timeline 16.1). For France and England, the Continental conflicts soon escalated into global commercial, territorial, and colonial rivalries that were resolved only with the outcome of the American Revolutionary War (1775–1783).

FRANCE: THE SUCCESSORS TO THE SUN KING   No French ruler was able to recapture the splendor of Louis XIV. Louis XV (r. 1715–1774), who succeeded to full political control at age thirteen and never acquired a strong will to rule, only compounded the problems of the French state. Those he chose as his subordinates were not always talented or loyal, and he permitted his mistresses, who were not trained in government, to influence his decisions about official matters. When Louis XV, despairing over a military defeat, expressed his misgivings about the future of France to his royal favorite, Madame de Pompadour (1721–1764), she reportedly replied with the prophetic *"Après nous le déluge"* ("After us, the flood").

Life at Louis XV's court could not be sustained in the grand manner of the late Sun King, and the nobles began to leave Versailles for Paris. Whether at Versailles or elsewhere, educated aristocrats were becoming fascinated by Enlightenment ideas, and they and their wives read the *Encyclopédie* and studied the writings of the philosophes. Upper-class women played influential roles in presiding over salons, where the enlightened thinkers and their admirers gathered to dine and converse. Two of the best-known salons were conducted by Madame du Deffand [day-FAHN] (1697–1780) and Julie Lespinasse [les-pee-NAHS] (1732–1776). For a number of years, Madame du Deffand (Marie de Marquise du Deffand) claimed Voltaire as her most prominent literary celebrity, and his presence ensured that other philosophes would attend her gatherings. Julie de Lespinasse, serving first as companion to Madame du Deffand, broke away to found her own salon, where Jean d'Alembert (1717–1783), coeditor of Diderot's *Encyclopédie,* was a favored guest.

Even though the French elite debated the merits of reform and the more controversial topics raised by the philosophes, Louis XV clearly did not accept the movement's call for change. It is ironic that the country where the Enlightenment began failed to undertake any of its progressive reforms. Indeed, when changes were finally introduced under Louis XVI (r. 1774–1792), they were too little and too late.

Handicapped by the weak Louis XV, France found its preeminent position in foreign affairs challenged by Great Britain, Austria, and Prussia. As a result of the Seven Years' War (1756–1763), France suffered defeats in Europe and lost its holdings in North America and India. During the American Revolution, France sided with the colonists against Great Britain, its foe at home and overseas. France's aid to the Americans further diminished the government's financial resources and forced the nation deeper into debt.

France's kings also failed to solve the nation's domestic problems, the consequence of their own failures of leadership and those of their royal officials. Matters worsened as the corrupt tax system moved the country closer to financial bankruptcy. And, most important, the crown was faced with a resurgent aristocracy determined to recover the feudal privileges it lost under Louis XIV. Rather than joining the king's efforts to reform the judicial system, the nobility blocked the crown at every step. The middle class joined forces with aristocratic rebels, transforming what had been a feudal issue into a struggle for freedom in the name of the people. In 1789, during the reign of Louis XVI, France started on a revolutionary path that united most of French society against the crown and culminated in the French Revolution (1789–1799) (see Chapter 17).

GREAT BRITAIN AND THE HANOVERIAN KINGS   To the philosophes, Great Britain was the ideal model of a nation. To them, Britain seemed more stable and prosperous than the states on the Continent, a success they attributed to the limited powers of the English monarchy imposed by Parliament during the Glorious Revolution of 1688. Britain's laws guaranteed to every Englishman certain political and social rights, such as free speech and fair and speedy trials. Britain's economy was strong as well. Prompted by enterprising merchants and progressive landowners, the nation was dominant in an expanding global market; at home, the standard of living was rising for the growing population.

After the death of Queen Anne in 1714, the English crown was inherited by George I, a great-grandson of James I and the Protestant ruler of the German principality of Hanover. The first two Hanoverian kings reigned in splendid isolation at the royal court, more interested in events in Germany than those in England. George I (r. 1714–1727) allowed Parliament to run the country. Under George II (r. 1727–1760), Britain was drawn into the Seven Years' War but emerged victorious, the dominant presence in world trade. From 1760 until the outbreak of World War I in 1914, Great Britain occupied center stage in international affairs.

Nevertheless, Great Britain faced serious domestic problems under George III (r. 1760–1820) because he sought to restore royal powers lost to Parliament by his predecessors. This internal struggle affected foreign policy when the king and Parliament offered differing proposals to control the economic development of the American colonies through export and import quotas, duties, and taxes. The differences between the two proposals hastened the onset of the American Revolution and probably contributed to Britain's eventual defeat.

ENLIGHTENED DESPOTISM IN CENTRAL AND EASTERN EUROPE
The system of European states underwent some modifications during the Age of Reason. Great Britain and France now dominated western Europe; the less populous countries of Holland and Sweden declined in power; Spain turned increasingly inward and all but disappeared from Continental affairs; and Italy, under Austrian and papal control, remained economically depressed. Meanwhile, Prussia, Austria, and Russia jockeyed for control of central and eastern Europe. Under their absolutist rulers, these states pursued aggressive policies, seizing territories from one another and their weaker neighbors. Although these rulers portrayed themselves as enlightened despots, their regimes were generally characterized by oppressive and authoritarian policies.

By 1740 Prussia, ruled by the Hohenzollern dynasty, had a solid economic base, a hardworking bureaucracy, and an efficient army. Capitalizing on these advantages, Frederick II, known as Frederick the Great (r. 1740–1786), turned Prussia into a leading European power. A pragmatic diplomat, skilled military tactician, and student of the Enlightenment and French culture, Frederick was an enlightened despot of the type beloved by the philosophes. He even attempted (though failed) to reform his state's agrarian economy and social system in accordance with the rational principle that all individuals have the natural right to choose for themselves the best way to live.

Prussia's chief rival in central Europe was Austria. Throughout the 1700s, Austria's rulers struggled to govern a multiethnic population that included large numbers of Germans, Hungarians, Czechs, and Slovaks along with Poles, Italians, and various Slavic minorities. At the same time, the emperors tried, with mixed success, to assert Austria's role as a great power, both politically and culturally. Schönbrunn Palace in Vienna, for example, was built as a rival to France's Versailles (Figure 16.4). Two rulers stand out—the Hapsburg emperors Maria Theresa and Joseph, her son, whose combined reigns lasted from 1740 to 1790.

Unlike Frederick II of Prussia, Maria Theresa (r. 1740–1780) was not attracted to the ideas of the philosophes. More important was her Roman Catholic faith, which led her to portray herself to her subjects as their universal mother. She was perhaps the most beloved monarch in this age of kings. Maria Theresa's reforming zeal sprang not from philosophic principle but from a reaction against Austria's territorial losses during military defeats. She used all her royal prerogatives to overhaul the political and military machinery of the state. Along with universal military conscription, increased revenues, and equitable distribution of taxes, she wanted a general reorganization of society that gave uniform treatment to all citizens. Her efforts were not wasted, for her son Joseph II took up her uncompleted task and became the ultimate personification of the enlightened despot. During his brief reign (1780–1790), Joseph II launched far-reaching changes

Figure 16.4 JOHANN FERDINAND HETZENDORF VON HOHENBERG. The Gloriette, or "The Temple of Fame." Schönbrunn Palace Gardens. 1768. Vienna. *The Gloriette, a triumphal arch flanked by colonnaded screens, is situated on the highest point within the vast gardens of Schönbrunn Palace. Designed by Johann Ferdinand Hetzendorf von Hohenberg (1732–1816), court architect to Empress Maria Theresa, it is the crowning touch of his beautification campaign for the palace grounds. It functioned as a theatrical backdrop for court rituals and receptions. Constructed partly from the ruins of a castle near the site, the Gloriette uses classical features (colonnades, balustrades, and statuary and urns) though its style is baroque (profuse decorative details and the reflecting pool).*

to raise farm production and to provide more economic opportunities for the peasants. Convinced that his country's economic and social institutions had to be fully modernized, he abolished serfdom and passed decrees guaranteeing religious toleration and free speech. In the 1790s, much of what he had accomplished was undone by his successors, who, fearing the excesses of the French Revolution, restored aristocratic and ecclesiastic control and privileges.

Russia was the newest member of the family of great powers, having achieved this stature during the reign of Peter the Great (r. 1682–1725). Abroad, Peter made Russia's presence known, and at home he began to reform political, economic, and social institutions along Western lines. Most of his eighteenth-century successors were ineffective, if not incompetent, until Catherine the Great (r. 1762–1796) became empress. She pursued the unifying policies of Peter, but unlike him she was able to win the powerful support of the large landowners. A patron of the Enlightenment, Catherine sought the advice of a few philosophes, including Diderot. She also attempted to increase farm productivity and improve the nearly enslaved condition of the peasants, but the vastness of Russia's problems and the reactionary autocratic government defeated any genuine reforms.

CULTURAL TRENDS IN THE EIGHTEENTH CENTURY: FROM ROCOCO TO NEOCLASSICAL

The Enlightenment dominated cultural life in this century, but two artistic styles also held sway. The rococo style in the arts mirrored the taste of the French nobility; the subsequent neoclassical style was adopted by progressive writers, artists, intellectuals, and ambitious members of the middle class. Meanwhile, new developments in literature were pointing the way toward the modern world.

The Rococo Style in the Arts

Conceived on a more intimate scale than the baroque style and committed to frivolous subjects and themes— the dominant ideas of a work—the **rococo style** arose in France in the waning years of the Sun King's reign. With his death in 1715 and the succession of his five-year-old heir, Louis XV, the nobility were released both from Versailles and from the ponderous baroque style. Paris once again became the capital of art, ideas, and fashion in the Western world. There, the rococo style

Figure 16.5 Jean-Antoine Watteau. *Departure from Cythera.* 1717. Oil on canvas, 4'3" × 6'4½". Louvre. *Watteau's aristocratic couples, savoring a last few moments of pleasure, represent the idealized image that the eighteenth-century elite wanted to present to the world. No hint of the age's problems is allowed to disturb this idyllic scene. From the court costumes to the hovering cupids, this painting transforms reality into a stage set—the ideal of rococo art.*

was created for the French elite almost single-handedly by the Flemish painter and decorator Jean-Antoine Watteau.

The rococo gradually spread to most of Europe, but its acceptance was tied to religion and class. It was embraced by the aristocracy in Germany, Italy, and Austria; Roman Catholic nobles in Austria developed a version of rococo that was second in importance only to that of France. The English, on the other hand, rejected the rococo, possibly because its erotic undercurrent and sexual themes offended Protestant middle-class sensibility. Consequently, rococo style is a purely Continental phenomenon; there is no English rococo.

ROCOCO PAINTING   Jean-Antoine Watteau [wah-TOE] (1684–1721) specialized in paintings that depict *fêtes galantes,* or aristocratic entertainments. In these works, Watteau portrays the intimate world of the aristocracy, dressed in sumptuous clothing, grouped in parks and gardens, and often accompanied by costumed actors, another of Watteau's favorite subjects. He filled these bucolic settings with air, lightness, and grace—a contrast to the occasionally heavy-handed baroque. Myth-

ological allusions made Watteau's works depictions of classical themes rather than merely scenes of aristocratic life.

In 1717 Watteau became the first rococo painter to be elected to membership in the Royal Academy of Painting and Sculpture in Paris. As required by the terms of election, he submitted as his diploma piece *Departure from Cythera* (Figure 16.5). The setting is Cythera, the legendary island of Venus, whose bust on the right is garlanded with her devotees' roses. Forming a wavering line, the lovers express hesitation as they make their farewells: the couple under the statue are lost in reverie as a clothed cupid tugs at the woman's skirt; beside this group a suitor assists his lady to her feet; and next to them a gentleman accompanies his companion to the waiting boat as she longingly gazes backward. This melancholy scene, signified by the setting sun and the departing lovers, represents Watteau's homage to the brevity of human passion.

In *Departure from Cythera,* many of the new values of the rococo style can be seen. Where the baroque favored tumultuous scenes depicting the passions and ecstasies of the saints, the rococo focused on smaller,

Figure 16.6   JEAN-ANTOINE WATTEAU. *The Sign for Gersaint's Shop.* Ca. 1720. Oil on canvas, 5'11⅝" × 10'1⅛". Stiftung Preussischer Kulturbesitz, Schloss Charlottenburg, Berlin. *This painting of a shop interior illustrates the social dynamics of the emerging art market in the eighteenth century. The aristocratic customers act as if they own the place, turning it into a genteel lounge. The shop employees, on the other hand, have clearly inferior social roles: one brings forward a heavy painting for inspection, another holds a miniature work up to view, and a third stands downcast at the left. Through such details, Watteau reveals the social gulf between classes that was implicit in the rococo style.*

gentler moments, usually involving love of one variety or another, whether erotic, romantic, or sentimental. Where the baroque used intense colors to convey feelings of power and grandeur, the rococo used soft pastels to evoke nostalgia and melancholy. The monumentality and sweeping movement of baroque art were brought down to a human scale in the rococo, making it more suited to interiors, furniture, and architectural details than to architecture itself. *Departure from Cythera* shows the rococo to be a refined, sensual style, perfect for providing a charming backdrop to the private social life of the eighteenth-century aristocracy.

In one of his last works, *The Sign for Gersaint's Shop,* Watteau removed all mythological and idyllic references (Figure 16.6). His subject, a shop where paintings are sold (François-Edmé Gersaint [1696–1750] was one of the outstanding art dealers of the eighteenth century), indicates the importance of the new commercial art market that was soon to replace the aristocratic patronage system. Art collecting in the age of Louis XIV had been restricted largely to kings, princes,

and nobles. Within Gersaint's shop, elegantly dressed customers browse, flirt, and study the shopkeeper's wares. The sexual motifs in the pictures on the walls and in the oval canvas on the right reinforce the sensuous atmosphere of this painting. But Watteau also makes this Parisian scene dignified by giving equal focus to the human figures and the role each plays in the overall composition.

Watteau's painting is a telling metaphor of the end of one age and the beginning of another. This meaning can be interpreted in the crating of the portrait of Louis XIV (on the left), a punning metaphor for the demise of the old political order and the style of Louis XIV. In effect, the painting shows that, in the rococo period, many new collectors came from the world of the upper bourgeoisie and shopped in commercial galleries like Gersaint's shop.

Watteau's paintings convey a dreamy eroticism, but those of François Boucher [boo-SHAY] (1703–1770) are characterized by unabashed sexuality. Boucher was the supreme exponent of the graceful Louis XV style,

Figure 16.7 FRANÇOIS BOUCHER. *Nude on a Sofa.* 1752. Oil on canvas, 23⅜ × 25⅜″. Alte Pinakothek, Munich. *The trend toward the secularization of consciousness that had been building since the late Middle Ages reached a high point in this nude by Boucher. Boucher's frank enjoyment of sensual pleasure and his desire to convey that feeling to the viewer represented a new stage in the relationship between artists and the public. By portraying his subject without any justification except eroticism, Boucher embodied a new artistic sensibility.*

becoming official painter to the French crown in 1765. His voluptuous nudes, which were made more titillating by their realistic portrayal without classical trappings, appealed to the king and to the decadent court nobility. Boucher's *Nude on a Sofa* is probably a study of one of Louis XV's mistresses (Figure 16.7). The casually suggestive pose, the rumpled bedclothes, and the delicate pastel shades are all designed to charm and to seduce. Boucher's art, though masterful, epitomizes the lax morals of French noble life that were becoming increasingly offensive even to other rococo artists.

A different focus is evident in the rococo portraits of Elisabeth-Louise Vigée-Lebrun [vee-ZHAY-luh-BRUHN] (1755–1842), who became the leading society painter of the later eighteenth century and one of the few women to gain fame as an artist. In 1787 she painted a famous family portrait of Louis XVI's queen, Marie Antoinette, whom she served as court painter (Figure 16.8). With this work, Vigée-Lebrun solidified her status as the equal of the best court portraitists of the century. Elements of the rococo style can be seen in this elegant portrait of the queen and her children in the dainty colors, the graceful gestures, and the feeling of domestic intimacy. The queen's role as mother is the focus as she sits with the baby Duke of Normandy in her lap, the small Madame Royale at her side, and the little Dauphin pointing at the empty cradle. Vigée-Lebrun's depiction of Marie Antoinette dressed as a lady of fashion instead of in the traditional trappings of royalty reflects the queen's well-known fondness for simplicity. Stifled by the formality of court

life, the queen promoted a relaxed social code at Le Hameau, a rustic hideaway she had built for herself at Versailles, where all rules of court etiquette were set aside.

The last great French rococo painter, Jean-Honoré Fragonard [frag-uh-NAHR] (1732–1806), revived Watteau's graceful, debonair themes, as in *The Pursuit* (Figure 16.9). A young woman, attended by two female servants, pauses in mock flight, as a suitor (on the left) offers her a rose. The subdued pastel colors of the man's shirt and the woman's dress cause their figures to stand out dramatically from the dark background. The sensuality of this encounter is heightened by an abundance of sexual symbols: a red rose (a symbol of love and courtship); a statue of two cupids in the background (attendants of the goddess Venus); a large vase on the left (a symbol of the female sex); and a fountain behind the woman (a symbol of sexual conquest).

What is fresh in Fragonard's art and prefigures romanticism is the luxuriant detail he lavishes on nature—an influence from Dutch landscape art. In *The Pursuit*, the vivid natural world seems to threaten the couple's romantic idyll. Despite his interest in nature, Fragonard remained faithful to the rococo style even after it fell out of fashion. His paintings continued to focus on the playful themes of flirtation and pursuit in a frivolous, timeless world.

ROCOCO INTERIORS The decorative refinement and graceful detail of the rococo style made it well suited to interior design. A major rococo design element was

Figure 16.8   Elisabeth-Louise Vigée Lebrun. *Marie Antoinette and Her Children*. 1787. Oil on canvas, 9′1¼″ × 7′5⅝″. Musée National du Château de Versailles. *Like the greatest court painters, Vigée-Lebrun was able to provide psychological insight into her highborn subjects while flattering them. Here, Marie Antoinette, though surrounded by adoring children, seems uncomfortable in a maternal role. Instead, with her head held in an imperious manner and her face a beautiful mask, she looks every inch the lady of fashion, which she indeed was. Vigée-Lebrun has muted this psychological insight by providing rich distractions for the viewer's eye, such as the shiny surfaces of the queen's attire (satin gown, pearls, and hat) and the elegant room (carpet, chest, and tasseled cushion).*

Figure 16.9   Jean-Honoré Fragonard. *The Pursuit*. 1771–1773. Oil on panel, 10′5⅛″. The Frick Collection, New York. *This painting was one of four panels known as* The Progress of Love, *commissioned by Madame du Barry, Louis XV's mistress and rival to Madame de Pompadour. Intended to adorn a pavilion at her palace, the panels were rejected for reasons unknown. Together, the four works constitute a symbolic allegory, covering the stages of love from first contact (here) through courtship and consummation to reverie. Fragonard's panels transform lovers' passion into works of art.*

rocaille: fanciful stucco ornaments in the shape of ribbons, leaves, stems, flowers, interlaces, arabesques, and elongated, curving lines applied to walls and ceilings. The effect of rocaille was to make solid surfaces look like fleeting illusions. Mirrors further deceived the senses, and chandeliers provided jewel-like lighting; all elements worked together to create a glittering, luxurious setting for an ultrarefined society.

Germain Boffrand [bo-FRAHN] (1667–1754), France's royal architect, helped to establish rococo's popularity with his Salon de la Princesse in the Hôtel de Soubise in Paris (Figure 16.10). Exploiting the room's oval shape,

Boffrand eliminated the shadows and omitted classical details such as pilasters and columns, which had been elements of decoration since the Renaissance. The floor-to-ceiling windows admit light freely, and the strategically placed mirrors reinforce the airy feeling. Instead of using a large overhead fresco, Boffrand divided the ceiling into many panel pictures. The characteristically nervous rococo line—seen in the intricate designs of the gold edging—integrates the interior into a harmonious whole. The overall effect of airiness, radiance, and grace is worthy of a Watteau setting of aristocratic revelry.

Figure 16.10 GERMAIN BOFFRAND. Salon de la Princesse, Hôtel de Soubise. Ca. 1735–1740. Paris. *The Salon de la Princesse was a reception room designed for the apartment of the Princess de Soubise. The graceful undulations of Boffrand's design represent the exquisite style of the Louis XV era. A typical rococo design element is the blurring of the line between the walls and the ceiling.*

German decoration followed the French lead. The Residenz, a palace commissioned by the prince-bishop of the German city of Würzburg, is an example of baroque architecture with rococo interiors. Designed chiefly by Balthasar Neumann [NOI-mahn] (1687–1753), the building's glory is the main reception room, called the Kaisersaal, or Emperor's Room (Figure 16.11). The ceiling frescoes are by Giovanni Battista Tiepolo [tee-AY-puh-loh] (1696–1770), an Italian-born rococo master. His paintings combine the theatricality of the Italian florid baroque and the love of light and color characteristic of Rubens and the Flemish school (see Chapter 14). But Tiepolo's frescoes are only one facet of the riotous splendor of this room, which abounds in crystal chandeliers, gilt ornamentation, marble statues, Corinthian capitals and arabesques, gold-edged mirrors, and cartouches, or scroll-like frames. In rooms such as this, the age's painters and decorators catered to their patrons' wildest dreams of grandeur.

Figure 16.11 BALTHASAR NEUMANN AND OTHERS. Kaisersaal, the Residenz. View toward the south wall. 1719–1744. Würzburg, Germany. *In this magnificent room, the ceiling fresco by Tiepolo is gorgeously framed with multicolored marble curtains pulled back by stucco angels. Other sumptuous details include ornate framed paintings, cartouches, and mirrors; gilded Corinthian capitals and arabesques; and crystal chandeliers suspended low over a polychrome marble floor.*

THE ENGLISH RESPONSE   In Great Britain, where the rococo was condemned as tasteless and corrupt, the painter William Hogarth (1697–1764) won fame as a social satirist, working in a style quite different from that of his French contemporaries. Even though his mocking works appealed to all social groups, the Protestant middle class most enthusiastically welcomed his biting satires. In the paintings, which sometimes ridicule idle aristocrats and always take a moralistic view of life, his bourgeois admirers discovered the same values that caused them to embrace the English novel. Taking advantage of his popularity, Hogarth made engravings of his paintings, printing multiple copies—the first major artist to take this step to reach a new clientele.

Among the most popular of Hogarth's moral works was the series of paintings that depict the course of a loveless marriage between a profligate nobleman and the daughter of a wealthy middle-class businessman. Titled *Marriage à la Mode,* this series comprises six scenes that show in exquisite detail the bitter consequences of an arranged marriage by following the husband and the wife to their untimely deaths. In the fourth episode, called *The Countess' Levée,* or *Morning Party,* Hogarth portrays the wife plotting a rendezvous with a prospective lover (Figure 16.12). In this scene, typical of the age's aristocratic entertainments, the hostess is having her hair curled while the would-be suitor lounges on a sofa, charming her with conversation. Nearby, guests, servants, and musicians play their supporting roles in this sad tale. Hogarth,

never willing to let the viewers draw their own conclusions, provides the moral lesson. In the right foreground, a black child-servant points to a small horned creature—a symbol of the cuckold, or the deceived husband—thus alluding to the wife's planned infidelity. Even the paintings on the walls echo Hogarth's theme of sexual abandon.

The Challenge of Neoclassicism

Soon after 1750, the rococo took a back seat to a new style, known as **neoclassical.** With its backward glance to the restrained style of antiquity, the neoclassical had its origins both in a rejection of the rococo and in a fascination with the new archaeological discoveries made at midcentury. Knowledge about Pompeii and Herculaneum—the Roman cities buried by Mount Vesuvius in 79 CE, with excavations beginning in 1738 and 1748, respectively—had greatly heightened the curiosity of educated Europeans about the ancient world. At the same time, scholars began to publish books that showed Greek art to be the original source of ancient classicism. The English authorities James Stuart and Nicholas Revett pointed out the differences between Greek and Roman art in *The Antiquities of Athens,* published in 1762. In 1764 the German Johann Joachim Winckelmann (1717–1768) distinguished Greek sculpture from the Roman in his *History of Art*—a study that led to the founding of the academic discipline of art

Figure 16.12   WILLIAM HOGARTH. *The Countess' Levée,* or *Morning Party,* from *Marriage à la Mode.* 1743–1745. Oil on canvas, 27 × 35″. Reproduced by courtesy of the Trustees, The National Gallery, London. *Hogarth's painterly techniques—learned in France—have transformed a potentially banal topic into a glittering social satire. On the left, a pig-snouted singer is used to ridicule the popular* castrati—*men who were emasculated as youths to preserve their boyish tenor voices. Hovering over the* castrato *is a flutist—his coarse features demonstrating the artist's loathing for this social type. Other rich details, such as the tea-sipping dandy in hair curlers and the female guest who is gesticulating wildly, confirm Hogarth's contempt for the entire gathering.*

INTERPRETING ART

Moral Vision
David's message is that sacrifice for one's country is better than family loyalty. (This theme is heightened by the knowledge that one sister will be killed because of her love for an enemy combatant.) This patriotic moral reflects the turbulent years just before the onset of the French Revolution, in 1789.

Anatomy The athletic bodies of the men show David's superb mastery of the human form—a classical feature of this painting.

Color The foreground figures, clad in bold shades of green, brown, pink, and red, stand out clearly against the shadowy and muted background.

Setting The classical setting—plain walls, three

arches with massive columns, and niches—reflects the ancient Roman style.

Balance The father, framed by the middle arch, divides the painting into two halves. On the left stand the three brothers—symbols of patriotic duty. On the right are three women and two children—symbols of love of family.

Patriarchal Values The brothers' bold arm and leg movements assert virile authority. The women, their faces averted and arms either hanging listlessly at their sides or shielding the two children, suggest helpless resignation. One child buries his or her face in one of the women's skirts, and the other child stares boldly at the unfolding drama.

Interpreting Art figure 16.1 JACQUES-LOUIS DAVID. *Oath of the Horatii.* 1785. Oil on canvas, 10'10" × 14'. Louvre. *David here depicts an episode from ancient Rome (7th century BCE): the three Horatii brothers pledge to fight to the death in defense of their city-state, while their father holds aloft their swords as tokens of their vows. With this work David returned grand history subjects to favor, a type of art that Poussin had pioneered in the 1600s (see Figure 14.16). So impressed were the philosophes by this painting that they urged artists to concentrate on neoclassical art with moral themes. Later, revolutionary leaders selected David to be the official artist of the Revolution (see Figure 17.5).*

history. The importance of neoclassicism is indicated by the decision made in 1775 by the Paris Salon—the exhibition (biennial to 1831 and annual thereafter) that introduced the latest paintings to the public—to rebuff works with rococo subjects and to encourage those with classical themes.

NEOCLASSICAL PAINTING In 1775, the same year the Paris Salon began to promote neoclassicism, Louis XVI appointed Joseph-Marie Vien [vie-AHN] (1716–1809) to head the Académie de France in Rome, a leading art school. A strict disciplinarian, Vien returned the study of art to the basics by instructing his students to focus on perspective, anatomy, and life drawing, efforts that resulted in the purified style of Jacques-Louis David [dah-VEED] (1748–1825), the principal exponent of the neoclassical style.

David's response to a commission from Louis XVI for a historical painting was *Oath of the Horatii,* a work that electrified the Paris Salon of 1785 (Interpreting Art

figure 16.1). Taking a page from the history of the early Roman republic, this painting depicts the brothers Horatii vowing to protect the state, even though their stand means killing a sister who loves one of Rome's enemies. The patriotic subject with its tension between civic duty and family loyalty appealed to the philosophes, who preferred neoclassicism, with its implicitly revolutionary morality, to rococo, with its frivolous themes.

David's *Oath of the Horatii* established the techniques and ideals that soon became typical of neoclassical painting. His inspirational model was the seventeenth-century French artist Poussin, with his classical themes and assured mastery of linear perspective. Rejecting the weightless, floating images of rococo painting, David portrayed his figures as frozen sculptures, painted in strong colors. The classical ideals of balance, simplicity, and restraint served as a basis for many of David's artistic choices.

David showed his mastery of these techniques and ideals in *The Death of Socrates,* which was exhibited

ENCOUNTER

Chinoiserie: Fantasy of the East

Cultural borrowing usually means cultural adaptation, rather than pure appropriation, because receiving cultures tend to process new ideas according to traditional tastes and habits of thought. Such was the situation in the eighteenth century, when the Chinese style took the West by storm. **Chinoiserie** *[shen-WAZ-uh-ree] (French, Chinois, "China"), as the Chinese style was called, was not a pure style but a Western fantasy of the East—an early version of what has come to be called Orientalism.*

In the 1700s, Chinoiserie became a fashionable style for the West's rich and powerful, including those in the English colonies in the New World. This style, with its elaborate decoration and intricate patterns, was used for interior design, furniture, pottery, textiles, and garden layout. While its roots dated from the age of Marco Polo (late thirteenth century), the heyday of Chinoiserie was about 1740 to 1770. The style lingered on until about 1850, dying out with the arrival in the West of more reliable information about Chinese culture.

Not historically accurate, Chinoiserie was inspired by travelers' accounts (see Encounter in Chapter 12), imported wares from the Far East, particularly in countries with East India companies—England (1600), Holland (1602), and France (1664)—or trade depots in China (Portugal, in Macao [1553])—and by the vivid imagination of Western craftspeople, artists, and designers, who drew freely on Chinese decorative design. In the 1600s, Chinese goods, such as cabinets, porcelain vessels, and embroideries, flooded the European market. Soon, new centers specializing in Chinese-style wares but cheaper than the imports sprang up across Europe. In Delft, the Netherlands, tin-glazed earthenware, sometimes called delftware, began to be manufactured in about 1600, and shortly thereafter, the blue-and-white pattern became the town's signature style, in imitation of blue-and-white Ming dynasty (1368–1644) porcelain. In Meissen, Germany, Europe's first hard-paste porcelain factory, using only hand labor, was established in 1710. Having mastered the secret Chinese formula for porcelain—clay fired into a vitrified, or glasslike, form—the Meissen workers created Chinese shapes for dishes, vases, and tea sets, handpainting them with fanciful designs, inspired by Chinese models.

The Chinoiserie fad influenced both interior and exterior design. Style-conscious people designated a Chinese room, with lacquered furniture, decorated screens, and precious objects, in their palaces or townhouses, as did France's King Louis XIV at Versailles in 1671. The Chinese garden, with its irregular shapes that imitate the irregularity of nature and its curved roof pagodas, or towers, and gazebos, influenced garden design. In England the homegrown English garden, so carefully planned to look unplanned, was merged with the Chinese version to create the Anglo-Chinese garden. Kew Gardens, outside London, is an elegant, surviving example of the Anglo-Chinese garden (Encounter figure 16.1).

LEARNING FROM THE ENCOUNTER

1. *Define Chinoiserie.* 2. *What* are the distinguishing characteristics of the Chinese style? 3. *Discuss* the impact of Chinese influence on Western interior design, garden design, pottery, and furniture. 4. *How* does pure Chinese style differ from Chinoiserie? 5. *Discuss* Chinoiserie today in the West, in films, commerce, and food.

Encounter figure 16.1   WILLIAM CHAMBERS. The Pagoda. 1761. Ht. 163'; lowest story 49' diameter. Kew Gardens, United Kingdom. © Copyright Colin Smith and licensed for reuse under this Creative Commons License. TQ1876. *The architect William Chambers (1723–1796) was unusual for this period, because he had traveled to the Chinese port of Guangzhou (Canton) in his youth. Thus, his design for this pagoda was actually based on firsthand knowledge, rather than the fanciful imaginings of other artists and designers of the time. An imitation of an actual Chinese pagoda, Chambers's pagoda stands ten stories tall, with projecting roofs on each level and dragons (eighty in all) positioned at each roof angle. The structure was heavily restored after damage during World War II. Originally a private preserve, Kew Gardens became a royal garden in 1759.*

Figure 16.13 JACQUES-LOUIS DAVID. *The Death of Socrates.* 1787. Oil on canvas, 4'11" × 6'6". Metropolitan Museum of Art. Wolfe Fund, 1931. *Neoclassicism usually relied on ancient literature and traditions for inspiration, as in this painting by David. The scene is based on Plato's dialogue* Phaedo, *though David has chosen to depict Plato present (at the foot of the bed), unlike in the literary account. Two of the domestic details, the lamp and the bed, are modeled on artifacts uncovered at Pompeii. The shackles and cuffs under the bed refer to the fact that Socrates was in chains just before drinking the hemlock.*

in the Paris Salon of 1787 (Figure 16.13). Like Jesus in scenes of the Last Supper, Socrates is portrayed shortly before his death, encircled by those men who will later spread his message. Just as in *Oath of the Horatii*, David's arrangement of the figures reflects the classical ideal of balance. Surrounded by grieving followers, the white-haired Socrates reaches for the cup of poison and gestures toward his heavenly goal—serene in his willingness to die for intellectual freedom.

THE PRINT As demands for art grew in England and France, prints became popular among the middle class. These new patrons wanted art for collecting and for decorating their homes, but they could not afford original paintings. Prints, which had been produced since the mid–fifteenth century (see Chapter 10), turned out to be the solution. The first prints were exclusively in black and white. Color prints dated from Rembrandt's

era, when Dutch printmakers pioneered the mezzotint and the aquatint. Both types of prints now came into their own.

The **mezzotint** (halftone), which requires several stages of cutting and scraping the metal plate with special tools to make an image, allows for subtle gradations of shadings along with precise lines to give greater definition. In the late 1600s, Dutch engravers arrived in London, where they trained a generation of artists in the mezzotint technique. In the 1700s, William Hogarth and other printmakers popularized mezzotint prints by making inexpensive reproductions of original paintings and copies of their own works. Connoisseurs and art patrons collected the more valuable, first-run mezzotints, while the middle classes bought the cheaper, mass-produced prints.

In comparison to the mezzotint, aquatints fell out of favor soon after their first appearance. However, in the

Figure 16.14 PHILIBERT-LOUIS DEBUCOURT. *The Public Promenade.* 1792. Etching, engraving, and aquatint, 14³/₈ × 23¼". The Elisha Whittelsey Collection, The Elisha Whittelsey Fund, Metropolitan Museum, New York. *Aquatints, such as this, appealed to the middle class, because the prints, besides being relatively inexpensive, were able to imitate the look of a watercolor painting, with their subtle shadings of color and shadow. The blues are set among spots of pink and white, and the darker trees around the periphery frame the scene. In the center, vivid colors highlight this gathering of fashionable society on parade. The artist Debucourt [de-BOO-cour] (1755–1832) satirizes his subjects, through their opulent dress and haughty manners, as they amuse themselves in the gardens of the Palais Royale—an eighteenth-century public area only in the sense that it was reserved for the social elite.*

late 1700s, Jean-Baptiste Le Prince (1734–1781) wrote a manual on the technique and began to print aquatints in France. Other printmakers soon joined him in Paris. Across the channel, Paul Sandby (1730–1809), a watercolorist—famous for his landscapes—was the first English painter to replicate his drawings in aquatints. An attempt to create the effect of a watercolor, **aquatints** were labor intensive and time-consuming to make. First, the image was cut into a copper plate with a metal tool. Then, the plate was dusted with resin and heated. As the resin melted, an irregular pattern of open and closed spaces was formed over the plate's image. Next, the plate was subjected to an acid wash (*aqua fortis,* nitric acid—the source of the name *aquatint*), etching only those areas around the solid resin and creating a fine, grainy pattern, capable of holding color. Finally, watercolor was applied by hand, either to the plate or to the print itself. By 1800, English and French collectors were

purchasing aquatints (Figure 16.14). However, with the rise of improved methods of color printing after 1830, the aquatint process soon faded away.

NEOCLASSICAL ARCHITECTURE No other painter could compare with David, but the Scotsman Robert Adam (1728–1792) developed a neoclassical style in interior decor that was the reigning favorite from 1760 until 1800. Classicism had dominated British architecture since the 1600s, and Adam reinvigorated this tradition with forms and motifs gathered during his archaeological investigations. Kenwood House in London shows his application of Roman design to the exterior of a domestic dwelling, combining Ionic columns, a running frieze, and a triangular pediment to form a graceful portico, or porch, in the manner of a Roman temple (Figure 16.15). In the library, Adam mixed classical elements with the pastel colors of the rococo to produce

Figure 16.15 ROBERT ADAM. Kenwood House. 1764. Exterior, the north front. London. *Adam's restrained style in the late eighteenth century represented a strong reinfusion of classical principles into the English tradition. His style, with its reliance on the classical orders and principles of balance and proportion, appealed to all classes but especially to the sedate middle class.*

an eclectic harmony (Figure 16.16). To continue this theme, he borrowed from Roman buildings to design his barrel-vaulted ceiling and adjoining apse.

French architects too began to embrace the neoclassical style in the late 1700s. The leader of this movement was Jacques-Germain Soufflot [soo-FLOH] (1713–1780), who designed buildings based on Roman temples. Soufflot's severe neoclassicism is characterized by its reliance on architectural detail rather than on sculptural decoration. Avoiding Adam's occasional intermingling of rococo and classical effects, Soufflot preferred pure Roman forms. The most perfect expression of Soufflot's style is the Pantheon in Paris. Soufflot's classical ideal is mirrored in the Pantheon's basic plan, with its enormous portico supported by huge Corinthian columns (Figure 16.17). Except for the statues in the pediment and a frieze of stone garlands around the upper walls, the building's surface is devoid of sculptural detail. For the dome, Soufflot found his inspiration not in Rome but in London. The Pantheon's spectacular dome,

Figure 16.16 ROBERT ADAM. Library, Kenwood House. 1767–1768. London. *Adam designed the library of Kenwood House with several basic elements of classical architecture: columns, pilasters, and apses. By and large, he followed the Renaissance dictum of letting the architectural elements determine the chamber's decorative details. Nonetheless, he achieved a dazzling effect by his daring addition of mirrors and color.*

Figure 16.17 Jacques-Germain Soufflot. The Pantheon. 1755–1792. Paris. *By 1789, advanced thinkers in France had begun to appropriate classical images for their movement, with David's neoclassical paintings leading the way. When the Revolution began, its leaders determined to build a suitable monument to house the remains of those philosophes whose works had furthered the cause of reform. Hence, it was natural that the revolutionary government turn Soufflot's classical church—with its portico modeled from Roman styles—into a patriotic shrine.*

with its surrounding Corinthian colonnade, is based on the dome of St. Paul's cathedral (see Interpreting Art figure 14.1).

Philosophy

The Age of Reason was a seminal period in the history of Western thought. Two landmark books in political science were published, along with the works of David Hume, one of the founders of modern philosophy.

POLITICAL PHILOSOPHY Modern political theory, which had been founded in the 1600s, continued to evolve in the Age of Reason. Absolutism, the reigning form of government, had many staunch defenders, such as Voltaire. Voltaire, convinced that the people lacked political wisdom, advocated enlightened despotism. But most other philosophes rejected absolutism and supported various forms of government.

The Enlightenment's chief political theorists were Baron de Montesquieu and Jean-Jacques Rousseau, whose contrasting social origins help explain their radically different definitions of the ideal state. Montesquieu, a titled Frenchman and a provincial judge,

believed that rule by an enlightened aristocracy would ensure justice and tranquillity. Rousseau, an impoverished citizen of the Swiss city-state of Geneva, advocated a kind of pure democracy. Rousseau's ideas about who should control the state were more far-reaching and revolutionary than Montesquieu's.

Montesquieu [mahnt-us-KYOO] (1689–1755) expressed his political ideas in *The Spirit of the Laws* (1748), a work that compares systems of government in an effort to establish underlying principles. He concludes that climate, geography, religion, and education, among other factors, account for the world's different types of laws as well as governmental systems. Despite his misunderstanding of the roles of climate and geography, Montesquieu's analytical approach identified influences on governments that had not been considered before. One enduring idea in *The Spirit of the Laws* is that a separation of governmental powers provides an effective defense against despotic rule. Montesquieu was an admirer of England's parliamentary democracy and of the work of the English political philosopher John Locke (see Chapter 15), whose influence is evident here. American patriots adopted this principle of the separation of powers in the 1780s when they framed the Constitution, dividing the federal government's power into executive, legislative, and judicial branches.

In contrast to the conservative Montesquieu, Jean-Jacques Rousseau [roo-SOH] (1712–1778) framed his political theories within a libertarian tradition. Rousseau set forth his model of the ideal state in *The Social Contract*, published in 1762. He agreed with John Locke that human beings are free and equal in nature, but he defined the "state of nature" as a paradoxical condition in which individuals can follow any whim and hence possess no moral purpose. On the other hand, the state, which is founded on a social contract (an agreement among people), gives its citizens basic civil rights (freedom, equality, and property) and a moral purpose—precisely the things that they lack in nature. That morality arises within the civil state is a function of the "general will," Rousseau's term for what is best for the entire community. If each citizen is granted the right to vote, and if each citizen votes on the laws in accord with the general will, then the laws will embody what is best for the whole society. Thus, in Rousseau's thinking, citizens who obey the laws become moral beings. (It should be noted that who defines and implements the general will and how it affects individual freedom remain ambiguous in *The Social Contract*.)

In contrast to Locke's form of democracy, whereby a representative group such as a legislature acts in the name of the people, Rousseau's asserted that the people themselves collectively personify the state through the general will. Rousseau's ideal state, therefore, has to be relatively small so that all citizens can know and recognize one another. His model for the ideal state was based on his experience as a citizen of the tiny Genevan republic. Nevertheless, Rousseau has had an incalculable influence on thinkers and politicians concerned about much larger states. Indeed, his impact in the nineteenth century extended far beyond democratic circles. Nationalistic philosophers such as G. W. F. Hegel borrowed Rousseau's theory of the all-encompassing state, and radical theorists such as Karl Marx adopted his doctrine of the general will (see Chapters 17 and 18).

DAVID HUME   David Hume (1711–1776), a close friend of fellow Scotsman Adam Smith (see page 466), was a philosopher and historian. His *History of England,* in six volumes, became the standard for generations. From 1763 to 1766, Hume served at the British embassy in Paris, where he was honored by the French philosophes. He later returned to Edinburgh, where he was the leader of the Scottish Enlightenment.

Hume first laid out his philosophy in *A Treatise of Human Nature* (1739–1740), which he continued to revise over the rest of his life. His argument in this treatise is subversive, as he undermines that which he claims to defend. He begins in the critical spirit of the Age of Reason and ends up advocating skepticism. He follows the empirical ("knowledge comes from experience") method of the English thinker John Locke. However, revising Locke's dictum that all ideas in the mind are first in the senses, he denies the existence of the mind, holding that it is simply a grab bag of mental images. He then shows that Locke's dictum leads, not to certainty, but to **solipsism,** the belief that all that can be known is one's own mental world. Hume reached this controversial conclusion by breaking down ideas into (a) sense impressions and (b) mental images formed as a result of these impressions. Thus, two worlds exist: the subjective world, which can be known and worked with but which contains no guarantee of its objective truth; and the external world, which is perceived, if at all, through a screen of ideas.

Hume also applied his empirical-skeptical method to **causality**—the idea that one event in the world causes another. He knew that such reasoning was typical of human thinking on empirical matters. In the end, he concluded that cause and effect is not communicated to the mind through the senses; it is merely an assumption made about the world. In other words, the notion of causality rests on habit. Later thinkers have found it difficult to refute Hume's skepticism.

Hume was also controversial for his religious views. His known skepticism kept him from a professor's chair at Edinburgh University. To live in peace, he arranged to have printed after his death the *Dialogues Concerning Natural Religion* (1779), an atheistic work that called God "an empty hypothesis."

Literature

Western literature in the Age of Reason was dominated by French authors and the French language, which now replaced Latin as the international language of scholarship, diplomacy, and commerce. French writers made common cause with the philosophes, sharing their faith in a glorious future. They wrote for the growing middle-class audience that was replacing the aristocratic patrons. Because these authors were under the constant threat of state censorship, they were often forced to disguise their barbed social criticisms or to sugarcoat their beliefs. Those restrictions did not, however, deter them from their mission: to liberate the consciousness of their readers and usher in an enlightened society.

FRENCH WRITERS: THE DEVELOPMENT OF NEW FORMS   The two political philosophers discussed earlier—Montesquieu and Rousseau—were also prominent figures in French literature. Early in his career Montesquieu wrote *Persian Letters,* a cleverly devised, wide-ranging critique of French institutions and customs in the guise of letters purporting to be written by and to Persian travelers during a trip to Paris. Through "Persian" eyes, Montesquieu ridiculed the despotism of the French crown, the idleness of the aristocracy, and the intolerance of the Roman Catholic Church. This device of using a detached observer of Western life was a safeguard against censorship, as was the decision to print *Persian Letters* in the Netherlands. Montesquieu's publication inspired a new type of literature, a genre in which a "foreign" traveler voices the author's social criticisms.

Rousseau foreshadowed the romantic sensibility of the next century with his intensely personal autobiography, *The Confessions.* Published after his death, this work was the frankest self-revelation that had yet been seen in print. It narrated Rousseau's lifelong follies and difficulties, including sexual problems, religious vacillation, a mismatched marriage, and his decision to place his five offspring in an orphanage as soon as each was born. Not only did he reveal his personal secrets, but he also tried to justify his failings, pleading with his audience that they not judge him too harshly. The revelations shocked many readers, but others praised him for his emotional truthfulness and were willing to overlook his self-serving treatment of a number of the facts of his own life. After Rousseau's candid admissions, the genre of autobiography was never the same again.

The third great French writer of the eighteenth century was François-Marie Arouet, better known by his pen name, Voltaire (1694–1778)—the outspoken leader of the Age of Reason and the philosophe who best personifies the Enlightenment (Figure 16.18). A restless genius, Voltaire earned success in many forms, including dramas, essays, poems, histories, treatises, novels, a philosophical dictionary, letters, and the first work of history—the *Essay on Customs*—to survey civilization from a world perspective.

Of Voltaire's voluminous writings, only one work is still widely read today: the novel *Candide,* published in 1759. The most popular novel of the Age of Reason, *Candide* exhibits Voltaire's urbane style, his shrewd mixture of philosophy and wit, and his ability to jolt the reader with an unexpected word or detail. Beneath its frivolous surface, this work has the serious purpose of ridiculing the fashionable optimism of eighteenth-century thinkers who, Voltaire believed, denied the existence of evil and insisted that the world was essentially good.

At one time an optimist himself, Voltaire altered his beliefs about evil after the 1755 Lisbon earthquake, a calamity that figures prominently in *Candide*. This comic adventure tale recounts the coming-of-age of the aptly named Candide, who is introduced to optimism by Dr. Pangloss, a caricature of a German professor. The naive hero suffers many misfortunes—war, poverty, religious bigotry, trial by the Inquisition, shipwreck—and through them all holds fast to Pangloss's teaching that "this is the best of all possible worlds." But finally, faced with mounting incidents of pain and injustice, Candide renounces optimism. The story ends with the hero's newly acquired wisdom for combating the evils of boredom, vice, and want: "We must cultivate our garden."

NEOCLASSICISM IN ENGLISH LITERATURE In England, the presence of a Protestant middle class, which was growing larger and increasingly literate, created a demand for a literature that was decorous, conservative, and basically moralistic and religious in tone, even if that religion were little more than deference to nature and nature's God. The poetry of Alexander Pope and the monumental historical work of Edward Gibbon are typical of this style of literature, which is referred to as neoclassical.

Alexander Pope (1688–1744) is the most representative voice of the English neoclassical style. His poems celebrate the order and decorum that were prized by the middle classes—the social group from which he sprang. He became his age's leading spokesman for humane values such as reason, classical learning, good sense and good taste, and hatred of hypocrisy and ostentation. His verses, marked by their satire and wit,

Figure 16.18 JEAN-ANTOINE HOUDON. *Voltaire.* 1780. Life-size. Bibliothèque Nationale, Paris. *Houdon's neoclassical portrait in plaster of Voltaire shows the sculptor's determination to portray his subject as an ancient Roman. Houdon seated Voltaire in an armchair copied from ancient models and draped him in an ample robe that suggested Roman dress (but was actually based on the robe worn by the great philosophe to keep out the cold). He endowed his sculpture with a vivid sense of life, as may be seen in the fine details and the expressive face.*

made Pope the supreme inspiration of the Age of Reason until the romantics, led by William Wordsworth in the 1790s, turned away from the neoclassical ideal.

Pope wrote many kinds of poetry—pastorals, elegies, and satires, among others—but the work closest to the spirit of the Age of Reason is his *Essay on Man,* a didactic work combining philosophy and verse, published in 1733–1734. Issued in four sections and composed in rhymed couplets, this poem brings together one of the age's central ideas, optimism, and some notions inherited from antiquity. In the first section of this poem, Pope argues that God in his infinite power has created the best possible world—not a perfect universe—and that God's design rests on the concept of the great chain of being: reaching from God to microscopic creatures, this chain links all living things together. Human beings occupy the chain's midpoint, where the human and animal species meet. Because of this position, two different natures fight in the human breast: "Created half to rise, and half to fall; / Great lord of all things, yet a prey to all." According to Pope, since humanity's place is unchanging, human reason is limited, and God does not make mistakes, humans should not question the divine plan. He concludes that "whatever is, is right." From this fatalistic principle it follows that what humans perceive as evil is simply misunderstood good. This qualified optimism was satirized by Voltaire in *Candide* through the character of Dr. Pangloss.

Having established a fatalistic outlook in the first section of *Essay on Man,* Pope became more optimistic in the remaining sections. Although God's ways may be unknowable, he reasoned that some truths may still be learned by human beings: "The proper study of mankind is man." From this belief he concluded that a paradise could be created on earth if human beings would think and act rationally—an attitude dear to the hearts of the philosophes.

Edward Gibbon's (1737–1794) *History of the Decline and Fall of the Roman Empire* appeared in six volumes between 1776 and 1788. Gibbon's recognition was instant and universal; he was hailed across Europe both for the breadth of his historical knowledge and for the brilliance of his style. His subject, the history of Rome, appealed to the age's classical interests, and his skepticism, notably regarding the Christian faith, echoed the sentiments of the philosophes. Although Gibbon's authority as a scholar was eclipsed in the next century because of the progress of historical science, his work remains one of the Enlightenment's genuine literary masterpieces.

Gibbon's massive work reflects both the ancient historical tradition and the ideals of the Enlightenment. Following the ancient historians, Gibbon wrote with secular detachment and offered reasons for historical change based on human motives and natural causes. From the Enlightenment, he determined that history should be philosophy teaching through example—that is, we should learn moral lessons from history. These influences come together in his history when he attributes Rome's decay to an unpatriotic and subversive Christian faith along with the Germanic invasions. In effect, Gibbon's history praises secular civilization and covertly warns against the perils of religious enthusiasm.

THE RISE OF THE NOVEL   Despite the contributions of Pope and Gibbon to Western letters, the most important literary development in England during the Age of Reason was the rise of the modern novel. The hallmark of the early English novel was its realism. In the spirit of the Scientific Revolution, the new authors broke with the past and began to study the world with fresh eyes. Previous writers had based their plots on historical events or fables, but now individual experience became the keystone of the writer's art, and authors turned away from traditional plots in favor of an accurate representation of real-life events.

The English novel was realistic in several ways. It focused on individual persons rather than universal types and on particular circumstances rather than settings determined by literary custom. Its plots also followed the development of characters over the course of minutely observed time. The sense of realism was complete when the author adopted a narrative voice that contributed to the air of authenticity.

The novel captured the wholehearted attention of the reading public, including many women. The works of Samuel Richardson and Henry Fielding especially appealed to these new readers. Their writings helped to define the modern novel and, at the same time, set the standards for later fiction. For centuries, tragedy, with its plots about aristocratic heroes and heroines, had been regarded as the highest literary form. But since the age of Richardson and Fielding, the novel, with its focus on ordinary people, has been and remains the dominant literary genre.

The novels of Samuel Richardson (1689–1761) focus on love between the sexes. For more than a thousand pages in *Pamela, or Virtue Rewarded* (1740) and almost two thousand pages in *Clarissa Harlowe* (1747–1748), he tells the contrasting stories of two young women whose virtue is tested by repeated seduction attempts. Pamela, a resourceful and calculating maidservant, eventually finds happiness in marriage to her prosperous would-be seducer. Clarissa, from a higher social class but of weaker mettle, runs off with her seducer and dies of shame.

In contrast to Richardson's sentimental domestic dramas, the novels of Henry Fielding (1707–1754) depict a robust world of comedy and adventure. His best work is *The History of Tom Jones, a Foundling* (1749), a comic masterpiece that has been called the finest English novel. Tom, the hero, is a high-spirited young man who makes little effort to resist the temptations that come his way. His wealthy guardian rejects him for his immoral behavior, but Tom is shown to be good-hearted and honest and thus worthy of the good fortune that befalls him at the novel's end when he has learned the virtues of moderation. The novel contains a great deal of amusing satire, aimed particularly at the upper classes.

Music

The standard in music in the early part of the eighteenth century was set by the French, as it was in art and decoration. Rococo music, like rococo art, represented a reaction against the baroque. Instead of the complex, formal structure of baroque music, French composers now strove for a light and charming sound with graceful melodies over simple harmonies. Known as the ***style galant*** ("gallant style"), this music was particularly fashionable during the reign of Louis XV.

SLICE OF LIFE
How to Manipulate the System

LADY MARY WORTLEY MONTAGU
Letter, 25 March 1744

Lady Montagu (1689–1762) was one of the great letter writers in the Western tradition. A free spirit and a keen observer, this Englishwoman lived apart from her husband, Lord Edward Wortley Montagu, for about twenty years, four of which were spent in Avignon, France. In this letter to her husband, Lady Mary explains how she was able to save a group of French Protestant Huguenots from being galley slaves.

I take this opportunity of informing you in what manner I came acquainted with the secret I hinted at in my letter of the 5th of Feb. The Society of Freemasons at Nîmes presented the Duke of Richelieu, governor of Languedoc, with a magnificent entertainment. It is but one day's post from hence, and the Duchess of Crillon with some other ladies of this town resolved to be at it, and almost by force carried me with them, which I am tempted to believe an act of Providence, considering my great reluctance and the service it proved to be to unhappy, innocent people.

The greatest part of the town of Nîmes are secret Protestants, which are still severely punished according to the edicts of Louis XIV whenever they are detected in any public worship. A few days before we came they had assembled; their minister and about a dozen of his congregation were seized and imprisoned. I knew nothing of this, but I had not been in the town two hours when I was visited by two of the most considerable of the Huguenots, who came to beg of me with tears to speak in their favour to the Duke of Richelieu, saying none of the Catholics would do it and the Protestants durst not, and that God had sent me for their protection, [that] the Duke of Richelieu was too well bred to refuse to listen to a lady, and I was of a rank and nation to have liberty to say what I pleased. They moved my compassion so much I resolved to use my endeavours to serve them, though I had little hope of succeeding.

I would not therefore dress myself for the supper, but went in a domino to the ball, a mask giving opportunity of talking in a freer manner than I could have done without it. I was at no trouble in engaging his conversation. The ladies having told him I was there, he immediately advanced towards me, and I found from a different motive he had a great desire to be acquainted with me, having heard a great deal of me. After abundance of compliments of that sort, I made my request for the liberty of the poor Protestants. He with great freedom told me that he was so little a bigot, he pitied them as much as I did, but his orders from Court were to send them to the galleys. However, to show how much he desired my good opinion he was returning and would solicit their freedom (which he has since obtained).

INTERPRETING THIS SLICE OF LIFE

1. *What* is Lady Mary Wortley Montagu's motive for acting as she does? 2. *What* is the religious situation in the town of Nîmes? 3. *How* does Lady Montagu prevent the Huguenots from becoming galley slaves? 4. *Compare* the tone and style of this letter with the way we write letters (or e-mails or text messages) today.

The perfect instrument for rococo music was the harpsichord, a keyboard instrument whose strings are plucked, giving it a delicate, refined sound. At the same time, improved instruments, such as brasses, woodwinds, and violins, were joining the musical family. The piano was invented in the first decade of the eighteenth century by Bartolomeo Cristofori, who installed a mechanism in a harpsichord that would strike the strings with hammers rather than pluck them. With this new instrument, a player could vary the loudness of the sound depending on the force exerted on the keys, something impossible to do on the harpsichord—thus the name **pianoforte**, from the Italian for "soft" and "loud."

The two outstanding composers of rococo music were the Frenchmen François Couperin and Jean-Philippe Rameau. Couperin [koop-uh-RAN] (1668–1733) set the tone in court society in the early 1700s. His finest works were written for the harpsichord; many contain dance pieces and are noted for their rhythmic virtuosity. His highly ornamented compositions are the perfect musical counterpart to Watteau's paintings.

Rameau [rah-MOH] (1683–1764) shared Couperin's fascination with the harpsichord and small-scale works, but his major achievement was as a composer of dramatic operas. Following in the footsteps of the French-Italian operatic composer Jean-Baptiste Lully (see Chapter 14), he made a ballet sequence with a large corps of dancers a central feature of his operatic works. The best of his operas was *Hippolyte and Aricie* (1733), based on the French playwright Racine's tragedy *Phèdre.* Rameau heightened the tension of the gripping plot through his expressive music, underscoring the sexual tension between the doomed heroine and her stepson.

Like rococo art, rococo music was supplanted after 1750 by the new **classical style,** in which more serious expression seemed possible. An important characteristic of classical music was its emphasis on form and structure. The most versatile and widely used form to emerge was the **sonata form,** in which a musical piece is written in three main sections, known as the exposition, the development, and the recapitulation. In the first, melodies and themes are stated; in the second, the same material is expanded and changed in various ways; and in the third, the themes are stated again but with richer harmonies and more complex associations for the listener.

The sonata form was also used as the basis for whole compositions, including the **symphony** (a composition for orchestra), the concerto (a piece for a solo instrument and orchestra), and the sonata (a work for a small group of instruments). Such pieces often have three movements varying in **key, tempo,** and **mood.** The first is usually the longest and has a quick tempo. The second is slow and reflective, and the third is as quick as the first if not quicker. If there are four movements, the third is either a minuet, based on a French dance, or a **scherzo** [SKAIRT-so], a lively Italian form. The sonata form provided general principles of composition that governed each movement and yet allowed composers to express their own ideas. Classical music retained the rococo love of elegant melodic lines and clear, simple harmonies, but by using the sonata form, composers were able to add length and depth to their works.

A second basic form that helped define the classical style was **theme and variations,** a technique in which a musical idea is stated and then repeated in variant versions. The theme and its variations are each about the same length, but each variation is unique and may vary in mood from the basic theme. Variations may diverge from the first theme in several ways, including changes in rhythm, dynamics, harmony, key, accompaniment, and **tone color**—the quality of the sound, determined by the overtones. The theme and a variation may be heard together, or played overlapping, or separated by pauses. Main themes may be inventions of a composer or a borrowed melody from an existing work. The theme and variations form has been used in independent works or for a single movement in a symphony, sonata, or **chamber work** (music for a small ensemble of instruments or voices).

Franz Joseph Haydn [HIDE-un] (1732–1809) was the first master of the classical style. Haydn spent almost thirty years as music director at the palace of a Hungarian noble family, where his status was that of a skilled servant of the reigning prince. At his death, however, he was both comfortably well-off and famous throughout Europe. He is largely responsible for the development of the sonata form, and his 104 symphonies helped to define the standard, four-movement symphony. Despite their formal regularity, the symphonies show Haydn's inventiveness and sense of freedom as he experimented with a large and imaginative variety of moods and structures.

Haydn's most popular symphony today is Symphony No. 94 in G Major, generally known as the *Surprise* Symphony. First performed during Haydn's first visit to London in 1791, this work helped to establish Haydn's name with the concertgoing public there. The second movement, marked *andante* (Italian, "moderate speed"), is in the theme and variations form. The opening theme, evocative of the children's nursery rhyme "Twinkle, Twinkle, Little Star," begins softly but ends with a crashing chord—the *surprise* that gives this symphony its nickname. Four variations follow, achieved through shifts in tone color, dynamics, rhythm, and melody. The movement concludes with a restatement of the core theme, as a dissonant accompaniment seems to mock the piece's lighthearted mood. Haydn's more than seventy string quartets, each composed for first and second violins, viola, and cello, became the accepted norm for this type of chamber music. His supreme innovation was to allow each instrument to show its independence from the rest. Although the first violin has the most prominent role, the musical effect of a Haydn quartet is of four persons conversing. His operas (about twenty), popular in his day, are now seldom performed (Figure 16.19).

However prodigious Haydn's efforts, they are overshadowed by the greatest exponent of the classical style, Wolfgang Amadeus Mozart (1756–1791). From the age of six, he wrote music, alternating composing with performing. His travels around Europe as a child prodigy exposed him to the musical currents of his day, which he eagerly adapted into his own works. For nine years of his adult life, he was a court musician in the service of the archbishop of Salzburg, a post that caused him great anguish because of its low social position. Unlike Haydn, he would not accept the conventional position of musician as a liveried (uniformed) servant of a wealthy patron. The last decade of his life was spent as a freelance musician in Vienna, where he died in extreme poverty. Despite his brief and tragic life, Mozart left a huge body of music that later generations have pronounced sublime.

Mozart's gift was not for creating new musical forms; Mozart already had at hand the sonata, the opera, the symphony, the theme and variations, and the quartet. Rather, his inimitable talent was for composing music with a seemingly effortless line of melody, growing naturally from the opening bars until the finale. His disciplined and harmonious works embody the spirit of the Enlightenment.

Figure 16.19 Performance of a Haydn Opera. *This anonymous print depicts a scene from Haydn's* L'incontro improvviso, *or* The Chance Meeting, *staged around 1775 at Esterháza, the summer castle of the Esterházy family, his patron and employer. Dignitaries and music lovers flocked to Esterháza to hear Haydn's latest works and to walk the grounds. In the print, the proscenium stage, the painted scenery, the costumed singers, and the orchestra below in the pit indicate that the presentations of operas have not changed much over the past 235 years. Some scholars assert that Haydn is playing the harpsichord, at the lower left. Although he was isolated at Esterháza, his reputation grew, and his symphonies and concertos were performed across Europe.*

The transparency of Mozart's composing technique allowed him to give a unique stamp to every type of music that he touched, and he composed in every genre available to him. In vocal music, he composed religious works (such as Masses, oratorios, and an unfinished Requiem Mass) and dramatic works (for example, operas and a ballet). In instrumental music, he wrote orchestral and ensemble music, including symphonies, serenades, **divertimentos** (instrumental works, performed as entertainment, as at social gatherings or banquets), marches, minuets, and German dances; concertos for piano, violin, horn, flute, trumpet, and clarinet; chamber music for strings and winds; violin sonatas; and keyboard sonatas.

The light touch, which makes Mozart such a beloved composer, is nowhere more evident than in his work for a small string orchestra, *Eine Kleine Nachtmusik* (*A Little Night Music*; 1787), K. 525, one of his most often heard works today. Classified as a **serenade,** this lighthearted piece, in four movements, was composed for an evening's entertainment. The third movement is a **minuet and trio,** a classical music form derived from a French court dance, also called the minuet. It begins with a stately melody whose loud staccato tones summon up images of the courtly bowings and curtsies of the dance's origin. As the minuet unfolds, each section is repeated. The minuet then yields to a quieter, smoothly flowing trio, also written as a dancelike melody with repeated phrases. The movement ends with a repeat of the opening stately melody and a concluding staccato phrase.

The fullest expression of Mozart's genius was reached in his operas, especially his comic operas, where he gave free rein to the playful side of his nature, blending broad humor with dramatic characterization. His masterpiece in this genre is probably *The Marriage of Figaro,* based on a play by the French philosophe Pierre Beaumarchais [boh-mahr-SHAY]

(1732–1799). Since its first performance in 1786, *Figaro*'s humor and rich musical texture have made it one of the most popular works in the entire operatic repertory. Beneath the farcical scenes and the enchanting melodies, however, lies a serious theme: by allowing the servant Figaro to outwit his arrogant master, Mozart joined the growing ranks of those who criticized the privileged classes and attacked the injustices of their times. In Mozart's other music, his personal presence was always obscured. But in *Figaro*, the servant-musician who chafes at his hard lot speaks with Mozart's authentic voice.

The Legacy of the Age of Reason

After the Enlightenment, Western civilization was never the same. By the end of the period, the prevailing form of government—absolutism—was on the defensive, facing condemnation from all sides. Supporters of absolutism argued for enlightened despotism, aristocratic critics advocated a division of centralized rule into rival branches, and democrats wanted to abolish monarchy and give the power to the people. Under these assaults, absolutist governments began to crumble.

Another development in the eighteenth century with long-term consequences was the emergence of the middle classes as a potent force for change. By and large, the Enlightenment reflected their political, social, and economic agenda, though their advocates claimed to speak for all people regardless of background. The rise of the middle classes also opened the door to popular forms of culture, such as the novel. Today, this democratizing tendency continues and is one of the hallmarks of modern civilization.

Many of the ideas and principles of the Enlightenment are now articles of faith in the Western heritage. From it come the beliefs that governments should rest on the consent of the people, that the least amount of state interference in the lives of citizens is best, and that all people are created equal. More fundamentally, from the Enlightenment come the views that human nature is good and that happiness is the proper goal of human life.

Although the Enlightenment pointed the way to the future, we must not be misled by the modern-sounding language of the times. The philosophes wrote endlessly in support of free speech and religious toleration, and yet censorship and bigotry remained the normal condition for most Europeans. Despite their brave words, most enlightened thinkers did not move from ideas to action, believing instead that ideas would triumph because of their inner logic and inherent justice. Moreover, they thought that the ruling classes would surrender their privileges once reason had shown them the error of their ways. The Enlightenment was the last era in which such simplistic beliefs were espoused. The world in 1789 stood poised on the brink of an era in which ideas became politicized through action, war, and social agitation. In the postrevolutionary world, the radical power of ideas would be understood by all.

KEY CULTURAL TERMS

Enlightenment	*style galant*
philosophes	pianoforte
Deism	classical style (in music)
Pietism	sonata form
First Great Awakening	symphony
Physiocrats	key
rococo style	tempo
fête galante	mood
rocaille	scherzo
neoclassical style	theme and variations
Chinoiserie	tone color
mezzotint	chamber work
aquatint	divertimentos
solipsism	serenade
causality	minuet and trio

QUESTIONS FOR CRITICAL THINKING

1. Identify and explain the four trends that characterize the Age of Reason. How do these trends influence the culture of this period?

2. Show how the Greco-Roman world, the Scientific Revolution, and the Renaissance affected the Enlightenment.

3. Using a specific painting from each style, compare and contrast the rococo with the neoclassical artistic style.

4. Compare and contrast the literary contributions of Montesquieu, Rousseau, Voltaire, Gibbon, and Alexander Pope to the Enlightenment.

5. What are the three most significant developments of the Age of Reason? Explain.

17

REVOLUTION, REACTION, AND CULTURAL RESPONSE
1760–1830

The Age of Reason was a time of radical talk and little action. However, during the years between 1760 and 1830 three revolutions so fundamentally changed the Western world that some historians consider this period the beginning of the modern era. The Industrial Revolution created the factory system, which replaced agriculture as the soundest basis for the economic well-being of a society. The American Revolution demonstrated that government by the people is a workable alternative to kingship. And the French Revolution swept away centuries-old monarchies and redistributed political power across Europe (Figure 17.1).

These changes were not welcomed by all classes, and those with vested interests tried to prevent the spread of revolutionary political ideas. However, the middle class, or the bourgeoisie, who benefited the most from these revolutions, asserted itself as the new standard-bearer of culture, first embracing neoclassicism and then the new spirit and style of the age—romanticism.

THE INDUSTRIAL REVOLUTION

Even before the Industrial Revolution, agricultural innovations in England made industrialization possible. The shift toward enclosure, whereby wealthy landowners fenced off common lands and consolidated them into large estates, brought hardship to smaller farmers but did result in increased farm productivity and converted land into a commodity. Improvements in farming techniques and the introduction of new crops increased yields and farm income. Technology also led to improved tools and farm implements, such as the iron plow and the reaper.

◀ **Detail** Jean-Auguste-Dominique Ingres. *Napoleon I.* 1806. Oil on canvas, 8′6″ × 5′4″. Musée de l'Armée, Paris.

Figure 17.1 Jean-Auguste-Dominique Ingres. *Napoleon I.* 1806. Oil on canvas, 8'6" × 5'4". Musée de l'Armée, Paris. *Napoleon, emperor of France, 1804–1815, is depicted on a throne in the style of an ancient ruler but with references that link him to the French monarchy. He wears a wreath, a Greek symbol of victory, and in his right hand he holds a long rod topped by a gold fleur-de-lis, or French lily—France's national symbol since the Middle Ages. His left hand holds the ivory hand of justice, an image adopted by France's kings in 1314 and revived by Napoleon at his coronation in 1804. Ingres' portrait helped to establish Napoleon's authority and image.*

Industrialization in England

By the mid–eighteenth century, changes at home and abroad had created conditions that steered England toward industrialization. An increasing population provided both a labor force and a consumer market. Money to invest was available because of surplus capital generated by sound fiscal practices. Several decades of peace had created an atmosphere conducive to economic growth, and the government's policies promoted further expansion. Free of internal tariffs or duties, goods moved easily throughout Britain's navigable waterways, and Britain's acquisition of colonies gave merchants access to raw materials and new overseas markets.

However, industrialization required three necessary changes: the substitution of machines for manual labor; the replacement of animal and human power with new sources of energy such as water and steam (the steam engine, patented by James Watt in 1769, transformed the generation of power); and the introduction of new and large amounts of raw materials, such as iron ore and coal (Figure 17.2).

The changes in the cotton cloth industry dramatically illustrate the phases of the Industrial Revolution. Local woolen producers, threatened by competition from cotton, persuaded Parliament to prohibit the importation of inexpensive cotton goods from India; but still the demand grew. The industry tried to meet the demand for cotton through the medieval putting-

Figure 17.2 MICHAEL ANGELO ROOKER. *The Cast Iron Bridge at Coalbrookdale.* 1782. Approx. 15½ × 24½″. Aberdeen Art Gallery, Aberdeen, Scotland. *The earliest iron bridges, made from the superior grade of iron that was being produced in the new factories, were molded and cast to look like wooden bridges. The first iron bridge, located at Coalbrookdale, became a favorite subject for many artists. Architects did not begin to use iron in building construction until the early 1800s.*

out system—a method of hand manufacture in which workers wove the fabric in their homes—but cottage production proved hopelessly outdated. As a result, industrialists developed the factory system to accelerate and control manufacturing; flying shuttles and power looms were located in one building, which was situated near a swiftly flowing stream that supplied the water for the steam engines that drove the textile machines.

The laborers had to adjust their lives to the demands of the factory system. No longer could rural workers stay at home and weave at their own pace. Towns near the factories rapidly expanded, and new ones sprang up in the countryside next to the mills. In both cases, employees were crowded into miserable living quarters, with little regard given for the basic amenities of human existence. With the factories came a realigned class system of capitalists and workers at either extreme, a transformed social order, new indicators of wealth and success, and new patterns of class behavior. The earlier cooperation between the country gentry and small farmers was replaced by increasingly strained relations between factory owners and the working class.

Classical Economics: The Rationale for Industrialization

Although industrialization did not produce a school of abstract theorizing, it did generate serious studies about the newly emerging economic system. Much of this thought could be interpreted as a rationale for industrialization and a justification for profit seeking. The French Physiocrats and the Scotsman Adam

Smith both advocated the abolition of mercantilism—the economy at the service of the state—and its replacement with a laissez-faire system—the economy at the service of the individual entrepreneur. In England, Smith's ideas attracted a band of thinkers who became known as the classical economists and included Thomas Malthus and David Ricardo.

Smith's key contribution to classical economics was his advocacy of a free-market system based on private property that would automatically regulate prices and profits to the benefit of all. He focused his *Wealth of Nations* (1776) on agriculture and commerce, while only glancing at manufacturing. However, as manufacturing came to dominate the English economy, businessmen found in his work verification for their activities. Smith argued that entrepreneurs, acting out of their enlightened self-interest, not only would get rich but also would raise the standard of living for all—provided the government did not interfere with the economy.

The writings of Thomas Malthus (1766–1834) and David Ricardo (1772–1823) also lent support to the changes wrought by the Industrial Revolution. In his *Essay on the Principle of Population* (1788), Malthus forecast a world burdened with misery that would worsen if the population continued to increase. Since population grows at a geometric rate and food supply advances at an arithmetical rate, the number of human beings will soon far exceed the amount of food, leading Malthus to conclude that famines, plagues, and wars are necessary to limit the world's population. His gloomy prediction persuaded most of the middle classes that laborers could not be helped, because they were responsible for their own thoughtless habits and deeds.

SLICE OF LIFE
Life Inside a "Satanic Mill" in 1815

ELIZABETH BENTLEY
Report of Parliamentary Committee on the Bill to Regulate the Labour of Children in Mills and Factories, 1832

The poet William Blake (1757–1827) was more truthful than poetic in describing England's factories as "dark, Satanic mills." In 1832 the British House of Commons convened a parliamentary commission to investigate factory conditions, and its report confirmed the hellish environment in which male, female, and child workers labored. The testimony of Elizabeth Bentley, a former child laborer, exposing working conditions about 1815, was part of the commission's final report.

What age are you?
Twenty-three.
What time did you begin work at the [flax] factory?
When I was six years old [in 1815].
What was your business in that mill?
I was a little doffer.
What were your hours of labour in that mill?
From 5 in the morning till 9 at night, when they were thronged [extremely busy].
What were the usual hours of labour when you were not so thronged?
From six in the morning till 7 at night.
Do you consider doffing a laborious employment?
Yes.
Explain what you had to do.
When the frames are full, they have to stop the frames, and take the flyers off, and take the full bobbins off, and carry them to the roller, and then put empty ones on, and set the frame going again.
Does that keep you constantly on your feet?
Yes, there are so many frames and they run so quick.
Your labour is very excessive?
Yes, you have not time for anything.
Suppose you flagged a little, or were late, what would they do?
Strap us.
Have you ever been strapped?
Yes.
Is the strap used so as to hurt you excessively?
Yes it is. . . . I have seen the overlooker go to the top end of the room, where the little girls hug the can to the backminders [hold water in a vessel for machine workers]; he has taken a strap, and a whistle in his mouth, and sometimes he has got a chain and chained them, and strapped them all down the room.
Had you a clock?
No, we had not.
Were you generally there in time?
Yes, my mother has been up at 4 o'clock in the morning, and at 2 o'clock in the morning; the colliers [coal workers] used to go to their work at 3 or 4 o'clock, and when she heard them stirring she has got up out of her warm bed. . . . I have sometimes been at Hunslet Car at 2 o'clock in the morning, when it was streaming down with rain, and we have had to stay till the mill was opened.
You are considerably deformed in person as a consequence of this labour?
Yes I am.
And what time did it come on?
I was about 13 years old when it began coming, and it has got worse since; it is five years since my mother died, and my mother was never able to get me a good pair of stays to hold me up, and when my mother died I had to do for myself, and I got me a pair.
Were you perfectly straight and healthy before you worked at a mill?
Yes, I was as straight a little girl as ever went up and down town.
Do you know of anybody that has been similarly injured in their health?
Yes, in their health, but not many deformed as I am.
Where are you now?
In the poorhouse.

INTERPRETING THIS SLICE OF LIFE

1. Based on this Slice of Life, *describe* factory conditions in England before the factory reform acts of the 1830s. 2. *Would* you expect Elizabeth Bentley to have attended school during her youth? 3. *Note* the absence of child labor laws, worker's compensation, factory safety legislation, and factory hour regulation. *Compare and contrast* factory conditions then and now.

Timeline 17.1   REVOLUTION, REACTION, AND CULTURAL RESPONSE

1760	1775	1783	1789	1799	1815	1830
Industrial Revolution in England	American Revolution		French Revolution	Napoleon and the French Empire	Restored Bourbon Monarchy in France	

1769 Watt's steam engine	**1776** Smith's *Wealth of Nations*			**1793** David's *Death of Marat*	**1803** Beethoven's *Symphony No. 3*	**1808** Goethe's *Faust* (Part 1)	**1818** Géricault's *Raft of the "Medusa"*	**1830** Berlioz's *Symphonie fantastique*
	1774 Goethe's *The Sorrows of Young Werther*			**1798** Wordsworth and Coleridge's *Lyrical Ballads*		**1813** Austen's *Pride and Prejudice*	**1821** Constable's *Hay Wain*	

In *Principles of Political Economy and Taxation* (1821), David Ricardo explained his "iron law of wages": laborers' wages will always hover around the subsistence level, and workers will never be able to improve their standard of living beyond that level. Tying Malthus's conclusion to his own, he argued that the working class is inevitably mired in poverty. Thus, Adam Smith and the classical economists provided the business classes with rationales to justify the methods of industrialization and their consequences.

POLITICAL REVOLUTIONS, 1760–1815

From the Treaty of Paris (1763) to the Battle of Waterloo (1815), Europe saw monarchies fall, new forms of government emerge, and old societies swept away. By 1830 Europe was divided into a conservative eastern Europe and a progressive western Europe that included the former colonies in the New World. This twofold division persisted well into the twentieth century (Timeline 17.1).

The American Revolution

Although Great Britain was leading the way to industrialization, it was also suffering from an outmoded tax structure and from debts contracted in the Seven Years' War. The royal ministers tried numerous schemes and taxes to make the American colonists share in the burden of empire. The colonists, calling the British government's new taxes on sugar, stamps, and tea unconstitutional, claimed immunity from imperial taxation because, they asserted, they were not represented in the British Parliament.

Protests and violence succeeded in nullifying the parliamentary taxes and uniting the colonies in a common cause. In 1774 the colonists convened a Continental Congress in Philadelphia, which spoke for the American people against the "foreign power" of Great Britain. In April 1775, conflict between British troops and colonists in Massachusetts triggered a war. The Continental Congress proclaimed the American goals in the Declaration of Independence, signed on July 4, 1776: government by consent of the governed and the rights to life, liberty, and the pursuit of happiness. The American Revolution lasted until 1783 and resulted in victory and independence for the colonies.

To realize their democratic goals, the Americans developed two new ideas: the constitutional convention and a written constitution. Wary of centralized power, and disappointed at their new nation's first efforts at governance, the framers of the United States Constitution met in Philadelphia in 1787 and created three coordinated branches of government—legislative, judiciary, and executive—with specified powers delegated to each. (The idea of a balance of powers is derived from the works of both the English political theorist John Locke and the French philosophe Montesquieu [see Chapters 15 and 16].) The central government could assess and collect its own taxes, regulate commerce, and make and enforce laws. But the framers limited the government's role in everyday life by incorporating a Bill of Rights for all citizens into the Constitution.

The framers failed to extend rights to slaves, whose existence was barely noted, and women were not given the right to vote. Still, the Constitution made America the most democratic society of its day and the first successful democracy since Athens in the fifth century BCE. As an exemplary democracy, the United States offered hope to the oppressed, and its successful

Table 17.1 SHIFTS IN THE FRENCH GOVERNMENT, 1789–1830	
July 1789–September 1792	Limited constitutional kingdom; the National Constituent Assembly
September 1792–August 1795	First Republic; Reign of Terror (1793–1794)
August 1795–November 1799	Directory
November 1799–May 1804	Consulate
May 1804–June 1815	First Empire
June 1815–July 1830	Restored Bourbon monarchy

struggle for independence provided a model for future revolution.

The French Revolution

Despite the importance of the American Revolution, the revolution in France overshadowed it. Because of its dramatic break with the past and its lasting world-wide effects, the French Revolution is a pivotal event in modern history.

When Louis XVI took the throne in 1774, the French crown was confronted with social unrest, economic inequalities, and financial crises. Both the aristocrats, who were resurgent after the death of Louis XIV, and the emerging bourgeoisie were clamoring for power. The affluent bourgeoisie aligned themselves with the nobles in supporting laissez-faire economics, but they joined the king in calling for an end to the feudal privileges of the aristocracy. The peasant farmers endured burdensome taxes and continued to be subjected to feudal claims. In cities and towns, the lower middle class—small shopkeepers, salaried workers, and semi-skilled artisans—had little opportunity to escape their bleak existence. Below them wage earners and menial workers barely earned subsistence wages, while some drifted in and out of the criminal world. Oppressed by high taxes and harboring ill-disguised hatred for the classes above them, the lower orders schemed to stay one jump ahead of the tax collector.

In the 1780s, France amassed a huge national debt, fueled by its support of the American Revolution. In 1789 Louis XVI agreed to convene the Estates-General, a representative body similar to the British Parliament, which had last met in the early 1600s. When this body gathered, the middle-class representatives shunted aside the nobles and the church leaders and formed the National Constituent Assembly, which proceeded to end royal despotism and turn France into a limited, constitutional kingdom similar to England (Table 17.1).

This first phase of the Revolution lasted from 1789 until 1792. Dominated by the well-to-do middle classes, the National Constituent Assembly embraced laissez-faire, restricted the vote to property owners, overhauled the legal system, and introduced representative government. Its approval of *The Declaration of the Rights of Man and Citizen* (1789), a document that guaranteed both natural and civil rights, has served as the basis of subsequent French regimes. In framing the constitution of 1791, the National Constituent Assembly attempted to embody the slogans of the Revolution—liberty, equality, and fraternity—but class hatred made fraternity more an ideal than a reality. This stage of the revolution failed, however, because Louis XVI proved to be untrustworthy. Forces inside France were also pressing its leaders for increasingly radical reforms, and a coalition of European states invaded France to restore the monarchy.

The Revolution entered its second and most violent phase, which lasted from September 1792 to August 1795. This phase was dominated by leaders from the lower bourgeois and working classes, who executed the king, founded the French Republic, and briefly replaced Christianity with a state religion organized on rational ideals (Figure 17.3). Full voting rights were given to all males, including blacks and Jews, state education was opened to all, conquered people were allowed to vote on their future, and the slave trade was abolished. Women, however, were denied the vote and citizenship, but they acquired certain rights, including equal treatment of both sexes in marital law and equal rights of inheritance for male and female children, and the legal age for marriage was raised to twenty-one. (These advances were short-lived, as they were all swept away later by the Napoleonic Code, after 1804.)

Such far-reaching reforms alarmed many who supported the monarchy, church, and old social order, and soon the fledgling republic faced civil war at home and invasions from abroad, which in turn set off more domestic political and financial crises. These events led to the yearlong Reign of Terror (1793–1794), when

Figure 17.3 Louis-Leopold Boilly. *Simon Chenard as a Sans-culotte.* 1792. Oil on canvas, 13⅛ × 8⅝". Musée Carnavalet, Paris. *As French workers came into their own during the second phase of the Revolution, their clothing became fashionable. The men dressed in short jackets and baggy trousers, rather than in the aristocratic costume of waistcoats and breeches, or culottes, with silk stockings. Because of the long trousers, these workers were known as* sans-culottes *("without breeches"). The artist Boilly, a supporter of the Revolution, sought to glorify the* sans-culottes *in this portrait of a typical worker—actually his friend, the actor Simon Chenard. Clad in worker's attire, including wooden shoes, and holding the tricolor (the red, white, and blue banner of the Revolution), Chenard strikes a heroic pose, as if ready to defend his newly won rights. Boilly has placed Chenard in the foreground so that he towers over the landscape, just as the newly enfranchised workers dominated the political scene.*

many suspected enemies of the Revolution were executed. Its excesses overshadowed many of the French Republic's accomplishments and discredited the Revolution's appeal among many of its early supporters. In August 1795, a more moderate republic, known as the Directory, was instituted, in which power was shared between two legislative houses and five directors.

The Directory lasted only four years. Although this government favored the commercial middle classes, it was committed to furthering the Revolution. However, its leaders faced nearly insurmountable problems, such as a growing counterrevolution, the collapse of the currency, and a breakdown in law and order. The directors appealed to the military for aid against their enemies, and in November 1799 General Napoleon Bonaparte staged a coup d'état (French, literally, "a stroke of state,"

a sudden, violent overthrow of government) that abolished the Directory and established the Consulate.

With the rise of Napoleon (1769–1821), events had come full circle, in effect returning France to a monarchy. Napoleon was a dictator and military genius who embodied the enlightened despotism of his century and, at the same time, anticipated modern totalitarianism. Above all, he was heir to the French Revolution.

Although the cost of Napoleonic rule between 1799 and 1815 was the loss of political liberty at home, France did receive internal stability and a consolidation of most of the Revolution's policies. Napoleon kept careers "open to talent" (Napoleon's term meaning jobs for the people with the proper ability, not for those with aristocratic connections), suppressed aristocratic privilege, rewarded wealthy property owners, and refashioned public education. He welcomed home revolutionaries who had emigrated—provided they were loyal to his regime. He restored relations with the papacy, though he failed to achieve religious harmony. He also ended the civil war that had raged for more than a decade, and he reformed the economy.

Napoleon's most enduring legacy was the law code he helped draft. Intended for universal application, the Napoleonic Code introduced rational legal principles and legitimized the idea of the lay state. The code rested on reforms of the revolutionary era, such as the abolition of serfdom, the guilds, and feudal property. Despite its reactionary ideas of paternal rule and the subservience of women—thus reversing the small gains made by women in the revolutionary era—the code remains the basis of civil law in both France and its former colonies.

Napoleon's military conquests and diplomatic successes soon eclipsed his domestic achievements. A brilliant field general before he seized power, Napoleon launched a series of victorious wars once he became emperor in 1804 (see Figure 17.1). When not winning battles, he managed to undermine the coalitions allied against him by exploiting his foes' basic distrust of one another. In particular, he worked to keep Great Britain out of Continental affairs while he crushed Prussia and Austria, which then sued for peace. Simultaneously, he annexed land for France and established satellite kingdoms ruled by members of his family or by his generals. As the self-proclaimed heir to the Age of Reason and the French Revolution, Napoleon reorganized his newly conquered territories along the lines of France. At first, many local reformers welcomed the French, but they soon learned the high costs of occupation and began to resist their "liberators" (Map 17.1).

Napoleon's empire upset the European balance of power at a basic level, so that ultimately the other nations united to defeat him once he was proven vulnerable in battle by the failure of his invasion of Russia in

LEARNING THROUGH MAPS

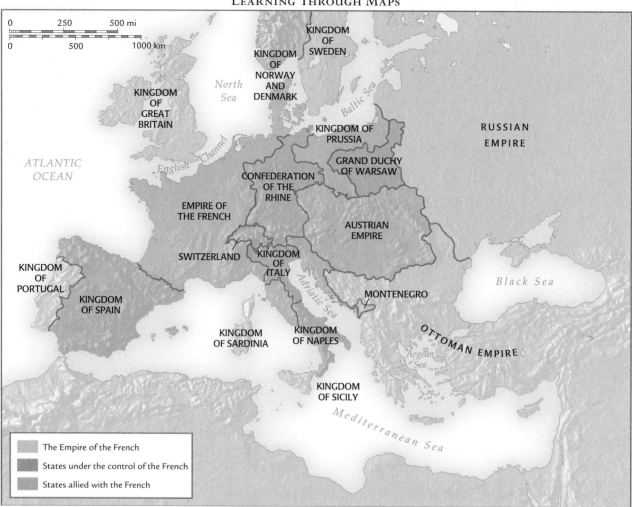

Map 17.1 EUROPE AT THE HEIGHT OF NAPOLEON'S POWER, 1810–1811
This map shows the maximum expansion of Napoleonic power across the map of Europe. 1. *Compare* the borders of the French Empire in this map with those of France in Map 16.1, Europe, 1763–1789. 2. *Identify* the states now under the control of, or allied with, France. 3. *Notice* the various states that appear in Map 14.1 but no longer exist or have new names in Map 17.1. 4. *Consider* the influence of geography in helping make Great Britain and Russia the enemies of Napoleon.

1812. An alliance of Great Britain and the European states defeated Napoleon in June 1815 at Waterloo (in modern Belgium). Exiled to an island in the South Atlantic, Napoleon died there in 1821, but his spirit hovered over France and Europe for much of the nineteenth century.

Technology

The American Revolutionary War, the French Revolutionary Wars, and the Napoleonic Wars were blends of the old and new. Waged with both proven and new weapons, they were fought with traditional and innovative tactics and strategies and subjected to varied influences, far from the scenes of battle. By about 1750, most of Europe's great powers (Great Britain, France, Austria, and Prussia) had created an early version of the military-industrial complex. While these systems varied by country, their basic infrastructure was the same: tax systems to pay for armies and navies, contracts to supply arms and materials, and bureaucracies to oversee funds, goods, and services. Officers still came from the upper class, with rank-and-file soldiers and sailors from the lower class. With most countries at military parity, victory often hinged on technology, innovative thinking, and resources as the scale and complexity of warfare increased.

CHANGES IN MILITARY WEAPONRY   The evolution of the artillery cannon exemplified the changing face of weaponry in this period:

- In the 1730s, the French improved the cannon, casting it as solid metal, out of which the barrel was bored; they also standardized the cannon's parts, thus making a failed part easy to replace. Most nations adopted the French cannon, but older-type siege guns also remained in use.
- By the 1770s, artillery had become more accurate and more powerful, more mobile and safer.

Despite the improved cannon, battlefield success still depended on how the generals placed their troops and managed their firepower, as Napoleon demonstrated in his victories.

COMPOSITION OF ARMIES   The makeup of European armies was transformed by the French Revolution:

- In 1793, France founded the first citizens' army through the *levée en masse*, or mobilization of all Frenchmen.
- From 1793–1815, other countries continued to rely on mercenary troops or those pressed or tricked into military service.
- By 1914, most Western nations had adopted the French model, using conscription of eligible male citizens to have large standing armies.

CHANGES TO NAVAL WARFARE   The rivalry between France and Great Britain changed the role of naval warfare in the imperial ambitions of states.

- In 1763, France entered a naval race with Great Britain after being defeated in the Seven Years' War. Nevertheless, for the rest of this period, France valued its army over its navy and did not built up its fleet strength.
- In contrast, Britain placed the Royal Navy first, giving it strong support from Parliament and the nation, which enhanced British national identity (Figure 17.4).
- Britain's naval superiority was evident in its better officer training and more powerful ships.
- Britain's Royal Navy defeated Napoleon's navy, after which Britain "ruled the waves" until World War I.

REACTION, 1815–1830

The victorious nations tried to restore Europe to its prerevolutionary status, but the forces of change had already altered the future of Western—and world—

history. The French, as heirs to the Enlightenment notion that they were citizens of the world, largely ignored the traditions of the peoples whom they had conquered, convinced that the principles of their revolutionary society represented what was best for humanity. However, the French were not as successful as they had hoped in exporting their revolution, because the victorious continental states and Great Britain shared a conservative agenda that aimed to suppress the advance of liberal ideas. At the Congress of Vienna in 1815, the victors stripped France of most of its conquests, restored the balance of power, halted or reduced reform programs, and inaugurated a period of reaction.

Despite this redesign of the map, many Napoleonic reforms remained in force until 1830 and beyond. Even in France, where the allies restored the Bourbons, Louis XVIII (r. 1815–1824) issued a charter that guaranteed a constitutional regime resembling the limited monarchy of 1791. Most western European states now had governments elected by male citizens and civil laws based on the Napoleonic Code. In contrast, Prussia, Russia, and Austria remained autocratic, and untouched by democracy and representative government.

The fate of reform in Europe between 1815 and 1830 varied from modest changes in England to repression in Russia. In the immediate postwar period in Great Britain, the government resisted attempts to reform Parliament or to institute free trade, but in the 1820s, Britain began to modernize. France regressed toward absolutism as the restored Bourbon monarchy chipped away at the revolutionary heritage. By 1830, resistance to the crown was mounting, and in the July Revolution the French replaced the Bourbon monarchy with Louis Philippe, the Duke of Orléans (r. 1830–1848). Constitutional government now put the middle class in power.

In central Europe, the Austrian Empire kept liberal sentiments from spreading among its subjects. Prussia, which had made important liberal reforms in the Napoleonic era, now seemed more interested in efficiency than in modernizing the state. Russia became increasingly reactionary and repressive. Until the 1860s, Russia's czarist regime and Austria's mastery of central Europe widened the gulf between eastern and western Europe.

REVOLUTIONS IN ART AND IDEAS: FROM NEOCLASSICISM TO ROMANTICISM

The makers of the French Revolution adopted an artistic style that was already in vogue and perfectly suited their purposes—the neoclassical. In contrast to

ENCOUNTER

Slavery and the French Revolution

Slavery and the slave trade are as old as civilization. In ancient Mesopotamia, Egypt, Israel, Greece, and Rome, men, women, and children fell into this terrible system in varied ways: by conquest (conquerors enslaved their captured enemies), by sale (parents could sell children for economic gain), by debt (to settle a debt), by court sentence (a judicial punishment), and by kidnapping (gangs of slave traders preying on the weak). Slaves were required to perform the most arduous and dangerous tasks, had no rights or privileges, and were entrenched at the bottom of society. Slavery and the slave trade remained unchallenged in the Western world until about 1750.

When African slaves were introduced into the West Indies and North America, many whites accepted slavery as embedded in history, sanctioned by the Bible, and necessary to large-scale agricultural production. After 1750 those attitudes were challenged, as thinkers and religious groups, especially the Quakers, began to question slavery's legitimacy. The turning point came, during the French Revolution, when whites, struggling to overthrow repressive regimes in France, inspired slaves in the French West Indies to fight for their freedom—and the ideals of the French Revolution: liberty, equality, and brotherhood.

By the 1780s, New World slave owners were importing nearly seventy-five thousand slaves a year, many of them destined for the sugar plantations in the French colony of Saint Domingue, or modern Haiti. Saint Domingue formed the western half of the island of Hispaniola; the eastern half was Spain's colony of Santo Domingo. The slaves in French Saint Domingue, with no rights, were at the bottom of a rigid social and racial system. Above them were the free people of color—those of mixed blood who had some rights but were still subject to discrimination. Next, constituting a group of second-class citizens, were less influential whites, who served as plantation overseers and ran the small businesses. At the top stood the white plantation owners, prosperous merchants, some French noblemen, the clergy, and government officials. In 1789, when news of the outbreak of the French Revolution reached Saint Domingue, the colony's old social and racial order began to crumble.

In the opening phases of the French Revolution, the upper-class whites on Saint Domingue set up their own government, sent delegates to the Estates-General in France (Encounter figure 17.1), and pressed for economic freedom. From 1790 to 1794, a series of revolts by the free people of color, the poorer whites, and the slaves occurred and spread to the Spanish side of the island. The island's revolutionary government abolished slavery in 1793, and the French government did likewise in 1794. By then, Toussaint L'Ouverture [TOO-san LOO-ver-tchur] (1743–1803), an ex-slave who was literate and familiar with the writings of the French philosophes, had emerged as a military and political leader. In 1801, after defeating both British and French forces, he ruled the island as a military dictator. A year later Toussaint was arrested and sent to France, where he died in prison.

---

the frivolous rococo, this style was high-minded, ethical, and serious. Neoclassical artists and architects followed the ancient Greco-Roman ideals of balance, simplicity, and restraint, principles that were thought to embody the underlying order of the universe. Truth was seen as eternal, unchanging, the same for one and all. Art and literature created according to classical principles were believed to be both morally uplifting and aesthetically satisfying.

In England, classicism lingered on in the novels of Jane Austen. Untouched by the revolutions that dominated this age, Austen created fictional works that took England's deep countryside for their setting and dealt with the lives of the less wealthy gentry, a middle-class world that appealed to her audience.

Advanced thinkers in France made the neoclassical paintings of David a symbol of the new rational order they wanted to introduce into the world. The Revolution intensified devotion to classical ideals, and David became its official artist. Later, when the Revolution lost its way and France began to see itself as a new Rome, Napoleon made David his court painter. After 1800, David transformed neoclassicism into an imperial style that lingered on in France and on the Continent long after the French emperor was exiled from Europe in 1815.

Even earlier, starting about 1770, a new movement was emerging across Europe, one that was to have lasting effects on the Western consciousness. **Romanticism,** a new way of thinking, came to dominate European arts and letters in the nineteenth century. Rejecting neoclassicism as cold and artificial, the romantics glorified unruly nature, uncontrolled feeling, and the mysteries of the human soul. They claimed that their

Encounter figure 17.1 *Jean-Baptiste Bellay [buh-LAY] joined the slave revolt led by Toussaint L'Ouverture before being elected as one of three delegates to the constitutional assembly, or Convention, in 1793. He lost his seat in 1797, returned to Haiti, and faded into history. Elegantly dressed and wearing the French tricolor in his sash and on his hat, Bellay leans against the bust of Abbé Raynal [re-NAHL], the French philosophe whose antislavery writings inspired Toussaint and probably Bellay. Including and relating a dead person to the individual in the portrait was a popular device in eighteenth-century paintings. The background on the right represents the Haitian countryside.*

Out of the mixing of an economic enterprise to supply slave labor for an expanding plantation system for Europeans, a debate among European intellectuals over human rights and freedom, and a series of revolutions in France and wars in Europe, an independent republic emerged, in 1803, on the island of Haiti. This government was the first black republic in history and the second republic in the New World. A new society had been born, and its future now rested in the hands of an emancipated and self-governing people.

LEARNING FROM THE ENCOUNTER

1. *What* was the socioeconomic system in the French West Indies at the end of the eighteenth century? 2. *How* did ideas and events of the French Revolution affect conditions in the French West Indies? 3. *What* were the outcomes of the Haitian revolt? 4. *Discuss* the issues raised by the revolt and its results. Have slavery and the slave trade been fully eliminated from the world today?

---

ideals were more in tune with human nature than the order, reason, and harmony of classicism. Some elements of romanticism have permeated the Western way of thinking to become articles of faith in the modern world.

Neoclassicism in Literature after 1789

During her brief life, Jane Austen (1775–1817) wrote six novels that together rank as the finest body of fiction produced in this period. Austen approached novel writing in a classical spirit, portraying her characters as inhabiting a serene environment reminiscent of the quiet domestic scenes of the seventeenth-century Dutch painter Vermeer (see Chapter 14). Calling herself a miniaturist, she concentrated her author's eye on a vanishing world where the smallest important unit was the family and the most significant problems involved the adjustment of social relationships.

In the hands of a lesser writer, such a literary program might have failed by being too narrow, but Austen transcended her limited framework. She did this through clear writing, ironic understatement, and, above all, beautifully realized descriptions of the polite manners and minute rituals of provincial life: the balls attended, the letters and conversations, the visits to relatives, and the unexpected social breakdowns, such as an elopement, a betrayed confidence, or a broken engagement. She was especially sensitive to the constraints her society imposed on women, depicting with great wit a world in which women were given little access to formal education, confined to the domestic sphere, kept economically dependent on men, and

Figure 17.4   JAMES GILLRAY. *John Bull Bother'd:—or—the Geese Alarming the Capitol.* 1792. Hand-colored etching and aquatint, 12¼ × 15¼". British Museum, London. *As the French Revolution grew more radical, British observers became increasingly alarmed. James Gillray (1756–1815), the master caricaturist of England's "golden age of caricaturing," shows William Pitt, the prime minister, peering through a telescope with John Bull—the symbol of Great Britain— standing beside him. At this time, national symbols were taking shape across the West. In this caricature, Pitt thinks the geese are the French sans-culottes about to descend on Great Britain and overthrow the government. John Bull, the personification of the common man, is bothered (a word derived from "both eared"), not knowing what to believe since he sees only geese, and, like many Englishmen in 1792, he is confused. To emphasize his dilemma, his hat reads "God Save the King" while his French cockade has "Vive la liberté" ("Long Live Liberty"). The balloons— a typical feature of these caricatures—above Pitt and John Bull convey Pitt's fears and John Bull's mixed feelings. This Gillray work typically has more than one meaning, as it is also a sly protest against the British government's campaign to whip up fear about events in France. When collected by admirers, prints like this became part of what has been called the public sphere of British life, which included coffeehouses and print shops, where public discourse occurred among the politically aware. This work also shows Gillray to be a master of the aquatint.*

socialized to be weak and sentimental. The best known of Austen's novels is *Pride and Prejudice* (1813), a gently satirical work whose plot revolves around the problems that arise when the Bennets—a shabby genteel family— try to find suitable husbands for five daughters.

Neoclassical Painting and Architecture after 1789

Jacques-Louis David founded neoclassicism in painting in the 1780s and remained its consummate exponent until his death in 1825. As official artist of the French Revolution, he rendered contemporary events in the

ancient manner. David's most successful painting from this period was his study of the Revolution's famous martyr Jean-Paul Marat [muh-RAH], who was assassinated while seated in his bath (Figure 17.5). Himself an ardent supporter of the Revolution, David meticulously planned this work to give universal meaning to a specific moment in French history. The setting is historically accurate because Marat suffered from a skin disorder and often conducted official business while seated in the bathtub. Once having established the scene, David suppressed every detail that did not contribute to the general impression of tragedy. As a result, the few details take on a highly charged quality. The figure of Marat resembles a piece of classical sculpture against the stark background. His torso is twisted so that the bleeding wound and the peaceful face are fully visible. The pen and the inkwell remind the viewer that Marat was killed while serving the Revolution. In effect, David has portrayed Marat as a secular saint.

Barely escaping the Revolution's most violent phase, David survived to become court painter to Napoleon, and modifications in the cause of political propaganda now appeared in his art. Napoleon, to enhance his image as a new Augustus, encouraged David to make his painting reflect the pomp and grandeur of the Napoleonic court. *The Coronation of Napoleon and Josephine* is typical of David's imperial paintings (Figure 17.6). This pictorial record of the investiture conveys the opulent splendor and theatrical ceremony that Napoleon craved as a way of validating his empire in the eyes of Europe's older monarchs, who regarded him as an upstart. Napoleon's family members, who had been made kings, princes, and princesses, or given lesser titles, are depicted in elaborate court dress. Earlier, in the coronation ritual, Napoleon, not the pope, had placed the crown on his own head, an act validating the modern conception of political power. In this painting, the standing Napoleon prepares to crown the kneeling empress. David portrays the pope as a mere spectator, seated behind Napoleon.

The only neoclassical painter comparable to David was his pupil Jean-Auguste-Dominique Ingres [ANG-gruh] (1780–1867). Ingres inherited the mantle of neoclassicism from David, but he lacked his teacher's moral enthusiasm. As a result, Ingres' classicism is cold-blooded and stark in its simple images. The finest expressions of Ingres' art are his portraits. Using clean lines drawn with a sure and steady hand, he created

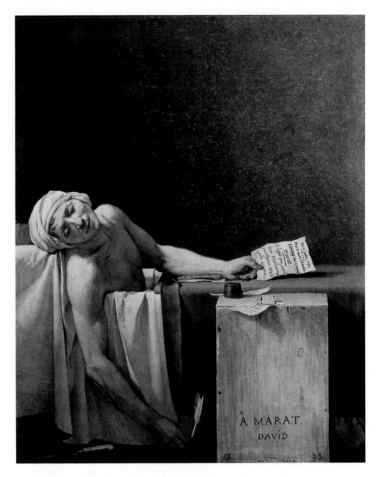

Figure 17.5 Jacques-Louis David. *Death of Marat.* 1793. Oil on canvas, 65 × 50½". Musées Royaux des Beaux-Arts, Brussels. *David's presentation of figures in the nude in his neoclassical history paintings was often denounced by literal-minded critics as unrealistic, but David defended this choice as consistent with "the customs of antiquity." The critics were silenced by David's depiction of the Marat murder scene, since in this case the nudity was true to life. In this painting, David's classical principles and the demands of realistic portrayal combined to produce a timeless image.*

Figure 17.6 Jacques-Louis David. *The Coronation of Napoleon and Josephine.* 1805–1808. Oil on canvas, 20' × 30'6½". Louvre. *Napoleon orchestrated his own coronation and then guided David in painting it. For instance, Napoleon's mother did not attend, probably because of her disapproval of her son's grandiose ambitions, but Napoleon insisted that David depict her seated prominently at the center of the festivities. David also shows the pope's hand raised in benediction, contrary to the report of eyewitnesses who described him sitting with both hands resting on his knees.*

Figure 17.7 Jean-Auguste-Dominique Ingres. *Madame Rivière.* 1805. Oil on canvas, oval, 45 × 36″. Louvre. *Ingres was the last great painter of portraits in a field that was taken over by the camera after 1840. A keen observer of the human face and form, Ingres was able to render intense, idealized but realistic likenesses, as evidenced in Madame Rivière's portrait. Ingres conveys his subject's physical presence by centering her in the foreground, highlighting her physical features and the color of her flesh, and depicting the gleaming surfaces of her clothing and the pillow on which she leans. The patterned shawl—probably an expensive accessory—accentuates the oval shape of the portrait by covering the subject's right arm, curling around her shoulders, and hanging over the chair.*

photographic images of his subjects. Of Ingres' many portraits, one of the most exquisite is that of Madame Rivière [reev-yehr], the wife of Philibert Rivière, an official in Napoleon's government (Figure 17.7). While not probing deeply into the inner self, this portrait does convey the sitter's high social position, stressing her poise and alluding to her wealth through her jewelry and dress. Madame Rivière's portrait and that of Napoleon (see Figure 17.1) were among those Ingres exhibited in the 1806 Paris Salon, where the public's acclaim elevated the young artist's reputation, at age twenty-six, to new heights. In his own way, Ingres gave the rising bourgeois class in the Napoleonic Empire the same glamorous treatment that had been accorded prerevolutionary aristocracy in rococo portraits.

After 1789 the neoclassical style in architecture spread to the European colonies, notably to the former British territories in North America. In the United States, the middle-class founders of the new republic made neoclassicism synonymous with their own time, which is known as the federal period. They graced their capital, Washington, with the classical architecture that symbolized devotion to republican and democratic sentiments.

The most profound influence on America's classical heritage was exercised by Thomas Jefferson (1743–1826), the coauthor of the Declaration of Independence and the third president of the United States. Jefferson was also a master architect. Like other architects in this era, he was deeply indebted to the principles of the Italian Andrea Palladio (1508–1580), whose book on architecture he had read. Palladio's Villa Rotonda near Vicenza served as the model for Jefferson's home at Monticello, near Charlottesville, Virginia (Figure 17.8). Like the Villa Rotonda (see Figure 12.23), Monticello is a country dwelling arranged around a domed central area, though it features only two symmetrical connecting wings. Executed in brick with wooden trim, Monticello has inspired so many imitations that it has come to symbolize the American dream of gracious living.

Likewise, Jefferson's design for Virginia's state capitol in Richmond has deeply influenced public architecture (Figure 17.9). From his plan for the Virginia statehouse arose the tradition of building public structures in the form of ancient temples. His model for the capitol was the Maison Carrée (see Figure 5.12), a Roman temple dating from the first century CE. Though small by today's standards for public buildings, Jefferson's statehouse has a strong presence and is a marvel of refined elegance and simple charm. The most pleasing part of his original design is the central building, with its perfectly proportioned features—columns, pediment, and windows. Even though two smaller wings were added later, they enhance rather than detract from Jefferson's symmetrical and harmonious plan.

Romanticism: Its Spirit and Expression

In contrast to neoclassicism, romanticism symbolized the unbounded and untamed. The romantics' patron saint was Rousseau, whose emotionalism and love of nature had made him out of step with his own time. Like Rousseau, the romantics preferred to be guided by emotion and intuition. Following these guides, they conjured up an image of the world that was deeply personal and alive with hidden meanings. Nature itself became God for many romantics, who spiritualized nature so that divinity was expressed through bucolic

Figure 17.8 THOMAS JEFFERSON. Monticello. 1770–1784; remodeled 1796–1806. Charlottesville, Virginia. *The Palladio-inspired architecture of Monticello reflected Jefferson's ethical vision. Its portico in the plain style of a Roman temple mirrored his admiration for the Roman republic and its ideals of simplicity and order. Its overall devotion to mathematical principles and unobtrusive details were expressions of his commitment to disciplined living. Though built for one of America's elite, Monticello was conceived on a modest scale as a visual rebuke to the luxurious palaces of Europe's aristocrats.*

Figure 17.9 THOMAS JEFFERSON. State Capitol of Virginia. 1785–1796. Richmond, Virginia. *Jefferson described the Maison Carrée, the model for this statehouse, as "the most perfect and precious remain of antiquity in existence." Political considerations also influenced Jefferson's choice, for he identified this Roman temple as a symbol of Roman republican values. Like Monticello, Jefferson's statehouse design was an outgrowth of his ethical vision.*

Figure 17.10 Philip Jacques de Loutherbourg. *Coalbrookdale by Night.* 1801. Oil on canvas, 26¾ × 42″. Science and Society Picture Library, London. *At first glance, this painting seems to portray the world engulfed in a flaming inferno. Only gradually does the meaning of the scene—a depiction of one of England's new industrialized towns— emerge. As a terrifying symbol of industrialism, the painting helps to explain what romantic art was rebelling against.*

scenes as well as terrifying natural spectacles. To characterize this force of nature, the romantics invented the term **sublime** to convey the awesome and majestic power of the sea, earthquakes, floods, and storms.

The romantic reverence for nature stemmed partly from a desire to escape from the effects of the Industrial Revolution, which was altering the countryside for the worse (Figure 17.10). Not surprisingly, England, the first home of industrialization, became the center of movements that exalted the Middle Ages and idolized nature, creating sentiments that existed only in the romantics' imaginations. Their rejection of the industrial world had other consequences, including a preoccupation with the exotic East and the domains of the imagination, dreams, drugs, and nonrational mental states.

Many early romantics willingly saw in the French Revolution a better future for Europe. They believed that the revolutionary watchwords "liberty," "rights of man," "the individual," and "equality" could become the basis of a moral and humanitarian viewpoint and could be applied beyond the orbit of the French Revolution. When Greece declared its independence from the feeble Ottoman Empire and fought for its freedom in the 1820s, for example, many Europeans, influenced by revolutionary principles, declared their solidarity with the rebels. Among them was the English romantic poet Lord Byron, who died in Greece while aiding in the cause of Greek independence.

The French Revolution also sparked a strong negative reaction among some romantics, who criticized its seemingly random violence. They likewise deplored Napoleonic imperialism, which squeezed the life out of other cultures by conquering them and then imposing French customs. These conservative romantics renounced the French Revolution's stress on abstract ideas and natural rights and focused their attention on history and the rights and traditions native to each country. They especially disagreed with the Revolution's international spirit and advocated instead a nationalistic point of view.

At first, romantic nationalism was little more than a reaction against foreign influences and a reverence for those unique aspects of culture that are created by the common people—folk dancing, folk sayings, folktales, folk music, and folk customs. This benign nationalism later developed into an aggressive attitude that insisted on the moral superiority of one people over all others and expressed unrelenting hostility toward outsiders. In its extreme form, militant nationalism encouraged the expulsion of "alien" groups who were not recognized as members of the national heritage. Aggressive nationalism in Europe lasted almost a century, from 1848 to 1945, climaxing in Nazi Germany, and still remains a potent force around the world.

The romantics also generated a cult of nonconformity and held in great esteem outlaws, gypsies, and those who lived outside middle-class society. This hostility toward middle-class life has an ironic twist because those who professed it generally came from this class and sought its patronage. The unruly presence of romanticism coincided with the rise to political dominance of the middle class. Out of the love-hate relationship between romantics and the middle class emerged another familiar emblem of modern life, the antibourgeois bourgeois—that is, middle-class people who scorn their own social origins. From the dawn of the romantic period until the present day, modern culture has been filled with middle-class rebels in revolt against their class.

France played a central role in romanticism because of its culturally strategic position, and England also produced major figures in romanticism, particularly in poetry and painting. Notwithstanding these achievements, the heart of romanticism was German-speaking Europe. The French writer Madame de Staël (1766–1817) helped popularize German culture with her book *On Germany* (1810). So great was the German cultural response that romanticism is often called a German invention.

The Romantic Movement in Literature

Romanticism in literature was foreshadowed in the German literary movement known as **Sturm und Drang,** or storm and stress. This movement flourished briefly in the 1770s and early 1780s, arising as a revolt against classical restraint and drawing inspiration from Rousseau's emotionalism. On a positive level, this literary movement idealized peasant life and the unconventional, liberated mind. The Sturm und Drang writers attacked organized religion because of its hypocrisy and followed Rousseau in finding God in nature. These middle-class authors objected to the formality and tedium of eighteenth-century life and letters and valued free expression in language, dress, behavior, and love. By the mid-1780s, the movement had settled down, drained of its rebelliousness. The most influential members became fully integrated into the German literary scene.

The Sturm und Drang movement's outstanding writer was Johann Wolfgang von Goethe [GUHR-tuh] (1749–1832), the greatest of German writers. In 1774, while still in his twenties, Goethe acquired a European-wide reputation with *The Sorrows of Young Werther,* a novel in which the young hero commits suicide because of disappointment in love. So successful was this novel that it led to Wertherism, the social phenomenon in which young men imitated the hero's emotionalism, sometimes even to the point of killing themselves. Werther is a complex character: passionate and excitable, given to inappropriate outbursts, moved by the innocence of children, attracted to social misfits, and overwhelmed by God's presence in nature. He embodies many characteristics of romanticism.

Literary romanticism truly began with the publication in England in 1798 of *Lyrical Ballads* by William Wordsworth (1770–1850) and Samuel Taylor Coleridge (1772–1834). The two poets rejected what they considered to be the artificiality of the neoclassicists and turned to natural types of verse, Coleridge to ballad forms and Wordsworth to simple lyrics of plain folks, voiced in the common language of the "middle and lower classes of society." Henceforth many Romantic writers, in both poetry and prose, sought to reproduce the language of customary speech—a literary revolution that was the equivalent of the coming of democracy.

The task Wordsworth assigned himself in *Lyrical Ballads* was to compose verses about the pleasures of everyday existence. He responded to this challenge with poems filled with deep feeling, which were mainly about finding wisdom in simple things. A poem from this collection titled "Lines Composed a Few Miles Above Tintern Abbey" shows Wordsworth's pantheism, or the belief that God lives in nature. In it, speaking to his sister Dorothy, he recalls the strong emotions he felt in his early life when he "bounded o'er the mountains, by the sides / of the deep rivers, and the lonely streams, / wherever nature led." Now he describes himself as subdued but still "a worshipper of Nature." Wordsworth's nature is a world of overgrown hedgerows, meadows, orchards, and peasant cottages. The beauty of the ordinary became Wordsworth's life-long preoccupation; he is regarded as the English language's most stirring poet of nature.

Soon after the appearance of *Lyrical Ballads,* Goethe published his verse play *Faust* (Part I, 1808). Goethe's Werther had been a social rebel, the prototype of the antibourgeois bourgeois. But his Faust was a universal rebel, unwilling to let any moral scruple stand in the way of his spiritual quest for the meaning of life. Faust's two distinguishing marks are his relentless pursuit of knowledge and his all-consuming restlessness. Having exhausted book learning, Faust hopes that experience will satisfy his spiritual hunger, and thus he turns to the devil (Mephistopheles), who proposes to give Faust all the exciting experiences that have been absent in his life. If Faust finds any of his adventures satisfying, then his immortal soul is forever condemned to hell. Under such conditions Faust signs the compact, in his blood, with Mephistopheles.

Mephistopheles helps Faust recover his youth and involves him in a series of escapades that include drunkenness, sexual excess, seduction, and murder. His mistress kills their illegitimate child and perishes in despair. *Faust,* Part I, concludes with Faust more dissatisfied than when he began and no nearer to his goal. Goethe later added Part II (1832), in which God redeems Faust because of his willingness to sacrifice his life for others, but because it lacked the emotional intensity of Part I, it failed to reach a large audience.

Goethe's *Faust,* Part I, became the most often performed German-language play in the world. It inspired numerous paintings and several works of music. The word **Faustian** now is used to characterize one who is willing to sacrifice spiritual values for knowledge, experience, or mastery.

Figure 17.11   RICHARD WESTALL. *George Gordon, Lord By-ron.* 1813. Oil on canvas, 36 × 28″. National Portrait Gallery, London. *Westall's portrait of Lord Byron captures the brooding and dark good looks that made him the exemplar of the romantic hero. Gazing intently into the distance while resting his chin on his hand, Byron seems lost in thought. His isolation is heightened by the overall darkness except for his face, hand, and shirt collar. It was this image of Byron—a person coiled tight as a spring—that caused one female admirer to describe him as "mad, bad, and dangerous to know."*

Another powerful voice in romantic literature was the English poet George Gordon, Lord Byron (1788–1824). Better known on the Continent than his compatriots Wordsworth and Coleridge, Byron was called by Goethe the "herald of world literature." The personality of Byron has fascinated successive generations of Western artists and thinkers. At a time when the middle classes were ruled by a restrictive code of respectability, he created a model for rebellious youth with his flowing hair, open shirt collar, and love of ungovernable forces (Figure 17.11). His greatest romantic creation was probably himself—the "Byronic hero," who was moody, passionate, absorbed in exploring and expressing his innermost self.

Yet the English treated Byron as a pariah and drove him into exile for his unconventional life. Perhaps in retaliation, Byron, in his most admired poem, *Don Juan* (1819–1824), presented the notorious seducer as a virtuous hero—a literary device intended to expose the hy-pocrisy of society. Like Goethe's *Faust,* Byron's *Don Juan* was a study in moral duality and reflected the author's fascination with subterranean drives in human nature.

Byron was the best known of the trio of romantic poets whose enduring lyrical works helped to define the period from 1810 to 1824 as England's great Age of Poetry. The other two were Byron's friend Percy Bysshe Shelley (1792–1822), famed for poetry that is often charged with radical politics, and John Keats (1795–1820), who drew on a tragic personal history to create works of quiet beauty and stoic calm. That all three led tragically shortened lives—Byron dying at age thirty-six, Shelley at twenty-nine, and Keats at twenty-five—contributed in later years to their romantic image as doomed poets.

English romanticism also produced two of the most pervasive figures of Western culture—Frankenstein and his manufactured monster. Made familiar through countless films and cartoons, these two fictional characters first appeared in the novel *Frankenstein* (1818) by Mary Wollstonecraft Shelley (1797–1851). Shelley was well connected to two of the most unconventional literary families of the day; she was the daughter of Mary Wollstonecraft, a founder of modern feminism (see Chapter 16), and she was the wife of Percy Bysshe Shelley. In Shelley's novel, Dr. Frankenstein, having thoughtlessly constructed a humanlike being with no prospect for personal happiness, is eventually hunted down and killed by his own despairing creature. Part of the romantic reaction against Enlightenment rationalism, which began with Rousseau (see Chapter 16), Shelley's novel presented Frankenstein as a man driven by excessive and obsessive intellectual curiosity and the monster as a tragic symbol of science out of control. Written in the optimistic dawn of the industrialized age, when humanity seemed on the verge of taming the natural world, Shelley's *Frankenstein* is one of the earliest warnings that scientific research divorced from morality is an open invitation to personal and social disaster.

Romantic Painting

Romanticism in painting was a European-wide art style, in which artists of all countries shared many subjects (landscape scenes and literary subjects) and themes (love of the exotic and the cult of the hero). But there were also national variations within this international style, as reflected in the images created by the leading painters in England, Germany, Spain, and France.

ENGLAND   Romanticism in painting appeared first in England, manifesting itself as part of a cult of nature

Figure 17.12 JOHN CONSTABLE. *The Hay Wain.* 1821. Oil on canvas, 51¼ × 73″. Reproduced by courtesy of the Trustees, The National Gallery, London. *Although the pastoral subject was alien to them at the time, French romantic painters recognized in Constable a kindred spirit when* The Hay Wain *was exhibited at the Paris Salon of 1824. The scene's informality, the strong colors, and the natural lighting converted them, and a later French school of landscape painters was influenced by Constable.*

with two distinct aspects, the pastoral and the sublime. Painters of pastoral scenes specialized in landscapes in which peasant life was equated with the divine order of things, thus forging a moral link between human beings and the natural environment. John Constable was the chief exponent of the pastoral. In contrast, painters of sublime subjects focused on devastating natural or human-made calamities, reflecting a world order beyond mortal control or understanding. The leading exponent of the sublime was J. M. W. Turner.

Like the Dutch masters of the 1600s, John Constable (1776–1837) preferred to paint simple country landscapes. But more important than the Dutch influence on his art was the romantic cult of nature. Constable's landscapes, like Wordsworth's poetry, reflected the sense of God's universal presence in nature. Wordsworth claimed that nature aroused feelings that "connect the landscape with the quiet of the sky." In his six-foot canvases, Constable tried to awaken the viewer

to the divinity in nature by focusing on ordinary scenes such as might be encountered on a country walk. Constable had an almost holy vision that was true to nature without using what he called tricks or crass emotional appeals.

Constable's landscapes often convey a feeling of having been painted on the spot. In actuality, he liked to sketch on a site and then transform his impressions in his studio into a finished painting that preserved the feeling of immediacy. This two-step method resulted in a style that was both solid and sensitive to the natural world and also conveyed the feeling that his vision sprang from a mystical communion with nature, rather than being an artificial scene conceived in an artist's workshop.

Although Constable's art was not fully appreciated by his contemporaries, a few works won acclaim and helped to redefine the way the public looked at nature. Of these the most famous is *The Hay Wain* (Figure 17.12).

Figure 17.13 JOHN CONSTABLE. *Cloud Study.* 1821. Oil on paper on panel, 8⅜ × 11½″. Yale Center for British Art, New Haven. Paul Mellon Collection. *As Constable made his cloud paintings, he kept precise records of the weather conditions. For example, in this* Cloud Study, *he recorded the date and time, September 21, 1821, between 2 and 3 P.M., and noted: "strong Wind at west, bright light coming through the Clouds which are laying one on the other." Thus, these paintings combine the scientist's meticulous eye with the artist's sensitive response to nature.*

Over the years, this painting has been reproduced so often that it is sometimes dismissed as calendar art, but when it first appeared, it excited admiration at home and in Paris. The freshness of the simple images attracted viewers to the beauty of the scene. *The Hay Wain* added many features of everyday rural life to the repertoire of romantic motifs, including a thatch-roofed cottage, a gently flowing stream, a dog running along a riverbank, cows grazing in the background, and overhead the ever-changing English sky.

The sky, for Constable, served as the unique source of light. In 1821–1822, he conducted a program that he called "skying," capturing on canvas the cloud-filled English sky as it moved from sunshine to rain and back again (Figure 17.13). Dissatisfied with earlier artists who used artificial means to represent nature, Constable worked as a naturalist to record the truth in nature. Constable's cloud studies echoed romantic poets, like Goethe and Wordsworth, who identified clouds as a symbol of various themes, such as loneliness and the fleeting quality of life. In his attempt to portray the out-of-doors in its lively colors and ever-changing light, Constable was an important influence on the nineteenth-century impressionists.

As for the sublime, Joseph Mallord William Turner (1775–1851) created a new type of subject, "the sublime catastrophe," in which he specialized from 1800 until about 1830. He was the most original artist of his age, prefiguring the impressionists with his virtuosic use of color and anticipating modern abstract painting in his depictions of wild nature. An example of

Turner's sublime catastrophes is *Snowstorm: Hannibal and His Army Crossing the Alps* (Figure 17.14). Although inspired by an episode from Roman history that appealed to the public's taste for historical themes, this painting is more about the fury of nature than it is about the Carthaginian general Hannibal. The actual subject is the snowstorm, whose sweeping savagery threatens to annihilate everything, including soldiers and horses. No artist before Turner had handled paint in the way that he does here. He turns the sky, which occupies at least three-fourths of the canvas, into an abstract composition, a series of interpenetrating planes of differently colored light.

Turner also dealt with another aspect of the sublime theme, the notion that all human endeavor is doomed, in *The Bay of Baiae, with Apollo and the Sibyl* (Figure 17.15). Inspired by his first visit to Italy, he portrays classical motifs in a romantic landscape. In ancient Rome, the imperial court built splendid villas and baths at the Bay of Baiae (near Naples), which by Turner's time stood in ruins. The painter, using artistic license, rearranged the actual scene to make this vista much more appealing. By placing Apollo and the Sibyl in the foreground, Turner alludes to a Greek myth associated with the nearby port of Cumae, the home of the Cumaean Sibyl.

GERMANY About the time the sublime developed in England, it also was launched in Germany by Caspar David Friedrich (1774–1840), a painter who specialized in brooding landscapes, usually with a few diminutive human figures to give them a spiritual

Figure 17.14   JOSEPH MALLORD WILLIAM TURNER. *Snowstorm: Hannibal and His Army Crossing the Alps.* 1810–1812. Oil on canvas, 4′9½″ × 7′9½″. Tate Gallery. *Hannibal and his troops, stretching from left to right in the bottom third of the painting, are almost invisible; above them and dominating the scene is a raging snowstorm, through which may be glimpsed a ghostly sun. This painting, based on a gothic novel of the time, was less about the ancient struggle between the Carthaginian general Hannibal and Rome than about the French general Napoleon and England in the 1800s; thus, this work implicitly reflects the period's political climate—a rare occurrence in Turner's art.*

Figure 17.15   JOSEPH MALLORD WILLIAM TURNER. *The Bay of Baiae, with Apollo and the Sibyl.* 1823. Oil on canvas, 57¼ × 94″. Tate Gallery. *Turner has deftly focused the viewer's eye on the painting's center by means of a circular arrangement of objects (boats, ruins, and rocks) and the use of shadows and light. Within this space, Turner places Apollo making overtures to the Sibyl, a tactic whose outcome is symbolized by the rabbit and the snake. The rabbit (center) represents love, referring to Apollo's pursuit of the Sibyl, and the snake (lower right) alludes to lurking evil, perhaps a reference to the Sibyl's fate for spurning Apollo. The god curses her so that she will grow old but never die—just as the ruins at the Bay of Baiae are reminders of Rome's former glory.*

Figure 17.16   CASPAR DAVID FRIEDRICH. *Monk by the Sea.* 1808–1810. Oil on canvas, 43¼ × 67½". Stiftung Preussischer Kulturbesitz, Schloss Charlottenburg, Berlin. *This painting is revolutionary in form and content. In form, it violates classical perspective by using a low horizon line to create a sky of limitless space; it also rejects traditional design by reducing figures and setting to a minimum level. In content, the meaning is left deliberately ambiguous. These simplifications make the painting a nearly abstract image, and thus it points the way to modern art (see Chapter 19).*

scale. A lifelong resident of Pomerania on northern Europe's Baltic coast, he drew artistic inspiration from his homeland's deserted beaches, dense forests, and chalky cliffs. What sets his landscapes apart from those of earlier artists on the same subject is his desire to turn natural scenes into glimpses of the divine mystery. Avoiding traditional Christian subjects, Friedrich invented his own symbols for conveying God's presence in the world.

In *Monk by the Sea* (Figure 17.16), the setting is the stark Baltic seacoast, where a hooded figure stands on the dunes before a great wall of sky. This figure—the monk of the title—forms the only vertical line in an otherwise horizontal painting. Below is the angry sea, but the sky is calm except for a bank of clouds lit by the moon or perhaps the coming dawn. By showing

the monk from the back—he rarely painted faces—Friedrich encourages the viewer to see what the monk sees and to feel what he feels. Perhaps, filled with optimism, he awaits a new day. Or perhaps, despairing, he watches the descent of night. Or perhaps he feels insignificant when confronted with the limitless sky and sea. Infrared photographs have revealed that Friedrich originally included two ships struggling against the waves in the painting. Ships are often present in Friedrich's works, symbolic of a divine messenger to the human realm. By painting them out, Friedrich removed an optimistic note that may have guided the viewer's interpretation. Nevertheless, the finished painting represents twin romantic themes and favorites of Friedrich's—love of solitude and fascination with the infinite.

Figure 17.17 Francisco Goya. *The Family of Charles IV.* 1800. Oil on canvas, 9'2" × 11'. Prado, Madrid. *Following a well-established Spanish tradition, Goya has painted himself into the canvas on the left, from which vantage point in the shadows he observes the royal family. Velázquez had followed this tradition 150 years earlier (see Figure 14.12), which this painting echoes. Goya portrayed the ravaged face of the king's sister on the left as a reminder of the fleeting nature of human beauty.*

SPAIN In Spain, romanticism flourished in the anti-classical paintings of Francisco Goya (1746–1828), a major figure in Spanish culture. Reflecting a nightmarish vision of the world, his art ranges from rococo fantasies to sensual portraits to grim studies of human folly to spiritual evil and finally to scenes of hopelessness. Various reasons have been suggested for Goya's descent into despair, but certainly his dashed hopes for the regeneration of Spain's political and social order were central to his advancing pessimism, as was his slow decline into deafness.

In the 1790s, Goya served as court painter to King Charles IV, and signs of the artist's political disaffection can be detected in his revealing portrait of the royal family (Figure 17.17). He depicts the queen (center) as a vain, foolish woman and the king (right, front) as a simpleton. History has judged Goya's interpretations to be accurate, for this was a corrupt and stupid court. Perhaps the lace-covered gowns, the glittering medals, and the general elegance of the ensemble allowed him to get away with such unflattering portraits and survive within this dangerous environment.

In 1799 Goya published a collection of etchings that set forth his savage indictment of the age's social evils and established him as an outstanding humanitarian artist. The title of this series was *Caprichos*, or *Caprices*, a romantic genre that allowed artists to express their personal feelings on any subject and to use irrational or imaginative scenes to plead for the use of reason in human affairs. One of the eighty *caprichos*, *Hasta la Muerte*, or *Until Death* (Figure 17.18), shows an old woman gazing admiringly in a mirror and adjusting

Figure 17.18 Francisco Goya. *Hasta la Muerte (Until Death).* 1797–1798. Etching and aquatint, approx. 7½ × 5¼". Galerie P. Proute, Paris. Bridgeman-Giraudon/Art Resource, NY. *Goya's artistic technique in the* Caprichos *series is aquatint, a process that uses acid on a metal plate to create subtle shades of light and dark. The absence of color in the resulting engravings heightens the moral message of these works. In this etching, the mirror and the bottles and jars of cosmetics on the table reinforce Goya's visual statement about vanity and aging.*

Figure 17.19   Francisco Goya. *The Execution of the Third of May, 1808.* 1814–1815. Oil on canvas, 8'9" × 13'4". Prado, Madrid. *A comparison of this painting by Goya with David's portrait of the assassinated Marat (see Figure 17.5) shows the difference in tone between romantic and neoclassical art. David makes Marat's death a heroic sacrifice despite its tragic circumstances. In contrast, Goya's passionate portrayal of the Spanish martyrs shows that there is nothing heroic about their deaths; their cause may be just, but the manner of their death is pitiless and squalid.*

her hat, while a young woman, perhaps her maid, and two young men look on. The young woman and one male attendant each cover their mouths, suggesting they are laughing at such a ridiculous scene; the other man gazes upward in a state of disbelief. In many of the *caprichos*, Goya probes the deeper meaning of life, but, here, he treats the theme of vanity with a touch of humor, at the expense of a clueless old lady.

Napoleon's conquest of Spain and the subsequent Spanish war of liberation form the background to Goya's masterpiece, *The Execution of the Third of May, 1808* (Figure 17.19). This protest against French imperialism—one of the world's most compelling depictions of the horrors of war—shows Spanish captives being executed by a French firing squad. The French troops are a faceless line of disciplined automatons, and the

Spanish a band of ill-assorted prisoners. The Spanish patriots are arranged in three groups: those covered with blood and lying on the ground are already dead, those facing the firing squad will be dead in an instant, and those marching forward with faces covered are scheduled for the next round. The emotional center of this otherwise somber-hued painting is the white-shirted man bathed in brilliant light. With his arms outstretched, he becomes a Christ figure, symbolizing Goya's compassion for all victims who die for a good cause.

FRANCE   Romantic painting arrived in France in 1818 with the appearance of *The Raft of the "Medusa,"* a work by Théodore Géricault [zhay-rih-KOH] (1791–1824) that was based on an actual incident (Figure 17.20). The *Me-*

Figure 17.20   THÉODORE GÉRICAULT. *The Raft of the "Medusa."* 1818. Oil on canvas, 16'1"
× 23'6". Louvre. *Other artists, including Turner and Friedrich, painted shipwrecks and their
victims (see Figure 18.3), but Géricault's enormous canvas is probably the best known. He so vividly caught his subjects' desperation and hope that his work received instant praise, regardless of
the controversies surrounding the subject and its relationships to social and political issues. With
his usual thorough preparation, Géricault made over fifty studies of the incident, rearranging the
figures on the raft until he had created a pyramidal structure, moving from the lower left corner
to the center and upper right.*

dusa, a sailing ship, had foundered in the South Atlantic, and it was believed that all aboard were lost. Then,
after almost two months, a handful of survivors were
rescued from a makeshift raft. From their story came
shocking details of mutiny, crimes by officers, murder,
cannibalism, and a government cover-up.

Géricault was attracted to this incident in which a
few men outwitted death against all odds. Focusing
on the moment of their rescue, he depicts ordinary humans as noble heroes nearly overwhelmed by the savage forces of nature. The nude and partially clad bodies
in the foreground convey a powerful sense of dignity
and suffering. From here, the figures surge upward
toward the black youth who is hoisted aloft and wav-
ing a flag at the unseen rescue ship. Géricault wanted
his painting to convey a political statement about the
government and to be as realistic as possible—he
interviewed survivors and had a replica of the raft

constructed—but at the same time, he imbued it with
expression and pathos. The result was a highly emotional work that embodied the spirit of romanticism.

Géricault's *Raft of the "Medusa"* also illustrates romanticism's connection to liberal political ideas. The
devastated humanity on the raft underscored the
breakdown in civilization that the entire *Medusa* incident came to represent. The painting itself became a
rallying point for the critics of the restored Bourbon
monarchy, who saw in the portrayal of a crew cast
adrift a metaphor for the French nation. Many of Géricault's ideas were taken up by Eugène Delacroix [del-
uh-KWAH] (1798–1863), who became the leader of a
school of romantic painting that was in open rivalry
with Ingres and the neoclassicists. Like Géricault, Delacroix was a humanitarian who drew artistic inspiration
from his violent times. In the 1820s, he identified with
Greek freedom fighters in their war of independence

Figure 17.21   Eugène Delacroix. *Massacre at Chios*. 1824. Oil on canvas, 13'10" × 11'7".
Louvre. *Delacroix used vivid colors and vulnerable bodies to express the horror of the historic
event—a typical technique for him. Dead and dying Greeks fill the foreground, while two Turkish soldiers (in turbans) continue to slaughter the innocents. In the middle background, another
group of Greeks is being killed, and, in the far left, distant smoke rises from a burning village.
The dark blue sea in the background and the yellowish blue sky overhead add a threatening mood
to the scene of carnage. The unearthly yellow of the sky is echoed in the skin tones of the victims
in the foreground.* Massacre at Chios, *when exhibited in the 1824 Paris Salon, was a popular
success. The French government bought it for six thousand francs—a common practice in this
period, which linked the art world and the state, creating a kind of "official art." When impressionism was born in the 1870s, it would be in reaction against "official art" (see Chapter 19).*

Figure 17.22   Eugène Delacroix. *Liberty Leading the People.* 1831. Oil on canvas, 8'6" × 10'8". Louvre. *Delacroix's canvas bears some meaningful resemblances to Géricault's* Raft of the "Medusa." *Each painting takes a contemporary event as its subject and transforms it into a symbol of France. Moreover, Delacroix's placement of two dead male figures, one partially nude and the other clothed, echoes similar figures in Géricault's work. Delacroix's portrayal of the people triumphant thus seems to be an optimistic response to Géricault's image of France adrift.*

against the Turks, expressing his support in *Massacre at Chios* (Figure 17.21). Delacroix painted it immediately after the Turks killed twenty thousand Greek inhabitants of the Aegean island of Chios in 1822. Chios, which claims to be the birthplace of Homer, was linked in European minds with the glories of classical culture. Delacroix's painting of this horrific scene is a rarity in the history of Western art: it is a great work of art and simultaneously a piece of political propaganda.

Delacroix's *Liberty Leading the People* was also inspired by a political incident, the July Revolution of 1830, which resulted in the establishment of a limited constitutional monarchy (Figure 17.22). The painting combines history and allegory, depicting revolutionar-

ies on the barricades led by an idealized, bare-breasted goddess of liberty. Surrounding Liberty are three central figures who symbolize the various classes that constitute "the People": the man in the tall hat represents the middle classes, the chief beneficiaries of the revolution; the kneeling figure in the cap stands for the working-class rebels; and the boy brandishing the twin pistols is an image of the street urchin, among the lowest social groups. The focal point of the painting is the tricolor, the Revolutionary flag adopted in the Revolution of 1789, outlawed from 1815 until 1830 and now restored as France's unifying symbol. The flag's red, white, and blue determine the harmony of color in the rest of this painting. Completed soon after the 1830 revolution, this work was purchased by the new king as a fitting tribute to the struggle that brought him to power. It was quickly hidden away, however, for the bourgeois establishment found the revolutionary heritage an embarrassment. Only later, with the creation of the Second Republic in 1848, did the French public see the painting.

Science and Philosophy

Science, having been part of natural philosophy since ancient Greece (see Chapter 2), grew more independent with each field of study going its separate way. Science, based on a blend of empiricism, experiment, and rationalism, now held sway in western Europe, especially among French and British thinkers. But east of the Rhine, German thinkers, rejecting what they judged to be the materialism and skepticism of the new science (see "David Hume," Chapter 16), began developing an alternative approach to truth—German idealism, which assigned a central role to spiritual values. Still, the vast majority in the West remained ignorant of these shifts in science and thought. They found comfort and assurance in popular religion, especially in those movements that had emerged in the early eighteenth century (see Chapter 16).

SCIENCE   Between 1760 and 1830, the educated classes of Europe embraced the Scientific Revolution, making its findings part of the bedrock of Western thought (see Chapter 15). Although this period did not witness dramatic breakthroughs equal to the Scientific Revolution or Newtonian synthesis, the world of science changed in many ways: better organization and diversity, new journals devoted to research, and public recognition of scientific achievements.

Instead of "science," it now became customary to speak of "the sciences." The sciences, as such, comprised the biological sciences, the physical sciences, and the natural sciences. Each area of scientific study, in turn, began to splinter into distinct and specialized disciplines, such as botany, zoology, chemistry, and electricity. As more scientific discoveries were made, the new knowledge was soon integrated into the mainstream of Western thought and culture and spread around the world (Figure 17.23)—a trend that continues today.

Modern chemistry, one of the new sciences born in the eighteenth century, was founded through the efforts of primarily one scientist—Antoine-Laurent Lavoisier [AN-twan-lo-RAHN lahv-WAHZ-yeh] (1743–1794). Trained as a chemist, he conducted experiments with air, gas, and heat, which led, in turn, to many discoveries, including his explanation for combustion. At about

the same time, the first chemical element—oxygen—was identified by the English scientist and theologian Joseph Priestly (1733–1804). Later, Lavoisier, through his experiments, discovered the life-sustaining role that oxygen played for plants and animals. Lavoisier also broke water down into its two basic elements, oxygen and hydrogen, though he did not identify hydrogen by name. For the discipline of chemistry, he coauthored its classification system and established the ground rules for conducting chemical experiments. Lavoisier also was active in governmental affairs and dedicated his expertise to improving the French economy and society. However, because of his government service for the French crown, he became a victim of the Reign of Terror and was guillotined.

The study of electricity, which began in the mid-1600s, advanced with the English physicist Robert Boyle (see Chapter 15). Boyle was one of the first to recognize that electricity has mutual attraction and repulsion characteristics. In the 1740s, the American Benjamin Franklin (1706–1790) conducted experiments with electric phenomena, testing the properties of what he called the "electric fluid." Soon he was able to distinguish between positive and negative charges and between conductors and nonconductors of electricity. His famous and dangerous 1752 kite episode proved that electricity is identical with lightning. Later, he invented the pointed iron lightning rod, which protected a building from lightning by transmitting an electrical charge by wire into the ground, thus reducing the number of fires in a city. Franklin wrote several articles explaining his experiments, which made his reputation as a man of science in Europe, and his contributions to the understanding of electricity made him a central figure in this field.

The Swedish botanist, explorer, and collector Carl Linnaeus [ley-NEE-eus] (1707–1778) laid out the modern taxonomic system for plants, animals, and minerals in his *Systema Naturae* (1753). Taxonomy is the science of the classification of living organisms or extinct beings. Linnaeus also established the basic botanical nomenclature (names), along with the rules for their use. In his system, the plant and animal worlds are divided into a hierarchy: beginning at the top, class, order, genus, and species. In his nomenclature, he used a binomial method (two names, both in Latin: first the genus and then the species—for example, *Equus caballus,* for the domestic horse). His system became part of modern science, though aspects of it have been updated, supplemented, and modified.

PHILOSOPHY   German thought stood in stark contrast to the Anglo-French Enlightenment. German idealism, which espoused a spiritual view of life, was closely related to the romantic spirit and its expressions. From

Figure 17.23 Frontispiece, *Journal du voyage fait par ordre du roi à l'Équateur (Journal of the Voyage to the Equator, by Order of the King).* 1751. *This frontispiece, taken from a thesis defense, was dedicated to three French scholars who set out to measure the equator in 1742. Such expeditions preceded the establishment of schools and colleges in Europe's South American colonies in the eighteenth century. The images in the frontispiece blend classical themes with the new science. Minerva, the Roman goddess of wisdom, sits enthroned and surrounded by* putti, *angelic figures associated with the Roman goddess Venus. The* putti *are using scientific instruments—microscopes and magnifying glasses—to examine plants, study the globe, calculate distances, and experiment with fire. In the left background is a telescope and, in the left foreground, a pendulum clock. The illustration's message is clear: scientific knowledge is spreading around the world.*

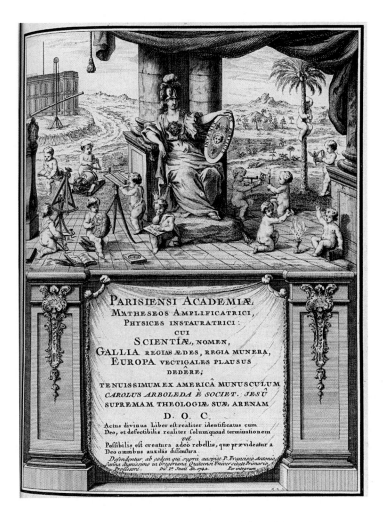

Kant through Hegel, German thinkers constructed idealism as a philosophic alternative to conventional religion.

In the 1790s, Immanuel Kant [KAHNT] (1724–1804) began the revolution in German thought when he distinguished the world of phenomena ("appearances") from the world of noumena ("things-in-themselves," or spirit). In Kantian terms, the phenomenal world can be understood by science, but the noumenal world can be studied only by intuitive means.

Kant's followers, nonetheless, tried the impossible when they began to map out the spiritual realm. Johann Gottlieb Fichte [FICK-tuh] (1762–1814) found reality in the World Spirit, a force having consciousness and seeking self-awareness. Friedrich Wilhelm Joseph von Schelling [SHEL-ing] (1775–1854) equated nature with the Absolute, his name for ultimate reality. He also was the first to espouse the romantic belief in the religion of art by claiming that artists reveal divine truths in inspired works. Schelling's teaching on art influenced the English poet Coleridge and through him the English romantic movement.

The climax of idealism came with Georg Wilhelm Friedrich Hegel [HAY-guhl] (1770–1831), who explained human history as the record of the World Spirit seeking to know its true nature. Self-knowledge for the World Spirit arose only through a dialectical struggle. In the first stage, the Spirit developed a thesis that in turn produced an antithesis; in the second stage, a conflict ensued between these two ideas that led to a synthesis, or a new thesis, which in turn gradually provoked new strife—a third stage, and so on. Hegel's theory of history ignored individuals because humans in the mass became tools of the World Spirit in its quest for freedom. In this view, wars, riots, and revolts were merely evidence of spiritual growth. For this reason, Hegel characterized Napoleon and his wars as embodiments of the World Spirit.

Hegelianism had a tremendous impact on later Western thought. Revolutionaries such as Karl Marx borrowed Hegel's dialectical approach to history. Conservatives, especially in Germany, used his thought as a justification for a strong centralized state, and nationalists everywhere drew inspiration from his thought. Other thinkers rejected his denial of human responsibility and founded existentialist philosophies that glorified the individual (see Chapter 20).

The Birth of Romantic Music

As the middle class gained political power between 1789 and 1830, they converted the musical scene into a marketplace; that is, laissez-faire economics and music became intertwined. Replacing elite forms of patronage, programs that the bourgeoisie now attended required admission fees and paid performers. Salaries and the demand for performances freed musicians from the patronage system. With their newly won independence, they became eccentric and individualistic—attitudes that were encouraged by the romantic cult of the artist. Music grew more accessible as democracy progressed, and new industrial techniques and production allowed more people to own inexpensive musical instruments.

The most gifted composer of this period, and one of the greatest musical geniuses of all time, was Ludwig van Beethoven [BAY-toe-vuhn] (1770–1827), a German who spent most of his life in Vienna. He personified the new breed of musician, supporting himself through concerts, lessons, and the sales of his music (Figure 17.24). His works represent both the culmination of classical music and the introduction of romantic music. Working with the standard classical forms—the sonata, the symphony, and the string quartet—he created longer works, doubling and even tripling their conventional length. He also wrote music that was increasingly expressive and that showed more warmth and variety of feeling than classical music, particularly his program music—that is, music that portrays a particular setting or tells a story. Beethoven made several other significant musical innovations, including the use of choral voices within the symphonic form and the composing of music that expressed the power of the human will.

Beethoven's career may be divided into three phases, but his extreme individualism left his unique stamp on everything that he composed. In the first phase, from the 1790s until 1803, he was under the shadow of Haydn, with whom he studied in Vienna. Beethoven's First Symphony (1800) may be termed a classical work, but in it he reveals a new spirit by lengthening the first and third movements and making the middle movement more lively than usual.

In the second phase, from 1803 until 1816, Beethoven's genius gave birth to romantic music. He began to find his own voice, enriching and deepening the older forms. The Third Symphony (1803), which Bee-

thoven called the *Eroica (Heroic),* is the most characteristic work from this second stage. The composer originally dedicated this symphony to Napoleon, whom he admired as a champion of democracy. But when the French ruler declared himself emperor in 1804, Beethoven angrily tore up the dedication page and dedicated the work instead "to the memory of a great man." In the Third Symphony, Beethoven substantially expanded the musical material beyond the limits characteristic of earlier symphonies, making it longer and more complex. The music is grand, serious, and dignified, a truly heroic work.

From the second phase also comes Beethoven's most famous work, Symphony no. 5 in C Minor, op. 67 (1808). The highly emotional Fifth Symphony, filled with bold harmonies and rich color contrasts, begins with a conflict-laden movement and concludes with an exultant final movement. The first movement opens with four notes—three short and one long—which have been described as the most memorable musical phrase of all time. During World War II their similarity to the Morse code made them symbolic of "V for Victory," and the Fifth Symphony was played at concerts to rally support for the Allied troops. In the first movement, this musical phrase is endlessly repeated, passed back and forth among the various instruments, played by a single instrument, or group of instruments, or the full orchestra. This phrase is also given shifting tone colors, ranging from harsh to lyrical, from soft to loud, along with dynamic changes in rhythm. The four notes function as a unifying motif in the first movement, and they return as a pervasive presence throughout the other three movements.

In his third phase, from 1816 until 1827, Beethoven's music became freer and more contemplative, reaching its culmination in the Ninth Symphony (1822–1824), the last of his large-scale works. In the last movement of this work, Beethoven included a choral finale in which he set to music the poem "Ode to Joy" by the German romantic poet Friedrich von Schiller [SHIL-uhr] (1759–1805). Despite a life of personal adversities that included deafness from the age of thirty, Beethoven affirmed in this piece his faith in both humanity and God—"Millions, be you embraced! For the universe, this kiss!" The magnificent music and the idealistic text have led to the virtual canonization of this inspirational work.

Across these three phases, Beethoven was a prolific composer in all musical genres; many of these works are unrivaled in their expressiveness and originality. Besides the nine symphonies, he wrote two Masses, two ballets, one opera *(Fidelio),* sixteen string quartets, thirty-two piano sonatas (most notably the *Pathétique* and *Moonlight* sonatas), five concertos for piano, one

Figure 17.24 FERDINAND GEORG WALDMÜLLER. *Ludwig van Beethoven*. 1823. Oil on canvas, approx. 28⅓ × 22⅝″. Archiv Breitkopf and Härtel, Leipzig, Germany. Original destroyed in World War II. *Beethoven in his later years was the embodiment of the romantic genius, disheveled, singing to himself as he strolled Vienna's streets, mocked by street urchins; once, he was even arrested by the police as a tramp. In this 1823 portrait, Waldmüller suggests Beethoven's unkempt appearance, but through the strong expression, fixed jaw, and broad forehead he also conveys the great composer's fierce determination and intelligence.*

concerto for violin, and numerous chamber and choral compositions.

Vienna contributed another outstanding composer in Franz Schubert [SHOO-bert] (1797–1828), who was famous for the beauty of his melodies and the simple grace of his songs. He lived a rather bohemian life, supporting himself, like Beethoven, by giving lessons and concerts. But unlike Beethoven, Schubert wrote mainly for the living rooms of Vienna rather than for the concert hall and is most famous for perfecting the **art song,** called *lied* (plural, *lieder*) in German. The emergence of this musical form in the Romantic period was tied to the revival of lyric poetry. Schubert composed the music for over six hundred *lieder*, with texts by Goethe ("Gretchen at the Spinning Wheel"), Shakespeare ("Who Is Sylvia?"), and other poets. His efforts raised the song to the level of great art.

One of Schubert's best-known songs is "Erlkönig" ("The Erlking"), a musical setting of a narrative ballad by Goethe. Filled with romantic imagery, the poem tells of a distraught father, carrying his dying son in his arms while riding horseback through a storm-filled night. During the hectic ride, the boy has visions of the Erlking—in German folklore, the king of the elves, and, in Goethe's poem, the symbol of death. Schubert sets the text against a musical background that represents

the horse's galloping hooves: pulsing, triplet rhythms. The song requires the soloist to give voice to each of four characters: narrator, father, son, and Erlking. Appropriate music is written for each, such as, for example, upper register, with discordant notes, for the boy; and cajoling tunes for the Erlking. Three times the boy cries out, "My father, my father!" The song ends with the narrator speaking in recitative: *"In seinen Armen das Kind war tot,"* ("In his arms the child was dead").

A final composer of significance in this first period of romanticism was the Frenchman Hector Berlioz [BAIR-lee-ohz] (1803–1869). His most famous work is the *Symphonie fantastique (Fantastic Symphony)* (1830), a superb example of program music. Subtitled "Episode of an Artist's Life," this symphonic work illustrates musically a story that Berlioz described in accompanying written notes. In the tale, which takes the form of an opium dream, an artist-hero hopelessly adores an unfaithful woman and eventually dies for her. Relatively conventional in form, the symphony is most original in its use of a recurring musical theme, called an *idée fixe*, or "fixed idea," that becomes an image of the hero's beloved. Because every section contains the *idée fixe* in a modified form, it unifies the symphony in an innovative way. For example, in the fifth movement, subtitled "Dream of a Witches' Sabbath," he uses the *idée fixe* to introduce the witches' dance—a favorite pseudo-gothic subject for romantic composers and artists. Berlioz based the dance on the *Dies Irae (Days of Wrath)* from the Catholic Mass, thus making it emblematic here of a black mass, or devil worship. The *Dies Irae* theme, made up of long, evenly sustained notes, is first stated by low woodwinds and horns, accompanied by chimes. The theme becomes part of a musical conversation, being played in a rapid staccato, by high woodwinds, giving it a mocking sound. Variations of the theme are played by various groups of instruments, sometimes overlapping, and with frequent shifts in rhythm and tone color. The success of this Berlioz symphony helped to strengthen the fashion for program music in the romantic period.

The Legacy of the Age of Revolution and Reaction

During this period of revolution and reaction, the West turned away from the past, with its monarchical forms of government, its hierarchical society dominated by aristocratic landowners, its glacial rate of change, and its patronage system ruled by social, ecclesiastical, and political elites. Three events in particular—the Industrial Revolution and the American and the French Revolutions—have left an indelible stamp on the modern world. The Industrial Revolution, which continues today, has gradually made humanity master of the earth and its resources while accelerating the pace of life and creating the two leading modern social groups, the middle class and the working class. The Industrial Revolution also spawned classical economics, the school of economists who justified the doctrine of laissez-faire that is still held to be the best argument for capitalism and continuous industrial growth. This same doctrine altered the patronage system, subjecting the creative works of modern artists, writers, musicians, and humanists to the law of the marketplace.

The American Revolution produced the first successful modern democracy, one that today stands as a beacon of hope for those oppressed by authoritarian regimes. The French Revolution contributed the idea of an all-encompassing upheaval that would sweep away the past and create a new secular order characterized by social justice and fairness. Although viewed with skepticism by some people, for multitudes of others the notion of such a revolution became a sustaining belief. From the French Revolution also arose the idea that race and religion should not be used to exclude people from the right to vote—a reflection of its emphasis on the "brotherhood of man." Further, the French Revolution contributed the idea of a citizens' army, based on national conscription—a development that led to the savagery of modern warfare. And the French Revolution gave birth to the Napoleonic Code, the law code that is used in the French-speaking world today.

Both the French and the American Revolutions contributed certain beliefs that have become basic statements of Western political life, such as the idea that constitutions should be written and that basic human liberties should be identified. Indeed, the progressive expansion of natural and civil rights to embrace all of society is an outgrowth of these two revolutions.

Other enduring legacies of this late-eighteenth- and early-nineteenth-century period are the neoclassical buildings in Washington, D.C., and in most of the state capitals of the United States, the body of music of the romantic composers, and the paintings of the neoclassical and early romantic schools. An ambiguous legacy of this period has been nationalism, the belief in one's own country and its people. At its best, nationalism is a noble concept, for it encourages people to examine their roots and preserve their collective identity and heritage. At its worst, it has led to brutal outbursts, dividing the people of a country against one another and culminating in the disintegration of nations. Both forms of nationalism remain potent forces in the world today.

On a more personal level, this period saw the development of the romantic view of life, an attitude that stresses informality, identification with the common people, the importance of feeling and imagination, and enjoyment of simple pleasures. Perhaps more than any other legacy of this period, the romantic outlook has helped to shape the way that most Western men and women live in today's world.

KEY CULTURAL TERMS

romanticism	sublime
Sturm und Drang	art song *(lied)*
Faustian	*idée fixe*

QUESTIONS FOR CRITICAL THINKING

1. Discuss the reasons why the Industrial Revolution occurred first in England. Describe its impact on English society.

2. What were the causes of the American Revolution? What were its goals? How successful were the American colonists in achieving their goals?

3. Some historians claim that the French Revolution is the most important political event in the modern world. Evaluate this claim. What were the Revolution's "good" and "bad" results?

4. What were the roots of neoclass icism? Compare and contrast the works of David and Ingres as expressions of neoclassicism.

5. What were the origins of romanticism? Explain it as a cultural movement, relying on the works of Goethe, Hegel, and Beethoven as the bases of your response.

18

THE TRIUMPH OF THE BOURGEOISIE
1830–1871

The French and American Revolutions offered the hope of political power to the disfranchised, and the Industrial Revolution promised material gains to the impoverished. Those expectations remained largely unfulfilled in Europe, however, as the nineteenth century unfolded. Benefits were reaped mainly by one group—the bourgeois class, especially its wealthiest sector.

Left behind was a new group created by industrialization—the proletariat, or working class. These urban workers expressed their frustrated hopes through political uprisings and social movements, and often the lower middle class joined in demanding universal suffrage and a fairer distribution of power and wealth. Against the liberalism of the bourgeoisie, some workers set forth the ideals of socialism. But reform was limited at best, and successive waves of revolutionary uprisings failed to win significant improvements (Figure 18.1).

These events were echoed in the cultural realm. From its peak in the 1820s, romanticism declined and slowly faded away. Embraced by the middle class, it became respectable and lost much of its creative fire. By midcentury, a new style, realism, was emerging that reflected the new social and political order. Realism focused on ordinary people and strove to depict in objective terms "the heroism of everyday life." At the same time, industrialization continued to spread, and traditional beliefs and values were being challenged by everything from the theories of Charles Darwin to the invention of the camera (Timeline 18.1).

◀ **Detail** FRANÇOIS RUDE. *The Departure of the Volunteers.* 1833–1836. Approx. 42 × 26′. Paris.

Timeline 18.1   THE AGE OF THE BOURGEOISIE

1830		1848	1851			1861	1865	1871
		Revolutions in Europe				American Civil War		
							Creation of German Empire	
Revolutions of 1830	**1839** Daguerre's camera	**1848** Marx and Engels's *Communist Manifesto*	**1851** Great Exhibition	**1854** Dickens's *Hard Times*	**1857** Flaubert's *Madame Bovary*	**1862** Hugo's *Les Misérables*		**1869** Tolstoy's *War and Peace*
1832 English Reform Bill; Sand's *Indiana*		**1847** Brontë sisters' *Wuthering Heights* and *Jane Eyre*		**1855** Courbet's *The Meeting*	**1859** Darwin's *On the Origin of Species*	**1863** Manet's *Olympia*		

Figure 18.1   FRANÇOIS RUDE. *The Departure of the Volunteers. 1833–1836. Approx. 42 × 26'. Paris. This sculptural group, depicting a crowd of warriors inspired by the winged Liberty, symbolizes the French people on the march during the revolution of 1830, the first of a series of revolutions in nineteenth-century Europe. Designed for the Arch of Triumph in Paris, the work came to be known affectionately as* La Marseillaise, *the name of the French national anthem.*

THE POLITICAL AND ECONOMIC SCENE: LIBERALISM AND NATIONALISM

The twin forces of liberalism and nationalism drove many of the period's events. The basic premise of liberalism—the individual should be free from external control—resonated with the American and French Revolutions as well as the bourgeois class's need to liberate itself from aristocratic society. The liberal political agenda included constitutionally guaranteed political and civil rights, especially free speech, religious toleration, and voting rights for property-owners. Perhaps most important, liberalism promoted laissez-faire economics, which allowed the wealthy classes to maximize their profits and justified their control of the workers. Liberalism was most successful in England, France, and Belgium, failed to take root in Italy and central and eastern Europe, and never affected czarist Russia.

In contrast, nationalism emphasized cooperation among all of a country's people who shared a common language and heritage. Overlooking class divisions, nationalists advocated humanitarian values, stressing the concept that all members of a nation are brothers and sisters. As nationalism spread, these values were often expanded to include liberal ideals, republican principles, and even democratic beliefs. Nationalism became a force in central, southern, and eastern Europe, where the states of what would become Germany and Italy were still little more than "geographic expressions" (Map 18.1). However, after 1848 nationalism grew increasingly militant and ethnocentric.

LEARNING THROUGH MAPS

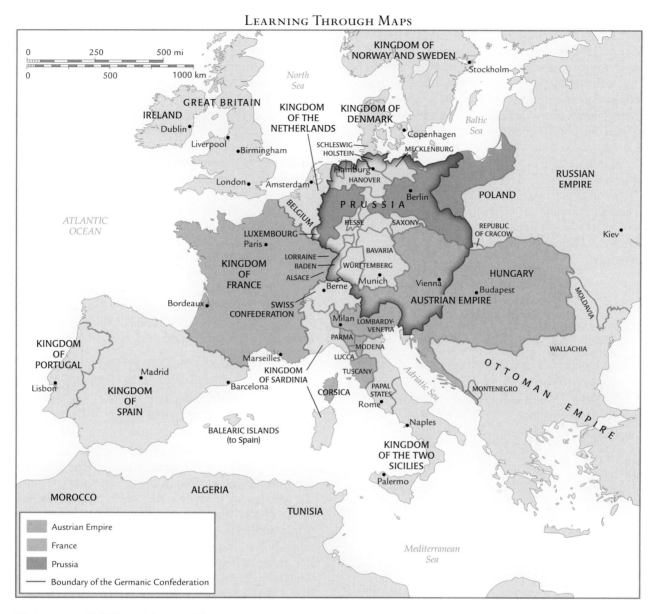

Map 18.1 EUROPE AFTER THE CONGRESS OF VIENNA, 1815
This map shows the political divisions of Europe after the defeat of Napoleon. 1. *Compare* this map with Map 17.1, Europe at the Height of Napoleon's Power. 2. *Notice* the trend toward larger but fewer states. 3. *Which* states improved their territorial holdings at the Congress of Vienna? 4. *Which* states were the losers at the congress? 5. *Identify* the German Confederation and its boundary. 6. *Which* state, Austria or Prussia, was better positioned to emerge as leader of the German Confederation?

The Revolutions of 1830 and 1848

The repressive policies imposed at the Congress of Vienna in 1815 were challenged by a series of uprisings, beginning in France with the July Revolution of 1830, which overthrew the last Bourbon king and installed Louis Philippe (r. 1830–1848) and a liberal constitution. This regime—known as the July Monarchy—

eventually became the tool of the rich middle class at the expense of the workers. Voting rights were limited to wealthy male property-owners, and laws favored an unregulated economy. The July Monarchy showed that the middle class, once empowered, refused to extend the benefits of liberalism to disfranchised groups.

Liberal revolutions followed France's lead, first in Belgium and then in central and southern Europe, but they all failed. In central Europe, local authorities backed by Austrian troops quickly crushed the liberal uprisings and punished rebels, imposed martial law, reinstituted censorship, and took control of the school systems. Although liberals continued to work for moderate reforms, conservatives dashed their hopes. Across central and eastern Europe, the one force emerging as a rallying point was nationalism, focusing on ethnic identity and common cultural heritage.

In 1848 accumulated dissatisfactions and frustrations erupted in another series of uprisings across Europe (Table 18.1), starting with demonstrations and riots in Paris in February. The rebellions were propelled by liberal ideals and nationalistic goals, but their immediate causes were declining production, rising unemployment, and falling agricultural prices. By spring, the path of revolution ran from Paris through Berlin to Vienna, and all along this route varied groupings of bourgeoisie, intellectuals, workers, students, and nationalists toppled kings and ministers. Temporary governments, led by liberals and reformers, drove out foreign troops and set up constitutional monarchies, republics, or democracies with universal male suffrage. A few governments—influenced by the new movement known as socialism—addressed economic problems by passing laws to stimulate productivity, improve working conditions, and aid the poor with relief or employment programs.

By fall, the conservatives—the army, the aristocrats, and the church—had rallied to defeat the disorganized revolutionaries, and by January 1849 many of the old rulers had reclaimed power. After the failed revolutions of 1848, the idealism of the liberals, social reformers, and nationalists gave way to an unsentimental vision of politics backed by the use of force. This perspective came to be known as *realpolitik*, a German term that means "practical politics," a tactful way of saying "power politics."

European Affairs in the Grip of Realpolitik

From 1850 to 1871, realpolitik guided the European states as conservative regimes turned to strong and efficient armies, short, fierce wars, and ambiguously written agreements to resolve the problems that surfaced in the 1848 revolts. Otto von Bismarck (1815–1898), the prime minister of Prussia and future architect of German unification, mocked the failure of the liberals' parliamentary reforms and asserted that his country's fate would be settled not with speeches but with "blood and iron." Nationalists in Austrian-occupied Italy learned that Italian unity could be achieved only by military force and clever diplomacy. The Russian czars, seldom supporters of any type of reform, became even more committed to the belief that if any change did come, it would begin at the top, not the bottom, of society.

LIMITED REFORM IN FRANCE AND GREAT BRITAIN   An astute observer of the 1848 revolutions was Louis-Napoleon Bonaparte, nephew of the former French emperor. He became Emperor Napoleon III (r. 1852–1870) of the Second French Empire by appealing to both the bourgeoisie and the working class. A benign despot, he ruled over a sham representative government supported by a growing middle class made prosperous by an expanding industrial base. He also provided the poor with social services; with an economic plan and subsidies, he enabled most urban workers and farmers to maintain a high standard of living.

Table 18.1   MAJOR POLITICAL EVENTS OF 1815–1871

EVENT AND DATE	OUTCOME
Congress of Vienna, 1815	Inaugurates an era of repression
July Revolution in France, 1830	Ends the Bourbon dynasty and installs the bourgeois monarchy
First English reform bill, 1832	Extends voting rights to wealthy middle-class males
Revolution in France, 1848	Ends the bourgeois monarchy and installs the Second Republic, with Louis-Napoleon as president
Revolutions in Europe, 1848–1851	Their failure leads to an era dominated by realpolitik
Creation of Second French Empire, 1851	Louis-Napoleon becomes Napoleon III and leads empire until 1870
Kingdom of Italy, 1860	Sicily joins Piedmont
Creation of German Empire, 1862–1871	Engineered by Bismarck using a policy of "blood and iron"; unites German states around Prussia
American Civil War, 1861–1865	Preserves national union and abolishes slavery
Second English reform bill, 1867	Extends voting rights to working-class males
Franco-Prussian War, 1871	Destroys the Second French Empire, proclaims the German Empire, and leaves a legacy of French bitterness toward Germany

Figure 18.2 CHARLES BARRY AND A. W. N. PUGIN. The Houses of Parliament. 1836–1860. Big Ben (right) 320' high; Victoria Tower (left) 336' high; riverfront width 800'. London. *In contrast to the revolutionary tradition on the Continent, Great Britain struggled to respond to changing political and social realities through debate and reform. To many observers in England and abroad, Parliament symbolized the success of liberalism and the representative legislative system. The Gothic spires of the Houses of Parliament rose in the mid–nineteenth century after the old buildings burned. Along with the neighboring clock tower known as Big Ben (a name applied originally only to the bell), they still stand today as the most recognizable image of modern London.*

In Great Britain, a liberal coalition of landed and business interests pushed a reform bill through Parliament in 1832 over the protests of the conservatives. This new law redrew Britain's political map to reflect the population shift resulting from industrialization. It also enfranchised thousands of new male voters by lowering the property qualifications for voting, although millions of citizens still could not vote. In 1867 a second reform bill extended voting rights to working-class males. Under Queen Victoria (r. 1837–1901), with political forces balanced evenly between liberals and conservatives, Great Britain reached its apex of economic power and prestige (Figure 18.2).

WARS AND UNIFICATION IN CENTRAL EUROPE Among the German-speaking states, the small principalities tended to discard liberalism and embrace militant nationalism. Their concerns were overshadowed, however, by the power struggle between Prussia and Austria for control of central Europe. William I became king of Prussia in 1861, and Bismarck was appointed his prime minister. Over the next few years, Bismarck built the Prussian army into a fierce fighting machine, at the same time ignoring liberal protests and the Prussian assembly and its laws. Nationalism replaced liberalism as the rallying cry of the Prussians, and Bismarck used this shift to unite the Germans around the Prussian state at the expense of France and Austria (see Map 18.1).

Bismarck achieved his goal by neutralizing potential enemies through deft diplomacy and, failing that, through force. By 1866 he had united the German states

into the North German Confederation, a union that excluded Austria. In 1870 he engineered a diplomatic crisis that forced France to declare war on Prussia. Costly French defeats brought the Franco-Prussian War to an abrupt end later that year, toppled the Second Empire of Napoleon III, and resulted in France's humiliation in the treaty signed at Versailles in 1871, proclaiming the German Empire. The seeds of World War I were sown by this crucial turn of events (Map 18.2).

On the Italian peninsula, most of which was ruled by Austrian princes, liberalism and nationalism were also causes of disruption. In the 1830s, Italian liberals inspired by the revolutionary writings of Giuseppe Mazzini [maht-SEE-nee] (1805–1872) banded together to form Young Italy, a nationalist movement, and the independent Italian state of Piedmont-Sardinia emerged as the hope of liberals. Piedmont was a constitutional monarchy that honored its subjects' civil and political rights. Its economy was well balanced between farming and trade, and under Prime Minister Count Camillo Benso di Cavour [kuh-VOOR] (1810–1861), the standard of living was raised for many Piedmontese, especially middle-class merchants and manufacturers.

Between 1859 and 1871, Piedmont expelled most of the Austrians. As part of his grand strategy to unite Italy, Cavour, with the encouragement of Napoleon III of France, annexed parts of central and southern Italy. Further assistance came from the fiercely patriotic soldier Giuseppe Garibaldi [gahr-uh-BAHL-dee] (1807–1882), who, with his personal army of a thousand "Red Shirts," invaded and liberated the Kingdom of the

Map 18.2   EUROPE IN 1871
This map shows the political divisions of Europe in the third quarter of the nineteenth century. 1. *Compare* this map with Map 18.1, Europe After the Congress of Vienna. 2. *Notice* the sacrifice of the small states in the German Confederation and on the Italian peninsula to the unified countries of Germany and Italy. 3. *Observe* the changes in the European holdings of the Ottoman Empire. 4. *Consider* how the unification of Germany threatened the dominance of France in Europe. 5. *Which* states divided Poland among themselves?

Two Sicilies (see Map 18.1) from its Spanish Bourbon ruler. In 1860 Sicilians voted overwhelmingly to join Piedmont in a Kingdom of Italy, and soon thereafter the Italian mosaic fell into place. In 1866 Austria gave up Venetia, and in 1870 Rome fell to nationalist troops and became Italy's capital.

Civil War in the United States

Paralleling the turbulent unification of the states of Italy and Germany, the United States was also undergoing expansion and centralization, processes that carried within themselves the seeds of conflict. The economy was mixed and regionally divided. On one side stood

the Northeast, the national leader in commerce, trade, and banking and the site of a growing factory system; on the other side was the South, dominated by huge cotton plantations cultivated by thousands of black slaves. The unsettled western lands formed a third region.

After 1830 the economic issues that divided the northern and southern states became intensified over the question of slavery (Figure 18.3). As settlers moved west, the debate over the spread of slavery into these new territories and states aggravated sectional interests. In 1861 the southern states seceded from the Union, provoking a civil war.

Unlike Europe's contemporaneous wars, which were short and resulted in relatively few deaths, the American Civil War lasted four years and resulted in

Figure 18.3 JOSEPH MALLORD WILLIAM TURNER. *The Slave Ship (Slavers Throwing Overboard the Dead and Dying, Typhoon Coming On). Ca. 1840. Oil on canvas, 35¾ × 48¼".* Courtesy, Museum of Fine Arts, Boston. Henry Lillie Pierce Fund. *Turner was motivated, in part, to paint* The Slave Ship *because of the famous* Zong *trial of 1783. The captain of the* Zong, *a British slave ship, in a ploy to collect insurance on his "property," claimed that because the ship was running out of water, he ordered the crew to throw the sick slaves overboard. At the trial, testimony proved that there was no water shortage on the ship. However, the court saw the incident as a civil insurance issue, not a criminal case, and the insurance company eventually had to pay for the loss of property—that is, the value of the slaves who had died. By the time he painted* The Slave Ship *(ca. 1840), Parliament had, in the 1830s, abolished slavery in the British colonies. Turner's terrifying image of natural calamity and human cruelty reflected the humanitarian values that had surfaced during the parliamentary and national debates about slavery. The ghoulish scene, painted in Turner's unique romantic style, depicts the castaway bodies of the dead and dying, encircled by hungry fish, as they sink into the stormy sea.*

huge losses on both sides (Figure 18.4). The Northern victory in 1865, engineered by President Abraham Lincoln (in office 1861–1865), saved the Union and guaranteed freedom for the slaves. But animosity between the North and the South continued to smolder during the war's aftermath, called Reconstruction (1865–1876), and relations remained strained, particularly over racial matters, for more than a century.

Industrialism, Technology, and Warfare

Underlying the political upheavals of this period were rapid changes in industrialism, technology, and warfare. The three became more closely intertwined as they spread across Europe and the Atlantic Ocean, affecting the daily lives of people at every social level.

INDUSTRIALISM: THE SHRINKING GLOBE   After its beginnings in England in the 1700s (see Chapter 17), industrialism started to take root in France in the 1830s, and a short time later Belgium entered the industrial age. For the next forty years, Belgium and France were the chief economic powers on the Continent, with factory and railway systems radiating from Paris and Brussels to Vienna and Milan by 1871. The expansion of rail lines meant that factories no longer needed to be near coal mines or clustered in urban areas. Inventions in communications, such as the telegraph, made it easier for industrialists to take advantage of distant resources and markets, and in 1866 engineers laid a transatlantic telegraph cable, linking Europe and America. Further shrinking of the globe occurred with the founding of national postal systems. The United Kingdom led the way (1839), creating the world's first postal service

Figure 18.4 ÉDOUARD MANET. *The Battle of the U.S.S.* Kearsarge *and the C.S.S.* Alabama. 1864. Oil on canvas, 54¼ × 50¾". Philadelphia Museum of Art. John G. Johnson Collection, 1917. *The American Civil War was also fought on the high seas. The C.S.S.* Alabama *was built in England in 1862 and, for twenty-two months, this commercial raider attacked Union merchant ships until the U.S.S.* Kearsarge *sank it off the French coast in 1864. Many bystanders on shore witnessed the battle, and reports quickly reached Paris, where Manet, after reading about the event, painted his imagined version of the conflict. He not only caught the drama of naval warfare but also documented its technological changes—the combining of steam with sail. His painting started a trend among French artists to travel to the coast and paint seascapes. In the 1870s, the impressionists (see Chapter 19) painted many marine scenes, which helped establish their reputation.*

with a uniform postage rate. Switzerland and Brazil soon followed with their own systems (1843). By 1878, a crazy quilt of competing national postal rates led to the formation of the Universal Postal Union (UPU); within ten years, the UPU numbered fifty-five independent countries.

NEW TECHNOLOGIES   Rapid technological advances confirmed the revolutionary nature of the industrial age.

The steam engine, invented in 1769, was used in the following transportation and manufacturing:

- Steamboats, with paddle wheels (1807); their heyday was 1816–1870, on the Ohio and Mississippi rivers
- Steam locomotives (1830); the Age of the Railroad was 1830–1945
- Water turbines (1820s) were used first in sawmills and textile mills and, after 1882, also in hydroelectric plants

Gas lighting, with coal gas, came into use in the early 1800s in Great Britain. It was used for lighting both streets and homes. By 1870, most European towns and cities were outfitted with gas lights. Oil, a new

power source discovered in Pennsylvania in 1859, was mainly a source of kerosene for lamps; gasoline was considered a waste by-product during this period.

New military technology included steam-powered boats and railway engines, to haul troops, horses, and supplies; and the "needle gun," a breech-loading rifle that fired a cartridge, instead of a muzzle-loading musket that shot a ball. The industrial-military complex, with weapons from arms manufacturers and orders from government procurement officials, continued to evolve. By 1870 Germany, now unified around Prussia, was setting the pace in strategy and weaponry in Continental Europe.

THE SPREAD OF INDUSTRIALISM   In 1830 Great Britain passed into another phase of the Industrial Revolution. While continuing to build ships and construct factories, its industrialists laid a network of rail lines linking all its major cities by 1850 (Figure 18.5). In Britain and on the Continent, the mining of new coal and iron deposits and the rise of imports in materials for textiles and other goods kept the machines of industry humming. British financiers, joined by Continental bankers, made

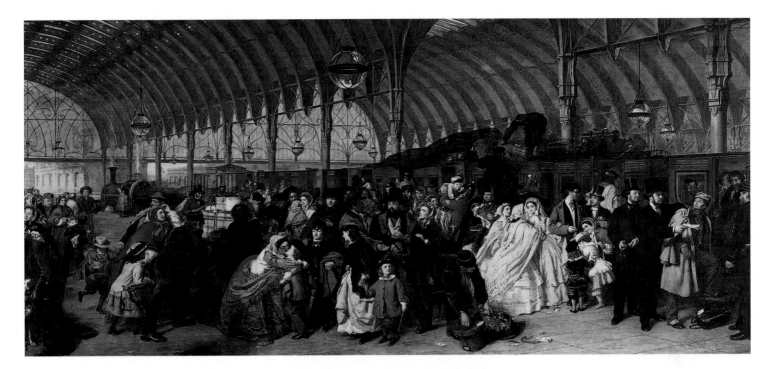

Figure 18.5 W. P. FRITH. *The Railway Station.* Ca. 1862. Oil on canvas, 3'10" × 8'5". Royal Holloway College and Bedford New College, Surrey, England. *London was the hub of England's economy long before the Industrial Revolution, and with the coming of the railroads its position was enhanced. The massive new railway stations, often constructed of glass and iron, symbolized the changing business and leisure habits of life. In this painting of one of London's new rail stations, Frith's well-dressed middle-class citizens convey the excitement of travel as well as its novelty and uncertainty.*

loans to fledgling companies for new factories, warehouses, ships, and railways, thereby generating more wealth for capitalists with surplus funds to invest.

SYMBOLS OF THE BOURGEOIS AGE: THE CRYSTAL PALACE AND THE SUEZ CANAL   As Europe's economy grew, two marvels of the industrial age—the Crystal Palace in London and the Suez Canal in Egypt—captured the world's imagination. The iron and glass Crystal Palace housed the Great Exhibition of 1851—in effect, the first world's fair (see Slice of Life, p. 540). There, the newest inventions and machine-made goods were displayed for everyone to see, rich and poor alike. Although many nations displayed products and inventions, Great Britain's exhibits were the most impressive, thereby proving that it was the world's leading industrial and agricultural power (Figure 18.6).

The second marvel, the Suez Canal, linked the Gulf of Suez and the Red Sea with the Mediterranean Sea. Funded by a French company and opened in 1869, the canal shortened the distance between Europe and India, thus enabling steamships to ferry passengers and goods around the globe more quickly and comfortably (Figure 18.7).

The Crystal Palace, the Suez Canal, and other wonders of the age were made possible by the labor of millions of workers—men, women, and children. On the Continent, the working and living conditions of this group were no better than the squalid circumstances found in Great Britain in the first stage of the Industrial Revolution. The social costs of industrialism, notably the rapid growth of cities that threw poor and ill-trained people into slums and ghettos, were part of its negative side. The slums became breeding grounds for class hatred and offered ready audiences for revolutionaries and socialists advocating revolt and social changes. The rebellions that flashed across the Continent in 1848 were caused partly by the mounting frustrations in these working-class areas.

Even a large segment of the middle class remained cut off from economic and political power. In the United States, all white males were granted suffrage in the 1820s, and in England voting rights were granted to working-class males in the Reform Act of 1867. The revolutions of 1830 and 1848 widened the franchise for French, Italian, German, and Austrian men, although important government posts were always reserved for aristocrats. Women still could not vote anywhere in

Figure 18.6 JOSEPH PAXTON. Crystal Palace, Hyde Park, London. 1851. Cast iron, wrought iron, and glass. Color lithograph with watercolor, by Joseph Nash. Approx. 21½ × 29⅝". Guildhall Library, London. *This illustration shows the splendor of the Great Exhibition, which so impressed visitors. When the fair closed, the Crystal Palace was disassembled and rebuilt in south London, where it stood as an arts and entertainment center until destroyed by fire in 1936. The "prefab" construction principles of the Crystal Palace foreshadowed modern building methods.*

Figure 18.7 A French Frigate in the Suez Canal. 1869. © The Hulton Picture Company, London. *Just as Great Britain showed the world what it could achieve through industry and agriculture, so France demonstrated its technological and engineering genius in digging the Suez Canal. The Suez Canal Company, headed by the French entrepreneur Ferdinand de Lesseps [duh lay-SEPS] (1805–1894), began its work in 1859 and completed the canal ten years later. The French vessel pictured here was one of the first to navigate this waterway linking the Mediterranean with the Orient.*

1871, nor could wage earners (except for British and American workers) and members of the lower middle class. Universal suffrage was not yet a reality.

NINETEENTH-CENTURY THOUGHT: PHILOSOPHY, RELIGION, AND SCIENCE

The period 1830 to 1870 was rich in intellectual discourse. Liberalism, based on the ideas of Locke, Montesquieu, Rousseau, and Voltaire, and tested and proven in the American and French Revolutions, was now redefined. Socialism, born in reaction to industrialism and liberal economic theory, emerged as a galvanizing force for change among the working classes. Popular religion, in protest against the embryonic secular state, gave rise to evangelicalism, a conservative movement dedicated to biblical authority. And breakthroughs in science and thought challenged traditional ways of understanding the world and history.

Liberalism Redefined

At the heart of the debate over liberalism was the question "Which is primary, the individual or the group?" Liberalism glorified free expression for each human being, and capitalists used liberal arguments to justify their economic policies. But the corollaries of these policies seemed to be poverty, degradation, and injustice for workers, and new voices began to be raised in support of approaches that promised antidotes to the injustices of industrial capitalism. Primary among these were a variety of socialisms, forms of political and social organization in which material goods are owned and distributed by the community or the government.

In the late 1700s, English philosopher and social theorist Jeremy Bentham (1748–1832) had developed a variant of liberalism known as **utilitarianism.** Bentham made "utility" his supreme moral principle, meaning that what gave pleasure to both the individual and society was right and what gave pain was wrong. Utility for society was always identified with "the greatest happiness for the greatest number"—a view that reflected Bentham's commitment to democracy. Accepting liberalism's laissez-faire ideal, yet tempering it with the principle of utility, Bentham pushed for a renovation of the repressive and outmoded governments of his time, including reform of the legal system, prisons, and education.

After 1830 Bentham's ideas were reinterpreted by bourgeois liberalism's strongest defender, the English philosopher John Stuart Mill (1806–1873). Growing to maturity in the second phase of the industrial age, Mill became increasingly fearful that the masses and a powerful state would ultimately destroy individual rights and human dignity. In his essay *On Liberty* (1859), Mill argued that the continued existence of the "civilized community" required the fullest freedom of speech, discussion, and behavior that was possible among all citizens, as long as no person was physically harmed. Mill's essay represents the high point of English liberalism.

After having advocated laissez-faire economics in his 1848 edition of the *Principles of Political Economy,* in later editions Mill embraced a mild form of socialism. Condemning unbridled economic competition, he reasoned that though production was subject to economic laws, distribution was not, and thus humans should divide the benefits of industrialism along rational lines. Mill also campaigned for religious toleration and minority rights and became a staunch supporter of women's right to vote and own property. In many of his writings, Mill collaborated with Harriet Taylor, his wife.

Socialism

Liberalism provided support for bourgeois values, but **socialism** seemed to many European workers and intellectuals to be the irresistible wave of the future. Socialism began as a reaction to industrialism and came to be its most severe critic, holding out a vision of what society might become if only certain fundamental reforms were made. Two main groups spoke for socialism in the 1800s: the utopian socialists and the Marxists. The utopians, who had their greatest impact before 1848, believed that the ills of industrial society could be overcome through cooperation between workers and capitalists. In contrast, the Marxists, who flourished after 1848, held the utopians in contempt as naive idealists and called for revolutions, violence, and the inevitable triumph of scientific socialism—a term coined by Marxists that reflects their faith in the inexorable laws of their theory of history.

The principal utopian socialists—Robert Owen (1771–1858) (himself a wealthy industrialist), Comte de Saint-Simon [san-see-MOH(N)] (1760–1825), and Charles Fourier [FOOR-ee-ay] (1772–1837)—shared the belief that a more just society could be introduced using the discoveries about society made in communal associations that served as laboratories for their philosophical ideas. All three thinkers were concerned more about the consumption of the fruits of industrialism than about the creation of goods. To them, the workers were simply not receiving a fair share for their efforts and were being victimized by a ruthless, competitive

ENCOUNTER

The Tragedy of the Cherokee Nation

Cultural encounters are unpredictable, with neither side able to foresee the long-range outcome of their meetings. Such was the case when the Cherokees, a tribe of Native Americans, decided to organize themselves and their lands, preparatory to petitioning to become a state in the United States. While they were amazingly successful in adopting American values and traditions, they failed in their ultimate goal.

When the first European settlers were establishing colonies on the Atlantic coast, the Cherokees lived farther inland, in farming villages surrounded by hunting and fishing lands, in western Virginia and the Carolinas, eastern Kentucky and Tennessee, and northern Alabama and Georgia. Their villages, composed of five hundred to two thousand people each and ruled by chiefs and priests, were fairly independent, though linked in loose regional federations. Although they had contact with the settlers, the Cherokees kept to the traditions of their ancestors.

However, as whites moved west after 1700, their impact on Cherokee landholdings was devastating. During the Revolutionary War, when the Cherokees sided with the British, American forces broke their power and forced them to surrender much of their land. Additional land was lost in the Georgia colony when the Cherokees were forced to give up two million acres to pay off debts to white traders. By 1800 they were confined to parts of northern Georgia, the western Carolinas, and eastern Tennessee. The

Cherokee population, however, remained the same—about twenty-two thousand people—as it had been in 1650.

Recognizing their inability to stem the tide of white settlement, Cherokee leaders devised a strategy for survival: they would forsake the old ways and Westernize their culture. Cherokee leaders and their people adopted white techniques of farming and home construction and began to acquire property. They fought alongside Americans in wars against other Native Americans and the British. Most important, Sequoyah (b. between 1760 and 1770, d. 1843), a Cherokee, invented a writing system, called a syllabary, for his native tongue (Encounter figure 18.1). The syllabary quickly enabled many Cherokees to read and write. In 1827 tribal leaders established the Cherokee Nation (northern Georgia), with separate legislative, executive, and judicial branches, a bill of rights, and a written constitution—based on the U.S. model. A bilingual newspaper, *The Cherokee Phoenix*, began publishing in 1828.

Despite their efforts to Westernize, the Cherokees soon learned that this was not enough. In 1830 the Cherokees, along with other tribes, were ordered to move to the Oklahoma Indian Territory. The Cherokee Nation sued to protect their lands, and the U.S. Supreme Court sided with them, but President Andrew Jackson (in office 1828–1836) refused to enforce the Court's decision. Jackson's refusal is bitterly ironic, for

---

system. To solve these problems, the utopian socialists proposed a number of alternatives, but their often impracticable schemes had little chance of succeeding in an age that was becoming more scientific and realistic.

The utopian socialists and their supporters quickly faded from view once Karl Marx (1818–1883) appeared on the scene. As a student at the University of Berlin, Marx studied Hegel's dialectical explanation of historical change, but as an atheist he rejected Hegel's emphasis on Spirit. Since his radical politics made a teaching post untenable in reactionary Prussia, Marx became editor of a Cologne newspaper. When the police shut down the paper, he sought refuge abroad. From Brussels, he and Friedrich Engels (1820–1895), his lifelong friend and coauthor, were asked to develop a set of principles for a German workers' society. The resulting pamphlet, *The Communist Manifesto* (1848), became the bible of socialism. Both men played minor roles in the 1848 revolts, seeing in them the first

steps of a proletarian revolution. Marx spent his last years in London, writing his major work, *Capital* (volume 1, 1867; volumes 2 and 3, completed by Engels, 1885–1894), and founding an international workers' association to implement his ideas.

Marx's approach to historical change differed radically from the utopian view. According to Marx, history moved in a dialectical pattern as the Hegelians had argued, but not in rhythm with abstract ideas, or the World Spirit. Instead, Marx thought that material reality conditioned historical development; the various stages of history, which were propelled by class conflicts, unfolded as one economic group replaced another. For example, the bourgeoisie, which had emerged out of the collapse of the feudal system, represented only a moment in history, destined dialectically to bring forth its own gravedigger, the proletariat, or the urban working class. Moreover, the institutions and ideas of a society constituted a superstructure

Encounter figure 18.1 HENRY INMAN, after Charles Bird King. *Sequoyah.* Ca. 1830. Oil on canvas, 35¼ × 30½″. National Portrait Gallery, Smithsonian Institution. NPG.79.174. *This portrait depicts Sequoyah dressed in white man's clothing, except for the exotic turban. Smoking a clay pipe, he wears a peace medal and holds a tablet displaying the Cherokee alphabet he invented—symbolic of his attempts to accommodate his people to mainstream society. Henry Inman's (1801–1846) portrait is a copy of one painted by Charles Bird King (1785–1862) in 1828 for the Commissioner of Indian Affairs in Washington, D.C., in an effort to create a record of prominent Native Americans. A legendary figure in American history, Sequoyah lives today through the name of the genus of California's giant redwood trees.*

he said his goal was "to reclaim [Native Americans] from their wandering habits and make them a happy, prosperous people"—the same goal sought by the Cherokees. In 1838–1839, American soldiers evicted the Cherokees from their homes and lands, and more than four thousand died on the 116-day journey to Oklahoma, a trek that became known as the Trail of Tears. In Oklahoma, the Cherokee joined with other southeastern tribes—the Creek, the Chickasaw, the Choctaw, and the Seminole—all of whom had been forcibly relocated earlier.

LEARNING FROM THE ENCOUNTER

1. *Compare and contrast* Cherokee life before and after the American Revolution. 2. *Identify* the steps taken by the Cherokees to emulate white settlers. 3. *Explain* the role of Sequoyah. 4. *What* happened to the Cherokee Nation? 5. *Why* did the Cherokees' plan fail? 6. Can you *relate* the ordeal of assimilation experienced by the Cherokees to the experiences of today's immigrants?

erected on the foundation of economic reality; governments, law, the arts, and the humanities merely reflected the values of a particular ruling class.

Marx then forecast a revolt by the proletariat, who would install a classless society. He believed that the workers' revolution would be international in scope and that communist intellectuals would assist in bringing an end to bourgeois rule. Elaborating on his political, economic, and social theories, Marx's followers created Marxism and, inspired by his ideal society, organized to abolish the capitalist system, although their impact before 1871 was minimal.

From the first, socialism appealed especially to women, because it condemned existing social relations and called for universal emancipation. The ideal classless society would be free of every inequality, including sexual inequality. Utopian socialists were the most welcoming to supporters of female rights. For example, Fourier claimed that female freedom was the touchstone for measuring human liberation everywhere; Owen espoused a new moral order in which sexual and class differences would be overcome in cooperative, loving communities; and Saint-Simon preached the moral superiority of women, though he preferred sexual complementarity to sexual equality.

Marx and Engels's views on women were ambiguous. They urged the full integration of women into the workforce as a condition of female emancipation but insisted that freedom for male workers was key to radical social change. So, they encouraged women to curb their aspirations in the name of the greater good—that is, for an ideal Marxian workers' society.

Religion and the Challenge of Science

The rise of **evangelicalism** was the major religious development of the Age of the Bourgeoisie. Evangelicalism, a distinctively Protestant movement, grew out of the Methodist tradition, with its focus on personal salvation (belief that one must be "born again") and sanctification (ability of the Holy Spirit to redeem sinners and create new lives) (see Chapter 16). In the United States, all mainline Protestant sects except the Lutherans and the Episcopalians became evangelicals, while, in England, the Methodists formed the movement's core, along with a strong wing of Anglicans. The evangelicals wanted to transform society, one person at a time, and their methods included revivalism and the **holiness** movement—which stressed sanctification, or a holy life, after being born again. They also were involved in the founding of nonsectarian self-help and personal uplift organizations, all in Great Britain: the Young Men's Christian Association (1844), the Young Women's Christian Association (1855), and the Salvation Army (1865).

The evangelicals were deemed conservative, because of their insistence on the paramount authority of the Holy Scriptures—a position that set them apart from liberal Protestants, who adopted many Deist ideas, and from traditional Protestants, such as Episcopalians and Lutherans, who stressed ritual and the sacraments. Grounded in their biblical faith, the evangelicals tried to hold the line against new developments in thought and science that contradicted their beliefs and values.

While the evangelicals worked to hold back the secular tide that was washing over the West, the Roman Catholic Church committed to a war against modernity itself. The once liberal Pius IX (pope 1846–1878), made captive briefly during the 1848 uprising in Rome, became one of the most reactionary popes in history. In 1864 he issued an encyclical, the *Syllabus of Errors*, in which he denounced, as contrary to the faith, about eighty modern ideas, including public schooling, liberalism, democracy, socialism, religious toleration, and civil marriage. Then, in 1870, he proclaimed the doctrine of papal infallibility, by which the pope cannot err when he speaks *ex cathedra* (Latin, "from the chair")—that is, when speaking officially as pope. This decree, which was made retroactive, led to a schism with some disaffected Catholics in the Netherlands, Germany, and Switzerland, but it slowly faded from prominence. Until 1963 the Catholic Church seemed self-isolated and opposed to all progressive ideas.

Meanwhile, in a development that alarmed some Christians, some German Protestant scholars began to study the Bible not as a divinely inspired book incapable of error but simply as a set of human writings susceptible to varied interpretations—a movement called **higher criticism.** These scholars began to try to identify the author or authors of each of the biblical books rather than relying on old accounts of their origins, to study each text to determine its sources rather than treating each book as a divine revelation, and, most important, to assess the accuracy of each account rather than accepting it as God's final word. By 1871 orthodox Christians across the West were engaged in intellectual battles with the higher critics, some of whom portrayed Jesus not as God's son but as a mythological figure or a human teacher.

While the higher critics chipped away at Christianity from within, science assaulted it from outside. Geologists first discredited the biblical story of creation, and then biologists questioned the divine origin of human beings. The challenge from geology was led by the Englishman Charles Lyell [LIE-uhl] (1797–1875), whose fossil research showed that the earth was much older than Christians claimed. By treating each of God's six days of creation as symbolic of thousands of years of divine activity, Protestant Christians were able to weather this particular intellectual storm. Not so easily overcome, however, was biology's threat to biblical authority.

Following the Bible, the church was clear in its explanation of humanity's origin: Adam and Eve were the first parents, having been created by God after he had fashioned the rest of the animate world. Paralleling this divine account was a secular argument for evolution. Based on Greek thought, but without solid proofs, it remained a theory and nothing more for centuries. In 1859, however, the theory of **evolution** gained dramatic support when the Englishman Charles Darwin (1809–1882) published *On the Origin of Species*. Marshaling data to prove that evolution was a principle of biological development rather than a mere hypothesis, Darwin showed that over the course of millennia modern plants and animals had evolved from simpler forms through a process of natural selection.

In 1871, in *Descent of Man*, Darwin applied his findings to human beings, portraying them as the outcome of millions of years of evolution. Outraged clergy attacked Darwin for his atheism, and equally zealous Darwinians heaped ridicule on those who adhered to the biblical story of creation for their credulity. Today, the theory of evolution is one of the cornerstones of biological science, despite some continuing criticism.

Other advances in science were helping to lay the groundwork for the modern world. In the 1850s, French scientist Louis Pasteur [pass-TUHR] (1822–1895) proposed the germ theory of disease, the notion that many diseases are caused by microorganisms. This seminal idea led him to important discoveries and proposals for change. Claiming that germs are responsible for the spread of disease, he campaigned for improved sanitation and sterilization and thus paved the way for antiseptic surgery. He demonstrated that food spoilage could be prevented by killing microorganisms through heating, a discovery that resulted in the "pasteurization" of milk. His studies of rabies and anthrax led him to the first use of vaccines against these diseases, thus laying the groundwork for the scientific study, immunology. As the founder of the science of bacteriology and an important figure in the development of modern medicine, Pasteur is the embodiment of Francis Bacon's seventeenth-century assertion that "knowledge is power."

In chemistry, a fruitful way of thinking about atoms was finally formulated, moving beyond the simplistic notions that had been in vogue since fifth-century BCE Greece. In about 1808 the Englishman John Dalton (1766–1844) invented an effective atomic theory, and in 1869 the Russian Dmitri Mendeleev [men-duh-LAY-uhf] (1834–1907) worked out a periodic table of elements, based on atomic weights, a system that, with modifications, is still in use. By 1871 other chemists had moved from regarding molecules as clusters of atoms to conceiving of them as structured into stable patterns. Nevertheless, without means and equipment for studying the actual atoms, atomism remained merely a useful theory until the twentieth century.

Advances in chemistry also led to changes in anesthetics and surgery. In the 1840s, chemists introduced nitrous oxide, chloroform, and other compounds that could block pain in human beings. Use of these new painkillers in obstetrics increased after Queen Victoria was given chloroform to assist her in childbirth in 1853. These desensitizers revolutionized the treatment of many diseases and wounds and made modern surgery possible.

CULTURAL TRENDS: FROM ROMANTICISM TO REALISM

In its triumph, the middle class embraced both neoclassical and romantic styles in the arts. In neoclassicism, the bourgeoisie found unchanging aesthetic rules that echoed their belief that the seemingly chaotic marketplace was actually regulated by economic laws. In romanticism, they found escape from the sordid and ugly side of industrialism.

But both styles slowly grew mundane and pretentious under the patronage of the middle class, partly because of the inevitable loss of creative energy that sets in when any style becomes established and partly because of the conversion of the cultural arena into a marketplace. Because they lacked the deep learning that had guided aristocratic patrons in the past, the new bourgeois audiences demanded art and literature that mirrored their less refined values. Catering to this need, artists and writers produced works that were spectacular, sentimental, and moralistic. Simply put, successful art did not offend respectable public taste.

Adding to this bourgeois influence was the growing ability of state institutions to control what was expressed in art and literature. The most powerful of these was France's Royal Academy of Painting and Sculpture, founded in 1648 for the purpose of honoring the nation's best painters. After 1830 its leaders became obsessed with rigid rules, thus creating what was called "official art." Those artists who could not obtain the academy's approval for exhibiting their works in the annual government-sponsored Paris Salons, or art shows, were virtually condemned to poverty unless they had other means of financial support. Rejected artists soon identified the Royal Academy as a defender of the status quo and an enemy of innovation. No other Western state had a national academy with as much power as France's Royal Academy, although in other European countries similar bodies tried to regulate both art and literature.

In reaction to the empty, overblown qualities of official art, a new style began to appear in the 1840s. Known as **realism,** this style focused on the everyday lives of the middle and lower classes (Interpreting Art figure 18.1) The realists depicted ordinary people without idealizing or romanticizing them, although a moral point of view was always implied. Condemning neoclassicism as cold and romanticism as exaggerated, the realists sought to convey what they saw around them in a serious, accurate, and unsentimental way. Merchants, housewives, workers, peasants, and even prostitutes replaced kings, aristocrats, goddesses, saints, and heroes as the subjects of paintings and novels.

Many forces contributed to the rise of realism. In diplomacy, this was the era of Bismarck's realpolitik, the hard-nosed style that replaced cautious and civilized negotiation. In science, Darwin demystified earthly existence by rejecting the biblical view of creation and concluding that the various species, including human beings, evolved from simpler organisms. The spread of democracy encouraged the realists to take an interest in ordinary people, and the camera, invented in the 1830s, inspired the realists in their goal of truthful accuracy. All these influences combined to make realism a style intent on scientific objectivity in its depiction of the world as it is.

Literature

In literature, the romantic style continued to dominate poetry, essays, and novels until midcentury, when it began to be displaced by realism. Romantic writers focused on their characters' emotions and showed great faith in the power of an individual to transform his or her own life and the lives of others. Realist writers, in contrast, tended to be determinists who let the facts

SLICE OF LIFE
Observing Human Behavior: The Classes and the Masses

This Slice of Life tells the tale of the two Englands: the world of the well-to-do classes, who were visiting the 1851 Great Exhibition—as reported by Charlotte Brontë (1816–1855), the novelist; and the world of the masses, the lower and *working classes, who were observed on the grounds at the annual Derby Day Horse Races, in 1861—as described by Hippolyte Taine (1828–1893), the French philosopher, historian, and critic.*

CHARLOTTE BRONTË
The First World's Fair, 1851

Yesterday I went for the second time to the Crystal Palace. We remained in it about three hours, and I must say I was more struck with it on this occasion than at my first visit. It is a wonderful place—vast, strange, new, and impossible to describe. Its grandeur does not consist in *one* thing, but in the unique assemblage of *all* things. Whatever human industry has created you find there, from the great compartments filled with railway engines and boilers, with mill machinery in full work, with splendid carriages of all kinds, with harness of every description, to the glass-covered and velvet-spread stands loaded with the most gorgeous work of the goldsmith and silversmith, and the carefully guarded caskets full of real diamonds and pearls worth hundreds of thousands of pounds. It may be called a bazaar or a fair, but it is such a bazaar or fair as Eastern genii might have created. It seems as if only magic could have gathered this mass of wealth from all the ends of the earth—as if none but supernatural hands could have arranged it thus, with such a blaze and contrast of colours and marvellous power of effect. The multitude filling the great aisles seems ruled and subdued by some invisible influence. Amongst the thirty thousand souls that peopled it the day I was there not one loud noise was to be heard, not one irregular movement seen; the living tide rolls on quietly, with a deep hum like the sea heard from the distance.

HIPPOLYTE TAINE
A Day at the Races, 28 May 1861

Races at Epsom: it is the Derby Day, a day of jollification; Parliament does not sit; for three days all the talk has been about horses and their trainers. . . .

Epsom course is a large, green plain, slightly undulating; on one side are reared three public stands and several other smaller ones. In front, tents, hundreds of shops, temporary stables under canvas, and an incredible confusion of carriages, of horses, of horsemen, of private omnibuses; there are perhaps 200,000 human heads here. Nothing beautiful or even elegant; the carriages are ordinary vehicles, and toilettes are rare; one does not come here to exhibit them but to witness a spectacle: the spectacle is interesting only on account of its size. From the top of the Stand the enormous antheap swarms, and its din ascends. But beyond, on the right, a row of large trees, behind them the faint bluish undulations of the verdant country, make a magnificent frame to a mediocre picture. Some clouds

speak for themselves. They rejected the bourgeois world as flawed by hypocrisy and materialism and denounced the machine age for its mechanization of human relationships. Realism in literature flourished between 1848 and 1871, chiefly in France, England, Russia, and the United States, especially among African American writers who found their voices during the slavery controversy preceding the Civil War.

THE HEIGHT OF FRENCH ROMANTICISM   In France the leading exponent of romanticism was the poet, dramatist, and novelist Victor Hugo (1802–1885). His poetry established his fame, and the performance of his tragedy *Hernani* in February 1830 solidified his position as the leader of the romantic movement. Enlivened with scenes of rousing action and by characters with limitless ambition, this play seemed with one stroke to sweep away the artificialities of classicism. Its premiere created a huge scandal. When the bourgeois revolution erupted in July 1830, many French people believed that Hugo's *Hernani* had been prophetic of the political upheaval.

Hugo became something of a national institution, noted as much for his humane values as for his writing. Because of his opposition to the regime of Napoleon III, he was exiled from France for eighteen years, beginning in 1851. While in exile, he published his most celebrated novel, the epic-length *Les Misérables*

as white as swans float in the sky, and their shadow sweeps over the grass; a light mist, charged with sun-shine, flits in the distance, and the illuminated air, like a glory, envelops the plain, the heights, the vast area, and all the disorder of the human carnival.

It is a carnival, in fact; they have come to amuse themselves in a noisy fashion. Everywhere are gypsies, comic singers and dancers disguised as negroes, shoot-ing galleries where bows and arrows or guns are used, charlatans who by dint of eloquence palm off watch chains, games of skittles and sticks, musicians of all sorts, and the most astonishing row of cabs, barouches, droskies, four-in-hands, with pies, cold meats, melons, fruits, wines, especially champagne. They unpack; they proceed to drink and eat; that restores the creature and excites him; coarse joy and open laughter are the re-sult of a full stomach. In presence of this ready-made feast the aspect of the poor is pitiable to behold; they endeavour to sell you penny dolls, remembrances of the Derby; to induce you to play at Aunt Sally,[1] to black your boots. Nearly all of them resemble wretched, hun-gry, beaten, mangy dogs, waiting for a bone, without hope of finding much on it. They arrived on foot dur-ing the night, and count upon dining off crumbs from the great feast. Many are lying on the ground, among the feet of the passers-by, and sleep open-mouthed, face upwards. Their countenances have an expression of stupidity and of painful hardness. The majority of them have bare feet, all are terribly dirty, and most absurd-looking; the reason is that they wear gentle-men's old clothes, worn-out fashionable dresses, small bonnets, formerly worn by young ladies. The sight of these cast-off things, which have covered several bod-ies, becoming more shabby in passing from one to the other, always makes me uncomfortable. To wear these old clothes is degrading; in doing so the human being shows or avows that he is the off-scouring of society. Among us [the French] a peasant, a workman, a la-bourer, is a different man, not an inferior person; his blouse belongs to him, as my coat belongs to me—it has clothed no one but him. The employment of ragged clothes is more than a peculiarity; the poor resign themselves here to be the footstool of others.

One of these women, with an old shawl that ap-peared to have been dragged in the gutter, with bat-tered head-gear, which had been a bonnet, made limp by the rain, with a poor, dirty, pale baby in her arms, came and prowled round our omnibus, picked up a castaway bottle, and drained the dregs. Her second girl, who could walk, also picked up and munched a rind of melon. We gave them a shilling and cakes. The humble smile of thankfulness they returned, it is impossible to describe. They had the look of saying, like Sterne's[2] poor donkey, "Do not beat me, I beseech you—yet you may beat me if you wish." Their coun-tenances were burned, tanned by the sun; the mother had a scar on her right cheek, as if she had been struck by a boot; both of them, the child in particular, were grown wild and stunted. The great social mill crushes and grinds here, beneath its steel gearing, the lowest human stratum.

---

[1] A game played at fairs, featuring an effigy of an old woman smoking a pipe, at which fairgoers threw missiles to win prizes.
[2] Laurence Sterne (1713–1768), British novelist.

INTERPRETING THIS SLICE OF LIFE

1. *Compare and contrast* what Brontë and Taine say about the different groups they meet. *Why* are their descriptions so different? 2. *What* do their observa-tions reveal about life in mid-nineteenth-century England and about their own attitudes? 3. *How* would you describe public behavior in the United States, and *what* does that tell us about our society?

(The Wretched) (1862), which expresses his revulsion at the morally bankrupt society he believed France had become after Napoleon I. The hero and moral center of the book is the pauper Jean Valjean, imprisoned for seventeen years for stealing a loaf of bread. He escapes and becomes a prosperous, respectable merchant, but the law is unrelenting in its pursuit of him, and he is forced into a life of hiding and subterfuge. Hugo makes Valjean a symbol of the masses' will to freedom, and his bourgeois readers were fascinated and horrified at the same time by Valjean's ultimate triumph.

Another popular romantic literary figure was the French novelist and playwright George Sand (1804–1876), who was forced by need to become a writer. Amandine-Aurore-Lucie Dupin took the name George Sand in part to keep from embarrassing her own and her estranged husband's families and in part to assert herself in the male literary world; she was addressed by her friends as Madame George Sand. Sand has been called the first modern, liberated woman. She courted controversy as she engaged in highly public sexual liai-sons with leading men of the times, including roman-tic composer and pianist Frédéric Chopin [SHO-pan] (1810–1849). She often dressed as a typical bourgeois gentleman: coat and vest, cravat, trousers, steel-tipped boots, and top hat. Sand was the first Western woman to play an active part in a revolutionary government. In the Paris uprising of 1848, she sat on committees,

INTERPRETING ART

Composition Five vertical forms (the human figures and the columns) and two horizontal forms (the bar counter and the panel behind the bar) are the main design elements. Manet creates an optical illusion with the background mirror, which is filled with images of patrons' heads and lighting fixtures.

Color The colors create rich optical effects. Black—Manet's favorite hue—is dominant (the barmaid's dress; the man's attire). The somber mood is relieved by bits of gold, orange, red, blue, and green. The splashes of white (the lighting; the barmaid's upper torso) make this an eye-popping image.

Mood The barmaid—surrounded by pleasure-seekers—stands alone, withdrawn, perhaps bored, as she works her monotonous job. In her unseeing gaze and stiff posture, Manet has captured the anonymity of life in the industrial age.

Artist's Vision Manet brings the viewer directly into the scene by (1) presenting the barmaid in close-up, standing in a confrontational pose—a method adapted from the new art of photography; and (2) by cropping the scene, as shown by the male figure (right) and the chandeliers (above)—a method adapted from Japanese prints (see Encounter in Chapter 19).

Spectacle Manet captures the spectacle of the new entertainments: the ghastly white light, the crush of customers, the stoic barmaid, the male customer who may be making a proposition, the trapeze artist whose green feet are visible in the top left corner.

Perspective The mirror distorts the traditional use of perspective, leaving the viewer puzzled by the placement of figures and objects. The barmaid appears to be looking outward but is also standing before the top-hatted man in the mirror.

Interpreting Art figure 18.1 ÉDOUARD MANET. *A Bar at the Folies-Bergère.* 1882. Oil on canvas, 3'1½" × 4'3". Courtauld Institute Galleries, London (Courtauld Collection). *This painting's setting—the Folies-Bergère, dating from 1869—was a café-concert, or glorified beer hall, which offered drinks and raucous stage acts. From the 1850s these venues initially catered to the lower classes, but in time, Parisians from all social strata began to spend time here. The barmaid, who posed in Manet's studio, actually worked at the Folies-Bergère. Manet drew inspiration from Courbet and the realists for subject matter and painting methods. In turn, he influenced the impressionists and postimpressionists (see Chapter 19) with his focus on urban life, new ways to apply paint, and his aesthetic ideal of art for art's sake.*

---

delivered speeches and debated issues, and wrote in support of the short-lived radical socialist regime.

Because her father was descended from Polish royalty and her mother was the daughter of a Parisian bird-seller, Sand found herself in a socially equivocal position in class-conscious France. Thus, she was predisposed to focus her writings on people without power, such as women, artists, and laborers. Her novels and plays, with their strong political undertones, illustrate Victor Hugo's claim that romanticism was "liberalism in literature." For Sand, idealism simply meant another way to call for social reform.

Sand's first novel, *Indiana* (1832)—perhaps her best—features multifaceted characters and accurately depicts the constraints on married women in her day. The nineteen-year-old heroine, Indiana, who is unhappily married to an older man, seeks true love, apart from her spouse and in a relationship of equals. Unfortunately, because of her lover's treachery and society's

inflexible marital code, she is forced to flee to Bourbon Island (modern Réunion), then a French colony in the Indian Ocean. There she finds a soul mate with whom she settles down in a Rousseau-like paradise. Critics read the work as an attack on France's Napoleonic Code, which placed wives under their husband's control (see Chapter 17). *Indiana* made Sand's reputation, and she followed it with about eighty more novels and twenty plays.

ROMANTICISM IN THE ENGLISH NOVEL In England, romanticism found its most expressive voices in the novels of the Brontë sisters, Charlotte (1816–1855) and Emily (1818–1848). Reared in the Yorkshire countryside far from the cultural mainstream, they created two of the most beloved novels in the English language. Their circumscribed lives seemed to uphold the romantic dictum: true artistic genius springs from the imagination alone.

Emily Brontë's *Wuthering Heights* (1847) creates a romantic atmosphere through mysterious events, ghostly apparitions, and graveyard scenes, but it rises above the typical gothic romance. The work is suffused with a mystical radiance that invests the characters and the natural world with spiritual meanings beyond the visible. A tale of love and redemption, the story focuses on a mismatched couple, the genteel Catherine and the outcast Heathcliff, who are nevertheless soul mates. In the uncouth, passionate Heathcliff, Brontë creates a Byronic hero who lives outside conventional morality. Her portrayal of him as a man made vengeful by cruel circumstances has led some to label this the first socio-revolutionary novel.

Charlotte Brontë published *Jane Eyre* in the same year *Wuthering Heights* appeared. A dark and melancholy novel, the work tells the story of a governess's love for her brooding and mysterious employer. Her hopes for happiness are crushed by the discovery that the cause of his despair is his deranged wife, kept hidden in the attic. Narrated in the first person, the novel reveals the heroine's deep longings and passions as well as her ultimate willingness to sacrifice her feelings for moral values. Recognized at the time as a revolutionary work that dispensed with the conventions of sentimental novels, *Jane Eyre* was attacked by critics but welcomed by readers, who made it a best seller.

ROMANTICISM IN AMERICAN LITERATURE   Romanticism reached a milestone with the American literary and philosophical movement known as **transcendentalism.** Flourishing in New England in the early and middle part of the 1800s, this movement was critical of formal religions and drew inspiration from the belief that divinity is accessible without the necessity of mediation. Unlike the God of traditional religion, the divine spirit (transcendence) manifests itself in many forms, including the physical universe, all constructive practical activity, all great cultural achievements, and all types of spiritual expression. In their goal of seeking union with the world's underlying metaphysical order, the transcendentalists followed in the steps of the German idealists (see Chapter 17). Of the transcendentalists, Henry David Thoreau (1817–1862) was probably the most influential. His most celebrated book, *Walden* (1854), the lyrical journal of the months he spent living in the rough on Walden Pond, is virtually the bible of today's environmental movement. Thoreau's *On the Duty of Civil Disobedience* (1849), an essay on the necessity of disobeying an unjust law, was one of the texts that inspired Martin Luther King Jr.'s protests of the 1950s and 1960s against the United States' segregated social system.

American poetry now became a major presence in Western literature with the writings of Emily Dickinson (1830–1886) and Walt Whitman (1819–1892). Both poets drew on their personal lives, in the manner of other romantic poets. They also adopted offbeat verse forms and punctuation, which have greatly influenced twentieth-century poets. Today, Dickinson and Whitman are regarded as two of the most innovative poets of nineteenth-century American literature. Dickinson, a recluse, published only seven poems during her lifetime. Since her death, her reputation has increased dramatically, based on about 1,800 poems that make up the Dickinson canon. Whitman, vilified at first by the establishment, lived long enough to see himself become an American icon, the model of the good gray-haired poet. During his career, he effected a revolution in American poetry by creating a body of works based on his experience as an American, written in a specifically American language.

REALISM IN FRENCH AND ENGLISH NOVELS   Realism began in France in the 1830s with the novels of Honoré de Balzac [BAHL-zak] (1799–1850). Balzac foreshadowed the major traits of realism in the nearly one hundred novels that make up the series he called *The Human Comedy.* Set in France in the Napoleonic era and the early industrial age, this voluminous series deals with the lives of more than two thousand characters, in both Paris and the provinces. Balzac condemns the hollowness of middle-class society, pointing out how industrialism has caused many people to value material things more than friendship and family, although there are virtuous and sympathetic characters as well.

France's outstanding realist was Gustave Flaubert [floh-BAIR] (1821–1880), who advocated a novel free from conventional, accepted moral and philosophical views. His masterpiece is *Madame Bovary* (1857), which caused a scandal with its unvarnished tale of adultery. In contrast to Balzac's broad sweep, Flaubert focused on a single person, the unhappy and misguided Emma Bovary. In careful detail, he sets forth the inner turmoil of a frustrated middle-class woman trapped by her dull marriage and her social standing. By stressing objectivity and withholding judgment, Flaubert believed he was following the precepts of modern science. As a social critic, he portrays everyday life among the smug members of a small-town, bourgeois society. Notwithstanding the scandal it caused, *Madame Bovary* was an instant success and established the new style of realism. For most readers, Emma Bovary became a poignant symbol of people whose unrealistic dreams and aspirations doom them to failure.

English novelists also wrote in the new realist style. Like French realists, they railed against the vulgarity, selfishness, and hypocrisy of the middle class, but unlike the French, who were interested in creating unique characters, they spoke out for social justice. England's most popular writer of realist fiction was Charles Dickens (1812–1870), who favored stories dealing with the harsh realities of the industrial age. Writing to meet deadlines for serialized magazine stories, Dickens poured out a torrent of words over a long literary career that began when he was in his twenties.

In early works, such as *Oliver Twist* (1837–1839) and *David Copperfield* (1849–1850), Dickens was optimistic, holding out hope for his characters and, by implication, for society in general. But in later novels, such as *Bleak House* and *Hard Times,* both published between 1851 and 1854, he was pessimistic about social reform and the possibility of correcting the excesses of industrialism. Dickens's rich descriptions, convoluted plots with unexpected coincidences, and topical satire were much admired by Victorian readers, and his finely developed and very British characters, such as Mr. Pickwick, Oliver Twist, and Ebenezer Scrooge, have survived as a memorable gift to literature.

Realist fiction in England was also represented by important female writers. The two most successful were Elizabeth Gaskell (1810–1865) and Mary Ann Evans (1819–1880), better known by her pen name, George Eliot. Both wrote novels about the hardships imposed on the less fortunate by England's industrial economy. Gaskell's *North and South* (1855) underscores the widening gap between the rich, particularly in England's urban north, and the poor, concentrated in the rural south, within the context of the rise of the labor unions. Typically, her themes involve contrasts, contradictions, and conflicts, such as the helplessness of the individual in the face of impersonal forces and the simultaneous need to affirm the human spirit against the inequalities of the factory system. Similarly, in *Middlemarch* (1872) and other novels, George Eliot explores the ways human beings are trapped in social systems that shape and mold their lives, for good or ill. Less deterministic in outlook than Gaskell, Eliot stresses the possibility of individual fulfillment despite social constraints as well as the freedom to make moral choices.

THE RUSSIAN REALISTS Russia now for the first time produced writers whose realist works received international acclaim: Leo Tolstoy [TOHL-stoy] (1828–1910) and Fyodor Dostoyevsky [duhs-tuh-YEF-skee] (1821–1881). Like English and French realists, these Russians depicted the grim face of early industrialism and dealt with social problems, notably the plight of the newly liberated serfs. Their realism is tempered by a typically Russian concern: Should Russia embrace Western values or follow its own traditions, relying on its Slavic and Oriental past? Significantly, Tolstoy and Dostoyevsky transcend Western realism by stressing religious and spiritual themes.

In his early works, Tolstoy wrote objectively, without moralizing. The novel *Anna Karenina* (1875–1877) describes the unhappy consequences of adultery in a sophisticated but unforgiving society. *War and Peace* (1865–1869), his greatest work, is a monumental survey of Russia during the Napoleonic era, portraying a huge cast of characters caught up in the surging tides of history. Although Tolstoy focuses on the upper class in this Russian epic, he places them in realistic situations without romanticizing them. In these works, he was a determinist, convinced that human beings were at the mercy of forces beyond them. But in 1876, after having a religious conversion to a simple form of Christianity that stressed pacifism, plain living, and radical social reform, he repudiated all art that lacked a moral vision, including his own. Tolstoy devoted the rest of his life to this plain faith, following what he believed to be Jesus's teachings and working for a Christian anarchist society.

Fyodor Dostoyevsky was a powerful innovator who introduced literary devices that have become standard in Western letters. For example, *Crime and Punishment* (1866), written long before Sigmund Freud developed psychoanalysis, analyzes the inner life of a severely disturbed personality. In *Notes from Underground* (1864), the unnamed narrator is the first depiction of a modern literary type, the antihero, a character who lacks the virtues conventionally associated with heroism but who is not a villain.

In *The Brothers Karamazov* (1879–1880), Dostoyevsky reaches the height of his powers. Like Flaubert in *Madame Bovary,* Dostoyevsky sets his story in a small town and builds the narrative around a single family. Each of the Karamazov brothers personifies certain traits of human behavior, though none is a one-dimensional figure. Using the novel to address one of life's most vexing questions—If God exists, why is there suffering and evil in the world?—Dostoyevsky offers no easy solution. Indeed, he reaches the radical conclusion that the question is insoluble, that suffering is an essential part of earthly existence and without it human beings can have no moral life.

REALISM AMONG AFRICAN AMERICAN WRITERS In the 1840s, as public opinion in the United States became polarized over slavery, a new literary genre, the **slave narrative,** emerged. The narratives, whether composed by slaves or told by slaves to secretaries who wrote them down, were filled with gritty, harsh details of the unjust slave system; these stories in turn influenced realist fiction and also fueled the fires of antislavery rhetoric. Many slave narratives were eventually published, but probably the most compelling was *Narrative of the Life of Frederick Douglass* (1845), written by Douglass

Figure 18.8 Jean-Auguste-Dominique Ingres. *The Turkish Bath.* Ca. 1852–1863. Oil on canvas, diameter 42½". Louvre. *Interest in Oriental themes was a continuous thread in France's nineteenth-century bourgeois culture. In his rendering of a Turkish bath, Ingres used a harem setting in which to depict more than twenty nudes in various erotic and nonerotic poses. The nudes nevertheless are portrayed in typical classical manner, suggesting studio models rather than sensual human beings.*

(1817–1895) himself, which launched this literary tradition. Douglass's narrative described a heroic struggle, starting from an early awareness of the burden of being a slave, continuing through successful efforts to educate himself, and concluding with a bolt to freedom and a new life as a spokesman for abolition. This eloquent narrative was one of the first great modern books in the West to be written by a person of color. Besides establishing a new genre, Douglass made a splendid addition to the old genre of autobiography and opened the door to an inclusive world literature free from the racial segregation that had characterized the varied literatures of the world since the fall of Rome.

Another African American who contributed to the realist tradition was Sojourner Truth (1795–1883). Given the slave name of Isabell ("Bell") Hardenberg at birth, she won her freedom and took a new name, symbolic of her vow to "sojourn" the American landscape and always speak the truth. Truth's voice, captured by her secretary, Olive Gilbert, is both colloquial and eloquent, teasing and sincere, homespun and filled with biblical knowledge. Her actual voice electrified listeners, causing Truth to be remembered as one of the most natural orators in the nineteenth-century United States. Sojourner Truth's "Ain't I a Woman?" speech, delivered in 1851 before the Women's Rights Convention in Akron, Ohio, shows the simple eloquence that made her a legend in her own time.

Art and Architecture

Realism in art grew up alongside an exaggerated version of romanticism that persisted well beyond mid-century. Even neoclassicism was represented in the official art of France throughout this period. Both styles found favor with the wealthy bourgeoisie.

NEOCLASSICISM AND ROMANTICISM AFTER **1830** Jean-Auguste-Dominique Ingres, who had inherited the position of neoclassical master painter from Jacques-Louis David, controlled French academic art until his death in 1867. He understood the mentality of the Paris Salon crowds, and his works catered to their tastes. What particularly pleased this audience—composed almost exclusively of the wealthy, educated middle class—were chaste nudes in mythological or exotic settings, as in *The Turkish Bath* (Figure 18.8). The women's tactile flesh and the abandoned poses, though superbly realized, are depicted in a cold, classical style and lack the immediacy of Ingres' great portraits.

Eugène Delacroix, Ingres' chief rival, remained a significant force in French culture with comparable artistic power. Delacroix perfected a romantic style filled with superb mastery of color and human feeling. One of his finest works from this period is *Hamlet and Horatio in the Graveyard,* based on act 5, scene 1, of Shakespeare's drama (Figure 18.9). In the painting, one of the

Figure 18.9 EUGÈNE DELACROIX. *Hamlet and Horatio in the Graveyard.* 1839. Oil on canvas, 32 × 26″. Louvre. *Shakespeare's* Hamlet, *a tragedy of doomed love, became a touchstone for romantic artists and poets. Delacroix, after having seen* Hamlet *performed in Paris, was so taken by the graveyard scene that he created at least three lithographs and two paintings of it. In this painting, he has reduced the scene to its bare essentials: the two gravediggers (foreground) confront Hamlet and Horatio (middle ground), while a cloud-filled sky takes up nearly half of the canvas. He makes the dark skull the focus of the painting by having all four figures gaze at it and placing it against the light sky. Dynamic tension is added by the diagonal line running from the upper right to the lower left side of the painting, a line made up of the descending hill and the gravedigger's upraised arm.*

gravediggers holds up a skull to Hamlet and Horatio. Delacroix, faithful to the Shakespearean text, captures the men's differing reactions: Hamlet, on the right, seems to recoil slightly, while Horatio appears more curious. In this and later paintings, Delacroix tried to work out the laws governing colors—especially the effects they have on the viewer. The results in *Hamlet and Horatio in the Graveyard* are somber hues that reinforce the melancholy atmosphere. Later, the impressionists based some of their color theories on Delacroix's experiments (see Chapter 19).

Romantic painting, especially of landscapes, became popular in the United States as Americans pushed westward. The grandeur, vastness, and beauty of the new country and God's presence in nature, as explained by the transcendental poet and essayist Ralph Waldo Emerson (1803–1882), inspired landscape artists to glorify nature, to portray nature as sublime, and to relate the individual to the natural world. One group of artists, known as the Hudson River school (ca. 1825–1870), specialized in images of the mountains and valleys of New England and New York. For them, following Emerson's teachings, God and nature were one, and they attempted to infuse their works with a mystical quality while also showing that the individual had a role to play in understanding and affecting nature. A second generation of the Hudson River school ushered

in **luminism,** an art movement that emphasized nature rather than the individual, whom they often depicted in small scale or omitted entirely from their paintings. Some luminists followed the American frontier as it was pushed westward, in search of spectacular landscapes (Figure 18.10).

Like romantic painting, nineteenth-century architecture tended to be nostalgic, intrigued by times and places far removed from the industrial present. Particularly appealing were medieval times, which were considered exotic and even ethically superior to the present. Patriotism also contributed to the trend among romantic architects to adapt medieval building styles, notably the Gothic, to nineteenth-century conditions, since the Middle Ages was when the national character of many states was being formed.

In London, when the old Houses of Parliament burned to the ground in 1834, a decision had to be made about the style of their replacement. Since English rights and liberties traditionally dated from Magna Carta in 1215, during the Middle Ages, a parliamentary commission chose a Gothic style for the new building (see Figure 18.2). Designed by Charles Barry (1795–1860) and A. W. N. Pugin (1812–1852), the Houses of Parliament show a true understanding of the essential features of the Gothic style, using pointed arches and picturesque towers. Nevertheless, this building is not

Figure 18.10 ALBERT BIERSTADT. *The Rocky Mountains, Lander's Peak.* 1863. Oil on canvas, 73½ × 120¾″. The Metropolitan Museum of Art. Rogers Fund, 1907 (07.123). *The German-American Albert Bierstadt (1830–1902) traveled, in 1859, with a government survey party, headed by Frederick W. Lander, to the Nebraska territory. This scene, the peak in the distance named for the survey leader, is in present-day Wyoming. Typical of luminism, the human world—men, horses, camping gear, and tents—is dwarfed by the sky and mountains. Based on sketches made on site, Bierstadt painted this work in his New York City studio.*

genuinely Gothic, for it adheres to classical principles in the regularity of its decorations and its emphasis on the horizontal.

THE RISE OF REALISM IN ART   Dissatisfied with the emotional, exotic, and escapist tendencies of romanticism, a new breed of painter began to depict real-life events. In 1848 the jury of the Paris Salon, influenced by the democratic feelings unleashed by the social revolutions of that year, allowed a new kind of painting to be shown. The artist most identified with this new style was Gustave Courbet [koor-BAY] (1819–1877), renowned for his refusal to prettify his works in the name of aesthetic theory. His provocative canvases outraged middle-class viewers and made him the guiding spirit

of militant realism. Until about 1900, most painters followed in his footsteps. Combative, largely self-taught, and a man of the people, Courbet first attracted notice in 1849 by painting common folk at work. Above all, he strove for an art that reflected ordinary life.

Courbet's art was not readily accepted under France's Second Empire (1852–1871). Salon juries rejected his pioneering works, such as *The Meeting, or "Bonjour Monsieur Courbet,"* a visual record of an encounter between the painter and his wealthy patron, Alfred Bruyas (1821–1877) of Montpellier (Figure 18.11). With an expansive gesture, the well-dressed Bruyas (center) greets Courbet (right), as a manservant (left) stands with head bowed. The painter's informal costume—with painting equipment and belongings strapped to his back—

Figure 18.11 GUSTAVE COURBET. *The Meeting, or "Bonjour Monsieur Courbet."* 1855. Oil on canvas, 50¾ × 58⅝". Musée Fabre, Montpellier. *This painting is an allegory of the artistic and financial pact made between Courbet and his wealthy patron, Bruyas. Deeply attracted to Fourier's socialist ideas, both men thought they had found the solution, a Fourierist term, to the problem of uniting genius, capital, and work for the benefit of all. Published letters between the two show them involved in a mutual compact: for Bruyas, greater access to art circles and society, and for Courbet, the gaining of spiritual and economic freedom. Despite their partnership, the figural placement in the painting proclaims the preeminence of the artist: with his head tilted haughtily, the painter is privileged, placed nearest the viewer and isolated from the other two figures.*

helped promote Courbet's image as a carefree artist serving the cause of realism. With Bruyas' financial backing, Courbet installed this painting at the Realism Pavilion, next door to the official Salon of 1855. Critics ridiculed *The Meeting,* claiming it had no narrative, dramatic, or anecdotal subject, and accused Courbet of self-promotion and narcissism. Relishing the controversy, Courbet remained true to his vision and continued to make art from his own life—an ideal that influenced Manet and the impressionists (see Chapter 19).

Another of Courbet's paintings rejected by the 1855 Salon jury and exhibited in the Realism Pavilion was his masterpiece, *Interior of My Studio* (Figure 18.12). An intensely personal painting that visually summarizes his approach to art until this time, this work uses actual people to convey allegorical meaning. Its subtitle suggests Courbet's intent: *A Real Allegory Summing Up Seven Years of My Life as an Artist.* At the center of this canvas sits the artist himself, in full light and painting a landscape while he is watched by a naked model and a small boy. The model and the fabric may be ironic references to the Salon's preference for nudes and still lifes. To the left of this central group, in shadow, are depicted those who have to work for a living, the usual subjects of Courbet's paintings, including peasants (the hunter and his dog) and a laborer. To the right, also in shadow, are grouped those for whom he

paints, including his friends and mentors, each representing a specific idea. For example, the man reading a book is the poet Charles Baudelaire [bohd-LAIR], a personification of lyricism in art. As a total work, *Interior of My Studio* shows Courbet as the craftsman who mediates between the ordinary people pursuing everyday lives and the world of art and culture, bringing both to life in the process.

Although Courbet is considered the principal founder of the realist style in art, he had a worthy predecessor in Honoré Daumier [DOH-m'yay] (1808–1879), a painter of realistic scenes before realism emerged as a recognized style. Daumier chronicled the life of Paris with a dispassionate eye. In thousands of satirical lithographs, from which he earned his living, and hundreds of paintings, he depicted its mean streets, corrupt law courts, squalid rented rooms, ignorant art connoisseurs, bored musicians, cowardly bourgeoisie, and countless other urban characters and scenes. His works not only conjure up midcentury Paris but also symbolize the city as a living hell where daily existence could be a form of punishment.

Daumier is a master of the lithograph print. Lithography, invented in 1798 in Germany, is based on the resistance between water and grease. In early lithography, the artist drew an image on a flat stone surface using a greasy substance—applied with brush or

Figure 18.12 GUSTAVE COURBET. *Interior of My Studio: A Real Allegory Summing Up Seven Years of My Life as an Artist.* 1855. Oil on canvas, 11′9¾″ × 19′6⅜″. Louvre. *Romanticism and realism are joined in this allegorical work. The subjects— the artist and artistic genius—were major preoccupations of the romantic era, as was the use of allegory. But undeniably realist is Courbet's mocking attitude toward academic art and society. This painting's fame rests on its deft three-part composition, its allegorical biography of the artist, and its painterly technique, which captures the sensuosity of different textures, such as the female model's skin, a lace shawl, and a dog's ruffled fur.*

Figure 18.13 HONORÉ DAUMIER. *The Freedom of the Press.* Caption: *"Ne vous y Frottez Pas!!"* ["Watch It!!"]. 1834. Lithograph, 16½ × 11½″. British Museum, Department of Prints and Drawings, London. *Daumier's career as a caricaturist was made possible by technological advances associated with the industrial era. After drawing a cartoon, he reproduced it for the ever-expanding popular market using the lithographic process, the first application of industrial methods to art. Daumier's prints reflect his liberal politics, as shown in this defense of a free press. And their design elements—a blend of figures and words, the use of metaphors, and the lack of reverence for authority—make them the progenitors of today's political cartoons.*

crayon—and then poured a special chemical to adhere the image to the stone. He then dampened the stone with water, which saturated the nongreasy areas. The artist next applied an oily ink with a roller, which held fast only to the greasy image, while the blank sections were protected by the thin layer of water. Next, paper was laid on the stone, which was then run through a press, thus transferring the image to the paper. Today's lithography makes use of zinc or aluminum surfaces instead of stone.

In Daumier's prints, no one and nothing was safe from his gaze. For example, in *The Freedom of the Press*, he depicts a muscular printer, symbolic of free ideas, ready to fight oppressive regimes (Figure 18.13). On the right, Charles X, attended by two ministers, has been knocked down—a reference to the role of the press in the king's fall from power in the revolution of 1830. On the left, top-hatted Louis Philippe threatens the printer with an umbrella, egged on by two attendants. For

Figure 18.14   HONORÉ DAUMIER. *The Third-Class Carriage.* Ca. 1862. Oil on canvas, 25¾ × 35½″. Metropolitan Museum of Art. Bequest of Mrs. H. O. Havemeyer, 1929. *Close study of this oil painting reveals Daumier's genius for social observation: the mother's doting expression, the old woman's stoicism, and the melancholy profile of the top-hatted man in the shadows at the far left. None of the figures is individualized, however, for all represent social types. Despite the cramped quarters, Daumier stresses the isolation of individual travelers.*

such satire, Daumier was awarded a six-month prison term in 1832, but to his adoring audience he was a hero. Daumier often included printers in his political drawings until tighter censorship laws were passed in 1835.

One of Daumier's well-known paintings is titled *The Third-Class Carriage* (Figure 18.14). In Paris, third-class coach was the cheapest sort of rail travel, and the resulting accommodations were cramped and plain. In Daumier's scene the foreground is dominated by three figures—a mother with her sleeping child, an old woman, and a sleeping boy. Behind them are crowded other peasants and middle-class businessmen, the latter recognizable by their tall hats. Although caricature is hinted at in this painting, it is a realistic portrayal of the growing democratization of society brought on by the railway.

Figure 18.15   JEAN-FRANÇOIS MILLET. *The Gleaners.* 1857. Oil on canvas, 33 × 44″. Musée d'Orsay, Paris. *Millet's realistic scenes of peasants were inspired in part by the biblical quotation "In the sweat of thy face shalt thou eat bread" (Genesis 3:19). In* The Gleaners, *Millet expresses this idea with controlled beauty, depicting the women with simple dignity despite their hard lot. The painting's earth tones reinforce the somber nature of the subject.*

Figure 18.16   ROSA BONHEUR. *The Horse Fair.* 1853. Oil on canvas, 8′ × 13′3″. Metropoli- tan Museum of Art. Gift of Cornelius Vanderbilt, 1867. *Artists specializing in animal scenes usually painted their subjects in loving detail but only sketched in the background—perhaps re- flecting lack of landscape technique. In contrast, Bonheur fully renders the setting of* The Horse Fair, *including the feathery trees and dusty cobblestones. So precise is her design that the cupola in the distance has been identified as that of La Salpêtrière hospital in Paris—a landmark near a midcentury horse market. Such realism led to the work's favorable reception from Napoleon III, which in turn helped promote Bonheur as one of France's best painters. In 1864 Bonheur became the first woman to receive the Legion of Honor, France's highest award. However, the award was bestowed privately by the empress, for the emperor refused to give the medal to a woman in a public ceremony.*

In contrast to Daumier with his urban scenes, Jean- François Millet [mee-YAY] (1814–1875) painted the countryside near Barbizon, a village south of Paris where an artists' colony was located in the 1840s. Mil- let and the Barbizon school were influenced by the English romantic Constable, whose painting *The Hay Wain* had been admired in the Paris Salon of 1824 (see Figure 17.12). Unlike Constable, who treated human be- ings only incidentally in his landscapes, Millet made the rural folk and their labors his primary subject.

One of Millet's most famous Barbizon paintings, *The Gleaners,* exhibited in the Salon of 1857, depicts three women gleaning—that is, scavenging grain left over from the harvest (Figure 18.15). The gleaners belonged to a depressed rural class that had fallen hopelessly behind in France's rush into industrialism. The com- position hints at their plight by depicting the women isolated from the world in a desolate landscape. Reject- ing any ties to socialism, Millet instead claimed that "it is the treatment of the human condition that touches me most in art." Salon critics nevertheless reacted by calling him a socialist, and seeing the threat of revolu- tion in these marginalized laborers.

However, realist painters could focus on rural life and not be accused of socialism, as the career of Rosa

Bonheur [boh-NURR] (1822–1899) reveals. Specializ- ing in animal subjects, Bonheur enjoyed success with critics and public alike, starting with the Salon of 1841, when she was nineteen. In 1848 the Salon jury awarded Bonheur a Medal First Class for an animal scene. In 1853 *The Horse Fair* (Figure 18.16)—portraying spirited horses and their handlers at a horse market—made her an international celebrity, after a lithograph copy sold well in France, Britain, and the United States. What makes Bonheur's horses different from those painted by the romantic Delacroix was her accuracy in depict- ing anatomy and movement—a reflection of her realist faith in science. To prepare for this painting, Bonheur, dressed as a man, visited a horse market twice a week for two years to make sketches. Today, the work is con- sidered her masterpiece, both for its impressive scale and for its knowledgeable portrayal of nineteenth- century country life.

If the Parisian art world was gratified by the paint- ings of Bonheur, it was outraged by the work of Éd- ouard Manet [mah-NAY] (1832–1883), a painter whose style is difficult to classify. He contributed to the events that gradually discredited the Salon and the Royal Academy, encouraging painters to express themselves as they pleased, and thus was a bridge between the

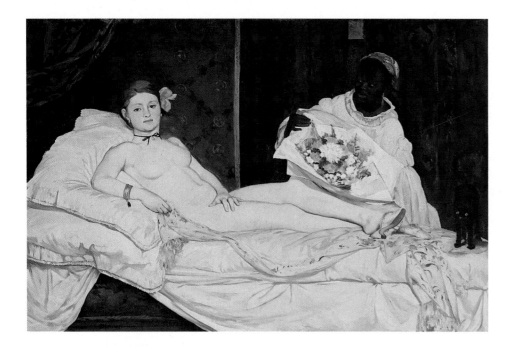

Figure 18.17 ÉDOUARD MANET. *Olympia.* 1863. Oil on canvas, 51¼ × 74¾". Musée d'Orsay, Paris. *Despite its references to traditional art,* Olympia *created a furor among the prudish and conservative public and critics. Parisian bourgeoisie expected to see nudes in the official Salon, but they were shocked by the appearance of a notorious prostitute, completely nude. The art critics, likewise, found the painting indecent and also condemned Manet's harsh, brilliant light, which tended to eliminate any details of the room's interior. Regardless of its initial negative reception,* Olympia *today is admired as a work that broke with traditional art practices and opened the way for a modern art centered on the painter's own theories.*

realists of the 1860s and the group that became known in the 1870s as the impressionists. His notoriety arose in 1863 when Napoleon III authorized a Salon des Refusés (Salon of the Rejects) for the hundreds of artists excluded from the official exhibit. An audacious painting by Manet in this first of the counter-Salons made him the talk of Paris and the recognized leader of new painting.

In the official Salon of 1865, Manet exhibited *Olympia*, painted two years earlier, which also created a scandal (Figure 18.17). The painting presents a nude woman on a bed, a subject established by the painter Titian in the sixteenth century, but which Manet now modernized. Titian presented his nude as the goddess Venus in an idealized setting, but Manet rejected the trappings of mythology and depicted his nude realistically as a Parisian courtesan in her bedroom. The name Olympia was adopted by many Parisian prostitutes at the time, and Manet portrayed her as being as imperious as a Greek goddess from Mount Olympus. Manet's Olympia is neither demure nor flirtatious; she gazes challengingly at the observer in a mixture of coldness and coyness. Her posture speaks of her boldness, as she sits propped up by pillows and dangles a shoe on her foot. She is attended by a black maid, whose deferential expression is in sharp contrast to Olympia's haughty demeanor. At her feet lies a black cat, an emblem of sexuality and gloom, perhaps inspired by a poem by the artist's friend Baudelaire.

More important than these historical connections, however, are Manet's artistic theories and practices, which strained the boundaries of realism. Unlike other realists, whose moral or ideological feelings were re-

flected in the subjects they painted, Manet moved toward a dispassionate art in which the subject and the artist have no necessary connection. Manet's achievement was revolutionary, for he had discarded the intellectual themes of virtually all Western art: reliance on anecdote, the Bible, Christian saints, politics, nostalgia, Greece and Rome, the Middle Ages, and sentimental topics. With his work, he opened the door to an art that had no other purpose than to depict what the artist chose to paint—that is, "art for art's sake." In sum, Manet was the first truly modern painter.

Photography

One of the forces propelling painting toward a more realistic and detached style of expression was the invention of the camera. Two types of camera techniques were perfected in 1839. In France, Louis-Jacques-Mandé Daguerre [duh-GAIR] (1787–1851) discovered a chemical method for implanting images on silvered copper plates to produce photographs called daguerreotypes. In England, William Henry Fox Talbot (1800–1877) was pioneering the negative-positive process of photographic images, which he called "the pencil of nature." Not only did the camera undermine the reality of the painted image, but it also quickly created a new art form, photography. From the beginning, many photographers began to experiment with the camera's artistic potential, though only since 1945 has photography received wide acceptance as serious art.

Among the early photographers were the American Mathew Brady (about 1823–1896) and the English Julia

Margaret Cameron (1815–1879). Both made important contributions to photography, but their techniques and results differed widely. Brady attempted, through a sharp focus, to capture his subject in a realistic manner, whereas Cameron, by using a soft focus, delved into the personality and character of the individual in a near-mystical way.

Brady's reputation today is based mainly on his pictorial record of the American Civil War. Before the war, he operated a spacious studio and gallery in New York City, and there, in February 1860, he photographed Abraham Lincoln, who was campaigning to be the Republican nominee for president (Figure 18.18). This portrait introduced Lincoln to the East Coast public, who previously had thought the midwesterner to be a coarse, backwoods politician. The original photograph achieved wide circulation when it was printed on a *carte-de-visite*, a 2½-inch print that was mounted as a calling card or collected as a personal memento. After Lincoln was elected president, he acknowledged to Brady that the photograph had been instrumental in securing his victory.

While Brady and his staff were photographing battlefield scenes as well as portraits, Cameron, in 1863, at age forty-eight, began to photograph her family and friends—many of whom were prominent Victorians (Figure 18.19). Within two years her talent was recognized, and soon she was exhibiting her works and winning awards. Her photographs document her

Figure 18.18 MATHEW BRADY. *Abraham Lincoln.* 1860. Library of Congress. *Urged by his supporters in New York City, Lincoln hastily arranged to have Brady photograph him. Typical of the* carte-de-visite, *Lincoln is shown standing in a three-quarter-length frontal pose, a position influenced by the Western tradition of portrait painting. Dressed in the proper attire of the successful attorney that he was, Lincoln looks steadily at the viewer while resting his left hand lightly on a stack of books. This photograph enhanced the Honest Abe image, with its dignity, seriousness, and air of calm resolve. On the left is the photographer's logo: Brady N.Y.*

Figure 18.19 JULIA MARGARET CAMERON. *Beatrice.* 1866. Victoria and Albert Museum, London. *Cameron photographed many women representing religious, historical, classical, and literary females. Turning to* The Divine Comedy, *Cameron tries to capture the compelling beauty of Beatrice, who was one of the guiding inspirations of Dante's famous work. The light, coming in from the upper right, accentuates Beatrice's contemplative pose and her allure. In 1864, eight years before Cameron took this picture and when she was beginning her career, she wrote that she wanted to ennoble photography "by combining the real & Ideal and sacrificing nothing of Truth by all possible devotion to Poetry and beauty."*

conventional views of a woman's place in society, her deep Christian faith, and the impact of the romantic movement. In her effort to catch the consciousness of each sitter, Cameron experimented with lighting, used props and costumes, tried different cameras, and often developed her own plates.

Music

Originating shortly after 1800, romantic music reigned supreme from 1830 until 1871. Romantic works grew longer and more expressive as composers forged styles reflecting their individual feelings. To achieve unique voices, romantic composers adopted varied techniques such as shifting rhythms, complex musical structures, discordant passages, and minor keys. In addition, with the spread of nationalistic feelings across Europe, especially after 1850, composers began to incorporate folk songs, national anthems, and indigenous dance rhythms into their music. Nonetheless, throughout this era romantic composers stayed true to the established forms of classical music composition—the opera, the sonata, and the symphony.

Although a baroque creation, opera rose to splendid heights under romanticism. The bourgeois public, bedazzled by opera's spectacle and virtuoso singers, eagerly embraced this art form. Operatic composers sometimes wrote works specifically to show off the vocal talents of particular performers. So prolific were these musicians that they wrote over half of the operas performed today.

Concerts also flourished under romanticism. As the middle class grew wealthier, they used culture, especially music, to validate their social credentials. They founded orchestras, whose governing boards they ran, turned concerts into social rituals with unwritten codes of dress and behavior, and made musical knowledge a badge of social worthiness (Figure 18.20).

Opera composers embraced the romantic style. Operatic orchestras became larger, inspiring composers to write long, elaborate works requiring many performers. Composers began to integrate the entire musical drama, creating orchestral music that accentuated the actions and thoughts of the characters onstage. Most important, the form of opera itself was transformed. At first, composers imitated the form they had inherited, writing operas in which a series of independent musical numbers—that is, **arias** (melodious songs)—alternated with recitatives (text either declaimed in the rhythms of natural speech with slight musical variations or sung with fuller musical support). The Italian composer Verdi brought this type of opera to its peak, advancing beyond the mechanical aria-recitative alternation. But even as Verdi was being lionized for his operatic achievements, a new style of opera was arising in Germany in the works of Wagner, which were written not as independent musical sections but as continuous musical scenes.

Giuseppe Verdi [VAYR-dee] (1813–1901), Italy's greatest composer of opera, followed the practice of the time and borrowed many of his plots from the works of romantic writers filled with passion and full-blooded emotionalism. One of the operas that brought him in-

Figure 18.20 Covent Garden Theater, London. 1846. Engraving. University of Southampton Library. *This engraving shows a concert at London's Covent Garden Theater, with the famous French conductor Louis Jullien (1812–1860) leading an orchestra and four military bands. Note the fashionable clothes: "poke" bonnets and elegant dresses with low necklines for the women; evening wear and "stovepipe" hats for the men; and formal or military dress for the musicians. An event such as this came to be called a "promenade" concert, or "proms," the equivalent of a pop concert, with a blend of lighter and classical music. Jullien is credited with introducing proms to London, and they remain an essential feature of musical life there today.*

ternational fame was *Rigoletto* (1851), based on a play by Victor Hugo. What make it such a favorite with audiences are its strong characters, its beautiful melodies, and its dramatic unity—features that typify Verdi's mature works. A study in romantic opposites, this work tells of a crippled court jester, Rigoletto, deformed physically but emotionally sensitive, coarse in public but a devoted parent in private. The jester's daughter, Gilda, is also a study in contrasts, torn between love for her father and attraction to a corrupt noble.

In *Rigoletto,* Verdi continues to alternate arias with sung recitatives, but overall his music for the orchestra skillfully underscores the events taking place onstage. In addition, he employs musical passages to illustrate the characters' psychology, using convoluted orchestral backgrounds to accompany Rigoletto's monologues, for example, or shifting from simple to showy musical settings to demonstrate Gilda's conflicted nature. In Act III, the lighthearted aria "La donna e mobile" ("Woman Is Fickle") is sung by the Duke of Mantua, expressing perfectly his cynical view of women. Following a brief orchestral section, the duke sings a four-line refrain, which is reprised two more times, in between two verses with different words. The theme of this tenor aria is "Woman is deceitful, always changeable in word and thought." Verdi underscores the irony by setting this famous aria in a low dive—a decaying inn—where the count has been lured by Maddalena, a loose woman. When the aria ends, Rigoletto, who has been eavesdropping on the Duke of Mantua, exchanges words, in recitative, with Maddalena's brother, a hired killer.

Other operas followed, enhancing Verdi's mounting celebrity: *La Traviata* in 1853, based on a play written by the French romantic writer Alexandre Dumas [doo-MAH] the younger, and *Aïda* in 1871, commissioned by Egypt's ruler and first performed in the Cairo opera house.

Romantic opera reached its climax in the works of Richard Wagner [VAHG-nuhr] (1813–1883), who sought a union of music and drama. A political revolutionary in his youth and a visionary thinker, Wagner was deeply impressed by the romantic idea that the supreme expression of artistic genius occurs only when the arts are fused. To that end, he not only composed his own scores but also wrote the **librettos,** or texts, frequently conducted the music, and even planned the opera house in Bayreuth, Germany, where his later works were staged.

Wagner's major musical achievement was the monumental project titled *The Ring of the Nibelung* (1853–1874), a cycle of four operas—or **music dramas,** as Wagner called them—that fulfilled his ideal of fusing music, verse, and staging. In these works, the distinction between arias and recitatives was nearly erased, giving a continuously flowing melodic line. This unified sound was marked by the appearance of recurring themes associated with particular characters, things, or ideas, known as **leitmotifs.**

Perhaps the best-known Wagnerian motif is that identified with the valkyrie—the mythic blond women warriors who administered to the fallen heroes in Valhalla, the Norse heaven. They were the subject of Wagner's second opera in the *Ring* cycle, *Die Walküre (The Valkyrie)* (1856). Act III of that opera begins with "Ride of the Valkyries," an exciting evocation of a wild cosmic ride, which builds to a thrilling climax, interspersed with quiet **pianissimos**—very soft sounds—and crashing **crescendos**—increases in volume—and shifts in rhythm and tone color. The work, written as an orchestral prelude, unfolds with the curtain rising before its finish, to reveal a stage filled with blond maidens carrying dead warriors to their heavenly rest. Today, it is sometimes heard in films, as in the helicopter scene in *Apocalypse Now,* Francis Ford Coppola's 1979 epic about the Vietnam War.

Based on a popular romantic source—the medieval Norse myths—the *Ring* also reflected Wagner's belief that opera should be moral. The *Ring* cycle warns against overweening ambition, its plot relating a titanic struggle for world mastery in which both human beings and gods are destroyed because of their lust for power. Wagner may have been addressing this warning to the Faustian spirit that dominated capitalism in the industrial age—a message that went unheeded.

Another German, Johannes Brahms (1833–1897), dominated orchestral and chamber music after 1850 in much the same way that Wagner did opera. Unlike Wagner, Brahms was no musical innovator. A classical romanticist, he took up the mantle vacated by Beethoven, and he admired the baroque works of Bach. In Vienna, his adopted home, Brahms became the hero of the traditionalists who opposed the new music of Wagner. Neglecting the characteristic romantic works of operas and program music, he won fame with his symphonies and chamber music. His characteristic sound is mellow, always harmonic, delighting equally in joy and melancholy.

Despite his conservative musicianship, Brahms's work incorporates many romantic elements. Continuing the art-song tradition established by Schubert (see Chapter 17), Brahms introduced folk melodies into his pieces. In his instrumental works, he often aimed for the expressiveness of the human voice, the "singing" style preferred in romanticism. He was also indebted to the romantic style for the length of his symphonies, the use of rhythmic variations in all his works, and, above all, the rich lyricism and songfulness of his music.

Despite the dominance of classical musical forms, this period was the zenith of romantic *lieder,* or art songs. The continuing popularity of lieder reflected bourgeois taste and power, since amateur performances of these songs were a staple of home entertainment for the well-to-do, especially in Germany and Austria. In the generation after Schubert, the best composer of lieder was the German Robert Schumann (1810–1856), a pianist who shifted to music journalism and composition when his right hand became crippled in 1832. Splendid fusions of words and music, his songs are essentially duets for voice and piano.

Schumann's lieder are often parts of song cycles held together with unifying themes. One of his best-known song cycles is *Dichterliebe (A Poet's Love)* (1840), set to verses by Heinrich Heine (1797–1856), Germany's preeminent lyric poet. This song cycle superbly illustrates the romantic preoccupation with program music. For instance, the song "Im Wunderschönen Monat Mai" ("In the Marvelously Beautiful Month of May") conveys the longing of Heine's text through ascending lines of melody and an unresolved climax. The passion in this song cycle was inspired by Schumann's marriage to Clara Wieck (1819–1896), a piano virtuoso and composer in her own right.

The Legacy of the Bourgeois Age

We today still live in the shadow of the bourgeois age. The failed revolutions of 1830 and 1848 are textbook examples of the limits of revolutionary change; they also inspired the amoral concept of realpolitik, a guiding principle in much of today's world. Realpolitik also contributed to the unification of Germany in 1871, which upset the balance of power on the Continent, unleashed German militarism, and led to France's smoldering resentment of Germany. The two world wars of the twentieth century had their seeds in these events.

With liberalism in the ascendant, the middle-class values of hard work, thrift, ambition, and respectability became paramount, as did the notion that the individual should take precedence over the group. However, the utopian socialists and the Marxian socialists, in criticizing liberalism and the industrial system, offered alternative solutions to social and economic problems. Their proposals foreshadowed approaches such as labor unions, mass political parties, and state planning. The intellectual and artistic developments of this age had far-reaching repercussions. There is still interest in Marx's controversial analysis of history, despite the collapse of global communism; Darwin's theory of evolution, though intensely debated, is central to modern thought; Pasteur's contributions in immunology and microbiology and to the development of modern medicine have helped make the world a safer place; higher criticism, by challenging the Hebrew Bible and the New Testament, has diminished the notion of religious revelation itself; and the evangelical movement, with its faith-based rejection of arguments grounded in science, history, and textual analysis, has become a fixture in the American political landscape.

Romanticism, although under siege from other modes of thought after 1850, has not disappeared from the West, even today. Realism, its immediate successor, became the reigning style until 1900, partly because of the development of the camera and the art of photography. London's Crystal Palace inaugurated the high-tech tradition in art and architecture, and inventions and new techniques in printing and publishing laid the foundation for a mass market in the visual arts. Perhaps the most significant artistic development during this time was Manet's adoption of the credo "art for art's sake," which terminated the debate over the representational nature of art. Most artists in the post-1871 period followed Manet's bold move.

KEY CULTURAL TERMS

utilitarianism
socialism
evangelicalism
holiness
higher criticism
evolution
realism
transcendentalism

slave narrative
luminism
aria
libretto
music drama
leitmotif
pianissimo
crescendo

QUESTIONS FOR CRITICAL THINKING

1. Discuss the major historical and cultural events be-tween 1830 and 1871 and show how they influenced the arts and humanities, particularly the neoclassical and romantic styles before 1848 and the realist style thereafter.

2. Discuss industrial developments in this era. What impact did these changes have on culture, especially on political philosophy?

3. What was Manet's innovation that laid the founda-tions of modern art? Explain.

4. Discuss realism as a cultural style, using an example from both literature and art as the basis of your essay.

5. What impact did the middle class and its ideology of liberalism have on nineteenth-century politics and culture? Explain the changed nature of liberalism in the mid-nineteenth century.

19

THE AGE OF EARLY MODERNISM
1871–1914

Between 1871 and 1914, Europe enjoyed unprecedented tranquillity, free of military conflict, which led many Westerners to consider this the new age predicted by Enlightenment thinkers. But hindsight exposes this age as one of rampant nationalism, aggressive imperialism, and growing militarism, culminating in the outbreak of World War I in 1914. At the same time, the phenomenon known as "modern life" was emerging, with people sharing in the benefits of the nation-state and the Second Industrial Revolution. In the cultural realm, **modernism** was born; this movement rejected both the Greco-Roman and the Judeo-Christian legacies and tried to forge a new perspective that was true to the modern secular experience.

Modernism lasted about one hundred years, going through three distinct stages. During its first phase (1871–1914), which is treated in this chapter, artists, writers, and thinkers established the movement's principles through their creative and innovative works. The second phase, the zenith of modernism (1914–1945), is the subject of Chapter 20; and the exhaustion and decline of the movement, the third phase (1945–1970), is covered in Chapter 21.

EUROPE'S RISE TO WORLD LEADERSHIP

The Age of Early Modernism, despite the prevailing moods of optimism and tranquillity, was an age of accelerated and stressful change. Dynamic forces—imperialism, nationalism, and militarism—were shaping the course of history that came to define life in the twentieth century (Figure 19.1). Acting as a catalyst on these powerful forces were the middle classes, whose political power grew daily across the West.

◄ **Detail** UMBERTO BOCCIONI. *Unique Forms of Continuity in Space.* 1913. Bronze (cast 1931). 43⅞ × 34⅞ × 15¾". The Museum of Modern Art, New York. Acquired through the Lillie P. Bliss Bequest. Photograph © 1997 The Museum of Modern Art, New York.

559

Figure 19.1 RAOUL DUFY. *July 14 in Le Havre.* 1906. Oil on canvas, 21½ × 14⅞". Collection of Mr. and Mrs. Paul Mellon. National Gallery, Washington, D.C. *This colorful depiction of Bastille Day, France's Independence Day, by Raoul Dufy (rah-uhl due-fee) (1877–1953), is a fitting symbol of nationalism and middle-class life in a provincial city. Dufy's blurred images of men and women hurrying down the street heighten the sense of hustle and bustle of small-town life. Above the figures' heads the French flag flies front and center with other flags and banners fluttering nearby—France's tricolored flag a reminder of its revolutionary heritage. Le Havre, founded in the sixteenth century, was a busy industrial port on the Seine River. Dufy, a native of Le Havre, experimented briefly with fauvism and cubism before establishing his own style as a painter of recreational and festive events. He also was famous for his watercolors and prints depicting similar subjects.*

Figure 19.2 UMBERTO BOCCIONI. *Unique Forms of Continuity in Space.* 1913. Bronze (cast 1931), 43⅞ × 34⅞ × 15¾". The Museum of Modern Art, New York. Acquired through the Lillie P. Bliss Bequest. Photograph © 1997 The Museum of Modern Art, New York. *Umberto Boccioni and his fellow futurists were members of an Italian-based literary and artistic movement that typified early modernism's rejection of the past and set out to create a new concept of art. The futurists called for the destruction of museums, libraries, and all existing art forms. In this striding bronze figure, Boccioni distorts form and space to create an airstreamed image of speed, the new modern icon.*

As imperialistic ambitions grew, Europe became a world power with a network of political and economic interests around the globe and competition among Europe's states intensified. Imperialism, combined with heightened nationalism and militaristic impulses, created an atmosphere of patriotism that eventually led rival states to war.

The Second Industrial Revolution, New Technologies, and the Making of Modern Life

The Second Industrial Revolution differed from the first in several significant ways. First, Great Britain, the world's industrial leader since 1760, faced competition from Germany and the United States. Second, science and research provided new and improved industrial products and influenced manufacturing much more than during the first revolution. Finally, steam and water power were replaced by newer forms of industrial energy, such as oil and electricity. The internal combustion engine replaced the steam engine in ships and, in the early 1900s, gave rise to the automobile and the airplane. Europeans and the world were entering an age of power and speed (Figure 19.2).

Technology, the handmaid of science, was also reshaping the world. The wireless superseded the tele-

Figure 19.3 MARY CASSATT. *Reading "Le Figaro."* 1878. Oil on canvas, 41 × 33". National Gallery, Washington, D.C. *Cassatt's woman reading a newspaper was a rare subject in the nineteenth century. Artists usually depicted women reading books rather than newspapers, which were identified with the man's world outside the home. The woman is the artist's mother, Katherine Cassatt, who is reading* Le Figaro, *one of Paris's leading newspapers. Rich and well educated, Mrs. Cassatt was a strong influence in her daughter's life and career. The formidable figure of the mother takes up much of the painting, and the mirror on the left reflects her and her surroundings. The artist has cropped the mirror, much in the style of a photograph, a popular technique among early modernist painters.*

graph, the telephone made its debut, and national and international postal services were instituted. Typewriters and tabulators transformed business practices. Rotary presses printed thousands of copies of daily newspapers for an increasingly literate public (Figure 19.3).

The Second Industrial Revolution affected almost every segment of the economy. In transportation, more efficient engines meant lower transportation costs and less expensive products. Refrigeration permitted perishable foods to be transported great distances without spoiling. Advertising became both a significant source of revenue for publishers and a persuasive force in the consumer economy. Increased wealth provided more people more leisure time and new recreations appeared, such as seaside resorts, music halls, movies, and bicycles—all contributing to what is now known as modern life.

Industrialized cities, with their promises of well-paying jobs, comfortable lives, and diverse entertain-

ments, drew residents of small towns and farms, and by 1900 nearly 30 percent of the people in the West lived in cities (Figure 19.4). As urbanization expanded, the standard of living improved. Consumers benefited from an overall decline in prices and consistent wages and salaries. From about 1900 to the outbreak of World War I in 1914, the middle and upper classes enjoyed unprecedented prosperity and leisure, but misery mounted among the urban working class. Urban slums grew more crowded, and living conditions worsened. The presence of squalor in the midst of plenty pricked the conscience of many citizens, who began to work for better housing and less dangerous working conditions for laborers. When these reform efforts proved inadequate and state-funded social welfare programs failed to alleviate the problems, labor unions thrived, along with their best weapon, the strike.

One reform did succeed: the founding of secular public education. Its advocates claimed that public schools, financed by taxes and supervised by state

Figure 19.4 CAMILLE PISSARRO. *The Great Bridge to Rouen.* 1896. Oil on canvas, 29³/₁₆ × 36½". Carnegie Museum of Art, Pittsburgh. Purchase. *Pissarro's painting captures the energy of Rouen and transforms this French river town into a symbol of the new industrial age. Contributing to the sense of vitality are the belching smokestack, the bridge crowded with hurrying people, and the dockworkers busy with their machinery. The fast pace is underscored by the impressionist technique of "broken color," giving immediacy to the scene.*

agencies, would prepare workers for jobs in industrialized society and create an informed and literate citizenry—two basic needs of modern life. An unanticipated result of the establishment of public school systems was that ties between children and their parents were loosened.

The status of women also changed dramatically. New employment opportunities opened for teachers, nurses, office workers, and salesclerks. Because some jobs required special skills, colleges and degree programs were developed to train women. Many young women still turned to domestic service, but new household appliances reduced the need for servants. Independent retail shopkeepers continued to work long hours in family businesses, but working conditions for women in factories were now regulated by laws (Figure 19.5).

Some women reformers, primarily from the middle class—Emmeline Pankhurst (1858–1928) and Susan B. Anthony (1820–1906), leaders in the women's suffrage movement in Great Britain and the United States, respectively—advocated more freedom for women, continuing a tradition that had begun on a limited scale before 1871. They launched successful campaigns to revise property and divorce laws, giving women greater

Figure 19.5 EYRE CROWE. *The Dinner Hour at Wigan.* 1874. Oil on canvas, 30 × 42¼". Manchester City Art Gallery, Manchester, England. *Social possibilities for English women expanded to some degree during this era. This painting depicts a factory scene in which the young female workers gain a brief respite from their tasks. A few talk together quietly, while others remain apart or finish a chore. They all seem dwarfed by the huge mill with the smokestacks in the background, a fitting symbol of industrial power.*

control over their wealth and their lives. In several countries, women reformers founded suffrage movements, using protests and marches to dramatize their situation. Following a vigorous, occasionally violent, campaign, women won the right to vote in Great Britain in 1918 and in the United States in 1920.

Response to Industrialism: Politics and Crisis

At the dawn of early modernism, the assumptions of liberalism were challenged in many quarters. Except in Great Britain and the United States, liberals were under siege in national legislatures both by socialists—who wanted more central planning and more state-funded services for workers—and by conservatives—who feared the masses and supported militant nationalism as a way to unify their societies. After 1900, political parties representing workers and trade unionists, which were strong enough to push successfully for laws to correct some social problems of industrialism, further threatened the liberals' hold on power.

Events also seemed to discredit liberal economic theories. Ideally, under free trade the population ought to decline or at least stabilize, and wages and prices ought to operate harmoniously, but neither happened. Population was surging and industrial capitalism was erratic, leading many critics of liberal capitalism to conclude that the so-called laws of liberal economics did not work.

DOMESTIC POLICIES IN THE INDUSTRIALIZED WEST Germany, France, Great Britain, and the United States all faced domestic problems during this period. Founded in 1871, the German Reich, or Empire, moved toward

unity under the astute leadership of its first chancellor, Otto von Bismarck, and the new kaiser, or emperor, William I (r. 1871–1888), former king of Prussia (Figure 19.6). Despite the illusion of parliamentary rule, the tone of this imperial reich was conservative, militaristic, and nationalistic.

In France, the Third Republic was founded after the humiliating defeat of the Second Empire by Germany in 1871. Even though the regime remained hopelessly divided between republicans and monarchists, it agreed on the need to correct the most glaring social injustices in an attempt to counteract the growing appeal of the workers' parties and socialism. France's liberal center gradually evaporated, creating bitter deadlocks between socialists and conservatives that no government could resolve.

Great Britain was more successful than Germany and France in solving its domestic problems. Controlled by political parties that represented the upper and middle classes, the British government passed social legislation that improved the working and living conditions of poorer families and created opportunities for social mobility through a state secondary-school system. As in Germany and France, these reforms did not prevent workers from forming their own political party, the Labour Party. By 1929, Labour had gained enough support to elect a majority of Parliament and the prime minister.

Across the Atlantic, the United States now challenged Great Britain's industrial supremacy. America's expanding economy allowed big business to dominate politics at all levels (Figure 19.7). But, in the early 1900s, reform movements, spurred by its democratic tradition, temporarily restrained the power of the business conglomerates, or trusts, particularly in transportation and oil.

Figure 19.6 ANTON VON WERNER. *Proclamation of the German Empire on January 18, 1871 at the Hall of Mirrors in Versailles.* 1885. Oil on canvas, approx. 65¾ × 79½". Bismarck Museum, Friedrichsruhe, Germany. *This painting commemorates the moment when the German Empire was proclaimed and King William of Prussia became its first emperor. Von Werner uses reflections from the famed Hall of Mirrors at Versailles to make the stirring scene more theatrical, and added drama comes from the raised swords of the officers. The strong presence of the army was prophetic of the dominant role the military was destined to play in the German Empire.*

SLICE OF LIFE
Winning the Right to Vote

LADY CONSTANCE LYTTON
Notes from a Diary

Lady Constance Lytton (1869–1923), the daughter of a former viceroy of India, was a leader of the women's suffrage movement in Great Britain. Arrested during a protest in Liverpool in 1910, she assumed the name and status of a working-class woman, Jane Warton, because she feared that her high social position would prompt the police to release her. As "Jane Warton," she went on a hunger strike and was force-fed by a doctor and wardresses (female guards), a horrifying tactic experienced by many suffragettes.

I was visited again by the Senior Medical Officer, who asked me how long I had been without food. I said I had eaten a buttered scone and a banana sent in by friends to the police station on Friday at about midnight. He said, "Oh, then, this is the fourth day; that is too long, I shall feed you, I must feed you at once," but he went out and nothing happened till about six o'clock in the evening, when he returned with, I think, five wardresses and the feeding apparatus. He urged me to take food voluntarily. I told him that was absolutely out of the question, that when our legislators ceased to resist enfranchising women then I should cease to resist taking food in prison. He did not examine my heart nor feel my pulse; he did not ask to do so, nor did I say anything which could possibly induce him to think I would refuse to be examined. I offered no resistance to being placed in position, but lay down voluntarily on the plank bed. Two of the wardresses took hold of my arms, one held my head and one my feet. One wardress helped to pour the food. The doctor leant on my knees as he stooped over my chest to get at my mouth. I shut my mouth and clenched my teeth. I had looked forward to this moment with so much anxiety lest my identity should be discovered beforehand, that I felt positively glad when the time had come. The sense of being overpowered by more force than I could possibly resist was complete, but I resisted nothing except with my mouth. The doctor offered me the choice of a wooden or steel gag; he explained elaborately, as he did on most subsequent occasions, that the steel gag would hurt and the wooden one not, and he urged me not to force him to use the steel gag. But I did not speak nor open my mouth, so that after playing about for a moment or two with the wooden one he finally had recourse to the steel. He seemed annoyed at my resistance and he broke into a temper as he plied my teeth with the steel implement. He found that on either side at the back I had false

teeth mounted on a bridge which did not take out. The superintending wardress asked if I had any false teeth, if so, that they must be taken out; I made no answer and the process went on. He dug his instrument down on to the sham tooth, it pressed fearfully on the gum. He said if I resisted so much with my teeth, he would have to feed me through the nose. The pain of it was intense and at last I must have given way for he got the gag between my teeth, when he proceeded to turn it much more than necessary until my jaws were fastened wide apart, far more than they could go naturally. Then he put down my throat a tube which seemed to me much too wide and was something like four feet in length. The irritation of the tube was excessive. I choked the moment it touched my throat until it had got down. Then the food was poured in quickly; it made me sick a few seconds after it was down and the action of the sickness made my body and legs double up, but the wardresses instantly pressed back my head and the doctor leant on my knees. The horror of it was more than I can describe.

I was sick over the doctor and wardresses, and it seemed a long time before they took the tube out. As the doctor left he gave me a slap on the cheek, not violently, but, as it were, to express his contemptuous disapproval, and he seemed to take for granted that my distress was assumed. At first it seemed such an utterly contemptible thing to have done that I could only laugh in my mind. Then suddenly I saw Jane Warton lying before me, and it seemed as if I were outside of her. She was the most despised, ignorant and helpless prisoner that I had seen. When she had served her time and was out of the prison, no one would believe anything she said, and the doctor when he had fed her by force and tortured her body, struck her on the cheek to show how he despised her! That was Jane Warton, and I had come to help her.

INTERPRETING THIS SLICE OF LIFE

1. *Why* did Lady Lytton assume the name of a working-class woman, and *what* does that reveal about English life? 2. *Describe* the procedures and techniques used in force-feeding. 3. *How* did Lady Lytton "see" Jane Warton at the end of her ordeal? 4. *Explain* why the suffragettes used the hunger strike in their civil rights battle. 5. *Compare and contrast* this battle for civil rights with recent civil rights struggles.

Figure 19.7 EDGAR DEGAS. *The Cotton Bureau in New Orleans.* 1873. Oil on canvas, 29⅛ × 36¼". Musée des Beaux-Arts, Pau, France. *By the third quarter of the nineteenth century, the United States was challenging English supremacy in world trade. The French painter Degas must have observed this scene—the interior of a cotton exchange in New Orleans—while visiting relatives in Louisiana. Whether consciously or not, Degas accurately depicted the social realities of this bourgeois work space: the capitalist idlers reading a newspaper or lounging against a wall and, in contrast, the paid employees intent on their work.*

In the late 1800s, eastern and central Europeans came to America in the largest migration of human population ever recorded. These immigrants—after painful adjustments, particularly in the crowded slums of the eastern cities—gradually entered the mainstream of American life. They provided much of the labor for the factories, and they transformed the United States into a much richer ethnic society, while making valuable contributions to the culture.

DOMESTIC POLICIES IN CENTRAL, SOUTHERN, AND EASTERN EUROPE   The less industrialized states of central, southern, and eastern Europe faced more difficult challenges. As the factory system spread to their regions, these countries had no well-defined political and economic policies for handling the problems of industrialism. In Italy, because regional leaders were often stronger than the prime minister, the government allowed the north to become industrialized while the south, including Sicily, remained in a semifeudal condition. As a result, the north, driven by an expanding middle class, moved far ahead of the agrarian south, where vast estates were worked by peasant labor. In the Austro-Hungarian Empire, the government's biggest problem was ethnic unrest, a direct outgrowth of the denial of political freedom to the Slavic minorities. Although the Austrian Germans granted political parity to the Hungarians, allowing them free rein within their land, they did not address the discontent among the Slavs. Even while the region seethed with ethnic

violence, the empire's capital, Vienna, became a glittering symbol of modernism. From *fin-de-siècle* ("end-of-the-century") Vienna came the cultural style called expressionism and the psychology of Sigmund Freud.

Farther east, the autocratic Russian Empire slowly entered the industrial age, hampered by its vast size, sluggish agrarian economy, and inefficient bureaucracy. Adding to Russia's woes were violent underground revolutionaries who despaired of any substantial reform at home. In 1881 an anarchist assassinated the reform-minded czar Alexander II (r. 1855–1881), and his reactionary successors dismantled his programs, as the economy worsened. In 1905 Japan defeated Russia in the Russo-Japanese War (1904–1905), setting off an abortive revolution led by underpaid factory workers and starving peasants. By promising relief, Czar Nicholas II (r. 1894–1917) weathered the storm, but few of his pledges were fulfilled. Instead, the state violently repressed dissent, and the imperial court grew dangerously isolated.

Imperialism and International Relations

In 1871 most European nations believed that domestic issues, such as internal law and order, were more important than foreign trade and overseas colonies. By 1914 those beliefs had been reversed: a state's primary national interests were now equated with its role in the global economy and foreign affairs.

Figure 19.8   G. W. BACON. *Battle of Omdurman.* 1898. Engraving. *In September 1898, an Anglo-Egyptian army of twenty-six thousand men, led by General H. H. Kitchener (1850–1916), annihilated Sudanese forces numbering about forty thousand, at Omdurman on the Nile River in Sudan. Within five hours, the British, armed with rifles, cannons, and machine guns, killed over ten thousand Sudanese troops and wounded about the same number, while losing fewer than four hundred soldiers. Leading one of the British units in the cavalry charge was the young Winston Churchill—whose glory days lay ahead. With this victory, the British extended their control of the Nile River farther south, and by 1914 they had solidified their position in Africa, controlling lands from Alexandria (in the north) to the Cape of Good Hope (in the south), and from the east to the west coast in sub-Saharan Africa (see Map 19.1).*

THE SCRAMBLE FOR COLONIES   Before 1875 the common wisdom was that a colony brought both benefits and problems to a modern state, but after that year Western thinking abruptly changed. Europe's industrialized states began to compete for colonies and for trade rights around the world. To maintain their high standard of living, they had to find new markets, underdeveloped areas in which to invest capital, and cheap sources of raw materials. Given these needs, product-rich Africa was an imperialist's dream. Acquiring African lands through various means, including treaties with local chiefs, claims by missionaries and explorers, or victories by superior armies, the European states set up colonial governments, opened trading companies, and extracted raw materials (Figure 19.8). France and Britain claimed the best lands; Germany

and Italy had to settle for the more barren, less commercially desirable areas (Map 19.1). In the Far East, the Europeans, the United States, and Japan competed for colonies in the South Pacific and trading rights in China (Map 19.2).

Imperialism fomented many crises, particularly in Africa, but none led to war on European soil. In this mostly tranquil climate, Europeans came to believe that peace depended on a complex set of secret alliances among the major powers. These diplomatic agreements, reinforced by powerful armies and navies, had originated after the Franco-Prussian War in 1871. By 1914 Europe was divided into two armed camps—France, Great Britain, and Russia (the Triple Entente) against Germany, Austria-Hungary, and Italy (the Triple Alliance) (Map 19.3).

LEARNING THROUGH MAPS

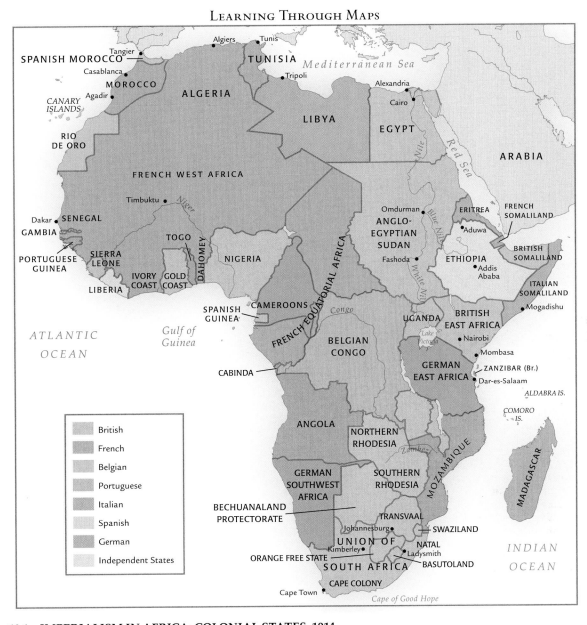

Map 19.1   IMPERIALISM IN AFRICA: COLONIAL STATES, 1914
This map shows Europe's colonies in Africa on the eve of World War I. 1. *Notice* the
movement of Europeans from the coastal lands of Africa in Map 15.1, Expansion of
Europe, to the founding of colonies across the continent in this map. 2. *Identify* the
holdings of the European powers. 3. *Which* country had the largest number of colonies?
Which country had the smallest number? 4. *Locate* centers of potential conflict among
the colonial powers. 5. *Which* two countries remained independent of European control?
Source: Felix Gilbert, *The End of the European Era, 1890 to the Present.* New York: Norton, 1970, p. 23.

THE OUTBREAK OF WORLD WAR I   In June 1914, an incident
took place in Sarajevo (in modern Bosnia and Herze-
govina) for which diplomacy had no peaceful remedy:
the assassination of the heir to the Austro-Hungarian
throne, Archduke Francis Ferdinand (1863–1914). The
Austrians were convinced that Serbia, a Balkan state
and an ally of Russia, was behind the murder of the

crown prince. They demanded a full apology and
punishment of the guilty parties. Serbia's reply proved
unsatisfactory and Austria declared war.

Austria's action set in motion the mobilization plans
required by the alliance system. Frantic efforts to restore peace failed. By August 4, 1914, Russia, France, and
Britain were fighting Germany and Austria-Hungary

LEARNING THROUGH MAPS

Map 19.2   IMPERIALISM IN ASIA: COLONIAL STATES, 1914
This map shows Europe's expansion into Asia on the eve of World War I. 1. *Compare* the small presence of Europeans in Asia in Map 15.1, Expansion of Europe, with their extensive holdings in this map. 2. *Identify* holdings of the European powers. 3. *Notice* that China, Japan, and the United States have become colonial powers. 4. *Which* country was the dominant colonial power? 5. *What* countries occupied islands in the Pacific Ocean? 6. *Which* continent, Africa in Map 19.1 or Asia in this map, was more subject to European occupation?
Source: Felix Gilbert, *The End of the European Era, 1890 to the Present.* New York: Norton, 1970, pp. 24–25.

LEARNING THROUGH MAPS

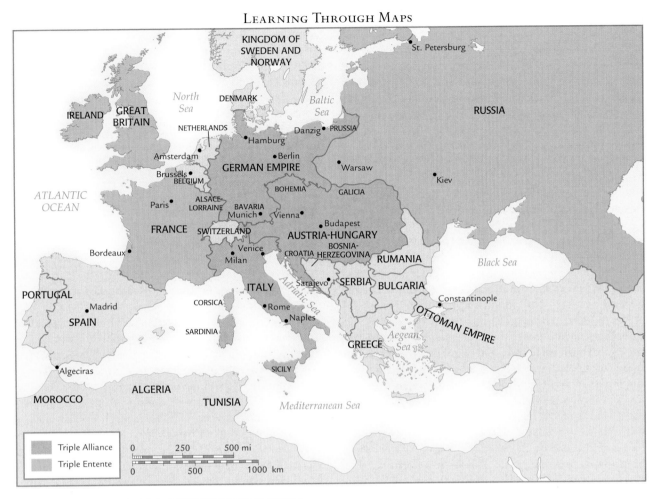

Map 19.3 EUROPE ON THE EVE OF WORLD WAR I
This map shows the political divisions in Europe in 1914. 1. *Identify* the member states of the Triple Alliance and the Triple Entente. 2. *Which* of the two alliances would have the geographic advantage when defending its member states? 3. *Which* small states might become battlegrounds if war broke out between the two alliances? 4. *Locate* Sarajevo, the city where an incident occurred that set off World War I. 5. *Notice* the lost lands of the Ottoman Empire and the creation of nation-states on this map, compared with the same territories in Map 18.2, Europe in 1871.

while Italy watched from the sidelines. Modern life—symbolized by huge armies, military technology, and industrial might—had plunged Europe and, later, much of the world into the bloodiest war that civilization had yet witnessed.

EARLY MODERNISM

As the age of modernism began, many in the West believed that a golden era had dawned. This sanguine outlook was fueled by the spread of self-government, advances in science and technology, and a rise in the standard of living that held the promise of unlimited moral and material progress for humanity. As a result,

a passion for novelty and a desire to cast off the dead hand of the past characterized the era.

However, a mood of uncertainty began to creep into early modernism and undermined its optimism. Artists and thinkers, for whom rebellion was a primary response to the world, questioned traditional Western ethics, religion, and values. They expressed their doubts chiefly through constant experimentation, through a desire to return to aesthetic fundamentals, and, especially among the painters, through a belief that the art process itself is more valuable than the completed work. As the pace of events accelerated around them, a vigorous **avant-garde,** or vanguard, of writers, artists, and intellectuals pushed Western culture toward an elusive, uncertain future (see Figure 19.2).

Philosophy, Psychology, and Religion

As the century closed, new directions in philosophy and psychology reshaped these disciplines, fostered the growth of modernism, and undercut cherished Western beliefs that dated from the Enlightenment— ideas about human rationality, universal moral order, and personal freedom. The creators of these seminal innovations were Friedrich Nietzsche, Sigmund Freud, and Carl Jung. At the same time, mainstream and popular religion, though largely impervious to these intellectual trends, struggled to hew to traditional values and beliefs as society grew more secular.

NIETZSCHE The German philosopher Friedrich Nietzsche [NEE-chuh] (1844–1900), a prophet of modernism, was notorious for his corrosive thought. He saw beyond the optimism of his times and correctly predicted the general disasters, both moral and material, that would afflict Western culture in the twentieth century. To him, the philosophies of the past were all false because they were built on nonexistent absolute principles. Denying moral certainty, Nietzsche asserted that he was the philosopher of the "perhaps," deliberately cultivating ambiguity. Nietzsche vehemently rejected middle-class and Judeo-Christian ideals, identifying them with "herd" or "slave" values. For the same reason, he heaped scorn on many of the "isms" of his day— liberalism, socialism, and Marxism—claiming that they appealed to humanity's lowest common denominator and were thus destroying Western civilization.

Nevertheless, there were affirmative, positive aspects to Nietzsche's thought. He believed in a new morality that glorified human life, creativity, and personal heroism. He forecast the appearance of a few *Übermenschen,* or supermen, who had the "will to power," the primeval urge to live beyond the herd and its debased values. He praised these supermen for living "beyond good and evil," for refusing to be bound by society's rules and mores.

Virtually unknown when he died, Nietzsche became one of the giants of twentieth-century thought. His radical thinking—notably in affirming that civilization itself is nothing more than a human invention—has touched nearly every phase of modern thought, including religion, philosophy, literary criticism, and psychology. His glorification of individualism was an especially powerful stimulus to artists, writers, and musicians. An extreme individualist, he was contemptuous of the strong German state, though the Nazis in the 1930s used his writings to justify their theory of Aryan supremacy.

FREUD AND JUNG Rather than making a blanket condemnation of human morality and behavior, the Austrian Sigmund Freud [FROID] (1856–1939) offered an approach to human psychology that could be used for further explorations into the study of the self. Part of the circle of intellectuals and artists who flourished in Vienna around 1900, Freud, a neurologist, invented a new way of thinking about human nature that profoundly affected Western society.

Freud's analysis of the human mind challenged the Enlightenment's belief that human beings are fully rational. Freud argued that the human personality is the product of an intense internal struggle between instinctual drives and social reality. According to Freud, each psyche, or self, is composed of an id, a superego, and an ego. The *id* is the source of primitive, instinctual drives and desires, notably sex and aggression. The *superego* corresponds to the will of society internalized as the conscience. The *ego* represents the conscious public face that emerges from the conflict between the inborn instincts and the conscience and acts as the balancing component that establishes inner resolutions. In Freud's view, a true, lasting equilibrium among the three components of the psyche cannot be reached; the internal struggle is constant and inescapable. Those in whom the imbalance is pronounced suffer varying degrees of mental illness, ranging from mild neurosis to extreme psychosis. Even though Freud's theory tends toward determinism, he had hope for human freedom. For those who accepted their inescapable limitations, he believed that the truth about the human condition would liberate them from damaging habits of thought and enable them to function as morally free individuals—that is, free to make moral choices in full knowledge of the consequences of their actions.

Freud's greatest achievement was the founding of psychoanalysis, a school of thought, which includes (1) a procedure for investigating the mind's processes that are otherwise unavailable, (2) a method, based on that investigation, for treating mental disorders, and (3) a body of psychological data obtained from these studies, which collectively establish a new scientific discipline. This school of thought is dedicated to the principle that once the roots of neurotic behavior are unraveled, a patient can lead a freer, healthier life. As part of psychoanalysis, Freud devised the "free association" therapy whereby his patients were asked to say, spontaneously and without inhibition, whatever came into their minds—memories, random observations, anything at all—and thus uncover traumas buried in their unconscious. He also studied his patients' dreams, which he thought were forms of wish fulfillment, a theory he set forth in *The Interpretation of Dreams* (1899). Freud's influence is pervasive today in Western culture, but critics have recently called into question not only his conclusions but his ethics as well.

A challenge was made to Freud's views by a former associate, the Swiss psychologist Carl Jung [YOONG] (1875–1961). Jung developed a theory of a universal, collective unconscious, shared by all humans, that exists in conjunction with each individual's "personal" unconscious. Jung speculated that the secrets of the unconscious could be revealed by studying archetypes, ancient images that occur again and again in human experience and appear in dreams, myths, and folktales. His conception of archetypes opened a rich source of images and subjects for many modernist artists and writers. Despite their differences, however, Freud and Jung agreed that the conscious mind is only a very small part of individual personality—a belief that is a cornerstone of modernism.

RELIGIOUS DEVELOPMENTS The 1870–1914 era was one of the last periods in which religious values continued to motivate all levels of society. Evangelicalism, with its focus on personal salvation and faith-based truth, remained in control of mainline American Protestantism—Baptist, Congregational, Methodist, and Presbyterian—along with English Methodism. However, that changed in the 1880s, when adherents to the **Social Gospel**—stressing social betterment rather than personal piety—began to dominate mainline faiths. Social reform, rooted in Jesus's social teachings and the Jewish prophets' call for social justice (see Chapter 5), had always been a secondary goal of the evangelicals (see Chapter 17), but now it became the primary tenet of the mainline churches. The religious equivalent of progressive politics, the Social Gospel taught Americans that the evils of industrialism could be ameliorated through social outreach projects, such as settlement houses and soup kitchens. In Europe, a similar development emerged in Inner Mission, a Lutheran program aimed at helping the industrial poor. Believers in the Social Gospel were called liberal Christians, because their optimistic outlook drew on key liberal ideas of the Enlightenment: free will, reason, and progress (see Chapter 16).

Contemporary evangelicals felt their faith betrayed by the rise of liberal Christianity in the United States. Thus, after 1880, a wing of the evangelical movement transformed itself, becoming the **fundamentalist** movement. The fundamentalists held fast to certain basic beliefs: the inerrancy of the Holy Bible, the need to be "born again," the truth of miracles, and the belief in the resurrection. In a broad sense, the fundamentalists are John Wesley's children, because like the founder of Methodism, they insisted on personal sanctification. Having lost control of mainline Protestantism, the fundamentalists founded an array of new sects, including the Church of God (1886), the Pen-tecostal Church (1901), the Church of God in Christ (1901)—a black Pentecostal church—and the Assemblies of God (1913). These churches, as well as other fundamentalist sects, shared the practice of "speaking in tongues," as a sign of the Holy Spirit's presence—derived from I Corinthians 12:8–10.

Meanwhile, in Europe the Roman Catholic Church's strong stance against modern ideas (see Chapter 18) helped bring on the *Kulturkampf* (German, "culture war"), from 1871 to 1878, between Germany and the Vatican. With Germany unified, the Protestant chancellor Otto von Bismarck feared meddling by the church, especially on the part of Bavaria, a Catholic-majority state in southern Germany. Thus, he pushed legislation through the Reichstag, or parliament, that was pointedly aimed at Catholic citizens, such as weakening church power over education, making civil marriages mandatory, and expelling the Jesuit order from Germany. His plan failed, as Catholic representatives increased their numbers in the Reichstag, and, on the election of a new pope, Bismarck made peace with the church. Still, some German laws stayed in effect, such as the state's oversight of priests and the expulsion of the Jesuits, until 1917.

Although the 1878 compromise ended Germany's *Kulturkampf*, the popes thereafter until 1914 pursued a wavering policy toward new ideas and the upheavals in politics, economics, and society. On the one hand, they held the line against innovative ideas, such as by condemning **Modernism** (1907), a liberal movement within Catholicism (1850–1910), which applied new findings in history, philosophy, and psychology to church teachings. And, on the other hand, while opposing both socialism and the excesses of laissez-faire capitalism, the popes encouraged specific social reforms that led to social action, conducted by priests and lay Catholics in both Europe and overseas.

Literature

Three overlapping and contradictory styles characterize early modern literature: naturalism, decadence, and expressionism. **Naturalism** was inspired by the methods of science and the insights of sociology to focus on such issues as working-class unrest and women's rights. Naturalistic writers, while striving for objectivity, tended to depict industrial society in harsh terms. **Decadent** writers rejected material values, scorned science, and mocked bourgeois society, which they identified with respectability and mediocrity. **Expressionism** was built on the premise that bourgeois culture had robbed the arts of their capacity to express the truth and thus new methods and forms of expression must

Timeline 19.1   EARLY MODERNISM

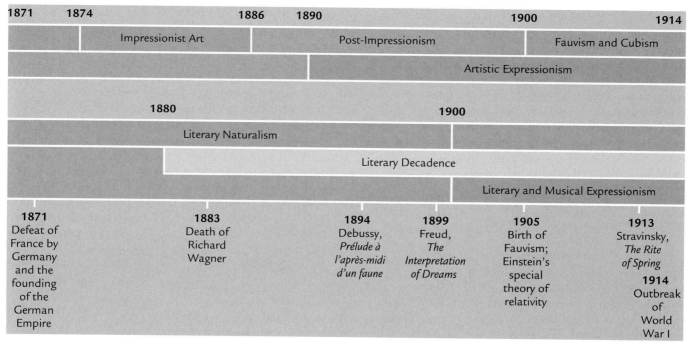

be found. To some degree, the three styles share a disdain for middle-class life and values (Timeline 19.1).

NATURALISTIC LITERATURE   The founder and chief exponent of naturalism was Émile Zola [ZOH-luh] (1840–1902), the French writer whose fame rests on the *Rougon-Macquart* series (1870–1893), twenty novels depicting the history of a single family under France's Second Empire. The novels treat socially provocative themes such as prostitution (*Nana,* 1880) and the horrifying conditions in the coal-mining industry (*Germinal,* 1884). They offer a richly detailed portrait of French society in the mid–nineteenth century and also illustrate Zola's belief in biological determinism. Whether the novels' characters became prostitutes or virtuous housewives, family men or drunken suicides, Zola traces their ultimate fates to inborn dispositions. Nevertheless, Zola was no rigid fatalist. His novels convincingly portray people fervently trying to control their destinies in an uncaring universe.

Another outstanding naturalist was the Norwegian playwright Henrik Ibsen (1828–1906), who pioneered the **problem play,** dealing with social issues. The problem play became the staple of the modern theater and Ibsen remains its most eloquent practitioner. Ibsen lived mainly in Germany and Italy, writing about the middle-class Norwegian world he had fled, treating with frankness such previously taboo themes as venereal disease, suicide, and the decay of Christian values.

In *A Doll's House* (1879), Ibsen questions a wife's subservient role in a traditional marriage. When the play begins, the wife Nora is treated by her husband Torvald as a charming child whose sole purpose is to amuse him. When Nora borrows money to save Torvald's life, she keeps it secret, because she knows how "painful and humiliating" it would be for him to know he owed her anything. But his reaction when he finds out—condemning her bitterly and then forgiving her like a father—makes her realize she is living with a stranger. Faced with such lack of understanding, she deserts both husband and family, closing the door on bourgeois "decency." The unconventional ending created a scandal when the play was first performed. Eventually, *A Doll's House* became an international success, and its liberated heroine became the symbol of the new woman of the late 1800s.

The preeminent naturalistic writer from eastern Europe was the Russian Anton Chekhov [CHEK-ahf] (1860–1904), a physician turned playwright and short-story writer, who found his subject in the suffocating life of Russia's small towns. He peopled his gently ironic plays with men and women in anguish over their ordinary lives, although his most arresting characters are those who endure disappointment without overt complaint. It is this latter quality that has made Chekhov's comedies, as these bittersweet plays are called, such favorites of both actors and audiences.

The Three Sisters (1901), a play that dramatizes the uneventful lives of a landowning family confined to the drab provinces, is characteristic of Chekhov's work. The characters conceal their depression behind false gaiety and self-deceit. His heroines, the three sisters, are bored, restless, and frustrated, not quite resigned to their mediocre existence. They talk constantly of a trip to Moscow, a journey longed for but never made. Today, Chekhov's plays suggest the dying world of Russia's out-of-touch ruling class, who were about to be swept away by the Marxist revolution of 1917.

An important naturalistic writer in the United States was Kate Chopin [SHO-pan] (born Catherine O'Flaherty; 1851–1904), a short-story writer and novelist whose fiction reflected the trend in nineteenth-century American literature away from romanticism and toward realism and naturalism. A frequent theme in Chopin's writings was a romantic awakening, usually by a female character. The setting was sketched out in **local color,** or regional details, and her method of tracking the action was naturalistic—that is, she based plot twists on biological and socioeconomic factors. A St. Louis native, Chopin focused her stories and novels on **Creole** and **Cajun** life in Louisiana, two ethnic groups rooted in the southern part of that state, a world that caught her imagination during a twelve-year-long marriage to a Creole planter and merchant.

The Awakening (1899) was Kate Chopin's masterpiece and the novel that abruptly ended her literary career, as she was stunned into silence by a hostile public reaction. A tale of adulterous passion, this novel is an American *Madame Bovary* (see Chapter 18). The story of Edna Pontellier, the Kentucky-born wife of a Creole husband, *The Awakening* explores a woman's passionate nature and its relation to self, marriage, and society. Edna rejects conventional morality, social duty, and personal obligations to her husband and children. She establishes her own home, earns money with her painting, accepts one lover, and pursues another. Ultimately, however, Edna's bid for freedom fails. She drowns herself—brought down by tradition, prejudice, and other societal pressures. Chopin's ending has been criticized for its shift to commonplace morality, but the novel nevertheless is an early attempt to deal with the issue of women's liberation. More than a simple naturalist, Chopin is hailed today as a precursor of postmodernism (see Chapter 22) because of her keen interest in marginal people and feminist themes.

DECADENCE IN LITERATURE The decadent movement began in France with Joris-Karl Huysmans [wees-MAHNS] (1848–1907), a follower of Zola's, who in 1884 broke with the social-documentary style of naturalism and wrote the perverse novel *À rebours (Against Nature)*. Paris was astonished by this partly autobiographical work. In it, Huysmans presents an exotic hero, Des Esseintes, bristling with eccentricity and neurotic feelings and yet filled with inexpressible spiritual yearnings. Des Esseintes, deploring modern life for its vulgarity and materialism, creates an encapsulated, silent world where he cultivates artificial pleasures. He collects plants whose very nature is to appear diseased. He stimulates his senses with unusual sounds, colors, and smells, orchestrating them to music so that he experiences a sensory overload. And, in a violent rejection of classicism, he embraces the crude Latin writings of late Rome.

In Great Britain, Oscar Wilde (1854–1900) was the center of the 1890s decadent movement, with its generally relaxed view of morals and cynically amused approach to life (Figure 19.9). As with Huysmans, Wilde's outrageous manner can scarcely be separated from his literary achievements. Dressed in velvet and carrying a lily as he sauntered down London's main streets, Wilde gained notoriety as an **aesthete**—one unusually sensitive to the beautiful in art, music, and literature—even before he achieved fame as a dramatist of witty comedies of manners, such as *The Importance of Being Earnest* (1895). Wilde's only novel, *The Picture of Dorian Gray* (1894), features a hero immersed in exotic pleasures and secret vices, his youth preserved while his portrait ages horribly.

Today's most widely admired Decadent writer, the Frenchman Marcel Proust [PROOST] (1871–1922), made his appearance at the end of this period. Starting in 1913 and concluding in 1927, Proust published a series of seven autobiographical novels collectively titled *À la recherche du temps perdu (Remembrance of Things Past)*. In this massive undertaking, he re-creates the world of upper bourgeois society that he had known as a young man but had deserted in 1903. Withdrawn into a cork-lined retreat reminiscent of Des Esseintes' silent hideaway in *À rebours*, Proust resurrected in the pages of his novels the aristocratic salons, the vulgar bourgeois world, and a sordid collection of mistresses, prostitutes, and rich homosexuals. Proust's wider concerns brilliantly echo the new scientific theories of his time: the inner workings of the human mind, as in Freudian psychoanalysis, and the relativity of time, as in Einstein's universe. Today, Proust's novels may be read in contradictory ways, as the supreme expression of a life lived for art or as the embodiment of a life empty of spiritual purpose.

EXPRESSIONIST LITERATURE Expressionism, unlike the other two styles, did not originate in France. Instead, it arose in Scandinavia in the works of the Swedish playwright August Strindberg and in central Europe in the fiction of Franz Kafka. Strindberg (1849–1912), having first earned fame through naturalistic plays, shifted to an expressionist style in the 1890s. *The Dream Play* (1907) is typical of his expressionist dramas in

Figure 19.9 Aubrey Beardsley. *Salomé with the Head of John the Baptist: The Climax.* Illustration from "Salome" by Oscar Wilde. 1893. Line block print. Private Collection. The Stapleton Collection. *The visual counterpart to Wilde's decadent style in literature was art nouveau, especially as practiced by Aubrey Beardsley. Typical of his work is this black-and-white illustration for Wilde's play-poem* Salomé, *based on the biblical story of the dancer. In this print, Salomé holds the severed head of John the Baptist, whose death she had ordered, and gazes into his face. While the print focuses on the heads of Salomé and John the Baptist, the viewer's attention is also drawn to the ghastly image in the lower-right corner where the dripping blood forms a pool in which two flowers grow. Blending organic shapes and flowing lines with perverse themes, Beardsley's artificial style reveals art nouveau's affinity with an underworld of depravity.*

employing generic figures with symbolic, all-purpose names ("Daughter," "Father," and so on), shadowy plots, and absurd fancies. In *The Dream Play,* time and place become meaningless, as, for instance, when a lovesick soldier suddenly becomes old and shabby and his bouquet of flowers withers before the audience's eyes. Strindberg's innovative techniques were meant not to obscure his meaning but rather to initiate the public into new ways of seeing and understanding life.

The finest exponent of expressionism was Franz Kafka (1883–1924), whose strange, symbolic stories question traditional views of reality. Perhaps Kafka's most striking work is the short story *Metamorphosis* (1919), in which the hero awakens to discover that he has been turned into a giant insect—a vivid image of an identity crisis and a gripping parable of what happens when a person is suddenly perceived to be different from other people.

Kafka's *The Trial,* a novel completed in 1914 and published in 1925, features a doomed main character with the generic name of Joseph K. An obscure government official, Joseph K. has his well-ordered world shattered when he is accused of a nameless crime. Unable to identify either his accusers or his misdeed and denied justice by the authorities, Joseph K. is eventually convicted by a mysterious court and executed by two bureaucrats in top hats. Kafka's faceless, powerless hero has become one of the most widely discussed figures of modernism. In effect, Kafka transformed his own alienation—as a German-speaking Jew from the Czech-speaking, Protestant section of predominantly Roman Catholic Austria—into a modern Everyman victimized by forces beyond human control (Figure 19.10).

The Advance of Science

Biology and chemistry made rapid advances during this period. In biology, the Austrian monk Gregor Johann Mendel (1822–1884) had finished his groundbreaking research in 1865, but his findings, the basis for the new science of genetics, were ignored until three researchers, working independently, rediscovered his reports in 1900. Mendel proved the existence of dominant and recessive traits, and using the laws of probability, worked out the pattern for offspring over the generations. Subsequent research showed that Mendelian laws applied to virtually all animals and plants.

The founder of the new discipline, radiochemistry, was Marie Sklodowska Curie (1867–1934), a Polish physicist and the first scientist to be awarded two Nobel Prizes. Working with her French husband, Pierre Curie (1859–1906), Madame Curie identified two new radioactive elements, polonium and radium. The isolation of radium stimulated research in atomic physics. Another contributor to radiochemistry was the German physicist Wilhelm Conrad Roentgen [RENT-guhn] (1845–1923), whose 1895 discovery of X-rays led to their use in diagnostic medicine.

The discoveries in genetics and radiochemistry boosted the period's optimism and faith in progress, but experimentations in physics had the opposite effect, adding to the undercurrent of uncertainty and doubt that also existed. Three brilliant scientists—Max Planck, Niels Bohr, and Albert Einstein—launched a

Figure 19.10 EDVARD MUNCH. *The Scream.* 1893. Oil on canvas, 36 × 29". Nasjonalgalleriet, Oslo. *The expressionists, whether writers, artists, or musicians, responded to the uncertainty of the modern world with images of despair, anxiety, and helplessness. The work of the Norwegian painter Edvard Munch provides a visual counterpart to the bleak and brooding plays of Strindberg and the terrifying stories of Kafka. Munch, whose paintings reflect a nightmarish vision of life as a tormented existence never free from pain, once said, "I hear the scream in nature." The Scream is a visual metaphor of modern alienation. The skull-headed, sexless figure, with mouth open and hands over ears, seems to be ignored by the couple walking away in the background. In a way typical of expressionism, Munch depicts the world as unnatural, as evidenced by the painting's swirling patterns of lines and colors. Masked and armed thieves stole Munch's* Scream *from its museum setting in 2004, and police recovered it, slightly damaged but repairable, in 2006.*

wave-theory physics, he realized the revolutionary nature of his discovery. Planck's quantum theory became a primary building block in the speculation of the second of the trio, Danish physicist Niels Bohr.

Bohr (1885–1962) was the prime mover in solving the mystery of the structure of the atom. When he began his research, the Greek idea of the indivisible atom had already been discarded. Scientists in the early 1900s had proved that each atom is a neutral body containing a positive nucleus with negatively charged particles called electrons. And one researcher had speculated that electrons orbit a nucleus in much the same way that the planets move around the sun—suggesting a correspondence with Newtonian theory.

Until Bohr's theory of atomic structure was set forth in 1912, however, no one could explain how these miniature solar systems actually worked. Bohr's solution was based on bold assumptions: that an electron could revolve about a nucleus only in certain privileged orbits and that, when it is in these orbits, it does not emit radiation. He concluded that an electron radiates only when it leaps from orbit to orbit. Using Planck's quantum theory, he called these leaps "quantum jumps," referring to the amount of radiative energy released. Bohr's discovery had tremendous consequences, leading eventually to the development of nuclear energy for weaponry and electrical generation.

German-born Albert Einstein (1879–1955) also did important theoretical work in atomic physics, but his most significant research in the early 1900s involved the relationship between time and space. Newton had maintained that there existed absolute rest and absolute velocity, absolute space and absolute time. Einstein asserted that the only absolute in the universe is the speed of light, which is the same for all observers. He concluded that all motion is relative and that concepts of absolute space and time are meaningless. If two systems move with relatively uniform motion toward each other, there exist two different spaces and two different times. He called this finding the special theory of relativity. This theory replaces Newtonian absolute space with a grid of light beams that in effect determines the meaning of space in each situation. Einstein's special theory was the first step in a reformulation of scientific concepts of space and time.

The Modernist Revolution in Art

After 1871 a revolution began in the arts and architecture that aimed to replace Renaissance ideals with modernist principles. Although there were many trends within this revolution, in painting and sculpture it generally meant a shift from an art that reflected the natural world to one rooted in the artist's inner vision, from

revolution that led other scientists to discard the previously accepted belief that Newton's laws of motion were universal.

Max Planck (1858–1947) laid the foundation for modern physics in 1900 with research in quantum theory. His research called into question the wave theory of radiation, which dated from the 1700s. Working with hot objects, Planck observed that the radiative energy that emanated from a heat source issued not in a smooth wave but in discrete bursts. He measured each burst of radiation and computed a mathematical formula for expressing the released energy, a unit that he called a *quantum*—a word meaning a specified amount, derived from the Latin *quanta*, or "how much." When Planck could not fit his quantum formula into traditional

an art based on representational or naturalistic images to one devoted to nonrepresentational or nonobjective forms, and from an art focused on content to one dedicated to the process of creation itself. By the time the revolution in painting and sculpture was complete, artists had given up realism and made abstraction their ideal. In architecture, the modernist revolution was less radical, though architects slowly turned away from Greco-Roman and Gothic styles and created functional buildings devoid of decoration.

IMPRESSIONISM   The stylistic innovation in painting known as **impressionism** began in the 1870s. Despite owing much to previous styles, "the new painting"—as one French critic labeled the new style—marked a genuine break with the realistic tradition that had dominated Western art since the 1300s. The impressionists chose to depict what they saw in nature, but they were inspired by the fast pace of modern life to portray transient moments. They concentrated on the play of light over objects, breaking up seemingly solid surfaces, stressing vivid contrasts between colors in sunlight and shade, and depicting reflected light in all its possibilities. Unlike earlier artists, they abandoned the studio, painting in the open air and recording spontaneous impressions of their subjects instead of making sketches outside and then moving indoors to complete the work from memory. Their painting methods were influenced by technological advances: the shift from the studio to the open air was made possible by the

advent of cheap rail travel, which allowed easy access to the countryside or seashore, and by the discovery of chemical dyes and oils that allowed paint to be kept in metal tubes, which artists could carry with them, along with portable easels.

Although impressionism was a product of industrial society, it was at the same time indebted to the past. From realism the impressionist painters learned to find beauty in the everyday world. From the Barbizon painters (a group of French landscape painters active in the mid–nineteenth century), they took the practice of painting in the open air. From the romantics they borrowed the techniques of "broken color"—splitting up complex colors into their basic hues—and of using subtle color shadings to create a shimmering surface effect (see Chapter 18).

Impressionism acquired its name not from supporters but from angry art lovers who felt threatened by the new painting. The term *impressionism* was born in 1874, when a group of artists organized an exhibition of their paintings. Reaction from the public and the press was immediate, and derisive. Among the 165 paintings exhibited was *Impression: Sunrise,* by Claude Monet [moh-NAY] (1840–1926). Viewed through hostile eyes, Monet's painting of a rising sun over a misty, watery scene seemed messy, slapdash, and an affront to good taste (Figure 19.11). Borrowing Monet's title, art critics extended the term *impressionism* to the entire exhibit. In response, Monet and his twenty-nine fellow artists in the exhibit adopted the name as a badge of their

Figure 19.11 CLAUDE MONET. *Impression: Sunrise.* 1872. Oil on canvas, 19½ × 25½". Musée Marmottan, Paris. *Monet's* Impression: Sunrise *illustrates the immediacy of impressionism. From his window overlooking Le Havre harbor, Monet painted what he recorded in a letter to a friend: "sun in the mist and a few masts of boats sticking up in the foreground." The artist has transformed the substantial world of nature into fragmented daubs of broken color.*

unity, despite individual differences. From then until 1886, impressionism had all the zeal of a "church," as the painter Renoir put it. The impressionists gave eight art shows. Monet was faithful to the impressionist creed until his death, although many of the other impressionists moved on to new styles.

Monet wanted to re-create the optical sensations he experienced. Rejecting traditional content, he focused on light and atmosphere, simulating the visual effects of fog, haze, or mist over a landscape and, especially, over water. That this approach succeeded so well shows the harmony between Monet's scientific eye and painterly hand. His studies of changing light and atmosphere, whether depicting haystacks, the Rouen cathedral, or water lilies (Figure 19.12), demonstrate Monet's lifelong devotion to impressionism.

Figure 19.12 CLAUDE MONET. *Waterlily Pond (Le Bassin des Nymphéas).* 1904. Oil on canvas, 34½ × 35¾". Denver Art Museum. *Knowledgeable about the art market and determined to escape a life of poverty, Monet produced nonthreatening works that appealed to conservative middle-class collectors. For these patrons, he painted natural scenes, such as water lilies, that evoked pleasant memories of simple rural values. Begun in 1899, the water lily series occupied him for the rest of his life. Setting up his easel in his splendid garden at Giverny and working at different times of the day, Monet captured the effect of changing sunlight on this beloved subject.*

Figure 19.13   AUGUSTE RENOIR. *The Luncheon of the Boating Party.* 1881. Oil on canvas, 51 × 68″. The Phillips Collection, Washington, D.C. *Renoir's return to traditional values is reflected in this vivid painting. He uses the restaurant's terrace to establish conventional perspective, the left railing forming a diagonal line that runs into the distance. He balances the composition, weaving the young men and women into a harmonious ensemble, painting some standing and others sitting. He also employs colors effectively, using orange, blue, and black to offset the expanses of white in the tablecloth and the men's shirts and women's blouses.*

Unlike Monet, Auguste Renoir [REN-wahr] (1841–1919) did not remain faithful to the impressionist movement. In the early 1880s, personal and aesthetic motives led him to move away from impressionism and exhibit in the official Salon (when he could get his work accepted). In his modified style, he shifted from a soft-focus image to a concentration on form, a move that brought quick support from art critics and wealthy patrons.

Painted about the time of his break with impressionism, *The Luncheon of the Boating Party* demonstrates Renoir's splendid mastery of form (Figure 19.13). Its subject is a carefree summer outing on a restaurant terrace on an island in the Seine, the company being composed of the painter's friends, including fellow artists, a journalist, the café owner, and an actress. *The Boating*

Party shows that Renoir had not given up—nor would he ever—his impressionist ties, for his stress in this work on the fleeting, pleasure-filled moment was basic to the style, as was his use of broken color in a natural background. Nevertheless, what remained central to Renoir's creed were the foreground figures, treated clearly and with substance.

In contrast to Monet and Renoir, whose careers bloomed in poverty, Berthe Morisot [mohr-ee-ZOH] (1841–1895) was a member of the upper middle class. Her wealth and artistic connections—Fragonard was her grandfather and Manet her brother-in-law—allowed her to apply herself to painting and play an important role in the founding of the impressionist movement. In her work, she focused on atmosphere and the play of light on the human form, although she never sacrificed

Figure 19.14   BERTHE MORISOT. *The Harbor at Lorient*. 1869. Oil on canvas, 17⅛ × 28¾″. National Gallery of Art, Washington, D.C. Ailsa Mellon Bruce Collection. *Morisot painted in open air this harbor scene at Lorient on the Bay of Biscay in Brittany, while visiting there. The sky, clouds, ships, and houses are reflected in the water. The lady, sitting alone and lost in thought, looks down at the wall while shading herself with a fashionable parasol. The muted browns of the seawall set off the woman's white dress with its pinkish overtone, and the darkish colors of her hat are repeated in the brown to black colors in the ships' hulls. The painting's design—the diagonal line of the seawall on the right; the parallel diagonal line of the houses and trees on the left; and the horizontal line of the ships' masts and house rooflines in the middle distance—creates a harbor pool in the foreground and reinforces the vastness of the sky. Morisot's quick brushwork gives the painting a feeling of immediacy and intimacy—the aim of impressionism. She signed her name, B. Morisot, on the seawall.*

her subjects to the cause of color alone. Her subjects were modern life, from urban workers to the confined world of domestic interiors and gardens and smartly dressed ladies out for a stroll (Figure 19.14).

A few Americans also made contributions to impressionism. The most important of them was Mary Cassatt [kuh-SAT] (1845–1926), a young woman who joined the impressionist circle while studying painting in Paris. Hailing from a prosperous, well-connected Philadelphia family, Cassatt urged her wealthy friends to collect the new art. Because of her influence, some of the most notable impressionist paintings are now in American museums. Cassatt, however, was not devoted exclusively to impressionism. Like other artists of this era, she was fascinated by Japanese prints that were on exhibit in Paris in 1890, and she was the first to imitate all aspects, including color, of the **ukiyo-e**

[oo-key-yoh-AY] prints—the woodcuts that had developed in Japan in the 1600s—as in *The Bath*, or *The Tub* (about 1891; Figure 19.15). A mother and child were a typical subject in Cassatt's art.

POST-IMPRESSIONISM   The rebellious, experimental spirit instilled by the impressionists had freed art from the tyranny of a single style. Artists now moved in varied directions, united only by a common desire to extend the boundaries of impressionism. This ambition signified the triumph of the modernist notion that art must constantly change in order to reflect new historical conditions—the opposite of the classical ideal of eternal truths. Impressionism was succeeded by **postimpressionism** (1886–1900), whose four most important artists were Georges Seurat, Paul Cézanne, Paul Gauguin, and Vincent van Gogh.

Figure 19.15 MARY CASSATT. *The Bath,* or *The Tub.* Ca. 1891. Soft-ground etching with aquatint and drypoint on paper, 12⅜ × 8⅞". National Museum of Women in the Arts, Washington, D.C. *This Cassatt print, in Japanese-inspired style, symbolizes the globalization of Western culture that was well under way in early modernism. The first of ten prints in a series, it is the only one that could be called a true imitation. It uses simple design, Japanese spatial pattern, flat areas of color, and a hint of Japanese facial features to create a Western version of a ukiyo-e print—except that it is made on a metal plate, not a woodblock. In the rest of this series, Cassatt adopted a more Western style, notably adding a complete background, such as wallpaper and windows. Her interest in Japanese prints coincided with Gauguin's experiments (see Figure 19.18) with Tahitian-inspired art. By drawing inspiration from non-Western sources, Cassatt and Gauguin are forerunners of postmodernism.*

Like the impressionists, Georges Seurat [suh-RAH] (1859–1891) painted the ordinary pleasures of Parisian life in a sunlit atmosphere, but his way of doing so was formulaic and theoretical, markedly different from the approach of, say, Monet. After studying scientific color theory, Seurat developed a technique known as **pointillism** (or divisionism), which meant applying to the canvas thousands of tiny dots of pure color juxtaposed in such a way that, when viewed from the proper distance, they merged to form a natural, harmonious effect of color, light, and shade. His most famous pointillist work is *A Sunday Afternoon on the Island of La Grande Jatte* (Figure 19.16), an affectionate, good-humored look at Parisians enjoying themselves. The technique may be novel and "scientific," but the composition is classical and serene, with carefully placed and balanced figures and repeated curved shapes, visible in the umbrellas, hats, and other objects. Seurat's style led to a minor school of painters, but his influence on later developments in art was overshadowed by that of Cézanne.

Paul Cézanne [say-ZAN] (1839–1906), a pivotal figure in Western art, was the prophet of abstraction in postimpressionism and a precursor of cubism. **Abstraction** is the trend in modern art that emphasizes shapes, lines, and colors independent of the natural world. With Édouard Manet, he was one of the founders of modern painting. He exhibited with the original impressionist group in 1874 but by 1878 had rejected the movement because its depiction of nature lacked substance and weight. He sought a new way to portray nature so as to reveal its underlying solidity and order. After experimentation, Cézanne concluded that nature is composed of such geometric forms as cylinders, spheres, cubes, and cones. By trying to reveal this idea in his works, he opened up a new way of painting that has influenced art to the present day.

Cézanne's greatest works came after 1886, when he left Paris for his quiet home in Aix-en-Provence in southern France. Among his favorite subjects was the nearby mountain Mont Sainte-Victoire (Figure 19.17). Like many later works, *Mont Sainte-Victoire* points toward abstraction but never quite gives up representation. Amid the geometric forms in the picture's lower half, house shapes peek through daubs of green foliage, reminding the viewer that this is a realistic landscape. Later artists took up Cézanne's challenge and

Figure 19.16 GEORGES SEURAT. *A Sunday Afternoon on the Island of La Grande Jatte.* 1884–
1886. Oil on canvas, 6′9″ × 10′1″. Art Institute of Chicago. Helen Birch Bartlett Memorial
Collection, 1926. *Unlike most impressionists, Seurat worked slowly and methodically. In the
case of* La Grande Jatte, *he spent years organizing the canvas and then painting the thousands
of dots required by the pointillist technique. Such painstaking attention to detail was necessary to
achieve the harmonious effect his finished paintings demonstrate.*

Figure 19.17 PAUL CÉZANNE. *Mont Sainte-Victoire.* Ca.
1900. Oil on canvas, 30¾ × 39″. Hermitage, St. Petersburg.
*Although Cézanne was the founder of the postimpressionist move-
ment that culminated in abstraction, he had a conservative approach to art. He wanted to create paintings that had the solidity
of the art in the museums, especially the works of the seventeenth-
century painter Nicolas Poussin. Hence, Cézanne continued to
rely on line and geometric arrangement as well as on color and
light, simplifying his paintings into austere images of order and
peaceful color. In this one of sixty paintings of Mont Sainte-
Victoire—visible from his studio in Aix-en-Provence—Cézanne's
closeness to abstract art may be seen. The distant mountain has
a solid presence, but the houses, foliage, fields, and road disappear into a set of ambiguous forms and color planes. Cézanne's
handling of the color planes, with their jagged edges and abrupt
juxtapositions, inspired the cubists to search for a new way to
represent the world.*

ENCOUNTER

The French Impressionists Meet Ukiyo-e Art

Japanese culture became an obsession among Europe's avant-garde in the late 1800s, once diplomatic and commercial relations were reestablished with the island kingdom. Soon there arose among cultural leaders the fashion Japonisme *[ja-pon-eas-muh], a French term meaning "the love of all things Japanese."*

Europeans, except for the Dutch, lost access to Japan in 1638, when Japan's military ruler, the shogun, closed the country to foreigners. Thereafter, the Dutch colony on Deshima, an island in Nagasaki harbor, operated as Japan's window on the world, conducting from there a highly regulated but lucrative two-way trade (see Encounter in Chapter 14). Japan's isolationist policy began to crumble in 1853, in response to American gunboats demanding trade relations. At first, five ports were opened; others soon followed.

With trade renewed, Japanese culture flowed into the West. Especially impressive were woodblock prints, or *ukiyo-e* [oo-key-yoh-AY] ("pictures of the floating world")—then unknown in the West. Executed at first in black and white, ukiyo-e prints entered a golden age with the introduction of color in about 1770. When these prints reached Europe, their simple design and bold colors fascinated the impressionist and postimpressionist painters.

Numerous artists, including Édouard Manet, Claude Monet, Pierre Renoir, Mary Cassatt (see Figure 19.15), Paul Cézanne, and Paul Gauguin, played with Japanese motifs in their works, but Vincent van Gogh had the greatest affinity with the ukiyo-e prints. Van Gogh especially admired and collected the prints of Andō Hiroshige [he-roh-SHE-ge] (1797–1858), with their flat areas of pure color and figures drawn with a few wispy lines. Hiroshige's *Sudden Shower at Ōhashi Bridge at Atake* (Encounter figure 19.1) inspired van Gogh's oil painting *The Bridge in the Rain (After Hiroshige)* (Encounter figure 19.2), one of three studies he made of Japanese prints. Van Gogh did more than "copy" the print; he transformed it by heightening the color contrasts and adding a decorative border. Learning from his ukiyo-e studies, van Gogh forged his own unique style of painting, thus establishing a link between Japanese and Western art.

LEARNING FROM THE ENCOUNTER

1. *What* historic event caused Japan to reopen its doors to the world? 2. *What* role did trade play in this artistic encounter? 3. *Define* ukiyo-e print. 4. *What* was the appeal of ukiyo-e prints to Western artists? 5. *Discuss* the influence of ukiyo-e prints on van Gogh's artistic style. 6. *How* does art contribute to globalization?

---

created the first truly abstract paintings, the most visible signs of twentieth-century art (see Chapter 20).

The postimpressionist Paul Gauguin [go-GAN] (1848–1903) began the movement known as **primitivism**—the term used to describe the West's fascination with non-Western culture as well as pre-Renaissance art. Gauguin's eccentric personal life also made him a legendary figure of modernism. Rejecting Parisian bourgeois life, he abandoned his career and family and exiled himself to the French colony of Tahiti, living a decadent, bohemian existence.

Before moving to the South Pacific, Gauguin lived and painted among Breton peasants, inhabitants of Brittany in western France. He developed a personal style that favored flattened shapes and bright colors and avoided conventional perspective and modeling. He also became interested in non-Western, "primitive" religions, and many of his Tahitian works refer to indigenous beliefs and practices, as in *Manao Tupapau: The Spirit of the Dead Watching* (Figure 19.18). When exhibited in Paris, this painting created an uproar, for Western audiences were not accustomed to seeing dark-skinned nudes in art, and certainly not presented reclining on a bed, a customary pose for female nudes since the Renaissance (see Figure 16.7). Furthermore, the seated ghost at the left was a direct challenge to a secular worldview. Since his day, Gauguin's role in art has been reevaluated. Today, Gauguin is recognized for his introduction of non-Western traditions into Western art, thus enriching its vocabulary, and for his expressive use of color.

With the postimpressionist Vincent van Gogh [van GO] (1853–1890), the tradition of expressionism began to emerge in Western art, although he was not part

Encounter figure 19.1 ANDŌ HIROSHIGE. *Sudden Shower at Ōhashi Bridge at Atake.* Ca. 1857. Woodcut, approx. 13²/₅ × 8⁷/₁₀". *Hiroshige created a new genre, the travelogue print, based on sketches made on the spot, in all weathers and at different times of day.* Sudden Shower at Ōhashi Bridge *is from the series* One Hundred Famous Views of Edo. *He boldly crops the composition, shows the human figures dwarfed by the setting, and uses unusual perspective—typical features of his art.*

Encounter figure 19.2 VINCENT VAN GOGH. *The Bridge in the Rain (After Hiroshige).* 1887. Oil on canvas, approx. 28¾ × 21¼". Van Gogh Museum, Amsterdam (Vincent van Gogh Foundation). *This painting shows the lessons van Gogh learned by copying Hiroshige's* ukiyo-e *print: strong, dark color to outline figures, bold color contrasts, cropping of the composition, and dramatic perspective. Van Gogh made these techniques his own in his later works.*

of any expressionist school. "Expressionism" in van Gogh's case meant that the painting served as a vehicle for his private emotions to an unprecedented degree. He sometimes allowed his moods to determine what colors to use and how to apply paint to canvas, a principle that led to an idiosyncratic style. Van Gogh's life was filled with misfortune, and even his painting had little recognition in his lifetime. In his youth, he was rebuffed in his efforts to do missionary work among poverty-stricken Belgian coal miners. His attempts at friendship ended in failure, including a celebrated episode in the south of France with the painter Gauguin. His overtures to women resulted in utter humiliation. In the end, he became mentally unstable and committed suicide.

From his personal pain, van Gogh created a memorably expressive style. Rejecting the smooth look of tra-

ditional painting and stirred by the colorful canvases of the impressionists, he sometimes applied raw pigments with his palette knife or fingers instead of with a brush. His slashing strokes and brilliant colors mirrored his mental states, giving the viewer a glimpse into his volatile personality. For instance, his *Self-Portrait* strongly suggests mental agitation, through the dominance of the color blue and the swirling lines of paint (Figure 19.19). The anguish in his eyes is reinforced by the vortex of color framing the head and the deep facial lines. As a result, the portrait seethes with emotion.

The most memorable of van Gogh's paintings is *The Starry Night* (Figure 19.20). Executed in the last year of van Gogh's life, the painting depicts a tranquil village under an agitated sky filled with pulsating stars, an unnatural crescent moon, and whirling rivers of light. Intensifying the strange imagery is the grove of cypress

Figure 19.18   PAUL GAUGUIN. *Manao Tupapau: The Spirit of the Dead Watching.* 1892. Oil on burlap mounted on canvas, 28½ × 36⅜". Albright-Knox Art Gallery, Buffalo. A. Conger Goodyear Collection, 1965. *Gauguin wrote of this painting that he wanted to convey the presence of* **tupapau,** *or "the spirit of the dead," as envisioned by the young girl on the bed. He implies her fear through the mixture of the yellow, purple, and blue colors; by the sparks of light, or phosphorescences, which symbolize the spirits of the dead; and by the ghost depicted as an old woman in the left background. He felt it necessary "to make very simple paintings, with primitive, childlike themes" and to use "a minimum of literary means" in order for western Europeans to understand how Tahitians viewed life and death.*

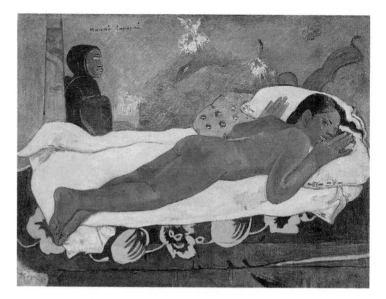

Figure 19.19   VINCENT VAN GOGH. *Self-Portrait.* 1889. Oil on canvas, 25½ × 21¼". Musée d'Orsay, Paris. *Van Gogh's self-absorption is reflected in the thirty-six self-portraits he painted during his eleven-year artistic career. Anguished and prone to mental breakdown, he must have found a measure of reassurance in recording the subtle changes in his own countenance. A constant in all his likenesses is the haunted eyes, showing the inner torment from which he could never quite escape. The very execution of this work demonstrates van Gogh's passionate mood, as in the aggressive brushstrokes that congeal into a radiating pattern of energy lines covering the painting's surface. He painted this self-portrait in 1889, a year before he took his own life.*

trees (left foreground), rendered in the shape of flames. The ensemble of convoluted shapes and bold colors expresses the artist's inner turmoil. In a sense, van Gogh's works constitute his psychological signature; his style is perhaps the most easily recognizable one in Western art.

FAUVISM, CUBISM, AND EXPRESSIONISM   The preeminence of Paris as the hub of Western culture was enhanced by the arrival of Henri Matisse and Pablo Picasso in about 1900. These innovative and prolific artists emerged as the leaders of the pre–World War I generation, later dominating the art world in the twentieth century in much the same way that Ingres and Delacroix had in the nineteenth century.

Henri Matisse [ma-TEES] (1869–1954) rose to fame in 1905 as a leader of **fauvism.** The fauves—French for "wild beasts," a name their detractors gave to them— were a group of loosely aligned painters who exhibited together. Matisse's work, like that of his colleagues, stemmed from the tradition of van Gogh, with color as its overriding concern. In *Open Window, Collioure,* Matisse painted a kaleidoscope of colors—pinks, mauves, bluish greens, bright reds, oranges, and purples—that derive not from the direct observation of nature but, rather, from the artist's belief that color harmonies can control the composition (Figure 19.21). The colors are "arbitrary" in the sense that they bear little resemblance to what one would actually see from the window, but they are far from arbitrary in their relation to one another—which was what interested Matisse.

Pablo Picasso [pih-KAH-so] (1881–1973), a talented young Spanish painter, was attracted to Paris's avant-garde art community in about 1900. In 1907 he proved his genius with *Les Demoiselles d'Avignon (The Young Ladies of Avignon),* perhaps the most influential painting of the twentieth century (Figure 19.22). This revolutionary work moved painting close to abstraction—the

Figure 19.20 VINCENT VAN GOGH. *The Starry Night.* 1889. Oil on canvas, 29 × 36¼". The Museum of Modern Art, New York. Acquired through the Lillie P. Bliss Bequest. Photograph © 1997 The Museum of Modern Art, New York. *Van Gogh's* The Starry Night *is a stunning symbol of the unstable world of early modernism. The whirling, luminous sky, formed with wild patches of color and tormented brushstrokes, reflects the psychic disturbance of the painter—an early example of expressionist art. But van Gogh was more than an artist beset by personal demons; he wanted to follow Delacroix (see Chapters 17 and 18) and depict nature, using color and drawing, without slavishly copying reality. In van Gogh—as in his contemporary, the philosopher Nietzsche—psychic turmoil and artistic vision were inseparable.*

Figure 19.21 HENRI MATISSE. *Open Window, Collioure.* 1905. Oil on canvas, 21¾ × 18⅛". National Gallery of Art, Washington, D.C. Courtesy Mrs. John Hay Whitney, New York. *Like van Gogh, Matisse resisted quiet surface effects, preferring the look of paint applied in thick daubs and strips of varying length. His dazzling optical art was created by his use and placement of vibrant colors. In this painting, Matisse interprets the glorious view from his studio overlooking the Mediterranean.*

Figure 19.22 PABLO PICASSO. *Les Demoiselles d'Avignon (The Young Ladies of Avignon).* Paris (June–July 1907). Oil on canvas, 8' × 7'8". The Museum of Modern Art, New York. Acquired through the Lillie P. Bliss Bequest. Photograph © 1997 The Museum of Modern Art, New York. *This painting's title derives from Picasso's native Barcelona, where Avignon Street ran through the red-light district. First intended as a moral work warning of the dangers of venereal disease (the figures still show provocative poses), the painting evolved over the months, changing as Picasso's horizons expanded. That he left the painting unfinished—like a scientist's record of a failed laboratory experiment—illustrates a leading trait of modernism, the belief that truth is best expressed in the artistic process itself. A recent survey reveals that this painting is the most often reproduced work in art history textbooks.*

realization of Cézanne's dream. An unfinished work, *Les Demoiselles* reflects the multiple influences operating on Picasso at the time—the primitivism of African masks, the geometric forms of Cézanne, and the ancient sculpture of pre-Roman Spain. Despite its radical methods, this painting still has a conventional composition: five figures with a still life in the foreground. Nevertheless, with this painting Picasso redirected objective art beyond abstraction and into the development of nonobjective painting—thus overturning a standard founded in the Renaissance.

Les Demoiselles was the prelude to **cubism,** one of the early-twentieth-century styles leading Western art toward abstraction. With his French colleague Georges Braque [BRAHK] (1882–1963), Picasso developed cubism. This style of painting, which went through different phases at the hands of different artists, basically fragments three-dimensional objects and reassembles them in a pattern that stresses their geometric structure and the relationships of these basic geometric forms. Braque and Picasso worked so closely together

that their paintings could sometimes not be separately identified, even, it is said, by the artists themselves.

With his adoption of cubist methods, Picasso gave up Renaissance space completely, representing the subjects from multiple angles simultaneously and shaping the figures into geometric designs. He later added a new feature to cubism when he applied bits and pieces of other objects to the canvas, a technique called **collage** (French for "pasting"). Collage nudged cubism closer to pure abstraction; the flat plane of the painting's surface was now simply a two-dimensional showcase for objects. *Man with a Hat* (also known as *Portrait of Braque*) shows Picasso's blend of cubist style with collage (Figure 19.23).

Although Paris remained the capital of Western art, other cities were also the scene of aesthetic experiment. Oslo, Munich, Vienna, and Dresden became artistic meccas, especially for expressionist painters who followed the path of van Gogh and the fauves. In Munich, expressionism led to the formation of an international school of artists known as Der Blaue Reiter ("The Blue

Figure 19.23 PABLO PICASSO. *Man with a Hat.* (Also known as *Portrait of Braque.*) Paris (after December 3, 1912). Pasted paper, charcoal and ink on paper, 24 × 19⅝". The Museum of Modern Art, New York. Purchase. Photograph © 1997 The Museum of Modern Art, New York. *This image alludes to the close working relationship between Picasso and Braque. Whether the portrait is of Braque is debatable, especially since Picasso denied it. He claimed he worked without a model and added, "Braque and I [afterwards] pretended it was his portrait." The anecdote stresses the point that both men were less interested in content than creating a new visual reality through nontraditional means.*

Rider"), named after a painting of the same name. Rejecting the importance of artistic content and refusing to paint "safe" objects, this group of painters concentrated on basics such as color and line, which were meant to express inner feelings. Founded by the Russian exile Wassily Kandinsky [kan-DIN-skee] (1866–1944) in 1911, this school made the first breakthrough to **abstract art**—nonrepresentational or nonobjective paintings that defy any sense of reality or connection to nature and are, as the artist himself put it, "largely unconscious, spontaneous expressions of inner character, nonmaterial in nature." Kandinsky's aesthetic vision was to create free forms, possessing no objective content, consisting only of meandering lines and amorphous blobs of color. For all their seeming randomness, however, his paintings were planned to look that way. He consciously worked out the placement of the lines and the choices of color, leaving nothing to chance. He also linked the fluidity of painting with the lyricism of music, a connection suggested in *Panel for Edwin R. Campbell No. 4* (Figure 19.24) by the meandering lines.

In this famous set of four panels representing the seasons of the year, Kandinsky used vivid colors to express his guiding belief that art has a spiritual quality.

NEW DIRECTIONS IN SCULPTURE AND ARCHITECTURE   Few sculptors of any consequence appeared in the 1871–1914 period and only one genius: Auguste Rodin [roh-DAN] (1840–1917). Rejecting the static classicism of the mid–nineteenth century, Rodin forged an eclectic style that blended romantic subject matter, Renaissance simplicity, and Gothic angularity with the radical changes under way in painting. In the sculpture *Eve* (Figure 19.25), he created a rough Gothic effect using modern means, torturing the surface, especially of the stomach and the head. The result was both impressionistic (the play of light on the scored surfaces) and expressionistic (the traces of Rodin's fingers on the bronze medium, which so dramatically suggest the intensity of the artist's involvement).

Having lagged behind the other arts for most of the century, architecture began to catch up in the 1880s.

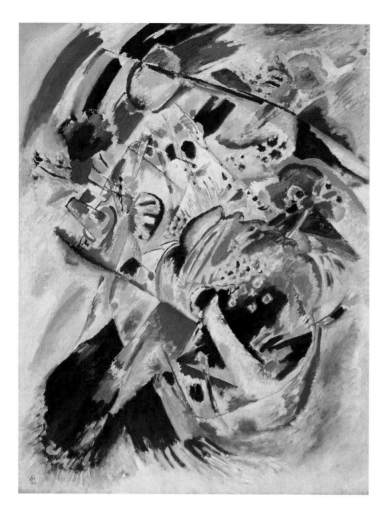

Figure 19.24 WASSILY KANDINSKY. *Panel for Edwin R. Campbell No. 4* (formerly *Painting No. 201, Winter*). 1914. Oil on canvas, 64¼ × 48¼". The Museum of Modern Art, New York. (Nelson A. Rockefeller Fund, by exchange.) *This panel is one of four commissioned by a founder of the Chevrolet Motor Car Company, to hang in his New York apartment. When Kandinsky painted this series, he moved from nonrepresentational to totally "nonobjective art," an expression he coined. His ideas rested on the romantic notion that serious art can be a substitute for religion; the artist serves as "priest," who, with mystical insight, can tap into the divine. Later artists, such as Robert Rauschenberg (see Chapter 21), ridiculed this idea as pretentious. Kandinsky, in this painting, achieves what he had set out to do—eliminate all representative imagery and express himself solely through line, color, and form. Red, the dominant color, is set off against blues, greens, and yellows, with accent colors of white and black to suggest winter—his only bow to representational aesthetics.*

Figure 19.25 AUGUSTE RODIN. *Eve.* 1881. Bronze, ht. 67". Rodin Museum, Philadelphia Museum of Art. *This life-size statue of Eve was originally conceived as half a pair, with Adam, to flank* The Gates of Hell, *Rodin's masterpiece, loosely based on Dante's* Inferno *(see Chapter 9). The figure of Eve owed much to Michelangelo's expressive forms, particularly that of Eve in* The Expulsion from the Garden of Eden *on the Sistine Chapel ceiling (see Chapter 12). Reflecting her dual roles as first mother and coauthor of original sin, Rodin's Eve is both voluptuous (beautiful face and curvaceous form) and ashamed (face averted and, in gestures of modesty, arms shielding breasts and left leg raised).*

The United States led the way, notably in the works of the Chicago school. The skyscraper, perfected by Chicago-based architects, became synonymous with modernism and modern life. Unlike modernist painting and sculpture, the new architecture arose for practical reasons: dense populations and soaring real estate values.

Using the aesthetic dictum that "form follows function," the Chicago school solved design problems without relying on past techniques and traditions. This dictum means that a building ought to be a workable organism where the pressure of daily existence is channeled into a harmonious, functioning whole; in practical terms, the pressure is called function, the resultant building, form. The author of this dictum, Louis Sullivan (1865–1924), produced a masterly example of the Chicago school's style in the Wainwright Building in St. Louis, Missouri. Here, Sullivan used a steel frame, joining the horizontal and vertical girders, to create a towering grid, which became the exterior's defining pattern (Figure 19.26). Rather than covering the exterior walls with ornamentation or design elements, as was done in earlier steel skyscrapers, Sullivan left the girders exposed in order to give a sense of unity to the building. Vertical columns extend up the sides of the building, connecting the base—the two first floors—with the top floor. By making the building's exterior a grid, it became a visual expression of the structural frame underneath. Although Sullivan rejected the rich ornamentation of the nineteenth-century Gothic as well as the balanced decorations of classicism, he nevertheless devised his own decorative scheme, which may be seen in the vertical and horizontal elements, for example, and the spaces (blocks) between the windows. In this building, Sullivan's one exception to his rule of pure functionality is in the decorative facade he used to "hide" the water tank and elevator machinery on its top floor.

Sullivan defined the public building for the twentieth century, and his disciple Frank Lloyd Wright (1869–1959) did the same for domestic architecture in about 1910. In the Victorian era, architects had discovered that the middle-class demand for comfortable, spacious housing was an excellent source of income. This same class of patrons continued to demand well-built homes, and for them Wright created a new type of dwelling he called "organic," a term he coined to describe a building that is constructed of local woods and stone and therefore harmonizes with the physical environment. Although unconventional in his own life, he was rather a romantic about his bourgeois patrons. To strengthen domestic values, he planned houses that encourage the inhabitants to identify with the natural surroundings; his structures also broke down the typical reliance on fixed interior walls to encourage fluid

Figure 19.26 Louis Sullivan. Wainwright Building. 1890–1891. St. Louis, Missouri. Photograph © Marvin Trachtenberg. *Purity became an identifying characteristic of modernist style. It was apparent in Matisse's color experiments, in Picasso's abstract cubist forms, and even in the expressionist goal of unvarnished truth. In architecture, Louis Sullivan introduced the purity principle with his artistic credo that "form follows function." Originally built for a wealthy St. Louis businessman, this early modernist architectural icon deteriorated until the National Trust for Historic Preservation purchased it (1973), thus saving it from the wrecking ball. Today, the Wainwright Building is part of a state of Missouri office complex.*

Figure 19.27   Frank Lloyd Wright. Frederick C. Robie House, 1910. Hyde Park Neighborhood, Chicago. *Between 1900 and 1910, Wright introduced his "prairie houses," named for the* Ladies Home Journal *article (1901) in which their designs first appeared. The Robie House, built in an affluent Chicago suburb for a wealthy client, is a fine example of this midwestern American style that became later the "dream house" for many middle-class homeowners. The style's strong focus on horizontal lines, resulting in shifting planes of light across the facade, may be compared to the multiple perspectives of cubism, the parallel development in painting.*

family relationships and a free flow of traffic. In time, Wright's style became standard for progressive architects throughout the United States, expressed in the exterior in strong horizontal lines, overhanging eaves, banks of windows, and a minimum of decorative detail (Figure 19.27).

Music: From Impressionism to Jazz

Richard Wagner died in 1883 (see Chapter 18), but in certain respects he is the commanding musical presence in early modernism. Most composers were either utilizing in their own way the harmonic advances he had made, working out the implications of those advances, or reacting to his influence by elaborately rejecting it. For example, a musical style influenced by Wagner was impressionism, which was in part inspired by his shimmering, constantly alternating chords. The impression-

ist composers did not stay under his tutelage, however. Where Wagner was philosophical and literary, seeking to fuse all the arts, the impressionists explored sound for its own sake. Like impressionist painters, impressionist composers thought that all moments—no matter how real—were fleeting and fragmentary, and their musical compositions illustrated this principle. Their music, without conventional thematic development or dramatic buildup and release, often sounds veiled or amorphous when compared with the music of, for example, Haydn.

Claude Debussy [duh-byoo-SEE] (1862–1918), a French composer, founded the impressionist style in music. He created constantly shifting colors and moods through such musical methods as gliding chords and chromatic scales derived from non-Western sources. Debussy's music represents the climax of the nineteenth-century interest in programmatic titles, large orchestras, rich chords, and relatively free rhythms and forms.

One of Debussy's programmatic works, *Prélude à l'après-midi d'un faune (Prelude to the Afternoon of a Faun)* (1894), is generally recognized as the first impressionist orchestral masterpiece. This work, a musical setting of the poem "The Afternoon of a Faun" (1876) by the French poet Stéphane Mallarmé (1842–1898), is a sensuous confection of blurred sounds and elusive rhythms. To achieve its mood of reverie, Debussy used a meandering musical line played by a soulful solo flute, backed by muted strings and delicately voiced brasses and woodwinds. Adding to the work's dreamy mood is its subtle **dynamics,** changes in the volume of sounds, as in the sudden shifts between *piano* (Italian, "soft") and *forte* (Italian, "loud").

Impressionist music produced a second major voice in France during this period: Maurice Ravel [ruh-VEL] (1875–1937), a composer loosely indebted to Debussy. Unlike Debussy, Ravel had a taste for the clear structure of classical musical forms as well as established dance forms. Perhaps the most impressionistic of Ravel's compositions is *Jeux d'eau (Fountains)* (1901), a programmatic work for piano marked by sounds evoking sparkling and splashing water. Even before Ravel wrote *Jeux d'eau,* his classical inclinations were evident in *Pavane pour une infante defunte (Pavane for a Dead Princess)* (1899), a work for piano with a melancholy quality; here, the music captured the stately rhythm of the baroque **pavane,** an English court dance of Italian origin. Dance also inspired Ravel's *Valses nobles et sentimentales (Waltzes Noble and Sentimental)* (1911), a work for piano based on the waltzes of Franz Schubert and the Parisian ballrooms of the 1820s, and *La Valse (The Waltz)* (1920), an orchestral work that is a sardonic homage to the waltzes of nineteenth-century Vienna. Ravel's best-known work, *La Valse* is in actuality an embittered metaphor in which the increasingly discordant sounds of the music represent the forces that generated the catastrophe of World War I.

A trend in opposition to Wagner was expressionism, which developed simultaneously with expressionist art in Vienna. Drawing on the insights of Freudian psychology, musical expressionism offered a distorted view of the world, focusing on anguish and pain. Its most striking feature was its embrace of **atonality,** a type of music without major or minor keys. To the listener, atonal music sounds discordant and even disturbing, because it offers no harmonious frame of reference. It is characterized by wide leaps from one tone to another, melody fragments, interrupted rhythms, and violent contrasts. Rejecting traditional forms, expressionist composers made experimentation central to their musical vision.

The founder and leader of the expressionist school was Arnold Schoenberg [SHUHN-burg] (1874–1951), who gave up a Wagnerian style in about 1907 and moved toward atonality. At first, Schoenberg employed traditional musical forms, as in the Second String Quartet (1908), although no string quartet had ever sounded like his dissonant creation. Scored without a designated key and filled with snatches of melody, this work offered the listener no recognizable frame of reference. Violinists were required on occasion to play the most extreme notes of which their instruments were capable.

Besides traditional forms, Schoenberg also established a favorite compositional method of expressionism: setting a literary text to music and following its changes in character and feeling. An influential example of expressionist music with text was *Pierrot lunaire* (1912), based on symbolist poems by a Belgian writer and scored for chamber quintet and (flute [and piccolo], clarinet [and bass clarinet], violin [and viola], cello, and piano) and voice. Though Schoenberg downplayed the source text's importance, the music's violent shifts and prevailing discord clearly complement the alienated psychology and shocking language of the symbolist text. Instead of conventionally singing the text, the solo vocalist declaims, or chants, the words by combining speech and song.

"Moonstruck Pierrot," one of the twenty-one songs in the *Pierrot lunaire* cycle, features the poet as clown, made drunk with the beauty of the moonlight. Schoenberg's music conveys the poet's hyperbolic thoughts, as in, for example, the use of a **cadenza**—a passage with an improvised feel—to represent the streaming moonlight. He also establishes the main motive, a seven-note sequence for piano and violin, in the first line, which begins with *"Den Wein"* (German, "the wine")—a poetic metaphor for moonlight. The main motive and the *Den Wein* line are repeated in lines 7 and 13. The poetic text, like other songs in this cycle, is a **rondeau,** a thirteen-line French verse form dating from the late Middle Ages.

Pierrot lunaire represents the extreme of Schoenberg's expressionism before World War I. This work made him one of the two most highly respected composers of early modernism. Unwilling to rest on his laurels, he continued to experiment with innovative musical techniques (see Chapter 20).

The other outstanding twentieth-century musical genius active during this period was the Russian Igor Stravinsky [struh-VIN-skee] (1882–1971). Untouched by Wagnerism but attuned to the revolutionary events unfolding in the arts and in literature, Stravinsky acquired his reputation at about the same time as Schoenberg. In 1913 Stravinsky wrote the music for *The Rite of Spring,* a ballet produced by Sergei Diaghilev [dee-AHG-uh-lef] (1872–1929) for the Ballets Russes in Paris. Stravinsky's music and the ballet's choreography tapped into the theme of primitivism in art that was currently the rage in the French capital. Stravinsky's pounding rhythms

Figure 19.28   Mathews Band. Lockport, Louisiana. Hogan Jazz Archive, Howard-Tilton Memorial Library, Tulane University. *Bands—both black and white—flourished in nineteenth-century America. Band concerts were part of town culture, as they played at local events, including picnics, holidays, and parades. For black musicians, playing in a band offered an opportunity to hone musical skills, earn cash, wear snappy clothes, and bask in the spotlight. Band culture, with its well-experienced musicians, became part of jazz culture, and in Dixieland jazz, the band component still remains strong today. The all-brass band pictured here was in Lockport, Louisiana, a village on Bayou Lafourche, near New Orleans. Note the region's vernacular-style building in the background: the wooden house, raised on blocks, for ventilation; the shallow porch with four plain wood supports; the central doorway with flanking windows; and the hinged wooden window covers.*

evoke a pagan ritual, using abrupt meter changes, a hypnotic beat, and furious **syncopation,** the musical technique of accenting a weak beat when a strong beat is expected. *The Rite of Spring* builds to an exhilarating—even frenetic—conclusion, titled "The Sacrifice," with time signature changes in almost every measure, explosive beats on the drums, and blaring brasses. A sudden shift in dynamics brings a brief quieter interlude, marked by thrumming chords and silent beats, followed by a raucous, throbbing climax of drums and brasses. The "savage" music coupled with the erotic dancing created a scandal that made Stravinsky the leading avant-garde composer in the world. Despite his innovative rhythms, Stravinsky was no relentless experimenter. After World War I, Stravinsky, though touched by modernism's influences, became the head of a classical school that was centered in France and opposed the more extreme theories being introduced by Schoenberg through his work in Vienna.

As Western music moved away from ancient and medieval sources, a new tradition, **jazz,** rooted in African American tradition, began to emerge in the United States (Figure 19.28). The word *jazz,* originally a slang term for sexual intercourse, reflects the music's origins in the New Orleans sexual underworld. Jazz combined West African and African-Caribbean rhythms with Western harmony, along with an improvisatory call-and-response style rooted both in African songs and in gospel songs of the urban Protestant revival in the 1850s. Jazz drew on two other African American musical forms as well—ragtime, which was chiefly instrumental, and the blues, which originated as a vocal art.

Ragtime flourished from 1890 to 1920. The word *ragtime* is derived from the phrase "ragged time," the original name for this type of syncopated music perfected by black pianist and composer Scott Joplin (1868–1917) and based on a blend of African American rhythms and Western harmony. The **blues** grew out of the rural African American tradition of work songs and spirituals and evokes the pain to be found in life, love, poverty, and hard work. Blues and jazz are both powerfully expressive musical forms, considered specifically American contributions to world music.

The Legacy of Early Modernism

From the period of 1871–1914 come many of the defining trends of the twentieth century. The legacy of militant nationalism gave birth to the two great world wars that devastated the century. Nationalism remains a potent force, threatening to overturn state boundaries and governments. Imperialism, another legacy, had radically contradictory consequences. On the one hand, it exported Western peoples, values, and technology around the globe, bringing a higher standard of living and greater expectations for the future. On the other hand, it disturbed if not destroyed traditional ways of life and led to a series of wars as colonial peoples struggled to cast off the yoke of Western oppression. And militarism, a third legacy, made rivalry among states a perpetual source of anxiety and destruction.

On the cultural scene, the era of early modernism set the stage for the twentieth century. The rise of the masses led to a growing proletarianization of culture. As a result, the middle classes were subjected to a cultural assault from urban workers in much the same way that aristocrats had been attacked and displaced by the middle classes. Technology fueled the rise of mass culture. A second legacy of this era was the avant-garde, whose leaders systematically tried to destroy the last vestiges of Judeo-Christian and classical Greco-Roman traditions. In rejecting the classical ideal of the search for eternal truths, artists followed the impressionists' lead and continued to strive for change as a reflection of the new historical conditions that surrounded them. And finally, early modernism established the emotional and aesthetic climate of the century—its addiction to experimentalism, its love-hate relationship with uncertainty and restlessness, its obsession with abstraction, its belief in the hidden depths of the human personality, and its willingness to think the unthinkable.

KEY CULTURAL TERMS

modernism
avant-garde
Social Gospel
Fundamentalist
    Movement, or
    fundamentalism
Modernism, in
    Catholicism
naturalism
decadent
expressionism
problem play
local color
Creole
Cajun
aesthete
impressionism
ukiyo-e
postimpressionism

pointillism
abstraction
primitivism
fauvism
cubism
collage
abstract art
dynamics
piano
forte
pavane
atonality
cadenza
rondeau
syncopation
jazz
ragtime
blues

QUESTIONS FOR CRITICAL THINKING

1. Define early modernism. Using an example of early modernism from literature and the visual arts, show how each represents the style.

2. Discuss the fundamental causes of World War I and also the immediate events that led to the outbreak of the war. Do you think war could have been prevented? Explain.

3. Define avant-garde and discuss what role the avant-garde played in late-nineteenth-century Western literature and art.

4. Compare and contrast impressionism, fauvism, cubism, and expressionism, noting the leading artists in each style and their representative works.

5. In which ways did militant nationalism, imperialism, and militarism affect the historical and cultural events during early modernism?

20

THE AGE OF THE MASSES AND THE ZENITH OF MODERNISM

1914–1945

The period between 1914 and 1945 was one of crisis, mainly because of four events: World War I (1914–1918), the Great Depression of the 1930s, World War II (1939–1945), and the arrival of the common people on the political stage. Today, we know that the making of the masses into a historically powerful force was the most significant event of this turbulent time. The rise of the masses heralded the onset of a new phase of culture—the Age of the Masses—in which ordinary men and women from the lower middle class and the working class challenged bourgeois dominance in much the same way that the bourgeoisie had earlier challenged and eventually overcome the aristocracy.

The needs of this new audience led to the birth of mass culture with its fresh forms of popular expression. Mass culture triggered negative responses from most serious artists, writers, and musicians, who preferred the difficult and remote modernist style. A few daring artists did appropriate ideas from mass culture, but the majority stayed true to modernist ideals, constantly testing the limits of the arts. Thus, this period saw both the rise of mass culture and the zenith of modernism.

THE COLLAPSE OF OLD CERTAINTIES AND THE SEARCH FOR NEW VALUES

Before 1914, liberal values guided most people's expectations. Between the outbreak of World War I and the end of World War II, however, these values were severely tested and in some cases overthrown. Wars, revolutions, and social upheavals often dominated both domestic and foreign affairs. To those

◄ **Detail** PABLO PICASSO. *The Three Musicians*. 1921. Oil on canvas, 6'8″ × 6'2″. Philadelphia Museum of Art. The A. E. Gallatin Collection.

Figure 20.1   PABLO PICASSO. *Guernica*. 1937. Oil on canvas, 11′5½″ × 25′5¾″. Prado, Madrid. *Picasso's* Guernica *is a vivid symbol of the violent twenty years between World War I and World War II. Depicting the bombing of the unarmed town of Guernica by Nazi planes during the Spanish Civil War, the painting transforms the local struggle into an international battle between totalitarianism and human freedom—the issue that also dominated the age's ideological debates.*

who clung to liberal ideals, the world seemed to have gone mad (Figure 20.1). In Russia, Italy, Germany, and Spain, individual rights became secondary to the needs of society or simply to the wishes of the ruling totalitarian party. The doctrine of laissez-faire also fell into discredit during the Depression of the 1930s, bringing capitalism itself into question and leading to the rise of state-controlled economies.

World War I and Its Aftermath

In 1914 came the war that nobody expected and that took an estimated ten million lives. On one side were the Central powers—Germany, Austria-Hungary (members of the Triple Alliance), Turkey, and Bulgaria. Their principal war aim was to assert the power of the central European region, which had been eclipsed by western Europe for almost two hundred years. This region's new sense of importance was due to the unification of Germany in 1871, which had made the German Empire the most powerful industrial and military state on the Continent.

Opposed to the Central powers were the Allied forces: France, Russia, and Great Britain (members of the Triple Entente), joined in 1915 by Italy (a former

member of the Triple Alliance). The Allies refused to allow the Central powers to revise the balance of power and, in particular, were determined to keep Germany from gaining new lands. Early on, fighting between the two sides bogged down into siege warfare with huge battlefield losses and appalling hardships at home (Figure 20.2). In the spring of 1917, this stalemate was upset by two events: the United States entered the war on the Allied side, promising fresh troops and supplies (Figure 20.3) and revolution broke out in Russia, interrupting its war effort and later causing the newly formed Communist regime to make peace with the Central powers in 1918. Then the Germans launched a massive assault on the western front. However, the Allies, supported by American troops, foiled the attack and forced the Germans to surrender in November 1918.

The peace that ended the war—the 1919 Treaty of Versailles—was based partly on a plan of the U.S. president, Woodrow Wilson (in office 1913–1921). Wilson's plan aimed to keep Europe safe from war, and it called for the self-determination of nations, democratic governments, and the establishment of the League of Nations, an international agency to maintain the peace. Despite the optimism surrounding its signing, the Versailles Treaty sowed the seeds of discord in Germany that contributed to World War II (Map 20.1). Defeated

Figure 20.2 PAUL NASH. *"We Are Making a New World."* 1918. Oil on canvas, 28 × 36". Imperial War Museum, London. *Paul Nash, one of Britain's official artists during World War I, made the reality of the war's destructive power evident to civilians at home. In his battle scenes, farmlands were turned into quagmires and forests into "no-man's lands." The artist's choice of the title for this painting mocks the politicians' promises that tomorrow will be better.*

Figure 20.3 CHILDE HASSAM. *Allies Day. May, 1917.* 1917. Oil on canvas, 36½ × 30¼". Gift of Ethelyn McKinney in memory of her brother, Glen Ford McKinney, National Gallery, Washington, D.C. *Patriotic rituals, such as Bastille Day in France (see Figure 19.1), expanded readily during wartime to recognize nations allied to fight a common enemy. Upon the United States' entry into World War I, French, British, and American flags were displayed along New York City's Fifth Avenue. This outpouring of unity among the Allied forces and support for the war contrasts markedly with Paul Nash's ironic imagery (see Figure 20.2). Childe Hassam (1859–1935) studied in Paris before returning home to become America's leading impressionist painter. In the style of a cropped photographic image, Hassam frames the flags with the tall buildings, on the left, which fade into the distance, and, on the right, only the thinnest edge of other buildings' facades. The painting's airy mood is heightened by the sunlight reflected on the buildings on the left.*

LEARNING THROUGH MAPS

Map 20.1   EUROPE AFTER WORLD WAR I
This map shows Europe's political divisions in the early 1920s. 1. *Notice* the territories
lost by Germany, Bulgaria, Russia, and Austria-Hungary. 2. *What* name was now given
to Russia? 3. *Which* countries lost the most territory? 4. *How* did these lost lands affect
European politics? 5. *Observe* the increase in the size of countries in southeastern Europe
in this map, as compared with their smaller size in Map 19.3, Europe on the Eve of World
War I. 6. *Notice* that the Ottoman Empire in Map 19.3 has become Turkey in this map.

German officials and officers would later rally nationalistic feelings by denouncing the treaty as a humiliation
for their country. The Versailles Treaty also prepared
the ground for future troubles in the Middle East, particularly in turning over Mesopotamia—that is, the
provinces of Mosul, Baghdad, and Basra in the defunct
Ottoman Empire—to British control. In Mesopotamia,
where no single modern country had been before, the
kingdom of Iraq would be formed in 1921, despite the
deep fault lines among Shia and Sunni Muslims, Arabs, Kurds, Persians, and Assyrians (Figure 20.4).

Peace brought boom times to the economies of the
victorious Allies, however. Britain and France returned
to business as usual. The United States reverted to its
prewar isolationism, and between 1924 and 1929 it
exhibited the best and the worst of free enterprise—
unprecedented prosperity and rampant greed.

The economies of the Central powers did not fare
as well. After a shaky start, Germany survived near
bankruptcy to regain its status as the leading industrial state on the Continent. Under the Weimar Republic, Germany's first democratic parliamentary regime,

Figure 20.4 *The First Oil "Gusher" in the Middle East.* Kirkut, Iraq. October 14, 1927. © The British Petroleum Company plc, London. *The West entered the Age of Oil after World War I, and Britain's designs on Ottoman lands rested on educated hunches that vast pools of oil lay beneath the desert sands there. Signs of oil could be interpreted in swamp fires in Mosul and black sludge oozing out of the ground to make pools in Baghdad. However, it was in 1927 that the existence of underground oil, perhaps the largest field in the world, was confirmed by the eruption of oil, rising 140 feet above the derrick, as this anonymous photograph commemorates. Maneuvering to control this underground oil has been the burden of the history of Iraq ever since.*

Figure 20.5 DOROTHEA LANGE. *Migrant Mother, Nipomo, California.* 1936. Library of Congress. *Migrant workers were increasingly attracted to the vegetable fields of California during the Great Depression. Seasonal laborers, they harvested crops for very low wages under miserable working conditions and usually lived in crowded, unsanitary camps. This photograph shows a migrant mother, surrounded by three children, whose bleak future has been made worse by the failure of the pea crop. Dorothea Lange's poignant photographs, collected in* An American Exodus: A Record of Human Erosion *(1939), reflected her strong sense of social justice, her sympathy for the downtrodden, and her own life as the child of a broken home.*

the country once again became a center for European culture, providing key leaders in avant-garde painting and literature. Conversely, Austria-Hungary was divided into separate nations, and its Slavic population dispersed among several states. Lacking a sound economic base, the onetime empire never fully recovered from its defeat.

As the 1920s drew to a close, a warning signal sounded: the crash of the New York Stock Exchange in October 1929. After the crash, the buoyant atmosphere of the twenties lingered for only a few months. Then economic depression in the United States, a key player in the world's economy, pulled down Europe's financial house.

The Great Depression of the 1930s

The Depression wiped out prosperity and brought mass unemployment, street demonstrations, and near starvation for many people (Figure 20.5). In Europe and the United States, governments were forced to take extreme measures to restore their economies. Great Britain and France chose to discard free trade and move toward government-controlled economies. Under President Franklin Delano Roosevelt (in office 1933–1945) and his New Deal program, the United States followed a policy of state intervention to revitalize the economy. Roosevelt started public works projects, sponsored programs such as Social Security and unemployment insurance to benefit working people, and moved to

ENCOUNTER

Civil Disobedience and the Campaign for Indian Independence

Warfare is the traditional method by which societies free themselves from foreign control. Such was the case in the American Revolution. However, during the period between World War I and World War II, a new method of resistance against foreign rule emerged in British India, known as civil disobedience.

In the 1600s, Great Britain's rule in India extended only to trade and commerce, under the supervision of the British East India Company (see Encounter in Chapter 15). Then, in 1857, the Sepoy Rebellion brought this phase of British-Indian history to an abrupt end. Brutally quelling the revolt, British leaders abolished the East India Company and placed India under the British crown (Raj, or Reign—a Hindu word from Sanskrit, "king"), including a secretary of state for India, a viceroy for India, and the Indian Civil Service. The Raj continued what the East India Company had begun: fostering agriculture, building railroads and harbors, linking the country by telegraph, trying to change Indian customs and rituals, which the English considered barbaric, and founding schools to train Indians for lower positions in the Indian Civil Service.

Thereafter, many Hindus and Muslims, who studied at Oxford and Cambridge, where they learned Western politics and ideas, returned home and called for economic and social reforms and demanded a larger role in Indian affairs. Modeled on Western political parties, the National Indian Congress, founded in 1885 as an assembly where grievances could be aired and passed on to British officials, soon emerged as India's most influential reform group. After 1900 the Congress allied itself with the All-India Muslim League, and after World War I their united front began to push for total independence. However, the British stood firm and the coalition frayed, as the Muslim minority held back, fearing that the Hindu-majority Congress would dominate India after independence.

The National Indian Congress lacked effective leadership, but that vacuum was filled with the return of Mohandas Karamchand Gandhi (1869–1948) to India in 1914. Gandhi, having studied law in London (1888–1891) and having become a civil rights lawyer in South Africa (1893–1914), was the leader that the movement required. While in South Africa, Gandhi experienced a moral and spiritual awakening, completing a process that began during his English sojourn. In his spiritual quest, he was influenced by a mixture of Western and Eastern sources, including the Russian Tolstoy's writings on Christianity, the American Thoreau's essay on civil disobedience, the Bible, the Qur'an, and, in particular, the Bhagavad-Gita, the Hindu religious classic on personal behavior. From these sources, Gandhi wove a creed, in which he repudiated materialism while embracing the doctrines of nonviolence (*ahimsa*) and civil disobedience (*satyagraha*, or "holding to the truth").

Gandhi turned the Indian National Congress into an effective political weapon. And he emerged as the voice and conscience of the Indian people. During the 1920s, he led a movement to boycott British goods and urged his countrymen to reject the British legal system and British-style education. He also opposed further industrialization, calling on Indians to return to cottage industries, such as spinning cloth for their clothes (Encounter figure 20.1).

India's hopes for self-rule were muddled by a 1937 British law, the Government of India Act, which made India a self-governing state within the British Empire, but it proved unworkable due to growing mistrust between Hindus and Muslims.

After World War II, Gandhi played a key role in the negotiations that culminated in the granting of inde-

---

regulate Wall Street and the banks. Depressed conditions hung on until World War II, however.

Germany suffered the most in Europe. Domestic problems, brought on in part by bank failures and rising unemployment, led to political crises that doomed the Weimar democracy and set the stage for the National Socialists, or Nazis, under Adolf Hitler.

While Europe suffered, Japan prospered. Since 1926 Japan had been ruled by Emperor Hirohito (r. 1926–1989), who was worshiped as a god, although actual power was wielded by military leaders and businessmen. In the 1930s, these groups pursued expansionist and militaristic policies, first taking over Manchuria and then making war on China. As Europe's situation worsened in the late 1930s, Japan was able to make a move into Southeast Asia.

The Rise of Totalitarianism

With the 1919 peace treaty, democracy seemed triumphant in the West. By 1939, a mere twenty years later, most of the new democracies—Germany, Austria, Hungary, Italy, Spain, Bulgaria, and Rumania—were totalitarian. Totalitarianism is a twentieth-century phenomenon, but its roots reach back to Robespierre dur-

pendence to the states of India (Hindu) and Pakistan (Muslim) in 1947. In this event's aftermath—as turmoil raged, caused by Muslims and Hindus migrating from one state to the other—Gandhi was assassinated. Nevertheless, his approach to solving social, political, and economic issues inspired Martin Luther King Jr. and the 1960s civil rights leaders (see Chapter 21), the Czechs and other central European peoples during the fall of communism (see Chapter 22), and proponents of civil disobedience around the world. During Gandhi's lifetime, Indian admirers conveyed on him the honorific title Mahatma (mah-HAAT-mah), or "great-souled."

LEARNING FROM THE ENCOUNTER

1. *Why* did the British crown take over India from the East India Company? 2. *Discuss* the events and ideas that shaped Mahatma Gandhi's life. 3. *Are* Gandhi's techniques useful in solving problems in the United States?

Encounter figure 20.1 MARGARET BOURKE-WHITE. *Gandhi at the Spinning Wheel.* 1946. *In the 1930s, Gandhi launched a program of village industries. He encouraged fellow countrymen to gain economic independence from Britain as well as to identify themselves with India's crafts heritage. A man of his time, Gandhi used the media to advance his political agenda against British colonialism, as this photograph testifies. He is depicted wearing a simple loincloth while quietly reading a book.*

ing the French Revolution (see Chapter 17). Totalitarian governments seek to control every aspect of the lives and thoughts of their citizens. Art, literature, and the press exist only in the service of the state. "Truth" itself becomes a matter of what the state says it is. Between the wars, totalitarianism emerged in two forms: Russian communism and European fascism.

RUSSIAN COMMUNISM   Russian communism was based on the writings of Karl Marx, whose theory was reinterpreted by the revolutionary leader V. I. Lenin. Lenin accepted Marx's basic premise that economic conditions determine the course of history and his conclusion that history leads inevitably to a communist society run by and for the workers. Unlike Marx, Lenin believed that radical reform could occur only when a small, elite group—rather than a mass movement—seized power in the name of the people.

In 1917 Russia was plagued by an incompetent ruler, an inefficient military staff, a weak economy, and rising social and political discord. Revolution broke out in February, and a small band of Marxist communists— the Bolsheviks—seized the reins of government in October. Led by Lenin (r. 1917–1924), the Bolsheviks began to reorder the economy and the political system. Under their plan, the state would control production and

Figure 20.6 Nuremberg Nazi Party Rally. 1933. *Under the skillful orchestration of their propaganda chief, Joseph Goebbels, the National Socialists staged massive demonstrations whose goal was to overpower the emotions of participants and observers alike. In this anonymous photograph, Nazi Party members and private army units pass in review. In the 1930s, such demonstrations succeeded in uniting the German masses with the Nazi leader.*

distribution, and soviets—or councils of workers, military personnel, and peasants—would restructure the social and economic order at the local level, as directed by the Communist Party under Lenin.

After Lenin's death, Joseph Stalin (r. 1928–1953) emerged as the sole ruler of the Union of Soviet Socialist Republics, as the Russian Empire was now called, and he proceeded to impose his will over the state. Production was increased and modernization accomplished through state-owned farms, factories, and heavy industry. No political party other than the Communist Party was permitted, however, and Stalin was ruthless in dealing with his opponents and critics. He had them either murdered or imprisoned in a vast network of forced-labor camps, known as the Gulag, in the Siberian wilderness. The number of his victims is beyond imagining: more than ten million men, women, and children met unnatural deaths in the period of forced collectivization of agriculture, 1929–1936, and millions more were murdered during purges and in the Gulag.

EUROPEAN FASCISM European fascism was based on the idea that the masses should participate directly in the state—not through a legislative or deliberative body such as a parliament, but through a fusion of the population into one "spirit." Fascism sought to bind the masses by appealing to nonrational sentiments about national destiny. Like communists, fascists believed that the individual was insignificant and the nation-state was the supreme embodiment of the destiny of its people.

In practice, fascism led to loss of personal freedom, as did communism, because its ideals of economic stability and social peace could be achieved only through dictatorship and tight control over the press, education, police, and the judicial system. Because of its idealistic nationalism, fascism was also hostile both to foreigners and to internal groups that did not share the majority's history, race, or politics. The movement's innate aggressiveness led to strong military establishments, which were used to conquer new lands in Europe and to win colonial empires. Fascism first appeared in Italy in the 1920s and then in Germany and Spain in the 1930s.

In Italy, a floundering economy led to national frustration, which, in turn, caused more and more people to follow the Fascists. Under Benito Mussolini [moo-suh-LEE-nee] (r. 1922–1945), the Fascists dreamed of a revitalized Italy restored to its ancient glory. After seizing power in 1922, Mussolini achieved some success with his programs, and as the rest of Europe suffered through the Depression, his pragmatic policies gained admirers elsewhere.

Germany in the early 1930s was wracked by the Depression, unemployment, and political extremism, and in 1933 the voters turned to the National Socialist (Nazi) Party. By 1936, the Nazis had restored industrial productivity, eliminated unemployment, and gained the support of many business leaders and farmers. The Nazis' success depended ultimately on their *Führer,* or "leader," Adolf Hitler (r. 1933–1945), a middle-class Austrian and veteran who had hammered together a strong mass movement built on anti-Semitism and anticommunism. With his magnetic personality, he attracted devoted followers with promises to restore Germany to prewar glory. From the outset, the Nazis' ruthless treatment of political enemies, of the Jews, and of any dissidents aroused fears, but most Europeans ignored these barbaric acts, preferring to focus on the regime's successes (Figure 20.6).

Monarchical Spain's farm economy and traditional institutions were strained by industrial growth in the 1920s, and in the early 1930s a coalition of reformers overthrew the king and created a secular republic with a constitution guaranteeing civil rights. Conservatives plotted to restore monarchical rule and the church's influence. In 1936 civil war broke out. General Francisco Franco (r. 1939–1975) led the conservatives to victory in 1939, defeating an alliance of reformers. During hostilities, Hitler and Mussolini supplied Franco's fascist army with troops and equipment, and Stalin backed the losing faction. For the Germans and the Italians, Spain's civil war was a practice run for World War II. For example, the bombing of unarmed towns such as Guernica (see Figure 20.1) foreshadowed the indiscriminate bombing and killing of civilians that characterized the later war.

World War II: Origins and Outcome

The origins of World War II lay in the Treaty of Versailles (denounced by many Germans as a "dictated peace" that brought the loss of lands in France and Poland), the Great Depression, and nationalism. In his first year in power, Hitler launched a propaganda campaign to revise the Versailles Treaty that focused on Germany's glorious past. His regime, he boasted, was the Third Reich, or empire, which would last for a thousand years—like the Holy Roman Empire (1000–1806) rather than the German Empire (1871–1918). In 1936 he marched troops into the Rhineland, Germany's industrial heartland, which had been demilitarized by the Versailles Treaty. When the world ignored this provocative act, he concluded that Germany's former enemies were weak, and he initiated a plan to conquer Europe. Over the next two years, Europe watched as Hitler seized Austria and Czechoslovakia. World War II began on September 1, 1939, when Germany invaded Poland; France and Britain responded with declarations of war.

Within nine months, the Nazis occupied most of western Europe. In fall 1940, the British, under their wartime leader Winston Churchill (in office 1940–1945), were bravely holding on, taking the brunt of the German air raids. Unable to defeat England by air, Hitler turned eastward and invaded the Soviet Union in 1941 (Figure 20.7). Shortly thereafter, the Soviet Union and Great Britain became allies against Nazi Germany. Then, on December 7, 1941, Japan attacked Pearl Harbor, an American military base in the Pacific, and a few days later Germany and Italy followed Japan in declaring war on the United States. Japan's war motive

Figure 20.7 MARGARET BOURKE-WHITE. *Russian Tank Driver. 1941. Photojournalism, a popular form in which the photograph rather than the text dominates the story, reached new heights during World War II, particularly in illustrated magazines such as* Life. *Margaret Bourke-White, one of the first women war journalists, was the only foreign correspondent–photographer present in the Soviet Union when the Germans invaded in June 1941. In this photograph, a Russian tank driver peers through his window with the cannon jutting out over his head—a vivid image of the integration of human beings into mechanized warfare.*

was to eliminate the United States' naval presence in the Pacific region in order to be able to conquer and control Southeast Asia.

The war in Europe lasted until May 1945, when the combined armies of the Allies—Britain, the Soviet Union, and the United States—forced Germany to surrender. Italy had previously negotiated an armistice with the Allies in September 1943 after anti-Fascists overthrew Mussolini and set up a republic. In the Pacific, where the Allies had captured key Japanese islands, the war against Japan was brought to an abrupt end in August 1945, when the United States dropped atomic bombs on the Japanese cities of Hiroshima and Nagasaki (Figure 20.8). The more than two hundred thousand Japanese killed in these two raids climaxed the death toll of World War II, adding to its estimated thirty to fifty million deaths.

By 1945 the world had witnessed some of the most brutal human behavior in history, but few people were prepared for the Nazi death camps. Gradually it became known that the Nazis had rounded up the Jews of Germany and eastern Europe and transported them in cattle cars to extermination camps, where they were killed in gas chambers. The Nazis referred to their plan to eliminate the Jewish people as the Final Solution, but the rest of the world called it the Holocaust. This genocidal policy involved the murder of six million Jews out of a population of nine million, along with millions of other people the Nazis deemed undesirable, such as Gypsies and homosexuals (Figure 20.9).

In 1945, after six years of war, Germany and Japan lay in ruins. Italy escaped with less damage. France, partly occupied by the Germans for most of the war, was readmitted to the councils of the Allies. England, though victorious, emerged exhausted and in the shadow of its former allies, the United States and the Soviet Union. The old European order had passed away. The Soviet Union and the United States were now the two most powerful states in the world.

THE ZENITH OF MODERNISM

Modernism was the reigning cultural style of this period. With an underlying spirit of skepticism and experimentation, it guided artists, writers, composers, filmmakers, designers, and architects in their labors. But this style had limited emotional appeal, and an ever-growing public felt isolated from avant-garde developments. When this wider audience was exposed to modernist works, they often responded negatively, considering them incomprehensible, obscene, or provocative in some way. They turned instead to the increasingly available and affordable pleasures offered by **mass culture.**

Mass Culture, Technology, and Warfare

From its late-nineteenth-century beginnings, modernism was both a product of and reaction against technology and warfare, and during the first half of the twentieth century, the three became even more intertwined. Technology and warfare often seemed inseparable as technology dictated how wars were fought and military planners, usually men whose experiences dated from an earlier time, seemed unable to adapt to the latest war technologies. And modernism, holding a mirror up to the age, recorded and reflected the devastating impact of technology and warfare on society, exposing, in effect, the shaky foundations and boundaries of modern life. However, even mass culture, despite its mass appeal, seemed unable at times to resist the corrosive antics of the modernist aesthetic.

MASS CULTURE AND THE NEW TECHNOLOGIES Like modernism, mass culture was a direct outgrowth of industrialized society. Its roots reached back to the late 1800s, when skilled workers began to enjoy a better standard of living than had previously been possible for the lower classes. This new generation of consumers demanded products and amusements that appealed to their tastes: inexpensive, energetic, and easily accessible.

In response, entrepreneurs using new technologies flooded the market with consumer goods and developed new entertainments. Unlike the folk culture or popular culture of earlier times, modern mass culture was also mass-produced culture. The untapped consumers' market led to the creation or expansion of new industries, in particular automobiles, household goods, and domestic appliances. Most forms of mass culture—radio, newspaper comic strips and cartoons, professional sports, picture magazines, recordings, movies, and musical comedies—had originated before World War I, but now, between the wars, they came into their own. The 1920s was the golden age of Broadway's musical comedies, and radio reached its peak in the years between 1935 and 1955.

The spread of mass culture heightened the prestige of the United States, as it was the source of the most vigorous and imaginative popular works. The outstanding symbol of America's dominant role in popular culture is Walt Disney (1901–1966), the creator of the famous cartoon figure of Mickey Mouse (1928). By 1945 mass culture was playing an ever-expanding role in the public and private lives of most citizens in industrialized societies. A few modernists now began to incorporate aspects of mass culture into their works, using jazz in "serious" music or film in theatrical performances, for example. But most artists, writers, and musicians stood apart from such influences. Their isolation reflected an almost sacred commitment to the

Figure 20.8 Carrier Planes over the U.S.S. *Missouri*. 1945. *Although the Japanese surrendered unconditionally on August 15, 1945, the formal signing of the surrender documents occurred in a ceremony on the deck of the U.S.S. Missouri, a battleship, in Tokyo Bay, on September 2, 1945—V-J Day. By then American troops were on the ground in Japan, and the supreme might of the Allies had been assembled to let the Japanese and the world know who had won the war. This message was delivered as squadrons of carrier planes flew over the victorious American fleet. The Allied forces, supplied with weapons and materials from the United States, proved that nations had to possess both military and industrial power if they expected to win wars.*

Figure 20.9 Nazi Death Camp in Belsen, Germany. 1945. *When the Nazis came to power in Germany in 1933, they secretly began to imprison their political enemies in concentration camps, where they were tortured or executed. By 1942 the Nazis had extended this secret policy across Europe to include minority civilians, particularly Jews. Photographs such as this one revealed to the world the atrocities committed by the Nazi regime.*

modernist ideals of experimentation, newness, and deliberate difficulty. And a handful of visual artists imbued these ideals with spiritual meaning.

WARFARE The interdependency of technology and warfare accelerated in this violent era. In every nation across the Western world, the powerful industrial-military-state complex ordered the new weapons, mass-produced goods, and mobilized citizen armies. A new dictum now emerged: only those states that successfully blend technology, warfare, and government can win wars. For example, the ties among the military, industry, and government were evident in the Anglo-German naval rivalry of the early 1900s. This race to build the strongest battleships was a manifestation of imperialism and militant nationalism. And in the buildup to World War I, the military came to play the dominant role in this three-way relationship. To paraphrase one historian, the "twin processes" that distinguish the twentieth century now became the industrialization of war and the politicization of economics. The end result was to create fighting machines, which neither politicians nor military leaders could control. Once elaborate preparations and detailed mobilization plans were set in motion, they could not be halted.

By 1914 industrialized nations had adopted new weapons—the 75 mm field cannon, machine guns, and breech-loading rifles—and had constructed rail systems for moving troops and supplies. Thinking of yesterday's wars (see Chapter 18), military leaders at first believed that World War I would be swift and short. But, instead, it turned out to be a war of indecisive battles, with huge losses on both sides. The lessons learned from this long, bitter struggle were that the next war would be fully mechanized with armored vehicles, tanks, and planes; and science and technology would play crucial roles.

Germany, Japan, and Italy—which heeded these lessons of World War I—had the advantage in the first three years of World War II. But their natural resources, productivity, organizational skills, and resolve failed to match those of the Allied forces. Ultimately, Allied victory was made possible because of the well-oiled industrial-military-state complex, in which labor and management worked together, with an occasional push from the state; bureaucracies smoothly supplied the logistics; states financed key scientific projects, such as the building of the first atomic bombs; and civilians willingly made sacrifices for the war effort.

Experimentation in Literature

Modernist writers between 1914 and 1945 remained dedicated to experimentation, a stance that reflected despair over their era's instability. By challenging the traditional norms and methods of literature through carefully composed experimental works, these writers were convinced that they could impose order on the seeming randomness and meaninglessness of human existence.

THE NOVEL Depiction of the narrator's subjective thoughts was a principal concern of modernist novelists, who otherwise differed markedly from one another. The most distinctive method that arose from this concern was **stream-of-consciousness** writing, a method in which the narrative consists of the unedited thoughts of one of the characters, through whose mind readers experience the story. Stream-of-consciousness fiction differs from a story told in the first person—the grammatical "I"—by one of the characters (for example, Dickens's *David Copperfield*) in that it is an attempt to reproduce the actual experience of thinking and feeling, even to the point of sounding fragmented, random, and arbitrary.

The Irish author James Joyce and the English writer Virginia Woolf were important innovators with the stream-of-consciousness technique. In his novel *Ulysses*, James Joyce (1882–1941) uses this device as a way of making the novel's characters speak directly to readers. For instance, no narrator's voice intrudes in the novel's final forty-five pages, which are the scattered thoughts of the character Molly Bloom as she sinks into sleep. This long monologue is a single run-on sentence without any punctuation except for a final period.

Despite *Ulysses'* experimental style, Joyce aspired to more than technical virtuosity. He planned this monumental work as a modern version of the *Odyssey*, contrasting Homer's twenty-four books of heroic exploits with an ordinary day in the lives of three Dubliners. Joyce's sexual language, although natural to his characters, offended bourgeois morals. *Ulysses*, first published in France in 1922, became the era's test case for artistic freedom, not appearing in America or England until the 1930s.

Rejecting traditional narrative techniques, Virginia Woolf (1882–1941) experimented with innovative ways of exploring time, space, and reality. Like her contemporaries Joyce and Freud, Woolf was interested in examining the realities that lie below surface consciousness. Many critics consider *To the Lighthouse* (1927) Woolf's finest novel. In it she uses stream of consciousness to strip the story of a fixed point of view and capture the differing realities experienced by the characters—in much the same way that cubist painters aimed at representing multiple views. Thus, she focuses on the characters' inner selves, creating diverse effects through interior monologues. For instance, one character's matter-of-fact mentality differs from his wife's emotional, free-ranging consciousness. A distinguished literary critic and the author of well-known feminist works such as *A Room of One's Own* (1929), Woolf gathered around her the avant-garde writers, artists, and intellectuals known as the Bloomsbury Group and founded, with her husband, Leonard Woolf, the Hogarth Press.

American writers also contributed experimental fiction to the modernist revolution. By and large, they made their first contacts with Europe during World War I and stayed on until the Great Depression drove them home (Figure 20.10). Ernest Hemingway (1899–1961) was the first of these Americans to emerge as a major literary star. His severely disciplined prose style relied heavily on dialogue, and he often omitted details of setting and background. His writing owed a debt to popular culture: from the era's hard-boiled detective fiction he borrowed a terse, world-weary voice to narrate his works, as in *The Sun Also Rises* (1926). In this novel, he portrays his fellow American exiles as a "lost generation" whose future was blighted by World War I—a modernist message. In Hemingway's cynical vision, politics is of little importance; what matters most are drinking bouts with male friends and casual sex with beautiful women.

William Faulkner (1897–1962) was another American who became a giant of twentieth-century fiction. The stream-of-consciousness technique is central to his 1929 masterpiece, *The Sound and the Fury*. With a story line repeated several times but from different perspectives, this novel is especially audacious in its opening section, which narrates events through the eyes of a mentally challenged character. More important than this modernist device was his lifelong identification with his home state of Mississippi, where, after a brief sojourn in Europe, he returned to explore themes about extended families bound together by sexual secrets. Faulkner's universe became the fictional county of Yoknapatawpha, which he peopled with decaying gentry, ambitious poor whites, and exploited blacks. His artistic power lay in his ability not only to relate these characters to their region but also to turn them into universal symbols.

Although experimentalism was central to modernist fiction, not all modernist writers were preoccupied with innovative methods. Other writers were identified with the modernists because of their pessimistic viewpoints or their explosive themes. The modernism of the British writer D. H. Lawrence (1885–1930), for example, was expressed in novels of sexual liberation. Frustrated by the

Figure 20.10 PABLO PICASSO. *Gertrude Stein.* 1906. Oil on canvas, 39¼ × 32". Metropolitan Museum of Art. Bequest of Gertrude Stein, 1946. *Talented Americans were introduced to Paris by American writer and expatriate Gertrude Stein, who made her studio a gathering place for the Parisian avant-garde. There she entertained Matisse and Picasso, composer Igor Stravinsky, writers Ernest Hemingway and F. Scott Fitzgerald, and many other brilliant exponents of modernism. Stein was shocked at first by the starkness and brooding presence of Picasso's portrait of her, but she came to regard it as an accurate likeness, saying, "For me it is I, and it is the only reproduction of me which is always I."*

sexual repression in bourgeois culture, Lawrence, the son of a miner, concluded that the machine age emasculated men. As an antidote, he preached a religion of erotic passion. He set forth his doctrine of sexual freedom most clearly in the 1928 novel *Lady Chatterley's Lover*, issued privately and quickly banned for its explicit language and scenes. Not until the 1960s, and only after bitter court battles, was this novel allowed to circulate freely. In the novel, the lovemaking episodes between Lady Chatterley, wed to an impotent aristocrat, and the lower-class gamekeeper Mellors were presented as models of sexual fulfillment with their mix of erotic candor and moral fervor.

Falling outside the modernist category is the English novelist and essayist George Orwell (1903–1950), who nevertheless was a major writer in this period. Born Eric Blair to a genteel middle-class family, Orwell changed his name, rejected his background, lived and worked among the poor and downtrodden, and became a writer. He also became the conscience of his generation because he remained skeptical of all the political ideologies of his day. In the allegorical novel *Animal Farm* (1945), he satirized Stalinist Russia. In the antiutopian novel *1984* (1948), he made totalitarianism the enemy, especially as practiced in the Soviet Union, but he also warned of the dangers of repression in capitalist society. What made Orwell remarkable in this age torn by ideological excess was his claim to be merely an ordinary, decent man. It is perhaps for this reason that today Orwell is claimed by socialists, liberals, and conservatives alike.

POETRY   Modern poetry found its first great master in William Butler Yeats (1865–1939). His early poems are filled with romantic mysticism, drawing on the myths of his native Ireland. By 1910 he had stripped his verses of romantic allusions, and yet he never gave up entirely his belief in the occult or the importance of myth. As Irish patriots grew more hostile to their country's continued submersion in the United Kingdom, climaxing in the Easter Rebellion of 1916, Yeats's poems took on a political cast. His best verses came in the 1920s, when his primary sources were Irish history and Greco-Roman myth. Perhaps his finest lyric is "Sailing to Byzantium," a poem that conjures up the classical past to reaffirm ancient wisdom and redeem the tawdry industrialized world.

T. S. Eliot (1888–1965) was another founder of modern poetry. Reared in St. Louis and educated at Harvard, Eliot moved to London in 1915, becoming an English citizen in 1927. He and Ezra Pound (1885–1972), another American exile, established a school of poetry that reflected the crisis of confidence that seized Europe's intellectuals after World War I. Like those of the poets of late Rome, Eliot's verses relied heavily on literary references and quotations.

"The Waste Land," published in 1922, showed Eliot's difficult, eclectic style; in 403 irregular lines, he quotes from or imitates thirty-five authors, including Shakespeare and Dante, adapts snatches from popular songs, and uses phrases in six foreign languages. Form matches content because the "waste land" itself represents a sterile, godless region without a future, a symbol drawn from medieval legend but changed by Eliot into a symbol of the hollowness of modern life. In 1927 he moved beyond such atheistic pessimism, finding solace by being received into the Church of England—a step he celebrated in the poem "Ash Wednesday," published in 1930.

The black American poet Langston Hughes (1902–1967) also belongs with the outstanding modernists. Hughes drew inspiration from many sources, including Africa, Europe, and Mexico, but the ultimate power of his poetry came from the American experience: jazz, spirituals, and his anguish as a black man in a white world. Hughes's emergence, like that of many African American writers, occurred during a population shift that began in 1914 when thousands of blacks from the American South settled in northern cities such as New York, Chicago, and Detroit in hopes of a better life (Figure 20.11).

At the same time that America's ethnographic map was being redrawn, a craze for Negro culture sprang up that was fueled by jazz and the avant-garde cult of primitivism (see Chapter 19). This craze sparked the Harlem Renaissance, a 1920s cultural revival in the predominantly black area of New York City called Harlem. Hughes was a major figure in this black literary movement. His earliest book of verses, *The Weary Blues* (1926), contains his most famous poem, "The Negro Speaks of Rivers." Dedicated to W. E. B. DuBois (1868–1963), the founder of the National Association for the Advancement of Colored People, Hughes's verse memorializes the deathless spirit of his race by linking black history to the rivers of the world.

Another outstanding figure of the Harlem Renaissance was Zora Neale Hurston (about 1901–1960), the most prolific African American woman writer of her generation. Poet, novelist, folklorist, essayist, Hurston made her literary task the exploration of what it means to be black and female in a white- and male-dominated society. Not a rabble-rousing polemicist, she drew from many traditions besides her experience as an African American, including American southern and American feminist literatures, along with the insights of anthropology from her graduate studies at Barnard College in New York. An excellent example of this approach is *Their Eyes Were Watching God* (1937), published after

Figure 20.11 Jacob Lawrence. *Migration Series, No. 58.* The original caption reads, "In the North the Negro had better educational facilities." 1940–1941. Tempera on gesso on composition board, 12 × 18″. The Museum of Modern Art, New York. Gift of Mrs. David M. Levy. *Jacob Lawrence's* Migration *series, a cycle of paintings commissioned by* Fortune *magazine, depicted the mass flight of African Americans from the American South to the North in their quest for a better life. Lawrence (1917–2000) was a Harlem resident and the son of black migrants. These works are simplistic in format (standard small size and common color scheme); nevertheless, they reveal Lawrence's knowledge of modernism, especially in the flatness and angularity of the figures and the unusual perspective. The painting titled* No. 58 *evokes a sense of rhythm by having the number sequence repeated by the young girls' arm and leg movements and their swaying dresses. This series established Lawrence as a serious artist, and in 1941 he became the first African American included in the permanent collection of New York's Museum of Modern Art.*

the heyday of the Harlem Renaissance. In this novel, Hurston portrays the African American heroine Janie Crawford as she seeks sexual and personal fulfillment in rural segregated Florida in the 1920s and 1930s. Speaking in heavy dialect, marked by pithy language and folk sayings, Janie Crawford narrates her life story, giving a richly evocative sense of time and place to the novel's events.

DRAMA Drama now moved in new directions in both Europe and America. The German Bertolt Brecht [BREKT] (1898–1956), an expressionist in aesthetics and a Marxist in politics, blended a discordant style learned from the Berlin streets with his hatred of bourgeois soci-

ety into what he called "**epic theater.**" Rebelling against traditional theater, which he thought merely reinforced class prejudices, he devised a radical theater centered on a technique called the "alienation effect," whose purpose was to make the bourgeois audience uncomfortable (Figure 20.12). Alienation effects could take any form, such as outlandish props, inappropriate accents, or ludicrous dialogue. By breaking the magic spell of the stage, Brecht's epic theater challenged the viewers' expectations and prepared them for his moral and political message. A victim of Nazi oppression, Brecht fled first to Scandinavia and then to America, where he lived for fifteen years before moving to East Berlin in 1952 to found a highly influential theater company.

Figure 20.12   Hannah Höch. *Cut with the Kitchen Knife Dada through Germany's Last Weimar Beer-Belly Cultural Epoch.* 1919–1920. Photomontage and collage with watercolor, 44⅞ × 35⅟₁₆". Staatliche Museen zu Berlin, Nationalgalerie. *The art of German artist Hannah Höch (1888–1978) is a visual counterpart to the dramas of Brecht. In this piece, Höch portrays her fellow Germans as morally and politically corrupt, a point she reinforces with the caustic title. Höch belonged to the art movement called Dada, which was imported into Berlin from Zurich at the end of World War I. Höch's artistic technique—*photomontage,* which mixed photographs cut from newspapers to send a message—was adapted from the collages invented by Picasso (see Chapter 19). Note the word* Dada *appears several times in this image.*

A year before he officially embraced Marxism, Brecht teamed with the German-born composer Kurt Weill [WILE or VILE] (1900–1950) to create one of the best-known musicals in modern theater, *The Threepenny Opera* (1928). Loosely based on an eighteenth-century English opera, Brecht and Weill's expressionist version was raucous, discordant, violent, and hostile to bourgeois values. The playwright, believing bourgeois audiences wanted goodness to triumph over evil, made the hero a small-time hoodlum ("Mack the Knife") and then saved him at the last moment from a hanging that he richly deserved.

Besides such pathfinders as Brecht, this period produced two major modernist playwrights: Jean Cocteau and Eugene O'Neill. The French dramatist Jean Cocteau [kahk-TOE] (1889–1963) helped launch the French trend for modernizing the Greek classics. His *The Infernal Machine* (1934), for example, updates Sophocles' *Oedipus* so that the story is filled with Freudian

overtones—Oedipus is portrayed as a "mother's boy"—and film clips are introduced for flashbacks. Eugene O'Neill (1888–1953) was the first American dramatist to earn worldwide fame. Like Cocteau, he wrote new versions of Greek tragedies, as in *Mourning Becomes Electra* (1931), modeled on Aeschylus's *Oresteia*. O'Neill's best plays, however, are family-conflict dramas, as in *Long Day's Journey into Night*, staged posthumously in 1956.

Philosophy, Science, and Medicine

The Age of the Masses was a fertile period in philosophy, science, and medicine, when old certainties were under fire from, respectively, new schools of thought, a revolutionary way of looking at the world, and medical advances. However, certainty still reigned supreme in one highly visible aspect of science—the practical application of science as a cure for social ills. Indeed, this was the last period when blind faith in science still ruled, a trend that began with the Scientific Revolution and was sanctified by the Enlightenment's optimistic perspective (see Chapters 15 and 16).

PHILOSOPHY   During this period, the idealist philosophy that had dominated Continental speculation since the early 1800s was replaced by two new schools of thought. First, in Austria and England, Ludwig Wittgenstein developed ideas that helped establish the logical positivist school, which became known after World War II as the analytical school. Second, in Germany, Martin Heidegger founded the existentialist school. Both schools tried to create new philosophies that were in harmony with modernist developments.

The Austrian Ludwig Wittgenstein [VIT-guhn-stine] (1889–1951) believed the West was in a moral and intellectual decline that he attributed to faulty language, for which, he surmised, current philosophical methods were to blame. Wittgenstein asserted that traditional philosophical speculation was senseless because, of necessity, it relied on language that could not rise above simple truisms.

Wittgenstein's solution to this intellectual impasse was to dethrone philosophy and make it simply the servant of science. He set forth his conclusion in his *Tractatus Logico-Philosophicus* in 1922. In this treatise, he reasoned that, although language might be faulty, there are mathematical and scientific tools for comprehending the world. He proposed that thinkers give up the study of values and morals and assist scientists in a quest for truth. This conclusion led to **logical positivism,** a school of philosophy dedicated to defining terms and clarifying statements.

Wittgenstein later rejected the idea that language is a flawed instrument and substituted a theory of language as games, in the manner of children's play. Nevertheless, it was the point of view set forth in the *Tractatus* that made Wittgenstein so influential in the universities in England between 1930 and 1960 and in America after World War II.

While Wittgenstein was challenging philosophy's ancient role, Martin Heidegger [HI-deg-uhr] (1889–1976) was assaulting traditional philosophy from another angle by founding modern **existentialism.** The result of Heidegger's critique was to restore philosophy to its primary role as the definer of values for culture. His major work, *Being and Time* (1927), focused on the peculiar nature of human existence (the source of the term *existentialism*) when compared with other objects in the world. For him, human existence leads to anxiety, because of the consciousness that there is a future that includes choices and death. He noted that most people try to avoid facing their inevitable fate by immersing themselves in trivial activities. For a few, though, Heidegger

thought that the existential moment offers an opportunity to seize the initiative and make themselves into authentic human beings. "Authenticity" became the ultimate human goal: to confront death and to strive for genuine creativity—a typical German philosophical attitude shared with Goethe and Nietzsche.

Although among this period's foremost thinkers, Heidegger's politics made him controversial. He used his post as a German university professor to support the rise of Nazism in the 1930s. To some critics, Heidegger's existential viewpoint—an individual, powerless to reshape the world, can only accept it—seemed to support his political position. Indeed, some commentators have condemned existentialism for this reason.

Heidegger's best-known disciple and one who rejected Nazism was the French thinker Jean-Paul Sartre [SAHR-truh] (1905–1980). Sartre's major philosophical work, *Being and Nothingness* (1943), was heavily indebted to his mentor's concepts. From Heidegger came his definition of existentialism as an attitude characterized by concern for human freedom, personal responsibility, and individual choices. Sartre used these ideas to frame his guiding rule: because human beings are condemned to freedom—that is, not free *not* to choose—they must take responsibility for their actions and live "without excuses." After 1945, Sartre rejected existentialism as overly individualistic and thereafter tended to support Marxist collectivist action.

SCIENCE   In the sciences, physics remained the field of dynamic activity. The breakthroughs made before World War I were now corroborated by new research that compelled scientists to discard the Newtonian model of the universe as a simple machine. They replaced it with a complex, sense-defying structure based on the discoveries of Albert Einstein and Werner Heisenberg (Figure 20.13).

Einstein was now the leading scientist in the West, comparable to Newton in the 1700s. His special relativity theory, dating from 1905, overturned the Newtonian concept of fixed dimensions of time and space (see Chapter 19). In Einstein's view, absolute space and time are meaningless categories, since they vary with the situation. In 1915 Einstein expanded this earlier finding into a general theory of relativity, a universal law based on complex equations that apply throughout the cosmos. The heart of the general theory is that space is curved as a result of the acceleration of objects (planets, stars, moons, meteors, and so on) as they move through undulating trajectories. The earth's orbit about the sun is caused not by a gravitational "force" but by the curvature of space-time around the sun. In 1919 a team of scientists observed the curvature of space in the vicinity of the sun and confirmed that space curves to the degree that Einstein's theory had forecast. Since then, his

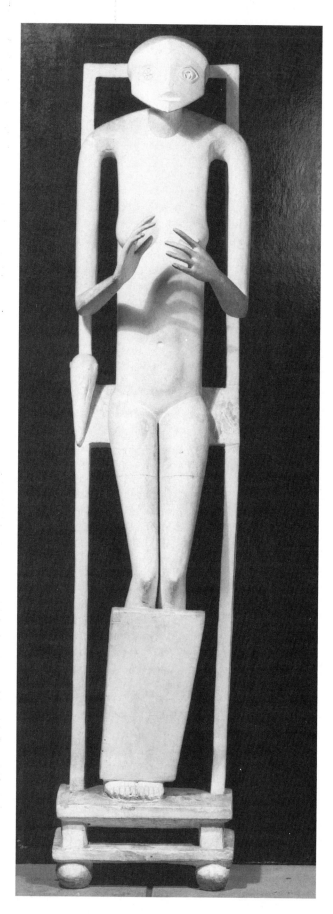

Figure 20.13 ALBERTO GIACOMETTI. *Hands Holding the Void.* 1934. Plaster sculpture, original cast, ht. 61½". Yale University Art Gallery, New Haven, Connecticut. Anonymous gift. *The uncertainty of the modern world—as demonstrated by both physics and the economic and social realities of daily life—is poignantly symbolized in Giacometti's sculpture. His melancholy figure, clutching an invisible object, evokes the anguish humans suffered in no longer being able to expect answers from traditional sources, such as science and philosophy. Giacometti personally shared these fears as he created, in this unusual work (inspired by his admiration for Egyptian sculpture), a semiseated female whose face is a mask. She seems to be, in the opinion of one critic, searching for what is truly human in a state of painful ignorance—the predicament of those in the modern world.*

general theory has survived many tests of its validity and has opened new paths of theoretical speculation.

The other great breakthrough of modern physics was the establishment of quantum physics. Before 1914, the German physicist Max Planck discovered the quantum nature of radiation in the subatomic realm (see Chapter 19). Ignoring the classical theory that energy is radiated continuously, he proved that energy is emitted in separate units that he called *quanta,* after the Latin for "how much" (as in *quantity*), and he symbolized these units by the letter h.

Working with Planck's h in 1927, which by now was accepted as a fundamental constant of nature, the German physicist Werner Heisenberg [HIZE-uhn-berg] (1901–1976) arrived at the uncertainty principle, a step that constituted a decisive break with classical physics. Heisenberg showed that a scientist could identify either an electronic particle's exact location or its path, but not both. This dilemma led to the conclusion that absolute certitude in subatomic science is impossible because scientists with their instruments inevitably interfere with the accuracy of their own work—the uncertainty principle. The incertitude involved in quantum theory caused Einstein to remark, "God does not play dice with the world." Nevertheless, quantum theory joined relativity theory as a founding principle of modern physics.

A practical result of the revolution in physics was the opening of the nuclear age in August 1945. The American physicist J. Robert Oppenheimer [AHP-uhn-hi-muhr] (1904–1967), having made basic contributions to quantum theory, was appointed head of the team that built the first atomic bomb. Oppenheimer's other role as a member of the panel that advised that the atomic bombs be dropped on Japan raised ethical questions that divided the scientific community then and continue to do so.

While debates divided the scientific community, many people in the rest of society forcefully expressed

SLICE OF LIFE
The Face of Evil: A Nazi Death Camp

ELIE WIESEL
Night (2006)

In this excerpt from his autobiographical novel, Night, *Wiesel (b. 1928) describes the arrival of his family at Auschwitz, a Nazi death camp, in 1944.*

The beloved objects that we had carried with us from place to place were now left behind in the wagon and, with them, finally, our illusions.

Every few yards, there stood an SS man, his machine gun trained on us. Hand in hand we followed the throng.

An SS came toward us wielding a club. He commanded:

"Men to the left! Women to the right!"

Eight words spoken quietly, indifferently, without emotion. Eight simple, short words. Yet that was the moment when I left my mother. There was no time to think, and I already felt my father's hand press against mine: we were alone. In a fraction of a second I could see my mother, my sisters, move to the right. Tzipora was holding Mother's hand. I saw them walking farther and farther away; Mother was stroking my sister's blond hair, as if to protect her. And I walked on with my father, with the men. I didn't know that this was the moment in time and the place where I was leaving my mother and Tzipora forever. I kept walking, my father holding my hand.

Behind me, an old man fell to the ground. Nearby, an SS man replaced his revolver in its holster.

My hand tightened its grip on my father. All I could think of was not to lose him. Not to remain alone.

The SS officers gave the order.

"Form ranks of fives!"

There was a tumult. It was imperative to stay together.

"Hey, kid, how old are you?"

The man interrogating me was an inmate. I could not see his face, but his voice was weary and warm.

"Fifteen."

"No. You're eighteen."

"But I'm not," I said. "I'm fifteen."

"Fool. Listen to what *I* say."

Then he asked my father, who answered:

"I'm fifty."

"No." The man now sounded angry. "Not fifty. You're forty. Do you hear? Eighteen and forty."

He disappeared into the darkness.

INTERPRETING THIS SLICE OF LIFE

1. *Summarize* the events set forth in this excerpt from Wiesel's book. 2. *What* is the significance of the inmate insisting that the son claim to be eighteen and the father to be forty? 3. *Explain* what the narrator means by the word *illusions* in the first sentence. 4. *Relate* the narrator's experience with that of children caught in contemporary political upheavals.

their unquestioning trust in the pseudoscience behind the racist theories that then flourished across the West. These theories, which blamed social ills on innate racial differences, were rooted in the writings of Joseph-Arthur, Comte (Count) de Gobineau [go-be-no] (1816–1882), a French social theorist. Gobineau's claim that the white race—which he labeled the "Aryans," that is, the Germanic peoples, including the English— was superior to all others resonated across the political and social spectrum. Many people in the West came to share his view that the future of civilization depended on maintaining the racial purity and dominance of Aryan culture. Over time, Gobineau's theory, dressed up in many guises and justified by scientific research, had a powerful impact on Western society and history.

Germany was probably the country most affected by racist thought, as expressed in the eugenics (Greek, *eugenes*, "of good stock") movement, which called for the selective breeding of human beings. Nazi ideology, rooted in the myth of Aryan supremacy, led to a full-fledged eugenics program and eventually to genocide. Seeking Aryan racial purity, the Nazis created a forced sterilization program in the 1930s, in which doctors sterilized more than four hundred thousand people who were deemed genetically defective, including the mentally unfit, severe alcoholics, and the handicapped. The Aryan supremacy claim resulted in the Holocaust, the Nazi plan to eliminate Jews, whom German doctors believed to be carriers of many genetic disorders (see Slice of Life). After World War II, knowledge of the Holocaust helped discredit the eugenics movement.

The eugenics movement in the United States did not lead to genocide, but it did spark varied governmental policies. In 1924 a federal law was passed closing immigration from southern and eastern Europe, the Balkans, and Russia. Vice President Calvin Coolidge (1872–1933)

Timeline 20.1   HIGH MODERNISM, 1914–1945

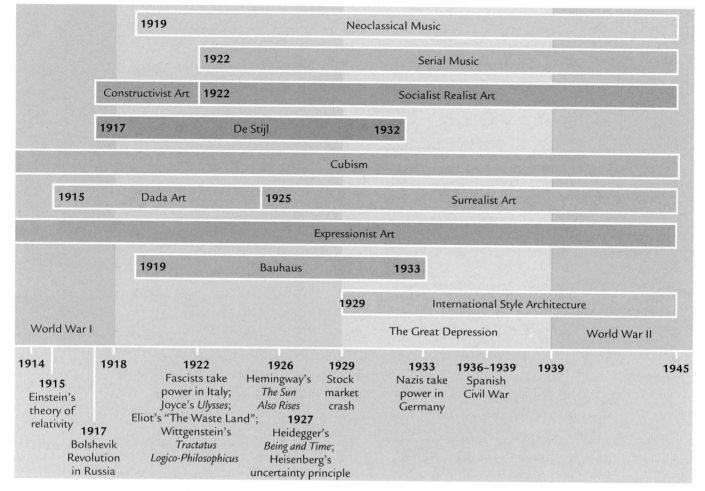

justified this legislation thusly: "America must be kept American. Biological laws show . . . that Nordics deteriorate when mixed with other races." Only six senators voted against this exclusionary law. Further, by 1930, twenty-seven states had laws that allowed involuntary sterilization of the feebleminded and others deemed unfit—with the surgery performed usually at state-run psychiatric hospitals or homes for the mentally challenged. Eugenics programs also thrived in England and France. And, earlier, in 1901, Australia closed its doors to non-European immigrants, making itself a citadel of white culture.

MEDICINE   Major medical events between 1900 and 1945 occurred in two areas: identification of disease pathogens and the development of pharmaceuticals. Medical researchers, following Pasteur's germ theory of disease (see Chapter 18), now identified these new pathogens—disease-causing agents: rickettsias, organisms that cause diseases such as typhus; protozoans, organisms that produce tropical illnesses such as malaria; and viruses,

organisms that cause mumps, measles, and polio. New pharmaceuticals included aspirin (1899), the world's universal pain remedy today; arsphenamine (1910), an arsenic-based preparation, which was the first effective treatment for syphilis and the first chemotherapy; sulfonamide (1936), an antibacterial agent, used to cure septicemia (blood infection) and other infections; penicillin (discovered in 1928 and made available in injectable form in 1941), probably the West's most popular antibiotic, used against syphilis, meningitis, and other ills, until the rise of penicillin-resistant bacteria; and streptomycin (1944), the first successful treatment for infectious tuberculosis. In World War II, penicillin helped save many lives on the battlefield.

Art, Architecture, Photography, and Film

The art, architecture, photography, and film of the interwar period were driven by the same forces that were transforming literature and philosophy. Mod-

THE ZENITH OF MODERNISM 615

ernism reached its zenith in painting and architecture, photography came into its own as part of the mass media, and movies became the world's most popular form of mass culture (Timeline 20.1).

PAINTING Painting now dominated the visual arts. Painters launched new art movements every two or three years, although certain prevailing themes and interests could be discerned as a foundation for the three shifting styles: abstraction, primitivism and fantasy, and expressionism. Picasso and Matisse, the two giants of twentieth-century art, continued to exercise their influence, yet they too worked within these three categories, all of which had arisen in the postimpressionist period.

Abstraction Picasso and Braque laid the platform for abstraction with their cubist paintings before World War I (see Chapter 19), but Soviet painters now moved beyond cubism to full abstraction, thus staking out claims as the founders of modern abstract art. The most influential of these Soviet artists was Kasimir Malevich [mahl-YAY-vich] (1878–1935).

Influenced by the cubists and the Italian futurists—the latter, a school of artists who depicted forms in surging, violent motion—Malevich was already working in an abstract style when World War I began. By war's end in 1918, he was painting completely nonobjective canvases. Believing that art should convey ethical and philosophical values, he created a painting style devoted to purity and devoid of content except for line, color, and shape. He called this style **suprematism,** named for his belief that the feelings are supreme over every other element of life—feelings, that is, expressed in a purely rational way.

Searching for a way to visualize emotions on canvas, Malevich adopted geometric shapes as nonobjective symbols, as in *Suprematist Composition* (Figure 20.14). In this painting, design has triumphed over representation. There are only geometric shapes of different sizes and varying lengths. The choice of the geometric shapes reflects their role as basic elements of composition with no relation to nature. The qualities shown in Malevich's painting—flatness, coolness, and severe rationality—remain central to one branch of abstract art today.

Malevich's suprematism helped to shape **constructivism,** the first art style launched by Lenin's regime in 1917. Malevich's philosophical views, rooted in Christian mysticism, ran counter to the materialism of the Marxist government, however, and the flowering of abstraction in the Soviet Union was abruptly snuffed out in 1922. In that year, Lenin pronounced it a decadent form of bourgeois expression, and its leaders were imprisoned or exiled. In place of constructivism, the Soviet leaders proclaimed the doctrine of **socialist**

Figure 20.14 KASIMIR MALEVICH. *Suprematist Composition.* 1916–1917. Oil on canvas, 29 × 36¼". The Museum of Modern Art, New York. Photograph © 1997 The Museum of Modern Art. *Malevich's geometric style reflected his belief that abstract images had a spiritual quality comparable to that of religious icons. Thus, if approached in the proper spirit, an abstract form could become a meditation device that could lead the viewer's thoughts beyond the physical realm. For Malevich, the physical realm was no longer of use, and painting was a search for visual metaphors (mainly geometric elements) that could evoke awareness of unconscious and conscious experiences in the individual. His belief was typical of thinking among the German and Russian avant-garde in the early 1900s.*

realism, which demanded the use of traditional techniques and styles and the glorification of the communist ideal. This type of realistic art also held greater appeal for the Soviet masses, who had been alienated by the abstract style of constructivism.

A movement similar to suprematism and constructivism, called **de Stijl** [duh STILE] ("the style"), originated in the Netherlands, lasting from 1917 to 1932.

INTERPRETING ART

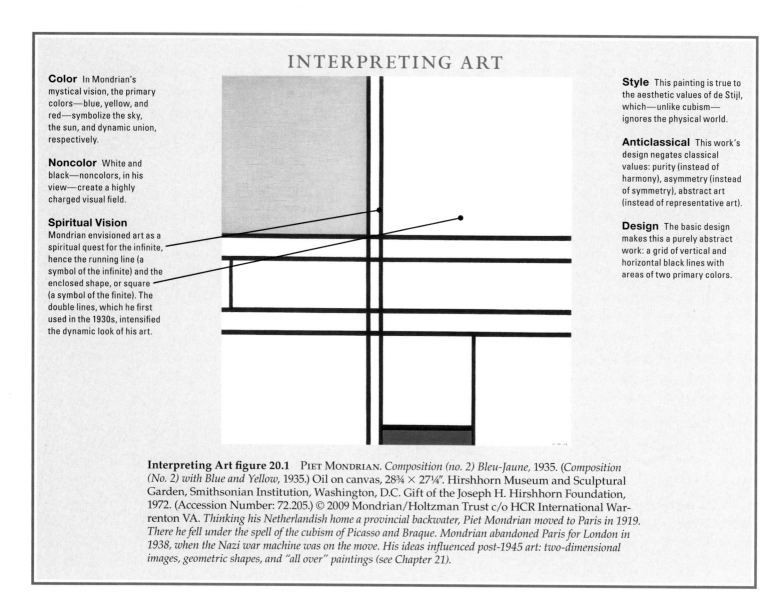

Color In Mondrian's mystical vision, the primary colors—blue, yellow, and red—symbolize the sky, the sun, and dynamic union, respectively.

Noncolor White and black—noncolors, in his view—create a highly charged visual field.

Spiritual Vision Mondrian envisioned art as a spiritual quest for the infinite, hence the running line (a symbol of the infinite) and the enclosed shape, or square (a symbol of the finite). The double lines, which he first used in the 1930s, intensified the dynamic look of his art.

Style This painting is true to the aesthetic values of de Stijl, which—unlike cubism—ignores the physical world.

Anticlassical This work's design negates classical values: purity (instead of harmony), asymmetry (instead of symmetry), abstract art (instead of representative art).

Design The basic design makes this a purely abstract work: a grid of vertical and horizontal black lines with areas of two primary colors.

Interpreting Art figure 20.1 Piet Mondrian. *Composition (no. 2) Bleu-Jaune*, 1935. (*Composition (No. 2) with Blue and Yellow*, 1935.) Oil on canvas, 28¾ × 27¼″. Hirshhorn Museum and Sculptural Garden, Smithsonian Institution, Washington, D.C. Gift of the Joseph H. Hirshhorn Foundation, 1972. (Accession Number: 72.205.) © 2009 Mondrian/Holtzman Trust c/o HCR International Warrenton VA. *Thinking his Netherlandish home a provincial backwater, Piet Mondrian moved to Paris in 1919. There he fell under the spell of the cubism of Picasso and Braque. Mondrian abandoned Paris for London in 1938, when the Nazi war machine was on the move. His ideas influenced post-1945 art: two-dimensional images, geometric shapes, and "all over" paintings (see Chapter 21).*

De Stijl artists shared the belief that art should have spiritual values and that artists have a social mission to improve the world by revamping society along rational lines, from town planning to private residences to eating utensils.

The de Stijl movement was led by the painter Piet Mondrian [MAHN-dree-ahn] (1872–1944), who after 1919 worked successively in Paris, London, and New York. He developed an elaborate theory to give a metaphysical meaning to his abstract paintings. A member of the Theosophists—a cult that flourished in about 1900—he adapted some of their mystical beliefs to arrive at a grid format for his later paintings, notably using the Theosophists' stress on cosmic duality, in which the vertical represented the male and the horizontal the female. To create the grid format, he used heavy black lines set against a white background. Into this highly charged field he introduced rectangles of the primary colors—blue, yellow, and red, as in *Composition with Blue and Yellow* (Interpreting Art figure 20.1).

Despite the pioneering work of suprematism and the de Stijl school, cubism remained the leading art movement of this period, and Pablo Picasso was still the reigning cubist. Picasso's protean genius revealed itself in multiple styles after 1920, but he continually reverted to his cubist roots, as in *The Three Musicians* (Figure 20.15). Like the rest of his works, this painting is based on a realistic source, in this case a group of masked musicians playing their instruments. The forms appear flattened, as if they were shapes that had been cut out and then pasted to the pictorial surface—the ideal of flatness so prized by modern painters.

The most famous work of Picasso's long career also dates from this period: the protest canvas *Guernica*,

Figure 20.15 PABLO PICASSO. *The Three Musicians.* 1921. Oil on canvas, 6′8″ × 6′2″. Philadelphia Museum of Art. The A. E. Gallatin Collection. *This cubist painting captures the energy of a musical performance. Here and there among the flattened shapes can be seen hints of musical instruments being fingered by disembodied hands. Only a little imagination is needed to bring this masked trio to life. The brilliant colors coupled with the broken and resynthesized forms evoke the jagged rhythms the musicians must have been playing.*

painted in a modified cubist style. Picasso named this painting for an unarmed town that had been bombed by Nazi air planes (in the service of Franco) during the Spanish Civil War. He used every element in the work to register his rage against this senseless destruction of human life (see Figure 20.1). The black, white, and gray tones conjure up newspaper images, suggesting the casual way that newspapers report daily disasters. An all-seeing eye looks down on a scene of horror made visible to the world through the modern media—as symbolized by the electric bulb that acts as a retina in the cosmic eye. Images of death and destruction—the mother cradling a child's body, the stabbed horse, the enraged bull, the fallen man, and the screaming woman—are made even more terrifying by their angular forms. In retrospect, *Guernica* was a watershed painting both topically and stylistically. The blending of cubism with social protest was new—as was Franco's type of unbridled warfare. *Guernica* forecast even more horrifying events to come.

The American painter Georgia O'Keeffe (1887–1986) refused to follow European painters down the path to pure abstraction. Instead, she pursued a distinctively American type of abstraction, using American subjects drawn from nature, which she pared to their pure form and color; at the same time, she kept representation of the natural world as a primary goal of her art. A native of Wisconsin, O'Keeffe found a spiritual home in the American Southwest—Texas and especially New Mexico—whose sun-drenched, stark landscapes inspired some of her most famous images. Sensitive to light, color, texture, and atmosphere, she registered in her paintings the previously hidden beauties of this high desert world, as in *Cow's Skull with Calico Roses* (Figure 20.16). As early as the Renaissance, painters had occasionally used death's-heads as *memento mori* (reminders of death), but no artist before O'Keeffe had thought of presenting a cow's skull as an art subject. The already abstract form of the cow's skull, stripped bare of flesh, became even more abstract as she simplified it

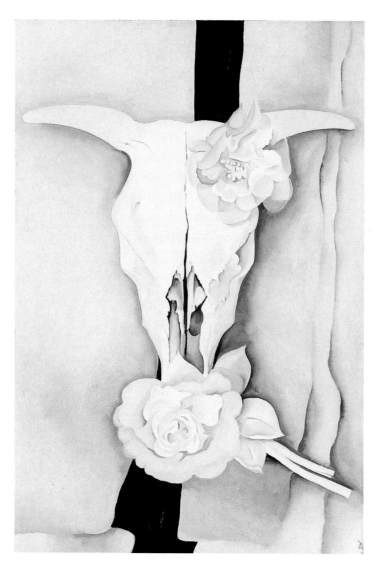

Figure 20.16 GEORGIA O'KEEFFE. *Cow's Skull with Calico Roses*. 1932. Oil on canvas, 36⁵/₁₆ × 24¹/₈″. Art Institute of Chicago. Gift of Georgia O'Keeffe. *The simplified forms—the skull and the rose—link this painting to the period's trend to abstraction, but their placement so as to suggest the image of a "face" devouring a rose implies a connection with another development of this period, surrealism, a style that delighted in realistic images with double meanings (see Figure 20.18). Whether intentional or not, O'Keeffe's overlapping of stylistic boundaries was typical of the fluid artistic scene in the years between the two world wars.*

and presented it close-up with two roses nearby. The result is an image of shocking beauty.

Primitivism and Fantasy The modernists' admiration for primitivism led to **Dada** [DAH-dah], the most unusual art movement of the twentieth century. Named for a nonsense word chosen for its ridiculous sound, Dada flourished in six cities—Zurich, Berlin, Cologne, Hannover, Paris, and New York—between 1915 and 1925, chiefly as unruly pranks by disaffected artists

who wanted to "hurl gobs of spit in the faces of the bourgeoisie." They staged exhibits in public lavatories, planned meetings in cemeteries, and arranged lectures where the speaker was drowned out by a bell. Slowly it became evident that these outrageous acts conveyed the message that World War I had made all values meaningless. Believing the spiritual claims and traditional beliefs of Western humanism were dead, the Dada group embraced antiart as the only ethical position for an artist in the modern era.

The most influential exponent of Dada was the French artist Marcel Duchamp [doo-SHAHN] (1887–1968), who abandoned cubism in about 1915. His best-known Dada piece is the "definitely incomplete" work called *The Bride Stripped Bare by Her Bachelors, Even,* a mixture of oil, wire, and lead foil on two glass panels made between 1915 and 1923, sometimes called *The Large Glass* (Figure 20.17). Although it is certainly enigmatic, and in the eyes of many viewers it looks like a giant swindle, much is clear about *The Large Glass.* It has an erotic theme, typical of Dada art. Duchamp makes this theme manifest in the sculpture by devoting the upper half to the bride (the amorphous shape floating on the left) and her "apartment" (the stretch of gauze with three holes) and populating the lower "chamber" with the bachelors (the nine objects to the left) and their sex organ (the contraption made of a watermill, grinder, and other bits of metal). Linking the bride with the bachelors are tiny capillaries, or thin tubes, filled with oil—symbolic of fertilization with sperm. Duchamp's point seems to be similar to that of the novelist D. H. Lawrence: sex in the machine age has become boring and mechanized.

Dada led to **surrealism,** an art movement that began in the 1920s. Unlike Dada, surrealism was basically a pictorial art. Inspired by Freud's teaching that the human mind conceals hidden depths, the surrealists wanted to create a vision of reality that also included the truths harbored in the unconscious. They portrayed dream imagery, fantasies, and hallucinations in a direct fashion that made their paintings more startling than those of Dadaist artists. Among the leading surrealists were Salvador Dali and Paul Klee.

The Spanish painter Salvador Dali [DAH-lee] (1904–1989) concentrated on subjects that surfaced from his lively imagination and often contained thinly disguised sexual symbols. Probably his most famous work is the poetically named painting *The Persistence of Memory,* which depicts soft, melting watches in a desertlike setting (Figure 20.18). Sexual themes may be read in the limp images of watches—perhaps a reference to sexual impotence. Regardless of its meaning, the painting gives a strange twist to ordinary things, evoking the sense of a half-remembered dream—the goal of surrealist art. Despite obvious painterly skills, Dali culti-

Figure 20.17 MARCEL DUCHAMP. *The Bride Stripped Bare by Her Bachelors, Even* (or *The Large Glass*). 1915–1923. Oil and lead wire on glass, 9′1¼″ × 5′9⅛″. Philadelphia Museum of Art. Bequest of Katherine M. Dreier. *Shortly after this legendary assemblage was built, the glass shattered. Duchamp repaired the work, replacing the glass with heavier panes and installing a reinforced frame. But effects of the accident are still apparent. Duchamp claimed to be delighted by these chance additions to his original design. In making this claim, he was the forerunner of the modernist idea that chance should play a guiding role in art. After World War II, many artists began to incorporate random effects into their works.*

vated a controversial, even scandalous, personal image. His escapades earned him the public's ridicule, and the surrealists even disowned him. From today's vantage point, however, Dali is admired for two reasons: for having created some of modernism's most fantastic images and for being a link with the pop artists of the 1960s (see Chapter 21).

The Swiss painter Paul Klee [KLAY] (1879–1940) may be grouped with the surrealists, but he was too changeable to be restricted to a single style. He is best known for an innocent approach to art, which was triggered by his fondness for children's uninhibited scrawls. The childlike wonder portrayed in his whimsical works has made him a favorite with collectors and viewers. A professor from 1920 until 1930 at the Bauhaus, Germany's leading art institute between the wars, Klee created poetic images, rich in color and gentle wit, as in *Revolution of the Viaduct* (Figure 20.19). This painting depicts the breakup of a viaduct—a series of arches built to carry a road across a wide valley—when each arch,

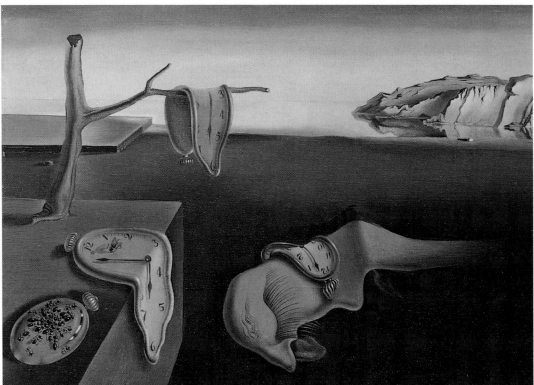

Figure 20.18 SALVADOR DALI. *The Persistence of Memory (Persistance de la mémoire)*. 1931. Oil on canvas, 9½ × 13". The Museum of Modern Art, New York. Given anonymously. Photograph © 1997 The Museum of Modern Art. *Dali liked to paint images that were actually optical illusions. In this painting, the watch depicted on the right is draped over an amorphous shape that, on inspection, appears to be that of a man. Dali's use of such optical effects reflected his often-stated belief that life is irrational.*

marching on thin "legs" and footlike bases, goes its own way. More than a cartoon, this whimsical work is Klee's allegorical response to Europe's growing fascist culture—an atypical gesture by this usually apolitical artist. Klee equates the viaduct with the neo-Roman buildings favored by the Nazis as an expression of a homogeneous community ideal. The viaduct's breakup into individualized arches forecasts the downfall of Nazism. Klee thus espouses a quiet faith that fascist mass conformity may be undermined by the subversive acts of cultural revolutionaries—such as himself.

Klee's poetic images deeply impressed the Argentinean painter Xul Solar (zool so-LAHR) (born Oscar Agustin Alejandro Schulz) (1887–1963). Xul Solar's encounter with European art began during a twelve-year stay in France and Italy, where he mingled with the avant-garde, especially the futurists (see Figure 19.2). But it was Klee and his childish sense of wonder that spoke directly to Xul Solar. When Xul Solar returned to Buenos Aires in 1924, his playfulness was soon evident in Neocriollismo ("new Creole-ism"), the movement he founded, along with its own Neocriollo language. Mixing Portuguese and Spanish, Neocriollo was in part a sly call for unity among the nations of South America and in part an expression of his spiritual quest for a universal tongue. The name he now adopted, Xul So-

lar, has several meanings, including "solar light" and "light from the south." From this period stems his lifelong friendship with the writer Jorge Luis Borges (see Chapter 22). Xul Solar's paintings, usually executed in watercolors, combined a childlike quality with a visionary's sense of reality, as in *Drago* (Figure 20.20).

The Mexican painter Frida Kahlo [KAH-low] (1907–1954), famed for her unsettling self-portraits, might be classified with the surrealists, though she is usually linked with the Mexican muralists, the politically motivated artists who flourished between the two world wars and who painted mural (wall) cycles in public buildings to dramatize their socialist vision and solidarity with Mexico's native peoples. For most of her life, she was involved in a tempestuous marriage to Diego Rivera (1886–1957), a leading Mexican muralist, but she was much more than the wife of a famous painter. Kahlo was an important artist in her own right, creating works that reflected her physical and spiritual suffering (she had polio at age six and was in a serious accident at eighteen). Today, she is known as an artist who turned private anguish into art with universal resonance.

Kahlo's *Self-Portrait Dedicated to Dr. Eloesser* (Figure 20.21) dates from a dark period in her life. Beset by marital and health problems and distraught over the assassination of her friend the Russian Marxist Leon Trotsky,

Figure 20.19 PAUL KLEE. *Revolution of the Viaduct.* 1937. Oil on canvas, 25⅝ × 19⅝″. Kunsthalle, Hamburg. *Klee painted this work in the aftermath of the* Degenerate Art *exhibition, which opened in Munich in July 1937. Mounted by the Nazis to showcase what they called subversive art—art that encouraged "political anarchy and cultural anarchy"—the show was a frontal assault on modernism. Klee, living in Switzerland after having been fired from his German teaching post in 1933, was represented by seventeen works in this show, displayed under the topics "confusion" and "insanity." Klee's* Revolution of the Viaduct *was part of the response of the international modernist art world to the Nazi challenge.*

who had been living in exile in Mexico, Kahlo was restored to health by the strict regimen of Dr. Eloesser of San Francisco. In gratitude, she dedicated this work to him, as indicated by the flying banner, which reads, in part, "to my doctor and my best friend, with all my love." Despite this upbeat motif, the portrait reflects Kahlo's obsession with death and suffering.

Expressionism The chief expressionist painters in this era were Henri Matisse, a founder of fauvism before World War I (see Chapter 19), and Max Beckmann, the heir to German expressionism. In the 1920s, Matisse's art was distinguished by its decorative quality, a tendency since his fauvist days. Tapping into the period's love affair with Orientalism, Matisse enlivened the painting surface with decorative patterns taken

Figure 20.20 XUL SOLAR. *Drago.* 1927. Watercolor, approx. 10 × 12⅔″. Museo Xul Solar, Buenos Aires. *This small painting, filled with tiny national flags, schematic images of the sun, moon, and stars, religious symbols, and a lizard-like creature with two legs where the tail should be, portrays an alternate universe to that of Einstein and Newton.* Drago *suggests a dreamscape—hence, Xul Solar's art is sometimes linked with that of the surrealists.*

Figure 20.21 FRIDA KAHLO. *Self-Portrait Dedicated to Dr. Eloesser.* 1940. Oil on masonite, 22¼ × 15¾". Private collection, U.S.A. *Kahlo reveals a modernist sensibility in this likeness, which draws on multicultural sources, including Christianity and her indigenous Mexican heritage. The necklace of thorns, which makes her neck bleed, refers both to Christ's crown of thorns worn during the Crucifixion and to the Aztec prophetic ritual that required self-mortification with maguey thorns. The earring in the form of a hand—a gift from Picasso—symbolizes the hand of fate, and the jungle of oversized leaves evokes an image of nature out of control.*

Figure 20.22 HENRI MATISSE. *Decorative Figure in an Oriental Setting.* 1925. Oil on canvas, 51⅛ × 38½". Musée National d'Art Moderne, Centre Georges Pompidou, France. *In this work, the subject and the implied setting—an odalisque, or female slave, in a harem room in some unknown sultan's palace—had been an important part of Matisse's repertoire since the founding of fauvism. The nude, or sometimes partially clothed, odalisques conveyed a not-so-subtle message: enjoy living in contrast to the daily grind and materialism of Western industrial society.*

from varied non-Western sources: wallpapers, carpets, and fabrics, as in *Decorative Figure in an Oriental Setting* (Figure 20.22). And, as the work's title suggests, the female subject is rendered as simply another decorative element in the overall design. Nevertheless, Matisse remains true to his fauvist roots with the richly saturated colors.

Matisse was rebuked for concentrating on decorative subjects while many nations slipped into anarchy in the 1930s. No such charge can be made against the German painter Max Beckmann (1884–1950), whose expressionist paintings register horror at the era's turbulent events. *The Departure* is typical of his works, being concerned with both personal and spiritual issues (Fig-

ure 20.23). The structure of the painting—divided into three panels (a triptych) like a medieval altarpiece—suggests that it has religious meaning. It was the first of nine completed triptychs. Influenced by the mystical teachings of the German thinker Arthur Schopenhauer (1788–1860), East Asian philosophy, and the Jewish kabbalah (medieval writings), *The Departure* represents a yearning to be free of the horrors of earthly existence. In the side panels, Beckmann depicts images of cruelty, including bound human figures, one of whom is gagged, being subjected to torture—perhaps reflecting his fears of the rise of Nazism. In contrast, the central panel, in which a man, woman, and child are ferried across a lake by a hooded boatman, evokes the theme of deliverance. When the Nazis came to power in 1933, they declared Beckmann a degenerate artist, confiscated his works, and fired him from his academic post. In 1937 he sought refuge in Amsterdam, where he managed to survive World War II.

Figure 20.23   MAX BECKMANN. *The Departure.* 1932–1935. Oil on canvas, center panel 7′ × 3′9″, side panels 7′ × 3′3″. The Museum of Modern Art, New York. *In* The Departure, *Beckmann's expressionism is revealed through the treatment of form and color. The flat, angular figures, arranged into awkward positions, and the unusual perspective reinforce the painting's disturbing theme. The dark hues of the side panel, appropriate for the violent images, contrast with the bright colors of the central panel and its message of salvation.*

ARCHITECTURE   In the 1920s and 1930s, architects continued their search for a pure style, free of decoration and totally functional. Their efforts resembled a mystical quest, stemming from the belief that new architecture could solve social problems by creating a new physical environment—a recurrent theme in European modernism.

This visionary ideal of architecture was best expressed in Germany's Bauhaus, an educational institution whose aim was to bring about social reform through a new visual environment, especially in the design of everyday objects. To that end, the school brought together artists, craftspeople, and architects. During a brief lifetime, from 1919 to 1933, when it was closed by the Nazis, the Bauhaus, under Walter Gropius [GROH-pee-uhs] (1883–1969), was the center of

abstract art in Germany. The Bauhaus affected later culture in two ways: it developed a spartan type of interior design characterized by all-white rooms and wooden floors, streamlined furniture, and lighting supplied by banks of windows by day and recessed lamps at night; and it introduced the **international style** in architecture—sleek, geometrical, and devoid of ornament (Figure 20.24).

The international style's most distinguished representative in this period was the Swiss architect Charles-Édouard Jeanneret, better known as Le Corbusier [luh kor-boo-ZYAY] (1887–1965), whose artistic credo was "A house is a machine for living." In pursuit of this ideal, he pioneered building methods such as prefabricated housing and reinforced concrete as ways to eliminate ordinary walls. His Savoye House, near Paris, became

Figure 20.24 WALTER GROPIUS. The Bauhaus, Workshop Wing. 1925–1926. Dessau, Germany. Architectural Association Photo. © Petra Hodgson. *The Bauhaus (German, Architecture House) was an applied arts, architecture, and design school that operated from 1919 to 1933, when it was closed by the Nazis because of its supposed Jewish connections. Founded in Weimar in 1919, it moved to Dessau in 1925. Aspiring architects and designers trained in sculpture, painting, architecture, and crafts workshops, learning to design objects for a mass society, which would be both functional and aesthetically pleasing. Among the distinguished teachers were Paul Klee (see Figure 20.19) and Wassily Kandinsky (see Figure 19.24). The Bauhaus workshop wing, part of a three-building complex, was designed in the international style. Its front wall, constructed of glass and metal, became a defining architectural feature of office skyscrapers in the postwar period (see Figure 21.1).*

Figure 20.25 LE CORBUSIER. Savoye House. 1929–1931. Poissy, near Paris. *Le Corbusier wanted to break with previous styles of architecture and create a new style in tune with the machine age. His design for the Savoye House realizes this ambition completely through its severe geometrical form, its absence of decoration except for architectural details, and its sparkling white walls. When finished, the Savoye House had the streamlined look associated with industrial machinery, an achievement much admired in the 1930s.*

the prototype of private houses for the wealthy after World War II (Figure 20.25). The Savoye House was painted stark white and raised on columns, its ground floor had a curved wall, and its windows were slits. A painter before becoming an architect, Le Corbusier designed architecture that combined cubism's abstractness (the raised box) with constructivism's purity (whiteness).

PHOTOGRAPHY Between 1900 and 1945, photography continued to evolve within the two areas that emerged at the time of its birth: the photograph as a historical record and the photograph as a work of art (see Chapter 18). History-minded photographers wanted direct and realistic images, which would serve as records of their era for future generations, including documentary photographs, combat photographs, landscape scenes, urban scenes, industrial culture, and records of endangered social life (for example, village life and Native American rituals). In contrast, artistic photographers manipulated their final images, using soft-focus lenses and techniques borrowed from art and film, to create, for example, impressionistic photographs, photomontages (mixing photographs with words cut from newspapers—see Figure 20.12), and photographs influenced by abstraction, cubism, Dada, surrealism, and other art styles of the era. Neither category is absolute, however, as aesthetic influences inevitably creep into historic photographs and artistic photographs do serve as historic records of the event that produced them.

Documentary photography, or photojournalism, was probably this period's most highly visible photographic genre. This was because newspapers and magazines, both part of the explosive growth of mass culture, seemed insatiable in their appetite for new images. Staid newspapers, like the *New York Times* and England's *The Times,* resisted placing photographs on the front page, but the tabloids and the regional press, eager to boost sales, plastered historic, lurid, and humorous photographs on the front page and sprinkled others liberally throughout their pages as a way to attract more readers. A milestone in photographic history occurred in 1936 with the founding of *Life* magazine— the brainchild of Henry Luce (1898–1967)—because it was the first general-audience magazine in which pictures dominated. With fifty-two issues each year, *Life* raised the demand for new photographs exponentially. *Life*'s success soon spawned rivals in the United States and similar-style magazines in Germany, England, France, and elsewhere.

Photojournalism, perhaps because it was still in its infancy and thus had little tradition, exerted a powerful attraction for women, including Margaret Bourke-White (1906–1971) and Dorothea Lange (1895–1965), two of the period's leading photojournalists. Bourke-White estab-

lished her reputation with the Henry Luce group, starting in 1930. When *Life* was founded, she became one of four staff photographers who routinely circled the globe in search of a scoop. Her subjects, presented straightforwardly and directly, with just a hint of compassion, included Dust Bowl victims, southern sharecroppers, Czech life on the eve of the Nazi takeover, World War II (see Figure 20.7), Gandhi (see Encounter figure 20.1) and the partition of India, and the Korean War. Lange's fame rests primarily on her photographs for the Farm Security Administration (FSA), part of President Roosevelt's New Deal. Her photographs, made in extreme close-up, depict in uncomfortable detail lives wasted during the Depression (see Figure 20.5). More than a documentary record, her photographs served a propaganda function, because they were commissioned by this federal agency to bring the plight of the rural poor to the attention of affluent America.

FILM Motion pictures—the movies—were immediately popular when they were introduced in the early 1900s, and by the mid-1920s they had become the most popular mass entertainment, drawing larger audiences than the theater, vaudeville, and the music halls. The American film director D. W. Griffith (1875–1948) showed in such pioneering works as *The Birth of a Nation* (1915) and *Intolerance* (1916) that it was possible to make movies that were serious, sustained works of art. His technical innovations, such as crosscutting and the close-up, made more complex film narratives possible, but such attempts to develop the medium were rare. Although other directors quickly appropriated Griffith's techniques, few went beyond them, and the movies remained resolutely lowbrow. The present-day distinction between movies (the widest possible audience) and films (appealing to more educated, intellectual audiences) had not yet arisen.

One of the era's most inventive directors was the Russian Sergei Eisenstein [IZE-uhn-stine] (1898–1948), who introduced techniques that had an enormous influence on the rise of art films. In *The Battleship Potemkin* (1925), he pioneered the **montage** technique, which consisted of highly elaborate editing patterns and rhythms. He developed the montage because he believed that the key element in films was the way the scenes were arranged, how they faded out and faded in, and how they looked in juxtaposition. By focusing on the material of the film itself instead of highlighting the plot or the characters' psychology, Eisenstein showed his allegiance to the artistic aspect of moviemaking.

Perhaps the most controversial director of this period was Leni Riefenstahl [LAY-nee REE-fen-shtahl] (1902–2003), the German dancer and actress, who became Hitler's favorite moviemaker. Her masterpiece was *Triumph of the Will* (1934), an almost-two-hour-long

Figure 20.26 Still, from *Citizen Kane*. 1941. RKO. *This still from* Citizen Kane *conveys the megalomania of the film's hero, Charles Foster Kane, played by its director and star, Orson Welles. Kane is depicted standing before a huge portrait of himself. Such extreme vanity as displayed here was a typical propaganda method in the Age of the Masses. Totalitarian leaders of both the right and the left, including Hitler and Stalin, cultivated the cult of the personality through huge public portraits. Reflecting his democratic values, Welles's film satirized the rise and fall of citizen Kane, a self-absorbed newspaper mogul modeled on the newspaper publisher William Randolph Hearst (1863–1951). Part of the film's appeal stemmed from its innovative cinematography, which permitted deep-focus imagery, so that extreme foreground and background could be viewed simultaneously with equal clarity—a breakthrough that is suggested by this still.*

documentary depicting the sixth Nazi Party Congress in Nuremberg, held in September 1934, which introduced the Nazi Party to the world (see Figure 20.6). The film's title was Hitler's own term, reflecting his borrowing from Nietzsche's philosophy (see Chapter 19). Made in black and white, this film depicted the Nazi pageant in all of its dramatic glory, including massed ranks of thousands of party members, torchlight parades, athletic displays by well-muscled young men, children marching in close ranks, and rituals involving flags emblazoned with swastikas. Riefenstahl made the film even more theatrical with new camera angles and creative editing. Although brilliant, this film showed how politics could subvert art, simply by making art the handmaid of a political agenda. After World War II, Riefenstahl was convicted as a war criminal for her Nazi propaganda and sentenced to four years in prison. Her career never recovered from the stigma of her support for the Nazi regime.

The United States (which eventually meant Hollywood, California) had dominated the motion picture industry since World War I, and the industry underwent important changes during these years. Sound movies became technically feasible in the late 1920s, and in the early 1930s three-color cinematography processes were developed. Both of these technical developments became basic to the movies throughout the world, but other experiments, such as wide-screen and three-dimensional photography, were less successful. Another important development in this period was the descent on Hollywood of many German filmmakers in flight from the Nazis. In the Hollywood of the 1930s, these exiles helped to create some of the outstanding achievements in world cinema.

A sign of the excellence of Hollywood movies in these years is Orson Welles's *Citizen Kane* (1941), often called America's best film (Figure 20.26). An American, Welles (1915–1985) had learned from the German exiles and borrowed their expressionist methods, such as theatrical lighting and multiple narrative voices. Welles's own commanding presence in the lead role also contributed to making this an unforgettable movie. But one of the hallmarks of the movie—its dark look, which underscores the theme of unbridled lust for power—was in actuality a money-saving device to disguise the absence of studio sets. Is *Citizen Kane* a "film" or a "movie"? It is a measure of Welles's genius that it is triumphantly both: its frequent showing both on television and in theaters attests to its popularity, yet its discussion and analysis in film journals and books points to its high prominence as a film.

Music: Atonality, Neoclassicism, and an American Idiom

During the 1920s and 1930s, Western music was fragmented into two rival camps. On one side was the Austro-German school headed by Arnold Schoenberg, who had introduced atonality before 1914 and in the 1920s pioneered serial music. On the other side was the French school led by Igor Stravinsky, who had experimented with primitive rhythms and harsh dissonances in the early 1900s but after World War I adopted a stern neoclassical style.

Having abandoned tonality in 1909, Schoenberg in the 1920s introduced **serial music,** a method of composing with a **twelve-tone scale**—twelve tones that are related not to a tonal center in a major or minor key but only to each other. Lacking harmonious structure, serial music sounded dissonant and random and tended to create anxiety in listeners. As a result, serial music appealed to cult rather than mass audiences. Lack of a responsive public did not halt Schoenberg's pursuit of atonality. His serial system culminated in *Variations for*

Orchestra (1928), a composition that uses the classical form of theme with variations. In 1933 he emigrated to America, where his devotion to atonality mellowed. Some of Schoenberg's later works mix twelve-tone writing with tonality.

Stravinsky, in exile from the Soviet Union after 1917, went to live in Paris, where he became the dominant figure of **neoclassicism** in music, borrowing features from seventeenth- and eighteenth-century music (Figure 20.27). In his neoclassical works, he abandoned many techniques that had become common to music since the baroque period, such as romantic emotionalism and programmatic composition as well as impressionism's use of dense orchestral sounds. Austere and cool, his neoclassical compositions used simple instrumental combinations and sounded harmonious. Stravinsky's works from this period made him the outstanding composer of the twentieth century.

Stravinsky originated neoclassicism in 1919 with the ballet *Pulcinella* and brought the style to a close in 1951 with the opera *The Rake's Progress*. Between these two works was one of his most admired compositions, the *Symphony of Psalms,* dating from 1930. *Pulcinella* and *The Rake's Progress* owe much to the music and comic operas of the classical composers Pergolesi [per-GO-lay-see] (1710–1736) and Mozart (see Chapter 16), respectively, and the *Symphony of Psalms* follows a baroque model in its small orchestra and musical structure. Despite borrowing forms and ideas, Stravinsky made them his own, introducing occasional dissonances and continuing to experiment with complex rhythmic patterns.

American music, meanwhile, was discovering its own idiom. Charles Ives (1874–1954) focused on American melodies, including folk songs, hymns, marches, patriotic songs, ragtime tunes, and music of his beloved New England. Working without models, Ives experimented with tonality and rhythm in ways similar to those of the European avant-garde. Typical of his work is the *Concord* Sonata for piano (1909–1915). Another American composer, Aaron Copland (1900–1990), had achieved some success by imitating European styles, but in the 1930s he began to develop a distinctive American style. His ballet scores *Billy the Kid* (1938), *Rodeo* (1942), and *Appalachian Spring* (1944), commissioned by choreographers Agnes de Mille (1909–1993) and Martha Graham (1893–1991), drew on hymns, ballads, folk tunes, and popular songs of the period. His delightful melodies, brilliant sound, jazzy experimentation, and upbeat rhythms ensured the popularity of these pieces.

Despite the overall folksy sound of *Appalachian Spring,* the only actual folk tune Copland used was "Simple Gifts," a hymn from the Shaker sect that expressed their faith in simple living. An eighteenth-century offshoot of the Quakers, known originally as "shaking Quakers," the Shakers showed religious

Figure 20.27 PABLO PICASSO. *Stravinsky.* 1920. Pencil on gray paper, 24⅜ × 19⅛". Musée Picasso, Paris. *Picasso's pencil sketch of Stravinsky is a perceptive character study. Long before Stravinsky became almost unapproachable, Picasso portrayed him as an aloof, self-absorbed young man. Stravinsky's cold demeanor is obvious in the tense posture, the harsh stare, and the clasped hands and crossed legs. Picasso's sketch also hints at Stravinsky's genius by exaggerating the size of his hands, perhaps to emphasize their role in the composer's creative life.*

fervor through ecstatic rituals, including speaking in tongues, dancing, and shaking of the body. Copland exploited this Shaker hymn, making it the theme of Section 7, "Simple Gifts," of his ballet score. Written in the classical form of theme and variations, "Simple Gifts," begins with the sweet melody of the hymn's first two lines, "'Tis the gift to be simple, 'tis the gift to be free / 'Tis the gift to come down where we ought to be." There are five variations, with the theme being varied through changes in key, tempo (slow to staccato), dynamics (soft to loud), instrument combinations, and tone color. In the concluding variation, Copland pulls out all stops, using the full orchestra playing *fortississimo* (a made-up term, "extremely loud"; abbreviated *fff*) to transform the simple melody into a majestic affirmation of the simple life.

A major American composer who cared less about developing a purely American idiom and more about exploring music's frontiers was George Antheil [an-TILE] (1900–1959). Living in Europe from 1922 to 1933, Antheil became part of the intellectual avant-garde who were intrigued by the machine-oriented culture of the Age of the Masses. In worshiping the machine, these artists and musicians followed in the steps of the futurists, the Italian group who had raised "speed" to an artistic principle before World War I (see Figure 19.2). As part of the 1920s European scene, Antheil was led to incorporate industrial sounds—the music of the masses—into his compositions. Hence, his *Ballet méchanique (Mechanical Ballet)* (1924; revised 1952) included scoring for unusual "instruments" (electric bells, small wood propeller, large wood propeller, metal propeller, siren, and sixteen player pianos) as well as more traditional instruments (piano and three xylophones). Antheil claimed this incorporation of urban and industrial sounds as his goal in composing this iconoclastic work: "It is the rhythm of machinery, presented as beautifully as an artist knows how. . . . It is the life, the manufacturing, the industry of today."

The African American composer William Grant Still (1895–1978), who was born in the heart of the Old South, in Mississippi, also left his defining mark on this period. Still was uniquely positioned to make a major contribution to serious music. He was educated in both black and white institutions of higher learning, a student first of medicine and then of music composition and steeped in Western musical styles, both traditional and radically avant-garde, along with jazz idioms created by both white and black performers. His eclectic musical style used traditional Western musical forms infused with elements of jazz and various other forms of black musical expression, as well as popular music and orchestration. He wrote ballets, five symphonies, orchestral suites, symphonic poems, chamber works, songs, arrangements of spirituals, and operas, including *The Troubled Island* (1938), with a libretto by Langston Hughes, the first opera by an African American to be staged by a professional opera company (the New York City Opera).

Still's most popular work today is the *Afro-American* Symphony (1931), the first symphony by a black American to be performed by a major symphony orchestra. Still's symphony, though composed in a Western musical form, draws on elements of the African American heritage for its themes, rhythmic structures, and instrumentation. In the first part of the symphony's third movement, for example, the main theme, which appears after a brief introduction, is a four-note phrase that Still called the *hallelujah* motive, thereby evoking the central role played by gospel singing in African American life. Accompanying the hallelujah theme is

a banjo playing on the offbeat—a jaunty reminder of the banjos in nineteenth-century black minstrel shows. The countermelody, a syncopated version of an African American spiritual, also was inspired by the African American church tradition. The playfulness of this section suggests a jubilant mood, based on the poem that Still quoted in a preface to this movement: "An' we'll shout ouah hallelujahs / On dat mighty reck'nin' day"—by Paul Laurence Dunbar (1872–1906), an African American poet. The "reck'nin' day" refers to the messianic hope for a day of jubilation at the time of Christ's second coming, when African Americans will be rewarded for their sufferings on earth. The jubilant mood is expressed through sudden shifts in dynamics, rhythm, tone color, register, and varied combinations of instruments.

During the Age of the Masses, jazz began to reach larger audiences, in part because of the development of the radio and the phonograph. Many jazz greats forged their reputations in these years. The fame of the finest jazz composer, Duke Ellington (born Edward Kennedy Ellington; 1899–1974), dated from 1927 at Harlem's Cotton Club. Ellington's songs balanced superb orchestration with improvisation and ranged from popular melodies, such as "Sophisticated Lady" (1932), to major suites, such as *Such Sweet Thunder* (1957), based on Shakespeare. Jazz's premier female vocalist, Billie Holiday (1915–1959), whose bittersweet style was marked by innovative phrasing, also appeared then.

Ellington's "Mood Indigo" (1930), now a standard in the American songbook, shows him to be a master of jazz composition. He usually wrote for a fifteen- or sixteen-piece **swing band** orchestra, with himself on piano, creating music marked by syncopation and lush tone color. In "Mood Indigo," he used his music expressionistically to convey a gentle air of melancholy—hence its title. Introduced with a swelling crescendo that builds to a crashing climax, which is then repeated, this piece unfolds in typical popular song format: refrain, verse, refrain. The delicate blend of jauntiness and sadness invoked by the minor key gives it a haunting quality, which is heightened by the slow fade to silence at the end.

Two jazz performers whose careers extended well beyond this period are Louis Armstrong (1901–1971) and Ella Fitzgerald (1918–1996). Armstrong, better known as Satchmo, became a goodwill ambassador for the United States with his loud and relaxed New Orleans–style trumpet playing. Ella Fitzgerald, a vocalist noted for her bell-like voice and elegant phrasing, became the peerless interpreter of jazz standards as well as pop tunes. In the next period, jazz fragmented into a host of styles and was a vital ingredient in the birth of rock and roll, the popular music form originating in the 1950s that has since dominated popular music.

The Legacy of the Age of the Masses and the Zenith of Modernism

The Age of the Masses has transformed material civilization in the West in both good and bad ways. It has given us the most destructive wars of history, the greatest economic depression since the 1300s, the most absolute forms of government since the late Roman Empire, the first modern attempt to eliminate an entire people, the fully formed industrial-military-state complex, and a weapon capable of destroying the planet. At the same time, it has brought a better standard of living to most people in the West and given millions of Westerners their first taste of democracy.

This age has also had a contradictory impact on cultural developments. On the one hand, it saw the growth of a worldwide mass culture, led by American ingenuity, which began to dominate public and private life for most people. On the other hand, it inspired a revolt by modernist artists, writers, and musicians to create works free of mass culture's influence. Their creations were experimental, perplexing, and often committed to what they defined as spiritual values. A few modernists refused to become mass culture's adversaries, and their moderating voices pointed toward a healthier relationship between mass culture and the elitist tradition after World War II.

Besides the polarization of mass and high culture, this period left other cultural legacies. Films became accepted as a serious art form, and they remain the great-est legacy of mass culture to the twentieth century. Photography was also beginning to be accepted as a legitimate art form. Advances in medicine, especially in new pharmaceuticals, were ending the threat from many diseases and thus adding years to the expected human life span. It was also during this period that America emerged as a significant cultural force in the West, partly because of the tide of intellectuals flowing from Europe, partly because of America's growing political, economic, and military power, and partly because of excellent native schools of writers, musicians, and artists. And finally, a questioning mood became the normative way of looking at the world, replacing the certainty of previous centuries.

The modernists had pioneered a questioning spirit in about 1900, and in this period the revolution in physics seemed to reinforce it. Einstein's conclusion that space and time are interchangeable was echoed by artists, writers, and musicians who focused on form to define content in their work. And Heisenberg's uncertainty principle seemed to reverberate everywhere—from Wittgenstein's toying with language to the highly personal narrative voices that dominated the novel to the constantly shrinking set of basic beliefs that characterized the period's religious thought and, ultimately, to the widespread belief that Western civilization had lost its course.

KEY CULTURAL TERMS

mass culture
stream of consciousness
epic theater
photomontage
logical positivism
existentialism
suprematism
constructivism
socialist realism
de Stijl

Dada
surrealism
international style
montage
serial music
twelve-tone scale
neoclassicism
fortississimo
swing band

QUESTIONS FOR CRITICAL THINKING

1. Explain how events between 1914 and 1945—the world wars, the Great Depression, totalitarianism, and the rise of the masses—influenced the modernist style.

2. What postimpressionist trends dominated the arts in this period? In each trend, identify a leading artist, a representative work of each, and traits of each artist's style.

3. Select an artistic or literary work that best symbolizes the Age of the Masses. Justify your selection.

4. What were the characteristics of modernism between the world wars—in the arts? in literature? in philosophy? in music? Name a key figure and an artwork in each area.

5. "The period between 1914 and 1945 represents the 'End of Certainty' in the West." Evaluate this statement (using five examples) in light of this period's developments in the arts, humanities, and science.

21

THE AGE OF ANXIETY AND LATE MODERNISM

1945–1970

Fear of nuclear war had a pervasive effect on attitudes and events after 1945 and led to an enormous buildup of weapons by the United States and the Soviet Union. This arms stockpiling in turn contributed to uncontrolled military spending at the expense of domestic programs. For many Westerners, anxiety about nuclear war produced moods of absurdity, futility, and despair. Against the backdrop of these harsh realities, the cultural style known as late modernism captured the anguish experienced by many artists, writers, and intellectuals.

TRANSFORMATIONS IN THE POSTWAR WORLD

The end of World War II brought the cold war period—an era of political and military rivalry, international tensions, and conflicting ideologies. World relations were governed by a bipolar balance of power between the United States and the Union of Soviet Socialist Republics (USSR). The American bloc included the United States, most of Western Europe, Great Britain and the British Commonwealth, and their former enemies Japan, West Germany, and Italy. The Soviet bloc embraced virtually all of Eastern Europe and, after 1949, when the Communists took power, China.

The cold war escalated for two main reasons. First, the superpowers extended their confrontations to the third world—developing countries in Africa (except South Africa), Asia (except Japan and parts of Southeast Asia), and Latin America—rushing in to influence events as the West's colonial empires fell and were replaced by struggling independent states. Second, the

◀ **Detail** Ludwig Mies van der Rohe and Philip Johnson. Seagram Building, New York City. 1954–1958. Ezra Stoller © Esto.

631

development of ballistic missiles capable of hurtling nuclear weapons across intercontinental distances raised the possibility of sudden strikes and mass destruction without warning.

By the 1970s, the West seemed balanced between the two superpowers and their respective blocs, and the cold war, with its threat of nuclear annihilation of the human race, loomed over the foreseeable future.

The Era of the Superpowers, 1945–1970

With Germany and Japan defeated, the ideological differences and geopolitical viewpoints between the USSR and the Western nations came to shape the future of the postwar world. The two opposed systems emerged as seemingly inevitable consequences of World War II. For the American bloc, democracy was the rule, social welfare was slowly expanded, and the economies were booming. For the Soviet bloc, collectivist regimes prevailed, social welfare was comprehensive, and the economies either stagnated or grew slowly.

POSTWAR RECOVERY AND THE NEW WORLD ORDER The chief Allied forces—the United States, Great Britain, and the Soviet Union—began to plan for the postwar era before World War II ended. They agreed to occupy Germany and Japan, giving those nations representative forms of government and drastically curbing their military systems. They joined with forty-eight other countries in 1945 to found the United Nations, a peacekeeping and human rights organization dealing with international disputes (Figure 21.1). They also prepared for worldwide economic recovery by establishing several transnational organizations, such as the World Bank, which provides funds and technical assistance to developing countries for large-scale building projects, and the International Monetary Fund (IMF), which fosters international monetary cooperation, encourages the expansion of international trade, and attempts to stabilize exchange rates. However, the Soviet Union refused to participate in these economic arrangements (Timeline 21.1).

In 1945 the Allies split Germany into four occupied zones. In 1949 Great Britain, France, and the United States united their zones into the Federal Republic of Germany (West Germany), and the USSR set up its zone as the German Democratic Republic (East Germany). By 1969 West Germany, led by moderates devoted to capitalism, had become Europe's chief industrial power, and East Germany, under a collectivist regime, lagged far behind.

In Japan the American victors imposed a democratic constitution that kept the emperor as a figurehead; introduced a parliamentary system; gave the vote to women, workers, and farmers; and virtually eliminated

Figure 21.1 WALLACE K. HARRISON INTERNATIONAL COMMITTEE OF ARCHITECTS. United Nations Headquarters. 1949–1951. New York. *The decision to locate the United Nations Headquarters in New York made that city the unofficial capital of the free world—a term that was applied to the United States and its allies during the cold war. And the choice of a "glass box" skyscraper for the United Nations Secretariat building helped to ensure that the international style would be the reigning style of architecture in the postwar period, until about 1970.*

the military. Between 1950 and 1973, under this renovated system, Japan's gross domestic product grew more than 10 percent a year on average, surpassing that of any other industrialized nation.

By the early 1950s, both Great Britain and France were enjoying moderate economic growth, although each was beset by endemic labor unrest. Left-wing governments in both countries nationalized major industries and founded national health-care systems, although conservatives periodically returned some businesses to private hands.

France and West Germany recognized that the era of the small state was over and it was necessary to cooperate to ensure economic stability. In 1957 they initiated a free-trade zone that also included Belgium, the Netherlands, Luxembourg, and Italy. Called the European Economic Community, or the Common Market,

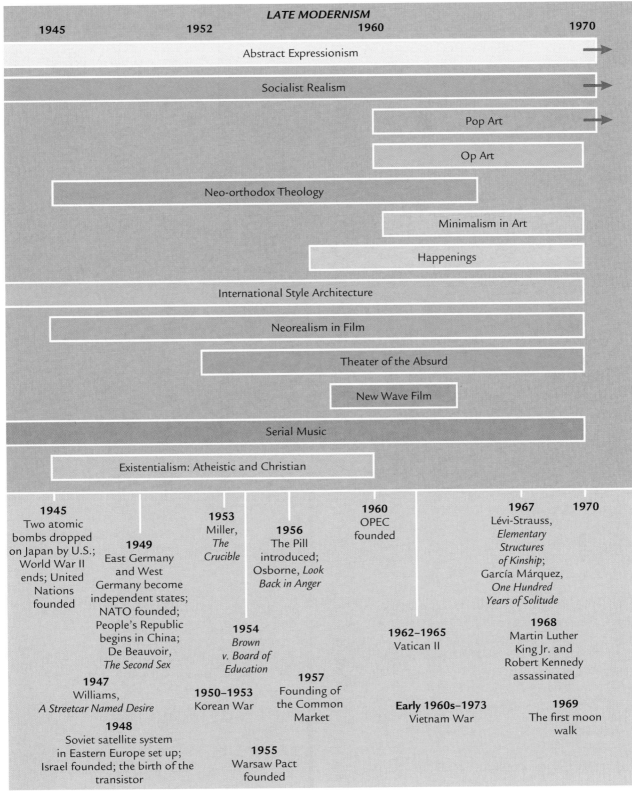

LATE MODERNISM

| 1945 | 1952 | 1960 | 1970 |

Abstract Expressionism

Socialist Realism

Pop Art

Op Art

Neo-orthodox Theology

Minimalism in Art

Happenings

International Style Architecture

Neorealism in Film

Theater of the Absurd

New Wave Film

Serial Music

Existentialism: Atheistic and Christian

1945
Two atomic bombs dropped on Japan by U.S.; World War II ends; United Nations founded

1947
Williams, *A Streetcar Named Desire*

1948
Soviet satellite system in Eastern Europe set up; Israel founded; the birth of the transistor

1949
East Germany and West Germany become independent states; NATO founded; People's Republic begins in China; De Beauvoir, *The Second Sex*

1950–1953
Korean War

1953
Miller, *The Crucible*

1954
Brown v. Board of Education

1955
Warsaw Pact founded

1956
The Pill introduced; Osborne, *Look Back in Anger*

1957
Founding of the Common Market

1960
OPEC founded

1962–1965
Vatican II

Early 1960s–1973
Vietnam War

1967
Lévi-Strauss, *Elementary Structures of Kinship*; García Márquez, *One Hundred Years of Solitude*

1968
Martin Luther King Jr. and Robert Kennedy assassinated

1969
The first moon walk

1970

this organization became the driving force in Europe's prosperity over the next decade.

Another reason for the formation of the Common Market was that the USSR threatened to dominate Europe. After World War II, Soviet troops occupied neighboring countries in Eastern Europe, ostensibly to provide a military shield for the USSR. By 1948 the

Soviets had converted these countries into Communist satellites, their industrial and agricultural systems tied to the Soviet economy.

Joseph Stalin, the architect of the Soviet Union's rise to superpower status, saw that the West's market economy and ideas of freedom posed a threat to the collectivist system. Thus, he imposed extreme sacrifices

LEARNING THROUGH MAPS

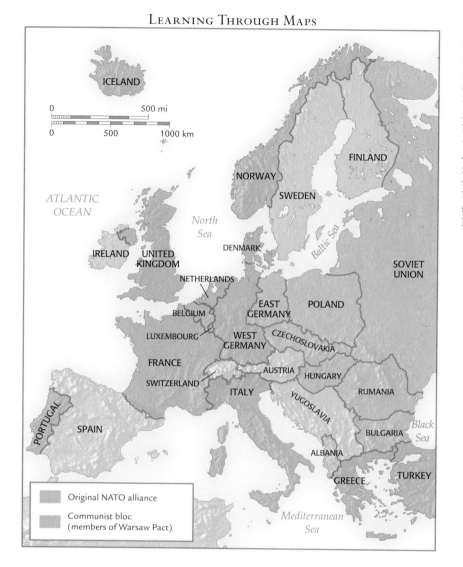

Map 21.1   EUROPE IN 1955
This map shows Europe at the height of the cold war. 1. *Notice* the division of Europe between NATO and the Communist bloc. 2. *Which* countries were not members of either alliance? 3. *Which* countries would most likely be battlegrounds if war occurred between the two power blocs? 4. *Notice* also the division between East Germany and West Germany. 5. *Observe* the westward expansion of the Soviet Union in this map, as compared with the smaller Soviet Union on Map 20.1, Europe after World War I.

on the Soviet citizenry to bring their war-shattered economy up to the level of that of the advanced industrialized countries. After Stalin's death in 1953, his successors were less brutal but they continued the policies of censorship and political repression.

The United States emerged as the leader of the free world in 1945, claiming to have earned this status because of crucial contributions to Allied victory. It believed that the war had been a moral crusade for human freedom and that it now had to protect the rights of people around the globe. On the basis of these beliefs, the United States justified an activist foreign policy, and between 1945 and 1970 it was probably the wealthiest and most powerful nation-state that ever existed.

During the 1950s American domestic life was characterized by complacency and blandness, but the 1960s proved to be a turbulent decade around the world, of which the American experience was only a part. In that decade, millions of people protested against the Vietnam War and racism and questioned the old ways

of thinking. Hippies cultivated a bohemian lifestyle and contributed to the emergence of a counterculture that rejected mainstream values and traditions.

Racial prejudice was the most pressing domestic problem in the United States after World War II because it was so embedded in the nation's history. In 1954 the Supreme Court declared segregation in public schools unconstitutional. The next year, Rosa Parks (1913–2005), a black Alabaman, refused to move to the back of a bus as required by state law and was jailed. The social protests following her arrest were a turning point in American race relations. Rejecting a historically passive role, black citizens began to use the tactics of civil disobedience to win their equal rights. However, the civil rights movement did not spread across the nation until the 1960s. After some stalling, the federal government instigated changes in education, living conditions, and voting rights for black Americans. In 1968 the civil rights struggle temporarily lost direction and momentum when its leader, Martin Lu-

Figure 21.2 ANDY WARHOL. *Mao.* 1973. Acrylic and silk-screen on canvas, 14′6⅞″ × 11′4½″. Art Institute of Chicago. Mr. and Mrs. Frank G. Logan Purchase Prize and Wilson L. Mead Funds. *A feature of totalitarian societies in the twentieth century was the personality cult, the practice of giving a political leader heroic dimensions, thus making the leader the personification of the state. In Communist China, the cult of Mao Zedong established Mao as a secular god. American pop artist Andy Warhol turned Mao's official photograph into a pop culture icon, suggesting that there is no difference between propaganda in a totalitarian state and media stardom in a free society.*

ther King Jr., was assassinated, but a new generation soon arose in America's black community to confront racism.

THE COLD WAR   Hope for peace and cooperation among the victorious powers disappeared after 1945 as the USSR and the United States defined their respective spheres of influence. By 1949 an "iron curtain" had descended in Europe, dividing the West from the East (Map 21.1). In 1949 fear of a Soviet invasion led the Western democracies to form a military alliance called the North Atlantic Treaty Organization (NATO) with the United States as its leader. The Eastern bloc countered with the Warsaw Pact (1955), an alliance led by the Soviet Union. By 1955 a balance of terror seemed to have been reached because both the United States and the USSR possessed enough bombs and missiles to destroy each other.

The East-West contest spread to other regions of the world. In 1949 Chinese Communists defeated the ruling Kuomintang Party and commenced to build a socialist system under Mao Zedong [MAU (D)ZE-DUHNG] (r. 1949–1976) (Figure 21.2). The confrontation between the superpowers now shifted to the Far East, with a limited war between North and South Korea. Alarmed at the possible expansion of Communism, the United States, supported by the United Nations, sent troops in support of the South Koreans. China then dispatched its soldiers to aid the North Koreans. A stalemate resulted, followed by an armistice in 1953, which guaranteed the borders between the two countries. From this conflict came two guiding principles of the nuclear age: (1) proxy wars between surrogate allies could replace actual hostilities between the superpowers, and (2) wars could be fought with conventional weapons rather than with nuclear arms.

In 1961 cold war tensions were heightened and refocused on Europe when the East Germans built the Berlin Wall to prevent its citizens from fleeing to West Berlin. Conceived as a way to save communism, the wall came to symbolize the divisions between Western and Eastern Europe (Figure 21.3). But the severest strain on the superpower system was the Vietnam War, which erupted in the early 1960s. Originating as a

Figure 21.3   The Brandenburg Gate. *More than 3.5 million refugees migrated to the West from the German Democratic Republic, or East Germany, between 1945 and 1961. In August 1961, East Germany constructed a wall of concrete and cinder blocks, reinforced with steel girders, and barbed wire strung on top that snaked through the city. From 1961 to 1989, the Berlin Wall stood as the dividing line between Communism and Western democracy. The Brandenburg Gate, in the background, is one of Berlin's historic landmarks.*

Figure 21.4 The National Guard at Kent State, Ohio. 1970. *This photograph bears a striking resemblance to Goya's* Execution of the Third of May, 1808 *(see Figure 17.19), a painting that protested the killing of Spanish civilians by French soldiers. In the tense days after the Kent State deaths, this photograph served a similar function in American society as many people began to think of the dead students as martyrs to the anti–Vietnam War cause.*

civil war, it became a cold war contest when the United States joined South Vietnam to repel the Communist troops invading from the north. For American soldiers, the war was difficult to wage because it was fought in unfamiliar jungle terrain against a guerrilla army and because it became so unpopular at home. Protests against the war culminated in confrontations at universities in Ohio and Mississippi, leaving six students killed in clashes with public authorities (Figure 21.4).

The Vietnam War proved to be a turning point in the cold war. The United States withdrew from South Vietnam in 1973, thereby allowing its conquest by North Vietnam in 1975. Two conclusions were drawn from the war: (1) America's superpower status was cast into doubt, and its leaders became reluctant to exercise military power; and (2) superpowers could not defeat small states by means of conventional warfare. Taken together, these post-Vietnam lessons suggested that the international influence of the United States was in decline, and that opened the door to global cooperation in the 1970s.

EMERGENCE OF THE THIRD WORLD   After 1945 Europe's overseas territories began their struggles for freedom and self-government, and by 1964 most of the colonial holdings had been transformed into independent countries—a process called decolonization. In 1946 the United States let go of the Philippines. In 1947 Great Britain agreed to divide India into a Hindu-dominated state—India—and a separate Muslim state—Pakistan. The Dutch gave up the East Indies, which in 1950 became Indonesia. France tried to retain Indochina but

in 1954 was driven out, and the former colony was divided into North and South Vietnam.

In the Middle East, Arab states were freed by France and Britain, which had dominated them since 1919. After 1945 the region was in continual turmoil because its oil was needed by the industrialized states, its geopolitical position in the eastern Mediterranean attracted the superpowers, and Islamic fundamentalism led to militant Arab nationalism. But the founding of the Jewish state of Israel, in 1948, contributed the most to an unstable Middle East. Israel expelled more than a half-million Arabs from Palestine, and the fate of these refugees has heightened the tensions in the region. The Israeli-Palestine conflict serves as a rallying cry for Arabs to destabilize and eliminate the state of Israel.

In Africa, nearly all colonies became free, although through often painful and costly transitions. In the 1960s, France concluded a bloody war in Algeria, relinquishing it and most of its West African colonies. The British withdrew gradually from East Africa, leaving behind bureaucracies that could serve the new states (Figure 21.5). In southern Africa, Rhodesia became Zimbabwe in 1980, achieving independence from Great Britain and gaining black majority rule.

One of the consequences of decolonization and the emergence of the third world was the so-called North-South divide. Relationships between industrialized countries, which have been generally north of the equator, and developing third world countries, many located south of the equator, became at this time a major issue in international politics. The newly inde-

Figure 21.5 Portraits of Queen Elizabeth II and Kwame Nkrumah, Accra, Ghana. 1961. *In 1957 Ghana was the first of Britain's African colonies to gain independence. In 1961 Queen Elizabeth visited the new nation. Five years later, its leader, Nkrumah (r. 1957–1966), was overthrown by the army. The towering size of the double portraits suggests that Nkrumah was under the spell of the cult of personality—the deliberate creation, using mass media techniques, of hero worship of a country's leader by the people.*

pendent but still developing countries quickly found themselves at a serious economic disadvantage. In 1964 the United Nations held a conference where plans were made to promote international trade to aid developing countries. Some progress was made in narrowing the North-South divide, but the gap has never been closed.

MASS CULTURE   In the postwar era, American mass culture began to serve as the common denominator of an emerging world civilization. With its democratic and energetic qualities, sexual content, and commitment to free expression, American mass culture attracted people around the globe. Scenes of American life, conveyed through television, movies, and advertising, mesmerized millions, who imitated these images. The popularity of American clothing, food, and music now began to influence lifestyles across the free world as well as in the Soviet bloc, the third world, and the Middle East. The rise of a worldwide mass culture, in its infancy during late modernism, produced an insatiable demand for popular entertainment, along with a fascination with celebrities. Of the existing media when the period began, movies were perhaps best positioned to address this demand. American movies transformed many actors and entertainers into iconic presences around the world, for example, Elvis Presley (1935–1977) (see Figure 21.16). New forms of amusements, such as watching television, carrying transistor radios, listening to record albums, and attending rock concerts, grew with the birth of new media. Contributing to this push for new types of entertainment

was the abrupt shift in musical taste that occurred in the 1950s (see Encounter on page 662).

THE END OF MODERNISM

In 1947 the British-American author W. H. Auden (1907–1973) published a poem titled "The Age of Anxiety," which expressed the melancholy spirit of his times. He described a period caught between a frantic quest for certainty and a recognition of the futility of that search. Responding to the unparalleled violence of World War II, Auden's anxious age was haunted by death and destruction, fueled by memories of the Holocaust in Europe and the two atomic bombs dropped on Japan. While relations between the Soviet Union and the United States deteriorated and World War III seemed inevitable, melancholy could and often did turn into despair. In this gloomy setting, modernism entered its final phase.

Late modernism, flourishing from 1945 until 1970, expressed the vision of a group of artists, writers, and thinkers who seemed overwhelmed by this despairing age. Existentialism—with its advice to forget the past and the future and to live passionately for the present—appeared to be the only philosophy that made sense. Paradoxically, diminished faith in humanity kept the modernists at their creative tasks and prevented them from falling into hopeless silence.

Like earlier modernists, late modernists thought of themselves as an elite. They were committed to saving what they considered worthwhile in Western culture while destroying all that was irrelevant, ignoring mass culture, and borrowing insights from depth psychology—the psychoanalytical study of the relationship between the conscious and the unconscious mind—and non-Western sources. Armed with this sense of mission, they stripped their works down to the most basic components, abandoning strict rationality and making randomness the rule. They cast aside subject matter and pressed experimentation to the extreme, reducing painting to lines and colors, sculpture to textures and shapes, and music to random collections of sound. Like earlier modernists, they invested their works with spiritual or metaphysical meaning by claiming that abstract paintings and sculptures are meditation devices and that music that mixes noise and harmony echoes the natural world.

Philosophy and Religion

Existentialism, born between the two world wars, dominated Western thought in the immediate postwar period. Two French writers, Jean-Paul Sartre and Albert Camus, were the leading voices of atheistic existentialism, who expressed their ideas through their novels and plays (see the section "The Literature of Late Modernism"). Theistic, or god-based, existentialism, also flourished, as a part of the religious thought of the times.

Postwar religious thought was dominated by **neoorthodoxy**, which had been founded by the Swiss Protestant thinker Karl Barth (1886–1968) in the aftermath of World War I. Claiming God is beyond human reason, Barth urged a return to traditional, or orthodox, Christian beliefs, such as original sin, the Trinity, the Resurrection, and even the Virgin Birth, and rejected the human-centered religion of liberal Protestantism, with its reliance on reason, which had been in ascendance since the late 1800s (see Chapter 19). Barth stressed the gulf between "wholly other" God and lowly humanity, a gulf only God could bridge—thus reviving the *via antiqua,* of late medieval theology, which argued for the separation of reason and faith (see Chapter 10).

After 1945 and following Barth's lead, neoorthodoxy prospered in Western religious circles, specifically in the writings of the German-born American Protestant Paul Tillich [TIL-ik] (1886–1965). Tillich's theology was forged in the crucible of twentieth-century calamities. His liberal Christian faith was shattered during World War I, while he served as a chaplain in the German army, and he fled Germany to the United States in 1933, after the Nazis barred him from university teaching. Once in the United States, he taught at prestigious divinity schools and eventually completed *Systematic*

Theology (1951–1963), a three-volume work that explores linkages between culture and Christianity.

At the heart of Tillich's thought is his notion of God. He begins where the German philosopher Nietzsche ends, with the "death of God" (see Chapter 19). However, for Tillich, the God who has died is the "personal" deity of liberal Christianity—an idea that led some critics to accuse him of agnosticism or atheism. But Tillich insists that the authentic God exists: this infinite being is the "God behind God," the "ground of all being"— that is, the source for all existence and meaning in life.

Tillich thought of himself as a "boundary man," who stood on the threshold of two eras, when one way of life was dying and a new one was being born—an observation that summed up the Age of Anxiety for many religious seekers. Catholics, Protestants, and existentialists, both atheistic and Christian, eagerly read his difficult works. Atheistic existentialists, while denying God's existence, accepted Tillich's description of the human condition as hopeless without God. Christian existentialists embraced his description of the gulf separating humans from the "God behind God" and made a "leap of faith" to embrace the full panoply of orthodox Christian beliefs. "Leap of faith" was coined by the Danish thinker Søren Kierkegaard (1813–1855), whose writings from the previous century thrived during late modernism because of the popularity of Christian existentialism.

Two other major postwar religious thinkers also attracted a wide-ranging audience: the Frenchman Jesuit Teilhard de Chardin [tah-yahr duh shahrdan] (1881–1955) and the German-Jewish religious philosopher Martin Buber (1878–1965). Teilhard, a geologist and paleontologist, blended science and religion in his philosophical writings, such as *The Phenomenon of Man* (1955), to set forth a Christianized view of evolution. For Teilhard, history is an evolutionary process with moral advances occurring at certain stages, such as the moment of Jesus's Incarnation, and the entire process is moving toward spiritual wholeness, when Jesus will return to earth—the Second Coming—to inaugurate the last stage of human redemption. Teilhard's most significant works were published after his death, because of their potential for controversy. In 1962 the Vatican warned believers against uncritical acceptance of his ideas.

Martin Buber was a commanding figure in the new state of Israel, having fled from Nazi Germany in 1938. Before leaving Germany, he and the theologian Franz Rosenzweig (1886–1929) had translated the Hebrew Bible into German (1926–1937). Shortly after arriving in Jerusalem, Buber was appointed professor of social philosophy at Hebrew University, and later he was made the first president of the Israeli Academy of Sciences and Art. His best-known work, *I and Thou,* though first published in 1923, was among the late modern period's top religious best sellers. In this work, using poetic language, Buber described the universe as comprising a three-tiered moral hierarchy: God, the Eternal Thou; the human, the I; and the rest of the world, the It—with the Eternal Thou making possible all human relationships. The ideal relation is that of I-Thou, between a human and God, a tie characterized by openness, mutuality, directness, and trust. He urged that all human-to-human relations be of the I-Thou type, to the fullest extent possible. The most problematic relation is that of I-It. A necessary evil when practiced between humans and the animal, plant, and natural worlds, the I-It relationship becomes morally wrong when used between humans, as it turns other people into objects for one's own advantage.

One remarkable milestone, with wide-ranging implications for religious culture, occurred under late modernism: reform of the Roman Catholic Church, initiated by Pope John XXIII (pope 1958–1963) and carried out by the Second Vatican Council (1962–1965), better known as Vatican II. Vatican II made dramatic changes within the church and the Catholic community, such as introducing vernacular language into the Mass, abolishing various dietary restrictions, and allowing greater lay participation in religious services. Even more dramatic changes were made in the church's views toward nonmembers: Eastern Orthodox and Protestant Christians were now no longer termed heretics but were regarded as brothers and sisters in Christ; friendly overtures were made to the Jews along with expressions of regret for the church's past anti-Semitism; other world religions were addressed with praise for their spiritual quests; and peoples, everywhere, were assured of the church's repudiation of coercion in matters of faith. With its reforms, Vatican II became the most significant church council since the Council of Trent in the sixteenth century (see Chapter 13).

Political and Social Movements

In the 1960s, political and social movements, notably structuralism, feminism, and black consciousness, eclipsed existentialism. Unlike existentialism, with its focus on freedom and choice, **structuralism** affirms the universality of the human mind in all places and times; thus, human freedom is limited. Structuralists maintain that innate mental patterns cause human beings to interact with nature and one another in consistent and recurring ways, regardless of the historical period or the social setting. It follows that civilization (as represented in governments, social relations, and lan-

guage) and ideas (e.g., freedom, health, and beauty) arise from deep-seated modes of thought instead of from the environment or progressive enlightenment. Structuralists reason not only that all knowledge is conditioned by the mind but also that civilization itself reflects the mind's inborn nature. By defining and analyzing the levels of culture, they attempt to garner some understanding of the elemental nature of the human mind.

The two leading structuralists are Noam Chomsky [CHAHM-skee] (b. 1928), an American linguist, and Claude Lévi-Strauss [lay-vee-STRAUS] (1908–2009), a French anthropologist. Chomsky's *Syntactic Structures* (1957) prompted a revolution in linguistics, the scientific study of languages. He argues that below the surface form of sentences (that is, the grammar) lies a deeper linguistic structure that is intuitively grasped by the mind and is common to all languages. Similarly, Lévi-Strauss made war on empirical thinking with his 1967 study, *The Elementary Structures of Kinship.* He claimed that beneath the varied relations among clans in different societies exist certain kinship archetypes with such common themes as the incest taboo and marriage patterns. Chomsky and Lévi-Strauss imply that common universal structures run through all minds and all societies and can be expressed as a general code. This conclusion gives a pronounced psychoanalytic cast to structuralist thought, because it leads researchers to focus on the subconscious mind.

Following Chomsky and Lévi-Strauss, other scholars have studied subsurface patterns in such disciplines as history, child development, and literature. No thinker has unified the various structuralisms into a coherent theory of mind. It is an intriguing coincidence, however, that the trend of thought that points to a universally shared mind-set parallels the rise of a global culture under postmodernism.

The revival of feminist thought was another significant development in philosophy after World War II. The French thinker and novelist Simone de Beauvoir [duh boh-VWAHR] (1908–1986) sparked this revival, following the dry spell that set in after many Western women won the right to vote in the 1920s. In her 1949 treatise, *The Second Sex,* de Beauvoir argued that women are treated by men as "the Other," an anthropological term meaning a person or group accorded a different and lower existence. Drawing on personal anecdote and existentialist thought, she advised women who want independence to avoid marriage and, like men, create their own immortality (Figure 21.6).

De Beauvoir's message was heard around the world, but it was especially in the United States that women heeded her. America's best-known feminist in the 1960s was Betty Friedan (1921–2006). She awakened the

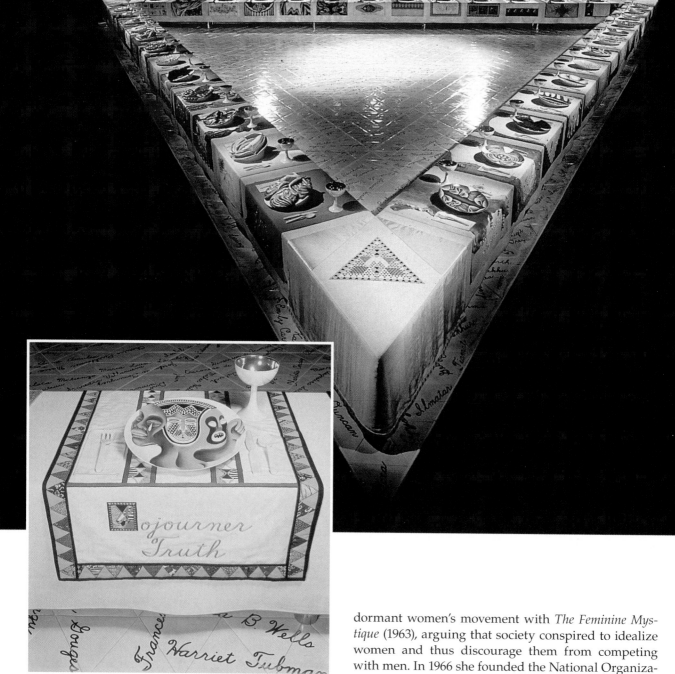

Figure 21.6 JUDY CHICAGO. *The Dinner Party.* 1979. Installation view. Multimedia, china painting on porcelain, needlework, 48 × 48 × 48' installed. © Judy Chicago. *The rebirth of feminism led some women artists to adopt explicit feminist themes in their art, as in the works of Judy Chicago (born Gerowitz, 1939). Chicago abandoned abstract expressionism in the late 1960s, at about the same time she changed her name, thereafter devoting her art to the feminist cause. The Dinner Party, her most ambitious project to date, is dedicated to leading historical and mythological women of Western civilization. In this work, she arranges a triangular-shaped dining table with thirty-nine places decorated in individual styles, honoring such famous women as Sappho and Sojourner Truth (inset; see also Chapter 18).*

dormant women's movement with *The Feminine Mystique* (1963), arguing that society conspired to idealize women and thus discourage them from competing with men. In 1966 she founded the National Organization for Women (NOW), an advocacy group that has attracted millions of members. According to its founding manifesto, NOW supports women's "equal partnership with men" and is committed to "integrating women into the power, privileges, and responsibilities of the public arena." Friedan did not always agree with the radical feminists of the 1970s, and in 1982 she showed that she was still a moderate in *The Second Stage,* a book that advocates men's liberation as a condition for women's equality.

Like feminism, the black consciousness movement grew after 1945 (Figure 21.7). The earliest sig-

Figure 21.7 ROMARE BEARDEN. *The Dove.* 1964. Cut-and-pasted paper, gouache, pencil and colored pencil on cardboard, 13⅜ × 18¾″. The Museum of Modern Art, New York. Art © Romare Bearden Foundation/Licensed by VAGA, New York, NY. *Romare Bearden (1914–1988), the United States' most honored post–World War II black painter, blended modernism with elements from his cultural heritage. In the 1960s, he developed a style reminiscent of cubism, which employed collage and flattened, angular figures to produce twenty collages that he labeled "projections"—enlarged images made through a photographic process, photostat, which was popular from the 1950s to the 1980s. In* The Dove, *Bearden has created a Harlem scene, with a dove perched above the comings and goings of people on a busy street along with idlers, who peer out of the window or smoke cigarettes. Bearden's collage, made from photographs, newspaper clippings, and colored paper, all pasted together, was inspired by personal history—his life in North Carolina and New York, his love of jazz, and his artistic training.*

nificant theorist of black identity was Frantz Fanon [fah-NOHN] (1925–1961), a psychiatrist from French Martinique who practiced medicine among the Arabs of Algeria. An eyewitness to French colonialism and oppression, Fanon became convinced that the West had doomed itself by abandoning its own moral ideals. By the late 1950s, Fanon began to justify black revolution against white society on the basis of existential choice and Marxism. In 1961, in *The Wretched of the Earth,* he issued an angry call to arms, urging nonwhites to build a separate culture. Some black leaders in America welcomed Fanon's message in the 1960s, as did third world thinkers who rejected Western ideologies in the 1970s.

America in the 1960s produced a radical black voice in Malcolm X (1925–1965), the pseudonym of Malcolm Little. A fiery personality, he made sharp ideological shifts, moving from advocacy of black separatism to a call for an interracial civil war and, after his conversion to orthodox Islam, to support of racial harmony. He remains a prophetic voice for many African Americans who want a clearer sense of their history, culture, and accomplishments in a predominantly white society.

In the turbulent 1960s, Malcolm X's voice was overpowered by that of Martin Luther King Jr. (1929–1968), a visionary who dreamed of a world free from racial discord. Probably the most famous black figure in Western history, King advocated civil disobedience—based on Christian teachings, the writings of the New England philosopher and abolitionist Henry David Thoreau, and the example of India's liberator, Gandhi (see Encounter in Chapter 20). An inspirational leader and a superb orator, King galvanized blacks, along with many whites, into the Southern Christian Leadership Conference, organized by ministers to end segregation in American life, notably in schools and universities. Though King's dream of an integrated society lives on, the civil rights movement took many directions after his assassination.

Science and Technology

Although important theories were developed in biology and physics during the postwar period, spectacular advances in applied science affected people more directly and immediately. From the 1940s through the 1960s, the lives of millions around the world were irretrievably altered by the inventions coming out of laboratories and research centers and by the scientific by-products of World War II and the cold war.

- Late 1940s: the transistor, a semiconductor for controlling electronic impulses, which gave birth to improved hearing aids and pocket radios. Mass-produced transistor radios, miniaturized and portable, ushered in the information age, starting in the 1960s.
- The 1950s: first commercial nuclear power stations; used to generate electrical power. By 1970, forty-two plants were producing about 4.5 percent of the United States' electricity. As the most promising alternative to fossil fuels, commercial nuclear power programs were established by many Western nations.
- In 1957: the Soviet Union launched the first globe-circling satellite, *Sputnik,* thus sparking a space race between the superpowers. In 1958, the United States countered with its first space satellite.
- In 1961: the Soviet Union sent the cosmonaut Yury Gagarin (1934–1968) around the earth. President John Kennedy (in office 1961–1963) promised that the United States would have a man on the moon before the end of the sixties. In 1962 the U.S. put John Glenn (b. 1921) into orbit, and, in July 1969, two astronauts walked on the moon's surface (see Slice of Life).

The moon walk, which climaxed the space race between the USSR and the United States, was made possible by advances in telecommunications, rocketry, and the miniaturization of controlling and guidance systems.

Medicine

As with science and technology, breakthroughs in medicine changed the patterns of behavior and raised the living standards for populations on every conti-

nent. While most discoveries saved lives, some had social and moral implications that spilled over into societal and gender issues.

The invention of a safe birth control pill in 1956 triggered a sexual revolution, which, by the late 1960s, was part of the social unrest and rejection of accepted moral codes and personal behavior patterns for many Americans. This newly found sexual freedom, popular in the 1960s and 1970s, grew more restricted in the 1980s with the advent of AIDS (see Chapter 22).

Other medical advances benefited the public without generating social and moral debates. In the 1950s, polio was eradicated through vaccines developed by the American physicians Jonas Salk (1914–1995) and Albert Sabin (1906–1993). Innovative surgical methods, radiation treatment, and chemotherapy drastically reduced cancer mortality. In the biological sciences, in 1953, Francis Crick (1916–2004) and James Watson (b. 1928) reported their discovery of the structure of DNA (deoxyribonucleic acid), the chemical substance ultimately responsible for determining individual hereditary characteristics. The implications of this discovery would not be fully understood until later (see Chapter 22).

The Literature of Late Modernism: Fiction, Poetry, and Drama

Despite late modernism's prevailing mood of despair, this period produced a veritable cacophony of voices in fiction, poetry, and drama. Literary culture flourished along the New York–London–Paris axis, though voices from beyond that axis occasionally broke through and were heard. African American writers continued to make their presence felt on the international stage. The avant-garde was still very much alive, as writers pushed the boundaries of literary art. There also emerged new schools of writing and theater, based on rival theories, seeking to connect with audiences. The names of many of these writers have become household names, and their works today are lauded as classics. In retrospect, this period was a golden age of literature.

FICTION The Frenchmen Jean-Paul Sartre and Albert Camus were among late modernism's leading postwar thinkers. In a trio of novels called *Roads to Freedom,* published between 1945 and 1950, Sartre interwove Marxist collectivist beliefs with existentialism's focus on the individual. Accepting the existentialist view that life is cruel and must be confronted, he portrayed his characters as cooperating for a new and better world, presumably one in which they would be able to live in harmony. Although Sartre wrote a series of plays that

SLICE OF LIFE

Humans in Space: "One Giant Leap for Mankind"

NEIL ARMSTRONG AND EDWIN E. ALDRIN
Recollections of the Moon Landing and Transmittals of the Astronauts' Voices

The intersecting of science, technology, and the human spirit was played out before a worldwide audience in July 1969 when the American astronauts Neil Armstrong (b. 1930) and Edwin E. Aldrin (b. 1930) walked on the moon. The event transcended cold war politics, as earthlings realized that Armstrong's first steps on the moon were monumental. His steps ushered in a new age that opened opportunities and raised fears about the future of the planet and space travel.

NEIL ARMSTRONG: The most dramatic recollections I had were the sights themselves. Of all the spectacular views we had, the most impressive to me was on the way to the Moon, when we flew through its shadow. We were still thousands of miles away, but close enough, so that the Moon almost filled our circular window. It was eclipsing the Sun, from our position, and the corona of the Sun was visible around the limb of the Moon as a gigantic lens-shaped or saucer-shaped light, stretching out to several lunar diameters. It was magnificent, but the Moon was even more so. We were in its shadow, so there was no part of it illuminated by the Sun. It was illuminated only by earthshine. It made the Moon appear blue-grey, and the entire scene looked decidedly three-dimensional. . . .

[*After touchdown*] The sky is black, you know. It's a very dark sky. But it still seemed more like daylight than darkness as we looked out the window. It's a peculiar thing, but the surface looked very warm and inviting. It was the sort of situation in which you felt like going out there in nothing but a swimming suit to get a little sun. From the cockpit, the surface seemed to be tan. It's hard to account for that, because later when I held this material in my hand, it wasn't tan at all. It was black, grey and so on. It's some kind of lighting effect, but out the window the surface looks much more like light desert sand than black sand. . . .

EDWIN E. ALDRIN [*On the moon*]: The blue color of my boot has completely disappeared now into this—still don't know exactly what color to describe this other than grayish-cocoa color. It appears to be covering most of the lighter part of my boot . . . very fine particles. . . .

[*Later*] The Moon was a very natural and pleasant environment in which to work. It had many of the advantages of zero gravity, but it was in a sense less *lonesome* than Zero G, where you always have to pay attention to securing attachment points to give you some means of leverage. In one-sixth gravity, on the Moon, you had a distinct feeling of being *somewhere*. . . . As we deployed out experiments on the surface we had to jettison things like lanyards, retaining fasteners, etc., and some of these we tossed away. The objects would go away with a slow, lazy motion. If anyone tried to throw a baseball back and forth in that atmosphere he would have difficulty, at first, acclimatizing himself to that slow, lazy trajectory; but I believe he could adapt to it quite readily. . . .

Odor is very subjective, but to me there was a distinct smell to the lunar material—pungent, like gunpowder or spent cap-pistol caps. We carted a fair amount of lunar dust back inside the vehicle with us, either on our suits and boots or on the conveyor system we used to get boxes and equipment back inside. We did notice the odor right way.

INTERPRETING THIS SLICE OF LIFE

1. *How* does Neil Armstrong describe the sights as they approach the moon? 2. *What* are some of the advantages and disadvantages of being on the moon? 3. In *what* ways did these landings and subsequent trips to the moon affect our society? 4. *What* are the implications in humans taking future trips to the moon and beyond? *Explain.*

are infrequently performed today, his most successful drama, and perhaps his most enduring literary work, is *No Exit* (1944), which shows how three characters turn their lives into living hells because they made unfortunate choices in desperate situations.

Like Sartre, the Algerian-born writer and thinker Albert Camus [kah-MOO] (1913–1960) wrote novels, plays, and philosophical works that mirrored his po-

litical thinking and personal values. His finest literary work was *The Fall* (1956), a novel published at the height of his reputation as one of the West's main moral voices. In 1957 he was awarded the Nobel Prize in Literature. Written as a single rambling monologue, *The Fall* portrays an anguished, self-doubting central character who accuses himself of moral fraud. When admirers recognized Camus in the narrator's voice, they were shocked because they were unwilling to accept this harsh self-judgment. Whether his self-mocking confession heralded Camus' move toward God—as some critics have maintained—can never be known, for he was killed prematurely in an auto accident.

Existentialism's rejection of bourgeois values and its affirmation of identity through action appealed to black writers in the United States. As outsiders in a white-dominated society, these writers identified with the French thinkers' call to rebellion. The first black author to adopt an existential perspective was Richard Wright (1908–1960), whose outlook was shaped by his birth on a Mississippi plantation. His works, such as his novel *Native Son* (1940) and his autobiography, *Black Boy* (1945), were filled with too much rage at racism to be accepted by white literary critics in the 1940s. His later years were spent in Paris, where he further developed his interest in existentialism.

The most successful black American author of this time was James Baldwin (1924–1987), who began to write during a self-imposed exile in France (1948–1957), where he had fled from racial discrimination. Baldwin's writings explored the consequences of growing up black in a predominantly white world, and in his first novel, *Go Tell It on the Mountain* (1953), he drew on his Christian beliefs to mute his anger against the injustices that he believed blacks daily endured. This novel, which held out hope for an integrated society, established the literary theme that he pursued until Martin Luther King Jr.'s assassination caused his vision to darken. In later novels, such as *No Name in the Street* (1972), Baldwin regretfully accepted violence as the only path to racial justice for black Americans.

In postwar fiction, existentialism sometimes took second place to a realistic literary style that concentrated on exposing society's failings. Three major writers who blended existential despair with realism's moral outrage were Norman Mailer (1923–2007), Doris Lessing (b. 1919), and Alexander Solzhenitsyn [solzhuh-NEET-suhn] (1918–2008). Their shared goal was to uncover the hypocrisy of their age.

Mailer, an American, drew on his experience as a soldier in World War II to capture the horror of modern war in his first and finest novel, *The Naked and the Dead* (1948). This work portrays a handful of enlisted men, a microcosm of America, as victims of their leaders' bad choices. He describes their officers as pursuing fantasies of glory, inspired by a notion that the world is godless and without lasting values. In the late 1960s, Mailer began to write as a journalist, eventually achieving so much fame that his essays overshadowed his novels. His best journalism is the book-length essay *The Armies of the Night* (1968), an account of the October 1967 peace march on Washington, D.C., in which he participated. This book won Mailer a Pulitzer Prize.

Lessing, a white eastern African writer, used realism to show the contradictions at work in her homeland, Rhodesia (modern Zimbabwe), between blacks and whites, British and Dutch, British and colonials, capitalists and Marxists, and, always, women and men. In the *Children of Violence* series (1950–1969), consisting of five novels, she presents the story of the rise of black freedom fighters and the diminishing of white control in what was then a British colony. This disintegrating world serves as a backdrop to the existential struggle for self-knowledge and independence by the main character, Martha Quest. In her best-known novel, *The Golden Notebook* (1962), Lessing addresses, among other issues, the socialization process that stifles women's creativity. Her concerns, however, are not just female identity but also the moral and intellectual fragmentation and confusion she sees in the modern world. Lessing received the Nobel Prize for Literature in 2008.

The Russian Solzhenitsyn wrote realistic novels that praise the Russian people while damning Marxism, which he regarded as a "Western heresy," opposed to Orthodox Christianity. His short novel *One Day in the Life of Ivan Denisovich* (1962) reflects his own rage at being unjustly imprisoned under Stalin. This novel, published during Nikita Khrushchev's (Soviet premier 1958–1964) de-Stalinization drive, offers an indelible image of the tedium, harassment, and cruelty of life in a forced-labor camp. And yet Ivan Denisovich remains a Soviet John Doe, dedicated to Marxism, his work, and his comrades (Figure 21.8).

When Solzhenitsyn's later books, which were banned in the Soviet Union until its fading years, revealed his hatred for Communism, he was deported, in 1974. Choosing exile in the United States, he settled in a Vermont hideaway from which he expressed moral disgust with the West for its atheistic materialism and softness toward the Soviet system. His values—Christian fundamentalism and Slavophilism, or advocacy of Russia's cultural supremacy—resemble those of Russia's great nineteenth-century preexistentialist novelist Dostoevsky. Believing that Communism was finally dead, Solzhenitsyn returned to his homeland in 1994, but he was an ineffective moral crusader in post–Soviet Russia.

POETRY Many late modernist poets used a private language to such a degree that their verses were often unintelligible to ordinary people and thus had a limited audience. A few who used conventional verse styles, however, earned a large readership. Of this latter group, the Welsh poet Dylan Thomas (1914–1953) was the most famous and remains so today. Thomas's poems mirror the obscurity favored by the modernist critics, but what makes his works so memorable is their glorious sound. With their strong emotional content, jaunty rhythms, and melodious words, they are perfect to read aloud.

Figure 21.8 Vitaly Komar and Aleksander Melamid. *Stroke (About March 3, 1953).* 1982–1983. Oil on canvas, 6′ × 3′11″. Collection of Evander D. Schley. Courtesy Ronald Feldman Fine Arts, New York. Photo credit: D. James Dee. *The two Russian émigré painters Komar (b. 1943) and Melamid (b. 1945)—who work as a team—painted this work,* Stroke, *soon after arriving in the United States. In it, they depict the lonely death of Stalin and the discovery of his body by a member of his inner circle. The artists subtly criticize both Stalin and the Soviet system in the way the official stares unmoved at the dead tyrant. Komar and Melamid show their postmodernist tendencies in their use of elements from earlier styles of art, such as the theatrical lighting and unusual perspective typical of Caravaggio (see Chapter 14).*

Better known than Thomas's poems, though, is his verse play *Under Milk Wood* (1954), arguably the best-loved poetic work of late modernism. Unlike the poems, this verse play is direct and imbued with simple emotions. Originally a play for radio, it presents a typical day in a Welsh village, a world Thomas knew well, having grown up in such a place. His portraits of the eccentric villagers with their colloquialisms reminded millions of listeners of their own youth.

A late modernist poet who was able to be experimental and yet win a popular audience was the American writer Allen Ginsberg (1926–1997), the most significant poet produced by the **beat generation** of the 1950s. Like Dylan Thomas, he had an ear for colloquial speech, and he was able to construct new forms to convey iconoclastic views as no other contemporary poet. "Howl" (1956),

his most famous poem, was an homage to rebel youth and illicit drugs and sex. Overcoming censorship, it opposed a capitalist, heterosexual, bourgeois society and became the anthem of the beat generation.

DRAMA Late modern drama spawned multiple trends. There were experimental plays, filled with theatrical innovations and philosophic allusions; "social problem" plays, written in the naturalistic tradition of Ibsen and Shaw; realist-style plays, dealing with class conflict; and lyrical plays, driven by poetic language and rich characterization.

Indeed, the most radical changes in literature took place in drama. Sharing existentialism's bleak vision and determined to find new ways to express that outlook, a group of dramatists called the **theater of the**

absurd emerged. The absurdists shifted the focus of their plays away from the study of the characters' psychology to stress poetic language and abandoned realistic plots to concentrate on outrageous situations. A typical absurdist play mixed tragedy with comedy, as if the playwright thought that the pain of existence could be tolerated only if blended with humor.

Samuel Beckett (1906–1989), an Irish writer who lived in Paris, was the best-known dramatist of absurdist theater. His *Waiting for Godot* (1952) is a play in which almost nothing "happens" in the conventional sense of that word. Combining elements of tragedy and farce, *Waiting for Godot* broke new ground with its repetitive structure (the second act is almost a replica of the first), its lack of scenery (the stage is bare except for a single tree), and its meager action (the characters engage in futile exchanges based on British music-hall routines). What plot there is also reinforces the idea of futility, as the characters wait for the mysterious Godot, who never appears.

In later years, Beckett's works explored the dramatic possibilities of silence, as in the one-act drama *Not I* (1973). In this play, a voice—seen only as a mouth illuminated in a spotlight—tries to, but cannot, stop talking. Beckett's plays portrayed human consciousness as a curse; yet, at the same time, his works affirmed the human spirit's survival in the face of despair.

Another member of the absurdist school was Eugene Ionesco [e-oh-NES-ko] (1909–1994), the Romanian-born French playwright, whose plays were absurdist in style and explored themes similar to Beckett's, such as social isolation and the breakdown in language. Rejecting naturalism, with its focus on ordinary folk struggling to bring order to their everyday lives, Ionesco created a nonnaturalistic theater, using surreal methods, bizarre speech patterns, and nonrational modes of thought. His plays were so hostile to the naturalistic style that they have been called antiplays. After establishing his reputation with a series of short, one-act plays, such as *The Lesson* (1952), he graduated to longer plays and became a leading light of the theater of the absurd. Ionesco's most enduring full-length play is *Rhinoceros* (1959), a play with conformity as its theme. In it, people in a small town are being turned into rhinoceroses. At first, this evokes horror—in themselves and in others—but, eventually, as the entire town is transformed, everyone takes delight in their new skins. Ironically, the play ends with the antihero, too stupid to become a rhinoceros, glorying in his humanity.

In the late 1950s, when his plays were first performed, England's Harold Pinter (1930–2008) was often grouped with the absurdist playwrights. However, it soon became apparent that he belonged to no particular school but was creating his own style. Today, **Pinteresque** is a term denoting a dramatic style marked by enigmatic plots, underwritten characters, and, especially, the liberal use of silences in the dialogue.

For Pinter, a play often begins with a room, occupied by one or more characters. Dramatic tension is introduced when a stranger arrives, throwing all into confusion, upsetting routines and calling relationships into question, as seen, for example, in *The Homecoming* (1965), perhaps Pinter's best-known play. A professor brings his wife home to meet his father and two brothers in London. The wife's presence sparks sexual tensions among family members, who compete for her attention. The play ends, surprisingly, with the wife joining the all-male household and the husband turning a blind eye. In 2005 Pinter was awarded the Nobel Prize for Literature.

In addition to the absurdist playwrights, other significant late modernist dramatists included the American Arthur Miller (1915–2005), the British John Osborne (1929–1994), and the American Tennessee Williams (1911–1983).

Arthur Miller was the master of the "social problem" play, a genre that originated with Ibsen in early modernism (see Chapter 19). Miller adapted Ibsen's 1881 play *Enemy of the People* into English in 1951, because of its passionate defense of minority rights. Most of Miller's early works addressed social concerns, including *All My Sons* (1947), about a corrupt factory owner in wartime; *Death of a Salesman* (1951), about false social values; and *The Price* (1968), about a failed relationship between two brothers. In his masterpiece, *The Crucible* (1953), Miller uses the story of a 1692 witch trial in Salem, Massachusetts, to symbolize the U.S. House of Representatives Un-American Activities Committee's search for Communists.

John Osborne's fame rests primarily on a single work: *Look Back in Anger* (1956). This realist drama, filled with working-class rage against the leaders of postwar British society, centers on a tormented hero, Jimmy Porter, and two compliant, apron-wearing, middle-class women, who cater to his every mood and whim. Osborne's play was the opening salvo in a movement that was quickly named the **angry young men.** Osborne's scathing words, uttered by Jimmy Porter, seemed to speak for a generation, who lamented their country's failure to maintain its empire and Great Britain's place in the sun. *Look Back in Anger* revolutionized the British stage, as elitist "society" plays gave way to works dealing with class conflict and working-class themes.

The lyrical dramas of Tennessee Williams (born Thomas Lanier Williams) addressed a wholly different set of issues: furtive sex and family secrets—reflecting perhaps his homosexuality—and pent-up anger—a legacy of his upbringing in the Deep South. Adding to the intensity of his plays is the romantic speech of his characters, many of whom are self-deluded. His many masterpieces include *The Glass Menagerie* (1944), about a domineering mother; *A Streetcar Named Desire* (1947), about forbidden sexual desire; *Cat on a Hot Tin Roof* (1955), about sexual frustration; and *The Night of the Iguana* (1961), about a wayward clergyman. Of these, *A Streetcar Named Desire* stands out for its indelible portraits of the fading southern belle Blanche, who uses gentility as both a veil and a weapon, and the crude Stanley, who is impatient with romantic drivel. Both of them are victims of a world in transition. By 1965, Williams's most creative period was over, but his lyrical drama made him the poet of late modernism.

Late Modernism and the Arts

The capital of the postwar art world shifted from Paris to New York. The end of Parisian dominance had been predicted since the fall of France to the Nazis in 1940; and the emerging economic and military superiority of the United States by 1945 guaranteed that America's largest city would be the new hub of Western culture. However, New York's cultural leaders were divided: one side wanted to build on the native school of American art, which was realistic and provincial; the other side was ready to take up the mantle of leadership of the West's avant-garde. The chief institutional ally of this latter group, which soon dominated the field, was New York's Museum of Modern Art (MOMA) founded principally by the Rockefeller family in 1929. New York's cultural community was also influenced by North Carolina's Black Mountain College (closed in 1956), whose experimental atmospheres nurtured many avant-garde painters (as well as poets, musicians, and dancers) on their road to success in New York.

In determining the direction of late modern art, the New York artists had to recognize their cultural situation: the domination of painting by Picasso, whose restless experimentation seemed to define art's leading edge; the prevalence of psychological theories that encouraged artists to experiment with spontaneous gestures and to seek insights from primitive peoples and from religious experience; and the cardinal need for constant newness. These forces had been shaping modernism since 1900, but the effects of World War II, the Holocaust, and the postwar arms race further dispelled illusions and raised the level of despair.

PAINTING Shortly after 1945, an energetic style of painting came to dominate late modernism: **abstract expressionism,** sometimes called **action painting.** Like earlier modernists, the abstract expressionists made spiritual claims for their work, saying their spontaneous methods liberated the human spirit. One of the founders of abstract expressionism was the American Jackson

Pollock (1912–1956), who launched this style with his "drip" paintings, between 1947 and 1950. Influenced by Jungian therapy to experiment with spontaneous gestures, Pollock nailed his canvases to the floor of his studio and dripped loops of house paint onto them from buckets with holes punched in their bottoms (Figure 21.9). The drip canvases led to a new way of looking at art in terms of randomness, spontaneity, "alloverness," and stress on the actual physical process of painting.

Figure 21.9 JACKSON POLLOCK. *White Light.* 1954. Oil, enamel, and aluminum paint on canvas, 48¼ × 38¼". The Museum of Modern Art, New York (Sidney and Harriet Janis Collection). *Pollock's refusal to use traditional methods reflects his belief that rational approaches to art are flawed and his faith that subconscious feelings, when released, reveal hidden truths—an attitude typical of the abstract expressionists. At first glance,* White Light *looks like a hodgepodge of lines and scrawls—painted without any pretense of design. But close study reveals an organization of yellows and oranges interspersed with blacks and whites, with white dominating the surface. The final effect is light—white light. Like Pollock's "drip" paintings,* White Light *has no center, no top, no bottom. With no single object or part of a picture on which to focus, the early viewers often became confused and angry, an attitude that made Pollock's works controversial and open to ridicule, but, by the time of his death, he was the most recognized and widely exhibited of the abstract expressionists.*

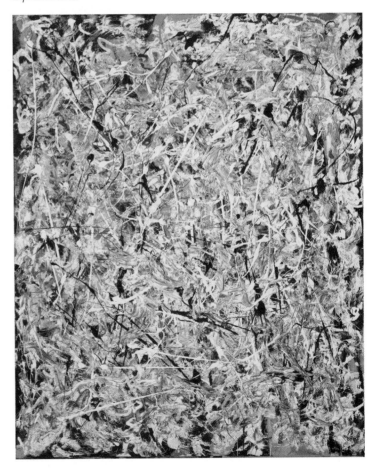

Pollock's tendency to move around the canvas during its execution also introduced the idea of the artist interacting with the artwork.

Another founder of abstract expressionism was the Dutch-born Willem de Kooning (VIL-uhm duh KOO-ning) (1904–1997). De Kooning studied art and worked as a commercial artist in Holland before coming to the United States as a stowaway in 1926. His earliest art—still lifes and figures—showed the influence of cubism and Picasso and, later, surrealism. By 1945 he had created a new style, using male figures and abstract elements. In 1948 he established his reputation with a one-man show of abstract black-and-white paintings, using enamel house paints—a revolutionary gesture. These were followed by more abstract works in which he introduced color. By then, de Kooning was defining himself as an action painter.

In 1950 de Kooning painted a controversial series on women. These paintings caused a furor, which has not fully subsided today. To other abstract expressionists, de Kooning seemed to be breaking ranks with their techniques and imagery, and many critics especially

Figure 21.10 WILLEM DE KOONING. *Woman and Bicycle*. 1953. Oil on canvas, 6'4½" × 4'1". Collection. Whitney Museum of American Art, New York. *De Kooning's female, with her bulging eyes, double set of exaggerated teeth, and extended breasts, fills over half the canvas. Her threatening appearance is heightened by the artist's slashing brushstrokes and vivid colors, especially in the flesh tones and dress. Feminist critics have observed that this painting alludes to one of a male's basic fears: large and monstrous women out to conquer and subdue him. Many women see this painting and the series as an insult to their bodies and female identity. Some art critics interpret this painting from a formalist perspective, viewing the image as secondary to the work's meaning and focusing more on de Kooning's handling of paint and use of colors.*

faulted his rendition of the female form and features (Figure 21.10). For the next ten years, the mid-fifties to the mid-sixties, de Kooning moved from painting women to landscapes and back to women again. His return to the female form—which some art critics and feminists read as satirizing women's bodies—generated more controversy.

The first generation of abstract expressionists was attracted by the movement's energy, rawness, and seriousness. An outstanding recruit to the new art was Mark Rothko [RAHTH-koh] (1903–1970), a Russian émigré who painted in a style very different from Pollock's. A mystic, Rothko envisioned eliminating pigment and canvas and suspending clouds of shimmering colors

in the air. After 1950 he settled for creating huge paintings that focused on no more than two or three fields of color (Figure 21.11).

By the mid-1950s, a new generation of abstract expressionists had emerged in New York, the most important of whom were Helen Frankenthaler [FRANK-un-thahl-uhr] (b. 1928), Frank Stella (b. 1936), Jasper Johns (b. 1930), and Robert Rauschenberg [RAU-shun-buhrg] (1925–2008). Following in Pollock's footsteps, Frankenthaler adopted a method of spilling pigment onto canvas from coffee cans. By guiding the paint's flowing trajectory, she stained the canvas into exquisite, amorphous shapes that, though completely flat, seem to suggest a third dimension (Figure 21.12).

Frank Stella, after graduating from Princeton University, began as an abstract expressionist but soon

Figure 21.11 MARK ROTHKO. Orange and Yellow. 1956. Oil on canvas, 91 × 71″. Albright-Knox Art Gallery, Buffalo, New York. © 1998 Kate Rothko Prizel and Christopher Rothko/ Artists Rights Society (ARS), New York. *Rothko layered his colors, one upon another, to create a radiance of blending at their intersections, giving* Orange and Yellow *an intensity of light as well as of color. In this and all of his paintings, Rothko aims to create secular icons for a nonreligious age, a spiritual theory inherited from the Russian constructivist tradition. Accordingly, he banishes all references to nature from his art and focuses on fields of color floating in space—timeless, universal images.*

Figure 21.12 HELEN FRANKENTHALER. *Interior Landscape.* 1964. Acrylic on canvas, 104⅞″ × 92⅞″. San Francisco Museum of Modern Art. Gift of the Women's Board (68.52). © 2011 Helen Frankenthaler/Artists Rights Society (ARS), New York. *Frankenthaler's staining method—pouring acrylic paint (a water-based paint) onto a canvas—illustrates the tension between spontaneity and control typical of abstract expressionism. On the one hand, this technique leads naturally to surprises because of the unpredictable flow of the paint. On the other hand, the artist exercises control over the process, from choosing the colors and thickness of the paint to manipulating the canvas during the staining. In effect, she becomes both a participant in and the creator of the final work of art.*

Figure 21.13 FRANK STELLA. *Tahkt-i-Sulayman I.* 1967. Polymer and fluorescent paint on canvas, 10'1¼" × 20'2¼". Menil Collection, Houston. *This painting, with its curving lines, is part of Stella's* Protractor *series—a term based on the drafting instrument, usually shaped as a semicircle. The outlines of the protractor are repeated horizontally and vertically across the canvas and interlace with one another. The warmer variations of reds and pinks are balanced by the cooler shades of blues and greens. Stella's subject is purely abstract, colors and lines only, with no hint of any natural or human forms. The name for this work is inspired by the name of a royal palace in medieval Persia.*

Figure 21.14 JASPER JOHNS. *Target with Plaster Casts.* 1955. Encaustic on canvas with plaster cast objects, 51 × 44 × 3½". Courtesy Leo Castelli Gallery, New York. Art © Jasper Johns/Licensed by VAGA, New York, NY. *Johns is a key figure in the transitional generation of painters between the abstract expressionists and the pop artists. He rebelled against the pure abstraction of the older movement, yet he shied away from embracing mass culture images as directly as did the younger school of painters. His* Target with Plaster Casts *is typical of his playful, witty style. In this work, he makes a visual play on words, juxtaposing a bull's-eye with plaster casts of body parts, each of which has been a "target"—that is, a subject for artists to represent throughout history.*

found the style too confining. While experimenting with various styles, he gave birth to a technique called **hard-edge**—a term used to describe the nonpainterly effect created by strips of color separated by precise clear edges. To achieve this, Stella made black paintings patterned at first with white stripes and then later with colored stripes. In the mid-1960s, he enhanced the visual effect of his hard-edge paintings by working with canvases that were fashioned into asymmetrical forms, called shaped canvases. These geometric shapes, curves, and intersecting patterns of bright colors established his reputation and made him one of the most popular artists of the late 1960s (Figure 21.13). Unlike many other late modernist artists, Stella became an important figure in postmodern art (see Chapter 22).

Jasper Johns and Robert Rauschenberg found abstract expressionism too constricting and overly serious. Although Johns did not abandon expressionism, he added ordinary objects to his works, as in *Target with Plaster Casts* (1955) (Figure 21.14). In this work, Johns painted a banal image below a row of wooden boxes enclosing molds of body parts. A basic feature of his art is the contrast between the precisely rendered human parts (above) and the painterly target (below). Johns's fascination with such tensions paved the way for the self-contradicting style of postmodernism. Similarly, Rauschenberg abandoned pure painting to become an **assemblage** artist, mixing found objects with junk and adding a dash of paint. In *Monogram*, he encircled a stuffed goat with a rubber tire and splashed the goat's head with color, thus turning ready-made objects into an abstract image (Figure 21.15).

Both Johns and Rauschenberg, with their playful attack on serious art, opened the door for the **pop art** movement. Rejecting the modernist belief that spiritual values may be expressed in nonrealistic works,

Figure 21.15 Robert Rauschenberg. *Monogram.* 1959. Multimedia construction, 4 × 6 × 6'. Moderna Museet, KSK, Stockholm. Art © Robert Rauschenberg/Licensed by VAGA, New York, NY. *In his glorification of junk, Rauschenberg helped to open the door to postmodernism. In works such as* Monogram, *he showed that anything, no matter how forlorn, even a stuffed goat and a discarded automobile tire, could be used to make art. Such irreverence reflected a democratic vision in which no object is seen as having greater artistic merit than any other.*

Figure 21.16 Andy Warhol. *Elvis I & II.* 1964. Two panels: synthetic polymer paint and silkscreen ink on canvas, each panel 82 × 82". © 2004 The Andy Warhol Foundation, Inc./Art Resource New York. Elvis I & II *is typical of Warhol's style, which placed little value on originality. His deadpan appropriation of pop culture images, such as this of Elvis Presley, could be interpreted as both an homage to celebrity culture and a representation of the cultural poverty of his era. Working from what could pass as a poster for one of Elvis's movies, he manipulates the image four times in what is a typical diptych form as if it were four photographs—or posters. Warhol's commercial approach to portraiture made him the most celebrated society artist of his generation.*

the pop artists frankly admitted that they had no spiritual, metaphysical, or philosophic purpose—they simply created two-dimensional images. Even though a kind of pop art developed in London in the 1950s, it was not until a new generation of New York artists began to explore commercial images in the early 1960s that the movement took off.

The most highly visible pop artist was Andy Warhol (1927–1987), a former commercial artist who was fascinated by the vulgarity and energy of popular culture. Warhol's deadpan treatment of mass culture icons became legendary, whether they were Campbell's Soup cans, Coca-Cola bottles, or Elvis Presley (Figure 21.16). By treating these icons in series, much in the same way that advertisers blanket the media with multiple images, he conveyed the ideas of repetitiveness, banality, and boredom. An artist who courted fame through his self-promotion stunts, Warhol recognized America's obsession with celebrity in his oft-quoted line, "In the future everyone will be famous for fifteen minutes."

With the New York school commanding the art world, European artists seemed to disappear into the shadows. One group, however, shared the stage with the New York group for a brief moment in the

1960s: the practitioners of **op art.** Embracing the abstract ideal of abstract expressionism, op art concentrated on abstract, mathematical forms, which were visually stimulating to the eyeball, such as whirling effects, moiré (patterned) silklike surfaces, or lingering afterimages. Perhaps the best-known op artist is Bridget Riley (b. 1931), a British painter whose theory of perception owes much to that of Georges Seurat, the founder of pointillism (see Chapter 19). Riley's *Drift No. 2, 1966* (Figure 21.17), made during her formative period, is executed in black and white, which was typical of her style at the time. The more steadily the viewer studies the image, the greater the vibrating effect on the eye.

SCULPTURE The British sculptor Henry Moore (1898–1986) was the only major sculptor working in the postwar period who did not attempt to translate into sculptural form what was taking place in the world of painting. Moore established his reputation in the 1930s, when he was identified with surrealism and constructivism (see Chapter 20). He was guided by the "truth to materials" argument and by the principle of exposing the complete sculptural form. Moore's "truth

Figure 21.17 BRIDGET RILEY. *Drift No. 2, 1966.* Acrylic on canvas, 91½ × 89½". Albright-Knox Art Gallery, Buffalo, New York. *Bridget Riley is typical of op artists in her reliance on prints—a strategy to democratize art by making it available to an extended audience, in contrast to the implied elitism of original oil paintings. Riley also seems to prefer silkscreen printing, a commercial method for reproducing art images, especially those with a so-called hard edge, as in her works. The result is a combination of visual sensation triggered by the complexities of patterns, forms, and light.*

to materials" meant that he often used a material in its natural state, such as wood or stone, and he left some of his bronze castings with a rough, unfinished and unpolished texture that made them seem more natural. In trying to reveal the complete sculptural form, Moore abandoned the traditional solid mass of a work to create, within his sculpture, "voids, holes, and hollows." He cut into the solid forms, to allow light and space to interplay between the solid mass and the hollowed-out areas.

In the 1930s, Moore slowly won over the skeptical public, who had initially rejected his works. During World War II, he continued to sculpt and, at the same time, sketched a series of "shelter" drawings, which depicted Londoners huddled in the underground subway stations during the blitz—the Nazi bombing of England. His sketches and sculptures enhanced his reputation in the United Kingdom and abroad.

After the war, Moore cast huge sculptures to be installed in sculpture gardens, in parks, and in front of public buildings (Figure 21.18). Many of them represented the humanistic tradition and images characteristic of his postwar sculptures—a mother and child, a reclining nude, a fallen warrior, and a family group. By the time of his death, Moore was considered one of the leading sculptors of the postwar period and his monumental works part of the urban landscape amid the era's prosperity and growth.

Abstract expressionist painting had its equivalent in sculpture in the works of several Americans, notably David Smith (1906–1965); Louise Nevelson (1899–1988), a Russian émigré; and Eva Hesse (1936–1970), a German émigré. David Smith's point of departure, however, differed from that of the painters in that he drew inspiration from the symbols of primitive cultures, as in *Cubi IX*, a geometric work that, according to the artist, represents an altar with a sacrificial figure (Figure 21.19). If the viewer is unaware of the intended meaning, however, this stainless steel work, although influenced by cubism, has the inaccessible look of a Pollock drip canvas. In contrast, the wooden sculptures of Louise Nevelson are not about representation at all but, instead, are simple compositions

Figure 21.18 HENRY MOORE. *Reclining Figure.* 1957–1958. Roman travertine, length 16'8". UNESCO Building, Paris. *Moore made the reclining female nude with her "open" body one of his trademarks. The UNESCO figure, with its rough surface, reflects Moore's appreciation for the effect of climate on natural stones and his admiration for ancient sculptures weathered over time. While most of his female figures are cast in bronze, this one is carved in marble.*

Figure 21.19 DAVID SMITH. *Cubi IX.* 1961. Stainless steel, 105¾ × 58⅝ × 43⅞". Collection Walker Art Center, Minneapolis. Gift of the T. B. Walker Foundation, 1966. Art © Estate of David Smith/Licensed by VAGA, New York, NY. *Smith's ability as a sculptor of enormous and rather destructive energies shines through in the monumental* Cubi *series, the last artworks he made before his accidental death. A machinist by training, Smith liked to work with industrial metals, welding and bending them into geometric units to meet his expressive needs. His desire to shape mechanical images into expressive forms related him to the abstract expressionist movement in painting.*

fashioned from old furniture and wooden odds and ends (Figure 21.20). The use of found objects allowed Nevelson to realize the abstract expressionist's goal of spontaneous art devoid of reference to the artist's life. Eva Hesse followed Nevelson in opposing representational art, but Hesse's art owed more to **minimalism,** a trend that stripped art to its basics and then worked on that. Hesse ultimately found that goal too simplistic. In her short career, she created a small body of abstract works, filled with wit, irony, and references to famous art such as *Laocoön* (1996) (Figure 21.21).

Pop art was an influence in the sculptures of George Segal (1924–2000) and Claes Oldenburg (b. 1929). Segal's ghostly works are plaster casts of live subjects, such as his *Parking Garage* (1968), which depicts a seated man, seemingly dejected and lost in his thoughts (Figure 21.22). Segal himself rejected the pop art label—pointing out that his sculptures have expressionistic surfaces, like Rodin's works (see Chapter 19)—but his method reduces the body to a cartoon form and thus relates it to popular culture. In contrast, Oldenburg embraced consumer culture while manufacturing sly, humorous reproductions of familiar objects—typewriters, electric fans, toilets, bathtubs, and pay telephones (Figure 21.23). These collapsed sculptures of ordinary objects—made of vinyl or canvas and stuffed with foam rubber or kapok—served as opposite images of the manufactured goods. Oldenburg's humor in depicting American productivity complemented the pop art painters who similarly were mocking material, consumer society.

While American sculpture flourished, the controversial German sculptor Joseph Beuys [BOYS] (1921–1986) was shaking up the art establishment at home and developing a theoretically based style, which helped shape the postmodernist movement after 1970 (see Chapter 22). Beuys's dramatic impact on sculpture was similar to that of John Cage's influence on Western music.

Beuys's first sculptures, made from animal fat and felt, reflected his miraculous escape during World War II, when he, a pilot in the German air force, was taken from his downed plane by rescuers who thrust his cold body into these substances for protection. His use of unconventional materials echoed artistic choices then being made by members of the abstract expressionist school. Beuys's greatest notoriety, and the source of his enduring influence, came in the 1960s with his staged performances—reminiscent of happenings then under way in New York and a forecast of the performance art of the 1970s (see Chapter 22). In the tradition of happenings, Beuys staged one of his most famous pieces, *Coyote, I Like America and America Likes Me* (Figure 21.24), at the René Block Gallery, in New York. In this 1974 masterwork, preserved on film, Beuys was wrapped in felt with a shepherd's crook sticking out of his felt "tent," while a live coyote wandered about the room. For a week, he and the coyote moved in unison around the gallery as if in a dance, emphasizing the connection between the human and animal worlds. One of his props—fifty copies of the *Wall Street Journal* delivered each day—symbolized the power wielded by money in the art world. Other symbols evoked his heroic rescue during World War II. This radical piece of performance art reflected Beuys's artistic credo: opposition to the old concept of art as a unique object and

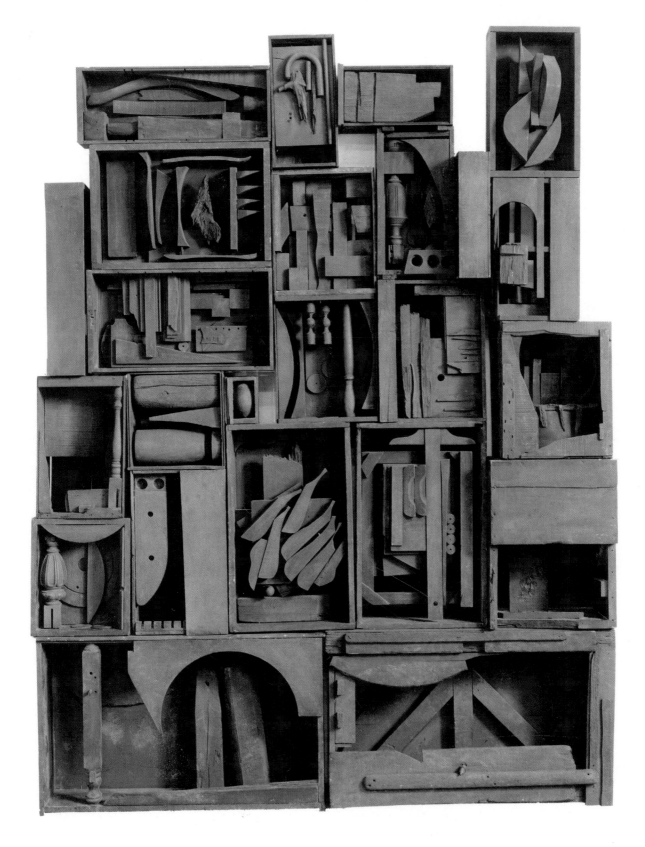

Figure 21.20 Louise Nevelson. *Black Wall.* 1959. Wood painted black. 24 units, 9'4"
× 7'¼". Tate Gallery, London. © 2005 Estate of Louise Nevelson/Artists Rights Society
(ARS), New York. *Though a modernist, Nevelson anticipated postmodernism by combining
genres, as in this freestanding wall that integrates architecture, sculpture, and painting. She
assembled boxes of various sizes, which she stuffed with found objects, such as a measuring T,
manuals, and carved pieces of wood; the whole assemblage was then painted black, giving the
finished work the appearance of a relief sculpture.*

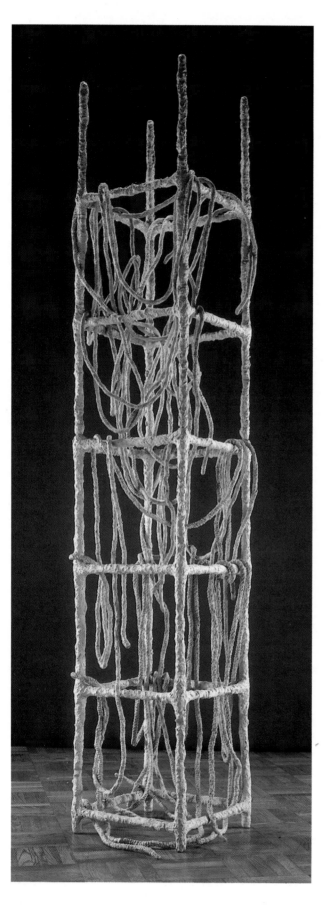

Figure 21.21 EVA HESSE. *Laocoön.* 1966. Acrylic paint, cloth-covered cord, wire, and papier-mâché over plastic plumber's pipe, 120 × 24 × 24″. Allen Memorial Art Museum, Oberlin College, Oberlin, Ohio. Fund for Contemporary Art and gift of the artist and the Fischbach Gallery, 1970. *Hesse's sculpture has created a humorous homage to one of the most famous classical works in Western art,* Laocoön and His Two Sons *or* The Laocoön Group *(see Interpreting Art Figure 4.1). Hesse's cords, while evocative of the snakes of the ancient sculpture, are actually used to bind together the covered pipes and open cubes. This playful sculpture suggests the death of myth in the modern world.*

support for the dismantling of the dealer-critic-museum system. A political radical whose views harkened back to early modernism, he sought to blend artistic freedom with social revolution. Beuys's visionary theatrics led to the revival of German expressionism—one of the major developments in Western art today (see Chapter 22).

ARCHITECTURE Two influential late modernist architects were the Finnish-born Eero Saarinen [E-ro SAAR-uh-nen] (1910–1961) and the German-born Ludwig Mies van der Rohe [mees van duh ROH] (1886–1969). Both made important, though quite distinct, contributions after World War II as they experimented with materials and designs.

Eero Saarinen came from a family of architects and sculptors. After graduating from Yale University, he joined, in the late 1930s, his father's architectural firm in Michigan. He followed the international style throughout his career, but, in the last decade of his life, he began to experiment with the style's basic rectilinear format, specifically by introducing eye-catching sculptural forms and designs. Reinforced and prestressed concrete, which had been available for many years (see Chapter 20), provided Saarinen with the materials to bring to fruition his sculptural-based buildings.

Saarinen's approach was to define a structure by its specific purpose, such as an organized sports arena (ice hockey rink) or a building for transportation (airline terminal), and then create a design that would both serve and symbolize the building's function. In the Dulles International Airport, outside Washington, D.C., and the TWA terminal at Kennedy International Airport in New York City (Figure 21.25), Saarinen achieved the sense and symbolism of flight. Two other powerful artistic legacies of Saarinen's creative genius were his 360-foot-high Gateway Arch in St. Louis (completed after his death) and his award-winning furniture designs.

Mies van der Rohe, in comparison with Saarinen, had a greater impact on late modernist architecture with his international style buildings in New York and

Figure 21.22 GEORGE SEGAL. *The Parking Garage.* 1968. Plaster, wood, electrical part, and light bulbs, 117¾ × 155". Collection of The Newark Museum, 68.191. The Newark Museum, Newark, NJ. Art © The George and Helen Segal Foundation/Licensed by VAGA, New York, NY. *Unlike other pop artists, George Segal views the world through existential eyes. While Warhol glamorized his celebrity subjects, Segal often portrays his subjects as lonely and beset by anxiety. He conveys their boredom and depression through fixed facial expressions and heavy limbs while keeping their appearances generalized. His modeling technique, which requires subjects not to move until the plaster dries, reinforces the melancholy image. By creating a suitable setting for his sculptures, he influenced the rise of installation art (see Chapter 22).*

Figure 21.23 CLAES OLDENBURG. *Soft Pay-Telephone.* 1963. Vinyl, filled with kapok, mounted on a painted wood panel, 46 × 19 × 9". Solomon R. Guggenheim Museum, New York. Gift, Ruth and Philip Zierler, in memory of their dear departed son, William S. Zierler. *Oldenburg claims that his soft forms possess many identities, thus allowing a variety of interpretations. His allusions to the sensual and erotic in the shape and contours of* Soft Pay-Telephone *are evident. The sagging vinyl, filled with material from the kapok tree, presents in a humorous way one of the most used objects in communication in the 1960s, which now is becoming a museum piece itself.*

Figure 21.24 Joseph Beuys in Performance. *Coyote, I Like America and America Likes Me.* 1974. René Block Gallery, New York. *This photograph of Joseph Beuys holding forth during a performance in 1974 is an iconic image of late modernism. More than an artist, Beuys considered himself a shaman, that is, a priest able to communicate with the gods and perform healing rituals—a view that harkened back to primitive times. Thus, his acts were, in effect, shamanistic rituals, mysterious to outsiders but therapeutic for the initiated. In this belief, he was part of the assault against consumer culture; he particularly denied that art should be a marketable commodity. Indeed, his artistic activity left no body of artworks to be sold. Beuys tapped into the period's longing for meaning, as he became in demand as a personality.*

Figure 21.26 LUDWIG MIES VAN DER ROHE AND PHILIP JOHNSON. Seagram Building. 1954–1958. New York City. Ezra Stoller © Esto. *Mies's decision to use bronze-tinted windows as virtually the only decorative feature of the Seagram Building's simple geometrical design had a profound impact on his contemporaries. Following his lead, other architects made the high-rise skeleton-frame building with tinted windows the most recognizable symbol of late modernism.*

other American cities. The last director of the Bauhaus, Germany's premier design school before World War II, Mies closed its doors in 1933 and moved to the United States in 1938 (see Chapter 20). In the 1950s, he captured the world's attention with a glass skyscraper, New York's Seagram Building (Figure 21.26). Based on the artistic creed "Less is more," this building's design is simple, a bronze skeletal frame on which tinted windows are hung—the building's only decorative feature. The implementation of his ideals of simplicity and restraint also led him to geometrize the building, planning its structural relationships according to mathematical ratios. So successful was Mies van der Rohe's "glass box" buildings, they became the prototype for skyscrapers built around the world until the early 1970s.

Happenings

Happenings was the term given to theatrical skits created by painters, sculptors, musicians, dancers, actors, and friends, performing odd and sometimes ridiculous actions. Happenings were planned so as to give the appearance of spontaneity; often involving chance elements, these experimental events—changeable, irreproducible, and explosive—were staged so as to make the audience a participant in the performance. Were they serious or meant to be viewed as satires? Or were they a "put-on"?—the much-abused critical term of late modernism inspired by the off-putting behavior of jazz performers toward unsophisticated fans. Whatever their meaning, happenings could have thrived only in the 1960s, when much of the West's traditional culture was under assault from within the establishment. Some older critics often sniffed at the entire concept, denying its originality and instead connecting it to Dada (see Chapter 20) and Dada's unrestrained cabaret shows during World War I in Europe. The first happening probably was held at Black Mountain College, in the early fifties, featuring the avant-garde artist Robert Rauschenberg. The artist credited with organizing the first happening in New York City was the painter Allan Kaprow (1927–2006), who, according

◄ **Figure 21.25** EERO SAARINEN. Trans-World Airline (TWA) Terminal, Kennedy International Airport. 1962. New York City. Ezra Stoller © Esto. *The terminal's exterior is designed to give the impression of a bird in flight. Saarinen accomplished this by installing a reinforced concrete roof anchored by two soaring beams, or cantilevers, which flare up and out on both ends and are connected by a lower center section, with the whole roof resting on giant Y-shaped pillars. Inside, curving stairways and supports add to the exterior's sense of a bird soaring. The sculptural design helped define the purpose of the building and enhanced the anticipation and adventure of flying. This terminal is no longer in use, and its future remains in doubt.*

Figure 21.27 ALLAN KAPROW. Scene, from *18 Happenings in 6 Parts*. 1959. *This photograph shows the artist Allan Kaprow playing a musical instrument in the first happening for which he wrote the script and John Cage the music. At the time, Kaprow was studying music with Cage, whose aleatory ideas are evident in the event's program. During each of the event's six parts, three happenings took place simultaneously, with the ringing of a bell signaling when to begin and end. Audience members were given cards of written instructions, which told them when to applaud and when to shift seats and move from gallery to gallery.*

to legend, staged *18 Happenings in 6 Parts* (1959) (Figure 21.27), along with the composer John Cage and Robert Rauschenberg. Kaprow is also credited with coining the term *happening.*

Late Modern Music

The major musical styles that were dominant before World War II persisted in late modernism. Musical styles were still polarized into tonal and atonal camps, led by Stravinsky and Schoenberg, respectively. After Schoenberg's death in 1951, however, Stravinsky abandoned tonality and adopted his rival's serial method. Stravinsky's conversion made twelve-tone serialism the most respected type of atonal music, though other approaches to atonality sprang up, notably in the United States. Under late modernism, this dissonant style became the musical equivalent of the spontaneous canvases painted by Pollock and other abstract expressionists.

Despite embracing the dissonance and abstraction of serialism, Stravinsky filled his late modernist works with energy and feeling, the touchstones of his musical style. Two of his finest serial works are *Agon* (1957), a score for a ballet with no other plot than a competition among the dancers, and *Requiem Canticles* (1968),

a religious service for the dead, marked by austere solemnity.

Dissonance also characterizes the music of Krzysztof Penderecki [pahn-duhr-ETS-key] (b. 1933), a member of the Polish school who is anything but a doctrinaire modernist. Committed to an older musical ideal, he believes that music, above all things, must speak to the human heart. Nevertheless, he has been a constant innovator, seeking to create new sounds through the unconventional use of stringed instruments and the human voice. Marked by classical restraint, his compositions are clearly structured works permeated by fluctuating clouds of sounds, as in *Threnody for the Victims of Hiroshima* (1960), scored for fifty-two stringed instruments. (A threnody is a song of lamentation.) Reflective of the melancholy mood of late modernism, this work conjures up the eerie minutes, in 1945 at Hiroshima, between the dropping of the atomic bomb and its detonation. Penderecki achieves unearthly effects through the use of **glissando** (the blending of one tone into the next in scalelike passages) in an extremely high register and by the string players bowing their instruments in abnormal ways.

The most influential late modernist was John Cage (1912–1992), whose unusual, even playful, approach to music opened the door to postmodernism. Briefly Schoenberg's student, Cage gained most of his controversial notions—in particular, his goal of integrating noise into music—from the enigmatic teachings of Zen Buddhism. A work that demonstrates this goal is called *4'33" (Four Minutes and Thirty-three Seconds)*. The title describes the time period for which the performer is to sit immobile before a piano keyboard so that the concert hall sounds, in effect, become the music during the performer's silence. Cage's spirited experiments made him the darling of the avant-garde who, with assemblage artists, choreographers, and sculptors, helped to break down the divisions among the art forms—in anticipation of a postmodernist development.

Film

Film was perhaps the most important art form of late modernism, holding its own against the upstart—television—though the outcome of the competition for market share between the two media continues to be in doubt. Filmmaking grew more international, moving toward a global cinema. Hollywood increasingly flexed its muscles as the period unfolded, but studios in Europe and elsewhere played major roles in this expanding world market of mass entertainment.

In Rome, Cinecittà—Italy's largest motion picture studio—was rebuilt, after the war. At Cinecittà, the first postwar film movement was born, **neorealism,** which trained an unforgiving eye on the gritty life of postwar Italy. The director Roberto Rosselini (1906–1977) founded this movement with *Open City* (1945), an unsparing portrait of Italy's chaotic capital in the war's last days, as the Italian underground fought the retreating Nazis. Perhaps the greatest of the neorealists was Federico Fellini (1920–1993), who adopted a satirical style as his art progressed, taking images from the circus and often using the actress Giulietta Masina (1921–1994), his wife, as his muse. This he did in the incomparable *Juliet of the Spirits* (1965), a hilarious romp through the consumer-driven, erotically charged Italy that had emerged in the 1960s.

Similarly, Japan's film industry was reestablished after the war, thus helping its national economy to recover and ensuring a Japanese presence in the emerging global culture. Daiei Films in Tokyo inaugurated a successful marketing campaign to export its films to the West through means of seeking awards in film festivals, which now functioned as international marketplaces for film distributors. Daiei's success began at the prestigious Venice Film Festival in 1951, when *Roshomon*—a dramatic film, directed by Akira Kurosawa [kur-uh-SAH-wah] (1910–1998), recounted a particular event from the shifting perspectives of its several characters. *Roshomon* won the top prize and, at the same time, introduced the world to Japanese

cinema. Other films followed, usually falling into the category of **art film,** featuring unusual narrative structures, blood and gore with an uplifting humanist message, and dramatic camera work, and the production suffused with the personal vision of the director.

Art films also dominated the French film industry. In the 1950s, France's influential journal of film criticism *Cahiers du Cinéma* began to use the term *auteur* ("author") to denote those directors who "wrote" with their cameras as they made their films. Auteurs were distinguished from mere directors, who simply made movies by collaborating with screenwriters, cinematographers, editors, costume designers, set designers, lighting technicians, and musicians. Auteurist theory inspired France's first postwar film movement, **Nouvelle Vague,** or the French **New Wave** (late fifties to early sixties). Adopting experimental methods, New Wave directors used "jump cuts" (rapid changes of scenes), freeze-frames, and ambiguous time sequences to create idiosyncratic films, such as *The 400 Blows* (1959), directed by François Truffaut (1932–1984). Unique among these directors was the politically minded Jean-Luc Godard (b. 1930), whose *Week End* (1967) is a seriocomic satire of "the weekend from hell."

Sweden, neutral during World War II, enjoyed a film boom, largely through the multilayered works of Ingmar Bergman (1918–2007). Bergman's angst-ridden characters, torn between love of life and the certainty of death, were consummate exemplars of late modernism. Drawing on his strict Lutheran upbringing, Bergman created a powerful series of films, set both in the bleak feudal past and in the equally bleak, though different, world of the modern middle class. The greatest of these are *The Seventh Seal* (1957), which presents a harrowing vision of the medieval plague, culminating in a chess game between the crusader knight and the devil (Figure 21.28), and *Winter Light* (1963), part of the *Silence of God* trilogy, which offers a portrait of a Protestant pastor adrift in the personal and political ambiguities of modern life.

Other important film centers during this period included Moscow, London, and Calcutta (today, Kolkata). Yet, while the rest of the world produced art films, Hollywood stayed with the tried and true: genre movies, defined by drama or setting, such as westerns (late forties to early fifties); *film noir* (French, "dark film"), a style of crime film marked by harsh lighting, hard-boiled heroes, and existential angst (late forties to early fifties); musicals (until 1967); social problems (entire period); and romantic comedies (entire period). Some of the genres, by their nature, produced escapist movies with formulaic plots, stereotyped characters, and predictable outcomes. One representative of Hollywood's creative genius, while still working within the confines of a genre—the musical—is the incomparable *Singing*

ENCOUNTER

The Globalization of Popular Music

Global music emerged between 1945 and 1970, powered by many forces, such as improved technology, international relations, and popular tastes. New media, including radio, film, and television, transformed the world into a "global village," a term dating from this era. The potential audience for this global village was broadened by rapid advances in the recording industry, which were fueled by a postwar economic boom in the West, Japan, and parts of the third world. After 1948 the superpowers fostered global music, with the Soviets exporting classical music and the Americans a mixture of classical, pop, and jazz.

In 1945 the big band sound dominated American popular music. Usually composed of about twenty musicians and led by an instrument-playing conductor, the big bands played love ballads, swing tunes, and jazzy pop, in concerts, at nightclubs, and in recording studios. As the big band era gave way to rock and roll in the mid-fifties, American popular music became infused with revolutionary styles and sounds. In rock and roll, music drew from both white and black roots, from country music and from rhythm and blues, from rockabilly and from gospel and jazz; and overlaying it all was an uninhibited sexual tone. The sound of rock and roll—gritty, loud, and urgent—reflected its mixed heritage outside the mainstream. Rock and roll's first outlets were bars, records, and radio, but soon small bands of five to eight musicians performed in concerts

and on tours, playing to hordes of screaming fans, especially teenagers.

In the mid-sixties, rock and roll evolved into rock, a more sophisticated but less sexy global style, embodied most famously by the Beatles (active 1959–1970). Soon, rock had wiped most other musical styles off the map, with its driving rhythms, wailing vocals, and youthful angst.

Even though most influences flowed outward, some rock stars, for example, the Beatle George Harrison (1943–2001), were drawn to non-Western music. Enamored of Eastern mysticism, Harrison persuaded the Beatles to fly to India in 1967 to meditate for a week—a fact loudly reported in the world's media. He studied the sitar with Ravi Shankar (b. 1920), India's most famous musician, and their friendship helped make Shankar one of the first non-Western superstars of global music. By the 1960s, global music was the cornerstone of a worldwide youth culture.

Two other musical forms also helped the rise of global music: folk music, especially non-Western, and dance music, mainly from Latin America with African rhythms. Non-Western folk music showed its power by creating a few global stars, for example, the South African Miriam Makeba (1932–2008), singing Xhosa and Zulu songs. Dance music contributed a Latin beat with African overtones to global music, including the *samba* (early 1940s), a Brazilian blend of syncopation with Af-

Figure 21.28 The Devil and the Knight. Still, from *The Seventh Seal.* Ingmar Bergman, director. 1957. *Various scenes in the film depict the ongoing chess match (as here) between the devil (Bengt Ekerot) and the returning crusader knight, Antonius Block (Max von Sydow). Antonius plays chess for his soul, even as he reveals much about his feelings for God, religion, and life. The title,* The Seventh Seal, *is taken from the biblical book of Revelation, where the opening of seven seals heralds the end of the world. Revelation 8:1 states: "The Lamb then broke the seventh seal, and there was silence in heaven for about half an hour." Bergman's allegorical movie vividly represents this dramatic passage with its depiction of a world beset by plague, violence, and death.*

rican steps; the *mambo* ("voodoo priestess") (1943), a mix of swing and Afro-Cuban rhythms; the *cha-cha-cha* (1954), a Cuban offspring of the mambo; and the *bossa* nova (Portuguese, "new wave") (late 1950s), a Brazilian blend of samba and jazz.

A fitting symbol of the global music then emerging is the African American jazz trumpeter Louis "Satchmo" Armstrong (Encounter figure 21.1), who toured the world tirelessly after 1947, earning the nickname "Ambassador Armstrong" (see Chapter 20). Ambassador Armstrong lives on in recordings such as "What a Wonderful World" (1968), which celebrates Satchmo's simple faith at the height of the 1960s rebellion.

LEARNING FROM THE ENCOUNTER

1. *What* forces contributed to the rise of a global music culture after 1945? 2. *Evaluate* the significance of each of these forces. 3. *What* role did rock and roll play in the rise of a global music culture? 4. *Discuss* the impact of folk music and dance music on global music culture. 5. *Why* is Louis Armstrong a fitting symbol of early global music? 6. *Who* today best represents global music in our contemporary culture?

Encounter figure 21.1   Louis Armstrong in Cairo. Louis Armstrong House Museum, New York City. 1961. *In this photograph, Louis Armstrong is pictured outside a hospital in Cairo, surrounded by laughing children. In appearances such as this, Armstrong was seen as the United States' goodwill ambassador to the world, showcasing a lively, home-grown art form.*

in the Rain (1952), codirected by Stanley Donen (b. 1924) and the film's star, Gene Kelly (1912–1996). While the movie breaks no new ground, it has become the gold standard by which other musicals are judged, because of the perfect ease with which it realizes each of the disparate elements of the filmic art.

Another trend in film in the United States, and elsewhere, was the rise of the documentary. The documentary style was made possible by the invention of the portable handheld camera in 1959, thus allowing the recording of ordinary people and events in real time. Documentaries attracted a cult following because of the immediacy of their subjects, which were often "ripped" from newspaper headlines. Two early examples by American directors are *Don't Look Back* (1967), directed by D. A. Pennebaker (b. 1925), about the 1965 concert tour of Great Britain by the then-emerging singer Bob Dylan (b. 1941), and *Titicut Follies* (1967), an exposé of the horrors of a mental hospital in Massachusetts, by Frederick Wiseman (b. 1930). American documentary

films appeared at the same time as the French movement called *cinéma vérité* ("direct cinema"). Both the French and the Americans shared values with the Italian neorealists, especially in their preference for truth over art.

A further development that changed film was the rise of film festivals for showcasing new releases. The Venice Film Festival came first, in 1932, but after the war, festivals were established in Cannes, France (1947), Berlin (1951), London (1956), and Karlovy Vary, in the Czech Republic (1965). In the United States, the film industry remained aloof from festivals during this period, preferring to market itself through traditional venues, but changes in the U.S. film industry were occurring as art house cinemas and university film societies began showing foreign films and catering to selected audiences. Around the globe, distributors set up systems to specialize in old films, and movie houses showing "classic" films grew in popularity.

The Legacy of the Age of Anxiety and Late Modernism

The Age of Anxiety began with a war-weary world hoping for peace and ended in a standoff between two superpowers capable of destroying the human race. This international rivalry, which permeated every phase of life, also helped shape the cultural style of late modernism—the final phase of modernism that had been the West's reigning style since about 1870.

In the mid-1950s, fear gripped the world as the United States and the Soviet Union, armed with atomic and hydrogen bombs and long-range missiles, seemed positioned to go to war. But as one crisis followed another, the adversaries found ways to avoid a military showdown. In the competition for economic supremacy, the USSR and its Eastern European satellites lost the race. By the early 1970s, the West had surged ahead in manufacturing, productivity, and marketing to produce a consumer society and a burgeoning middle class that were the envy of the world.

In the immediate postwar era, some Western intellectuals embraced existentialism, while others turned to Christian existentialism or neoorthodoxy. The vast majority of believers remained with traditional religious faiths, seeking answers and solace in an increasingly secular society. Protestant churches confronted the changing world in their separate denominations, while the Roman Catholic Church convened a council. By the late 1960s, structuralism and a materializing hedonism in popular culture, which were challenging the tenets of Christian and middle-class values, indicated future unrest.

Scientific discoveries and inventions were, as they always had been, a mixed blessing. Most were beneficial in their initial stages, raising the standard of living or, in the case of medicine and medical practices, improving the lives of people in many societies. The United States, in its desire to be a world leader, added universities and research centers to the already existing industrial-military-state complex, creating a military establishment capable of wielding huge economic, political, and even spiritual influence—as President Dwight Eisenhower (in office 1953–1961) famously cautioned. This amalgamation of knowledge and power for the benefit of a nation, a trait of Western societies since the Scientific Revolution, has become an accepted way of life in most industrialized countries and has increasingly shaped contemporary society.

Late modernism, like bipolar international relations and rising economic trends, emerged out of the traumas and experiences of World War II. The United States, with New York City as the hub, became the West's cultural leader, as the "arts capital" label shifted from Europe to America. Painting, sculpture, architecture, and literature flourished in the United States with only an occasional voice from Western Europe or the Soviet Union being heard on the international level. Abstract expressionism was the first art style of the restless and rebellious postwar generation of New York painters and sculptors, followed by an ever-changing series of styles: pop art, op art, minimalism, and other schools. Films witnessed a rebirth after the war and, along with television, competed for a worldwide audience, whose attention spans were growing shorter and shorter. In the arts and popular culture, the United States was outdistancing the Soviet Union, as American clothes, music, movies, and celebrities won the hearts of young people around the world. The United States, with its materialistic society, relaxed lifestyle, and rock-and-roll music, was now the force driving the emergent global culture.

Regardless of events in the arts and elsewhere, the cold war defined the Age of Anxiety. The crises that brought both superpowers to the brink of war, the efforts of the United States and the Soviet Union to gain support among third world countries, and the deep-seated ideological differences between their political and economic systems seemed to indicate that the cold war would last for decades. Likewise, the divide between rich and poor countries, which had begun in the 1960s, signaled more widening in the future. Finally, innovations in the arts foreshadowed more changes to come in styles, techniques, and materials after 1970.

KEY CULTURAL TERMS

late modernism
neoorthodoxy
structuralism
beat generation
theater of the absurd
Pinteresque
angry young men
abstract expressionism
action painting
hard-edge
assemblage art

pop art
op art
minimalism
happening
glissando
neorealism
art film
auteur
Nouvelle Vague
    (New Wave)

QUESTIONS FOR CRITICAL THINKING

1. Discuss the impact of military armaments and modern technology on the culture of the world between 1945 and 1970.

2. Late modernism has been called the "Age of Anxiety." Defend or refute this observation, drawing on the literature and art from this period.

3. Discuss how the rise of modern feminism helped shape the culture (literature, thought, and art) from 1945 to 1970.

4. Describe the major developments in late modern literature and give representative examples of writers working in this field.

5. How have painters made social issues a central concern in the art since 1945? What causes attracted them? How have they been expressed in their works?

22

THE CONTEMPORARY WORLD
Globalization, Terrorism, and Postmodernism
1970–

In the early 1970s, the West entered a period marked by three events: the second phase of the cold war; a growing world economy, known as globalization; and the rise of postmodernism. In reaction to these events, the next twenty years, until 1990, was a period of extremes, oscillating between optimism and pessimism.

Politically, these gyrations manifested themselves at the end of the Soviet Union. Some scholars proclaimed the collapse of Communism to have ended the Age of Extremism, or the Long War—two terms used to describe the twentieth century's extended conflicts between totalitarian regimes (Fascism, Nazism, and Communism) and parliamentary-democracies (England, France, and the United States). Elation quickly gave way to pessimism, as ethnic hatreds revived in the post-Communist world, leading to outbreaks of violence and localized wars.

Economically, higher oil prices in the early 1970s raised the standard of living in the oil-producing countries but, at the same time, endangered the affluence enjoyed by the industrialized world. Hopes and fears were also raised across the world as Western nations shifted manufacturing to cheaper labor markets in the Far East.

Social problems, formerly localized, grew more global: the specter of food shortages and famines sparked by exploding populations; the threat of job losses caused by new technologies; and the potential for environmental calamities produced by both the industrialized states and the developing countries.

In the 1990s, these shifting moods and challenges helped define postmodern culture, with its drive to globalization and its vision of a unified,

◀ **Detail** REM KOOLHAAS. Seattle Central Library. 2004. Seattle. © Ron Wurzer/Getty Images.

667

multicultural world. But any renewed sense of hope quickly disappeared at the onset of the twenty-first century, when conflicts between the West and Islamic radicals, which had been sporadic for decades, moved to a higher level. The recent history of this period can be divided into two phases: toward a new global order, 1970–2001; and the Age of Terrorism, or the beginning of another Long War, 2001–present.

TOWARD A NEW GLOBAL ORDER, 1970–2001

The early 1970s marked a turning point, not only for Western civilization but for the world as well. The balance of global power began to shift from the bipolar, superpower model to a multipolar system that included Japan, China, and Western Europe. This political realignment started when the superpowers moved toward *détente*, a French term meaning "a waning of hostility." By the early 1970s, détente had produced several arms-limitation treaties between the USSR and the United States, creating a favorable climate for a reappraisal of cold war attitudes and a reduction of other global ideological battles. China, a previously closed country, began to interact with the United States and other Western countries. In addition, as the industrialized nations became increasingly dependent on the oil-producing countries, the latter exerted more influence on world events.

Economic, National, and International Developments

During the 1970s the world's economy underwent several changes. The standard of living declined for most citizens in Western Europe and the United States when the Organization of Petroleum Exporting Countries (OPEC), a cartel of the oil-rich states of the Middle East, raised prices. As a result, most Western nations went into a recession that resulted in rising unemployment and inflation. Also, the migration of Turks, North Africans, and Arabs to Europe as guest workers restructured the labor market and intensified socioeconomic tensions in many European countries. And the Soviet Union, with its state-controlled economy, could no longer produce both arms and consumer goods.

The 1970s was a time of political drift in the United States in the wake of the Watergate scandal and President Richard Nixon's (in office 1969–1974) resignation; in contrast, the 1980s brought dramatic changes both nationally and internationally. Under President Ronald Reagan (in office 1981–1989), the government adopted laissez-faire economic policies, which led to an economic turnaround. The nation paid for this prosperity, however, with increased spending, a huge national debt, and a shift in foreign trade from creditor to debtor status. The gap between rich and poor also widened, leading to increasing polarization in American society.

On the international scene, détente suffered two setbacks: the Soviet invasion of Afghanistan in 1979 in support of local Communist leaders; and the Polish government's suppression of Solidarity—a labor movement founded in 1980 that pushed for economic reforms. Cold war sentiments revived, ongoing disarmament talks between the superpowers broke down, and an intensified arms race seemed imminent.

The international tension dissipated in 1985 with the appearance of Mikhail Gorbachev [GOR-bah-chof] (in office 1985–1991) as the new moderate leader of the Soviet Union, which had fallen behind the more-productive capitalist nations. Gorbachev introduced a new era of détente with his overtures to the United States, which opened communication between the two superpowers.

The Fall of Communism

Within the Soviet Union, Gorbachev initiated reforms in the state bureaucracy and the Communist Party that were designed to raise the standard of living. His plans dramatically altered the course of history in the USSR, Eastern Europe, and the world. Gorbachev's domestic reforms contributed to the breakup of the centralized structure of the USSR, as some member states declared their independence and others gained local control. From the old Soviet system, following more than seventy years of Communism, a severely weakened Russia reemerged, shorn of its vast empire yet still managing to retain some ethnic republics through a commonwealth arrangement (Map 22.1).

Gorbachev's policies toward the satellite states led to the dissolution of the Communist bloc in Eastern Europe, symbolized by the destruction of the Berlin Wall (Figure 22.1). Newly independent, these former Communist states struggled to maintain their social welfare programs and worker protection system and at the same time to move toward democratic government and a market economy. However, Russia, with its ethnic and regional crises on the rise, Boris Yeltsin (in office 1991–1999) tried to steer a course in uncharted political waters. Russia's future seemed to be in the hands of either the nationalists and Communists, who wanted to restore their country's former imperial and economic systems, or the reformers, who wanted a marketplace economy and political freedom.

Under Vladimir Putin, president (1999–2008) and now prime minister (2008–), Russia began to dismantle its earlier democratic reforms, to centralize political control, and to reinvigorate a nationalist agenda. Exercising

LEARNING THROUGH MAPS

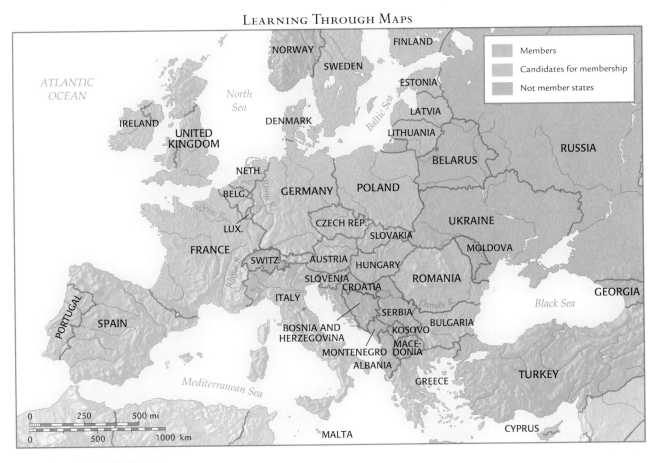

Map 22.1   EUROPE IN 2009
This map shows the member countries of the European Union as of 2009. 1. *Note* those countries that are candidates for membership. 2. *Observe* which current member states of the EU are former members of the Communist bloc, as shown on Map 21.1, Europe in 1955. 3. Excluding Norway and Switzerland, which are special cases, *identify* those countries that are not currently members of the EU. 4. *Why* do you think these countries are not yet members of the EU? 5. *Speculate* on Russia's attitude toward the expansion of the EU to the borders of Russia.

newly found economic power—based on oil and natural gas resources—it is today more involved globally in diplomacy and European and international trade. At the same time, Russia sees new threats to its national security, as its former satellites rush to join either the European Union or the North Atlantic Treaty Organization.

Beyond Russia's borders, the downfall of the Soviet system set off a chain of events that ended Soviet control of eastern and central Europe and rebalanced the power structure in Europe, marked the demise of Communism, and left the United States the "winner" of the cold war. The euphoria generated by the fall of Communism and the expectancy of a "new world order" quickly became linked with market-based economies, which replaced the discredited state-run models. The implications of these political and economic transformations gave further proof that the world was shrinking and that globalization would be the defining trend in the 1990s (Timeline 22.1).

The Post–Cold War World

After 1989 the United States emerged as the world's lone superpower, while many other countries faced nearly intractable problems. The United States basked in its unique position because of its military superiority, its central role in international affairs, and its consumer society, which helped propel the global economic boom. Complicating America's preeminence was its unwillingness to work in full harmony with the United Nations. Convinced that the UN was dominated by third world interests, the United States preferred to act alone, through coalitions of its own choosing, or to work with established regional alliances. Other nations, such as Japan, failed to recover from the 1990s downturn of its financial markets, while China, in spite of its phenomenal economic growth rate of 8 to 12 percent a year, faced a number of domestic crises. Some of its citizens, particularly students and workers, called for a more

Figure 22.1 Fall of the Berlin Wall. 1989. *Given the Soviet Union's previous use of force in Eastern Europe, no one had predicted that the collapse of the Communist states would be so quick and bloodless. The most symbolic event of this extraordinary period was the dismantling of the wall that separated East Berlin from West Berlin.*

open and democratic society. Public demonstrations led Chinese authorities to crack down on protesters in Beijing's Tiananmen Square in June 1989 (Figure 22.2).

Throughout the 1990s, economic globalization intensified because of the spread of free-market systems. However, volatility in financial markets led to social and political unrest, thus hinting at what might happen during a global financial crisis and calling into question many assumptions of laissez-faire capitalism. At first, for example, the economies of the Pacific Rim countries, except for Japan, boomed, but by 1998, the euphoria had waned. Paralleling globalization was the rise of regional economic alliances, such as the European Union as a free-trade zone and the North Atlantic Free Trade Association (Nafta) among Canada, the United States, and Mexico. The Internet and electronic commerce were, at the same time, revolutionizing the way the world conducts its business.

The World Trade Organization (WTO), founded in 1994 to promote free trade, has helped settle trade dispute among its member states. The WTO, along with the World Bank, the International Monetary Fund (IMF), and regional trade associations, has increased global wealth and reduced global poverty. However, not all countries have benefited from globalization and free trade, and a few have been openly critical of free-market economics. In these disaffected countries, globalization is usually identified with the United States,

giving rise to anti-American and antiglobalization sentiments and generating a new form of populism—that is, advocating the rights of a nation's citizenry against the power of multinational corporations and the developed world.

From the mid-1990s to 2001, the world's economy was driven by developments in the United States. First, the American stock market climbed because of the dot-com companies—communications and technology businesses, funded by venture capitalists. Speculation and greed ran the market up to new heights, until the bubble burst in 2001. Second, American businesses outsourced many white-collar jobs to developing nations, following the lead of factory owners who had earlier moved plants to countries with cheap labor.

In addition to the economic fallout from the end of the cold war, regional nationalism and ethnic violence, which had been suppressed during the era of the superpowers (1945–1970s), now resurfaced. In the 1990s, with the disintegration of Yugoslavia, wars broke out among the newly formed states along ethnic and religious lines. Eventually, as Europe dithered over what to do, the United States decided to act. After a series of air strikes, the fighting ended and the warring factions were brought to the peace table, where they accepted a series of accords, thus bringing a wary peace to the region. The changes taking place in the United States and Europe were matched by events in the Middle

Timeline 22.1 CULTURAL STYLES, 1970–PRESENT

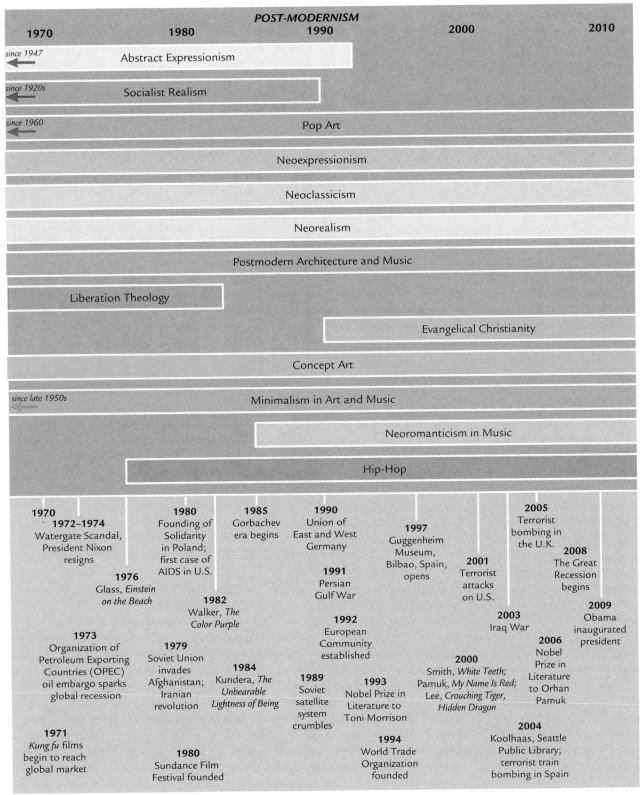

East. Tensions and wars in that region had mounted during the cold war. Israel, for example, won wars against its neighbors in 1967 and 1973. In the late 1970s, conditions seemed to improve when Egypt and Israel signed peace treaties. Just when it seemed that conditions might improve, the Iranian Revolution occurred. In 1979 a theocratic Islamic government was established in Iran, which, while heartening to the faithful, let the world know that a militant, radical movement had been born.

The Middle East was further destabilized when Iraq, under Saddam Hussein [sa-DAHM hu-SANE]

Figure 22.2   Protester Standing in Front of Tanks. Tiananmen Square, Beijing, China, 1989. *In the 1980s, the Chinese government abandoned its isolationist policy, engaged in international trade, and sent its young people to study abroad to prepare them to be future leaders of China. Having seen life outside China, they returned home and began to demand more freedom, which the authoritarian government would not permit. This struggle, between the government and the youth, climaxed in Tiananmen Square, the symbol of Chinese Communist power, during the prodemocracy demonstrations that were watched, as they unfolded, on television around the world.*

(r. 1979–2003), invaded Iran in 1980. Believing Iran weak under its new revolutionary government, Hussein calculated a quick and easy victory. However, the war, with high casualties on both sides, dragged on until 1988. Two years later, the Iraqis invaded Kuwait, which soon led to the 1991 Gulf War. A coalition of Western and Muslim states, led by the United States, drove the Iraqis from Kuwait. Although defeated, Hussein remained in power throughout the decade.

THE AGE OF TERRORISM, 2001–

Two iconic American buildings—symbolic of the superpower's far-reaching economic, military, and cultural power—became the target of anti-Americanism on September 11, 2001. Previous terrorist attacks had tar-

geted overseas military bases, the World Trade Center (1993), and embassies in Africa (1998), but those paled in comparison to the devastating assault on the Twin Towers of the World Trade Center in New York City (Figure 22.3) and the Pentagon in Washington, D.C. The attacks, commonly referred to as 9/11, were organized by al Qaeda [al KAY-duh], a small radical Islamic sect, who capitalized on America's lax immigration policies and their own technological know-how for their destructive scheme.

The United States, convinced that Afghanistan's government—the Taliban, an Islamic fundamentalist group—was harboring al Qaeda and its head, Osama bin Laden [o-SAH-mah bin LAHD-en] (b. 1957), invaded the country in October 2001. The Taliban-led government fell in a few weeks, and America and its NATO allies occupied the capital and sections of the country.

A new constitution was drafted, and elections held as a first step toward democracy, but Afghanistan, plagued by ethnic rivalries, systemic poverty, and a resurgent Taliban, remains a perplexing challenge to the West.

In March 2003, the United States, supported by Britain and a few other nations, invaded Iraq. President George W. Bush (in office 2001–2009) reasoned that Saddam Hussein's dictatorship had to be overthrown, claiming Hussein possessed weapons of mass destruction, which were about to be unleashed on the world. Although the initial fighting lasted only weeks and Saddam Hussein was captured in December 2003, the war has dragged on for over six years, proving costly in lives and expenditures (Figure 22.4). The U.S. public has remained deeply divided over the war, and, despite a decline in the fighting and a more stable Iraq, the final outcome of the war and Iraq's future is uncertain.

Unlike the cold war, which was a by-product of twentieth-century events, the war in Iraq must be set in its historical context—back to the twelfth-century Crusades (see Chapter 9). After the flowering of Islamic civilization (see Chapter 8), the Muslims experienced centuries of humiliation as they fell victims to European power. In the past decade, some Islamic religious and political leaders have capitalized on the ensuing resentment, calling on their followers to avenge past misdeeds by "the Western infidels" and to reestablish a theocratic Muslim empire. Whether recent events will result in a clash of civilizations and a second Long War remains to be seen. Whatever its final resolution, tensions between the West and Islam are now more intense than ever before, and more violence and bloodshed seem likely in the near future (Figure 22.5).

The wars in Iraq and Afghanistan, which served as the backdrop to the almost two-year-long runup to the 2008 U.S. presidential election, were overshadowed by a rapidly spreading global economic downturn that rivaled the Great Depression (see Chapter 20). This current crisis—called by some economists, the Great Recession—spurred many nations to take unprecedented steps, both nationally and internationally, to bring stability to the financial system and establish effective regulatory agencies. This Great Recession, brought about by the near-collapse of a market-driven global economy, has called into question the benefits of free-market capitalism, which has held sway for the past two decades. The global downturn and its aftermath will mark another turning point in history. America's new president, Barack Obama (b. 1961) (in office 2009–), will assume the reins of power at this historic moment.

Figure 22.3 Proposed World Trade Center Project. 2004. New York. *The 2001 destruction of the Twin Towers of the World Trade Center presented a challenge and an opportunity to rebuild the area. After years of public debates, political pressures, and lawsuits, the authorities chose the plan of the Berlin-based Studio Libeskind in 2004. The Polish-born American Daniel Libeskind's (LEE-behs-kihnd) (b. 1946) model shows Freedom Tower to the left, an open area and plaza for the memorial to the 9/11 victims, and a cluster of five surrounding buildings. Freedom Tower, the centerpiece of the project, will be a 1,500-foot skyscraper with a 276-foot-tall spire, making it taller than the Twin Towers. Construction of the subway station and transportation hub started in late 2005. A 9/11 museum and a performing arts center, designed by Frank Gehry, are being planned.*

Figure 22.4   American Soldiers Examine an Iraqi Child. 2005. *This scene—American soldiers examining a wounded Iraqi child during a U.S. government–sponsored community health outreach program—recalls similar images from the United States' recent wars—from World War II to the Vietnam War. This picture also illustrates the dilemma of an army fighting on foreign soil. The soldiers are warriors waging a war against the enemy and, at the same time, protectors of the innocent victims of warfare. Throughout history, armies have come as liberators and remained as occupiers, which often turns them from friend to foe.*

Figure 22.5   An Anti-American Painting. 2006. Tehran, Iran. *The United States' "stars and stripes," in the shape of a revolver, expresses the growing hostility against America in Iran and other parts of the Muslim world. The contrast between the painted protest and the arabesque patterns on the wall is heightened by the woman strolling down the street. Her traditional attire emphasizes the cultural gulf between American women and Muslim women. The shadows of the trees frame the photograph, giving it an artistic touch that catches the eye while sending an obvious message to the viewer.*

THE BIRTH OF POSTMODERNISM

In the 1970s, late modernism (see Chapter 21) was challenged by a new movement: **postmodernism.** With its optimistic view of history—as shown by its desire to reinterpret earlier styles—postmodernism reflected a more positive outlook than that of late modernism. Having grown to maturity after World War II and believing that late modernism's anxiety was outdated, the postmodernists embraced mass culture and, in general, displayed a playful approach to creativity (Figure 22.6). As witnesses to the world-ranging rivalry between the two superpowers, the postmodernists envisioned a global culture, free from military threat.

The United States and postmodernism have been closely intertwined. American artists and scholars played a key role in establishing the culture of postmodernism because the United States is unique in being a microcosm of global society, and because affluence made its consumers the driving force in the world economy. The cold war's end in 1990, which left the United States as the only superpower, also enhanced America's presence in postmodernism. However, the globalization of postmodernism has produced a paradox: American culture, especially popular culture, values, and technology, is eagerly adopted everywhere, but alongside adoption come voices denouncing America's cultural imperialism as well as American military might and economic power.

Postmodernism's cultural vision looks in two directions: forward to a global, democratic, many-voiced civilization, and backward to the roots of the Western tradition. This double vision embraces the works of women, minority group members, and representatives of the third world, even as it reexamines both classical and preclassical civilizations. The events of 9/11 cast this global vision into doubt, when the day's tragic events inaugurated the Age of Terrorism. Nevertheless, the vision endures, despite the threats posed by war, terrorist acts, and, since 2008, a global recession.

Medicine, Science, and Technology

In today's world, advances in science and technology have had a greater impact than in the past. Not only have science and technology accelerated and directed change around the globe, but they have also become integral parts of the world's economy, international affairs, and the military-industrial complex of most nations.

MEDICINE   The health and well-being of most humans have improved since 1970. New drugs and surgical procedures have saved and prolonged life for millions in industrialized nations. Governments and international organizations have worked together to educate the populace, to distribute drugs and build medical facilities, and to eradicate childhood diseases around the world.

Organ transplants and the use of artificial organs have prolonged life for many people otherwise without hope. However, these practices have also embroiled the medical profession in ethical controversy, including charges that only a few people can afford these procedures and that they drain the financial resources of the health-care system. Likewise, new methods in human reproduction, while helping a few, have led to court cases, involving such moral dilemmas as: When a couple divorces, which of the two has a legal right to a fertilized egg? With surrogate parenting, does a surrogate mother have parental rights? When a sperm donor is used, does the donor have a legal right to protect his identity from his offspring?

Despite medical breakthroughs that have saved millions of lives, some locales are still threatened by fatal diseases, and worldwide epidemics are always possible. In the 1980s, AIDS (acquired immune deficiency syndrome) arrived and quickly spread to certain sections of society. AIDS, along with an increase of other sexually transmitted diseases, not only slowed down the sexual revolution but also wiped out segments of the population. In sub-Saharan Africa, AIDS has devastated many communities where there are few hospitals or clinics; local attitudes have exacerbated the problem either by denying the existence of the disease or by rejecting modern medical practices. In some areas, the most productive age groups have been decimated, leaving behind a generation of orphans, many probably infected with the disease (Figure 22.7).

Fatal infectious diseases, easily transmitted and with millions of international travelers as potential carriers, have spread rapidly around the world. Especially worrisome have been the influenza viruses, such as "bird flu" and "swine flu," originating and moving out of Asia. The World Health Organization (WHO) and national health units work together, monitoring the paths of these diseases and cooperating to contain and eradicate them.

SCIENCE   Advances in genetics, based on the discovery of DNA, have revealed basic information about the origins of life. Researchers have decoded the human genome, composed of perhaps three billion units of DNA, arranged into twenty-three pairs of chromosomes. In

Figure 22.6 NAM JUNE PAIK. *My Faust-Channel 5-Nationalism.* 1989–1991. Twenty-five Quasar 10-inch televisions, three Sony laser disc players, Neogothic wood frame with base, 104 × 50 × 32″. Private Collection, Seoul. *Designed by the Korean American artist Nam June Paik, this artwork is a playful commentary on war as a form of national religion. Housed in a Neogothic frame, inspired by medieval altarpieces, the art is filled with military objects, such as bombs, jackboots, and helmets, as well as television screens and laser disc players. By covering the top and sides of the frame with flags from many of the world's nations, Paik suggests that all countries make sacred cults of their military establishments.*

biogenetics, scientists have cloned animal and plant products and organs, as well as whole sheep and mice, their most spectacular achievement. As in medicine, these breakthroughs raise serious ethical questions, such as: What use will be made of the genome map? Should attempts be made to clone humans? Are genetically modified fruits and vegetables safe for human consumption? Just as in medicine, the resolution of these questions will probably be determined within the courts.

TECHNOLOGY   The inventions and improvements in machine technology have had a more direct and immediate impact on public and private life than advances in medicine and science. New devices have evolved from the miniaturized integrated circuit invented around 1959, which had its origins in transistors (see Chapter 21), and from the founding of the microchip industry, starting in the 1970s. The microchip replaced the transistor and its components with a single integrated circuit, or chip, thus making it possible to further reduce the size of machines, in particular, the computer.

Figure 22.7 AIDS Patient Dies from Kidney Failure While Surrounded by Family Members. Mission Hospital, Southern Africa. 2002. Gideon Mendel/Network—Saba. *According to one study, two million people died of AIDS in 2007. One and one-half million of them were from sub-Saharan Africa. The United Nations and some of its members, including the United States, have increased their efforts to combat AIDS. However, the approach of the United States' faith-based organizations—no condoms and sexual abstinence—has stirred up controversies among Americans and world health authorities. About thirty-three million humans are living with AIDS or HIV (human immunodeficiency virus), which affects the immune system and leads to AIDS.*

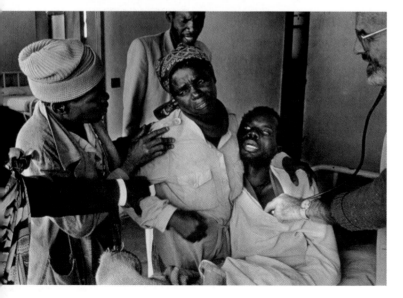

Communication satellites, adapted from the 1960s U.S. space program, made an interlinked global culture possible. Multinational corporations now depend on these satellites, and people everywhere watch televised events at the same time thanks to satellite communication.

But the computer and the Internet have revolutionized life even more, making previously unimaginable quantities of data immediately accessible, simplifying complex tasks, and transforming traditional habits of personal and public life around the globe. Consumers, through e-commerce, purchase goods and services directly and, through e-trade, buy and sell stocks and bonds without brokers. Scholars, researchers, and students, through IT (information technology), access journals, books, libraries, and databases to keep up with areas of expertise. From Web sites, businesses place orders, restock inventories, and sell to customers. Individuals e-mail friends and family, keep pace with current events, pay bills and do their banking, and design their own Web sites, where they pursue varied interests and hobbies, such as watching movies and playing video games. These developments have led to "cocooning," a mode of stay-at-home living in which people surround themselves with electronic devices and seldom venture into the public sphere, even for amusement and social contact.

In contrast, the cell, or mobile, telephone has changed social behavior by allowing people to discuss business and personal matters, while also providing them with varied forms of entertainment. At the same time, the cell phone has tethered the wandering individual to the communication network, like a puppet on a string.

The microchip further revolutionized the entertainment industry, which now produced many new products, including portable TVs, radios, CD players, and media players. However, some buyers with alternate agendas, such as terrorists, have utilized these inventions to construct an effective and sophisticated global network that allows them to carry on their destructive work and to deliver their messages to a worldwide audience. For better and for worse, e-mails, blogs, and text messages whiz around the world in seconds. These instant forms of communicating can galvanize opinions, appeal for international aid in time of crisis, or stir up groups and set off riots or demonstrations.

Another breakthrough is under way in nanotechnology, which seeks to manipulate materials on the atomic level, with the aim of building microscopically small devices. This breakthrough follows the post-1945 trend toward miniaturization (see Chapter 21). (*Nano* [Greek, "dwarf"] in the international scientific vocabulary means "one-billionth part of.") Research in the United States and East Asia is still in its infancy, though stain-resistant textiles, cosmetics, and improved media players, using nanotechnology, are already available. Current research indicates future benefits in varied fields, including health care, the environment, and communications.

Technological know-how is central to the growth of many emerging economies. Technology, since the Industrial Revolution, has given developing nations the means to catch up with the more advanced ones. Just as Germany and the United States eventually bypassed Great Britain (see Chapter 19), today poor countries with access to models of productivity and technology can close the gap and sell their manufactured goods to richer, consumer nations. The Pacific Rim countries did this in the 1970s and 1980s. China and India, both rapidly moving up the technology ladder, have emerged as major players in international trade and commerce.

Since 1995, the interfacing of technology with climate has become a global issue. In the 1980s, studies showed that the emission of certain gases, including carbon dioxide, were creating a greenhouse effect, or the warming of the earth's surface, which might melt the polar ice and raise sea levels. Alarmed at this prospect, 141 countries ratified the Kyoto Protocol (1997), which mandated specific reductions of industrial emissions by the signatory nations. However, the United States refused to sign, asserting that the treaty's demands would cripple its economy. Meanwhile, corroboration of global warming continues to come from reports of historic levels of polar ice melting in both the Arctic and Antarctic regions.

Philosophy and Religion

Since the 1970s, most intellectual trends have been confined to academic circles and small groups of thinkers, while religious ideas and movements have caught the attention of the world. The two primary subjects of academic and literary debate have been poststructuralism and deconstruction. **Poststructuralism,** growing out of structuralism (see Chapter 21), offers varied ways to understand and interpret all texts, not just literary ones. **Deconstruction** is a method of criticism that focuses on reading, rhetoric, and aspects of language. In contrast, organized religious groups across the world have entered the political arena, often playing a pivotal role in domestic and international affairs, while advocating their views on economic, social, and cultural issues.

PHILOSOPHY Thomas Kuhn, Roland Barthes, and Jacques Derrida were leading thinkers in the postmodern era, though most of their writings appeared earlier. Their ideas gave rise to ongoing debates about timeless issues, such as how humans communicate, understand, and explore the unknown and comprehend their own

existence and the meaning of life. Kuhn's ideas were easily understood and quickly adopted by the intellectual community, but the nuanced arguments of Barthes and Derrida were not as accessible and remain unfamiliar to the general public.

The American Thomas Kuhn (1922–1996) was a student of the history of science, exploring the assumptions and methods of scientific research. In *The Structure of Scientific Revolutions* (1962), Kuhn reasoned that throughout the history of science, research has been framed by a paradigm—an unconsciously agreed-on pattern of thought in each scientific discipline—that limits scientists to operating within its boundaries. For Kuhn, no basic changes can occur in science until a series of findings are made that render the existing paradigm unworkable, resulting in a **paradigm shift.** When a paradigm shift occurs, one worldview is exchanged for another, as occurred, for example, when earth-centered astronomy gave way to sun-centered astronomy (see Chapter 15). A paradigm shift, in turn, sparks new experiments that test basic assumptions and generate more questions. Kuhn's paradigm-shift argument was soon adopted by other disciplines, including the social sciences, economics, and business-school curriculums, and has now entered the mainstream of Western thought.

While Roland Barthes [BART] (1915–1980) bridged the structuralism and poststructuralism movements, he, in contrast to Kuhn, attracted a select group of followers and his influence was confined to a small audience. In books on linguistics and language, Barthes, as a structuralist, asserted that every language has its own structure, or code, capable of being decoded. In later works, Barthes, as a poststructuralist, argued that any theory or explanation, such as that used in understanding or decoding a language or literary work, requires its own theory of meaning or explanation. This necessitates a further set of codes and explanations or a series of discourses. Although his quirky style, wit, and allusions and his eclectic interests made Barthes difficult to understand, his ideas profoundly impacted literary and cultural criticism in France and the United States. But many of his critics were bothered by the implications of his thought. Since Barthes reasoned that there were no certainties in understanding a text, there were, therefore, no overarching concepts (such as science) or political or economic systems (such as democracy or socialism or capitalism). Critics charged that his analysis led to extreme relativism or even **nihilism**—the denial of objective truth.

Jacques Derrida [deh-RE-dah] (1930–2004), a French philosopher and linguist, was another voice of postmodernism and the founder of deconstruction. His book *Of Grammatology* (1967) established his reputation as a seminal thinker. Derrida defined deconstruction as a new type of reading practice, which "deconstructed" a text, claiming that a text, whether it be a novel, philosophical essay, or history book, could be read in many ways and could have so many meanings that it possessed no ultimate meaning. He argued that speech and writing, as they were deconstructed, could not be analyzed as they were subject to how they were read and who was the reader. Deconstruction became another way to destabilize and displace the former methods of understanding what was said or read or thought to be the "truth." Like the critics of poststructuralism, the enemies of deconstruction concluded that it was one more assault on the West's self-evident truths and fundamental principles—which were rooted in scientific methods, empiricism, and rationalism.

RELIGION AND RELIGIOUS THOUGHT   After 1970, religious organizations tried, as in the past, to adjust to a rapidly changing world. Many of the faithful utilized the latest technology for learning purposes, to spread the faith, and to defend themselves, but others rejected or attacked scientific and cultural changes that they believed to be threats to their values and beliefs. Christianity and Islam, the world's most popular religions, adopted similar patterns of acceptance or repudiation, but they varied in their respective strategies and tactics for accommodating their faiths to modernity and the postmodern world.

In Latin America in the late 1960s, **liberation theology** became a driving force for change in the struggle against poverty and the oppression of the poor. Roman Catholic intellectuals, inspired by Vatican II (see Chapter 21), founded this school of thought, which appealed especially to the clergy who lived and worked among the dispossessed. Mixing Christian social justice with Marxist analysis, advocates called for reform of the economic and political systems along with planned Christian-based communities that allowed the poor to work together to improve their living and working conditions. As liberation theology took root, its revolutionary ideas appeared to threaten the stability of some Latin American countries. In the 1980s, the Catholic Church withdrew its support for the movement and military regimes wiped out many of its communities, killing some priest-leaders. But liberation theology has survived as an underground movement in poverty-stricken regions of the world.

In the United States, appeals for Christian social justice reached new heights in the late 1960s. But the assassination of Martin Luther King Jr. in 1968, the acceleration of the Vietnam War, and cultural upheaval at home ended this phase of religious activism. Partly in reaction to these events, and partly due to the revival and restructuring of the evangelical wing of Protestantism (see Chapter 19), institutionalized religion in the United States took a different direction. In the 1960s

and 1970s, a number of charismatic, fundamentalist preachers, led by Billy Graham (b. 1918), capitalized on the rapid growth of television to deliver their revival messages. Some of these TV evangelists reached celebrity status, and their followers donated generously to build campus-style religious centers, large sanctuaries, and colleges. These preachers attracted believers, who were disenchanted with mainstream culture, which they saw as a double threat: to their personal faith and to their vision of a Christian America.

By the 1990s, these groups—now called evangelicals—had coalesced into the National Association of Evangelicals and, through their political activity, were affecting the outcome of elections. Known variously as the Religious Right or the Christian Conservatives, they joined with the Republican Party to become a powerful force in American politics. Through the media and the ballot box, they have proclaimed their beliefs on many issues of modern life: stem cell research, evolution, abortion, homosexuality, and same-sex marriages. Their political activity has sparked controversy over the relationship between government and faith and has raised, once again, concerns about the "wall" that has separated church and state in the United States for more than two hundred years.

Unlike in the United States, organized religion in western Europe has continued to decline as a social and cultural force. Many urban churches have been converted to secular uses, the ranks of Roman Catholic priests and nuns are in steep decline, and membership in Protestant churches has dwindled. However, in Africa and Asia, both the Roman Catholic and Protestant churches, especially the evangelicals, have won millions of converts by expanding mission programs and building churches, schools, and hospitals. African and Asian bishops and cardinals make up an increasingly large percentage of the Roman Catholic hierarchy, which indicates that the Roman Catholic Church will be less Eurocentric in the future.

The papacy of John Paul II (pope, 1978–2005) typified the challenges facing not only the Roman Catholic Church but all organized religion during this period. A cardinal from then-Communist Poland, he was the first non-Italian pope in 455 years. An engaging, bright, and energetic man, he took advantage of the news media and the jet plane, making highly publicized visits to nearly every country on the globe. He reached out to other faiths and played a key role in bringing down the Communist regime in his native Poland, which turned out be the opening phase of the fall of the USSR (Figure 22.8). He also strengthened papal power, undermined some Vatican II reforms (see Chapter 21), and held firm to the church's traditional stands on most gender and social issues. The humanity and political acumen so evident in his early years gave way to a more autocratic style and a conservative theology, which reflected not only his aging but also the church's response to its more globalized membership and an increasingly secular world.

Islam, the world's other major religion, has also been under siege in the contemporary world, particularly with the rise of Islamic radicalism. In 1979, in Iran, the ayatollahs—learned Shiite scholars—led a revolution against the shah's regime and set up the Islamic Republic of Iran. In Afghanistan, after an Afghani victory against the Soviets (1988) and an inconclusive civil war (1992–1996), the Taliban (r. 1996–2001), a local Islamist movement, emerged the winner and established a strict Muslim theocracy. The Taliban gave Osama bin Laden a safe haven from which to operate his al Qaeda network. Other radical Muslim groups—such as the Muslim Brotherhood in Egypt, Hezbollah in Lebanon, and Hamas, which won political power in Palestine in early 2006—attract Muslims who see them as alternatives to dysfunctional regimes, the sworn enemies of Israel, or as the strident voices of anti-Americanism who are willing to take on the "Great Satan" (the United States).

These Muslim fringe groups have been further radicalized by the historic memory of European Crusaders conquering and humiliating their ancestors (see Chapter 9), by geopolitics and the recognition of their pivotal location on the globe, by the oil that has enriched their countries and raised Arab national pride, and by recent reinterpretations of the Qur'an. The most influential of these commentaries was by the Egyptian thinker Sayyid Qutb [si-YID KU-tahb] (1906–1966), the father of modern Islamic terrorism. In his works—*In the Shade of the Qur'an* (thirty volumes, starting in 1954) and *Milestones* (1964)—Qutb advised Muslims on how Allah wanted them to live in the modern world. Most important, Qutb called for a *jihad*, an armed struggle against the Infidels (the West) and their puppets, the secular Muslim regimes. In this struggle, the Near Enemy (secular Muslim rulers) and the Far Enemy (the United States and its European allies) would have to be destroyed. The terrorist leader Osama bin Laden answered this call to arms and urged many Muslims to his version of Qutb's ideology. After expelling the Infidels, this modern-day jihad must purify their homelands of erring communities, kill the Far Enemies, and found a new Islamic empire based on the past, back to the time of the Prophet. Whatever ultimate fate awaits bin Laden and al Qaeda, the "franchising" of al Qaeda cells has spread throughout the world.

The Literature of Postmodernism

Postmodernist literature is notable for the inclusion of new literary voices drawn from diverse sources, including Latin America, central and eastern Europe, and the Islamic world, as well as minorities, assimi-

Figure 22.8 Pope John Paul II in Poland. 1979. *Soon after being elected pope, Karol Wojtyla [voy-TIH-wah] returned to his homeland. His June 1997 visit to Poland was a bold gesture. The leader of the Roman Catholic Church was warmly received, and he met with many organizations, including Solidarity, the underground labor movement that, in 1989, helped overthrow the Communist government in Poland. In retrospect, the pope's trip was seen as an important step in the ending of the cold war.*

lated colonial peoples, and new immigrants. Taken together, these new voices signal a shift away from the dominance of the New York–London–Paris cultural axis and the rise of a global culture.

FICTION In the late 1960s, Latin American authors attracted international acclaim. Most of these writers held left-wing political opinions and practiced a literary style called **"magic realism,"** which mixed realistic and supernatural elements. The ground had been prepared for the magic realists by the Argentine author Jorge Luis Borges [BOR-hays] (1899–1986), whose brief, enigmatic stories were concerned with language itself. The outstanding representative of the magic realist school is Gabriel García Márquez [gahr-SEE-uh MAHR-kays] (b. 1928) of Colombia, who received the 1982 Nobel Prize in Literature—the first Latin American novelist to be so honored. His *One Hundred Years of Solitude* (1967) is among the most highly acclaimed novels since 1945. Inspired by William Faulkner's (see Chapter 20) fictional county of Yoknapatawpha, Mississippi, García Márquez invented the town of Macondo as a symbol of his Colombian birthplace. Through the eyes of an omniscient narrator—probably an unnamed peasant—who sees Macondo as moving toward a predestined doom, he produced a hallucinatory novel that blends details from Latin American history with magical events, such as a character's ascent into heaven. The novel's pessimism is typical of the magic realist school.

While Latin America's authors were enjoying international renown for the first time, the writers of central and eastern Europe—another new center of postmodernism—were renewing an old tradition. From the early 1800s until Communist regimes were installed in the early twentieth century, the finest writers of central and eastern Europe had often been honored in the West. The revival of the literature of this region was heralded by the 1950s cultural thaw initiated by Soviet leader Khrushchev (see Chapter 21), but this thaw proved premature, since controversial writers were either silenced or forced to seek refuge in the West. Exile was the choice of the novelist Milan Kundera [KOON-deh-rah] (b. 1929) of Communist Czechoslovakia, who moved to France after his first novel, *The Joke* (1969), put him in disfavor with Czech authorities. Kundera's style has affinities with magic realism, notably the blending of fantasy with national history, but unlike the Latin American authors, he uses fantasy to emphasize moral themes, never for its own sake. He is also more optimistic than the magic realists, hinting that the power of love can lead to a different and better life. Indeed, Kundera tends to identify sexual freedom with political freedom.

The equation of sexual and political freedom is certainly the message of Kundera's finest novel to date, *The Unbearable Lightness of Being* (1984). He made the center of this work two historic events—the coming of Communism to Czechoslovakia in 1948 and its reimposition after the 1968 uprising. He describes the obsessive and ultimately destructive behavior of his main characters as they try to define their sexual natures in the repressive Czech state. Although his novel shows how insignificant human existence is in the face of political repression, he refuses to despair. That his characters struggle for sexual fulfillment, even when faced with overpowering odds, is his way of affirming a humanist message: the human spirit can be diminished but never broken.

A belief in the power of the human spirit, similar to Kundera's, is apparent in the work of the American writer Alice Walker (b. 1944). In her poetry, essays, and fiction, she brings a positive tone to her exploration of the African American experience. Her novel *The Color Purple* (1982) is the story of a black woman abused by black men and victimized by white society. The literary device she uses to express this woman's anguish is an old one, a story told through an exchange of letters. What is unique is that in some letters the suffering woman simply pours out her heart to God—an unexpected but moving twist in the skeptical atmosphere of the postwar world. *The Color Purple* also draws on Walker's feminist consciousness, showing that the heroine's survival depends on her solidarity with other black women. Winner of the 1983 Pulitzer Prize, *The Color Purple* was transformed into an award-winning film in 1985, and in 2005 it became a successful Broadway musical.

Toni Morrison (b. 1931), whose novels explore the plight of black Americans, was the first African American to win the Nobel Prize in Literature (1993). Except for *The Song of Solomon* (1977), which has a male narrator, her novels focus on female characters victimized by racism. In *The Bluest Eye* (1970), for example, a young black girl, attracted by the standard of white beauty, yearns to have blue eyes. Morrison also shows that violence is a central part of black life, as, for instance, in *Sula* (1973), when a grandmother, wanting to support her family, deliberately injures herself in order to collect insurance money. Inspired by her African heritage, she draws on folklore, mythology, and the supernatural, as in *Beloved* (1987), in which a ghost is the central character. Despite the racism and violence, Morrison imbues her novels with spiritual longing, thus offering hope for a more just society in the future. Her latest novel, *A Mercy* (2008), expresses that hope more directly, by focusing on a multicultural household in colonial America where race plays only a minor role.

Maxine Hong Kingston (b. 1940) enriched postmodernism by bringing Chinese Americans into American literature through her autobiographical books, a novel, short stories, and articles. Her avowed literary aim has been to "claim America," that is, to show that the Chinese have the right to belong through their labor in building the country and their own communities. In staking out this claim, she was influenced by the modernist poet William Carlos Williams (1883–1963), who envisioned an American culture distinct from Europe and fashioned from indigenous materials and forms. Kingston's writings not only celebrate Chinese strength and achievement but also serve to avenge wrongs—by calling exploitation, racism, and ignorance by their true names.

The daughter of Chinese immigrants whose language was Say Yup, a dialect of Cantonese, Kingston has used her own life as a paradigm of the Chinese American experience. Drawing on childhood stories told in the immigrant community, she wrote two works that draw on her Chinese heritage: *The Woman Warrior: Memoirs of a Girlhood Among Ghosts* (1976), dealing with matriarchal influence, and *China Men* (1980), telling of the patriarchal side. In 2008 Kingston was awarded the Medal for Distinguished Contribution to American Letters.

Postmodern literature grew more pluralistic with the rise of writings crafted from the experience of overseas peoples, drawn to Europe from former colonies. One of the most commanding voices in this new writing is the English-born Zadie Smith (born Sadie Smith) (b. 1975). Smith, educated within the British establishment at Cambridge University, made a stunning debut with *White Teeth* (2000), an evocative novel about multicultural London. In highly ironic prose, Smith presents the lives of three families—all outsiders in a way—over three generations: a working-class family of Muslim Bengalis; a working-class family similar to the author's, with a white English father and a Jamaican-born wife; and an educated, middle-class family of British Jews. A hugely ambitious work, *White Teeth* addresses many of today's major topics, such as ethnic and racial identity, terrorism, and assimilation.

The 2001 terrorist attacks on New York and Washington, D.C., made Westerners eager for knowledge about Islamic culture, by writers from within that world. Previously, translations of Islamic fiction had appeared regularly in the West, though their style and themes usually echoed Western models, as in *The Cairo Trilogy* (1956–1957), about three generations of Egyptians between World War I and the early 1950s, by the Nobel laureate Naguib Mahfouz [MAH-fooz] (1911–2006). Now, after 9/11, the audience expanded dramatically, to address the burgeoning desire for Islamic books.

The most profound voice yet to emerge in Islam for many Westerners is that of the controversial Turkish writer Orhan Pamuk [PAH-muk] (b. 1952). His first novel, *The White Castle* (1985), about the ironies of modernization, made him a writer to watch. Later works confirmed that judgment. Today, Western readers often hail him as the "conscience of his nation," because his themes echo basic Turkish dilemmas: Western or Islamic identity, secularism or religion, and freedom or authority.

Of Pamuk's novels, *My Name Is Red* (2000) has excited the most global attention. Although events revolve around a murder, the novel is learned, ironic, erotic, and deeply steeped in the literary methods of the modernist novel. *My Name Is Red* focuses on a circle of artists—all miniaturists—at the court of the Ottoman sultan Murat III (r. 1574–1594), a generous patron of the arts. When one artist goes missing, a chain of events is unleashed, ending with the death of the murderer. Adding to the novel's allure are tidbits of Ottoman history, references to miniaturist styles across the Islamic world, and, of special note, meditations on the stir that arose when Western painting was introduced to the Ottoman court (see Encounter figure 11.1). The novel's narrative unfolds in a modernist style, as each of its fifty-nine chapters is told from a shifting perspective, including those of several characters, a dog, a gold coin, and the color red. In 2006 Pamuk received the Nobel Prize in Literature, the first Turkish writer to be honored with this award.

POETRY Poetry has, by and large, experienced a fallow period after 1970. The already tiny audience for poetry has grown smaller still, in response to the explosive growth of mass media, shifting demographics, and the obscurity of most verse. It has also thus far resisted globalization, largely because, as is often said, "Poetry in translation does not travel well." However, one major poet, writing in English, has emerged: Derek Walcott (b. 1930), the West Indian poet.

Walcott's writings reflect his personal situation, first as a youth on the remote volcanic island of Saint Lucia, and second as a mature black writer, torn between island culture and his new American homeland. Author of numerous plays and books of poetry, Walcott became world famous with *Omeros* (1990), a book-length poem that revisited Homer's *Iliad* and *Odyssey*, transposing their setting to the Caribbean in the 1900s and drawing on their themes of war and homecoming, respectively. Dante's *Divine Comedy* also influenced Walcott, providing him with the theme of salvation and the three-line verse form in which the poem is composed. In *Omeros,* Walcott blended imagery and diction, redolent of the lush tropics, with anguish for the paradisiacal world he had lost. Walcott was awarded the Nobel Prize in Literature in 1992.

DRAMA Drama, like poetry, has not become global. Avant-garde theater has all but disappeared. Few outstanding dramatists have emerged since the politicized 1960s, when they made sociopolitical issues central to their works. Thus, the theater, often diagnosed as "the glorious invalid," has been ailing over the past few decades. However, there have been two rays of hope: the comedies of the Italian team Dario Fo (b. 1926) and Franca Rame (b. 1929) and the rise of comedy troupes.

In Fo-Rame, from 1959 to 1970, Fo was the leader, writing, directing, designing sets and costumes, and, sometimes, composing music. Rame, his wife, muse, and leading lady, assisted at all levels. Nurtured in socialist families in Italy, the pair were drawn to popular theater, which catered to ordinary people. Their early plays were little more than comic revues, satirizing postwar Italy. In response, the church and the state began a continuing campaign to censor them. Over time, as their satire became fiercer, their fame grew, along with controversy. In the 1960s, Fo and Rame became sensations on Italian television. From 1970 to 1985, they performed with a theatrical collective in Milan, for which Fo wrote plays, including *Accidental Death of an Anarchist* (1970), which established his international reputation. This provocative play, based on a real-life event, raised the question "Did a police suspect leap

ENCOUNTER

Continental Drift: Demography and Migration

From prehistoric times, the size and density of human populations (demography) and their movement from one geographic area to another (migration) have always been part of the human experience. Thus, today's migrations and demography, while closely linked to the Age of Globalization, are not new habits and traditions.

While the world's expanding population and shifting patterns of migration are continuations of past trends, they also indicate the global community's future destiny. Today's migrants are exerting strong pressures on national and local governments, along with human service agencies, and increasing tensions within countries and between nations. These pressures are made more acute due to the earth's constricted livable areas, the finite supply of natural resources, and the varied ethnic, racial, cultural, religious, and ideological differences between the migrants and their adopted lands.

Since the 1500s, migrations, both voluntary and forced, have accelerated over time, with each new generation affecting the growth of commerce and the ethnic and racial character of the destination nation. Migrations in the 1600s and 1700s were closely tied to the first phase of global expansion, and immigrants were mainly slaves from Africa shipped to the New World and a smaller number of white Europeans sent to convict settlements overseas, as in Australia. The Great Migration occurred between 1845 and 1914, when forty-one million immigrants settled in North and South America, though most came from Europe to the United States. In the twentieth century, some nations placed restrictions on immigration, but desperate people, especially those seeking work and political asylum, continued to find new homelands.

Since the 1970s, the patterns of immigration have varied: Vietnamese war refugees to the United States and some Asian nations following the Vietnam War; legal and illegal workers from Latin America to the United States (Encounter figure 22.1); ex-colonials returning home to Europe as the colonial system disappeared; guest workers from southern Europe and Muslim countries to Europe; Asian temporary workers to the oil-exporting countries; and eastern Europeans to western Europe after the collapse of Communism. These migration patterns have put pressures along many borders, such as between eastern and western European nations, among some Asian countries, and along the Mexican–United States border. Many immigrants have recorded their stories in fiction, plays, and films—thus contributing to the multiculturalism of postmodernism.

Demographic studies show that the world's population is approaching seven billion, and the projection is for over nine billion by 2050. However, diseases, such as AIDS in Africa, flu epidemics from Asia, or some other lethal illness, could change these forecasts. Twenty of the most populous cities are on the five largest landmasses: twelve in Asia, five in Latin America, two in Europe, and one in North America (New York). Other demographic shifts are taking place that will

---

to his death or was he pushed?" Blending drama with comedy, this full-length, tragic farce used techniques from **commedia dell'arte** (Italian, "comedy of art"), a theatrical form from the sixteenth to the eighteenth century, involving clowns, puppets, and stock figures; absurdist drama; and Fo's own imagination. In 1997 Dario Fo was awarded the Nobel Prize in Literature.

Theater troupes, offering evenings of inventive wit, social satire, and music, originated in England. The British group that pioneered this trend was Beyond the Fringe (1960–1963), a four-person team, featuring the actor and musician Dudley Moore (1935–2002). Their example later inspired the Monty Python Flying Circus (1969–1974), led by the hilarious John Cleese (b. 1939). The success of Beyond the Fringe was confined mainly to concert halls and television, whereas Monty Python's reach extended into mass culture. Both groups satirized religion, the state, and popular fads. But what set Monty Python apart was its surreal-

ism, an influence from absurdist theater. The current popularity of sociopolitical satire in the West is a testament to the enduring influence of these two groups.

Postmodernism and the Arts

After 1970, artists and architects moved beyond late modernism, which dissolved into weak minimalist schools (see Chapter 21). In postmodernism, the shock of the new gave way to the shock of the old. Abandoning the pessimism of late modernism, with its focus on abstraction and purity, postmodern artists grew more optimistic and revived earlier styles, although always with added layers of meaning, nuance, or irony. Realism made a triumphant return to art, flourishing as **neorealism**, a style based on photographic clarity of detail; as **neoexpressionism**, a style that offers social criticism and focuses on nontraditional painting

Encounter figure 22.1 Mexican Migrants. 1986. *Mexican migrants, desperately seeking work, travel across deserts or pay smugglers to get them across the U.S.-Mexican border. The United States faces a growing dilemma with the large influx of illegal immigrants from Central and Latin America, and politicians cannot agree on how to solve the problem. Agribusiness, many farmers, and low-paying companies need these migrants, legal or illegal, as cheap laborers. But their arrival has overloaded state and local welfare agencies, aroused suspicion and distrust, and heightened prejudices.*

bring more challenges. In rich countries, the population is aging and the working population is declining, while in poor countries, the population is growing and a larger percentage of this population is young people.

These demographic and migration trends are changing the face of the West. National identities are being challenged today, and these debates can be polarizing in an ethnically and racially mixed society. For example, France in 2006, with a population that is 10 percent Muslim, has been beset by urban unrest among Arab youth and divisive protests over the ban of religious headscarves in public schools and the lack of economic opportunities. The future of the West will be determined in part by how Westerners respond to globalization and two of its most powerful stimulants: demography and migrations.

LEARNING FROM THE ENCOUNTER

1. *What* are some of the broad issues brought about by demographic changes and immigration? 2. *How* have the major migrations since the seventeenth century affected the growth of nations? 3. *Discuss* the patterns of migrations since the 1970s. 4. *What* do the demographic studies tell us about the world's populations? 5. Give *examples* of how these developments affect American society and your life.

---

methods; and as **neoclassicism** (not to be confused with the neoclassicism of the late eighteenth century), which had been dormant since the early twentieth century and pronounced dead by the late modernists.

Neoclassicism is the most striking style within postmodernism, in both painting and architecture, perhaps because it looks so fresh to modern eyes. But modernist abstraction still remains a significant facet of postmodernism. The postmodernists, in their openness to artistic possibilities and their refusal to adopt a uniform style, resemble the postimpressionists of the late nineteenth century.

PAINTING The American neorealist painter Philip Pearlstein (b. 1924) has kept the human figure a part of postmodern art. Starting in the 1960s, he made his chief subject human bodies beyond their prime, perhaps as a way of reflecting the melancholy of the age. He rendered his nonidealized nudes in stark close-up, their bodies at rest like hanging meat, and with cropped heads and limbs as in a photograph (Figure 22.9). His works seem to parody the "centerfold sexuality" that accompanied the sexual revolution brought on in part by the birth control pill.

Whereas neorealism tends to neutrality or moral subtlety, neoexpressionism uses realism to create works with overtly sociopolitical messages. The outstanding neoexpressionist is the German artist Anselm Kiefer [KEE-fuhr] (b. 1945), whose expressive tendencies owe much to his older countryman Joseph Beuys (see Chapter 21). Kiefer's works have blazed new trails with nontraditional materials, including dirt, tar, and copper threads (Interpreting Art figure 22.1). In his apocalyptic vision, personal references, and historical allusions, Kiefer is perhaps the contemporary artist closest to the German expressionists of the early 1900s.

In the United States, a leading neoexpressionist is Susan Rothenberg [ROTH-en-berg] (b. 1945). Sensing the tidal shift under way in art circles, she abandoned 1960s minimalism for a more expressive style in 1973. Until 1980 she painted one subject: the horse. Her horse paintings evoke a contrived sensibility as they are not so much living creatures as a representation of her feelings—an artistic credo she shares with van Gogh (see Chapter 19). In *Butterfly* (1976), the horse appears flattened against the giant X at its midsection (Figure 22.10). The handling of paint—to give an agitated feel to the work's surface—links her style to that of Willem de Kooning (see Figure 21.10).

A painter who embraced elements of neorealism and neoexpressionism, along with other artistic trends, to forge a unique style is the Colombian artist Fernando Botero (b. 1932). Like the neorealists, Botero populates his canvases with human and animal shapes, though he makes each figure grossly overweight. Like the neo-expressionists, he adopts exaggerated effects—the inflated figures—to reveal his negative feelings for his middle-class subjects, but, unlike the neoexpressionists, he creates highly varnished canvases, devoid of visible brushstrokes and textured surfaces. The rotund figures are flat, brightly colored, and boldly outlined—as in Colombian folk art. And he gives each work a political subtext, a mission he borrowed from the Mexican muralist Diego Rivera (see Chapter 20). *Dancing in Colombia* (1980), with its robust musicians, is typical of Botero's style, but the dancers, rendered in a smaller scale, are fairly unusual (Figure 22.11). This scene mocks the smug middle class, who party while drug lords destroy their country.

A painter who uses neoclassicism to make subtle commentary on art history is Peter Blake (b. 1920). In *The Meeting, or "Have a Nice Day, Mr. Hockney,"* he depicts a meeting of three 1960s British pop artists who in the 1980s joined the ranks of postmodernism (Figure 22.12). This new version of Courbet's *The Meeting, or "Bonjour Monsieur Courbet"* (see Figure 18.11) is both an ironic comment on contemporary neoclassicism and a classical composition in itself. The three artists depicted are, from left to right, Howard Hodgkin (b. 1932), Peter Blake, and David Hockney (b. 1937), the last-named grasping a huge paintbrush. Blake's *Meeting* abounds in ironic juxtapositions: age versus youth, Old World versus the New, the aesthetic life versus consumerism, work versus play, and timeless present versus fleeting moment. Blake's postmodernism fuses rival traditions, the eternal values of classicism and the transience of pop art.

Modernist abstraction remains a force in postmodernism. The most famous abstractionist working today is Frank Stella (b. 1936), an American painter with a varied career. A minimalist in the 1950s, painting striped canvases (see Figure 21.13), he became a forerunner of neoexpressionism in the 1970s, using gaudy color and decorative effects. Since the 1980s,

Figure 22.9   PHILIP PEARLSTEIN. *Female on Eames Chair, Male on Swivel Stool.* 1981. Watercolor, 60 × 40″. Collection of Eleanor and Leonard Bellinson. Courtesy Donald Morris Gallery, Birmingham, Michigan. *Pearlstein's refusal to glamorize his nude subjects is part of a democratizing tendency in postmodernism. Just as some postmodernist authors borrow freely from mass-circulation genres such as mystery and science fiction, so Pearlstein focuses attention on bodily features like sagging breasts and bulging veins that had been overlooked by realist painters.*

he has stayed true to abstract ideals, as in *Norisring,* one of the *Shard* series, which uses the scraps left over from other works (Figure 22.13). Abstract and non-representational, this work is nevertheless postmodernist, since it combines genres, in this case, painting and sculpture—an ambition of many postmodernist artists.

Another devotee of late modern abstraction is the African American artist Samuel Gilliam (b. 1933). Gilliam began as an abstract expressionist and a color field painter, covering the entire canvas with color and emphasizing solid areas of color on a monumental scale. Through a series of artistic experiments, he was led to create multicolored soaked and stained canvases, draping and wrapping them in space, and shaping them

INTERPRETING ART

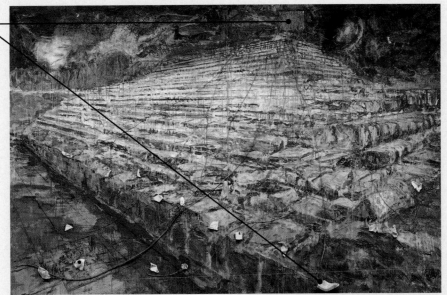

Materials
Nontraditional materials: copper wires, bits of broken pottery, and a fragmented circuit board.

Setting The massive copper colored pyramid evokes the step pyramid of Sakkareh (see Figure 1.13), thus establishing a link to ancient Egypt. The pyramid, presumably, is Osiris's tomb.

Egyptian Myth
Osisris, one of Egypt's chief gods, was dismembered by his enemy-brother, Set. Isis, the devoted sister-wife of Osiris, reassembled his body, except for the penis, and restored him to eternal life. In time, Isis became Egypt's chief goddess and Osiris, the ruler of the underworld.

Allegory The circuit board, atop the pyramid, stands for Isis, and the pottery shards symbolize Osiris's body parts. The copper wires, linking the circuit board to the pottery shards, represent both Isis's love and a nuclear reactor.

Ambiguous Message Kiefer uses the Osiris-Isis image (see Figure 4.11) to give shape to his fears of modern technology: technology has become a deity with the capacity either to destroy or to create.

Existentialism
Created at the end of the cold war, this artwork, with its apocalyptic image of a blasted earth, is a chilling reminder of the threat of nuclear destruction that hovered over the period.

Interpreting Art figure 22.1   ANSELM KIEFER. *Osiris and Isis*. 1985–1987. Diptych, mixed media on canvas, 12′6″ × 18′4½″ × 6½″. Courtesy Marian Goodman Gallery, New York. *Unlike modernist artists, whose goal was an art purified of national markers and symbols, Anselm Kiefer is very much a postmodernist in embracing his German roots, particularly in coming to terms with the calamitous Nazi period. Thus, his artistic mission: to explore his German heritage and identity. A secondary theme in his art has been the continuity of Western culture from its earliest stages to the present. Kiefer has lived and worked in France since 1995.*

Figure 22.10   SUSAN ROTHENBERG. *Butterfly*. 1976. Acrylic on canvas, 69½ × 33″. National Gallery, Washington, D.C. Gift of Perry R. and Nancy Lee Bass. 1995.6.1. *While Rothenberg's choice of the horse as a subject may reflect her personal feelings, the horse is among the oldest images in the Western canon, dating from the prehistoric cave art of France. The horse was revered as a noble beast in aristocratic cultures that have flourished from antiquity until modern times, and their art has reflected that view. Even in the modern liberal democracies of the 1800s, the horse, while no longer prized as in the past, was still judged valuable as a work animal or a romantic beast and was represented as such in art. Only with the coming of modernist abstraction did the horse cease to appeal to artists. Rothenberg's art thus restores the horse to a central place in the canon, with the image now purged of elitist and utilitarian overtones.*

Figure 22.11 FERNANDO BOTERO. *Dancing in Colombia.* 1980. Oil on canvas, 74 × 91". Metropolitan Museum of Art, New York. Anonymous Gift, 1983 (1983.251). *Botero's use of "fatness" to depict Colombia's ruling middle class springs from the socialist belief that the wealthy feast while the poor starve—a visual equivalent of the English slang "fat cat." Because famine has largely ended in the industrialized world, Botero's symbolism may be meaningless for some people. Yet, many can still resonate to the rotund shapes, viewing them simply satirically, because of the obesity epidemic in the United States and elsewhere in the West.*

into three-dimensional sculptural works (Figure 22.14). These large "draped" paintings, which are part of the installation art movement (see below), have been hung in various public places—subway stations, airports, and libraries. He continues to experiment in diverse media, using computers to create images, combining colors, textures, spaces, and materials, such as plastics and aluminum, and linking his earlier styles with his latest innovations. Gilliam and Romare Bearden (see Chapter 21) are considered the leading African American painters after World War II.

Defying easy categorization is the German painter Gerhard Richter (b. 1932), whose style-shifting images make him the art world's chameleon. This protean artist's paintings range over the postmodernist spectrum, from abstraction to a kind of realism, with stops in between, including photo-realism (a painting style that mimics the clarity of a photograph) and op art, often working in two styles at once. Richter further complicates his art through varied means, such as choosing banal subjects (two lighted candles) and blurring realistic images (to suggest faded photographs). Perhaps his most arresting image is *Betty* (1988) (Figure 22.15), a portrait of a woman whose face is hidden from the artist's (and the viewer's) gaze. This perverse image, with its slightly blurred effect, while charming, forces the viewer to question the artistic intent of this most enigmatic of postmodern artists.

SCULPTURE   Like painters, postmodernist sculptors began to work with realistic forms. For example, serving as complements to the neorealist paintings of Philip Pearlstein are the sculptures of the American John De Andrea (b. 1941). Typically, De Andrea uses traditional poses, as in *Sphinx* (Figure 22.16). But his human figures are fully contemporary, suggestive of young, upwardly mobile professionals ("yuppies") who have taken off their clothes. Whether or not his works are satirical, De Andrea manages to capture in sculptural form the erotic quality considered so desirable by modern advertising, movies, and mass media.

Minimalism, an art movement that originated in the 1950s and 1960s (see Chapter 21), showed great staying power after 1970, particularly among sculptors who drew inspiration from its tendency to reduce artistic elements to the simplest forms. Minimalist sculptors explored issues of medium, form, and meaning, as in the works of Dan Flavin (1933–1996). Flavin, rejecting the traditional materials of sculpture, made light the principal medium in his art (Figure 22.17). Because his usual light source was fluorescent tubes, this choice impacted the final form of his works. Because of the centrality of technology in his art, each work's meaning is literal and not personal—a pervasive feature of minimalism.

The minimalist aesthetic also inspired the spare form of the Vietnam Veterans' Memorial, in Washington, D.C., designed by Maya Ying Lin (b. 1959), the

Figure 22.12 PETER BLAKE. *The Meeting, or "Have a Nice Day, Mr. Hockney."* 1981–1983. Oil on canvas, 39 × 49". Tate Gallery. *Blake brings classicism up-to-date by applying its features and principles to a contemporary California setting. He fills the sun-drenched scene with double-coded references, including the pose of the girl in the right foreground (borrowed partly from a skating magazine and partly from classical sculpture), the dog (an allusion to American youth culture and Alberti's Renaissance artistic theory), and the winged hat of the person in the Dodgers shirt (a contemporary sports emblem and a symbol of the god Mercury). The result is a hybrid scene, marked by the ironic contrast between the grave and self-contained central figures and the "cool" teenagers in the background.*

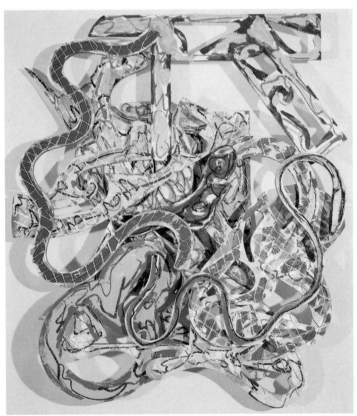

Figure 22.13 FRANK STELLA. *Norisring (XVI, 3X).* 1983. Mixed media on etched aluminum, 6'7" × 5'7" × 1'3". Collection of Ann and Robert Freedman. Courtesy Knoedler & Company, New York. *Largely because of his lively intelligence, Stella has stayed on the cutting edge of postmodernism. He has kept abstraction alive almost single-handedly at a time when realist styles are dominant. His 1960s innovation, the shaped canvas, allowed him to replace the rectilinear canvas with an abstract form (see Figure 21.13). By the early 1980s, he had transformed the shaped canvas into a blend of sculpture and painting, as in Norisring.*

Figure 22.14 SAM GILLIAM. *All Cats Are Grey at Night.* 1996. Acrylic on canvas, 65 × 44 × 8″ (installed, variable). Collection of Patrick Everett. Photo: Mark Gulezian/Quicksilver. *Gilliam, who was a member of the Washington color school of the 1960s, moved beyond abstract expressionism, redefining its traditions and techniques to experiment and create his own style. According to one critic, Gilliam has brought back "the pleasure of texture and the optical qualities of painting." In his "drapes"—as these works are called—he blends colors, softening them on the surface and balancing them in the hanging of the canvas, thus combining colors and texture.*

Figure 22.15 GERHARD RICHTER. *Betty.* 1988. Oil on canvas, 40¼ × 28½″. St. Louis Art Museum. © Gerhard Richter. *Richter's jarring portrait of Betty—with face averted—sparks a multilayered interpretation. In existential terms, the subject expresses the isolation of modern life. In an art historical sense, the depiction of the back of the head evokes the method of Renaissance sculptors in fully finishing their figures in the round (see Figure 11.11). In modernist terms, the provocative pose is a challenge to viewers' basic assumptions about art. A feminist reading could interpret the subject as rejecting the "male gaze" of the painter. And in Freudian terms, the pose could reflect an estrangement between subject (his wife?) and artist. Richter's silence about his motives here leaves the meaning of the work open. Thus, Richter's Betty stands as a masterpiece of postmodernist ambiguity.*

daughter of Chinese immigrants. Winner of a national contest for the design—two highly polished black granite walls set at angles so as to form a giant V— Lin rejected traditional images of fallen warriors (see Figure 4.15) and chose instead an unconventional and understated tribute to those who had died. In her artistic vision, the memorial was to appear "as a rift in the earth," which would lift up and then recede—a hint of the environmental art principles then being born. On its two walls are carved the names of the Vietnam War's casualties, the more than fifty-eight thousand American men and women killed or missing, arranged not alphabetically but by the war year for each death. Perusing the names gives a striking representation of

the rhythm of the conflict, as the fighting intensified in the late 1960s and early 1970s and then wound down to its end, in 1974. Built on the northwest side of the National Mall, this monument has become one of the most hallowed and visited places in the United States (Figure 22.18).

In contrast to the solemnity and timelessness of Lin's outdoor sculptures are the entertaining and transitory works of Christo (b. 1935) and his wife, Jeanne-Claude (1935–2009). Their creations are often identified with environmental art, a type of art that is related to nature, usually site specific and sometimes ephemeral (see the

Figure 22.16 JOHN DE ANDREA. *Sphinx.* 1987. Polyvinyl, oil paint, life-size. Courtesy ACA Galleries, New York. *Unlike Pearlstein, who uses nudity to register his disgust, De Andrea designs his polyvinyl nudes to celebrate the glossy lives of the upper middle class. The bodies of his nude subjects convey what today's consumer culture urges everyone to be: healthy, sleek, athletic, and sexy.*

section "Environmental Art"), and also with **conceptual art,** a type of art in which the idea or concept is more important than the means employed to complete it. Conceptual art, which began in the 1960s, is often a vehicle for sociopolitical ideas. Regardless of the definition, Christo and Jeanne-Claude's works overawe the viewer, relate to the landscape, bring out crowds and the media, and stir up controversy (Figure 22.19).

Their monumental projects require years of planning, the cooperation and approval of government agencies and private institutions, the employment of hundreds of workers, and the purchase of vast quantities of materials, usually roping, steel rods, and fabrics. Christo and Jeanne-Claude accept no funding or donations for these events and pay for them from the sales of their own works, including postcards, scale models, and other personalized items. Their wrapping a building, stringing a nylon fence along a coastline, or decorating a park or environmental site becomes a public spectacle. Each art event lasts for only a few weeks and is then dismantled—to be remembered through photographs, on film, or in the minds of those who witnessed it. The environment returns to its pre-event state and the art disappears—thus, only the idea or the memory remains of this transitory happening.

A postmodernist sculptor, whose mysteriously seductive works have earned him a strong presence in global culture, is Anish Kapoor (b. 1954), an Indian artist born in Mumbai (Bombay), who has lived and worked in the United Kingdom since 1972. Drawing on his Indian roots and his Western training and inspired by the aesthetic of the German artist Joseph Beuys (see Chapter 21), Kapoor has produced a varied body of works, using an eclectic stew of materials: raw pigment, chalk, dirt, fiberglass, stones, gourds, concrete,

Figure 22.17 DAN FLAVIN. *Untitled (For Ellen).* 1975. Pink, blue, and green fluorescent light, ht. 88¼". As installed at the Des Moines Art Center, Des Moines. 1994. *Just as video art added a new medium—sound—to the sculptural art, so did Dan Flavin's works in light. By making light his medium, Flavin shifted the aesthetic focus from sculpture's traditional concerns— texture and presence—to mood and atmosphere. In* Untitled, *which is installed in a corner niche of an otherwise empty gallery, the glowing lights evoke feelings of safety and pleasure. Adding a personal touch to this abstract piece is the subtitle,* For Ellen, *whose memory presumably has inspired the cheery colors of pink, blue, and green.*

Figure 22.18 MAYA YING LIN. Vietnam Veterans' Memorial. 1982. Black granite, 250' length (each wing). Washington, D.C. *The vertex of the V-shaped memorial is set in such a way that makes it possible to view the Washington Monument and then turn to see the Lincoln Memorial—the shrines that honor America's two most admired presidents. The Vietnam Veterans' Memorial, although controversial when built, has had a healing effect, bringing the nation together after a war that bitterly divided its citizens. Every day, visitors come to pay their respects, leaving flowers, photographs, letters, and military medals. The seemingly endless list of names reminds the viewer of the terrible costs of war.*

Figure 22.19 CHRISTO AND JEANNE-CLAUDE. Image, from *The Gates*. 2005. Central Park, New York. *The Gates in Central Park lasted for two weeks, a typical time period for a Christo project. Seventy-five hundred gates—free-hanging, saffron-colored fabric panels—were positioned ten to fifteen feet apart along the footpaths for a total of twenty-three miles. The winter landscape, with the bare trees and blanket of snow, and the rows of saffron-colored panels, gave the effect of a brightly colored river running through Central Park where an individual could walk for miles enjoying the interplay between nature and art. The artists, who developed the concept in 1979, worked with government and civic groups to gain their approval. Christo and Jeanne-Claude, according to their arrangements, paid for the 21-million-dollar project.*

aluminum, stainless steel, bronze, felt, acrylic, and wax. Of his prolific sculptures, perhaps his most famous is *Cloud Gate* (2004), installed in Chicago's Millennium Park (Figure 22.20). Weighing 110 tons, this monumental work nevertheless is scaled to fit easily into the vast park setting—thus blurring the boundaries between architecture and sculpture.

Another important postmodernist sculptor is Rachel Whiteread (b. 1964), one of the "Brit Pak" or, more seriously, the YBA, Young British Artists. The YBA has traded in the low-key style of older British art for an art that is attention grabbing and often associated with scandal. Unlike the works of many of this British school, Whiteread's sculptures are deeply serious and modest in execution. Inspired by American minimalist art of the 1960s and 1970s, her works usually represent simple ideas using familiar, everyday objects (Figure 22.21). She works in various media, including plaster, concrete, resin, and rubber.

INSTALLATION ART **Installation art** is a boundary-challenging art born in the 1960s that specializes in architectural tableaux [tah-BLOZ]—depictions of a scene, as on a stage, with silent and motionless characters—drawing and quoting from both artistic sources (such as music, painting, sculpture, and theater) and the workaday world (such as everyday tasks, media images, and

foodstuffs); the finished work often includes a human presence. One of the most gifted installation artists is the American Ann Hamilton (b. 1956), who is known for sensory works filled with meaning. The piece *mantle*, installed in a second-floor gallery at the Miami Art Museum in 1998 (Figure 22.22), had as its human focus a woman performing a simple household task at an open window—an homage to Dutch genre art, which pictured women in similar poses. The woman's task—sewing sleeves onto the bodies of wool coats—gives the piece its name (a mantle is, among other things, a sleeveless garment). Wires dangle down the gallery's wall into a mound of sixty thousand cut flowers displayed on a 48-foot-long table behind the woman. The decaying flowers are a memento mori, or a reminder of death—a frequent theme of Renaissance art. In 1999 Hamilton represented the United States at the prestigious Venice Art Biennale, and in 2008 she received the Heinz Award for the Arts and Humanities.

ENVIRONMENTAL ART A new art form that emerged after 1970 was **environmental art.** Environmental structures were fashioned from native materials, such as stone, mud, water, and plants, so as to appear as if made by nature. Part landscape design, part engineering, and part

Figure 22.20 Anish Kapoor. *Cloud Gate.* 2004. Stainless steel, 33 × 66 × 42'. Millennium Park, Chicago. *Inspired by blobs of liquid mercury, Cloud Gate has an elegant curvilinear shape, whose mirrorlike surface captures the fleeting changes in its urban environment, both on the ground and in the sky. Designed to be interactive, this accessible artwork is literally experienced by visitors as they walk around it and through its arch. Cloud Gate's abstract form echoes Western modernist ideals, while its ever-changing surface, according to Kapoor, is a metaphor for a state of becoming—a typical worldview of Indian thought.*

minimalist art, this sculpture began in response to modernism's wish to erase the boundary between art and life, as in *Spiral Jetty (1970)* by Robert Smithson (1938–1973) (Figure 22.23). What made environmental sculpture postmodern was its politics, as the works, in effect, expressed solidarity with the environmental cause.

VIDEO ART Nam June Paik (1932–2006) founded video art in the late 1950s and, during his lifetime, became the best-known artist working in this new art form. **Video art** is made with a video monitor, or monitors, and may be produced using computerized programs or with handheld cameras; the work may be ephemeral or permanent. Over time, Paik evolved from an artist intent on being entertaining into one devoted to serious issues and, starting in the 1980s, embracing political ideas. *My Faust (Stations): Religion* (1989–1991), a sophisticated work representing

his political beliefs, is part of a series of thirteen individual multimonitor installations (see Figure 22.6). Rich in allusions, this work refers to the thirteen channels available at the time on Manhattan television, and the word *stations* in the title, reinforced by the Neogothic altarpieces, suggests Christianity's Stations of the Cross, the thirteen stages of Jesus's journey to his crucifixion. The character Faust was a symbol of both restlessness and relentless seeking of knowledge, even to the loss of the soul (see Chapter 17). Thus, Paik's *My Faust* suggests humanity's pact with the devil for secular power and glory.

ARCHITECTURE By the mid-1960s, architecture was moving away from late modernism toward postmodernism, as avant-garde architects experimented with new forms and built with new materials. In particular, the unadorned "glass box"—the centerpiece of late

692

Figure 22.21 RACHEL WHITEREAD. *Untitled (Yellow Bath).* 1996. Cast made of rubber and polystyrene, ht. 31½ × w. 81½ × d. 45⅓". Luhring Augustine Gallery, New York. *Whiteread's wide-ranging eye has led her to sculpt many household objects, including mattresses, chairs and tables, bookshelves, and bathtubs. Her works are more than mere representations; she makes a cast of the spaces around an object, trying to capture traces of a human presence. In its new incarnation, Whiteread's bathtub has been compared to a sarcophagus. Such an interpretation is acceptable to the artist, as she is on record as comparing her casting technique to the making of a death mask. Indeed, there is a faint air of melancholy about Whiteread's sculptures, since they seem to affirm human mortality.*

modernist design—was cast aside in favor of decorative exteriors and various **claddings,** or covers or overlays on the exterior walls.

Contributing to the rise of postmodern architecture was a new way of thinking about a building. In late modernism, a building was usually a monument, a timeless structure like a painting or a sculpture. But in postmodernism, a building is one piece of a historic urban landscape, for good or ill. If the setting is thriving, then a new building should harmonize with its neighbors, but if the area is in decline, then the new edifice can act as a catalyst to help revitalize the urban space. Thus, performing arts centers, opera houses, athletic arenas, and museums became agents of change, the nucleus around which restaurants, theaters, shops, apartments, and condominiums were built. A building itself becomes a place not only to see but also to experience urban life. For example, a new museum can not only function as a repository for art, but also serve as an educational center, house an auditorium for lectures, films, and performances, and offer a fancy on-site restaurant.

One of the earliest exponents of postmodern architecture is the American Robert Venturi (b. 1925), whose ideas are summarized in his book *Complexity and Contradiction in Architecture* (1966). Rejecting modernist architecture, which he thinks inhuman because of its starkness, he attempts to create buildings that express the energy and ever-changing quality of contemporary life. Fascinated by mass culture, he is inspired by popular architecture, such as Las Vegas casinos and

Figure 22.22 ANN HAMILTON. View of *mantle.* Miami Art Museum. 1998. *Installation art has affinities with other innovative art forms, but it lacks the centrality of the videotaped image, as in video art, or a strong musical component, as in performance art. In* mantle, *there was a minor musical aspect: radio receivers, placed amid the flowers, transmitted musical and other sounds during the event. Feminist in perspective, this installation may be interpreted as an ironic comment on the male-dominated art world, because, until the mid-twentieth century, this world discouraged women from becoming artists and limited their artistic choices mainly to domestic chores, such as making clothes. In the photograph, Ann Hamilton is the woman sewing; volunteers and paid attendants performed this task when the artist was absent.*

Figure 22.23 Robert Smithson. *Spiral Jetty.* 1970. Rock, salt crystals, earth, and water, diameter 1,500'. Great Salt Lake, Utah. Art © Estate of Robert Smithson/Licensed by VAGA, New York. *Smithson's mission, derived from minimalist aesthetics, was to blur the boundary between art and nature, as in* Spiral Jetty. *Constructed of materials native to the Great Salt Lake region, the jetty gives little hint of its human origin, except for the spiral form. And even that form has altered over time, as the lake's water levels have risen and fallen. By creating art that is subject to the same climatic and geologic forces as its site, Smithson reminds viewers of the transience of all human endeavor. Thus, an air of gentle melancholy pervades his works.*

motels in the form of Indian tepees—a kitsch style sometimes called "vernacular." A work that enshrines his love of the ordinary is Guild House, a retirement home in a lower-middle-class section of Philadelphia (Figure 22.24). Faceless and seemingly artless, this building is indebted to popular culture for its aesthetic appeal; for instance, the wire sculpture on the roof resembles a television antenna, and the recessed entrance and the sign evoke memories of old-time movie houses. Venturi's playful assault on modernism opened the door to the diversity of postmodernism. In 1991 Venturi received the Pritzker Architecture Prize, considered the profession's highest honor.

Among the architects who have spanned both late modernism and postmodernism and who recognize the relationships between urban life and architecture is I. M. Pei [PAY] (b. 1917). Pei, born in China, came to the United States in his teens to study architecture. Among his teachers was Walter Gropius [GROH-pe-us] (1883–1969), of Bauhaus fame, who had fled from Nazi Germany (see Chapter 20). Beginning in 1955, Pei and his partners designed some of the most significant buildings of the late twentieth century, including the John F. Kennedy Library in Boston, the Morton H. Myerson Symphony Center in Dallas, the East Building of the National Gallery in Washington, D.C., the Rock and Roll Hall of Fame and Museum in Cleveland, and his latest project, the Museum of Islamic Art in Doha, Qatar (Figure 22.25). Pei has designed museums not just to be repositories for art but as educational and social centers, and to make them more accessible and welcoming for a broader audience—a postmodern trend to democratize the arts. Pei was awarded the Pritzker Architecture Prize in 1983.

A prominent strain in postmodern architecture is **high tech,** a style that uses industrial techniques and whose roots stretch back to the Crystal Palace (see Figure 18.6) and the Eiffel Tower. Richard Rogers (b. 1933) of England and Renzo Piano (b. 1937) of Italy launched this revival with the Georges Pompidou Centre in Paris, which boldly displays its factory-made metal parts and transparent walls (Figure 22.26). Commissioned by France to restore Paris's cultural position over New York, the Pompidou Centre has spawned many imitations as well as a style of interior decoration. Piano was awarded the Pritzker Architecture Prize in 1998.

One of the most controversial buildings in postmodern architecture is the thirty-seven-story, pink granite headquarters building of American Telephone and Telegraph, executed in a neoclassical style (Figure 22.27). Designed by Philip C. Johnson (1906–2006), an American disciple of Mies van der Rohe, this building was a slap in the face to the modernist ideal because it used classical forms. AT&T Headquarters has a base, middle, and top, corresponding to the foot, shaft, and capital of a Greek column—the basic element of Greco-Roman building style. As a final blow to modernist purity, Johnson topped his building with a split pediment crown (a triangular shape whose apex is split, usually so as to form a semicircle—a typical feature of classical architecture), causing a hostile critic to compare it to an eighteenth-century Chippendale highboy (a tall chest of drawers set on a legged base). Notwithstanding the furor surrounding its creation, this building heralded the resurgence of the neoclassicist wing of postmodernism. Johnson was the first recipient of the Pritzker Architecture Prize, in 1979.

The Guggenheim Museum in the Basque city of Bilbao, Spain, designed by the American Frank Gehry (b. 1929), was recognized immediately as a classic when it opened in 1997. Hired by city officials to build the museum as part of a civic rejuvenation project, Gehry chose a site on the Nervion River, which has played a major role in the city's history. Gehry's design is in the form of a rose, or "metallic flower," with a rotunda at its center and the petals spiraling in waves of centrifugal force (Figure 22.28). Typical of Gehry's expressionist handling of flexible materials, strips of metal ripple and flare outward into the city. Within the baroque interior are exhibition spaces, an auditorium, a restaurant,

Figure 22.24   Robert Venturi. Guild House. 1965. Philadelphia. *Venturi's aesthetic aim is to transform the ordinary into the extraordinary. He followed this democratic ideal in Guild House, where he took a "dumb and ordinary" (his term) concept and tried to give it a monumental look. His ironic intelligence and his perverse delight in mass culture have made him a guiding spirit of postmodernism.*

Figure 22.25   I. M. Pei. Museum of Islamic Art. 2008. Doha, Qatar. Corbis. *Pei, who seldom takes on new major projects, designed this museum, with its geometric forms and soaring cubic dome, as a blend of Eastern and Western architecture. He was inspired by the Ibn Tulun Mosque in Cairo (see Figure 8.12), with its domes and ablution fountain resting on three receding squares. The museum, sited on an artificial island accessible by a pedestrian bridge lined with trees, includes galleries, a library, a conservation center, and an auditorium. It is part of Qatar's Education City, where several American universities have schools of medicine, engineering, computer science, design, and diplomatic service.*

Figure 22.26 RICHARD ROGERS AND RENZO PIANO. *The Georges Pompidou Centre for Art and Culture.* 1971–1977. Paris. *Designed in a gaudy industrial style and erected in the heart of a quiet section of Paris called Beaubourg, the Pompidou Centre was controversial from the start, as it was planned to be. Its showy appearance sharply contrasted with the historic styles of neighboring structures—a contrast that has become a guiding ideal of postmodernist architects. The furor that greeted the Pompidou Centre on its opening has occurred in other places where city governments have placed colorful and brash high-tech temples amid their traditional buildings.*

a café, retail space, and an atrium that functions as a town square. The choice of a rose, the symbol of the Virgin Mary, was appropriate for Catholic Spain. Gehry, by shifting this emblem from a church to a museum, transformed it into an ambiguous sign of the postmodern period. In 1989 Gehry was awarded the Pritzker Architecture Prize.

Two of architecture's brightest new stars are Rem (born Remmet) Koolhaas (b. 1944), of the Netherlands, and Zaha Hadid (b. 1950), an Iraqi-born British citizen. Both were awarded the Pritzker Architecture Prize, Koolhaas in 2000 and Hadid in 2004, the first woman to receive it. Their lives overlapped in London, when Hadid worked at the Office for Metropolitan Architecture (OMA), which Koolhaas cofounded in 1975. Koolhaas moved OMA to Rotterdam in the early 1980s, but Hadid remained in London, now her home.

Rebelling against the late modernist ideal that architecture could be an agent for social transformation, Koolhaas and Hadid created nonutopian styles that connected with their urban settings. For both, a building is one part of a city, but cities, not buildings, are the

Figure 22.27 PHILIP C. JOHNSON AND JOHN BURGEE. *American Telephone and Telegraph Headquarters.* 1979–1984. New York. © Peter Mauss/Esto. *Although classical rules were followed in the planning of Johnson and Burgee's AT&T Headquarters, it was built using modernist methods. Like modernist structures, the building has a steel frame to which exterior panels are clipped. Despite its modernist soul, the physical presence of this postmodernist building conveys the gravity and harmony customarily associated with classical architecture.*

Figure 22.28   FRANK O. GEHRY. Guggenheim Museum. 1997. Bilbao, Spain. *Gehry is famed for pushing the boundaries of architecture, which has often been confined by set rules, because he, as a friend of painters and sculptors, sees himself as both an artist and an architect. Thus, the Bilbao Guggenheim has been labeled sculptural architecture, considered a work of art in itself. Gehry relied on a sophisticated computer program to achieve the building's dramatic curvature, and he chose metal titanium to sheathe the exterior, thereby giving it a gleaming, wavy-in-a-strong-wind appearance.*

basic units of the emerging global culture. Koolhaas set these ideas in motion in his 1975 treatise, *Delirious New York, A Retroactive Manifesto for Manhattan*—a call to arms to refashion the urban landscape. Koolhaas's Seattle Central Library (2004) (Figure 22.29), set atop one of the hills overlooking Puget Sound, is a beautiful realization of his ideal: a building should harmonize with its immediate urban context. Hadid pursued a similar goal in the Rosenthal Center for Contemporary Art (2003), in Cincinnati, which fits seamlessly into its setting (Figure 22.30).

Film

After 1970 the film industry, now globalized, was under siege from many, often interrelated forces, including technological innovations, a volatile marketplace,

evolving film tastes, and the steady loss of audiences to new forms of entertainment. Although the American film remained paramount globally, the Hollywood studio system, ailing since 1955, transformed itself over the next three decades.

Old Hollywood soon gave way to the new, as film studios shrank and movie screens grew wider, to counter the assault from television. Studios devised creative strategies to lower costs, such as shooting films abroad or sharing expenses with foreign companies. New film distribution systems arose, offering new formats, such as videos and DVDs, both for rent and for sale, and television showed an unquenchable demand for movies on the small screen. A few small companies made a specialty of art films. For example, Miramax Films (1979–2005), with appealing works such as the historic comedy *Shakespeare in Love* (1998), directed by John Madden (b. 1949), became a leading global brand. The new Holly-

Figure 22.29 REM KOOLHAAS. Seattle Central Library. 2004. Seattle. *Despite a restless facade, Seattle's Central Library is meant to be used rather than viewed as a monument, according to the architect, Koolhaas. In his aesthetic vision, the cascading levels and thrusting angles echo the hilly terrain of the city's downtown. Inside, a soaring atrium welcomes visitors and psychedelic green-yellow escalators beckon patrons to explore. Besides escalators and elevators, an innovative pathway spirals through the eleven-level structure. Generous windows overlook the surrounding cityscape and allow interplay between the indoors and outside. Koolhaas's masterpiece reinvents the modernist "glass box," making the library's exterior and interior into an exuberant fantasy, but, like many postmodern libraries, a place to enjoy and to meet.*

wood also spawned auteurist directors, including the New York–based Woody Allen (b. 1935), who directed urban neurotic art films such as *Annie Hall* (1977), and Clint Eastwood (b. 1930), who directed the postmodern western *Unforgiven* (1992). A strong sign that Hollywood had changed was the founding of what is now the Sundance Film Festival, in 1980, by the actor Robert Redford (b. 1937). The festival has become a national and international showcase for art films, independent films, and documentaries. In today's competitive mass culture and in these lean economic times, the production of such venturesome films is increasingly at risk.

Meanwhile, in the new Hollywood, filmmakers continue to make genre films, keeping them fresh with new technologies, such as DTS Digital Sound in *Jurassic Park* (1993), directed by Steven Spielberg (b. 1946); computer-generated graphics in *Toy Story* (1995), a collaboration between Pixar Studios and Disney; and

digital video cameras in *Star Wars: Episode II—Attack of the Clones* (2002), directed by George Lucas (b. 1944). Of special note is *Titanic* (1997), the disaster film directed by James Cameron (b. 1954), which shows Hollywood's newest quandary: it was the most expensive film ever made and the highest-grossing film of all time.

A final major change in Hollywood after 1970 was that films began to represent more closely the ethnic and racial pluralism of the United States. The trend began with *Sweet Sweetback's Baadasssss Song!* (1971), directed by Melvin Van Peebles (b. 1932), which led, in turn, to the **blaxploitation film** genre—crime films featuring a swaggering black hero and catering to black audiences. Van Peebles's commercially successful works paved the way for other black directors, such as Spike (born Shelton) Lee (b. 1957), with his urban drama *Do the Right Thing* (1989), a study of racially charged violence. As African Americans joined the Hollywood mainstream,

Figure 22.30 Zaha Hadid. Rosenthal Center for Contemporary Art. 2003. Cincinnati. *Hadid's bold design—dramatic color contrasts, elongated horizontal lines, and interplay of shadow and light—gives a fresh look to the corner site of the Rosenthal Center. Yet the building fits easily into the Cincinnati setting, as its dramatic facade makes linkages with the nearby buildings (right, left, and rear). The street-level floor, articulated by a combination of glass walls and columns, is reminiscent of early modernism.*

Hispanics and Asian Americans followed suit. However, after 9/11, Arab Americans and other Americans of Middle Eastern descent were rarely depicted favorably in films—a source of grievance for these groups.

The seismic shifts shaking the American film industry were felt around the globe. Although audiences declined sharply, those viewers who remained were more youthful. As Asia's economies soared (in Japan, from the 1970s to the 1990s, and in China, India, and South Korea, from the 1990s to the present), their youthful audiences became a driving force in the market, as in the rise of the martial arts film genre. Japanese cinema retained a strong hold on world cinema. For example, Akira Kurosawa's (1910–1998) *Ran* (1985), Shakespeare's *King Lear* transposed to feudal Japan, experienced international acclaim and technicians there introduced the IMAX wide-screen format

(1970)—a popular format for movies in most large cities today.

Film industries in Australia and China also joined the global film community. Australia's film boom produced art films of exquisite beauty, often based on real-life events, mixing gritty details with magic realism, such as *Picnic at Hanging Rock* (1975), a haunting tale of a school outing that ends tragically, directed by Peter Weir (b. 1944). Weir later was summoned to Hollywood—a path now taken by many foreign directors. Australian film remains highly influential today, as in *Moulin Rouge* (2001), directed by Baz Luhrmann (b. 1962), which almost single-handedly revived the musical genre. And Australia's top directors and actors move easily between Australia and Hollywood.

China's rise to global eminence in film was equally spectacular, despite the use of a lowly genre inspired by ancient fighting rituals—the martial arts film. The revival began in Hong Kong, where martial arts films were entrenched by 1955. The regional genre went global in *The Big Boss* (1971), starring Bruce Lee (born Lee Jun Fan, in San Francisco) (1940–1973) and directed by Wei Lo (1918–1996). This film featured fighting with bare fists—*kung fu*, a Cantonese term, hence, the kung fu genre. With Hong Kong's films burgeoning, mainland China's film world reawakened in the mid-1980s, when a new generation of filmmakers emerged who preferred art films to genre films. The group's leader was Zhang Yimou (b. 1951), whose films, while controversial in China, were greeted as revelations and earned many awards abroad, as, for example, *Raise the Red Lantern* (1991), a heartbreaking tale of forced marriages, multiple wives, and intrigue. The proof that China's films were truly global came when *Crouching Tiger, Hidden Dragon* (2000), a martial arts film directed by Taiwan's Ang Lee (b. 1954), won the Academy Award for Best Foreign Language Film (Figure 22.31).

Postmodern Music

In the 1960s, some innovative composers rejected late modernist atonality for its unemotional quality and harsh sounds. In place of atonality, they founded a postmodern musical style that was more emotionally appealing, though they remained committed to experimental methods. The most notable composer working in this style, the American Philip Glass (b. 1937), has made it his mission to return exuberance to music. Working in a minimalist mode, he draws on varied sources, including classical Indian music, African drumming, and rock and roll. Much of his music is written for **synthesizer,** a machine with a simple keyboard that can duplicate the sounds of up to twelve instruments simultaneously. Glass composes with simple tonal harmonies, pulsating rhythms, unadorned scales, and, above all, lilting arpeggios, the cascading sounds produced by playing the notes of a chord in rapid sequences.

A Glass piece is instantly recognizable for its obsessive, repetitive quality, as in "Vessels," from the score for the documentary film *Koyaanisqatsi* (1983), a Hopi word meaning "life out of balance." In this choral work, sung without a text, Glass manipulates human voices into a thrilling dialogue, much as earlier composers had used groups of instruments. A cluster of higher voices creates a constantly shifting pattern of undulating tones, against which a group of lower voices forges a forward-moving wall of sound. Glass's kaleidoscopic music provides a haunting accompaniment to the time-lapse photography used in the documentary film.

A composer of symphonies, chamber works, film scores, and dance pieces, Glass has gained the widest celebrity for his operas. His first opera, *Einstein on the Beach* (1976), produced in collaboration with the equally controversial American director Robert Wilson (b. 1941), was staged at New York's Metropolitan Opera, a rarity in recent times for a living composer. In their kaleidoscopic work, Glass and Wilson redefined the operatic form, staging a production lasting four and one-half hours without intermission and with Glass's driving music set to Wilson's texts with no recognizable plot, no formal arias, and no massed choruses. So successful was this venture that Glass followed it with operas based on other remarkable figures, *Satyagraha* (1978), dealing with the life of Gandhi, India's liberator (see Encounter in Chapter 20), and *Akhnaten* (1984), focusing on the Egyptian pharaoh who is sometimes called the first monotheist (see Chapter 1). Glass's interests took an even more multicultural turn in 1998

with the premiere and world tour of his multimedia opera *Monsters of Grace,* with a libretto based on the thirteenth-century mystical poetry of the Persian poet Jalal ad-Din ar-Rumi (see Chapter 8). In 2000 Glass returned to Western themes with *In the Penal Colony*—a "pocket opera" he terms it, that is, a short, compact opera with few characters and simple staging—based on Kafka's short story. Western themes became intensely political in his opera *Waiting for the Barbarians* (2005), with a libretto based on the 1980 novel by Nobel laureate John M. Coetzee [KUUT-zee] (b. 1940), a South African novelist of German and English descent, who now lives in Australia. The opera's setting and plot— a frontier town of an unnamed "Empire," which is awaiting the attack of the "barbarians"—evokes the Iraq War and the threat of terrorism.

One of the best-known living composers is the American John Adams (b. 1947). Like many other composers of his generation, Adams is a minimalist, but he stands out for his resonant sounds and firm grasp of musical form. He has written for a wide range of media, including orchestra, opera, video, film, and dance, and he has composed both electronic and instrumental music. His operas, *Nixon in China* (1987), *The Death of Klinghoffer* (1991), *I Was Looking at the Ceiling and Then I Saw the Sky* (1998), and *Doctor Atomic* (2005; revised 2008), based on historical events, have been viewed by more audiences than any other operas in recent history. Two orchestral works, *The Chairman Dances,* adapted from *Nixon in China,* and *Shaker Loops* (1996), have been called "among the best known and most frequently performed of contemporary American music" by one critic. In 2001 Adams returned to his minimalist roots with *Guide to Strange Places,* a twenty-minute pulsing orchestral work, divided into five

Figure 22.31 Still, from *Crouching Tiger, Hidden Dragon.* 2000. Crouching Tiger, Hidden Dragon *featured several Asian superstars, along with relative unknowns, such as Zhang Ziyi (b. 1979) (pictured above, center). Zhang plays a young woman, a runaway, who is on a quest involving honor and revenge. Her character—central to the complex story—blends Eastern martial arts with Western feminist aspirations—a mixture that appealed to a global audience. Ironically, while Westerners were drawn to the over-the-top fighting scenes—actors on wires, moving in seemingly gravityless space—Chinese viewers were critical, finding the spectacle unrealistic.*

Figure 22.32   Scene, from *Le Grand Macabre*. *By blithely mixing periods and styles, Ligeti's Le Grand Macabre has established itself as a satiric work that plays fast and loose with operatic tradition. The setting, to quote the composer, is "the run-down but nevertheless carefree and thriving principality of Breughelland [Ligeti's term] in an 'anytime' century." The hero is Death (Le Grand Macabre) and the subject is living in the shadow of the apocalypse. In this world, Death gets no respect, as the cunning peasant inhabitants pursue sex, alcohol, and political advancement. In the scene above, an astrologer peers through a telescope—a device not yet invented in Bruegel's time.*

sections with alternating fast and slow movements. Two years later, this piece became the score for a ballet of the same name, choreographed by Peter Martins (b. 1946), the Danish-born ballet master of the New York City Ballet, the eighth collaboration between Adams and Martins.

Three major composers with reputations for bold inventiveness and diverse influences demonstrate the multiple styles of postmodern music. They are the Hungarian-born Austrian Gyorgy Ligeti [LIG-uh-tee] (1923–2006), the American John Corigliano [koh-RIG-li-ah-no] (b. 1938), and the Chinese-born Tan Dun (b. 1957).

Ligeti's music, rooted in the minimalist aesthetic, evolved over the course of his career. In his early works, he showed the mischievous spirit of John Cage, as in *Future of Music* (1961), a piece in which the performer and the audience simply gaze at one another for a set time. Later, he experimented with **electronic music** (music involving electronic processing, picked up from varied sound sources and requiring the use of loudspeakers in concert), pioneered by the French-born American composer Edgar Varese (1883–1965). In the mid-1960s, Ligeti abandoned melody, rhythm, and harmony to fashion a unique sound, as in *Atmospheres* (1966)—his most frequently heard work to date. In *Atmospheres*, he invented "micropolyphony," to create shifting masses of sound, notable for their density and texture. In 1968 the director Stanley Kubrick (1928–1999) used passages from this work to evoke the future in the film *2001: A Space Odys-*

sey. A restless genius, Ligeti continued to experiment, as in the opera *Le Grand Macabre* (1976; revised 1999), blending pop culture, satire, mock operatic music, and the peasant paintings of Pieter Bruegel (see Chapter 13). This ironic valentine to postmodernism has been called by critics an "antiopera," a "musical comedy of the absurd," and an "apocalyptic romp" (Figure 22.32).

Corigliano belongs to the **neoromantic** wing of postmodern music. His works, composed in varied mediums, including orchestral, chamber, opera, and film, show an ever-evolving style, filled with rich expressiveness and innovative technique. He is perhaps best known today for the film score of *The Red Violin* (1999), directed by the Canadian François Girard (b. 1963). Following the 300-year-history of "the red violin," Corigliano's haunting score (finished in 1997) draws on diverse musical styles, such as classical, pop, and folk, covering a global odyssey from Italy to Austria to Britain to China to Canada. Using the score's central motif, Corigliano expanded it into *The Red Violin Chaconne* (1997), an independent work for violin and orchestra. (A chaconne, originally an eighteenth-century Spanish court dance, is a musical form that features variations on a harmonic progression, rather then variations on a melody.)

Tan Dun (surname, Tan) is a rising presence on the global music scene. Or, as John Cage has said, Tan is a musical force "as the East and the West come together as our one home." A graduate of Beijing's Central Con-

Figure 22.33 WILLIAM STRUHS. Laurie Anderson performing at the Spoleto Festival U.S.A., June 1999. *Laurie Anderson, second from left, whose works define performance art, is pictured here in the midst of a performance of* Songs and Stories from "Moby Dick" *at the Spoleto Festival U.S.A., held in Charleston, South Carolina. Her nineteenth-century costume, the stovepipe top hat and frock coat, reflects the time period of Melville's famous novel. The setting of the performance, with its alienating effects created by electronic means, suggests the technological world that is the principal concern of her art. For example, on a background screen are projected, among other things, constantly shifting lines and words of Melville's text, letters of the alphabet, blown-up images of the performers, and dictionary definitions; similarly, in addition to instrumental music, there are songs, chanted passages, and spoken words, some of whose sounds are deliberately distorted by electronic means.*

servatory (1981) and of New York's Columbia University (PhD, 1993), he developed an eclectic style that reflects deep familiarity with the music of both cultures. In orchestral and chamber music, opera, and film scores, he blends Chinese musical, historical, and cultural traditions with historic Western styles, including classical, minimalist, and popular music forms. Global audiences first became acquainted with Tan's dramatic music in Ang Lee's film *Crouching Tiger, Hidden Dragon* (2000), for which his score was awarded an Oscar. His most ambitious work to date, the opera *Marco Polo* (1995), fuses a Western avant-garde musical form—an opera within an opera—with pan-Asian multicultural elements: Peking Opera from China, kabuki theater from Japan, shadow puppet theater from Indonesia, and face painting from Tibetan ritual. Period musical instruments from Europe, India, Tibet, and China add to the multicultural fusion. In this multilayered story, the travel of Marco Polo from West to East is symbolic of the real-life trip of the Italian adventurer, the global encounter now under way within the postmodern world, and Tan Dun's own spiritual journey.

Performance Art

Laurie Anderson (b. 1947) is a key artist in **performance art**—a democratic type of mixed-media art born in the 1960s that ignores artistic boundaries, happily mixing high art (such as music, painting, and theater) and popular art (such as rock and roll, film, and fads) to create a unique, irreproducible artistic experience.

Anderson's performance art consists of sing-and-tell story-songs about mundane events of daily life, which somehow take on unearthly significance. These monologues are often tinged with humor and are delivered in a singsong voice backed up by mixed-media images, strange props, and varied electronic media, including electronic musical instruments, photo projection, manipulated video, and devices that alter the sound of her voice. Central to the performance is her stage persona, rather like Dorothy in *The Wizard of Oz*, in which she gazes with wide-eyed wonder on the modern technological world. A gifted violinist, she intends her music to play only a supporting role in her art, though her recordings—for example, *The Ugly One with the Jewels* (1995), based on a work called *Readings from the New Bible* (1992–1995)—have found eager listeners. In *Songs and Stories from "Moby Dick"* (1999), based on Herman Melville's nineteenth-century novel, she broke new ground by composing for male voices as well as her own (Figure 22.33).

The American Cindy Sherman (b. 1954) has also created a body of performance art, but without music. Sherman first attracted notice in the 1970s with photographs of herself in elaborately staged poses, evocative of old movie scenes or fan-magazine images of a fictional actress (Figure 22.34). These photographs seemed to present women as sex objects, trapped in gender roles, and their ambiguous nature made her controversial, especially to feminists. In the eighties, she made a series called *History Portraits*, in which she impersonated famous art subjects. In the nineties, she made photographs using pornographic subjects, mock

Figure 22.34 CINDY SHERMAN. *Untitled #50.* Photograph. 1979. Collection The Museum of Modern Art, New York. *In this black-and-white photograph from the* Film Still *series, Sherman impersonates an ice-cold sophisticate, a stereotypical role in the movies of her youth. The room's furnishings—low sofa, matching chairs, flowing draperies, abstract sculptures, and square coffee table with three ashtrays—are directly from the 1950s—the period that established Sherman's artistic sensibility. She sits ramrod upright on the sofa, ready for an evening at the theater or, perhaps, an upscale restaurant. The low brim of the hat, which obscures her eyes, adds an air of mystery. Sherman's aesthetic intent is unclear: Is she simply presenting a straight-ahead image, à la Warhol? Or is she ironically nudging the viewer with her nostalgic wink at the past?*

fashion images, and fairy-tale characters. Sherman's art, with its staged and rather tacky quality, seeks to dethrone high art and bring it down to earth for today's audiences.

Mass Culture

The information boom has spread American culture around the world and transformed it into a global village. Television provided the initial means of communication, but the videocassette recorder, the compact-disc player, the digital recorder, the camcorder, the computer, the Internet, the cell phone, and the World Wide Web have connected the globe's peoples with unforeseen consequences.

With this information explosion has come the Age of Infotainment, that is, a blend of information and entertainment, a phenomenon that can be observed across the mass media. Older mass media—newspapers, magazines, and radio—have declined, while newer outlets, such as television and computers, have grown. Even new types of media are under siege; for example, the nightly televised news has taken second place to the 24-hour news network format pioneered by CNN in the early 1980s. CNN itself is now challenged by a pan-African news channel, using French and English, and Qatar-based Al Jazeera, the global voice of the Arabs, broadcasting in English.

Similar changes are under way in entertainment. Old types of amusements, such as radio and comic strips, have been joined by innovative means of media coverage, including cable television with MTV, and all-sports channels. These changes have given birth to extravagantly popular figures: Michael Jack-

son (1958–2009), superstar of the mid-1980s; Madonna (b. 1959), queen of popular songs in the early 1990s; and Eminem (born Marshall Mathers III in 1972), a white rapper and the king of pop music in the new millennium. As entertainment continues to evolve, probably the most highly visible and influential development in recent years has been the birth of hip-hop—the voice of the people in the street.

The rise of hip-hop began in the 1970s. With origins in break dancing, graffiti art, rap rhyming, and disc jockeys playing with turntables and "scratch" effects, **hip-hop** music emerged in black and Hispanic America, spoken in either English or Spanish. By 2001, hip-hop was paramount in American pop music, largely because of the same forces mainstreaming African Americans in Hollywood films and on television. Hip-hop has spread to Mexico, much of Latin America, parts of Canada, the Far East, and Europe, especially within immigrant communities.

SUMMING UP

Since the dawn of history, humans have discovered that understanding their own times, while necessary, can be difficult and unpredictable. Few have had either the ability to make sense of their own history or the wisdom to know what will endure. Predicting how today's events and trends will determine the course of history for the rest of this century is well nigh impossible.

Nonetheless, considering the current breathtaking changes in the political, social, and economic realms, we offer two contradictory interpretations of the near future. On the one hand, in our postmodern era, we see a new vision of the world—global and democratic,

SLICE OF LIFE
How Did We Get Here? Where Are We Going?

Amin Maalouf

Amin Maalouf (b. 1949), whose native language is Arabic but who writes in French, is both an exemplar and a keen observer of the emerging global culture. Born in Lebanon as a Roman Catholic Arab, he wrote articles for a Beirut newspaper, traveling to India, Bangladesh, Ethiopia, Somalia, Kenya, Yemen, and Algeria. Driven out of Lebanon by the 1975 civil war, he moved to France where he has written a series of prizewinning novels that have made him world renowned. The following excerpt is from the introduction to Origins (2004), *a multigenerational memoir of the Maalouf family.*

Someone other than I might have used the word "roots" [for the title to this memoir]. It is not part of my vocabulary. I don't like the word, and I like even less the image it conveys. Roots burrow into the ground, twist in the mud, and thrive in darkness; they hold trees in captivity from their inception and nourish them at the price of blackmail: "Free yourself and you'll die!"

Trees are forced into resignation; they need their roots. Men do not. We breathe light and covet the heavens. When we sink into the ground, we decompose. The sap from our native soil does not flow upward from our feet to our heads; we use our feet only to walk. What matters to us are roads. Roads convey us from poverty to wealth or back to poverty, from bondage to freedom or to a violent death. Roads hold out promises, bear our weight, urge us on, and then abandon us. And we die, just as we were born, at the edge of a road not our choosing.

Roads, unlike trees, do not sprout from the ground wherever the seeds happen to fall. Like us, they have origins—illusory origins, since roads don't have real starting points. Before the first curve, just behind us, there was a prior curve, and another one behind that one. The origin of every road is elusive because at every crossroad other roads have merged, with other

origins. If we were to take into account all these tributaries, the earth would be encircled a hundred times.

In my family, these tributaries must be taken into account. I come from a clan that has been nomadic from time immemorial in a desert as wide as the world. Our countries are oases that we leave when the spring goes dry; our houses are tents clad in stone, our nationalities a matter of dates and ships. The only thing connecting us to one another, beyond the generations, the seas, and the Babel of languages, is the soft sound of a name.

Is a family name a homeland? Yes, that's the way it is. And instead of religious faith, an old-fashioned faithfulness.

I've never had a true religious affiliation. If anything, I've had several incompatible ones. Nor have I ever felt an overriding loyalty to one nation. It is true, I don't have just one country. On the other hand, I willingly identify with the history of my large family—with its history and its legends. Like the ancient Greeks, I ground my identity in a mythology; I know it is fictitious, but I revere it as though it reveals truth.

Interpreting This Slice of Life

1. *Compare and contrast* Maalouf's distinction between "roots" and "roads" as metaphors to define oneself and one's family. 2. *What* lesson does "roads" as a metaphor for identity have for troubled regions of the world beset by ethnic, racial, and religious tensions? 3. *What* lesson does "roads" as a metaphor for identity have in the United States, as a way of addressing the question of illegal immigrants? 4. *Can* the concept of "roads" be applied to your family history? *Explain* your answer.

embracing the contributions, tastes, and ideas of men and women from many races and countries and borrowing freely from high culture and mass culture. In this optimistic view, the world continues to take its lead from Western civilization, largely because of its proven capacity to adapt and survive. On the other hand, in light of the mounting tensions around the world, these trends toward unity seem mere illusions. In our pessimistic view, the future may be filled with renewed disruptions and clashes among societies, which could manifest themselves in various ways, ranging from economic sanctions to armed conflicts to terrorist campaigns.

When we consider our past, as we have in this book, one major lesson is clear: The long term in history is unpredictable. For example, five thousand years ago in 3000 BCE, who could have predicted that the fledgling Egyptian and Mesopotamian societies would become cradles of civilization, leaving enduring cultural forms before falling into decay? Or in 2000 BCE, who could have foreseen that a rejuvenated Egypt and Mesopotamia would eventually be undermined by Iron Age invaders? Or would it have been possible to guess in 1000 BCE, a time of disarray and decline in the eastern Mediterranean, that first Greece and later Rome would evolve into the civilizations that became the standard in the West? Or at the dawn of the Christian era, with the Roman Empire at its height, who would have dared forecast that Roman power would spread so widely but then collapse, to be succeeded by three separate and distinct civilizations—Islam, Byzantium, and the West? Or in 1000 CE, who could have anticipated that the backward West would become the constantly revolutionizing industrial giant whose culture would dominate the world? Drawing a lesson from this quick survey, we readily admit that we cannot know what the long-term future will bring. Perhaps all we can say is that, based on past history, civilization as we know it is likely to undergo fundamental change, as a consequence of some unforeseen technological, political, religious, economic, or social crisis and its response.

Underneath these tensions, uncertainties, conflicts, and daily crises flows the challenge of modern life and below that current what makes us human: the search for spiritual guidance, the curiosity to explore, the satisfaction to comprehend, the genius to express our creative talents, and the past to guide us. These common threads of human existence, like an abiding faith, prove that the human spirit survives and, ultimately, prevails. The Mesopotamians and Greeks recognized these immortal qualities in mortals. Whatever the future, we will continue to hold to these humanistic values.

The Legacy of the Contemporary World

From our present perspective it seems that after 1970 the world turned a corner, leaving the immediate past behind. Old traditions, habits, and principles, in place for generations, fell by the wayside and were quickly replaced by new truths, arrangements, and loyalties. The cold war ended and the Age of Terrorism was born. Instead of rivalry between two superpowers, the world now faces a war between the West and Islam, which threatens to become a clash of civilizations. The triumph of one superpower—the United States—after the fall of communism also fragmented the Western bloc, as fissures emerged between the U.S. and Europe. Also, oil-rich Russia, China, India, and Iran have presented challenges to America's hegemony and security. Nevertheless, the United States, with its democratic institutions and free-market economy, is widely imitated across the world. However, the revival of militant nationalism and ethnic warfare, the reaction against globalization in poorer countries in the form of populism, the spread of terrorism, and, since 2008, the dramatic worldwide credit crisis and depression threaten the triumph of liberal democracy and free-market economics. Taking the long view, the prospect of endless progress stretching into the unforeseeable future has given way to the hope of modest growth limited by the earth's dwindling natural resources. The division of the world into three parts after World War II—the West, the Soviet bloc, and the Third World—has now evolved into an emerging global civilization, interconnected via technology, the United Nations and its various agencies, multinational corporations, film, mass media, mass culture, tourism, and assorted nongovernmental organizations (NGOs).

KEY CULTURAL TERMS

postmodernism
poststructuralism
deconstruction
paradigm shift
nihilism
liberation theology
magic realism
commedia dell'arte
neorealism
neoexpressionism
neoclassicism
conceptual art
installation art
environmental art
video art
cladding
high tech
blaxploitation film
synthesizer
electronic music
neoromanticism
performance art
hip-hop

QUESTIONS FOR CRITICAL THINKING

1. Define postmodernism. Explain the impact of historical events on the rise of postmodernism.

2. Identify three trends in postmodern art. Discuss a work of art that exemplifies each of these trends.

3. Identify three postmodern thinkers and their key ideas. Show how each of these ideas represents postmodernism.

4. Write a brief essay showing the relationship between social issues and the postmodern arts and humanities, using examples from five of the following areas: philosophy, religion, literature, the arts, architecture, film, music.

5. Discuss the forces and issues that led to a new global order after 1970.

SUGGESTIONS FOR FURTHER READING AND LISTENING

1 PREHISTORY AND NEAR EASTERN CIVILIZATIONS

Suggestions for Further Reading

KASTER, J., ed. and trans. *The Literature and Mythology of Ancient Egypt*. London: Allen Lane, 1970. An anthology that includes creation myths, rituals, stories, songs, proverbs, and prayers.

KRAMER, S. N. *History Begins at Sumer: Thirty-nine Firsts in Recorded History*. Philadelphia: University of Pennsylvania Press, 3rd revised edition, 1981. A lively account based largely on Sumerian documents translated by a master.

PRITCHARD, J. B. *Ancient Near Eastern Texts Relating to the Old Testament*. Princeton: Princeton University Press, 1969. For the serious student, a collection of the most important non-biblical texts, including myths, histories, prayers, and other types of writing.

SANDARS, N. K., ed. *The Epic of Gilgamesh*. New York: Penguin, 1972. The editor's informative introduction sets the tone for this famous ancient epic.

2 AEGEAN CIVILIZATIONS: THE MINOANS, THE MYCENAEANS, AND THE GREEKS OF THE ARCHAIC AGE

Suggestions for Further Reading

BARNSTONE, W., ed. and trans. *Greek Lyric Poetry*. New York: Bantam Books, 1962. Selections from literary fragments dating from the seventh century BCE to the sixth century CE; includes helpful biographical notes.

HOMER. *Iliad*. Translated by R. Fagles. New York: Viking Penguin, 1998. The best recent modern translation of the story of the Trojan War.

———. *Odyssey*. Translated by R. Fagles. New York: Viking Penguin, 1996. The epic of Odysseus's adventures after the fall of Troy, again in Fagles's well-received translation.

Sappho, a Garland: The Poems and Fragments of Sappho. Translated by J. Powell. New York: Farrar, Straus & Giroux, 1993. This slim volume contains all of Sappho's existing verses, both whole and fragments, rendered into contemporary language.

WHEELWRIGHT, P., ed. *The Presocratics*. New York: Bobbs-Merrill, 1966. A collection of quotations from early philosophers that captures the flavor of sixth-century Greek thought.

Of all the many translations of Greek literature, the Loeb Classical Library (Harvard University Press) is probably the best.

3 CLASSICAL GREEK CIVILIZATION: THE HELLENIC AGE

Suggestions for Further Reading

AESCHYLUS. *Oresteia*. Translated by R. Fagles. New York: Penguin, 1986. A good modern version of the only dramatic trilogy that survives from ancient Greece.

ARISTOPHANES. *Lysistrata*. Translated by J. Henderson. New York: Oxford University Press, 1987. This modern version captures the antiwar spirit and bawdy humor of the original comedy.

EURIPIDES. *The Bacchae and Other Plays*. Translated by P. Vellacott. New York: Penguin, 1972. An excellent collection of Euripides' dramas, in each of which strong-minded women play major roles.

HERODOTUS. *The Histories*. Translated by A. de Sélincourt. New York: Penguin, 1972. Prefaced with an informative introduction, this translation captures both the language and the narrative of the first history book in Western literature.

KAPLAN, J., ed. *The Pocket Aristotle*. New York: Washington Square Press, 1966. Edited selections from the *Physics*, the *Nicomachean Ethics*, *Politics*, and *Poetics* give a sense of Aristotle's method of inquiry.

ROUSE, W. H. D., trans. *Great Dialogues of Plato*. New York: New American Library, 1963. Includes the full text of the *Republic*, the *Apology*, *Phaedo*, and the *Symposium*.

SOPHOCLES. *The Theban Plays*. Translated by E. F. Watling. New York: Penguin, 1974. The three plays about the misfortunes of King Oedipus and his family; includes *Oedipus Rex* and *Antigone*. Unlike Aeschylus's Oresteian trilogy, Sophocles' Theban plays do not constitute a unified work; each was originally performed with other plays (now lost).

THUCYDIDES. *The Peloponnesian War*. Translated by R. Warner. New York: Penguin, 1970. A translation that captures the sweep and drama of the original.

4 HELLENISTIC CIVILIZATION AND THE RISE OF ROME

Suggestions for Further Reading

APOLLONIUS OF RHODES. *The Voyage of Argo*. Translated by E. V. Rieu. Baltimore: Penguin, 1959. A rollicking tale of adventure and romance.

AUSTIN, M. M., ed. *The Hellenistic World from Alexander to the Roman Conquest: A Selection of Ancient Sources in Translation*. Cambridge: Cambridge University Press, 1981. Letters, decrees, and official pronouncements from the Hellenistic period; provides a real sense of the time.

CATULLUS. *The Poems of Catullus*. Translated by P. Whigham. Baltimore: Penguin, 1966. Superbly crafted, these poems range from the moving to the ribald.

CICERO. *Selected Works*. Translated by Michael Grant. New York: Penguin, 1960. An excellent selection of philosophical and forensic works by Rome's most influential writer.

LUCRETIUS. *On the Nature of the Universe*. Translated by R. Latham. Baltimore: Penguin, 1971. A prose translation of this complex and fascinating work.

MENANDER. *Plays and Fragments*. Translated by P. Vellacott. Baltimore: Penguin, 1967. Helpful introduction and lively translations bring Menander's humor to life.

PLAUTUS. *The Pot of Gold and Other Plays*. Translated by E. F. Watling. Baltimore: Penguin, 1965. Five of Plautus's most humorous plays, exhibiting Roman cultural indebtedness to the Hellenistic world.

SHAPIRO, H., and CURLEY, E., eds. *Hellenistic Philosophy: Selected Readings*. New York: Modern Library, 1965. Selections from writings on Epicureanism, Stoicism, Skepticism, and Neo-platonism, with short introductions.

TERENCE. *Phormio and Other Plays*. Translated by B. Radice. Baltimore: Penguin, 1967. Three elegant and demanding plays by a comedian more austere than funny.

5 JUDAISM AND THE RISE OF CHRISTIANITY

Suggestions for Further Reading

Early Christian Writings. Translated by M. Staniforth. Baltimore: Penguin, 1968. An excellent collection of letters, primarily from the second century, that reveal the spread of Christianity and the elaboration of its ideas.

Holy Bible, New Testament, Old Testament. There are many translations of these sacred books, ranging from the "Authorized Version," popularly known as the King James version of the early seventeenth century, to various twentieth-century translations based on recent scholarship. The New American Bible is the version approved for the lectionary in the Catholic Church in the United States.

JOSEPHUS. *The Jewish War.* Translated by G. A. Williamson. New York: Penguin, 1974. Josephus, a Jew who served Rome, wrote one of the few surviving accounts of this period.

6 ROMAN IMPERIAL CIVILIZATION AND THE TRIUMPH OF CHRISTIANITY

Suggestions for Further Reading

AMMIANUS MARCELLINUS. *The Later Roman Empire (A.D. 354–378).* Translated by W. Hamilton. New York: Penguin, 1986. The primary surviving record of the tumultuous mid-fourth century by the last of Rome's truly great historians.

AUGUSTINE, SAINT. *The City of God.* Edited by D. Knowles. New York: Penguin, 1972. A monumental work that illustrates Augustine's blending of classical and Christian thought.

———. *The Confessions of St. Augustine.* Translated by R. Warner. New York: Mentor, 1963. Augustine's great, introspective account of his intellectual and spiritual journey.

APULEIUS. *The Golden Ass.* Translated by R. Graves. New York: Farrar, Straus & Giroux, 1951. A sound translation of one of the most lively and entertaining tales in ancient literature.

Early Christian Lives. Translated by C. White. New York: Penguin, 1998. An exceptional anthology of Christian lives, including the essential St. Anthony by Athanasius and St. Martin by Sulpicius Severus.

EUSEBIUS. *The History of the Church from Christ to Constantine.* Translated by G. A. Williamson. New York: Penguin, 1965. Though a partisan account written by a credulous observer, this work is the major source of early Christian history.

HORACE. *The Complete Works of Horace.* Introduction by C. Kraemer. New York: Modern Library, 1936. Masterly translations of the works that made Horace Rome's outstanding lyric poet.

JUVENAL. *The Sixteen Satires.* Translated by P. Green. New York: Penguin, 1970. Superb vernacular versions of Juvenal's bitter works.

MARCUS AURELIUS. *Meditations.* Translated by G. Hays. New York: Modern Library, 2002. By means of this readable translation, the brooding Roman emperor lays bare his soul in perhaps the greatest literary monument to Stoicism.

SENECA. *Letters from a Stoic.* Translated by R. Campbell. Baltimore: Penguin, 1969. These selections from the author's *Moral Epistles* reveal first-century Stoicism as both idealistic and practical.

VIRGIL. *The Aeneid.* Translated by R. Fitzgerald. New York: Vintage, 1981. An exceptionally readable verse translation that captures the rhythm and majesty of the original.

WHITE, CAROLINNE. *Early Christian Latin Poets.* London: Routledge, 2000. Expertly selected and translated selections from twenty Christian poets.

7 THE HEIRS TO THE ROMAN EMPIRE: BYZANTIUM AND THE WEST IN THE EARLY MIDDLE AGES

Suggestions for Further Reading

BEDE. *A History of the English Church and People.* Translated by L. Sherley-Price. New York: Penguin, 1955. Written in 731, this account of the church in Saxon England is an important source for understanding early Christian society and attitudes in England.

BOETHIUS. *The Consolation of Philosophy.* Translated by V. E. Watts. New York: Penguin, 1969. An account, combining verse and prose and written in the early sixth century, that shows how Christian faith and pagan philosophy enabled the author to accept both his fall from power and death.

Charlemagne and Louis the Pious: Five Lives. Translated by T. F. X. Noble. State College: Penn State University Press, 2009. In addition to Einhard's and Notker's versions of Charlemagne's life, this volume has three lives of his son and successor Louis. Introductory material and annotations guide the reader.

COMNENA, ANNA. *The Alexiad of Anna Comnena.* Translated and with a brief introduction by E. R. A. Sewter. New York: Penguin, 1979. A fresh, modern translation of this Byzantine classic work of history, with notes, a map, appendixes, and genealogical tables; some of the author's digressions are consigned to footnotes.

GREGORY, BISHOP OF TOURS. *History of the Franks.* Translated by L. Thorpe. New York: Penguin, 1974. An engrossing account of this chaotic time by an eyewitness.

HROSVITHA. *The Plays of Hrotsvit [Hrosvitha] of Gandersheim.* Translated and with an introduction by K. Wilson. New York: Garland, 1989. A lively and authoritative translation of these early medieval plays, with scholarly notes.

MOSCHOS, J. *The Spiritual Meadow.* Translated by J. Wortley. Kalamazoo, Mich. Cistercian Publications, 1992. A moving work beautifully translated and usefully introduced and annotated.

PSELLUS, M. *Fourteen Byzantine Rulers.* Translated by E. R. A. Sewter. New York: Penguin, 1966. An exciting and fascinating narrative of more than a century of Byzantine history.

8 THE WORLD OF ISLAM, 630–1517

Suggestions for Further Reading

Arabian Nights. Translated by J. Zipes. New York: Dutton Signet, 1991. Selections from the *Arabian Nights,* the alternative name for *The Thousand and One Nights,* by a noted authority on world folktales.

Assemblies of al-Hariri. Translated and with an introduction by A. Shah. London: Octagon Press, 1981. An up-to-date translation of this classic of Arabic literature, telling of the adventures of the charming and learned rogue Abu Zayd. All fifty episodes, or "assemblies," are included.

The Essential Rumi. Translated by C. Barks and others. San Francisco: Harper San Francisco, 1997. Excellent American English free-verse renderings of the difficult poetry in the *Masnavi,* the masterpiece of the Sufi mystic Rumi. Includes selections of Rumi's love poems and teaching parables, along with Barks's insightful introductions.

Ibn Hazm. *The Ring of the Dove: A Treatise on the Art and Practice of Arab Love.* Translated by A. J. Arberry. London: Luzac & Company, 1953. A didactic work that blends a study of the characteristics and meaning of love, including examples, anecdotes, and poems, with a moral discourse on sinning and the virtues of abstinence.

Ibn Khaldun. *The Muqaddimah: An Introduction to History.* Translated by F. Rosenthal. Edited by N. J. Dawood. Princeton, N.J.: Princeton University Press, 1969. Introduces the student to Ibn Khaldun's study of the origins and characteristics of civilization. An abridged edition of Rosenthal's three-volume translation.

The Koran [Qur'an]. Translated by N. J. Dawood. New York: Penguin, 2003. Easy-to-read, authoritative translation of Islam's holy book. Follows the Qur'anic tradition of arrangement of suras, or chapters.

The Seven Odes: The First Chapter in Arabic Literature. Translated by A. J. Arberry. London: George Allen & Unwin, 1957. An analysis, history, and modern translation of the earliest Arabic literary works—the seven odes, or "hanged poems," which hung on the walls of the Kaaba before the time of Muhammad and the rise of Islam.

Suggestion for Listening

Islamic Call to Prayer. Perhaps the most familiar prayer in Islamic religion, the Call to Prayer is chanted five times daily, echoing around the world. Performed by a single male voice, according to traditional rules of expression.

9 THE HIGH MIDDLE AGES: THE CHRISTIAN CENTURIES

Suggestions for Further Reading

Abelard, P. *The Story of Abelard's Adversities.* Translated by J. T. Muckle. Toronto: Pontifical Institute of Mediaeval Studies, 1964. Brief but revealing account by one of the medieval period's most colorful and influential characters.

Chrétien de Troyes. *The Complete Romances of Chrétien de Troyes.* Translated and with an Introduction by David Staines. Bloomington: Indiana University Press, 1990. An accurate and contemporary prose translation based on the best manuscripts.

Cole, P. *The Dream of the Poem: Hebrew Poetry from Muslim and Christian Spain, 950–1452.* Princeton, N.J.: Princeton University Press, 2007. This anthology contains a brilliantly translated version of some of the most enthralling, haunting, moving poetry one is likely to encounter.

Dante. *The Divine Comedy. The Inferno. The Purgatorio. The Paradiso.* Translated by J. Ciardi. New York: New American Library, 1982. The best contemporary English translation.

Hildegard of Bingen. *Scivias.* Translated by C. Hart and J. Bishop. New York: Paulist Press, 1990. A modern, readable translation of Hildegard's writings.

The Lais of Marie de France. Translated and with an introduction by R. Hanning and J. Ferrante. Durham, N.C.: Labyrinth Press, 1982. A modern, free-verse translation of these Old French poems; with notes and an extremely useful introductory essay.

The Song of Roland. Translated by F. Golden. New York: Norton, 1978. A readable and modern translation that still captures the language and drama of the original.

St. Thomas Aquinas. *Summa Theologica.* 3 vols. Translated by Fathers of the English Dominican Province. New York: Benziger, 1947. A good English version of St. Thomas's monumental work, which underlies Roman Catholic theology.

Tierney, B. *The Crisis of Church and State, 1050–1300.* Englewood Cliffs, N.J.: Prentice-Hall, 1964. Primary documents linked by sound interpretations and explanations.

Suggestion for Listening

Hildegard of Bingen (mid–twelfth century). *O Pastor Animarum.* A plainsong setting of a prayer to God the Father, as part of the church's liturgy.

10 THE LATE MIDDLE AGES, 1300–1500

Suggestions for Further Reading

Boccaccio, G. *The Decameron.* Translated by M. Musa and P. E. Bondanella. New York: Norton, 1977. An updated translation of the hundred stories—some learned, some coarse, but all humorous—that make up this work; first published about 1351.

Chaucer, G. *The Canterbury Tales.* Edited by N. Coghill. New York: Penguin, 1978. Of many versions of these bawdy and lighthearted tales, Coghill's is one of the most readable and enjoyable; the original work dates from 1385.

Christine de Pizan. *The Book of the City of Ladies.* Translated by E. J. Richards. New York: Persea Books, 1982. An accessible, modern translation of this late medieval work, which argues that the political and cultural dignity of women depends on their being educated properly, just as men are; first published in 1405.

Langland, W. *The Vision of Piers Plowman.* Translated by H. W. Wells. New York: Sheed and Ward, 1959. A good modern version of Langland's work criticizing the religious establishment of his day and calling for a new order; written between 1362 and 1394.

Petrarch. *The Canzoniere.* Translated into verse with notes and commentary by M. Musa. Bloomington: Indiana University Press, 1996. Exquisite poetry beautifully presented.

Suggestion for Listening

Guillaume de Machaut. Machaut's innovations in rhythm helped inaugurate the *ars nova* style. His *Notre Dame* Mass, which employed isorhythms, is the first setting of the Mass Ordinary by a known composer.

11 THE EARLY RENAISSANCE: RETURN TO CLASSICAL ROOTS, 1400–1494

Suggestions for Further Reading

Cassirer, E., Kristeller, P. O., and Randall, J., eds. *The Renaissance Philosophy of Man.* Chicago: University of Chicago Press, 1948. Selections from Pico, Valla, and other Renaissance scholars accompanied by a useful text.

Pico della Mirandola. *On the Dignity of Man.* Indianapolis: Bobbs-Merrill, 1956. A succinct statement on Renaissance thought by one of its leading scholars.

Pius II. *Reject Aeneas, Accept Pius.* Selected letters of Aeneas Silvius Piccolomini. Introduced and translated by T. Izbicki, G. Christianson, and P. Krey. Washington, D.C.: Catholic University of America Press, 2006. A wonderful selection of letters that reveals the fascinating life and times of the humanist pope.

Suggestions for Listening

DUNSTABLE (or DUNSTAPLE), JOHN. Dunstable's sweet-sounding harmonies helped inaugurate early Renaissance music. Predominantly a composer of sacred music, he is best represented by motets, including *Veni Sancte Spiritus—Veni Creator Spiritus* and *Sancta Maria, non est similis.* He also wrote a few secular songs, of which the two most familiar are *O Rosa bella* and *Puisque m'amour.*

JOSQUIN DES PREZ. Josquin's Masses, motets, and chansons all illustrate his skill at combining popular melodies with intricate counterpoint and his use of harmonies commonly heard today. The motet *Ave Maria,* the chanson *Faulte d'argent,* and the Mass *Malheur me bat* are good examples of his style.

12 THE HIGH RENAISSANCE AND EARLY MANNERISM, 1494–1564

Suggestions for Further Reading

CASTIGLIONE, B. *The Book of the Courtier.* Translated by G. Bull. New York: Penguin, 1967. A flowing translation; includes a helpful introduction and descriptions of characters who participate in the conversations recorded by Castiglione; first published in 1528.

MACHIAVELLI, N. *The Prince.* Translated by G. Bull. New York: Penguin, 1971. The introduction covers Machiavelli's life and other writings to set the stage for this important political work; written in 1513.

Suggestion for Listening

WILLAERT, ADRIAN. Willaert is particularly noted for his motets, such as *Sub tuum praesidium,* which reflect the Renaissance humanist ideal of setting the words precisely to the music. His *Musica nova,* published in 1559 and including motets, madrigals, and instrumental music, illustrates the complex polyphony and sensuous sounds that made him a widely imitated composer in the second half of the sixteenth century.

13 NORTHERN HUMANISM, NORTHERN RENAISSANCE, RELIGIOUS REFORMATIONS, AND LATE MANNERISM, 1500–1603

Suggestions for Further Reading

CALVIN, J. *Institutes of the Christian Religion.* Translated by F. L. Battles. Philadelphia: Westminster Press, 1960. A translation of Calvin's theological masterpiece.

CERVANTES, M. DE. *Don Quijote [Quixote].* Translated by B. Raffel with volume edited by D. de Armas Wilson. New York: Norton, 1999. An up-to-date translation of the first modern novel with accompanying commentary; another excellent volume in the Norton Critical Edition series.

ERASMUS, D. *Praise of Folly.* Translated by B. Radice. New York: Penguin, 1971. A lively translation of Erasmus's satire that ridiculed the hypocrisy of the age, especially in the church; originally published in 1509.

LUTHER, M. *Three Treatises.* Translations by various authors. Philadelphia: Fortress Press, 1960. Good versions of the short works that helped to make Luther an outstanding and controversial public figure in his day.

MONTAIGNE, M. DE. *Essays and Selected Writings.* Translated and edited by D. Frame. New York: St. Martin's Press, 1963. The *Essays* reveal Montaigne as one of the founders of French Skepticism.

RABELAIS, F. *The Histories of Gargantua and Pantagruel.* Translated by J. M. Cohen. Franklin Center, Pa.: Franklin Library, 1982. An excellent modern version of this lusty masterpiece.

SHAKESPEARE. *Hamlet. Othello. King Lear. Romeo and Juliet. Antony and Cleopatra. Macbeth.* One of the best editions available of Shakespeare's tragedies is the New Folger Library, published by Washington Square Press. This series is inexpensive and profusely illustrated, and it offers extensive editorial notes.

Suggestions for Listening

PALESTRINA, GIOVANNI PIERLUIGI DA. A prolific composer of Masses, Palestrina is the major musical figure of the Counter-Reformation. Unlike the highly emotional style of Josquin, Palestrina's music is noted for its tightly controlled quality and its perfection of detail, as illustrated in such Masses as *Hodie Christus natus est, Assumpta est Maria,* and *Ave Maria.*

WEELKES, THOMAS. An English composer and organist, Weelkes is an important figure in late Renaissance music. A composer of sacred vocal music and instrumental works for viols and harpsichord, he is best known for introducing the Italian madrigal to England and adapting it to the tastes of his compatriots. His madrigals are characterized by clever word paintings, as in "O, care, thou wilt despatch me" and "The Andalusian merchant" (both 1600).

14 THE BAROQUE AGE I: GLAMOUR AND GRANDIOSITY, 1600–1715

Suggestions for Further Reading

BEHN, A. *Oroonoko and Other Stories.* Edited and introduced by M. Duffy. London: Methuen, 1985. An edition of Behn's stories, with a useful introduction; these short works prepared the way for the novel genre, born after 1700. *Oroonoko* was first published in 1678.

CORNEILLE, P. *The Cid.* Translated by V. J. Cheng. Newark: University of Delaware Press, 1987. A version of Corneille's drama, recounting the story of a hero torn between honor and love; imitates the poetic form of the original, first staged in 1636.

MILTON, J. *Paradise Lost.* New York: Norton, 1975. Milton's baroque epic about rebellion—Lucifer's revolt in heaven and Adam and Eve's defiance on earth; Scott Elledge provides a useful introduction and notes to the text, which was first published in 1667.

MOLIÈRE (POQUELIN, J. B.). *The Misanthrope.* Translated by R. Wilbur. London: Methuen, 1967. A good translation by a leading American poet. Useful English versions by various translators of Molière's other frequently performed comedies are also available, including *The Miser* (New York: Applause Theatre Book Publishers, 1987), *Tartuffe* (London: Faber and Faber, 1984), and *The Bourgeois Gentleman (The Would-Be Gentleman)* (New York: Applause Theatre Book Publishers, 1987).

RACINE, J. B. *Phaedra [Phèdre].* Translated by R. Wilbur. New York: Harcourt Brace Jovanovich, 1986. A solid translation of this French tragic drama.

SOR JUANA INÉS DE LA CRUZ. *Poems, Protest, and a Dream.* Translated by M. S. Peden. New York: Penguin, 1997. A selection of Sor Juana's writings, including ironic, courtly poems and the first defense by a New World author of the right of women to be educated, *La Respuesta de la poetisa a la muy ilustre Sor Filotea de la Cruz (Response to the Most Illustrious Poetess Sor*

Filotea de la Cruz), first published in 1691. With a helpful
introduction by I. Stavans.

Suggestions for Listening

BACH, JOHANN SEBASTIAN. The greatest composer of the baroque
era, Bach is best known for his sacred music, which has tremendous emotional power. His church music for voices includes more than two hundred cantatas, or musical settings
of biblical and choral texts, such as *Jesu der du meine Seele
(Jesus, Thou Hast My Soul), Wachet Auf (Sleepers Awake),* and
O Haupt voll Blut und Wunden (O Sacred Head Now Wounded);
six motets, such as *Jesu meine Freude (Jesus, My Joy);* two Passions, or musical settings of biblical passages and commentaries on the Easter season (the *St. Matthew Passion* and the
St. John Passion); and a Mass, the Mass in B Minor. He also
composed instrumental church music, notably about 170
organ chorales required by the liturgy for the church year.
Besides sacred music, Bach wrote secular music, including
the "Little" Fugue in G Minor, the *Brandenburg Concertos,*
and *The Well-Tempered Clavier* (1722; 1740), a collection of
works for keyboard that consisted of one prelude and fugue
for each of the twelve major and minor keys.

HANDEL, GEORGE FRIDERIC. The German-born Handel, who
lived and worked mainly in England, made eighteenth-
century England a center of baroque music. Of the thirty-six
Italian-style operas that he composed and produced in London, three of the best known are *Rinaldo* (1711), *Giulio Cesare*
(1724), and *Serse* (1738). His oratorios—including *Messiah*—
were performed in public theaters rather than churches and
especially appealed to the rising middle classes. Handel also
produced a body of instrumental music, of which the most
significant are the two suites known as the *Fireworks Music*
(1749) and the *Water Music* (about 1717) and six concertos for
woodwinds and strings.

LULLY, JEAN-BAPTISTE. Lully's eleven operas helped to define the
operatic genre in France, giving it an opening overture and a
ballet movement. Of his operas, the best known are probably
Theseus (1675) and *Amadis* (1684). Especially appealing to
modern ears are the massed choruses and rhythmic dances
of his operas.

MONTEVERDI, CLAUDIO. A prodigious composer of madrigals
and sacred music, Monteverdi is best remembered as a pioneer of opera. He composed his operas in a highly expressive style that matched the spirit of the music to the meaning
of words in the text, as in *Orfeo* (1607) and *The Coronation of
Poppea* (1642).

VIVALDI, ANTONIO LUCIO. Vivaldi's concertos—scored for a solo
instrument (including violin, bassoon, cello, oboe, or flute)
and orchestra—perfected the form for later composers.
Rhythmical and full of feeling, these works often were given
picturesque or evocative titles, as in *The Four Seasons* (1725),
a cycle of four violin concertos, named for the seasons of the
year. One of the most popular works of serious music, *The
Four Seasons* was part of a larger suite of twelve, known as
The Trial Between Harmony and Invention.

15 THE BAROQUE AGE II: REVOLUTIONS IN SCIENTIFIC AND POLITICAL THOUGHT, 1600–1715

Suggestions for Further Reading

BACON, F. *The Essays.* New York: Penguin, 1985. Judiciously
edited version of Bacon's highly readable text, dating from
1625, which contributed significantly to the rise of modern
scientific thinking.

BAYLE, P. *Historical and Critical Dictionary: Selections.* Translated
by R. H. Popkin and C. Brush. Indianapolis: Bobbs-Merrill,
1965. Typical and controversial excerpts from one of the first
modern dictionaries, originally published in 1697.

DESCARTES, R. *Discourse on Method.* Edited and translated by
E. Anscombe and P. T. Geach. Indianapolis: Bobbs-Merrill,
1971. A lucid translation of one of the key tracts of modern
philosophy; Descartes' arguments and evidence are relatively easy to understand. First published in 1637.

GALILEI, G. *Dialogue Concerning the Two Chief World Systems—
Ptolemaic and Copernican.* Translated by S. Drake, foreword
by A. Einstein. Berkeley: University of California Press, 1953.
Written in a conversational style, this work—first published
in 1632—aligned Galileo with the supporters of the Copernican system and led to his trial by the Roman Catholic
authorities.

HOBBES, T. *The Leviathan.* Buffalo, N.Y.: Prometheus Books,
1988. Hobbes's most important work—first issued in 1651—
advocating absolutist government without any restraint by
the people; this work has inspired many modern forms of
authoritarian rule.

LOCKE, J. *An Essay Concerning Human Understanding.* New York:
Collier Books, 1965. A good edition, introduced by M. Cran-
ston, of Locke's essay arguing that the mind is shaped by the
environment, an assertion that made the progressive theories of the modern world possible; first published in 1690.

———. *Two Treatises of Government.* Cambridge: Cambridge
University Press, 1967. An excellent edition with introduction and notes by the distinguished scholar P. Laslett;
Locke's *Second Treatise,* making the case for the doctrine of
government by consent of the governed, has become the
bible of modern liberalism.

16 THE AGE OF REASON, 1700–1789

Suggestions for Further Reading

DIDEROT, D. *The Encyclopedia: Selections.* Edited and translated
by S. J. Gendzier. New York: Harper & Row, 1967. Well-
chosen selections from the most influential work of the Enlightenment; originally published between 1750 and 1772.

FIELDING, H. *The History of Tom Jones, a Foundling.* Middletown,
Conn.: Wesleyan University Press, 1975. The rollicking novel
about an orphan who through personal charm, good looks,
and honesty survives misadventures and is finally restored
to his rightful inheritance; first issued in 1749.

GIBBON, E. *The History of the Decline and Fall of the Roman Empire.*
Abridged by M. Hadas. New York: Putnam, 1962. One of the
landmarks of the Enlightenment, Gibbon's history attributes
the fall of Rome to the rise of Christianity; published between 1776 and 1788.

HARDT, U. H. *A Critical Edition of Mary Wollstonecraft's "A Vindication of the Rights of Woman, with Strictures on Political and
Moral Subjects."* Troy, N.Y.: Whitston, 1982. An authoritative
text of one of the books that helped launch the modern
feminist movement.

MONTESQUIEU, BARON DE. *The Persian Letters.* Translated by G. R.
Healy. Indianapolis: Bobbs-Merrill, 1964. An excellent English version of this epistolary novel that satirizes European
customs through the eyes of fictional Persian travelers; the
original dates from 1721.

———. *The Spirit of the Laws.* Translated and edited by A. M.
Cohler, B. C. Miller, and H. S. Stone. New York: Cambridge
University Press, 1989. A good English version of this

groundbreaking work that claims people's choices are influenced by such matters as climate, geography, and religion.

POPE, A. *An Essay on Man*. Edited by M. Mack. London: Methuen, 1964. A poetic statement of the ideals of the Enlightenment by the leading English poet of the age.

RICHARDSON, S. *Pamela*. London: Dent, 1962. A modern edition of one of the earliest novels in the English language, recounting the tale of a servant girl whose fine moral sense enables her to prevail over adversity and rise to the top of aristocratic society.

ROUSSEAU, J.-J. *Basic Political Writings*. Translated and edited by D. A. Cress. Indianapolis: Hackett, 1987. Includes selections from *First Discourse* (1750), *The Social Contract* (1762), *Émile* (1762), and other writings.

———. *Confessions*. Translated by J. M. Cohen. New York: Penguin, 1954. A highly original book, the first in the tradition of confessional autobiographies; bridges the Enlightenment and the romantic period.

SMITH, A. *The Wealth of Nations: Representative Selections*. Indianapolis: Bobbs-Merrill, 1961. The basic writings that set forth the theory of free-market economics; first published in 1776.

VOLTAIRE. *Candide*. Translated by L. Bair. New York: Bantam Books, 1981. The most popular novel of the eighteenth century; first published in 1759.

Suggestions for Listening

COUPERIN, FRANÇOIS. The harpsichord, with its delicate and lively sounds, was the signature instrument of rococo music; Couperin's more than two hundred harpsichord works, composed usually in highly stylized and stately dance rhythms, helped to define the rococo musical style. Typical works are *La visionaire* (The Dreamer) and *La mystérieuse* (The Mysterious One), both from 1730.

HAYDN, FRANZ JOSEPH. Over a long and laborious career, Haydn honed his approach to music, moving from late baroque forms until he established the sonata form of composition as the basic ingredient of the classical musical style. Of the string quartets, those in Opuses 17 and 20, composed respectively in 1771 and 1772, show his pure classical style; the quartets he wrote in the 1790s (Opuses 76 and 77) illustrate his later style, bursting with rhythmic vitality and harmonic innovation. Good examples of his more than one hundred symphonies are Symphony No. 45 (*Farewell*) (1772), Symphony No. 85 (*La reine*, or *The Queen*) (1785), Symphony No. 94 (*Surprise*) (1791), and Symphony No. 103 (*Drum Roll*) (1795). Besides instrumental music, Haydn composed religious works, notably the oratorios for orchestra and massed chorus, *The Creation* (1798) and *The Seasons* (1801)—inspired by Handel's *Messiah*.

MOZART, WOLFGANG AMADEUS. The most gifted composer of the period, Mozart helped to define the classical style in virtually all forms of musical expression, including the symphony, the piano sonata, the concerto for piano and orchestra, the string quartet, and the comic opera. Mozart's religious music includes Masses, motets, and settings of sacred songs, such as *Solemn Vespers of the Confessor* (1780), with its serene "Laudate Dominum" section, as well as the *Epistle Sonatas* for organ and orchestra, composed between 1767 and 1780 as part of the Mass. Among his best-loved compositions are his last two symphonies, Nos. 40 and 41, composed in 1788; the six concertos for piano and orchestra written in 1784; the six string quartets in Opus 10 (1785), dedicated to Haydn; the opera *Don Giovanni* (1787) in Italian, combining comic and dramatic elements; and the comic operas *The Marriage of Figaro* (1786) and *Cosi fan Tutte* (They All Do It This Way) (1790) in Italian and *Die Zauberflöte* (The Magic Flute) (1791) in German.

RAMEAU, JEAN-PHILIPPE. Rameau's musical fame rests largely on his operas, which combine late baroque forms with rococo elegance and grace. His best-known operas include *Hippolyte et Aricie* (1733), *Les Indes galantes* (The Gallant Indies) (1735), and *Castor et Pollux* (1737).

17 REVOLUTION, REACTION, AND CULTURAL RESPONSE, 1760–1830

Suggestions for Further Reading

AUSTEN, J. *Pride and Prejudice. Sense and Sensibility*. Introduction by D. Daiches. New York: Modern Library, 1950. Both novels deal with English provincial life. *Pride and Prejudice* (1813) focuses on the proud Mr. Darcy, who must be humbled before the "prejudiced" Elizabeth Bennet can take his marriage proposal seriously; *Sense and Sensibility* (1811) uses practical-mindedness ("sense") to expose the self-indulgence of the "picturesque" spirit ("sensibility"), an aspect of genteel taste in the late eighteenth century.

BYRON, G. G., Lord. *Don Juan*. Edited by T. G. Steffan, E. Steffan, and W. W. Pratt. New York: Penguin, 1973. One of Byron's most admired works, full of autobiographical references; dates from 1819–1824.

FICHTE, J. G. *Addresses to the German Nation*. Translated by R. F. Jones and G. H. Turnbull. Chicago: Open Court, 1923. The work that helped to launch German nationalism when first published in the early 1800s.

GOETHE, J. W. v. *Faust*. Part I. Translated by M. Greenberg. New Haven, Conn.: Yale University Press, 1992. A good English version of Goethe's drama of a man prepared to sacrifice his soul for the sake of knowledge based on feeling; originally published in 1808.

———. *The Sorrows of Young Werther*. Translated by E. Mayer and L. Bogan. Foreword by W. H. Auden. New York: Vintage, 1990. The 1774 romantic novel that brought Goethe his earliest European-wide fame, translated by modern poets.

HEGEL, G. W. F. *Reason in History*. Translated and with an introduction by R. S. Hartman. New York: Liberal Arts Press, 1953. The best source for Hegel's theory that history moves through a dialectical process; first published in 1837.

KANT, I. *Critique of Pure Reason*. Introduction and glossary by W. Schwarz. Aalen, Germany: Scientia, 1982. A good version of Kant's difficult work that tried to establish what human reason can know apart from experience; dates from 1781.

MALTHUS, T. *On Population*. Edited and with an introduction by G. Himmelfarb. New York: Random House, 1960. This influential essay, first published in 1788, identified the modern dilemma of keeping population growth in equilibrium with food production.

RICARDO, D. *On the Principles of Political Economy and Taxation*. New York: Penguin, 1971. Ricardo's "iron law of wages"—that wages tend to hover around the subsistence level—became a central tenet of nineteenth-century laissez-faire theory.

SCHELLING, F. W. J. v. *Ideas for a Philosophy of Nature*. Translated by E. E. Harris. New York: Cambridge University Press, 1988. An excellent translation of Schelling's 1799 work, which helped shape romantic thinking by claiming to find God both in nature and in the human intellect.

SHELLEY, M. *Frankenstein*. With an introduction by D. Johnson. New York: Bantam Books, 1991. The original source of the

Frankenstein legend, published in 1818 when Shelley was twenty-one years old; inspired by an evening of reading and discussing ghost stories.

WORDSWORTH, W. *Lyrical Ballads.* Edited by R. L. Braett and A. R. Jones. London: Routledge and Kegan Paul, 1988. A well-annotated edition of the original volume (1798) by Wordsworth and Coleridge that initiated the age of romantic poetry in England; contains informative introductory material.

Suggestions for Listening

BEETHOVEN, LUDWIG VAN. Composing mainly in classical forms, notably the symphony and the string quartet, Beethoven moved from a classical style in the manner of Haydn and Mozart to a romantic style that was his own. The First Symphony (1800) shows his classical approach; the Third Symphony, the *Eroica* (1803), inaugurated his romantic style with its intense emotionalism and rich thematic variations. Of special note is the Ninth Symphony (1822–1824), a semi-mystical work whose final section blends full orchestra with a massed chorus. The emotional nature of the Violin Sonata No. 9 (*Kreutzer* Sonata, 1803) inspired the Russian writer Leo Tolstoy to use the piece as a catalyst for murder in his story "The Kreutzer Sonata." Beethoven's stylistic development can also be traced in his sixteen string quartets: the first six quartets, dating from 1800, reflect the grace of Haydn and Mozart, and the last five, Nos. 12 through 16 (1823–1826), are technically difficult to play, enormously long, and characterized by mood shifts from light to tragic and unusual harmonic juxtapositions. The familiar piano piece "Für Elise" (1808) is a fine example of the rondo form.

BERLIOZ, HECTOR. Berlioz was typically romantic in going beyond the forms of classicism and stressing the emotional possibilities of his music. For example, his *Requiem* (1837) is less a religious work than a dramatic symphony for orchestra and voices; its inspiration was the tradition of patriotic festivals originated during the French Revolution. Similarly, his opera *Damnation of Faust* (1846) is not an opera in a conventional sense but a series of episodes based on Goethe's play, a form that allowed the composer to focus on those scenes that seemed full of theatrical potential. Finally, the *Symphonie fantastique* (1830) is more than a symphony; it has been called "a musical drama without words"—the prototype of romantic program music.

SCHUBERT, FRANZ. Though a prolific composer of symphonies, operas, and piano sonatas, Schubert is most famous for perfecting the art song, or *lied*. Two of his best-known songs, with texts by Goethe, are "Gretchen am Spinnrade" ("Gretchen at the Spinning Wheel," 1814) and "Erlkönig" ("The Erlking," 1815). One of Schubert's most celebrated chamber works, a quintet for piano and strings, is "Die Forelle" ("The Trout," 1821), in which the lively, fluid music suggests the energetic movements of a swimming fish.

18 THE TRIUMPH OF THE BOURGEOISIE, 1830–1871

Suggestions for Further Reading

BALZAC, H. DE. *Cousin Bette.* Translated by M. A. Crawford. New York: Penguin, 1972. A representative novel from the *Human Comedy* series, Balzac's monumental commentary on French bourgeois society in the post-Napoleonic era.

———. *Père Goriot.* Translated by J. M. Sedgwick. New York: Dodd, Mead, 1954. Another of the best known of Balzac's almost one hundred novels in the *Human Comedy* series.

BRONTË, C. *Jane Eyre.* Edited and with an introduction by M. Smith. London: Oxford University Press, 1973. A classic of romanticism, this novel deals with a theme dear to the hearts of nineteenth-century women readers, the life and tribulations of a governess.

BRONTË, E. *Wuthering Heights.* Edited and with an introduction by I. Jack. New York: Oxford University Press, 1983. A classic of romanticism, this novel recounts the doomed affair of the socially mismatched but passionate soul mates Heathcliff and Catherine.

DICKENS, C. *Hard Times.* London: Methuen, 1987. A depiction of life in the new industrialized cities, this grim tale of forced marriage and its consequences reveals what happens when practical, utilitarian thinking replaces human values.

———. *Oliver Twist.* London: Longman, 1984. Dickens's moving tale of the orphan Oliver and his experiences among London's poor in the sordid conditions of the 1830s.

DICKINSON, E. *Complete Poems of Emily Dickinson.* Edited by T. H. Johnson. Boston: Little Brown, 1976. Excellent gathering of the complete corpus—all 1,775 works—of Dickinson's poetry, arranged in chronological order from awkward juvenilia to the morbid, hell-obsessed verses of her later years. Compiled by a respected Dickinson scholar.

DOSTOYEVSKY, F. *The Brothers Karamazov.* Translated by D. Magarshack. New York: Penguin, 1982. In his novel, Dostoyevsky deals with broad metaphysical and psychological themes, such as the right of human beings to reject the world made by God because it contains so much evil and suffering. These themes are dramatized through the actions and personalities of the brothers and their father.

———. *Crime and Punishment.* Translated by S. Monas. New York: New American Library, 1980. A masterpiece of psychological insight, this gripping tale of murder explores the themes of suffering, guilt, redemption, and the limits of individual freedom.

DOUGLASS, F. *Narrative of the Life of Frederick Douglass, an American Slave, Written by Himself.* Introduction by Henry Louis Gates. Bedford Books in American History. Bedford Press, 1993. A heartbreaking, but ultimately uplifting, autobiography of perhaps the most influential and celebrated African American of the nineteenth century. Originally published in 1845, this work launched the literary genre known as the slave narrative. A reprint of the 1960 Harvard University Press publication.

ELIOT, G. *Middlemarch.* New York: Penguin, 1965. This classic of realist fiction explores the psychology and growth in self-understanding of the principal characters, Dorothea Brooke and Dr. Lydgate.

FLAUBERT, G. *Madame Bovary.* Translated by A. Russell. New York: Penguin, 1961. One of the first realist novels, and possibly the finest, Flaubert's work details Emma Bovary's futile attempts to find happiness in a stifling bourgeois world.

GASKELL, E. C. *North and South.* New York: Dutton, 1975. A portrait of economic and social disparities in mid-nineteenth-century England.

GILBERT, O., and TRUTH, S. *The Narrative of Sojourner Truth.* Dover Thrift Editions, 1997. This autobiography, as told to a secretary, recounts the amazing life story of the nineteenth-century African American woman who endured thirty years of slavery in upstate New York, after which she became a leading abolitionist and a fighter for various reforms, including women's suffrage. Originally published in 1850.

HUGO, V. *Les Misérables.* Translated by L. Wraxall. New York: Heritage Press, 1938. A good English version of Hugo's epic novel of social injustice in early-nineteenth-century France.

Marx, K., and Engels, F. *Basic Writings on Politics and Philosophy*. Edited by L. Feuer. Boston: Peter Smith, 1975. A representative selection of their prodigious writings, which challenged industrial capitalism in the mid–nineteenth century and provided the theoretical basis for socialism and communism.

Mill, J. S. *On Liberty*. New York: Norton, 1975. Mill's examination of the relationship between the individual and society.

———. *Utilitarianism*. Indianapolis: Hackett, 1978. A defense of the belief that the proper goal of government is to provide the greatest happiness for the greatest number.

Sand, G. *Indiana*. Translated by G. B. Ives. Chicago: Academy Chicago, 1977. Sand's first novel, with its romantic themes and feminist message, established her as a writer of great promise.

Tolstoy, L. *War and Peace*. Translated by L. and A. Maude. London: Oxford University Press, 1984. Tolstoy's epic novel traces the impact of the Napoleonic Wars on the lives of his Russian characters and explores such themes as the role of individual human beings in the flow of history.

Whitman, W. *The Complete Poems*. Edited by F. Murphy. New York: Viking Press, 1990. The complete poems of arguably the best poet yet produced in the United States. An authoritative edition compiled by a longtime Whitman scholar.

Suggestions for Listening

Brahms, Johannes. Brahms's four symphonies (1876, 1877, 1883, and 1885) demonstrate the disciplined style and majestic lyricism that made him the leader of the anti-Wagner school. Brahms also excelled in chamber music, a genre usually ignored by romantic composers. His chamber works show him to be a worthy successor to Beethoven, especially in the Piano Quartet in G Minor, Op. 25 (late 1850s), the Clarinet Quintet in B Minor, Op. 115 (1891), and three string quartets, composed between 1873 and 1876.

Schumann, Robert. Continuing the art-song tradition perfected by Schubert, Schumann composed song cycles such as *Dichterliebe (A Poet's Love)* (1840) and *Frauenliebe und Leben (A Woman's Love and Life)* (1840), both filled with heartfelt passion and set to verses by romantic poets. Schumann also had much success with his works for solo piano, including the delightful *Kinderszenen (Scenes from Childhood)* (1839), which he called "reminiscences of a grown-up for grown-ups." Unlike the *lieder* and piano music, Schumann's other works are often neglected today, such as his four symphonies (1841, 1845–1846, 1850, 1851); two choral offerings, *Das Paradies und die Peri (Paradise and the Peri)* (1843) and *Der Rose Pilgefahrt (The Pilgrimage of the Rose)* (1851); incidental music for the stage (Byron's *Manfred*); and assorted chamber works.

Verdi, Giuseppe. Primarily a composer of opera, Verdi worked exclusively in the romantic tradition, bringing to perfection the style of opera that alternated arias and recitatives. His operatic subjects are based mainly on works by romantic authors, such as *Il Corsaro (The Corsair)* (1848), adapted from Lord Byron, and *La Traviata (The Lost One)* (1853), adapted from Alexandre Dumas the younger. Shakespeare, whom the romantics revered as a consummate genius, inspired the librettos for *Otello* (1887) and *Falstaff* (1893). Like the romantics generally, Verdi had strong nationalistic feelings that he expressed in, for example, *Les Vêpres Siciliennes (The Sicilian Vespers)* (1855) and *La Battaglia di Legnano (The Battle of Legnano)* (1849).

Wagner, Richard. Wagner created a new form, music drama, that fused all the arts—a development that reflected his theory that music should serve the theater. His early style may be heard in *Der Fliegende Holländer (The Flying Dutchman)* (1842), which alternates arias and recitatives in the traditional way. By 1850, in *Lohengrin*, he was moving toward a more comprehensive operatic style, using continuously flowing music and the technique of recurring themes called *leitmotifs*. He reached his maturity with *Der Ring des Nibelungen (The Ring of the Nibelung)*, written between 1853 and 1874; in this cycle of four operas, he focuses on the orchestral web, with the arias being simply one factor in the constantly shifting sounds. His works composed after 1853 pushed the limits of classical tonality and became the starting point for modern music.

19 THE AGE OF EARLY MODERNISM, 1871–1914

Suggestions for Further Reading

Chekhov, A. P. *Plays*. Translated and edited by E. K. Bristow. New York: Norton, 1977. Excellent versions of Chekhov's most memorable plays: *The Sea Gull, Uncle Vanya, The Three Sisters,* and *The Cherry Orchard.*

Chopin, K. *The Awakening*. Edited by M. Culley. New York: Norton, 1976. The story of a sensual woman's coming-of-age that shocked the American public, whose outrage then silenced its author; with notes, excerpts from contemporary reviews, and essays in criticism. The novel was first published in 1899.

Freud, S. *Civilization and Its Discontents*. Translated and edited by J. Strachey. New York: Norton, 1962. Freud's ideas about history and civilization, based on his psychological findings and theories; Strachey is the editor of the Standard Edition of Freud's complete works.

———. *The Interpretation of Dreams*. Translated and edited by J. Strachey. New York: Basic Books, 1955. Freud's seminal work about the role of the unconscious in human psychology and his new theory of psychoanalysis; considered by many scholars his most important work.

Huysmans, J.-K. *Against Nature*. Translated by R. Baldick. New York: Penguin, 1966. A superb English version of this curious work, first published in 1884.

Ibsen, H. *A Doll's House*. Translated by C. Hampton. New York: S. French, 1972. An excellent English version of Ibsen's most often performed play, the story of a woman's awakening to the facts of her oppressive marriage.

Jung, C. G. *Basic Writings*. Edited with an introduction by V. S. de Laszlo. New York: Modern Library, 1959. A good selection of the most important works of the Swiss psychiatrist who explored the importance of myths and symbols in human psychology.

———. *Memories, Dreams, Reflections*. Edited by A. Jaffé. New York: Vintage, 1963. Jung's highly readable autobiography, in which he describes the origins of his theories.

Kafka, F. *The Metamorphosis, The Penal Colony, and Other Stories*. Translated by W. and E. Muir. New York: Schocken Books, 1988. This volume contains the best of Kafka's brilliant short prose works, all concerned with anxiety and alienation in a hostile and incomprehensible world.

———. *The Trial*. Translated by W. and E. Muir. New York: Schocken Books, 1968. A definitive edition of Kafka's nightmare novel in which the lead character is tried and convicted of a crime whose nature he cannot discover.

Nietzsche, F. W. *The Portable Nietzsche*. Selected and translated by W. Kaufmann. New York: Penguin, 1976. A collection of the most important writings of the German philosopher, compiled by the American scholar who rescued Nietzsche from the charge of proto-Nazism into which his philosophy had fallen during the Nazi era.

PROUST, M. *Remembrance of Things Past.* Translated by C. K. Scott Moncrieff, T. Kilmartin, and A. Mayor. London: Chatto & Windus, 1981. Contains all seven volumes of Proust's monumental work, which portrays the early twentieth century as a transitional period with the old aristocracy in decline and the middle class on the rise.

WILDE, O. *The Picture of Dorian Gray.* New York: Oxford University Press, 1981. Wilde's only novel recounts the story of a man whose portrait ages and decays while he remains young and handsome despite a dissolute life; the most enduring work of the Decadent school of late-nineteenth-century English literature.

ZOLA, É. *Germinal.* Translated and with an introduction by L. Tancock. New York: Penguin, 1954. A realist novel that exposes the sordid conditions in the French mining industry.

Suggestions for Listening

DEBUSSY, CLAUDE. Debussy's veiled, subtly shifting harmonies helped to found impressionist music. Excellent examples of his style may be heard in the orchestral works *Prélude à l'après-midi d'un faune (Prelude to the Afternoon of a Faun)* (1894) and *Nocturnes* (1899); in the collections for piano called *Estampes (Prints)* (1913) and *Préludes* (1910–1913); and in the opera *Pelléas et Mélisande* (1902). Not all of his music was impressionistic, however; for example, in the piano music called *Children's Corner* (1908), he blended classical values with his typical harmonic structures.

JOPLIN, SCOTT. Typical of Joplin's ragtime compositions with a syncopated beat are "Maple Leaf Rag" (1899), "Sugar Cane Rag" (1908), and "Magnetic Rag" (1914). He also wrote a ragtime opera, *Treemonisha* (1911), a failure in his lifetime but a modest success in recent revivals.

RAVEL, MAURICE. Working in the shadow of Debussy, Ravel was an impressionist with classical inclinations; where Debussy was rhapsodic, Ravel was restrained. The work for solo piano *Jeux d'eau (Fountains)* (1901) shows Ravel's impressionist style to perfection. His classicism is most evident in compositions indebted to dance forms, including two works for solo piano, *Pavane pour une infante defunte (Pavane for a Dead Princess)* (1899) and *Valses nobles et sentimentales (Waltzes Noble and Sentimental)* (1911), and two works for orchestra, *La Valse (The Waltz)* (1920) and *Boléro* (1928).

SCHOENBERG, ARNOLD. By the end of this period, in 1914, Schoenberg was recognized as the leader of expressionist music, particularly with the atonal work *Pierrot lunaire (Moonstruck Pierrot)* (1912), scored for chamber quintet and voice. In earlier works, he was less radical, as in the Second String Quartet (1908), which fused classical forms and fragmentary melodies. Only after 1923 did Schoenberg make a breakthrough to serial composition, the type of music with which he is most identified (see Chapter 20).

STRAVINSKY, IGOR. Stravinsky, who along with Schoenberg dominated twentieth-century music, also began writing music during this period, principally as a composer of ballet scores based on Russian folk tales and traditions. These were *The Firebird* (1910), *Petrushka* (1911), and *Le Sacre du printemps (The Rite of Spring)* (1913). With *Le Sacre,* he established his originality as a composer, especially in his innovative rhythms and his handling of folk themes.

20 THE AGE OF THE MASSES AND THE ZENITH OF MODERNISM, 1914–1945

Suggestions for Further Reading

BRECHT, B. *The Threepenny Opera.* English version by D. Vesey and English lyrics by E. Bentley. New York: Limited Editions Club, 1982. An excellent adaptation of Brecht's biting drama about the underworld in Victorian England; Bentley's lyrics capture the slangy flavor of the German play first staged in 1928.

COCTEAU, J. *The Infernal Machine and Other Plays.* Norfolk, Conn.: New Directions, 1964. Cocteau fuses classicism with experimental methods in his modernist plays; he updates the Oedipus legend, for example, by introducing Freudian ideas and using film clips to present flashbacks.

ELIOT, T. S. *Collected Poems, 1909–1962.* New York: Harcourt, Brace & World, 1963. Eliot, a pillar of modernism, portrayed his times as exhausted and abandoned by God.

FAULKNER, W. *The Sound and the Fury.* New York: Modern Library, 1946. The most admired novel from the Yoknapatawpha series, Faulkner's monumental study of post–Civil War Mississippi society.

HEIDEGGER, M. *Being and Time.* Translated by J. Macquarrie and E. Robinson. New York: Harper, 1962. First published in 1927, this work helped launch the existentialist movement by portraying the universe as a meaningless place and human existence as a never-ending quest for authenticity.

HEMINGWAY, E. *The Sun Also Rises.* New York: Scribner's, 1970. Hemingway's semiautobiographical first novel, set in France and Spain in 1925.

HUGHES, L. *Selected Poems of Langston Hughes.* London: Pluto, 1986. Poetry by one of the twentieth century's outstanding writers.

JOYCE, J. *Ulysses.* New York: Penguin, 1986. This classic of modernism uses a tapestry of narrative styles to portray a day in the lives of three middle-class citizens of Dublin.

LAWRENCE, D. H. *Lady Chatterley's Lover.* New York: Modern Library, 1983. A controversial work that poses sex as a panacea for the ills of contemporary industrialized life.

O'NEILL, E. *Three Plays: Desire Under the Elms, Strange Interlude, Mourning Becomes Electra.* New York: Vintage, 1961. O'Neill's trilogy of plays based on Aeschylus's *Oresteia* and involving a contemporary New England family.

ORWELL, G. *Animal Farm; Burmese Days; A Clergyman's Daughter; Coming Up for Air; Keep the Aspidistra Flying; 1984.* New York: Octopus/Heinemann, 1980. This volume contains Orwell's most significant writings, most of which convey the author's hatred of tyranny and his skepticism about the future of humanity.

SARTRE, J.-P. *Being and Nothingness: An Essay in Phenomenological Ontology.* Translated and with an introduction by H. E. Barnes. Abridged. New York: Citadel Press, 1956. Sartre sets forth his existentialist philosophy, focusing on such key ideas as individual freedom and personal responsibility.

WALKER, A., ed. *I Love Myself When I Am Laughing . . . And Then Again When I Am Looking Mean and Impressive: A Zora Neale Hurston Reader.* Introduction by M. H. Washington. Old Westbury, N.Y.: The Feminist Press, 1979. A judicious collection of Hurston's writings, including excerpts from novels (*Their Eyes Were Watching God,* 1936) and autobiography (*Dust Tracks on a Road,* 1942); essays ("How It Feels to Be Colored Me," 1928, "Crazy for Democracy," 1945); and short stories ("The Gilded Six-bits," 1933); with an admiring "afterword" by the celebrated writer Alice Walker.

WITTGENSTEIN, L. *Tractatus Logico-Philosophicus.* Translated by D. F. Pears and B. F. McGuiness, with an introduction by B. Russell. London: Routledge and Kegan Paul, 1974. An excellent English-language version of the treatise that led to logical positivism in philosophy.

WOOLF, V. *To the Lighthouse.* London: Hogarth Press, 1974. A typical Woolf novel in its stream-of-consciousness technique and its exquisitely detailed observations of contemporary thinking.

YEATS, W. B. *The Collected Poems of W. B. Yeats.* Edited by R. J. Finneran. New York: Collier Books, 1989. One of modernism's leading voices, Yeats wrote poetry devoted to such themes as Celtic myth, the tragic violence of Irish history, and the mystical nature of human existence.

Suggestions for Listening

ANTHEIL, GEORGE. An American composer who worked in both experimental and traditional forms, Antheil lived in Europe in the 1920s and 1930s. His best-known experimental work is *Ballet mécanique (Mechanical Ballet)* (1924; revised 1952), scored for airplane propellers and other industrial noises. Recognizing that his mechanical aesthetic was at a dead end with this work, Antheil spent the rest of his career searching for a personal style: from neoclassicism (1925–1927), as in the lyrical *Piano Concerto* (1926); to Americana experiments (1927–1942), as in the opera *Transatlantic* (1927–1928), a political farce about an American presidential election; to neo-romanticism (see Chapter 22), as in Symphony No. 4 (1942) and Symphony No. 5 (1947–1948), which blend melodic and rhythmic experiments with classical forms.

COPLAND, AARON. Copland's most popular works incorporate folk melodies and pay homage to the American way of life. Copland used cowboy songs in the ballet scores *Billy the Kid* (1938) and *Rodeo* (1942); he incorporated variations on the Shaker hymn "Simple Gifts" in *Appalachian Spring* (1944), originally a ballet score that was later rearranged as a suite for symphony orchestra. His faith in the future of democracy is expressed most fully in the short, often-performed work "Fanfare for the Common Man."

ELLINGTON, EDWARD KENNEDY ("DUKE"). Ellington's jazz style blended careful orchestration with ample opportunity for improvisation. Many of his songs have become standards in the popular music repertory, such as "Creole Love Call" (1928), "Mood Indigo" (1934), "Don't Get Around Much Anymore" (1940), and "Sophisticated Lady" (1932). Less well known are his serious longer compositions, such as *Such Sweet Thunder* (1957) and *In the Beginning God* (1965), a religious work.

IVES, CHARLES. America's first great composer, Ives experimented with atonality, clashing rhythms, and dissonant harmony long before they became a standard part of twentieth-century music. He frequently drew on American themes, as in the *Concord Sonata* for piano (1909–1915) and the orchestral *Three Places in New England* (1903–1914; first performed in 1931), works that evoked the landscape of his native region. A good example of one of his atonal works is *The Unanswered Question* (1908), a short work for trumpet, four flutes, and strings.

SCHOENBERG, ARNOLD. During this period, Schoenberg, the leader of the school of atonality, originated serialism as a method of composing, as may be heard in *Variations for Orchestra* (1928), the unfinished opera *Moses and Aaron* (1932), and *Violin Concerto* (1936).

STILL, WILLIAM GRANT. Still's eclectic style usually relied on traditional Western musical forms while drawing on diverse elements of his African American background and hybrid educational experience, including jazz, popular music and orchestration, Negro spirituals, and Western avant-garde music. Notable achievements include the ballet *Lenox Avenue* (1937), the opera *The Troubled Island* (1938), with a libretto by Langston Hughes, and the *Afro-American Symphony* (1931).

STRAVINSKY, IGOR. Schoenberg's rival Stravinsky became the leader of neoclassicism in music with the ballet *Pulcinella* (1919) and continued this musical style in such works as *Symphony of Psalms* (1930), the opera-oratorio *Oedipus Rex (Oedipus the King)* (1927), the Symphony in C (1940), and the opera *The Rake's Progress* (1951).

21 THE AGE OF ANXIETY AND LATE MODERNISM, 1945–1970

Suggestions for Further Reading

The Autobiography of Malcolm X. With the assistance of A. Haley. Secaucus, N.J.: Castle Books, 1967. In his own words, Malcolm X describes his rise from obscurity to become a powerful figure posing radical solutions to racial problems.

BALDWIN, J. *Go Tell It on the Mountain.* New York: Grossett and Dunlap, 1953. A novel representative of Baldwin's early optimism about reconciliation of the black and white races.

———. *No Name in the Street.* New York: Dial Press, 1972. A novel representative of Baldwin's bitterness after the murder of Martin Luther King Jr.

BECKETT, S. *Waiting for Godot.* Edited and with an introduction by H. Bloom. New York: Chelsea House Publishers, 1987. The central image of Beckett's absurdist play—pointless waiting—has become a metaphor for the disappointed hopes of late modernism.

CAMUS, A. *The Fall.* Translated by J. O'Brien. New York: Knopf, 1957. Camus' most autobiographical novel, dealing with self-deceit and spiritual yearning.

CHOMSKY, N. *Syntactic Structures.* The Hague: Mouton, 1957. The work that revolutionized linguistics by claiming that there is a structure that lies hidden beneath the surface of language.

DE BEAUVOIR, S. *The Second Sex.* Translated and edited by H. M. Parshley. New York: Vintage, 1974. One of the books that helped launch the feminist revival by arguing that women must abandon "femininity" and create their own immortality just as men do.

FANON, F. *The Wretched of the Earth.* Translated by C. Farrington. New York: Grove Press, 1968. Fanon's groundbreaking study of racism and colonial liberation; a classic of modern revolutionary theory.

FRIEDAN, B. *The Feminine Mystique.* New York: Norton, 1963. The first acknowledgment of housewives' dissatisfaction with their role and desire for a career, this work was a milestone in the rebirth of feminism in the United States.

GINSBERG, A. *Collected Poems, 1947–1980.* New York: Harper & Row, 1984. A late modernist, Ginsberg wrote poetry that reflected his openness to diversity and his passion for freedom.

KING, M. L., JR. *A Testament of Hope: The Essential Writings of Martin Luther King, Jr.* New York: Harper & Row, 1986. A good introduction to the thought of the most influential black American in history.

LESSING, D. *Children of Violence.* (Includes *Martha Quest, A Proper Marriage, A Ripple from the Storm, Landlocked.*) New York:

Simon and Schuster, 1964–1966. *The Four-Gated City.* New York: Knopf, 1969. Covering the period between the 1930s and 1960s, this series is Lessing's literary meditation on the transformation of her colonial homeland, Rhodesia, into the black state of Zimbabwe. Martha Quest, the focal point of this quintet of novels, is the author's surrogate witness to these turbulent events.

LÉVI-STRAUSS, C. *The Elementary Structures of Kinship.* Translated by J. H. Bell and others. Boston: Beacon Press, 1969. A classic of social anthropology, this work established that there are only a few basic patterns of kinship relationships in all societies.

MAILER, N. *The Naked and the Dead.* New York: Rinehart, 1948. Mailer's novel of World War II, his first and best work.

SARTRE, J.-P. *The Age of Reason* and *The Reprieve.* Translated by E. Sutton. *Troubled Sleep.* Translated by G. Hopkins. New York: Knopf, 1947, 1947, and 1950. Sartre's trilogy of novels, called *The Roads to Freedom,* demonstrates existentialism in action.

———. *No Exit and Three Other Plays.* Translated by L. Abel and S. Gilbert. New York: Vintage, 1976. *No Exit* is Sartre's most famous drama, illustrating his idea that "hell is other people" because they strive to define us and see us as objects; also includes *Dirty Hands, The Respectful Prostitute,* and *The Flies.*

SOLZHENITSYN, A. *One Day in the Life of Ivan Denisovich.* Translated by R. Parker. New York: Dutton, 1963. Published with permission of the Soviet authorities, this novel revealed the existence of Stalin's slave labor camps.

THOMAS, D. *The Collected Poems of Dylan Thomas.* New York: New Directions, 1953. The finest lyric poet of the late modern period, Thomas wrote on such themes as sex, love, and death.

———. *Under Milk Wood, A Play for Voices.* New York: New Directions, 1954. A verse play set in a mythical Welsh village that comes to symbolize a lost world in an urbanized age.

WRIGHT, R. *Black Boy: A Record of Childhood and Youth.* New York: Harper, 1945. Wright's description of his rise from share-cropper status to international renown.

———. *Native Son.* New York: Grossett and Dunlap, 1940. Wright's most celebrated novel, the powerful story of the violent consequences of racism in the life of a young black man.

Suggestions for Listening

CAGE, JOHN. After the late 1950s, Cage's music came to be characterized by wholly random methods that he called *aleatory* (from the Latin *alea,* "dice"), as represented by 4'33" (*Four Minutes and Thirty-three Seconds*) (1952), *Variations IV* (1963), and *Aria with Fontana Mix* (1958).

PENDERECKI, KRZYSZTOF. Penderecki, an eclectic composer, draws inspiration from diverse sources, including Stravinsky and classical and church music. Reflective of the turbulent history of Poland, his music centers on themes of martyrdom, injustice, and persecution. The first work that made him an international musical star was *Threnody for the Victims of Hiroshima* (1960), a piece for orchestra that uses stringed instruments and human voices in unusual ways. Perhaps his masterpiece is the more traditional oratorio *Passion and Death of Our Lord Jesus Christ According to St. Luke,* more commonly called "The St. Luke Passion" (1966), which incorporates Gregorian chant, folk music, nonverbal choral sounds, and modified serialism. He also has had success with operas, as in the simultaneously dissonant and lyrical *Paradise Lost* (1978), based on Milton's epic poem (see Chapter 14).

STRAVINSKY, IGOR. After 1951, Stravinsky replaced his neoclassical style with the technique of serial music, as in the song *In Memoriam Dylan Thomas* (1954), the ballet *Agon* (1954–1957), and the orchestral works *Movements* (1959) and *Orchestral Variations* (1964).

22 THE CONTEMPORARY WORLD: GLOBALIZATION, TERRORISM, AND POSTMODERNISM, 1970–

Suggestions for Further Reading

BARTHES, R. *Elements of Semiology.* London: Cape, 1967. Translated by A. Lavers and C. Smith. Semiology, the study of signs and their meaning, was an invention of Barthes, used by him in the reading and interpretation of texts.

DERRIDA, J. *Of Grammatology.* Baltimore: Johns Hopkins University Press, 1997. Translated by G. C. Spivak. An updated version of Derrida's difficult 1967 work, which established deconstructionist theory.

FO, D. *Accidental Death of an Anarchist.* New York: S. French, 1987. Translated by S. Cowan. A deeply political play, Fo's tragic farce entertains even as it raises questions about Italy's police and court system.

GARCÍA MÁRQUEZ, G. *One Hundred Years of Solitude.* New York: Cambridge University Press, 1990. A classic of postmodernism that mixes magical happenings with realistic events in the mythical Colombian town of Macondo.

KINGSTON, M. H. *China Men.* New York: Knopf, 1980. Dealing with Kingston's patriarchal heritage, this autobiographical work complements *The Woman Warrior,* which focuses on matriarchal influences.

———. *The Woman Warrior: Memoirs of a Girlhood Among Ghosts.* New York: Knopf, 1976. A novel dealing with the confusion of growing up Chinese American in California; the "ghosts" of the subtitle refer to both the pale-faced Americans and the legendary female avengers brought to life by immigrant tales.

KUHN, T. *The Structure of Scientific Revolution.* Chicago: University of Chicago Press, 1996. Kuhn's thesis, now an established principle, is that revolutions occur in science only after sufficient discrepancies arise to challenge the ruling paradigm in a scientific field. First published in 1970.

KUNDERA, M. *The Unbearable Lightness of Being.* Translated by M. H. Heim. New York: Harper & Row, 1984. A novel that explores the anguish of life under communism in Eastern Europe.

MORRISON, T. *Beloved.* New York: Plume, 1998. First published in 1987, *Beloved* widened Morrison's audience after it was made into a movie. Morrison transformed a true incident from pre–Civil War America into a haunting and complex story with the dimensions of a Greek tragedy.

PAMUK, O. *My Name Is Red.* New York: Vintage, 2002. Translated by E. M. Goknar. A literary tour de force, set in the sixteenth-century Ottoman Empire, that blends murder mystery, court intrigue, and art history, with a meditation on differences between Western and Muslim civilizations.

SMITH, Z. *White Teeth.* New York: Vintage, 1990. Using story lines from three families of diverse ethnic, racial, and religious heritages, which intersect and overlap, this novel uncovers the melting pot that postimperial Britain is today.

WALCOTT, D. *Omeros.* New York: Farrar, Straus & Giroux, 1990. An epic treatment of Caribbean culture, drawing on Homer's *Iliad* (war) and *Odyssey* (homecoming) and Dante's

Divine Comedy (salvation), composed in a Dante-esque verse form.

WALKER, A. *The Color Purple.* New York: Harcourt Brace Jovanovich, 1982. An uplifting novel that describes the central black female character's rise from degradation to modest dignity. The heroine's awkward but poignantly moving letters reveal the difficulty and the ultimate heroism of her victory.

Suggestions for Listening

ADAMS, JOHN. Adams, a minimalist, has emerged as one of the freshest composers working today. Noted for resonant sounds and strong mastery of form, especially orchestral music, as in *Harmonium* (1997) and *Guide to Strange Places* (2005), and opera, as in *Nixon in China* (1987), *The Death of Klinghoffer* (1991), *I Was Looking at the Ceiling and Then I Saw the Sky* (1998), and *Doctor Atomic* (2005).

ANDERSON, LAURIE. The premier performance artist of our time, Anderson has come a long way since 1973's *Duets on Ice,* when, dressed in a kilt and skating on ice, she played duets with herself on the violin (it had been altered to play a prerecorded solo) on Manhattan street corners, the duration of the piece dependent on the melting ice. More recent performances are memorialized through records such as *Mister Heartbreak* (1984); *Sharkey's Day* (1984), based on a Bauhaus work by Oskar Schlemmer; *Strange Angels* (1989), taken from the performance piece titled *Empty Places; The Ugly One with the Jewels* (1995), generated by the performance called *Stories from the New Bible* (1992–1995); and *Life on a String* (2001), inspired by the material in *Songs and Stories from "Moby Dick"* (1999), based on Herman Melville's novel. Her most popular work to date—almost 900,000 copies sold—is *O Superman* (1980), a single record that was later incorporated into the epic-length *United States I–IV* (1983).

CORIGLIANO, JOHN. Corigliano's deeply emotional music evokes the romantic era, with its soaring themes, lush tones, and rhythmic energy. A prolific award-winning composer, he has written orchestral works (such as *Concerto for Clarinet and Orchestra* [1977]), chamber pieces (such as *Phantasmagoria,* for cello and piano [2000]), one opera (*Ghosts of Versailles* [1999]), and film scores (such as *Altered States* [1997]) and was awarded the 2001 Pulitzer Prize in music for his Symphony No. 2. In his most famous work for orchestra, Symphony No. 1 (1999), Corigliano registered his anger and sorrow over the loss of friends to AIDS; the piece's third movement includes a twelve-minute cantata—thus evoking the choral singing in Beethoven's Ninth Symphony (see Chapter 17). Corigliano's most mainstream work remains the film score for *The Red Violin* (1999)—for which he won an Oscar.

GLASS, PHILIP. Glass's pulsating rhythms and cascading sounds have made him a popular and successful figure in postmodern music. He is best known for his operas, including *Einstein on the Beach* (1976), *Satyagraha* (1978), *Akhnaten* (1984), *Monsters of Grace* (1998), and *Waiting for the Barbarians* (2005), and for his film scores, such as those for *Koyaanisqatsi* (1983), *Mishima* (1985), *Kundun* (1998), the classic silent film *Dracula* (1999), *The Hours* (2002), and *The Illusionist* (2006).

LIGETI, GYORGI. Ligeti's eclectic range extends over the postmodern landscape, including the Cage-like *Future of Music* (1961), the electronic music of *Articulation* (1958), the New Age music of *Atmospheres* (1966) and *Lux Aeterna (Eternal Light),* the "anti-opera" *Le Grand Macabre* (1976; rev. 1999), the pulsing *Clocks and Clouds* (1972–1973), and the world music–inspired *Études for Piano* (3 vols., 1985–2001).

TAN DUN. Tan Dun, trained in music in both China and the United States, is the most global composer working today. His music draws on varied styles: from the West, classical, experimental, and popular; and from China, Peking opera and traditional and folk music. He is also multicultural in his instrument choices, ranging over the musical history of both cultures, including nontraditional and organic instruments, such as bowls of water amplified to make sounds, as in *Water Passion After St. Matthew* (2000). His eclectic output includes the operas *Marco Polo* (1995) and *The First Emperor* (2006), the orchestral piece *Tea: A Mirror of Soul* (2002), and for multimedia, *The Map: Concerto for Cello, Video and Orchestra* (2002). His fame rests primarily on his film scores: *Crouching Tiger, Hidden Dragon* (2000) and *Hero* (2004).

GLOSSARY

Italicized words within definitions are defined in their own glossary entries.

abstract art Art that presents a subjective view of the world—the artist's emotions or ideas—or art that presents *line, color,* or shape for its own sake.

abstract expressionism Also known as *action painting,* a nonrepresentational artistic style that flourished after World War II and was typified by randomness, spontaneity, and an attempt by the artist to interact emotionally with the work as it was created.

abstraction In modern art, nonrepresentational or non-objective forms in sculpture and painting that emphasize shapes, *lines,* and *colors* independent of the natural world.

a cappella [ah kuh-PEL-uh] From the Italian, "in chapel style"; music sung without instrumental accompaniment.

action painting Another name for *abstract expressionism.* Action painting referred to an artist's use of agitated motions while applying paint to canvas, such as Jackson Pollock's "drip paintings" or Willem de Kooning's slashing strokes. Inspired by *surrealism's* reliance on automatic responses as a way to release the creative unconscious.

adab [ah-DAHB] An Arabic term. Originally, it meant good manners or good conduct. In the eighth century, it appeared as a literary *genre;* later, it indicated the possession of athletic skills and literary knowledge and applied especially to the elite. Today, *adab* refers to the whole of literature.

aesthete One who pursues and is devoted to the beautiful in art, music, and literature.

aisles The side passages in a church on either side of the central *nave.*

ambulatory [AM-bue-la-tor-e] A passageway for walking found in many religious structures, such as outdoors in a *cloister* or indoors around the *apse* or the *choir* of a church.

Anglicanism The doctrines and practices of the Church of England, which was established in the early sixteenth century under Henry VIII.

angry young men A late 1950s and early 1960s literary movement in Great Britain, composed of novelists and playwrights, whose works expressed frustration and anger over their country's loss of empire and declining status on the world's stage. Most of the angry young men were part of an emerging meritocracy, having been born in the lower classes but educated in the universities, including Oxford and Cambridge.

anthropomorphism [an-thro-po-MOR-fizm] The attributing of humanlike characteristics and traits to nonhuman things or powers, such as a deity.

antiphon [AN-te-fon] In music, a short prose text, chanted by unaccompanied voices during the Christian *liturgy.*

apocalypse [uh-PAHK-uh-lips] In Jewish and early Christian thought, the expectation and hope of the coming of God and his final judgment; also closely identified with the last book of the New Testament, Revelation, in which many events are foretold, often in highly symbolic and imaginative terms.

apologists From the Greek *apologia,* "in defense of." Christian writers (about 150–300) who differentiated between Christianity, Judaism, and pagan philosophies, and who discussed ways in which Christians could be good citizens of the Roman Empire.

apostolic succession A term for the idea in the Catholic Church that the authority of bishops descends from the authority of the apostles, Christ's twelve followers.

apse In architecture, a large projection, usually rounded or semicircular, found in a *basilica,* usually in the east end; in Christian *basilicas,* the altar stood in this space.

aquatint An early type of color print, made with a metal plate, which attempted to replicate the effect of a watercolor; originated in the Netherlands in about 1650. The golden age of the aquatint was from about 1770 to 1850. The print's name derives from nitrous oxide *(aqua fortis),* a chemical used in the printmaking process.

arabesque [air-uh-BESK] Literally, "Arabian-like"; decorative lines, patterns, and designs, often floral, in Islamic works of art.

arcade A series of arches supported by *piers* or columns, usually serving as a passageway along a street or between buildings.

Archaic style The *style* in Greek sculpture, dating from the seventh century to 480 BCE, that was characterized by heavy Egyptian influence; dominated by the *kouros* and *korē* sculptural forms.

architectural paintings A type of wall painting, which created the optical illusion of either a wall opening or the effect of looking through a window; popular in imperial Rome.

architrave [AHR-kuh-trayv] The part of the *entablature* that rests on the *capital* or column in classical *post-beam-triangle construction.*

aria [AH-ree-uh] In music, an elaborate *melody* sung as a solo or sometimes a duet, usually in an *opera* or an *oratorio,* with an orchestral accompaniment.

ars nova Latin, "new art"; a style of music in fourteenth-century Europe. It used more secular themes than the "old art" music of earlier times, which was closely identified with sacred music.

art film A film *genre* marked by unusual narrative structures, violent action, and uplifting themes; associated with directors indebted to *auteurist* theory.

art song *(lied)* In music, a *lyric* song with *melody* performed by a singer and instrumental accompaniment usually provided by piano; made popular by Schubert in the nineteenth century.

ashlar [ASH-luhr] A massive hewn or squared stone used in constructing a fortress, palace, or large building.

assemblage art An art form in which the artist mixes and/or assembles "found objects," such as scraps of paper, cloth, or junk, into a three-dimensional work and then adds paint or other decorations to it.

ataraxia [at-uh-RAK-see-uh] Greek, "calmness"; in *Hellenistic* philosophy, the state of desiring nothing.

atonality [ay-toe-NAL-uh-tee] In music, the absence of a *key* note or tonal center and the use of the *tones* of the chromatic *scale* impartially.

atrium [AY-tree-uhm] In Roman architecture, an open courtyard at the front of a house; in Christian *Romanesque* churches, an open court, usually colonnaded, in front of the main doors of the structure.

attic The topmost section or crown of an arch.

audience The group or person for whom a work of art, architecture, literature, drama, film, or music is intended.

aulos In music, a reed woodwind instrument similar to the oboe, usually played in pairs by one player as the double aulos; used in Greek music.

autarky [AW-tar-kee]   Greek, "self-sufficient"; in *Hellenistic* thought, the state of being isolated and free from the demands of society.

auteur [oh-TURR]   French, "author"; a film director who imposes a personal style. The *auteurist* director "writes" with the camera to express a personal vision.

avant-garde [a-vahn-GARD]   French, "advance guard"; writers, artists, and intellectuals who push their works and ideas ahead of more traditional groups and movements.

baldacchino [ball-duh-KEE-no]   An ornamental structure in the shape of a canopy, supported by four columns, built over a church altar, and usually decorated with statues and other ornaments.

balustrade   In architecture, a rail and the row of posts that support it, as along the edge of a staircase or around a dome.

baptistery   A small, often octagonal structure, separated from the main church, particularly in Europe, where baptisms are performed.

bard   A tribal poet-singer who composed and recited works, often of the *epic poetry* genre.

baroque [buh-ROKE]   The prevailing seventeenth-century artistic and cultural *style*, characterized by an emphasis on grandeur, opulence, expansiveness, and complexity.

barrel vault   A ceiling or *vault* made of sets of arches placed side by side and joined together.

basilica [buh-SILL-ih-kuh]   A rectangular structure that included an *apse* at one or both ends; originally a Roman building used for public purposes, later taken over by the Christians for worship. The floor plan became the basis of nearly all early Christian churches.

bay   A four-cornered unit of architectural space, often used to identify a section of the *nave* in a *Romanesque* or *Gothic* church.

beat generation   A literary movement in the United States, from about 1950 to 1970, made up of poets, novelists, and playwrights, who stood apart from the mainstream literary establishment, as reflected in their use of street language, experimental forms of literary expression, and liberal use of alcohol and drugs. While expressing solidarity with society's downtrodden—the source of the term *beat*—the beats criticized capitalism, bourgeois society and values, and the nuclear arms race.

bel canto [bell KAHN-toe]   Italian, "beautiful singing"; a style of singing characteristic of seventeenth-century Italian *opera* stressing ease, purity, and evenness of *tone* along with precise vocal technique.

blank verse   Unrhymed iambic pentameter (lines with five feet, or units, each consisting of an unaccented and an accented syllable).

blaxploitation film   A crime film *genre* that features a swaggering black hero, catering to black audiences.

blind arcade   A decorative architectural design that gives the appearance of an open *arcade* or window but is filled in with some type of building material such as stone or brick.

blues   A type of music that emerged around 1900 from the rural African American culture, was originally based on work songs and religious spirituals, and expressed feelings of loneliness and hopelessness.

Byzantine style [BIZ-uhn-teen]   In painting, decoration, and architecture, a *style* blending Greco-Roman and oriental components into a highly stylized art form that glorified Christianity, notably in domed churches adorned with *mosaics* and polished marble; associated with the culture of the Eastern Roman Empire from about 500 until 1453.

cadenza [kuh-DEN-zah]   In music, a *virtuoso* passage, usually for a solo instrument or voice, meant to be improvised or to have an improvised feeling.

Cajun   A descendant of French pioneers, chiefly in Louisiana, who in 1755 chose to leave Acadia (modern Nova Scotia) rather than live under the British crown.

calligraphy   Penmanship or handwriting, usually done with flowing lines, used as a decoration or as an enhancement of a written work; found in Islamic and Christian writings.

Calvinism   The theological beliefs and rituals set forth in and derived from John Calvin's writings, placing emphasis on the power of God and the weakness of human beings.

campanile   From the Latin *campana*, "bell"; a bell tower, especially one near but not attached to a church; an Italian invention.

canon   A set of principles or rules that are accepted as true and authoritative for the various arts or fields of study; in architecture, it refers to the standards of proportion; in painting, the prescribed ways of painting certain objects; in sculpture, the ideal proportions of the human body; in literature, the authentic list of an author's works; in religion, the approved and authoritative writings that are accepted as divinely inspired, such as the *scriptures* for Jews and Christians; and in religious and other contexts, certain prescribed rituals or official rules and laws. In music, a canon is a *composition* in which a *melody* sung by one voice is repeated exactly by successive voices as they enter.

canzone [kan-ZOH-nee]   Latin, "chant"; a type of love poem popular in southern France during the twelfth and thirteenth centuries.

capital   In architecture, the upper or crowning part of a column, on which the *entablature* rests.

capitularies   From the Latin *capitula* (chapters), a term meaning quasi-legislative documents of varying lengths issued by Carolingian kings on a variety of secular and ecclesiastical topics. Some capitularies flowed from the kings, while others emerged from general assemblies of the Franks.

Carolingian minuscule   A new, highly legible script that originated in the reign of Charlemagne (768–814). The script served the king's desire for accurate copies of key ancient and contemporary books. It gradually replaced earlier scripts that were difficult to read and led to errors in transcription.

cathedral   The church of a bishop that houses a cathedral, or throne symbolizing the seat of power in his administrative district, known as a diocese.

causality   The idea that one event "causes" another; the relation between a cause and its effect.

cella [SELL-uh]   The inner sanctum or walled room of a *classical* temple where sacred statues were housed.

chamber work   Music for a small ensemble of instruments or voices.

chanson [shahn-SAWN]   French, "song"; a fourteenth- to sixteenth-century French song for one or more voices, often with instrumental accompaniment. Similar to a *madrigal*.

chanson de geste [shahn-SAWN duh zhest]   A poem of brave deeds in the *epic* form developed in France during the eleventh century, usually to be sung.

character A person in a story or play; someone who acts out or is affected by the *plot*.

chiaroscuro [key-ahr-uh-SKOOR-oh] In painting, the use of dark and light contrast to create the effect of modeling of a figure or object.

Chinese rococo A variation of the European *rococo*, characterized by oriental shapes, materials, techniques, and design elements.

Chinoiserie [shen-WAZ-uh-ree] French, "Chinois," China. A *style* and taste in the West for Chinese culture, embracing the decorative arts and, to a lesser extent, Chinese writings; most influential from 1740 to 1770, but lingering until about 1850.

chivalric code The rules of conduct, probably idealized, that governed the social roles and duties of aristocrats in the Middle Ages.

chivalric novel A late medieval literary form that presented romantic stories of knights and their ladies; the dominant literary form in Spain from the late Middle Ages into the *Renaissance*.

choir In architecture, that part of a *Gothic* church in which the service was sung by singers or clergy, located in the east end beyond the *transept*; also, the group of trained singers who sat in the choir area.

chorus In Greek drama, a group of performers who sang and danced in both *tragedies* and *comedies,* often commenting on the action; in later times, a group of singers who performed with or without instrumental accompaniment.

Christian humanism An intellectual movement in sixteenth-century northern Europe that sought to use the ideals of the *classical* world, the tools of ancient learning, and the morals of the Christian *scriptures* to rid the church of worldliness and scandal.

chthonian deities [THOE-nee-uhn] In Greek religion, earth gods and goddesses who lived underground and were usually associated with peasants and their religious beliefs.

civic humanism An Italian *Renaissance* ideal, characterized by dedicated and educated citizens who served as administrators and civil servants in their cities; inspired by the period's *classical* revival.

civilization The way humans live in a complex political, economic, and social structure, usually in an urban environment, with some development in technology, literature, and art.

cladding In architecture, a covering or overlay of some material for a building's exterior walls.

classic, or classical Having the forms, values, or standards embodied in the art and literature of Greek and Roman *civilization;* in music, an eighteenth-century style characterized by simplicity, proportion, and an emphasis on structure.

classical baroque style A secular variation of the *baroque* style that was identified with French kings and artists, was rooted in *classical* ideals, and was used mainly to emphasize the power and grandeur of the monarchy.

classicism A set of aesthetic principles found in Greek and Roman art and literature emphasizing the search for perfection or ideal forms.

clavier [French, KLAH-vyay; German, KLAH-veer] Any musical instrument having a keyboard, such as a piano, organ, or harpsichord; the term came into general usage with the popularity of Bach's set of studies titled *The Well-Tempered Clavier.*

clerestory windows [KLEER-stor-ee] A row of windows set along the upper part of a wall, especially in a church.

cloister In architecture, a covered walkway, open on one side, which is attached to the four walls of buildings that face a quadrangle; originated in medieval church architecture. Also, a monastery or convent dedicated to religious seclusion.

collage [koh-LAHZH] From the French *coller,* to "glue"; a type of art, introduced by Picasso, in which bits and pieces of materials such as paper or cloth are glued to a painted surface.

color Use of the hues found in nature to enhance or distort the sense of reality in a visual image.

comedy A literary *genre* characterized by a story with a complicated and amusing *plot* that ends with a happy and peaceful resolution of all conflicts.

comedy of manners A humorous play that focuses on the way people in a particular social group or class interact with one another, especially regarding fashions and manners.

commedia dell'arte [kuh-MAY-de-uh del-AR-teh] Italian, "comedy of art"; an Italian theatrical *genre* from the sixteenth century, using puppets and stock characters, with a strong streak of improvisation. Highly influential later on live theater in Italy and elsewhere.

composition The arrangement of constituent elements in an artistic work; in music, composition also refers to the process of creating the work.

conceptual art A *late modern* art movement in which the concept or idea of the proposed art is more important than the means for its execution.

concerto [kuhn-CHER-toe] In music, a *composition* for one or more soloists and *orchestra,* usually in a symphonic *form* with three contrasting movements.

conch The rounded semi-dome that topped the half-*drum* of an *apse.*

congregational or Friday mosque A type of *mosque* used for Friday prayers, inspired by the prophet Muhammad's original example. Characterized by a central courtyard along with a domed fountain for ablutions; found across the Islamic world.

consort A set of musical instruments in the same family, ranging from bass to soprano; also, a group of musicians who entertain by singing or playing instruments.

constructivism A movement in nonobjective art, originating in the Soviet Union and flourishing from 1917 to 1922 and concerned with planes and volumes as expressed in modern industrial materials such as glass and plastic.

content The subject matter of an artistic work.

context The setting in which an artistic work arose, its own time and place. Context includes the political, economic, social, and cultural conditions of the time; it can also include the personal circumstances of the artist's life.

contrapposto [kon-truh-POH-stoh] In sculpture and painting, the placement of the human figure so the weight is more on one leg than the other and the shoulders and chest are turned in the opposite direction from the hips and legs.

convention An agreed-upon practice, device, technique, or form.

Corinthian The third Greek architectural order, in which temple columns are slender and *fluted,* sit on a base, and have *capitals* shaped like inverted bells and decorated with carvings representing the leaves of the acanthus bush; this style was popular in *Hellenistic* times and widely adopted by the Romans.

cornice In architecture, the crowning, projecting part of the *entablature.*

cosmopolitan From Greek, *cosmos,* "world," and *polis,* "city"; a citizen of the world, that is, an urban dweller with a universal, or world, view.

Counter-Reformation A late-sixteenth-century movement in the Catholic Church aimed at reestablishing its basic beliefs, reforming its organizational structure, and reasserting itself as the authoritative voice of Christianity.

countersubject In music, in the *fugue,* a contrasting variant to the *subject;* played in tandem with the *subject,* either below or above it.

covenant In Judaism and Christianity, a solemn and binding agreement or contract between God and his followers.

Creole An ambiguous term, sometimes referring to descendants of French and Spanish settlers of the southern United States, especially Louisiana; used by Kate Chopin in her short stories and novels in this sense. In other contexts, *Creole* can refer either to blacks born in the Western Hemisphere (as distinguished from blacks born in Africa) or to residents of the American Gulf states of mixed black, Spanish, and Portuguese ancestry.

crescendo [krah-SHEN-doh] In music, an increase in volume.

cruciform [KROO-suh-form] Cross-shaped; used to describe the standard floor plan of a church.

Crusades A series of military campaigns launched in 1095 by Pope Urban II to recover the Holy Land from its Muslim conquerors. The name derives from *crucesignati,* Latin for "signed by the cross," signifying the cross that crusaders stitched onto their clothing. The First Crusade (1097–1099) captured Jerusalem and established some small "Crusader States" in the eastern Mediterranean but the movement as a whole failed, over the centuries, in its stated objective.

cubism A *style* of painting introduced by Picasso and Braque in which objects are broken up into fragments and patterns of geometric structures and depicted on the flat canvas as if from several points of view.

culture The sum of human endeavors, including the basic political, economic, and social institutions and the values, beliefs, and arts of those who share them.

cuneiform [kue-NEE-uh-form] Wedge-shaped characters used in writing on tablets found in Mesopotamia and other ancient *civilizations.*

Cynicism A *Hellenistic* philosophy that denounced society and its institutions as artificial and called on the individual to strive for *autarky.*

Dada [DAH-dah] An early-twentieth-century artistic movement, named after a nonsense word that was rooted in a love of play, encouraged deliberately irrational acts, and exhibited contempt for all traditions.

decadence A late-nineteenth-century literary *style* concerned with morbid and artificial subjects and themes.

deconstruction In *postmodern* literary analysis, a set of practices for analyzing and critiquing a text in order to "deconstruct" its actual meaning and language.

deductive reasoning The process of reasoning from the general to the particular—that is, beginning with an accepted premise or first statement and, by steps of logical reasoning or inference, reaching a conclusion that necessarily follows from the premise.

Deism [DEE-iz-uhm] A religion based on the idea that the universe was created by God and then left to run according to *natural laws,* without divine interference; formulated and practiced in the eighteenth century.

de Stijl [duh STILE] Dutch, "the style"; an artistic movement associated with a group of early-twentieth-century Dutch painters who used rectangular forms and primary colors in their works and who believed that art should have spiritual values and a social purpose.

devotio moderna [de-VO-tee-oh mo-DER-nuh] The "new devotion" of late medieval Christianity that emphasized piety and discipline as practiced by lay religious communities located primarily in northern Europe.

Diaspora [dye-AS-puhr-uh] From the Greek, "to scatter"; the dispersion of the Jews from their homeland in ancient Palestine, a process that began with the Babylonian Captivity in the sixth century BCE and continued over the centuries.

Dionysia [DYE-uh-NYSH-ee-ah] Any of the religious festivals held in ancient Athens honoring Dionysus, the god of wine; especially the Great Dionysia, celebrated in late winter and early spring in which *tragedy* is thought to have originated.

divertimento Instrumental work, performed as entertainment, as at social gatherings or banquets.

divining Predicting the future by "reading," or interpreting, the entrails of an animal or the behavior of birds; practiced by ancient Roman priests and religious leaders.

dominate Term applied to the Roman imperial regime inaugurated by Diocletian (284–305) implying that the emperor was *dominus,* "lord and master," instead of "first citizen" (see *principate*). The dominate persisted in the East into the Byzantine era but became meaningless in the West after the death of Theodosius (395), Rome's last sole emperor.

Doric The simplest and oldest of the Greek architectural orders, in which temple columns have undecorated *capitals* and rest directly on the *stylobate.*

drum In architecture, a circular or polygonal wall used to support a dome.

drypoint In art, the *technique* of incising an image, using a sharp, pointed instrument, onto a metal surface or block used for printing. Also, the print made from the technique.

dynamics In music, changes in the volume of a sound.

early Renaissance style A *style* inspired by *classical* rather than *Gothic* models that arose among Florentine architects, sculptors, and painters in the late fourteenth and early fifteenth centuries.

electronic music Music produced using electronic means, usually with a *synthesizer* and/or a computer.

empiricism The process of collecting data, making observations, carrying out experiments based on the collected data and observations, and reaching a conclusion.

engraving In art, the *technique* of carving, cutting, or etching an image with a sharp, pointed instrument onto a metal surface overlaid with wax, dipping the surface in acid, and then printing it. Also, the print made from the *technique.*

Enlightenment The eighteenth-century philosophical and cultural movement marked by the application of reason to human problems and affairs, a questioning of traditional beliefs and ideas, and an optimistic faith in unlimited progress for humanity, particularly through education.

entablature [en-TAB-luh-choor] In architecture, the part of the temple above the columns and below the roof, which, in *classical* temples, included the *architrave,* the *frieze,* and the *pediment.*

entasis [EN-ta-sis] In architecture, convex curving or enlarging of the central part of a column to correct the optical illusion that the column is too thin.

environmental art   A *postmodern* art form that uses the environment, including stone, earth, and water, so as to create a natural-looking artwork. Environmental art is ephemeral, as it tends to revert to its primary elements over time—thus echoing the ever-changing world of nature.

epic   A poem, novel, or film that recounts at length the life of a hero or the history of a people.

epic poetry   Narrative poetry, usually told or written in an elevated style, that recounts the life of a hero.

epic theater   A type of theater, invented by Brecht, in which major social issues are dramatized with outlandish props and jarring dialogue and effects, all designed to alienate middle-class *audiences* and force them to think seriously about the problems raised in the plays.

Epicureanism [ep-i-kyoo-REE-uh-niz-uhm]   A *Hellenistic* philosophy, founded by Epicurus and later expounded by the Roman Lucretius, that made its highest goals the development of the mind and an existence free from the demands of everyday life.

episode   In music, a short transitional section played between the *subject* and the *countersubject;* used in *fugal* composition.

epistemology   The branch of philosophy that studies the nature, extent, and validity of knowledge.

eschatology [es-kuh-TAHL-uh-jee]   The concern with final events or the end of the world, a belief popular in Jewish and early Christian communities and linked to the concept of the coming of a *Messiah.*

evangelicalism   Historically, a nineteenth-century Protestant movement, mainly in the United States, which grew out of the Methodist tradition and emphasized personal piety and the working of the Holy Spirit. Evangelicalism dominated mainline Protestant America until about 1870. Today, evangelicalism is a term used for describing Protestants who emphasize *fundamentalism,* biblical inerrancy, and conservative social values.

evangelists   From the Greek *evangelion,* a term generally used for those who preach the Christian religion; more specifically, the four evangelists, Matthew, Mark, Luke, and John, who wrote about Jesus Christ soon after his death in the first four books of the New Testament.

evolution   The theory, set forth in the nineteenth century by Charles Darwin, that plants and animals, including humans, evolved over millions of years from simpler forms through a process of natural selection.

existentialism [eg-zi-STEN-shuh-liz-uhm]   A twentieth-century philosophy focusing on the precarious nature of human existence, with its uncertainty, anxiety, and ultimate death, as well as on individual freedom and responsibility and the possibilities for human creativity and authenticity.

expressionism   A late-nineteenth-century literary and artistic movement characterized by the expression of highly personal feelings rather than of objective reality.

fan vaulting   A decorative pattern of *vault* ribs that arch out or radiate from a central point on the ceiling; popular in English *Perpendicular* architecture.

Faustian [FAU-stee-uhn]   Resembling the character Faust in Goethe's most famous work, in being spiritually tormented, insatiable for knowledge and experience, or willing to pay any price, including personal and spiritual integrity, to gain a desired end.

fauvism [FOH-viz-uhm]   From the French *fauve,* "wild beast"; an early-twentieth-century art movement led by Matisse and favoring exotic colors and disjointed shapes.

fête galante [fet gah-LAHNN]   In *rococo* painting, the *theme* or scene of aristocrats being entertained or simply enjoying their leisure and other worldly pleasures.

feudalism   The customary name for the political regime in much of the medieval West, beginning in the Carolingian period. The term basically pertains to honorable relationships between lords and vassals. Vassals promised to give their lords homage and fealty (i.e, respect and fidelity), as well as aid and counsel (i.e., military service and legal advice). In return, lords promised their vassals protection and maintenance (i.e., military cover and a landed estate), or fief (*feudum* in Latin, whence the name "feudalism."). The term also signifies the exploitation of peasants by landowners.

First Great Awakening   The period of religious revivalism among Protestants that placed emphasis on a direct and personal relationship with God and undermined the traditional role and power of the established churches; centered mainly in the British American colonies during the 1730s and 1740s.

First Romanesque   The first stage of *Romanesque* architecture, about 1000–1080. First Romanesque churches had high walls, few windows, and flat wooden roofs, and were built of stone rubble and adorned with *Lombard bands* and *Lombard arcades.* Begun along the Mediterranean, in the area ranging from Dalmatia, across Northern Italy and Provence, to Catalonia.

Flamboyant style [flam-BOY-uhnt]   A late French *Gothic* architectural style of elaborate decorations and ornamentation that produce a flamelike effect.

florid baroque style   A variation of the *baroque* style specifically identified with the Catholic Church's patronage of the arts and used to glorify its beliefs.

fluting   Decorative vertical grooves carved in a column.

flying buttress   An external masonry support, found primarily in *Gothic* churches, that carries the thrust of the ceiling, or *vault,* away from the upper walls of the building to an external vertical column.

forms   In music, particular structures of arrangements of elements, such as *symphonies,* songs, concerts, and *operas.* In painting and sculpture, **form** refers to the artistic structure rather than to the material of which an artwork is made.

forum   In Rome and many Roman towns, the public place, located in the center of the town, where people gathered to socialize, transact business, and administer the government.

forte [FOR-tay]   Italian, "loud." A musical term.

fortissismo [fawrh-tis-ISS-e-moh]   In music, extremely loud; abbreviated fff.

fourth-century style   The sculptural *style* characteristic of the last phase of the *Hellenic* period, when new interpretations of beauty and movement were adopted.

fresco   A painting done on wet or dry plaster that becomes part of the plastered wall.

friars   Members of a thirteenth-century mendicant (begging) monastic order.

frieze [fREEz]   A band of painted designs or sculptured figures placed on walls; also, the central portion of a temple's *entablature* just above the *architrave.*

fugue [FEWg]   In music, a *composition* for several instruments in which a *theme* is introduced by one instrument and then repeated by each successively entering instrument so that a complicated interweaving of themes, variations, *imitations,* and echoes results; this compositional technique began in the fifteenth century and reached its zenith in the *baroque* period in works by Bach.

fundamentalism Historically, an American Protestant movement that broke free of the *evangelicals* from about 1870 to 1970, stressing biblical inerrancy, "speaking in tongues," and opposition to certain modern scientific trends, such as evolution and higher criticism. Today, fundamentalism is often aggregated with *evangelicalism* and other socially conservative religious movements.

gallery In architecture, a long, narrow passageway or corridor, usually found in churches and located above the *aisles,* and often with openings that permit viewing from above into the *nave.*

gargoyle [GAHR-goil] In architecture, a water spout in the form of a grotesque animal or human, carved from stone, placed on the edge of a roof.

genre [ZHON-ruh] From the French, "a kind, a type, or a class"; a category of artistic, musical, or literary composition, characterized by a particular *style, form,* or *content.*

genre subject In art, a scene or a person from everyday life, depicted realistically and without religious or symbolic significance.

geocentrism The belief that the earth is the center of the universe and that the sun, planets, and stars revolve around it.

ghazal [GUZ-l] A short *lyric,* usually dealing with love, composed in a single rhyme and based on the poet's personal life and loves.

glissando [gle-SAHN-doe] (plural, **glissandi**) In music, the blending of one *tone* into the next in scalelike passages that may be ascending or descending in character.

goliards [GOAL-yuhrds] Medieval roaming poets or scholars who traveled about reciting poems on topics ranging from moral lessons to the pains of love.

Gospels The first four books of the New Testament (Matthew, Mark, Luke, and John), which record the life and sayings of Jesus Christ; the word itself, from Old English, means "good news" or "good tales."

Gothic style A *style* of architecture, usually associated with churches, that originated in northern France and whose three phases—early, High, and late—lasted from the twelfth to the sixteenth century. Emerging from the *Romanesque* style, Gothic is identified by *pointed arches, ribbed vaults, stained-glass* windows, *flying buttresses,* and carvings on the exterior.

Greek cross A cross in which all the arms are of equal length; the shape used as a floor plan in many Greek or Eastern Orthodox churches.

Gregorian chant A *style* of *monophonic* church music sung in unison and without instrumental accompaniment and used in the *liturgy;* named for Pope Gregory I (590–604).

groined vault, or cross vault A ceiling, or *vault,* created when two *barrel vaults,* set at right angles, intersect.

happening A *late modern* theatrical development, combining skits with outrageous events and involving performances by painters, actors, musicians, and audience members, so as to give the impression of spontaneity.

hard-edge In *late modern* painting, a technique used in color paintings, by which the areas of *color* are precisely delineated from one another.

harmony The simultaneous combination of two or more *tones,* producing a chord; generally, the chordal characteristics of a work and the way chords interact.

heliocentrism The belief that the sun is the center of the universe and that the earth and the other planets revolve around it.

Hellenic [hell-LENN-ik] Relating to the time period in Greek civilization from 480 to 323 BCE, when the most influential Greek artists, playwrights, and philosophers, such as Praxiteles, Sophocles, and Plato, created their greatest works; associated with the *classical* style.

Hellenistic [hell-uh-NIS-tik] Relating to the time period from about 323 to 31 BCE, when Greek—and later Roman—and oriental or Middle Eastern cultures and institutions intermingled to create a heterogeneous and *cosmopolitan civilization.*

henotheism The worship of one god without denying the existence of other gods. Sometimes called "monolatry." Associated with Akhenaten in Egypt.

heresy Greek, literally "to choose," "a choice." In Christian *theology,* any church teaching deliberately chosen that is deemed unacceptable by the majority, by the popes, or by the bishops sitting in a council. By extension, any unorthodox belief or teaching in politics, philosophy, or science.

hieroglyphs [HI-uhr-uh-glifs] Pictorial characters used in Egyptian writing, which is known as hieroglyphics.

high classical style The *style* in Greek sculpture associated with the ideal physical form and perfected during the zenith of the Athenian Empire, about 450–400 BCE.

higher criticism A rational approach to Bible study, developed in German Protestant circles in the nineteenth century, that treated the biblical *scriptures* as literature and subjected them to close scrutiny, testing their literary history, authorship, and meaning.

High Renaissance The period from about 1495 to 1520, often associated with the patronage of the popes in Rome, when the most influential artists and writers of the *Renaissance,* including Michelangelo, Raphael, Leonardo da Vinci, and Machiavelli, were producing their greatest works.

high tech In architecture, a *style* that uses obvious industrial design elements with exposed parts serving as decorations.

hip-hop In *postmodern* popular culture, after 1970, an eclectic trend among African Americans and Hispanic Americans, drawing on break dancing, graffiti art, rap rhyming, and disc jockeys playing with turntables and "scratch" effects; highly influential on today's youth culture, popular music, film, and dance styles.

holiness A nineteenth-century American Protestant movement, which came out of the Methodist tradition, emphasizing holy living and the need to be "born again" as a true disciple of Jesus Christ; part of the *fundamentalist* movement after 1870.

Homeric epithet A recurring nickname, such as "Ox-eyed Hera," used in Homer's *Iliad* or *Odyssey.*

hubris [HYOO-bris] In Greek thought, human pride or arrogance that leads an individual to challenge the gods, usually provoking divine retribution.

humanism An attitude that is concerned with humanity, its achievements, and its potential; the study of the *humanities;* in the *Renaissance,* identified with *studia humanitatis.*

humanities In the nineteenth century, the study of Greek and Roman languages and literature; later set off from the sciences and expanded to include the works of all Western peoples in the arts, literature, music, philosophy, and sometimes history and religion; in *postmodernism,* extended to a global dimension.

hymn From the Greek and Latin, "ode of praise of gods or heroes"; a song of praise or thanksgiving to God or the gods, performed both with and without instrumental accompaniment.

idealism In Plato's philosophy, the theory that reality and ultimate truth are to be found not in the material world but in the spiritual realm.

idée fixe [ee-DAY FEEX] French, "fixed idea"; in music, a recurring musical *theme* that is associated with a person or a concept.

ideogram [ID-e-uh-gram] A picture drawn to represent an idea or a concept.

idyll A relatively short poem that focuses on events and *themes* of everyday life, such as family, love, and religion; popular during the *Hellenistic* period and a standard form that has been periodically revived in Western literature throughout the centuries.

illuminated manuscript A richly decorated book, painted with brilliant colors and gold leaf, usually of sacred writings; popular in the West in the Middle Ages.

illusionism The use of painting *techniques* in *florid baroque* art to create the appearance that decorated areas are part of the surrounding architecture, usually employed in ceiling decorations.

imitation In music, a *technique* in which a musical idea, or motif, is presented by one voice or instrument and is then followed immediately by a restatement by another voice or instrument; the effect is that of a musical relay race.

impasto [ihm-PAHS-toe] In painting, the application of thick layers of pigment.

impressionism In painting, a *style* introduced in the 1870s, marked by an attempt to catch spontaneous impressions, often involving the play of sunlight on ordinary events and scenes observed outdoors; in music, a style of *composition* designed to create a vague and dreamy mood through gliding melodies and shimmering *tone colors.*

impressionistic In art, relating to the representation of a scene using the simplest details to create an illusion of reality by evoking subjective impressions rather than aiming for a totally realistic effect; characterized by images that are insubstantial and barely sketched in.

incunabula (singular, **incunabulum**) The collection of books printed before 1500 CE.

inductive reasoning The process of reasoning from particulars to the general or from single parts to the whole and/or final conclusion.

installation art A boundary-challenging type of art born in the 1960s that creates architectural tableaux, using objects drawn from and making references to artistic sources (such as music, painting, sculpture, and theater) and the workaday world (such as everyday tasks, media images, and foodstuffs) and that may include a human presence. Associated with the work of Ann Hamilton.

international style In twentieth-century architecture, a *style* and method of construction that capitalized on modern materials, such as ferro-concrete, glass, and steel, and that produced the popular "glass box" skyscrapers and variously shaped private houses.

investiture controversy The long quarrel between the medieval popes and the German emperors over their respective rights and responsibilities. The struggle sprang from the denial by the church, especially by the eleventh century popes, of the right of laypeople to invest clerics with the symbols of their church offices.

Ionic The Greek architectural order, developed in Ionia, in which columns are slender, sit on a base, and have *capitals* decorated with scrolls.

isorhythm In music, a unifying method based on rhythmic patterns rather than *melodic* patterns.

Italo-Byzantine style [ih-TAL-o-BIZ-uhn-teen] The *style* of Italian *Gothic* painting that reflected the influence of *Byzantine* paintings, *mosaics,* and icons.

iwan [eye-van] In Islamic architecture, a vaulted hall. In the 4-*iwan mosque,* one *iwan* was used for prayers and the other three for study or rest.

jazz A type of music, instrumental and vocal, originating in the African American community and rooted in African, African American, and Western musical forms and traditions.

Jesuits [JEZH-oo-its] Members of the Society of Jesus, the best-organized and most effective monastic order founded during the *Counter-Reformation* to combat Protestantism and spread Roman Catholicism around the world.

jihad [JEE-HAD] Originally, this Arabic term meant "to strive" or "to struggle" and, as such, was identified with any pious Muslim combating sin and trying not to do evil. In modern times, radical Islamic states and groups have given the term new meaning as "Holy War" and have used it to justify military and other violent action against their enemies. A central belief in Islam.

key In music, a tonal system consisting of seven *tones* in fixed relationship to a tonic, or keynote. Since the *Renaissance,* key has been the structural foundation of the bulk of Western music, down to the *modernist* period.

keystone The central stone at the top of an arch that locks the other stones in place.

Koine [KOI-nay] A colloquial Greek language spoken in the *Hellenistic* world that helped tie together that *civilization.*

korē [KOH-ray] An *Archaic* Greek standing statue of a young draped female.

kouros [KOO-rus] An *Archaic* Greek standing statue of a young naked male.

late Gothic style A *style* characterized in architecture by ornate decoration and tall cathedral windows and spires and in painting and sculpture by increased refinement of details and a trend toward naturalism; popular in the fourteenth and fifteenth centuries in central and western Europe.

late mannerism The last stage of the *mannerist* movement, characterized by exaggeration and distortion, especially in painting.

late modernism The last stage of *modernism,* characterized by an increasing sense of existential despair, an attraction to non-Western cultures, and extreme experimentalism.

lay A short *lyric* or narrative poem meant to be sung to the accompaniment of an instrument such as a harp; based on Celtic legends but usually set in feudal times and focused on courtly love *themes,* especially adulterous passion. The oldest surviving lays are those of the twelfth-century poet Marie de France.

leitmotif [LITE-mo-teef] In music, and especially in Wagner's *operas,* the use of recurring *themes* associated with particular characters, objects, or ideas.

liberalism In political thought, a set of beliefs advocating certain personal, economic, and natural rights based on assumptions about the perfectibility and autonomy of human beings and the notion of progress, as first expressed in the writings of John Locke.

liberation theology A reform movement, which began in the late 1960s among Roman Catholic priests and nuns in Latin America, blending Christian teachings on social and economic justice with Marxist theory. After this movement went global, the Vatican withdrew its support in the 1980s, though liberation theology remains an underground force in some parts of the world today.

libretto [lih-BRET-oh] In Italian, "little book"; the text or words of an *opera,* an *oratorio,* or a musical work of a similar dramatic nature involving a written text.

line The mark—straight or curved, thick or thin, light or dark—made by the artist in a work of art.

Linear A In Minoan *civilization,* a type of script still undeciphered that lasted from about 1800 to 1400 BCE.

Linear B In Minoan *civilization,* an early form of Greek writing that flourished on Crete from about 1400 until about 1300 BCE and lasted in a few scattered places on the Greek mainland until about 1150 BCE; used to record commercial transactions.

liturgical drama Religious dramas, popular between the twelfth and sixteenth centuries, based on biblical stories with musical accompaniment that were staged in the area in front of the church, performed at first in Latin but later in the *vernacular languages;* the mystery plays (*mystery* is derived from the Latin for "action") are the most famous type of liturgical drama.

liturgy A rite or ritual, such as prayers or ceremonies, practiced by a religious group in public worship.

local color In literature, the use of detail peculiar to a particular region and environment to add interest and authenticity to a narrative, including description of the locale, customs, speech, and music. Local color was an especially popular development in American literature in the late nineteenth century.

logical positivism A school of modern philosophy that seeks truth by defining terms and clarifying statements and asserts that metaphysical theories are meaningless.

logos [LOWG-os] In *Stoicism,* the name for the supreme being or for reason—the controlling principle of the universe—believed to be present both in nature and in each human being.

Lombard arcades In architecture, a sequence of decorative *arcades* beneath the eaves of a building. First used in churches in Lombardy (North Central Italy). A defining feature of the *First Romanesque.*

Lombard bands In architecture, a web of vertical bands or buttresses along the sides of a building. First used in churches in Lombardy (North Central Italy). A defining feature of the *First Romanesque.*

luminism In nineteenth-century American landscape painting, a group of artists, who were inspired by the vastness of the American west and influenced by *transcendentalism,* approached their work by consciously removing themselves from their paintings.

lute In music, a wooden instrument, plucked or bowed, consisting of a sound box with an elaborately carved sound hole and a neck across which the (often twelve) strings pass. Introduced during the High Middle Ages, the lute enjoyed a height of popularity in Europe from the seventeenth to eighteenth century.

Lutheranism The doctrine, *liturgy,* and institutional structure of the church founded in the sixteenth century by Martin Luther, who stressed the authority of the Bible, the faith of the individual, and the worshiper's direct communication with God as the bases of his new religion.

lyre In music, a handheld stringed instrument, with or without a sound box, used by ancient Egyptians, Assyrians, and Greeks. In Greek culture, the lyre was played to accompany song and recitation.

lyric A short subjective poem that expresses intense personal emotion.

lyric poetry In Greece, verses sung and accompanied by the *lyre;* today, intensely personal poetry.

Machiavellianism [mahk-ih-uh-VEL-ih-uhn-iz-uhm] The view that politics should be separated from morals and dedicated to the achievement of desired ends through any means necessary ("the end justifies the means"); derived from the political writings of Machiavelli.

madrasah [mah-DRASS-ah] An Arabic term meaning a religious school for advanced study; a forerunner of the Islamic university. Today, madrasahs are schools for Islamic youth, and their curriculum is based on the Qur'an.

madrigal [MAD-rih-guhl] A *polyphonic* song performed without accompaniment and based on a secular text, often a love *lyric;* especially popular in the sixteenth century.

maenad [MEE-nad] A woman who worshiped Dionysus, often in a state of frenzy.

magic realism A literary and artistic *style* identified with Latin American *postmodernism* that mixes realistic and supernatural elements to create imaginary or fantastic scenes.

mannerism A cultural movement between 1520 and 1600 that grew out of a rebellion against the *Renaissance's* artistic norms of symmetry and balance; characterized in art by distortion and incongruity and in thought and literature by the belief that human nature is depraved.

maqamah [mah-kah-mah] In Arabic, "assembly." A Muslim literary *genre,* intended for educated readers, that recounted stories of rogues and con men; filled with wordplay, humor, and keen usage of Arabic language and grammar. Created by al-Hamadhani in the tenth century.

Mass In religion, the ritual celebrating the Eucharist, or Holy Communion, primarily in the Roman Catholic Church. The Mass has two parts, the Ordinary and the Proper; the former remains the same throughout the church year, whereas the latter changes for each date and service. The Mass Ordinary is composed of the Kyrie, Gloria, Credo, Sanctus, and Agnus Dei; the Mass Proper includes the Introit, Gradual, Alleluia or Tract, Sequence, Offertory, and Communion. In music, a musical setting of certain parts of the Mass, especially the Kyrie, Gloria, Credo, Sanctus, Benedictus, and Agnus Dei. The first complete Mass Ordinary was composed by Guillaume de Machaut [mah-SHOH] (about 1300–1377) in the fourteenth century.

mass culture The tastes, values, and interests of the classes that dominate modern industrialized society, especially the consumer-oriented American middle class.

matriarchy Greek, literally "mother-rule"; term for historical or mythical societies in which political and social power is in the hands of women.

medallion In Roman architecture, a circular decoration often found on triumphal arches enclosing a scene or portrait; in general architectural use, a tablet or panel in a wall or window containing a figure or an ornament.

medium The material from which an artwork is made.

melisma In music, in *plainsong,* a style of singing in which a group of notes is sung to the same syllable; the opposite of *syllabic* singing.

melody A succession of musical *tones* having a distinctive shape and rhythm.

Messiah A Hebrew word meaning "the anointed one," or one chosen by God to be his representative on earth; in Judaism, a savior who will come bringing peace and justice; in Christianity, Jesus Christ (*Christ* is derived from a Greek word meaning "the anointed one").

metope [MET-uh-pee]   In architecture, a panel, often decorated, between two *triglyphs* on the *entablature* of a *Doric* Greek temple.

mezzotint   Also known as halftone. An early type of color print, made with a metal plate, characterized by subtle gradations of shadings and clear definition of *line*; developed in about 1650 in the Netherlands.

microtone   In music, an interval, or distance between a sound (pitch) on a scale, that is smaller than a semi*tone*—the smallest interval in mainstream Western music prior to *jazz*. Muslim music uses a microtonal system.

minaret   In Islamic architecture, a tall, slender tower with a pointed top, from which the daily calls to prayer are delivered; located near a *mosque.*

minbar [min-bar]   In Muslim *mosque* architecture, a pulpit with steps, sometimes on wheels for portability; used by a cleric for leading prayers and giving sermons.

miniature   A small painting, usually of a religious nature, found in *illuminated manuscripts*; also, a small portrait.

minimalism   A trend in *late modern* and *postmodern* art, architecture, and music that found beauty in the bare essentials and thus stripped art, buildings, and music to their basic elements. The minimalist aesthetic was a strong influence in the architecture of Mies van der Rohe, many art styles, including *conceptual art, environmental art,* and *op art,* and the music of Philip Glass.

minstrel   A professional entertainer of the twelfth to seventeenth century; especially a secular musician; also called "jongleur."

minuet and trio   In music, a *classical* music form, based on two French court dances of the same name, dating from the seventeenth and eighteenth centuries; often paired in the third section of *symphonies* in the *classical* period. Typically, the minuet was in ¾ time and with a moderate *tempo*, while the trio provided contrast but had no standard form.

modernism   A late-nineteenth- and twentieth-century cultural, artistic, and literary movement that rejected much of the past and focused on the current, the secular, and the revolutionary in search of new forms of expression; the dominant style of the twentieth century until 1970.

Modernism   In Roman Catholic Church history, a liberal movement among progressive churchpeople, 1850 to 1910, which applied new findings in history, philosophy, and psychology to traditional church teachings; condemned by the Vatican in 1907.

modes   A series of musical *scales* devised by the Greeks and believed by them to create certain emotional or ethical effects on the listener.

monophony [muh-NOF-uh-nee]   A *style* of music in which there is only a single line of melody; the *Gregorian chants* are the most famous examples of monophonic music.

monotheism   From the Greek *monos*, "single, alone," and the Greek *theos*, "god"; the belief that there is only one God.

montage   In film, a technique consisting of highly elaborate editing patterns and rhythms.

mood   In music, the emotional impact of a *composition* on the feelings of a listener.

mosaic   An art form or decoration, usually on a wall or a floor, created by inlaying small pieces of glass, shell, or stone in cement or plaster to create pictures or patterns.

mosque   A Muslim place of worship, often distinguished by a dome-shaped central building placed in an open space surrounded by a wall.

motet   A multivoiced song with words of a sacred or secular text, usually sung without accompanying instruments; developed in the thirteenth century.

mural   A wall painting, usually quite large, used to decorate a private or public structure.

muse   In Greek religion, any one of the nine sister goddesses who preside over the creative arts and sciences.

music drama   An *opera* in which the action and music are continuous, not broken up into separate *arias* and *recitatives*, and the music is determined by its dramatic appropriateness, producing a work in which music, words, and staging are fused; the term was coined by Wagner.

myth   A traditional story about gods, heroes, or ancestors that serves to exemplify essential moral, political, social, or psychological characteristics believed to exist in a given society.

narrative voice   In literature, the *narrator,* a key element in fiction. An omniscient narrator, usually in the third person, knows everything about the *plot* and *characters,* regardless of time and place—typical of nineteenth-century novels. In *modernist* fiction, the narrative voice tends to be disjointed, unreliable, and often in the first person.

narrator   The speaker whose voice we hear in a story or poem.

narthex   The porch or vestibule of a church, usually enclosed, through which worshipers walk before entering the *nave.*

naturalism   In literature, a late-nineteenth-century movement inspired by the methods of science and the insights of sociology, concerned with an objective depiction of the ugly side of industrial society.

natural law   In *Stoicism* and later in other philosophies, a body of laws or principles that are believed to be derived from nature and binding on human society and that constitute a higher form of justice than civil or judicial law.

natural philosophy   Science based on philosophical speculation and experiments or data, founded in Ionian Greece in the sixth century BCE; a term that embraced both science and philosophy until about 1800 CE.

nave   The central longitudinal area of a church, extending from the entrance to the *apse* and flanked by *aisles.*

neoclassical style   In the late eighteenth century, an artistic and literary movement that emerged as a reaction to the *rococo* style and that sought inspiration from ancient *classicism.* In the twentieth century, between 1919 and 1951, *neoclassicism* in music was a style that rejected the emotionalism favored by *romantic* composers as well as the dense orchestral sounds of the *impressionists*; instead, it borrowed features from seventeenth- and eighteenth-century music and practiced the ideals of balance, clarity of texture, and non-programmatic works.

neoclassicism   In the late third century BCE, an artistic movement in the disintegrating *Hellenistic* world that sought inspiration in the Athenian Golden Age of the fifth and fourth centuries BCE; and, since 1970, *neoclassicism* has been a highly visible submovement in *postmodernism*, particularly prominent in painting and architecture, that restates the principles of *classical* art—balance, harmony, idealism.

neoexpressionism   A submovement in *postmodernism*, associated primarily with painting, that offers social criticism and is concerned with the expression of the artist's feelings.

Neolithic   Literally, "new stone"; used to define the New Stone Age, when human *cultures* evolved into agrarian systems and settled communities; dating from about 10,000 or 8000 BCE to about 3000 BCE.

neoorthodoxy   A twentieth-century Protestant movement, dedicated to recentering orthodox theology in Christian thought and emphasizing the central role played by God in history. Founded after World War I in opposition to the *Social Gospel.*

neoplatonism   A philosophy based on Plato's ideas that was developed during the Roman period in an attempt to reconcile the dichotomy between Plato's concept of an eternal World of Ideas and the ever-changing physical world; in the fifteenth-century *Renaissance,* it served as a philosophical guide for Italian humanists who sought to reconcile late medieval Christian beliefs with *classical* thinking.

neorealism   A submovement in *postmodernism* that is based on a photographic sense of detail and harks back to many of the qualities of nineteenth-century *realism.*

neoromanticism   A *postmodern* movement in music, starting after 1970, which rejects *atonality* and draws inspiration from the music of the *romantic* period.

neumes   From the Greek *neuma,* a "gesture," or "sigh"; a system of musical notation, used from the Carolingian period to the fourteenth century, inserted into *plainchant* manuscripts to signal pitch and to a lesser degree the shape of the *melody.*

New Comedy   The *style* of comedy favored by *Hellenistic* playwrights, concentrating on gentle satirical *themes*—in particular, romantic *plots* with stock *characters* and predictable endings.

nihilism   The denial of any objective ground of truth and, in particular, of moral truths.

nominalism [NAHM-uh-nuhl-iz-uhm]   In medieval thought, the school that held that objects were separate unto themselves but could, for convenience, be treated in a collective sense because they shared certain characteristics; opposed to *realism.*

northern Renaissance   The sixteenth-century cultural movement in northern Europe that was launched by the northward spread of Italian *Renaissance* art, culture, and ideals. The northern Renaissance differed from the Italian Renaissance largely because of the persistence of the *late Gothic style* and the unfolding of the *Reformation* after 1520.

Nouvelle Vague   French, "New Wave"; a *late modern* movement in French film, featuring innovative narrative structures and various experimental cinematic techniques. French word for "New Wave" films in the post–World War II period that experimented with new ways to capture scenes and events.

octave   In music, usually the eight-tone interval between a note and a second note of the same name, as in C to C.

oculus [AHK-yuh-lus]   The circular opening at the top of a dome; derived from the Latin word for "eye."

Old Comedy   The *style* of *comedy* established by Aristophanes in the fifth century BCE, distinguished by a strong element of political and social satire.

oligarchy   From the Greek *oligos,* "few"; a state ruled by the few, especially by a small fraction of persons or families.

Olympian deities   In Greek religion, sky gods and goddesses who lived on mountaintops and were worshiped mainly by the Greek aristocracy.

op art   A *late modern* art movement, using *abstract,* mathematically based forms to create stimulating images for the eyes, such as optical patterns, lingering images, and whirling effects.

opera   A drama or play set to music and consisting of vocal pieces with *orchestral* accompaniment; acting, scenery, and sometimes *choruses* and dancing are used to heighten the dramatic values of operas.

oratorio   A choral work based on religious events or *scripture* employing singers, *choruses,* and *orchestra,* but without scenery or staging and performed usually in a church or a concert hall.

orchestra   In Greek theaters, the circular area where the *chorus* performed in front of the audience; in music, a group of instrumentalists, including string players, who play together.

organum [OR-guh-nuhm]   In the ninth through the thirteenth centuries, a simple and early form of *polyphonic* music consisting of a main *melody* sung along with a *Gregorian chant;* by the thirteenth century it had developed into a complex multivoiced song.

Orientalizing style   A phase of Greek art, particularly Greek vase painting, lasting from about 700 to 530 BCE, which drew inspiration from Near Eastern art, including artistic techniques, vessel forms, decorative motifs, and subjects.

Paleolithic   Literally, "old stone"; used to define the Old Stone Age, when crude stones and tools were used; dating from about 2,000,000 BCE to about 10,000 BCE.

pantheism   The doctrine of or belief in multitudes of deities found in nature; a recurrent belief since prehistoric times. Prominent in nineteenth-century *romanticism.*

pantomime   In Roman times, enormous dramatic productions featuring instrumental music and dances, favored by the masses; later, a type of dramatic or dancing performance in which the story is told with expressive or even exaggerated bodily and facial movements.

paradigm shift   The exchange of one worldview or perspective for another, as, for example, the shift from earth-centered astronomy to sun-centered astronomy between 1550 and 1700; a **paradigm** is an unconsciously agreed-on pattern of thought in a scientific discipline and, by extension, any shared set of beliefs and habits of thought; a term coined by Thomas Kuhn.

parchment   A writing surface, prepared from calf-, sheep-, and goatskins, developed in ancient Pergamum. Parchment's supple surface allowed the storing of writing on both sides of a page and thus opened the door to the first books.

pastoral   A type of *Hellenistic* poetry that idealized rural customs and farming, especially the simple life of shepherds, and deprecated urban living.

pavane [puh-VAHN]   A sixteenth- and seventeenth-century English court dance of Italian origin; the dance is performed by couples to stately music. Ravel based *Pavane for a Dead Princess* (1899) on this *baroque* dance form.

Pax Romana   Latin, the "Roman Peace." A term applied to the first two centuries of the Roman Empire when the Mediterranean was at peace, albeit on Roman terms.

pediment   In *classical*-style architecture, the triangular-shaped area or gable at the end of the building formed by the sloping roof and the *cornice.*

pendentive [pen-DEN-tiv]   In architecture, a triangular, concave-shaped section of *vaulting* between the rim of a dome and the pair of arches that support it; used in Byzantine and Islamic architecture.

performance art   A democratic type of mixed-media art born in the 1960s that ignores artistic boundaries, mixing high art (such as music, painting, and theater) and popular art (such as rock and roll, film, and fads), to create a unique, nonreproducible, artistic experience. Associated with the work of Laurie Anderson.

peristyle [PAIR-uh-stile] A colonnade around an open courtyard or a building.

Perpendicular style The highly decorative *style* of *late Gothic* architecture that developed in England at the same time as the *late Gothic* on the European continent.

Persian miniature A *style* of *miniature* painting that flourished in Persia from the thirteenth to seventeenth century; characterized by rectangular designs, the depiction of the human figure as about one-fifth the height of the painting, and refined detail.

perspective A technique or formula for creating the illusion or appearance of depth and distance on a two-dimensional surface. **Atmospheric perspective** is achieved in many ways: by diminishing color intensity, by omitting detail, and by blurring the lines of an object. **Linear perspective,** based on mathematical calculations, is achieved by having parallel lines or lines of projection appearing to converge at a single point, known as the *vanishing point,* on the horizon of the flat surface and by diminishing distant objects in size according to scale to make them appear to recede from the viewer.

Petrine Idea In Catholic *theology,* the idea that as Christ had made St. Peter the leader of the apostles (Matthew 16:18–19), his successors, the bishops of Rome (or popes), inherited his authority.

philosophes [FEEL-uh-sawfs] A group of European thinkers and writers who popularized the ideas of the *Enlightenment* through essays, novels, plays, and other works, hoping to change the climate of opinion and bring about social and political reform.

phonogram A symbol used to represent a syllable, a word, or a sound.

photomontage An art *medium,* in which photographs, from varied sources, but especially from newspapers, are cut up, rearranged, and pasted onto a surface, such as a poster board. When done, the photomontage usually sent a political or social message. Starting in 1918, the photomontage was part of the *Dada* movement's assault against traditional art.

Physiocrats [FIZ-ih-uh-kratz] A group of writers, primarily French, who dealt with economic issues during the *Enlightenment,* in particular calling for improved agricultural productivity and questioning the state's role in economic affairs.

piano Italian, "soft." In music, softly. Also, the usual term for *pianoforte.*

pianissimo Italian, "very softly," a musical term.

pianoforte [pee-an-o-FOR-tay] A piano; derived from the Italian for "soft/loud," terms used to describe the two types of sound emitted by a stringed instrument whose wires are struck with felt-covered hammers operated from a keyboard.

picaresque novel From the Spanish term for "rogue." A type of literature, originating in sixteenth-century Spain, that recounted the comic misadventures of a roguish hero who lived by his wits, often at the expense of the high and mighty; influenced novel writing across Europe, especially in England, France, and Germany, until about 1800; the anonymous *Lazarillo de Tormes* (1554) was the first picaresque novel.

pictogram A carefully drawn, often stylized, picture that represents a particular object.

pier In architecture, a vertical masonry structure that may support a *vault,* an arch, or a roof; in *Gothic* churches, piers were often clustered together to form massive supports.

Pietà [pee-ay-TAH] A painting or sculpture depicting the mourning Virgin and the dead Christ.

Pietism A religious reform movement among German Lutherans, which stressed personal piety, along with support for social programs for the poor; part of the general religious ferment of western Europe in the late 1600s and early 1700s and a catalyst for the *First Great Awakening* in British Colonial America in the 1700s.

pilaster [pih-LAS-tuhr] In architecture, a vertical, rectangular decorative device projecting from a wall that gives the appearance of a column with a base and a *capital;* sometimes called an applied column.

Pinteresque In the theater, a dramatic style, attributed to the British playwright Harold Pinter; characterized by enigmatic *plots* and, especially, long pauses in the dialogue.

Platonism The collective beliefs and arguments presented in Plato's writings stressing especially that actual things are copies of ideas.

plainsong Also called *plainchant.* In music, the *monophonic* chant sung in the *liturgy* of the Roman Catholic Church.

plot The action, or arrangement of incidents, in a story.

podium In architecture, a low wall serving as a foundation; a platform.

poetry Language that is concentrated and imaginative, marked by meter, rhythm, rhyme, and imagery.

pointed arch A key element of *Gothic* architecture, probably introduced from the Muslim world, which permitted the joining of two arches of identical height but different width. Pointed arches led to complex designs and reduced the need for thick walls to support the massive *vaults* and roofs typical of the *Romanesque style.*

pointillism [PWANT-il-iz-uhm] Also known as divisionism, a *style* of painting, perfected by Seurat, in which tiny dots of paint are applied to the canvas in such a way that when they are viewed from a distance they merge and blend to form recognizable objects with natural effects of color, light, and shade.

polyphony [puh-LIF-uh-nee] A style of musical *composition* in which two or more voices or melodic lines are woven together.

polytheism [PAHL-e-the-iz-uhm] The doctrine of or belief in more than one deity.

pop art An artistic *style* popular between 1960 and 1970 in which commonplace commercial objects drawn from *mass culture,* such as soup cans, fast foods, and comic strips, became the subjects of art.

portico In architecture, a covered entrance to a building, usually with a separate roof supported by columns.

porticus A covered, usually colonnaded, porch or walkway. A porticus might complement one building or serve to join two or more buildings together.

post-and-lintel construction A basic architectural form in which upright posts, or columns, support a horizontal lintel, or beam.

post-beam-triangle construction The generic name given to Greek architecture that includes the post, or column; the beam, or lintel; and the triangular-shaped area, or *pediment.*

postimpressionism A late-nineteenth-century artistic movement that extended the boundaries of *impressionism* in new directions to focus on structure, composition, fantasy, and subjective expression.

postmodernism An artistic, cultural, and intellectual movement, originating in about 1970, that is more optimistic than *modernism*, embraces an open-ended and democratic global *civilization*, freely adapts elements of high culture and *mass culture*, and manifests itself chiefly through revivals of earlier styles, giving rise to *neoclassicism*, *neoexpressionism*, and *neorealism*.

poststructuralism In analytical theory, a set of *techniques*, growing out of *structuralism*, which were used to show that meaning is shifting and unstable.

Praxitelean curve [prak-sit-i-LEE-an] The graceful line of the sculptured body in the *contrapposto* stance, perfected by the *fourth-century style* sculptor Praxiteles.

primitivism In painting, the "primitives" are those painters of the Netherlandish and Italian schools who flourished before 1500, thus all Netherlandish painters between the van Eycks and Dürer and all Italian painters between Giotto and Raphael; more generally, the term reflects modern artists' fascination with non-Western art forms, as in Gauguin's Tahitian-inspired paintings. In literature, primitivism has complex meanings; on the one hand, it refers to the notion of a golden age, a world of lost innocence, which appeared in both ancient pagan and Christian writings; on the other hand, it is a modern term used to denote two species of cultural relativism, which either finds people isolated from civilization to be superior to those living in civilized and urban settings, as in the cult of the noble savage (Rousseau), or respects native peoples and their cultures within their own settings, yet accepts that natives can be as cruel as Europeans (the view expressed by Montaigne).

principate Term applied to the Roman imperial regime inaugurated by Augustus Caesar (31 BCE–14 CE), who was designated "princeps," meaning "first citizen." The principate lasted until the death of Emperor Alexander Severus in 235 CE.

problem play A type of drama that focuses on a specific social problem; the Swedish playwright Ibsen was a pioneer of this *genre*, as in *A Doll's House* (1879), concerning women's independence.

program music Instrumental music that depicts a narrative, portrays a *setting*, or suggests a sequence of events; often based on other sources, such as a poem or a play.

prose The ordinary language used in speaking and writing.

prosimetric A literary work in both *prose* and verse. Developed in antiquity, this literary *genre* was popularized in the Middle Ages by Boethius's *Consolation of Philosophy* and adapted for the vernacular by Dante's *La Vita Nuova* (*The New Life*).

proverb A pithy saying, thought to convey folk wisdom or a general truth.

Puritanism The beliefs and practices of the Puritans, a small but influential religious group devoted to the teachings of John Calvin; they stressed strict rules of personal and public behavior and practiced their beliefs in England and the New World during the seventeenth century.

qasida [kah-SEE-dah] In Arabic, "ode." An ode composed in varied meters and with a single rhyme; that is, all lines end in the same rhyming sound. The leading poetic *genre* in Muslim literature.

qiblah [kee-blah] In Islamic *mosque* architecture, a niche, often richly decorated, pointing the direction for prayer, that is, toward the Kaaba in Mecca.

ragtime A type of instrumental music, popularized by African Americans in the late nineteenth and early twentieth centuries, with a strongly syncopated rhythm and a lively *melody*.

Rayonnant [ray-yo-NAHNN] A decorative *style* in French architecture associated with the High *Gothic* period, in which walls were replaced by sheets of *stained glass* framed by elegant stone *traceries*. Also called "Radiant."

realism In medieval philosophy, the school that asserted that objects contained common or universal qualities that were not always apparent to the human senses but that were more real or true than the objects' physical attributes; opposed to *nominalism*. In art and literature, a mid- to late-nineteenth-century style that focused on the everyday lives of the middle and lower classes, portraying their world in a serious, accurate, and unsentimental way; opposed to *romanticism*.

recitative [ress-uh-tuh-TEEV] In music, a rhythmically free but often stylized declamation, midway between singing and ordinary speech, that serves as a transition between *arias* or as a narrative device in an *opera*.

Reformation The sixteenth-century religious movement that looked back to the ideals of early Christianity, called for moral and structural changes in the church, and led ultimately to the founding of the various Protestant churches.

refrain In music, a recurring musical passage or phrase; called *ritornello* in Italian.

regalia Plural in form, often used with a singular verb. The emblems and symbols of royalty, as the crown and scepter.

relief In sculpture, figures or forms that are carved so that they project from the flat surface of a stone or metal background. **High relief** projects sharply from the surface; **low relief**, or **bas relief**, is more shallow.

Renaissance [ren-uh-SAHNS] From the French for "rebirth"; the artistic, cultural, and intellectual movement marked by a revival of *classical* and *humanistic* values that began in Italy in the mid–fourteenth century and had spread across Europe by the mid–sixteenth century.

representational art Art that presents a likeness of the world as it appears to the naked eye.

restrained baroque style A variation of the *baroque* style identified with Dutch and English architects and painters who wanted to reduce *baroque* grandeur and exuberance to a more human scale.

revenge tragedy A type of play popular in sixteenth-century England, probably rooted in Roman *tragedies* and concerned with the need for a family to seek revenge for the murder of a relative.

ribbed vault A masonry roof with a framework of arches or ribs that reinforce and decorate the *vault* ceiling.

rocaille [roh-KYE] In *rococo* design, the stucco ornaments shaped like leaves, flowers, and ribbons that decorate walls and ceilings.

rococo style [ruh-KOH-koh] An artistic and cultural *style* that grew out of the *baroque* style but that was more intimate and personal and emphasized the frivolous and superficial side of aristocratic life.

romance A story derived from legends associated with Troy or Celtic culture but often set in feudal times and centered on *themes* of licit and illicit love between noble lords and ladies.

Romanesque style [roh-muhn-ESK] A *style* of architecture, usually associated with churches built in the eleventh and twelfth centuries, that was inspired by Roman architectural features, such as the *basilica*, and was thus Roman-like. Romanesque buildings were massive, with round arches and *barrel* or *groined vault* ceilings, and had less exterior decoration than *Gothic* churches.

romanticism   An intellectual, artistic, and literary movement that began in the late eighteenth century as a reaction to *neoclassicism* and stressed the emotional, mysterious, and imaginative side of human behavior and the unruly side of nature.

rondeau [RON-doh], (plural, **rondeaux**)   A French verse form, consisting of thirteen lines, or sometimes ten lines, dating from the late Middle Ages.

rose window   A large circular window, made of *stained glass* and held together with lead and carved stones set in patterns, or *tracery,* and located over an entrance in a *Gothic cathedral.*

sacred music   Religious music, such as *Gregorian chants, Masses,* and hymns.

sarcophagus [sahr-KAHF-uh-guhs] (plural, **sarcophagi**)   From the Greek meaning "flesh-eating stone"; a marble or stone coffin or tomb, usually decorated with carvings, used first by Romans and later by Christians for burial of the dead.

satire   From the Latin, "medley"—a cooking term; a literary *genre* that originated in ancient Rome and was characterized by two basic forms: (a) tolerant and amused observation of the human scene, modeled on Horace's style, and (b) bitter and sarcastic denunciation of all behavior and thought outside a civilized norm, modeled on Juvenal's style. In modern times, a literary work that holds up human vices and follies to ridicule or scorn.

satyr-play [SAT-uhr]   A comic play, often featuring sexual *themes,* performed at the Greek drama festivals along with the *tragedies.*

scale   A set pattern of *tones* (or notes) arranged from low to high.

scenographic [see-nuh-GRAF-ik]   In *Renaissance* architecture, a building style that envisioned buildings as composed of separate units; in the painting of stage scenery, the art of *perspective* representation.

scherzo [SKAIRT-so]   From the Italian for "joke"; a quick and lively instrumental *composition* or movement found in *sonatas* and *symphonies.*

Scholasticism   In medieval times, the body or collection of knowledge that tried to harmonize Aristotle's writings with Christian doctrine; also, a way of thinking and establishing sets of arguments.

Scientific Revolution   The seventeenth-century intellectual movement, based originally on discoveries in astronomy and physics, that challenged and overturned medieval views about the order of the universe and the theories used to explain motion.

scripture   The sacred writings of any religion, as the Bible in Judaism and Christianity.

Second Romanesque   The second and mature stage of *Romanesque* architecture, about 1080–1200. Second Romanesque churches were richly decorated and built on a vast scale, including such features as double *transepts,* double *aisles,* crossing towers, and towers at the ends of the *transepts;* associated with Cluniac monasticism.

secular music   Nonreligious music, such as *symphonies,* songs, and dances.

serenade   In music, a lighthearted piece, intended to be performed outdoors in the evening; popular in the eighteenth and nineteenth centuries.

serial music   A type of musical composition based on a *twelve-tone scale* arranged any way the composer chooses;

the absence of a tonal center in serial music leads to *atonality.*

setting   In literature, the background against which the action takes place; in a representational artwork, the time and place depicted.

seven liberal arts   Essentially, the curriculum of the ancient schools. Canonized by Martianus Capella in *The Marriage of Mercury and Philology* (late fifth century CE), the arts were grammar, rhetoric, dialectic (logic), arithmetic, geometry, astronomy, and music. In medieval schools, the arts were often divided into the Trivium (grammar, rhetoric, and dialectic) and the Quadrivium (arithmetic, geometry, astronomy, and music).

Severe style   The first sculptural *style* of the *classical* period in Greece, which retained stylistic elements from the *Archaic* style.

sfumato [sfoo-MAH-toh]   In painting, the blending of one *tone* into another to blur the outline of a form and give the canvas a smokelike appearance; a technique perfected by Leonardo da Vinci.

shaft graves   Deep pit burial sites; the dead were usually placed at the bottom of the shafts; a burial practice in Mycenaean Greece.

skene [SKEE-nee]   A small building behind the *orchestra* in a Greek theater, used as a prop and as a storehouse for theatrical materials.

Skepticism   A *Hellenistic* philosophy that questioned whether anything could be known for certain, argued that all beliefs were relative, and concluded that *autarky* could be achieved only by recognizing that inquiry was fruitless.

slave narrative   A literary *genre,* either written by slaves or told by slaves to secretaries, which emerged prior to the American Civil War; the genre was launched by the *Narrative of the Life of Frederick Douglass, an American Slave* (1845); the harsh details of the inhumane and unjust slave system, as reported in these narratives, contributed to *realist* literature.

social contract   In political thought, an agreement or contract between the people and their rulers defining the rights and duties of each so that a civil society might be created.

Social Gospel   A Protestant movement, mainly in the United States, whose heyday was from 1880 to 1945, which stressed social improvement rather than personal piety; the religious equivalent of *liberal* politics.

socialism   An economic and political system in which goods and property are owned collectively or by the state; the socialist movement began as a reaction to the excesses of the factory system in the nineteenth century and ultimately called for either reforming or abolishing industrial capitalism.

socialist realism   A Marxist artistic theory that calls for the use of literature, music, and the arts in the service of the ideals and goals of socialism and/or communism, with an emphasis in painting on the realistic portrayal of objects.

solipsism   In philosophy, the sense that only one's self exists or can be known.

sonata [soh-NAH-tah]   In music, an instrumental *composition,* usually in three or four movements.

sonata form   A musical *form* or structure consisting of three (or sometimes four) sections that vary in *key, tempo,* and *mood.*

squinch   In architecture, an arch, or a set of gradually wider and projecting arches placed diagonally at the internal angles of towers in order to mount a round or polygonal superstructure on a square plan, used in Gothic, Byzantine, and Islamic architecture (cf. *pendentives*).

stained glass   An art form characterized by many small pieces of tinted glass bound together by strips of lead, usually to produce a pictorial scene of a religious theme; developed by *Romanesque* artists and a central feature of *Gothic* churches.

stele [STEE-lee]   A carved or inscribed vertical stone pillar or slab, often used for commemorative purposes.

stereobate   In Greek architecture, the stepped base on which a temple stands.

Stoicism [STO-ih-sihz-uhm]   The most popular and influential *Hellenistic* philosophy, advocating a restrained way of life, a toleration for others, a resignation to disappointments, and a resolution to carry out one's responsibilities. Stoicism appealed to many Romans and had an impact on early Christian thought.

stream-of-consciousness   A writing technique used by some modern authors in which the narration consists of a *character's* continuous interior monologue of thoughts and feelings.

structuralism   In *postmodernism*, an approach to knowledge based on the belief that human behavior and institutions can be explained by reference to a few underlying structures that themselves are reflections of hidden patterns in the human mind.

studia humanitatis [STOO-dee-ah hu-man-ih-TAH-tis] **(humanistic studies)**   The Latin term given by *Renaissance* scholars to new intellectual pursuits that were based on recently discovered ancient texts, including moral philosophy, history, grammar, rhetoric, and poetry. This new learning stood in sharp contrast to medieval *Scholasticism*.

Sturm und Drang [STOORM oont drahng]   German, "storm and stress"; a German literary movement of the 1770s that focused on themes of action, emotionalism, and the individual's revolt against the conventions of society.

style   The combination of distinctive elements of creative execution and expression, in terms of both *form* and *content*.

style galant [STEEL gah-LAHNN]   In *rococo* music, a *style* of music developed by French composers and characterized by graceful and simple *melodies*.

stylobate [STY-luh-bate]   In Greek temples, the upper step of the base that forms a platform on which the columns stand.

subject   In music, the main *theme*.

sublime [suh-BLIME]   In *romanticism*, the term used to describe nature as a terrifying and awesome force full of violence and power.

suprematism [suh-PREM-uh-tiz-uhm]   A variation of *abstract art*, originating in Russia in the early twentieth century, characterized by the use of geometric shapes as the basic elements of the composition.

surrealism [suh-REE-uhl-iz-uhm]   An early-twentieth-century movement in art, literature, and theater, in which incongruous juxtapositions and fantastic images produce an irrational and dreamlike effect.

swing band   A fifteen- or sixteen-member orchestra, which plays ballads and dance tunes; dominated popular music in the United States and in large cities in western Europe, from the early 1930s until the early 1950s.

syllabic   In music, in *plainsong*, a style of musical setting in which one note is set to each syllable.

symbolic realism   In art, a *style* that is realistic and true to life but uses the portrayed object or person to represent or symbolize something else.

symphony   A long and complex *sonata*, usually written in three or four movements, for large *orchestras*; the first movement is traditionally fast, the second slow, and the third (and optional fourth) movement fast.

syncopation [sin-ko-PAY-shun]   In music, the technique of accenting the weak beat when a strong beat is expected.

syncretism [SIN-kruh-tiz-uhm]   The combining of different forms of religious beliefs or practices.

synthesizer [SIN-thuh-size-uhr]   An electronic apparatus with a keyboard capable of duplicating the sounds of many musical instruments, popular among *postmodernist* composers and musicians.

tabula rasa [TAB-yuh-luh RAH-zuh]   "Erased tablet," the Latin term John Locke used to describe the mind at birth, empty of inborn ideas and ready to receive sense impressions, which Locke believed were the sole source of knowledge.

technique   The systematic procedure whereby a particular creative task is performed.

tempera   A permanent, fast-drying painting *medium* consisting of colored pigment and a water-soluble binder, usually egg yolk; widely used in early Christian art and then continuously used until the development of oil paints in the fifteenth century.

tempo   In music, the relative speed at which a *composition* is to be played, indicated by a suggestive word or phrase or by a precise number such as a metronome marking. (A metronome is a finely calibrated device used to determine the exact tempo for a musical work.)

tenebrism   In painting, a style of *chiaroscuro* that uses bright, sweeping light to illuminate figures against an intense dark background.

terza rima [TER-tsuh REE-muh]   A three-line stanza with an interlocking rhyme scheme (*aba bcb cdc ded*, and so on), used by Dante in his *Divine Comedy*.

tetrarchy   Greek, "rule by four." A term applied to the institutional arrangements created by Diocletian, in which rule in the Roman Empire was shared among two Augustuses and two Caesars.

texture   In a musical composition, the number and nature of voices or instruments employed and how the parts are combined.

theater of the absurd   A type of theater that has come to reflect the despair, anxieties, and absurdities of modern life and in which the characters seldom make sense, the plot is nearly nonexistent, bizarre and fantastic events occur onstage, and *tragedy* and *comedy* are mixed in unconventional ways; associated with *late modernism*.

theme   The dominant idea of a work; the message or emotion the artist intends to convey; used in music, literature, and art.

theme and variations   In music, a *technique* in which a musical idea is stated and then repeated in variant versions, with modifications or embellishments; used in independent works or as a single movement in a *symphony*, *sonata*, or chamber work.

theocracy   From the Greek *theos*, "god"; a state governed by a god regarded as the ruling power or by priests or officials claiming divine sanction.

theology   The application of philosophy to the study of religious truth, focusing especially on the nature of the deity and the origin and teachings of an organized religious community.

tone   A musical sound of definite pitch; also, the quality of a sound.

tone color   In music, the quality of a sound, determined by the overtones; used for providing contrasts.

tracery   Ornamental architectural work with lines that branch out to form designs, often found as stone carvings in *rose windows.*

tragedy   A serious and deeply moral drama, typically involving a noble protagonist brought down by excessive pride (hubris) and describing a conflict between seemingly irreconcilable values or forces; in Greece, tragedies were performed at the festivals associated with the worship of Dionysus.

transcendentalism   A literary and philosophical movement that emphasized the spiritual over the material, the metaphysical over the physical, and intuition over empiricism. Its central tenet identified God or the divine spirit (transcendence) with nature; popular in early- and mid-nineteenth-century New England.

transept   In church architecture, the crossing arm that bisects the *nave* near the *apse* and gives the characteristic *cruciform* shape to the floor plan.

tremolo   In music, the rapid repetition of two pitches in a chord, so as to produce a tremulous effect.

triclinium   In the Roman world, a dining room with three couches for diners to recline on while eating. In the Middle Ages, the term for a formal reception chamber, which could be used for dining or other festive occasions.

triconch   A prestigious building type developed by the Romans and inherited by medieval builders. The three (tri-) *conches* constituted an *apse* at one end and two *apse*-like extrusions along the building's long sides.

triglyph [TRY-glif]   In Greek architecture, a three-grooved rectangular panel on the *frieze* of a *Doric* temple; triglyphs alternated with *metopes.*

trill   In music, the rapid alternation of two notes, a step apart; used as a musical embellishment.

triptych [TRIP-tik]   In painting, a set of three hinged or folding panels depicting a religious story, mainly used as an altarpiece.

trope [TROHP]   In *Gregorian chants,* a new phrase or *melody* inserted into an existing chant to make it more musically appealing; also called a turn; in literature, a figure of speech.

troubador [TROO-buh-door]   A composer and/or singer, usually an aristocrat, who performed *secular* love songs at the feudal courts in southern France.

twelve-tone scale   In music, a fixed *scale* or series in which there is an arbitrary arrangement of the twelve *tones* (counting every half tone) of an octave; devised by Arnold Schoenberg.

tympanum [TIM-puh-num]   In medieval architecture, the arch over a doorway set above the lintel, usually decorated with carvings depicting biblical themes; in *classical* style architecture, the recessed face of a *pediment.*

ukiyo-e [oo-key-yoh-AY]   A type of colorful Japanese print, incised on woodblocks, that is characterized by simple design, plain backgrounds, and flat areas of color. Developed in seventeenth century Japan; admired by late-nineteenth-century Parisian artists, who assimilated it to a Western style that is most notable in the prints of Mary Cassatt.

utilitarianism [yoo-til-uh-TARE-e-uh-niz-uhm]   The doctrine set forth in the social theory of Jeremy Bentham in the nineteenth century that the final goal of society and humans is "the greatest good for the greatest number."

vanishing point   In linear *perspective,* the point on the horizon at which the receding parallel lines appear to converge and then vanish.

vault   A ceiling or roof made from a series of arches placed next to one another.

vernacular language [vuhr-NAK-yuh-luhr]   The language or dialect of a region, usually spoken by the general population as opposed to the wealthy or educated elite.

vernacular literature   Literature written in the language of the populace, such as English, French, or Italian, as opposed to the language of the educated elite, usually Latin.

via antiqua [VEE-uh ahn-TEE-kwah]   The "old way," the term used in late medieval thought by the opponents of St. Thomas Aquinas to describe his *via media,* which they considered outdated.

via media [VEE-uh MAY-dee-ah]   The "middle way" that St. Thomas Aquinas sought in reconciling Aristotle's works to Christian beliefs.

via moderna [VEE-uh moh-DEHR-nah]   The "new way," the term used in late medieval thought by those thinkers who opposed the school of Aquinas.

video art   A type of art made with a video monitor or monitors; produced using either computerized programs or handheld cameras; can be ephemeral or permanent.

virtuoso [vehr-choo-O-so]   An aristocratic person who experimented in science, usually as an amateur, in the seventeenth century, giving science respectability and a wider audience; later, in music, a person with great technical skill.

voussoir [voo-SWAR]   A carved, wedge-shaped stone or block in an arch.

Vulgate   Name for the edition and translation of the Bible into Latin prepared by St. Jerome (345–420). The term derives from Latin *vulgus,* meaning "the crowd" or "the people generally," but specifically those who spoke Latin, not Greek.

westwork   The exterior western end of a church; originated by the Carolingians, whose churches were given tall, impressive western ends. *Romanesque* and *Gothic* builders retained Carolingian height but added sculptural and architectural details so as to create ornate, intricate facades.

woodcut   In art, the technique of cutting or carving an image onto a wooden block used for printing; originated in the late Middle Ages. Also, the print made from the technique.

word painting   In music, the illustration of an idea, a meaning, or a feeling associated with a word, as, for example, using a discordant *melody* when the word *pain* is sung. This technique is especially identified with the sixteenth-century *madrigal;* also called word illustration or madrigalism.

ziggurat [ZIG-oo-rat]   A Mesopotamian stepped pyramid, usually built with external staircases and a shrine at the top; sometimes included a tower.

CREDITS

Chapter 1 CO-1, © Erich Lessing/Art Resource, NY; 1.1, © Copper Age/ The Bridgeman Art Library/Getty Images; 1.2, © Jean-Marie Chauvet/ Corbis Sygma; 1.3, © Naturhistorisches Museum, Wien. Photo: Alice Schumacher; 1.5, © The British Museum; 1.6, © Erich Lessing/Art Resource, NY; 1.7, © University of Pennsylvania Museum, #150029; 1.8, © University of Pennsylvania Museum, #150848; 1.9, © Erwin Böhm, Mainz; 1.10, © Carolyn Clark/Color Spectrum Library, London; 1.12, © The British Museum; 1.13, © Tim Schermerhorn; 1.14, © Inge Morath/ Magnum Photos, Inc.; 1.15, © AKG Images; 1.16, © Erich Lessing/Art Resource, NY; 1.17, The Metropolitan Museum of Art, Rogers Fund and contribution from Edward S. Harkness, 1929. (29.3.2) Photograph © 1997 The Metropolitan Museum of Art; 1.18, © Margarete Büsing/Bildarchiv Preußischer Kulturbesitz/Art Resource, NY; 1.19, © Bildarchiv Preußischer Kulturbesitz/Art Resource, NY; 1.20, © The British Museum; 1.21, © Werner Forman/Art Resource, NY; 1.22, © Boltin Picture Library/ Bridgeman Photos, Inc.; 1.23, © Giraudon/Art Resource, NY; 1.24, © Bildarchiv Preussischer Kulturbesitz/Art Resource, NY; 1.25, © Fred J. Maroon/ Photo Researchers, Inc.; 1.26, Persepolis, Iran/© Bridgeman Art Library **Chapter 2** CO-2, © Vanni/Art Resource, NY; 2.1, © Cornucopia/Susanna Hickling ; 2.2, 2.3, © Erich Lessing/Art Resource, NY; 2.4, © SEF/Art Resource, NY; 2.5, © Nimatallah/Art Resource, NY; 2.6, © Craig and Marie Mauzy, Athens, Greece; 2.7, © George Grigoriou/Getty Images/Stone; 2.8, © AAAC/Topham/The Image Works; 2.9, © The Granger Collection, New York; Interpreting Art 2.1, © The British Museum; Encounter 2.1, © Réunion des Musées Nationaux/Art Resource, NY; 2.12, © Vanni/Art Resource, NY; 2.13, © Erich Lessing/Art Resource, NY; 2.14, The Metropolitan Museum of Art, Fletcher Fund, 1932. (32.11.1) Photograph © 1997 The Metropolitan Museum of Art; 2.15, © Nimatallah/Art Resource, NY; 2.16, © Hirmer Fotoarchiv, Munich; 2.17, © Craig and Marie Mauzy, Athens, Greece; 2.18, © Staatliche Antikensammlung und Glyptothek München; 2.19, © Vanni Archive/Corbis **Chapter 3** CO-3, © The Granger Collection, New York; 3.1, Courtesy of the Arthur M. Sackler Museum, Harvard University Art Museums, Bequest of David M. Robinson. Photo by Michael Nedzweski, © President and Fellows of Harvard College, Harvard University; 3.2, 3.3, © Hirmer Fotoarchiv, Munich; 3.4, © Bildarchiv Preussischer Kulturbesitz/Art Resource, NY; 3.5, © Hirmer Fotoarchiv, Munich; 3.6, © Ara Guler/Magnum Photos, Inc.; 3.8, © Erich Lessing/Art Resource, NY; Encounter 3.1, © Staatliche Museen zu Berlin/ Preußischer Kulturbesitz Antikensammlung. Photo by Johannes Laurentius/Art Resource, NY; 3.9, © Ronald Sheridan/Ancient Art & Architecture Collection; 3.10, © Kunsthistorisches Museum; 3.11, © The British Museum; 3.12, © The Granger Collection, New York; 3.13, © C.M. Dixon/Ancient Art & Architecture Collection; 3.14, © Ronald Sheridan/ Ancient Art & Architecture Collection; 3.15, © Scala/Art Resource, NY; 3.16, © René Burri/Magnum Photos, Inc.; 3.17, Robert Harding/Getty Images/Digital Vision; 3.18, © Hirmer Fotoarchiv, Munich; 3.19, 3.20, © Scala/Art Resource, NY; 3.21, © Hirmer Fotoarchiv, Munich; 3.22, © The British Museum; 3.24, © Nimatallah/Art Resource, NY; 3.25, © Hirmer Fotoarchiv, Munich; 3.26, © Staatliche Antikensammlung und Glyptothek München **Chapter 4** CO-4, The Metropolitan Museum of Art, Rogers Fund, 1909. (09.39) Photograph © The Metropolitan Museum of Art/Art Resource, NY; 4.1, The Metropolitan Museum of Art, Rogers Fund, 1918. (18.145.10) Photograph © 1999 The Metropolitan Museum of Art.; 4.2, © Bildarchiv Preussischer Kulturbesitz/Art Resource, NY; 4.3, © Art Resource, NY; 4.5, © Alinari/Art Resource, NY; 4.6, © Scala/Art Resource, NY; 4.7, © Erich Lessing/Art Resource, NY; 4.8, © AKG Images; 4.9, © Alinari/Art Resource, NY; 4.10, The Metropolitan Museum of Art, Rogers Fund, 1911. (11.90); 4.11, © The British Museum; 4.12, © C.M. Dixon/Ancient Art & Architecture Collection; 4.13, © Art Resource, NY; Encounter 4.1, © Bildarchiv Preussischer Kulturbesitz/Art Resource, NY; 4.14, © Foto Marburg/Art Resource, NY; 4.15, Pinacoteca Capitolina, Palazzo Conservatori, Rome, Italy/Index/© Bridgeman Art Library; 4.16, The Metropolitan Museum of Art, Rogers Fund, 1909. (09.39) Photograph © The Metropolitan Museum of Art/Art Resource, NY; 4.17, Louvre, Paris, France/© Lauros-Giraudon/Bridgeman Art Library; Interpreting Art 4.1, Araldo de Luca **Chapter 5** CO-5, © Scala/Art Resource, NY; 5.1, © Israel Museum, Jerusalem; 5.2, © Oriental Institute Museum, University of Chicago; 5.3, © The Jewish Museum, NY/Art Resource, NY; 5.4, © Zev Radovan/www.BibleLandPictures.com; 5.5, © Richard T. Nowitz; 5.6, © The Jewish Museum/Art Resource, NY; 5.7, © Israel Museum, Jerusalem; 5.8, Courtesy of Nancy L. Lapp; 5.9, 5.10, © Zev Radovan/www .BibleLandPictures.com; 5.11, © Carl Purcell/Words & Pictures; 5.12, © Zev Radovan/www.BibleLandPictures.com; Encounter 5.1, © Erich

Lessing/Art Resource, NY; 5.13, © Phototheque André Held; 5.14, 5.15, © Scala/Art Resource, NY; 5.16, © Hirmer Fotoarchiv, Munich; 5.17, © Scala/Art Resource, NY; 5.18, © Erich Lessing/PhotoEdit **Chapter 6** CO-6, Pinacoteca Capitolina, Palazzo Conservatori, Rome, Italy/© Index/ The Bridgeman Art Library; Encounter 6.1, © Scala/Art Resource, NY; 6.1, © Fototeca Unione, Rome. American Academy in Rome; 6.2, © Superstock; 6.3, © F1online digitale Bildagentur GmbH/Alamy; 6.4, © C.M. Dixon/Ancient Art & Architecture Collection; 6.5, 6.6, © Scala/Art Resource, NY; 6.8, © Giraudon/Art Resource, NY; 6.9, © Scala/Art Resource, NY; 6.10, © Paul Chesley/Getty Images/Stone; 6.11, Rome, Italy/Index/ © Bridgeman Art Library; 6.12, © Guido Rossi/TIPS Images USA; 6.13, © Williams A. Allard/Getty Images/National Geographic; 6.14, © Foto Marburg/Art Resource, NY; 6.15, 6.17, © Scala/Art Resource, NY; 6.18, © Nimatallah/Art Resource, NY; 6.19, © Ronald Sheridan/Ancient Art & Architecture Collection; 6.20, © Alinari/Art Resource, NY; 6.21, © Vanni/ Art Resource, NY; Interpreting Art 6.1, © Scala/Art Resource, NY; 6.22, © Scala/Art Resource, NY; 6.23, © Biblioteca Apostolica Vaticana (MS Vat. Cat 3867 fol 100); 6.24, © R. Sheridan/Ancient Art & Architecture Collection; 6.25, © Erich Lessing/Art Resource, NY; 6.26, © Phototheque André Held; 6.27, 6.28, 6.29, © Scala/Art Resource, NY **Chapter 7** CO-7, Aachen Cathedral, Aachen, Germany/Bildarchiv Steffens/The Bridgeman Art Library; 7.1, © Yann Arthus-Bertrand/Corbis; 7.2, © State Historical Museum, Moscow; 7.3, © English Heritage Photo Library; 7.4, © Bildarchiv Preussischer Kulturbesitz/Art Resource, NY; 7.5, © Bibliothèque Nationale de France, Paris; 7.6, © The Art Archive/Gianni Dagli Orti; 7.7, © The Art Archive/Monastery of Saint Catherine Sinai Egypt/ Gianni Dagli Orti; 7.8, © The Art Archive/Gianni Dagli Orti; 7.9, © Dumbarton Oaks, Image Collections and Fieldwork Archives, Washington, DC; 7.10, © Scala/Art Resource, NY; 7.11, © AKG Images; 7.12, © Bibliotheque Nationale, Paris, France/The Bridgeman Art Library; 7.13, © Ian Berry/Magnum Photos, Inc.; 7.14, © Scala/Art Resource, NY; 7.16, © The Art Archive/Gianni Dagli Orti; 7.17, © Snark/Art Resource, NY; 7.18, © The Board of Trinity College, Dublin, Ireland/The Bridgeman Art Library; 7.19, © Scala/Art Resource, NY; 7.20, © The Art Archive/Bibliothèque Nationale Paris; 7.21, © Biblioteca Nationala a Romaniei, MS R II 1, folio 18 verso; 7.22, © Snark/Art Resource, NY; 7.23, © Bayerische Staatsbibliothek, Munich, Germany/The Bridgeman Art Library; 7.24, Archives Larousse, Paris, France/© Giraudon/The Bridgeman Art Library; 7.25, Aachen Cathedral, Aachen, Germany/Bildarchiv Steffens/ The Bridgeman Art Library; 7.28, Erich Lessing/Art Resource, NY **Chapter 8** CO-8, © Sylvain Grandadam/Photographer's Choice/Getty Images; 8.1, © AP/Wide World Photos; 8.2, Reproduced by kind permission of the Trustees of the Chester Beatty Library, Dublin; 8.3, © Vanni Archive/Corbis; 8.4, The Nelson-Atkins Museum of Art, Kansas City, Missouri. Purchase: Nelson Trust. (44-40/2); 8.5, © Bibliotheque Nationale de France, Paris (Ms Arabe 5847 fol 5v); 8.6, Minbar from Kutubiyya Mosque, Marrakesh, Morocco. Islamic. Woodwork. 12th C., 1137-ca.–1145. H. 12 ft. 10 in.; W. 2 ft. 10¼ in.; D. 11 ft. 4¼ in. Three quarter view from the right. Photography by Bruce White. Photograph © 1998, The Metropolitan Museum of Art8.7, Used by permission of the Edinburgh University Library. Or Ms. 161, folio 16r; Encounter 8.1, © The Granger Collection, New York; 8.8, © Victoria & Albert Museum, London/Art Resource, NY; 8.9, © J. Pate/Robert Harding Picture Library; 8.10, © Werner Foreman Archive/Art Resource, NY; 8.11, © Werner Forman/Art Resource, NY; 8.12, © Ronald Sheridan/Ancient Art & Architecture Collection; 8.13, Courtesy of the World of Islam Festival Trust; 8.14, © Adam Lubroth/Art Resource, NY; 8.15, © Bibliothèque Nationale de France, Paris. AR. 5847. Fol. 95; Interpreting Art 8.1, © Art Resource, NY; 8.16, © Erich Lessing/ Art Resource, NY **Chapter 9** CO-9, © Scala/Art Resource, NY; 9.1, © Erich Lessing/Art Resource, NY; 9.2, © British Library Board, Cott Claud B IV f.79v; 9.3, © Scala/Art Resource, NY; 9.4, © Erich Lessing/Art Resource, NY; 9.5, © Snark/Art Resource, NY; Encounter 9.1, © English Heritage Photograph Library; 9.6, © The Granger Collection, New York; 9.7, © AKG Images/Stefan Diller; 9.8, © Bibliotheque Nationale, Paris, France/The Bridgeman Art Library; 9.9, © Erich Lessing/Art Resource, NY; 9.10, © Catherine Karnow/Woodfin Camp and Associates; 9.11, © Giraudon/Art Resource, NY; 9.12, © Jean Bernard; 9.14, © AKG Images/Schütze/Rodemann; 9.15, © AKG Images/Stefan Drechsel; 9.16, © Lee Snider Photo Images; 9.17, © Photographie Bulloz/Art Resource, NY; 9.18, 9.19, © Réunion des Musées Nationaux/Art Resource, NY; 9.20, Courtesy the Master and Fellows of Corpus Christi College, Cambridge. © Corpus Christi College, Cambridge; 9.22, © Hirmer Fotoarchiv, Munich; 9.25, © Brian Lawrence/Superstock; 9.26, 9.27, © Ronald Sheridan/

Ancient Art & Architecture Collection; 9.28, 9.29, © Hirmer Fotoarchiv, Munich; 9.30, Jean Feuillie, © Centre des Monuments Nationaux, Paris; 9.31, © Scala/Art Resource, NY; 9.33, 9.34, © Hirmer Fotoarchiv, Munich; 9.35, © Snark/Art Resource, NY; 9.36, University Library of Munich, Cim. 15, Cod. Ms. 24   **Chapter 10** CO-10, © Scala/Art Resource, NY; 10.1, Ampliaciones y Reproducciones MAS (Arxiu Mas), Barcelona; 10.2, Library of Congress, Law Library (s65p7); 10.3, © Giraudon/Art Resource, NY; 10.4, © Bibliotheque Royale de Belgique; 10.5, © The Art Archive/Corbis; Encounter 10.1, © Réunion des Musées Nationaux/Art Resource, NY; 10.6, © Art Resource, NY; 10.7, © Foto Marburg/Art Resource, NY; 10.8, 10.9, 10.10, 10.11, 10.12, 10.13, © Scala/Art Resource, NY; 10.14, © Art Resource, NY; 10.15, © AKG Images; 10.16, © Bildarchiv Preussischer Kulturbesitz/Art Resource, NY; 10.17, 10.18, Galleria degli Uffizi, Florence, Italy/© Bridgeman Art Library; 10.19, © Alinari/Art Resource, NY; 10.20, © Giraudon/Art Resource, NY; 10.21, St. Bravo Cathedral, Ghent/© Giraudon/Art Resource, NY; Interpreting Art 10.1, © The National Gallery, London/Art Resource, NY; 10.22, Photograph © Board of Trustees, National Gallery of Art, Washington, DC; 10.23, © AKG Images   **Chapter 11** CO-11, © Nimatallah/Art Resource, NY; 11.1, © Scala/Art Resource, NY; 11.2, © Museo Thyssen-Bornemisza. Madrid; 11.3, © Scala/Art Resource, NY; Encounter 11.1, © The National Gallery, London/Art Resource, NY; 11.4, © Scala/Art Resource, NY; 11.5, © Vatican Museums and Galleries, Vatican City, Italy/The Bridgeman Art Library; 11.6, © Scala/Art Resource, NY; 11.8, © Bill Chaitkin/Architectural Association, London; 11.9, 11.10, 11.11, © Scala/Art Resource, NY; 11.12, © Erich Lessing/Art Resource, NY; 11.13, 11.14, 11.15, 11.16, © Scala/Art Resource, NY; 11.17, © Corbis/Karen Tweedy-Holmes; 11.18, © AKG Images/Rabatti-Domingie; 11.19, 11.20, 11.21, © Scala/Art Resource, NY; 11.22, Galleria degli Uffizi Florence, Italy/© Bridgeman Art Library, London; 11.23, © AKG Images; 11.24, © The Frick Collection, New York; 11.25, © Bibliotheque Royale de Belgique   **Chapter 12** CO-12, © DeA Picture Library/Art Resource, NY; 12.1, © Erich Lessing/Art Resource, NY; 12.2, © AKG Images; 12.3, © Hans Hinz/Artothek; 12.4, © Scala/Art Resource, NY; 12.5, © Hamburger Kunsthalle/Bildarchiv Preussischer Kulturbesitz/Photo: Elke Walford/Art Resource, NY; Encounter 12.1, © Museu Nacional de Arte Antigua, Lisbon, Portugal, Giraudon/The Bridgeman Art Library; 12.6, © Scala/Art Resource, NY; 12.7, Canali Photobank, Milan, Italy; 12.8, © Réunion des Musées Nationaux/Art Resource, NY; 12.9, Courtesy of the Vatican Museum. Photo by A. Bracchetti and P. Zigrossi; Interpreting Art 12.1, © Erich Lessing/Art Resource, NY; 12.11, 12.12, Courtesy of the Vatican Museum. Photo by A. Bracchetti and P. Zigrossi; 12.13, © Scala/Art Resource, NY; 12.14, © Alinari/Art Resource, NY; 12.15, © Scala/Art Resource, NY; 12.16, © Cameraphoto/Art Resource, NY; 12.17, Galleria degli Uffizi Florence, Italy/© Bridgeman Art Library, London; 12.18, © Scala/Art Resource, NY; 12.19, Galleria dell'Accademia, Florence/© Bridgeman Art Library, London; 12.20, © Scala/Art Resource, NY; 12.21, © SEF/Art Resource, NY; 12.22, © Stephen Studd/Stone/Getty Images; 12.23, © Alinari/Art Resource, NY; 12.25, © Scala/Art Resource   **Chapter 13** CO-13, © Bildarchiv Preussischer Kulturbesitz/Art Resource, NY; 13.1, © Erich Lessing/Art Resource, NY; 13.2, © Art Resource, NY; 13.4, © AKG Images/Dieter E. Hoppe; 13.5, © Blauel/Gnamm/Artothek; 13.6, Courtesy of the Fogg Art Museum, Harvard University Art Museums. Gift of William Gray from the collection of Francis Calley Gray; 13.7, Musée d'Unterlinden, Colmar, France/© Giraudon/Bridgeman Art Library, London; 13.8, © Scala/Art Resource, NY; 13.9, © Bildarchiv Preussischer Kulturbesitz/Art Resource, NY; 13.10, © The Detroit Institute of Arts, USA/City of Detroit Purchase/The Bridgeman Art Library; 13.11, © Erich Lessing/Art Resource, NY; Encounter 13.1, © The Granger Collection, New York; 13.12, © Nationalmuseum, Stockholm, Sweden/The Bridgeman Art Library; 13.13, 13.14, © Bildarchiv Preussischer Kulturbesitz/Art Resource, NY; 13.15, © Erich Lessing/Art Resource, NY; 13.16, © Scala/Art Resource, NY; 13.17, © National Portrait Gallery, London; 13.18, Courtesy Curia Generalizia, Society of Jesus; 13.19, 13.20, Toledo, S. Tome, Spain/Index/© Bridgeman Art Library, London; 13.21, © Scala/Ministero per i Beni e le Attività culturali/Art Resource, NY; 13.22, © Art Resource, NY; 13.23, © Scala/Art Resource, NY; 13.24, © Foto Marburg/Art Resource, NY   **Chapter 14** CO-14, 14.1, © Réunion des Musées Nationaux/Art Resource, NY; 14.2, © Erich Lessing/Art Resource, NY ; 14.3, © The National Gallery, London/Art Resource, NY; 14.4, Courtesy Dordrechts Museum and The Netherlands Institute of Cultural Heritage; 14.6, © Bettmann/Corbis; Encounter 14.1, Folding Screens Showing Nagasaki in the Kanbun Era (1661–1673).Courtesy Nagasaki Museum of History and Culture; 14.7, 14.8, 14.9, © Scala/Art Resource, NY; 14.10, © The De-troit Institute of Arts, USA/City of Detroit Purchase/The Bridgeman Art Library; 14.11, © Scala/Art Resource, NY; 14.12, © Erich Lessing/Art Resource, NY; 14.13, © Réunion des Musées Nationaux/Art Resource, NY; 14.14, © Photographie Bulloz/Art Resource, NY; 14.15, © Erich Lessing/Art Resource, NY; 14.16, © Erich Lessing/Art Resource, NY; 14.17, © Rijksmuseum, Amsterdam; 14.18, © Bildarchiv Preussischer Kulturbesitz. Photo by Jörg P. Anders. Gemäldegalerie/Art Resource, NY; 14.19, Mauritshuis, The Hague/© Bridgeman Art Library, London; 14.20, © Rijksmuseum, Amsterdam; 14.21, Louvre, Paris, France/© Lauros-Giraudon/Bridgeman Art Library, London; 14.22, © Réunion des Musées Nationaux/Art Resource, NY; 14.23, © The National Gallery, London/Art Resource, NY; Interpreting Art 14.1, © A.F. Kersting; 14.24, © Erich Lessing/Art Resource, NY; 14.25, © The Granger Collection, New York   **Chapter 15** CO-15, Courtesy Department of Library Services. American Museum of Natural History. Photo by Craig Chesek. Neg. #4825(2); 15.1, © The Granger Collection, New York; 15.2, Courtesy Department of Library Services. American Museum of Natural History. Photo by Craig Chesek. Neg. #4825(2); 15.3, © Bettmann/Corbis; 15.4, © The Granger Collection, New York; 15.5, © Scala/Art Resource, NY; 15.6, © National Portrait Gallery, London; 15.7, © Erich Lessing/Art Resource, NY; 15.8, © Science & Society Picture Library/The Image Works; 15.9, © Erich Lessing/Art Resource, NY; 15.10, © Bettmann/Corbis; 15.11, © The New York Public Library/Art Resource, NY; 15.12, © The Granger Collection, New York; 15.13, © Réunion des Musées Nationaux/Art Resource, NY; 15.14, © Bibliothèque Nationale de France, Paris; Encounter 15.1, Courtesy Freer Gallery of Art, Smithsonian Institution, Washington, DC, Purchase F1942.15   **Chapter 16** CO-16, © Erich Lessing/Art Resource, NY; 16.1, © Superstock; 16.2, From A Diderot Pictorial Encyclopedia of Trades and Industry, Dover Publications, © 1959, plate #34 (upper), New York; 16.3, © The Barber Institute of Fine Arts, University of Birmingham/The Bridgeman Art Library; 16.4, © Daniel Zupac/Bruce Coleman, Inc./Photoshot; 16.5, © Erich Lessing/Art Resource, NY; 16.6, © AKG Images; 16.7, © Scala/Art Resource, NY; 16.8, © Réunion des Musées Nationaux/Art Resource, NY; 16.9, © The Frick Collection, New York; 16.10, © Réunion des Musées Nationaux/Art Resource, NY; 16.11, © Erich Lessing/Art Resource, NY; 16.12, © The National Gallery, London/Art Resource, NY; Interpreting Art 16.1, © Erich Lessing/Art Resource, NY; Encounter 16.1, © Patrick Ward/Corbis; 16.13, Courtesy The Metropolitan Museum of Art, Catherine Lorillard Wolfe Collection, Wolfe Fund, 1931 (31.45). © The Metropolitan Museum of Art/Art Resource, NY; 16.14, The Metropolitan Museum of Art, The Elisha Whittelsey Collection, The Elisha Whittelsey Fund, 1961 (61.531) Photograph © 1978 The Metropolitan Museum of Art.; 16.15, 16.16, © English Heritage Photographic Library; 16.17, © Giraudon/Art Resource, NY; 16.18, © Réunion des Musées Nationaux/Art Resource, NY; 16.19, © AKG Images   **Chapter 17** CO-17, © Musée de l'Armee/Dist. Réunion des Musées Nationaux/Art Resource, NY; 17.1, © Réunion des Musées Nationaux/Art Resource, NY; 17.2, City of Aberdeen Art Gallery and Museums Collections; 17.3, © The Art Archive/Musée Carnavalet Paris/Dagli Orti/Picture Desk; Encounter 17.1, © Giraudon/Art Resource, NY; 17.4, © Courtesy of the Warden and Scholars of New College, Oxford/The Bridgeman Art Library; 17.5, © Réunion des Musées Nationaux/Art Resource, NY; 17.6, Louvre, Paris, France/© The Bridgeman Art Library; 17.7, © Erich Lessing/Art Resource, NY; 17.8, © Robert C. Lautman Photography/Monticello; 17.9, © 1995 Bob Leek; 17.10, © Science & Society Picture Library/The Image Works; 17.11, © National Portrait Gallery, London; 17.12, © The National Gallery, London/Art Resource, NY; 17.13, Yale Center for British Art, Paul Mellon Collection, USA/© Bridgeman Art Library; 17.14, 17.15, © Clore Collection, Tate Gallery, London/Art Resource, NY; 17.16, © Jörg P. Anders/Bildarchiv Preussischer Kulturbesitz/Art Resource, NY; 17.17, © Scala/Art Resource, NY; 17.18, Private Collection/© Index/The Bridgeman Art Library; 17.19, 17.20, © Erich Lessing/Art Resource, NY; 17.21, © Réunion des Musées Nationaux/Art Resource, NY; 17.22, © AKG Images; 17.23, Courtesy of the John Carter Brown Library at Brown University; 17.24, © AKG Images   **Chapter 18** CO-18, 18.1, © Réunion des Musées Nationaux/Art Resource, NY; 18.2, © Ronald Sheridan/Ancient Art & Architecture Collection; 18.3, © Museum of Fine Arts, Boston, Massachusetts, USA/Henry Lillie Pierce Fund/The Bridgeman Art Library; 18.4, © The Philadelphia Museum of Art/Art Resource, NY; 18.5, Royal Holloway and Bedford New College, Surrey/© Bridgeman Art Library; 18.6, © Guildhall Library, City of London /The Bridgeman Art Library; 18.7, © Hulton Archive/Getty Images; Encounter 18.1, © National Portrait Gallery, Smithsonian Institution/Art Resource, NY; Interpreting Art 18.1, The Courtauld Institute

Gallery, Somerset House, London; 18.8, Louvre, Paris, France/Lauros-Giraudon/© The Bridgeman Art Library; 18.9, © Réunion des Musées Nationaux/Art Resource, NY; 18.10, © The Art Archive/Metropolitan Museum of Art New York; 18.11, © Réunion des Musées Nationaux/Art Resource, NY; 18.12, © Erich Lessing/Art Resource, NY; 18.13, © Bibliotheque Nationale, Paris, France/The Bridgeman Art Library; 18.14, The Metropolitan Museum of Art, Bequest of Mrs. H.O. Havemeyer, 1929. The H.O. Havemeyer Collection. (29.100.129). Photograph © 1992 The Metropolitan Museum of Art; 18.15, © Scala/Art Resource, NY; 18.16 The Metropolitan Museum of Art, Gift of Cornelius Vanderbilt, 1887. (87.25). © The Metropolitan Museum of Art/Art Resource, NY; 18.17, © Réunion des Musées Nationaux/Art Resource, NY; 18.18, Library of Congress (62-5803); 18.19, © Victoria & Albert Museum/Art Resource, NY; 18.20, © Private Collection/Bridgeman Art Library **Chapter 19** CO-19, Umberto Boccioni (1882–1916). *Unique Forms of Continuity in Space.* 1913. Bronze. 43⅞ × 34⅞ × 15¾". Acquired through the Lillie P. Bliss Bequest. (231.1948). The Museum of Modern Art, New York. Digital Image © The Museum of Modern Art, NY/Licensed by Scala/Art Resource, NY; 19.1, Collection of Mr. and Mrs. Paul Mellon, Image © 2006 Board of Trustees, National Gallery of Art, Washington, 1906, oil on canvas, .546 × .378 (21½ × 14⅞); framed: .638 × .473 × .036 (25⅛ × 18⅝ × 1⁷⁄₁₆). 1985.64.13. © 2009 Artists Rights Society (ARS), New York/ADAGP, Paris; 19.2, Umberto Boccioni (1882–1916). *Unique Forms of Continuity in Space.* 1913. Bronze. 43⅞ × 34⅞ × 15¾". Acquired through the Lillie P. Bliss Bequest. (231.1948). The Museum of Modern Art, New York. Digital Image © The Museum of Modern Art, NY/Licensed by Scala/Art Resource, NY; 19.3, © Christie's London/Artothek; 19.4, © Carnegie Museum of Art, Pittsburgh, Museum Purchase; 19.5, Eyre Crowe, The Dinner Hour at Wigan, © Manchester City Art Galleries; 19.6, © The Granger Collection, New York; 19.7, © Erich Lessing/Art Resource, NY; 19.8, © The Art Archive/Ellen Tweedy/Picture Desk; 19.9, Private Collection/© The Stapleton Collection/Bridgeman Art Library; 19.10, Photo: J. Lathion, © Nasjonalgalleriet. © 2009 The Munch Museum/The Munch-Ellingsen Group/Artists Rights Society (ARS), New York; 19.11, © Réunion des Musées Nationaux/Art Resource, NY; 19.12, Claude Monet, Le Bassin des Nympheas, 1904. Funds from Helen Dill bequest, 1935.14. Photograph courtesy of the Denver Art Museum; 19.13, The Phillips Collection, Washington, D.C.; 19.14, Berthe Morisot, *The Harbor at Lorient.* 1869. Ailsa Mellon Bruce Collection, Image courtesy of the Board of Trustees, National Gallery of Art, Washington.; 19.15, Mary Cassatt (American, 1844–1926) *The Bath,* 1891. Soft-ground etching with aquatint and drypoint on paper. 12⅜ × 9⅜. National Museum of Women in the Arts. Gift of Wallace and Wilhelmina Holladay; 19.16, © Erich Lessing/Art Resource, NY; 19.17, © Scala/Art Resource, NY; Encounter 19.1, The Whitworth Art Gallery, The University of Manchester; Encounter 19.2, Amsterdam, Van Gogh Museum (Vincent Van Gogh Foundation); 19.18, Albright-Knox Art Gallery, Buffalo, NY. A. Conger Goodyear Collection, 1965; 19.19, © Réunion des Musées Nationaux/Art Resource, NY; 19.20, Vincent van Gogh, *The Starry Night,* (1889). Oil on canvas. 29 × 34¼" (73.7 × 92.1 cm). Acquired through the Lillie P. Bliss Bequest. The Museum of Modern Art, NY. Digital image © The Museum of Modern Art, NY/Licensed by Scala/Art Resource, NY; 19.21, Henri Matisse. *Open Window, Collioure,* Collection of Mr. and Mrs. John Hay Whitney, Image © 2006 Board of Trustees, National Gallery of Art, Washington, 1905, oil on canvas, .553 × .460 (21¾ × 18⅛); framed: .711 × 6.22 × .051 (28 × 24½ × 2). © 2009 Succession H. Matisse/Artists Rights Society (ARS), New York; 19.22, Pablo Picasso (1881–1973). *Les Demoiselles d'Avignon.* 1907. Oil on canvas, 8' × 7' 8". Acquired through the Lillie P. Bliss Bequest. (333.1939). The Museum of Modern Art, New York. Digital Image © The Museum of Modern Art, NY/Licensed by Scala/Art Resource, NY. © 2009 Estate of Pablo Picasso/Artists Rights Society (ARS), New York; 19.23, Digital Image © The Museum of Modern Art/Licensed by Scala/Art Resource, NY. © 2009 Estate of Pablo Picasso/Artists Rights Society (ARS), New York; 19.24, Digital Image © The Museum of Modern Art/Licensed by Scala/Art Resource, NY . © 2009 Artists Rights Society (ARS), New York/ADAGP, Paris; 19.25, Augustine Rodin. *Eve.* 67 × 18½ × 23¼". The Rodin Museum, Philadelphia. Gift of Jules E. Mastbaum; 19.26, © Marvin Trachtenberg; 19.27, Photo © Richard Bryant/Arcaid/Corbis. © 2009 Frank Lloyd Wright Foundation, Scottsdale, AZ/Artists Rights Society (ARS), New York; 19.28, The William Ransom Hogan Archive of New Orleans Jazz, Tulane University **Chapter 20** CO-20, © The Philadelphia Museum of Art/Art Resource, NY. © 2009 Estate of Pablo Picasso/Artists Rights Society (ARS), New York; 20.1, Photo © AKG Images. © 2009 Estate of Pablo Picasso/

Artists Rights Society (ARS), New York; 20.2, © Imperial War Museum, London/The Bridgeman Art Library; 20.3, Gift of Ethelyn McKinney in memory of her brother Glenn Ford McKinney, © 2006 Board of Trustees, National Gallery of Art, Washington, 1917, oil on canvas, .927 × .768 (36½ × 30¼); framed 1.108 × .943 x .064 (43⅝ × 37⅛ × 2½). 1943.9.1; 20.4, © British Petroleum Company plc, London; 20.5, Courtesy Library of Congress, 62-95653; Encounter 20.1, © Margaret Bourke-White/Time Life Pictures/Getty Images; 20.6, © AP/Wide World Photos; 20.7, © Margaret Bourke-White/Time Life Pictures/Getty Images; 20.8, © Corbis; 20.9, © AP/Wide World Photos; 20.10, The Metropolitan Museum of Art, Bequest of Gertrude Stein, 1947 (47.106). Photo © The Metropolitan Museum of Art/Art Resource, NY. © 2009 Estate of Pablo Picasso/Artists Rights Society (ARS), New York; 20.11, Jacob Lawrence (1917–2000). "In the North the African American had more educational opportunities." Panel 58 from *The Migration Series.* (1940–41; text and titled revised by the artist, 1993) Tempera on gesso on composition board, 12 × 18" (30.5 × 45.7 cm). Gift of Mrs. David M. Levy. The Museum of Modern Art, New York. Digital Image © The Museum of Modern Art, NY/Licensed by Scala/Art Resource, NY. © 2009 The Jacob and Gwendolyn Lawrence Foundation, Seattle/Artists Rights Society (ARS), New York; 20.12, Photo © Bildarchiv Preussischer Kulturbesitz/Art Resource, NY. © 2009 Artists Rights Society (ARS), New York/VG Bild-Kunst, Bonn; 20.13, Photo: Yale University Art Gallery. © 2009 Artists Rights Society (ARS), New York/ADAGP/FAAG, Paris; 20.14, © The Malevich Society; Interpreting Art 20.1, Hirshhorn Museum and Sculpture Garden, Smithsonian Institution. Gift of the Joseph H. Hirshhorn Foundation, 1972. (72.205). Photography by Lee Stalsworth. © 2009 Mondrian/Holtzman Trust c/o HCR International Warrenton VA; 20.15, © The Philadelphia Museum of Art/Art Resource, NY . © 2009 Estate of Pablo Picasso/Artists Rights Society (ARS), New York; 20.16, Georgia O'Keeffe, American, 1887–1986, *Cow's Skull with Calico Roses,* 1931, oil on canvas, 36 × 24 in. (91.4 × 61 cm), Alfred Stieglitz Collection, gift of Georgia O'Keeffe, 1947.712, The Art Institute of Chicago. Photography © The Art Institute of Chicago; 20.17, Photo © The Philadelphia Museum of Art/Art Resource, NY. © 2009 Artists Rights Society (ARS), New York/ADAGP, Paris/Succession Marcel Duchamp; 20.18, Salvador Dali (1904–1989). The Persistence of Memory. 1931. Oil on canvas, 9½ × 13". (162.1934). Given anonymously. The Museum of Modern Art, New York. Digital Image © The Museum of Modern Art, NY/Licensed by Scala/Art Resource, NY. © 2009 Salvador Dali, Gala-Salvador Dali Foundation/Artists Rights Society (ARS), New York; 20.19, Photo © Artothek. © 2009 Artists Rights Society (ARS), New York/VG Bild-Kunst, Bonn; 20.20, All rights reserved by Pan Klub Foundation. Museo Xul Solar; 20.21, Courtesy of Mary-Anne Martin/Fine Art, New York. © 2009 Banco de México Diego Rivera Frida Kahlo Museums Trust, Mexico, D.F./Artists Rights Society (ARS), New York; 20.22, Photo © CNAC/MNAM/Dist. Réunion des Musées Nationaux/Art Resource, NY. © 2009 Succession H. Matisse/Artists Rights Society (ARS), New York; 20.23, Max Beckmann (1884–1950). Departure. 1932–33. Oil on canvas, triptych, center panel, 7' ¾" × 45⅜"; side panels each 7' ¾" × 39¼". Given anonymously (by exchange). (6.1942.a-c). The Museum of Modern Art, New York. Digital Image © The Museum of Modern Art, NY/Licensed by Scala/Art Resource, NY. © 2009 Artists Rights Society (ARS), New York/VG Bild-Kunst, Bonn; 20.24, © Michael Nicholson/Corbis; 20.25, Photo © Anthony Scibilia/Art Resource, NY. © 2009 Artists Rights Society (ARS), New York/ADAGP, Paris/FLC; 20.26, © Underwood & Underwood/Corbis; 20.27, Photo © AKG Images. © 2009 Estate of Pablo Picasso/Artists Rights Society (ARS), New York **Chapter 21** CO-21, © Vanni/Art Resource, NY; 21.1, © Robert Brenner/PhotoEdit; 21.2, Andy Warhol, American, 1928–1987, *Mao,* 1973, Synthetic polymer paint and silkscreen ink on canvas, 448.3 × 346.7 cm (176½ × 136½ in.), Mr. and Mrs. Frank G. Logan Purchase Prize and Wilson L. Mead funds, 1974.230, The Art Institute of Chicago. Photography © The Art Institute of Chicago. © 2009 The Andy Warhol Foundation for the Visual Arts, Inc./Artists Rights Society (ARS), New York; 21.3, © Fritz Henle/Photo Researchers, Inc.; 21.4, © John Darnell/Ohio Historical Society; 21.5, © Express Newspapers/Getty Images; 21.6, Photo © Judy Chicago, 1979/TTF Archives. © 2009 Judy Chicago/Artists Rights Society (ARS), New York; 21.6 inset, Sojourner Truth place setting, from The Dinner Party, © Judy Chicago, 1979, mixed media, 5' × 3'. Collection: The Dinner Party Trust. Photo © Donald Woodman. © 2009 Judy Chicago/Artists Rights Society (ARS), New York; 21.7, Digital Image © The Museum of Modern Art/Licensed by Scala/Art Resource, NY. Art © Romare Bearden Foundation/Licensed by VAGA, New York, NY; 21.8, Courtesy Ronald

Text Credits

Chapter 1 p. 12, Samuel Noah Kramer, "A Sumerian Father Lectures His Son," excerpt from *History Begins at Sumer* (New York: Doubleday/Anchor, 1959); p. 21, Miriam Lichtheim, excerpt from "The Man Who Was Tired of Life" from *Ancient Egyptian Literature: Volume I.* Copyright 1973–1980 by the University of California Press;   **Chapter 2** p. 46, Sappho, "He Seems to Be a God" from *Seven Greeks* by Guy Davenport, copyright © 1995 by Guy Davenport. Reprinted by permission of New Directions Publishing Corp; Alceus, "Longing for Home" from *Greek Lyric Poetry* translated by M. L. West (Oxford University Press 1993);   **Chapter 3** p. 77, Xenophon, from *Oeconomicus: A Social and Historical Commentary*, translated by Sarah B. Pomeroy (Clarendon Press 1994);   **Chapter 4** p. 97, from *The Idylls of Theocritis: A Verse Translation by Theocritis*, translated by Thelma Sargent. Copyright © 1982 by Thelma Sargent. Used by permission of W. W. Norton & Company, Inc.;   **Chapter 5** p. 120, Flavius Josephus, excerpt from *History of the Jewish War*, trans. G. A. Williamson. Revised with an introduction, notes, and appendices by E. Mary Smallwood. Copyright © G.A. Williamson, 1959, 1969. Introduction and editorial matter copyright © E. M. Smallwood, 1981. Reproduced by permission of Penguin Books Ltd.; p. 132, Vibia Perpetua, excerpt from *The Acts of the Christian Martyrs*, edited by Herbert Musurillo, copyright 1972;   **Chapter 7** p. 190, Liudprand of Cremona, "Marriage Diplomacy Nets a Diplomatic Insult" from *The Works of Liudprand of Cremona*, translated by F. A. Wright (London: Routledge, 1930);   **Chapter 9** p. 247, from *The Letters of Abelard and Heloise*, translated and introduced by Betty Radice (Penguin Classics, 1974). Copyright © Betty Radice, 1974. Reproduced by permission of Penguin Books Ltd.;   **Chapter 11** p. 311, Laura Cereta, excerpt from "Defense of the Liberal Instruction of Women" from *Her Immaculate Hand: Selected Works by and about the Women Humanists of Quattrocentro Italy*, edited by Margaret King & Albert Rabil, 1992. Pegasus Press, #13;   **Chapter 12** p. 359, from *The Lives of the Artists, Volume I*, translated by George Bull (Penguin Classics, 1987). Copyright © George Bull, 1965. Reproduced by permission of Penguin Books Ltd.;   **Chapter 13** p. 388, from Bartolomé de las Casas, *A Short Account of the Destruction of the Indies*, edited and translated by Nigel Griffin. Introduction by Anthony Pagden (Penguin Classics, 1992). Translation and Notes copyright © Nigel Griffin, 1992. Introduction copyright © Anthony Pagden, 1992. Reproduced by permission of Penguin Books Ltd.;   **Chapter 14** p. 408, from *The Century of Louis XIV*, pages 71-72, edited by Orest Ranum and Patricia Ranum. Copyright © 1972 by Orest Ranum and Patricia Ranum. Reprinted by permission of HarperCollins Publishers, Inc.; Duke of Saint-Simon, *Memoirs de Saint-Simon*, reprinted in *The Century of Louis XIV*, edited by Orest and Patricia Ranum (p. 87, copyright 1972);   **Chapter 15** p. 451, Suzanne Gaudry, excerpt from *Witchcraft in Europe, 1100–1700: A Documentary History*, edited by Alan C. Kors and Edward Peters, pages 274–75, © 1972. Reprinted by permission of the University of Pennsylvania Press;   **Chapter 20** p. 613, excerpt from *Night* by Elie Wiesel, translated by Marion Wiesel. Translation copyright © 2006 by Marion Wiesel. Reprinted by permission of Hill and Wang, a division of Farrar, Straus and Giroux, LLC;   **Chapter 22** p. 703, excerpt from *Origins: A Memoir* by Amin Maalouf, translated by Catherine Temerson. Copyright © 2004 by Éditions Grasset & Fasquele. Translation copyright © 2008 by Catherine Temerson. Reprinted by permission of Farrar, Straus and Giroux, LLC.

INDEX

Page numbers in *italics* indicate pronunciation guides; page numbers in **boldface** indicate illustrations. For readers using the two-volume set of *The Western Humanities*, page numbers 1–367 (Chapters 1–12) refer to material in Volume I: *Beginnings through the Renaissance,* and page numbers 304–704 (Chapters 11–22) refer to material in Volume II: *The Renaissance to the Present.*